FALSE DAWN

THE UNITED RELIGIONS INITIATIVE, GLOBALISM, AND THE QUEST FOR A ONE-WORLD RELIGION

Lee Penn

FALSE DAWN

*THE
UNITED RELIGIONS
INITIATIVE, GLOBALISM,
AND THE QUEST FOR A
ONE-WORLD RELIGION*

SOPHIA PERENNIS

HILLSDALE NY

First published in the USA
by Sophia Perennis
© Lee Penn 2004

For information, address:
Sophia Perennis, P.O. Box 611
Hillsdale NY 12529
sophiaperennis.com

Printed in the
United States of America

Library of Congress Cataloging-in-Publication Data

Penn, Lee.
False dawn : the United Religions Initiative, globalism,
and the quest for a one-world religion / Lee Penn.

p. cm.

Includes bibliographical references and index.
ISBN 1 59731 000 x (pbk: alk. paper)
1. Religions (Proposed, universal, etc.) 2. United Religions
Initiative. I. Title.

BL390.P375 2004
299'.93—dc22   2004021510

CONTENTS

FOREWORD • 1

EDITOR'S FOREWORD: THE "COUNTER-INITIATION"
    DOCUMENTED—A TRADITIONALIST PERSPECTIVE • 3

AUTHOR'S INTRODUCTION, WITH AN APOLOGIA • 5

    The Argument, in Brief • 5
    Apologia: Replies to a Skeptic's Questions • 8
    A Road Map for Readers • 14
    The Intellectual Precursors of Today's New Age Movement • 18
    Present-Day New Age Supporters of the United Religions Initiative • 21
    Globalist Politicians and Businessmen • 23

ACKNOWLEDGMENTS • 28

METHODS • 29

PART I: HONORING THE "SPIRIT OF THE AGE":
    THE UNITED RELIGIONS INITIATIVE (URI)

    Point : Counterpoint • 33

CHAPTER 1: ONE ANGLICAN BISHOP'S DREAM • 35

CHAPTER 2: THE RISE OF THE UNITED RELIGIONS INITIATIVE • 39

    The Interfaith Movement of the 20th Century: Seed-bed of the URI • 39
    Founding the URI: 1993–1996 • 44
    Laying the Groundwork: 1997–1999 • 45
    Establishing Global Presence: 2000–2002 • 47
    The URI in 2004: "We Are Everywhere" • 53
    URI's Global Leadership: Diversity in Action • 55
    URI Funding: Secular Foundations, Billionaires, and Theosophists • 57
    "Appreciative Inquiry": Molding Minds For A Post-Modern Religion • 63
    Flexible Response: URI's Changes in Strategy Since 1996 • 66

CHAPTER 3: THE IDEALS AND THE PRACTICE OF THE URI • 69

    The URI Charter • 69

Good Fruit: Works of Mercy by URI Cooperation Circles • 73
    Africa • 73
    Asia • 75
    United States • 76
Seven Bad Fruit: URI Activists' Cultural Radicalism • 76
    Equivocation on Radical Islam • 77
    Hospitality for a Convicted Rapist and Terrorism Suspect • 79
    SIECUS and the Sexual Revolution • 82
        The Dog That Did Not Bark: The "Gay Agenda" Goes Missing
        From The URI • 83
    *Huston Smith and "Entheogens"—Proposing Better Religion
    Through Chemistry* • 84
        Bishop Swing's Condemnation of "Entheogens" • 86
    Interfaith Indoctrination for Children • 87
    "Peacebuilding" by Muzzling the Press in Zimbabwe • 89
    Other Oddities: From Pseudo-Shamanism to the "Lowerarchy" • 90

CHAPTER 4: THE URI'S FRIENDS IN HIGH PLACES • 93

The United Nations • 93
    The UN Environmental Program (UNEP) • 96
    UNESCO • 97
    The United Nations Population Fund (UNFPA) • 98
Politicians: From the White House to the State House • 99
George Soros • 101
Movements for "Global Governance" • 102
    The State of the World Forum • 102
    The Earth Charter Movement • 104

CHAPTER 5: AMONG THE NATIONS: THE NON-CHRISTIAN SUPPORTERS OF THE URI • 105

Traditional Religions and the URI • 105
    Jews • 105
    Muslims • 106
    Non-Abrahamic Faiths • 107
The Interfaith Movement and the URI— "Unity in Diversity"
  in Practice • 109
New Religious Movements and the URI • 115
    Sects and Cults • 115
        The Unification Church • 115
            The Strange Religion of the Rev. Sun Myung Moon • 116
            The Unificationists' Work with the URI • 124
        Scientologists and the "New Cult Awareness Network" • 126
        ISKCON—The "Hare Krishna" movement • 126

Wicca and the Goddess Movement • 127
    The Benign Public Face of Wicca • 128
    Transgressive Religion: From Polyamory to "Root-Based Sorcery" • 129
Theosophy and the New Age Movement • 131
    The Lucis Trust: Followers of Alice A. Bailey • 132
    Corinne McLaughlin and Gordon Davidson • 132
    Robert Muller • 133
    Barbara Marx Hubbard • 134
    Neale Donald Walsch • 135
Spiritual Odds and Ends • 136

CHAPTER 6: A DIVIDED VERDICT — THE CHURCHES AND THE URI • 140

The Anglican Communion • 140
    Mainstream Anglicanism • 140
    New Age Anglicanism • 146
        Lauren Artress and the Labyrinth Movement • 146
        James Parks Morton and the Cathedral of St. John the Divine • 150
        Matthew Fox and the "Techno Cosmic Mass" • 152

Other Protestants • 156

Latter-Day Saints • 157

Eastern Orthodoxy and the Oriental Orthodox Churches • 158

The Catholic Church • 158
    Vatican Opposition • 158
    Catholic Dissent—Standing With the United Religions • 160
        The Archdiocese of San Francisco • 161
        Catholics on the URI Global Council • 165
        Other Catholic URI Leaders and Activists • 166

CHAPTER 7: FOURTEEN REASONS TO STAND AGAINST THE UNITED RELIGIONS INITIATIVE • 175

[I] The URI Versus Christian Evangelism • 175

[II] Stigmatizing "Exclusive Religions" and Orthodoxy as "Fundamentalism" • 182

[III] Laying the Ground for a New Religion of the "Sacred Earth" • 188
    Bishop Swing • 189
    Other URI Leaders and Proponents • 191
    The United Communities of Spirit • 197
    Lex Orandi, Lex Credendi: The Syncretic Language and Symbols of the URI • 198
    Syncretism in Stone: Designing an Interfaith Temple • 201
    The Implications of Religious Syncretism • 203

[IV] Fostering Dissent Within Traditional Religions • 205

[V] A "New Ethic" for the New World Order: Hans Küng's Global Ethic • 206

[vi]   Secular Millenarianism • 211

[vii] A Fanciful View of History • 214

[viii] Religious Relativism • 215

[ix]   Population Control • 217

[x]   A Worldly, Utilitarian View of Religion • 222

[xi]   The Political Agenda of the URI • 224

[xii] Feminism and the Ordination of Women • 226

[xiii] Promotion of the New Age Movement, Pantheism, and
        Theosophy • 227

[xiv] The United Religions Is Not Required by the Christian
        Call to Unity • 229
        The Documents of Vatican II • 230
        Papal Teachings Since Vatican II • 232

CHAPTER 8: CLOSING THE CASE AGAINST THE URI • 235

PART II: SERVANTS OF THE SHINING DARKNESS: THE
        ANTI-GOSPEL OF THE NEW AGE MOVEMENT

        Point : Counterpoint • 239

CHAPTER 9: THE NEW AGE MOVEMENT: FRIVOLOUS IN APPEARANCE,
        SINISTER IN SUBSTANCE • 246

CHAPTER 10: HELENA BLAVATSKY AND THE THEOSOPHICAL SOCIETY • 248

        Mankind and Nature as "Gods" • 249

        Sympathy for the Devil • 249

        Inverting Christian Tradition • 251

        Population Control—in 1888 • 252

        Evolutionary Racism • 252

        The Theosophical Swastika • 253

        Dragon-Worship: The Religion of the Ancients—and of the Future • 255

        Hatred for the Christian Churches • 256

        The Worldwide Influence of Blavatsky and of Theosophy • 256

CHAPTER 11: ALICE A. BAILEY AND THE LUCIS TRUST • 259

        Continuing Blavatsky's Work • 260

        Praising the Fallen Angels and Re-defining "666" • 260

        Proclaiming Human Divinity and Denying Christ • 262

        Population Control • 263

        Astrological Racism • 264

Human Inequality in the New Age • 265

Anti-Semitism • 265

Equal-Opportunity Contempt for Traditional Religions • 269

The Coming New Religion • 270

Updating Freemasonry for the New Religion • 273

Dealing With "Reactionary Forces" • 274

Bailey's New World Order: "A New Power of Sacrifice" • 274

World Wars and Atom Bombs: Engines of Human Evolution • 276

Praise for Communism: From Lenin to Mao • 279

Human Civilization: Destruction and Rebirth • 282

The End of the Theosophical Road: "The Center of Pure Darkness" • 283

CHAPTER 12: PRESENT-DAY FOLLOWERS OF ALICE BAILEY • 284

Pathways to Peace and its Theosophical Associates • 284

Corinne McLaughlin and Gordon Davidson • 285

CHAPTER 13: PIERRE TEILHARD DE CHARDIN • 286

The Emerging "Common Soul of Humanity" • 287

The Bleak Eschatology of the "Omega Point" • 288

"Faith in Progress" • 288

Apologetics for Totalitarianism • 289

Balancing "Laissez Faire" with "Firmness" • 293

A Pragmatic, Evolutionary Case for Euthanasia and Eugenics • 294

Darwinian Racism • 296

World War II as a "Crisis of Birth" for Humanity • 299

Atom Bombs: Heralding the Coming of the "Spirit of the Earth" • 300

The Coming "Separation" of Reactionaries and Progressives • 301

"The Age of Nations Has Passed" • 302

Exalting "Planning" and Use of Man's Power • 302

Evolutionary Utopia: "War in a Naturally Sublimated Form" • 303

The Vatican's 1962 Warning Against Teilhard's Works • 304

A Present-day Vatican "Compromise" With Teilhard? • 304

CHAPTER 14: ROBERT MULLER • 306

Heterodox Theology and Cosmology • 306

Building a New World Order and Establishing "Proper
    Earth Government" • 308

The Fate of Opponents: "A Special Corral of the Universe" • 312

Muller's Theosophical Connections • 313

CHAPTER 15: BARBARA MARX HUBBARD • 316

    Inverted Theology: "We Are Gods!" • 316

    New Morality, From the Womb to the Tomb • 319

    The Coming "Selection" of Mankind • 320

    Atom Bombs and "Conscious Evolution" • 323

    The New Order: "The Next Stage of Individualism" • 324

    Barbara Marx Hubbard and Theosophy • 324

    A Well-Connected "Futurist" • 326

CHAPTER 16: NEALE DONALD WALSCH • 327

    Walsch's Blob God, an Evolving "God" of Good and Evil • 327

    Demoting Jesus to "Highly Evolved Being" • 328

    Denying Death, Praising the "Cosmic Wheel" • 329

    "Hitler Went To Heaven" • 330

    A Relativist, Utilitarian "God" • 331

    Libertine Theology • 332

    Libertine Practice: Free Love, Communal Parenting, and Euthanasia • 333

    The Judgments of Walsch's Tolerant God • 336

    Grains of Truth Amidst the New Age Sewage • 337

    Overthrowing the Churches and Proclaiming the New Gospel • 339

    The Apocalyptic Choice: Utopia or Doom • 341

    Communism and World Government, as the Extraterrestrials Do It • 342

    Walsch's Heroes and Allies • 346

    Neale Donald Walsch and Theosophy • 347

CHAPTER 17: THE INVERTED SPIRITUALITY AND POLITICS OF THE NEW AGE MOVEMENT • 348

PART III: LEVIATHAN RISING: THE GLOBALIST ALLIES OF THE URI

    Point : Counterpoint • 355

    The Coercive Utopians of the 21st Century • 358

CHAPTER 18: MIKHAIL GORBACHEV, "MAN WITH A STILL-UNFULFILLED DESTINY" • 359

    "The Socialist Idea is Inextinguishable" • 359

    "Nature Is My God" • 361

    Gorbachev's Smallpox Hoard • 361

The "Last Remaining Global Leader"? • 362

CHAPTER 19: THE STATE OF THE WORLD FORUM • 365

Aims: "Re-inventing the World" and "Global Governance" • 365

Out With Traditional Religions; In With the New Age • 366

"Progressive" Global Governance • 370

Implementing the "Population Plan" • 372

The Lighter Side of the Forum: Nude Marches, Tantric Sex,
    and Entheogens • 373

"Simple Living" for the Global Elite • 375

Post-modern Shamanism • 376

The Forum's Elite Supporters • 378

CHAPTER 20: THE EARTH CHARTER • 380

The Earth Charter: a Velvet Glove • 384

The Green Cross Philosophy: The Earth Charter's Iron Fist • 386

CHAPTER 21: MAURICE STRONG • 389

CHAPTER 22: THE WORLD ECONOMIC FORUM • 393

**CHAPTER 23: ARE THE NEW AGE AND GLOBALIST MOVEMENTS A
    CONSPIRACY? • 396**

**PART IV: IN CONCLUSION: FROM THE "ANTI-TRADITION"
    TO THE "COUNTER-TRADITION"**

Point : Counterpoint • 401

CHAPTER 24: THE ASCENDANCY OF THE "ANTI-TRADITION" • 404

**CHAPTER 25: A SPECULATIVE POSTSCRIPT: AFTER THE "ANTI-TRADITION,"
    THE FINAL "COUNTER-TRADITION"? • 409**

An Advisory • 409

Abnormal Times • 409

The End of the Age?—Papal Warnings Against the Left • 410

An Apocalyptic Threat From the Right, as Well? • 413

The Two-Fold Threat: Lessons From History • 415

The Two-Fold Threat: Warnings From Scripture and Patristic   Tradition • 417

A False Hope: the "Great King" of the West and a Future "Holy Pope" • 419

Religious Sectarianism: Laying the Foundation for the Final   Deception • 421

Spiritual Vulnerability: the Fetishes of Authority and Obedience • 431

Outside the Church, Two Witnesses to the Dual Peril • 432

The Nihilist's Dark Prophecies: Friedrich Nietzsche • 432

The Warnings of a Sufi Metaphysician, René Guénon • 436

What Is To Be Done? • 438

Sed Contra: Against Extreme-Right "Solutions" to the Crisis • 440

A Challenge: Is Orthodoxy Better Than Heresy? • 447

APPENDIX I: THE URI CHARTER'S "PREAMBLE, PURPOSE, AND PRINCIPLES" • 449

APPENDIX II: URI'S GLOBAL LEADERSHIP • 452

A SELECTIVE BIBLIOGRAPHY • 455

AUTHOR'S BIOGRAPHY • 479

INDEX • 481

FOREWORD

False Dawn may be the most important book you read this year. Everyone, whether you consider yourself liberal or conservative, secular or devout, should heed its warning.

At a time when many of the religions are at war with each other, a simple notion is gaining popularity: that what humankind needs to save itself is a single über-religion and global governance that will bring humanity together in life-saving global harmony.

To understand why the idea of a one-world religion is such a bad idea, it may help to first understand why it can sound so good. Many supporters of a "one-world religion" have aims that, in fact, appear to be both visionary and vitally necessary. Throughout history, there have been endless divisive, bloodthirsty edicts from rabbis, Popes, ministers, and imams—demands for life-or-death allegiance to Yahweh, Christ, or Allah.

Now, our world is armed to the teeth, and members of all the great religions have access to nuclear weapons—weapons that we can use to act out the Apocalypse ourselves. There are teenaged Saudi fundamentalists who would happily immolate themselves to truck-nuke the White House, in order to avenge the Crusades. As some people see these dangers, they are creating a movement to unite the nations and the religions of the world, establishing a religious and political form of Esperanto in the hope for peace.

In *False Dawn*, Lee Penn reveals the history of this movement and its key contemporary champions—among whom are Mikhail Gorbachev and global power broker George Soros. (Strange bedfellows, indeed: Gorbachev, who seemingly fell on his sword to save Western civilization—and now wants to remake the world as a Green, and Soros, the tycoon who tanked the British pound and the Southeast Asian stock markets.) He also explains in chilling detail why the development of a "one-world religion" would be a disaster for us all.

I first became aware of *False Dawn* after reading Lee Penn's stories about the threat of a "one-world religion," articles that he had written for *New Oxford Review*, *Touchstone Magazine*, and the *Journal* of the Spiritual Counterfeits Project. I had known Lee for many years as a very perceptive and fair-minded scholar of religious issues, as someone who was suspicious of easy answers and who was not afraid to take unpopular stands. When I first read his accounts of the new world religion and its architects, Lee was helping me research a book, soon to be published by Grove-Atlantic, that traced mankind's concepts of immortality and the hereafter. During our collaboration, he reminded me that typically faiths that were meant to serve God end up serving men—after the original beliefs are corrupted by the very leaders who had vowed to protect them.

A one-world religion is only the latest, and certainly the greatest, example of this corruption of faith. In the new global village of Gorbachev and Soros, there would be only one chapel—an "interfaith temple" where worshippers would take spiritual direction from a new, alloyed sacred text. Such a "Scripture" would, presumably, combine all the best aspects of the Torah, the Bible, the Koran, and the wisdom of the East. In the broadest sense, *False Dawn* speaks to the worst aspect of the communications age: the destruction of all cultures through homogenization. We live in a time that may soon see kids in Modesto, California and kids in Calcutta, India all wearing the same clothes, playing the same sports, watching the same movies, and even using the same slang. In this same vein, we can see a world approaching in which these children all come together to worship some great amalgamated "savior."

Notwithstanding the tortuous compromises of faith that would be required, the idea that one could create a single, superior global spirituality makes no more sense than the notion of making a "perfect automobile" by combining the best parts from a Mercedes, a Cadillac, a Ferrari, and a Rolls-Royce. In either case, the result would be a jalopy that goes nowhere. However, to understand why so many powerful world leaders, from the political left and right alike, feel that a one-world religion is a world-saving panacea, you will have to take up *False Dawn*.

Lee Penn explains how a religion meant to satisfy everyone will be doomed to satisfy no one; he also suggests some vital solutions.

MARK CHRISTENSEN

(Mark Christensen is the author of two novels, *Aloha* and *Mortal Belladaywic*, and of nonfiction books, including *Build The Perfect Beast*, *The Sweeps: Behind the Scenes of Network TV*, and *Wildlife*. He has been a media columnist for *Rolling Stone*, and his work has appeared in other national publications, from *Playboy* to *Wired*. He is completing *Forever Young*, a book to be published by Grove-Atlantic, about man's search for spiritual and bodily immortality.)

EDITOR'S FOREWORD:

THE "COUNTER-INITIATION" DOCUMENTED
—A TRADITIONALIST PERSPECTIVE

LEE PENN, A TRADITIONAL EASTERN CHRISTIAN, is a rare workman of difficult and necessary information. Both his background in Marxist political activism, and his heartfelt and intelligently reasoned repentance of that ideology, have uniquely fitted him to be a first-rank religious investigative reporter of the latter days, a sort of religious Noam Chomsky. He retains the ability to gaze at the monstrous distortion and destruction of the human spirit in these times, without descending into "paranoia"—i.e., simplistic explanations for the purpose of allaying anxiety.

I hold to the doctrines of the Traditionalist School, as found in the writings of René Guénon and Ananda Coomaraswamy (often called the "founders" of the School), Frithjof Schuon, Titus Burckhardt, Martin Lings, Seyyed Hossein Nasr, Rama Coomaraswamy, James Cutsinger, et. al. The Traditionalists are "esoterists" who understand that esoterism cannot be a religion in itself; consequently, they emphasize the need for affiliation with one of the great world religions—in particular, Judaism, Christianity, Islam, Hinduism, or Buddhism. The Traditionalists are "universalists" in the sense that they believe that God has established more than one path (under the diverse forms of these religions) by which the human soul may return to Him. However, the Traditionalists are enemies of syncretism. The reason is this: since each world religion possesses all that the soul requires, mixing elements from different traditions denies the sufficiency of each, and creates a Frankenstein monster sewn together out of organically unrelated elements which God has not willed to unite. Traditionalists say that the unity of religions is present in the transcendent mystery and Oneness of the Divine Nature, and is not to be made manifest by human attempts to unite religions on Earth.

Lee Penn is not a Traditionalist in the sense that I have described, though in the years I have known him he has shown no tendency to proselytize me to Christianity (I am a Muslim), beyond making one formal invitation as is required of him by Christ's Great Commission. He also has shown a real understanding that, just as the ideologies of both "left" and "right" are equally bankrupt and equally likely to contribute, from their polarized perspectives, to the worst cultural, political and technological developments, so also the stance of the "promiscuous ecumenist" and that of the "rabid religious exclusivist" are destined to be equally of baleful use to the rulers of the darkness of this world.

So, I believe it is fitting that this book appear on the list of Sophia Perennis publications, a list that includes the twenty-three titles of the Collected Works of René Guénon in a new English translation. Of all the Traditionalists, Guénon was most able to unite pure metaphysics and comparative religion with social criticism—and even with investigative reporting, insofar as it related to the subversive pseudo-esoteric societies of his day. Two of his earliest books, *The Spiritist Fallacy* and *Theosophy: History of a Pseudo-Religion* (both available from Sophia Perennis), are exposés of the occult underworld of the first half of the 20th century. Guénon saw the occultists, Theosophists and spiritualists of that era as expressions of the "Anti-Tradition," those forces working in our time to destroy all valid religious expression so as to prepare the way for the regime of Antichrist. He believed that most of them were *unconscious* of the role they were playing (seeing that "the road to Hell is paved with good intentions"), but that a small number of them formed a conscious elite who knew very well what they were up to. Members of this elite acted as agents of the "Counter-Tradition;" their activities have been destined to lead to the "Counter-Initiation"—the satanic perversion not simply of religious doctrine and morality, but also of contemplative spirituality itself. Guénon's prophetic masterpiece, *The Reign of Quantity and the Signs of the Times*, draws the ultimate eschatological conclusions relative to the "Anti-Tradition," the "Counter-Initiation," and the mass breakthrough of malign "infra-psychic forces" that these spiritual movements have unleashed into the human world.

My own book, *The System of Antichrist: Truth and Falsehood in Postmodernism and the New Age* (Sophia Perennis, 2001), was a conscious attempt to update *The Reign of Quantity*. If Lee's book had been available to me when I wrote it, I would have quoted from it at length, since it provides, in so many areas, documented support for my own findings.

In *False Dawn*, with the help of over 3,000 footnotes, we finally have the "Counter-Tradition" *documented*—at least in terms of its visible religious and political expression. Lee Penn's research into the United Religions Initiative and allied movements demonstrates with the blinding clarity of "mere facts" that the pseudo-esoteric underworld of Guénon's time has mushroomed, and is now poised to make itself of great and terrible use to the global power elite. He also demonstrates how, as the influence of the New Age movement wanes on a popular level, it is progressively being adopted as a "contingency ideology" by elements of that same worldwide elite.

In our time, the political and economic ideologies of left and right, the doctrines of traditional religion, and even the dogmas of materialist science are losing cultural force. As the old belief systems wither, their fading power leaves a vast void of meaning in the mind of the human race. Nature, however, abhors a vacuum. So, we had better be very clear—if we can stand to look—about the nature and the intentions of those groups and forces that are poised to leap into this mental and spiritual void while claiming to fill it. In making this leap, the forces of the "Anti-Tradition" and the "Counter-Initiation" would (if God were to allow it) usher in a *post-human* age.

CHARLES UPTON

AUTHOR'S INTRODUCTION, WITH AN APOLOGIA

A NEW RELIGIOUS MOVEMENT, the United Religions Initiative (URI), is rising worldwide. This interfaith movement's stated aims are peace among religions and creation of "cultures of peace, justice and healing" for all. In the midst of a global "War on Terror" that may become an all-out war between the Islamic and Western world, such a movement has undeniable appeal.

The URI has attracted a disparate group of activists, and seems to be remarkably skillful in defusing tensions among them. Its proponents have included the Dalai Lama and churchmen from the state-approved churches in the People's Republic of China, pro-gay Episcopalians and anti-gay followers of the Rev. Sun Myung Moon, radical Muslims and radical feminists, as well as rich capitalist foundations and those who announce the spiritual bankruptcy of capitalism. Both George Soros and President George Bush have, in different ways, supported the URI. The movement's founder, Episcopal Bishop William Swing, is an avowed Republican, and voted for George W. Bush in 2000; that same year, at the end of a URI global conference, he raised his arms to join a Wiccan's invocation of Hekate and Hermes. Such is the URI's "unity in diversity." If it could create such a microcosm of unity among its followers since 1996, how might the URI unify the world in future years?

THE ARGUMENT, IN BRIEF

I am writing to warn the public worldwide against the activities of the United Religions Initiative, against its supporters within the New Age movement, and against the URI's globalist, utopian allies within the State of the World Forum, the World Economic Forum, and the Earth Charter movement.

The URI, which Bishop Swing of the Episcopal Church's Diocese of California launched in 1995, describes itself as "a growing global community dedicated to promoting enduring, daily interfaith cooperation, ending religiously motivated violence and creating cultures of peace, justice and healing for the Earth and all living beings."[1] The introduction to the URI Charter sets out the movement's planetary ambitions: "Working on all continents and across continents, people from different religions, spiritual expressions and indigenous traditions are creating unprecedented levels of enduring global cooperation.... The URI, in time, aspires to have the visibility and stature of the United Nations."[2]

Unfortunately, the URI has a grandiose agenda that goes far beyond its principal, publicly stated aim of promoting peace, tolerance, and non-violence among all religions and spiritual movements. As shown by the repeated, public speeches and writings of URI leaders and activists since the movement began in 1995, the URI and its allies propose the following:

• Squelching Christian evangelism, in the name of promoting inter-religious peace.

---

1. United Religions Initiative, "The United Religions Initiative Charter," http://www.uri.org/resources/publications/Charter%20PC%20format.doc, p1; downloaded 07/07/04 (cited below as URI, "Charter").

2. Ibid.

• Marginalizing orthodox Christians as "intolerant" and "fundamentalist."

• Preparing the way for a new, global spirituality that can accommodate domesticated forms of all current religions and spiritual movements.

• Promoting a new, collectivist "global ethic."

• The idea that the main goal of religion is social reform, rather than service to God.

• The idea that all religions and spiritual movements are equally true, and equally efficacious as ways to attain communion with God.

• Population control—especially in Third World countries.

• Providing a global podium and respectability for cultism, occultism, witchcraft, Theosophy, and other spiritually harmful religious movements.

This agenda isn't written directly into the Charter of the URI. However, it is plainly evident in the public statements and actions of URI leaders and their allies.

The URI arose out of, and is the culmination of, the interfaith movement that began with the 1893 Parliament of World Religions. Beginning with that conclave, the interfaith movement has facilitated the spread of non-Christian religions in the West, and has undermined Christian evangelization efforts in the rest of the world. The interfaith movement was, until the 1990s, primarily the province of religious reformers and political liberals. Since then, some Western government and corporate interests (such as those that participate in the State of the World Forum and the World Economic Forum) have been promoting the interfaith movement. Traditional religion, it seems to them, is bad for prosperity and stability.

The URI is not yet widely known; it is nevertheless important for these reasons:

• The URI's vision and mission are broader in scope than those of other interfaith organizations, and the URI collaborates with most of these groups.

• The URI has grown from a California-based movement of 55 people in the mid-1990s to a global movement of over 26,000 activists[1] in 56 countries,[2] with backing from prominent foundations and from Federal officials.

• The URI has gained significant support in the Third World—unlike other interfaith movements, whose support has been concentrated among liberal reformers in Europe and North America. (The appeal of the URI in the Third World appears to be its call for peace among religions; it is unlikely that members there are aware of the New Age, globalist, and utopian baggage that the URI carries.)

• The URI is building an ever-closer relationship with the UN and its agencies.

• In its documents, by the writings and speeches of its activists and leaders, and by the alliances it builds, the URI makes manifest the agenda of liberal globalists. Understanding the URI therefore sheds light on a social and political movement that is far more influential than the URI alone. The URI is a case study in a global pathology that may soon affect us all.

---

1. Charles Gibbs and Sally Mahé, *United Religions Initiative, Birth of a Global Community: Appreciative Inquiry in Action*, Lakeshore Publishers, 2004, p 289 (cited below as Gibbs/Mahé, *Birth of a Global Community*).

2. Statistics are from an analysis by Lee Penn of two URI documents from September 2004; see United Religions Initiative, "Cooperation Circles of the URI," http://www.uri.org/regionalnews/cclisting.asp, printed 09/23/04, and United Religions Initiative, "Affiliates," http://www.uri.org/regionalnews/affiliates/index.asp, printed 09/23/04. There are Cooperation Circles or Affiliates in 56 different countries as of September 2004, based on these two lists.

Associated with the URI are various organizations and movements that propose construction of a New World Order, in which global governance and globalized economics will supersede the national regimes and traditional societies that we have hitherto known. There are left-wing and right-wing factions among the globalists, but they agree that the Old World Order—including the sovereign nation-state and traditional religions—must go. To that end, some left-wing globalists (George Soros, among others) and some right-wing globalists (President George W. Bush, the U.S. State Department, and the Rev. Moon's Unification Church, among others) have supported the URI.

To a significant extent, New Age spirituality informs the leftist supporters of the New World Order. Prominent supporters of the URI and of globalism include Robert Muller, a former UN assistant secretary-general, best-selling metaphysical author Neale Donald Walsch, and futurist Barbara Marx Hubbard. These New Age writers have drawn inspiration from Theosophy, an occult spiritual movement that took its current form in 1875 with the founding of the Theosophical Society in New York City by Helena Blavatsky. The Lucis Trust (disciples of Alice A. Bailey, a Theosophist writer of the mid-20th century) and other Theosophists and occultists are on the record as supporters of the URI.

The writings of Blavatsky, Bailey, Muller, Marx Hubbard, and Walsch are a comprehensive anti-Gospel, setting forth a vision of spiritualized totalitarianism, moral chaos, and a politically correct form of Social Darwinism. These authors' teachings, repeated within their lengthy, sleep-inducing books, include the following:

• Praise for Lucifer, the light-bearer and giver of "Wisdom," because he awoke mankind in the Garden of Eden from its primal unconsciousness. For these New Age theorists, the Fall was really mankind's Ascent into knowledge and freedom.

• Proclaiming that we humans are gods, and that death is not real.

• Advocacy for population control—especially for the poor in the West and for the underdeveloped countries. This advocacy goes back to the late 1800s, when world population was a fraction of its current level.

• Support for eugenics and euthanasia.

• Contempt for traditional religions—with concentrated scorn directed at Judaism, evangelical Protestantism, and Roman Catholicism.

• Support for a new world order, a spiritualized form of Communism in which everyone will "share" everything.

• Apologetics for various and sundry dictators and authoritarian movements, of the extreme Right as well as the extreme Left.

• Acceptance of war and atomic weapons as instruments of human evolution.

• Forecasting a pending (and for them, desirable) "selection" of mankind, in which the progressives enter the New Age and the reactionaries face extinction. For the New Age apostles of "progressive" Social Darwinism, these casualties are a necessary price to pay for human evolution.

Many New Age and liberal Catholic supporters of the URI claim Pierre Teilhard de Chardin, a dissident 20th century Catholic priest and paleontologist, as a source of their own beliefs. Teilhard promoted some of the aberrant ideas listed above, and upheld "the right of the earth to organize itself by reducing, even by *force*, the reactionary and backwards elements."[1]

It should be noted that many New Age believers are unaware of the negative aspects of their mentors' teachings. Many people never study these writings at all; others pay attention only to what they agree with, ignoring their teachers' "hard sayings."

---

1. Pierre Teilhard de Chardin, *Letters to Léontine Zanta*, intro. by Robert Garric and Henri de Lubac, tr. by Richard Wall, Harper and Row, 1969, p 116, letter of January 26, 1936.

~

My own perspective is that of an orthodox Christian; I was Episcopalian until 1995, and have since made my spiritual home among Eastern Catholics and Eastern Orthodox. In this book, I discuss the problems with the URI, the New Age movement, and the globalists, issues that may be of interest to orthodox Christians of all confessions and denominations.

In 1907, Pope St. Pius X issued an encyclical letter, *On the Doctrines of the Modernists*, denouncing a theological movement within the Catholic Church that sought to accommodate the Spirit of the Age. The Pope said,

> But since the Modernists (as they are commonly and rightly called) employ a very clever artifice, namely, to present their doctrines without order and systematic arrangement into one whole, scattered and disjointed one from another, so as to appear to be in doubt and uncertainty, while they are in reality firm and steadfast, it will be of advantage, Venerable Brethren, to bring their teachings together here into one group, and to point out the connexion between them, and thus to pass to an examination of the sources of the errors, and to prescribe remedies for averting the evil.[1]

Regarding the beliefs of the URI, the globalists, and their New Age supporters, my intent is the same: to show their teachings in an organized fashion, and to show how their disparate views form a consistent—and grossly misguided—whole.

APOLOGIA: REPLIES TO A SKEPTIC'S QUESTIONS

Given this standpoint, some readers who are not Christian or "traditional" in any sense may wonder whether this book should be of interest to them. Here is how I would answer such skeptics:

Skeptic: I am not an orthodox Christian; why should I care about, or oppose, a movement that is against orthodox Christianity?

Author: For these reasons:

• You may be a liberal Christian, and believe that ancient understandings of scripture and tradition should be revised to meet the knowledge and requirements of the present day. Nevertheless, spiritual freedom is indivisible; the denial of liberty to one endangers the liberty of all. (That's why civil liberties groups often defend extremists and crazies.) The laws and precedents that are used now to suppress the people you fear and loathe can be used later to suppress you when power changes hands (which it always does, sooner or later).

• You may be a follower of Judaism, Islam, Hinduism, Buddhism, or of one of the indigenous religious movements. As I am not a practitioner or a scholar of these faiths, I cannot step inside your shoes to understand what concerns the world-view and agenda of the URI and the globalists may raise for you. However, it may be that some of the concerns of orthodox Christians are those that traditional believers in your own faith will share.

---

1. Pope St. Pius X, Encyclical Letter *Pascendi Dominici Gregis* (*On the Doctrines of the Modernists*), http://www.vatican.va/holy_father/pius_x/encyclicals/documents/hf_p-x_enc_19070908_pascendi-dominici-gregis_en.html, Paragraph 4.

• In addition, all believers in all religions should note that the URI and its globalist and New Age allies propose radical social and spiritual change that would affect everyone on the planet. If orthodox Christianity is taken out of the picture—as some of the New Age authors propose—who will the reformers take on next? Will the traditions that you cherish, the memories of which may grace your childhood, survive? Will your children be free to believe and live as you and your ancestors, of blessed memory, have done?

• In the name of pluralism and diversity, URI activists and their New Age allies mix and match beliefs and practices from a wide range of religions and spiritual movements. As a rule, these reformers take attractive items out of context, redefine them, and put them to use in a way that no traditional believer in other religions ever would. (My editor Charles Upton—a Sufi Muslim scholar and an expert on comparative religion—has identified some of these distortions; read the footnotes as well as the main text.) To put it crudely: the syncretists are spiritual magpies. These scavengers steal what they want, put it to selfish use, and befoul what they touch. Will you trust such people to shape a new spirituality for the new millennium?

Skeptic: So what are you, some kind of fundamentalist?

Author: I believe what is set forth in the Creed of the ancient and undivided Church:

I believe in one God, the Father Almighty, Maker of heaven and earth, and of all things visible and invisible; And in one Lord Jesus Christ, the Son of God, the Only-Begotten, begotten of the Father before all worlds, Light of Light, Very God of Very God, begotten not made; of one essence with the Father, by Whom all things were made: Who for us men and for our salvation came down from heaven, and was incarnate of the Holy Spirit and the Virgin Mary, and was made man; And was crucified also for us under Pontius Pilate, and suffered and was buried; The third day He rose again, according to the Scriptures; And ascended into heaven, and sits at the right hand of the Father; And He shall come again with glory to judge the living and the dead; Whose Kingdom shall have no end. And I believe in the Holy Spirit, the Lord and Giver of Life, Who proceeds from the Father, Who with Father and Son together is worshipped and glorified, Who spoke by the prophets. And I believe in One Holy, Catholic and Apostolic Church. I acknowledge one Baptism for the remission of sins. I look for the Resurrection of the dead and the Life of the world to come. Amen.[1]

I am a Christian, baptized and chrismated to serve Christ, who is my Lord and Savior. I am obliged to share the Faith with those who might be receptive to it—recognizing that my deeds provide a witness (for good or for ill) that is louder than any words that I utter.

All mankind was created by God, and all are held in existence by Him. Just as all the creation that there is, is by and through Christ, so also all salvation is by and through Christ. Nevertheless, I do not, and dare not, judge the salvation or spiritual state of non-Christians. God is loving, merciful, and just, and will do all things possible to bring all to Him. As Christ said, "And I have other sheep, that are not of this fold; I must bring them also, and they will heed my voice. So there shall be one flock, one shepherd." (John 10:16). Christ continues, "And I, when I am lifted up from the earth, will draw all men to myself." (John 12:32). God is in charge of evangelization, and does not need televangelists or door-to-door salesmen to complete the job.

The Apostle Paul testifies likewise: "When Gentiles who have not the law do by nature what the law requires, they are a law to themselves, even though they do not have the law. They show that what the law requires is written on their hearts, while their conscience also bears witness and their conflicting thoughts accuse or perhaps excuse them on that day when, according to my gospel, God judges the secrets of men by Christ Jesus." (Rom. 2:14–16)

---

1. The Nicene Creed, as printed in the *Orthodox Study Bible: New Testament and Psalms*, Thomas Nelson Publishers, 1993, pp755–756.

In this spirit, the Catholic Church teaches,

Those who, through no fault of their own, do not know the Gospel of Christ or his Church, but who nevertheless seek God with a sincere heart, and, moved by grace, try in their actions to do his will as they know it through the dictates of their conscience—those too may achieve eternal salvation. Nor shall divine providence deny the assistance necessary for salvation to those who, without any fault of theirs, have not yet arrived at an explicit knowledge of God, and who, not without grace, strive to lead a good life. Whatever good or truth is found amongst them is considered by the Church to be a preparation for the Gospel and given by him who enlightens all men that they may at length have life.[1]

I can affirm where I have found grace; it is not my job to state where grace is not. Furthermore, I accept—fully—what the Catholic Church declared at Vatican II:

The Vatican Council declares that the human person has a right to religious freedom. Freedom of this kind means that all men should be immune from coercion on the part of individuals, social groups and every human power so that, within due limits, nobody is forced to act against his convictions nor is anyone to be restrained from acting in accordance with his convictions in religious matters in private or in public, alone or in associations with others. The Council further declares that the right to religious freedom is based on the very dignity of the human person as known through the revealed word of God and by reason itself.[2]

You, dear skeptic, get to decide: is this fundamentalism? Are those who believe as I do a threat to peace?

Skeptic: Are you in favor of religious division, then?

Author: There are two very different movements for religious unity, and many people confuse them. I believe orthodox Christians should respond differently to these movements.

The movement for unity among Christians is the ecumenical movement. I believe that Christ wills that Christians should be united. At the Last Supper, He prayed for unity among the Apostles, and for unity among those who would follow them, through the centuries: "I do not pray for these only, but also for those who believe in me through their word, that they may all be one; even as thou, Father, art in me, and I in thee, that they also may be in us, so that the world may believe that thou hast sent me." (John 17:20–21) Division among Christians is a scandal: a stumbling-block for those who seek truth, and a witness against the Gospel. This book does not criticize, or pertain to, the ecumenical movement. I desire to see the day that all Christians can receive the Eucharist at any Christian altar, but do not venture any suggestions (aside from prayer and love) on how this might be brought about.

The interfaith movement, the quest for unity among all religions and spiritual expressions, is a different matter altogether. As the movement has taken shape since 1893, it is inextricably tied to the quest for a New Spirituality that would unify the planet in a New World Order. The URI is the fullest expression of this movement now. This movement is a foe of traditional Christianity; it seeks to domesticate the other ancient religions as well, subordinating all faiths to seek a "Kingdom" of this world. Followers of traditional religions who embrace the present-day interfaith movement will find themselves in the position of sheep who negotiate with wolves about the dinner menu.

That said, there are some forms of interfaith cooperation that would be desirable:

• Collaboration on corporal works of mercy: negotiating an end to wars, feeding the hungry, care for the sick, housing the homeless, and the like.
• Collaboration on behalf of human rights and justice, building on the Natural Law, the morality that is built

---

1. Vatican II; *Lumen Gentium*, section 16, in Austin Flannery, O.P., General Editor, *Vatican Council II: The Conciliar and Post-Conciliar Documents*, 1992 rev. ed., Costello Publishing Company, Northpoint, New York, pp 367–368.
2. Vatican II; *Dignitatis Humanae*, 7 December 1965, section 2, in ibid., p800.

into the conscience of all men. (C.S. Lewis illustrated this shared tradition, the *Tao*, in his appendix to *The Abolition of Man*, using instances from sacred texts worldwide.)[1] Obviously, people of different faiths should cooperate to oppose abortion, human cloning and human trafficking, sweatshops, torture, and aggressive war; likewise, all should support religious freedom.

• Education is beneficial—not in order to "prove" that all religions really are the same, but to dispel false or inadequate information that people may have about other faiths and their adherents.

None of these activities require or promote the utopian, syncretic beliefs that are integral to the URI and other present-day interfaith organizations.

In any case, no interfaith umbrella group is needed for religious leaders and teachers to tell their own followers to be peaceful and charitable toward members of other faiths. Nor is an interfaith movement needed for religious leaders to exercise their authority to ensure that this is done.

Note also that this book is, in its own way, an interfaith effort in support of Tradition,[2] the *Tao* that C.S. Lewis illustrated. I am Byzantine Catholic; my editor is Sufi Muslim; I have received essential insights and aid from Jews and from Christians in all the major confessions: Catholic, Eastern Orthodox, Anglican, and Reformed Protestant alike.

Skeptic: Do you believe in use of force, bribery, or "holy deception" to advance the Christian cause?

Author: No, not at all. Opposition to force, fraud, enticement, and manipulation in the name of religion is the one thing that the URI is *right* about. As the *Catechism of the Catholic Church* says, "One may not do evil so that good may result from it."[3]

Christ himself firmly rebuked his disciples for considering use of force against those who rejected him:

And it came to pass, when the time was come that he should be received up, he steadfastly set his face to go to Jerusalem, And sent messengers before his face: and they went, and entered into a village of the Samaritans, to make ready for him. And they did not receive him, because his face was as though he would go to Jerusalem. And when his disciples James and John saw this, they said, 'Lord, wilt thou that we command fire to come down from heaven, and consume them, even as Elias did?' But he turned, and rebuked them, and said, 'Ye know not what manner of spirit ye are of. For the Son of man is not come to destroy men's lives, but to save them.' And they went to another village." (Luke 9:51–56, KJV)

Skeptic: Do you believe that the adherents of the URI are all misguided? Do you think that the movement is entirely evil?

Author: No, to both questions.

Many people who turn to the URI seek peace among religions, and are distressed—rightly—by the epidemic spread of religious hatred and violence. These seekers mean well and have a good goal. However, some people within the URI and its globalist, utopian allies have a far wider, and far worse, agenda in mind.

As for the URI itself: despite the movement's many errors, some of its chapters are doing valuable works of mercy—caring for the sick and the poor, and negotiating cease-fires in civil wars. The movement's leaders and activists are a mixed bag; peacemakers work side-by-side with globalists, utopians,

---

1. C.S. Lewis, "Illustrations of the *Tao*," in *The Abolition of Man*, Macmillan Publishing Co., Inc., 1947, paperback ed. 1955, pp 95–121.

2. For further discussion of this Tradition, see the Editor's Foreword.

3. *Catechism Of The Catholic Church*, Second Edition, Libreria Editrice Vaticana, 1997, section 1756, p 435 (cited below as *Catechism*).

cultists, and occultists. Bishop Swing, the founder of the URI, himself sometimes speaks a sober, vital message of peace—while at other times raising his hands with the Wiccans[1] and hailing "a spirit of colossal energy" being "born in the loins of the earth."[2]

Skeptic: You're against global governance. But humanity's problems are worldwide, and need a global solution. What, other than a global government, can deal with global corporations, global warming, and emerging plagues?

Author: This is part of mankind's predicament. Our problems are indeed worldwide. However, those who seek to govern and re-make the world are, by reason of that dark lust for power, unfit to do so. Nation-states are not a perfect way to run the world; far from it. My task is to remind everyone that no matter how hot this particular frying pan is, leaping into the fire is no solution.

Skeptic: You're against the Earth Charter and other plans to equitably redistribute wealth from the rich to the poor. How can any spiritual person be for capitalism?

Author: An individualist, capitalist, market economy does indeed rely on mankind's greed to work; from the Christian perspective, it's a bad system. The others are worse. Socialism and collectivism have been tried, in many forms around the world. National Socialism, Communism, Peronism, Fascism, Francoism, and other authoritarian social experiments have claimed tens of millions of victims—the dead, the imprisoned, the tortured, the exiled, the dispossessed—since 1914. Nor is European-style social democracy the answer, even though it is far more benign than the aforementioned dictatorial systems. The key question is this: if European social democracy is so good materially and spiritually, why aren't Europeans having enough children to replace (let alone increase) their population? In economics as with international relations, I see no humanly attainable solutions that bring us to Utopia, or anywhere near it.

Skeptic: Why do you see the patterns that you do? The participants in these movements deny that they intend what you claim. You're a conspiracy theorist!

Author: Often, those who are committed to a movement—whether it be the interfaith movement, the movement for globalism, or a religious sect—are totally committed to their party's presuppositions and goals. Theirs is the viewpoint of a lover, not that of an analyst, a scholar, or a critic. An outsider can often readily see what the committed activists cannot. (In similar fashion, neighbors and relatives might immediately perceive the neuroses of a dysfunctional family—maladies that the members themselves might not see until they have experienced a crisis and received intensive counseling.)

As for the conspiracy question: I do identify common beliefs and goals among the "progressive" religious and secular globalists; their shared world-view and mutual sympathies are obvious. I am not attempting to identify some central organization that governs these movements; I do not believe that such a conspiracy exists. Neither the Federal Reserve Bank nor the Council on Foreign Relations, two common targets of conspiracy theorists, appear in this book.

Skeptic: All of this sounds like the Republican Party line. Is this a public relations effort for them?

1. Donald Frew, Covenant of the Goddess, "1999–2000 Interfaith Report," http://www. cog.org/interfaith/cogdf00.html, printed 2/8/03.

2. Bishop William Swing, "Opening Address," United Religions Initiative, Stanford University, June 23–27, 1997, http://www.united-religions.org/youth/welcome/swingspeech.htm, printed 1997; no longer on the Net at this address. This passage is also cited in Gibbs/Mahé, *Birth of a Global Community*, p107. Swing's speech may, as of 2004, be found on-line with the "Wayback Machine," a web archive research tool, at http://web.archive.org/web/19991023022803/http://www.united-religions. org/youth/welcome/swingspeech.htm, printed 08/02/04.

Author: No, not at all. I am not active in any political party. By contrast, Bishop Swing, the founder of the URI, said in the summer of 2004 that "I'm a Republican. I voted for George W. Bush."[1] In turn, President Bush has congratulated Swing for his interfaith work, and praised the URI.[2] Opposition to the URI, and to globalism and other utopian ideologies, does not fit into present-day "left/right" categories.

Skeptic: If you're not a Republican, you must be a fascist. You certainly talk like a reactionary!

Author: Here's what I believe about government and human rights, directly out of the *Declaration of Independence*:

> We hold these truths to be self-evident, that all men are created equal, that they are endowed by their Creator with certain unalienable Rights, that among these are Life, Liberty and the pursuit of Happiness.—That to secure these rights, Governments are instituted among Men, deriving their just powers from the consent of the governed,—That whenever any Form of Government becomes destructive of these ends, it is the Right of the People to alter or to abolish it, and to institute new Government, laying its foundation on such principles and organizing its powers in such form, as to them shall seem most likely to effect their Safety and Happiness.[3]

As for the purpose of politics, C. S. Lewis sums it up in *Mere Christianity* better than I could:

> The State exists simply to promote and to protect the ordinary happiness of human beings in this life. A husband and wife chatting over a fire, a couple of friends having a game of darts in a pub, a man reading a book in his own room or digging in his own garden—that is what the State is there for. And unless they are helping to increase and prolong and protect such moments, all the laws, parliaments, armies, courts, police, economics, etc., are simply a waste of time.[4]

I altogether reject Utopianism, of the Left or of the Right. It is a lethal political and spiritual disease, an error which the *Catechism of the Catholic Church* condemns as "secular messianism" and "intrinsically perverse."[5]

Such acceptance of human limitations leaves plenty of room for any of us to undertake the corporal and spiritual works of mercy that God asks of us. C. S. Lewis puts this into perspective in his essay "The World's Last Night." In bidding us to remember that Christ is coming again to judge the living and the dead (and that the Second Coming could happen at any time), Lewis says,

> Frantic administration of panaceas to the world is certainly discouraged by the reflection that 'this present' might be 'the world's last night'; sober work for the future, within the limits of ordinary morality and prudence, is not. For what comes is Judgment: happy are those whom it finds laboring in their vocations, whether they were merely going out to feed the pigs or laying good plans to deliver humanity a hundred years hence from some great evil. The curtain has indeed now fallen. Those pigs will never be fed, the great campaign against White Slavery or Governmental Tyranny will never in fact proceed to victory. No matter; you were at your post when the Inspection came.[6]

---

1. Bob Williams, "Swing marks 25th year as Bay Area bishop (Daybook)," *Episcopal News Service* (*ENS*) interview of Bishop Swing, August 9, 2004, http://ecusa.anglican.org/3577_4 8087_ENG_HTM.htm, printed 08/10/04 (cited below as Williams, "Swing Marks 25th year," *ENS*, 08/09/04).

2. International Diplomacy Council, letter from President Bush, November 6, 2002, http://www.diplomacy.org/idc1140101.html, printed 02/17/03 and 08/16/04.

3. The National Archives, "Declaration of Independence," http://www.archives.gov/national_archives_experience/declaration_transcript.html, viewed 02/27/04.

4. C. S. Lewis, *Mere Christianity*, Macmillan Publishing Co., 1960, ch. 8, p169.

5. *Catechism*, section 676, p177.

6. C. S. Lewis, "The World's Last Night," ch. 7 of *The World's Last Night And Other Essays*, Harcourt Brace Jovanovich, 1973, pp111–112.

I have used this dialogue with a skeptic to make clear the principles and beliefs that led me to write this book, and have guided its composition.

In addition, there was motivation from a Biblical admonition against silence in the face of evil. The LORD had said to Ezekiel: "If I say to the wicked, 'You shall surely die,' and you give him no warning, nor speak to warn the wicked from his wicked way, in order to save his life, that wicked man shall die in his iniquity; but his blood I will require at your hand. But if you warn the wicked, and he does not turn from his wickedness, or from his wicked way, he shall die in his iniquity; but you will have saved your life." (Ezek. 3:18–19)

A ROAD MAP FOR READERS

This foreword is impressionistic, without an attempt to prove my case in detail.

Those who venture into the main text will find an abundance of documentation for the argument that I make against the URI, its globalist allies, and the pro-URI "gurus" in the New Age movement. These movements' own literature makes the case against them, for those who have eyes to see and ears to hear. I have paid the URI and its associates the compliment of taking them seriously; those who have "a mouth speaking great things" (Dan. 7: 8) deserve such scrutiny and exposure.

At the end of the book is a postscript, speculating on the aftermath of the movements now in train for economic, political, and religious globalization. The postscript, like this foreword, is impressionistic. I offer it not as a prophecy, but as a way to get readers to consider some of the unexpected side effects and complications that the current drive for a New World Order may pose for mankind. Evil may come at us from the Right as well as from the Left—or from both directions simultaneously. Those who fail to scan the entire horizon for political and spiritual peril may find themselves unexpectedly overwhelmed.

Anyone who has not examined the interfaith, New Age, and globalist movements previously might find the participants and their activities to be confusing, and may need orientation. My answers to the following questions are brief. For the details, complexities, nuances, and "hot parts" (of which there are many), proceed to the body of this book.

- *Is this book fiction or non-fiction? Real-life or satire?*

Alas, it is all non-fiction. I would rather that the bizarre activities and beliefs that I have uncovered were confined to the pages of light thrillers and inane, preachy end-times novels. The reality is otherwise. And nothing herein is satire—although some of the words and deeds of the New Age enthusiasts make it appear that they are parodying themselves.

- *What organizations are involved, and how are they associated?*

The following organizations form a loose network of associates with a shared world-view. Mutual sympathy and common belief, not a chain of command or a shared directorate, bring them together. (As you look over this list of movements, consider the scope of their ambition. Isn't it reassuring to know that so many well-connected *bien-pensants* want to create a "new civilization" for us all? In any case, we won't need to worry about *voting* on these reformers' ideas; it will all be done for us, and for our own good.)

⌇ THE UNITED RELIGIONS INITIATIVE (URI)

The United Religions Initiative (URI) is a fast-growing interfaith movement launched in 1995 by William E. Swing, one of the Episcopal Church's prominent liberal bishops. The movement describes itself as "a growing global community dedicated to promoting enduring, daily interfaith cooperation, ending religiously motivated violence and creating cultures of peace, justice and healing for the Earth and all living beings."[1] The URI Charter says, "The URI, in time, aspires to have the visibility and stature of the United Nations."[2] The URI grew out of the post-1893 interfaith movement, and exemplifies that broader movement's utopian, anti-traditional world-view.

In mid-2004, Bishop Swing glowed with optimism about the prospects for the URI: "Our cooperation circles [URI local chapters] have gone from none at charter signing, to having 100, to having 200; now we're almost having 300, and we'll soon have 1,000. We're in 50 countries in the world; we have people from 80 different religions; we have offices on five continents—and we get more than 1 million hits a month on our website."[3]

⌇ THE LUCIS TRUST

The Lucis Trust is a Theosophical organization with offices on Wall Street in New York, in London, and in Geneva. It was founded by Alice and Foster Bailey in 1922. (Its publishing house was initially the Lucifer Publishing Company,[4] until it was renamed Lucis Publishing Company). In 1923, the Baileys established the Arcane School, "a correspondence school presenting the principles of the Ageless Wisdom through esoteric meditation, study and service as a way of life" for those who wish to pursue the path of "new age discipleship."[5] More than 80 years later, the Trust keeps the Arcane School in operation, and ensures that Alice Bailey's 24 long-winded books remain in print.

The Lucis Trust supports the URI, the Temple of Understanding, and other spiritual and political movements for a "New World Order."

⌇ THE GORBACHEV FOUNDATION AND GREEN CROSS INTERNATIONAL

Mikhail Gorbachev, the last premier of the Soviet Union, founded the Gorbachev Foundation in January 1992, within a month of the December 1991 dissolution of the USSR. The Foundation's stated goal is "to help assert democratic values and moral, humanistic principles in the life of society. In a globalizing world, the search for guidelines in building a new, more equitable international order is increasingly important. The overall motto of the Gorbachev Foundation is *Toward a New Civilization*."[6]

Gorbachev also founded Green Cross International, a global environmentalist movement. Green Cross, established in 1993, "promotes legal, ethical and behavioral norms that ensure basic changes in the values, actions and attitudes of government, the private sector and civil society, necessary to build

---

1. URI, "Charter," p1.

2. Ibid.

3. Williams, "Swing Marks 25th Year," *ENS*, 08/09/04.

4. See, for example, the title page of Alice A. Bailey, *Initiation, Human and Solar*, First Edition, Lucifer Publishing Co., 135 Broadway, New York City, 1922.

5. Arcane School, "Frequently asked questions about the Arcane School," http://www.lucistrust.org/arcane/faq.php, printed 08/09/04.

6. The Gorbachev Foundation, "About Us," http://www.gorby.ru/en/rubrs.asp?rubr_id =302, printed 08/09/04.

a sustainable global community."[1] As part of their quest for "basic changes" worldwide, Green Cross supports the Earth Charter Initiative, a drive for UN adoption of a far-reaching environmental ethical code. Gorbachev has said, "My hope is that this charter will be a kind of Ten Commandments, a 'Sermon on the Mount,' that provides a guide for human behavior toward the environment in the next century and beyond."[2]

There are no direct ties between either of Gorbachev's organizations and the URI, but the URI supports the Earth Charter. All of these movements share the goal of building a "new civilization," as envisioned by affluent Western liberals and by ex-Communist leftists.

ཉྫྫ THE STATE OF THE WORLD FORUM

The State of the World Forum (SWF) is a spin-off from the Gorbachev Foundation.[3] It was intended by Mikhail Gorbachev to establish "a kind of global brain trust to focus on the present and future of our civilization."[4] Since its founding in 1995, the SWF has drawn crowds of current and has-been political leaders, corporate CEOs, social change activists, and New Age "gurus" to its luxurious meetings. There, they discuss creation of "an ever more inclusive and holistic approach to global governance."[5] At SWF conclaves, shamanism and tantra are "in," and traditional monotheism is definitely "out."

The SWF co-sponsored the URI's first global summit meeting in 1996. Since then, there have been no formal links between the two organizations. However, they do have donors and activists in common. By this means, these organizations promote what URI Global Council member Donald Frew describes as "the Western liberal social agenda. It covers many groups, and those who are in one group are likely to be in another. It is a world-view, *not* a conspiracy."[6]

ཉྫྫ THE EARTH CHARTER INITIATIVE

The URI is one of many liberal organizations that has lined up to support the Earth Charter, a revolutionary set of ecological principles put forward in 1994 by Mikhail Gorbachev, Maurice Strong, Steven

1. Green Cross International, "Mission," http://www.greencrossinternational.net/greencrossFamily/index.html, printed 08/09/04.

2. Green Cross International, "Interview—Environment: 'Act Globally, not Nationally,'" *Los Angeles Times*, May 8, 1997, http://www.greencrossinternational.net/GreenCrossFamilygorby/newspeeches/interviews/laTimes.html, printed 05/09/03. In recent years, Gorbachev has said the same, in less picturesque fashion: "The Earth Charter opens a new phase not only in ecological movement, but also in the world's public life. We must do everything we can, so that this Charter is accepted exactly as it was designed: a set of vitally important rules." (Mikhail Gorbachev, as quoted in The Earth Charter Initiative, *Biannual Report* 2002–2003, Earth Charter International Secretariat, http://www.earthcharter.org/files/resources/Biannual%20Report.pdf, p10, printed 06/22/04.)

3. The Gorbachev Foundation/USA convened the first SWF in San Francisco in 1995; the SWF has since become a separate non-profit organization. (State of the World Forum, "Gorbachev Foundation USA 10th Anniversary Celebration," http://www.worldforum.org/home/fmsd_2.htm, printed 2/6/03).

4. State of the World Forum, "The World's Religions and The Emerging Global Civilization: An Interfaith Summit Conference June 24–28, 1996 San Francisco," *Pacific Church News*, April/May 1996, p33. A note at the end of the article says, "All quotes are from material distributed by the State of the World Forum."

5. State of the World Forum—Commission on Globalisation, "Commission Overview: Strategic Context—The Challenge of Globalisation," http://www.commissiononglobalization.org/overview/main.htm, printed 05/23/03.

6. Interview of Donald Frew by Lee Penn, 3/28/03.

Rockefeller, and others. (Rockefeller had told ecological activists in 1998 that "One can think of the Earth Charter with its tripartite structure as a Tree of Life."[1])

Among the many supporters of the Earth Charter are the US Conference of Mayors, the Sierra Club, the Rosicrucians, the School of Ageless Wisdom, the Florida Cannabis Action Network, and about 100 Catholic religious orders. The Earth Charter Initiative seeks UN passage of the Earth Charter, and hopes that its principles will be written into binding international treaties. The killer idea—literally—in the Charter's "green" rhetoric is the call to "Ensure universal access to health care that fosters reproductive health and responsible reproduction."[2] In UN circles, "reproductive health" includes artificial contraception, abortion, and sterilization.

☶ The World Economic Forum

The World Economic Forum (WEF), founded in 1971, considers itself to be critical in setting each year's global agenda:

> It has become the premier gathering of international leaders from business, government, academia, media, non-governmental and other civil organizations. From its origins as a small business conference in the Swiss Alps, the Annual Meeting has grown to become the event where the leading issues confronting humanity are discussed and debated at the start of each calendar year. . . . The Forum believes that progress can best be achieved when governments and business can freely and productively discuss challenges and work together to mold solutions. The unique atmosphere of the Annual Meeting creates opportunities for the formation of global partnerships and alliances.[3]

Forbes reported that the 2004 annual meeting had "2,280 participants from 94 countries, including some 800 chairmen and chief executives, billionaires like Michael Dell and Bill Gates, 203 ambassadors and 31 heads of state and government."[4] WEF leaders—who include Earth Charter activist Maurice Strong—have made it clear that they support "global governance."[5]

There are no direct ties between the URI and the WEF. However, to the extent that the WEF meetings address religion, they support New Age rather than traditional beliefs.

· *Who are the leaders of these movements, and how are they related to each other?*

☶ Bishop William E. Swing, founder of the URI

William E. Swing (1936—) has been the Bishop of the Episcopal Diocese of California since 1979; he plans to retire in 2006 to give full time to the URI.[6] His jurisdiction, fittingly, includes San Francisco,

---

1. Steven Rockefeller, "Update on Earth Charter Drafting Process," October 14, 1998; this is on the web page "International Environment Forum," 6–8 November 1998, http://www.bcca.org/ief/dchar98c.htm, printed 07/02/04. The same sentence is in the Earth Charter discussion, and is stated as "Adapted from Earth Council documents," in Gerald O. Barney et al., *Threshold 2000: Critical Issues and Spiritual Values for a Global Age*, Millennium Institute and CoNexus Press, 1998, p146.

2. The Earth Charter Initiative, "The Earth Charter," "II. Ecological Integrity"—Article 7, http://www.earthcharter.org/files/charter/charter.pdf, printed 03/24/04.

3. World Economic Forum, "About the Annual Meeting," http://www.weforum.org/site/homepublic.nsf/Content/Annual+Meeting+2003%5CAbout+the+Annual+Meeting, printed 01/03/03.

4. Michael Freedman, "World Economic Forum: Sunny Days in Snowy Davos," *Forbes.com*, January 21, 2004, http://www.forbes.com/2004/01/21/cz_mf_0121econdavos.html, printed 01/23/04.

5. World Economic Forum, "Global Governance: What Needs to Change?," http://www.weforum.org/site/knowledgenavigator.nsf/Content/Global%20Governance:%20Wh at%20Needs%20to%20Change%3F, printed 03/15/03.

6. Episcopal News Service, "Bishop Swing of California announces retirement," October 26, 2004, http://www.episcopalchurch.org/3577_53388_ENG_HTM.htm, printed 11/05/04.

Marin County, Berkeley, and most of the remainder of the San Francisco Bay Area. Swing's avocation is golf, and he made the championship cut for the 1994 AT&T Pebble Beach Pro-Am tournament. (In this respect, he followed in his father's footsteps. In 2004, Swing said, "My father was a professional golfer, and we lived at a country club."[1]) Swing conceived the idea of the URI in 1993, and has vowed "to commit the rest of my life to an initiative that would create a United Religions."[2] He has been married since 1961, and has two children.

Bishop Swing had long been a low-key liberal within the Episcopal Church, the U. S. branch of the Anglican Communion. Until the mid-1990s, he had avoided the public controversies associated with James Pike, Jack Spong, and other flamboyant, gadfly Episcopal bishops. In 1990, he ran for election in the Diocese of Washington DC, but was not chosen.[3] In 1996, Swing turned down nomination to run for Presiding Bishop of the Episcopal Church.

With Swing's acceptance of Matthew Fox as a priest in 1994, and with his launch of the URI in 1995, he has taken a higher profile on the left wing of the Anglican Communion. In 1997, he boasted to a San Francisco-based gay activist that "I've probably ordained more gays and lesbians than the rest of the Anglican church put together."[4] And in early 2003, he told the Patriarch of Constantinople that "I have ordained more women than any other bishop in the history of the Church and would be glad to talk about my experience;" the Patriarch replied, "I don't want to know your experience."[5]

Swing nevertheless continues to present himself as conservative. During the mid-2004 celebration of his 25th anniversary as Bishop of California, Swing said,

> I'm a conservative person. I'm a Republican. I voted for George W. Bush. Yet I am seen as a raving liberal throughout the church. I'm very conservative about marriage. I'm very conservative about hard work. I'm very conservative that you celebrate the sacraments; if you're going to preach, you say your prayers, and you read the Bible and you do your homework. Inside myself, I have an awful lot of conservative tendencies, and I serve a constituency that is primarily liberal, and we get along just fine. And so, I'm really glad I'm not a raving liberal in San Francisco, because I think we'd all go off the deep end."[6]

THE INTELLECTUAL PRECURSORS
OF TODAY'S NEW AGE MOVEMENT

≈ HELENA PETROVNA BLAVATSKY

Helena Petrovna Blavatsky (1831–1891), was born in Ukraine. She had two brief marriages. The first, in July 1849 to General Nikifor Blavatsky, a Russian governor of Armenia, lasted until her flight that September, and was never consummated. After Helena abandoned her husband, she began a quarter-

1. Williams, "Swing Marks 25th Year," *ENS*, 08/09/04.

2. Bishop William E. Swing, August 10, 1996 speech before the North American Interfaith Network Conference, p1.

3. Bishop William E. Swing, "The Swing Shift: 25 Years of the 155 Years of the Diocese of California," *ENS*, August 9, 2004, http://www.episcopalchurch.org/3577_48075_ ENG_ HTM.htm, printed 08/10/04 (cited below as Swing, "The Swing Shift," *ENS*, 08/09/04).

4. Christian de la Huerta, *Coming Out Spiritually: The Next Step*, Tarcher/Putnam, 1999, p 4.

5. Bishop William E. Swing, "2003 Ecumenical Pilgrimage to London, Canterbury, Rome, Istanbul: Day 9, Thursday April 10—Constantinople/Haiki," http://diocal.org/modules.php?op=modload&name=EasyContent&file=index&menu=122101 &page_id=110, printed 08/09/04. Swing repeated both boasts in his celebratory article on the occasion of the 25th anniversary of his consecration: "The Bishop of California has not only ordained more women than any bishop in Church history, but he also has ordained more openly gay and lesbian priests and deacons than any bishop in Church history" (Swing, "The Swing Shift," *ENS*, 08/09/04).

6. Williams, "Swing Marks 25th Year," *ENS*, 08/09/04.

century of travel through Europe, Asia, and North America. While in the US, she undertook a biga-mous second marriage in 1875 to a follower, Michael Betanelly. (Mr. Blavatsky was still alive at the time in Russia.) The new marriage too was abortive; within several months Blavatsky abandoned him, and Betanelly obtained a divorce in 1878.

Helena Blavatsky was profoundly influenced from her childhood onward by Freemasonry and occultism. At her grandparents' home, she studied the occult library of her maternal great-grandfa-ther, Prince Pavel Dolgorukii, "a prominent Rosicrucian Freemason in the years before Catherine II closed the lodges. In her adolescence, she admired Prince Aleksandr Golitsyn, a magician and Freema-son who encouraged her growing interest in esotericism."[1]

Blavatsky visited Paris in the early 1850s, and "astonished the Freemasons there with her knowl-edge" of the secrets of Scottish Rite and Egyptian Rite Masonry.[2] In her travels through Europe, Amer-ica, and Asia, "everywhere she was involved with Freemasonry, Oriental secret societies, occult fraternities, and with the spiritualists who constituted, as it were, the exoteric 'church' from which doors opened to the more esoteric circles."[3] Blavatsky said in *Isis Unveiled* that she hoped for Masonry to return to its ancient, occult roots,[4] and averred that the Masonic quest for knowledge and under-standing would remain "empty words" for "as long as they neglect their mother Magic, and turn their backs upon its twin sister, Spiritualism."[5] She also praised Grand Orient Masonry for allowing atheists to join their Lodges.[6]

Blavatsky "smoked her first hashish, which she used for many years, in 1850 in Cairo."[7] She told an associate, "Hasheesh multiplies one's life a thousand fold. My experiences are as real as if they were ordinary events of actual life. Ah! I have the explanation. It is a recollection of my former existences, my pervious incarnations. It is a wonderful drug, and clears up a profound mystery."[8]

Blavatsky was wounded in battle at Mentana in 1867; she was fighting against the Pope, and on the side of Garibaldi, for the unification of Italy.[9] Another biographer says that during the 1850s, Blavatsky was probably a member of Mazzini's *Jeune Europe*, a revolutionary Carbonari secret society.[10] "In 1871, while in Cairo, Egypt, she founded a spiritualist group which disbanded because of its inept, fraudu-lent attempts to create psychic phenomena."[11]

Blavatsky's next stop was the United States. While in New York City, Blavatsky founded the Theo-sophical Society in 1875. In 1878, she moved to India, where she remained until scandal forced her to leave the country in 1885. In 1884, the Society for Psychical Research, which had been friendly to The-osophy, investigated her claims to paranormal abilities and to receiving mystical messages from

---

1. K. Paul Johnson, *Initiates of Theosophical Masters*, State University of New York Press, 1995, p 1 (cited below as Johnson, *Initiates of Theosophical Masters*).

2. Joscelyn Godwin, *The Theosophical Enlightenment*, State University of New York Press, 1994, pp 280, 281.

3. Ibid., p 281.

4. H. P. Blavatsky, *Isis Unveiled: Vol. II, Theology*, Theosophical University Press, 1988 reprint of 1877 ed., pp 376–377. (cited below as Blavatsky, *Isis Unveiled: Vol. II*).

5. H. P. Blavatsky, *Isis Unveiled: Vol. I, Science*, Theosophical University Press, 1988 reprint of 1877 ed., p 30.

6. Blavatsky, *Isis Unveiled: Vol. II*, p 377, and a letter from Charles Sotheran that she cites with approval, ibid., p 390.

7. J. Gordon Melton, Jerome Clark, and Aidan A. Kelly, *New Age Almanac*, Visible Ink Press, 1991, p 16 (cited below as Mel-ton, *New Age Almanac*).

8. Tim Maroney, *The Book of Dzyan*, Miskatonic University Archives, 2000, p 15. Original source: A.L. Rawson, "Mme. Blavatsky: A Theosophical Occult Apology," *Frank Leslie's American Magazine* 33 (February 1892), reprinted in *Theosophical History*, vol. 2, no. 6 (April 1988), p 211.

9. Sylvia Cranston, *HPB: The Extraordinary Life & Influence of Helena Blavatsky*, Putnam, 1994, pp 78–79; K. Paul Johnson, *The Masters Revealed: Madame Blavatsky and the Myth of the Great White Lodge*, State University of New York Press, 1994, pp 39–40.

10. Johnson, *Initiates of Theosophical Masters*, p 4.

11. Melton, *New Age Almanac*, p 16.

ascended spirit masters. In 1885, their report deemed her a charlatan. "Other close associates of Blavatsky would confirm the report in later years."[1] Blavatsky spent the remainder of her life in Europe.

Blavatsky died in 1891 in London, having written *Isis Unveiled* (1877) and *The Secret Doctrine* (1888), two massive, soporific texts still revered by her present-day followers. She claimed that these books were channeled from the Mahatmas, her spirit guides, but "large sections of her books which purport to be her own words are in fact duplications of passage in other, earlier books to which she had access. From the very first appearance of *Isis*, charges of plagiarism have swirled around HPB's writing."[2]

According to the *New Age Almanac*, "she will be remembered as the person most influential in creating the modern occult movement in the West."[3] Worldwide, the Theosophical Society has about 35,000 members in 37 countries.[4]

≈ ALICE A. BAILEY AND FOSTER BAILEY

Alice A. Bailey (1880–1949) was born in England. During her youth, she was an Evangelical Christian missionary working with the British Army in India—or, as she later described herself in her autobiography, a "rabid, orthodox Christian worker."[5] She married Walter Evans in 1907; they moved to the US, where he became an Episcopal priest. The family had three daughters, but the marriage was destroyed by Evans' bad temper. Alice separated from him in 1915 and obtained a divorce in 1919. With the end of her first marriage, she began her journey into occultism.

Bailey became a member of Annie Besant's Theosophical Society (the movement that Helena Blavatsky had founded); she broke off from them to found her own school of Theosophy after she began receiving "messages" from "Tibetan Master" Djwhal Khul in 1919. Alice met Foster Bailey, who had been the national secretary of the Theosophical Society, around this time. They married in 1921.

The Baileys founded Lucifer Publishing Company in 1922 (later renaming it Lucis Publishing Company). They also established the Arcane School in 1923, and World Goodwill in 1932. As of 1978, the Arcane School claimed that it had had 200,000 students over its lifetime.[6] A scholarly study of the New Age movement says, "Bailey's influence on the New Age movement, especially in its early phase, is pervasive."[7]

By the time she died, Alice Bailey had produced 24 volumes of Theosophical musings; she claimed that most of these were dictated to her by her Tibetan spirit guide. Two historians specializing in the New Age movement said that the books "are extremely dense. Bailey's husband, Foster, once admitted that in the first edition of *A Treatise on White Magic*, the printers had inadvertently typeset twenty pages twice and included them in the published volume. It was two years before anyone noticed, including the Baileys themselves."[8]

Foster Bailey (1888–1977), a 32nd degree Mason,[9] continued the work of the Lucis Trust after Alice Bailey died. He said that Masonry "is all that remains to us of the first world religion which flourished

1. Ibid., p17.

2. Philip G. Davis, *Goddess Unmasked: The Rise of Neopagan Feminist Spirituality*, Spence Publishing Co., 1998, p220.

3. Melton, *New Age Almanac*, p18.

4. Anthony Aveni, *Behind the Crystal Ball: Magic, Science, and the Occult from Antiquity Through the New Age*, 2002, rev. ed., University Press of Colorado, p171.

5. Alice A. Bailey, *The Unfinished Autobiography of Alice A. Bailey*, Lucis Publishing Company, 1951, p1.

6. Bruce F. Campbell, *Ancient Wisdom Revived: A History of the Theosophical Movement*, University of California Press, 1980, p152.

7. Wouter J. Hanegraaff, *New Age Religion and Western Culture: Esotericism in the Mirror of Secular Thought*, State University of New York Press, 1998, p95.

8. Richard Smoley and Jay Kinney, *Hidden Wisdom: A Guide to the Western Inner Traditions*, Penguin/Arkana, 1999, p291.

9. Foster Bailey, *The Spirit of Masonry*, Lucis Publishing Company, 1957, p135.

in an antiquity so old that it is impossible to affix a date. It was the first unified world religion. Then came the era of separation of many religions, and of sectarianism. Today we are working again towards a world universal religion. Again then, Masonry will come into its own, in some form or another."[1] His book, *The Spirit of Masonry*, is still available from New Age and Masonic book sellers.

Alice Bailey's present-day followers at the Lucis Trust are avowed supporters of the URI.

♒ PIERRE TEILHARD DE CHARDIN, S. J.

Pierre Teilhard de Chardin (1881–1955) was a French Jesuit priest, paleontologist, and theologian. He was ordained as a priest in 1911, and served as a stretcher-bearer during World War I; he received the Legion of Honor and other awards for valorous performance. During the early 1920s, his evolutionary theological writings gained unfavorable notice at the Vatican; Teilhard was forbidden to publish these and later works during his lifetime. He obeyed, but circulated his writings privately. After his death, Teilhard's friends saw to their publication between 1955 and 1970. From 1923 to 1945, Teilhard spent much of his time doing paleontological research in China; he participated in the 1929 discovery of Peking Man. Teilhard's final years were in France and the United States.

Teilhard's theology anticipated themes common among present-day New Age writers, although he disavowed Theosophy and what he deemed to be world-denying Asian religious philosophies. URI supporters Robert Muller, Barbara Marx Hubbard, and Matthew Fox acknowledge Teilhard as one of their mentors.

PRESENT-DAY NEW AGE SUPPORTERS OF THE UNITED RELIGIONS INITIATIVE

♒ ROBERT MULLER

Robert Muller (1923–) was born in Belgium, and was raised in Alsace-Lorraine. During World War II he was a refugee, and participated in the French Resistance movement. Muller obtained a Doctorate of Law from the University of Strasbourg, and began his career with the United Nations in 1948. By his retirement in 1986, he had risen through the ranks to be an Assistant Secretary-General of the UN, and his World Core Curriculum earned a UNESCO prize in 1989. He later served as Chancellor of the UN University for Peace in Costa Rica. He met his first wife, Margarita Gallo, at the UN in the late 1940s; after her death in the 1990s, he remarried.

Muller has been a public supporter of the URI since its inception. He also has cooperated with Theosophists for decades, and the World Core Curriculum—now being used in 43 private "Robert Muller Schools"—acknowledges the work of Alice A. Bailey as one of its sources. In turn, Dale McKechnie, a vice president of the Lucis Trust, said in 1998, "Robert Muller apparently has been influenced by Alice Bailey's works. . . . He did speak at some of our conferences. . . . We have been a great supporter of his work. We've tried to support him and the United Nations and his current work at the Peace University in Costa Rica."[2]

1. Ibid., p 29.
2. Telephone interview, April 24, 1998, by Lee Penn of Dale McKechnie, Vice-President of the Lucis Trust.

♒ Barbara Marx Hubbard

Barbara Marx Hubbard (1929–) is a New Age futurist. One of her supporters says, "She has spent the last thirty years identifying options and people contributing to a creative, sustainable future. In the 1970s and 1980s, she worked on designing and producing major synergistic conferences, bringing together opposing factions to seek cooperative solutions, such as the Soviet-American Citizen Summits to develop joint-nation projects. In 1984, her name was placed in nomination for the Vice Presidency of the United States with her 'campaign for a positive future.'"[1] Marx Hubbard is a board member of the World Future Society and the Society for the Universal Human, and is co-founder of the Foundation for Conscious Evolution. She collaborates with Neale Donald Walsch, saying, "I see that we have different functions toward the same goal. Our function has been to provide an evolutionary context and a developmental path toward the next stage of evolution that includes the best of the teachers and thinkers now transforming our world."[2]

Barbara Marx Hubbard was heir to the Marx family toy fortune, and was raised without religious affiliation.[3] Her teenage spiritual search took her through the Episcopal Church, but she found the priest to be uninspiring, "affable, pallid, correct, traditional."[4] She was already convinced that God's "behavior toward His children was unacceptable."[5] Barbara married an artist, Earl Hubbard, in 1951; she had five children, and divorced after her consciousness expanded. In 1980, she visited an Episcopal monastery in Santa Barbara, Mount Calvary, for a spiritual retreat. At this time, she began receiving channeled messages from "the Christ voice,"[6] an entity that told her that the "brave congregation of souls attracted to the future of the world are my avant-garde—the New Order of the Future."[7] These communications have continued since then. The *New Age Almanac* says, "During the last two decades, Hubbard has become one of the major spokespersons of the New Age Movement and of the goals of planetary consciousness."[8]

Barbara Marx Hubbard assisted in the drafting of the URI Charter, and still supports this movement. She also has attended meetings of Gorbachev's State of the World Forum. Barbara Marx Hubbard closed a section of her 1998 book *Conscious Evolution* with part of the "Great Invocation," a Theosophical prayer from the Lucis Trust: "When asked what I choose to be the outcome of the book, my answer is that it serve the fulfillment of the plan. 'May Light and Love and Power restore the plan on Earth.' That is my prayer."[9] The prayer comes directly from the works of Alice A. Bailey.

♒ Neale Donald Walsch

Neale Donald Walsch (1943–) is the best-selling author of the *Conversations With God* books, a series of channeled dialogues with "God." His career path has been diverse: managing editor of a newspaper,

1. Infinite Health, "Barbara Marx Hubbard," http://www.infinitehealth.net/speakers-organizations/barbara-marx-hubbard.aspx, printed 08/10/04.

2. Miriam Knight, "Agent of Evolution: Interview with Barbara Marx Hubbard," *New Connexion*, September 2003, http://www.newconnexion.net/article/09-03/hubbard.html, printed 08/10/04.

3. Barbara Marx Hubbard, *The Revelation: Our Crisis Is A Birth*, Foundation for Conscious Evolution, Sonoma CA, 1993, p 21 (cited below as Marx Hubbard, *Revelation/Crisis*).

4. Ibid., p 24.

5. Barbara Marx Hubbard, *The Hunger of Eve*, Stackpole Books, 1976, p 13.

6. Marx Hubbard, *Revelation/Crisis*, p 61.

7. Ibid., p 64.

8. Melton, *New Age Almanac*, p 410.

9. Barbara Marx Hubbard, *Conscious Evolution: Awakening the Power of Our Social Potential*, New World Library, Novato, California, 1998, p 216.

program director for a radio station, public information officer for a large public school system, founder of an advertising and marketing firm, and nationally syndicated radio talk show host. All of this—including jobs with New Age luminaries Elisabeth Kübler-Ross and Terry Cole Whitaker— preceded a time of disaster for Walsch.

In the midst of a crisis, in February 1992, Walsch says that he wrote an angry letter to God, asking why his life was such a struggle. "God" responded, and the result—three years later—was the first book of the *Conversations With God* series. Since then, Walsch claims to have reached a readership of more than 25 million people with his message that we are one with God. Walsch now spends all his time pursuing "his vision of a world in which people no longer live in fear of God, or of each other."[1]

Walsch was raised Roman Catholic, but left the Catholic Church at age 20. (Walsch's oft-repeated recollections of his childhood religious training read like a real-life version of *Sister Mary Ignatius Explains It All For You*.) He then passed through various Protestant denominations, but now has his own religion, a feel-good faith in which "*Hitler went to heaven*."[2] Walsch's spirit guide explained, "There is no hell, so there is no place else for him to go."[3] Walsch has been married five times,[4] and so was ready to hear "God's" admonition to us all that "Your marriage vows, as you presently construct them, have you making a very un-Godly statement."[5]

Walsch was active in the URI in the late 1990s, and remains a public supporter of the movement. He and Barbara Marx Hubbard praise each other's work, and they seek the same goals.

GLOBALIST POLITICIANS AND BUSINESSMEN

☰ MIKHAIL GORBACHEV

Mikhail S. Gorbachev (1931–) was the last ruler of the Soviet Union, from 1985 to 1991. He joined the Communist Party in 1952, became First Secretary for Agriculture in 1970, and joined the Politburo in 1979. Gorbachev had the patronage of Yuri Andropov, the KGB boss who ruled the USSR from 1982 to 1984. After his 1985 election as General Secretary of the Communist Party, Gorbachev attempted to reform the Soviet system; his slogans were *glasnost* (openness) and *perestroika* (restructuring). He was married to Raisa Gorbachev from 1953 until her death in 1999.

Soon after assuming power, Gorbachev signed

a five-year plan, for 1985 to 1990, that brought the Soviet Union to its high point of developing an arsenal of deadly pathogens, including plague, brucellosis, tularemia, anthrax, and smallpox. . . . At the same time U.S. scientists were collaborating with Russian counterparts to eradicate any trace of smallpox from the world (from which some 300 million people died during the twentieth century), the Soviet Union was secretly hoarding twenty tons of the germ for military use. New strains were being created. All this during glasnost.[6]

---

1. Evolve, "Neale Donald Walsch—Biography," http://www.evolve.org/pub/doc/walsch_bio.html, printed 08/11/04.

2. Neale Donald Walsch, *Conversations with God: An Uncommon Dialogue, Book* 2, Hampton Roads Publishing Company, Inc., 1997, p 35 (cited below as Walsch, *Conversations/Book* 2); also, Neale Donald Walsch, *Conversations with God: An Uncommon Dialogue, Book* 1, Hampton Roads Publishing Company, Inc., 1995, p 61.

3. Walsch, *Conversations/Book* 2, p 42.

4. Neale Donald Walsch and Dr. Brad Blanton, *Honest to God: A Change of Heart That Can Change the World*, Sparrowhawk Publications, 2002, p 79.

5. Neale Donald Walsch, *Conversations with God: An Uncommon Dialogue, Book* 3, Hampton Roads Publishing Company, Inc., 1998, p 223.

6. Derek Leebaert, *The Fifty-year Wound: How America's Cold War Victory Shapes Our World*, Little, Brown, and Co., 2002, p 516.

In 1988, Gorbachev announced that the USSR would abandon the "Brezhnev doctrine" that had decreed that no country would be allowed to leave the Soviet orbit. The next year, revolutions swept across Eastern Europe, and Soviet rule collapsed. Gorbachev did not respond with invasion, as the USSR had done in Hungary in 1956 and in Czechoslovakia in 1968. The collapse of the Warsaw Pact ended the Cold War in Europe; Gorbachev received the Nobel Peace Prize in 1990 for this. The Soviet Union dissolved at the end of 1991, after the secession of member republics, and after a comic-opera coup by hard-line Communists in August 1991, in which Gorbachev had been held under house arrest for three days.

Gorbachev is a friend of President George H. W. Bush (1989–1993), and remains politically active worldwide, via the Gorbachev Foundation, Green Cross International, the Club of Rome, and other globalist movements. He is unpopular in Russia, having received one-half of 1% of the votes cast in the June 1996 presidential election there. Many Russians blame Gorbachev for the chaos and privation that followed the fall of the USSR.

Gorbachev is not affiliated with the URI, but his theology is compatible with it. He told a Gorbachev Foundation/Netherlands interviewer, "nature is my god. To me, nature is sacred. Trees are my temples and forests are my cathedrals."[1] He still avows, *The socialist idea has not lost its significance or its historical relevance.*"[2] Therefore, "I am convinced that a new civilization will inevitably take on certain features that are characteristic of, or inherent in, the socialist ideal."[3]

♒ MAURICE STRONG

Maurice Strong (1929–), a divorced and remarried Canadian businessman, made a multimillion-dollar fortune in the oil and utility industries. For decades, Strong has been a zealous environmentalist and a supporter of "global governance." In recent years, he has been Senior Advisor to UN Secretary General Kofi Annan, Senior Advisor to the President of the World Bank, President of the UN's University for Peace in Costa Rica, Co-Chairman of the Council of the World Economic Forum, and a member of Toyota's International Advisory Board. Since 2003, Strong has been sent to North Korea by Kofi Annan to mediate the ongoing nuclear crisis.

Strong became friends with George H. W. Bush while the elder Bush was US Ambassador to the UN; as a result, in 1992, President Bush did not oppose Strong's appointment as the Secretary-General of the 1992 UN environmental summit meeting in Rio de Janeiro. Strong and Mikhail Gorbachev then began the Earth Charter movement to rectify what they saw as the excessively "anthropocentric emphasis" of the Declaration on the Environment produced at this UN conference.[4] Strong says, "The **real goal** of the Earth Charter is that it will in fact become like the *Ten Commandments*, like the *Universal Declaration of Human Rights*. It will become a symbol of the aspirations and the commitments of people everywhere."[5] He has urged that it be implemented quickly, saying at the 1995 State of the World Forum that "We shouldn't wait until political democracy paves the way. We must act now."[6]

1. Fred Matser, "Nature Is My God," an interview with Mikhail Gorbachev, *Resurgence* 184, http://resurgence.gn.apc.org/184/gorbachev.htm, printed 05/20/03 and 08/11/04.

2. Mikhail Gorbachev, *On My Country And The World*, Columbia University Press, 2000, p67; the emphasis was as given in the original text.

3. Ibid., p74.

4. The Earth Charter Initiative, "About Us: The Earth Charter Project, 1945–1992," http://www.earthcharter.org/aboutus/overview1945_1992.htm, printed 05/13/03.

5. The Earth Council, "Papers and Speeches: Interview—Maurice Strong on a 'People's Earth Charter,'" March 5, 1998, http://www.ecouncil.ac.cr/about/speech/strong/mstrong.htm, printed 05/09/03.

6. Anita Coolidge, "Ecology—the ultimate democracy: A report from the State of the World Forum," *San Diego Earth Times*, November 1995, http://www.sdearthtimes.com/et1195/et1195s3.html, printed 05/08/03.

Strong has described himself as "a socialist in ideology, a capitalist in methodology."[1] He also says, "We are gods now, gods in charge of our own destiny, and gods can't be capricious."[2] As for his own spirituality, Strong says, "Universalist expressions of religious belief have always attracted me ... I have found the development of my inner spiritual resources one of my most constant challenges, and my connection with the cosmic forces that shape all existence has become central to me."[3]

♒ GEORGE SOROS

George Soros (1930–) is a billionaire investor and currency speculator. He is divorced and remarried, with 5 children.[4] Soros gave $15.5 million to the 2004 campaign against the re-election of President George W. Bush,[5] saying "It would be too immodest for a private person to set himself up against the president. . . . But it is, in fact . . . the Soros Doctrine."[6] With similar grandiosity, in 1997 he had said, "It is a sort of disease when you consider yourself some kind of god, the creator of everything, but I feel comfortable about it now since I began to live it out."[7]

Soros' resources to be "creator of everything" have increased; according to the annual billionaire list issued by *Forbes* magazine, his wealth increased from $3.5 billion in 1997 to $7.2 billion in 2004. Soros has been an investor in the Carlyle Group, a privately held firm with a major stake in the US defense industry; other participants in the group have included former President George H. W. Bush, James Baker (secretary of state for the elder Bush), Frank Carlucci (Secretary of Defense under Reagan), and—until the aftermath of the 9/11 attack—the bin Laden family from Saudi Arabia.[8] In 1992, Soros made $1 billion by betting against the British pound, forcing it out of the European exchange system. Soros' speculation has been blamed for starting the Asian financial crisis of 1997, but he lost $2 billion in the 1998 Russian financial panic. Soros was convicted of insider trading in France in December 2002; if the resulting € 2.2 million fine is upheld on appeal, he would disgorge his gains from speculating on a 1988 French bank merger.[9]

Soros gave money to the URI in 1997,[10] and has been an active participant in the World Economic Forum and the State of the World Forum. He is an ardent supporter of "reproductive rights" and other liberal causes. In eastern Europe, according to *Forbes*, he has "spent freely to help return ex-communists to power."[11]

1. William Baue, "Rio + 10 Series: A Brief History of the Earth Summits—From Stockholm to Rio," SocialFunds.com, June 7, 2002, http://www.socialfunds.com/news/article.cgi /article858.html, printed 06/18/04.

2. Maurice Strong, *Where on Earth Are We Going*, Vintage Canada, 2001, p 29.

3. Ibid., pp 181–182.

4. "Forbes 400" listing, *Forbes Magazine*, October 6, 2003, p 174.

5. *Forbes Magazine*, "The Forbes 400," "Big Wheels," listing for George Soros, October 11, 2004, p 142.

6. Laura Blumenfeld, "Billionaire Soros takes on Bush," *MSNBC News*, November 11, 2003, http://www.msnbc.com/news/991865.asp?cp1=1, printed 06/17/04.

7. Peter Newcomb et al., "The Forbes 400," article on George Soros, *Forbes*, October 13, 1997, p 181 (cited below as Newcomb, "The Forbes 400," 10/13/97).

8. Oliver Burkeman and Julian Borger, "The ex-president's club," *The Guardian*, October 31, 2001, http://www.guardian.co.uk/wtccrash/story/0,1300,583869,00.html, printed 08/16/04.

9. John Tagliabue, "French court convicts Soros," *International Herald Tribune*, December 21, 2002, http://www.iht.com/articles/81091.html, printed 12/31/02.

10. Dennis Delman, "Second United Religions Summit Conference," *Pacific Church News*, June/July 1997, p 28, and United Religions Initiative, "Foundation Grants Enable URI Youth Leadership on Worldwide Net," *URI News Update*, March 1997, no. 2, p 1.

11. Newcomb., "The Forbes 400," 10/13/97, p 181.

≈ TED TURNER

Ted Turner (1938–), a media billionaire from Atlanta, Georgia, has been divorced 3 times and has 5 children.[1] His most recent wife was actress Jane Fonda; they divorced in 2001. According to a BBC report in 2001, "Turner, who once described Christianity as 'a religion for losers' says, in an interview with *New Yorker* magazine, 'She just came home and said: 'I've become a Christian.' That's a pretty big change for your wife of many years to tell you. That's a shock.'"[2]

Turner founded the Cable News Network (CNN), and pledged in 1997 to donate $1 billion to the UN. His wealth rose during the 1990s boom, reaching $5 billion in 1998. With reverses in his media empire since 2000, "America's largest private landowner" has $1.9 billion left.[3] In 1999, Turner nevertheless described himself as "a socialist at heart."[4]

Turner has not associated himself with the URI, but he is one of the 21 co-chairs of Gorbachev's State of the World Forum. He sponsored an interfaith meeting at the UN in 2000, and has said that "Christianity is an eco-unfriendly religion."[5] He added, "You've got to be hopeful because I think that we're smarter than the opposition, because we are thinking long term. We're better educated and I put my money on the smart minority rather than the dumb majority. Wouldn't you?"[6]

One of Turner's solutions for the world's problems is a "voluntary" global one-child policy for the next century, since "the world's population should be about two billion, and we've got about six billion right now.... Personally, I think the population should be closer to when we had indigenous populations, back before the advent of farming. Fifteen thousand years ago, there was somewhere between 40 and 100 million people. But Paul and Anne Ehrlich have convinced me that if we're going to have a modern infrastructure, with commercial airlines and interstate highways around the world, we're going to need about two billion people to support it."[7] Turner did not specify how his plan would be implemented.

- *Are the "players" described in this book the only ones seeking a New World Order?*

No. There are other contenders for global power, and other wanna-be "Messiahs," in addition to those mentioned in this book. I have investigated the URI and its allies; movements and spiritual leaders not tied to the URI (for example, Sai Baba and Share International's camera-shy "Maitreya") get little attention here. This area of research remains wide open for those who wish to pursue it.

- *Where are the URI and its globalist, New Age allies headed from here?*

As of 2004, it might have seemed that these movements are merely weird California-style sideshows. The reality is otherwise. The URI—and more ominously, the associated globalist movements—are well-connected to the UN, to some major foundations and corporations, and to sympathizers in schools, the Western media, and much of the middle management of mainline Protestant and Roman

1. "Forbes 400" listing, *Forbes Magazine*, October 6, 2003, p161.
2. Andrew Walker, "Jane Fonda: Not so plain," *British Broadcasting Company*, April 20, 2001, http://news.bbc.co.uk/1/hi/uk/1287787.stm, printed 08/11/04.
3. *Forbes Magazine*, "The Forbes 400," "Spotlights," listing for Ted Turner, October 11, 2004, p130.
4. Drudge Report, "Ted Turner: I Am A Socialist At Heart," September 29, 1999, http://www.drudgereport.com/matt2.html, printed in 1999; no longer on the Net. The same information is still accessible at John Howard, "Ted Turner's A Socialist?," Scoop Headlines, *The New Zealand Edge*, October 1, 1999, http://www.scoop.co.nz/stories/HL9910/S0 0001.htm, printed 05/21/03.
5. Tracey C. Rembert, "Ted Turner: Billionaire, Media Mogul... And Environmentalist" (Interview), *E Magazine*, January/February 1999, Volume X, number 1, p10.
6. Ibid., p12.
7. Ibid., pp10–11.

Catholic churches. These movements are ambitious, and growing, and may be able to put themselves forward as "saviors" if the current world order becomes unstable.

Most unfortunately, "unstable" is an optimistic description of the present political and economic outlook. As I discuss in detail in the last two chapters of the book ("The Ascendancy of the 'Anti-Tradition'" and the "Speculative Postscript"), I believe that we are in the early years of a global Time of Troubles, at least equal in severity to that of 1914-1945. In this environment, radical movements— Utopians of the extreme Left and the extreme Right alike—can win mass support and political power with little warning. Who would have said in 1904 that Russia would have a Communist revolution in 13 years; who in 1913 predicted anything like the Third Reich? We need to be alert, and not ignore those who have written the present era's equivalents to Hitler's *Mein Kampf* and Lenin's *What Is To Be Done?* (Do you rebel at my use of these analogies for some aspects of the present day New Age and globalist movements? Go to Part II and Part III of this book, and examine the details.)

• ***What can we do about this?***

I am not a political strategist, nor a seasoned organizer, nor a financier. I do not, therefore, have a political or social or economic program to propose that might delay, mitigate, or forestall the present global trends toward war and new forms of "spiritual" tyranny. Among the readers of this book, there may be those who have such ideas; let them come forward and do their best. Everyone's vocations, abilities, and circumstances are different; the appropriate response to the warnings in this book will vary accordingly.

There is one answer that I propose, something that anyone who believes in God (or desires to have such faith) can do. Let us all seek God's aid to examine our consciences, and renounce any wrongful acts, attitudes, or negligence that we discover thereby. Then, pray for God to have mercy upon and to bless our foes, whoever they may be; ask that He grant them the gifts of amendment of life and of sanctity, that they may be saved. Just as everyone has different gifts, everyone will perceive a different set of enemies. Pray for them all, especially those most in need of God's mercy. These prayers can be brief and to the point: for example, "Lord Jesus Christ, Son of the Living God, have mercy upon [name of enemy]."

This might seem to be an impractical and pious response to a real, and dire, worldly predicament. However, I believe that the root of our present crisis is spiritual; the start of the solution must be spiritual, as well.

I have written previously about the URI, globalism, and the New Age movement for various magazines and Internet sites, especially between 1998 and 2000. The research and analysis in this book supersedes my prior work on the URI, the New Age movement, and the globalists. Much has changed in the last four years, and this book reflects those changes.

I close this foreword with an exhortation: Be alert! When reformers of the Left or the Right propose a political or spiritual New Order that will lead us all to a brighter tomorrow, question them closely. If what is proposed involves breaking the laws that are written on our hearts in order to build an earthly New Jerusalem, then show the would-be "saviors" swiftly to the door.

LEE PENN

ACKNOWLEDGMENTS

I OWE A PARTICULAR DEBT to the magazines and organizations who have published my earlier works on the United Religions Initiative (URI) and related matters: *The Christian Challenge, Foundations, Human Life International Reports, New Oxford Review,* the *Journal* and *Newsletter* of the Spiritual Counterfeits Project, *World Net Daily, The Wanderer,* and *Touchstone.* Additionally, in February 2005, the Catholic Family and Human Rights Institute published a booklet by me on the URI, titled "The United Religions Initiative: An Organization Seeking to Undermine Traditional Religious Faith and Evangelization."

I have benefited greatly from the work undertaken by the writers associated with the *Journal* of the Spiritual Counterfeits Project. My analysis, although done independently of theirs, corroborates and expands upon their assessment in the 1980s and 1990s of the movements for religious syncretism and global government. However, neither they, nor my other prior publishers, are responsible for what I am saying in this book.

I have used several images from medieval manuscripts in this book. These images were collected by James L. Matterer and his associates, and are made available for public use through the "Medieval Macabre" web site.[1]

Since 1995, many people have helped me in the work that led up to this book: providing research assistance, story leads, and access to rare documents, reviewing and criticizing drafts of my writing, allowing me to call upon them for emotional and spiritual support, sending notes of encouragement, providing financial assistance, and praying for me. Without their aid, I could not have begun, continued, or completed this book. Many of these allies have requested anonymity, and I respect that wish. You know who you are; please accept my gratitude.

Various URI staff members and supporters also have given me documents and have allowed me to interview them (in person, by phone, or by e-mail) since 1997. The information they provided was essential, and I am grateful to them. Chief among them, in recent years, is Donald Frew, a Neopagan elder and long-time URI activist who has been on its board of directors since 2002. Mr. Frew has been very generous with his time, even though he knows that I am an opponent of the URI and related movements. His actions exemplify the best in religious liberalism: a willingness to listen to opponents and grasp their arguments, without the expectation that either side will surrender their convictions.

LEE PENN

---

1. Medieval Macabre, "Supernatural and Fantastic Imagery of the Middle Ages," http://www.godecookery.com/macabre/macabre.htm, printed 06/11/04.

METHODS

Most of this book's data are from documents, tapes, and books prepared by the URI and its allies, from mainstream and New Age press coverage of the URI and related groups' activities, and from interviews of people associated with these organizations. I have reviewed other critiques of the New Age and globalist movements; these books provided useful research leads and identified possible areas of concern. However, I have not depended on other authors' reporting and analysis. I have based my work on information that I was able to obtain and verify myself in its original form; see the footnotes as evidence of this.

Quotations are verbatim from original sources; grammar, punctuation, spelling, and typography are as given therein. In a few cases, I have inserted an explanatory word or phrase into a quote; these insertions are marked by square brackets, "[ ]." Occasionally, I have inserted "[sic]" into quotations, to show that the apparent error in the quote is from the original source. I have shortened some quotations, and these abridgments are noted with ellipses within the quotation. Some quotations contain ellipses in their original form; I document this in the associated footnote.

In view of the controversial nature of this material, I have chosen to footnote the text profusely. With the aid of these notes, anyone may review, repeat, and build upon the research that I have done. I identify each source fully when I first cite it in a chapter; later references are in an abbreviated form. When I cite the same source in successive footnotes, the first reference is in full form; the immediately following notes use "ibid."

The majority of the footnotes document my sources; some also provide background data, or offer additional commentary from me or from Charles Upton. If any item sparks particular curiosity, take a side trip into the notes. Commentary in the footnotes is there because I believe it adds value, or may be of general interest. Nevertheless, those who read the book straight through, without making detours into the footnotes, will see the whole argument as I intend to present it.

Throughout the book, I have capitalized "Theosophy" and its variants when referring to the occult spiritual movement founded in 1875 by Helena Blavatsky, and carried forward by Annie Besant and Alice Bailey. (The exception is direct quotes, where I have left all capitalization as I found it.) The word "theosophy" also has a broader meaning, "belief about God and the world, held to be based on mystical insight."[1] I have not used "theosophy" in that sense; my criticism of Theosophy pertains specifically to the ideas and activities of Blavatsky and her spiritual descendants.

All Internet references include the date that the document was viewed, printed, or downloaded. The on-line source of each such document is accurate as of that date. However, the Internet is ever-changing; any on-line document may have been deleted, revised, re-named, moved, or placed in a secure, pay-per-view archive since then. I have retained paper or electronic archives of all Internet documents cited in this book, even if they are no longer on the Internet. (Likewise, I have a file of all magazines, reports, and books cited in this book.)

In addition, I have used the "Wayback Machine," an Internet research tool, to point to an on-line archive of some Web pages that have been revised or removed from the Net since I had initially viewed them. The footnotes show the instances in which I have used this system. To use this archive, go to the Web address http://www.archive.org/web/web.php, and in the "Wayback Machine" data entry area, enter the Web address of the page that you are seeking. If the page exists in their archive, the "Wayback

---

1. *Webster's Seventh New Collegiate Dictionary*, G. & C. Merriam Company, 1970, p 916.

Machine" will show a complete copy of the page. (This archive shows Web pages that are more than six months old, and does not include password-protected or pay-per-view pages, or sites in which the Webmaster has blocked access by archival systems. Therefore, not all old Web sites can be recovered with this system.)

Unless otherwise noted, all Scripture quotations are from the *Revised Standard Version* of the Bible.[1] (I have used the King James Version in a few instances; these citations are noted by "KJV.")

1. Herbert G. May and Bruce M. Metzger, eds., *The New Oxford Annotated Bible With the Apocrypha*, Revised Standard Version, New York: Oxford University Press, 1977.

PART I

HONORING THE "SPIRIT OF THE AGE": THE UNITED RELIGIONS INITIATIVE (URI)

The Lord and Satan vying for the soul of a man, who is navigating the ocean of vices and sin. From *Le grant kalendrier et compost des Bergiers*, printed by Nicolas Le Rouge, Troyes, 1496.

"For whoever is ashamed of me and of my words in this adulterous and sinful generation, of him will the Son of man also be ashamed, when he comes in the glory of his Father with the holy angels."

Jesus, in Mark 8:38

"Truly, truly, I say to you, unless one is born anew, he cannot see the kingdom of God."

Jesus, in John 3:3

POINT : COUNTERPOINT

The world's agenda is the agenda of the church.[1]

————Anglican Bishop James Ottley, 1997

In the past our glorious visions of the future—heaven, paradise, nirvana— were thought to happen after death. The newer thought is that we do not have to die to get there! We are not speaking here of life after death in some mythical heaven, but life more abundant in real time in history. We are speaking of the next stage of our social evolution.[2]

————Barbara Marx Hubbard, 1998

It is, indeed, among Christians themselves that the final decisive assault on Christianity has been mounted; led by the Protestant churches, but with Roman Catholics eagerly, if belatedly, joining in the fray. All they had to show is that when Jesus said that His kingdom was not of this world, He meant that it was. Then, moving on from there, to stand the other basic Christian propositions similarly on their heads. As, that to be carnally minded is life; that it is essential to lay up treasure on earth in the shape of a constantly expanding Gross National Product; that the flesh lusts with the spirit and the spirit with the flesh, so that we can do whatever we have a mind to; that he who loveth his life in this world shall keep it unto life eternal. And so on.[3]

Malcolm Muggeridge, "The Great Liberal Death Wish"————

If there's a United Religions pursuing a dialogue in depth, it begins to ask larger questions and force religions to make larger statements.[4]

————Bishop William Swing, 1997

Almost every contemporary proposal to bring freedom into the church is simply a proposal to bring tyranny into the world. For freeing the church now does not even mean freeing it in all directions. It means freeing that peculiar set of dogmas loosely called scientific, dogmas of monism, of pantheism, or of Arianism, or of necessity. And every one of these . . . can be shown to be the natural ally of oppression.[5]

G. K. Chesterton, *Orthodoxy*————

---

1. Anglican Communion Office at the United Nations, "The Ministry of the Anglican Communion Office at the United Nations—Annual Report 1997," http://www.aco.org/united-nations/annual97.htm, printed 1998; no longer on the Net at this address. As of 2004, this document may be found at http://web.archive.org/web/19980202045506/http://www.aco.org/united-nations/annual97.htm, printed 08/02/04.

2. Barbara Marx Hubbard, *Conscious Evolution: Awakening the Power of Our Social Potential*, New World Library, Novato, California, 1998, p18 (cited below as Marx Hubbard, *Conscious Evolution*).

3. Malcolm Muggeridge, "The Great Liberal Death Wish," reprinted in *The Portable Conservative Reader*, ed. Russell Kirk, Viking Penguin Inc., 1982, p615.

4. Don Lattin, interview with William Swing, "Bishop's Idea for a Leap of Faiths," *San Francisco Chronicle*, 06/22/97, p3/Z1.

5. G. K. Chesterton, *Orthodoxy*, Image Books, 1959, p125.

I must acknowledge that, throughout the centuries, in seeking to love God and express the unity that is in God, many Christians have not honored the distinctness and validity of other religions, but have sought to make the whole world Christian.[1]

―――――CHARLES GIBBS, EXECUTIVE DIRECTOR OF THE URI, 1999

All authority in heaven and earth has been given to me. Go therefore and make disciples of all nations, baptizing them in the name of the Father and of the Son and of the Holy Spirit, teaching them to observe all I have commanded you.

JESUS, IN MATT. 28:18–20―――――

For whoever is ashamed of me and of my words in this adulterous and sinful generation, of him will the Son of man also be ashamed, when he comes in the glory of his Father with the holy angels."

JESUS, IN MARK 8:38―――――

We long not for a new religion, but for the evolution of religion, such that we embody the qualities of our master teachers and become conscious cocreators with the divine universal intelligence ourselves.[2]

―――――BARBARA MARX HUBBARD, 1998

New objects in religion, new systems and plans, new doctrines, new preachers, are necessary to satisfy that craving which the so-called spread of knowledge has created. The mind becomes morbidly sensitive and fastidious; dissatisfied with things as they are, desirous of a change *as such*, as if alteration must of itself be a relief.[3]

JOHN HENRY NEWMAN, "THE RELIGION OF THE DAY"―――――

This grand vision is unfolding as a natural part of social evolution, and simply reflects an avant garde attunement with the 'zeitgeist'—the 'spirit of the times'.[4]

―――――BRUCE SCHUMAN, COMMENTING ON THE 1997 URI GLOBAL SUMMIT

Do not be conformed to this world.

ST. PAUL, ROM. 12:2―――――

1. Charles Gibbs, "An Ethical Mandate for the United Religions," *Journal of the United Religions Initiative*, Issue 5, p11.
2. Marx Hubbard, *Conscious Evolution*, pp89–90.
3. John Henry Newman, *Parochial and Plain Sermons*, Vol. 1 (1834), Sermon 24, "The Religion of the Day," Ignatius Press, 1997, p200.
4. Bruce Schuman, "All One People: A Common Flame burns for all," *The Light and Life Journal: An Exploration of the Spiritual Universe*, Autumn 1997, p6.

1

ONE ANGLICAN BISHOP'S DREAM

Bishop William Swing, of the Episcopal Church's Diocese of California, has built a religious bridge to the future; he wants everybody on Earth to cross it with him. The United Religions Initiative (URI), which Swing launched in 1995, describes itself as "a growing global community dedicated to promoting enduring, daily interfaith cooperation, ending religiously motivated violence and creating cultures of peace, justice and healing for the Earth and all living beings."[1] The introduction to the URI Charter sets out the movement's planetary ambitions: "Working on all continents and across continents, people from different religions, spiritual expressions and indigenous traditions are creating unprecedented levels of enduring global cooperation.... The URI, in time, aspires to have the visibility and stature of the United Nations."[2] As Bishop Swing said in 1996, "the religions of the world should aspire to be as moral as the nations of the world and meet regularly to strive for global good."[3]

Swing told the Congressional Human Rights Caucus in 1997 that the URI was part of the effort to "shape a new world order following the end of the Cold War," and that "a United Religions could offer the world a powerful new vision of hope—the vision that the deepest stories we know can now cease to be causes of separation between people, and become instead the foundation for a reunited humanity."[4]

In November 2002, URI Executive Director Charles Gibbs hailed the growth of the movement: "Since 1996, the URI has grown from a small group of 55 visionary people to a global organization with nearly 200 Cooperation Circles engaging over 15,000 interfaith activists from 88 faith traditions and 46 countries.... In six years, URI has established itself as an innovative and respected global organization."[5] (Cooperation Circles are local chapters of the URI.)[6] The URI continues to grow. It

---

1. United Religions Initiative, "The United Religions Initiative Charter," http://www. uri.org/resources/publications/Charter%20PC%20format.doc, p1; downloaded 07/07/04 (cited below as URI, "Charter").

2. Ibid.

3. Bishop William Swing, "The United Religions Initiative," document issued in April 1996, p3 (cited below as Swing, "The United Religions Initiative," 04/96).

4. Rep. Tom Lantos, "Bishop William Swing Of The Episcopal Diocese Of California Discusses The United Religious Initiative, An Effort To Encourage Peace And Respect For Human Rights," *Congressional Record*: November 4, 1997 (Extensions), found through a Google search of news group postings, printed 06/11/04.

5. Charles Gibbs, URI fund raising letter, November 14, 2002, pp1, 2.

6. "At the heart of URI are Cooperation Circles (CC's), self-organizing groups with seven people or more from at least three religions, spiritual expressions or indigenous traditions. Established organizations such as interfaith councils, as well as new associations, are equally welcome. Our CC's make URI's vision a reality. Every day and throughout the world URI members are engaged in initiatives such as: microcredit lending circles for women in Kenya, interfaith art & sacred spaces [sic] gatherings in the UK, youth radio broadcasting in Malawi, interfaith sharing among women in Israel and enabling communities of worship to be more energy efficient in the USA." (United Religions Initiative, "Membership in URI: Cooperation Circles," http://www.uri.org/abouturi/membership/, printed 06/03/04).

stated that in 2003, its work "engaged hundreds of thousands of people around the world."[1] As of early 2004, the movement stated that its Cooperation Circles had 26,000 members.[2] By the fall of 2004, the URI had 270 Cooperation Circles.[3]

In its 2003 Annual Report, the URI boasted of its growing international influence: "URI's successful grassroots engagement and its role as a catalyst for positive change is having an impact around the world and is engaging experts in Organizational Development, Conflict Transformation and International Relations—from the United Nations, NGOs and the international interfaith movement."[4]

The URI invites believers in *all* "religions, spiritual expressions and indigenous traditions"[5] to join. Bishop Swing also wishes to include "earnest agnostics"[6] and those who say, "I'm not religious but I'm into spirituality."[7]

The URI works regularly with most other interfaith organizations, and is developing ever-closer ties to the United Nations. Its supporters come from the long-established religions, as well as from the new religious movements and cults that arose in the 20th Century. With this base of support, and with global annual revenue of about $2.2 million to $3 million,[8] the URI has assured itself of survival. It is in a position to benefit from the unsettling spiritual aftermath of globalization, social upheaval, economic distress, and war.

When Bishop Swing and other URI leaders seek public support for the URI, their primary pitch is one with almost universal appeal: the desire for peace, and the fear of terrorism and nuclear war. In 1998, Swing wrote, "Religions need a United Religions. Bombs are exploding in the name of God in cities throughout the world, religious persecution is more prevalent now than ever before, religious extremists are demanding and obtaining nuclear weapons, and still there is no neutral arena where all of the religions can engage each other."[9] He said in 1999, "What is a bigger terrorist threat than religion in the world today? There is none. . . . We now have a Hindu bomb, and an Islamic bomb. So now we translate atomic weapons into religion. And if that happens, then there's a proliferation of religious fundamentalists who get their hands on the atomic weapon. What we're looking at is religion is taking over the atomic bomb."[10] Swing wrote in October 2001 that "There will be an ultimate nuclear holocaust inspired by religions unless religions wake up to their whole responsibility toward all the life that God created. . . . We must grant dignity to other faiths and learn a common vocation for the good of all."[11]

To call forth our courage and imagination on behalf of the URI, Bishop Swing has quoted from the

1. United Religions Initiative, "Circles of Light 2004," text from an invitation to a URI fund raising banquet held on January 24, 2004.

2. Charles Gibbs and Sally Mahé, *United Religions Initiative, Birth of a Global Community: Appreciative Inquiry in Action*, Lakeshore Publishers, 2004, p 289.

3. United Religions Initiative, "Letter from Executive Director," October/November 2004, http://www.uri.org/abouturi/edrreport/index.asp, printed 11/03/04.

4. United Religions Initiative, 2003: *Compassionate Actions for a Better World*, annual report; http://www.uri.org/resources/URI_Anual_Report_2003.pdf, viewed 09/24/04.

5. URI, "Charter," p 1.

6. Jennifer Shaw, "Bishop Offers New Religious Vision for 21st Century," *Contra Costa Sun*, news section, page 6, March 26, 1997.

7. Bishop William Swing, "Keynote address for URI Global Assembly," August 19, 2002; http://pcn.diocal.org/uriaddress.html, printed 03/06/03.

8. Based on data from URI annual reports for 2000, 2001, 2002, and 2003, covering funding for the headquarters, and an estimate by URI Global Council member Donald Frew of $1 million per year spent by URI Cooperation Circles.

9. Bishop William Swing, "Let's Pursue Peace With Islam," *San Francisco Chronicle*, Wednesday, October 14, 1998, p A21.

10. Coleen O'Connor, "Uniting Religions: Bishop Swing talks about religious terrorism, atomic bombs, and why we need a United Religions now," http://www.gracecathedral.org/enrichment/interviews/int_19990107.shtml, printed 2/4/03.

11. Bishop William Swing, "A Swing Through the Diocese," *Pacific Church News*, October/November 2001, p 5.

prologue of Goethe's *Faust*: "Whatever you can do, or dream you can, begin it. Boldness has genius, power, and magic in it."[1]

In part, the URI's aims reflect traditional morality and common sense. People should never kill each other in the name of God, and everyone ought to be civil and charitable to those of other faiths. Some URI Cooperation Circles, the local chapters of the movement, do hands-on work for the poor and the sick; others are negotiating peace settlements to end wars in Third World countries.

Unfortunately, the URI is tainted by New Age utopianism and by its leaders' habitual affinity for leftist causes. Therefore, the URI agenda is far broader, and far stranger, than putting an end to religiously motivated violence.

From the beginning of the movement, URI leaders—from Bishop Swing on down—have set forth a grandiose, messianic vision. In 1996, Bishop Swing explained that "The nature of the United Religions would be to focus on: 1) the whole human family; 2) the whole health of our planet; and 3) the whole realm of living species, and to offer the unique gifts of religions."[2] In 1995, Bishop Swing had said that the world is moving toward "unity in terms of global economy, global media, global ecological system. What is missing is a global soul."[3]

How would Swing's "global soul" be created? Thus far, it has been primarily by means of conferences, dialogues, interfaith liturgies, networking, fund raising, public declarations, and press releases.[4] However, if radicals within the URI and among its New Age, globalist, and utopian allies realize their full ambitions, the global soul would have lion's teeth.

Theosophists, cultists, and the leaders of Gorbachev's State of the World Forum and Earth Charter movements have set forth their dreams in detail. There would be a New Religion for the "new civilization"[5] of the new millennium. Its code would be the Earth Charter (which Gorbachev likens to "a kind of Ten Commandments, a 'Sermon on the Mount'");[6] its creed would be "unity in diversity;" its cult

---

1. Goethe, from the Prologue of *Faust*, as quoted by Bishop William Swing, *The Coming United Religions*, United Religions Initiative and CoNexus Press, 1998, p 28.

2. Swing, "The United Religions Initiative," 04/96, p 1.

3. Bishop William Swing, "What is missing is a global soul," *Pacific Church News*, August/September 1995, p 5. Regarding Bishop Swing's notion that the world is now moving toward "unity in terms of . . . global ecological system," Charles Upton (a Sufi Muslim scholar and an expert on comparative religion) comments, "Haven't we always had a unified ecological system? Haven't the winds and the ocean currents, the sun and moon been in existence as long as there has been life on earth? Is nature another network or organization we are in the process of creating via some kind of United Species Initiative? To attempt to impose an artificial unity on a pre-existing natural one is to fragment the natural one, not unite it—and that's exactly what technological society is doing." (Charles Upton, e-mail to Lee Penn, 09/09/04).

4. The URI's own description of its activities is consistent with this characterization:
"What Does URI Do?
• Creates safe opportunities for dialogue, sharing and action
• Pilots innovative approaches to peacebuilding
• Supports youth and leadership development
• Contributes seed funds for local initiatives and encourages indigenous philanthropy
• Produces and distributes interfaith educational materials
• Convenes regional and global interfaith gatherings to extend best practices
• Provides a global communications and knowledge sharing network
• Offers a community of hope and a positive vision for the future."
(United Religions Initiative, "Introduction," http://www.uri.org/abouturi/welcome/, printed 07/16/04.)

5. "The Gorbachev Foundation from the very beginning of its activity set as one of its main tasks the goal of working out the problems of a transition to a new paradigm of development—or, as we call it, a new civilization." Mikhail Gorbachev, in Mikhail Gorbachev and Zdeněk Mlynář, *Conversations with Gorbachev: On Perestroika, the Prague Spring, and the Crossroads of Socialism*, Columbia University Press, 2002, p 172.

6. Green Cross International, "Interview—Environment: 'Act Globally, not Nationally,'" *Los Angeles Times*, May 8, 1997, http://www.greencrossinternational.net/GreenCrossFamily/gorby/newspeeches/interviews/laTimes.html, printed 05/09/03.

would be the "sacred Earth."[1] The seven new capital sins would be pollution, overpopulation, over-consumption, nationalism, patriarchy, capitalism, and "fundamentalism" (which in most cases simply means daring to evangelize for Christ). The only heresy would be religious orthodoxy. As Fr. Richard Neuhaus, editor of *First Things* magazine has warned, "Where orthodoxy is optional, orthodoxy will sooner or later be proscribed."[2]

It remains to be seen whether the URI and its allies can "co-create" a spiritual New World Order that would depart so radically from the wisdom that mankind has passed through all traditional cultures and all long-established religions. It is my hope that exposure of the radical agenda of the URI and its allies will help to forestall these developments.

1. In 1997, URI Executive Director Charles Gibbs said that a URI planning conference held in New York City discussed how to "support sacred earth values in a variety of ways." (Charles Gibbs, "Regional Conferences Prepare for URI Global Summit," *Pacific Church News*, August/September 1997, p23). While at St. John the Divine, URI supporter James Parks Morton said, "The language of the 'Sacred Earth' has got to become mainline." (Alan AtKisson, "The Green Cathedral: An Interview with the Rev. James Parks Morton," IN CONTEXT # 24, http://www.context.org/ICLIB/IC24/Morton.htm, printed 04/08/03.) On March 2, 2003, at a URI-sponsored interfaith peace service at Grace Cathedral, there was "a huge globe centered on the Cathedral's main altar." (Diocese of California, "In Time of War: March 2nd Interfaith Prayer Service Sought to Head Off War Effort," *Pacific Church News On-Line*, April/May 2003, Vol. 141, no. e3, http://pcn.diocal.org/PCNO/pcn003-3/index.html, printed 05/08/03).

2. Fr. Richard John Neuhaus, "The Public Square," *First Things*, January 1996, http://www.firstthings.com/ftissues/ft9601/public.html, printed 03/29/03; see also Fr. Richard John Neuhaus, "The Public Square," *First Things*, January 1997, http://www.firstthings.com/ftissues/ft9701/public.html, printed 11/04/03.

2

THE RISE OF THE
UNITED RELIGIONS INITIATIVE

THE INTERFAITH MOVEMENT OF THE 20TH CENTURY: SEED-BED OF THE URI

THE GLOBAL INTERFAITH MOVEMENT, which seeks spiritual and ethical common ground among the world's religions, began with the 1893 Parliament of World Religions, a Chicago meeting of 400 leaders from 41 denominations and religions.[1] Interfaith scholar Marcus Braybrooke said, "The Parliament has been called by Sidney Ahlstrom a watershed in American life—marking the change from the dominance of Anglo-Saxon Protestantism to the start of a multi-religious society.... The Parliament did not of itself destroy the Protestant hegemony, but contributed to this by symbolizing the changes taking place."[2] The effects were felt overseas, as well. The Parliament "provided Asian religions with an apologetic to resist Christian missionary pressure and indeed to suggest that the wisdom of the East is superior to Christianity."[3]

The "prime movers" of the 1893 Parliament were Charles Carroll Bonney (a member of the Swedenborgian church), the Rev. John Henry Barrows (a Presbyterian minister and "self-confessed Liberal Christian,") and the Rev. Jenkin Lloyd Jones (a Unitarian minister).[4]

The Theosophical Society was well-represented, having received two days of the 17-day Parliament to propound its own beliefs at a Theosophical Congress.[5] A historian of Theosophy says that the Parliament gave Theosophists "a breakthrough into public acceptance and awareness which had hardly seemed possible a few years before."[6] Crowds of up to 3,000 gathered to listen to Theosophical speakers.[7] Several of the World Parliament's speakers on behalf of non-Christian religions had been

---

1. Peter Occhiogrosso, *The Joy of Sects: A Spirited Guide to the World's Religious Traditions*, Image Books, 1996, p xiv (cited below as Occhiogrosso, *The Joy of Sects*). In its on-line history, the Council for a Parliament of the World's Religions says, "The 1893 Parliament had marked the first formal gathering of representatives of eastern and western spiritual traditions. Today it is recognized as the occasion of the birth of formal interreligious dialogue worldwide." (Council for a Parliament of the World's Religions, "Who We Are: Our History," http://www.cpwr.org/who/history.htm, printed 08/03/04.)

2. Marcus Braybrooke, *Pilgrimage of Hope: One Hundred Years of Global Interfaith Dialogue*, Crossroad, 1992, pp 41–42 (cited below as Braybrooke, *Pilgrimage of Hope*).

3. Ibid., p 42.

4. Ibid., pp 12, 13, 14, 17.

5. René Guénon, *Theosophy: History of a Pseudo-Religion*, tr. by Alvin Moore et al., Sophia Perennis, 2001, p 152 (cited below as Guénon, *Theosophy*). See also Sylvia Cranston, *HPB: The Extraordinary Life and Influence of Helena Blavatsky, Founder of the Modern Theosophical Movement*, G. P. Putnam's Sons, 1994, pp 426–427 (cited below as Cranston, *HPB*).

6. K. Paul Johnson, *Initiates of Theosophical Masters*, State University of New York Press, 1995, p 97.

7. Michael Gomes, *The Dawning of the Theosophical Movement*, The Theosophical Publishing House, 1987, pp 16–17 (cited below as Gomes, *The Dawning of the Theosophical Movement*).

Theosophists—Kinza Hirai and Dharmapala, who spoke for Buddhism, Mohammed Webb, who upheld Islam, and Chakravarti, who was one of the Hindu representatives.[1] In his 1921 history of the Theosophical movement, René Guénon wrote that after the 1893 Parliament, "the Theosophists seemed very satisfied with the excellent occasion for propaganda afforded them in Chicago, and they even went so far as to proclaim that 'the true Parliament of Religions had been, in fact, the Theosophical Congress.'"[2]

The Parliament brought women religious leaders to the fore, as well; one of the nineteen women to address the gathering was Antoinette Brown Blackwood, the first Christian woman to be ordained as a minister in the US.[3]

In this respect, little has changed in the last 111 years. Liberal Protestants, Unitarians, social reformers, Theosophists, adherents of other heterodox "New Religious Movements," and proponents of Westernized, modern variants of non-Christian religions have provided much of the leadership of the interfaith movement since 1893. Interfaith publisher Joel Beversluis characterized interfaith activists as "the liberals, those who are not afraid to think outside the box."[4]

With the first Parliament of World Religions, Hinduism and Buddhism began their missionary efforts in Western countries.[5] Soyen Shaku introduced Zen Buddhism to the US at the Parliament; his students popularized this faith in the West.[6] The Hindu holy man Vivekananda, who spoke at this conference, led the first yoga class on American soil in 1895; he also popularized reincarnation and other ideas that had been introduced into the US in the 1870s by Theosophists.[7] Vivekananda called for an end to religious conversions and for each religion to "assimilate the spirit of the others." He said, "The Christian is not to become a Hindu or a Buddhist, nor a Hindu or a Buddhist to become a

1. Cranston, *HPB*, p426. Another historian notes, "Dharmapala, who represented Buddhism at the World Parliament of Religions held in Chicago in 1893, had earlier been recruited to Theosophy by Blavatsky and Olcott." (Kay Alexander, "Roots of the New Age," in James R. Lewis and J. Gordon Melton, eds. *Perspectives on the New Age*, State University of New York Press, 1992, p32.)

2. Guénon, *Theosophy*, p155.

3. Blackwood was ordained in 1853 to serve as pastor to the South Butler congregation of the Congregationalist Church. (Martin Forward, *Inter-Religious Dialogue: A Short Introduction*, Oneworld Publications, 2001, p127.) For additional background on Blackwood, see Office of the County Historian, "Butler, New York," http://www.co.wayne.ny.us/Departments/historian/HistButler.htm, printed 03/24/04.

4. Interview of Joel Beversluis by Lee Penn, October 2002.

5. Charles Upton says, "It should be noted that orthodox Hindus view as charlatans all teachers who attempt to spread Hinduism among non-Indians, since the only path of admission into Hinduism is to be born into one of the castes. [See Dr. Rama Coomaraswamy, MD, "The Desacralization of Hinduism for Western Consumption," http://www.coomaraswamy-catholic-writings.com/Hinduism%20for%20Western%20Consumption.htm, printed 03/03/04.] From the strictly orthodox Hindu standpoint, 'Hindu proselytization' is an impossibility." (E-mail from Charles Upton to Lee Penn).

6. Occhiogrosso, *The Joy of Sects*, p113.

7. Philip Jenkins, *Mystics and Messiahs: Cults and New Religions in American History*, Oxford University Press, 2000, pp71–72. In his 1921 exposé of Theosophy, René Guénon excoriated Vivekananda: "Thus, this 'Parliament' was the appearance of Swāmi Vivekānanda, who completely distorted the Hindu doctrine of 'Vedānta' under the pretext of adapting it to the Western mentality. If we mention him here, it is because Theosophists have always regarded him as one of their allies, even calling him 'one of our brothers of the Elder race' (a designation which they also applied to their 'Mahātmās') and 'a prince among men'. The pseudo-religion invented by Vivekānanda had a certain success in America. . . ." (Guénon, *Theosophy*, p151.) Likewise, journalist Peter Occhiogrosso says that Vivekānanda "gave a dramatic and influential address that sought to counter the stereotype of Hindus as superstitious and intolerant. In so doing, he probably also painted a rather idealized mural of Hinduism that was closer to the conception of the British Orientalists—scholars who studied the religion without participating—than to the swarming reality of Indian life. For better or worse, Vivekānanda's intellectualized and spiritualized version of Hinduism is the one that caught the modern Western imagination. Even today, the aspects of Hindu belief practiced by Americans bear only a nominal resemblance to the sectarian worship of the average Indian." (Occhiogrosso, *The Joy of Sects*, p63.)

Christian. But each religion must assimilate the spirit of the others and yet preserve its own individuality and grow according to its own law of growth."[1] (A century later, URI leaders would repeat these themes.) Vivekananda's compatriots praised his stance; "when Vivekananda returned to India in 1896, he was welcomed as a hero who had reversed the tide of Christian proselytization by winning American converts to Hinduism."[2]

Theosophists held that the Parliament vindicated their beliefs in religious unity. In 1894, Professor Max Müller told an audience at Oxford University,

> Such a gathering of representatives of the principal religions of the world has never before taken place; it is unique; it is unprecedented; nay, we may truly add, it could hardly have been conceived before our own time. . . . It established a fact of the greatest significance, namely, that there exists an ancient and universal religion, and that the highest dignitaries and representatives of all the religions in the world can meet as members of one common brotherhood, can listen respectfully to what each religion had to say for itself, nay, can join in a common prayer and accept a common blessing, one day from the hands of a Christian archbishop, another day from a Jewish rabbi, and again another day from a Buddhist priest.[3]

After the 1893 Parliament of the World's Religions, a legion of interfaith groups attempted to unite the world's religions. The principal interfaith groups as of 1993 were the World Congress of Faiths, the Temple of Understanding, the World Conference on Religion and Peace, and the International Association for Religious Freedom.[4] There have, as yet, been few tangible results of their activities.

However, this may now be changing. Marcus Braybrooke, an interfaith leader and scholar who is now active in the URI, said: "The main brake on the growth of interfaith understanding has been the conservatism of the religious communities. Happily, now, those at the leadership level in many religious traditions recognize the vital importance of interreligious cooperation."[5] With this new attitude, the ground has been prepared for the spread of movements such as the URI.

After the 1893 conclave, the next Parliament of World Religions occurred in 1993 in Chicago. Since then, Marcus Braybrooke noted that there has been "rapid growth of interfaith activity throughout the world."[6] As Donald Frew (a Wiccan Neopagan member of the URI Global Council) said: "In 1893, America met the Hindus and Buddhists. In 1993, they met us. We were now officially part of the American religious scene; we wouldn't be written off anymore as just a bunch of weirdos in California. After that, anytime a global interfaith event happened, we would be invited."[7] Thus, the 1993 Parliament marked the entry of Neopaganism into the religious mainstream. The URI carries this tradition forward, offering a platform and global networking opportunities to a kaleidoscopic array of religions and spiritual movements.

---

1. Swami Vivekānanda, 1893 Parliament of Religions, as quoted in Celia and David Storey, eds., *Visions of an Interfaith Future*, International Interfaith Centre, 1994, p39 (cited below as C. and D. Storey, *Visions of an Interfaith Future*).

2. Catherine Wessinger, "Hinduism Arrives in America: The Vedanta Movement and the Self-Realization Fellowship," in Timothy Miller, ed., *America's Alternative Religions*, State University of New York Press, 1995, p177.

3. As quoted by Gomes, *The Dawning of the Theosophical Movement*, p17; the ellipsis is as it was in the text.

4. Marcus Braybrooke, *Faith and Interfaith in a Global Age*, CoNexus Press, 1998, p19. (cited below as Braybrooke, *Faith and Interfaith*).

5. Ibid., pp20–21.

6. Ibid., p89.

7. Anneli Rufus, "Every Witch Way," *East Bay Express*, October 6–12, 2000; http://www.eastbayexpress.com/archive/100600/cover5_100600.html, printed 01/04/01; no longer on the Net at this address. As of 2004, this document may be found at http://web.archive.org/web/20001019032040/http://www.eastbayexpress.com/archive/100600/cover5_100600.html, printed 08/02/04.

Donald Frew said in 2002, "it was the enthusiasm for interfaith generated by the 1993 Parliament that helped the early success of the URI."[1] In 2003, he wrote, "Everyone who attended the Parliament went home transformed and enthused. . . . Not one of us was willing to wait another hundred years for such a life-transforming experience. This need was answered by Bishop William Swing, the Episcopal Bishop of California, in 1995."[2] Thus, URI is the direct descendant of the Parliament of World Religions.

Utopian, globalist thinking is a standard part of the world-view of the interfaith movement. Brother Wayne Teasdale, a "Christian *sannyasi*" and a trustee for the Council for a Parliament of the World's Religions, said,

> We are rapidly entering an axial time, a new age which may well be decisive for humanity and the Earth. It will be an age unlike any other in the issues it will resolve, in the directions it assumes, in the consciousness that guides it, and in the truly global civilization it will fashion. Nationalism and fanaticism will diminish before the human family's discovery of a more universal identity. Humankind will come of age, and will outgrow these forms of association as doubtful luxuries no longer desirable or affordable.[3]

Teasdale said that the 1993 Parliament was "so radically significant as to be a catalyst into the next age. . . . The Parliament was a transcendent moment in history animated by a spirit of genuine openness, mutual listening, and respect. . . . During those momentous days at the end of summer 1993, a revelation was given to humanity."[4] This revelation included "a Global Ethic, a Universal Spirituality."[5] Likewise, Marcus Braybrooke said that "a new world order based on love and compassion is being born, although as yet those who hold political and economic power seem scarcely aware that such a new age is coming into being."[6]

This search for a religious basis for world unity has long been part of the interfaith movement. Globalists and interfaith activists understand that religion is the basis of an enduring civilization. As the historian Christopher Dawson stated, "It is the religious impulse which supplies the cohesive force which unifies a society and a culture. The great civilizations of the world do not produce the great religions as a kind of cultural by-product; in a very real sense, the great religions are the foundations on which the great civilizations rest."[7] Lally Lucretia Warren, a leader of the 2004 Parliament of World Religions from Botswana, reiterated this insight in 2004: "Religion is the chief instrument through which order is established in the world."[8]

Thus, a stable global "new civilization" must be built upon a new global religion. Sir Francis Younghusband, who founded the World Congress of Faiths in 1936, wrote during World War II that "A new world order is now the dream of men, but for this a new spirit will be needed."[9] Regarding a "Congress on Science and Religion," Teilhard de Chardin said in 1941, "The purpose of the New York meetings, if I understand it aright, is not merely to seek a superficial reconciliation between the diverse forms of

1. E-mail from Donald Frew to Lee Penn, 11/18/02.

2. Donald Frew, "The Covenant of the Goddess & the Interfaith Movement," December 23, 2003, http://www.witch-vox.com/white/coginterfaith.html, printed 08/04/04.

3. Brother Wayne Teasdale, "Sacred Community at the Dawn of the Second Axial Age," in Joel Beversluis, ed., *Sourcebook of the World's Religions: An Interfaith Guide to Religion and Spirituality*, New World Library, 2000, p238.

4. Ibid., pp239–240.

5. Ibid., p240.

6. Braybrooke, *Faith and Interfaith*, p28.

7. Christopher Dawson, *Progress and Religion*, Image Books, 1960, p184.

8. Geneive Abdo, "Can a parliament of leaders from traditional religions and those with a more New Age flavor save the world from itself?," *Jewish World Review*, July 8, 2004, http://www.jewishworldreview.com/0704/religious_globalization_spiritual_summit.php3, printed 07/08/04.

9. Sir Francis Younghusband, as quoted in Braybrooke, *Pilgrimage of Hope*, p70.

Faith which divide the human spirit and make it at odds with itself, but to find what they have fundamentally in common. We seek a new spirit for a new order."[1] At a 1993 interfaith conference in India, held to carry forward the work of the 1893 Parliament of World Religions, the Executive Secretary of the National Spiritual Assembly of the Baha'is in India said, "The new world order, as one can perceive, will need a world religion. It will seek a new orientation, a new conception of morals, applicable not only to the individual, but also to society as a whole."[2]

Patricia Mische, of Global Education Associates, set out the linkage between religion and a new world order in detail:

the very fact that organized religion can and sometimes has been such a powerful force in war and conflict also suggests that it can play a powerful role in building and helping to maintain systems of peace, human rights, social justice and ecological balance. Just as there is ample evidence of human destructiveness being perpetrated in the name of religion, so is there evidence of religion and spirituality inspiring creative solutions and energizing new directions in history. In his explorations of the rise and fall of great civilizations, the historian Arnold Toynbee found that spirituality and religion played a significant role in bridging the time/space between the fall of one civilization and the rise of another. The 'creative minorities' that helped build new civilizations from the ashes of the old were often motivated by a strong spiritual vision. In contrast, civilizations that lost their spiritual core were not long sustained. If we accept Toynbee's conclusions about the importance of spirituality and religion in the rise and fall of civilizations, then we are led to certain conclusions about the importance of spirituality in the development of any truly new world order or global civilization of our time. Inner spiritual growth and transformation may be as, or even more, important than external political changes in global systems. Put another way, inner, spiritual growth, and the development of more democratic, effective, and humane global systems, may be inseparable parts of a holistic world order. They develop in conformity to one another and are mutually reinforcing. The nurturing of a deeper, global consciousness, and the harnessing of spiritual and moral energies for a more just and humane world order, are vital aspects of its healthy development.[3]

It should be no surprise that the Global Education Associates supports the URI; they participated in the preparation of the URI draft Charter in 1998–2000, and helped to facilitate the 1999 URI annual global conference.[4]

Many experienced interfaith leaders expect the URI to go much further than previous efforts at interfaith unity. The Rev. James Davis, an interfaith minister from New York, said of the URI conference he attended in 1997: "We've never seen any organization build coalitions as quickly or as successfully as the United Religions Initiative."[5] In 1998, comparative religion scholar Huston Smith deemed the URI the "most significant" interfaith effort.[6] In 2002, New Age author Neale Donald Walsch said that the URI is "more global in scope, and more universal in reach" than other interfaith organizations, adding that "I am not sure that any other interfaith organization casts that wide a net."[7] Interfaith activist and publisher Joel Beversluis described the URI in October 2002 as "the most energetic of the interfaith organizations, with the broadest reach.... It does stand out as the most dynamic umbrella organization for existing and new groups."[8] David Cooperrider, a professor of management

---

1. Pierre Teilhard de Chardin, "Some Reflections on Progress," *The Future of Man*, translated by Norman Denny, Harper & Row, 1964, p76.

2. A.K. Merchant, "Inter-Religious Dialogue—The Challenge of Building Mutual Trust and Friendship—A Baha'i Perspective," in C. and D. Storey, *Visions of an Interfaith Future*, p168.

3. Patricia Mische, "Religion and World Order: Introduction and Overview," *Religion and World Order* 1994 *Symposium*, Global Education Associates, http://www.globaleduc. org/RWO3.pdf, printed 08/03/04.

4. Global Education Associates, "About GEA," http://www.globaleduc.org/About2.shtml, printed 08/03/04.

5. The Rev. James Davis (Wittenberg Center for Alternative Resources), telephone interview by Lee Penn, 12/10/97.

6. Carolina Wolohan, "Group uses U.N. as its model," *San Jose Mercury News*, June 22, 1998; printed 6/29/98.

7. E-mail from Neale Donald Walsch to Lee Penn, 11/20/02.

8. Interview of Joel Beversluis by Lee Penn, October 2002.

at Case Western Reserve University—whose "Appreciative Inquiry" system has been used by the URI since 1996—said in 2002 that the URI "continues to enjoy an annual growth rate of 100 percent, which, Prof. Cooperrider estimates, will bring them to about 1,000 centers in the next five to eight years. He also predicts that URI might garner a Nobel Peace Prize before its first decade is complete."[1]

If these predictions are accurate, the URI will prove to be the culmination of the global interfaith movement.

FOUNDING THE URI: 1993–1996

Bishop Swing conceived the idea of the URI in February 1993, after Gillian Sorenson, then the deputy secretary of the UN, invited him to sponsor an interfaith service at Grace Cathedral in 1995 to celebrate the 50th anniversary of the signing of the UN Charter.[2] Swing wondered why the nations of the world could meet for peace on an ongoing basis, while the religions of the world could not. He took his vision of United Religions to interfaith leaders in June 21, 1993,[3] and received support from them. Swing then unveiled the plan for the URI to the public during the UN anniversary interfaith service, held at Grace Cathedral on June 25, 1995.

In 1995 and 1996, Bishop Swing traveled to the UN headquarters in New York City, China, Taiwan, Korea, Japan, India, Pakistan, Egypt, Jordan, Israel, Rome, England, Turkey, Germany, and Switzerland to seek support from religious leaders and interfaith activists for the URI.[4] Some Christians, Jews, and Muslims expressed interest, as did many representatives of Asian religions and interfaith organizations.[5] Nevertheless, Swing said that most of these leaders would not help to build the URI. Swing concluded that "A United Religions is never going to happen if you start at the top. . . . It's gotta be a grassroots movement."[6]

Bishop Swing returned to the United States, remaining "determined to commit the rest of my life to an initiative that would create a United Religions."[7] This dream was so compelling that in 1996, Bishop Swing turned down a nomination to run in the 1997 election for Presiding Bishop of the Episcopal Church.[8] Swing told the 1997 diocesan convention that his diocese is now the world: "I intend to keep thinking globally and acting locally. Now my diocese is Pinole and Padua. Kyoto and Concord. Oxford and Ohlhoff House."[9] In 2004, Bishop Swing reaffirmed his global commitment: "Each morning I say the same prayer: 'O God in whom we live and move and have our being. . . .' The 'we' in

1. Christopher Johnston, "The Best Possible World," *CWRU Magazine*, Spring 2002, http://appreciativeinquiry.cwru.edu/intro/timeline.cfm, printed 02/19/03.

2. Nina Wu, "If it's about oil, just say so," [Interview with Bishop Swing], *The Examiner*, Jan. 7, 2003, http://www.examiner.com/examiner_qa/default.jsp?story=n.qa.0107w, printed 02/19/03.

3. Bishop William Swing, "What is missing is a global soul," *Pacific Church News*, August/September 1995, p5.

4. Swing, August 10, 1996 speech before the North American Interfaith Network Conference, pp2–3 (cited below as Swing, speech to NAIN Conference, 08/10/96).

5. Bishop William Swing, "Reactions from Religious Leaders," document released in the summer of 1996 by the URI (cited below as Swing, "Reactions from Religious Leaders," summer 1996). In an e-mail to Lee Penn on 11/18/02, URI Global Council member Donald Frew said of the Bishop's contacts in 1995 and 1996, "Earlier on, URI folks were casting far and wide for interest and support. Many of these early contacts did not amount to much and did not last."

6. Transcribed by Lee Penn from a tape of the speech by Bishop Swing at the Commonwealth Club, April 25, 2001 (cited below as Swing, Commonwealth Club speech, 04/25/01).

7. Swing, speech to NAIN Conference, p1.

8. Bishop William Swing, "One Dream Too Many," *Pacific Church News*, June/July 1996, p5.

9. Bishop William Swing, "Excerpts: Bishop's Address" [to 1997 Diocesan convention], *Pacific Church News*, December 1997/January 1998, p35. Pinole and Concord are cities in Swing's diocese; Ohlhoff House is a charitable organization that the Episcopal diocese runs.

my daily petition is (1) my family, (2) the Diocese of California, and (3) peacemakers of the United Religions Initiative scattered throughout the world. In my heart there is a oneness, a unity in each of these three. I have been consecrated by God to serve the unity in all three areas."[1] After his retirement as Diocesan Bishop in 2006, Swing "plans to dedicate himself full-time to furthering the development of the United Religions Initiative."[2]

From 1996 to 2000, the URI held global summit conferences each summer in the US. The first of these occurred at the Fairmont Hotel, atop San Francisco's Nob Hill. It was attended by 56 people,[3] whom Bishop Swing described as "religious leaders, international interfaith leaders, CEOs, leaders of institutions and interested individuals."[4] This series of meetings culminated in the June 2000 URI global summit in Pittsburgh, Pennsylvania, at which the URI Charter was signed. After 2000, URI summit meetings occurred worldwide—five regional meetings in different parts of the world in 2001 and early 2002, capped by the first Global Assembly meeting in Rio de Janeiro, Brazil in August 2002.

LAYING THE GROUNDWORK: 1997–1999

From 1997 through 1999, the URI prepared the Charter that its members would sign in 2000, established working relationships with other interfaith organizations, and organized a Y2K event, the 72-hour "Global Cease-Fire." URI activists met worldwide, from Argentina to Zimbabwe, to build support for the movement. Bishop Swing took the interfaith gospel to the Congressional Human Rights Caucus, a planning committee for the 2002 Olympics in Salt Lake City, and the European Commission.

The 1997 conference, held at Stanford University, included 200 people from 40 countries,[5] selected by URI organizers from among 1,200 candidates.[6] The "vast majority" of the delegates were from the United States.[7] Neither the Vatican nor the Southern Baptist Convention (the largest Protestant denomination in the US) sent representatives.[8] Participants issued a call for a 24-hour worldwide religious cease-fire starting on December 31, 1999.[9] Representatives of several interfaith groups (including the Council for a Parliament of the World's Religions, the World Congress of Faiths, Global Education Associates, the Temple of Understanding, and the Center for World Thanksgiving) signed a memorandum of understanding to support closer cooperation among those groups.[10] Bruce Schuman, a

1. Bishop William Swing, "Episcopacy, Episcopal Diocese, and the *San Francisco Chronicle*," web site of the Episcopal Diocese of California, http://www.diocal.org/article.php?sid=248&mode=thread&order=0, printed 05/18/04. The ellipse in the quotation is as it was in the original.

2. Episcopal News Service, "Bishop Swing of California announces retirement," October 26, 2004, http://www.episcopal-church.org/3577_53388_ENG_HTM.htm, printed 11/05/04.

3. United Religions Initiative, "Letter From the URI's Founder, Bishop William E. Swing," *Annual Report* 2000, p2; cited below as URI, *Annual Report* 2000. In his 1998 book, Swing stated that 56 people attended this meeting; 55 "pledged themselves to become the United Religions Initiative (one person declined)." (Bishop William Swing, *The Coming United Religions*, United Religions Initiative and CoNexus Press, 1998, pp18–19, cited below as Swing, *The Coming United Religions*). Both attendance figures, 55 and 56 people, have appeared in URI documents pertaining to the 1996 summit meeting.

4. Bishop William Swing, "Seeking Peace Among Religions," *San Francisco Chronicle*, pA-17, August 22, 1996.

5. Charles Gibbs and Sally Mahé, *United Religions Initiative, Birth of a Global Community: Appreciative Inquiry in Action*, Lakeshore Publishers, 2004, p111 (cited below as Gibbs/Mahé, *Birth of a Global Community*).

6. Paul Chaffee, "Ring of Breath Around the World: A Report of the United Religions Initiative Global Conference," issued in the summer of 1997 by the United Religions Initiative, p7.

7. Don Lattin, "Religious Violence Decried At Gathering," *San Francisco Chronicle*, June 26, 1997, pA-19.

8. Ibid.

9. Charles Gibbs, "Report from the Executive Director," *Journal of the United Religions Initiative*, Fall 1997, p2.

10. Paul Andrews, "this issue:," *Journal of the United Religions Initiative*, Fall 1997, Issue 4, p1; the names of the groups were provided by Paul Andrews in a conversation on December 5, 1997.

New Age activist, said of the 1997 conference: "The net result was a complex and quite vital creative process that sustained a constant creative excitement, and a sense that this grand vision is unfolding as a natural part of social evolution, and simply reflects an avant garde attunement with the 'zeitgeist'—the 'spirit of the times.'"[1]

From 1997 through 1999, interfaith meetings to build support for the URI occurred in Great Britain, New York City, Argentina,[2] Brazil, India, South Africa, Ethiopia, Belgium, Los Angeles,[3] Japan, the Netherlands, Romania,[4] Uganda, Germany,[5] the Philippines, Pakistan, Malawi, Zimbabwe, Mozambique,[6] Venezuela,[7] Austria, Switzerland, Washington DC,[8] Kenya,[9] and Sudan.[10] Thus, the URI boasted of "an active presence on every continent."[11] In 1998, Bishop Swing spoke in Washington DC to the Congressional Human Rights Caucus; in Salt Lake City, he discussed plans for URI involvement in the 2002 Olympics.[12] He also "spoke in Shanghai, Kyoto, Bucharest and London, and presented a paper at the European Commission in Brussels."[13]

Meanwhile, the URI began to draft its Charter. Bishop Swing said, "We hired Dee Hock, the inventor of the VISA card, to try to invent a structure for the URI," with the goal of creating "an organizational design where the greatest amount of authority is invested in the smallest unit, which is un-bureaucratic, which is un-centralized."[14] Swing reported that Dee Hock "and 14 others sat in a room for 3 years"[15] to prepare the Charter that the URI signed in 2000.

The 1998 URI summit conference, held in June at Stanford University, drew 208 participants from 38 countries;[16] 128 (61%) were from North America.[17] In cooperation with the Temple of Understanding, the Council of the Parliament of World Religions, and other interfaith organizations, the URI made plans to "create a multi-cultural global youth service project for people 20-30 years of age on every continent."[18] URI delegates issued a call for a 72-hour "Global Cease-Fire" from December 31, 1999 through January 2, 2000; they also adopted the first draft of a charter, and began circulating it worldwide for comment and revision.[19]

1. Bruce Schuman, "All One People: A Common Flame burns for all," *The Light and Life Journal: An Exploration of the Spiritual Universe*, Autumn 1997, p 6.

2. Charles Gibbs, "Regional Conferences Prepare for URI Global Summit," *Pacific Church News*, August/September 1997, p 22.

3. United Religions Initiative, "Building a Worldwide Movement," *URI News Update*, Fall 1997, pp 5–6.

4. United Religions Initiative, "News Updates from Around the World," *URI Update*, Spring 1998, pp 3–6.

5. United Religions Initiative, "URI in the world," *URI Update*, Fall 1998, pp 6–7.

6. United Religions Initiative, "URI in the world," *URI Update*, Spring 1999, pp 3–5.

7. United Religions Initiative, "72 Hours: Unprecedented Acts of Peace Among Religions And Spiritual Communities," *URI Update*, Fall 1999, p 3.

8. United Religions Initiative, "URI in the world," *URI News Update*, Fall 1998, pp 6–7.

9. Gibbs/Mahé, *Birth of a Global Community*, p 138.

10. "United Religions Initiative: Building spiritual partnerships for a just, sustainable, and peaceable world," URI leaflet issued 9/15/98 (cited below as URI, "Building spiritual partnerships," 9/15/98 leaflet).

11. Ibid.

12. Dennis Delman, "Bishop's Address to Diocesan Convention—Lambeth Erred: Diocese to Tackle Lambeth Statement: 'Homosexual Practice Incompatible With Scripture'," *Pacific Church News*, December 1998/January 1999, p 43.

13. Ibid.

14. Swing, Commonwealth Club speech, 04/25/01.

15. Ibid.

16. Gibbs/Mahé, *Birth of a Global Community*, p 139.

17. Annie Imbens-Fransen, "The United Religions Initiative: From an inspiring, idealistic and ambitious initiative toward a realistic possibility," *Journal of the United Religions Initiative*, Issue 5, p 16.

18. United Religions Initiative, "Highlights URI Global Summit III," leaflet issued July 1998, back page.

19. Dennis Delman, "Third URI Summit Plans 72 Hour Global Cease Fire," *Pacific Church News*, August/September 1998, p 22.

About one hundred delegates from 30 countries attended the fourth URI summit, held in June 1999 at Stanford University.[1] (Attendance was lower than it had been in 1997 and 1998 because of financial problems that beset the URI in 1999[2]—including a cumulative debt of $700,000.[3]) The 1999 summit meeting prepared for the 72-hour cease-fire, revised the draft URI charter, and planned for "the inauguration of a truly global URI."[4] At this conference, Prafultabai Jaintilal, a Hindu delegate from Mozambique, said that "the president of Mozambique had attended a recent URI meeting in Maputo and that local people looked to the URI's work to bring positive change and stability" to Mozambique after many years of war.[5]

ESTABLISHING GLOBAL PRESENCE: 2000–2002

The URI claimed that "over 1,000,000 participants" in more than 60 countries participated in its 3-day global "religious cease-fire" from December 31, 1999 through January 2, 2000[6]—a 72-hour millennial bash dedicated to what the URI called "commitments of service, peacebuilding, reconciliation, and consciousness transformation."[7]

According to the URI, "over 300 representatives from 39 faith traditions and 44 countries"[8] attended the fifth global summit meeting of the URI, held at Carnegie-Mellon University in Pittsburgh from June 25-30, 2000.[9] URI leaders had expected "tens of thousands of leaders of the world's religions, spiritualities, and indigenous traditions" to attend this "momentous occasion;"[10] they did not. Swing's liberal colleague in Canada, Anglican Bishop Michael Ingham of New Westminster, predicted in April 2000 that the Secretary-General of the UN and the Dalai Lama would show up for the charter signing.[11] They did not. Nevertheless, Swing remained enthusiastic about URI's prospects.

1. Dennis Delman, "4th Global Summit Begins Transition To United Religions," *Pacific Church News*, October/November 1999, p37.

2. United Religions Initiative, "A glimpse from the Sacred Mountain," http://www. united-religions.org/newsite/ resources/summit99.htm, printed mid-1999; no longer on the Net at this address. As of 2004, the Web page is available at http://web.archive.org/web/20000815213125/http://www.united-religions.org/newsite/resources/summit99.htm. For the Executive Director's accurate prediction of lower summit meeting attendance, see Charles Gibbs, introductory article, *URI Update*, no. 5, spring 1999, p1.

3. Gibbs/Mahé, *Birth of a Global Community*, p155.

4. Charles Gibbs, introductory article, *URI Update*, no. 6, fall 1999, p1.

5. Gibbs/Mahé, *Birth of a Global Community*, p160.

6. URI, *Annual Report 2000*, "URI Milestones 2000," p3.

7. URI, *Annual Report 2000*, "72 Hours of Peacebuilding: Three Days to Change the World," p4.

8. URI, *Annual Report 2000*, "URI Milestones 2000," p3.

9. On June 26, the day of the Charter signing, the 2 main Pittsburgh newspapers featured stories about 1,100 Catholics attending the first Tridentine Latin Mass offered in St. Paul Cathedral since 1970, and gave this far more prominent coverage than they gave to the URI. The worshippers at the Latin Mass outnumbered the URI delegates by about 4 to 1. (David Conti, "1,100 faithful celebrate first Tridentine Mass in 30 years, Pittsburgh *Tribune-Review*, June 26, 2000, http://www.triblive.com/ news/plato626.html; printed 06/30/00; no longer on the Net.) The home pages of the two papers (http://www.post-gazette.com/main.html and http://triblive.com/main.html) featured the Mass story on June 26; their URI coverage was buried within the papers' Web sites.)

10. E-mail message dated 10/29/99 by a person who attended and reported upon Bishop Swing's 10/28/99 URI presentation in Pittsburgh.

11. Kathy Blair, "United Religions gets Canadian start in B.C.," *Anglican Journal/Canada*, http://www.anglicanjournal. com/126/04/canada11.html, printed 06/02/01.

Bishop Swing, an avid golfer, said he felt like "Tiger Woods on the 18th hole at Pebble Beach." [1] He exulted, "This is the spirit's property . . . and no one owns it. Fifty years from now, people from all over the world will flock to Pittsburgh in tribute of this signing." [2] Delegates signed the URI charter and recognized 85 cooperation circles worldwide as URI chapters. Additionally, "more than 6,000 people"[3] signed the Charter over the Internet.[4]

An array of odd spiritual movements made their appearance at the conference. Andrew Nesky, host of the radio program "Science and the Outer Streams," provided Internet access to the URI charter-signing ceremony.[5] Nesky's web page says that

Science and the Outer Streams provides a forum to express eclectic ideas and expand people's conscious [sic], and approaches the unexplained from an intellectual and non-judgmental standpoint. Join us in discussing esoteric studies, spirituality, psychology, speculative science, religions, artificial intelligence and mysticism. Also featured is a section on the United Religious Iniative [sic] (URI), which brought together faiths as diverse as Christianity, Buddhism, Islam, and Wicca in an effort to end religiously motivated violence. Host Andrew Nesky is the president of the Theosophical Society in Pittsburgh, PA. He has twice been elected Master of a Masonic Lodge and is a published writer.[6]

This marked the URI's first acknowledged link with Freemasonry and with Theosophy (a faith system that combines aspects of Buddhism, Hinduism, and Western occultism).

Rowan Fairgrove, an avowed Wiccan long active in the URI,[7] reported that the chant which opened the URI meeting was:

Gathered in here in the mystery of the hour
Gathered in one strong body
Gathered here in our unity and power
Spirit draw near.[8]

(At this gathering, Bishop Swing said that the URI was "the spirit's property,"[9] and the meeting's opening chant asked that "Spirit draw near." Neither Fairgrove nor Bishop Swing named the spirit that owns the URI, and that the URI invoked.)

The religious ceremony that started the conference on June 25 was a potpourri. As the Pittsburgh *Post-Gazette* reported,

1. Ervin Dyer, "Charter signed for religious coalition," Pittsburgh *Post-Gazette*, June 27, 2000, http://www.post-gazette.com/regionstate/20000627unitedreligion7.asp, printed 06/28/2000. (cited below as Dyer, "Charter signed," *Post-Gazette*, 06/27/00).

2. Ibid.

3. URI, *Annual Report* 2000, "URI Milestones 2000," p3.

4. URI, *Annual Report* 2000, "Letter from Interim Global Council Chair Rita Semel and Executive Director Charles Gibbs," p4.

5. These programs are on-line at Science and the Outer Streams, "Episode List," with links from the following web pages: http://www.inecom.com/outer/list.asp?iPage=2, http://www.inecom.com/outer/list.asp?iPage=3, and http://www.inecom.com/outer/list.asp?iPa ge=4; printed 02/19/03. The main page of the URI web site in mid-2000 said, "View the webcast of the Global Signing Ceremony. Thank you to Andrew Nesky of Science and the Outer Streams, Technimedia for making this webcast possible." (United Religions Initiative, http://www.united-religions.org/newsite/index.htm, printed in 2000. This version is no longer on the Net at this address, but may be found at http://web.archive.org/web/20000815062848/http://www.united-religions.org/newsite/index.htm, as of 2004.)

6. Science and the Outer Streams, "About the show," http://www.inecom.com/outer/default.asp; printed 10/8/02.

7. Fairgrove is currently a URI affiliate member. (United Religions Initiative, "Affiliates," http://www.uri.org/regional-news/affiliates/index.asp, printed 09/23/04, cited below as URI, "Affiliates").

8. URI discussion forum [for 2000 summit meeting], "Message 91: Gathering Chant," http://www.safnet.com/uri/forum/messages/91.html, printed 06/26/00.

9. Dyer, "Charter signed," *Post-Gazette*, 06/27/00.

Drummers from Manipur, India, in their egg yolk-golden robes, beat out a call to assemble. Native Americans, representing the Haudenosaunee, drew the celebrants into a wide circle on the lawn at Carnegie Mellon as sacred sage was burned to attract the spirits during a ritual earth blessing. When it was over, participants from Senegal, Brazil, South Korea, Canada, Pakistan, Israel and other countries strode into a university auditorium, singing 'Marching in the Light of God,' for a rousing round of storytelling and testimony.[1]

On June 26, when the charter was signed, the *Post-Gazette* reported that the Carnegie Music Hall "was turned into a celebration of spirit. African drummers and Indian musicians mixed with Muslims, Wiccans, Christians and lay people, singing and clapping in a circle of hope and diversity."[2] On July 1, the *Post-Gazette* reported that Swing had stayed up "past midnight watching a Mayan contingent performing spiritual rituals."[3]

Donald Frew, who has been a member of the URI Global Council, was asked to perform a "traditional Wiccan foundation blessing" at the closing ceremony; he said, "In this one, I specifically invoked Hekate and Hermes by name, and Bishop Swing was right there raising his arms in invocation with the rest of the Circle! We have, indeed, come a long way."[4]

Bishop Swing has come a long way, as well; the prayers in the Eastern Orthodox vespers service for Pentecost explicitly disavow his behavior. The ancient liturgy says, "Against Thee alone do we sin, but Thee alone do we also adore. We know not how to worship a strange god, nor how to stretch forth our hands to any other god, O Master."[5]

Additionally, there could be questions about the character of the gods whom Donald Frew invoked (with Swing's participation). A standard encyclopedia describes Hermes as one who "conducted the souls of the dead to the underworld" and as "the god of commerce, and the protector of traders and herds. As the deity of athletes, he protected gymnasiums and stadiums and was believed to be responsible for both good luck and wealth. Despite his virtuous characteristics, Hermes was also a dangerous foe, a trickster, and a thief."[6] Hekate (or Hecate) was worse. The same reference book says, "Unlike Artemis, who represented the moonlight and splendor of the night, Hecate represented its darkness and its terrors. On moonless nights she was believed to roam the earth with a pack of ghostly, howling dogs. She was the goddess of sorcery and witchcraft and was especially worshiped by magicians and witches, who sacrificed black lambs and black dogs to her. . . . In art Hecate is often represented with either three bodies or three heads and with serpents entwined about her neck."[7] In *A History of Witchcraft*, Jeffrey B. Russell says, "The three faces of Hecate are one source for Dante's idea that Satan has three faces in hell."[8]

In reply to these questions about Hekate and Hermes, Frew said,

What matters is the understanding of the invoker. The Hermes I invoked was like the Hermes you mention. However, Hekate is a very complex goddess, encompassing many more concepts than those mentioned in the standard references. I was invoking the Hekate of the late Neoplatonists, *not* a 'demonic' Hekate. Hermes

1. Ervin Dyer, "Religious summit focuses on ending violence worldwide," Pittsburgh *Post-Gazette*, June 27, 2000, http://www.post-gazette.com/regionstate/20000626unitedreli gion8.asp, printed 06/27/2000.

2. Dyer, "Charter signed," *Post-Gazette*, 06/27/2000.

3. Ervin Dyer, "Religious cooperative to spread message," Pittsburgh *Post-Gazette*, July 1, 2000, http://www.post-gazette.com/headlines/20000701uninat2.asp, printed 07/01/2000.

4. Donald Frew, Covenant of the Goddess, "1999–2000 Interfaith Report," http://www.cog.org/interfaith/cogdf00.html, printed 2/8/03.

5. Department of Religious Education, Orthodox Church in America, *The Vespers of Pentecost: Introduction and Text*, 1974, p34, from the second kneeling prayer.

6. Microsoft® Encarta® Reference Library 2003, entry for "Hermes;" © 1993–2002 Microsoft Corporation.

7. Ibid., entry for "Hecate".

8. Jeffrey B. Russell, *A History of Witchcraft: Sorcerers, Heretics, and Pagans*, Thames & Hudson, 1980, p48.

represents liminal[1] time and Hekate represents liminal space—both appropriate for a moment of transition like the founding of the URI. My intent was beneficial, whatever the prejudices of others about my gods.[2]

Bishop Swing said in June 2000 that the reason for having the URI charter-signing meeting in Pittsburgh was that "URI is a bridge building organization, and Pittsburgh is the city with the most bridges in North America."[3] There was a more practical reason, however. Donald Frew said, "We moved the 2000 Summit to Pittsburgh because the URI needed money and there were promised donors in Pittsburgh who wanted the summit to be there. . . . The funding in question was in the low hundreds of thousands."[4] A source in close contact with the Episcopal hierarchy indicated in late 1999 that the funding was "being sponsored by some foundations with deep pockets and a strong liberal agenda that includes putting pressure on the Episcopal diocesan structure."[5] One of these foundations was the Hillman Foundation, which is associated with a wealthy, nationally prominent liberal Republican family and with Calvary Church, "one of the few remaining liberal parishes in Pittsburgh."[6] (According to the *Post-Gazette*, "Locally, more than $400,000 was raised through private foundations and individuals. Calvary Episcopal Church in Shadyside, a longtime supporter, took up a collection."[7])

After the meeting, Robert Muller—a former assistant UN Secretary-General—praised the URI:

The Charter of a United Religions Organization . . . was adopted June 2000, in Pittsburgh. That organization can then help the peaceful resolution of the several religious conflicts we still have on this planet, develop a common modern global science of spirituality, a strategy and a methodology of spirituality (e.g. prayer, forgiveness, sanctity, thanksgiving, confession and so many other helpful practices). It will create a different, better, spiritual world, with religions united in a wonderful, non-fundamentalist diversity.[8]

The next major URI-related event was the World Millennium Peace Summit of Religious and Spiritual Leaders, held at the UN and the Waldorf-Astoria Hotel in New York City from August 28 through August 31, 2000. The URI stated that "many members" participated in this gathering, and that it was involved in planning the meeting as a member of the Advisory Council of Interfaith Organizations.[9] Additionally, Bawa Jain, the Secretary-General of the meeting, has been active in the URI, the World Economic Forum, the Earth Charter movement, and the Interfaith Center of New York.[10]

1. "Liminal" refers to the point of awareness below which events cannot be consciously felt or perceived. It is thus the lower border of consciousness. (By contrast, *sub*liminal advertising is promotional material that delivers its message without the conscious awareness of its targets.)

2. E-mail from Donald Frew to Lee Penn, 07/01/04.

3. PR NEWSWIRE release from the United Religions Initiative, "Local and Global Participants Gather in Pittsburgh June 25–30 to Focus On Ending Religiously Motivated Violence," June 20, 2000, http://bahai-library.org/newspapers/062000.html, printed 12/09/02.

4. E-mail from Donald Frew to Lee Penn, 11/18/02. Charles Gibbs and Sally Mahé corroborated this, saying that during the summer of 1999, "the possibility of holding this historic event in Pittsburgh, Pennsylvania was put forward by Bishop Swing. The hope of new sources of funding in Pittsburgh, a growing group of locally influential people committed to leadership roles in helping to produce the charter signing and summit, the symbolic importance of Pittsburgh as the city in the United States with the most bridges, and the pressure that had been growing over the years to move the URI global gathering out of San Francisco's Bay area led to a decision in October [1999] to hold the event in Pittsburgh." (Gibbs/Mahé, *Birth of a Global Community*, pp179–180.)

5. E-mail message dated 11/29/99, from a source associated with Trinity Episcopal Seminary, an Evangelical Episcopal seminary in Pittsburgh.

6. Ibid.

7. Dyer, "Charter signed," *Post-Gazette*, 06/27/00.

8. Robert Muller, *Ideas And Dreams for a Better World: 2501–3000, Volume VII*, Idea 2600, Annex, http://www.robertmuller.org/volume/ideas2501.html, viewed 06/21/04.

9. URI, *Annual Report* 2000, "URI Milestones 2000," p3.

10. For biographical data, see Millennium Peace Summit, "About Us: Bawa Jain, Secretary-General," http://www.millenniumpeacesummit.org/contact_bios_jain.html, printed 01/02/03.

About 800 religious leaders and 1,000 observers from 100 countries attended the World Millennium Peace Summit,[1] which had financial backing from Ted Turner, the Ford Foundation, and other private donors.[2] (The Dalai Lama, the spiritual leader of Tibetan Buddhists and a winner of the Nobel Peace Prize, was not invited to the Peace Summit, due to pressure from the People's Republic of China.)[3] Most of those in attendance signed a "Commitment to Global Peace,"[4] but plans to establish a UN-affiliated "International Advisory Council of Religious and Spiritual Leaders" to work with the UN Secretary-General went nowhere. The religious summit ended, moreover, with mutual feelings of victimization among the participants. Christians, Muslims, and Hindus[5] all complained of inadequate representation.[6] These tensions led to an event that Austin Ruse, the head of the Catholic Family and Human Rights Institute[7] (who covered the Peace Summit on-site), described as "a rugby scrum of ten mostly far eastern clerics"[8] who were fighting to get access to a microphone during a forum on conflict resolution. Six security guards broke up the "shoving match;"[9] when order was restored, the chairman ended all audience participation.[10] No resolutions—on poverty, the environment (including a proposal to endorse the Earth Charter), or anything else—were passed by the summit meeting.

At the summit, Christian hopes for peace encountered harsh reality. Bawa Jain explicitly rejected any claims of any religion—such as Christianity, Judaism, or Islam—to "absolute truth," saying "we will recognize there is not just one claim of absolute truth, but there is truth in every tradition."[11] Ted Turner's address to the summit harshly criticized Christianity. He said, "What disturbed me is that my religious Christian sect was very intolerant. . . . We thought that we were the only ones going to heaven."[12] Turner added, "We are all one race, and there is only one God that manifests himself in

1. The information about the Millennium Peace Summit is—except where otherwise documented—from Austin Ruse, "Summit of the Gods: Ted Turner's Millennium World Peace Summit," *Touchstone*, November 2000, http://www.touch-stonemag.com/docs/issues /13.9docs/13-9pg48.html, printed 05/07/03 (cited below as Ruse, "Summit of the Gods"); also, Austin Ruse, "Religious and Spiritual Leaders meet to form Permanent UN Advisory," *Friday FAX*, July 28, 2000, http://www.c-fa m.org/FAX/Volume_3/faxv3n35.html, printed 09/14/2000.

2. Bill Broadway, "A Full House For World Peace," *Washington Post*, September 2, 2000, p9. (Internet version, printed 09/20/2000; no longer on the Net.)

3. Ibid.

4. Chris Herlinger, "Historic Meeting Shows Religions at Their Best and Worst," *Beliefnet.com*, http://www.beliefnet.com/story/40/story_4097.html, printed 09/10/2000 (cited below as Herlinger, "Historic Meeting"). One who did not sign the "Commitment to Global Peace" was Cardinal Francis Arinze, then serving as president of the Vatican's Pontifical Council for Interreligious Dialogue. He did not sign because some of its provisions—such as the assertion that all religions are equal—contradict Catholic teachings. (Interview with Austin Ruse, September 2000; see also Catholic World News, "UN Summit Attendees Declare All Religions Equal," http://www. cwnews.com/Browse/2000/08/13726.htm, printed 05/07/03).

5. Herlinger, "Historic Meeting."

6. On Christian and Muslim complaints of under-representation, see Ruse, "Summit of the Gods".

7. The Catholic Family and Human Rights Institute (C-FAM) is a pro-life lobbying organization and think tank that works full-time with the UN and related organizations. Their web site is http://www.c-fam.org.

8. Ruse, "Summit of the Gods."

9. Ibid.

10. Interfaith leader Robert Traer reported similar events that occurred during the debate at the 1993 Parliament of the World's Religions about adoption of a draft of Hans Küng's "Global Ethic:" "What occurred on the last day of the Assembly was hardly spiritual or even ethical, as at times those who shouted the loudest and longest from the floor were given the microphone." (Robert Traer, *Quest For Truth: Critical Reflections on Interfaith Cooperation*, The Davies Group, 1999, p131; cited below as Traer, *Quest for Truth*).

11. James Harder, "U.N. Faithful Eye Global Religion," *Insight Magazine*, October 2, 2000, http://www.hvk.org/articles/1000/3.html, printed 05/07/03.

12. Reuters, "Religious Leaders Start Signing Peace Declaration," ABC News.com, printed 08/31/2000 (no longer on the Net). Another copy of this story is on-line at http://www.tibet.ca/wtnarchive/2000/9/1_1.html, printed 05/07/03 (cited below as Reuters, "Religious Leaders Start Signing Peace Declaration").

different ways."[1] In response, summit delegates "hooted and hollered like it was an old-time revival meeting,"[2] and gave Turner a standing ovation for remarks that the mainstream press described as "often irreverent."[3] Religious summit delegates gave an icy reception to a plea from the Patriarch of Ethiopia for protection of unborn children, and likewise sat in silence when a leader of the Muslim World Conference said that marriage could only occur between a man and a woman. By contrast, the delegates gave a standing ovation to a Buddhist "master" when he condemned all attempts at religious conversion. Joan Brown Campbell, of the National Council of Churches, joined the condemnation of "proselytizing," and got cheers from the assembly. Austin Ruse reported—courtesy of a "Vatican source"—that Cardinal Arinze was "furious" about the anti-Christian speeches given at the Peace Summit.[4]

Bishop Swing's first response to the 2001 terrorist attack on America—a sermon given the next day, on September 12, 2001—included a plug for the URI. In his sermon to the "Interfaith Service of National Mourning" at Grace Cathedral, Swing said, "We have to object when a religious group announces its spiritual superiority over other religious groups.... On the other side, we have to come together to find a common vocation for religions to work for the common good.... Ultimate security comes from the process of healing the scars and the brokenness and pointing people toward a unifying hope."[5] Bishop Swing ended his address to the assembled mourners thus: "September 11, 2001, a 911 call to end the day with a more united humanity, a wiser United States of America, and a more resourceful United Religions. Oh, One! Amen."[6] (Regarding the effect of 9/11 on the URI, Global Council member Donald Frew said in 2003, "More people see the need for interfaith dialogue and want to do it, but fewer have the time and resources."[7])

Between the June 2000 URI summit meeting in Pittsburgh and the summer 2002 URI Global Assembly, five regional URI assemblies occurred in Africa, Asia, Europe, the US, and South America; about 520 interfaith activists participated in them.[8]

The first URI global assembly occurred in Rio de Janeiro in August 2002. The URI stated that "320 people from 57 different traditions and 39 countries" attended[9]—the largest such annual meeting since it was founded. The theme of the meeting was "Sharing the Sacred, Serving the World."[10] Paul Chaffee, who had served on the URI Board until 2002, noted these accomplishments of the Assembly:

1. Colum Lynch, "U.N. Summit Hears Plea For Religious Tolerance," *Washington Post*, August 30, 2000, p A-16; Internet version printed 09/20/2000; no longer on the Net.

2. Ruse, "Summit of the Gods."

3. Reuters, "Religious Leaders Start Signing Peace Declaration."

4. Ruse, "Summit of the Gods." A Christian interfaith activist, who wishes to remain anonymous, attended the summit and confirms this report. In an e-mail to Lee Penn on 02/07/01, he said that Arinze had "spoken out against the persecution of Christians in India and in African countries;" in response, "Hindu monks and other eastern religious people . . . made many strong verbal attacks on him and tried to keep him from speaking."

5. Bishop William Swing, "Interfaith Service of National Mourning: Reflection," *Pacific Church News*, October/November 2001, p 33.

6. Ibid.

7. Interview of URI Global Council member Donald Frew by Lee Penn, 10/14/02 and 03/28/03.

8. Paul Chaffee, "United Religions Initiative Comes of Age in Rio," September 2002 e-zine, InterfaithNews.net, http://www.interfaithnews.net/index.php?page=uri, printed 11/25/02 (cited below as Chaffee, "United Religions Initiative Comes of Age in Rio"). The US conference was in Salt Lake City in May 2001, with "over 175" participants. The Latin American conference was in Oaxtepec, Mexico in January 2002, with 80 participants. The Africa conference was in Nairobi, Kenya in October 2001, with 128 participants. The Asia/Pacific conference was in Bali, Indonesia in December 2001, with 94 in attendance. The European conference was in Berlin, Germany in April 2002, with 42 participants. Source: United Religions Initiative, "Weaving the URI Region by Region," *Annual Report* 2001, pp 6–7; cited below as URI, *Annual Report* 2001.

9. Charles Gibbs, URI fund raising letter, November 14, 2002, p 2.

10. Chaffee, "United Religions Initiative Comes of Age in Rio."

selection of a new board with worldwide representation, the beginning of programs to implement the six-point "Guidelines for Action" in the URI charter (including "Ecological Imperatives" and "Sustainable, Just Economics"),[1] new programs for interfaith and intra-faith dialogue, and closer ties between the URI and the Council for a Parliament of the World's Religions.[2]

The next URI global assembly had been planned for Seoul, South Korea, starting on June 26, 2005. URI Executive Director Charles Gibbs noted the significance of the date: "the fifth anniversary of the signing of URI's Charter and the sixtieth anniversary of the signing of the United Nations Charter. June 25, 2005, the day before, will mark the fifty-fifth anniversary of the beginning of the Korean War."[3] However, in the fall of 2004, the URI scaled back these meeting plans due to a shortage of funds. Instead of a full-scale global assembly in Korea, there will be a meeting of the URI's "outgoing and incoming Global Councils."[4]

THE URI IN 2004: "WE ARE EVERYWHERE"

The URI has grown far beyond its Northern California roots, and now is active worldwide. As of September 2004, the URI web site listed 238 chapters ("Cooperation Circles") in 47 countries in the following regions:[5]

- 53 in Africa—1 in Angola, 1 Ethiopia, 1 in the Great Lakes region (Central Africa), 2 in Kenya, 10 in Malawi, 10 in Mozambique, 3 in Nigeria, 1 in the Republic of Benin, 2 in Senegal, 1 in Sierra Leone, 1 in South Africa, 3 in Swaziland, 1 in The Gambia, 14 in Uganda, 1 in Zambia, and 1 in Zimbabwe. (The URI has minimal presence in South Africa, despite support for the Initiative by Anglican Archbishop Desmond Tutu.)
- 61 in Asia—31 in India, 12 in Korea, 1 in Nepal, 15 in Pakistan, and 2 in Sri Lanka.
- 13 in Europe—1 in Belgium, 2 in Finland, 3 in Germany, 1 in Romania, 1 in Russia, 1 in Spain, and 4 in the United Kingdom.
- 16 in Latin America—5 in Argentina, 5 in Brazil, 1 in Chile, 1 in Haiti, 1 in Mexico, 1 in Peru, 1 in Panama, and 1 in Venezuela.
- 16 in the Middle East—1 in Egypt, 10 in Israel, 3 in Jordan, 1 in the Palestinian Territory, and 1 in Tunisia.
- 48 in North America—3 in Canada, and 45 in the US.
- 11 in the Pacific region—2 in Indonesia, 1 in Malaysia, 1 in New Zealand, 5 in the Philippines, and 2 in Vietnam.
- 20 multi-regional cooperation circles.

1. The URI described this as "Spiritual Agenda 21," a six-year vision that "will be revised and revisited by the next Global Assembly in 2005 and made into a public document by 2008." (Dennis Delman, "Peacebuilding Permeates First Global Assembly," *Pacific Church News*, Winter 2003, p5.) Global Council member Donald Frew said that Spiritual Agenda 21 "was accepted as a work in progress and a Global Council Committee—the Action Agenda Committee—was created to pursue this. The result has been that the 6 points of the Action Agenda (as it is now known) are priorities in our ongoing activities. However, to date, no final declaration or statement has been proposed." (E-mail from Donald Frew to Lee Penn, 07/01/04.)

2. Chaffee, "United Religions Initiative Comes of Age in Rio."

3. Charles Gibbs, "Letter from Executive Director: November 2003," United Religions Initiative, http://www.uri.org/about uri/edrreport/november.asp, printed 11/10/03.

4. Information provided by Donald Frew to Lee Penn, October 2004, and e-mail from Frew to Lee Penn, 11/03/04.

5. United Religions Initiative, "Cooperation Circles of the URI," http://www.uri.org/regionalnews/cclisting.asp, printed 09/23/04; analysis by Lee Penn.

This represents steady growth for the movement—3 new Cooperation Circles per month since June 2000.[1] (In June 2000, the URI had 85 Cooperation Circles.[2] The total had grown to "nearly 150" by the end of 2001,[3] and to 185 by the end of 2002.[4])

As of late fall 2004, the URI continued to grow. In his October/November 2004 newsletter, URI Executive Director Charles Gibbs stated that the URI then had "270 circles around the world. For the first time, URI has circles in Turkey, Tajikistan, Denmark, China, Bangladesh, and in Kashmir Valley, Jammu and Himachal Pradesh in India. . . . Upcoming URI activities include an assembly focusing on capacity building for the URI in Brazil in Curitiba, Brazil and an assembly for Spanish speaking Latin America hosted by the Indigenous community in Ayacucho, Peru, both in November."[5]

Based on a 2003 survey of its Cooperation Circles, the URI claims to be "doing a remarkable job with equal participation" of the sexes; 51% of its members are male, and 49% female.[6] The religious breakdown of members in 2003 was:

- 41% Christian
- 18% Buddhist
- 11% Muslim
- 6% Jewish
- 5% Indigenous
- 3% Baha'i
- 3% Hindu
- 13% Other religions.[7]

A majority of the Cooperation Circles—156 out of 238, or 66%—are based in Asia, Africa, Latin America, the Middle East, and the non-English-speaking nations of the Pacific Rim. It appears that the URI's base of support has expanded well beyond affluent Western liberals, the usual supporters of interfaith movements.[8] Donald Frew stated, "In North America, we comfortably talk about interfaith relationships. In other parts of the world, people are desperate to find ways to stop daily interreligious violence."[9] Bishop Swing said the same in early 2004: "when I've been in countries around the world where there is clear and evident religious violence, URI makes abundant sense and I have been warmly welcomed."[10]

In addition, individuals and organizations that "support the values of the URI"[11] may become URI Affiliates, subject to approval by the Global Council of the URI or by an existing Cooperation Circle.

1. Growth from 85 CCs in June 2000 to 238 CCs in September 2004, an increase of 153 CCs in 51 months, averages out to 3 new CCs per month. Cooperation Circles may be local, regional, or international.

2. URI, *Annual Report* 2000, "Letter from Interim Global Council Chair Rita Semel and Executive Director Charles Gibbs," p 4.

3. URI, *Annual Report* 2001, "Letter From Executive Director and Chair of the Interim Global Council," p 2.

4. United Religions Initiative, "2002 Year in Review," *Annual Report* 2002 leaflet; cited below as URI, *Annual Report* 2002.

5. United Religions Initiative, "Letter from Executive Director," October/November 2004, http://www.uri.org/abouturi/ edrreport/index.asp, printed 11/03/04. (cited below as URI, Oct./Nov. 2004 letter from Executive Director).

6. United Religions Initiative, *CC Survey Report* 2003, http://www.uri.org/ccsurveyrep ort2003/Section_Three.pdf, p 12.

7. Ibid., p 14.

8. Robert Traer, who led the International Association for Religious Freedom during the 1990s, said, "A more critical appraisal of interfaith activities would reveal that, at least in the West, they involve primarily affluent individuals who have the time and the means to chat about spirituality and religion. Many of these individuals are very critical of traditional religion, because in their eyes churches, mosques, synagogues and temples seem preoccupied with their own parochial concerns." (Traer, *Quest For Truth*, p 80.)

9. E-mail from Donald Frew to Lee Penn, 06/04/03.

10. Dennis Delman, "Interview with Bishop William E. Swing, Founder and President of the United Religions Initiative," *Pacific Church News online*, February/March 2004, http: //pcn.diocal.org/PCNO/pcn004-1/index.html, printed 02/24/04.

11. URI, "Affiliates."

As of September 2004, the URI web site listed 92 individual affiliates and 77 organization-level affiliates from 25 countries: 10 organizations and 9 individuals in Africa; 12 organizations and 5 individuals in Asia; 1 organization and 6 individuals in Europe; 6 organizations and 3 individuals in Latin America; 47 organizations and 66 individuals in North America; and 1 organization and 3 individuals in the Pacific Rim area.[1]

The URI has ambitious plans for growth. The URI said in early 2003 that over the next three years, it "fully expects to grow from 15,000 members to more than 30,000, building traditions of cooperation and giving hope to hundreds of thousands of people in conflict-sensitive areas of the world. We hope to engage 3 million people and many partner organizations in a global action research project— Visions for Peace Among Religions, designed to create peace among religions for the 21st century."[2] (Since then, its claimed membership has increased to 26,000.)[3] In May 2004, URI Executive Director Charles Gibbs said that the Global Council seeks to "grow from our current membership of 241 Cooperation Circles in 50 countries to 1,000 CCs in 100 countries, with 1,000,000 individual members by 2010," in order to "deepen its capacity to act effectively on local, regional and global levels."[4] In his July 2004 letter, Gibbs reported that the URI had 260 Cooperation Circles worldwide,[5] and in the fall of 2004, he reported an increase to 270.[6]

URI members are activists, so 26,000 people can have an effect disproportionate to their numbers. Additionally, URI "partner organizations" include many other interfaith groups, as well as the UN. Thus, the URI appears to have a good chance of meeting its membership targets.

URI's GLOBAL LEADERSHIP:
DIVERSITY IN ACTION

URI headquarters are in the Presidio, a former military base in San Francisco. There is a URI branch office in Ethiopia, its first outside San Francisco.[7]

There were 11 URI staff at the San Francisco headquarters as of September 2004,[8] and two URI "NGO Representatives"[9] at the UN.[10] In addition, there were 20 "Regional Staff and Support" worldwide;[11] 11 of them were also members of the URI Global Council.[12] Thus, as of the fall of 2004 the URI

---

1. Ibid.; analysis by Lee Penn. This is a small increase from the October 2002 affiliation levels: 89 individuals and 72 organizations.

2. United Religions Initiative, "Programs," http://www.uri.org.abouturi/programs/index.asp, printed 05/28/03.

3. Gibbs/Mahé, *Birth of a Global Community*, p 289.

4. Charles Gibbs, "Letter from Executive Director: May/June 2004," United Religions Initiative, http://www.uri.org/abouturi/edrreport/index.asp, printed 05/26/04.

5. Charles Gibbs, "Letter from Executive Director: July 2004," United Religions Initiative, http://www.uri.org/abouturi/edrreport/index.asp, printed 07/03/04. The URI web site listed 238 Cooperation Circles as of 09/23/04; it appears that their detailed list had not been updated to match Gibbs' tally.

6. URI, Oct./Nov. 2004 letter from Executive Director.

7. United Religions Initiative, "URI in the World," *URI Update*, Spring 2001, p 4.

8. United Religions Initiative, "URI Global and Regional Support," "URI Global staff," http://www.uri.org/abouturi/globalcouncil/globalstaff.asp, printed 09/23/04 (cited below as URI, "Global staff").

9. An NGO is a non-governmental organization that works with the UN.

10. United Religions Initiative, "Contact Us," "URI NGO Representatives," http://www.uri.org/abouturi/contact/, printed 09/23/04 (cited below as URI, "Contact").

11. URI, "Global staff," Regional Staff & Support.

12. United Religions Initiative, "URI Global Council," http://www.uri.org/abouturi/globalcouncil, printed 06/30/04 (cited below as URI, "Global Council").

had 33 staff—an increase from the 26 staff (13 at the headquarters, [1] and 13 "Regional Coordinators" worldwide[2]) that the URI had in May 2003.

The highest-paid URI staff member is Canon Charles Gibbs, who in 2002 earned $109,250 (plus $22,990 in benefits), for a total pay package of $132,240.[3]

Aside from Bishop Swing, the best-known URI staff have been the Rev. William Rankin, who joined the URI in 1998, and Dee Hock, founder and CEO Emeritus of VISA U.S.A. and Visa International.[4] Rankin was formerly the President and Dean of the Episcopal Divinity School, a major liberal Episcopal seminary in Cambridge, Massachusetts.[5] Rankin remained at URI headquarters until 2000, when he left to head a URI Cooperation Circle, the Global AIDS Interfaith Alliance (GAIA).[6]

Dee Hock began working with the URI in 1997,[7] and helped to prepare the URI Charter that was signed in 2000. Hock contributed to the URI in 2001, indicating his ongoing interest in the movement.[8] The URI says, "Led by Dee Hock and thanks to the Chaordic Alliance and its evolved Chaordic Commons, URI's chartering process moved from vision to concrete design. Through this partnership, URI's dream became reality."[9]

In the past, the URI has included Dr. David Cooperrider and three other members of Case Western Reserve University's Center for Social Innovation in Global Management (SIGMA project) on its list of staff and leaders.[10] The URI describes its relationship to SIGMA as "one of URI's earlier and most enduring partnerships."[11] Cooperrider and his staff have applied the Appreciative Inquiry management process to URI regional and global meetings since 1996.

From 1995 through early 2002, the leadership of the URI was predominantly American. A majority of the 23 URI board members and officers serving in 1998 were from the San Francisco Bay area.[12]

In July 2002, the URI elected a "Global Council," a board with representation from every continent. Their initial meeting was at the URI Global Assembly in August 2002. The board includes Bishop Swing, Executive Director Charles Gibbs, and 3 representatives from each of the major regions: Africa, Asia, Europe, Latin America and the Caribbean, the Middle East, North America, and the Pacific Islands. (The Middle Eastern board members include an Israeli Jew, a Palestinian Christian, and an Egyptian Muslim.) There are also 3 representatives for multi-regional cooperation circles, 3 members of the "transition advisory committee," and 9 "At-Large Trustees." Global Council elections are to occur every 3 years.

1. United Religions Initiative, "URI Staff," *URI Update*, December 2002, p8; also URI, "Contact."

2. United Religions Initiative, "Creating Cooperation Circles: A Practical Guide," p ii, issued August 2002; also URI, "Contact."

3. Form 990 for 2002, filed with the IRS by the URI; part V, schedule 6. This is available on-line (after registration) through a charity watchdog organization, Guidestar.org, at http://documents.guidestar.org/2002/680/369/2002-680369482-1-9.pdf (printed 09/27/04; cited below as URI, Form 990, 2002).

4. URI, "Building spiritual partnerships," 9/15/98 leaflet, with list of staff and board members.

5. Regarding the abortive ecclesiastical trial of Episcopal Bishop Walter Righter for ordaining an openly homosexual deacon, Rankin had said in 1995, "Heresy implies orthodoxy, and we have no such thing in the Episcopal Church." (Rankin was quoted by *Witness*, a liberal Episcopal magazine, December 1995, p36.)

6. The Global AIDS Interfaith Alliance, "Advisory Board," http://www.thegaia.org/aboutus/advisory.htm, printed 02/11/04.

7. "The United Religions Initiative," *The Chaordic Commons of Terra Civitas*, Summer 2001, Vol. 1, no 1, p14 (cited below as "URI," Chaordic Commons).

8. URI, *Annual Report* 2001, "Honoring Our Donors," p9.

9. United Religions Initiative, "Other Partnerships," http://www.uri.org/abouturi/partnerships/partners_other.asp, printed 07/17/04 (cited below as URI, "Other Partnerships").

10. URI, "Building spiritual partnerships," 9/15/98 leaflet, with list of staff and board members.

11. URI, "Other Partnerships."

12. URI, "Building spiritual partnerships," 9/15/98 leaflet, with list of staff and board members.

URI Council member Donald Frew has described many of the Council members as "theologians or leaders of interfaith groups."[1] As of 2004, four current and former URI trustees had participated in the Goldin Institute for International Partnership and Peace, a project established in Chicago in 2002 to support the interfaith work of the URI, the Parliament of World Religions, and similar movements.[2]

The 38 board members as of 2004 had the following religious affiliations:

- Baha'i—2
- Buddhist—4
- Christian—15[3]
- Hindu—4
- Indigenous—2
- Jewish—4
- Muslim—4
- Sikh—1
- Wiccan—1
- Zoroastrian—1

The names and religious affiliations of each of the 38 board members are listed in the appendix "URI's Global Leadership."

The Board has a majority, 22 of 38, of its members from outside the US and other "Anglosphere" nations.[4] Nineteen, half of the Global Council members, are from Asia, Africa, Latin America, the Middle East, and the non-English-speaking nations of the Pacific Rim:

- US—14
- New Zealand—1
- Great Britain—1
- Europe, outside of the UK—3
- Latin America—3
- Middle East—3
- Africa—4
- Asia, including the Philippines and Indonesia—9

URI FUNDING: SECULAR FOUNDATIONS, BILLIONAIRES, AND THEOSOPHISTS

Much of the URI's growth has happened in the Third World, where the least money is available. As a result, the URI has found it difficult to outgrow its dependence on a few major donors.

In late 1998, Bishop Swing acknowledged that secular support is critical for success of the URI. He said, "there is just enough help from non-religious resources: Case Western School of Management in Cleveland, Ohio; Dee Hock, founder of the Visa Card; the Presidio Trust in San Francisco, where the

---

1. URI Global Council member Donald Frew, e-mail to Lee Penn on 11/18/02.
2. Council for a Parliament of the World's Religions, "Reflections by Rev. Paul Chaffee," November 4, 2002, http://www.cpwr.org/what/programs/chaffeereflects.htm, printed 07/15/04.
3. Based on the data provided in the Appendix below: 9 Protestants (4 Episcopalians/Anglicans, 2 Presbyterian, 2 Lutherans, and 1 Protestant whose affiliation is unknown), 1 Eastern Orthodox, and 5 Catholics.
4. URI, "Global Council," with corrections provided by Donald Frew on 06/30/04.

URI office is located; plus individuals from around the world who produce 99.4% of all contributions that URI receives."[1]

In August 1999, the URI received one of its largest gifts, $1 million, from a recent inheritor of wealth; this allowed the URI to retire its remaining $400,000 debt.[2] In early 2004, the URI held a banquet to honor William K. Bowes, Jr., a Silicon Valley venture capitalist, "whose visionary philanthropy has provided an essential financial foundation for URI for the past seven years."[3] They also announced a $250,000 endowment grant from his brother and sister-in-law, John and Frances Bowes,[4] to fund awards to exemplary URI Cooperation Circles.

URI Global Council member Donald Frew stated in March 2003, "The vast majority of money comes from eight individuals and associated foundations; they are all Christian or Jewish."[5] These donors make contributions in the $100,000-$400,000 range.[6] URI contributions were "fairly localized in California and Texas" as of 2002.[7] Swing is alarmed by this trend. He said at the 2002 Global Assembly, "I figured that at the very beginning I could raise major funds from a few people. I figured that as we grew and matured the majority of funding would come from all segments of the URI family. What is at stake here is the very essence of the URI. We intend for the greatest amount of authority to be invested in the broadest unit. But if this money comes from a few people, those people will have the authority because wherever the money comes from will be the place of power."[8]

Donors to the URI have included the following foundations and organizations:

- Aes Corporation[9]
- Ale Petrol Company[10]
- Bank of New York and the George Link Jr. Foundation[11]
- Barbara and Carl D. Arnold Jr. Foundation[12]
- Alben F. and Clara G. Bates Foundation[13]

1. "Bishop Swing Addresses World Congress of Faiths: Raises Possibility That URI Might Play A Role in Salt Lake City Olympics Opening Ceremony," *Pacific Church News*, December 1998/January 1999, p39.

2. Gibbs/Mahé, *Birth of a Global Community*, p180.

3. Charles Gibbs, "Letter from Executive Director: February 2004," United Religions Initiative, http://www.uri.org/abouturi/edrreport/feb2004.asp, printed 03/05/03.

4. Ibid.

5. Interview of Donald Frew by Lee Penn, 3/28/03. The URI "Form 990" report, filed annually with the IRS, confirms this. The 2002 URI Form 990 shows that 53.2% of URI revenue for 1998–2001 was from major donors, those whose donations exceeded $137,365 during the 4-year period. This report for 2001 shows that over the 1997–2000 period, 53.8% of URI revenue was from those whose donations during the period exceeded $119,860. (Form 990 for 2001, filed with the IRS by the URI; part IV-A, lines 15–26f; this statistic was derived by dividing line 26b by line 26c. The 2001 Form 990 report is available on-line through the California Attorney General's office, at the URL http://justice.doj.ca.gov/charitysr/trust_list.asp?CT_INT=99867&intPageT=1, as of September 28, 2004.) 1999 and 2000 reports showed a similar degree of URI dependence on major donors.

6. Bert Williams, "Religious leaders meet in Healdsburg to work for peace," *Sonoma West Times & News*, May 14, 2003, http://www.sonomawest.com/articles/2003/05/14/healdsburg/news/nws-1.txt, printed 07/15/05.

7. Dennis Delman, "Interim Global Council Makes Transition to Elected Global Council," *Pacific Church News online*, October 2002, http://pcn.diocal.org/PCNO/pcn002-9/main.html, printed 01/06/03.

8. Bishop William Swing, Keynote address for URI Global Assembly, August19, 2002; http://pcn.diocal.org/uriaddress.html, printed 03/06/03 (cited below as Swing, URI keynote address, 08/19/02).

9. URI, *Annual Report* 2001, "Honoring Our Donors," p8.

10. United Religions Initiative, "Peace Resources," *URI Update*, November 2003, Issue 14, p3. The corporation funded the second stage of development of a peace curriculum; the initial phase had been funded by UNESCO.

11. URI, *Annual Report* 2002, "Honoring URI Donors and Volunteers."

12. URI, *Annual Report* 2001, "Honoring Our Donors," p8, and United Religions Initiative, 2003: *Compassionate Actions for a Better World*, annual report; http://www.uri.org/resources/URI_Anual_Report_2003.pdf, viewed 09/24/04 (cited below as URI, *Annual Report*, 2003).

13. URI, *Annual Report*, 2003.

- William K. Bowes Jr. Foundation[1]
- Cabell and Shirley Brand Charitable Trust[2]
- Camp Younts Foundation[3]
- Stacey B. Case Living Trust[4]
- Charity Enablers Foundation[5]
- Christopher Columbus Foundation[6]
- Community 2000 Charitable Trust[7]
- Community Foundation of Monterey County[8]
- Community Foundation of Silicon Valley[9]
- Community Wholistic Growth Center, Inc.[10]
- Copen Family Foundation[11]
- Cow Hollow Foundation[12]
- Nathan Cummings Foundation[13]
- Arthur Vining Davis Foundation.[14]
- Leonard and Shirley Ely Pass-Through Fund[15]
- Farrell Family Fund[16]
- Firedoll Foundation[17]
- Fraternite Notre Dame, Inc.[18]
- Bill and Melinda Gates Foundation—which gave $1 million in early 2003 to the Global AIDS Interfaith Alliance, a URI Cooperation Circle[19]

1. URI, *Annual Report*, 2000, "Honoring Our Donors," p7, and URI, *Annual Report*, 2001, "Honoring Our Donors," p8, and URI, *Annual Report*, 2002, "Honoring URI Donors and Volunteers," and URI, *Annual Report*, 2003.

2. Ibid., from the above annual reports for 2000–2003.

3. Ibid., from the above annual reports for 2000–2003.

4. URI, *Annual Report*, 2003.

5. URI, *Annual Report*, 2001, "Honoring Our Donors," p8.

6. List provided on November 20, 1997 by Paul Andrews, a URI staff member.

7. URI, *Annual Report*, 2002, "Honoring URI Donors and Volunteers."

8. List provided on November 20, 1997 by Paul Andrews, a URI staff member, also, URI, *Annual Report*, 2000, "Honoring Our Donors," p7.

9. Community Foundation of Silicon Valley, "Annual Report 2000"—list of grants in FY 1999–2000, p35; HTML version of the document http://www.cfsv.org/documents/annual_report_00.pdf, printed 03/18/03.

10. URI, *Annual Report*, 2003.

11. United Religions Initiative, "Foundation Grants Enable URI Youth Leadership on Worldwide Net," *URI News Update*, March 1997, no. 2, p1. (cited below as URI, "Youth Leadership," *URI News Update*, March 1997).

12. URI, *Annual Report*, 2002, "Honoring URI Donors and Volunteers."

13. URI, *Annual Report*, 2003.

14. The Vanderbilt Center for the Study of Religion and Culture, "Appendix H—Center for Religion and Culture"—The Arthur Vining Davis Foundation, p222, http://www.vanderbilt.edu/AnS/strategic/pdf/SAPCAS_Final_Report_2001_06_27-3_Appendix_ H.pdf, printed 04/21/03. (The document lists a $133,796 grant made by the Arthur Vining Davis Foundation "for the June 2000 Global Summit" of the URI.)

15. URI, *Annual Report*, 2000, "Honoring Our Donors," p7, and URI, *Annual Report*, 2001, "Honoring Our Donors," p8, and URI, *Annual Report*, 2002, "Honoring URI Donors and Volunteers."

16. URI, *Annual Report*, 2003.

17. Ibid.

18. Ibid.

19. Diocesan Digest, "Global AIDS Interfaith Alliance Receives $1 million from Gates Foundation," *Pacific Church News online*, February 2003, vol. 141 no. e2, http://pcn.diocal.org/PCNO/pcn003-2/index.html, printed 03/22/03. This grant is for "a 3-year program that serves 25 villages in Malawi's southern region. Through this program, 135 women brought HIV prevention and care to 3000 men, women, and children." (Global AIDS Interfaith Alliance, *Annual Report*: 2003, http://www.the-gaia.org/resources/AnnualReport03.pdf, p2; printed 07/15/04.)

- Fred Gellert Family Foundation[1]
- Global Peace Foundation[2]
- Richard and Rhoda Goldman Fund[3]
- Greenville Foundation of Northern California[4]
- Edward E. Hills Fund[5]
- George Hornstein Family Foundation[6]
- David Hyatt Memorial Philanthropic Fund for Interfaith Understanding[7]
- Ik Onkar Peace Foundation[8]
- International Education and Resource Network (I*EARN)[9]
- William R. and Gretchen B. Kimball Fund[10]
- Koret Foundation[11]
- Kramer Family Foundation[12]
- George Link, Jr. Foundation, Inc.[13]
- James J. Ludwig and Eileen D. Ludwig Foundation[14]
- Lucis Trust World Service Fund[15]
- Joseph L. and Sarah S. Marcum Foundation[16]
- McBean Family Foundation[17]
- McCune Foundation[18]
- Meadows Charitable Trust[19]
- Richard King Mellon Foundation[20]

1. URI, *Annual Report*, 2001, "Honoring Our Donors," p8.

2. URI, *Annual Report*, 2003.

3. List provided on November 20, 1997 by Paul Andrews, a URI staff member; Richard and Rhoda Goldman Fund, "2001 Grants—Education," ($500,000 over the 6 years from 1997 through 2002); http://goldmanfund.org/grants/01grants_edu.phpx, printed 12/13/02. The foundation made an additional $75,000 grant to the URI in 2003. (United Religions Initiative, "URI in the World—Announcements," *URI Update*, August 2003, Issue 13, p7; cited below as URI, "URI in the world," *URI Update*, August 2003). Their contributions are also acknowledged in URI, *Annual Report*, 2002, "Honoring URI Donors and Volunteers," and in URI, *Annual Report*, 2003.

4. URI, "URI in the World," *URI Update*, August 2003, p7; the foundation donated $17,000 to the URI for further development of the URI "Interfaith Peacebuilding Curriculum." Their donations are also acknowledged in URI, *Annual Report*, 2003.

5. URI, *Annual Report*, 2000, "Honoring Our Donors," p7, and URI, *Annual Report*, 2001, "Honoring Our Donors," p8.

6. URI, *Annual Report*, 2002, "Honoring URI Donors and Volunteers," and URI, *Annual Report*, 2003.

7. URI, *Annual Report*, 2001, "Honoring Our Donors," p8.

8. URI, *Annual Report*, 2003.

9. URI, "Youth Leadership," *URI News Update*, March 1997, p1.

10. URI, *Annual Report*, 2000, "Honoring Our Donors," p7, and URI, *Annual Report*, 2001, "Honoring Our Donors," p8.

11. URI, *Annual Report*, 2000, "Honoring Our Donors," p7, and URI, *Annual Report*, 2001, "Honoring Our Donors," p8, and URI, *Annual Report*, 2003.

12. URI, *Annual Report*, 2000, "Honoring Our Donors," p7, and URI, *Annual Report*, 2001, "Honoring Our Donors," p8, and URI, *Annual Report*, 2002, "Honoring URI Donors and Volunteers," and *Annual Report* 2003.

13. URI, *Annual Report* 2003.

14. URI, *Annual Report*, 2000, "Honoring Our Donors," p7, and URI, *Annual Report*, 2001, "Honoring Our Donors," p8, and URI, *Annual Report*, 2002, "Honoring URI Donors and Volunteers," and URI, *Annual Report*, 2003.

15. URI, *Annual Report*, 2000, "Honoring Our Donors," p7.

16. URI, *Annual Report* 2003.

17. URI, *Annual Report* 2000, "Honoring Our Donors," p7, and URI, *Annual Report* 2001, "Honoring Our Donors," p8, and URI, *Annual Report* 2002, "Honoring URI Donors and Volunteers," and URI, *Annual Report* 2003.

18. URI, *Annual Report*, 2000, "Honoring Our Donors," p7.

19. URI, *Annual Report*, 2001, "Honoring URI Donors," p8, and URI, *Annual Report*, 2002, "Honoring URI Donors and Volunteers."

20. URI, *Annual Report*, 2000, "Honoring Our Donors," *Annual Report* 2000, p7.

- Menke Foundation[1]
- Emil Mosbacher Jr. Foundation[2]
- Outrageous Foundation[3]
- Joe and Lois Perkins Foundation[4]
- Perkins-Prothro Foundation[5]
- David and Laura Perry Philanthropic Fund[6]
- Philanthropic Collaborative, Inc.[7]
- Iva and Jerome Preston Charitable Trust[8]
- San Francisco Foundation[9]
- Shafran Family Foundation[10]
- Sierra Club[11]
- Sierra Health Foundation[12]
- James R. and Donna H. Simanton Foundation[13]
- Soros Foundation[14]
- Rudolf Steiner Foundation[15]
- Strong Foundation for Environmental Values[16]
- Surdna Fund[17]
- Tara Center[18]
- John Templeton Foundation's Local Societies Initiative[19]
- Tides Foundation[20]

1. URI, *Annual Report, 2003: Compassionate Actions for a Better World,* annual report; http://www.uri.org/resources/URI_Anual_Report_2003.pdf, viewed 09/24/04.

2. URI, *Annual Report,* 2000, "Honoring Our Donors," p7.

3. URI, *Annual Report,* 2002, "Honoring URI Donors and Volunteers."

4. URI, *Annual Report,* 2000, "Honoring Our Donors," p7, and URI, *Annual Report,* 2001, "Honoring Our Donors," p8.

5. URI, *Annual Report,* 2003.

6. URI, *Annual Report,* 2000, "Honoring Our Donors," p7.

7. URI, *Annual Report,* 2002, "Honoring URI Donors and Volunteers."

8. URI, *Annual Report,* 2000, "Honoring Our Donors," p7, and URI, *Annual Report,* 2003.

9. List provided on November 20, 1997 by Paul Andrews, a URI staff member. A foundation report states that it donated $250 to the URI in fiscal year 2000. (The San Francisco Foundation, "Advised Grants," http://www.sff.org/giving/advised.html, printed 04/27/04.) Also, URI, *Annual Report,* 2003.

10. URI, *Annual Report,* 2003.

11. URI, *Annual Report,* 2002, "Honoring URI Donors and Volunteers."

12. URI, *Annual Report,* 2000, "Honoring Our Donors," p7.

13. URI, *Annual Report,* 2000, "Honoring URI Donors and Volunteers," and URI, *Annual Report,* 2003.

14. URI, "Youth Leadership," *URI News Update,* March 1997, p1; Dennis Delman, "Second United Religions Summit Conference," *Pacific Church News,* June/July 1997, p28.

15. Rudolf Steiner Foundation, "Client profiles—designated funds," http://www.rsfoundation.org/clientprofiles/project-descriptions.html, printed 11/13/02.

16. URI, *Annual Report,* 2001, "Honoring Our Donors," p8, and URI, *Annual Report,* 2002, "Honoring URI Donors and Volunteers."

17. List provided on November 20, 1997 by Paul Andrews, a URI staff member.

18. URI, *Annual Report,* 2001, "Honoring Our Donors," p8.

19. United Business Media, PR Newswire, "$80,000 Awarded to Groups Acting Locally to Foster Science and Religion Dialogue," June 4, 2003, http://www.prnewswire.com/news/, printed 06/06/03. The URI in Kampala, Uganda received a $10,000 grant for the "Center for Dialogue in Religion and Science." Grants were made by the Local Societies Initiative, which is funded by the John Templeton Foundation.

20. Tides Foundation, *Annual Report* 2001–2002, http://www.tidesfoundation.org/annReport01-02.pdf, printed in 2004. The Foundation listed a $3,000 grant to the URI. It is not known whether this is separate from, or the same as, one of the Tides grants that the URI acknowledges in its annual reports (from the Kieschnick Family Fund, the Tara Fund, and the Work-in-Progress Fund of the Tides Foundation).

- Kieschnick Family Fund of the Tides Foundation[1]
- Tara Fund of the Tides Foundation[2]
- Work-in-Progress Fund of the Tides Foundation[3]
- Travelers Foundation[4]
- Emily Hall Tremaine Foundation[5]
- United States Institute of Peace[6]
- Weiser Family Foundation[7]
- Worldwide Education and Research Institute [8]

Of the 72 donors listed above, 50 donated once to the URI, and 22 donated in two or more years. With new, high-profile donors such as Gates and Templeton, the URI may be able to obtain significant future income from other blue-ribbon givers who follow the lead of these high-prestige foundations.

URI staff member Paul Andrews said in the fall of 1997, "We do not want to be funded by any one particular source. We want a broad base of support for the URI, so that there is no question of a funding source setting a religious agenda."[9] By the same logic, a critic could say that URI dependence on "private, non religious"[10] benefactors has allowed non-religious donors to promote a secular agenda for the URI.

To assure broad-based, long-term funding for the URI, Bishop Swing made plans in 2002 to lead a 3-year, 14-member international fund raising group.[11] Donald Frew stated in June 2003 that "the URI is considering 're-thinking' its policy against accepting funds from religious organizations, provided that no single religious group wields influence thereby. A cap on acceptable donations from an individual group is one possibility."[12] Frew also said that the URI Global Council was working with regional and local URI activists worldwide so that they could raise more funds themselves, rather than relying on grants from the headquarters.[13]

1. URI, *Annual Report*, 2002, "Honoring URI Donors and Volunteers."
2. URI, *Annual Report*, 2001, "Honoring Our Donors," p8.
3. URI, *Annual Report*, 2002, "Honoring URI Donors and Volunteers."
4. URI, *Annual Report*, 2001, "Honoring Our Donors," p8.
5. URI, *Annual Report*, 2000, "Honoring Our Donors," p7.
6. United States Institute of Peace, "About the United States Institute of Peace," http://www.usip.org/aboutusip.html, printed 02/17/03; United States Institute for Peace, "PeaceWatch Online: Grant Awards," April 2002, http://www.usip.org/peacewatch/2002/4/grant2. shtml, printed 09/04/02 (announcing a $30,000 grant to the URI). This donation is also acknowledged in URI, *Annual Report*, 2002, "Honoring URI Donors and Volunteers." Additionally, the USIP appears to have donated to the URI during the reporting period for its 2003 annual report; see URI, *Annual Report*, 2003.
7. URI, *Annual Report*, 2002, "Honoring URI Donors and Volunteers," and URI, *Annual Report*, 2003.
8. Worldwide Education and Research Institute, "Philanthropic and Emergency Projects," http://weri.org/projects/philanth.htm, printed 09/29/98; no longer on the Net.
9. Interviews by Lee Penn of Paul Andrews, URI staff member, October 7 and December 11, 1997.
10. Carol Barnwell, "'United Religions' is Bishop Swing's goal," *The Lambeth Daily*, Issue 4, 22 July 1998, http://justus.anglican.org/resources/Lambeth1998/Lambeth-Daily/22/UR.html, printed 04/22/03, cited below as Barnwell, "United Religions." In 1997, Swing said that one of the things that "makes the URI different" is that it is "funded by non-religious sources, 'to create a common meeting ground that is paid for by ordinary people who have global hope for religions.'" ("Bishop Swing Asks for Religious Cease Fire at Japan Conference," *Pacific Church News*, December 1997/January 1998, p26.)
11. Chaffee, "United Religions Initiative Comes of Age in Rio."
12. E-mail from Donald Frew to Lee Penn, 06/04/03.
13. Interview with Donald Frew by Lee Penn, 06/03/03.

Since 1998, annual funding for the URI San Francisco headquarters has remained in the $1.2–$2.0 million range.[1] Donald Frew has estimated that URI Cooperation Circles raise an additional $1 million per year for their own activities.[2] Thus, the URI currently has about $2.2 million to $3 million per year available for its activities worldwide.

The 2002 Annual Report indicated that the URI spent about 14% of its budget on fund raising; this proportion increased to 17% in 2003.[3]

"APPRECIATIVE INQUIRY": MOLDING MINDS FOR A POST-MODERN RELIGION

Since April 1996, URI summit meetings and regional workshops have been run using the consensus-building principles of "Appreciative Inquiry" (AI), the management technique developed by Dr. David L. Cooperrider, co-chair of the Center for Social Innovation in Global Management (SIGMA), and Associate Professor of Organizational Behavior at the Case Western Reserve University School of Management.[4] In 2002, Donald Frew stated that Cooperrider and AI remain "very important" for the organization.[5]

Here's how Dr. Cooperrider describes "Appreciative Inquiry":

We have reached 'the end of problem solving' as a mode of inquiry capable of inspiring, mobilizing and sustaining human system change … The future (of organizational development) belongs to methods that affirm, compel, and accelerate anticipatory learning involving larger and larger levels of collectivity. These new methods 'are distinguished by the art and science of asking powerful, positive questions … view realities as socially constructed, and … become more radically relational, widening the circles of dialogue to groups of 100s, 1000s, and perhaps more—with cyberspace relationships into the millions. AI seeks out the best of 'what is' to ignite the collective imagination of 'what might be.' The aim is to generate new knowledge which expands 'the realm of the possible' and helps members of an organization to envision a collectively desired future; then to carry that vision in ways that successfully translate images into realities.[6]

1. In the summer of 1998, Bishop Swing told *Lambeth Daily* that the URI annual budget was roughly $1.5 million. (Barnwell, "United Religions"). Since then, annual spending for the URI headquarters in San Francisco has fluctuated in the $1.2–$2.0 million range: $1.9 million in 2000 (URI, *Annual Report*, 2000, "Statement of Activities, year ended December 31, 2000—Expenses," p11), $1.5 million in 2001 (URI, *Annual Report*, 2001, "Statement of Activities, year ended December 31, 2001—Expenses," p11), and $2.0 million in 2002 (URI, *Annual Report*, 2002, "Funds Received/Funds Spent 2002"). In 2003, the URI headquarters raised $1.4 million, and spent $1.2 million (URI, *Annual Report*, 2003). However, the annual reports list only donations made through the San Francisco headquarters (2001 *Annual Report*, p8, and 2000 *Annual Report*, p7). With the global spread of the movement, these San Francisco totals are less than the total annual expenditures for all URI-affiliated organizations worldwide.

2. Interview with Donald Frew by Lee Penn, 03/28/03. Additionally, a URI survey of its Cooperation Circles in 2003 indicated that the chapters had raised $922,000 in 2002–2003. (United Religions Initiative, *CC Survey Report* 2003, http://www.uri.org/ccsurveyreport 2003/Section_Four.pdf, p24.)

3. In 2002, the *Annual Report* stated that the URI spent $285,518 on fund raising, 14.4% of their total 2002 expenditures, $1,976,269 (URI, *Annual Report*, 2002, "Funds Received/Funds Spent 2002"). In 2003, the Annual Report stated that the URI spent $195,577 on fund raising, 16.5% of their total 2003 expenditures, $1,183,275 (URI, *Annual Report*, 2003). In 2001 the URI stated that they spent $213,599 on fund raising, 15.2% of their $1,406,378 annual expenditures for that year. (Form 990 for 2001, filed with the IRS by the URI; part II, line 44). 1999 and 2000 reports showed that about 10% of URI expenditures were for fund-raising.

4. Bishop William Swing, "The United Religions Initiative," document issued in April 1996, p7.

5. Interview of URI Global Council member Donald Frew by Lee Penn, 10/14/02.

6. Dennis Delman, "United Religions Initiative Advances With Appreciative Inquiry" *Pacific Church News*, February/March 1998, p22; all ellipses are as given in the original article (cited below as Delman, "URI Advances With Appreciative Inquiry").

When this process is applied to interfaith work, Cooperrider says participants will "see the best of each other's faith. . . . There is something good, strong, and wise about every tradition.[1]

The URI is being run with a process that, in Cooperrider's own words, views "realities as socially constructed" and seeks to "affirm, compel, and accelerate anticipatory learning" with the objective of "mobilizing and sustaining human system change" among "larger and larger levels of collectivity."[2] The agenda—post-modernist relativism, social engineering, and collectivism—could hardly be clearer.

In *The Coming United Religions* (a history of the URI as of 1998), Bishop Swing confirmed the critical role that Cooperrider's management consultants have played in the movement. With the involvement of the SIGMA team starting in 1996, Bishop Swing said,

> Our destiny changed dramatically. . . . In many ways they transformed us and continue to do so. No help was more important to us than the quality of spiritually alert people that SIGMA brought to our tables. This was the first clue that if there is to be a United Religions, the original impetus and expertise will have to come from fields other than religion. Left to their own devices, religions will not meet each other. But given outside assistance from multiple disciplines which are already functioning on a global basis and have learned to work around and beyond existing roadblocks, religions can move toward common ground.[3]

The "common ground," discovered with "outside assistance from multiple disciplines," will be defined on the world's terms, will use the world's money, and will reflect the world's priorities.

In addition to the URI, other users of AI have included the Adventist Development and Relief Agency International, CARE, Catholic Relief Services, the Christian Reformed World Relief Committee, the Environmental Law Institute, Lutheran World Relief, the Pearl S. Buck Foundation, the Salesian Society, the Salvation Army World Service Office, Save The Children, the United Nations Development Program, the US Agency for International Development, the US Department of Agriculture, the US Peace Corps, and World Vision Relief and Development,[4] GTE/Verizon, Motorola, BP America, Touche Ross, Seattle Group Health Cooperative, Imagine Chicago, United Way of America, Hunter Douglas, SmithKline Beecham, New York Power Authority, Sandia National Laboratories, Johnson & Johnson, Philadelphia Electric Company, Motorola/Teledesic, the Vermont state government,[5] and the US Navy.[6]

According to Cooperrider, SIGMA has "probably generated more funding for Weatherhead than any other research project in its history," including a grant of $6.5 million from the US Agency for International Development "to help establish a center for management and leadership development for international nonprofit organizations."[7] (The Weatherhead School of Management is the business

1. "A Conversation with David Cooperrider," *Pacific Church News*, February/March 2001, p 42.

2. Delman, "URI Advances with Appreciative Inquiry."

3. Swing, *The Coming United Religions*, p 18.

4. Case Western Reserve University, "GEM Alumni and Partners from 1994–2001," http://appreciativeinquiry.cwru.edu/gem/alumni.html, printed 05/09/03. "Global Excellence in Management (GEM) was a university-based program of learning that worked in partnership with U.S. private and voluntary organizations (PVOs) and international non-governmental organizations (NGOs) to conduct capacity building programs that promoted organizational excellence from 1994 until 2001. Today, a similar program is being carried out by AI Consulting." (Case Western Reserve University, "The GEM Initiative," http://appreciativeinquiry.cwru.edu/gem/index.html, printed 05/09/03.)

5. Client lists for David Cooperrider and Diana Whitney, who were among the founders of the Taos Institute, "More About the Workshop Leaders, AI, and the Workshop," http://www.ausl.re.it/ausl/meeting/ai/more.htm, printed 05/09/03.

6. Center for Executive Education, "The Leadership Summit—Bold and Enlightened Naval Leaders at Every Level," http://www.cee.nps.navy.mil/NewSite/leadership_summit/press_release.htm, printed 04/08/03. "Appreciative Inquiry is a process designed to create positive dialogue and was the pilot tool that the Navy used to improve leadership and align our individual self-talk."

7. Jeff Bendix, "Weatherhead, international religious group forge relationship," http://www.cwru.edu/pubs/cnews/1999/2-4/sigma.htm, printed 05/09/03.

school at Case Western Reserve University, where Cooperrider teaches.)

Appreciative Inquiry is rife within the Catholic Church. Susan Star Paddock, author of *Appreciative Inquiry in the Catholic Church*,[1] says,

> Where AI is being used it's really bringing the Church to life, but many Catholics who stumble on it by accident don't know about the others who are trying it. For example, in the Diocese of Cleveland Bishop Pilla has a whole initiative called Vibrant Parish Life that fully incorporates AI. AI is the planning methodology at Catholic Relief Services, is used in spiritual retreats, leadership development of new priests, ecumenical outreach, transitions, marital and family ministries, and stewardship development. It is the primary philosophy taught at Benedictine University School of Organization Development. Numerous religious communities are using AI and my book includes interviews with Benedictines, Dominicans, Vincentians, Sisters of Mercy and many others.[2]

Cooperrider is one of the co-founders of the Taos Institute,[3] which was established in 1991 on the belief that

> Social constructionist dialogues—of cutting edge significance within the social sciences and humanities—concern the processes by which humans generate meaning together. Our focus is on how social groups create and sustain beliefs in the real, the rational, and the good. We recognize that as people create meaning together, so do they sow the seeds of action. Meaning and action are entwined. As we generate meaning together we create the future.[4]

The Institute has "held international conferences in Taos, as well as provided consultation grounded in social constructionist theory to individuals and organizations and access to social constructionist literature."[5]

Gervase Bushe, a professor of organizational development who is friendly to AI, offers this synopsis of Appreciative Inquiry and social constructionism:

> Appreciative inquiry, however, is a product of the socio-rationalist paradigm . . . which treats social and psychological reality as a product of the moment, open to continuous reconstruction. Cooperrider and Srivastva argue that there is nothing inherently real about any particular social form, no transcultural, everlasting, valid principles of social organization to be uncovered. . . . Socio-rationalists argue that the theories we hold, our beliefs about social systems, have a powerful effect on the nature of social 'reality.' Not only do we see what we believe, but the very act of believing it creates it. . . . Conscious evolution of positive imagery, therefore, is a viable option for changing the social system as a whole.[6]

URI activist Paul Chaffee says, "Appreciative Inquiry is an expression of postmodern social constructionism. As such it is preoccupied with language, learning, relationship, and generativity in living

1. Susan Star Paddock, *Appreciative Inquiry in the Catholic Church*, Thin Book Publishing Co., 2003. (This publisher specializes in books about Appreciative Inquiry.)

2. Kathryn Lively, "Writer to Writer: An interview with Susan Star Paddock," *The Write Stuff: The Monthly E-Letter of Catholic Writing*, September 2002, Vol. 4, Issue 9, http://www.petersnet.net/cwa/ws/october2002.txt, printed 05/09/03.

3. Taos Institute, "Previous Conferences," http://www.taosinstitute.net/about/previous conferences.html, printed 05/09/03. At a conference on "The Spirit of Social Construction: Spirituality in Organizations, Therapy, and Social Construction," "The following Taos Institute Founders were there in full presence leading, facilitating and participating in this spiritual experience: Harlene Anderson, David Cooperrider, Kenneth Gergen, Mary Gergen, Sheila McNamee. There will be no tapes or papers available after this conference due to the nature of the conference."

4. Taos Institute, "Theoretical Background," http://www.taosinstitute.net/about/theoreticalbackground.html, printed 05/09/03.

5. Taos Institute, "Brief History," http://www.taosinstitute.net/about/briefhistory.html, printed 05/09/03.

6. Gervase R. Bushe, Ph.D., "Advances in Appreciative Inquiry as an Organization Development Intervention," (originally published in the *Organization Development Journal*, Fall 1995, Vol. 13, no. 3, pp 14–22); http://www.gervasebushe.ca/aiodj.htm, printed 04/29/03.

systems—and spends little if any time with 'objective reality' or 'absolutes,' including ultimate truth or the 'right' way to do something."[1] Thus, AI incorporates the notions that tradition is of little lasting value, commonly perceived reality is an illusion, morality is relative, we can collectively create new realities, and that acting upon all of this nonsense represents "conscious evolution."[2]

The promoters of AI offer reading lists for inquirers; the titles of the books and articles show that AI is a practical application of liberal, feminist, post-modern ideology. A resource list from the International Institute for Sustainable Development (IISD), developed by David Cooperrider and the executive director of the Taos Institute, includes works such as "Generative Metaphor Intervention: A New Approach to Intergroup Conflict," "Appreciating Diversity and Modifying Organizational Cultures: Men and Women at Work," "Social Construction and Appreciative Inquiry: A Journey in Organizational Theory" (published in *Management and Organization: Relational Alternatives to Individualism*), "The 'Child' As Agent of Inquiry," *No Limits to Cooperation: The Organization Dimensions of Global Change*, "Affect and Organization in Postmodern Society," Barbara Marx Hubbard's *Conscious Evolution: Awakening the Power of Our Social Potential*, "Partnering To Build And Measure Organizational Capacity: Lessons From NGOs Around The World," and "Constructionist Leadership in the Global Relational Age."[3]

A list of AI publications offered by the Appreciative Inquiry Commons at Case Western University includes similar fare: *Integrating Aboriginal Values into Land Use and Resource Management*, "Circles of Hope: Creating Social Change at the Speed of Light," *An Invitation to Social Constructionism*, "Is Diagnosis a Disaster?: A Constructionist Trialogue," another listing for Barbara Marx Hubbard's *Conscious Evolution*, and "Global integrity: Beyond instrumental relationality in transnational organizing."[4] Papers listed on the Taos web site include "Positionings in Gendered Relations: From Constructivism to Constructionism," *Toward a New Psychology of Gender*, and "Corpo-(un)reality; Embodied Specieous," [sic];[5] all were written by Mary Gergen, one of the co-founders of the Taos Institute.

FLEXIBLE RESPONSE: URI'S CHANGES IN STRATEGY SINCE 1996

The URI has grown markedly since 1996, when its first 55 members completed their summit meeting at the Fairmont Hotel in San Francisco. Nevertheless, the movement has taken a path different from what Swing had anticipated before 1998. The URI has growing numbers of adherents and allies among interfaith activists, religious liberals, and globalist organizations, but it has not captured the public's imagination in the US and Western Europe.

Bishop Swing originally planned that the URI would be a UN-style assembly of representatives of the world's major religions,[6] meeting at a 10-acre "United Religions complex, including a Hall of

1. Paul Chaffee, "Claiming the Light: Appreciative Inquiry & Corporate Transformation," December 12, 2001, http://www.givingspace.org/papers/may2002/Chaffee.doc, printed 05/09/03.

2. Barbara Marx Hubbard praises AI; see, for example, Barbara Marx Hubbard, *Conscious Evolution: Awakening the Power of Our Social Potential*, New World Library, 1998, pp134–136.

3. International Institute for Sustainable Development, "Appreciative Inquiry Resources: Literature," http://iisd1.iisd.ca/ai/resources.htm, printed 05/09/03.

4. Appreciative Inquiry Commons, "Research: Annotated Bibliography," http://ai.cwr u.edu/research/bibPublished.cfm#B, printed 05/09/03.

5. Taos Institute, "Manuscripts for Downloading," http://www.taosinstitute.net/manuscripts/manuscripts.html, printed 05/09/03.

6. "The URI," *Chaordic Commons*, p15. For a draft Charter that expressed this vision, see Peter Hart, "The United Religions Organization: A proposal for the 50th Anniversary of the Signing of the United Nations Charter at San Francisco, California, June 26, 1995" (cited below as Hart, draft United Religions charter, 1995).

Speaking, Hall of Listening, Hall of Action, and Hall of Meeting" in San Francisco's Presidio.[1] Swing said that this model was soon rejected: "Obvious questions surfaced: Who would be represented? Who needs another global bureaucracy? Why create a religious General Assembly, further politicizing existing institutions?"[2] Instead, the URI is a decentralized global network of activists from many of the world's religions, spiritual expressions, and indigenous traditions; the San Francisco headquarters is modest in size.

Swing said, "In 1993, I thought that by the year 2000 the United Religions Initiative would transition into The United Religions. I have come to see that such an all-encompassing title would be presumptuous. . . . we have been moving in the opposite direction: from a United Religions vision to the creation of a United Religions Initiative."[3] Therefore, the movement has retained its original name. Swing told the URI Global Assembly in 2002, "someday in the future there will be a United Religions but it will be made up of far more bodies than our own. . . . We see ourselves as a strong catalyst to collect religions and other interfaith groups in a process that leads ultimately to the creation of a United Religions. Therefore we left our own organizational design open-ended, so that someday in the future we can partner with others to create United Religions."[4]

A URI staff member said in late 1997 that by 2000, the URI would begin to seek organization-level endorsements.[5] However, in 1998 Bishop Swing stated that the URI strategy was to build support among the "grassroots faithful," creating a movement with enough momentum to convince religious leaders to join.[6] This strategy was still in force as of 2004. URI Global Council member Donald Frew said, "Ever since the URI shifted gears and went for a grass-roots approach rather than a top-down approach, it hasn't sought high-level endorsements from any religious bodies."[7]

In 1995, Swing's vision was that the URI would include representatives of the world's "great religions."[8] A Charter proposal written that year suggested that "in order to be entitled to a representative in the assembly, a member [religion] *must have more than two million believers and have been in continuous existence for more than 50 years*."[9] The scope of the URI had already broadened to include "spiritual movements" by the time of Bishop Swing's spring 1996 pilgrimage.[10] Now, people from all "religions, spiritual expressions and indigenous traditions"[11] are invited to participate.

In 1997, the URI hoped to "build a Worldwide Movement to create the United Religions as a lived reality locally and regionally, all over the world. The goal is to enroll 60,000,000 people by June 2000."[12] Reality fell drastically short of the URI's hope; during 2000, six thousand people signed the URI Charter.[13]

1. Don Lattin, "Bishop Pushes Presidio Interfaith Group," *San Francisco Chronicle*, January 23, 1996, p A-13.

2. Bishop William E. Swing, "United Religions—Keeping the Initiative," *Pacific Church News*, June/July 2000, p 29.

3. Ibid., p 30.

4. Swing, URI keynote address, August 08/19/02.

5. Interview with Paul Andrews, URI staff member, October 7 and December 11, 1997.

6. Swing, *The Coming United Religions*, p 19.

7. E-mail from Donald Frew to Lee Penn, 11/18/02.

8. Bishop William Swing, "The Creation of the United Religions: An Overview," document released by the URI in 1995, p 1.

9. Hart, draft United Religions charter, 1995, p 8.

10. Swing, "Reactions from Religious Leaders," summer 1996 (comment by the Rev. John Buehrens criticizing this decision), p 4.

11. United Religions Initiative, "The United Religions Initiative Charter," http://www. uri.org/resources/publications/Charter%20PC%20format.doc, p 1; downloaded 07/07/04.

12. United Religions Initiative, "URI Global Conference: In the spirit of service," *URI News Update*, No. 3, Fall 1997, p 3.

13. URI, *Annual Report* 2000, "URI Charter Signings 2000," p 6.

Despite the growth of the URI in recent years, two indices of a movement's mass appeal—book sales and press coverage[1]—indicate that the URI has not captured Americans' hearts and minds. During the first few years of its existence, the URI drew some attention from national media, and gained significant space in San Francisco-area newspapers. However, the 2002 URI "Global Assembly" in Rio de Janeiro received no coverage from the *New York Times*, the *Los Angeles Times*, or the *Washington Post*, which consider themselves to be national newspapers of record. Nor did the national and global URI meetings in 2001 and 2002 receive coverage from Bishop Swing's "hometown" papers, the *San Francisco Chronicle* and the *San Jose Mercury News*. Reuters, the Associated Press, *Time* magazine, and *Newsweek* magazine have likewise ignored the URI. Bishop Swing's 1998 book, *The Coming United Religions*, has been a slow seller at Amazon.com, with a sales rank of 321,532 as of November 5, 2004.[2] A new book about the URI, written by two URI staffers and published in December 2003, was an even slower seller on Amazon, ranking at 447,753 as of the same date.[3]

1. Based on search of publications' on-line archives as of 01/04/03, 06/13/03, and 06/02/04 by Lee Penn.

2. Search of Amazon web site, http://www.amazon.com, for data on Bishop Swing's book, *The Coming United Religions*, as of November 5, 2004.

3. Search of Amazon web site, http://www.amazon.com, for data on the book by Charles Gibbs and Sally Mahé, *Birth of a Global Community: Appreciative Inquiry in Action*, as of November 5, 2004.

3

THE IDEALS AND THE
PRACTICE OF THE URI

THE URI CHARTER

THE URI CHARTER, adopted in 2000, lays out the movement's agenda. After an introductory statement, there are these sections:

Preamble—the call that inspires us to create the URI now and continue to create it everyday;
Purpose—the statement that draws us together in common cause;
Principles—the fundamental beliefs that guide our structure, decisions and content;
Organization design—the way we organize to enhance cooperation and magnify spirit;
Guidelines for Action—an action agenda to inspire and guide our worldwide URI community.[1]

According to the Charter, "The purpose of the United Religions Initiative is to promote enduring, daily interfaith cooperation, to end religiously motivated violence and to create cultures of peace, justice and healing for the Earth and all living beings."[2]

URI proponents are quick to refer the movement's critics to the "Preamble, Purpose, and Principles" in the Charter, asking them what specific disagreements they have with these guidelines.[3] Donald Frew states that the document's guidelines should be evaluated as a group; "none of the principles are in isolation from each other."[4] However, the URI's founding document is written in the most general of terms; its interpretation and use will be determined by the beliefs of those reading the document.

The Preamble commits the URI to "create cultures of peace, justice and healing for the Earth and all living beings"[5]– assuming that human action can create such a utopia, and that there is not a conflict of interest between humans and any other "living beings." The Preamble promises, "We respect the uniqueness of each tradition, and differences of practice or belief."[6] However, part of the "uniqueness" of some religions (notably, Christianity and Islam) is the belief that their own teachings are uniquely

---

1. United Religions Initiative, "The United Religions Initiative Charter," http://www. uri.org/resources/publications/ Charter%20PC%20format.doc, p1; downloaded 07/07/04 (cited below as URI, "Charter").

2. Ibid., "Purpose," p3.

3. Interview between Lee Penn and Donald Frew, member of the URI Global Council, October 2002. The "Preamble, Purpose, and Principles" are printed in full as Appendix I of this book.

4. Interview between Lee Penn and Donald Frew, member of the URI Global Council, October 2002 and 03/28/03.

5. URI, "Charter," "Preamble," paragraph 1, p2.

6. Ibid., "Preamble," par. 2, p2. According to URI Global Council member Donald Frew, this means that URI members are "free not to participate in URI events that they are uncomfortable with." (Interview with Lee Penn, October 2002.)

inspired by God, and that their own way is the best—if not the only—way for mankind to be faithful to God.[1]

The Preamble proclaims, "We unite to build cultures of peace and justice."[2] These values are indeed essential, and Jesus made them part of the Beatitudes: "Blessed are those who hunger and thirst for righteousness, for they shall be satisfied. Blessed are the merciful, for they shall obtain mercy. . . . Blessed are the peacemakers, for they shall be called sons of God." (Matt. 5:6–7, 9). However, partisans of the Left often view "peace" as a call for pacifism and against patriotism, and see "justice" as requiring government-enforced egalitarianism. When activists (of the Left or the Right) interpret "cultures of peace and justice" in an ideological manner, they needlessly pit these social goals against other real human values, such as preserving or strengthening traditional cultures, national sovereignty, family stability, virtue, and individual liberty.

The Preamble says, "We unite to support freedom of religion and spiritual expression, and the rights of all individuals and peoples as set forth in international law."[3] However, international law does not offer the same protection of religious freedom that the First Amendment of the US Constitution has hitherto done. Many members of the United Nations, signers of UN human rights treaties and declarations, persecute Christians or impose government control of churches in their countries.

The UN "Declaration on the Elimination of All Forms of Intolerance and of Discrimination Based on Religion or Belief," adopted by the UN General Assembly in 1981, sets forth a broad view of religious freedom. However, its recognition of this right includes—in several places—the following restriction: "Freedom to manifest one's religion or beliefs may be subject only to such limitations as are prescribed by law and are necessary to protect public safety, order, health, or morals or the fundamental rights or freedoms of others."[4] These restrictions can easily be used to justify limits on religious freedom—for example, when the Chinese Communists invoke "order" as their reason for insistence on government control of churches. If the UN accepts abortion and artificial contraception as "fundamental rights," this clause will justify an assault on the Catholic Church and on other faiths which oppose these practices.

With the Preamble statement that "We unite in responsible cooperative action to bring the wisdom and values of our religions, spiritual expressions and indigenous traditions to bear on the economic, environmental, political and social challenges facing our Earth community,"[5] the URI commits itself to social and political action. The Preamble closes with a clear commitment to nonviolence: "We unite to use our combined resources only for nonviolent, compassionate action, to awaken to our deepest truths, and to manifest love and justice among all life in our Earth community."[6]

---

1. Sufi Muslim scholar Charles Upton comments, "Islam has certainly often been interpreted in this exclusivist manner, especially in modern times. Yet the Prophet Muhammad (peace and blessings be upon him) openly expressed his admiration for Christian monks, while making it clear that Islam was not to be a monastic religion; when some of his followers fled from Arabia to Africa to avoid persecution, they were given shelter by the Negus, Christian ruler of a kingdom somewhere in the area of present Ethiopia and Sudan. Seyyed Hossein Nasr recounts that in his childhood in Persia, Islamic discrimination against Christians and Jews was unknown. Furthermore, when the Communist regime of Ethiopia tried to close some of the ancient Christian churches of that nation, Christians and Muslims prevented this by massing together on the steps of these holy buildings. In truth, the Holy Qur'an grants validity to the religion of any 'people of the Book'—any people, that is, who possess a revealed scripture. And the Prophet himself said, 'I make no distinction between the prophets,' which from the Muslim point of view would include Abraham, Moses and Jesus." (E-mail from Charles Upton to Lee Penn, 03/13/04).

2. URI, "Charter," "Preamble," para. 6, p2.

3. Ibid., "Preamble," para. 9, p2.

4. Article 1, paragraph 3, "Declaration on the Elimination of All Forms of Intolerance and of Discrimination Based on Religion or Belief," in Joel Beversluis, ed., *Sourcebook of the World's Religions: An Interfaith Guide to Religion and Spirituality*, New World Library, 2000, p219. This clause is invoked in the two sections of the Declaration that specify the nature and scope of religious freedom.

5. URI, "Charter," "Preamble," paragraph 10, p2.

6. Ibid., "Preamble," para. 13, p2.

The first of the URI's 21 "Principles" is that "The URI is a bridge-building organization, not a religion."[1] This constitutes the URI's denial of opponents' charges that it is seeking to lay the foundation for a New Religion. The fourth principle states, "We encourage our members to deepen their roots in their own tradition"[2]—even though most Christian participants in the URI are liberal critics of their own tradition.

Other principles commit the URI to "respect the differences among religions, spiritual expressions and indigenous traditions," "welcome the gift of diversity," "practice equitable participation of women and men," "resolve conflict without resorting to violence," and "protect and preserve the Earth for both present and future generations."[3] All of these principles are the norm for Western-influenced, modern liberal organizations.

By design, the URI fosters local autonomy and fiscal responsibility for activists who accept the movement's goals and beliefs. Any individual or organization may join the URI if they "subscribe to the Preamble, Purpose and Principles."[4] Decisions are to be made "at the most local level that includes all the relevant and affected parties."[5] Participants have the "right to organize in any manner, at any scale, in any area, and around any issue or activity which is relevant to and consistent with the Preamble, Purpose and Principles."[6] Each part of the URI "shall relinquish only such autonomy and resources as are essential" to the pursuit of URI goals; in turn, each part of the movement has "the responsibility to develop financial and other resources to meet the needs of our part, and to share financial and other resources to help meet the needs of other parts."[7] The URI commits itself to "maintain the highest standards of integrity and ethical conduct, prudent use of resources, and fair and accurate disclosure of information."[8] These organizational principles embody norms from the classical liberal, constitutional regimes of North America and Western Europe. Most orthodox Christians would not quarrel with these management standards.

Individuals or groups that wish to join the URI do so by forming a Cooperation Circle (CC), or by joining an existing CC. Every URI CC "determines its own unique purpose, membership, and ways of making decisions,"[9] as long as these are consistent with the URI Charter. CCs that wish to coordinate their efforts with other Cooperation Circles may form a Multiple Cooperation Circle (MCC). The Charter says, "To provide initial stability and interfaith diversity, Cooperation Circles must have at least seven (7) members who represent at least three (3) different religions, spiritual expressions or indigenous traditions."[10]

Each CC is responsible to "take actions to encourage and ensure that its own members act in accordance with the Preamble, Purpose and Principles" of the URI, "to adhere to the by-laws and operating procedures as they evolve in the life of the URI;" "to communicate best practices and stories and highlights of activities with other parts of the URI;" "to develop financial resources to meet its own needs" *and* the needs of the rest of the URI, "to keep accurate and current records of its members, financial transactions and activities," and to hold the URI and its leaders and staff "harmless from any liabilities . . . in any way caused by a URI Circle's breach" of URI principles and procedures.[11] In the

1. Ibid., "Principles," principle 1, p3.
2. Ibid., "Principles," principle 4, p3.
3. Ibid., "Principles," principles 3, 7, 8, 9, and 10, p3.
4. Ibid., "Principles," principle 12, p3.
5. Ibid., "Principles," principle 13, p3.
6. Ibid., "Principles," principle 14, p3.
7. Ibid., "Principles," principles 16 and 17, p3.
8. Ibid., "Principles," principle 18, p4.
9. Ibid., "Organization Design," para. 2, p4.
10. Ibid., "Organization Design," para. 3, p4.
11. Ibid., "Responsibilities of Members," points 3, 5, 6, 7, 8, 10, and 11, p5.

application to join the URI, each Cooperation Circle pledges to "only use the name and related images of the United Religions Initiative in connection with our work as a member of the United Religions Initiative and in furtherance of the Preamble, Purpose, and Principles," and to "hold the name and related images of the United Religions Initiative as a sacred trust for all members."[1] Each CC is free to begin projects that it sees as compatible with URI principles, and does not have to seek prior approval from the Global Council or the Global Assembly for these activities.

In addition, individuals and groups who support the URI but do not wish to form a CC may become Affiliates, with the approval of the Global Council or of a URI CC. Fees may be assessed by the Global Council in order for Affiliates "to participate in URI activities and the communication network."[2] Affiliates do not vote for the Global Council, but may attend all URI meetings.[3]

The URI Global Council "will inspire and support the URI worldwide community in cooperative global action."[4] It is "responsible to develop financial and other resources to meet the needs of the URI," accepts membership applications, and manages "the affairs of the URI, Inc."[5] The Global Council includes up to 41 members—24 delegates elected every three years[6] by URI Cooperation Circles (3 from each of the world's 8 regions), up to 12 at-large delegates selected by the Global Council "to meet the need for greater diversity or a particular expertise," up to 3 members of the pre-2002 Board of Directors (to assist in the transition to the new Global Council), URI founder Bishop Swing, and the Executive Director of the URI.[7] (As of June 2004, 38 members of the URI Global Council had been announced, including 9 at-large members; they are listed in the Appendix.)

URI Global Council member Donald Frew stated that Swing left Rio de Janeiro before the first meeting of the Global Council in the summer of 2002. Frew added, "The organization is much more than Bishop Swing. It's not his own thing any more."[8]

At the 2002 Global Assembly, Swing stated that the URI office is often contacted "to see what the URI position is on a particular matter. Unfortunately we have no way of responding,"[9] because authority is decentralized among the cooperation circles. Swing said, "The URI staff doesn't have the voice for the URI. The Global Council is not a representative body empowered to speak for the whole. This case of the 'voice of URI' is left to a future day for us to decide. As pressure mounts for us to speak to the world with a strong voice, we will have to come to a conclusion about this matter, as soon as possible."[10] By early 2004, Swing deemed it necessary to delay resolving "the issue of voice" until after the 2005 URI global meeting in Seoul: "We're not even going to attempt that during this three years. That will have to be addressed and solved after the next meeting in Korea."[11]

Global Assembly meetings, gatherings of all the members of the URI, are to occur every three

1. United Religions Initiative, "Cooperation Circle Application for Membership," "Member's Statement Regarding Name Use," in application form issued in 2000 by the URI.

2. UR, "Charter," "Affiliates," p6.

3. United Religions Initiative, "Creating Cooperation Circles: A Practical Guide," p10, issued August 2002.

4. URI, "Charter," "The Global Council," p6.

5. Ibid.

6. The three-year term, which is different from the 2-year term stated in documents on the URI web site, was confirmed in a telephone conversation with Global Council member Donald Frew, 3/17/03.

7. URI, "Charter," "Composition of the Global Council," p6.

8. Interview of URI Global Council member Donald Frew by Lee Penn, 10/14/02.

9. Bishop William Swing, Keynote address for URI Global Assembly, August 19, 2002; http://pcn.diocal.org/uriaddress.html, printed 03/06/03.

10. Ibid.

11. Dennis Delman, "Interview with Bishop William E. Swing, Founder and President of the United Religions Initiative," *Pacific Church News online*, February/March 2004, http://pcn.diocal.org/PCNO/pcn004-1/index.html, printed 02/24/04.

years.[1] (The first of these meetings was in Rio de Janeiro, Brazil in August 2002.) The Global Assembly is not designed as a legislative or policy-making body. Rather, according to the Charter, "The Global Assembly will magnify everyone's capacity to carry forward their dreams and initiatives, address visions of collective actions for service in the world, and give voice to collective hopes and aspirations. The Global Assembly will align strengths and call forth unprecedented cooperation. The Global Assembly will celebrate the totality of the URI."[2] In other words, it is a world-wide interfaith networking party.

In the final section of the Charter, an "Agenda for Action is offered as guidance for URI activities."[3] The Charter states:

> the URI seeks to serve as a moral voice and a source of action grounded in contemplation in each of the following areas:
> Sharing the Wisdom and Cultures of Faith Traditions—actions to promote dialogue, education and kinship among the diverse religions and spiritual traditions of the world.
> Nurturing Cultures of Healing and Peace—actions to develop cultures in which all people can live without fear of violence.
> Rights and Responsibilities—actions to uphold human rights.
> Ecological Imperatives—actions to uphold the welfare and healing of the entire Earth community.
> Sustainable Just Economics—actions to bring a spiritual perspective to the tremendous gap between rich and poor.
> Supporting the Overall URI—local, regional and global actions to support all URI activities.[4]

With this Charter, the URI has set a broad but vaguely defined agenda for itself. The publicly stated opinions and actions of URI leaders and supporters clarify the practical application of the "Agenda for Action," in the same way that the *Federalist Papers*, the acts of Congress in the 1790s, and early Supreme Court decisions reveal the original intent of the authors of the US Constitution.

GOOD FRUIT: WORKS OF MERCY BY URI COOPERATION CIRCLES

Some of the activities reported by URI Cooperation Circles are practical works of mercy, deeds that any Christian could approve.

AFRICA

A Cooperation Circle in Angola, the "Comfort CC" in Luanda, aims to "comfort and counsel women undergoing domestic violence," as well as "visiting and comforting the sick and the elderly."[5] The chapter donated food and clothing to a refuge for lepers and their families, and "has determined that this is a worthy community to be involved with and support in whatever way that it can."[6]

1. The 3-year time between Global Assemblies, confirmed in a 3/17/03 telephone conversation with Global Council member Donald Frew, is a change from the 2-year interval stated in the "Global Assembly" section of "The United Religions Initiative Charter," p7.
2. URI, "Charter," "Global Assembly," p7.
3. Ibid., "Guidelines for Action," p7.
4. Ibid., "Guidelines for Action," p7.
5. United Religions Initiative, "URI in the World—New Treasures!," *URI Update*, August 2003, Issue 13, p6.
6. United Religions Initiative, "Building the Kingdom of God—a visit to a Leprosy Center in Angola," http://www.uri.org/regionalnews/africa/leprosy.asp, printed 07/13/04.

A URI Cooperation Circle in Kenya runs a micro-credit bank for women. Donald Frew said that in Kenya, war and AIDS have left many women without husbands, and in need of a livelihood. The Cooperation Circle "gives them small loans, at exceedingly easy terms, to start home businesses and become self-supporting. The typical loan is about 80 Kenyan schillings—or $1 US! I immediately thought of the American phone service ad campaign that is based around the idea of a dollar being worthless and here it was enough to completely turn a woman's life around."[1]

The Global AIDS Interfaith Alliance (GAIA), was established in 2000 "to prevent HIV in developing countries by working within religious and spiritual communities in high incidence areas;" the current focus is "the empowerment of women and the prevention of mother-to-infant HIV transmission in sub-Saharan Africa, India, and other regions."[2] GAIA-associated Cooperation Circles in Malawi are active in "assisting orphans whose parents have died from the AIDS epidemic,"[3] as well as supporting in-home care for AIDS patients.[4] By the end of 2003, 1,789 orphans in Malawi had received food, blankets, clothing, school supplies, and other necessities through GAIA, and 150 patients' families were given food, gloves, soap, pain relievers, and vitamins.[5]

The Forum of Religions, a Cooperation Circle in Mozambique, "is developing activities for the well-being of people such as giving food and clothing to flood victims, visiting hospitals to give moral support to cancer and pediatric patients, and by visiting people in jail and senior centers. This CC was consulted by the government about its role in improving living conditions in Mozambique."[6].

The Acholi Religious Leaders' Peace Initiative (ARLPI) was founded in February 1998 and is "an interfaith forum which brings together Muslim and Christian (Catholic, Orthodox & Anglican) leaders in Acholiland, Northern Uganda" to seek a negotiated end to a 15-year civil war in that region.[7] (The insurgents, the Lord's Resistance Army, are based in southern Sudan and are supported by the

1. E-mail from Donald Frew to Lee Penn, 01/02/03.

2. "URI's Cooperation Circles Exhibit Great Diversity of Needs," *Pacific Church News*, June/July 2001, p35. However, it appears that GAIA's strategy includes promotion of condom use in AIDS prevention. A report by GAIA founder William Rankin on an AIDS prevention conference in Tanzania in November 2000 indicates—with approval—that the Anglican Church of Tanzania now accepts condom use to prevent AIDS. Rankin said, "I was told in Dar es Salaam that the Anglican Church of Tanzania has now become the first religious organization nationwide to break the silence, to de-stigmatize infected persons, to approve the use of condoms, and to align itself broadly with the government's efforts to prevent HIV infection." (The Global AIDS Interfaith Alliance, "News & Updates: December, 2000," http://www.thegaia.org/news/01.01.01.asp, printed 01/07/03). Another report by Rankin also contained pro-condom quotations by an Anglican bishop from Tanzania, in the bishop's report on a GAIA-supported conference (The Global AIDS Interfaith Alliance, "News & Updates: May 2001," http://www.thegaia.org/news/5.01.01a.asp, printed 01/07/03). GAIA's training course for clinic nurses in Kenya included "de-stigmatization of persons living with HIV/AIDS, home care of HIV+ people, and how to deliver instruction to relatives of patients on toileting, feeding, washing, etc. The nurses will also be taught strategies for incorporating home care visits and home based education into their regular weekly duties. They will be given updated information on HIV/AIDS prevention and treatment practices in general, treatment of AIDS-related opportunistic infections, and instruction on condom distribution and accessibility issues." (The Global AIDS Interfaith Alliance, "News & Updates: 12–20–00," http://www.thegaia.org/news/12.20.00.asp, printed 01/07/03) Other GAIA AIDS education efforts support abstinence to prevent disease (Global AIDS Interfaith Alliance, *Annual Report*, 2003, http://www.thegaia.org/resources/AnnualReport03.pdf, p8, printed 07/15/04; cited below as GAIA, *Annual Report*, 2003) Thus, Catholics who accept Vatican teaching (against any use of artificial contraceptive devices, whether for birth control or for disease prevention) could approve of some GAIA activities, such as nursing care and drug assistance, but could not accept others. Because money is fungible, donations to GAIA are likely to allow the organization to fund some activities that are against Vatican norms—as well as funding activities that the Catholic Church would support.

3. United Religions Initiative, "Africa," http://www.uri.org/regionalnews/africa/ma lawi.asp, printed 05/28/03.

4. GAIA, *Annual Report*, 2003.

5. Ibid.

6. United Religions Initiative, "URI in the World," *URI Update*, Spring 2001, p5.

7. Acholi Religious Leaders' Peace Initiative (ARLPI), "Welcome to Acholipeace," http://www.acholipeace.org, printed 12/03/02.

Sudanese regime.)[1] The ARLPI has become a URI Cooperation Circle.[2] Sheik Abdulai Hussein, of the ARLPI, said that "several religious leaders came together, supported by the UN Development Programme. We now have programs for peace workers, and in some areas have negotiated cease-fires."[3] *Catholic World News* reported in April 2004 that since 1998, the ARLPI "has been actively involved in efforts to promote a peaceful settlement, sometimes opening its own negotiations with rebel leaders, and sometimes facing death threats from Kony's lieutenants. [Kony is the leader of the Lord's Resistance Army rebels.] The Ugandan government, too, has had a stormy relationship with the religious leaders, sometimes accepting their initiatives and sometimes describing the ARLPI as an impediment to the peace process."[4] The URI reports that the ARLPI has rescued "hundreds" of children abducted by the rebels.[5] Additionally, the CC's "latest internationally reported accomplishment has been to mediate between the presidential peace team and the leaders of the rebel army, bringing an invitation from the President to the leaders of the Lord's Resistance Army to make direct contact with the presidential peace team within a period of cease-fire."[6]

The Kashi Cooperation Circle in the US and a Cooperation Circle in Uganda provide orphanages and agricultural support for widows and orphans in Uganda.[7] Additionally, the "Body and Soul Development Cooperation Circle in Kampala, Uganda trains unemployed youth," teaching them "skills in starting and running small business enterprises."[8]

ASIA

The "Society for Awareness and Prevention of HIV/AIDS," a URI Cooperation Circle in India, is leading the effort to set up the "Indian Children's Medical Institute (ICMI), a 200-bed state-of-the-art, multi-specialty pediatric center" for children with HIV and other diseases. The Society was recently granted land at a discounted price by the government.[9]

The Executive Director of the URI reported in mid-2004 that the Ektaan Cooperation Circle in West Bengal, India "recently hosted a two-day clinic during which volunteer doctors, using donated supplies and medicine, provided health care for 300 people. The CC also hosted a five-day program that drew 5,000 participants to help supply housing and food for the poor. During this program,

1. Acholi Religious Leaders' Peace Initiative (ARLPI), "Background on the War in Northern Uganda," http://www.acholi-peace.org/backgroundtothewar.htm, printed 12/03/02.

2. United Religions Initiative, "Cooperation Circles of the URI," http://www.uri.org/regionalnews/cclisting.asp, printed 09/23/04.

3. United Religions Initiative, "Peacebuilding Stories from Africa Regional Assembly," *URI Update*, fall 2001, no. 10, p12.

4. Fredrick Nzwili, "The Forgotten War," *The Catholic World Report*, April 2004, p39. The article, on pp36–40, gives an overview of the history of the Ugandan war against the Lord's Resistance Army.

5. United Religions Initiative, "Acholi Religious Leaders facilitating political dialogue in war torn Uganda," http://www.uri.org/regionalnews/africa/acholi.asp, printed 07/16/04.

6. Ibid.

7. United Religions Initiative, "Multiregional," http://www.uri.org/regionalnews/multiregion/kashicc.asp, printed 10/12/02. However, the Kashi ashram, led by "Guru Ma," has come under public criticism as a cult. Former members accuse the ashram of brainwashing and deceit; the responses of the defenders of the ashram appear to place the controversy in the "he said/she said" category. For an index of articles covering this controversy, see "Ma's ashram: A special report," *TCPalm.com*, May 2, 2004, http://www.tcpalm.com/tcp/living/article/0,1651,TCP_1043_2841122,00.html, printed 05/07/04. One of the articles mentions the connection between the URI and the ashram. (Jayne Hustead, "Profiles of some Kashi ashram members," *TCPalm.com*, May 4, 2004, http://www.tcpalm.com/tcp/living/article/0,1651,TCP_1043_2841122,00.html, printed 05/07/04.) The liaison to the URI is "Kali Ma;" the story mis-names the URI as "United Religious Initatives."

8. United Religions Initiative, 2003: *Compassionate Actions for a Better World*, annual report; http://www.uri.org/resources/URI_Anual_Report_2003.pdf, viewed 09/24/04.

9. Regional Report: Society for Awareness and Prevention of HIV/AIDS CC, India," *Pacific Church News*, Spring 2002, p38.

people of all castes, including Brahmins and Untouchables, broke bread together in a historic recognition of their common humanity."[1] Elsewhere in India, the Chandigarh Interfaith Forum CC is organizing a blood bank at a local hospital.[2]

In Pakistan, a Cooperation Circle in Lahore "offers an alternative to child labor by running a school for girls that combines academic coursework with practical vocational training."[3]

The Vietnamese Interfaith Council, a US Cooperation Circle, has raised funds to help the Humanity Club of Vietnam provide food and medical care to the poor. According to the URI, "Money has already been raised to supply a vehicle for a much needed village ambulance and to build a footbridge so children can safely walk to school."[4]

UNITED STATES

A Cooperation Circle in North Carolina has conducted energy audits on homes and churches, to promote conservation.[5]

The Cooperation Circle in Washington DC has formed a partnership with Habitat for Humanity, and has organized an interfaith team to build a house in a low-income neighborhood.[6]

The Interfaith Circle of Love, a Seattle, Washington Cooperation Circle, has raised more than $5,000 per year for the last seven years on behalf of a boys' orphanage.[7]

SEVEN BAD FRUIT:
URI ACTIVISTS' CULTURAL RADICALISM

The aforementioned works of mercy deserve praise.

However, other activities and public statements by leaders, chapters, and prominent supporters of the URI throw a disturbing light on the practical meaning of the URI Charter's promise to "create cultures of peace, justice and healing for the Earth and all living beings."[8] These deeds and words include soft-pedaling the crimes of radical Islam, allowing a convicted multiple rapist to remain a URI "associate," signing a manifesto that gives religious leaders' support to the Sexual Revolution, propagating curricula that teach children to "create their own religion" and ask them to wonder whether God is "just a slob like us," excusing press censorship in the Third World, and engaging in faux-shamanism. The leaders and chapter-level activists in the URI who have done these things might be expected to understand the movement's founding principles and the intent of the URI Charter. It seems that they believe that the Charter allows for what they have done.

Nor does the URI have the defense that these activities are the work of people acting without an official connection to the URI. The press censorship forum in Zimbabwe and the shamanic rituals in North Carolina were carried out by local URI Cooperation Circles and were reported in the URI's

1. Charles Gibbs, "Letter from Executive Director: July 2004," United Religions Initiative, http://www.uri.org/abouturi/edrreport/index.asp, printed 07/03/04.

2. United Religions Initiative, "URI CCs Shine Brightly in India," http://www.uri.org/regionalnews/asia/india_ccs.asp, printed 07/16/04.

3. Bishop William Swing, et al., United Religions Initiative fund raising letter, November 2003.

4. United Religions Initiative, "Local URI Fundraising," *URI Update*, Spring 2000, p2.

5. United Religions Initiative, "URI in the World," *URI Update*, fall 2001, no. 10, p7.

6. United Religions Initiative, "URI in the World," *URI Update*, spring 2002, no. 11, p6.

7. United Religions Initiative, "URI in the World," *URI Update*, Spring 2001, p8.

8. United Religions Initiative, "URI's Charter," Preamble, http://www.uri.org/abouturi/charter, printed 07/17/04.

own documents. As of 2004, the URI's own web site included the interfaith curriculum for children ages 8–12. Various URI leaders have made public excuses for the acts of radical Islam and have signed the manifesto of the Sexual Information and Education Council of the US. If the ideals of the URI allow movement leaders and activists to act and speak in this fashion, then the ideals are flawed. (URI Global Council member Donald Frew avers that "most of the things that seem problematic" to URI opponents are "things of which most URI members are never aware.")[1]

EQUIVOCATION ON RADICAL ISLAM

In some forums, Bishop Swing has spoken clearly against *all* forms of religious violence and intolerance. At a sermon given during the 1999 meeting of the Parliament of World Religions, Swing said, "If someone of our faith inflicts terror on people of other faiths, it is incumbent upon us to repudiate heinous acts."[2] This denunciation of religious violence, like others issued by URI leaders since then, allows *no* justification for such behavior by believers of *any* faith. Indeed, it calls upon religious leaders to strongly condemn violence committed by members of their own faith.

However, Swing and other URI leaders have repeatedly made excuses for Islamic violence, alibis of a kind that they never propose on behalf of other faiths.

In his April 2001 speech before the San Francisco Commonwealth Club, Swing was asked whether Islamic governments should be forced to secularize. In reply, Swing described the Shari'a law against blasphemy in Pakistan, stating that it provided for executions on the testimony of one witness.[3] He said, "I think we're a long, long, long, long way away from having Islamic countries change. They have a high doctrine of not wanting to get sucked into contemporary values which they think have led a lot of people astray. They feel like the closer they stay with the teachings of the Prophet, and Allah through the Prophet, the closer they are to real law and the closer they are to real justice."[4]

Swing likewise took an understanding view of the destruction of Buddhist statues by the Taliban regime in Afghanistan:

> Because it's a shrine, it brings up a whole question of idolatry. They were saying, 'It's an idol.' What is an idol? When you go into a church and there's a statue, is that an idol? When you look at a stained glass window, is that an idol? If you look at your stock options, are they idols? There are a lot of things that have the potential to be idols, and some of those need to be blown up. . . . I'm not taking their side; I'm *not* taking the side of the Taliban. . . . It raises the whole question of idolatry in this world. I think the Taliban were surprised at the cultural impact and the religious impact of what they had done.[5]

When an audience member asked, "If one group practices violence in the name of religion, to what extent is violence justified in order to stop them?," Swing said, "I don't know the answer to that one. I have to go to the next question."[6]

---

1. Interview of Donald Frew by Lee Penn, 06/08/04.
2. Dennis Delman, "Bishop Swing Preaches at Cape Town Cathedral: Urges 'New Day and New Way of Peacemaking,'" *Pacific Church News*, February/March 2000, p 25.
3. Charles Upton states, "Such extreme and unbalanced interpretations of the Shari'a are a product of contemporary 'fundamentalist' Islam, which departs radically from tradition. A traditional principle in Islamic jurisprudence is that the more severe the punishment, the more stringent should be the rules of evidence." (E-mail from Charles Upton to Lee Penn, 06/26/03).
4. Transcribed by Lee Penn from a tape of the speech by Bishop Swing at the Commonwealth Club, April 25, 2001 (cited below as Swing, Commonwealth Club speech, 04/25/01).
5. Ibid.
6. Ibid.

At a URI-sponsored meeting held on October 10, 2001 at the United Nations Church Center, [1] Swing said that the September 11 hijackers did not hold a corrupted version of Islam, because *all* religions are guilty of fostering terrorism. "There is a lot of terror and violence in a lot of scripture. There has to be a critique of that. We have to hold the religions' feet to the fire for the violence and terror within them."[2] As a response to terrorism, Swing said that "we must address the brokenness at the root of the terrorist attacks by bridging the chasm between the 'haves' and the 'have-nots.'" [3] (Swing appeared not to know that some terrorist leaders—including Osama bin Laden—are millionaires, and that some wealthy Arab princes subsidize suicide bombers.)

Bishop Swing is not the first URI leader to justify the crimes of Islamic states. In September 1998, William Rankin (who was URI vice-president from 1998 through 2000) told The Claremont School of Theology that "In North Sudan the government, in some measure, is forced into strong Muslim identity by the history of overthrows when a more tolerant attitude was promulgated."[4]

URI outreach has included the Iranian Islamic regime, a government that the US has long listed as a sponsor of state terrorism.[5] A document on the URI web site in late 1999 stated that "Zimbabwe URI has formed a unique and innovative Partnership with the Iranian Embassy in Harare. The URI convened a meeting to be funded by the Iranian Embassy at which the URI Preamble, Purpose & Principles was discussed, and more members received into the URI community. They officially launched the 72 Hours Project at that meeting which took place [at the] end of October."[6] This collaboration between the URI in Zimbabwe and the Iranian Embassy is ongoing. A mid-2002 report to the URI by Tendai Chikuku, an activist in the Zimbabwe National Forum for Interfaith Dialogue (a URI Cooperation Circle) said: "Within the Zimbabwe context, strong network links have been forged with the Iranian Embassy as well as with the Palestinian Embassy. We are now being invited to all their official events and this is helping in forging other new relationships with other diplomatic corps."[7]

The strange accommodation between radical Islam and the URI goes back to the early days of the movement. From the start, Swing hoped to bring Muslim members and money into the URI. In January 1996, the *San Francisco Chronicle* reported that "Swing has gotten $150,000 in seed money for the project from private foundations, which he declined to identify. 'Ultimately, we are talking about

---

1. The URI Cooperation Circle at the UN sponsored this event. (United Religions Initiative, "URI Milestones, 2001," *Annual Report* 2001, p4).

2. C-FAM, "UN Religious Meeting Blames Religions for Terror Attack on US," *Friday FAX*, October 12, 2001, Vol. 4, no. 42; http://www.c-fam.org/FAX/Volume_4/faxv4n42.html, printed 02/19/03.

3. Ibid.

4. William Rankin, "The United Religions Initiative," The Center for Progressive Christianity, http://www.tcpc.org/resources/articles/united_religions.htm, printed 04/24/03; excerpts from lecture that he gave at the Claremont School of Theology, September 10, 1998. However, Hashim El-Tinay, a Sudanese refugee who has been active in the URI in Washington DC, said in an e-mail to Lee Penn on 10/24/01 that "I know of no supporters of the current Sudanese government or a member of the NIF participating in URI-DC meetings." (The NIF is the National Islamic Front, the ruling party in Sudan.)

5. For example, in a report issued in May 2002, the State Department said, "Iran remained the most active state sponsor of terrorism in 2001." (U.S. Department of State, "Patterns of Global Terrorism: 2001," May 21, 2002, http://www.state.gov/s/ct/rls/pgtrpt/20 01/html/10249.htm, printed 04/22/03).

6. United Religions Initiative, "Africa," http://www.united-religions.org/newsite/regions/africa/index.htm, printed in late 1999; no longer on the Net at this address. (This page may be found at http://web.archive.org/web/20000417180059/http://www.united-religions.org/newsite/regions/africa/index.htm, as of 2004.) The "72 Hours Project" was the 3-day religious cease-fire at Y2K. The "Country Coordinator" listed for the Zimbabwe URI was Elias Masicame, who has since served on the URI Interim Global Council (URI, *Annual Report* 2000, p8; it lists him as a member of the Christian Council of Mozambique).

7. United Religions Initiative, *Taking Our Experience Home: A Journey in URI Peacebuilding—A Report to the URI CC Community*, June 2002, http://www.uri.org/resources/publications/URI%20Peacebuilding.pdf, p26, printed 07/16/04.

hundreds of millions of dollars, but there is Arab money, Jewish money, Christian foundations, and other foundations that have come and expressed interest already,' he said."[1]

In his global pilgrimage in the spring of 1996, Bishop Swing obtained statements of support for the URI, as well as assistance in making contacts within the Muslim world, from two radical Muslim leaders who since became vocal supporters of the Taliban. These leaders were Syed Ahmed Bukhari, Imam of the Jama Masjid (India's largest mosque), in New Delhi,[2] and Qazi Hussain Ahmed, the leader of the Islamic fundamentalist party Jama'at-e-Islami in Pakistan.[3] After his return from the pilgrimage in 1996, Swing told the *Christian Science Monitor*, "When I talked with Muslim leaders I was amazed, even among radical fundamentalists, how many people were ready."[4] Likewise, in June of 1997, Swing told the *San Francisco Chronicle* that "We had some interesting responses, say, from fundamentalist Muslims in Pakistan and India— areas where we thought that the fundamentalists would say: 'We want nothing to do with this.' They said it would be a wonderful thing to be able to be at the table and speak from the heart about their faith."[5]

Canon Charles Gibbs, URI Executive Director, said that these two Muslim leaders have had no involvement with the URI since their 1996 contacts with Swing.[6] Gibbs stressed that the URI's work is "antithetical to terrorism of any sort. The URI as a whole and Muslim members of the URI as a group universally condemn the distortion of religion for violent ends so tragically manifested in the actions of September 11."[7]

HOSPITALITY FOR A CONVICTED RAPIST AND TERRORISM SUSPECT

In 2001, Swing stood by the URI's policy of wide-open inclusivity: "If we're going to open the door, let's just open the door all the way, and say that anybody from religion, indigenous traditions, or spiritual expressions can come to the table."[8] David Cooperrider acknowledged that an organization structured like the URI can be an "out of control" organization; he said, "It can't be supervised . . . you can't supervise the Internet."[9]

---

1. Don Lattin, "Bishop Pushes Presidio Interfaith Group," *San Francisco Chronicle*, January 23, 1996, p A-13.

2. On Bukhari's support for the Taliban: The Muslim News Online, "Bukhari Supports Taliban, asks PM to shut up," September 29, 2001, http://www.muslimnews.co.uk/news/news.php?article=1160, printed 10/29/2001. In April 1996, Swing wrote that Bukhari "saw how the United Religions would be an independent voice to speak to the United Nations. A United Religions Initiative 'would be a place we could speak from our hearts.' He gave his endorsement and asked to be sent an invitation for June 1997" (Bishop William Swing, "The United Religions Initiative," document issued in April 1996, p 4; cited below as Swing, "The United Religions Initiative," 04/96).

3. On Ahmed's support for the Taliban: Jamaat-e-Islami Pakistan, "The Leadership You Can Trust: Qazi Hussain Ahmad," http://www.jamaat.org/leadership/qha.html, printed 02/17/03; also, Yossef Bodansky, "Islamabad's Road Warriors," part 2 of 4, Freeman Center for Strategic Studies, http://www.americanfriends.org/nuclear/islam_war2N32.html, printed 10/28/2001. In April 1996, Swing wrote, "Senator Qazi Hussain Ahmed kindly outlined a plan for approaching Islam worldwide on behalf of United Religions. He also encouraged me to visit his closest ally who is the head of Islamic Fundamentalism in Egypt." (Swing, "The United Religions Initiative," 04/96, p 4).

4. Daniel Sneider, "United Nations of Clerics?: Religious Leaders Envision 'Spiritual UN'," *Christian Science Monitor*, July 18, 1996, p 3.

5. Don Lattin, interview with William Swing—"Bishop's Idea for a Leap of Faiths," *San Francisco Chronicle*, June 22, 1997, p 3/Z1.

6. E-mail from URI Executive Director Charles Gibbs to Auburn Traycik (editor of *The Christian Challenge*), 12/04/01.

7. Ibid.

8. Swing, Commonwealth Club speech, 04/25/01.

9. "A Conversation with David Cooperrider," *Pacific Church News*, February/March 2001, p 42.

As the URI has found since its 2001 US regional assembly, diversity and inclusiveness have their risks. Criteria for participation in the URI are so open-ended that a convicted multiple rapist and al-Qaida terror suspect can join, and can remain listed as an "Affiliate" on the URI web site.

Ghulam Rasool Chisthi, a Muslim cleric from Islamabad, Pakistan, attended the URI/USA summit conference in Salt Lake City in June 2001. At the end of the meeting, he was jailed on Federal charges that he lied on his visa application for entry into the US; Chisthi pleaded guilty to these charges in August 2001.[1] According to the *Salt Lake City Tribune*, Chisthi's visa application had concealed the fact that "in 1991, a London jury found Chisthi guilty of raping eight female followers. He was sentenced to 11 years in prison for the rapes and three counts of indecent assault. He served 6 years."[2] Chisthi's victims included teenagers, "young female worshippers at the Jamia Mosque in the Southall section of London."[3] In January 2002, Chisthi was deported to Pakistan.[4]

Chisthi's defenders painted a different picture of his offense. In August 2001, the *Salt Lake Tribune* reported that URI Executive Director Charles Gibbs defended Chisthi, saying that the British conviction that led to Chisthi's jailing "appears to have been a collision between his Islamic beliefs and English law."[5] The "Islamic belief" in question was polygamy, which is legal in Pakistan but illegal in England. David Randle, head of the URI in Salt Lake City, said that "one of Chisthi's wives—an underage teen and a British citizen—leveled an accusation of statutory rape against him in the early 1990s."[6] Randle added that Chisthi "once had multiple wives, but now says he has learned his lesson."[7]

The 2001 URI assembly in Salt Lake City was held at a facility that was used in February 2002 for the Olympic Games. The Pakistani URI delegate had aroused intelligence agents' suspicion by asking about living arrangements for Olympic athletes, security plans for President Bush's planned visit to the Winter Olympics, and which venues would draw the largest crowds during the Games.[8]

In July 2002, Italian newspapers revealed that Chisthi had been "part of the Salafi Group for Call and Combat, an Italian cell of al-Qaida operatives that plotted a 'spectacular terrorist attack' against the Vatican, described as a 'massacre having a great number of casualties.'"[9] (The assault, planned for 2001, was called off by Osama bin Laden. It appears that he did not wish to put the world on alert

---

1. Michael Vigh, "Pakistani Visitor Cleared in Terrorism Probe, Will Be Deported," *The Salt Lake Tribune*, January 9, 2002, http://www.sltrib.com/2002/jan/t01092002.htm, printed 11/13/02 (cited below as Vigh, "Pakistani Visitor Cleared," *Salt Lake Tribune*, 01/09/02).

2. Michael Vigh, "Pakistani Visitor Cleared," *Salt Lake Tribune*, 01/09/02.

3. Michael Vigh, "Muslim Cleric Denies Role in Terror Plans," *The Salt Lake Tribune*, August 17, 2002, reprinted at http://www.polygamyinfo.com/plygmedia%2002%2097trib. htm, printed 08/05/04 (cited below as Vigh, "Muslim Cleric Denies Role," *Salt Lake Tribune*, 08/17/02).

4. Vigh, "Pakistani Visitor Cleared," *The Salt Lake Tribune*, 01/09/02.

5. August 9, 2001 story from *The Salt Lake Tribune*, "Polygamous Past May Cost Pakistani Cleric Dearly in Utah," as reprinted by an anti-polygamy advocacy site, at http://www.polygamyinfo.com/plygmedia%2001%2096%20trib.htm; printed 11/13/02; cited below as "Polygamous Past," *Salt Lake Tribune*, 08/09/01. Charles Upton states, "Gibbs is implying here that rape is allowed under Islamic law, or that Islamic marriage is a form of rape. This is absurd. Rape is a crime, and Islamic marriage, including polygamous marriage, is explicitly defined as a mutual contract between two parties." (E-mail from Charles Upton to Lee Penn, 06/26/03.)

6. "Polygamous Past," *The Salt Lake Tribune*, 08/09/01.

7. Ibid.

8. Michael Vigh and Kevin Cantera, "Al-Qaida Agent in Utah?," *The Salt Lake Tribune*, August 9, 2002, http://www.sltrib.com/2002/aug/t08092002/utah/760260.htm, printed 11/12/02; cited below as Vigh/Cantera, "Al-Qaida Agent in Utah?" *Salt Lake Tribune*, 08/09/02. Also Associated Press, "Muslim Cleric Deported From U.S. May Have Been Al Qaeda Member," August 10, 2002, http://www.foxnews.com, printed 11/13/02.

9. Vigh/Cantera, "Al-Qaida Agent in Utah?," *The Salt Lake Tribune*, 08/09/02; Associated Press, "Muslim Cleric Deported From U.S. May Have Been Al-Qaeda Member," Fox News Channel, August 10, 2002, http://www.intellnet.org/news/2002/08/10/10826-1.html, printed 03/28/03.

prior to the September 11, 2001 attacks.)[1] Chisthi had been "briefly detained" in Italy in May 2001, but "weeks later arrived in Utah" for the URI conference.[2]

Chisthi and his supporters firmly deny that he is a terrorist, or sympathetic to terrorism. A week after the September 11, 2001 attack, Chisthi had said, "I am not a terrorist. . . . I have nothing to do with Osama bin Laden."[3] David Randle stood by him, and continued to correspond with Chisthi by phone and e-mail. Randle said that Chisthi "hates the terrorists. . . . He certainly doesn't fit the terrorist profile."[4] In 2002, after publication of allegations of his involvement in a plan to bomb the Vatican, Chisthi continued to deny that he was a terrorist. He wrote an e-mail from Pakistan to David Randle saying, "If I be found guilty of the crime of terrorism then they should shoot me dead, because I prefer to be dead than to be called a terrorist. . . . So far as the allegation against me of being a terrorist, I would say that this is absolutely baseless."[5] In September 2002, he stated, "We feel sorry for the innocent people from different nations who had become victims of the terrorist attack last year and pray to Almighty Allah, to rest their souls in peace."[6]

After Chisthi returned to Pakistan in early 2002, he remained active in the URI. URI Global Council member Donald Frew stated that Chisthi appeared—uninvited, and without having registered for the meeting—on the last day of the URI Global Assembly at Rio in the summer of 2002, seeking support and giving away copies of his book.[7]

Also, Chisthi was—as of November 2004—still listed on the URI web site as the contact person for the Universal Interfaith Peace Mission in Pakistan, a URI Affiliate.[8] Those who wish to be URI affiliates must apply to the URI for approval by the Global Council or by an existing Cooperation Circle. However, Frew described "affiliate" membership as "merely equivalent to joining the Sierra Club, i.e. paying dues and getting publications. Affiliate status is for those who do not meet the requirements for, or do not wish to assume the responsibilities that go with, full membership in the

1. Ibid.

2. Vigh, "Muslim Cleric Denies Role," *The Salt Lake Tribune*, 08/17/02.

3. Vigh/Cantera, "Al-Qaida Agent in Utah?," *The Salt Lake Tribune*, 08/09/02.

4. Ibid.

5. Vigh, "Muslim Cleric Denies Role," *The Salt Lake Tribune*, 08/17/02.

6. Staff reporter, "9/11 incident marked by releasing pigeons," *DAWN* Internet edition, September 12, 2002, http://www.dawn.com/2002/09/12/nat19.htm, printed 08/04/04; cited below as "9/11 incident marked by releasing pigeons," *DAWN*, 09/12/02.

7. Conversation between Lee Penn and Donald Frew, 12/09/02 and 03/28/03.

8. United Religions Initiative, "Affiliates—Asia," http://www.uri.org/regionalnews/affiliates/index.asp, printed 05/28/03 and 11/05/04. In an e-mail of 3/20/03 to Lee Penn, URI Global Council member Donald Frew confirmed that Chisthi, who is listed on the URI web site as "Allama Abul Fateh Chishti," the contact person for the Universal Interfaith Peace Mission (UIPM) in Pakistan, "is indeed the same Chisthi from Salt Lake." Additionally, a Pakistani newspaper report of September 2002 tied Ghulam Rasool Chishti to the UIPM: "Meanwhile, the universal international peace mission (UIPM), an body comprising members of different faiths and religions, on Wednesday presented a memorandum to the United Nations asking it to consider September 11 attack as an attack on UN and not on the US alone. The memorandum was presented to the UN representative here at Islamabad. The chairman of the UIPM, Ghulam Rasool Chishti, said the Holy Quran had described the act of killing of an innocent individual as the worst crime and that of a killing of the entire community. 'All the religions teach morality and consider terrorist attack against the humanity.' The UIPM, in its letter to Kofi Annan, the UN secretary general, condemned the attack on World Trade Centre and Pentagon, as it was absolutely against the moral teachings of all religions of the world. The letter said: 'We feel sorry for the innocent people from different nations who had become victims of the terrorist attack last year and pray to Almighty Allah, to rest their souls in peace.' The letter also suggested to the UN to launch an inter-religious educational programme to eradicate fanaticism." ("9/11 incident marked by releasing pigeons," *DAWN*, 09/12/02.)

URI."[1] Frew acknowledged that the URI's openness has made it difficult for the movement to screen out adherents that might be "problematic,"[2] such as Chisthi. He has also said, "If the URI runs into problems from being too inclusive, it will learn."[3]

These odd relationships between a liberal interfaith organization and radical Islamic activists raise questions about judgment of URI leaders. It may be—as happened in the 1960s, when white leftists supported Black Panther thugs—that the URI is being used skillfully by radical Muslims for their own ends. URI leaders may have described the URI to the Muslims as a "religious equivalent to the UN." Since the UN General Assembly is dominated by anti-US and anti-Israel forces, it may be that radical Muslims have seen the URI as a way to reduce Western predominance in world affairs—even if these Muslims otherwise abhor the beliefs of Western liberals.

SIECUS AND THE SEXUAL REVOLUTION

In 2000, two high-level URI executives—Canon Charles Gibbs, URI Executive Director, and the Very Rev. William Rankin, then serving as URI Vice-President[4]—signed a religious manifesto issued in January 2000 by the Sexual Information and Education Council of the US (SIECUS).[5] The "Religious Declaration on Sexual Morality, Justice, and Healing" opposes "unsustainable population growth and over-consumption," and favors "full inclusion of women and sexual minorities in congregational life, including their ordination and the blessing of same sex unions," "lifelong, age appropriate sexuality education in schools, seminaries, and community settings," and "a faith-based commitment to sexual and reproductive rights, including access to voluntary contraception, abortion, and HIV/STD prevention and treatment."[6] That's the whole agenda for the Sexual Revolution in the West. The "Declaration" does not address the injustices and human misery that are associated with widespread pornography, adultery, fornication, and divorce. URI leaders joined about 2,200 other liberal American religious leaders in signing the document.

URI executives' endorsement of the SIECUS manifesto belies the URI claim that its goal is limited to ending religiously motivated violence. It is ironic that with one hand, URI executives signed a manifesto promoting the "do it" agenda of SIECUS—and with the other hand, they formed a global alliance against AIDS—a disease that is usually spread by prostitution, fornication, adultery, sodomy, and recreational drug use.

In 2002, URI Global Council member Donald Frew stated that the current board "could not

---

1. E-mail from Donald Frew to Lee Penn, 06/04/03. However, the URI itself appears to attach more significance to "Affiliate" status. Their web site states: "URI Affiliates are vital to our dynamic community. Individuals, groups and organizations that support the values of the URI may join as Affiliate members. This membership offers opportunity for those who may not want to be active in a CC but who are willing to be called upon to offer expertise or for project cooperation. We are grateful to all of our Affiliates who share their skills and resources with URI CC's and at the regional or global levels. CC's may invite individuals or organizations to be Affiliates. People may also apply directly to the URI global office for membership." In other words, all affiliates attain that status after review by a local or global URI body. (United Religions Initiative, "Membership in URI: Affiliates," http://www.uri.org/abouturi/membership/, printed 07/05/04).

2. Conversation between Lee Penn and Donald Frew, 12/15/02 and 3/28/03.

3. Interview of Donald Frew by Lee Penn, 06/08/04.

4. Fr. Rankin is the founder and the current president of a major URI Cooperation Circle, the Global AIDS Interfaith Alliance. (The Global AIDS Interfaith Alliance, "Advisory Board," http://www.thegaia.org/aboutus/advisory.htm, printed 02/11/04.

5. The Religious Institute on Sexual Morality, Justice, and Healing, "List of Endorsements," http://www.religiousinstitute.org/endorsement.html, printed 01/04/03; a copy of this list dated June 26, 2000 is in Lee Penn's files, and contains the signatures of Gibbs and Rankin—indicating that the two URI leaders signed the manifesto within 6 months of its release.

6. The Religious Institute on Sexual Morality, Justice, and Healing, "The Religious Declaration on Sexual Morality, Justice, and Healing," http://www.religiousinstitute.org/declaration.html, printed 01/04/03.

endorse" external groups' declarations, such as the one issued by SIECUS. If that were to occur, he said that "we would be deluged by complaints from people who want us to endorse their own political agenda."[1] In early 2004, Frew stated that "the development of a comprehensive policy on URI endorsements is in progress, and is a high priority."[2]

The Dog That Did Not Bark:
The "Gay Agenda" Goes Missing From the URI

It is noteworthy that the URI, as an organization, has sidestepped the question of homosexuality. URI documents do not mention controversies or causes related to sexual orientation, and the gay caucuses that are active in many U.S. and European religious groups have not had an organized or visible presence at global URI meetings.[3]

The first time that homosexuality was addressed on the floor of a global URI summit meeting was during a speech in 1997 by Christian de la Huerta, from Q-Spirit, a group founded by de la Huerta to "promote personal growth and spiritual development in the gay/lesbian/queer community."[4] That year, he got a standing ovation from 80% of the delegates; 20% remained seated, and did not applaud.[5] When de la Huerta encountered Swing later that day, the bishop told him, "I want you to know that I'm very glad you were here and did what you did. I also want you to know that I've probably ordained more gays and lesbians than the rest of the Anglican church put together. And if you ever want to be a priest, call me."[6]

In 1998, however, de la Huerta reported a chilly reception from many delegates, especially from Muslims and Christians from Africa and Asia.[7] An official history of the URI describes de la Huerta's 1998 speech thus:

> Sometimes the unexpected was particularly challenging, as when one participant interjected into the plenary session a passionate demand for religious communities to stop persecuting homosexuals and to support their rights. Many of those attending agreed with the sentiments. Many disagreed. What made the action polarizing was not as much what was said as how and when it was said. The summit planners had built into the agenda many opportunities for people to speak to and with others about concerns they held passionately. . . . The primary concern about this gay rights statement was not that it challenged some people's beliefs, but that it had been one person imposing his will on the whole.[8]

This appears to have been the last discussion of gay-related issues at URI global meetings.

In May 2004, Bishop Swing declared his deep, ongoing commitment to the "peacemakers of the

---

1. Interview of URI Global Council member Donald Frew by Lee Penn, 10/14/02 and 03/28/03.

2. Interview of URI Global Council member Donald Frew by Lee Penn, 01/08/04.

3. The only public involvement of the Metropolitan Community Church (MCC), a predominantly gay church, in the URI was the attendance of an MCC pastor at a 1997 URI planning meeting in Buenos Aires, Argentina. (Charles Gibbs and Sally Mahé, *United Religions Initiative, Birth of a Global Community: Appreciative Inquiry in Action*, Lakeshore Publishers, 2004, p95, cited below as Gibbs/Mahé, *Birth of a Global Community*). A Google search by Lee Penn on 07/07/04 did not reveal any further MCC involvement with the URI.

4. Christian de la Huerta, *Coming Out Spiritually: The Next Step*, Tarcher/Putnam, 1999, p2.

5. Ibid., p4.

6. Ibid., p4.

7. Ibid., pp147, 152–154.

8. Gibbs/Mahé, *Birth of a Global Community*, pp144–145.

United Religions Initiative scattered throughout the world,"[1] equaling his devotion to his family and to his own diocese. In the same letter, Swing explained his decision to discipline Otis Charles, the retired Episcopal Bishop of Utah, for marrying another man and for having this ceremony publicized in the *San Francisco Chronicle*.[2] It appears that Swing—in his capacity as URI founder, and as a diocesan bishop in the Episcopal Church—did not wish to position himself at the leading edge of the gay marriage revolution in the US.[3]

HUSTON SMITH AND "ENTHEOGENS":
PROPOSING BETTER RELIGION THROUGH CHEMISTRY

The URI has attracted a few prominent supporters with odd ideas about the place of drugs in religious practice. A case in point is the world-renowned scholar Huston Smith. One of his avocations is supporting use of "entheogens"—taking hallucinogens in a controlled manner as a way to have a direct experience of the Divine.

Smith, author of *The World's Religions* (a text on comparative religion which has sold 2.5 million copies worldwide), has taught at Washington University, MIT, Syracuse University, and the University of California at Berkeley.[4] He has long favored the interfaith movement—including Bishop Swing's United Religions Initiative. Smith hailed the URI in June 1998 as "the most significant" ongoing interfaith effort, saying that "I think it is a much-needed move in our time."[5] In 1999, he "made commitments to specific action" on behalf of the 72-hour religious cease-fire observances that the URI planned for Y2K.[6] Smith donated to the URI in 2000.[7] In 2003, Smith said, "The United Religious [sic] Initiative, founded and presided over by Bishop Swing in San Francisco, is a large and flourishing meeting, doing practical things."[8] Smith's commitment to religious syncretism goes beyond public pronouncements. In 1999, Smith said that Christianity and his family formed his character; "throughout my life it has continued to be my meal," he said, "but I am a strong believer in vitamin supplements—spiritual insights gleaned from other religions."[9]

One of Smith's more offbeat spiritual "vitamin supplements" is use of entheogens, taking mescaline, psilocybin, or LSD[10] to attain mystical experiences. Smith acknowledges that he was "initiated to the entheogens through Timothy Leary and psilocybin in his home in Newton on New Year's Day,

---

1. Bishop William Swing, "Episcopacy, Episcopal Diocese, and the *San Francisco Chronicle*," web site of the Episcopal Diocese of California, http://www.diocal.org/article. php?sid=248&mode=thread&order=0, printed 05/18/04.

2. Bishop Otis Charles has a web site with pictures from the ceremony, and the text used for the service, at http://www.otischarles.com/ourwedding.html (viewed 09/15/04).

3. Bishop Swing said as much, himself, in the "marriage of a bishop" section of his letter in response to a public protest by Oasis, a gay advocacy group in the Diocese of California. (Bishop William Swing, "A Response to the Oasis/California Advisory Board," web site of the Episcopal Diocese of California, May 18, 2004, http://www.diocal.org/article.php? sid=250, printed 05/23/04; cited below as Swing, "A Response to Oasis/California," 05/18/04).

4. Council on Spiritual Practices, "Huston Smith," http://www.csp.org/cdp/smith.html, printed 01/16/03.

5. Carolina Wolohan, "Group uses U.N. as its model," *San Jose Mercury News*, June 22, 1998; printed 6/29/98.

6. North American Interfaith Network, "72 HOURS: An Interfaith Peace-Building Project," *NAINews & Interfaith Digest*, Spring 1999, http://www.nain.org/news/n99spring. htm, printed 06/01/04.

7. URI, *Annual Report* 2000, "Honoring Our Donors," p9.

8. Huston Smith, "Can Religion Save Us," interview by Jessica Roemischer, *What Is Enlightenment?* magazine, Spring/ Summer 2003, p75.

9. Worldwide Faith News, "Interfaith Dialog Deepens Beliefs, Say World Parliament Presenters," November 9, 1999, http://www.wfn.org/1999/11/msg00066.html, printed 01/15/03.

10. Huston Smith, *Cleansing the Doors of Perception: The Religious Significance of Entheogenic Plants and Chemicals*, Jeremy P. Tarcher/Putnam, 2000, p9; cited below as Smith, *Cleansing the Doors of Perception*. Smith lists these specific drugs as entheogens, and describes them as "virtually nonaddictive mind-altering chemicals."

1961."[1] Smith advocates use of entheogens, even though he acknowledges that they yield diminishing spiritual returns, are "capricious," and may open doors "onto the demonic." He says, "Even among those who are religiously responsible, entheogens appear to have (in the parlance of atomic decay) a half-life; their revelations decline. They are also capricious. Opening the gates of heaven at the start, there comes a time—I can attest to this myself—when they begin to open either to less and less or onto the demonic."[2] In the final chapter of *Cleansing the Doors of Perception*, Smith claims that "With the exception of peyote, which I took in the line of duty while working with the Native Americans . . . it has been decades since I have taken an entheogen."[3]

At the end of his essay "Do Drugs Have Religious Import? A Thirty-Five-Year Retrospect," Smith laid out his vision for better religion through chemistry:

> My personal, very tentative suggestion is to see if the drug authorities would be willing to approve of a duly monitored experiment on the issue. Find a church or synagogue, presumably small, that is sincerely open to the possibility that God might, in certain circumstances, work through selected plants or chemicals (as I personally believe he did through Soma and Newman's typhoid fever and continues to work through the peyote of the Native American Church). Permit this church to legally include a psychoactive as sacramental, perhaps once a month in its Eucharist. And finally, commission professional social scientists to observe what happens to this congregation in respect to religious traits—notably compassion, fervor, and service. A variant on this proposal would be to obtain legal permission for seminary students to have at least one entheogen experience in a religious setting. I was fortunate in being introduced to the entheogens as part of Harvard University's 1960–63 research program when they were not only legal, but respectable. I support the effort of the Council on Spiritual Practices to afford others the same opportunity.[4]

Smith's essay "Do Drugs Have Religious Import" was in a book published by the Council on Spiritual Practices (CSP), an organization which promotes use of "plant sacraments" as a way to obtain "primary religious experience."[5] Smith hailed the CSP in his own book, *Cleansing the Doors of Perception*:

> Though this book is being published as a free-standing volume in its own right, it is also listed as number five in a series of books on the entheogens—virtually nonaddictive drugs that seem to harbor spiritual potentials—that the Council on Spiritual Practices is issuing. I am comfortable with this, for not only did that Council instigate this book by asking me to pull its essays together; I support its objectives, which include working cautiously toward carving out a space where serious students of the entheogens can pursue their interests carefully and lawfully.[6]

In her 1998 book *Conscious Evolution*, URI supporter Barbara Marx Hubbard put "mind-expanding substances" on a par with the civil rights movement as a way to foster social change: "The environmental movement, the antiwar movement, the Apollo space program, the women's movement, the civil rights and human rights movements, new music, transcendental meditation, yoga, and

---

1. Huston Smith, "Do Drugs Have Religious Import? A Thirty-Five-Year Retrospect," in Thomas B. Roberts, ed., *Psychoactive Sacramentals: Essays on Entheogens and Religion*, Council on Spiritual Practices, 2001, p14. Smith's essay (cited below as Smith, "Do Drugs Have Religious Import?") is based on a talk that he gave at a 1995 conference at the Vallambrosa Conference Center in Menlo Park, California. This week-long gathering was sponsored by the Chicago Theological Seminary and the Council on Spiritual Practices, and involved "a group of theologians, clergy, mental health professionals, transpersonal psychologists, and other professionals who shared an interest in entheogens." (Roberts, ibid., p ix).
2. Smith, *Cleansing the Doors of Perception*, p63.
3. Ibid., p130.
4. Smith, "Do Drugs Have Religious Import?" in Roberts, *Psychoactive Sacramentals*, p16.
5. Council on Spiritual Practices, "About CSP," http://www.csp.org/about.html, printed 06/10/03.
6. Smith, *Cleansing the Doors of Perception*, pxv, "Preface."

mind-expanding substances all encouraged a young generation to act as instruments of social transformation —striving to birth the still-invisible societal butterfly."[1]

Bishop Swing's Condemnation of "Entheogens"

We must hope that Electric Kool-Aid does not find its way into URI interfaith services. It will never do so, as long as Bishop Swing has anything to say about the matter. He acted with dispatch and firmness to suppress supporters of entheogens when they became active in the Episcopal Diocese of California. Furthermore, no official URI documents have ever expressed approval of entheogen use.

Bishop Swing learned in late 2002 that there had been illegal drug use and a non-fatal overdose at an all-night dance held at an Episcopal parish in his diocese by the Rhythm Society (RS)[2]—a rave group[3] whose leaders were suspected of promoting use of entheogens. Swing intervened; the congregation's rector and the RS soon agreed to leave the parish.[4] The parish's entire vestry, its governing body, resigned; no more RS gatherings are to occur anywhere on Episcopal Church property in Swing's diocese.[5]

Soon thereafter, Swing issued a clear condemnation of entheogens. In 2003, he said,

> The time has come for us to be as specific as possible about drug use. Some teaching is heard among the theologically trained and ordained in our Diocese that certain drugs taken in appropriate quantities can be beneficial to spiritual growth. In former days Timothy Leary would tout the use of LSD. Today people are touting 'Ecstasy' or 'entheogens' as the threshold that opens human beings to supernatural realms. The Hopi Indians and their use of peyote are cited as beneficial models. What are not mentioned in these endorsements are the ravages of countless lives that trusted in drugs as a path to paradise. There are probably some very sincere pilgrims of the Spirit who have gone on a quest for the Transcendent, and certain drugs may have seemed to advance them. Their individual quests, as vivid as they may have been, will not be given an official platform in the Diocese of California. We have seen too many drug disasters, too many drug-imprisoned souls … Rumor has it that the Diocese of California is liberal about matters. Not always so. On the use of drugs in our buildings, at our

1. Barbara Marx Hubbard, *Conscious Evolution: Awakening the Power of Our Social Potential*, New World Library, Novato, California, 1998, pp 10-11.

2. Robert Jesse, of the Council on Spiritual Practices, is a co-founder of the Rhythm Society. (Excerpts from Rhythm Society Friends e-mail list, item 4; included as Exhibit N of a dossier prepared by a member of the Episcopal Parish of St. John the Evangelist, seeking Bishop Swing's intervention. See also the following web log: Jason Jay, "The Daily Drool: July 16, 2003—Hiatus," http://www.jasonjay.com/blog/000085.html, printed 03/20/04. Jay said, "Then this weekend I flew out to San Francisco for the Altered States and Spiritual Awakening conference that my friends in San Francisco organized. The whole weekend was incredible, particularly getting acquainted with Robert Jesse, the founder of The Rhythm Society. I think he will be an incredible contact and potential mentor for me around building communities of spirit and contexts for primary religious experience.") Jesse has also headed the Council on Spiritual Practices, the pro-entheogen organization that Huston Smith praises. (Council on Spiritual Practices, "Tripping: An Anthology of True-life Psychedelic Adventures," http://www. csp.org/chrestomathy/tripping_an.html, printed 03/20/04. The article states, "Bob Jesse left his position as a vice president of business development at Oracle, the world's second-largest software company after Microsoft, to head the Council on Spiritual Practices, a nonprofit organization that advocates (among other things) the responsible use of entheogens (divine-manifesting drugs) for religious purposes.")

3. Rave parties are large dance events for young adults, often lasting all night; there is loud music, flashing light, and (in some cases) abundant use of Ecstasy and other designer drugs. Some enthusiasts say that these parties have social and religious significance, fostering community, sharing, and the lowering of artificial barriers among the participants.

4. Lisa Leff, "Progressive Church Finds New Age Ties Unsettling," *Washington Post*, February 22, 2003, page B09; downloaded 3/26/03 from http://www.washingtonpost.com/ac2/wp-dyn?pagename=article&node=&contentId=A39186-2003Feb21&notFound=true. See also Don Lattin, "From rhythm and blues: Fight over dances and drugs tearing S. F. church apart," *San Francisco Chronicle*, February 4, 2002, page A-15; http://www.sfgate. com/cgi-bin/article.cgi?file=/chronicle/archive/2003/02/04/BA210350.DTL, printed 3/26/03.

5. Lee Penn, "ECUSA's Bishop Swing Denounces Drugs, and Dogma," *The Christian Challenge*, July/September 2003, p 30.

functions, this is absolutely forbidden. No wink, wink. Drug use in our churches will be absolutely forbidden. There is a higher path to God, i.e., the path of Jesus Christ. The cross is not a needle. The bread and wine are ordinary, not a hallucinogen. Ecstasy is a path, not a pill. Our drug policy will reflect this.[1]

In the spring of 2004, Swing explained the background for this statement. Otis Charles, a retired Episcopal bishop from Utah who had moved to Swing's diocese in 1993, had openly supported the unorthodox, pro-drug ideas and practices of the Rhythm Society. Swing said, "When I discovered that he is an advocate for taking enthogens [sic] such as Ecstasy and for taking hallucinogenic mushrooms to have a closer experience of God and for encouraging Christians to do the same, I was deeply disappointed. I wrote an anti-drug statement to the Diocese to distance myself from his position."[2]

Interfaith Indoctrination for Children

The URI web site contains a "Kids" section, with an interfaith curriculum for children ages 8-12.[3] These lessons were prepared by two teachers at the Marin Country Day School, a private school in Marin County for kindergarten through eighth grade children.[4] This curriculum illustrates the URI world-view with precision.

There are four lesson plans, ranging in length from 5 to 20 days; all four plans include in-class meditation[5] and creation of a "multicultural shrine" that will allow students to "connect spirituality to themselves" and to "create a sacred space within the classroom."[6] Teachers may begin the meditation exercises by "discussing with students what meditation is and how it can benefit people of all ages, regardless of their religious or spiritual beliefs. You might share some examples of how different religions use meditation."[7]

There is also an exercise called "Create Your Own Religion"—an apt preparation for life in California. As the URI says,

For this assignment, students will be writing a paper or story in which they will create their own religion. It should include the major components they have studied, including sacred texts, basic beliefs, holy places and

---

1. Bishop William Swing, "A Swing Through The Diocese: Drugs and the Diocese of California," *Pacific Church News*, Spring 2003, Vol. 141, No. 2, p5.

2. Swing, "A Response to the Oasis/California," 05/18/04.

3. United Religions Initiative, "Youth," "URI Kid's Website—for young people ages 8–12," http://www.uri.org/youth/, printed 05/27/03. Another document, still on the URI web site as of July 2004, says, "URI has developed an interfaith resource for children ages 8–12 and teachers about world religions, interfaith and an introduction to URI for young people. Kid tested and approved!" (United Religions Initiative, "Frequently Asked Questions," "What about children and the URI?," http://www.uri.org/abouturi/faq/, printed 07/17/04.)

4. The "Kids" section of the URI web page is at http://www.uri.org/kids (printed 07/14/04). The Marin Country Day School says that it "asks children to become skilled learners and ethical human beings, motivated to make a difference in the world" (Marin Country Day School (MCDS), "Welcome to MCDS," http://www.mcds.org, printed 05/26/03). The school says, accurately, that it is "steeped in the distinctive culture that characterizes Northern California" (MCDS, "Mission Statement," http://www.mcds.org, printed 05/26/03). According to URI Global Council member Donald Frew, one of the two authors of the curriculum is the wife of the URI Executive Director. (The authors, Debbie Gibbs and Dana Isaacs, are listed at United Religions Initiative, "URI Kids—Activities," "Introduction to Teacher Unit Plans," http://www.uri.org/kids/act_unit plan_intro.htm, printed 07/14/04.)

5. United Religions Initiative, "URI Kids—Activities," "Individual Spiritual Growth: Meditation Practice," http://www.uri.org/kids/act_indiv_meditation.htm, printed 07/14/04 (cited below as URI, Kids—"Meditation Practice").

6. The four lesson plans are linked to United Religions Initiative, "URI Kids—Activities," "Introduction to Teacher Unit Plans," http://www.uri.org/kids/act_unitplan_intro.htm (printed 07/14/04). The in-class shrine is discussed at United Religions Initiative, "URI Kids—Activities," "Individual Spiritual Growth: Creating a Multicultural Shrine," http://www.uri.org/kids/act_indiv_shrine.htm, printed 07/14/04.

7. URI, Kids— "Meditation Practice."

spaces, as well as holidays or festivals. It could also include special passages, symbols, icons, and whatever concept of God or holy guides the religion has, and it might need a geographical and/or cultural context. It could be in the past, or in the future. The possibilities are endless—their imaginations and your boundaries are the limits. Depending on your age level and time flexibility, students could spend time outlining their religion, or mind-mapping the different areas named above in order to organize their thoughts. The final draft might be a straight-forward essay, or it might be written as a story (i.e., as a day in the life). Another possibility would be for students to make presentations for their class about their religion and answer questions as if they are the leader of the religion.[1]

Indeed, having elementary and middle school children role-play themselves as leaders of their own religion is an instance of what the URI considers to be "spiritual growth"—and proof that "spiritual growth" (as the URI defines it) is not the same thing as advancement in holiness, humility, charity, and virtue.

In like fashion, when the children study the creation stories of different religions and spiritual traditions, the homework assignment is "let students create their own 'creation story.' Have them include elements that these stories seem to have in common but give them freedom to interpret the assignment their own way."[2] This exercise in reducing the religions to their common denominator is, according to the lesson plan, "the major assessment for this lesson."[3]

Students are given new songs to sing, with associated interfaith lessons. For "There'll Be Peace," teachers are to "ask students to explore how they might be a part of helping faiths become united and/or healing the earth. . . . If it is appropriate, this might be a good time to introduce students to interfaith work in your area, resources available from the United Religions Initiative."[4] The URI curriculum also incorporated "One of Us," a Grammy award-winning 1995 hit song by Joan Osborne.[5] The URI curriculum states that teachers may use this song "for students to gain a greater understanding of their feelings about God."[6] "One of Us" includes these deathless lyrics:

If God had a face, what would it look like?
And would you want to see
If seeing meant that you would have to believe
In things like heaven and in Jesus and the saints
And all the prophets?

Yeah, yeah, God is great.
Yeah, yeah, God is good.
Yeah, yeah, yeah, yeah, yeah.

What if God was one of us?
Just a slob like one of us?
Just a stranger on the bus
Trying to make his way home?
Back up to heaven all alone

1. United Religions Initiative, "URI Kids—Activities," "Individual Spiritual Growth: Create Your Own Religion," http://www.uri.org/kids/act_indiv_createrelig.htm, printed 07/14/04.
2. United Religions Initiative, "URI Kids—Activities," "Passage Comparison: Creation Stories," http://www.uri.org/kids/act_pass_creat.htm, printed 07/14/04.
3. Ibid.
4. United Religions Initiative, "URI Kids—Activities," "Songs and Music: There'll Be Peace," http://www.uri.org/kids/act_songs_peace.htm, printed 07/14/04.
5. Infoplease.com, "Joan Osborne," http://www.infoplease.com/ipea/A0883278.html, printed 08/02/04.
6. United Religions Initiative, "URI Kids—Activities," "Songs and Music: One of Us," http://www.uri.org/kids/act_songs_one.htm, printed 07/14/04.

Nobody calling on the phone
'cept for the Pope maybe in Rome."[1]

Of course, there is *no* religious bias *whatsoever* built into the song.

The glossary for the children's' interfaith curriculum defines *jihad* as "In Islam, the struggle to live a good life;"[2] a *messiah* is merely "someone treated as a savior of a country, a religion, or a group of people"[3]—with no allowance for a traditional Christian definition of this term. No traditional Christian books or web sites—from Protestants, Catholics, or Eastern Orthodox—are cited among the resources for users of this curriculum.[4] Other exercises in the lesson plan—visiting "various places of worship" to gain "first hand knowledge of what it feels like to be in a sacred space,"[5] or "interviewing a religious person," someone who "considers religion an important part of their life"[6]—seem to be aimed at a youthful audience raised without religious instruction or allegiance; they present religious practice and belief as inherently exotic. Such might be the case for children raised by the yuppies, atheists, and materialist magicians of Marin County; it is not true for most of the world.

There is no hint in the URI web pages that these activities might, if offered in a US public school, violate the prevailing doctrine of separation of church and state—but then, the ACLU only sues to stop *Christian* prayer.

"Peacebuilding" by Muzzling the Press in Zimbabwe

In December 2002, the URI Cooperation Circle in Zimbabwe held a workshop on "Promoting Non-violent Language in Reporting,"[7] at a time when the dictator of that country was violently repressing opposition press, politicians, and church activists. Speakers made excuses for censorship. One of the workshop leaders, from the University of Zimbabwe, said: "journalists must be sensitive to the cultural context within which they operate, and to [sic] tell the truth in a socially acceptable language context.... He pointed out that mutual respect between the two constituencies of the Media and the

1. Ibid.

2. Charles Upton, a Sufi Muslim, indicates that the curriculum's definition of *jihad* is inadequate. He says, "This definition is in danger of confusing the Islamic concept of *jihad* with two specifically western ideologies: epicureanism and the Calvinist identification of spiritual aspiration with worldly ambition. *Jihad* literally means 'struggle in the way of God.' It can take the form of the armed defense of the religion when an Islamic nation or group is attacked (which does *not* include conversion secured by force), vigorous public criticism of anti-religious ideas, trends and institutions, and—in the case of the 'greater *jihad*'—struggle against one's own passions, making the 'greater *jihad*' strictly synonymous with the Greek word *askesis* and the Russian *podvig*. Indiscriminate terrorism against unarmed civilians, women, children and other Muslims has nothing to do with *jihad* in the traditional sense; such crimes can in no way be characterized as 'struggle in the way of God.' The same must also be said of suicide, which is expressly forbidden in the *ahadith*." (E-mail from Charles Upton to Lee Penn, 04/27/04.)

3. United Religions Initiative, "United Religions Initiative Kids—Activities," "Glossary," http://www.uri.org/kids/activities_glossary.htm, printed 07/14/04.

4. Analysis by Lee Penn of United Religions Initiative, "URI Kids," "World Religions—Online Resource List for World Religions Unit," http://www.uri.org/kids/world_links.htm, printed 07/14/04, and United Religions Initiative, "URI Kids," "World Religions—World Religion Books for Young People and Their Elders," http://www.uri.org/kids/world_book.htm, printed 07/14/04.

5. United Religions Initiative, "URI Kids—Activities," "Encountering Others: Field Trips," http://www.uri.org/kids/act_ecn_field.htm, printed 07/14/04.

6. United Religions Initiative, "URI Kids—Activities," "Encountering Others: Interviewing a Religious Person," http://www.uri.org/kids/act_ecn_interview.htm, printed 07/14/04.

7. A report on this workshop, with the same information cited below, is at United Religions Initiative, *URI Peacebuilding Projects: Report to the United States Institute for Peace*, http://www.uri.org/resources/URIreporttoUSIP.pdf, pp 4–5, printed 07/16/04.

State is called for, with recognition that both are called to serve the public."[1] A representative of the Zimbabwe Broadcasting Corporation said that the media should give the people of Zimbabwe hope, "by reminding the people that despite all the problems there are many positive things going on and an abundance of resources in the country."[2] "Speaking on the professional standards and ethics on reporting, Dr. Tafatoaona Mahosa noted that there is need to regulate the media for the public good. He also pointed out that the African vision of media morality is based on the *ubuntu* concept,[3] therefore having a much broader application which is more circular in its thinking than the more commonly accepted linear framework."[4]

Thus, the peace-building workshop was an extended apologia for government control of the press, and for press-State collaboration. URI Global Council member Donald Frew said in response: "As an American, I often shudder when I see situations in other countries that go against my understanding of the Bill of Rights. But they have to be looked at in context. It's not ideal, but might lead to an improvement in a bad situation. We'll have to wait and see if they move the treatment of the press in the right direction."[5]

OTHER ODDITIES: FROM PSEUDO-SHAMANISM TO THE "LOWERARCHY"

Other URI activities in the US and overseas show what some URI activists mean by the movement's mission to "create cultures of peace, justice and healing for the earth and all living beings."

The URI Cooperation Circle in Asheville, North Carolina "held the Council of All Beings for people to experience being part of a ritual where the human species is only one voice among many."[6] This pseudo-shamanic ritual, invented in 1985 by "deep ecology" activists John Seed and Joanna Macy, has spread worldwide since then.[7]

Macy describes the ritual: "Participants begin by letting themselves be chosen by another life-form, be it animal, plant, or natural feature like swamp or desert. We use the passive verb, *be chosen*, in order to encourage people to go with what first intuitively occur to them, rather than selecting an object of previous study."[8]

---

1. United Religions Initiative, "Africa," http://www.uri.org/regionalnews/africa/zimb. asp, printed 05/28/03; cited below as URI, Zimbabwe conference, 12/02.

2. Ibid.

3. The "*ubuntu* concept" emphasizes the common good and collective action, rather than the rights and advancement of individuals. A business consultant friendly to *ubuntu* says, "'There is much to be learned from the African concept of *ubuntu.*' *Ubuntu*, Lawson points out, has been defined as the spirit of collective unity or solidarity. The opposite of being selfish and self-centred, it empowers everyone in the community to be valued: to reach their full potential in accord with all around them. 'It has been said that by using the solidarity spirit of *ubuntu* it is possible to build co-operation and competitive strategies by allowing teamwork to permeate a whole organization. In practice the *ubuntu* concept means the decision of the team is more important than the individual's.'" (Frank Heydenrych Consultants, "Using the spirit of ubuntu for team collaboration," Software Futures Press Office, *Techforum*, http://www.itweb.co.za/office/softwarefutures/9911151045.htm, printed 05/19/04.) Another writer from Zambia, while also supportive of ubuntu, warns: "In short, although it articulates such important values as respect, human dignity and compassion, the Ubuntu desire for consensus also has a potential dark side in terms of which it demands an oppressive conformity and loyalty to the group." (Dirk Louw, "Ubuntu: An African Assessment of the Religious Other," *Philosophy in Africa*, University of the North, http://www.bu.edu/wcp/Papers/Afri/AfriLouw.htm, printed 12/15/04).

4. URI, Zimbabwe conference, 12/02.

5. E-mail from Donald Frew to Lee Penn, 06/04/03.

6. United Religions Initiative, "URI in the World," *URI Update*, fall 2001, no. 10, p7.

7. Joanna Macy, "The Council of All Beings," http://www.rainforestinfo.org.au/deep-e co/Joanna%20Macy.htm, printed 04/15/03; cited below as Macy, "Council of All Beings."

8. Ibid.

John Seed reiterated the need for participants in the Council of All Beings to open themselves to spirits of nature: "Each of us is going to find an ally, or more accurately we are going to be found by an ally because this is not done in a direct and purposeful kind of way, but it's done in a way where we just be in nature and invite something to come to us. The spirit of something will come."[1]

Macy describes the next step:

Then we take time to behold this life-form in our mind's eye, bestowing upon it fullness of attention, imagining its rhythms and pleasures and needs. Respectfully, silently, we ask its permission to speak for it in the Council of All Beings. If time allows and supplies are available, we make simple masks, working together in companionable silence with paper and paints, twigs and leaves. Then, briefly clustering in small groups, we practice taking on the identity of our chosen life-form. This helps us let go of our self-consciousness as humans, and become more at ease in imagining a very different perspective on life. Then, with due formality, the participants assemble in a circle and the Council of All Beings commences. To create a sense of sacred space, prayers and invocations are spoken. Native American practices, such as smudging with sage or cedar, and calling in the blessings of the four directions, are often used here to good effect.[2]

When all the assembled life forms have spoken,

the assembled often break into singing, drumming, exultant dancing—releasing energy after the long, attentive listening. Sometimes the group just sits in stillness, silently absorbing what has been learned or writing in journals. Care is taken to thank the life-forms, who have spoken through us, and to dispose of the masks in a deliberate fashion. The masks may be formally burned, or hung on a tree or wall, or taken home with us as symbolic reminders of the ritual. On occasion, at the close of a Council, wanting to stay identified with the other life-forms, we fancy that we are putting on human masks, the better to work for them as we re-enter the world of the two-leggeds.[3]

Macy adds, "Here no fasting or drugs or arduous disciplines are needed to awaken the inner shaman."[4]

This exercise is, at best, a chance for tree-huggers to put on a drama, play-acting at being a tribal shaman. At worst, if real spirits are contacted, the "Council of All Beings" may involve willful contact with unclean, deceptive, preternatural entities.

In Washington DC, a URI Cooperation Circle planned "a one-day event—Animal Blessings/Animal Ethics: Science challenges Religion on the Animal-Human Hierarchy by cracking the Human Genome

---

1. John Seed, "IV Council Introduction (finding an ally)," from the *Council of All Beings Workshop Manual*, http://www.rainforestinfo.org.au/deep-eco/cabtran3.htm, printed 04/16/03.

2. Macy, "The Council of All Beings."

3. Ibid.

4. Ibid. Against this superficial view of shamanism, Charles Upton comments, "Shamanism possesses 'a highly developed cosmology . . . that might suggest concordances with other traditions in many respects,' including 'rites comparable to some that belong to traditions of the highest order,' says René Guénon in *The Reign of Quantity and the Signs of the Times*. However, the shamanic emphasis on 'inferior traditional sciences, such as magic and divination' means that 'a very real degeneration must be suspected, such as may sometimes amount to a real deviation, as can happen all too easily to such sciences whenever they become over-developed.' Nonetheless, shamanism may still in some cases be a true spiritual Way. Mircea Eliade, in *Shamanism: Archaic Techniques of Ecstasy*, describes it as both monotheistic and 'patriarchal' in its commonest forms, given that it conceives of God as a male figure inhabiting the highest point of the sky. The spirit powers, usually in animal form, that the shaman encounters are not simply the spirits of various life-forms on the plane of nature, but are closely analogous to the Jewish, Christian, Islamic and Zoroastrian idea of angels: messengers from the Transcendent God. To believe that the 'inner shaman' can be 'awakened' during an afternoon workshop is like believing that a valid Eucharist can be administered by children 'playing Mass.' It shows a terribly condescending and trivializing attitude to both the dangers and the positive powers of the religion of many primal peoples, which the interfaith movement claims to respect. This attitude also makes light of the fierce ascetic discipline, often at the risk of life, that is common among true shamans everywhere." (E-mail from Charles Upton to Lee Penn, 09/11/04).

Code," an event organized by the Committee on the Environment of the Diocese of Washington.[1] Such attempts to minimize the differences between animals and humans seem to be an odd way to promote "peace, justice and healing"—concepts unique to mankind.

At the 1999 URI Global Summit, participants offered what they considered to be "their highest vision for the URI Global Council." One of these visions was that the URI leadership "encourages a lowerarchy, not a hierarchy."[2] Perhaps the URI enthusiast did not know that "lowerarchy" is not an original term; it was used by the senior devil Screwtape to refer to Hell's ruling powers in C. S. Lewis' *Screwtape Letters.*[3]

1. United Religions Initiative, "URI in the World," *URI Update*, fall 2001, no. 10, p 8.
2. Sally Mahé, "Trustee Selection Process," *URI Update*, Issue 10, p 3.
3. C. S. Lewis, *The Screwtape Letters*, Macmillan Publishing Co., 1959, ch. xx, p 91.

4

THE URI'S FRIENDS
IN HIGH PLACES

THE URI'S QUEST FOR A "GLOBAL SOUL" has allies among those who favor radical social change and the establishment of global governance. Unfortunately, some influential people and powerful international agencies are heeding the messages of these reformers. Therefore, we all may suffer from the results of their utopian social experiments.

THE UNITED NATIONS

The URI and the UN are inextricably linked to each other. As URI Executive Director Charles Gibbs said in late 2004, "As many people know, the United Nations has played a key role in URI's life."[1] With time, this cooperative relationship grows.

From the beginning of the URI, Bishop Swing has upheld the example of the United Nations, and has decried the lack of similar united action among the world's religions. In 2001, he said, "All the nations of the world have been together every day for 50 years, struggling together with a common vocation, struggling for global good, and in the same 50 years, the religions of the world haven't spoken to each other, have no common vocation together to serve the world. . . . Who is more moral, the nations of the world, or the religions of the world?"[2] In 2004, Swing said that the URI "would, in spiritual ways, parallel the United Nations."[3]

The idea of an affinity between the URI and the UN is not just Swing's private opinion. According to the URI Charter, "The URI, in time, aspires to have the visibility and stature of the United Nations."[4] In January 2001, former UN Assistant Secretary General Robert Muller told Bishop Swing that the URI "will go very, very far, even beyond the United Nations."[5]

Prominent URI supporters have long assigned a quasi-religious role to the UN. Robert Muller said: "At the beginning the UN was only a hope. Today it is a political reality. Tomorrow it will be the world's religion."[6] He added, "The UN must be the mother and teacher—*mater et magister*—of the

---

1. United Religions Initiative, "Letter from Executive Director," October/November 2004, http://www.uri.org/abouturi/edrreport/index.asp, printed 11/03/04 (cited below as URI, Oct./Nov. 2004 letter from Executive Director).

2. Transcribed by Lee Penn from a tape of the speech by Bishop Swing at the Commonwealth Club, April 25, 2001.

3. Bishop William E. Swing, "The Swing Shift: 25 Years of the 155 Years of the Diocese of California," Episcopal News Service, August 9, 2004, http://www.episcopalchurch.org/3577 _48075_ENG_HTM.htm, printed 08/10/04.

4. United Religions Initiative, "The United Religions Initiative Charter," http://www. uri.org/resources/publications/Charter%20PC%20format.doc, introductory statement, paragraph 2, p1; downloaded 07/07/04.

5. United Religions Initiative, "Letter from the URI's Founder, Bishop William E. Swing," *Annual Report* 2000, p2 (cited below as URI, *Annual Report* 2000).

6. Robert Muller, *My Testament to the UN: A Contribution to the 50th Anniversary of the United Nations*, World Happiness and Cooperation, 1994, p4.

peoples of the world, concerned not only with the fullness of their lives, but also with their soul. The UN will become the world's common religion, a universal spirituality of which existing religions will be diverse cultural members and manifestations."[1] Fr. Luis Dolan, who was the coordinator of the URI effort in Latin America until his death in 2000,[2] said: "The UN 'extends the power of our hearts and souls.' The UN thus has become 'a cathedral where we can worship what is best in each other.' 'Little by little a planetary prayer book is being composed (at the UN) by an increasingly united humanity seeking its oneness.'"[3]

In the meantime, pending the apotheosis of the UN, the URI has successfully built many ties to the United Nations.

• Swing met with interfaith leaders at the UN in June 1993, "when the URI was nothing more than a vision looking for counsel and support."[4]
• In April 1998, UNESCO cooperated with the URI to sponsor a regional inter-religious and inter-cultural conference in Caracas, Venezuela.[5]
• In December 1999, the URI signed an "International Partnership" agreement with UNESCO. [6]
• Dr. Karen Plavan, president of the United Nations Association of Pittsburgh, spearheaded the local planning for the URI summit conference and charter-signing in June 2000.[7]
• In June 2000, URI supporters gathered at the UN headquarters in New York to publicly sign the URI Charter.[8]
• In August 2000, the URI assisted in planning the World Millennium Peace Summit of Religious and Spiritual Leaders at the UN, as a member of the Advisory Council of Interfaith Organizations.[9]
• In January 2001, the URI was recognized by the UN as a Non-Governmental Organization (NGO) by the UN Department of Public Information, giving the URI greater access to UN international conferences.[10]
• In May 2001, "guests from the United Nations" spoke to the URI/North America meeting on plans for the UN Environmental Sabbath.[11]
• The URI has a UN Cooperation Circle in the UN headquarters in New York City, as well as a multi-regional UNESCO Cooperation Circle.[12] The group at the UN headquarters says, "The dream of the URI-UN is to bring the principles and visions of the URI Charter into the work of the UN, and to integrate the voices of the world's

1. Ibid., p171.

2. United Religions Initiative, "United Religions Initiative: Building spiritual partnerships for a just, sustainable and peaceable world," leaflet issued September 15, 1998, "Board of Directors" and "Staff & Leadership" sections.

3. Fr. Luis Dolan, "Development and Spirituality: Personal Reflections of a Catholic," (Global Education Associates), http://www.globaleduc.org/dolan.htm, printed 5/14/99. It is no longer on the Net at this address, but a copy of this page is in a Web archive at http://web.archive.org/web/19991109094845/http://www.globaleduc.org/dolan.htm, printed 11/05/04.

4. Canon Charles Gibbs, "Father Luis Dolan Remembered," *Pacific Church News*, December 2000/January 2001, p47.

5. "A Chronological List Of National and International Presentations of the United Nations Spiritual Forum for World Peace," http://www.peacenvironment.net/1sforum/sfcrono.html, printed 1/13/03; item 52, April 19–23 1998.

6. URI, *Annual Report* 2000, "URI Milestones 2000," p3.

7. Marc Lukasiak, "Religious charter a global peace effort," Pittsburgh *Tribune-Review*, June 27, 2000, http://www.triblive.com/news.relg0627.html; printed 06/27/00; no longer on the Net. Plavan is still listed by Pittsburgh activists as a contact person for the URI. (The Thomas Merton Center, "Justice, Peace and Ecology Directory: T through Z," http://www.thomasmertoncenter.org/Directory_Justice_Groups/JPE_T-Z.htm, printed 04/23/03.)

8. URI, *Annual Report* 2000, "URI Charter Signings 2000," p6.

9. URI, *Annual Report* 2000, "URI Milestones 2000," p3.

10. United Nations Department of Public Information, Non-Governmental Organizations Section, NGO directory listing, http://www.un.org/dpi/ngosection/asp/form.asp?RegID=--&CnID=all&AcID=0&kw=United%20Religions%20Initiative&NGOID=24 98 printed November 25, 2002; United Religions Initiative, "URI Milestones 2001," *Annual Report* 2001, p4.

11. Paul Chaffee, "URI-NA: Circles in Motion," report on May 2001 Salt Lake City conference, http://www.uri.org/regions/namerica/story.htm, printed 10/18/01; no longer on the Net at this address. As of 2004, this page may be found at http://web.archive.org/web/20011128102810/http://www.uri.org/regions/namerica/story.htm.

12. United Religions Initiative, "Cooperation Circles of the URI," http://www.uri.org/regionalnews/cclisting.asp; printed 09/23/04.

faith communities into the arena of governance."[1]

• UNESCO and UNICEF were among the sponsors of the URI Global Assembly held in August 2002 in Rio de Janeiro.[2]

• In his July 2003 report to the URI, Executive Director Charles Gibbs urged URI "observance of the United Nations' International Day of Peace on September 21st," and suggested that members "collaborate with UN offices and missions in your area in commemorating the Day;"[3] he reiterated this call in his September 2003 letter.[4] In August 2003, Gibbs described the plans that the URI Cooperation Circle in Santiago, Chile had made to observe this "Day of Peace" in conjunction with the UN Regional Headquarters in Chile.[5] In September 2004, Gibbs again urged "observance of the United Nations' International Day of Peace on September 21st—an inspiring opportunity for collective global action within the URI community, and in solidarity with the UN and our sisters and brothers in other peace seeking organizations around the world."[6] He also cited plans by URI Cooperation Circles in Sri Lanka, the Philippines, and Chile to join this UN observance. [7]

• During 2004, the URI continued its collaboration with the Values Caucus at the United Nations, a coalition of Non-Governmental Organizations that seeks to bring "values shared by all of humankind" into the activities of the UN.[8] The Caucus held a 10th anniversary event "with guest speakers, Alfredo Sfeir Younis from the World Bank, our old friend and champion, and Carol Zinn, a member of the Values Caucus Coordinating Council from 2000 to 2002. Deborah Moldow, past chair of the Values Caucus, facilitated on behalf of URI-UN. The subject was The Ethical & Spiritual Dimensions of the Millennium Development Goals."[9]

• In May 2004, URI Global Council member Donald Frew stated that the URI has applied for consultative Non-Governmental Organization (NGO) status with the UN Economic and Social Council.[10] This would be in addition to the URI's present recognition by the UN Department of Public Information as an accredited NGO.

• In September 2004, "representatives of the URI participated in the UN's annual NGO conference—The Millennium Development Goals: Civil Society Takes Action. At the conference, the URI UN CC presented a workshop—The Ethical and Spiritual Dimensions of the Millennium Development Goals—that invited people to reflect more deeply on the implications of these goals for their work in the world."[11] Also, "the Standing Committee of URI's Global Council unanimously passed a resolution urging the URI community to observe the United Nations Fifth International Day for the Elimination of Violence Against Women, November 25, 2004."[12]

In the fall of 2004, URI Executive Director Charles Gibbs summed up this history of URI/UN cooperation in a letter to the URI community:

1. United Religions Initiative, "The United Religions Initiative at the United Nations," http://www.uri-un.org/, printed 06/12/04.

2. United Religions Initiative, "First Global Assembly to Convene in Rio de Janeiro in August," *Pacific Church News online*, July/August 2002, http://www.diocal.org/pcn/PCNO/pcno02-7.html, printed 10/12/02.

3. Charles Gibbs, "Letter from Executive Director: July 2003," United Religions Initiative, http://www.uri.org/abouturi/edrreport/july2003.asp, printed 07/15/03.

4. Charles Gibbs, "Letter from Executive Director: September 2003," United Religions Initiative, http://www.uri.org/abouturi/edrreport/september2003.asp, printed 09/26/03.

5. Charles Gibbs, "Letter from Executive Director: August 2003," United Religions Initiative, http://www.uri.org/abouturi/edrreport/august2003.asp, printed 09/05/03.

6. Charles Gibbs, "Letter from Executive Director: September 2004," United Religions Initiative, http://www.uri.org/abouturi/edrreport/index.asp, printed 09/19/04.

7. Ibid.

8. The Values Caucus at the United Nations, "An Evolving Mission Statement," http://www.valuescaucus.org/, printed 06/30/04.

9. The Values Caucus at the United Nations, "Time Line of Highlights—2004," http://www.valuescaucus.org/timeline04.html, printed 06/30/04.

10. As stated to Lee Penn by Donald Frew on 05/08/04.

11. URI, Oct./Nov. 2004 letter from Director.

12. Ibid.

URI's vision of enduring, daily interfaith cooperation to end religiously motivated violence and create cultures of peace, justice and healing was inspired by an interfaith service commemorating the 50th anniversary of the signing of the UN Charter. This vision took life through four years of global gatherings developing URI's charter and global community, held during the week that included the anniversary of the UN charter signing. URI's charter was signed on the 55th anniversary of the UN charter signing. URI is a Non-governmental Organization (NGO) formally affiliated with the UN's Department of Public Information. Following the inspiration of the URI UN cooperation circle, for the past two years, the URI community around the world has joined with the UN community in observing the International Day of Peace on September 21. . . . Also, many cooperation circles around the world work closely with local UN organizations. As URI's global community grows, it is critical that we honor our connection with the UN and allow its work for a more peaceful world to challenge and inspire ours. Together, we can build the world we want to live in.[1]

In addition, the URI and its leaders have cooperated with some of the principal specialized agencies of the UN.

THE UN ENVIRONMENTAL PROGRAM (UNEP)

In August 2002, the URI Global Assembly in Rio de Janeiro voted unanimously to endorse a "Call to Global Healing," which asks the world's religions to "partner with the United Nations Environment Programme (UNEP) to bring ethical and spiritual values to public policy decisions for sustainable development."[2] The director of UNEP, Adnan Z. Amin, said: "I would like to express my great appreciation to United Religions Initiative (URI)."[3]

The Call to Global Healing asks nations

to faithfully implement the principle of Respect for Nature of the UN Millennium Declaration; the call for Sustainable Development found in the UNEP GEO 3 report; and the agreed upon program of the upcoming World Summit on Sustainable Development. As people of faith, we support the agenda outlined by UNEP in the book *Earth and Faith*. As Klaus Topfer states in this publication, 'We have entered a new age—an age where all of us will have to sign a new compact with our environment and enter into the larger community of all living beings. A new sense of our communion with planet Earth must enter our minds.'"[4]

The "Call" adds,

To build this new Culture of Global Healing, we call upon a partnership between UNEP and faith communities to develop new leadership to guide this culture change initiative. We encourage partnerships between faith communities and other NGOs, business and industry and indigenous people, each bringing important dimensions to creating the culture of Global Healing. In addition, we avow our support of documents drafted by international consensus among multi-stakeholder, non-governmental groups, including but not limited to the Charter of the United Religions Initiative and the Earth Charter and the Four Worlds Principles for Building a Harmonious World.[5]

With the adoption of this "Call" and a declaration of support for the Earth Charter, the URI avowed its support for a radical environmentalist vision. Since then, URI leaders have continued their support for the Earth Charter. In April 2003, URI Executive Director Charles Gibbs was the moderator for a panel discussion on "Science, Religion, and Caring for the Environment: A Personal and Global

---

1. Ibid.
2. David Randle, "Utah Initiative Approved at Global Summit: URI Global Assembly Adopts Utah URI and UN URI Call to Global Healing," http://www.utahpop.org/utahinitiative.htm, printed 11/12/02 (cited below as Randle, "Utah Initiative Approved," 2002); also, United Religions Initiative, "Global Assembly Report," *Annual Report* 2002 leaflet.
3. Randle, "Utah Initiative Approved," 2002.
4. Ibid.
5. Ibid.

Responsibility," co-sponsored by the Club of Budapest and the International Diplomacy Council.[1] This event, which had New Age authors Ervin Laszlo and Brian Swimme as speakers, was "held in commemoration of: Earth Charter." [2]

In 2004, the URI stated that it is engaged in "an ongoing exploration of partnership possibilities between URI and UNEP."[3]

UNESCO

Since signing a partnership agreement with UNESCO in December 1999, the URI has cooperated with several high-profile UNESCO projects.

UNESCO and several Nobel Peace Prize laureates had issued a "Manifesto 2000 for a Culture of Peace and Non-Violence" in March of 1999.[4] The URI says, "URI and UNESCO (United Nations Educational, Scientific and Cultural Organization) are partners in the International Decade for the Culture of Peace and the Manifesto 2000. Everyone can act in the spirit of the culture of peace in the context of one's own family, workplace, neighborhood, town, or region, by becoming a messenger of tolerance, solidarity and dialogue."[5] During 2000, the URI web page solicited signatures for the UNESCO document.[6] By June 17 2004, the URI had contributed 301 signatures to the Manifesto[7] out of a total of 75,266,584.[8]

Manifesto signers pledged themselves to

> Respect the life and dignity of each human being without discrimination or prejudice; Practise active non-violence, rejecting violence in all its forms … Share my time and material resources in a spirit of generosity to put an end to exclusion, injustice, and political and economic oppression; Defend freedom of expression and cultural diversity, giving preference always to dialogue and listening without engaging in fanaticism, defamation and the rejection of others; … Contribute to the development of my community, with the full participation of women and respect for democratic principles.[9]

These Manifesto commitments are "an individual commitment and responsibility" of the signers.[10] The meaning of these pledges is open to question. Democratic heads of state, Nobel laureates, and dictators alike signed the Manifesto.[11] Signers and supporters of this UNESCO manifesto included Tony Blair, Jacques Chirac, Vaclav Havel, Ehud Barak, and other current and former democratic heads

---

1. International Diplomacy Council and Club of Budapest, USA, "Science, Religion, and Caring for the Environment: A Personal and Global Responsibility," http://www.earthcharter.org/files/CLUB_OF_BUDAHPEST_MEETING.doc, printed 05/13/03.

2. Ibid.

3. United Religions Initiative, "URI & United Nations," http://www.uri.org/abouturi/partnerships/partners_un.asp, printed 07/17/04. (cited below as URI, "URI & United Nations").

4. URI, *Annual Report* 2000, "URI Milestones 2000," p3.

5. URI, "URI & United Nations."

6. UNESCO, "Peace on the Move—News/articles: United Religions Initiative," http://www3.unesco.org/iycp/uk/uk_tb_national_articles.asp?CodeContact=12834, printed 12/14/02.

7. UNESCO, "Information Board—United Religions Initiative," http://www3.unesco. org/iycp/uk/uk_tb_perso.asp?CodeContact=12834, printed 06/17/04.

8. UNESCO, daily count of signers of "Manifesto 2000," http://www3.unesco.org/manifesto2000/uk/uk_compteur.asp, printed 06/17/04.

9. UNESCO, "Manifesto 2000 for a Culture of Peace and Non-Violence," http://www3. unesco.org/manifesto2000/uk/uk_manifeste.htm, printed December 14, 2002.

10. UNESCO, "Manifesto 2000—Who Is At The Source," http://www3.unesco.org/manifesto2000/uk/uk_pour_en_savoir_plus.htm, printed December 14, 2002.

11. Ibid.; analysis and summary by Lee Penn.

of state, as well as the Dalai Lama, Rigoberta Menchu Tum, Mikhail Gorbachev, Elie Wiesel, Desmond Tutu, and other Nobel laureates. Signers and supporters also included heads of state from authoritarian regimes: Alexander Lukashenko of Belarus, Khamtay Siphandone of Laos, Jiang Zemin of the People's Republic of China, Seyyed Mohammed Khatami of Iran, and Phan Van Khai of Vietnam.[1]

The European Executive Committee of the URI and the European Buddhist Union organized a conference, "Unity in Diversity—Ethical and Spiritual Visions for the World," at UNESCO's Paris headquarters in November 2000.[2]

In December 2000, a UNESCO/URI Cooperation Circle was launched in Barcelona, Spain, in a ceremony attended by over 600 people.[3] This Cooperation Circle has helped organize the summer 2004 meeting of the Parliament of the World's Religions.[4]

In its annual report for 2001, the UNESCO Centre of Catalonia stated that its UNESCO Association for Interreligious Dialogue is "a founder member of the United Religions Initiative."[5]

In 2003, the Rio de Janeiro URI Cooperation Circle received a $15,000 grant from UNESCO to create a "Peace Kit" to establish a "Peacemakers Network" to train teachers for two UNESCO programs in Rio in public schools and youth prisons.[6] According to the URI, "the project will provide 52 hours of training to 1,800 peace educators from different walks of life."[7] The Latin American coordinator for the URI said, "With the prototype in hand it is expected to be much easier to raise funds for accomplishing the rest of the project. It is also great that UNESCO itself is sponsoring the project. They really loved it and want to see it spreading worldwide. Two Brazilian ministries, Education and Justice, are also looking forward to sending one representative each to the workshop in order to follow up and observe the initiative more closely."[8] Thus, this small grant may be a seed for much larger programs in the future that will link the URI with the UN and with national governments. (Later in 2003, the project received second-stage funding from the Ale Petrol Company.)[9]

THE UNITED NATIONS POPULATION FUND (UNFPA)

The director of the URI in Zimbabwe joined an April 2002 petition to President Bush, urging full US funding for UNFPA programs; this petition cited the Dalai Lama and Anglican Archbishop Tutu as supporters of "modern family planning."[10]

---

1. UNESCO, "Manifesto 2000—Personalities Who Have Signed," http://www3.une sco.org/manifesto2000/uk/uk_pour_ en_savoir_plus.htm#personnalités, printed 03/20/04.

2. URI, *Annual Report* 2000, "URI Milestones 2000," p3.

3. Ibid.

4. URI, "URI & United Nations": "Our UNESCO Cooperation Circle (CC) in Barcelona—Association for Interreligious Dialogue CC—is one of several with strong connections to UNESCO. This CC will help organize the next edition of the Parliament of the World's Religions as Barcelona has been chosen as the site for its 2004 gathering."

5. Centre UNESCO de Catalunya, "Interreligious Dialogue," *Annual Report* 2001, p94.

6. Andre Porto (Regional Coordinator, Latin America), "United Religions Initiative: Circles Around the Globe: Rio CC receives UNESCO grant," *Pacific Church News On-Line*, April/May 2003, vol. 141, no. e3, http://pcn.diocal.org/PCNO/ pcn003-3/index.html, printed 05/08/03 (cited below as Porto, "Rio CC receives UNESCO grant," *PCN on-line*, April/May 2003). See also, United Religions Initiative, "Latin America & the Caribbean," http://www.uri.org/regionalnews/lamerica/brazil.asp, printed 05/28/03 (cited below as URI, "Latin America & the Caribbean," 2003).

7. United Religions Initiative, "Developing Resources for Peace in Brazil," *URI Update*, August 2003, Issue 13, p2.

8. Porto, "Rio CC receives UNESCO grant," *PCN-on-line*, April/May 2003. See also, URI, "Latin American & the Caribbean," 2003.

9. United Religions Initiative, "Peace Resources," *URI Update*, November 2003, Issue 14, p3.

10. International Committee of Religious Leaders for Voluntary Family Planning, news release, "International Committee of Religious Leaders for Voluntary Family Planning Calls on President Bush to Release $34 Million for UNFPA," April 30, 2002, http://www.co mmondreams.org/news2002/0430-05.htm, printed 06/11/03.

The UNFPA has, by its own account, spread "modern family planning" worldwide. In November 2000, the outgoing Executive Director Nafis Sadik, who had held that post for 14 years, "said that when the agency started, few countries had family planning programs, because it was simply not acceptable in many areas. But 'now every country in the developing world has family planning as part of its health service, and today every country now has a reproductive health program.'"[1] Sadik also admitted that "her agency has been responsible for tying developmental assistance to population control. 'I think we've been able to make the consensus . . . that population issues are part of developmental issues, that they're not separate, that they link with all facets of social life and economic and developmental life. . . . Without pursuing social policies and social goals, you can't really have economic development.'"[2]

POLITICIANS:
FROM THE WHITE HOUSE TO THE STATE HOUSE

President George W. Bush has publicly praised the URI and its founder, Bishop Swing.

In a November 6, 2001 letter from the White House, Bush congratulated Swing for receiving the 2001 Citizen Diplomacy Award from the International Diplomacy Council, a private organization that works closely with high-level State Department officials to assist overseas leaders and groups who visit the US. At the end of the letter, Bush said, "Both the United Religions Initiative and the International Diplomacy Council exist to foster a greater understanding among peoples. I salute these organizations for their roles in facilitating interaction among people and nations."[3] By contrast, neither President Clinton nor Hillary Clinton ever commented publicly on the URI. Previous recipients of the Citizen Diplomacy Award include former ambassador Shirley Temple Black, retired Bank of America chairman A. W. Clausen, and former Secretary of State George Schultz. [4]

Frank Dammann, manager of membership for the International Diplomacy Council (IDC), said in 2001 that Secretary of State Colin Powell is familiar with the work of IDC.[5] In addition, George P. Shultz, Secretary of State in the Reagan administration, is a member of the IDC Advisory Council.[6] Dammann stated that Bush's commendation of the IDC and the URI was at the suggestion of "higher level" officials in the State Department. [7]

This is not the only tie between the URI and the Federal government. The United States Institute of Peace (USIP), which is funded by Congress and whose Board of Directors is chosen by the President,[8] ran an article praising the URI in October 2001.[9] In 2002, the USIP published *Interfaith Dialogue and Peacebuilding*, a book containing "The United Religions At Work," an essay by URI Executive Director

1. *Catholic World News*, News Brief, "Outgoing UNFPA Head Admits Responsibility For Abortion Spread," November 28, 2000, http://www.cwnews.com/Browse/2000/11/143 46.htm, printed 05/08/03.

2. Ibid.

3. International Diplomacy Council (IDC), letter from President Bush, November 6, 2001, http://www.diplomacy.org/idc1140101.html, printed 08/16/04.

4. Dennis Delman, "Bishop Swing Given International Diplomacy Council Award," *Pacific Church News*, Winter 2002, p 46.

5. Interview of Frank Dammann (IDC) by Lee Penn, December 2001.

6. International Diplomacy Council, "Advisory Council," http://www.diplomacy.org/board.html, printed 10/21/04.

7. Interview of Frank Dammann (IDC) by Lee Penn, December 2001.

8. United States Institute of Peace, "About the United States Institute of Peace," http://www.usip.org/aboutusip.html, printed 02/17/03.

9. United States Institute of Peace, "Faith-Based NGOs and International Peacebuilding," October 22, 2001, http://www.usip.org/pubs/specialreports/sr76.html, printed 02/17/03.

Charles Gibbs.[1] USIP also made a $30,000 grant to the URI for a "Peace Building Training Program" in early 2002.[2] The URI has offered a link to the USIP on its web page, saying, "They are an independent and non-partisan federal institution and they specialize in providing the best peace education and training."[3]

In December 2001, URI Executive Director Charles Gibbs attended a US Navy leadership summit; he was invited as an "outside participant who could help bring some perspective . . . based on the URI's work around the world."[4]

In April 2004, an essayist in *Public Interest* magazine explained the apparent incongruity of an evangelical Protestant president, George W. Bush, supporting religious syncretism. It comes down to a strategic necessity in the global "War on Terror":

> All the more ironic, then, that in the most important policy and riskiest gamble of his presidency, Bush has embraced willy-nilly the view that liberal democracy is one thing, Protestant Christianity (or Christianity of any sort, or even Judeo-Christianity) entirely another. He has chosen to present America to the world not as the Christian nation for which his religious supporters take it, but as the universal sponsor of liberal democracy, which as such is impartial in principle as between Christianity and Islam. Thus must Bush present America not just to the world but to itself. It is said that John Foster Dulles helped desegregate American society by persuading a reluctant Eisenhower to send federal troops to Little Rock lest inaction hand the Soviets a propaganda windfall. Bush finds himself similarly trapped in the glare of global headlights. However trying the struggle with Islamism may prove, whatever sacrifices it may demand, he cannot revive Lincoln's appeal to Christianity, no matter how nondenominational that appeal would be. His religious rhetoric must be 'inclusive,' anodyne, and sterile. His administration must become America's first genuinely Methodist Taoist Native American Quaker Russian Orthodox Buddhist Jewish (and Muslim) one. And so the challenge of Islamic terror will collaborate with other forces to drive official America to ever greater lengths of secularism or syncretism.[5]

With this imperative, it seems likely that Federal support for the URI and similar ventures will increase.

Gray Davis, the then-incumbent governor of California, joined Bush's tribute to the URI and the IDC. In a November 14, 2001 letter from his office in Sacramento, Davis said, "By promoting peace and tolerance through the United Religions Initiative, you have made a positive and lasting impact. Your outstanding dedication to fostering international goodwill is an inspiration to us all."[6] (Davis, a liberal Democrat, was recalled by the voters in November 2003. He was replaced by a Republican, Arnold Schwarzenegger.)

In October 1997, Bishop Swing spoke to "a briefing of the Congressional Human Rights Caucus" to

1. United States Institute for Peace Press, advertisement for *Interfaith Dialogue and Peacebuilding*, http://www.usip.org/pubs/catalog/interfaith.html, printed 02/17/2003.

2. United States Institute for Peace, "PeaceWatch Online: Grant Awards," April 2002, http://www.usip.org/peacewatch/2002/4/grant2.shtml, printed 09/04/02.

3. United Religions Initiative, "Peacebuilding Training Links," http://www.uri.org/peacebuilding/links/peacetrnlinks.asp, printed 10/12/02 and viewed 07/16/04.

4. Charles Gibbs, "Executive Director's Report—December 2001," http://www.uri.org/urinews/edr1209, printed 01/14/02; no longer on the Net. Gibbs is listed as a participant in the summit—and his URI affiliation is noted—at Center for Executive Education, "Leadership Summit Attendees," http://www.cee.nps.navy.mil/NewSite/leadership_summit/attendee_list.htm, printed 04/08/03.

5. Clifford Orwin, "The Unraveling of Christianity in America," *The Public Interest*, Spring 2004, Issue #155, http://www.thepublicinterest.com/previous/article2.html, printed 08/03/04.

6. IDC, "Governor Gray Davis—Commendation: Reverend William Swing," http://www.diplomacy.org/idc11140102.html, printed 02/17/03.

discuss the URI with members of Congress and their staff.[1] Representative Tom Lantos (D-California) introduced Swing to the Caucus, and several days later made laudatory comments on Swing's behalf for inclusion in the Congressional Record, calling him "one of the outstanding religious leaders of our Nation.... Bishop Swing is an extraordinary man who is dedicated to promoting peace and respect for human rights around the globe.... I urge my colleagues to give thoughtful and serious considerations to the ideas of this dedicated man of God."[2]

The URI has established a multi-regional Cooperation Circle to support the proposal of Dennis Kucinich (a member of the House of Representatives and a candidate for the 2004 Democratic nomination as President of the US), for the creation of a Cabinet-level "Department/Ministry of Peace" in the US. The new agency would be "dedicated to peacemaking and the study of conditions that are conducive to peace."[3] The Cooperation Circle also will support similar moves in other countries. The URI is thus seeking enactment of one of the ideas proposed by Robert Muller, a prominent New Age supporter of the URI: "I dream that each country shall create a Ministry of Peace and an academy or institute for peace, with local branches, in order to guide and co-ordinate the efforts of citizens, schools, and local institutions and associations working for peace, non-violence, and a better world."[4] (The proponents of this agency have made an infelicitous name choice; in Orwell's *1984*, the "Ministry of Peace" was Big Brother's war department.)[5]

GEORGE SOROS

Billionaire currency speculator George Soros has contributed money to the URI Youth Network.[6] This is only one of his many grants on behalf of "progressive" causes. Soros has funded Choice in Dying and other groups that lobby for legalizing physician-assisted suicide.[7] He also supports needle exchange programs for drug addicts,[8] aids campaigns for legalization of marijuana for medical purposes,[9] and funds groups that will "support the protection of minor's [sic] rights to reproductive

1. Rep. Tom Lantos, "Bishop William Swing Of The Episcopal Diocese Of California Discusses The United Religious Initiative, An Effort To Encourage Peace And Respect For Human Rights," *Congressional Record*: November 4, 1997 (Extensions), found through a Google search of news group postings, printed 06/11/04.

2. Ibid.

3. United Religions Initiative, "Multi-Regional CC: Establishment of the Department/Ministry of Peace," http://www.uri.org/regionalnews/multiregion/ministry.asp, printed 05/27/04.

4. Robert Muller, "My Dreams for Peace Education," item 17, in "Volume 1, The First Five Hundred Ideas Of Two Thousand Ideas For A Better World," http://www.robertmulle r.org/voladnl/v1adnl.htm, viewed 06/21/04.

5. George Orwell, *1984*, New American Library edition, 1961, p8.

6. Dennis Delman, "Second United Religions Summit Conference," *Pacific Church News*, June/July 1997, p28, and United Religions Initiative, "Foundation Grants Enable URI Youth Leadership on Worldwide Net," *URI News Update*, March 1997, no. 2, p1.

7. Project Death In America (PDIA), "Transforming the Culture of Dying: The shaping of governmental and institutional policy," http://www.soros.org/death/governmental_policy.htm, printed 12/31/02. Choice in Dying is the latest incarnation of the Euthanasia Society of America, founded in 1938. (See Rita Marker, "Dying for the Cause: Foundation funding for the 'right-to-die' movement," *The Philanthropy Roundtable*, January 200, http://www.philanthropyroundtable.org/magazines/2001/january/marker.html, printed 12/31/02). Choice in Dying is linked to the June 1999 issue of the PDIA newsletter, where its publications are offered as "an exploration of the values that guide end-of-life decisions." (http://www.soros.org/death/news5.htm, printed 12/31/02).

8. William Shawcross, "Turning Dollars Into Change," *Time*, September 1, 1997, p54.

9. Peter Newcomb et al., "The Forbes 400," article on George Soros, *Forbes*, October 12, 1998, p184.

health care" and "expand women's access to abortion and family planning services."[1] Recent Soros grant recipients have included Catholics for a Free Choice, the publishers of *Our Bodies, Ourselves*, the National Abortion Federation, the Center for Reproductive Law and Policy ("$1,500,000 for a four-tiered strategy to defend against 'partial birth' abortion legislation and other threats to reproductive rights"), the National Abortion Rights Action League (NARAL), Planned Parenthood, the Religious Coalition for Reproductive Choice, and the Public Media Center's PR efforts on behalf of the State Family Planning Commission of China.[2]

Soros's ambitions, like Bishop Swing's, are large, but the financier is not daunted. Describing his multimillion-dollar effort to oust George W. Bush from the White House in the 2004 elections, Soros said, "'It would be too immodest for a private person to set himself up against the president,' ... 'But it is, in fact'—he chuckled—'the Soros Doctrine.'"[3] Likewise, in 1997, Soros had said, "It is a sort of disease when you consider yourself some kind of god, the creator of everything, but I feel comfortable about it now since I began to live it out."[4] Despite this claim to Olympian status, Soros was convicted of insider trading in France in December 2002; if the resulting €2.2 million fine is upheld, he would disgorge his gains from speculating on a 1988 French bank merger.[5]

New Age author and URI supporter Neale Donald Walsch praises Soros' work: "Ted Turner and George Soros have given away millions of dollars. They've empowered the dreams of humanity with the rewards of their own dreams, lived."[6] No mention, however, of the innocent victims of abortion, who have no chance to live *their* dreams.

MOVEMENTS FOR "GLOBAL GOVERNANCE"

From the time that the URI was founded, there has been cross-fertilization between it and other utopian, globalist movements. Many of the same people have led multiple organizations, or shared podiums with each other, or endorsed each others' manifestoes, or praised each others' books. By such means, without formal organizational ties, these organizations promote what URI Global Council member Donald Frew describes as "the Western liberal social agenda. It covers many groups, and those who are in one group are likely to be in another. It is a world-view, *not* a conspiracy."[7]

THE STATE OF THE WORLD FORUM

The State of the World Forum (SWF) is a spin-off from the Gorbachev Foundation[8] which promotes networking among high-level politicians, global business leaders, and New Age spiritual adepts.

1. Soros Foundation Network, "US Programs—Reproductive Rights," "Our Work," http://www.soros.org/usprograms/reproductive.htm, printed 12/31/02.

2. Open Society Institute, "Program on Reproductive Health and Rights—Grants 1997–2004," http://www.soros.org/repro/grants.htm, printed 12/31/02.

3. Laura Blumenfeld, "Billionaire Soros takes on Bush," *MSNBC News*, November 11, 2003, http://www.msnbc.com/news/991865.asp?cp1=1, printed 06/17/04.

4. Newcomb, "The Forbes 400," 10/13/97, p181.

5. John Tagliabue, "French court convicts Soros," *International Herald Tribune*, December 21, 2002, http://www.iht.com/articles/81091.html, printed 12/31/02.

6. Neale Donald Walsch, *Friendship with God: An Uncommon Dialogue*, G.P. Putnam's Sons, 1999, p34.

7. Interview of Donald Frew by Lee Penn, 3/28/03.

8. The Gorbachev Foundation/USA convened the first SWF in San Francisco in 1995; the SWF has since become a separate non-profit organization. (State of the World Forum, "Gorbachev Foundation USA 10th Anniversary Celebration," http://www.worldforum.org/home/fmsd_2.htm, printed 2/6/03).

The SWF has been a de facto ally of the URI. There is no formal link between the SWF and the URI, but URI staff member Paul Andrews said in 1997, "We are friendly colleagues. Some people go to both meetings."[1] Prominent URI supporters who have advised the State of the World Forum, or attended and spoken at Forum events, include Charles Gibbs (URI Executive Director),[2] Fr. Alan Jones (Dean of Grace Cathedral, Bishop Swing's parish),[3] Robert Muller (former Assistant Secretary-General of the UN),[4] Barbara Marx Hubbard (a New Age futurist),[5] Dee Hock (who assisted in drafting the URI Charter),[6] Lauren Artress (founder of the Labyrinth Project),[7] Anglican Archbishop Desmond Tutu,[8] James Parks Morton (of the Interfaith Center of New York),[9] Bawa Jain (of the Millennium World Peace Summit of Religions and Spiritual Leaders),[10] and Avon Mattison (of Pathways to Peace).[11] Eight foundations (the William K. Bowes Jr. Foundation, the Copen Family Foundation, the Koret Foundation, the Philanthropic Collaborative, Inc., the San Francisco Foundation, the Rudolf Steiner Foundation, the Surdna Foundation, and the John Templeton Foundation) have contributed to the URI as well as to the SWF.[12]

The SWF was a co-sponsor of the 1996 URI summit conference, along with the World Conference on Religion and Peace and the Foundation for Religious Understanding.[13] According to the SWF's 1996 statement,

We stand on the threshold of a new world order that may be defined either by an increasing polarization that fuels a spiral of escalating conflict and violence, or by a growing global cooperation that calls the human race to work across national, ethnic and religious boundaries to serve a larger global good. In response to this situation

1. Interview with Paul Andrews, URI staff member, October 7 and December 11, 1997. URI Global Council member Donald Frew said in an 11/18/02 e-mail to Lee Penn, "There will be a lot of people who will be attracted to the URI and to other groups, attending both. . . . In the vast majority of cases, we have no clue whatsoever which other groups our people go to."

2. State of the World Forum, *Toward a New Civilization*, May 1997; "1996 Participant List," p30 (cited below as SWF, *Toward a New Civilization*, 05/97).

3. State of the World Forum, *The 5th Annual State of the World Forum*, October 1–6, 1999, p14 (cited below as SWF, *5th Annual State of the World Forum*, October 1999).

4. State of the World Forum, "International Coordinating Council," http://worldforum.percepticon.com/network/inter_coord_council.html, printed 02/12/04; SWF, *Toward a New Civilization*, 05/97, "International Coordinating Council," p5, and "1996 Participant List," p33, and "1995 Participant List," p24.

5. 1997 participation: State of the World Forum, "Forum Program Schedule 1997," *Quarterly*, July-September 1997, Vol. 2, no. 3, p5; 1997 State of the World Forum, "Participants," http://www.worldforum.org/1997forum/1997_Participants.html, printed in 1997; no longer on the Net; cited below as SWF, 1997 participants. 1995–1996 participation: SWF, *Toward a New Civilization*, 05/97, "1996 Participant List," p31, and "1995 Participant List," p23.

6. State of the World Forum, "Schedule" for Wednesday, October 29, 1998, http://www.worldforum98.org/schedule/day_wednesday.html, printed in 1998; no longer on the Net.

7. SWF, 1997 participants.

8. State of the World Forum, *Registry of Accomplishments: 1995–2000*, p14 (cited below as SWF, *Registry of Accomplishments*).

9. SWF, *The 5th Annual State of the World Forum*, October 1999, p14.

10. State of the World Forum, "Forum 2000 Speakers and Participants," http://www.worldforum.org/forum2000/speakers.html, printed 02/04/01; no longer on the Net at this address. As of 2004, this web page may be found at http://web.archive.org/web/20010117072100/http://www.worldforum.org/forum2000/speakers.html.

11. SWF, *Registry of Accomplishments*, p6.

12. State of the World Forum, "Supporters," http://www.worldforum.org/about/supporters.htm, and State of the World Forum, "Partners," http://www.worldforum.org/about/partners.htm, printed 06/29/04. Donors to the URI are documented above in this book, in the section "URI Funding: Secular Foundations, Billionaires, and Theosophists."

13. "An Invitation to Share the Vision; An Invitation to Change the World," *Pacific Church News*, April/May 1996, p7. See also Don Lattin, "Bishop Pushes Presidio Interfaith Group," *San Francisco Chronicle*, January 23, 1996, pA-13; Lattin wrote that Swing "is working on the project with the World Conference on Religion and Peace, the Gorbachev Foundation, and San Francisco businessman Richard Blum."

and to help the world's religions serve the cause of global cooperation, we will cosponsor an interfaith summit conference this June in San Francisco. Specifically, the work of this conference will be to develop further the concept of a United Religions Organization and to develop an agenda for the State of the World Forum in October 1996.[1]

THE EARTH CHARTER MOVEMENT

At its Global Assembly in 2002, the URI called for adoption of the Earth Charter,[2] as the leaders of the State of the World Forum had done in 1995.[3] The reason is that, as Gorbachev said in 1993, "the balance in relations between man and nature has been upset and the very survival of mankind is in jeopardy. Indeed, the planet is slowly dying."[4]

1. State of the World Forum, "The World's Religions and The Emerging Global Civilization: An Interfaith Summit Conference June 24–28, 1996 San Francisco," *Pacific Church News*, April/May 1996, p33. A note at the end of the article says, "All quotes are from material distributed by the State of the World Forum."

2. Randle, "Utah Initiative Approved," 2002.

3. Mahbub ul Haq, Convener, "The Environment: Final Report on the Working Roundtables," September 30, 1995, http://www.well.com/user/wforum/transcripts/themes/6enviro1.html; printed 03/28/98; no longer on the Net.

4. Green Cross International, "The Hague Speech by Mikhail Gorbachev," the Hague, 24 May 1993, "Extracts," http://www.greencrossinternational.net/GreenCrossFamily/gorby/hague.html, printed 05/13/03.

5

AMONG THE NATIONS: THE NON-CHRISTIAN SUPPORTERS OF THE URI

TRADITIONAL RELIGIONS AND THE URI

THE URI HAS GAINED WIDE SUPPORT and participation from members and leaders of long-established non-Christian religions.

JEWS

Jews who have been URI leaders, or have participated in its public events, include:

- Rabbi Stacy Laveson Friedman.[1]
- Rabbi Fruman, of the Teqoa settlement near Bethlehem and a founder of the Gush Emunim.[2]
- Rabbi Joseph Gelberman, "founder of an interfaith seminary," participated in a URI planning meeting in New York in 1997.[3]
- Rabbi Doug Kahn, executive director of the San Francisco-based Jewish Community Relations Council, who has served on the URI board since 1998.[4]
- Rita Semel has served on the URI board since 1997; she has been vice-president of Jewish Family and Children's Services, and a member of Temple Emmanuel.[5]

1. United Religions Initiative, "Honoring URI Donors and Volunteers," *Annual Report* 2002 leaflet (cited below as URI, *Annual Report* 2002).

2. Fruman's party, Gush Emunim (the "Bloc of the Faithful"), opposes Israeli withdrawal form the Occupied Territories. In 2001, he participated in prayer and dialog with a Sufi sheikh, at an event sponsored by the Israel Interfaith Association CC. ("URI's Cooperation Circles Exhibit Great Diversity of Needs," *Pacific Church News*, June/July 2001, p34 (cited below as "URI Cooperation Circles," *PCN*, June/July 2001).

3. Charles Gibbs and Sally Mahé, *United Religions Initiative, Birth of a Global Community: Appreciative Inquiry in Action*, Lakeshore Publishers, 2004, p88 (cited below as Gibbs/Mahé, *Birth of a Global Community*).

4. URI leaflet with list of board members, dated 9/15/98. The list of members of the URI Interim Global Council (which served until 2002, when the Global Council was elected) is from United Religions Initiative, *Annual Report* 2000, p8, cited below as URI, *Annual Report* 2000. This body served until 2002. In 2003, Kahn re-joined the Board as a member of the Transition Advisory Committee. (United Religions Initiative, "URI Global Council," http://www.uri.org/abouturi/globalcouncil/, printed 06/30/04; cited below as URI, "Global Council").

5. 1997 list of Board members provided by URI staff member Paul Andrews, November 20, 1997. List of members of the URI Interim Global Council (which served until 2002, when the Global Council was elected) is from URI, *Annual Report* 2000, p8. Semel remains on the Global Council as part of the Transition Advisory Committee.

- Rabbi Zalman Schacter-Shalomi.[1]
- Rabbi Bernard Zlotowitz.[2]

In 1996, Swing had made a global pilgrimage, seeking support for the URI from religious leaders in Asia, Africa, and Europe. Jewish leaders who stated their support at that time included:[3]

- Rabbi Hugo Gryn, of the West London Synagogue.
- Richard Hirsch, Executive Director of the World Union for Progressive Judaism.
- Rabbi Mordechai Peron, former Chief Rabbi of the Israeli Army.
- Rabbi David Rosen, President of the World Conference on Religion and Peace.
- Sir Sigmund Sternberg, of the International Council of Christians and Jews.

MUSLIMS

American Muslim URI supporters have included:

- Iftekhar Hai, director of the United Muslims of America (UMA), who has served on the URI board since 1997[4]—as well as Dr. Waheed Siddiqee and Shafi Refai, other members of the UMA Interfaith Committee.[5]
- Kamilat, an organization of feminist Muslims in the US[6]
- W. D. Mohammed, of the Nation of Islam, described by the URI as a "leading Black American proponent of traditional Islam."[7]
- Ghazala Munir, from Michigan.[8]

Other Muslims who have supported the URI, or participated in its events, include:

- Haji Katende Abdu, from Makere University, Uganda.[9]
- Dr. Zeenat Ali, from St. Xavier's College, in Bombay, India.[10]
- Dr. Nahid Angha, co-director of the International Association of Sufism and director of the International Sufi Women organization.[11]

1. United Religions Initiative, "Some Early Supporters...," http://www.united-religions.org/72hours/supporters.htm; printed 1999, no longer on the Net (cited below as URI, "Some Early Supporters").
2. URI, *Annual Report* 2002, "Honoring URI Donors and Volunteers."
3. Bishop William Swing, "Reactions from Religious Leaders: United Religions International Tour," URI document issued in the summer of 1996, pp1–4 (cited below as Swing, "Reactions from Religious Leaders," summer 1996).
4. 1997 list of Board members provided by URI staff member Paul Andrews, November 20, 1997. List of members of the URI Interim Global Council (which served until 2002, when the Global Council was elected) is from URI, *Annual Report* 2000, p8. Hai remains on the Global Council as a member of the Transition Advisory Committee.
5. Iftekhar A. Hai, "American Muslims and the Global Interfaith Movement," *Pakistan Link*, http://www.pakistanlink.com/community/2000/Apr/07/08.html, printed 10/28/01.
6. URI is listed among Kamilat's "Alliances, Community Partnerships & Endorsements." (Kamilat, "Network," http://www.kamilat.org/fr_network.htm, printed 04/21/03.) In addition, they state that they participated in the 1998 URI summit meeting at Stanford University. (Kamilat, "Kamilat Participates in Global Interfaith Conference," http://www.kamilat.org/News/URI.htm, printed 04/21/03). A description of Kamilat's mission is at Kamilat, "About Kamilat," http://www.kamilat.org/fr_about.htm, printed 04/21/03.
7. Paul Chaffee, "URI Global Conference Begins Work Toward June 2000 Charter Ceremony," *Pacific Church News*, October/November 1997, p32 (cited below as Chaffee, "URI Global Conference," *PCN*, Oct./Nov. 1997). Charles Upton says of this description of the Nation of Islam, "The abysmal *religious ignorance* of the URI is here demonstrated again: The Nation of Islam is the furthest thing from traditional Islam, either Sunni or Shi'ite. It is, rather, an eccentric and anti-traditional ideology invented by Elijah Muhammad, which bears approximately the same relationship to Islam as Mormonism does to Catholicism or Eastern Orthodox Christianity." (E-mail from Charles Upton to Lee Penn, 04/27/04.)
8. Waheed Siddiqee, "UMA Pursues the Issue of Global Economic Disparity in Stanford Religious Conference," http://pakistanlink.com/community/98/july/10/05.html, printed in 1998; no longer on the Net; cited below as Siddiqee, "UMA Pursues," July 1998. Participated in the 1998 global summit meeting.
9. Ibid.
10. Ibid.
11. URI, "More Reflections From Stanford," *Journal of the United Religions Initiative*, Fall 1997, Issue 4, p8.

- Dr. Zaki Badawi, "President, The Muslim College, London."[1]
- Yousuf Bhailok, from the Muslim Council of Britain—who was elected as Patron of the URI in the UK in September 2002.[2]
- Bashir Ahmed Dultz, from Germany.[3]
- Maulana Abdul Khabir, the Grand Imam of the Badshahi Mosque in Lahore, Pakistan.[4]
- Rehama Namuburu, from Uganda.[5]
- Budya Pradipta, from the University of Indonesia.[6]
- The Sufi Sheikh Abu Salih, of Deir Qaddis (near Ramalla).[7]
- Shah Nazar Seyed Dr. Ali Kianfar.[8]
- P. K. Shamsuddin, a retired Justice from Kerala, India.[9]
- Sheikh Gamal M. A. Solaiman, Professor of Islamic law at the Muslim College in London.[10]
- Karimah Stauch, a Sufi Muslim from Germany.[11]

In 1996, Swing also gained endorsements for the URI from these Muslim leaders:[12]

- Dr. Javid Iqbal, a Pakistani former supreme court justice whom the URI describes as the "son of the founder of Pakistan."[13]
- Senator Kamel S. Abu Jaber and Randa Muqhar, of the Royal Institute for Interfaith Studies in Jordan.
- Dr. Mohammed Syed Tantawi, who was then the Grand Mufti of Egypt and Grand Sheik of Alazhar[14]

Non-Abrahamic Faiths

Numerous leaders of Asian and other non-Abrahamic religions—most notably, the Dalai Lama[15]—have been active in the URI, or have participated publicly in its events:

1. URI, "Some Early Supporters."
2. The Muslim Council of Britain, "United Religions Initiative AGM," in the September 13, 2002 on-line newsletter, http://www.mcb.org.uk/e31.html, printed 02/11/03.
3. Siddiqee, "UMA Pursues," July 1998. Participated in 1998 global summit meeting.
4. Charles Gibbs, "Letter from Executive Director: January 2004," United Religions Initiative, http://www.uri.org/abouturi/edrreport/january2004.asp, printed 03/13/04. He invited a Christian to speak in the mosque, for the first time in 400 years, and is "following the footsteps of his father as a URI leader and an ardent promoter of dialogue among religions," according to Gibbs' letter.
5. Siddiqee, "UMA Pursues," July 1998. Participated in 1998 global summit meeting.
6. Ibid.
7. In 2001, Abu Salih participated in prayer and dialog with a founder of Gush Imunim, an Israeli fundamentalist party, at an event sponsored by the Israel Interfaith Association CC. ("URI Cooperation Circles," *PCN*, June/July 2001, p34).
8. International Association of Sufism, "Featured Past Events," http://www.ias.org/featured/innerglobal_sfpresidio.html, printed 2/18/03; Kianfar has had "speaking engagements" at the URI.
9. Siddiqee, "UMA Pursues," July 1998. Participated in 1998 global summit meeting.
10. Gibbs/Mahé, *Birth of a Global Community*, p75. He gave a meditation at a URI planning meeting at Oxford in April, 1997.
11. Jane Lampman, "Interfaith effort for global problems," *Christian Science Monitor*, June 29, 2000, http://csmweb2.emcweb.com/durable/2000/06/29/p14s2.htm, printed 2/20/03; at the time, Stauch was a member of the URI European executive committee.
12. Swing, "Reactions from Religious Leaders," summer 1996, pp1–4.
13. Chaffee, "URI Global Conference," *PCN*, Oct./Nov. 1997, p32.
14. Bishop William Swing, "The Surprise Factor," *Pacific Church News*, June/July 1996, p9.
15. Swing, "Reactions from Religious Leaders," summer 1996, p2; see also Chuck Salter, "We're Trying To Change World History," *Fast Company*, November 2000, p232; Dennis Delman, "Peace Projects Proliferate for 72 Hours at the Millennium," *Pacific Church News*, June/July 1999, p21.

- Swami Agnivesh, a Hindu from India.[1]
- Robert Aitken, an American Buddhist roshi.[2]
- Sister Chandru Desai (a member of the Brahma Kumaris order, a movement that arose from Hinduism).[3]
- His Holiness Bhakti Svarup Damodara Swami, a Hindu educator in India.[4]
- Dr. Homi Dhalla, a "Zoroastrian interfaith leader" who hosted a URI planning meeting in Mumbai, India in 1998.[5]
- Arun Gandhi, a grandson of Mohandas Gandhi and a director of a non-violence institute in Memphis, Tennessee[6] and the board chairman for The Interfaith Alliance.[7]
- Maha Ghosananda, "patriarch of Cambodian Buddhism."[8]
- Philip Lane, "Chief of the Dakota Nation of Indians." [9]
- Mumi Lea, "head priestess of the Hawaiian religion."[10]
- Angaangaq Lybreth, an Inuit elder now living in Canada. He "heads the Indigenous International Earth Restoration Corps, is on the Board of the Club of Budapest, is an advisor to the Jane Goodall Institute, and represents the Indigenous community to the North American United Religions Initiative."[11]
- Members of the Guru Gobind Singh Foundation, a Sikh organization.[12]
- Guru "Ma," "who has an 87-acre ashram in Florida."[13]
- Dr. Usha Mehta, described by the URI as "the foremost Gandhian in India."[14]
- Gedong Oka, "a revered Gandhian from Bali, Indonesia." [15]
- Sri Ravi Peruman, a Hindu who served from 1998 through 2002 on the URI board.[16]
- Rohinton Rivetna, "a Zoroastrian who played a leadership role at the Parliament of the World's Religions."[17]

1. Agnivesh and the Religions for Social Justice CC in New Delhi led an anti-globalization protest march. ("URI Cooperation Circles," *PCN*, June/July 2001, p34).

2. Chaffee, "URI Global Conference," *PCN*, Oct./Nov. 1997, p33.

3. Board member list from "United Religions Initiative: Building spiritual partnerships for a just, sustainable, and peaceable world," URI leaflet issued in the fall of 1998; cited below as URI, "Building spiritual partnerships," 09/15/98 leaflet. Organizational affiliations provided by Paul Andrews, URI staff person, November 20, 1997.

4. Vedic Cultural Fellowship, "Board of Directors," http://www.vedicworld.org/directors.html, printed 07/27/01; he is described as "actively involved with the United Religions Initiative."

5. Canon Charles Gibbs, "URI Update," *URI News Update*, Spring 1998, p1.

6. Richard Scheinin, "Faith in Dialogue: Leaders From World's Myriad Religions Gather at Stanford in Hopes of Transcending Beliefs, Borders With 'Spiritual UN'," *San Jose Mercury News*, June 23, 1997, front section, page 1A.

7. The Interfaith Alliance, "Board of Directors," http://www.interfaithalliance.org/about-us/board/, printed 02/19/03.

8. Chaffee, "URI Global Conference," *PCN*, Oct./Nov. 1997, p32.

9. Gard Jameson, "The United Religions Initiative," *The Mighty Messenger*, Summer 1997 issue, http://www.ubfellowship.org/archive/newsletters/mmsu97.htm#initiative, printed 01/13/03; cited below as Jameson, "URI," summer 1997. Lane attended the 1997 and 1998 URI summit meetings at Stanford. (Gibbs/Mahé, *Birth of a Global Community*, pp123 and 140.)

10. Jameson, "URI," summer 1997.

11. Metro DC Committee of Correspondence for Democracy and Socialism, "Speakers," http://www.redandgreen.org/Information/Speakers.htm, printed 03/05/03.

12. Guru Gobind Singh Foundation, http://www.ggsfusa.org/interfaith.html, printed 02/11/03.

13. "Voices of the Light," No. 15, July 1, 1997; electronic newsletter of the United Communities of Spirit; http://www.origin.org/ucs/text/urii.cfm, printed 10/3/02.

14. Canon Charles Gibbs, "URI Update," *URI News Update*, Spring 1998, p1.

15. United Religions Initiative, "Global Charter Signing and Summit," *URI Update*, Fall 2000, p1; she died in the fall of 2002. (United Religions Initiative, "In Memorium [sic]," *URI Update*, December 2002, p7).

16. URI leaflet with list of board members, 9/15/98. List of members of the URI Interim Global Council (which served until 2002, when the Global Council was elected) is from URI, *Annual Report* 2000, p8; this body served until 2002.

17. Paul Chaffee, "Ring of Breath Around the World: A Report of the United Religions Initiative Global Conference," issued in the summer of 1997 by the United Religions Initiative, p3 (cited below as Chaffee, "Ring of Breath Around the World," summer 1997).

- Jehangir Sarosh, a Zoroastrian who was head of the UK and Ireland chapter of the World Conference on Religion and Peace.[1]
- Dharma Senya Senanayake, vice president of the Sarvodaya Shramadana Movement in Sri Lanka.[2]
- Natubhai Shah, "founder of the Jain academy of the UK."[3]
- Charanjit Singh, "a Sikh educator from the UK."[4]
- Dr. Karan Singh, "President, Temple of Understanding."[5]
- Dr. Mohinder Singh, described by the URI as a "Sikh interfaith leader."[6] He is a current member of the URI Global Council.
- Dr. Thoudam Singh, "Bhaktivedanta Institute, India."[7]
- Sulak Sivaraksa, an "internationally recognized Buddhist teacher and peace and justice activist" from Thailand.[8]
- Rev. Heng Sure, of the Dharma Realm Buddhist Association, in Berkeley, California.[9]
- Ven. Pandit Madampagama Assaji Thero, from the Interreligious Peace Foundation in Sri Lanka.[10]
- Thomas One Wolf,[11] a shaman from the "Northwest Salish people of Chief Seattle."[12]

Those who offered statements of support to Swing during his 1996 pilgrimage included:[13]

- Prime Master Chwasan, of the Won Buddhists in Korea.
- Swami Gokulananda of the Ramakrishna Ashrama in Delhi.
- Sri Jagadguru Shankaracharya Mathasamsthanam, a Hindu.
- General Sethna and Keki Gandhi, Sikh leaders.
- Dr. Ramnik Shah, Secretary of the National Assembly of the Baha'i in India.
- Shankaracharya of Kancheepuram, a Hindu from India.

THE INTERFAITH MOVEMENT AND THE URI—"UNITY IN DIVERSITY" IN PRACTICE

The URI promises in its Charter that "We seek and offer cooperation with other interfaith efforts."[14] Since its establishment, the URI has worked closely with the major interfaith organizations worldwide. Here are the highlights of this collaborative effort:

1. Gibbs/Mahé, *Birth of a Global Community*, p79. He participated in the April 1997 URI planning meeting at Oxford.
2. "News Updates from Around the World," *URI News Update*, Spring 1998, p3; *URI News Update*, Spring 1999, p3.
3. Charles Gibbs, "Regional Conferences Prepare for URI Global Summit," *Pacific Church News*, August/September 1997, p22.
4. Gibbs/Mahé, *Birth of a Global Community*, p82; participated in the April 1997 URI planning meeting at Oxford.
5. URI, "Some Early Supporters."
6. Canon Charles Gibbs, "URI Update," *URI News Update*, Spring 1998, p1.
7. URI, "Some Early Supporters."
8. Chaffee, "Ring of Breath Around the World," summer 1997, p5.
9. Don Lattin, "Religious Violence Decried at Gathering," *San Francisco Chronicle*, June 26, 1997, pA-19 (cited below as Lattin, "Religious Violence Decried," 06/26/97).
10. "URI Cooperation Circles," *PCN*, June/July 2001, p35.
11. URI, "Some Early Supporters"; also, The Supreme Master Ching Hai News, "Sharing Master's Love At the World Vision Conference—Learning From The Prophecies Of The Native Americans," http://www.chinghai.org.tw/eng/news/96/b-2.htm, printed 04/22/03.
12. International Peace Prayer Day, "Sacred Healing Walk," http://www.peacereal.com/ppd/sacred.html, printed 11/6/98; no longer on the Net.
13. Swing, "Reactions from Religious Leaders," summer 1996, pp1–4.
14. United Religions Initiative, "The United Religions Initiative Charter," http://www. uri.org/resources/publications/Charter%20PC%20format.doc, "Principles," principle 11, p3; downloaded 07/07/04.

• Numerous interfaith activists gave the green light to the concept of the URI when Bishop Swing brought the idea to them on June 21, 1993. These leaders included "Marcus Braybrooke, Bill Vendley, Daniel Gomez-Ibanez, Luis Dolan, Chung Ok Lee, Bawa Jain, Jim Morton, and many others."[1]
• Marcus Braybrooke, of the World Congress of Faiths, Sister Joan Kirby, of the Temple of Understanding, and Deborah Moldow, of the World Peace Prayer Society, were co-hosts of URI planning meetings in England and the US in 1997. [2] At the meeting in England, Braybrooke said that Swing's "dream fills me with enthusiasm, his energy and commitment with boundless admiration."[3]
• In India in 1997, the URI co-sponsored interfaith events with the Gandhi Smarak Nidhi, the World Conference on Religion and Peace (WCRP), and the Inter-Religious Federation for World Peace (IRFWP),[4] an interfaith group founded by the Rev. Sun Myung Moon.[5] The North American Interfaith Network sent three representatives to the URI summit in 1997—Peter Laurence, Gard Jameson, and Bettina Gray.[6]
• The URI said in 1999 that "At the recent WCC [World Council of Churches] assembly in Harare, URI reps Mac Kiiru, the East Africa Coordinator, Kelvin Sauls, URI Board Member, Godwin Hlatshwayo, African coordinator, and Andre Porto, URI Brazilian coordinator, participated in the WCC forums," and that "the URI Draft Charter and the 72 Hours of Peace building [sic] stirred enthusiasm and interest" among those who attended the WCC meeting in December, 1998.[7] However, Faith McDonnell, of the Institute for Religion and Democracy, a conservative organization that attended and reported on the 1998 WCC meeting, said that URI presence and influence at the meeting did not extend beyond the small discussion group attended by URI representatives.[8]
• The Interfaith Alliance of California co-hosted a "summit on Civility" in San Francisco in April 1999; this event was co-sponsored by the URI.[9]
• As a result of a June 1999 conference co-sponsored by the URI, the Council for a Parliament of the World's Religions, and the Interfaith Center of New York, a new organization for young interfaith activists emerged—the Interfaith Youth Core.[10]
• URI executives led four workshops at the 1999 session of the Parliament of the World Religions in Cape Town, South Africa.[11]
• URI Global Council member Donald Frew stated in 2002 that the URI and the Council for a Parliament of the World's Religions (CPWR) have "by far the closest relationship" in comparison with other interfaith groups.[12] One URI Cooperation Circle, "The Bridge," supports ongoing cooperation between the URI and the CPWR.[13]

The URI worked closely with the CPWR at the July 2004 Parliament of World Religions in Barcelona, Spain, a gathering which attracted about 8,000 participants. According to the Executive Director of the URI, "Over 150 URI leaders from around the world attended the Parliament. . . . Our members

1. Bishop William Swing, opening speech for the United Religions summit meeting, June 24–28, 1996, p1.
2. United Religions Initiative, "Regional Conferences Update," URI News Update, March 1997, p2.
3. "United Religions Initiative," http://hknrp.tripod.com/religions.htm, printed 11/25/02.
4. United Religions Initiative, "Building a Worldwide Movement," URI News Update, Fall 1997, p6 (cited below as URI, "Worldwide Movement," URI News Update, Fall 1997).
5. Rev. Sun Myung Moon, "Inaugural Address: Inter-Religious and International Federation for World Peace," http://www.unification.net/1999/990206.html, printed 01/10/03 (cited below as Moon, "Inaugural Address," 1999).
6. Jameson, "URI," summer 1997.
7. "URI in the world," URI Update, no. 5, spring 1999, p3.
8. Telephone interview by Lee Penn of Faith McDonnell, of the Institute for Religion and Democracy, June 22, 1999.
9. The Interfaith Alliance, "Grassroots Highlights," The Light (newsletter of the Interfaith Alliance), Summer 1999, http://www.interfaithalliance.org/Newsroom/Narchive/light _0799_fa.html, printed 06/06/01.
10. United Religions Initiative, "Interfaith Youth Core," URI Update, Spring 2001, p11. The "Core" spelling for the organization reflects the group's own usage. The web site for the Interfaith Youth Core is http://www.ifyc.org (printed 11/05/04).
11. Dennis Delman, "Parliament of the World Religions: Mandela, Dalai Lama at Plenaries; Bishop Swing, URI Staff Take United Religions Vision to Cape Town Meeting," Pacific Church News, February/March 2000, p23.
12. E-mail from Donald Frew to Lee Penn, 11/18/02.
13. E-mail from David Ponedel, Bishop of the Church of Divine Man, to Lee Penn, 11/11/02.

were a highly visible and substantial presence."[1] URI members "helped lead at least 70 of the 400 workshops offered" at the Parliament.[2] The URI hosted the July 11 evening session on regional networking.[3]

At the Barcelona Parliament, prominent speakers proclaimed universal inclusion *and* scorn for traditionalists, two common themes for interfaith meetings. As a reporter for the *Chicago Tribune* noted,

Deepak Chopra, the author of 29 books who has made the transformation from a holistic health expert to an Eastern guru, drew a packed audience. With his closing remark, 'When we heal the rift in our collective soul . . . we will be filled with love,' the crowd gave him a standing ovation. For Chopra's admirers, his charm lies in his disdain for traditional religion, which he described as 'idiotic' at the parliament. . . . Hans Küng, a Swiss Catholic theologian who is president of the Global Ethic Foundation in Tubingen, Germany, said the parliament should accept all organizations that consider themselves religious communities. 'You can't say this religion is real and this one is false,' he said. 'Religion is a personal thing.'[4]

Sir Sigmund Sternberg, a British founder of the Three Faiths Forum, is Patron of the URI in the UK; he spoke at their initial meeting in August 2000.[5] Sidney L. Shipton, the coordinator of the Three Faiths Forum, is a member of the URI Cooperation Circle there. The Three Faiths Forum is active in interfaith work at the United Nations and the World Economic Forum, and has cooperated with numerous overseas ambassadors and British Commonwealth officials.

The URI was active in planning the August 2000 World Millennium Peace Summit of Religious and Spiritual Leaders, as a member of the Advisory Council of Interfaith Organizations.[6]

The New York-based Temple of Understanding works extensively with the URI. The Temple's founder, Juliet Hollister, attended the URI summits in 1996[7] and 1997,[8] and gave the venture her public support in 1996.[9] Sister Joan Kirby, who was Executive Director of the Temple from 1994 to 2000,[10] has been active in the URI since 1996.[11] Fr. Luis Dolan, who had represented the Temple at the UN,[12] was the Latin American Coordinator for the URI until his death in 2000.[13] URI supporters Robert

1. Charles Gibbs, "Letter from Executive Director," August 2004—"URI—A Powerful Presence at the 4th Parliament of the World's Religions," http://www.uri.org/abouturi/edrreport/index.asp, printed 08/08/04.

2. Ibid.

3. United Religions Initiative, "URI: A Powerful Presence at the Parliament of the World's Religions," http://www.uri.org/regionalnews/multiregion/mosaico.asp, printed 07/15/04.

4. Geneive Abdo, "Defining the meaning of it all—Parliament of the World's Religions debates, celebrates faith," *Chicago Tribune* online edition, July 10, 2004, http://www.chicagotribune.com/news/nationworld/chi-0407100135jul10,1,4083875.story, printed 07/15/04.

5. Information in this paragraph is from The Three Faiths Forum, "2000: Another Excellent Year for Three Faiths Forum," http://www.threefaithsforum.org.uk/Press%20 Releases/report.htm, printed 12/09/2002.

6. URI, *Annual Report* 2000"URI Milestones 2000," p 3.

7. Bishop William Swing, "United Religions: It's Been Just One Grand Opening After Another," *Pacific Church News*, October/November 1996, p 24.

8. Letter from Bruce Schuman to Juliet Hollister, July 28, 1997; http://origin.org.uri/files/uri010.cfm, printed in 1997; no longer on the Net. Schuman wrote, "It was an honor to briefly meet you at the recent United Religions conference at Stanford."

9. URI pamphlet, "Dear Brothers and Sisters. . . ," fall 1996, page 1. The first page was signed by Bishop William Swing, Juliet Hollister, and Robert Muller.

10. Temple of Understanding, "Who We Are: Temple of Understanding Board of Trustees and Staff 2002–2003," http://www.templeofunderstanding.org/who_we_are_m.htm, printed 05/06/03.

11. United Religions Initiative, *URI News Update*, December 1996, p 3.

12. Temple of Understanding, "In Memoriam: Father Luis Dolan," http://www.templeofunderstanding.org/articles.htm, printed 05/06/03.

13. "The Temple of Understanding," pamphlet provided by them in the summer of 1997, p 12; also URI, "Building spiritual partnerships," 9/15/98 leaflet.

Muller, the Dalai Lama, and Hans Küng have been on the Temple's "International Council."[1] The Temple's stated goals are "To promote understanding among the world's religions; To recognize the Oneness of the human family; To achieve 'A Spiritual United Nations'."[2] Dale McKechnie, Vice President of the Lucis Trust (a Theosophist organization), said in 1998 that although there has been no organizational association between the Lucis Trust and the Temple of Understanding, "Their representative spoke at one of our conferences; we view them as a kindred spirit kind of group."[3]

The URI cooperated with other interfaith groups, and with liberal Catholics and Protestants, to "present the input of faith-based groups" to the 2003 meeting of the World Social Forum.[4] According to the URI Cooperation Circle in Rio de Janeiro,

> URI, the Interfaith Group of Porto Alegre and the Ecumenical Coalition (a group of Brazilian progressive Catholics and Protestant Churches and networks linked with CLAI—Latin American Council of Churches and WCC—World Council of Churches) organized a program and created a common space at the university's campus.... The program and production were designed and conducted collectively and the funds were provided by Christian networks such as Caritas, Red Cono Sur de Centros Laicos, Amerindia and the World Council of Churches.[5]

The URI joined the National Council of Churches, the San Francisco Interfaith Council, Grace Cathedral, and the California Council of Churches in co-sponsoring an interfaith prayer service in March 2003 against the war in Iraq.[6] The URI has also cooperated with the California Council of Churches to prepare an interfaith curriculum, "Building Bridges of Understanding."[7]

The URI is a member of a consortium of interfaith groups, the International Interfaith Organization (IIO). Aside from the URI, the following groups are members of the IIO: [8]

- Council for a Parliament of the World's Religions
- International Association for Religious Freedom
- International Interfaith Centre
- Interfaith Youth Core
- Millennium World Peace Summit of Religious and Spiritual Leaders
- Minorities of Europe
- Peace Council
- Temple of Understanding
- United Nations Spiritual Forum for World Peace Initiative
- World Conference on Religion and Peace

1. "The Temple of Understanding," 1997 pamphlet cited above, p 11 overleaf.

2. Ibid., p 2.

3. Telephone interview, April 24, 1998, between Lee Penn and Dale McKechnie, Vice-President of the Lucis Trust.

4. United Religions Initiative, "Latin America & the Caribbean," http://www.uri.org/regionalnews/lamerica/porto.asp, printed 07/15/04.

5. Ibid.

6. National Council of Churches, "Many Faiths, Joined Together for Prayer in San Francisco, Call for End to Unjust War on Iraq—and on America's Poor," *News from the National Council of Churches*, March 2, 2003, http://www.ncccusa.org/news/03news18. html, printed 3/16/03.

7. California Council of Churches, *Building Bridges of Understanding: A Study Guide for Congregations*, http://www.cal-churches.org/publication_pdfs/BBU-edition2.pdf, p 2, viewed 07/01/04. The document states, "The Rev. Kathy Cooper-Ledesma, Southern California Field Director for the California Council of Churches, has served as Project Coordinator and assisted in writing parts of the curriculum. Other team members include: Scott Anderson from the California Council of Churches; Rev. Dr. John Orr from the USC Center for Religion and Civic Culture; Nancy Nielsen from the United Religions Initiative, San Francisco; David Thompson, Video Producer, from Cumulus Productions; and Marcia Beauchamp, Curriculum Writer."

8. United Religions Initiative, "International Interfaith Organisations," *URI Update*, fall 2001, no. 10, p 11.

- World Congress of Faiths
- World Faiths Development Dialogue[1]
- World Fellowship of Inter-Religious Councils

URI leaders disavow any desire to "swallow" other interfaith groups. Donald Frew said, "There was a concept early on that the URI was so inclusive that other interfaith groups could be subsumed into it. This idea was quickly abandoned."[2] David Ponedel, who helped to form the URI/CPWR Cooperation Circle, says: "Usurping the work of another is redundant, pointless, and antithetical to the URI's stated purpose of daily interfaith cooperation. . . . If other interfaith organizations deem it in their best interests to associate themselves with the URI . . . I feel sure they would be welcome as CCs [Cooperation Circles], however, they would be autonomous organizations if they so choose."[3]

Despite the URI's history of collaboration with other interfaith movements, Swing alluded to continuing difficulties at the Global Assembly in 2002. He said,

It is central to the purpose of all international interfaith organizations that they be of assistance in relieving hostilities between religions. But what if the relationship between international interfaith groups is marred by hostilities? How can there be healing among faiths without first having healing among interfaith groups? A profound change must take place. Thank heaven that members of the Council for the Parliament of World Religions are here tonight. They want to collaborate with us and we want to collaborate with them. I hope that this generosity and our partnership will start in motion something good beyond our highest hopes.[4]

Swing said the same in early 2004, indicating that there is strife within the interfaith movement:

When I was first getting started, there were a few interfaith people who were kind towards me. Most saw me as a potential competitor, and some of the most influential have been very active in sabotaging the URI, and trying to ruin us with various religious groups. I might add that they have been very successful. . . . I can say with assurance that we have wonderful relationships with Marcus Braybrooke and the Center at Oxford, with the Temple of Understanding folks, and with the Council of the Parliament of World Religions. We have a decent speaking relationship with the IARS. I think the WCRP (World Conference on Religion and Peace) has a very tough time with us, and in some high places, sees us as a threat. We do not see ourselves as a threat and always want to work with the WCRP. Maybe in the future there will be leadership that is open to collaboration with us. I hope so. In the meantime we're doing fine in terms of collaboration with international interfaith groups.[5]

In mid-2004, Swing raised the possibility that the interfaith movement might break up into "denominations:" "I think we're at a crossroads with international interfaith work. We're all going to either break up into denominations or groups comparable to denominations, or we are going to figure out a way to complement each other and present a united front so that some day there will be a veritable United Religions, not just URI blown large, but something that will be created by the Holy Spirit that's way beyond our imaginations right now."[6]

Donald Frew explained these problems in June 2003:

1. United Religions Initiative, "Cooperation Circles Around the World," *URI Update*, Fall 2000, p5.

2. Interview of Donald Frew by Lee Penn, 3/28/03.

3. E-mail from David Ponedel, Bishop of the Church of Divine Man, to Lee Penn, 11/11/02.

4. Bishop William Swing, Keynote address for URI Global Assembly, August 19, 2002; http://pcn.diocal.org/uriaddress.html, printed 03/06/03.

5. Dennis Delman, "Interview with Bishop William E. Swing, Founder and President of the United Religions Initiative," *Pacific Church News online*, February/March 2004, http://pcn.diocal.org/PCNO/pcn004-1/index.html, printed 02/24/04. "IARS" may refer to the International Association of Religious Studies, or it may be an interviewer's misprint of the IARF, the International Association for Religious Freedom.

6. Bob Williams, "Swing marks 25th year as Bay Area bishop (Daybook)," *Episcopal News Service* interview of Bishop Swing, August 9, 2004, http://ecusa.anglican.org/3577_48087_ENG_HTM.htm, printed 08/10/04.

I think there was a general sense among some of the established interfaith groups, not uncommon among non-profits, that 'the funding pie is only so big, I have to guard my piece of it, and let's work together to keep anyone else from getting a slice.' In other words, more a sense of competition than cooperation. The CPWR and URI are actively working together to be a model of a better way of collaboration. . . . As some groups apparently pointed out when the URI was starting—and, no, I was never given the name of any particular group—there was a perceived scarcity not only of money, but of the time of religious dignitaries. For example, the Archbishop of Canterbury only has so much time to give to interfaith events. The more groups competing for that time, the less each one gets. A strange form of competition.[1]

As a parallel effort with the URI, in 1998 Bishop Swing formed the "Inter-Religious Friendship Group" (IRFG). Other leaders of the IRFG were the Dalai Lama and Richard Blum, a wealthy San Francisco investment banker (and the husband of Dianne Feinstein, a Democratic U.S. Senator from California).[2] Blum has supported the URI since early 1996.[3] Additionally, according to the *San Francisco Examiner*, "Blum has been a close associate of the Dalai Lama's for more than two decades, and has traveled extensively with the Tibetan leader, particularly to meetings with major world religious figures. . . . The Friendship Group is designed as a loosely knit organization of more than a dozen spiritual leaders, theologians and lay activists from around the world."[4] The founders of the IRFG said that their goal is to "create a confidential and relatively unstructured forum where the leaders of the world's religions can have regular conversations with one another."[5]

The IRFG met three times in 1998-1999, with its final meeting in November 1999 at the Carter Center in Atlanta, Georgia. The Rev. Dr. Gary Gunderson, then the director of the Carter Center's Interfaith Health Program,[6] said in 1999 that the URI "is one of the most promising global initiatives," a "long term alignment that will bear fruit for decades."[7] Gunderson has remained very supportive of the URI. He said in 2003 that the Interfaith Health Program, which is now at Emory University, has "two major cooperative agreements with the federal government including an 'Institute for Public Health and Faith Collaborations.'"[8] He added that in these efforts, "our continuing relationship with URI is highly valuable to us. . . . I think they are a nearly unique organization with a profoundly smart organizational logic and structure that offers the interfaith community a way forward in this difficult time."[9]

In 1999, Gunderson stated that, "While not a formal member of the URI, President Carter stressed how much the Center valued the role of religious leaders in conflict situations … He asked the group to request his involvement in the future as specific interventions or projects crystallize."[10] However, URI Global Council member Donald Frew says that the IRFG has not been active in the URI since 1999,[11] and there has been no public statement by Carter on behalf of the URI since then.

1. E-mail from Donald Frew to Lee Penn, 06/04/03.

2. Elaine Ruth Fletcher, "S.F. group's interfaith meeting draws Dalai Lama to Jerusalem," *San Francisco Examiner*, June 11, 1999, page A-2; Internet version; downloaded from http://www.sfgate.com. Printed 10/12/02 (cited below as Fletcher, "S.F. group's interfaith meeting," 06/11/99).

3. Don Lattin, "Bishop Pushes Presidio Interfaith Group," *San Francisco Chronicle*, January 23, 1996, p A-13.

4. Fletcher, "S.F. group's interfaith meeting," 06/11/99.

5. Ibid.

6. The Carter Center, Gary Gunderson, M. Div., "Biography," http://www.cartercenter.org/gunderson.html; printed in 1999; no longer on the Net at this address. As of 2004, this web site is available at http://web.archive.org/web/19991009125614/ http://www. cartercenter.org/gunderson.html.

7. E-mail from Gary Gunderson, of the Interfaith Health Program (formerly at the Carter Center, and now at Emory University), to Lee Penn, 12/02/99.

8. E-mail from Gary Gunderson to Lee Penn, 04/25/03. This Institute's web site is http://www.ihpnet.org/iphfc.htm, as of 11/05/04.

9. E-mail from Gary Gunderson to Lee Penn, 04/25/03.

10. E-mail from Gary Gunderson to Lee Penn, 12/02/99.

11. Interview between Lee Penn and Donald Frew, October 2002.

NEW RELIGIOUS MOVEMENTS AND THE URI

Bishop Swing decided in early 1996 to open the door of the URI to members of new "spiritual movements."[1] His intent was to increase the diversity of people involved in the URI, and to ensure more female participation and leadership.[2] This choice, which is now integral to the self-understanding of the URI, paved the way for participation in the URI by cultists, Theosophists, Wiccans, and New Age authors such as Neale Donald Walsch and Barbara Marx Hubbard.[3] Interfaith leader Marcus Braybrooke said of the URI in 1998 that "at this stage much of the energy comes from spiritual movements and highly-motivated individuals rather than from organized religions;"[4] this still appears to be true. (Nevertheless, Donald Frew said in October 2002 that the "vast majority" of URI participants are from the major, long-established religions.[5])

Bishop Swing stands by his decision to open the URI to new spiritual movements and "cults"– and to keep it open to them. He told the Commonwealth Club of San Francisco in May 1999 that the three principles agreed upon by the founders of the URI in 1996 were:

'1. we will be a grass roots movement; 2. it has to be men and women together; 3. invite religions and spiritual movements together—right from the beginning'. . . . Asked how the URI would handle cults, Bishop Swing answered that the United Religions would probably look a little like Alcoholics Anonymous: 'very diffuse.' He added that 'In United Religions, if you can abide by the purpose and principle, then you can get together. Once you open the door, you have to keep it open.'[6]

Given the beliefs of some of these spiritual movements, it seems that Bishop Swing and the URI did the theological equivalent of throwing a keg party and leaving the front door unlocked—at which point the theological equivalent of the Hell's Angels motorcycle gang joined the festivities.

SECTS AND CULTS

Numerous new religious movements, including organizations with reputations as sects or cults, have aligned themselves with the URI.

The Unification Church

Members of the Unification Church, and organizations aligned with it, have been active within the URI since 1997.

---

1. Bishop Swing, August 10, 1996 speech before the North American Interfaith Network Conference, p3.
2. See, for example, Jennifer Shaw, "Bishop Offers New Religious Vision for 21st Century," *Contra Costa Sun*, news section, page 6, March 26, 1997. This was a report on a Commonwealth Club speech by Bishop Swing.
3. In their book on the URI, Charles Gibbs and Sally Mahé describe a critical decision made by the URI in 1997. At a planning meeting in New York City in 1997, Deborah Ann Light, a Wiccan, and Taj Hamad, a staffer for the interfaith arm of the Unification Church, stated their desire to attend the 1997 URI summit meeting at Stanford. "There seemed to be every reason to invite them—every reason except fear of the consequences. It was easy to imagine the press getting wind of these people's [sic] involvement, with headlines reading: 'WITCH AND MOONIE AT URI SUMMIT!' And that would be the end of the URI. But the staff realized that once you caved into such fear, once you caved into prejudice against one group by others, you lost something precious. . . . The Moonie and the witch were invited, and it was a great victory." (Gibbs/Mahé, *Birth of a Global Community*, pp103–104.)
4. Marcus Braybrooke, *Faith and Interfaith in a Global Age*, CoNexus Press, 1998, p95.
5. Interview of Donald Frew by Lee Penn, October 2002.
6. Dennis Delman, "'For the Sake of the Children, We've Got to Talk,' Bishop Swing Tells Commonwealth Club Gathering," *Pacific Church News*, August/September 1999, p25.

• The Strange Religion of the Rev. Sun Myung Moon •

The Unification Church is a messianic movement, "claiming more than two million members in nearly 200 countries, with extensive holdings in real estate, commercial enterprises and even a recording studio."[1] The church and its allies have created a bewildering array of front groups, each with its own acronym; several of these organizations promote interfaith dialogue.

Hitherto, the Unification Church has had a reputation as a right-wing organization.[2] This church was a staunch, hawkish opponent of Communism during the Cold War. It has endorsed Republican politicians in the US, and military rulers in Bolivia and Honduras, and the right-wing nationalist Jean-Marie le Pen in France. Unificationists own the *Washington Times*, a conservative paper in Washington DC, and *Tiempos Del Mundo*, a major Latin American paper based in Buenos Aires. President George H. W. Bush had participated in the 1996 dedication of this newspaper for a $100,000 fee, according to Reuters:

> The former U.S. president, guest speaker at a banquet Saturday to launch Moon's new publication . . . was full of praise for the controversial evangelist's best-known newspaper, the *Washington Times*, and referred to Moon as 'the man with the vision.' Bush then travelled with Moon to neighboring Uruguay Sunday to help him inaugurate a seminary in the capital Montevideo to train 4,200 young Japanese women to spread the word of his Church of Unification across Latin America. Moon already owns a major newspaper, bank and hotel in Uruguay and is buying up land in the Argentine province of Corrientes, where he plans to construct what his followers call 'ideal cities.'[3]

The movement's founder, the Rev. Sun Myung Moon, declared on August 24, 1992 that "he and his wife are the Messiah and True Parents of all humanity."[4] (His conviction and 13-month imprisonment in the 1980s for tax evasion in the US[5] was not, it appears, a disqualification for this exalted role.) A follower of Moon's explains that since "Jesus could not fulfill his entire mission, Heavenly Father had to rebuild the foundation for True Parents, by sending the Third Adam, Sun Myung Moon. Rev. Moon fulfilled the mission of True Parents that Adam and Jesus had failed to fulfill. By uniting with Rev. and Mrs. Moon humanity can fulfill their purpose of creation and enter the Kingdom of Heaven both spiritually and physically."[6]

Moon had been building up for this Messianic announcement long before. Moon had said in 1973, "Are you better than Jesus? You must be better than him. . . . The whole world is in my hand, and I will conquer and subjugate the world. I will go beyond the boundary of the U. S., opening up the toll gate, reaching out to the end of the world. I will go forward, piercing through everything."[7] In 1976, he had said, "What about me, am I a son of God or a son of Satan? [The audience replied: GOD!] From a worldly viewpoint I may look like a son of Satan. What makes me a son of God? It is because

1. K.E. Grubbs, Jr., "Moon Over Washington," *The Wall Street Journal Online*, July 2, 2004, http://www.opinionjournal.com/taste/?id=110005298, printed 08/07/04.

2. Information in this paragraph is from David V. Barrett, *The New Believers: A Survey of Sects, 'Cults' and Alternative Religions*, Cassell & Co., 2001, pp202–211 (cited below as Barrett, *The New Believers*).

3. Reuters, "Bush Praises Sun Myung Moon as 'Man of Vision,'" November 25, 1996, as quoted by John Gorenfeld, *Where in Washington D.C. is Sun Myung Moon*, web log entry of December 2, 2003, http://www.gorenfeld.net/blog/2003/12/flash-back-bush-praises-sun-myung-moon.html, printed 08/07/04. See also Catholic World News, "Former US President Praises Sect Leader Moon," http://www.cwnews.com/news/viewstory.cfm?recnum=3 061, printed 08/07/04.

4. Unification Church, "Who is Reverend Moon," http://www.unification.org/rev_mrs_moon.html, printed 1/16/03 (cited below as Unification Church, "Who is Rev. Moon?").

5. Barrett, *The New Believers*, p205.

6. True Parents Organization, "Who are True Parents Page," http://www.tparents.org/Tp-WhoAre.htm, printed 01/21/03.

7. Rev. Sun Myung Moon, "Significance of the Training Session," May 17, 1973, http://www.tparents.org/Moon-Talks/sunmyungmoon73/SM730517.htm, printed 06/28/04 (cited below as Moon, "Significance of the Training Session," 05/17/73).

everything I do is 180 degrees opposite of what Satan would do. What Satan likes, I hate. I am 100 percent, 180 degrees absolutely different. That's why I am the son of God."[1]

On March 23, 2004, Moon and his wife were crowned as mankind's "True Parents" by their followers at a banquet at the Dirksen Senate Office Building. On that occasion, Moon told his followers,

A new era has arrived today. The number of people around the world who have received my teaching and are standing resolutely for the sake of building the Kingdom of Peace is growing by leaps and bounds. . . . But in the context of Heaven's providence, I am God's ambassador, sent to earth with His full authority. I am sent to accomplish His command to save the world's six billion people, restoring them to Heaven with the original goodness in which they were created. The five great saints and many other leaders in the spirit world, including even Communist leaders such as Marx and Lenin, who committed all manner of barbarity and murders on earth, and dictators such as Hitler and Stalin, have found strength in my teachings, mended their ways and been reborn as new persons. Emperors, kings and presidents who enjoyed opulence and power on earth, and even journalists who had worldwide fame, have now placed themselves at the forefront of the column of the true love revolution. Together they have sent to earth a resolution expressing their determination in the light of my teaching of the true family ideal. They have declared to all Heaven and Earth that Reverend Sun Myung Moon is none other than humanity's Savior, Messiah, Returning Lord and True Parent. This resolution has been announced on every corner of the globe.[2]

The "Congressional co-chairs" claimed by the Unificationists for this event included Representatives Danny K. Davis (D-Illinois), Harold Ford, Jr. (D-Tennessee), Roscoe Bartlett (R-Maryland), Curt Weldon (R-Pennsylvania), Chris Cannon (R-Utah), and Sanford Bishop (D-Georgia).[3] According to the Unificationists,

The event's main sponsor was the Interreligious and International Peace Council (IIPC), a project of the Interreligious and International Federation for World Peace (IIFWP) founded by Rev. and Mrs. Sun Myung Moon. IIFWP has a global network of some 50,000 Ambassadors for Peace in more than 160 nations, who are leaders from diverse professional and faith backgrounds dedicated to overcoming barriers of religion, race and ethnicity.[4]

Photos from a video of the ceremony produced by Moon's church show Rep. Davis as one of the two people carrying a crown toward the Rev. Moon and his wife, as a prelude to their dual coronation. When interviewed by *The Christian Challenge*, an Anglican magazine, Davis confirmed his role in the event. He said, "I was attempting to provide an accolade to the Rev. Moon and his wife for promoting visions of world peace," as well as for their "visions of family structure." He added, "From my vantage point, it did not have anything to do with religion. I am a practicing Baptist, and have been a Protestant all my life."[5] Davis said that Moon's speech "was similar to a baseball team owner telling team

1. Rev. Sun Myung Moon, "Untitled Address to Conference of U.S. and International Leaders," September 20, 1976, http://www.unification.net/1976/760920.html, printed 06/28/04.

2. Rev. Sun Myung Moon, "Declaring the Era of the Peace Kingdom—Address to the United States Congress," March 23, 2004, *FFPWU News*, http://www.familyfed.org/board/uboard.asp?id=ffwpu_news&skin=board_urim_simple&color=eng&page=8&u_no=516, printed 05/05/04.

3. Interreligious and International Peace Council (IIPC), "Host Committee—Congressional Co-Chairs," http://www.familyfed.org/usa/photo2004/20040323b_3.jpg, printed 05/05/04. The document is no longer on the Net at this location. (A copy of it was at this web page, as of 08/07/04: http://www.gorenfeld.net/blog/2004/05/back-from-memory-hole.html.) Cited below as IIPC, "Host Committee," March 2004.

4. Rev. Michael Leone, "Statement on the March 23rd, 2004 'Crown of Peace' Program," http://www.unification-study.com/SVFC/text/AwardStatement.htm, printed 08/07/04 (cited below as Leone, statement on the "Crown Peace" program).

5. Lee Penn, "Several Lawmakers Ambushed For 'Coronation' Of Unification Church Leader, Wife," *The Christian Challenge*, June 15, 2004, http://www.challengeonline.org/modules/news/article.php?storyid=38, printed 9/21/04 (cited below as Penn, "Lawmakers Ambushed for Coronation").

members that 'we are the greatest team on earth'" just before a game. Davis' reason for supporting Moon is that "if we try to bring people from different races, religions, and ethnic groups back together, this becomes good for the world order." [1]

The other Congressional participant in the coronation ceremony, Rep. Bartlett, likewise defended his participation—which included "holding Moon's robes, bowing to Moon and his wife, and participating in a four-way handshake with the couple"[2] and with Rep. Davis. Bartlett said, "What was so strange? ... I'm not rude, and if I was there and asked to do something that was benign, handing a robe to an old person and honoring him for his contribution to world peace and fundamental morality, now why wouldn't I do that if I was asked to?"[3]

Other lawmakers denied that they supported Moon and the Unificationists. Those who attended the event said that they were there briefly to honor constituents who were receiving awards, or to receive a peace award themselves.[4] The press secretary for Sen. Mark Dayton (D-Minn.) said that the meeting planners 'were not being up front as to who was sponsoring the event. We would never have been there if we knew what the event really was."[5]

Senator John Warner (R-Virginia) obtained permission for the March 23 gathering to be held in the Senate office building.[6] His spokesman, John Ullyot, stated that the request for rooms in the Dirksen building came from a constituent whom the Senator knew—but that there was no indication that this was a Unificationist event, or that Rev. Moon would be attending. Ullyot said, "Our office felt misled" when they learned what had occurred. (However, it is probable that Warner and his staff knew who the Unificationists are. In September 2002, Warner had—according to the Moonies—issued a proclamation that "congratulated True Mother" (Moon's wife) during her "peace tour" of the US.[7] In May 1993 Warner had commended Rev. Moon "with great admiration" for his "constructive activity," and said that "your accomplishment sets the example for others to follow. I wish you the very best in all your future endeavors."[8])

Meanwhile, the Unificationists have "denied tricking the congressmen, saying those invited" to the March 23 coronation "knew Moon would be there."[9] In response to the controversy about the event, a Unificationist spokesman said, "an invitation letter sent initially to every Congressional office clearly identified Rev. and Mrs. Moon as the founders of the IIFWP, and stated that they would participate and be honored at this event. The organizers are proud to honor Rev. and Mrs. Moon for their lifetime achievements and sacrificial efforts to promote world peace, and no effort was made to hide their involvement."[10]

Other sponsors claimed by the Unificationists for the March 23 rite, members of the "Invitational Committee," included Dr. Stephen Covey, a well-known motivational speaker who has also made

1. Ibid.

2. CBS Worldwide, Inc., "Maryland Representative Defends Unification Church Ceremony," WJZ 13—Baltimore News, July 2, 2004, http://wjz.com/localstories/local_story_ 184181645.html, printed 07/05/04 (cited below as CBS, "Maryland Rep. Defends Unification Church Ceremony," 07/02/04).

3. Ibid.

4. Penn, "Lawmakers Ambushed For Coronation."

5. Ibid.

6. Information in this paragraph is from: Charles Babington, "Warner Linked to the Rev. Moon," *Washington Post*, July 21, 2004, p A02; printed from http://www.washingtonpost.com, July 20, 2004.

7. Rev. Michael Jenkins, "12 City North American Speaking Tour—Washington D. C.," *Unification News* for October 2002, http://www.tparents.org/UNews/Unws0210/tm_wash_dc.htm, printed 08/26/04.

8. John Gorenfeld, "Senator Warner's warm 1993 welcome to Reverend Moon," web log entry for Friday, August 20, 2004, http://www.iapprovethismessiah.com/2004/08/senator-warners-warm-1993-welcome-to.html, printed 08/26/04 and 09/22/04. The post includes a photo image of Warner's May 15, 1993 letter greeting the Rev. Moon.

9. CBS, "Maryland Representative Defends Unification Church Ceremony," 07/05/04.

10. Leone, statement on the "Crown of Peace" program.

presentations for the State of the World Forum,[1] Rep. Philip M. Crane (R-Illinois), Rep. Thomas M. Davis III (R-Virginia), Rep. Eddie B. Johnson (D-Texas), and Sen. Lindsey Graham (R-South Carolina).[2] Staff for Johnson and Crane denied that these Congressmen had any involvement whatsoever in the March 23 coronation.[3] Capitol Hill sources have said that it is a common practice among special interest groups in Washington DC to invite VIPs to events, and then to claim—without further evidence of support—that the invitee endorses the special interest group's agenda.[4]

Within a month of the coronation, Rep. Charlie Rangel (D-New York) wrote a letter hailing Moon: "I, CHARLES B. RANGEL, Member of Congress, 15th Congressional District, by the power and authority vested in me, this 16th day of April, 2004, do recognize you as 'True Parents' exemplifying self-giving service and leadership and as 'King of Peace' in the key areas of reconciliation and peacemaking over fifty (50) years."[5]

The day after his coronation, March 24 2004, Moon told members of his church,

Yesterday the Crowning Ceremony was a great historical turning point. . . . Look at America, homosexuality and lesbianism is a violation of God. Many states have said they will allow Gay marriage. This is a Satanic position. This is not the will of God. . . . Now is the time for women to go to the front line. Invisible God is Father's position, visible God is the Mother's position. This is the age of Women. The Women must stand up and bring the movement of reconciliation and love. . . . 192 nations must become one. . . . Christianity must rise up and embrace Islam and Judaism. . . . America gave Father the crown as the King. However you must really be serious to desire to practice this. Otherwise the crown from America has no meaning for me. . . . From now on all Women must stand up. God loves Christianity, Judaism and Islam. America must stand up to unite these three. . . . Yesterday the Senate and House together offered the Crown as Peace King to True Parents. . . . Christianity centering on America must unite and lead the way by embracing all religions.[6]

Karen Smith, director of the UN office of the Interreligious and International Federation for World Peace, explained the meaning of the coronation for Unificationists:

in effect, the crowning means America is saying to Father 'Please become my king'. . . . To some extent then America is beginning to take its true providential position before God and will then 'find' its correct way forward, a way that is not seen by those blocked by Satan's thinking etc. Our work in the USA will need to expand this foundation, quickly, eventually to the point where America is central to the establishment of CIG [Cheon Il Guk, the movement's term for the "Kingdom of Heaven on Earth"[7]] by 2012.[8]

The Moonies said otherwise to the general public. A spokesman claimed, "Rev. Moon is concerned about the prevalence of conflict, violence, injustice and moral breakdown in our world, and wants to

---

1. State of the World Forum, "Forum 2000," "Presentation by Stephen Covey, Co-Chairman, Franklin Covey; Author, *The Seven Habits of Highly Effective People*," http://www.simulconference.com/clients/sowf/plsimcasts/plenary8.html, printed 05/28/04.

2. IIPC, "Host Committee," March 2004.

3. Penn, "Lawmakers Ambushed For Coronation."

4. Ibid.

5. John Gorenfeld, "Where in Washington D. C. is Sun Myung Moon?," "Rangel letter recognizes far-right publisher Sun Myung Moon as the 'True Parent'," April 17, 2004, http://www.gorenfeld.net/blog/2004/04/rangel-letter-recognizes-far-right.html, printed 05/28/04.

6. Rev. Sun Myung Moon, "The Crowning Ceremony Was A Great Historical Turning Point," *True Parents News*, http://www.familyfed.org/board/uboard.asp?id=tp_news&skin=board_urim_simple&color=eng&page=1&s1=0&s2=2&s3=4&sn=&find_word=crown&u_no=354, printed 05/28/04.

7. John Doroski, "Notes on Rev. Dong Woo Kim's Sermon," *The Words of the Kim Family*, January 12, 2003, http://www.tparents.org/Library/Unification/Talks/Kim/Kim-030112. htm, printed 08/07/04.

8. Unification News for April 2004, "Notes concerning Father's Comments and Rev. Kwak's guidance concerning the Crown," http://www.tparents.org/UNews/Unws0404/coron_tf_kwak_notes.htm, printed 08/07/04.

convey those concerns to leaders everywhere. The IIFWP events on Capitol Hill were intended to focus attention on these concerns and inspire participants to pursue peace through interreligious reconciliation, not to seek any temporal power."[1]

Moon's rambling speeches in March 2004 were consistent in style and content with his prior teaching.

In 1986, Moon proposed replacing democracy with "Godism": "Democracy has been tried, but it too has been exhausted. Godism is the one alternative which the people of the world will view and say, 'Surely, this is the solution.' However, people have only scratched the surface of Godism; they haven't plumbed it to the depths. It will take many more years to do that. People have just started paying attention to Reverend Moon. They will have to study the 120 volumes of my speeches in order to find out what Godism is all about!"[2] More than a decade previously, he had said the same. In 1973, Moon declared,

But when it comes to our age, we must have an automatic theocracy to rule the world. So, we cannot separate the political field from the religious. Democracy was born because people ruled the world, like the Pope does. Then, we come to the conclusion that God has to rule the world, and God loving people have to rule the world—and that is logical. We have to purge the corrupted politicians, and the sons of God must rule the world. The separation between religion and politics is what Satan likes most.[3]

Moon continues to exalt absolute obedience as the alternative to democracy. He said in 2004,

Democracy will no longer work. Do you think America is a country that is centered on God? America doesn't understand God's concept of kingship. . . . Absolute faith, absolute love and absolute obedience are now the most crucial virtues to bring about the kingdom. . . . Jesus is the ancestor of love, and the Lord of the Second Advent is the ancestor of absolute obedience. . . . Religion must guide the political parties, or they will fail. . . . We must save America.[4]

In 1997, Moon had written, "Homosexuals and fornicators are like dirty dung eating dogs. . . . Those people who love dung eating dogs must have some problem. Especially American people, and American leaders. If they truly love such dogs, they also become like dung eating dogs and produce that quality of life."[5] On January 1, 2004, Moon warned, "There will be a purge on God's orders, and evil will be eliminated like shadows. Gays will be eliminated, the three Israels will unite. If not then they will be burned. We do not know what kind of world God will bring but this is what happens. It will be greater than the communist purge but at God's orders."[6]

In 1997, Moon said, "The country that represents Satan's harvest is America."[7] In 2004, he added,

1. Leone, statement on the "Crown of Peace" program.

2. Rev. Sun Myung Moon, "The Standard of the Unification Church," August 10, 1986, http://www.unification.net/1986/860810.html, printed 06/15/04.

3. Moon, "Significance of the Training Session," 05/17/73.

4. Rev. Sun Myung Moon, as quoted in "Welcome back, True Parents!—True Parent's Return to America," October 15, 2004, http://www.familyfed.org/board/uboard.asp?id=tp _news&skin=board_urim_simple&color=eng&page=1&u_no=479, printed 10/18/04; cited below as Family Federation, "Welcome back, True Parents," 10/15/04. "Lord of the Second Advent" is one of the titles that Moon claims for himself, saying in August 2004, "The words 'True Parents' thus signify the Savior, Messiah and Lord of the Second Advent." (Rev. Sun Myung Moon, "Declaration of the Advent of the Revolution of True Heart and the Era of True Liberation and Complete Freedom. (Part 1)," True Parents News, August 20, 2004, http://www.family-fed.org/board/uboard.asp?id=tp_news&skin= board_urim_simple&color=eng&page=1&u_no=468, printed 10/02/04).

5. Rev. Sun Myung Moon, "The Family Federation For Cosmic Peace And Unification And The Cosmic Era Of Blessed Family," May 4, 1997, http://www.unification.net/1997/970504.html, printed 05/28/04.

6. Rev. Sun Myung Moon, "God's Day Speech," January 1, 2004, http://www.tparents. org/Moon-Talks/SunMyungMoon04/SM040101-Service-c.htm, printed 06/28/04 (cited below as Moon, "God's Day Speech," 01/01/04).

7. Rev. Sun Myung Moon, "A New Form of Church," May 1, 1997, http://www.tparents.org/UNews/unws9706/SM970501.htm, printed 06/15/04.

"Now we have the proclamation of God's Fatherland in the era of the Peace Kingdom. Everything that I am saying is being sent to the CIA, saying that True Father will bring down America."[1] (The "True Father," of course, is Moon himself.)

In 2001, Moon offered some unique advice on sexual health and temptation:

You sisters, I have seen you for 15 years. Where do you hold on? Your sexual organ is like the head of a poisonous snake. If you use it wrongly, it may destroy your family or even your nation. . . . The meaning of the human fall is the contamination of the blood lineage through sexual intercourse. Because of that, God has been incarcerated for thousands of years. . . . As a man, in your right front pants pocket is a small inside watch pocket. Keep pliers there, and when you go to the bathroom, once a day, pinch your love organ. Cut the skin a little bit as a warning. If your love organ does not listen to your conscience, then you should cut off the tip. Even if it takes that extreme measure, we have to make sure our mind and body become one. . . . We were told to love our enemy. What is our enemy? Our lineage and love organ. Love your enemy. . . . Unless we can constantly control our love organ, there is no hope to cleanse our lineage. Particularly you young men and ladies. There is a lot of temptation in the world. Temptation always stems from sexual desire. Women should carry a razor blade or a small pistol to protect your lineage.[2]

Likewise, in 1994 Moon said,

Do you love your spouse to the extent that the five major organs of your body go crazy? You should feel that once you begin talking with your spouse about love, that nothing can stop you. If there was a way to attach your wife to your hip so that no matter where you went or what you did, she would be welded to you, would you do that or not? If you are a husband that is equipped with True Love, you would love that idea, but if you refuse it then it means you are not filled with True Love. . . . Do you like the smell of your husband's semen? Answer to Father. Does it smell good or bad? You may not like the smell of your wife's stool, but do you smell your own? Why don't you smell your own but you smell your wife's? Because you are not totally one. You don't smell your own because it is part of you.[3]

Moon continued dispensing unusual theories of human physiology in 2004: "A Korean lady is a champion golfer. Many are wondering why. Americans have power in their shoulders, but the power of the Korean woman is in the lower part of her body: the hips and bottom. A strong bottom supports lineage and bearing children."[4]

In 2003, Moon blamed the Jews for the Holocaust, demanding they follow his form of "Christianity:" "Who are the Jewish members here, raise your hands! Jewish people, you have to repent. Jesus was the King of Israel. Through the principle of indemnity Hitler killed 6 million Jews. That is why. God could not prevent Satan from doing that because Israel killed the True Parents. Even now, you have to determine that you will repent and follow and become one with Christianity through Rev. Moon."[5] In 2001, he said that Hitler's victims benefited spiritually from the experience: "It is true that many Christians and Jews were killed by Hitler. Their potential to enter the K of G [Kingdom of God] increased (because of their experience). Hitler increased their chance of entering the K of G."[6]

Moon claims to have had the late North Korean dictator Kim Il Sung among his supporters. According to the Unification Church, "Risking his life, Reverend Moon traveled to North Korea in

1. Moon, "God's Day Speech," 01/01/04.

2. Rev. Sun Myung Moon, "Purity, Lineage, and the Love Organ (of Life)," February 18, 2001, http://www.unification.net/news/news20010218_2.html, printed 06/15/04 (cited below as Moon, "Purity, Lineage," 02/18/01).

3. Rev. Sun Myung Moon, "Who Was I," February 13, 1994, http://www.tparents.org/Moon-Talks/sunmyungmoon94/940213.htm, printed 08/07/04.

4. Family Federation, "Welcome back, True Parents," 10/15/04.

5. Rev. Sun Myung Moon, "Lead America Back to God," March 2, 2003, http://www.tparents.org/Moon-Talks/SunMyungMoon 03/SM030302_dc.htm, printed 05/28/04.

6. Moon, "Purity, Lineage," 02/18/01.

December 1991, and met with President Kim Il Sung, under whose regime he had been tortured and sent to a labor camp.... The North Korean ruler, who had suppressed religion for forty years, completely welcomed Reverend and Mrs. Moon."[1]

Since then, Moon has strengthened his ties with the Stalinist regime—including establishing an automobile plant in North Korea. A South Korean newspaper reported in August 2003 that there is a

strong relationship between the North Korean government and the Unification Church, or Family Federation for World Peace and Unification. The church, which owns Pyonghwa and such companies as the Tongil Group, the *Washington Times,* and UPI news service, among others, has had close ties with the North. The church and its business empire have engaged in not only North Korean business projects, but also many inter-Korean cultural exchange programs since the early 1990s. They have held inter-Korean art exhibitions, scholarly exchange programs and sports exchange programs. Recently, the Moon empire has established a hotel, a park and a church in the North.... Hwang Sun-jo, chairman of the Tongil Group, the largest business operation of the church, says, 'The West during the Cold War saw the North as a more closed and problematic country than it actually was. Mr. Moon then worked to improve the image of the North. He, for example, sent a Washington Times reporter to the North and made the country known to the West with a better image. Since then, the North has confided in the church.' The church's effort to build close ties with the North started in 1991 when Mr. Moon met with the late North Korean founder, Kim Il-sung. There, Mr. Kim reportedly asked Mr. Moon to take care of North Korean projects, including the Mount Geumgang project. Kim Chong-suh, professor of religion at Seoul National University, says, 'The church approached the North not so much from the perspective of religion as business.' It has been suggested that the church gave large sums to the Pyeongyang [sic] regime to gain an economic foothold in the country.[2]

In short, the erstwhile anti-Communist Moon is now trading profitably with one of the world's most repressive Marxist-Leninist regimes.

An ecclesiastical member of the "Invitational Committee" for the March 23, 2004 crowning of Moon was Archbishop G. Augustus Stallings, Chairman of the Executive Committee of the American Clergy Leadership Conference (ACLC), a Unificationist organization.[3] Stallings has a colorful past. As Jason Berry, an expert on the Catholic sex-abuse scandal, reports: "In 1989, *The Washington Post* began coverage of the flamboyant George Stallings, who quit the [Catholic] priesthood rather than follow Cardinal Hickey's request to enter a treatment facility after abuse accusations by former altar boys. He, too, was never prosecuted. Stallings launched his own religion, with drums, dancing, and stem-winding sermons that bestirred a tongue-in-cheek profile by 60 *Minutes*'s Morley Safer."[4] Stallings

1. Unification Church, "Who is Rev. Moon."

2. Min Seong-jae, "Pyonghwa Motors, Unification Church Do a Deal," *Joong Ang Daily*, Politics, August 31, 2003, http://joongangdaily.joins.com/200308/31/200308312358 096809900090309031.html, printed 06/15/04.

3. IIPC, "Host Committee," March 2004.

4. Jason Berry and Gerald Renner, *Vows of Silence: The Abuse of Power in the Papacy of John Paul II*, 2004, Free Press, p73. In his groundbreaking 1994 book *Lead Us Not Into Temptation*, Berry provided further detail on Stallings. Berry wrote, "A priest who had known Stallings for years told me that his flamboyant lifestyle was well known among gay priests in the archdiocese. In the mid-seventies, under Cardinal Baum, Stallings had been a vocational director, recruiting young men for the seminary. The priest did not know whether Stallings had molested two young people (as the *Washington Post* would later report) or how much Archbishop Hickey knew. 'Nothing about George would surprise me,' the priest chuckled." (Jason Berry, *Lead Us Not Into Temptation: Catholic Priests and the Sexual Abuse of Children*, Image Books, 1994, p214) Berry also reported, "Ordained in Washington in 1974, Stallings proved a charismatic orator. As his inner city parish flourished, Stallings filled the rectory with antiques. When parish council members protested he flew into a rage. He also held back a portion of Sunday collections which was due the archdiocese.... In a 1990 series in the *Washington Post*, reporters Bill Dedman and Laura Sessions Stepp found that in 1979 a parishioner complained 'that Stallings held parties at St. Theresa rectory and had men visit at odd hours.' An archdiocesan official said that 'the source of the complaints was unable or unwilling to specify allegations regarding possible sexual misconduct.' In 1982, a pastoral assistant had quit after finding Stallings and a fourteen-year-old boy naked in a rectory bedroom. Stallings claimed they were taking a bath after jogging. His pulpit charisma made

founded the Afro-centric Imani Temple in 1989 in Washington DC,[1] and accused the Catholic Church of racism. However, as *Christianity Today* reported, in May 2001, Stallings participated in one of the Rev. Moon's trademark mass weddings;

> strangely enough, though Stallings has repeatedly said that the world's Jesus isn't black enough (he once burned a portrait of 'the white Jesus'), he didn't want his wife to be African-American. Instead, he asked Moon for a Japanese wife because they're 'gentle,' 'take care of the kids,' and don't 'party all the time.' Needless to say, several of the black women in his congregation took offense at the comments.[2]

Stallings and the ACLC, meanwhile, have been involved in a campaign to remove crosses from Christian churches. As a writer for the ACLC magazine says, "In a recent international campaign, openhearted Christian ministers have courageously been taking down their church crosses. This is being done as acknowledgement that the crucifixion should not be the ultimate symbol of Christian faith, and also as atonement for the past oppression of Jews and Muslims through the cross as a symbol of political and religious domination."[3]

Unificationists say that Moon was inspired to begin the "take down the cross" campaign in June 2001, when lightning destroyed the cross that had been atop the chapel for 70 years at the Unification Theological Seminary in Barrytown, New York. A seminary official said in July 2001,

> As a symbol of Christ's suffering and salvific love for all humankind, the cross is heroic and magnificent. But as a symbol of humankind's malice toward God expressed by crucifying His son, the cross induces pain and sorrowful grief to God. While a symbol of God's victory, it is also a symbol of human sin. In 1974, Father Moon directed that the cross remain atop our Seminary. Upon hearing of its demise this June, he said that it is now time for all crosses to come down. In its place, the Unification Theological Seminary will help raise up a banner of the oneness of God and humankind, culminating the expectations of all religions, beyond the cross into the resurrection and life eternal on earth and in Heaven.[4]

The effort to develop a "theology" for this movement continues; in mid-2004, "the Theologians Club at the Unification Theological Seminary is hosting the UTS Theologians' Conference to begin to

Stallings a commanding figure to his flock. When Hickey twice asked him to take a new parish, parishioners protested and he remained pastor. . . . He also accepted into his rectory a priest who had been suspended from his religious order for making sexual advances to adolescent males. In 1989, when Hickey ordered Stallings to enter the Paraclete monks' hospital in New Mexico, Stallings blasted the church for being racist and launched the breakaway Imani Temple. The *Post* subsequently reported statements by two young men that Stallings had molested them while they were altar boys. Accusing the *Post* of racism, Stallings trumpeted his support of Marion Barry in the then mayor's unsuccessful battle against drug charges and emerged as a folk hero to many embittered blacks." (Berry, *Lead Us Not Into Temptation*, ibid., pp 218–219)

1. Ind-Movement.org, "Denominations: African American Catholic Congregation," December 27, 1999, http://www.ind-movement.org/denoms/aacc_imani.html, printed 05/31/04.

2. "Archbishops Wed in Moonie Wedding," *Christianity Today* web log, week of May 28, 2001, http://www.christianitytoday.com/ct/2001/122/32.0.html, printed 05/31/04.

3. Robert Selle, "Revolution of Love," *American Clergy Magazine*, April 27, 2004, http://www.americanclergy.com/index.php?file=fullarticle&iArticleId=102, printed 05/31/04.

4. Dr. Tyler Hendricks, "Liberating the Cross," "Unification News for July 2001," http://www.tparents.org/UNews/Unws0107/UTS_report.htm, printed 06/15/04. The Unificationists still regard this event as the reason for the "take down the cross" campaign. The "Theologians Club" at the Unification Theological Seminary wrote on June 1, 2004, "On June 11, 2001, lightning struck down the cross decorating the front of the Unification Theological Seminary. In view of this act of God, our True Father initiated the 'taking down the cross' movement. Unificationist leaders and diverse theologians have presented many profound reasons for the taking down of the cross." (Theologians Club of UTS, "Theologians' Conference at UTS," June 1, 2004 posting, http://www.familyfed.org/board/uboard.asp?id=announcements&skin=board_urim_simple&color=eng&page=2&u_no= 272, printed 06/03/04; cited below as "Theologians' Conference at UTS," 06/01/04.)

delineate a clear Unification theology on the cross as a symbol and why it should be removed from churches at this time."[1]

Unificationist spokesmen claimed that 300 Christian congregations had removed the cross from their churches between April and August 2003.[2] In a Good Friday 2003 press release, at the start of this Unificationist campaign, Stallings said that since Constantine, "the cross was a symbol of conquest and forced conversions, as expressed in the Crusades, the Inquisition, the Conquistadores, the forced conversions of Native Americans and colonialism in Africa and elsewhere in the name of Christ. These were all carried forward under the sign of the cross. To Muslims, Jews, Buddhists and many others, the cross is a symbol of intolerance and domination, not love and forgiveness."[3] Thus, to foster religious unity, Christians should "take down the cross," under the leadership of the ACLC—and, according to a Unificationist clergyman, "when Christianity takes down the cross a massive revival will break out in Christianity. 120 founded ACLC, now 120 set the condition to remove the cross and lift up Jesus in the resurrection. This will lead to the unity of Christianity, Islam and Judaism and soon a massive 'family' movement that will bless marriage removing the stained blood lineage from the earth."[4]

· *The Unificationists' Work with the URI* ·

Moon's bizarre beliefs and activities notwithstanding, some of his followers worldwide are active in the URI. In 2002, the URI accepted an "Interreligious Cooperation Award" from a Unificationist front group.

Taj Hamad, a representative of the "interfaith arm of the Unification Church," attended the 1997 URI global summit meeting at Stanford.[5] The same year in India, the URI co-sponsored interfaith events with—among other groups—the Inter-Religious Federation for World Peace (IRFWP),[6] which was founded by the Rev. Sun Myung Moon.[7]

In Mumbai, India in September 1998, the URI co-sponsored a "Dialogue on Conversion from Hindu and Christian Perspectives" with the World Conference on Religion and Peace (WCRP), a mainstream interfaith organization—and, yet again, with the IRFWP.[8] In December 2000, the URI office for the Horn of Africa (Ethiopia and neighboring countries) was given "a certificate of appreciation and a trophy for its activities in Ethiopia by the Family Federation for World Peace (FFWP)" at the Sheraton hotel in Addis Ababa;[9] the FFWP promotes Moon's teachings.[10]

The World Association of NGOs[11] (WANGO), founded by Moon,[12] gave Bishop Swing and the

---

1. "Theologians Club at UTS," 06/01/04.

2. Rev. Philip Schanker, "After 300 Crosses Taken Down in Churches across America, Muslim, Jewish & Christian Scholars, Leaders Confront Barriers to Peace," press release from the Family Federation for World Peace, August 20, 2003, http://releases.usnewswire. com/GetRelease.asp?id=140-08202003, printed 05/31/04.

3. Rev. Philip Schanker, "Christian Leaders To Carry Cross, Then Take It Down In Effort For Peace And Reconciliation," press release from the Family Federation for World Peace, April 18, 2003, http://www.ffwpu.asn.au/news/crown.htm, printed 05/31/04.

4. Rev. Michael Jenkins, "Christianity and the Cross," April 14, 2003, http://www.unification.net/news/2003/news20030414 _1.html, printed 06/01/04.

5. Gibbs/Mahé, *Birth of a Global Community*, p103.

6. URI, "Worldwide Movement," *URI News Update*, Fall 1997, p6.

7. Moon, "Inaugural Address," 1999.

8. United Religions Initiative, "URI In the World," *URI News Update*, Fall 1998, p7.

9. *URI—Horn of Africa Newsletter*, September 2001, p2.

10. See the US home page for the FFWP at http://www.familyfed.org/usa/, printed 02/17/03.

11. NGOs are Non-Governmental Organizations, private charities and advocacy groups recognized by the UN.

12. Moon stated that WANGO should "embrace the more dedicated and principled actors in the entire NGO community." (WANGO, "History of WANGO," http://www.wan go.org/about/history.html, printed 11/22/02). The Rev. Philip

URI the "WANGO Interreligious Cooperation Award" in October 2002 at a banquet in Washington DC.[1] The Rev. Sanford Garner, a founding member of the URI in Washington DC and the former Dean of the Episcopal National Cathedral, accepted the award on behalf of Swing.[2] Garner also offered an acceptance speech written by Bishop Swing.[3] In a 2004 article celebrating his 25th anniversary as Bishop of California, Swing listed this award from WANGO among 16 honors that he has received.[4]

This award sparked controversy within the URI. A URI activist expressed "horror and deep disappointment" at these events, and described the Unification Church as a cult that engages in "threats, brainwashing techniques, marriages to pre-arranged strangers," and lying to outsiders.[5] Charles Gibbs, the Executive Director of the URI, said: "I don't believe there has been as much passion and opposition expressed since we were struggling to finalize the Purpose statement in 1999."[6] Nevertheless, Gibbs reiterated the decision of the URI Standing Committee (which he described as "the equivalent of a Board's Executive Committee") to have Garner accept the WANGO award on Swing's behalf.[7]

Karen Smith, a Unificationist who has worked with the Interreligious and International Federation for World Peace (IIFWP)[8] at the UN, stated in 2002 that "some individuals who are now significant in IIFWP did attend some of the early meetings" of the URI, and that some IIFWP members are also active in URI Cooperation Circles (CCs).[9] Charles Gibbs has said, "I know of CCs who have valued members who come from the Unification Church."[10] As of 2003, the home page of the IIFWP offered links to "Other Peace Organizations"—including the UN, the URI, the Action Coalition for Global Change (a gathering of "progressive" globalist organizations) and the UN-sponsored University for Peace in Costa Rica.[11] The home page of the Religious Youth Service, a youth interfaith service group under the IIFWP, likewise linked to the URI and the North American Interfaith Network.[12]

Nevertheless, URI Global Council member Donald Frew stated that the Unification Church is "just one of scores of local groups 'co-sponsoring' events all around the world," so that "its impact and influence are seriously diluted."[13]

Schanker, speaking for the "Family Federation for World Peace and Unification" (popularly known as the Unification Church), and Karen Smith, speaking for the IIFWP, both acknowledged Moon as the founder of WANGO. (Interview of Schanker and Smith by Lee Penn, 11/6/02; e-mail from Smith to Lee Penn, 11/08/02).

1. World Association of NGOs, "History of WANGO: 2002, Beyond Boundaries," http: //www.wango.org/about_WAN GO/history_wango_2002.htm, printed 06/02/04.

2. World Association of NGOs, "Annual Conference 2002 and Awards Banquet," pp 1, 4; document faxed from WANGO to Lee Penn, 11/06/02.

3. E-mail from Charles Gibbs to URI members; forwarded to Lee Penn by an anonymous source, 11/15/02. URI Global Council member Donald Frew said, "The URI came up with the compromise of having someone else accept on the Bishop's behalf" (E-mail from Donald Frew to Lee Penn, 1/29/03). Frew characterized this compromise as an effort to make the award less of a high-profile news event (interview of Donald Frew by Lee Penn, 03/28/03).

4. Bishop William E. Swing, "The Swing Shift: 25 Years of the 155 Years of the Diocese of California," Episcopal News Service, August 9, 2004, http://www.episcopalchurch.org/3577_48075_ENG_HTM.htm, printed 08/10/04.

5. E-mail from Beverley Britton to Charles Gibbs, October 19, 2002; forwarded to Lee Penn by an anonymous source, 11/15/02.

6. E-mail from Charles Gibbs to URI members; forwarded to Lee Penn by an anonymous source, 11/15/02.

7. Ibid.

8. The IIFWP is an interfaith group founded by Moon. (See IIFWP, "Founders of the IIFWP," http://www.iifwp.org/About/Founders.shtml, printed 11/22/02.)

9. E-mail from Karen Smith to Lee Penn, 11/8/02.

10. E-mail from Charles Gibbs to URI members; forwarded to Lee Penn by an anonymous source, 11/15/02.

11. Interreligious and International Federation for World Peace, "Related Sites: Other Peace Organizations," http://www.iifwp.org/Links.shtml, printed 01/15/03.

12. Religious Youth Service, "Sites of Interest," http://www.rys.net/sites.htm, printed 1/15/03.

13. E-mail from Donald Frew to Lee Penn, 1/29/03.

WANGO also actively supports adoption of the Earth Charter.[1] The Unificationists' activism with the URI thus appears to be part of a strategy to broaden the conservative image that they have had in the past, so that the Rev. Moon and his followers can make a new appeal to the Left as well as to the Right.

Scientologists and the "New Cult Awareness Network"

The "New Cult Awareness Network" (NCAN)—dominated by Scientologists since they sued the former Cult Awareness Network out of existence in 1996[2]—has repeatedly praised the URI in its online publications.[3] Nancy O'Meara, a Scientologist and the treasurer of NCAN, stated that NCAN works with the URI, the North American Interfaith Network, and other interfaith groups.[4] She said that NCAN "representatives have been involved in local URI meetings since . . . 1999, and one member attended the URI conference in Salt Lake City. . . . URI has great potential as a grass-roots, localized, yet international movement."[5] Jeff Quiros, a spokesman for the Church of Scientology, says that the Church of Scientology is not a member of the URI, but that it "admires any efforts to promote and protect religious freedom and tolerance and interfaith dialog toward these ends."[6]

ISKCON—The "Hare Krishna" Movement

Members of ISKCON (the International Society for Krishna Consciousness, the "Hare Krishnas") have been active in the URI since the late 1990s.[7]

---

1. WANGO, "History of WANGO: 2002," http://www.wango.org/about/history2002. html, printed 1/15/03.

2. George D. Chryssides, *Exploring New Religions*, Cassell, 1999, p348; see also Barrett, *The New Believers*, pp101, 472; see also Richard Cimino and Don Lattin, *Shopping for Faith: American Religion in the New Millennium*, Jossey-Bass, 2002, p176.

3. See the newsletters of the New Cult Awareness Network (NCAN). The Foundation for Religious Freedom, which runs NCAN, distributed its book *Tolerance* 2000 at the URI summit meeting in Pittsburgh in 2000; Ravi Peruman, who served on the URI board in the late 1990s, praised the book on a San Francisco radio program. (NCAN, *Update*, Vol. IV, no. IV, http://www.cultawarenessnetwork.org/update/004.004.html, printed 02/18/03; also, NCAN, Update, Vol. IV, No. III, http://www.cultawarenessnetwork.org/update/004. 003.html, printed 02/18/03, for further praise of the URI.) An earlier newsletter (Cult Awareness Network, "CAN Update Archive," Vol. II, Issue I, http://cultawarenessnetwork.org/Can_Update/0201.html, printed in 1999; no longer on the Net) stated that CAN "is affiliated with many other religious tolerance groups—such as the United Religions Initiative and the World Parliament of Religions;" "representatives of the new CAN" were also invited to participate in a December 1998 conference led by Rev. Moon's IRFWP. Another CAN newsletter (CAN Update Archive," Vol. II, Issue III, http://www.cultawarenessnetwork.org/Can_Update/0203.htm, printed 11/12/99; no longer on the Net) stated that "CAN representatives have been part of the on-going worldwide activity to create a charter" for the URI. Tolerance For All, an NCAN-related organization, has a web page titled "Links to Our Friends," and includes a link to the URI. (http://www.toleranceforall.org/links/htm, printed 02/18/03.)

4. New Cult Awareness Network, "Who We Are," http://www.cultawarenessnetwork. org/WhoWeAre.html, printed 03/26/03.

5. E-mail from Nancy O'Meara to Lee Penn, 11/07/02.

6. E-mail from Jeff Quiros to Lee Penn, 11/15/02.

7. In July 1999, Rasikanandadas represented ISKCON at "Blessings for the Balkans," an interfaith event organized by the URI and the Brahma Kumaris. (The International Society for Krishna Consciousness, "Interfaith," *Temple Bulletin*, July-August 1999, p3). In October 2000, a newsletter that describes itself as "ISKCON-friendly" ("Chakra Mission Statement and Editorial Policy," http://chakra.org/contactus/mission.html, printed 12/09/02) ran a story in which an ISKCON leader promoted two URI events scheduled for November 2000—a "Culture of Peace" conference in Manipur India, and a ceremony for signing the URI Charter. (Bhaktisvapura Damodara Swami, "Invitation to All Devotees," http://www.chakra.org/articles/2000/10/25.manipur, Google cached copy, printed 12/05/02). In an article on the URI web site, the regional coordinator for the URI's Pacific region noted that Sundarananda Das, Prema Manjari, Gunadika, and other members of the local ISKCON community "did a wonderful job of assuring that our delegates were well attended to" at the December 2001 URI conference

WICCA AND THE GODDESS MOVEMENT

Wiccans and Neopagans[1] have been actively involved in the URI since 1997.[2] The Wiccan pentagram is among the array of 15 religious symbols that appeared on the cover of Bishop Swing's 1998 book *The Coming United Religions*, and still is used on many URI publications.[3] One of the three URI Global Council members elected in 2002 from the US is Donald Frew, a prominent Wiccan Neopagan.[4]

Neo-pagan groups that have expressed support for the URI have included:

- Coven of the Stone and the Mirror.[5]
- Covenant of the Goddess.[6]
- Goddess Holding the World Mural Project.[7]
- Hippo Haven Wiccan Community.[8]
- Pagan Educational Network.[9]
- the Pagan Sanctuary Network.[10]
- the 2001 "Pagan Summit" held in Bloomington, Indiana.[11]
- the "SerpentStone" coven in North Carolina.[12]

in Bali, Indonesia. (Marites Africa, "Pilgrims of Peace in Bali," http://www.uri.org/regionalnews/asiapacificassembly.asp, printed 12/5/2002). Donald Frew, a member of the Global Council, stated that a few ISKCON members participated in the URI Global Assembly in 2002, and that a sizable ISKCON contingent participated in the peace march associated with the conference. (Conversation between Lee Penn and Donald Frew, December 9, 2002.)

1. For further information on Wicca and Neopaganism, see Tal Brooke, "Spellbinding a Culture: The Emergence of Modern Witchcraft," *Journal* of the Spiritual Counterfeits Project, Vol. 23:4–24:1, 2000, pp4–17, and in the same issue, Tony Carnes, "The Witches of Harvard & MIT," pp30–41; obtainable through http://www.scp-inc.org.

2. Interview of Donald Frew by Lee Penn, 03/28/03.

3. In several URI publications issued in the fall of 2002, and on some of their Web pages posted in the same period, the 15 symbols are in a line, superimposed on a map of the globe.

4. URI, "Global Council."

5. "About Coven of the Stone and Mirror," http://www.geocities.com/Athens/Agora/2416/cosminfo.html, printed 1/11/03; the "High Priestess," Brigantia Stone, "has recently been involved with the Interfaith Council of Greater New York in projects related to the United Religions Initiative."

6. URI Global Council member Donald Frew is a "national interfaith representative" for the Covenant of the Goddess. (OakGrove Archive, "Past News and Issues: 3rd Quarter 2002," cites Covenant of the Goddess press release, http://oakdancer. com/archives/oga3q02.htm, printed 01/11/03).

7. Rowan Fairgrove, "Holy Brighid Holding the World in her Hands," http://www.conjure.com/inspired.html, printed 1/ 11/03.

8. Hauen Ypotame, "Hippo Haven Wiccan Community," http://moss.witchesgathering.com/, printed 02/19/03; the site says, "We are involved in United Religions Initiative, an effort to put an end to struggle between the world's religions, endorsed by the United Nations. The Greater Asheville Cooperation Circle has been growing steadily, and our High Priest represents the SerpentStone Family in this group."

9. Pagan Educational Network, "Links to Groups," http://www.paganednet.org/linktog.html, printed 1/11/03. After listing many pagan groups, they list the URI among activist groups that are "making a difference."

10. "United Religions Initiative Webring," http://a.webring.com/hub?ring=uri, printed 1/11/03; includes the Pagan Sanctuary Network and the Northern California Local Council of the Covenant of the Goddess.

11. Pagan Summit, "Who Attended," http://www.bloomington.in.us/~pen/summit/whoattend.html, printed 1/11/03. One of the attendees was Deborah Light, and she listed her affiliation as "United Religions Initiative."

12. H. Byron Ballard is a priestess of Inanna, an elder of SerpentStone, and is active in the URI; see her biographical information at H. Byron Ballard, "Pagan Festivals and Events: Free Spirit Gathering XVII," http://www.witchvox.com/festivals/ fest_fsg_02.html, printed 1/11/03.

- Spirit of the North Gathering, a "network of Druids in locality" in the UK.[1]
- Temple of Isis, in Isis Oasis, California.[2]

The Benign Public Face of Wicca

Defenders of Wicca present this religion as a benign way to connect with one's self and with the Earth. Starhawk, author of the Wiccan classic *The Spiral Dance*, says, "We're drawn to an earth-based spirituality out of a longing for some true, intimate connection with the earth."[3] Margot Adler, a Wiccan priestess for over 25 years and author of *Drawing Down The Moon*, says that

> when the altar is set, the candles lit, the circle cast, you know it is ritual time. Your deep self knows that you are ready to enter what Wiccans call 'the place between the worlds,' the place we often reach in dreams, or in art. . . . Through dance, chant, gesture, breath, candles, incense, the experience of speaking our concerns and truths, and sharing food and drink together, we can reconnect with each other. At these moments, we understand once again that we are connected to the cycles of life, to the rhythms of birth, growth, death, and rebirth. . . . Ultimately, everything that happens in ritual takes place in your own mind and heart, and in the minds and hearts of those you do ceremony with. The props are wonderful; they can deepen an experience, and sometimes they are great fun. But at the center of things, they are totally unnecessary.[4]

The URI's educational material for children describes Wicca thus:

> Wiccan spirituality is focused on the earth and its seasons and the forces and rhythms of nature and human beings. Its roots are in the ancient pre-Christian indigenous religions of Europe. . . . Wiccans see divinity in all living things and see divinity as being both male and female. All of life is perceived as sacred and interconnected. . . . Modern Wiccan practice is a creative and dynamic force. Spiritual insight is achieved through living in harmony with the earth.[5]

The Neopagan Elder Donald Frew addressed the 1993 Parliament of World Religions with an answer to the question "How can we achieve salvation, then?" His reply was as sanguine as the perspectives offered by Starhawk and the URI interfaith curriculum for children:

> We're not even trying to. We don't understand what there is to be saved from. The idea of salvation presupposes a Fall of some kind, a fundamental flaw in Creation as it exists today. Witches look at the world [around] us and see wonder, we see mystery. The death and destruction that frighten some we see as a necessary part of the wheel of life, exaggerated and exacerbated when life is lived out of balance with Nature. And while many of us believe in reincarnation, we do not seek to escape the wheel of rebirth. We can't imagine anything more wonderful than to come back to this bounteous and beautiful Earth, except perhaps to come back to an Earth freed from Man's environmental depredations.[6]

---

1. Spirit of the North Gathering, "Introduction," http://www.yewgrove.demon.co.uk/, printed 2/20/03; the group lists the URI among the "Friends of SONG," at http://www.yewgrove.demon.co.uk/song4.htm, printed 2/20/03.

2. United Religions Initiative, "Archive of 72 Hours Projects—Geographical Listing," http://www.united-religions.org/newsite/72hours/projects.htm, printed 6/22/00; no longer on the Net at this address. (A copy of this document may be found at http://web.archive.org/web/20010624201820/http://www.united-religions.org/newsite/72hours/projects.htm as of 2004.) Cited below as URI, "Archive of 72 Hours Projects."

3. Starhawk, "Sacred Ground: Listening to the Land," http://www.beliefnet.com/story/27/story_2715.html, printed 05/06/03.

4. Margot Adler, "Spirit & Matter: At the Center of Things," http://www.beliefnet.com/story/24/story_2407.html, printed 05/06/03.

5. United Religions Initiative, "Kids," description of Wicca, http://www.uri.org/kids/other_wicc.htm, printed 10/14/02.

6. Donald H. Frew, "Pagans In Interfaith Dialogue: New Faiths, New Challenges," http://www.cog.org/pwr/don.htm, printed on 07/01/04.

Transgressive Religion: From Polyamory to "Root-Based Sorcery"

The public face of Wicca *seems* benign; the reality can be quite otherwise. Wicca is a big tent, a non-dogmatic faith that has room—among its most extreme practitioners—for sex rituals, "holy" drug use, occultism, and black magic.

Each February in the San Francisco Bay Area, the Neo-pagan Ancient Ways bookstore hosts a 3-day "PantheaCon" convention for witches; the February 2004 gathering was attended by "about 1,500 people."[1] Those who offer convention workshops are the same ones who publish books on Wicca, speak at interfaith gatherings,[2] and lead classes for the public. At the 2003 PantheaCon, 3 URI activists—Rowan Fairgrove, Donald Frew, and Paul Chaffee—led the session "Paganism & the Interfaith Movement—A Conversation."[3] Frew and Fairgrove offered a similar workshop at the 2004 Panthea-Con.[4]

Frew said, "the intellectual cutting edge of the movement presents at PantheaCon, but there is also a lot of crap at the convention. It's a mixed bag."[5] The workshops offered at the PantheaCon conventions since 1999 have included a full menu of ways to explore transgressive spirituality.

Unusual sex-related workshops at the 2001 PantheaCon included a "queer sexmagick" class on oral sex (titled "Slip of the Tongue," with an unprintable course description), "Sacred Whore: Sexuality for Love, Healing and Fun," "Queer Magic," a nude workshop on "The Magic of Sexual Empowerment" ("a powerful workshop for men and women to explore their sexual energy within safe sacred space,") "Magick Mouth II" ("a playful and interactive women's workshop on oral sex magick for the men in your world"), and "Sex Writing: Pursuing the Goddess with Words."[6] The 2003 PantheaCon included classes on "Bouquet of Lovers: Polyamory for Pagans" (offered by "a five-person poly[7] Family who have been living together for the past five years"),[8] a "Pombagira Dance" in honor of the "sacred harlot of Rio,"[9] "The Use of Essential Oils as Aphrodisiacs,"[10] "Magick for Lovers,"[11] "Sex and Drugs: The Darkness and the Light,"[12] and "A Fun Social Mixer/Party, for Singles, Poly, Etc."[13] These offerings continued at the 2004 PantheaCon: "devotional for PombaGira, the sacred Harlot," "Polyamory: Ways of Loving More Than One," "Sacred Marriage: A Queer Feri Dance Ritual" (which was promised to be "sacred, ecstatic, and multisexual"), and "Dionysian Ritual in Ancient Greece."[14]

In case these workshops failed to provide sufficient spiritual darkness, those who attended the 2001 PantheaCon could attend classes on the "five points of the Iron Pentacle," "The scales of the serpent:

1. "PantheaCon 2004," *Ancient Ways Newsletter*, Spring 2004, vol. 9, issue 2, p 2.

2. Since the 1997 PantheaCon convention, Rowan Fairgrove and Donald Frew—elders in the Covenant of the Goddess, "the largest Wiccan religious organization in the world," and active participants in the URI—offered workshops about pagans in the interfaith movement.

3. 2003 *PantheaCon*, program, p 13, "Saturday morning schedule."

4. "Pantheacon 2004 Schedule," http://www.snugharbor.com/~ajb/longlist.php, printed 03/11/04 (cited below as "Pantheacon 2004 Schedule").

5. Interview of Donald Frew by Lee Penn, 03/28/03.

6. Ancient Ways, PantheaCon 2001 schedule, http://www.ancientways.com/html/schedule01.html, printed 02/26/01; no longer on the Net at this address (cited below as "Pantheacon 2001 Schedule"). (A copy may be found as of 2004 at http://web.archive.org/web/20010223215333/http://www.ancientways.com/html/schedule01.html.)

7. "Poly" refers to those who practice "polyamory," ongoing relationships with multiple partners.

8. 2003 *PantheaCon*, program, p 8, "Friday schedule."

9. Ibid., p 10, "Friday schedule."

10. Ibid., p 16, "Saturday afternoon schedule."

11. Ibid., p 18, "Saturday afternoon schedule."

12. Ibid., p 17, "Saturday afternoon schedule."

13. Ibid., p 20, "Saturday evening schedule."

14. "Pantheacon 2004 Schedule."

Aleph," two Labyrinth workshops, "Blending Toltec and Witch Wisdom,"[1] "Experiential Exploration of Shamanic Divination," "Ancient Hebrew Totems," "Inner Archetypes and the Ecstatic Path of Eternal Tantra," "The Path of the Dragon," "SpellCasting," "root-based sorcery in European folk magic," and "New, Improved Sex & Drugs" (led by a self-described "pagan, poly, psychedelic psychiatrist" and by her husband, "fungophile and student of shamanism").[2] The opening ritual of the 2001 Panthea-Con was led by the owner of the Ancient Ways store, a founder of the Covenant of the Goddess who is also the mistress of the Sirius Oasis, a lodge of the Ordo Templi Orientalis (OTO).[3] (The OTO practices the occult rites espoused by Aleister Crowley, the English Satanist of the early 1900s.[4])

The 2003 PantheaCon offered similar fare—classes on "Toltec and Wiccan Shamanism,"[5] "Children of a Darker God: Death is Only the Beginning,"[6] "Protection Magick and Psychic Self-Defense,"[7] "Energy Communication With Animals,"[8] "Gardner, Crowley, and Witchcraft,"[9] "Eyewitness to Isis,"[10] "Mary Magdalene, Priestess of the Goddess, Bride of Jesus,"[11] "Hepatoscopy or Liver Divination,"[12] "European Bear Worship as a Precursor to Christianity" (led by a "former Unitarian minister"),[13] "Witches' Cradle: The Psychic Centrifuge" (led by Fakir Musafar, a "shaman, artist, master piercer and body modifier," and by Cléo Dubois, whose "Academy of SM arts teaches bondage and SM to couples, Dominants, and switches,")[14] "The Truth about Yah: Debunking the Myth of Hebrew Monotheism,"[15] "Invocation of Kali,"[16] and a Gnostic Mass of the Ordo Templi Orientalis.[17]

The 2004 PantheaCon offered more of the same—or worse: "Chaos Magic Within the Hypnosis Paradigm," the "Ritual of the Mark of the Beast" (a "group performance of Aleister Crowley's ritual . . . designed to invoke the energies of the Aeon of Horus"), "Kali Maa: Tradition, Devotion, and Puja," a Gnostic Mass presented by the Ordo Templi Orientalis, "Understanding Aleister Crowley's Thoth Tarot," "Teonanácatl—The Visionary Mushroom Transforming Global Culture," "Nuit—The Limitless Goddess," and a participatory "Druid Underworld Ritual."[18]

1. The "wise" Toltecs practiced large-scale human sacrifice and worshipped the sun. "Their religion, centering on the god Quetzalcoatl, incorporated human sacrifice, sun worship, and a sacred ball game." ("Toltec," *The Concise Columbia Encyclopedia*, 1995.)

2. PantheaCon 2001 Schedule.

3. Ibid.

4. A biographer says, "Crowley, in taking the name Baphomet, was linking himself not only to the Templar tradition, but also to the blasphemous, even Satanic, connotations of Baphomet." (Lawrence Sutin, *Do What Thou Wilt: A Life of Aleister Crowley*, St. Martin's Griffin, 2002, p227). By 1914, Crowley "had crafted O.T.O. rituals to reflect his own erotomagical discoveries. . . . Crowley also added a new degree of his own devising—an XI° magical working utilizing anal sex which was, in practice, primarily homosexual." (Sutin, ibid., p228) Another biographer said, "Remove Christianity—or anti-Christianity—and Crowley stops making sense. Just as he treasured the title of the Great Beast 666, he also insisted in calling his many mistresses 'Scarlet Women'—after the monstrous whore in 'Revelations'." (Gavin Baddeley, *Lucifer Rising: sin, devil worship & rock'n'roll*, Plexus, 1999, p29).

5. 2003 *PantheaCon*, program, p9, "Friday schedule."

6. Ibid., p9, "Friday schedule."

7. Ibid., pp10–11, "Saturday morning schedule."

8. Ibid., p16, "Saturday afternoon schedule."

9. Ibid., p17, "Saturday afternoon schedule."

10. Ibid., p22, "Sunday morning schedule."

11. Ibid., p24, "Sunday morning schedule."

12. Ibid., pp24–25, "Sunday morning schedule."

13. Ibid., p27, "Sunday afternoon schedule."

14. Ibid., p28, "Sunday afternoon schedule."

15. 2003 *PantheaCon*, program, "PantheaCon Newsletter," Issue 2, Saturday, February 15, 2003.

16. 2003 *PantheaCon*, program, p30, "Sunday evening schedule."

17. Ibid., p27, "Sunday afternoon schedule."

18. "Pantheacon 2004 Schedule."

Among the classes offered in 2001[1] and again in 2003 were sessions for pagan children and teenagers, such as the "Eris Ritual," described as "Traditional Discordian Ritual & Sacred High Mass of Eris . . . Kid-friendly. Loud."[2] In 2003, the convention included a workshop titled "Sacred, Safe, and Sensual: Discussing Sexuality Education for Pagan Teens."[3] The presenters invited adult pagans to "discuss a 27-session, sex-positive, comprehensive sexuality education program available for our teens."[4] The leader of the 2004 "Open-to-All Discordian Ritual" said that he "had a happy Episcopalean [sic] upbringing, is now perpetually unsure, follows Pagans like a groupie, and is fairly tall."[5]

The uninhibited atmosphere at PantheaCon has led convention organizers to issue "Ritual Etiquette" warnings about illegal drug use and the need to practice safe sex. "The presence of illegal substances can jeopardize everyone participating in the Convention. So please don't!"[6] "Sex: It can be a powerful force, especially in an atmosphere of freedom. Respect it, and remember the following: among pagans, nudity is an affirmation, not an invitation! Be sure you interpret signals correctly. . . . *Practice Safe Sex!* Condoms will be available at the convention—use them, and if you have a STD (sexually transmitted disease) be responsible and tell your partner. With a little imagination you can probably think of something to do."[7] And finally, "Don't let anyone pressure you into joining a group or doing anything you are not ready for."[8] Such is the new religion that the URI has given a place at the table.

THEOSOPHY AND THE NEW AGE MOVEMENT

In 1997, URI staffer Paul Andrews said that "Theosophists are welcome as part of the conversation" in the URI.[9] Indeed, they have been. Theosophists have been active in the URI since the movement was founded.

The Lucis Trust World Service Fund, led by followers of Theosophist writer Alice Bailey, has given money to the URI.[10] In December 2002, the president of the Lucis Trust said of this donation, "we were happy to be able to make a contribution to URI's work."[11] Likewise, the Rudolf Steiner Foundation[12]—which promotes Anthroposophy, a variant of Theosophy—has donated to the URI.[13]

In addition, several prominent New Age writers whose ideas are strongly influenced by Theosophy—Robert Muller, Barbara Marx Hubbard, and Neale Donald Walsch—are enthusiastic supporters of the URI. Other Theosophists are following their lead, and actively support the URI. The

1. "PantheaCon 2001 schedule."
2. 2003 *PantheaCon*, program, p32, "Sunday evening schedule."
3. Ibid., p25, "Sunday morning schedule."
4. Ibid., p25, "Sunday morning schedule."
5. "Pantheacon 2004 Schedule."
6. 2003 *PantheaCon*, program, p4, "PantheaCon Ritual Etiquette."
7. Ibid., pp4–5.
8. Ibid., p5.
9. Interview with Paul Andrews, URI staff member, October 7 and December 11, 1997.
10. URI, *Annual Report* 2000, "Honoring Our Donors," p7.
11. Sarah McKechnie, letter to Lee Penn, December 5, 2002.
12. Rudolf Steiner Foundation, "Client profiles—designated funds," http://www.rsfoundation.org/clientprofiles/project-descriptions.html, printed 11/13/02.
13. Steiner led the Theosophical Society in Germany, but left in 1912—in part, because he disagreed with Annie Besant's promotion of Krishnamurti as a potential World Teacher, and in part because he gave Christ a greater cosmic role than other Theosophists were willing to accept. Steiner's Christology, however, is heterodox; no mainstream Christian church has accepted his views. (See Christopher Partridge, ed., *New Religions: A Guide—New Religious Movements, Sects, and Alternative Spiritualities*, Oxford University Press, 2004, pp210, 325.)

URI web site includes a link to "Spirit of Goodwill,"[1] a Theosophical organization that promoted Alice Bailey's "Great Invocation" and said, "you will be introduced to the ideals of the New World Religion which will unite people of all faiths."[2]

Collaboration between Theosophists and the URI should raise an alarm for all orthodox Christians. The cultural and political ideas of the Theosophists active in the URI are akin to Communism, with a spiritual gloss. (This is discussed in detail in Part II of this book.) There is a real danger that Theosophists will use the respectability and the organizational platform provided by the URI to spread their seductive, anti-Christian ideology.

The Lucis Trust: Followers of Alice A. Bailey

The Lucis Trust newsletter *World Goodwill* praised the URI in two of its 1999 issues,[3] citing it as part of a "global shift in consciousness," one of many actions that could usher in "an era of true peace, an era in which the glory of the One will be free to shine forth in all human actions."[4] In 2000, another Lucis Trust publication praised the URI (and the UNESCO Manifesto 2000 drive, which was endorsed by the URI) as part of a "planetary network" that counteracts "separative tendencies" and helps "construct an era of peace and stability impulsed [sic] by right relationships."[5] As of 2004, the Lucis Trust web site offered a link to the URI, as well as to the UN and many New Age organizations.[6]

Corinne McLaughlin and Gordon Davidson

New Age authors McLaughlin and Davidson describe themselves as "members and supporters of URI."[7] McLaughlin (who had been coordinator of President Clinton's National Task Force on Sustainable Development)[8] said, "I have the highest regard for URI and think it has an important influence today and tremendous future potential."[9] Gordon Davidson has hailed the emergence of the URI as a manifestation of the "descent of the Avatar of Synthesis, increasingly conditioning the mental plane, and aligned closely with the Christ."[10] Both Davidson and McLaughlin donated to the URI in

1. United Religions Initiative, "Research and Resources," http://www.uri.org/peacebuilding/links/peaceresourcelinks.asp, printed 05/28/03 and viewed 06/04/04. This is one of 12 links given on this URI web page.

2. Spirit of Goodwill, "Introduction," http://www.spiritofgoodwill.com/introduction.asp, printed 05/28/03. (As of 06/04/04, this site was down, and it has remained un-available since then. As of 11/05/04, an archive copy of the page was at http://web.arch ive.org/web/20030412180412/http://spiritofgoodwill.com/introduction.asp.)

3. World Goodwill, "Invoking the Spirit of Peace," reference to the URI 72-hour religious ceasefire on Y2K, *Newsletter*, 1999 issue 3, http://www.lucistrust.org/goodwill/wgnl993.shtml, printed 3/15/03 (cited below as World Goodwill, "Invoking the Spirit of Peace"), and World Goodwill, "Transition Activities," article on the URI, Newsletter, 1999 issue 1, http://www.lucistrust.org/goodwill/wgnl991.shtml, printed 02/08/03.

4. World Goodwill, "Invoking the Spirit of Peace."

5. Lucis Trust, "The Planetary Network," *Triangles Bulletin*, no. 133, September 2000, http://www.lucistrust.org/triangles/bulletin/2000/0009_network.shtml#uri, printed 12/16/02.

6. Lucis Trust, "World Goodwill—links," http://www.lucistrust.org/goodwill/links.shtml, viewed 11/05/04.

7. E-mail from Corinne McLaughlin to Lee Penn, November 1, 2002.

8. Biographical statement on McLaughlin, "Conference Speakers," for a June 2004 conference, "The Alchemy of Democracy: Restoring Soul to Culture;" also, The Center for Visionary Leadership, "Board of Directors," http://www.visionarylead.org/cvl-dirs.htm, printed 06/04/04.

9. E-mail from Corinne McLaughlin to Lee Penn, November 1, 2002.

10. Gordon Davidson, "The Significance of Intergroup Work for the Externalization of the Hierarchy," World Service Intergroup, http://www.synthesis.tc/IntergroupWork.htm, printed 11/23/02. On December 19, 1998, Davidson also said, "Religions are beginning to clean house with a growing universal spirit, the development of United Religions with spiritual leadership from Bishop Swing and Robert Muller." (Gordon Davidson, "Spiritual Foundations of Leadership," printed in Arcana Workshops, "Thoughtline," March 1999, http://www.meditationtraining.org/thoughtline/tl-9903.htm#2, printed 11/23/02).

2001,[1] 2002,[2] and 2003.[3] Davidson and McLaughlin, authors of *Spiritual Politics: Changing the World From the Inside Out*, dedicate the book to "DK" (Djwhal Khul, a Theosophical spirit being that supposedly dictated to Alice Bailey),[4] and say that the teachings of Alice Bailey "provided much of the inspiration for *Spiritual Politics*."[5]

Robert Muller

Robert Muller, a former Assistant Secretary-General of the UN and former Chancellor of the UN University for Peace in Costa Rica,[6] was present at the birth of the URI in the mid-1990s. He had proposed creation of a United Religions organization in the 1970s and 1980s,[7] and spoke publicly on behalf of Swing's organization as soon as the URI was announced to the public in 1995.[8] Muller also provided "editorial assistance" for a workbook used in URI planning meetings in 1996 and 1997,[9] and attended the 1996 URI summit meeting.[10] In October 2002, Muller claimed credit for the founding of the URI; he wrote, "In 1995, during the 50th Anniversary of the UN, I convinced San Francisco Bishop Swing to create the United Religions."[11]

The URI *Annual Report* for 2000 begins with a letter from Bishop Swing, avowing a 15-year spiritual relationship between himself and Muller. Swing said that Muller

> was the main speaker at a United Nations event at Grace Cathedral, San Francisco. I was so impressed by the scope of his remarks and his spiritual content that I requested a copy of his speech and quoted it on many occasions. Almost a decade later, Dr. Muller was one of the fifty-six people who attended the first Global Summit of the United Religions Initiative, in June 1996. . . . In late January 2001, he read the proposed draft of the URI's '21st Century Vision of Peace Among Religions,' and he responded immediately. 'Congratulations! What a distance covered since our first meeting in San Francisco. . . . God bless URI. . . . It will go very, very far, even beyond the United Nations'.[12]

Muller has also hailed Swing as a sage equivalent to Plato and Aristotle. In a vision of the world as it might be in 2013, Muller wrote,

> Humanity is now a united world community of nations, not only economic and political, but also spiritual, following the path opened in the last century by Dag Hammarskjöld and U Thant in the United Nations, by Robert Schuman in Europe, and also throughout the millennia by prophets and founders of religions, and by great sages

1. United Religions Initiative, "Honoring Our Donors," *Annual Report* 2001, p8.

2. URI, *Annual Report* 2002, "Honoring URI Donors and Volunteers."

3. United Religions Initiative, 2003: *Compassionate Actions for a Better World*, annual report; http://www.uri.org/resources/URI_Anual_Report_2003.pdf, viewed 09/24/04; cited below as URI, *Annual Report*, 2003.

4. Corinne McLaughlin and Gordon Davidson, *Spiritual Politics: Changing the World from the Inside Out*, Ballantine Books, 1994, dedication, p v.

5. Ibid., p16.

6. "About Robert Muller," http://www.robertmuller.org/p01.html, printed 10/15/02.

7. URI pamphlet, "Dear Brothers and Sisters. . . ," fall 1996, page 3—"A brief and incomplete history of proposals for a United Religions 1893–1996"; the same history is on-line at http://globalforum.org/research/history1.html, printed 04/09/03.

8. Don Lattin, "Religions of World Celebrated With Prayers to Dozen Deities," *San Francisco Chronicle*, June 26, 1995, p A11, front page section.

9. United Religions Initiative, *Draft Workbook For Pilot Groups*, p2.

10. Gibbs/Mahé, *Birth of a Global Community*, p32.

11. Note from Robert Muller to Lee Penn, October 2002.

12. URI, *Annual Report* 2000, "Letter from the URI's Founder, Bishop William E. Swing," p2. The ellipses in the quotation are exactly as they appeared in the original.

such as Plato, Aristotle, Maimonides, Huxley, Albert Schweitzer, Teilhard de Chardin, Thomas Berry, Bishop William Swing and others.[1]

Muller assigns an ambitious role to the URI: "The role and responsibility of the new United Religions Organization and of the World Parliament of Religions . . . will be no less than to give humanity a new spiritual, planetary, cosmic ideology to follow the demise of communism and capitalism."[2] The UN should lead "vigorous action" against "religious fundamentalism," a problem which Muller includes among a litany of grave evils such as "violence in all its forms," "extreme poverty," and "Earth destruction."[3] He adds that one of mankind's goals should be "to see the religions globalize themselves urgently in order to give us a universal, cosmic meaning of life on Earth and give birth to the first global, cosmic, universal civilization; the recent initiative to create the United Religions can do that."[4] Ultimately, the United Religions should become a specialized agency of the United Nations.[5] With the URI, Muller says that "My dreams and proposals in *New Genesis, Shaping a Global Spirituality* . . . are being fulfilled."[6]

Barbara Marx Hubbard

Another New Age supporter of the URI is Barbara Marx Hubbard, who Paul Chaffee (then serving on the URI board) praised in 1997 as an "internationally recognized futurist preoccupied with peacemaking."[7] Marx Hubbard introduced Dee Hock, the founder of VISA, to the URI and to Bishop Swing; she was also a member of the "URI Organizational Design Team" that worked in early 1998 on preparation of the draft URI Charter.[8] In 1998, Marx Hubbard wrote: "I recently attended an extraordinary conference of 200 religious and spiritual leaders hosted by the United Religions Initiative. . . . It is just possible that this group, joining with other comparable efforts, will effect such a great awakening" of the planet, a "Planetary Birth Day."[9] In November 2002, Marx Hubbard said that she had not been active in the URI since 1998, but added, "I believe that URI is extremely important," and "other interfaith organizations, I hope, will merge with them."[10]

1. Robert Muller, *Ideas And Dreams For A Better World*, "Additional information of each volume—Volume III," "PART IV THE FOURTEENTH ONE HUNDRED IDEA (IDEAS 1301 TO 1400) INTRODUCTION: The State of the World on Earth Day 2013," http://www.robertmuller.org/voladnl/v3adnl.htm, viewed 06/21/04.

2. Robert Muller, *Ideas And Dreams for a Better World: 1001–1500, Volume III*, Idea 1128, 12 August 1997, http://www.robertmuller.org/volume/ideas1001.html, viewed 06/21/04.

3. Ibid., Idea 1486, August 5, 1998.

4. Ibid., Idea 1101, 16 July 16, 1997.

5. Ibid., Idea 1151, September 4, 1997.

6. Robert Muller, *Ideas And Dreams for a Better World: 3501–4000, Volume IX*, Idea 3645, http://www.robertmuller.org/volume/ideas3501.html, viewed 06/21/04.

7. Chaffee, "URI Global Conference," *PCN*, Oct./Nov. 1997, p32. Hubbard attended the 1997 URI summit meeting.

8. URI on-line archive, e-mail from Sally Ackerly to URI leadership, February 27, 1998, http://origin.org/uri/txt/Org2Design.txt. Printed 1998; no longer on the Internet; cited below as Ackerly e-mail to URI leadership, 02/27/98. Barbara Marx Hubbard confirmed these activities in a message to Lee Penn on 11/11/02.

9. Barbara Marx Hubbard, *Conscious Evolution: Awakening the Power of Our Social Potential*, New World Library, Novato, California, 1998, pp193, 194.

10. Barbara Marx Hubbard, telephone message to Lee Penn, recorded and transcribed November 11, 2002.

Neale Donald Walsch

Better known than Muller and Marx Hubbard is Neale Donald Walsch, whose cozy, best-selling *Conversations with God* books have made him a celebrity of the New Age.[1] In 1998, Rabbi Michael Lerner—who formerly provided spiritual advice to Hillary Clinton—praised Walsch's books: "All three volumes of *Conversations With God* turn out to be a brilliant work of spiritual discourse, a powerful critique of spiritually dead versions of contemporary religion, and a challenge to those who imagine themselves secular to rethink the metaphysical foundations of their deepest beliefs."[2] Since then, Walsch has continued his chats with the spirit that he calls "God." Walsch hailed his 2002 book, *The New Revelations: A Conversation With God*, as "a life-altering book. It contains New Revelations . . . lifting the whole human race to a new level of experience, to a new understanding of itself, to a new expression of its grandest vision."[3] Over 7 million copies of Walsch's books have been sold in 27 languages.[4] Walsch claims that each of his books "finds its way into the hands of at least three other people," so that he has a readership of "something over 25 million."[5]

Walsch is a consistent, long-time proponent of the URI.

In 1997, Walsch attended the URI summit meeting at Stanford,[6] and the URI gave Walsch the leadership of its "Committee on Spirituality and the Global Social Agenda,"[7] a task force that assisted in URI planning in 1997-1998. At the 1997 URI summit conference, "Walsch said he represents the one million truth seekers who have purchased his books and made him the latest superstar on the spiritual circuit. 'If anything, I represent the new paradigm of a religionless religion—a religion without structure—a spirituality that transcends all boundaries,' he said."[8] Walsch was also involved in the early 1998 discussion of the draft URI Charter.[9]

In 1999, Walsch told readers of *Magical Blend* magazine to expect "the creation of a United Religions organization, similar to the United Nations, with delegates from each of the world's religions, spiritual movements, and indigenous cultures"[10] between 2000 and 2015.

In 2000, an interviewer asked Walsch to "name a few enterprises in the world you believe are working toward goals which are similar to yours."[11] Walsch's first response was to praise the URI:

Well, there is the United Religions Initiative out of San Francisco, undertaken by Bishop William Swing, the Episcopal Archbishop of California.[12] He has had a vision of a one-world religion—not a single religion, but a

---

1. For further information on Neale Donald Walsch, see Lee Penn and Tal Brooke, "Neale Donald Walsch: Conversations With Myself," *Journal* of the Spiritual Counterfeits Project, Vol. 26:4–27:1, 2003, pp4–19; see also John Moore, "Conversations With the God of This Age," *Journal* of the Spiritual Counterfeits Project, Vol. 22:2–22:3, 1999, pp34–47; obtainable through http://www.scp-inc.org.

2. Rabbi Michael Lerner, "God Tells Neale Walsch Some Interesting Stuff," (review of books 1, 2, and 3 of *Conversations With God*), *San Francisco Chronicle*, December 20, 1998, p10; downloaded from http://www.sfgate.com, 03/20/03.

3. Neale Donald Walsch, *The New Revelations: A Conversation With God*, Atria Books, 2002, pviii.

4. Don Lattin, "Chatting up the man who talks with God," *San Francisco Chronicle*, November 17, 2002, page E-2, downloaded 11/21/02 from http://www.sfgate.com.

5. E-mail from Neale Donald Walsch to Lee Penn, 11/20/02.

6. Chaffee, "URI Global Conference," *PCNews*, Oct./Nov. 1997, p32.

7. Neale Donald Walsch, "Ending Religious Conflict," *Magical Blend*, Issue 58, December 1997, p40.

8. Lattin, "Religious Violence Decried," June 26, 1997.

9. Ackerly, e-mail to URI leadership, 02/27/98.

10. Neale Donald Walsch, "Welcome to the New Millennium," *Magical Blend*, Issue 64, May 1999, p46.

11. Ravi Dykema, "Communicating with God: An interview with Neale Donald Walsch," *Nexus*, March/April 2000, http://www.nexuspub.com/articles/2000/mar2000/walsch.htm, viewed 06/19/04, cited below as Dykema, "Communicating with God."

12. It seems that Walsch gave the Bishop of California an ecclesiastical promotion. There are no Archbishops in the Episcopal Church in the US.

united religions organization to which delegates from all the world's religions would come, much as they do to the United Nations. They would discuss the world's issues and challenges from a religious perspective and then present to the governments of the world the viewpoints of the world's religions meeting collectively. The point is to see what would happen if we applied spiritual principles, the highest spiritual principles held in common by man, to the deepest problems being faced by the human race.[1]

In 2002, Walsch said "I support the initiative," although all his time is taken by his own writing and speaking engagements.[2]

In 2004, Walsch and his spirit guide gave their public nod, once again, to the URI. The spirit guide predicted, "More international conferences and congresses will be held, such as those which have already been held in recent years, inviting representatives of the world's religions to come together in one place to explore the path of mutual respect and cooperation."[3] Walsch replied, "I am aware of a number of such endeavors right now, including the United Religions Initiative."[4] Walsch's familiar spirit replied, "The discussions at these important gatherings will not focus on eliminating the differences between religions, for it will be recognized that diversity of spiritual expression is a *blessing*, not a problem. Rather, the focus will be on finding ways to honor those differences, seeing what they can further reveal to humanity about the Totality of God, and looking to see whether the *combination of all these different views* might produce a Whole that is Greater than the Sum of Its Parts."[5]

SPIRITUAL ODDS AND ENDS

Various other odd religious and utopian groups have entered the open door offered by the URI. There are enough of these to fill all the hot tubs in Marin County, California—including:

- Aetherius Society.[6]
- Aquarian Tabernacle Church International.[7]
- Association for Global New Thought.[8]
- Center for Inner Peace.[9]
- Church of Divine Man.[10]

1. Dykema, "Communicating with God."
2. E-mail from Neale Donald Walsch to Lee Penn, 11/20/02.
3. Neale Donald Walsch, *Tomorrow's God: Our Greatest Spiritual Challenge*, Atria Books, 2004, p234.
4. Ibid., p234.
5. Ibid., p235.
6. URI, *Annual Report* 2002, "Honoring URI Donors and Volunteers," and URI, *Annual Report* 2003. The Society says, "The Aetherius Society is a group of dedicated people cooperating with Ascended Masters to help usher in a New Age of Peace and Enlightenment upon our world." (The Aetherius Society, "What is the Aetherius Society," http://www.aetherius.org/NewFiles/Aetherius_Society.html, printed 07/05/04).
7. URI, *Annual Report* 2000, "Honoring Our Donors," p8; United Religions Initiative, "Affiliates—North America," http://www.uri.org/regionalnews/affiliates/index.asp, printed 09/23/04.
8. "Association for Global New Thought," http://www.new-thought.org/agnt.html, printed 03/27/03. The document states, "To date, our Leadership Council members have been invited to such distinguished gatherings as the United Religions Initiative, the Assembly of Religious and Spiritual Leaders for the Parliament of the World's Religions, and the Interfaith Action Network for Tibet with his Holiness, the Dalai Lama."
9. URI, *Annual Report* 2002, "Honoring URI Donors and Volunteers."
10. David Ponedel, Bishop of the Church of Divine Man (a self-described "psychic church" offering services in 4 cities in the San Francisco Bay area) assisted in planning the liturgy for the interfaith service at Grace Cathedral in 1995 at which the URI was announced to the public. He also helped form a URI cooperation circle, "The Bridge," which is a liaison between the URI and the Council for the Parliament of the World's Religions. (e-mail from Ponedel to Lee Penn, 11/11/02). Ponedel is a member of the Board of Directors of the San Francisco Interfaith Center, another URI Cooperation Circle. (interview with Lee Penn, November 2002).

- Church of Religious Science.[1]
- Cosmic Trybe, Gypsies.[2]
- Course in Miracles.[3]
- Common Ground Labyrinth Project.[4]
- Creative Living Fellowship.[5]
- Fetzer Institute.[6]
- Foundation Teilhard de Chardin, in the Netherlands.[7]
- Great White Fraternity.[8]
- International New Thought Alliance.[9]
- Masters Group.[10]
- Mastery Foundation.[11]

1. URI, *Annual Report* 2000, "Honoring Our Donors," p7.

2. URI, *CC Survey Report* 2003, http://www.uri.org/ccsurveyreport2003/Section_Three.pdf, p13 (cited below as URI, *CC Survey*, section 3, 2003); there were 4 adherents among those who responded to the 2003 URI membership survey.

3. URI, "North America," listing of participants in a January 2, 2001 "global peacemaking event" sponsored by the Alliance for Spiritual Community CC, http://www.united-religions.org/newsite/regions/namerica/index.htm, printed 06/01/2001; no longer on the Net at this address. The "peacemaking event" was described thus: "**The Alliance for Spiritual Community URI CC**—Laguna Niguel, California—sponsored a global peacemaking event January 2 from 10 AM to 12 noon. Prayers, chanting, blessings and song were offered from the Tushmal Singers, Ajacheman Nation, A Course in Miracles, Soka Gakkai Buddhist, Jewish, Taize Meditation, Baha'i, Muslim and Hindu traditions. We sat in a circle, and began with a ritual lighting of a candle. The Native American Singers led us in a blessing of the six directions. . . . The URI is alive and well in Laguna Niguel, California." (As of 2004, this web page may also be found at http://web.archive.org /web/20010619191721/ http://www.united-religions.org/newsite/regions/namerica/index.htm, printed 09/27/04.)

4. URI, "Archive of 72 Hours Projects," project in Erie, Pennsylvania.

5. URI, *Annual Report*, 2003. The Fellowship says, "We base our teachings on the principles of Religious Science, using The Science of Mind written by Dr. Ernest Holmes as our foundational text as well as the Bible and other sacred writings." (Creative Living Fellowship, "Welcome," http://www.creativelivingcenter.com/CLF_welcome.htm, printed 09/24/04.)

6. Synthesis Dialogues II, "Members," http://www.synthesisdialogues.org/members. htm, printed 02/19/03. Penny Williamson, "a Founding Facilitator and advisor for the Fetzer Institute Courage to Teach Program," was a facilitator at the URI Global Summit in 2000 and at the URI/North America summit in 2001. In addition, the Fetzer Institute and the URI co-sponsored speeches by Robert Inchausti and Jacob Needleman on May 18, 2004. Fetzer Institute publications are intended to "explore and describe the many ways, as individuals, communities, and nations, that we can illuminate and inhabit the essential qualities of the global citizen who seeks to live with the authenticity and grace demanded by our times." (Source: invitation issued by the URI and the Fetzer Institute, 2004.)

7. Foundation Teilhard de Chardin, "Allied Organisations," http://home.worldonline.nl/~sttdc/alli.htm, printed 2/20/03; they list the URI and the International Association for Religious Freedom as allies.

8. URI, *CC Survey*, section 3, 2003, p13; there were 3 adherents among those who responded to the 2003 URI membership survey.

9. International New Thought Alliance (INTA) press release, "89th INTA Leaders Highlights," *Baltimore Times Online*, July 15, 2004, http://www.btimes.com/News/article/article.asp?NewsID=46124&sID=4, printed 07/15/04. The INTA is an umbrella organization of New Thought organizations, including Religious Science, Unity, Divine Science, and the Universal Foundation for Better Living. The INTA Congress gave an award to Bishop Swing on July 22, 2004 for his work on the URI.

10. The Masters Group promotes "Personal Transformational Technologies specifically designed to open the individual into more expanded states of awareness. The methods used have been chosen for their simplicity, purity, ease, and effectiveness. Many of the experiences involve reconnecting with nature. . . . Sponsorship of programs providing synergistic action toward a transformed society. . . . Sponsorship of events designed to produce individual transformation through the direct transfer of a higher level of awareness." The head of the group, Gerry Eitner, describes herself as a "visionary coach," and says that she is "holds board positions on United Religions-DC, One Day in Peace, and is the focus person for peace for the North American section of the United Religions Initiative." She also has "orchestrated events for peace at "the US Capitol, the Masonic Temple, the Pentagon, various churches, and the Smithsonian Mall." (The Masters Group, "Who We Are," http://www.themastersgroup.org/brochure.html, printed 02/18/03).

11. Kay Lindahl is a member of the board of directors for the URI, other interfaith groups, and the Mastery Foundation. (The Listening Center, "The Sacred Art of Listening," http://www.sacredlistening.com/sal_author_illustrator.htm, printed 2/20/03). The Mastery Foundation has involved Werner Erhard from its beginning. "In 1983, Werner accepted the request of

- Mile Hi Church.[1]
- New Thought Center.[2]
- Pathways to Peace.[3]
- Planetary Educational Center.[4]
- Several Reiki circles.[5]
- Followers of Sai Baba.[6]
- Followers of "Supreme Master Ching Hai."[7]
- Unity Church.[8]
- Universal Oneness United.[9]
- Urantia Book Fellowship.[10]
- Wittenberg Center for Alternative Resources.[11]

---

the newly formed Mastery Foundation to consult in the creation of a transformational program for those who minister. Since then, he has continued to donate his expertise and services to the Foundation, at times developing new program material and leading courses, including one in Ireland in 1993." (The Mastery Foundation, "Ireland Initiative," http://www.masteryfoundation.org/ireland.htm, printed 2/20/03).

1. URI, Annual Report, 2003. The Church says, "Mile Hi Church is an affiliated member of the United Church of Religious Science based in California. Religious Science churches teach the Science of Mind and Spirit and are now located all over the world. Ernest Holmes, author of The Science of Mind, founded Religious Science in the 1920s. Religious Science is often referred to as a "New Thought" teaching along with Unity and Divine Science." (Mile Hi Church, "Who We Are," http://www.milehichurch.org/believe/whoweare.asp, printed 09/24/04.)

2. URI, Annual Report 2000, "Honoring Our Donors," p7.

3. URI, Annual Report 2002, "Honoring URI Donors and Volunteers."

4. URI, CC Survey section 3, 2003, p13; there were 7 adherents among those who responded to the 2003 URI membership survey.

5. URI, "Archive of 72 Hours Projects," projects in Long Island and Hampton Bays, NY. Reiki Circles operate independently, so the activities of these Circles does not necessarily represent the position of the Reiki movement as a whole.

6. URI, CC Survey, section 3, 2003, p13; there were 2 adherents among those who responded to the 2003 URI membership survey.

7. "Sharing Master's Love at the World Vision Conference: Learning from the Prophecies of the Native Americans," http://www.godsimmediatecontact.net/news/news96/b-2.htm, printed 1/11/03. Thomas and Sherri One Wolf, followers of Ching Hai, attended one of the URI summit meetings at Stanford in the late 1990s. The "godsimmediatecontact" site is the home page for Ching Hai. In Singapore, members of the Mahaguru Ching Hai Association joined members of other faiths in signing the URI charter and forming a URI Cooperation Circle in 2000. (Bahai News, "Interfaith Group Aims To End Violence, http://bahai-library.org/newspapers/100300.html, printed 1/11/03).

8. Unity of Salt Lake, "The Staff," biography of Marsha Pilgeram, board president, who says, "my heart is with URI and Unity," http://www.unityslc.org/staff_board.html, printed 2/11/03.

9. Universal Oneness United ("Mission Statement," http://www.uou.to/mission.htm, printed 1/11/03), runs the Light-Haven Interfaith Seminary. The Seminary is affiliated with the URI and the World Federation of Unity Churches, among others. (LightHaven InterFaith Seminary, "Affiliation's" [sic], http://www.lighthaven.to/afiliation.htm, printed 1/11/03).

10. "The Urantia Book Fellowship is an international spiritual communion of readers devoted to the study and dissemination of The Urantia Book." (The Urantia Book Fellowship, "The Urantia Book: A Revelation," http://www.ubfellowship.org/index_fef.htm, printed 02/22/03. The 1998 Annual Report of the Fraternal Relations Committee of the Fellowship (FRC) stated that the Fellowship is a member organization in the North American Interfaith Network (NAIN), and that five of NAIN's nineteen directors were Urantia Book readers, including its Chair and Vice Chair. Also, the FRC stated that "several readers are also working closely with more than two hundred religious leaders from around the world on the development of a United Religions Charter." (Marvin Gawryn, "Fraternal Relations Committee: 1998 Annual Report," http://www.ubfellowship.org/archive/admin/doc760. htm, printed 02/22/03). Gard Jameson, a member of the FRC, attended the 1997 URI summit at Stanford (Jameson, "URI," Summer 1997).

11. URI, Annual Report 2000, "Interim Global Council Membership in 2000," p8; Betsy Stang, who was then a Council member, is the Executive Director of the Wittenberg Center for Alternative Resources (Wittenberg Center, "Advisory Board," http://www.wittenbergcenter.org/Boardofdir.html, printed 01/11/03). Stang's private practice "utilizes clairvoyant counseling for personal and planetary transformation" (Wittenberg Center, "As the Medicine Wheel Turns," http://www.wittenbergorg/medicine. html, printed 01/11/03). She runs the Center's Interfaith Seminary. Its "Core Program" emphasizes "a strong foundation in comparative religion," "earth based spirituality, intuitive training, community service and multi-leveled mastery for the twenty-first century." Readings include "The Bible, The Bhagvad Gita, The Tao Te Ching, The Koran, as well as material

• World Federalist Association.[1]

Perhaps the most far-out of the URI's adherents is the Western Federation Church and Tribe, "a Church and a Tribe of people" led by Dr. Chief Swift Eagle.[2] The Tribe has twice decreed:

The Western Federation Church and Tribe, this seventh day of August 1999, and this nineteenth day of March 2001, does hereby adopt, in full, the United Religions Initiative and Declaration of the United Nations Conference On The Human Environment as part of the Western Federation Church and Tribe's by-laws and tenets and does adopt said documents as the religious and legal foundation of Mars and of the Earth's Moon which are entirely owned by the Western Federation Church and Tribe.[3]

For the URI, the sky is indeed the limit.

Regarding New Age advocates' influence on the URI, former board member Fr. Gerard O'Rourke has said, "No one person has that kind of dominance in this organization. If our board thought that they were creating a platform for the New Age movement, they would hit the ceiling."[4] Maybe, then, the URI Global Council should now meet in a room with a padded ceiling.

When asked whether the URI could separate itself from the New Age and Theosophical organizations and leaders discussed above, Donald Frew said, "There is no way that an organization that is trying to be inclusive, like the URI, can show these people the door just because they are 'New Age.' Groups can only be expelled from the URI for violating the Preamble, Purpose, and Principles expressed in the Charter—to which each new member agrees."[5] In other words, the URI Charter is broad enough to cover these groups—and their teachings.

"As the twig is bent, so grows the tree." The strong New Age and Theosophical influence in the URI makes it likely that this movement, when mature, will be very bent indeed.

from Joseph Campbell's The Masks of God, Jung's Man and his Symbols, Starhawk's Truth or Dare, Matthew Fox's Original Blessing, and Brian Swimme's The Universe Is A Green Dragon." (Wittenberg Center, "The Center for the Living Earth: Interfaith Seminary Program," http://www.wittenbergcenter.org/seminary.html, printed 01/11/03).

1. URI, "Archive of 72 Hours Projects," project in Washington DC.

2. Western Federation Church and Tribe, "Home Page," http://www.education-1.net/tribe.htm, printed 12/17/02.

3. Ibid.; see also the Western Federation's web page "United Religions Initiative Benchmark Draft Charter (for circulation through June 1999)", http://www.education-1.net/uri.htm (printed 11/12/02)—which contains a similar declaration, followed by a full copy of the draft Charter which the URI circulated in 1998.

4. Telephone interview by Lee Penn of Fr. Gerard O'Rourke, April 24, 1998.

5. E-mail from Donald Frew to Lee Penn, 03/07/04.

6

A DIVIDED VERDICT:
THE CHURCHES AND THE URI

URI GLOBAL COUNCIL MEMBER DONALD FREW said in 2003 that "75 percent of the people in the URI are Christians. They are often not forthcoming about their denominational affiliation. They are struggling with the issue of asserting their identity, versus bending over backward to be inclusive."[1]

Notwithstanding this self-effacement on the part of liberal Christians in the URI, the movement has widespread support among mainline Protestants and liberal Catholics. The Vatican, the Eastern Orthodox, and Evangelical Protestants have not associated themselves with the URI.

THE ANGLICAN COMMUNION

MAINSTREAM ANGLICANISM

Bishop Swing has held office for 25 years, and is the longest-serving active Diocesan bishop in the Episcopal Church's current House of Bishops.[2] He has boasted, "No diocese in the country is more in sync with the National Episcopal Church than the Diocese of California. . . . We have a high doctrine of the Church as the Body of Christ, so we are good team players at every turn."[3] In 2004, Swing avowed that his diocese is loyal to him, and he is loyal to the national Episcopal Church: "Money clearly measures this unity. Each year 99% of congregational and financial assessments has been paid in full. Each year 100% of the Diocese's assessment to the National Episcopal Church has been paid in full."[4] Swing's organizational fidelity has been amply repaid. Within the Episcopal Church in the United States and within the Anglican Communion, public supporters of the URI far outnumber public opponents.[5]

The URI obtained a low-key endorsement from Episcopal Presiding Bishop Frank Griswold in mid-1999. When he visited San Francisco for the celebration of the 150th anniversary of the Episcopal

1. Interview of Donald Frew by Lee Penn, 03/28/03.

2. Episcopal News Service, *Daybook*, September 23, 2004, "Grace Cathedral Sunday Forum to Salute Bill Swing's 25 Years as Bishop," http://www.wfn.org/2004/09/msg00225. html, printed 09/28/04.

3. Bishop William E. Swing, "A Swing Through the Diocese," *Pacific Church News*, October/November 2000, p5.

4. Bishop William E. Swing, "The Swing Shift: 25 Years of the 155 Years of the Diocese of California," *Episcopal News Service*, August 9, 2004, http://www.episcopalchurch.org/3577_48075_ENG_HTM.htm, printed 08/10/04.

5. Bishop Swing nevertheless alleges widespread opposition to the URI among Anglican bishops. In early 2004, he said, "There has always been a small cadre of bishops in the Episcopal Church who have been supportive. Most bishops just think I'm nuts or an infidel or a heretic. The same thing goes with the Anglican Communion." (Dennis Delman, "Interview with Bishop William E. Swing, Founder and President of the United Religions Initiative," *Pacific Church News online*, February/March 2004, http://pcn.diocal.org/PCNO/pcn004-1/index.html, printed 02/24/04.) Whatever other bishops may tell Swing in private, *public* support for the URI among Anglican bishops far outweighs *public* opposition.

Diocese of California, Griswold said "determined farsightedness is a characteristic I particularly associate with this diocese and many of its bishops across the years ... as well as your present bishop's vision of the potential force of the world's religions to bind up and bring together, rather than divide and turn the people of the earth against one another."[1] (Griswold appears not to have spoken publicly about the URI since then.)

In addition to Bishop Swing and Presiding Bishop Frank Griswold, nineteen other Anglican bishops are avowed supporters of the URI:

- Robert M. Anderson, the retired Bishop of Minnesota, currently an Assisting Bishop in the Diocese of Los Angeles.[2]
- Frederick H. Borsch, former Bishop of the Episcopal Diocese of Los Angeles.[3]
- Joseph Jon Bruno, Bishop of the Episcopal Diocese of Los Angeles—Borsch's successor.[4]
- C. Christopher Epting, head of the Office of Ecumenical and Interfaith Relations for the Episcopal Church's national headquarters.[5]
- Celso Franco de Oliveira, Bishop of the Anglican Diocese of Rio de Janeiro.[6]
- Bishop J. Clark Grew, the retired Bishop of the Diocese of Ohio[7]—and during 2000, one of 11 members of the "Council of Advice" for the Episcopal Church's Presiding Bishop.[8]
- Michael Ingham, Bishop of the Diocese of New Westminster, in British Columbia, Canada.[9]
- Bob Gordon Jones, the retired Bishop of Wyoming.[10]
- Samir Kafity,[11] former Anglican Bishop of Jerusalem and the Middle East.

1. Dennis Delman, "Morning Prayer at Trinity, Eucharist at Grace Cathedral Open Diocese's 150th Anniversary Celebration," *Pacific Church News*, October/November 1999, p21. In the fall of 2002, Griswold did not respond to several requests made to his staff for an updated statement about the URI.

2. URI, 2003: *Compassionate Actions for a Better World*, annual report; http://www.uri.org/resources/URI_Anual_Report _2003.pdf, viewed 09/24/04; cited below as URI, *Annual Report*, 2003. Identification is from a database on Episcopal bishops at http://newark.rutgers.edu/~lcrew/bishops/0006.html (printed 09/24/04), and from his listing with Millennium-3, an organization of liberal Episcopal bishops, at "About Millennium-3," http://www.millennium3.org/WhoWeAre.html, printed 09/ 24/04.

3. United Religions Initiative, "Honoring Our Donors," *Annual Report* 2000, p8 (cited below as URI, *Annual Report* 2000) and United Religions Initiative, "Honoring Our Donors," *Annual Report* 2001, p8 (cited below as URI, *Annual Report* 2001).

4. United Religions Initiative, "Affiliates," http://www.uri.org/regionalnews/affiliates/index.asp, printed 09/23/04 (cited below as URI, "Affiliates"). Diocesan Bishop since February 2002; see http://www.ladiocese.org/BishopsOffices.htm, printed 12/15/02.

5. E-mail from Christopher Epting to Lee Penn, 11/06/02. He said, "I have been in this office for eighteen months and have made a visit to the URI office in California, have seen to it that URI has a link to our new web page ... and have invited Bill [Swing] twice to address the House of Bishops, along with me on interfaith matters." He added, "I support URI, the World Parliament of Religions, the World and US Conference of Religions for Peace (on whose Board I serve), and other national and grassroots organizations which promote such understanding and cooperation."

6. URI board member Donald Frew stated that he marched alongside de Oliveira in the URI-sponsored peace march at the URI Global Assembly in Rio de Janeiro in the summer of 2002; e-mail from Donald Frew to Lee Penn, 12/10/02. On 11/18/ 02, Frew stated in an e-mail to Lee Penn that de Oliveira "participated in some of the Global Assembly events."

7. Bishop Clark Grew, "Episcopal Address to the 1999 Diocesan Convention," http://dohio.org/convention/episcaddress.html, printed late 1999; no longer on the Net. Grew said, "I ask each parish" to participate in the URI's "72 hour Initiative for Peace over New Years, from Friday December 31 to January 2nd, 2000."

8. List of members of Council of Advice provided by Jim Solheim, press officer for ECUSA, 4/17/2000 e-mail to Lee Penn.

9. URI, *Annual Report* 2001, "Honoring Our Donors," p9.

10. URI, *Annual Report* 2000, "Honoring Our Donors," p9; identification is from a database of Episcopal bishops in the US—"Jones, Bob Gordon, Wyoming," http://newark.rutgers.edu/~lcrew/bishops/0146.html, printed 12/15/02. He and Mary Page Jones are listed as URI affiliate members in Europe (URI, "Affiliates").

11. Bishop William Swing, "The United Religions Initiative," document issued in April 1996, pp5–6 (cited below as Swing, "The United Religions Initiative, 04/96).

- Robert L. Ladehoff, the retired Bishop of the Episcopal Diocese of Oregon.[1]
- The Most Rev. Alexander Mar Thoma, the Metropolitan of the Mar Thoma Syrian Church in Kerala, India.[2]
- Richard Millard, the retired Bishop Suffragan of Europe, and assisting Bishop of California.[3]
- McLeod Barker Ochola II, the retired Bishop of the Diocese of Kitgum, in Uganda.[4] Ochola is one of the leaders of the ARPLI, a URI Cooperation Circle that is attempting to negotiate an end to the civil war in Northern Uganda.
- James Ottley,[5] who served as the Anglican Observer at the United Nations from 1995[6] through 1999, and is currently an Assisting Bishop in the Diocese of Southeast Florida.[7]
- Mano K. Rumalshah, the former Bishop of Peshawar, Pakistan.[8]
- Bennett Sims, the former Bishop of Atlanta, Georgia.[9]
- K. H. Ting,[10] who has served as Chairman of the China Christian Council (CCC), the state-approved Protestant church in China,[11] and as Chair of the Chinese Christian Three-Self Patriotic Movement.[12]

1. URI, "Honoring Our Donors," *Annual Report* 2001, p 9, and United Religions Initiative, *Annual Report* 2000, "Honoring Our Donors," p 9, and United Religions Initiative, "Honoring URI Donors and Volunteers," *Annual Report* 2002 leaflet (cited below as URI, *Annual Report* 2002).

2. Swing, "The United Religions Initiative," 04/96, pp 3–4. This church has been in communion with Canterbury since 1974. It arose as a result of a 19th Century breakaway from its parent Church, the Malankara Orthodox Syrian Church. The split occurred due to the activity of Anglican missionaries, and a resultant spread of Protestant beliefs. (See Ronald G. Roberson, CSP, *The Eastern Christian Churches: A Brief Survey*, 5th ed., 1995, Edizioni Orientalia Christiana, p 35, and Rev. Dr. T. P. Abraham, "The Mar Thoma Church—A Historical Sketch," http://www.marthomachur ch.com/articles/history-sketch.htm, printed 04/23/03.) The Metropolitan died in 2000.

3. Bishop William Swing, "A Swing Through the Diocese," *Pacific Church News online*, March 2002, http://www.diocal.org/pcn/PCNO/pcn002-3.html, printed 10/12/02; Swing said, "When I started working on the United Religions Initiative, he backed me without wavering."

4. Charles Gibbs, "Letter from Executive Director," August 2004—"URI—A Powerful Presence at the 4th Parliament of the World's Religions," http://www.uri.org/abouturi/edrreport/index.asp, printed 08/08/04.

5. Telephone interview by Lee Penn of Bishop James Ottley, April 24, 1998; also, Anglican Communion Office at the United Nations, "The Ministry of the Anglican Communion Office at the United Nations—Annual Report 1997," http://www.aco.org/united-nations/annual97.htm, printed 1998; no longer on the Net.

6. "Bishop Ottley of Panama—Anglican Observer to U.N.," *Pacific Church News*, February/March 1995, p 33.

7. "Callings," *Pacific Church News*, June/July 1999, p 14; listing for James H. Ottley, http://newark.rutgers.edu/~lcrew/bishops/0203.html, printed 04/08/03.

8. "URI Global Summit III," *URI News Update*, Fall 1998, p 5; he attended the 1998 URI summit meeting, and was among those who "formally requested that the URI establish a Forum for Indo-Pakistani Dialogue." For his church affiliation, see Anglican Communion, "Mission at the Heart of the Church," May 2002, http://www.anglicancommunion.org/mission/events/200205/finalpressrelease.html, printed 01/13/02.

9. United Religions Initiative, "Donor Dialogue: A Conversation with John Moore," *URI Update*, November 2003, Issue 14, p 5. Sims and his wife "are deeply involved in URI, and Bennett is founder of the Institute for Servant Leadership and a strong peace advocate."

10. Bishop William Swing, "Reactions from Religious Leaders: United Religions International Tour," URI document issued in the summer of 1996, p 4 (cited below as Swing, "Reactions from Religious Leaders," summer 1996).

11. Ting is China's last Anglican bishop, and no priests in China function as Anglicans. Ting says, "The mission of the church in China will be fruitless if it adopts anti-communism as our mission, especially these days;" the church does not make public statements on human rights "because we are too small. . . . And if we do such a thing it will not be good for the church in the long run." ("China's Last Anglican Bishop Sees Unclear Future for Christians," *Pacific Church News Bulletin*, April 2001, http://www.diocal.org/pcn/PCNO/pcnb4-01.html, printed 10/12/02. The *Washington Post* reports that Ting "wrote that ardent Communist Party members could go to heaven because they were good people, too"—but added that Ting "has lobbied behind the scenes" for relaxation of repressive anti-religious policies. (John Pomfret, "Evangelicals on the Rise in Land of Mao," *Washington Post*, December 24, 2002, page A01; http://www.washingtonpost.com/ac2/wp-dyn?pagename=article&node=&contentId=A31459-2002Dec23&notFound=true, printed 03/18//03.)

12. Amity News Service, "Bishop Ting Retires; New Leadership Chosen," *Pacific Church News*, April/May 1997, p 29.

- Desmond Tutu, the Nobel laureate and retired Archbishop of Cape Town, South Africa.[1]
- David Young, CBE, the former bishop of Ripon and Leeds in the UK.[2]

The Episcopal Bishops who support the URI are on the Left on other issues, as well. During the 2003 General Convention, a conservative Episcopal bishop introduced a resolution reaffirming that "Holy Scripture containeth all things necessary to salvation," and re-stating other classical Anglican statements of faith.[3] Five US bishops who support the URI voted against the resolution, as did the majority of the House of Bishops; one pro-URI bishop voted for it; one abstained.[4] None of the above-listed pro-URI American bishops voted against the confirmation of Gene Robinson, the openly gay Bishop of New Hampshire; five voted for him.[5] (Voting was limited to active Diocesan bishops, and excluded those who were retired at the time of General Convention). Frank Griswold, the Presiding Bishop for the Episcopal Church in the USA, was the chief consecrator of Robinson in November 2003; Michael Ingham, the pro-URI Bishop of the Canadian Diocese of New Westminster, also participated in the ceremony.[6]

In 2001, a group of liberal Christians formed the FaithFutures Foundation (FFF), to encourage "re-framing Christian beliefs and practice since the results of critical scholarship perhaps impact most acutely on that faith tradition at present."[7] Later on, they will take aim at other religious traditions. They say, "As resources develop and its membership expands to include significant numbers of people from other religions and spiritual traditions, the Foundation anticipates that the focus on re-visioning Christianity will become just one among several lines of activity."[8] FFF has explicitly modeled its own organization on the Cooperation Circle design of the URI,[9] and has linked its own web site to the URI.[10] One of its trustees is Peter Lawson, a retired priest from the Diocese of California. Members of the panel of advisors include Marcus Borg, John Dominic Crossan, and John Shelby Spong, the retired Bishop of the Episcopal Diocese of Newark.[11] Thus, the URI appears to have gained some admirers who are celebrities among liberal Christians—including the gadfly Bishop Spong, who has denied the Virgin Birth, the Resurrection, and the Ascension of Jesus.[12]

---

1. Bishop William E. Swing, *The Coming United Religions*, United Religions Initiative and CoNexus Press, 1998; foreword, p6.

2. United Religions Initiative UK, "People @ URI—Trustees," http://www.uri.org. uk/about/people.html, printed 02/19/03;on his posting, see "CBE for Bishop who battled with the government over church schools," http://members.aol.com/jhg-carter/press291.htm, printed 02/20/03.

3. Louie Crew, "Tallies on Resolution B001 at General Convention 2003," http://newark.rutgers.edu/~lcrew/03_b001.html, printed 09/06/03; includes the text of the resolution.

4. Ibid. Voting for the resolution: Epting. Abstaining: Borsch. Voting against the resolution: Bruno, Grew, Ladehoff, Ottley, Swing.

5. Louie Crew, "Vote on Blessings (C051) and Consent to a Gay Bishop (C045) at GC 2003," http://newark.rutgers.edu/~lcrew/2003_c045.html, printed 08/16/03. Bishops who voted for Robinson were Bruno, Grew, Griswold, Ladehoff, and Swing.

6. American Anglican Council, "'Official' List of Bishops Participating in Gene Robinson's Consecration," January 6, 2004, http://www.americananglican.org/News/News.cfm? ID=927&c=21, printed 06/04/04. This list was as issued by the Episcopal News Service. Aside from Griswold and Ingham, no other pro-URI bishops appeared on this list.

7. Faith Futures Foundation, "A World of Many Faiths," http://www.faithfutures.org/multifaith.html, printed 06/04/04 (cited below as FFF, "A World of Many Faiths").

8. Ibid.

9. Faith Futures Foundation, *FFF Update* #1, June 2001, http://www.faithfutures. org/Newsletter/fffu062001.pdf, pp1–2, printed 06/04/04.

10. FFF, "A World of Many Faiths."

11. Faith Futures Foundation, "Leadership," http://www.faithfutures.org/Members/trustees.html, printed 06/04/04.

12. Bishop John S. Spong, "A Call for a New Reformation," http://www.dioceseofnewark.org/vox20598.html, Theses 4, 7, and 8, printed 06/19/04.

Episcopal dioceses that have acted in support of the URI include Central Gulf Coast[1] and Western Massachusetts,[2] which have donated to the URI. In 1999, the Diocese of Los Angeles passed a pro-URI resolution at its Diocesan Convention.[3] More recently, members of the diocesan "Commission on Ecumenical and Interreligious Ministries" have participated in the URI in Washington DC.[4] In 2003, the Episcopal Peace and Justice Commission of Oklahoma donated to the URI.[5]

The worldwide body of 800 Anglican bishops, meeting at the Lambeth Conference in Canterbury, England in July and August 1998, unanimously endorsed a URI call for a global religious cease-fire for December 31, 1999 to January 2, 2000.[6] The Lambeth resolution matched the text that the URI had adopted at its 1998 global conference, stating that the 72-hour cease-fire "will allow the world to end the old age in peace, and to begin the new millennium in the spirit of reconciliation, healing and peacemaking."[7] A report associated with the Lambeth resolution named the URI as the coordinator of the cease-fire project.[8] Bishop Swing introduced the resolution, and the North American and Caribbean bishops unanimously placed the cease-fire call in a package of non-controversial "agreed resolutions." The entire Conference then adopted all the "agreed resolutions" without debate on the last day of the meeting.[9] The URI has since used this endorsement as evidence of its own global influence.[10] In other respects—such as sexual morality and interpretation of Scripture—the 1998 Lambeth Conference upheld traditional Christian teaching. How many of the Lambeth bishops knew that they had supported a millennial call to "end the old age in peace"?[11]

The leading Anglican primate, Archbishop George Carey of Canterbury, did not speak publicly about the URI at any time after its unveiling in 1995. Rowan Williams, who was selected in 2002 as Carey's successor, has been similarly silent.[12] (Both, however, have participated in other, less

1. URI, *Annual Report 2001*, "Honoring Our Donors," p 8.

2. Ibid.

3. The 1999 diocesan convention adopted a resolution to "support the efforts of the United Religions Initiative in promoting the '72 Hours Project,' and encourage all parishes and missions in the Diocese to consider ways in which they might participate in this program." (Episcopal Diocese of Los Angeles, "Diocesan Convention 1999: Resolutions Adopted from Diocesan Convention," http://www.ladiocese.org/resolutions.html, printed late 1999; no longer on the Net).

4. Episcopal Diocese of Washington, "Annual Report (2003) of the Commission on Ecumenical and Interfaith Ministries," http://www.edow.org/diocese/governance/committees/comm_ecumenical.html, printed 06/04/04. The bishop of this Diocese is John B. Chane.

5. URI, *Annual Report 2003*.

6. "Lambeth Bishops Join Global Cease Fire," *Pacific Church News*, October/November 1998, p 31 (cited below as "Lambeth Bishops Join Global Cease Fire," *PCN*, Oct./Nov. 1998).

7. Ibid.

8. August 6, 1998 e-mail from Doug LeBlanc, a journalist for Episcopalians United, who was covering the Lambeth Conference on-site in 1998.

9. August 6, 1998 and August 8, 1998 e-mails from Doug LeBlanc.

10. *URI News Update*, "URI in the world," Fall 1998, p 6; "Lambeth Bishops Join Global Cease Fire," *PCN*, Oct./Nov. 1998, p 31; Paul Andrews, "URI 72 Hours Project: To End One Millennium & Begin Another With a World At Peace," *Pacific Church News*, February/March 1999, p 26; Dennis Delman, "Peace Projects Proliferate for 72 Hours at the Millennium," *Pacific Church News*, June/July 1999, p 21 (cited below as Delman, "Peace Projects Proliferate," *PCN*, June/July 1999).

11. Dr. Peter Toon, an Anglican priest who is a seasoned observer of these events, stated in 1999 that most Lambeth resolutions are adopted with little scrutiny or debate. In a September 18, 1999 e-mail to Lee Penn, he said, "Unless there is a topic that is debated what happens is a few activists write a paper and the group endorses it (usually with little or no careful reading) and then it gets into the full report of Lambeth and from it a resolution is passed, usually without any opposition. Most subjects therefore are not examined carefully and people who know the ropes there do not take the vast majority of Lambeth resolutions seriously. What is described here is a case in point. . . thus the only influence that can be shown is on the actual writers of the section report—perhaps two or three at the most. . . . most people including bishops are in the activist mood and simply go with the flow unless it is too painful or difficult."

12. Based on a Google search by Lee Penn, October 4 2002 and February 11 2003, on Rowan Williams and the URI.

controversial interfaith activities.) However, the Church of England newspaper criticized the URI in October 1999 and July 2001.[1]

At the General Conventions of the Episcopal Church in the US in 1997, 2000, and 2003, there were no resolutions, favorable or negative, about the URI. No press reports on these three Episcopal Conventions indicated that either the URI or Bishop Swing suffered any public criticism from Episcopal participants.[2]

In the October 2001 *Pacific Church News*, Swing wrote that he saw a positive change in the attitude of the Episcopal Church's House of Bishops, who met in Burlington, Vermont a week after the 9/11 attack. "The profound change that took place at this meeting was the full arrival of interfaith awareness. . . . For the first time in the history of the Episcopal Church, we have an interfaith officer, Bishop Christopher Epting, working daily at the national office. By popular request, I was asked to teach a class on the work of the United Religions Initiative. Last year I volunteered for the same task, but not one bishop showed up."[3]

Current and former Episcopal cathedral deans and rectors who publicly approve of the URI include:

- Sanford Garner, former Dean of the Episcopal National Cathedral in Washington DC.[4]
- Alan Jones, current Dean of Grace Cathedral in San Francisco.[5]
- James Parks Morton, former Dean of the Cathedral of St. John the Divine in New York City.[6] (He donated to the URI in 2003.)[7]
- H. Lawrence Whittemore Jr.,[8] the Dean Emeritus of the Cathedral Church of the Nativity in the Episcopal Diocese of Bethlehem, Pennsylvania.[9]

Numerous Episcopal parishes across the country have also supported the URI—including Trinity Cathedral Church, in Sacramento, California.[10] In October 2003, the Church Divinity School of the Pacific, an Episcopal seminary in Berkeley California, gave URI Executive Director Charles Gibbs an honorary doctorate to acclaim him for his URI work; Bishop Swing presented the award to Gibbs.[11]

1. The Church of England Newspaper, "Editorial," October 21, 1999, http://www.churchnewspaper.com/edit.htm, printed in 1999, no longer on the Net; Andrew Carey, "Behind the Spin: The creeping influence of the United Religions Initiative," http://www.churchnewspaper.com/feat1.htm, printed 7/20/01; no longer on the Net. Andrew Carey is the son of George Carey, the former Archbishop of Canterbury.

2. Analysis based on eyewitness reports from Episcopal journalists who attended these conventions.

3. Bishop William Swing, "A Swing Through the Diocese," *Pacific Church News*, October/November 2001, p5.

4. URI, *Annual Report* 2001, "Honoring Our Donors," p8. In addition to donating to the URI in 2001, in 2002 Garner accepted an award on behalf of Bishop Swing from a group established by the Rev. Sun Myung Moon—as shown in chapter 5 of this book.

5. URI, *Annual Report* 2000, "Honoring Our Donors," p9.

6. Morton also has been President of the Temple of Understanding from 1985 to 1997, and founder and president of the Interfaith Center of New York since then. Both organizations have been members of the URI, and Morton states that he has been active in the URI "since the URI's beginning as a 'member.'" (E-mail from Morton to Lee Penn, 11/07/02).

7. URI, *Annual Report* 2003.

8. URI, *Annual Report* 2000, "Honoring Our Donors," p10, and URI, *Annual Report* 2001, "Honoring Our Donors," p10 and URI, Annual Report 2003.

9. Cathedral Church of the Nativity, "Church Staff," http://www.nativitycathedral.org/ChurchStaff.htm, printed 12/13/02.

10. URI, *Annual Report* 2001, "Honoring Our Donors," p8 for Trinity Cathedral's donation. The URI annual reports for all years, 2000–2003, list other ECUSA parishes as donors to the URI.

11. United Religions Initiative, "Resources," *URI Update*, November 2003, Issue 14, p7.

One Anglican bishop—Archbishop Harry Goodhew, of Australia, who retired in 2001—publicly criticized the URI in 2000;[1] the retired Bishop of South Carolina, FitzSimons Allison, did the same.[2] No other Anglican Bishop in communion with Canterbury has stood publicly against the URI and Bishop Swing.

Bishop Charles Murphy, consecrated for the "Anglican Mission in America" in 2000 in Singapore by two conservative Anglican Archbishops, has denounced the URI as part of the "crisis of faith"[3] in the Episcopal Church in the US. However, George Carey (then serving as the Archbishop of Canterbury) never recognized Murphy as a bishop, denouncing the Singapore consecration as "irresponsible and irregular."[4]

Some Evangelical activists in the Episcopal Church have publicly denounced the URI, including David Anderson, of the American Anglican Council.[5] However, such activism on this matter is the exception rather than the rule. By 2000, it had become clear that many of the conservative Episcopal laity did not want to know what is happening with regard to the URI, and had become fatalistic if they did know. As one member of a large, conservative Anglican mailing list said regarding stories about the URI: "I would prefer you not send any more of this stuff to me.... [We] ... can't even keep our parish together ... There are many more wolves closer to the sled. What Swing does is also seen by God, and He will judge. If URI is the instrument by which the Revelation come true [sic], I say, Come Lord Jesus!"[6]

NEW AGE ANGLICANISM

Several prominent New Age Episcopalians—Matthew Fox, Lauren Artress (the popularizer of the present-day Labyrinth movement), and James Parks Morton (the former dean of the Cathedral of St. John the Divine in New York City)—are public supporters of the URI. With the public activities of Artress and Fox, the New Age movement has a strong, public presence in Bishop Swing's diocese and at his cathedral.

Lauren Artress and the Labyrinth Movement

Grace Cathedral is the center of the modern-day Labyrinth-walking fad that has spread through New Age workshops, mainline Protestant churches, and Roman Catholic retreat centers and convents. Bishop Swing's Cathedral has two labyrinths. One, a large rug with the labyrinth design, is inside the cathedral, near the baptismal font. The other, made of terrazzo stone and open 24 hours a day, is on

1. Archbishop Harry Goodhew, "The cross of Christ in a pluralistic world," *Southern Cross Online*, April 2000, http://www.anglicanmedia.com.au/old/april2000/abwrites.html, printed 02/19/03.

2. "A letter from +FitzSimons Allison, Retired Bishop of South Carolina," as received by e-mail from David Virtue, 03/20/2000.

3. Bishop Charles Murphy, statement to *The Living Church*, February 13–20, 2000, interviewed by Patricia Nakamura, as received by e-mail from David Virtue, 03/20/00.

4. Kathryn McCormick and James Solheim, "Singapore consecration provokes strong response throughout the church," *Episcopal News Service*, February 18, 2000, http://www. episcopalchurch.org/ens/2000-030xD.html, printed 04/08/03.

5. Concerned Episcopalians of St. Lawrence Deanery, "American Anglican Council Meeting Summary," November 24, 2003, http://www.cesld.org/aacmeeting.html, printed 03/05/04. According to this report from a liberal group that supports the current leadership of ECUSA, Anderson told an AAC meeting in Atlanta, "the same Bishops who supported Bishop Swing's United Religions Initiative were the ones who supported Bishop Robinson's confirmation. He condemned the United Religions Initiative as akin to polytheism. And stated that Jesus is not 'A way, a truth, and a life. He is the way, the truth, and the life.'"

6. E-mail forwarded from Fr. Kim to Lee Penn, 4/17/2000.

an outdoor plaza between the cathedral and the Diocesan office. The leader of the Labyrinth movement is Lauren Artress, an Episcopal priest. She runs Veriditas,[1] an organization that now calls itself "The Voice of the Labyrinth Movement."[2]

Artress, Canon for Special Ministries at Grace Cathedral,[3] says that she first encountered the Labyrinth in January 1991, when she decided to "return to a Mystery School seminar with Dr. Jean Houston, an internationally known psychologist, author, and scholar whom I studied with in 1985."[4] (In the 1990s, Houston was best known to the public as the "guru" who helped Hillary Clinton contact the spirit of Eleanor Roosevelt.[5] In 1966, Houston and her husband Robert Masters had published *The Varieties of Psychedelic Experience*, a book that hailed the "transformative effects" of properly guided use of psychedelic drugs.[6]) Artress says, "as soon as I set foot into the labyrinth I was overcome with an almost violent anxiety;" the next morning, she "awoke, distressed from a dream of having a heart attack."[7] Nevertheless, she has devoted herself since then to spreading the labyrinth walk as a "spiritual tool"[8] for all faiths.

Labyrinths were built into some medieval Cathedrals in Western Europe before 1500, but no documentation survives to show how, or whether, Catholics used labyrinths as part of their public liturgies or private devotions.[9] After 1500, most labyrinths were removed from cathedral floors; many were destroyed during the French Revolution.[10] The Chartres labyrinth is one of the few that has survived from the Middle Ages to the present day. The Chartres labyrinth went unused—and was usually covered with chairs for worshippers—until Artress began taking pilgrims to the site in the 1990s. Those

---

1. Lauren Artress, "The Birth of Veriditas," *Veriditas*, Winter 1996, Vol. 1, No. 1, p1. According to Artress, this word—spelled viriditas in classical Latin—means "springtime;" "Hildegard of Bingen adapted it to mean *greening power*. In her generous cosmic theology Hildegard defined the Holy Spirit as the *greening power of God*."

2. Grace Cathedral, "Veriditas," http://www.gracecathedral.org/labyrinth/, printed 06/01/04; see also Veriditas, "Veriditas: The Voice of the Labyrinth Movement," http://www.veriditas.net/, printed 06/01/04.

3. http://www.gracecathedral.org/labyrinth/index.shtml, printed 02/08/03.

4. Lauren Artress, *Walking a Sacred Path: Rediscovering the Labyrinth as a Sacred Tool*, Riverhead Books, 1995, pp1–2. (cited below as Artress, *Walking a Sacred Path*).

5. For more information on Jean Houston, see Craig Branch, "Jean Houston: Profile of the New-Age Advisor to Hillary Clinton," *Journal* of the Spiritual Counterfeits Project, Vol. 22:2–22:3, 1998, pp64–69, available through http://www.scp-inc.org.

6. J. Gordon Melton, Jerome Clark, and Aidan A. Kelly, *New Age Almanac*, Visible Ink Press, 1991, pp408–409.

7. Lauren Artress, *Walking a Sacred Path*, p2.

8. Lauren Artress, "Q and A with Lauren," *Veriditas*, Vol. 1, no. 2, Summer 1996, p18.

9. This historical background is from Mark Tooley, "Maze Craze: Labyrinths Latest Fad for Spiritual Seekers," *Touchstone Magazine*, September 2000, http://www.touchstonemag. com/docs/issues/13.7docs/13-7pg46.html, printed 06/02/04. A 1922 reference book on the history of mazes and labyrinths takes a similarly skeptical view: "It has often been asserted, though on what evidence is not clear, that the larger examples [of labyrinths in churches] were used for the performance of miniature pilgrimages in substitution for the long and tedious journeys formerly laid upon penitents. . . . Whether such practices ever obtained or not, most writers who have had occasion to mention church labyrinths during the last century have adopted, more or less without question, the view that not only were the labyrinths used in this way, but that they were in fact designed for this purpose" (W. H. Matthews, *Mazes and Labyrinths: Their History and Development*, Dover Publications, 1970 reprint of 1922 ed., p67; cited below as Matthews). After describing various conjectures about how labyrinths were used in medieval and ancien régime churches, Matthews said, "It is strange if, amongst all the great mass of medieval ecclesiastical literature, there is actually no indication of the use or significance of these monuments in the service of the Church; but no light appears to be forthcoming from this source, and certainly the writings of the chief authorities of these times give no support to any of the theories mentioned above. It is noteworthy that in none of the known examples [of church labyrinths] do any distinctively Christian images occur, and that, amongst all the myriad inscriptions, paintings, and carvings of the early Christians, in the catacombs of Rome and elsewhere, the labyrinth never once figures." (Matthews, ibid., p69) Matthews' comment about the absence of labyrinths from early Christian art and symbolism is a telling one, since the labyrinth symbol was well-known in the classical world.

10. Matthews, ibid., pp58 and 62.

who resurrect the Labyrinth now are making up a new religious tradition in ancient costume, as the Neopagans have done since World War II and as the Freemasons did after 1717.

The labyrinth movement has long been intertwined with the URI. Barbara Hartford, a URI staff member in San Francisco,[1] accompanied Artress on her first visit to the labyrinth at Chartres Cathedral in the early 1990s.[2] Artress acknowledged URI staffer Sally Ackerly[3] as one of those who provided "help in launching the labyrinth."[4] Since 1995, labyrinth walks have been common at URI events—from many of the URI-sponsored "religious cease fire" events held at the time of Y2K,[5] to the URI Global Assembly in Rio de Janeiro in the summer of 2002.[6]

As promoted by Artress, the Labyrinth movement is New Age in form and content.[7] In *Walking a Sacred Path*, her foundational book on the movement, Artress says, "The labyrinth introduces us to the idea of a wide and gracious path. It redefines the journey to God: from a vertical perspective that goes from earth up to heaven to a horizontal perspective in which we are all walking the path together."[8] "When I am in the center of the labyrinth . . . I pause to honor and bring into my being first the mineral consciousness, then the vegetable, then animal, human, and angelic. Finally I come to rest in the consciousness of the Unknown, which is the mystery, the divine pattern of evolution that is unfolding."[9] "When walking the labyrinth, you can feel that powerful energies have been set in motion. The labyrinth functions like a spiral, creating a vortex in its center."[10]

With Artress' New Age cosmology comes unorthodox theology. "The labyrinth is a large, complex spiral circle which is an ancient symbol for the Divine Mother, the God within, the Goddess, the Holy in all of creation. Matriarchal spirituality celebrates the hidden and the unseen. . . . For many of us the feminine aspect of the Divine has been painfully absent from our lives, our spirituality, and our Western culture. The Divine feminine is often the missing piece for which both women and men are searching."[11] "This Yahweh is supposed to have been the God that created all of the natural order, usurping the role of the Mother, the creator of life. Yahweh, God the Father, is the only version of the Transcendent God that is offered in Western Christianity. He is seen as the first cause of all things, the God of history. He is a faraway God whom we do not know personally. He does not seem to want to

1. United Religions Initiative, "URI Staff," *URI Update*, December 2002, p8.

2. Artress, *Walking a Sacred Path*, p4.

3. Ackerly was listed as a project manager for URI in a URI leaflet dated 9/15/98. As Sally Mahé, she is co-author of a new book on the URI (Charles Gibbs and Sally Mahé, *United Religions Initiative, Birth of a Global Community: Appreciative Inquiry in Action*, Lakeshore Publishers, 2004; cited below as Gibbs/Mahé, *Birth of Global Community*).

4. Artress, *Walking a Sacred Path*, p198; 13 people, including Ackerly, were acknowledged for this assistance.

5. United Religions Initiative, "72 Hours Global Action," *URI Update*, Spring 2000, p13—photo of labyrinth walk as part of the "72 Hours." Labyrinth walks in occurred as part of the 72 hours observance at Villa Maria Pennsylvania, Erie Pennsylvania, Pittsburgh Pennsylvania, Cleveland Ohio, Seattle Washington, and San Francisco California. (United Religions Initiative, "Archive of 72 Hours Projects—Geographical Listing," http://www.united-religions.org/newsite/72hours/projects.htm, printed 6/22/00; no longer on the Net; cited below as URI, "Archive of 72 Hours Projects"). The Labyrinth Project described its "Global New Year's Eve Gathering" as "Grace Cathedral's contribution to the United Religions Initiative for the 72 hour interfaith peace building project." ("The Global New Year's Eve Gathering: Symphony of Souls 2000," *Source: A Veritidas Publication*, Fall 1999, p7.)

6. "Sharing Wisdom" (photographs of 2002 URI Global Assembly), *Pacific Church News*, Winter 2003, p30; the large background photo shows a conference participant walking a Labyrinth at the URI meeting.

7. Labyrinths were built into the floors of some European cathedrals during the Middle Ages; most of these were removed after 1500—with the noteworthy exception of the labyrinth at Chartres. There is little or no surviving documentation on how the Church used and understood the medieval labyrinths. Thus, the modern-day re-discoverers of this devotional tool have been free to assign their own meaning to this symbol.

8. Artress, *Walking a Sacred Path*, p43.

9. Ibid., p60.

10. Ibid., p67.

11. Ibid., p67.

know us, either."[1] "The Virgin Mary represents the collective images of the feminine aspect of divinity."[2] "In my mind there is no doubt that the Holy Spirit captures the essence of the feminine side of God. It is the cosmic oneness, the receptive part of the Godhead that allows and understands the flow of our lives."[3] "May we lead a spiritual revolution that includes us all, relies on inner wisdom, accepts the guidance of a wisdom tradition, and recognizes compassion as its guiding principle. Let us allow the Father and Mother God to unite in sacred mystery. Let us build a world community in which all people have the opportunity to create meaning in their own lives."[4]

The literature produced by Veriditas since 1995 is as heterodox as Artress' book.[5] The project's publications assiduously avoid providing the specific Christian content that anyone could get from the Lord's Prayer, the Creed, the Rosary, the Stations of the Cross (a Catholic walking meditation on the Passion of Our Lord), or the Jesus Prayer. Some forms of labyrinth spirituality are supposedly based on a devotion to the Virgin Mary—not, however, as the type of the human soul in perfect receptivity to God's will, but as a goddess in her own right, whose worshippers invoke her for "the transformation of society and the preservation of the planet."[6]

In the Labyrinth Project newsletters published in between 1996 and 2001, there is no mention of the Trinity, the Crucifixion, the Resurrection, the Empty Tomb, God the Father, or God as Lord and King. The words—and the concepts—of sin, divine judgment, heaven, hell, repentance, redemption, and salvation are likewise absent. The Project's newsletters rarely mentioned Jesus.

This is no accident; the mission of Veriditas is *not* to promote a specifically Christian use of the labyrinth. Instead, as Artress said in 1995, "the labyrinth is a universal devotional tool. Anyone from any faith can walk it and find refreshment for the soul and renewal of spirit."[7] In 1996, Artress proposed weekend Labyrinth retreats as a way for "all to find healing, self-knowledge and our soul assignments and to continue weaving the Web of Creation."[8] She added that the Labyrinth is "a perfect spiritual tool for helping our global community to order chaos in ways that take us to the vibrant center of our being. You walk to the center of the labyrinth and there at the center you meet the Divine."[9] In 2000, Artress wrote of the effects of this tool: "I'm surprised by how perfect the labyrinth is for our times. It provides a fluid pattern that allows the structure between body, mind and spirit to break down. That is a tremendous offering at this time, because we are so divided in this world. The fact that people who walk the labyrinth can loosen their strictures and soften their boundaries is truly amazing."[10]

This all-purpose spiritual tool has the approval of the highest authorities in the Episcopal Church. In 1999, 2000, and 2001, Phoebe Griswold—the wife of the Presiding Bishop of the Episcopal Church in the USA—led Labyrinth pilgrimages to Chartres Cathedral, under the auspices of the Labyrinth Project;[11] she also published an article on the labyrinth of Chartres in the Winter 2001 issue of

1. Ibid., p67.
2. Ibid., p120.
3. Ibid., p161.
4. Ibid., p161.
5. Based on an analysis by Lee Penn of the content of Labyrinth Project newsletters published in 1996–2001.
6. Grace Cathedral, "Walking a Sacred Path™ 2004," session offered from June 7–13 by Andrew Harvey, *A Celebration of Mary: The Return of the Mother Archetype*, http://www.gracecathedral.org/labyrinth/events/wasp/cycles.shtml#cycle1, printed 03/08/04.
7. Lauren Artress, "The New Outdoor Labyrinth," *Grace Cathedral Magazine*, Spring 1995, pp6, 10.
8. Lauren Artress, "The Launching of the Labyrinth Network: Restoring the Web of Creation," *Veriditas*, Vol. 1, no. 2, Summer 1996, p1.
9. Lauren Artress, "Q and A with Lauren," *Veriditas*, Vol. 1, no. 2, Summer 1996, p18.
10. California Institute for Integral Studies, "*Sage Perspectives*: Lauren Artress," INNEReye ONLINE, August 24, 2000, http://www.ciis.edu/innereye/innereye082400.html, printed 10/18/01.
11. "Phoebe W. Griswold," http://buffalolore.buffalonet.org/taskforce/phoebe.htm, printed 05/08/03.

Anglican Theological Review.[1] As of 2001, thirteen Episcopal cathedrals had labyrinths, "including St. John the Divine in New York, National Cathedral in Washington and St. Mark's in Seattle."[2] There were Labyrinths at the Episcopal General Conventions in 2000 and 2003.[3]

Artress has long had other prestigious supporters. In 1987, she had founded "Quest: Grace Cathedral Center for Spiritual Wholeness;" this program was funded by Laurance S. Rockefeller's Fund for the Enhancement of the Human Spirit.[4] (Artress' project was only one of Rockefeller's New Age interests. He also funded research into crop circles (patterns in open fields supposedly created by space aliens),[5] Matthew Fox,[6] Grace Cathedral,[7] and Barbara Marx Hubbard. In turn, Barbara Marx Hubbard described Rockefeller as her "beloved patron,"[8] and said that Rockefeller's "intuition about 'the Christ of the 21st Century' deeply inspired me."[9])

The Labyrinth movement has gained many followers outside the Episcopal Church, as well. In early 2003, the *San Francisco Chronicle* reported, "Millions of people have walked 1,800 labyrinths around the country, with 1,100 people trained specifically to teach others how to walk them. Dozens of labyrinths have been built in the Bay Area."[10] For six years, Artress has been leading Labyrinth workshops at the Catholic cathedral of Chartres.[11]

Whether they know it or not, these who walk the Labyrinth under the tutelage of Artress and her colleagues are being led away from the Holy Trinity, and toward an alternative spirituality.

James Parks Morton and the Cathedral of St. John the Divine

Another New Age Anglican supporter of the URI is the Very Rev. James Parks Morton, formerly the Dean of the Episcopal Cathedral of St. John the Divine in New York City, and now President of the Interfaith Center of New York.[12]

1. Phoebe Griswold, "The Labyrinth of Chartres," *Anglican Theological Review*, Winter 2001, Vol. LXXXIII, no. 1; Lauren Artress provided an introduction to this story. (The journal table of contents was on-line at http://www.swts.nwu.edu/atr/wn01_issue.htm, printed 03/07/02; no longer on the Net at this address. As of 2004, this page is available at http://web.archive.org/web/20010629211940/http://www.swts.nwu.edu/atr/wn01_issue.htm.)

2. Don Lattin, "Leader of labyrinth movement builds new empire upon sand," *San Francisco Chronicle*, May 13, 2001, page B-8; downloaded from http://www.sfgate.com on 05/13/01.

3. For the 2003 Convention: E-mail from David Virtue to Auburn Traycik, August 1, 2003; Virtue was a journalist covering the convention on-site. For the 2000 Convention: Episcopal News Service photo of the Labyrinth at the Convention, as printed in *The Christian Challenge*, July-September 2003, p 28.

4. Veriditas, "Veriditas Staff: The Reverend Dr. Lauren Artress," http://www.veriditas.net/about/staff.html, printed 06/01/04.

5. Peter Carlson, "Fertile Imaginations: The Real Story of Those Mysterious Circles Runs Rings Around the Movie," *Washington Post*, Saturday, August 10, 2002, page C01.

6. Matthew Fox, *The Coming of the Cosmic Christ: The Healing of Mother Earth and the Birth of a Global Renaissance*, Harper San Francisco, 1988, p xi.

7. Donor list, *Grace Cathedral Magazine*, Spring 1995, p 9; covers donations made to the Cathedral capital campaign as of March 1, 1995; Rockefeller donated at least $10,000, according to this listing.

8. Barbara Marx Hubbard, *Conscious Evolution: Awakening the Power of Our Social Potential*, New World Library, Novato, California, 1998, p viii.

9. Barbara Marx Hubbard, *The Revelation: A Message of Hope for the New Millennium*, Nataraj Publishing, Novato, CA, 1995, p 350.

10. Heather Knight, "The peaceful path: In troubled times, more people turn to labyrinths to walk their worries away," *San Francisco Chronicle*, Feb. 28, 2003, page E-6.

11. Grace Cathedral, "Walking a Sacred Path™ 2004," "Faculty Bios—Lauren Artress," http://www.gracecathedral.org/labyrinth/events/wasp/cycles.shtml#cycle3, printed 06/01/04.

12. The Interfaith Center of New York, "Administration," http://www.interfaithcenter.org/contact.shtml, printed 05/06/03. Morton states that he has been active in the URI "since the URI's beginning as a 'member'" (e-mail from Morton to Lee Penn, 11/07/02).

While at St. John the Divine, Morton said, "The language of the 'Sacred Earth' has got to become mainline."[1] He acted on this belief by holding a St. Francis Day communion service in 1993 that invoked the gods Yemanja, Ra, Ausar, and Obatala during a chant just before the bread and wine were brought to the altar for consecration; the celebrant was Richard Grein, then incumbent as the Episcopal Bishop of New York.[2] (Yemanja is an Afro-Brazilian goddess of the sea;[3] Ra is the Egyptian sun god;[4] Ausar, also known as Osiris, is the Egyptian god of the dead, as well as a symbol of resurrection and eternal life;[5] Obatalá is a Yoruba Nigerian deity who is the patron saint of deformed people.[6])

The Cathedral's syncretism still has the approval of the local Episcopal bishop. In 2002, a group of Episcopalians from an Evangelical-oriented parish in South Carolina visited the Cathedral of St. John the Divine after doing some ministry at Ground Zero in New York City. The visitors

found expressions of various religious groups, including a Shinto altar. Many in our group felt a spiritual oppression in the place, so they left the Cathedral and had prayers on the bus. When Al Zadig, our clergy leader for the group, wrote to the Bishop of New York to comment on the Cathedral's mixed religious message, he got back a scathing letter saying, specifically, that the problem in the Episcopal Church was narrow-minded people like those in our group who couldn't appreciate all the wonderful ways to God.[7]

It was from the pulpit of Morton's cathedral in 1979 that James Lovelock first publicly announced the Gaia Hypothesis—that the earth as a whole is a living, conscious organism.[8]

Morton has worked to spread the Green gospel worldwide; he "co-founded the National Religious Partnership for the Environment, a group that has reached over 53,000 congregations of every faith across America with the ideas of sacred ecology and environmental responsibility."[9] He has also been a board member of the Earth Charter Project[10] and of Global Green, USA[11]—the US affiliate of

1. Alan AtKisson, "The Green Cathedral: An Interview with the Rev. James Parks Morton," IN CONTEXT #24, http://www.context.org/ICLIB/IC24/Morton.htm, printed 04/08/03 (cited below as AtKisson, "Interview with James Parks Morton").

2. Terry Mattingly, "Liturgical Dances With Wolves (1993): Ten Years As An Episcopalian—A Progress Report," http://tmatt.gospelcom.net/tmatt/freelance/wolves. htm, printed 04/08/03. Mattingly quoted the printed worship booklet for "Liturgy and Sermon, Earth Mass—Missa Gaia," distributed on October 3, 1993, at the Cathedral of St. John the Divine.

3. "Yemanja," http://www.wigmag.com/culture/stories-yemanja.html. This document was printed in 1998, and is no longer on the Net. See also "Tribute: In Honor of: Yemanja—Queen of the Oceans," http://www.geocities.com/Athens/6415/yemanja.html, printed 03/03/04.

4. "Ra," http://www.radiant.org/bubastis/deity/ra.html. This document, printed in 1998, is no longer on the Net. The Microsoft® Encarta® Reference Library 2003 states that "Ra or Re, in ancient Egyptian mythology" is a "sun god depicted with a human body and the head of a hawk. Ra was usually considered the creator and controller of the universe, his chief symbols being the sun disk and the obelisk."

5. "Ausar (Osiris) King of the Dead," http://www.africawithin.com/kmt/osiris.html, printed 03/03/04. This document describes Ausar's attributes thus: "Supreme god and judge of the dead. The symbol of resurrection and eternal life. Provider of fertility and prosperity to the living."

6. According to the Microsoft® Encarta® Reference Library 2003, Obatalá "had a role in creating the world, but drank too much palm wine, became drunk, and began making deformed people. All those with deformities are sacred to Oxalá [an alternate spelling for Obatalá], and his initiates do not drink alcohol or wear dark-colored clothing." See also "Obatala," http://www.pantheon.org/areas/mythology/africa/african/articles.html?/article s/o/obatala.html, printed 03/03/04.

7. The Rev. Richard I. H. Belser (Rector, St. Michael's Church, Charleston SC), "A Sermon," July 13, 2003, http://www.stmichaelschurch.net/BestandWorst.html, printed 07/30/03.

8. AtKisson, "Interview with James Parks Morton."

9. Temple of Understanding bulletin, "The First Annual Juliet Hollister Awards," December 16, 1996, United Nations, NYC.

10. Interfaith Center of New York, "Bio: The Very Reverend James Parks Morton," http://www.interfaithcenter.org/JPM-Bio.html, printed in 1998; no longer on the Net at this address. As of 2004, a copy of this web page is at http://web.archive.org/web/199910212 24340/http://www.interfaithcenter.org/JPMBio.html (cited below as "Bio of James Parks Morton").

11. Global Green USA, "About Global Green—Global Green Board of Directors," http://www.globalgreen.org/about/staff_board.html, printed 05/06/03.

Gorbachev's Green Cross International.[1] Morton was a co-chair of the Parliamentary Earth Summit, held in 1992 in conjunction with the UN Conference on Environment and Development, and of the "Wisdom Keepers II" conference, held in conjunction with the 1996 UN Conference on World Settlement.[2]

Matthew Fox and the "Techno Cosmic Mass"

Matthew Fox, a former Dominican priest who was received as an Episcopal priest by Bishop Swing in December 1994,[3] supports the URI. In an essay published in 2000, he wrote, "The work of the United Religions movement, begun by Bishop William Swing of California, is a living example of this quest for deep ecumenism, reaching into an effort to reconnect faith traditions that have been abysmally narrow and particularized for too long."[4] Fox says that Vatican opposition to the URI is an instance of anti-ecumenical envy.[5]

Fox has enjoyed unswerving support from Bishop Swing. In 1995, Swing told the Diocesan Convention, "this year Matthew Fox and I are gathering an ecumenical group to create an alternative liturgy for young adults."[6] Then, Swing lent $85,000 of Diocesan funds to help Fox establish the University of Creation Spirituality,[7] and he joined former Gov. Jerry Brown in dedicating the new university in August 1996.[8] In November 2003, Matthew Fox said that the school's Doctor of Ministry program has had "over 400" students since its inception.[9]

At the 1997 Diocesan Convention, Bishop Swing praised Fox's "total exploration of the power of God in the goodness of creation" at the University of Creation Spirituality, adding that "The experiment is worthwhile and aims at tomorrow and forever."[10] In his speech to the Diocesan Convention in 2000, Swing cited Fox's ventures as an example of God's Jubilee: "Matthew Fox starting a University of Creation Spirituality and buying a city block of downtown Oakland. Outrageous! . . . but Jubilee."[11]

Fox leads syncretic worship services that are consistent with the ideology of the URI. He says,

The Techno Cosmic Mass (TCM) has been up and running for five years in Oakland. . . . By altering the form of worship through taking in the elements of rave celebrations three things happen: First, new life flows through the ancient liturgical formulas and second, ravers are relieved of the drug aspect of raves and learn they can get high on worship itself. Third, the priesthood is not projected so exclusively onto a single minister but everyone participates in midwifing the grace of the event (no vicarious prayer!). Because everyone dances, everyone offers the priestly sacrifice. . . . Themes for the Mass, which attracts not only many kinds of Christians but also Buddhists, Hindus, Muslims, Taoists, Jews, pagans and goddess people, are chosen consciously. They include: The Green Man; Imagination, Dreams and Visions; the Return of the Divine Feminine (where we dance in the context of 400 images of the goddess from all the world's traditions including of course the Black Madonna and

---

1. Global Green USA, "About Global Green," http://www.globalgreen.org/about/about.html, printed 05/06/03.
2. "Bio of James Parks Morton."
3. "December 3 Ordinations," *Pacific Church News*, February/March 1995, p33.
4. Matthew Fox, "Creation Spirituality: The Deep Past and the Deep Future of Christianity," in Deborah A. Brown Ph.D., ed., *Christianity in the 21ˢᵗ Century*, The Crossroad Publishing Company, 2000, p151.
5. Matthew Fox, *Sins of the Spirit, Blessings of the Flesh*, Three Rivers Press, 1999, p317.
6. Bishop William Swing, "Diocesan Convention Address," October 21, 1995, p6.
7. "ECUSA Diocese Helps Fund 'Creation Spirituality' School," *The Christian Challenge*, May 1996, p18.
8. Bishop William Swing, "Reaching One Hundred Fifty," *Pacific Church News*, October/November 1996, p5.
9. Edie Weinstein-Moser, "Interview with: Matthew Fox—Creation Spirituality," *New Visions Magazine*, November 2003, http://www.newvisionsmagazine.com/november2003/fox1103.html, printed 06/17/04.
10. Bishop William Swing, "Excerpts: Bishop's Address" [to 1997 Diocesan convention], *Pacific Church News*, December 1997/January 1998, p34 (cited below as Swing, 1997 address to Diocesan convention, *PCN*, Dec. 97/Jan. 98).
11. Bishop William E. Swing, "Excerpts from Bishop Swing's Convention Address," *Pacific Church News*, December 2000/January 2001, p21.

Mary from the West); the Celebration of the Sacred Masculine, Gaia (usually on Mother's Day); the African Diaspora, the Wisdom of Rumi and the Sufi Tradition, Kabbalah and the Jewish Mystical Tradition, Feast of Lights (in December), Celtic Spirituality, Flowers, Plants and Trees, the Holiness of Animals, Our Lady of Guadalupe, The Sacredness of Our Bodies and more. The themes are of universal attraction just as dancing is and worship is. Dancing of course takes us into our lower charkas [sic] where we literally connect with the earth and so this kind of worship truly serves an ecological era.[1]

Several years previously, Fox had said the same: "'Dancing is the oldest forms [sic] of prayer,' says Fox, 'which you see in the African, and native American traditions, the Jewish and Christian traditions as well. Dance gets people into their lower chakras, the direct link with the life force.'"[2]

Fox is not the first to envision worship services that would get people "into their lower chakras." In his 1932 novel *Brave New World*, Aldous Huxley had prophesied sensual, high-tech liturgies that go even further than the Techno Cosmic Mass. As Huxley's "Solidarity Service" moved to its peak, "a sensation of warmth radiated thrillingly out from the solar plexus to every extremity of the bodies of those who listened; tears came into their eyes; their hearts, their bowels seemed to move within them, as though with an independent life."[3] (Huxley's service in *Brave New World*, however, climaxed in a manner that does *not* occur in Fox's services.)

Each month, about 500 people attend these services, which are held in a former ballroom in Oakland, California.[4] Two observers of trends in American religion—one of whom is the religion reporter for the *San Francisco Chronicle*—say that Fox's "creation spirituality" has "found an eager audience among lapsed Catholics of the baby-boom generation."[5]

Matthew Fox described the Planetary Mass that occurred at Grace Cathedral on Reformation Sunday, October 29, 1994—Fox's public debut with the Episcopal Diocese of California. At the service, there was a sun altar and a moon altar, used in a "Mass" where sin was "renamed:"

It was like being in a forest, where every direction one turned there was beauty and something interesting to behold. This included not only the singers, dancers, and rappers . . . but also the projections on large video screens, on television sets, on a huge globe suspended over the beautiful altars (one a sun altar, the second a crescent moon altar). On the screens were hummingbirds hovering, galaxies spinning, flowers opening, humans marching, protesting, embracing and polluting (sin was present and indeed renamed for us at the Mass). Life was there in all its panoply of forces, good and not so good, human and more than human.[6]

Perhaps it's just as well that Fox did not name the "more than human," "not so good" forces that attended this service.

Bishop Swing was present at Fox's 1994 liturgy, and loved it. The bishop said,

the Mass reminds him 'of an experience I had as a 9-year old boy in West Virginia, coming to a sense of God through Nature. That gets so layered over by generations of study and theology, but this Mass leads one back

1. Matthew Fox, "The Techno Cosmic Mass: A New Home for an Ancient Ritual," *Pacific Church News online*, November–December 2002, http://www.diocal.org/pcn/PCNO /pcn002-10/main.html, printed 01/06/03.

2. Elaine Cohen, "Matthew Fox: Techno Cosmic Mass Heralds New Spirituality," *Conscious Life*, July 1999, p11 (cited below as Cohen, "Matthew Fox," July 1999).

3. Aldous Huxley, *Brave New World*, 1932, Harper Perennial (1989 ed.), p83; see the description of the remainder of this liturgy on pp78–86 (chapter V, part 2).

4. The estimated attendance of 500 is from: Yehudit Steinberg, "Program Director—Skill Set," http://www.mysticscave.com/resume.html.htm, printed 06/22/04. Steinberg lists as a current post, "Consulting as Musical Director for Techno Cosmic Mass executive team with Rev. Matthew Fox, to streamline the dance music for an alternative prayer service with an attendance of 500." A 1999 report placed attendance at 1,200; no other attendance estimates from other sources have been this high (Cohen, "Matthew Fox," p11.)

5. Richard Cimino and Don Lattin, *Shopping for Faith: American Religion in the New Millennium*, Jossey-Bass, 2002, p25.

6. Matthew Fox, "Experiencing the First Planetary Mass in America," *Creation Spirituality*, Spring 1995, Vol. XI, no. 1, p32.

toward that great awe.' Swing, who has been bobbing to the techno-music, says it's 'so nice to see the church with a new song and a new language,[1]

and added

The whole business of having the Eucharist in the context of Nature, and the planets, and the unfolding of life is a context that has to happen. This is probably around the time of the genesis of liturgies like this, and I'm sure that there will be more and more. It's coming . . . So we brought a lot of people in their twenties and thirties who don't go to church, and they were struck by this. I love it. I think we're on our way.[2]

In early 2003, Swing reiterated his support for Matthew Fox, praising his drug-free postmodern liturgies: "It is possible to get high on healthy religion. My hero and pioneer in all of this is the Rev. Matthew Fox. He took the old 'Rave Mass'[3] and converted it to a 'Techno Mass.' No drugs. Period. Yet there is an openness to new forms of liturgy and common life that allow young people to tap into the brilliance of being with God."[4]

Fox continues to acknowledge Swing's backing for his new form of worship. He says,

Certain ecclesial guardians of the ancestral powers feel the forms we have are just fine—even if no one shows up; at the other extreme we have new agers who want to throw the past out entirely. In the middle there is the Techno Cosmic Mass movement wherein we are deconstructing and reconstructing the worship [of] our ancestors with the able leadership of the first post-modern generation. Fortunately, there are some religious figures like the Episcopal Bishop of California, Bishop Swing, who get in it [sic] and are supportive of this work.[5]

Fox's teachings have led Anglican prelates to greater sympathy for New Age beliefs. George Carey, who was Archbishop of Canterbury from 1991 through 2002, "said he had initially been 'hostile' to New Age ideas but had come to appreciate their emphasis on creation and the environment. He told a conference on new religious movements at the London School of Economics that the Church had much to learn from New Age spirituality. He first thought New Age was a muddle of beliefs at odds with mainstream Christianity until he read Christian writers such as Matthew Fox on the subject."[6]

Here follow some examples of Fox's theology, in his own words. As you read them, recall that he is an Episcopal priest in good standing in the Diocese of California.

1. Richard Scheinin, "Multimedia imagery Techno-ambient [sic] music It's the Planetary Mass," *Creation Spirituality*, Spring 1995, Vol. XI, no. 1, p 28.

2. Richard Scheinin and Matthew Fox, "The Planetary Mass Nine O'Clock Service: Reactions," *Creation Spirituality*, Spring 1995, Vol. XI, no. 1, p 30.

3. This appears to be a generalized reference to the rave movement of the 1980s and early 1990s. Christopher Partridge wrote, "It is not difficult to trace the continuity between the psychedelic hippie culture of the 1960s and the rave culture of the 1980s and 1990s. That said, while Buddhist and Hindu beliefs were central to much earlier psychedelic mystical experience, and although their influence is still important, contemporary psychedelia tends to be more eclectic and certainly more Pagan in orientation" (Christopher Partridge, "Psychedelic Spirituality," in Christopher Partridge, ed., *New Religions: A Guide— New Religious Movements, Sects, and Alternative Spiritualities*, Oxford University Press, 2004, p 377; cited below as Partridge, *New Religions*). An Australian commentator says, "The 'rave' began as a British phenomenon and was first reported in Australia in Melbourne in 1988. . . . While the aim is essentially one of pleasure through dance, sound, music and the use of hallucinogenic drugs, there is a sociopolitical component to these events. Participants talk of the failure of government and the Australian people in general to address the traumatizing legacies of colonialism, such as its effects on the Aborigines and the destruction of the environment." (Lynne Hume, "Doofs and Raves in Australia," in Partridge, *New Religions*, pp 416–417.)

4. Bishop William Swing, "A Swing Through The Diocese: Drugs and the Diocese of California," *Pacific Church News*, Spring 2003, Vol. 141, No. 2, p 5.

5. Matthew Fox, "Some Reflections on Community and the Techno Cosmic Mass," *Techno Cosmic Mass*, http://www.technocosmicmass.org/pages/about_tcm/tcm_articles.html, printed 05/05/04.

6. Victoria Combe, "Carey 'has learned' from the New Age," *London Telegraph*, April 20, 2001, http://www.telegraph.co.uk/news/main.jhtml?xml=/news/2001/04/20/ncarey20.xml, printed 05/19/03.

In his *Creation Spirituality* magazine, Fox has said that his theological agenda is to overturn Christian doctrine as it has been understood since the first ecumenical Council at Nicaea: "What is the rediscovery of the Cosmic Christ if not a deconstruction of the 'power Christology' that launched the Christian empire in the Nicean [sic] Council in the fourth century and an effort to reconnect to the older, biblical tradition, of Christ as cosmic wisdom present in all beings?"[1]

In his cornerstone book *The Coming of the Cosmic Christ*, Fox quotes Shiva, "creator and destroyer of things"[2] and "lord of the dance," as saying: "The phallos is identical with me. It draws my faithful to me and therefore must be worshipped;" Fox adds, "This is Cosmic Christ language."[3]

Fox has now published his own "Taoist inspired" version of the Lord's Prayer:

O Mother of the Universe,
Our Great Mother, the Tao,
You dwell in nature, in the sky, and in the heavens.

Empty yet inexhaustible,
You give birth to infinite worlds
You flow through all things, inside and outside,
May you give birth through us.

Sacred is your unnameable name.
Open our hearts like the sky.

May each being in the universe
Return to the common source that is You and that is serenity.
Then, realizing where we come from,
Earth will be like heaven
and we will become naturally tolerant,
Disinterested, amused,
Kindhearted as a grandmother,
Dignified as a king.

May we, immersed in your order,
Deal with whatever life brings us
Knowing that when death comes, we will be ready.

May we heed your teaching that violence,
Even when well intentioned,
Always rebounds upon itself.

May we learn that our enemies are not demons
But human beings like ourselves.

Help us to remain centered in you
So that all things will be in harmony.
Then the world would become a paradise.

---

1. Matthew Fox, "Creation Spirituality: Here Come the Postmoderns," *Creation Spirituality*, Autumn 1995, Vol. XI, no. 3, p5.

2. Charles Upton identifies an error in Fox's description of Shiva: "Brahma, *not Shiva*, is the creator-god of the Hindu trinity. Shiva is the destroyer, both in the outer sense of bringing the material world to an end, and in the inner one of representing the Transcendent Godhead, the realization of Whom destroys the world-illusion."

3. Matthew Fox, *The Coming of the Cosmic Christ*, Harper San Francisco, 1988, p176; his quote from "Shiva" is from Eugene Monick, *Phallos: Sacred Image of the Masculine*, Toronto, Inner City Books, 1987, pp29–30.

All people would be at peace
And the law would be written in our hearts.

As we learn to accomplish the great task
By a series of small acts
May we be patient with friends and enemies,
Compassionate toward ourselves
In order to reconcile all beings in the world.
Amen[1]

Matthew Fox also has identified the Virgin Mary as a goddess: "As far as the Goddess tradition goes, for years I've recognized that the Goddess in the Catholic tradition was, of course, Mary. . . . Recently, I taught a class entitled the 'Goddess and the City,' about how things were in the 12th century. As Mary, the Goddess sat on a throne, ruling the universe with justice and compassion, as well and the intellectual and artistic life of the medieval European city."[2] (Leave it to a radical ex-Catholic to lend support to the anti-Catholic canard that Catholics *worship* the Theotokos, the Mother of God.)

OTHER PROTESTANTS

In the US and overseas, liberal Protestant support for the URI is widespread:

• Dr. Glenn Bucher, who was president of the Graduate Theological Union in Berkeley, California at the time, was a member of the URI Board of Directors in 1997 and 1998.[3] The Graduate Theological Union donated funds to the URI in 2001[4] and 2002,[5] and is helping the URI and the Interfaith Center at the Presidio set up an Interfaith Academy to provide graduate-level classes for seminarians and religious leaders.[6]
• Paul Chaffee (a minister in the United Church of Christ, and executive director of the Interfaith Center in the Presidio) served as Secretary of the URI board through 2000.[7]
• Andrea Zaki Stephanous, from the Coptic Evangelical Organization for Social Services (CEOSS) in Egypt, participated in the April 1997 URI planning meeting in Oxford.[8] (The CEOSS was founded by the Egyptian Evangelical Church, but is now an independent social service organization.)[9]
• The Rev. Dr. Gary R. Gunderson, from the Interfaith Health Program of Emory University, donated to the URI in 2000 and 2001.[10] (He had worked for eight years with the Carter Center in Atlanta, Georgia[11])
• Dr. Wenzao Han, who has been General Secretary of the Amity Foundation (AF) and Chairman of the China

1. Techno Cosmic Mass, "The Lord's Prayer—Taoist Inspired Version by Matthew Fox," http://www.technocosmicmass.org/pages/about_tcm/lords_prayer_taoist.html, printed 05/20/04.
2. Virginia Lee, "Science and Spirit: Conversations with Matthew Fox, Ph.D. & Rupert Sheldrake, Ph.D.", *Common Ground On-Line*, http://www.commongroundmag.com/fox.html, printed 03/27/03.
3. List provided by Paul Andrews, URI staff person, November 20, 1997; URI leaflet with list of board membership, dated 9/15/98.
4. URI, *Annual Report* 2001,"Honoring Our Donors," p8.
5. URI, *Annual Report* 2002, "Honoring URI Donors and Volunteers."
6. Interfaith Center at the Presidio, "The Interfaith Center Academy," http://www.inter faith-presidio.org/academy.html, printed 05/28/03.
7. URI, *Annual Report* 2001, "Honoring Our Donors," p8; list of board members provided by Paul Andrews 11/20/97; URI leaflet with list of board members, dated 6/9/00.
8. Gibbs/Mahé, *Birth of a Global Community*, pp82–83.
9. Coptic Evangelical Organization for Social Services, "History," http://www.ceoss. org.eg/Histoy.htm, printed 07/07/04. The URL is as stated on the web site.
10. URI, *Annual Report* 2000, "Honoring Our Donors," p8, and URI, *Annual Report* 2001, "Honoring Our Donors," p9.
11. Gary Gunderson, biography, http://www.garygunderson.org/About_Us.html, printed 12/13/02.

Christian Council (CCC), has supported the URI since 1996.[1] (The AF and the CCC represent the state-approved Protestant church in China).
• The Rev. Dr. Sherman Hicks, a retired bishop of the Evangelical Lutheran Church in America (ELCA), and pastor of First Trinity Lutheran Church, Washington DC.[2]
• Jack Lundin, a Lutheran minister who has been on the URI board since 1997.[3]
• Bishop Robert Mattheis,[4] of the Sierra Pacific Synod of the Evangelical Lutheran Church in America.[5]
• Scotty McLennan, a Unitarian minister who is one of the Deans of Religious Life at Stanford University.[6] McLennan is the real-life inspiration for Scot Sloan, the "fighting young priest" who has been a character since the early 1970s in Gary Trudeau's *Doonesbury* comic strip.[7]
• The California-Pacific Annual Conference of the United Methodists decided in 1999 to become "a supporter of the United Religions Initiative."[8]
• At their General Conference in 2000, the United Methodists were offered a resolution to "reject/oppose overtures from United Religions Initiative"—and the delegates voted against this, by 766-19.[9]
• The Pacific Center for Spiritual Formation donated to the URI in 2003.[10]
• Presbyterian Homes donated to the URI in 2000.[11]
• Several Presbyterian and United Methodist congregations donated to the URI in 2001[12] and 2002.[13]

No Evangelical Christian leaders and no well-known American black Protestants have publicly supported the URI.

LATTER-DAY SAINTS

At the URI North America summit in late May 2001, Bishop Swing claimed that "Both in Utah and

1. Swing, "Reactions from Religious Leaders," summer 1996, p4; Delman, "Peace Projects Proliferate," *PCN*, June/July 1999, p21.
2. Hicks was chairman of the Washington DC URI delegation to the 1997 URI summit meeting. (Washington DC United Religions Initiative, "Renewing the Spirit of Community," http://web-wiz.com/origin/uri/dc-uri.htm, printed 1997; no longer on the Net.) He also was chairman of the Executive Committee of the URI in Washington DC in the late 1990s. (United Religions Initiative, "Where is the URI: United States," http://www.united-religions.org.connect/where/usa.shtml, printed 1998; no longer on the Net.)
3. List of URI board members provided by Paul Andrews, 11/20/97; URI leaflets with lists of board members, dated 9/15/98 and 6/9/00; United Religions Initiative, "URI Global Council," http://www.uri.org/abouturi/globalcouncil, printed 06/30/04.
4. URI, *Annual Report* 2000, "Honoring Our Donors," p7.
5. "ULC and the Sierra Pacific Synod," http://www.univelutch.org/ulcsps.html, for identification of Mattheis; printed 12/15/02.
6. URI, *Annual Report* 2001, "Honoring Our Donors," p10; for his biography, see Stanford University Office for Religious Life, "Who We Are: The Reverend Scotty McLennan," http://religiouslife.stanford.edu/about/who_we_are/mclennan.ht ml, printed 12/13/02.
7. Elizabeth Khuri, "People: Scotty McLennan: finding his religion," *Palo Alto Weekly*, March 7, 2001, http://www.paweek ly.com/PAW/morgue/news/2001_Mar_7.PEOPLE07.html, printed 12/13/02.
8. United Religions Initiative, *URI Update*, No. 6, Fall 1999, p8.
9. The United Methodist Church, "General Conference 2000," "Calendar: 1137–NonDis," http://www.gc2000.org/pets/CAL/info/c1137i.asp, printed 12/19/00.
10. URI, *Annual Report*, 2003. The Center says, "Our mission is to enable individuals, groups and congregations to experience a deeper awareness of God. We are rooted in the Christian contemplative tradition. We explore spiritual practices from our own and other faith traditions" (Pacific Center for Spiritual Formation, "About Pacific Center," http://www.pcentersf.org/aboutpcsf.html, printed 09/24/04.) They have recently affiliated with the URI. (Pacific Center for Spiritual Formation, "Twentieth Year Celebration," http://www.pcentersf.org/index.html, printed 09/24/04).
11. URI, *Annual Report* 2000, "Honoring Our Donors," p7.
12. URI *Annual Report* 2001, "Honoring Our Donors," p8.
13. URI, *Annual Report* 2002, "Honoring URI Donors and Volunteers."

around the world, the URI has received 'lots of cooperation' from The Church of Latter-Day Saints" (LDS).[1] Paul Chaffee, then a member of the URI Interim Global Council, stated that LDS President Hinckley "sent a letter of support" to the URI conference.[2] However, Mormon spokesman Dale Bills stated that the LDS has declined to participate in the URI, and that the letter that LDS President Hinckley had sent to the URI was merely a courtesy greeting.[3] Donald Frew stated that the only Mormons he has met personally in URI activities are those who are part of a Cooperation Circle at the Interfaith Center at the Presidio in San Francisco.[4]

EASTERN ORTHODOXY AND THE ORIENTAL ORTHODOX CHURCHES

No Eastern Orthodox bishops have been active in the URI since its founding.[5] However, two prelates of Oriental Orthodox, non-Chalcedonian Churches have endorsed URI activities. (These prelates are not in communion with mainstream, canonical Eastern Orthodoxy.) In 1996, Bishop Swing received a statement of support from Shenouda III, Pope of the Coptic Orthodox Church.[6] His Beatitude Mesrob II, Patriarch of Istanbul and All Turkey in the Armenian Apostolic Church, supported the URI "global cease fire" project in 1999.[7] There is no evidence that they, or their Churches, have been involved in the URI since then.

THE CATHOLIC CHURCH

Within the Catholic Church, opinion about the URI is divided. Rome stands firm against it. Nevertheless, Catholic support for the URI has spread worldwide, beyond the usual array of dissident Catholic theologians, priests, and religious orders.

VATICAN OPPOSITION

At Rome in 1996, Bishop Swing met with Cardinal Arinze, who was then the head of the Pontifical Council for Inter-Religious Dialogue.[8] Bishop Swing reported a firm rebuff from the Cardinal, the strongest "no" that he got from anyone during his global pilgrimage: [Cardinal Arinze] "Emphatically

---

1. Wayne Parry, "Inter-Faith Conference Comes to U," *The Daily Utah Chronicle*, May 2001, http://www.utahchronicle.com/main.cfm?include=detail&storyid=79102&, printed 07/05/2001; no longer on the Net.

2. Cheryl Buchta, "Religious groups gather in Salt Lake," *StandardNET*, June 1, 2001; http://www.standard.net, printed 6/1/2001; no longer on the Net.

3. Interview of Dale Bills, LDS spokesman, by Lee Penn—July 2001.

4. E-mail from Donald Frew to Lee Penn, 11/18/02.

5. This observation was confirmed in mid-2004 by Bishop Dimitrios of Xanthos, Director of the Office of Ecumenical and Interfaith Relations for the Greek Orthodox Archdiocese of America. In an e-mail to Lee Penn on 07/09/04, he said, "As far as I know, no Canonical Eastern Orthodox Bishop has engaged in activity either for or against the URI."

6. Swing, "The United Religions Initiative," 04/96, p5.

7. United Religions Initiative, "Some Early Supporters. . . ," http://www.united-religions.org/72hours/supporters.htm; printed 1999, no longer on the Net (cited below as URI, "Some Early Supporters"). See also North American Interfaith Network, "72 Hours: An Interfaith Peace-Building Project," in the *NAINet* newsletter, spring 1999, http://www.nain.org/news/n99spring.htm, printed 04/23/03 (cited below as NAIN, "72 Hours," spring 1999 newsletter).

8. Cardinal Arinze held this post from 1985 until October 2002, when he was appointed prefect of the Congregation for Divine Worship.

he said that he did not want my words to reflect that he was excited about the United Religions. He said that a United Religions would give the appearance of syncretism and it would water down our need to evangelize. It would force authentic religions to be on equal footing with spurious religions."[1] Swing said that the "most scintillating meeting" he had at the reception on the evening of his April 2003 papal audience was with Cardinal Francis Arinze. "In the past we haven't always seen eye-to-eye on interfaith matters. Now he has moved on from Interreligious to Divine Worship so our paths no longer cross," the bishop wrote.[2]

Archbishop Michael Fitzgerald, who worked under Cardinal Arinze (and is now his successor), ignored Bishop Swing's 1996 invitation to attend the 1997 URI summit conference.[3] Swing reported that Fitzgerald "said that his thoughts coincide with the thoughts of Cardinal Arinze" in opposition to the URI.[4]

Since then, the Vatican has restated its opposition to the URI. In a letter to the editor published in the June 1999 issue of *Homiletic & Pastoral Review*, a magazine for Catholic priests, Fr. Chidi Denis Isizoh, of the Pontifical Council for Interreligious Dialogue, said:

Religious syncretism is a theological error. That is why the Pontifical Council for Interreligious Dialogue does not approve of the United Religions Initiative and does not work with it. Indeed, when Bishop Swing came to the Vatican City in 1996 to solicit support from the Council, Cardinal Arinze clearly expressed his reservations about the proposal. As the United Religions Initiative develops, the reasons for not collaborating with it become more evident.[5]

As the *San Francisco Chronicle* reported in June 2000, "Swing found that the Vatican wanted nothing to do with his organization."[6]

In 2003, the Vatican document analyzing the New Age movement made an unfavorable reference to movements such as the URI: "Some international institutions are actively pursuing campaigns which

1. Swing, "The United Religions Initiative," 04/96, p7. Cardinal Arinze reiterated his concern about "spurious religions" in 2002: "there are sects and pseudo-religious or esoteric groups which are striving for recognition on a par with long-established religions" (Francis Cardinal Arinze, *Religions for Peace: A Call for Solidarity to the Religions of the World*, Doubleday, 2002, p136; cited below as Arinze, *Religions for Peace*).

2. Bishop William Swing, "2003 Ecumenical Pilgrimage to London, Canterbury, Rome, Istanbul," "Day 6—Monday, April 7—Vatican City/Janiculum Hill," http://diocal.org/modules.php?op=modload&name=EasyContent&file=index&menu=122101&page_id=107, printed 06/03/04 (cited below as Swing, "Ecumenical Pilgrimage").

3. Swing, "The United Religions Initiative," 04/96, p7.

4. Ibid. It is, nevertheless, possible that Archbishop Fitzgerald may change his position on the URI in the future. John Allen, the Rome correspondent for the liberal *National Catholic Reporter*, said in October 2002, "Broadly speaking, both Fitzgerald and Martino are theological moderates and social progressives. Assuming both become cardinals, which usually goes with the territory, it would strengthen the small center-left wing in the College of Cardinals, what I call in my book *Conclave* the 'Reform Party.' Fitzgerald, a member of the Missionaries of Africa ('White Fathers'), is a widely respected expert on Islam. He is known inside the Vatican as a man of wit, integrity, with an open mind and a deep sense of loyalty. His theological orientation can be glimpsed from a seminar in April 2001 at the Gregorian University, where Fitzgerald praised Jesuit Fr. Jacques Dupuis, the Jesuit theologian whose attempts to assign positive theological significance to religious diversity had been criticized by the Congregation for the Doctrine of the Faith. Fitzgerald said he wished 'to put on the record a debt of gratitude to Fr. Dupuis and his pioneering work.' 'I had the honor of being present in this hall during a presentation of Fr. Dupuis' book,' Fitzgerald said. 'Some have spoken of ambiguities, but since theology is a developing science, it is only natural that various theories will be presented, discussed, and brought into a synthesis.' It was a polite, loyal way of registering dissent." (John Allen, "Insta-analysis of papal appointments," October 4, 2002 (vol. 2, no. 6) installment of Allen's column "The Word From Rome," *National Catholic Reporter*, on-line edition, http://www.nationalcatholicreporter.org/word/word1004. htm, printed 05/10/04.) However, contrary to Allen's expectations, Fitzgerald had not (as of May 2004) been made a Cardinal.

5. Fr. Chidi Denis Isizoh, letter to the editor, *Homiletic & Pastoral Review*, Vol. XCIX, June 1999, p60.

6. Don Lattin, "Episcopal Bishop Seeks To Unite World Faiths," *San Francisco Chronicle*, June 19, 2000, pA1 (cited below as Lattin, "Bishop Seeks To Unite World Faiths," 06/19/00).

promote respect for 'religious diversity', and claim religious status for some questionable organisations. This fits in with the *New Age* vision of moving into an age where the limited character of particular religions gives way to the universality of a new religion or spirituality. Genuine dialogue, on the other hand, will always respect diversity from the outset, and will never seek to blur distinctions in a fusion of all religious traditions."[1]

As Archbishop Michael Fitzgerald explained in 2004,

> there is a great difference between our work in the interreligious dialogue and ecumenism. We are not looking for a theological consensus, at all, because we will not achieve a theological consensus. . . . I don't think we should be aiming at a universal theology in any way. . . . The challenges are that there are many, many, many initiatives around the world, interreligious initiatives, that take place. Some of these, I would say, lack a degree of discernment. Any type of religious movement is put together, even someone who has decided to create his own religion, he's there.[2]

Monsignor James Reinert, who is with the Vatican's mission to the UN, has had "no contact with the URI" and said that "it is my opinion that the position of Cardinal Arinze . . . is the position of the Holy See," and that he will "allow those comments [by Cardinal Arinze and Fr. Isizoh] to guide my work."[3]

Bishop Swing reported that Mother Teresa endorsed the URI in 1996.[4] However, there is no indication that she had any further involvement with the URI later in her life.[5] Nor has her order, the Missionaries of Charity, been active on behalf of the URI.[6] In a 1989 interview, Mother Teresa affirmed that she evangelized for Christ:

> I'm evangelizing by my works of love. . . . I'm evangelizing the way God wants me to. Jesus said go and preach to all the nations. We are now in so many nations preaching the Gospel by our works of love. 'By the love that you have for one another will they know you are my disciples.' That's the preaching that we are doing, and I think that is more real. . . . I love all religions, but I am in love with my own. No discussion. That's what we have to prove to them. Seeing what I do, they realize that I am in love with Jesus. . . . if they want peace, if they want joy, let them find Jesus. If people become better Hindus, better Moslems, better Buddhists by our acts of love, then there is something else growing there. They come closer and closer to God. When they come closer, they have to choose.[7]

CATHOLIC DISSENT—STANDING WITH THE UNITED RELIGIONS

Despite Vatican opposition, many Catholics have aligned themselves with the URI. Open Catholic supporters of the URI in the episcopate have included:

1. Pontifical Council For Culture and Pontifical Council For Interreligious Dialogue, "Jesus Christ The Bearer Of The Water Of Life: A Christian reflection on the "New Age," 2003, section 6.2, http://www.vatican.va/roman_curia/pontifical_councils/interelg/documents/rc_pc_interelg_doc_20030203_new-age_en.html, printed 02/3/03.
2. John Allen, "Interview with Archbishop Michael Fitzgerald," *National Catholic Reporter*, May 14, 2004, http://ncronline.org/mainpage/specialdocuments/fitzgerald.htm, printed 05/27/04.
3. E-mail from Msgr. James Reinert, Attaché with the Vatican's Permanent Observer Mission to the UN, to Lee Penn, 11/11/02.
4. Swing, "The United Religions Initiative," 07/96, p4.
5. Based on Google search done by Lee Penn, 02/11/03.
6. Based on Google search done by Lee Penn, 07/06/04.
7. Edward W. Desmond, interview with Mother Teresa—as it appeared in 1989 in the *National Catholic Register*, http://www.catholic.net/RCC/people/mother/teresa/interview.html, printed 10/01/02.

- Cardinal Paul Evaristo Arns, the retired Archbishop of São Paulo, Brazil.[1]
- Thomas Gumbleton, the auxiliary Bishop of Detroit.[2]
- Archbishop John Baptist Odama, of Gulu in Uganda.[3]
- Archbishop John Quinn of San Francisco, the retired predecessor of the incumbent Archbishop Levada.[4]
- Archbishop Anthony Pantin, bishop in Trinidad from 1967 until his death in 2000.[5]

The Archdiocese of San Francisco

William Levada, the Archbishop of San Francisco, has not officially stated support for the URI.[6] Nevertheless, the Archdiocese of San Francisco is—*de facto*, if not *de jure*—cooperating closely with the URI. As the *San Francisco Chronicle* reported in June 2000, "Locally, United Religions has the support of the Roman Catholic Church."[7] Diocesan spokesman Maurice Healey agreed that "through its actions, the Archdiocese has viewed the URI positively."[8]

Fr. Gerard O'Rourke, director of the Office of Ecumenical and Interreligious Affairs for the Catholic Archdiocese of San Francisco, has been an enthusiastic supporter of the URI from its beginning. He took a prominent part in the 1995 interfaith service that announced the URI to the public,[9] attended the 1996 URI summit meeting,[10] and served actively on the URI Board of Directors until 2002 (when

1. Information received by Lee Penn during a telephone conversation with Barbara Hartford, May 11, 1998; confirmed by Paul Andrews, May 14, 1998; they described him as a "strong supporter" of the URI.

2. In 1999, Bishop Gumbleton publicly endorsed the URI's Y2K "Global Cease-Fire" project (NAIN, "72 Hours," spring 1999 newsletter).

3. Archbishop Odama was elected in April 2002 to head the Acholi Religious Leaders' Peace Initiative (ARLPI), an interfaith movement seeking an end to the civil war in Northern Uganda. ("John Baptist Odama is new ARLPI Chairperson," http://www.acholipeace. org/newchairperson270402.htm, printed 12/03/02). The ARLPI is a URI Cooperation Circle.

4. Patrick Joyce, "United Religions: Growing interfaith movement has roots in San Francisco," *Catholic San Francisco*, October 18, 2002, p5 (cited below as Joyce, "United Religions," 10/18/02). She wrote, "The United Religions Initiative traces its roots to [the] 1995 celebration of the 50th anniversary of the founding of the United Nations in San Francisco. U.N. officials asked religious communities to join in the celebration. That request inspired Bishop Swing, Catholic Archbishop John Quinn and the other religious leaders, mostly from the Bay Area, 'to create something comparable to the United Nations in the religious field,' Father O'Rourke said. That led to the creation of the URI in 1996."

5. "News Updates from Around the World," *URI News Update*, Spring 1998, p5; they reported that he formed a URI group in Trinidad (cited below as URI, "News Updates," spring 1998 newsletter).

6. Nevertheless, it appears that Archbishop Levada spoke favorably of the URI to the Pope in a 2003 audience attended by Levada and Swing. He elicited a personal blessing from the Pope for Swing, but not a Papal blessing specifically for the URI. According to Bishop Swing, "Archbishop Levada spoke into his right ear, introducing [Greek Orthodox Bishop] Anthony and me as well as presenting a menu of topics unique to each of us. When he mentioned the United Religions Initiative and how we were working around the world seeking peace among religions, the Pope spun around toward me moving his hands up and down, saying, 'Blessings, blessings!'. . . The rest of the delegation came in and met the Pope one on one. . . . As we were leaving, he held my hand and said, 'Bless you, Anglican. All the best!'" The Pope's April 7 message to the ecumenical pilgrims, as reported by Bishop Swing, praised their "commitment to the growth of Christian unity through sincere dialogue, common prayer and fraternal cooperation in the service of the Gospel;" it praised Christian ecumenism, without mentioning the URI or other interfaith activities. (Swing, "Ecumenical Pilgrimage," 04/07/03). John Allen, the Rome correspondent for the National Catholic Reporter, covered this pilgrimage, as well. He said, "Levada's offhand reference to the URI in our conversation was seemingly quite positive." (E-mail from John Allen to Lee Penn, April 13, 2003.)

7. Lattin, "Bishop Seeks To Unite World Faiths," 06/19/00, pA5.

8. Interview of Maurice Healey, executive editor of *Catholic San Francisco*, 11/7/02, by Lee Penn.

9. List of people performing the "reading from the Parliament of World Religions' Declaration Towards a Global Ethic," service sheet for June 25, 1995 interfaith service celebrating the 50th anniversary of the UN and the launch of the United Religions Initiative.

10. Gibbs/Mahé, *Birth of a Global Community*, p31.

the URI selected a new board with global representation).[1] Fr. O'Rourke said in early 1997, "I am totally in support of Bishop Swing and the work that he is doing and the admirable team that he has created to reach out . . . all across the world."[2] In 1996 and 1997, Fr. O'Rourke served as the "convenor" of a URI task force that had been set up in 1996 with the duty of "Enrolling leaders of the different religious and faith traditions; mastering the articulation of the core message; locating leaders; reaching out; getting them on board."[3] At the Archdiocesan official "Religious Education Institute," held on February 2, 2002 at Mercy High School in San Francisco, most of the information at the literature table for O'Rourke's department was URI literature, including the URI charter, a URI advertising brochure, a URI newsletter, URI donation envelopes, and the year 2000 annual report for the URI.[4] O'Rourke's annual report for his office in 2001 noted the growth of the URI, and offered no Catholic criticism of the organization.[5]

In a 2004 profile of Fr. O'Rourke, *Catholic San Francisco* (the weekly paper for the Archdiocese) said that O'Rourke "has made himself open and welcoming to humankind's diverse ways of worshiping the Divine."[6] His welcome extended to Wicca and Neopaganism. As the paper says, "Wicca, a nature/goddess based religion, still remains one of the least understood spiritual paths for many people. But not by Gerry O'Rourke. In 1998, Father O'Rourke told [Wiccan elder Donald] Frew, 'You absolutely have to be here at the table.'"[7]

O'Rourke's spiritual interests range even further. As *Catholic San Francisco* reports,

A large influence on the priest was his experience of studying with Werner Erhard, who he met in 1973. Father Gerry says this relationship was important because of Erhard's insights and analysis of language, both in listening and in speaking. The priest saw that communication is one of the essentials for peace making, and love is a form of communications. That's one of Erhard's most important lessons, he said. 'Erhard empowered me to see things in a more contextual and inclusive way.' Inspired by Erhard, Father O'Rourke founded the Mastery Foundation with a group of people interested in empowering people working in religious ministry.[8]

In his work on the Mastery Foundation, O'Rourke has collaborated from the start with Otis Charles, the retired Episcopal bishop disciplined in 2004 by Bishop Swing for publicly marrying another man. A 1994 story by a reporter (who had taken *est*—Erhard Seminar Training—and enjoyed it) said,

Bishop Otis Charles, who retired last June [1993] as dean of the Episcopal Divinity School in Cambridge, Massachusetts, also wanted 'to make the 'technology of transformation' available to people in the Church, many of whom found *est* to be a stumbling block.' Bishop Charles, who did *est* in 1977, considers Werner Erhard and Ignatius of Loyola 'the two individuals most influential in shaping my manner of grappling with work and life in the last 15 years,' because although 'the two are separated by about 400 years, each had a gift of being able to put together a way of creating a space in which your own life and gifts were able to be clearly manifested.' In 1983 Bishop Charles met with Father Pennington, Father Gerry O'Rourke, and other ministers, priests, and rabbis in New York to form the Mastery Foundation; they conceived a program for clergy that combined Erhard's

---

1. List of board members provided 11/20/97 by Paul Andrews; list of board members from URI pamphlet dated 9/15/98; list of members of the "Interim Global Council" from United Religions Initiative, "Interim Global Council Membership in 2000," *Annual Report* 2000, p8.

2. Transcribed by Lee Penn from tape of the January 19, 1997 URI forum.

3. United Religions Initiative, "Resource Groups Structured At the Conclusion of the June 1996 URI Summit in San Francisco," *Journal of the United Religions Initiative*, Spring 1997, p5.

4. As witnessed by Lee Penn, who attended the event.

5. Archdiocese of San Francisco, "Annual Report of the Office of Ecumenical and Interreligious Affairs," 2001.

6. Sharon Abercrombie, "Interfaith advocate for including everyone at the table," *Catholic San Francisco*, May 14, 2004, p5.

7. Ibid.

8. Ibid.

'technology' with Pennington's teaching of 'centering prayer.' Father Pennington and Erhard led the first workshop the next year in Massachusetts, creating the course as they went along.[1]

In 1994, O'Rourke said that he had "left his vocation in 1973 and credits Erhard and his programs with enabling him to 'begin again' as a priest in 1979."[2] The Catholic priest said, "Werner's made mistakes in life, like the rest of us, and he's made efforts to try to correct them and bring harmony. His willingness to forgive under colossal fire and not retaliate, especially with family members, is heroic—it's the kind of stuff saints are made of."[3]

The Archdiocesan newspaper has continued to give favorable publicity to the URI. In May 2002, *Catholic San Francisco* carried an article about an interfaith festival at the Presidio; it ended with a plug for the URI, delivered by URI leader Paul Chaffee.[4] An October 2002 article in the same paper provided laudatory coverage of the URI's history and of its recent Global Assembly.[5] At a February 2004 ecumenical outreach program for young adults, co-sponsored by the Catholic and Episcopal dioceses in San Francisco, Bishop Swing was the featured speaker—and he "spoke passionately about his work with United Religions Initiative."[6]

The 2001 annual report of the Archdiocesan Office of Ecumenical and Interreligious Affairs noted that Fr. O'Rourke was one of 22 board members of the Interfaith Center at the Presidio, and that "many interreligious events take place in the historic chapel," including Taizé prayer sessions.[7] A leaflet for a 2002 Taizé prayer session at the Interfaith Center offered this version of the Lord's Prayer to the people:

Heavenly Mother, Heavenly Father, holy and blessed is your true name. We pray for your reign of peace to come, we pray that your good will be done, let heaven and earth become one. Give us this day the bread we need, give it to those who have none. Let forgiveness flow like a river through us, from each one to each one to each one. Lead us to holy innocence beyond the evil of our days. Come swiftly Mother, Father, come! For yours is the power and the glory and the mercy—Forever your name is All in One. Amen.[8]

The Interfaith Center at the Presidio has been a URI Cooperation Circle (a local chapter) since 2000, and its director, Paul Chaffee, was on the URI Board until 2002.[9]

On the evening of January 24, 2002, there was an "Interreligious Prayer Service" at the Catholic Cathedral of St. Mary of the Assumption in San Francisco. The service bulletin showed that there were

---

1. Dan Wakefield, "Erhard in Exile," *Common Boundary*, March/April 1994, on-line reprint at http://www.esatclear.ie/~dialogueireland/landmark/lifeafterest.htm, printed 06/03/04.

2. Ibid.

3. Ibid.

4. Sharon Abercrombie, "Getting to know you: Followers of many faiths share their beliefs at the Presidio," *Catholic San Francisco*, May 17, 2002, p 8.

5. Joyce, "United Religions," 10/18/02.

6. Jayme George, "'Theology on Tap' brings talk of faith to where young adults are," *Catholic San Francisco*, February 6, 2004, p 8.

7. Archdiocese of San Francisco, "Annual Report of the Office of Ecumenical and Interreligious Affairs," 2001, p 2. (The Taizé community was founded in 1940 in France by Brother Roger. It is a community of over 100 religious brothers, from Protestant and Catholic backgrounds; one of its goals is fostering Christian unity. See their web site, http://www.taize.fr/en/index.htm, for details on the community—which has received visits from "Pope John Paul II, three Archbishops of Canterbury, Orthodox metropolitans, the fourteen Lutheran bishops of Sweden, and countless pastors from all over the world." (Web page printed 03/03/04).

8. Leaflet obtained in early 2002: "Taizé At The Chapel: Festival of the Light of Christ," "with heartfelt thanks to our sponsor Interfaith Center at the Presidio."

9. 1997 list of board members: United Religions Initiative, "New Board," *URI News Update*, March 1997, p 3; 2000 list of Interim Global Council members: URI, *Annual Report* 2000, "Interim Global Council Membership in 2000," p 8.

eight URI leaders[1] who offered public prayer or participated in the ceremonial lighting of candles for peace. The *Catholic San Francisco* coverage of the service began with a large front page photo of Bay Area religious leaders, with Levada standing next to Swing, as they obeyed a call from the Rev. Alan Jones, Canon of Grace Cathedral, to "reach out and tell each other, 'you are beautiful, and may the spirit of peace fill your soul.'"[2]

On that same day, the Pope led an interfaith prayer meeting at the shrine of St. Francis in Assisi; leaders of Christian churches and representatives from the major non-Christian religions gathered to pray for peace and to hear a message from the Pope. In an article about the 2002 Assisi interfaith gathering in the Vatican newspaper *L'Osservatore Romano*, Cardinal Walter Kasper, president of the Pontifical Council for Promoting Christian Unity, had said, "Christians and followers of other religions 'cannot pray together' because their prayers are an expression of a faith they do not share."[3] Accordingly, at Assisi all the Christians prayed together; the members of 11 other religions went to separate rooms for their own prayer services.[4] This arrangement was done to avoid giving the appearance of religious syncretism.[5]

By contrast, in San Francisco, the interfaith service involved side-by-side prayers and readings of holy books by members of many faiths. In his homily, Archbishop Levada said, "Who can be here tonight in prayer for peace, side by side, hearing the scriptures, the songs, and the prayers of our different traditions give voice to the deepest aspirations of our hearts, and not be moved to say, 'Here is a soul-mate, a neighbor, a friend?'"[6]

Other pro-URI Catholic officials in the San Francisco Bay Area have included Rick Murray, a Catholic layman who served in 1998 as URI treasurer[7] and as an Interim Global Council member from 2000 through 2002.[8] Catholic deacon William Mitchell was on the URI board in 1998.[9] In 1998, Fr. O'Rourke said that Fr. Gene Boyle, from the Diocese of San Jose, was also active in the URI.[10] Regarding local Catholic participation in URI leadership, Fr. O'Rourke said, "None of us and especially myself are representing the Archdiocese or the Church in any liable sense to the institution."[11]

Along with the Archdiocese of San Francisco, the Jesuit leaders of the University of San Francisco actively support the URI. Fr. John Lo Schiavo, S.J., Chancellor of the University of San Francisco (USF), served through 2000 on the URI board of directors,[12] and donated to the URI in 2003.[13] Fr.

1. These were Bishop William Swing, Sr. Chandru Desai (a Hindu nun), the Rev. Heng Sure (a Buddhist), the Rev. Paul Chaffee (leader of the Interfaith Center at the Presidio), the Rev. Charles Gibbs (an Episcopal priest and the executive director of the URI), Iftekhar Hai (a Muslim), Rabbi Douglas Kahn, and Rita Semel (of the San Francisco Interfaith Council). Thus, eight of the 29 US-based URI board members were prominent participants in the prayer service. (Tally of board members is from URI, *Annual Report* 2000, "Interim Global Council Membership in 2000," p 8.)

2. "Religions join in prayer for peace," *Catholic San Francisco*, February 1, 2002, p 2.

3. Cindy Wooden, "Half of participants in pope's Assisi peace pilgrimage to be Muslim," *Catholic San Francisco*, January 18, 2002, p 17.

4. Cindy Wooden, "Day of Prayer for Peace: Pope, other leaders join to scatter 'shadows' of suspicion," *Catholic San Francisco*, February 1, 2002, p 8.

5. Sandro Magister, "Disputed Questions—Like Salvation Outside of the Church," *L'espresso*, www.chiesa, July 16, 2003, http://213.92.16.98/ESW_articolo/0,2393,41819,00. html, printed 05/10/04.

6. Archbishop William J. Levada, "Ordinary Time: Day of Prayer for World Peace," *Catholic San Francisco*, February 1, 2002, p 3.

7. United Religions Initiative, "Board of Directors," as listed in pamphlet dated 9/15/98.

8. URI, *Annual Report* 2000, "Interim Global Council membership in 2000," p 8.

9. United Religions Initiative, "Board of Directors," as listed in pamphlet dated 9/15/98.

10. Interview by Lee Penn of Fr. Gerard O'Rourke, May 4, 1998.

11. Fr. Gerard O'Rourke, "United Religions Initiative: Perspective of Father Gerry O'Rourke," April 7, 1998, p 2.

12. URI, *Annual Report* 2000, "Interim Global Council Membership," p 8; also, list of URI board members provided by URI staff member Paul Andrews to Lee Penn, 11/20/97.

13. URI, *Annual Report* 2003.

Steven A. Privett S.J., the current president of USF, gave Bishop Swing a glowing introduction at Swing's Commonwealth Club speech in April 2001, praising him as a "bishop for all peoples and all seasons."[1] Privett said,

> At the Jesuit University of San Francisco, we aim to educate students to change the world. It may sound corny, but Bishop Swing really *has* changed the world, and not just the world of the Episcopal Diocese of California, which he has presided over for 21 years. Bishop Swing's vision and spirit are the driving force behind the United Religions Initiative. His realization that dogma divides and action unites is the foundation of this worldwide, loosely knit union of religious persons of all persuasions who work together on the local level for peace, justice, and healing.[2]

The Rev. John P. Schlegel, S.J., President of the University of San Francisco from 1991 through 2000, donated to the URI in 2000.[3]

The Archdiocese of San Francisco has approved of the URI—and the interfaith affairs staff of the United States Conference of Catholic Bishops (USCCB) leaves such decisions to the interfaith staff of local dioceses. John Borelli, Associate Director of the Secretariat for Ecumenical and Interreligious Affairs of the USCCB, said in November 2002, "Since the Archdiocese of San Francisco is involved in the URI, the Catholic Church is involved. . . . Decisions about Catholic participation in the URI have been made at the local level, since URI events have been local."[4] In March 2003, Borelli said, "My advice to Gerry O'Rourke from the start is that all kinds of interfaith activities are beneficial and he should be involved in the URI if he feels it is a worthwhile project."[5] As of this writing, the URI has not come before the Bishops' Committee for Ecumenical and Interreligious Affairs for program approval or for acceptance of related expenses. Borelli also stated that there has been "no formal communication from the Vatican to the USCCB about the URI."[6] It appears that the USCCB bureaucracy is a *de facto* supporter of the URI.

Catholics on the URI Global Council

Nor is support for the URI limited to U. S. Catholics. The following five Catholics were elected to the URI "Global Council"—its board of directors—in 2002:[7]

- Fr. James Channan, of Pakistan, a Consultor for the Vatican Commission on Religious Relations with Muslims, and prior Vice-Provincial of the Dominican "Sons of Mary" order in Pakistan.[8]
- Dr. Gerardo Gonzalez Cortes, from Chile.

1. Transcribed by Lee Penn from a tape of the speech by Bishop Swing at the Commonwealth Club, April 25, 2001.
2. Ibid.
3. URI, *Annual Report* 2000, "Honoring Our Donors," p9; for biographical information, see San Francisco State University, "SFSU to Award Honorary Degree To The Rev. John P. Schlegel, President Of The University Of San Francisco," http://www.sfsu.edu/~news/prsrelea/fy99/105.htm, printed 12/15/02.
4. Interview of John Borelli by Lee Penn, 11/7/02.
5. E-mail from John Borelli to Lee Penn, 03/28/03.
6. Interview of John Borelli by Lee Penn, 11/7/02. In an e-mail to Lee Penn on 3/30/03, Borelli confirmed the quotations provided in this paragraph.
7. Data on religious affiliation of board members were provided by URI Global Council member Donald Frew, in an e-mail to Lee Penn, 11/18/02 and subsequently; this was supplemented by on-line research on the Council members, as shown in the footnotes after the Council members' names.
8. *Catalogus generalis familiæ Dominicanæ*, "Vice-Province of the Son of Mary in Pakistan," listing for Fr. James Channan, http://catalogus.op.org/activity.php?ent_type =PROVINCE&entity_id=2258, printed 11/25/02; see also James Channan OP, Prior Vice-Provincial of Pakistan, Dominican News Service, "Restoration of Joint Electorate in Pakistan," 1/28/02, http://news.op.org/justice/355.html, printed 11/25/02.

• Mrs. Annie Imbens-Fransen, of the Netherlands, who describes herself as a "feminist theologian."[1]
• Fr. Dr. George Khoury, President of the Ecclesiastical Tribunal of the Greek Catholic Church, in Israel.[2]
• Mr. Bonifacio Amado M. Quirog, Jr., President of the Bohol Goodwill Volunteers, Inc., Philippines.[3]

Other Catholic URI Leaders and Activists

Other Catholics worldwide—from Belgium, Brazil, Ethiopia, Hungary, India, Israel, Kenya, Mexico, Nepal, the Philippines, Uganda, Zimbabwe, and other countries—have been active in the URI. They include:

• Marites Africa, a Catholic from the Philippines, is the regional coordinator for the URI in the Pacific region.[4]
• Brother Eli Andrade, in Manila.[5]
• According to the URI, "the Mexican Cardinal's secretary Padre Arriaga, the Bishop of Cuernavaca and the representative of the president of Mexico attended the official opening ceremony" of the URI Regional Assembly held in Oaxtepec, Mexico in January 2002.[6]
• Sister Laetitia Borg, described by the URI as "a leader of the URI effort in Ethiopia"[7] and as that country's "leader for Franciscans International."[8]
• Sister Maribel Carceller, from the Philippines, is listed by the URI as the contact for the Asia-South Pacific RSCJ (Religious of the Sacred Heart) Peace and Justice Commission, a URI Affiliate.[9]
• Fr. Alejandro Castillo, a Franciscan priest from Mexico, facilitated a workshop on the "URI Agenda for Action" at the URI Latin America Regional Assembly, held in Mexico in January 2002.[10]
• Sister Joan Chatfield, a Maryknoll nun from Hawaii, attended the URI summit conferences in 1996[11] and 1997,[12] and assisted at the 2001 URI/North America conference.[13] She also contributed to the URI *Workbook*[14]

1. Annie Imbens-Fransen, "Foundation for Pastoral Care for Women and United Religions Initiative," http://www.dwcw.org/e-symposium_1/cgi/wwwbbs.cgi?Symposium&194, printed 11/25/2002.

2. Jewish-Christian Relations, "Reports 2000," information on Fr. Khoury is in the June 18, 2000 news release; http://www.jcrelations.net/res/reports00.htm, printed November 26, 2002; see also Interfaith Encounter Association, "Upcoming Events," for the same identification of Fr. Khoury; http://www.interfaith-encounter.org/upevents.htm, printed 11/26/02.

3. SojoNet, "Get Connected," http://www.sojo.net/get_connected/index.cfm/mode/detail_name/directory_id/946/action/directory.html, printed 11/25/02; the organization is a URI Cooperation Circle.

4. United Religions Initiative, "News & Events—Pacific," http://www.uri.org/regionalnews/pacific/, printed 07/07/03; her denominational affiliation is from a photo caption at the start of the October 2002 issue of Pacific Church News online, http://www.diocal.org/pcn/PCNO/pcn002-9/main.html, printed 01/06/03. See also Christian V. Esguerra, "Diverse faiths, one language of the heart," INQ7.net, http://www.inq7.net/nat/2001/oct/21/nat_13-1.htm, printed 02/19/03; the article in a Filipino paper identifies Africa as a Catholic, and states that she was introduced to the URI by Mario Fungo, a Catholic who had just attended the 1998 URI global summit meeting.

5. "URI in the world," *URI Update*, no. 5, spring 1999, p4; he is described as a member of the "URI core group."

6. United Religions Initiative, "Latin America & the Caribbean," http://www.uri.org/regionalnews/lamerica/lareg.asp, printed 3/20/03. I was unable to identify which Cardinal's secretary participated, and the see of the diocese of Cuernavaca was vacant at the time of the URI conference. (www.CatholicHierarchy.org, "Diocese of Cuernavaca," http://www.catholic-hierarchy.org/diocese/dcuer.html, printed 3/20/03.)

7. Canon Charles Gibbs, "URI Summit Delegates Move From Vision to Action Following Historic Charter Signing," *Pacific Church News*, October/November 2000, p37.

8. URI, "News Updates," spring 1998 newsletter, p4.

9. URI, "Affiliates."

10. United Religions Initiative, "Latin America Regional Assembly: Celebrating Our Identity, We Build Bridges," http://www.uri.org/regionalnews/lamerica/lareg.asp, printed 07/16/04.

11. Gibbs/Mahé, *Birth of a Global Community*, p32.

12. "Voices of the Light," No. 15, July 1, 1997; electronic newsletter of the United Communities of Spirit; http://www.origin.org/ucs/text/uri1.cfm, printed 10/3/02.

13. Paul Chaffee, "URI-NA: Circles in Motion," report on May 2001 Salt Lake City conference, http://www.uri.org/regions/namerica/story.htm, printed 10/18/01; no longer on the Net.

14. United Religions Initiative, *Draft Workbook For Pilot Groups*, p2.

that the URI used in planning sessions in 1996 and 1997.

• Lucien F. Cosijns had spent 14 years in Japan as a member of a missionary congregation.[1] He said, "After my study in Japan of Buddhism in general, with many contacts and discussions with Buddhist friends, clerics as well as lay people, and after having become part of the Japanese way of life, I did not see the sense anymore of converting the Japanese to the Christian faith."[2] He went into business in 1965, and has devoted himself full-time to the interfaith movement since 1997.[3] He has been active in the URI and other interfaith movements, and urges the URI, the Council for a Parliament of the World Religions, and the World Congress of Faiths to merge.[4] His goal is "the creation of a powerful one-voice forum of the world faith communities as a supranational body and as a worthy partner to the UN. This will be an important further step in the evolution of the growing unifying religious/political globalisation of our world."[5]

• Maria Eugenia Crespo de Mafia, from Brazil, is one of the two URI regional coordinators for Latin America.[6]

• Sr. Lilian Curaming,[7] of the Franciscan Missionaries of Mary in the Philippines,[8] was one of the leaders of a 2002 URI workshop on "Interfaith Dialogue for Nation-Building."[9]

• Fr. Christopher DeGiovine, director of campus ministry and chaplain for The College of Saint Rose in Albany New York, is listed by the URI as the contact person for the Albert Lectureship Board, a URI-affiliated organization.[10]

• Fr. Luis Dolan, a Passionist priest, served as URI Coordinator for Latin America until his death in the fall of 2000; he organized 6 URI conferences in the region, and "attracted the Catholic clergy in his territory."[11] He was also active in the Temple of Understanding, a New York-based interfaith organization with close ties to the United Nations.[12] In a document published in 1997 by Global Education Associates, Fr. Dolan said, "I believe that the UN offers us the first scripture written by communities rather than by a single inspired author. This scripture is the composite of all the basic documents of the UN, starting with the Charter."[13] Dolan said that to create "the future world order," the "Church of the future needs to come across primarily as a community of believers, rather than as an institution with a hierarchical structure;" he also opposed what he called the "belligerent attitude" of the Vatican at UN conferences.[14] Dolan stated that "all Church members need to be better educated on all aspects of human sexuality" in order to give the world "more future-oriented norms on human sexuality" as "the new world order takes concrete forms."[15]

1. Lucien F. Cosijns, "C.V.," http://users.online.be/interfaith_guidelines/paginas/6andere%20teksten/my%20cv.htm, printed 07/01/04.

2. Ibid.

3. Ibid.

4. Lucien F. Cosijns, "Global Changes in the Faith Communities," http://users.on line.be/interfaith_guidelines/paginas/3gemeensch/global%20changes%20in%20the%20faith%20communities.htm, printed 05/31/04.

5. Ibid.

6. United Religions Initiative, "URI Global staff," http://www.uri.org/abouturi/globalcouncil/globalstaff.asp, printed 07/05/04; this version of the document listed her "faith tradition" as "Christian Catholic." The version of the same document on the web as of 09/23/04 did not list the religious affiliation of the URI regional staff.

7. "URI in the world," URI Update, no. 5, spring 1999, p4; she is described as part of the "URI core group."

8. Sister Curaming's affiliation is listed in: Carmen N. Pedrosa, "Conversations on World Peace—part 1," Interreligious and International Federation for World Peace, http://www.iifwp.org/Ambassadors/conversations.shtml, printed 03/04/03.

9. United Religions Initiative, "Pacific," http://www.uri.org/regionalnews/pacific/phil. asp, printed 05/28/03.

10. URI, "Affiliates." His role as a Catholic pastor is stated by Paul Quirini, "College Chaplains Minister On-Line," http://www.evangelist.org/archive/htm/0827raic.htm, printed 12/15/02.

11. Sister Joan Kirby, Temple of Understanding, "In Memoriam, Father Luis Dolan," http://www.templeofunderstanding.org/archive/luis_dolan_rip.htm, printed 11/05/02.

12. For more information about the Temple of Understanding, see Lee Penn, "The United Religions Initiative—Foundations for a World Religion," SCP Journal, Vol. 22:4–23:1, 1999, p65.

13. Fr. Luis Dolan, "Development and Spirituality: Personal Reflections of a Catholic," (Global Education Associates), http://www.globaleduc.org/dolan.htm, printed 5/14/99.

14. Ibid.

15. Ibid.

• Professor Paul H. Gundani, a Roman Catholic, was the "Director of the United Religions Initiative, Zimbabwe" as of April 2002.[1]

• Fr. Patrick Hanjoul, a Catholic priest in Belgium, served as the chairman of "URI/Europe" until April 2002.[2]

• Sister Rosemary Huber, of the Maryknoll order, is active in a URI-associated interfaith group in Katmandu, Nepal.[3]

• Sister Joan Kirby, of the Temple of Understanding and the Religious of the Sacred Heart (RSCJ),[4] has been active in the URI since 1996.[5] URI Global Council member Donald Frew wrote in 1999 that "Sister Joan has been a strong promoter of Pagan involvement in the United Religions Initiative."[6]

• Sister Bridget Clare McKeever, director of the Office of Spirituality for the Catholic diocese of Salt Lake in Utah,[7] publicly endorsed the URI in 2001, at the time of the URI/North America meeting.[8]

• Sister Mhuire McLoughlin, an affiliate member of the URI,[9] is a member of the School Sisters of Notre Dame order, and is Pastoral Associate at the Sacred Heart Parish in Calumet, Michigan.[10]

• Thomas Michel SJ is director of the Jesuit Secretariat for Interreligious Dialogue,[11] and is a former member of the Pontifical Council for Interreligious Dialogue.[12] He endorsed the URI 72-hour religious ceasefire as "one way local interreligious groups might work for peace. The Five Commitments of the URI are concrete actions that local groups might decide to pursue."[13]

• Nestor Muller, a Roman Catholic from Brazil,[14] attended the 1999 URI global summit meeting. He

1. International Committee of Religious Leaders for Voluntary Family Planning, news release, "International Committee of Religious Leaders for Voluntary Family Planning Calls on President Bush to Release $34 Million for UNFPA," April 30, 2002, http://www. commondreams.org/news2002/0430-05.htm, printed 06/11/03.

2. Anne V. Roth, "Facing Violence as a Way to Peace: URI Europe/Middle East Regional Summit, April 6–10 2002," *Awakened Woman e-magazine*, http://www.awakenedwoman, com/May/uri_summit.htm, printed 12/18/02; he is identified as a Belgian priest in "Possible Board of Advisers," *Global Vision: Science & the Sacred*, http://www.global-vision.org/sacred/people.html, printed 12/18/02.

3. Maryknoll Mission Faces, "Day of Prayer for Peace in the World," http://www.maryknoll.org/MARYKNOLL/SOCIETY/mm_pope_peace1.htm, printed 3/21/03.

4. Charles Gibbs, "Report from the Executive Director," *Journal of the United Religions Initiative*, issue 3, Summer 1997, p2; for Kirby's religious order affiliation, see RSCJ, "Food for Thought," http://www.rscj.org/vocationrscj/tidbits.html, printed 12/15/02.

5. United Religions Initiative, *URI News Update*, December 1996, p3.

6. Donald Frew, "Report on the 1999 Parliament Assembly Preparatory Conference—Day 2—Wednesday," http://www.cog.org/pwr/Chicagointerfaith2.html, printed 03/26/03.

7. Judy Magid, "Hand Up, Not Handout, Theme of CHOICE Dinner and Bazaar," *The Salt Lake Tribune*, November 10, 2002, http://www.sltrib.com/2002/nov/11102002/Arts/15090.htm, printed 2/17/03; CHOICE is an acronym for Humanitarian Center for Outreach and Inter-Cultural Exchange.

8. Peggy Fletcher Stack, "Person-to-Person Interfaith Summit Opens in SLC," *The Salt Lake Tribune*, November 10, 2002, http://www.sltrib.com/2001/may/05312001/utah/101821.htm, printed 6/5/2001; no longer on the Net.

9. URI, "Affiliates."

10. Catholic Diocese of Calumet, "Calumet," http://www.dioceseofmarquette.org/pcalumet.htm, printed 07/06/04.

11. Thomas Michel SJ, "Our Comments on the Initiative," Issue 5 of the newsletter *Jesuits in Dialogue: The Interreligious Dimension*, http://puffin.creighton.edu/jesuit/dialogue/documents/news/news5.html, printed 2/11/03 (cited below as Michel, "Our Comments on the Initiative").

12. John Allen, "Fox on Asia in Rome," December 6, 2002 installment of Allen's column "The Word From Rome,", vol. 2, no. 15, *National Catholic Reporter* on-line edition, http://www.nationalcatholicreporter.org/word/word1206.htm, printed 05/10/04.

13. Michel, "Our Comments on the Initiative."

14. Charles Gibbs, United Religions Initiative, "Letter from Executive Director," February 2003, http://www.uri.org/abouturi/edreport/feb2003.asp, printed 05/26/03. Gibbs described Muller as "a passionate, deeply committed Roman Catholic," and noted that he attended the 1999 URI global summit meeting.

also helped plan URI and other interfaith gatherings in Brazil.[1] Since then, he has been active in the São Paulo URI Cooperation Circle.[2]

• Fr. Albert Nambiaparambil, who served in the 1990s as Secretary of Interreligious Dialogue for the Catholic Bishops' Conference of India,[3] is a URI affiliate[4] and a contact person for a URI Cooperation Circle, the World Fellowship of Inter-Religious Councils.[5]

• Fr. Dr. David Neuhaus, S. J., a priest in Israel who is associated with the Pontifical Biblical Institute,[6] prepared a seminar in conjunction with the Interfaith Encounter Association, a URI CC in Israel.[7]

• Fr. Centurio Olaboro, pastor of the 14,000-member Our Lady of Lourdes parish in Uganda,[8] is listed by the URI as the contact person for the Uganda Joint Christian Council, a URI-affiliated organization.[9]

• Raimundo Panikkar, a Catholic priest and theologian, spoke before a URI/UNESCO gathering in December 2000, and offered a public blessing to the URI.[10]

• Szabolcs Sajgo, a Jesuit priest and head of a retreat center in Hungary, attended the spring 1997 European URI conference; he said, "Religion no longer means the religious authorities but all the mature members of that specific religion also count, to reach the goals of UR. Humanity lives more and more in a world which is created by himself or herself and this world reflects the human being as a creator."[11]

• Fr. Joseph Wainaina, who has been the National Pastoral Coordinator for the Kenya Episcopal Conference, was elected treasurer of a URI Steering Committee in East Africa in May 1998.[12]

• Dr. Carol Zinn SSJ, a staff member of Global Education Associates (GEA),[13] said that the "creative and challenging work of the United Religions Initiative resonates with the mission and goals of the GEA, while the expertise and capacity-building of GEA found a welcome place in the URI."[14]

Recent URI documents list the following Catholic organizations as contributors, affiliates, or supporters of its projects:

1. United Religions Initiative, "The Brazilian/URI Interfaith Gathering," May 28–31, 1999, http://www.uri.org/rio2002/english/mir_itatiaia.htm, printed 05/26/03. Nestor Muller was a member of the organizing commission for this meeting, which was initially proposed by Fr. Luis Dolan.

2. United Religions Initiative, "Cooperation Circles Around the World," Latin America and the Caribbean, *URI Update*, Fall 2000, p5.

3. "Chapitre VIII: Visites Plus Récentes—Un Grand Échange Spirituel: Moines Chrétiens et Moines Buddhistes Se Recontrent En Inde," http://www.scourmont.be/degive/tibet /chap8.htm, printed 03/04/03.

4. URI, "Affiliates."

5. URI, "URI in the World," *URI Update*, fall 2001, no. 10, p5.

6. The Elijah Interfaith Institute, "Lecturers in Elijah School Programs," http://www. elijah.org.il/participants/lecturersn.shtml, printed 07/17/04; lists Fr. Nauhaus' affiliation and country of residence.

7. URI, "Middle East—Cooperation Circle: The Interfaith Encounter Association," http://www.uri.org/regionalnews/mideast/ieacc.asp, printed 07/16/04.

8. The River Fund, "Uganda—Ma's Orphans Providence Center," http://www.riverfund.org/programs/uganda_orphanage.htm, printed 12/15/02.

9. URI, "Affiliates."

10. URI, *Annual Report* 2000, "URI in Partnership," p5.

11. "United Religions Initiative," http://hknrp.tripod.com/religions.htm, printed 11/25/02. His status as a priest is documented in Gibbs/Mahé, *Birth of a Global Community*, p82.

12. "URI In the World," *URI News Update*, Fall 1998, p7; information on his Church position is from Andrea Useem, "Coming together: Interview with Fr. Joseph Wainaina," *Wajibu: A Journal of Social and Religious Concern*, Vol. 13, no. 3, 1998, http://www.peacelink.it/wajibu/4_issue/p2.html, printed 01/14/03.

13. Global Education Associates (GEA), "Religious Orders Partnership," http://www.globaleduc.org/rop.htm, printed 3/17/03 (cited below as GEA, "Religious Orders Partnership").

14. Global Education Associates, "United Religions Initiative," http://www.globaleduc.org/uri.htm, printed 3/17/03.

- Benet Hill Monastery.[1]
- Catholic Diocese of Oakland, California.[2] The Diocese donated to the URI in 2000, and is the only Catholic diocese thus far to have gone on record as doing so.
- Catholic Relief Services.[3]
- Franciscan Sisters of the Poor in Brooklyn, New York.[4]
- ICM Missionary Sisters.[5]
- Jesuit Community of Addis Ababa, Ethiopia.[6]
- Loretto Community in Denver, Colorado.[7]
- New Camaldoli Hermitage in Big Sur, California.[8]
- School Sisters of Notre Dame[9]—including the Mankato Province, Minnesota, which donated in 2000.[10]
- Sisters of the Blessed Sacrament in Atlanta, Georgia (Maisha House of Prayer).[11]
- Sisters of Charity, New York.[12]
- Sisters of the Humility of Mary, Villa Maria, Pennsylvania.[13]
- Sisters of Loretto.[14]
- Sisters of St. Francis of the Holy Cross.[15]
- Sisters of St. Francis in Oldenburg, Indiana and Philadelphia, Pennsylvania,[16] and the order's Leadership Team.[17]

1. URI, *Annual Report* 2002, "Honoring URI Donors and Volunteers." This is a Benedictine order of nuns founded in 1965, based in Colorado Springs, Colorado. Their web page is http://www.benethillmonastery.org/, as of 07/05/04.

2. URI, *Annual Report* 2000, "Honoring Our Donors," p7.

3. Catholic Relief Service (CRS) assisted in fundraising for youth workshops sponsored by a URI Cooperation Circle in Ethiopia in 2001 and 2002. The workshops covered "Respecting Diversity, Communications & Leadership Skills, Cultivating Non-Violent Thinking, The Role of Religious Reconciliation, Culture of Peace, and Connecting Faith and Action." (United Religions Initiative, "URI-Ethiopia: A Symbol of Peace," http://www.uri.org/regionalnews/africa/addis.asp, printed 02/17/03.

4. URI, *Annual Report* 2000, "Honoring Our Donors," p7. In addition, the Franciscan Sisters of the Poor in Warwick and the Bronx, New York and in Hoboken, New Jersey supported the URI's "global religious cease-fire" at Y2K. (URI, "Archive of 72 Hours Projects," projects in New York and New Jersey).

5. URI, *Annual Report* 2000, "Honoring Our Donors," p7.

6. *URI—Horn of Africa Newsletter*, September 2001, p4; Aba Grum Tesfaye facilitated a workshop on "Respecting Diversity" under the auspices of URI-Ethiopia, in May 2001.

7. URI, *Annual Report* 2000, "Honoring Our Donors," p7; Sister Mary Peter Bruce is listed as a donor. For her affiliation to the sisters in Denver, see *Denver Catholic Register*, "Religious sisters' exchange builds relationships," September 5, 2001, http://www.archden.org/dcr/archive/20010905/2001090514ln.htm, printed 12/15/02.

8. URI, *Annual Report* 2000, "URI Charter Signings 2000," p6. The Hermitage held a URI charter-signing event in June 2000 "attended by more than 25 religious and spiritual leaders from Catholic, Trappist, Jesuit, Benedictine, Chinese Chan Buddhist, Japanese Zen Buddhist, Korean Buddhist, Taoist, Confucian and Hindu traditions."

9. URI, *Annual Report* 2001, "Honoring Our Donors," p8.

10. URI, *Annual Report* 2000, "Honoring Our Donors," p7.

11. Ibid. The donor listing is "Sr. Loretta McCarthy and Maisha House of Prayer." McCarthy, the Maisha House of Prayer, and her order—the Sisters of the Blessed Sacrament, are listed in "Nuns and Sisters Serving within the Archdiocese of Atlanta," http://www.serraatlanta.org/sisters.htm, printed 12/15/02.

12. URI, *Annual Report* 2001, "Honoring Our Donors," p8, and United Religions Initiative, "Honoring URI Donors and Volunteers," *Annual Report* 2002 leaflet.

13. URI, *Annual Report* 2000, "Honoring Our Donors," p7, and URI, *Annual Report* 2001, "Honoring Our Donors," p8. The URI lists the "Sisters of the Humility of Mary" as donors for 2002, without specifying which convent was the donor (URI, *Annual Report* 2002 "Honoring URI Donors and Volunteers"). In addition, the Sisters of the Humility of Mary supported the URI "global religious cease-fire" at Y2K (URI, "Archive of 72 Hours Projects").

14. URI, *Annual Report* 2002, "Honoring URI Donors and Volunteers."

15. URI, *Annual Report* 2002, "Honoring URI Donors and Volunteers," and URI, *Annual Report* 2003.

16. URI, Annual Report 2000, "Honoring Our Donors," p7. The URI also lists the Sisters of St. Francis of Philadelphia as donors in 2002. (URI, *Annual Report* 2002, "Honoring URI Donors and Volunteers.") The Sisters of St. Francis in Philadelphia also supported the URI "religious cease fire" project at the beginning of 2000. (URI, "Archive of 72 Hours Projects.")

17. URI, "Affiliates"—North America.

- Sisters of St. Francis of Tiffin.[1]
- Sisters of St. Joseph,[2] including their house in Philadelphia.[3]
- Sisters of the Transfiguration.[4]

In addition, the following Catholic hierarchs, religious, and organizations supported the URI's global "religious cease-fire" for the New Year holiday of 2000:

- Mary Christine Fellerhoff, "CSA, Leadership Conference of Women Religious."[5]
- Franciscan Missionaries of Mary in Quezon City in the Philippines,[6] and in England, Scotland, Ireland, Malta, Hungary, Slovenia, and Bosnia.[7]
- Franciscan Sisters of Little Falls, Minnesota.[8]
- Sister Mary Margaret Funk, of Monastic Inter-Religious Dialogue.[9]
- Holy Redeemer Retreat Center in Oakland, California.[10]
- Institute of the Sisters of Mercy of Australia.[11]
- Leadership Conference of Women Religious, a US-based organization of Catholic nuns.[12]
- Medical Mission Sisters in Philadelphia.[13]
- Notre Dame Sisters in Omaha, Nebraska.[14]
- Pakistani Catholic Bishops National Commission for Christian Muslim Relations.[15]
- Pax Christi of Cleveland, Ohio.[16]
- Pax Christi USA and the Los Angeles Catholic Worker.[17]
- Religious Orders Partnership,[18] (encompassing more that 150 Catholic religious orders, who work with Global

1. Ibid. The URI also lists this order as donors in 2002 (URI, *Annual Report* 2002, "Honoring URI Donors and Volunteers").

2. URI, *Annual Report* 2000, "Honoring Our Donors," pp7, 9; three different nuns are listed as URI donors—Ss. Judith Cole, Pamela Owens, and Mary Ann Mulzet. In addition, the Sisters of St. Joseph in Wheeling, West Virginia and in Philadelphia supported the URI "religious cease-fire" at Y2K (URI, "Archive of 72 Hours Projects").

3. URI, "Affiliates"—North America.

4. URI, *Annual Report* 2002, "Honoring URI Donors and Volunteers."

5. URI, "Some Early Supporters."

6. URI, "Archive of 72 Hours Projects."

7. Gibbs/Mahé, *Birth of a Global Community*, p190. The Missionaries of Mary "organized interfaith prayer vigils for peace" as part of the URI's "72 Hours" project.

8. URI, "Archive of 72 Hours Projects." This order also supports the Earth Charter. (Franciscan Sisters of Little Falls, Minnesota, "Earth Charter: The Way Forward for Our Planet," http://www.fslf.org/peace.htm, printed 04/10/03.)

9. URI, "Some Early Supporters."

10. Holy Redeemer Center, "Multi-faith, Multicultural Peacebuilding Retreat," http://www.zone11.net/oakland/, printed 2/18/03. The Holy Redeemer Retreat Center promoted a retreat from 12/30/99 through 1/1/00 as "A URI Millineum [sic] Event," provided a link to the URI, and included a Labyrinth dedication as part of the retreat.

11. Institute of the Sisters of Mercy of Australia, "72 Hours," *Mercy-Justice Newsletter*, October 1999, http://www.mercy. org.au/NATIONAL/justice_news/9910.html, printed in 1999; no longer on the Net.

12. Leadership Conference of Women Religious, "Update", http://www.paulist.org/lcwr/Newsltr.html, printed in 1999; no longer on the Net. See also their July 1999 newsletter, http://lcwr.org/Newsletter/july.htm, in which they state that "many LCWR members will participate in the upcoming 72–hour peace-building project of the United Religions Initiative." (This document is no longer on the Net.)

13. URI, "Archive of 72 Hours Projects."

14. Ibid.

15. United Religions Initiative, "Building spiritual partnerships for a just, sustainable and peaceable world," leaflet issued 5/15/99.

16. URI, "Archive of 72 Hours Projects."

17. Ibid.

18. GEA Religious Orders Partnership, "1999–2002 Platform for Action," http://www.globaleduc.org/platform.htm, printed 02/20/03. They agreed to "use materials from the United Religions" to "promote the wisdom of all cultures and traditions."

Education Associates to "effect global systemic change.")[1]
• Sisters of Charity of St. Augustine in Richfield, Ohio.[2]
• Sisters of the Holy Name, in Santa Clara, California (Justice and Peace Committee of the California province).[3]
• Sisters of the Immaculate Heart of Mary in Saco, Maine.[4]
• Sisters of Providence in St. Mary-in-the-Woods in Indiana.[5]
• Fr. Ruben J. Villote, from the Philippines, urged widespread Catholic participation in the URI "Global Cease Fire."[6]

Catholic academic theologians who support the URI include an array of dissenters from the teachings of the Catholic Church.

Roger Corless donated to the URI in 2000.[7] He is "Emeritus Professor of Religion at Duke University, where he taught for thirty years, has published four books and more than fifty articles on Buddhism, Christianity, Buddhist-Christian Dialogue, and Queer Studies."[8] He

attends Mass and gives Dharma talks, but he does not consider himself to be a hybrid Buddhist-Christian. He feels more like a symbiont, hosting the two traditions and allowing them to interact. He was on the faculty of Duke University for thirty years and has recently retired to the Bay Area where he teaches at the Institute of Buddhist Studies. He writes for the newsletter of the San Francisco based Gay Buddhist Fellowship under the nom de plume Dharma Daddy.[9]

Paul Knitter, senior editor at Orbis Books and professor of theology at Xavier University, attended the URI summit conference in 1997.[10] Knitter, an ex-priest, favors artificial birth control and the ordination of women as priests, denies that Jesus is the unique Savior, the Son of God,[11] and finds the Resurrection to be "problematic."[12] Along with Daniel Maguire of Marquette University and Fr. Richard

1. GEA, "Religious Orders Partnership."

2. URI, "Archive of 72 Hours Projects."

3. Ibid.

4. Ibid.

5. Sisters of Providence, "General Officer Sister Joan Slobig elected to lead branch of international organization," Jan. 21, 2000 press release, http://www.spsmw.org/news/releases/joan.htm, printed 03/10/02; no longer on the Net at this address. (As of 2004, a copy of this web page is at http://web.archive.org/web/20020118135040/http://www.spsmw.org/news/releases/joan.htm). "Sisters of Providence General Officer Sister Joan Slobig has been elected chairperson of the Religious Orders Partnership (ROP), a prominent branch of Global Education Associates. . . . The Sisters of Providence hosted the ROP annual meeting in April 1999 at Saint-Mary-of-the-Woods, the first time the meeting occurred outside New York City in its 20-year history. A Platform for Action for 1999–2002 was adopted. The platform follows: . . . . Support the 72 Hours for Peace project of the United Religions Initiative. Encourage each member congregation to hold Global Spirituality and Education for Global Citizenship Workshops."

6. URI, "72 Hours: Unprecedented Acts of Peace Among Religions And Spiritual Communities," *URI Update*, Fall 1999, p4. See also, Fr. Ruben J. Villote, "Like The Wind Blowing Where It Pleases," *Philippine Daily Inquirer*, May 16, 1999, http://www.inquirer.net/mags/may99wk4/mag_9.htm, printed 1999; no longer on the Net at this address. (As of 2004, a copy of this web page is at http://web.archive.org/web/19991206141429/http://www.inquirer.net/mags/may99wk4/mag_9.htm.)

7. URI, *Annual Report* 2000, "Honoring Our Donors," p8.

8. Stanford Continuing Studies, "The Spirituality of the Great Religions" (course taught by Corless), http://continuing-studies.stanford.edu/academic_programs/campus_courses/courses/REL45.asp, printed 12/15/02.

9. *Queer Berkeley News*, "Buddhism and Christianity: Rivals and Allies" (title of course taught in the fall of 2002 at the Harvey Milk Institute by Corless), http://queer.berkeley.edu/news/display.php3?newsid=844, printed 12/15/02.

10. Paul Chaffee, "Ring of Breath Around the World: A Report of the United Religions Initiative Global Conference," issued in the summer of 1997 by the United Religions Initiative, p3.

11. *St. Catherine Review*, "Theology of Dr. Paul F. Knitter," 1999, http://www.aquinas-multimedia.com/catherine/theoknitter.html, printed 03/29/03; the document includes quotations from a textbook (*Faith, Religion, and Theology*) of which Knitter was co-author, and which is used in the introductory theology course required of all undergraduates at Xavier University.

12. Bob Buse, "Xavier Theology Professor's Threefold Denial," *St. Catherine Review*, July/August 1998, http://www.aquinas-multimedia.com/catherine/knitter.html, printed 03/29/03.

McBrien of Notre Dame, Knitter has said that he will not seek a *mandatum,* a statement from his bishop that his teaching is in accord with the doctrines of the Catholic Church.[1]

Leonard Swidler, professor of "Catholic Thought and Interreligious Dialogue" at Temple University, likewise attended the 1997 URI global meeting.[2] Swidler's prodigious track record includes such writings as "Jesus Was a Feminist" (1971), "God the Father: Masculine, God the Son: Masculine, God the Holy Spirit: Feminine" (1975), "Seven Reasons for Ordaining Women" (1977), "God, Father and Mother" (1984), "Dissent an Honored Part of Church's Vocation" (1989), *After the Absolute: The Dialogical Future of Religious Reflection* (1990), and "Yeshua, Feminist and Androgynous: An Integrated Human" (1991). He has also offered a lecture titled, "Why Christians Need to Dialogue With—NOT Proselytize—Non-Christians" (1992).

Brother Wayne Teasdale has supported the URI and other interfaith organizations,[3] and attended the 1997 URI summit meeting at Stanford.[4] He is an adjunct professor at the Catholic Theological Union,[5] describes himself as a "lay monk who combines the traditions of Christianity and Hinduism in the way of Christian sannyasa"[6] and proposes that the Church become "a welcoming place for all the religions."[7]

Last but not least among the theologians, Hans Küng supports the URI.[8] Bishop Swing hailed Küng as "the prime spokesperson for Vatican II and the single most important person who has written volumes on interfaith and ecumenical matters."[9] However, since 1979, Küng has been banned from teaching as a Catholic theologian.[10] (Küng continued to teach at Tübingen University, which moved him from the religious faculty to the secular faculty.) Cardinal Ratzinger (now Pope Benedict XVI), head of the Congregation for the Doctrine of the Faith at the Vatican, says of Küng that since 1979, "in Christology and in trinitarian theology he has further distanced himself from the faith of the Church."[11] Küng is not a representative of the Catholic Church or "the prime spokesperson for Vatican II"; he speaks only for himself.

The prominence of these dissenters among the Catholic supporters of the URI limits the ability of the URI to support interreligious dialogue based on truth rather than compromise of religious principle. Cardinal Arinze explains,

Interreligious dialogue is a sincere meeting of a person deeply convinced of his own faith, with a believer in another religion. It presupposes peaceful possession of one's religious identity card, and membership in such good standing in one's religious community that one can be named an ambassador of that community. Interreligious dialogue is therefore not for religious indifferentists, not for those who are problem children in their faith

1. Patricia Lefevere, "Implementing license to teach worries theologians," *National Catholic Reporter*, February 16, 2001, http://www.natcath.com/NCR_Online/archives/021601/021601h.htm, printed 03/26/03.

2. Information in this paragraph is from the curriculum vitae of Leonard Swidler, http://astro.temple.edu/~dialogue/Swidler/swidvit.html, printed 06/17/04. Swidler attended the 1997 URI summit meeting ("Section VIII—Special Projects," item 156, on Swidler's curriculum vitae).

3. Wayne Teasdale, "From Tolerance to Communion: The Parliament of the World's Religions," *Conscious Choice*, November 1999, http://www.consciouschoice.com/culture/tolerance1211.html, printed 12/10/02.

4. Gibbs/Mahé, *Birth of a Global Community*, 2004, p123.

5. Synthesis Dialogues II, "Members," http://www.synthesisdialogues.org/members.htm#Teasdale, printed 12/10/02.

6. Soul to Spirit, "Authors: Brother Wayne Teasdale," http://www.soultospirit.com/traditions/book_excerpts/religion/comparative/teasdale/teasdalebio.asp, printed 03/18/03.

7. Wayne Teasdale, "The Church as Matrix," *The Golden String*, Vol. 8, no. 1, http://www.bedegriffiths.com/Golden/gs_15.htm, printed 12/09/02.

8. Swing, "The United Religions Initiative," 04/96, p6.

9. Bishop William Swing, "The Surprise Factor," *Pacific Church News*, June/July 1996, p10.

10. Helen Hull Hitchcock, "Hans Küng: Vatican Rehab or Challenge to Change?," *Adoremus Bulletin*, May/June 1998, Vol. IV, no. 3, p7.

11. Joseph Cardinal Ratzinger, *Salt of the Earth: Christianity and the Catholic Church at the End of the Millennium—An Interview with Peter Seewald*, translated by Adrian Walker, Ignatius Press, San Francisco, 1997, p96.

community, not for academicians who entertain doubt about some fundamental articles of their own faith, nor for religious iconoclasts who have already shattered sacred statues and shaken some of the pillars on which their religion is built. It would be a mistake to allow such doubters into the arena of interreligious dialogue.[1]

Why would any Christians support the URI? For some Christians, the desire for peace and for an end to violence committed in the name of religion is so compelling a motive that they overlook the broader agenda of the URI and its New Age allies.

Other Christians accept a view of "religion" offered in 1998 by URI executive William Rankin, that religion is "a system of beliefs and practices by means of which a group of people struggles with ultimate problems of human life. It expresses their refusal to capitulate to death, to give up in the face of frustration, to allow hostility to tear apart their human aspirations."[2] "Human aspirations," rather than following and obeying God, are the ultimate concerns for such URI adherents.

Some Christians—such as Bishop Swing—see the URI as part of the revelation of "tomorrow's Christ," an evolutionary, universalist messiah:

The revelation of Jesus Christ whom we first met in the Middle East, our children will meet in some middle galaxy. Yes, the same Jesus Christ, but understood in tomorrow's terms. Not just the 1798 Jesus Christ, not the 1954 Jesus Christ, but tomorrow's Jesus Christ who is ascending and on his way to eternity, forever. Oh, how I'd love to live through the next spiritual revolution. It is coming and it is vast and worth all the pain. The God of the Universe will create a more universal church, more catholic, tomorrow while we wait for eternity.[3]

Pope St. Pius X anticipated these tendencies among 21st Century reformist Christians when he criticized the activities of the Sillon, a radical Catholic movement in early 20th Century France. He said, "The exaltation of their sentiments, the undiscriminating good-will of their hearts, their philosophical mysticism, mixed with a measure of illuminism, have carried them away towards another Gospel which they thought was the true Gospel of Our Savior."[4]

1. Arinze, *Religions for Peace*, p 51.
2. Bill Rankin, "URI Fundraising—What is Our Role," *URI News Update*, fall 1998, p 2.
3. Swing, 1997 address to Diocesan convention, *PCN*, Dec. 1997/Jan. 1998, p 34.
4. Pope St. Pius X, *Notre Charge Apostolique (Our Apostolic Mandate)*, encyclical of August 25, 1910, section 41, http://www.catholicculture.org/docs/doc_view.cfm?recnum=5456, printed 05/27/04.

7

FOURTEEN REASONS
TO STAND AGAINST THE
UNITED RELIGIONS INITIATIVE

DESPITE CONCERNS ARISING from the Twilight Zone aspects of the agenda of the URI (and some of its leaders and allies), shouldn't orthodox Christians cooperate with the URI? After all, "The earth is the LORD's and the fulness thereof" (Ps. 24:1), and Jesus has commanded us to "Love your enemies" (Mt. 5:43). So, isn't this movement for peace, religious tolerance, and environmental protection—even if imperfect—worth supporting?

In one word: No.

The URI is gravely flawed, from its foundation up. Christians should not assist the growth of this movement, though they should monitor its activities closely. The words of Bishop Swing, other URI executives and activists, and prominent URI allies make the case against the movement from an orthodox Christian perspective. Many other venues exist within which Christians can perform the works of mercy, spiritual and corporal, that the Gospel requires.

URI Global Council member Donald Frew has downplayed the significance of Swing's statements, saying: "The organization is much more than Bishop Swing. It's not his own thing any more."[1] Frew later added, "When members of the URI express an opinion, that's not the URI speaking officially."[2] Nevertheless, URI leaders and activists *do* shape the agenda of the movement, and their speeches, writings, and public actions consistently oppose orthodox Christianity.

[1] THE URI VERSUS CHRISTIAN EVANGELISM

The first reason to stand against the URI is that many leaders of the URI, including Bishop Swing himself, consistently equate Christian evangelism—preaching the Gospel—with conquest and manipulative proselytism.

The 21st and last of the URI's founding "Principles" is that "Members of the URI shall not be coerced to participate in any ritual or be proselytized."[3] Donald Frew explains that this is a ban on proselytizing *at URI events*.[4] Frew added, "I do not have a problem with proselytizing; I have a problem with

---

1. Interview of URI Global Council member Donald Frew by Lee Penn, 10/14/02.

2. Interview of Donald Frew by Lee Penn, 3/28/03.

3. United Religions Initiative, "The United Religions Initiative Charter," http://www.uri.org/resources/publications/Charter%20PC%20format.doc, "Principles," principle 21, p 4; downloaded 07/07/04 (cited below as URI, "Charter").

4. Interview of URI Global Council member Donald Frew by Lee Penn, 10/14/02.

coercive or unwanted proselytizing."[1] Robert Traer, who headed the International Association for Religious Freedom in the 1990s, said, "In interfaith dialogue it is helpful to clarify that opposition to proselytism does not mean opposing religious witness that seeks conversion."[2]

So far, so good; coercing, bribing, manipulating, or deceiving anyone so that they participate in any kind of religious observance anywhere is wrong. As Cardinal Arinze has written:

> Proselytism is the effort to persuade a person to embrace a religion by methods that offend against human dignity or that exploit the weakness or difficult situation of that person. Examples would be to try to 'convert' a person to a religion by force or pressure, whether such pressure be physical, psychological, political, economic, or otherwise. To entice a person to a religion in order to give that person a study scholarship, or a job opportunity, or promotion, or simply food or money, is also proselytism. This is wrong because it does not respect the God-given dignity and freedom of the human person. Religious unity arrived at by means of force, or pressure, or clever maneuvering, is not worthy of humanity and is not a suitable gift for Almighty God.[3]

Furthermore, it makes sense that those who participate in interfaith movements should *not* seek converts at interfaith meetings.

However, URI opposition to "proselytizing" is far broader than this. Many leaders of the URI, including Bishop Swing himself, habitually equate evangelism—preaching the Gospel—with conquest and manipulative proselytism. If these leaders have their way, the open proclamation of traditional Christian belief will be increasingly stigmatized as "hate speech;" legal repression could follow. As Cardinal Arinze said in 1997, "There is, however, a use of the word proselytism that is unacceptable. Some people use the word to refer to every effort to propose one's religion to others, even when the means used are noble, honest, and respectful. It is wrong and confusing to use the term in this sense. It is like giving a dog a bad name in order to hang it."[4]

Bishop Swing, the founder of the URI (and a permanent member of its Global Council) has spoken consistently since 1996 against "proselytizing." He gives that term a very broad, and altogether negative, meaning.

In his opening speech to the 1996 URI summit conference, Bishop Swing said, "There is not going to be a time in the near future when one religion converts, conquers, subjugates all of the other religions to itself."[5] He thus equated religious conversion with conquest and subjugation.

In his 1998 book *The Coming United Religions*, Bishop Swing defined Christian evangelization as "proselytizing." In February 1996, when he preached the United Religions message to a Bible study class at the Maramon, a week-long mission revival meeting of the Mar Toma Church in Southern India,

> In an instant, the little Bible study turned into a wild scene of interrogative and declarative assertions. Hundreds of energized people with Bibles in their hands came hurrying out of the jungle. They had come together at the Maramon in order to excite a passion to go out and convert every Hindu and Moslem possible. And here I

---

1. Interview of Donald Frew by Lee Penn, 3/28/03.

2. Robert Traer, *Quest For Truth: Critical Reflections on Interfaith Cooperation*, The Davies Group, 1999, p18 (cited below as Traer, *Quest for Truth*).

3. Francis Cardinal Arinze, *Religions for Peace: A Call for Solidarity to the Religions of the World*, Doubleday, 2002, pp139–140 (cited below as Arinze, *Religions for Peace*).

4. Francis Cardinal Arinze, *Meeting Other Believers: The Risks and Rewards of Interreligious Dialogue*, Our Sunday Visitor Publishing Division, 1997, p68 (cited below as Arinze, *Meeting Other Believers*).

5. Bishop William Swing, opening speech for the United Religions summit meeting, June 24–28, 1996, p5 (cited below as Swing, opening speech for 1996 URI summit).

was stating that the religions, themselves, need to come together and discover a new level of interacting. This, clearly, was perceived to be a threat to proselytizing.[1]

Despite Swing's pejorative description of evangelical zeal as "proselytizing," there's no indication whatsoever that the revival participants planned to use deceit, bribes, or violence to win converts.

In *The Coming United Religions*, Bishop Swing says,

As the first of the Ten Commandments says, 'Thou shalt have no other gods but me.' Is any dimension of religion deeper than that? This is the first commandment according to Jews and Christians. It is not foreign to Muslims, or, in fact, to more than half the people on earth. Yet if billions of people from exclusive religions are commanded to oppose the godly claims of other exclusive religions, what hope is there for peace among religions? In order for a United Religions to come about and for religions to pursue peace among each other, there will have to be a godly cease-fire, a temporary truce where the absolute exclusive claims of each will be honored but an agreed upon neutrality will be exercised in terms of proselytizing, condemning, murdering, or dominating. These will not be tolerated in the United Religions zone.[2]

Here's Bishop Swing's logic: connect "proselytizing" to "condemning, murdering, or dominating"— and then say that none of these will be tolerated in "the United Religions zone"—potentially, the whole world.

What Bishop Swing excoriates as "proselytizing" is evangelism, the God-given duty of faithful Christians and of the Church. As Jesus said, "Go therefore and make disciples of all nations, baptizing them in the name of the Father and of the Son and of the Holy Spirit, teaching them to observe all that I have commanded you." (Mt. 28:19-20) In scorning Christian evangelism, Bishop Swing belied his statement that the URI "seeks to honor the ancient and recent wisdom and good works"[3] of each of the world's religions.

In late 1999, Swing continued his attack on "the covert strategy of gentle conversion" used by religions: "1. Each religion must face a reality check of violence at the core of its story. 2. Religions cannot keep competing against each other or try to win superiority by out-populating people of other religions. 3. Religions cannot hide behind the covert strategy of gentle conversion, while in reality using every subtle economic and cultural harassment to gain conquest over other faiths."[4] The second count of this indictment seems to condemn having large families, implying that this is an unfair religious practice.

When an audience member at Swing's April 2001 Commonwealth Club speech asked how Christians and Muslims could reconcile practice of their "one true faith" with "acceptance of other religions," Swing said, "If you are a member of a religion that's a missionary religion, how do you hold on, on the one hand, to being on mission, rightfully so for your faith, and at the same time hold onto a vision of a generous God who holds everything together? How do you keep this stridency and this tolerance together inside yourself? . . . I think you live into the question, till you come to a new internal change in your own heart." This equation of missionary zeal with "stridency" echoed throughout Swing's presentation. All of his references to Christian evangelism were negative—including repeating a charge made by a South American tribal leader at a URI meeting, that missionaries had cut the

1. Bishop William E. Swing, *The Coming United Religions*, United Religions Initiative and CoNexus Press, 1998, p33 (cited below as Swing, *The Coming United Religions*).
2. Ibid., p31.
3. Ibid., p70.
4. Dennis Delman, "Bishop Swing Preaches at Cape Town Cathedral: Urges 'New Day and New Way of Peacemaking,'" *Pacific Church News*, February/March 2000, p25 (cited below as Delman, "Swing Preaches at Cape Town," *PCN*, Feb./March 2000).

tongues out of his father and grandfather because they continued to preach their own "pagan religion" to the tribe, in defiance of the missionaries' order that they "shut up."[1]

In a fall 2001 interview with a liberal Episcopal magazine, Swing again linked claims of religious truth to violence:

There is in religion itself, usually, a deep sense of terrorism that we manufacture. I don't think we're ever going to get toward a solution until we go back to the religions to say, 'How many times have we been encouraged to take the jawbone of an ass and slay all the Philistines for the sake of God? Or encouraged to believe that we need to kill every man, woman and child in the village or else we'll be haunted in our dreams like King Saul?' There's enough violence and terrorism in our own tradition that we've never come to terms with. Secondly, there's a sense of superiority in religions that we're going to have to take care of some day. You know, Nazi Germany would say, 'We're the superior race.' Well, religions get by with saying almost that, that we're really God's people and the others aren't, that we're going to heaven and the others aren't, that we're of great worth and the others aren't unless they become like us. So some day religions are going to have to become accountable for their own contribution to terrorism.[2]

In January 2003, Swing again insinuated that religions who claim to be "the true religion" are using "master race thinking":

Most religions have been founded upon (the concept) that God has chosen us, and we are the true religion: Anybody who's not part of us is not part of the true religion. If you come with the idea that you're part of a superior race of religious people, that gives you a lot of temptation to go after people who are not part of you—and you can do whatever you want to. It gets into the 'master race' thinking.... There's great competition among religions for who controls the greatest number of human beings.... And religions are out there in the world trying to corner the market for themselves. As long as we are trying to corner the market for ourselves, that makes it possible to turn your face away and not look while things are being done to other people.[3]

Nevertheless, Swing has also recently favored the export of an American model of religious freedom, which allows room for evangelization. In the Winter 2003 issue of *Pacific Church News*, Swing wrote,

What if the United States of America's chief religious export were religious freedom and its undergirding assumptions? In the eyes of the state, all religions are created equal. That is not to say that in the eyes of God or the eyes of believers of various faiths all religions are equal. But in order to avoid the bloodthirstiness of political

1. Transcribed by Lee Penn from a tape of the speech by Bishop Swing at the Commonwealth Club, April 25, 2001 (cited below as Swing, Commonwealth Club speech, 04/25/01). Rosalia Gutierrez, of the Kolla tribe, told a URI planning meeting in 1997 in Buenos Aires, Argentina, that "she could barely speak her native language; her grandparents had had their tongues cut out so they couldn't teach the language to their children!" (Charles Gibbs and Sally Mahé, *United Religions Initiative, Birth of a Global Community: Appreciative Inquiry in Action*, Lakeshore Publishers, 2004, p97; cited below as Gibbs/Mahé, *Birth of a Global Community*).

2. Julie A. Wortman, "Promoting 'Franchises' To End Religious Violence: an interview with William Swing," *The Witness*, December 2001, p10 (cited below as Wortman, Interview with Swing, *Witness*, 12/01).

3. Nina Wu, "If it's about oil, just say so," [Interview with Bishop Swing], *The Examiner*, Jan. 7, 2003, http://www.examiner.com/examiner_qa/default.jsp?story=n.qa.0107w, printed 02/19/03. However, Frithjof Schuon, a Traditionalist proponent of the "transcendent unity of religions" says, "Every religion by definition wants to be the best, and 'must want' to be the best, as a whole and also as regards its constitutive elements; this is only natural, so to speak, or rather 'supernaturally natural' ... religious oppositions cannot but be, not only because forms exclude one another ... but because, in the case of religions, each form vehicles an element of absoluteness that constitutes the justification for its existence; now the absolute does not tolerate otherness nor, with all the more reason, plurality.... To say form is to say exclusion of possibilities, whence the necessity for those excluded to become realized in other forms." (Frithjof Schuon, *Christianity/Islam: Essays in Esoteric Ecumenism*, p15; reference provided by Charles Upton.)

dominance by one religion, all religions will be treated equally and provided with freedom to flourish. We try to encourage democracy around the world. What if we encouraged our version of religious freedom?[1]

In early 2004, the URI joined a San Francisco protest against the proposed French law banning the wearing of conspicuous religious attire, including the Muslim *hijab*, in French schools.[2] The open question is, which vision guides the policies of Swing and the URI—the *peaceful* export of the traditional American vision of religious freedom,[3] or the opposition to religious evangelization?

Swing's slurs against "proselytizing" are in contrast with his oft-repeated pleas for Church growth in his own diocese, such as this exhortation in his address to the Diocesan Convention in 2000: "This past year we closed St. Matthias', San Ramon. And we have not started one surviving new congregation at a time when the Bay Area has undergone a rapid expansion of population. Doesn't this bother us, we who are called to spread the Good News of Jesus Christ? What is going on here?"[4] What is going on may be easy to explain. Bishop Swing has been giving his flock a mixed message, and "if the trumpet give an uncertain sound, who shall prepare himself to the battle?" (1 Cor. 14:8, KJV)

Despite the foregoing attacks on traditional Christianity, Swing still considers himself to be "called by God," and a follower of Christ. In 2004, on the occasion of his 25th anniversary as Bishop of California, Swing said, "I do believe that I was called by God to be Bishop of California. I have felt Divine Presence whispering, yearning, beckoning, and enduring. Jesus Christ is the only bishop of our souls, and we prelates are only pitiful pretenders who willingly serve our time, get our portraits painted, and move along as bishop VI fades into bishop VII, who fades into bishop VIII. The real bishop stays. Jesus, Good Shepherd!"[5]

URI board members and executives have agreed with Swing that religious evangelism is an evil—presumably, making an exception for their *own* proselytizing on behalf of religious syncretism.

In 1999, Charles Gibbs, the Executive Director of the URI, apologized for two millennia of Christian evangelism. His *mea culpa* was not limited to religious violence; he also regretted "proclaiming that Jesus Christ is Lord and Savior of all" and seeking "to make the whole world Christian":

> I must acknowledge that, throughout the centuries, in seeking to love God and express the unity that is in God, many Christians have not honored the distinctness and validity of other religions, but have sought to make the whole world Christian. I confess that a tremendous amount of violence has been visited on the world by Christians aflame with the conviction that the only path to salvation is through proclaiming that Jesus Christ is Lord and Savior of all, and that it is the responsibility of Christians to make Christians of all people. I profoundly regret that violence.[6]

---

1. Bishop William Swing, "The Import-Export of U.S. Religion," *Pacific Church News*, Winter 2003, p5. (cited below as Swing "The Import-Export of U.S. Religion," *PCN*, Winter 2003).

2. Jessie Mangaliman, "S. F. religious rally decries French plan," *San Jose Mercury News*, January 18, 2004; printed 01/18/04 from the Internet.

3. I refer to the "traditional American vision of religious freedom," recognizing that this tradition has been under sustained attack in the US for the last 50 years. In the name of "equal rights" and preventing "establishment of religion," courts have outlawed prayer in public schools, banned the display of Nativity scenes and the text of the Ten Commandments in public buildings and parks, and—in California—required Catholic charitable organizations to provide insurance coverage for employees' use of artificial contraceptives (the use of which is against the teaching of the Catholic Church). I would add that the current attempts to export American values and institutions to the Middle East and elsewhere by force are a latter-day form of Jacobinism, and make a travesty of the very values that the proponents of "remaking the world in our image" claim to uphold.

4. Bishop William E. Swing, "Excerpts from Bishop Swing's Convention Address," *Pacific Church News*, December 2000/January 2001, p21.

5. Bishop William E. Swing, "The Swing Shift: 25 Years of the 155 Years of the Diocese of California," Episcopal News Service, August 9, 2004, http://www.episcopalchurch.org/3577_48075_ENG_HTM.htm, printed 08/10/04.

6. Charles Gibbs, "An Ethical Mandate for the United Religions," *Journal of the United Religions Initiative*, Issue 5, p11.

In 2001, Gibbs told a federally supported conference on faith-based Non-Governmental Organizations that "URI recognizes the right of people to share and promote their faith but it also recognizes the destructiveness of proselytizing when it is conducted insensitively."[1] Given the extreme sensitivity of opponents of Christianity to public manifestation of the Christian faith, Gibbs' criticism of "insensitive proselytizing" leaves much room for infringement of religious freedom for Christians.

In 2004, Gibbs told an interfaith gathering that when religions make claims to be the exclusive bearers of truth, the result is violence. As the *San Francisco Chronicle* reported, "Gibbs said the problem seems to be that people of all three faiths [Christians, Jews, and Muslims] limit themselves with a narrow interpretation of religious law, with their own exclusive version of the truth. 'That,' the priest said, 'has led to incredible bloodshed.' According to Gibbs, the solution is spirituality, not religion."[2]

During the 1997 URI summit conference at Stanford, the gay activist Christian de la Huerta had made a statement on gay spirituality to a plenary session. Afterward, in response, Rosalia Gutierrez—a member of the Kolla tribe[3] in Argentina, and on the URI Global Council since 2002—told de la Huerta, "When you go out and tell others about this experience, ask them to remember us Indigenous people. Ask them to stop the evangelization. Tell them that we don't wish to be evangelized. For if you do away with our traditions, who will tell you about the Earth or remind you of nature?"[4]

At a public April 1997 URI forum at Grace Cathedral, Sri Ravi Peruman (who was on the URI board from 1997 through 2002)[5] said that religions have "invaded and crusaded," "subverted and converted."[6] *Pacific Church News* reported: "Calling statements about 'authentic religious freedom' for everyone, 'the freedom to proselytize,' Peruman said that there should be a universal *Declaration of Rights* not to be converted to another religion."[7] In 2000, Swing explained this statement (which was made at a *public*, URI-sponsored event) to a Sufi Muslim critic of the URI. Swing said that Peruman "is a Hindu who, like many Hindus of India, sees the issue of proselytizing to be a major obstacle to interfaith dialogue. Your quote was a private quote from Ravi. Your implication that the URI is calling for a Declaration of Rights not to be converted to another religion is absolutely not the case."[8]

The Dalai Lama, exiled leader of Tibetan Buddhism and a public supporter of the URI, has joined India's Hindu nationalist leaders in condemning "proselytism" by Christians and Muslims. On January 25 2001, after a meeting with leaders of the World Hindu Council (a group which wants to make India a Hindu state), the Dalai Lama said, "Whether Hindu or Muslim or Christian, whoever tries to convert, it's wrong, not good . . . I always believe it's safer and better and reasonable to keep one's own tradition or belief."[9] The Dalai Lama added, "The methods adopted by Christian missionaries for religious conversions are wrong and they, instead of indulging in conversions, should make efforts to preserve their own traditions. . . . Conversion is an outdated concept and it is harmful as it results in

1. United States Institute of Peace, "Faith-Based NGOs and International Peacebuilding," October 22, 2001, http://www.usip.org/pubs/specialreports/sr76.html, printed 02/17/03.

2. Don Lattin, "INTERFAITH GATHERING IN S.F.: Seeking common ground—Christians, Muslims, Jews told spirituality, not religion, is key," *San Francisco Chronicle*, May 25, 2004, http://www.sfgate.com/cgi-bin/article.cgi?file=/chronicle/archive/2004/05/25/BAGMH6R5LI1.DTL, printed 05/26/04.

3. Gibbs/Mahé, *Birth of a Global Community*, p 97.

4. Christian de la Huerta, *Coming Out Spiritually: The Next Step*, Tarcher/Putnam, 1999, p 4.

5. 1997 list of board members: United Religions Initiative, "New Board," *URI News Update*, March 1997, p 3; 2000 list of Interim Global Council members: United Religions Initiative, "'Interim Global Council Membership in 2000," *Annual Report 2000*, p 8.

6. Dennis Delman, "Grace Cathedral Satellite Conference," *Pacific Church News*, June/July 1997, p 27.

7. Ibid.

8. Letter from Bishop Swing to Charles Upton, November 6, 2000; provided to Lee Penn by Charles Upton.

9. Associated Press (AP), "Dalai Lama condemns Christian, Muslim practice of seeking converts," January 26, 2001, http://www.cnn.com/2001/WORLD/asiapcf/south/01/25/india.lama/, printed 03/29/03.(cited below as AP, "Dalai Lama condemns seeking converts,"01/26/01).

clashes between different religions."[1] (The Dalai Lama also warned against "countering conversions through use of force.")[2] The Associated Press reported that "The Dalai Lama and others signed a statement saying: 'We oppose conversions by any religious tradition using various methods of enticement.'"[3]

India's Hindu radicals are outraged by conversions to Christianity among tribal peoples and untouchables, and define "enticement" very broadly—including Christian provision of education, health care, and social services. In recent years, Hindu nationalists have attacked many Christians, laymen and clergy alike, in pogroms throughout India. Despite their opposition to Christian evangelism, modern-day Buddhist and Hindu leaders proselytize aggressively in the West.

Sister Jayanti, the European director of the Brahma Kumaris (a primarily female order with Hindu roots),[4] was asked at a 1998 meeting of 20 world religious leaders: "Thinking 5 or 10 years from now, what will have made this worthwhile for you"?[5] Jayanti, a URI supporter,[6] stated her dream that there will be no more religious conversions: "The leaders of religions will be trusting each other and encouraging their organisations to function from a position of peace and friendship not from competition, mistrust or conversion. There will be a recognition that each person is on the path that is right for them."[7]

URI supporter Brother Wayne Teasdale, a Catholic, likewise holds that interreligious dialogue trumps evangelization and proclamation of the Gospel. He acknowledges that this view is contradictory to the teachings of the Catholic Church as stated "in so many of her documents, especially *Redemptoris Hominis* and the more recent, *Dominus Iesus*."[8] Teasdale says, "The notion that dialogue is subordinate to evangelization is not acceptable to the other traditions, and the Church's insistence on it too much can complicate her relationships with these traditions. The Church's twin values of evangelization and dialogue might be seen in a new way, that is, in terms of the value of sensitivity and discipline in the use of our language and how we speak of the other religions."[9]

By contrast, Article 18 of the UN's *Universal Declaration on Human Rights* recognizes that everyone has "the right to freedom of thought, conscience, and religion; this right includes freedom to change his religion or belief" and freedom "either alone or in community with others and in public or private, to manifest his religion or belief in teaching, practice, worship, and observance."[10]

As Cardinal Arinze said, "We must acknowledge the right of every believer to propose his religion to

---

1. "Christian missionaries' methods for conversion wrong: Dalai Lama," *Daily Excelsior*, http://www.dailyexcelsior.com/01jan27/news.htm, printed 3/29/03. The Excelsior describes itself on its home page (http://www.dailyexcelsior.com/) as "The largest circulated daily of Jammu and Kashmir."

2. Ibid.

3. AP, "Dalai Lama condemns seeking converts,"01/26/01.

4. According to Charles Upton, the Brahma Kumaris are "a quasi-monastic order of hybrid Hindu-New Age lineage." Another observer says, "Unlike traditional forms of Hinduism, their teachings come not so much from the ancient scriptures, as from revelations given in trance states." (David V. Barrett, *The New Believers: A Survey of Sects, 'Cults' and Alternative Religions*, Cassell & Co., 2001, p 265; cited below as Barrett, *The New Believers*).

5. Anne Radford, "Appreciative Inquiry Newsletter," Appreciative Inquiry Resource Centre, Issue 5, May 1999, http://www.aradford.co.uk/Pagefiles/05newsletter.htm, printed 05/09/03 (cited below as Radford, "Appreciative Inquiry Newsletter," 05/99).

6. United Religions Initiative, "72 Hours Global Action," *URI Update*, No. 7, Spring 2000, p 6; Jayanti and the Brahma Kumaris nuns worldwide participated actively in the "72 Hours." She also attended the 1996 URI global summit meeting. (Gibbs/Mahé, *Birth of a Global Community*, p 32.)

7. Anne Radford, "Appreciative Inquiry Newsletter," 05/99.

8. Wayne Teasdale, "The Church as Matrix," *The Golden String*, Vol. 8, no. 1, http://www.bedegriffiths.com/Golden/gs_15.htm, printed 12/09/02.

9. Ibid.

10. "Universal Declaration of Human Rights," as adopted by the UN General Assembly in 1948, in Joel Beversluis, ed., *Sourcebook of the World's Religions: An Interfaith Guide to Religion and Spirituality*, New World Library, 2000, p 327.

others with the hope that they may welcome it, believe in it, and embrace it."[1] He emphasized: "For the Christian it is not only a right but a duty to share the faith. It is therefore unacceptable that some people should oppose the right of Christians, or indeed of any other believers, to propose their religion to others in all freedom. Such a stand should be regarded as religious fanaticism or fundamentalism and should be rejected."[2]

While Swing and others allied with the URI condemn Christian "proselytization," they evangelize with zeal on behalf of the URI. This is the usual behavior of religious leaders: promoting their own faith and their own organization, while belittling the competition. The URI leaders quoted above appear to understand—consciously or otherwise—the incompatibility of traditional Christianity with the new interfaith world-view that they propose. And these URI leaders appear to have grasped the traditional principle that all enduring civilizations have a religious basis. If there is to be a global "new civilization,"[3] there must also be a new global faith to complement it. Therefore, URI opposition to Christian evangelization is not accidental; it is consistent with, and integral to, the aims of this movement and its globalist allies.

[11] STIGMATIZING "EXCLUSIVE RELIGIONS" AND ORTHODOXY AS "FUNDAMENTALISM"

The second reason to stand against the URI is that many URI leaders, from Bishop Swing on down, view orthodox Christians (as well as traditional Muslims and Jews) as "fundamentalists" who are a threat to religious peace.

Some URI leaders and staff—a minority—are tolerant of conservative and "fundamentalist" religious believers. URI staff member Paul Andrews had said in 1997, "It is my hope that our organization will not just be a network of religious liberals, but will include people who have real differences. . . . We need the power of what the fundamentalists bring as part of the religious conversation. There is no requirement that people who come into the United Religions stop believing that their faith is true."[4] URI Global Council member Donald Frew said in 2003, "I do not have a problem with fundamentalists. I have a problem with the violent behavior that is sometimes done by fundamentalists."[5] In early 2004, he added, "the groundwork for cooperation between conservative Christians and the URI is there; I would like to see it implemented through ongoing conversations."[6]

Nevertheless, many URI leaders—including Bishop Swing—see orthodox Christians and other traditional adherents of the Abrahamic faiths as "fundamentalists" who put peace at risk.

In April 2001, Bishop Swing offered a psychological diagnosis of the origin of fundamentalism and the "exclusive claims" of religions:

> Fundamentalism from my point of view, comes about where people feel more and more insecure, and grab harder and harder to the exclusive claims of one religion or another. And that cuts off the circulation of the blood flow, so that the sense of the freedom that there must be in God, and the generosity of God, and the compassion of God, gets frozen out with the exclusive claims. So, fundamentalism is a real issue. But I think fundamentalism isn't just a group of people; I think it's the human heart. How much freedom can you stand? And how much does your lack of security cause you to grip at life so hard that you squeeze the life out of it?[7]

1. Arinze, *Meeting Other Believers*, p66.
2. Arinze, *Religions for Peace*, p138.
3. Mikhail Gorbachev, in Mikhail Gorbachev and Zdeněk Mlynář, *Conversations with Gorbachev: On Perestroika, the Prague Spring, and the Crossroads of Socialism*, Columbia University Press, 2002, p172.
4. Interviews by Lee Penn of Paul Andrews, URI staff member, October 7 and December 11, 1997.
5. Interview of Donald Frew by Lee Penn, 3/28/03.
6. Interview of Donald Frew by Lee Penn, 01/08/04.
7. Swing, Commonwealth Club speech, 04/25/01.

He added, "Most of us have learned religion through war. We go back and read our stories, and our group, with our god, fought their group with their god, and we won, and we slaughtered them, and that proves that god loves us and god hates them. That's the kind of story that's in the psyche of children who learn religion all over the world. The great, guiding, exciting stories are not about peace-making; they are about who won the war."[1]

At the October 10, 2001 URI meeting at the UN, Swing said that the URI seeks to address the problem of "fundamentalists in our own groups," an issue that traditional religion "wimps out on."[2] Swing said the same in the October 2001 issue of *Pacific Church News*, his diocesan magazine: "So much harm is done worldwide by so many religions, e.g., poisoning the wells of spirituality and teaching adherents to marginalize, paganize, and plain old despise people of other beliefs, that interfaith becomes a practical necessity."[3]

In the spring of 2003, while denouncing all drug use, Swing equated "dogma" to use of mind-bending drugs. He said, "When human beings are alert, we yearn for an experience of the Divine, with the Divine. That is not the problem. That is to be encouraged. The question then is how to have a transcendent experience without having your brain fried . . . by drugs or dogma?"[4]

Two people who served as URI board members in the late 1990s made it clear that they had no sympathy for fundamentalism, a term that they defined broadly indeed. At a February 1997 URI forum at Grace Cathedral, Paul Chaffee (who was then URI Board Secretary) said, "We can't afford fundamentalists in a world this small."[5] At the same forum, Rita Semel (who was then, as now, URI board Chair) said that fundamentalism "comes out of fear and ignorance. So many things are out of our control now that were much simpler when I was growing up."[6]

Other prominent URI supporters express the same disdain for "fundamentalism."

In 2000, the Episcopal Church's Presiding Bishop, Frank Griswold, denounced the irregular Singapore consecrations of two evangelical bishops to serve conservative Episcopalians in the United States. Griswold condemned "the dangerous fundamentalism—both within Islam and our own Christian community—which threatens to turn our God of compassion into an idol of wrath."[7]

Michael Ingham, an Anglican bishop from Canada, rejects the view that salvation comes only through Jesus. As journalist Terry Mattingly reported, "The bishop doesn't mince words. Traditionalists

---

1. Ibid.

2. C-FAM, "UN Religious Meeting Blames Religions for Terror Attack on US," *Friday FAX*, October 12, 2001, Vol. 4, no. 42; http://www.c-fam.org/FAX/Volume_4/faxv4n42.html, printed 02/19/03.

3. Bishop William Swing, "A Swing Through the Diocese," *Pacific Church News*, October/November 2001, p5 (cited below as Swing, "A Swing Through The Diocese," *PCN*, Oct./Nov. 2001).

4. Bishop William Swing, "A Swing Through The Diocese: Drugs and the Diocese of California," *Pacific Church News*, Spring 2003, Vol. 141, No. 2, p5. The ellipsis was in the original text. For Christians, this leaves open the question: which articles of the Creeds, or which dogmatic definitions by the Ecumenical Councils of the Church, cause the brain to fry? Charles Upton comments, "Dogma is among the necessary means by which dogma is transcended—which does not mean discarded. You can't go beyond dogma if you haven't gotten there yet." (Charles Upton, e-mail to Lee Penn, February 3, 2004.)

5. Transcribed by Lee Penn from URI-provided tape of URI forum at Grace Cathedral, held on 02/02/97, cited below as URI forum, Grace Cathedral, 02/02/97. In a November 21, 2000 letter to Bishop Swing, Charles Upton described this as "inflammatory language," an instance of using "buzz-words denoting large, ill-defined categories of humanity." (Letter from Charles Upton to Bishop Swing, November 21, 2000; provided by Charles Upton to Lee Penn.) In reply, Swing said Upton's criticism of Chaffee's statement was "well-ordered." (Letter from Bishop Swing to Charles Upton, December 7, 2000; provided by Charles Upton to Lee Penn.)

6. URI forum, Grace Cathedral, 02/02/97.

7. Presiding Bishop Frank Griswold, statement of January 31, 2000 "For the primates of the Anglican Communion," in response to the consecration in Singapore of Bishops Rodgers and Murphy, http://www.episcopalchurch.org/episcopal-life/SingLett.html, printed 04/08/03. (This document was at http://arc.episcopalchurch.org/episcopal-life/SingLett.html, as of 02/12/04.)

who defend 'Christian exclusivism' and other judgmental ancient dogmas may, in fact, worship a different god than the interfaith deity who inspires modern pluralists, he said."[1] Ingham continued, "The problem with exclusivism is that it presents us with a god from whom we need to be delivered, rather than the living God who is the hope of the world. . . . The exclusivist god is narrow, rigid, and blind. Such a god is not worthy of honor, glory, worship or praise."[2]

Bishop Ingham also excoriated fundamentalism and those he describes as "mainstream conservatives:"

Religious fundamentalism is on the rise all over the world, in every major tradition. It is a reaction of fear to modernity, to the rapid speed of change in modern societies. It is a nostalgic longing for simplicity, both intellectual and political, a deep impulse to stem the tide of change that is sweeping away social and cultural traditions right across our globalized world. Hardly anyone today underestimates the force or danger of fundamentalism. There is scarcely a more toxic combination than religion and fear. There is no limit to its barbarity and intolerance. One of the characteristics of fundamentalism, whether Christian, or any other, is its endless capacity for rationalization and self-justification in the name of sacred text or sacred tradition. The power of fundamentalism lies precisely in its ability to claim divine authorization, the imprimatur of God, and its ability to manipulate the anxieties of people by dogmatic and unquestioning use of ancient and holy myths. Fundamentalism is not the only obstacle, however. Mainstream conservatives, who must be distinguished from fundamentalists, exhibit the same motives of anxiety. . . . Both fundamentalism and mainstream conservatism see a common enemy in religious pluralism.[3]

Hans Küng has denounced the Pope's call for the re-evangelization of Europe, scorned Papal denunciations of Western hedonism, and stood for "the modern values of freedom, pluralism, and tolerance"—including revision of the Catholic Church's teachings about sex:

And much as a spiritual renewal of Europe is necessary, one form of it may be doomed to failure from the start. That is the backward-looking utopia of a 'spiritual unity of Europe' in which the confessional walls between Catholics, Protestants, and Orthodox are retained, leading to the restoration programme of a 're-evangelization of Europe' in a Roman Catholic direction which John Paul II proclaimed in 1982 in the mediaeval pilgrimage centre of Santiago di [sic] Compostela and again in 1990 in Prague (at the same time insisting on the need for obedience to the church.) For such a programme is accompanied by a constant denunciation of Western democracy as consumerism, hedonism, and materialism, not by an unambiguous affirmation of the modern values of freedom, pluralism, and tolerance—right into the sphere of the Pope's own church (questions of birth control and sexual morality!).[4]

Küng made a threat, as well: "To put it bluntly: no regressive or repressive religion—whether Christian, Islamic, Jewish or of whatever provenance—has a long-term future."[5] When Küng denounced "regressive or repressive religion," it was the monotheistic religions that he named specifically as not having "a long-term future." These are the same religions which Bishop Swing describes as "exclusive religions."[6]

The *San Jose Mercury News* reported that at the 1996 URI summit conference, former UN official Robert Muller "said that fundamentalism, resting on inflexible belief systems, tends to play an

1. Terry Mattingly, *On Religion*, "Can today's church veto the saints?," http://tmatt.gospelcom.net/column/1998/10/07/, printed 06/11/04.

2. Ibid. Mattingly has quoted Ingham's *Mansions of the Spirit: The Gospel in a Multi-Faith World*.

3. Michael Ingham, "Is Tolerance Enough? New Hopes and New Obstacles to Religious Unity," http://www.cyberus.ca/~stjohns/ingham2.html, printed 04/08/03 (cited below as Ingham, "Is Tolerance Enough?").

4. Hans Küng, *Global Responsibility: In Search of a New World Ethic*, Continuum Publishing Company, 1996, p 23.

5. Ibid.

6. Swing, *The Coming United Religions*, p 31.

incendiary role in global conflicts. Peace will be impossible, Muller said, without the taming of fundamentalism through a United Religions that professes faithfulness 'only to the global spirituality and to the health of this planet.'"[1] (At that time, Bishop Swing disagreed with Muller, saying, "When the fundamentalists join the family of the world, they will bring great gifts . . . They are not the enemy.")[2]

URI supporter Bishop K.H. Ting, who has been President of the China Christian Council (CCC), likewise disdains fundamentalists. In 1997, he said, "Although there were no denominational differences, there are disagreements among the Christians in China. Those who show the tendency of being fundamentalists often question the faith of others who do not agree with them. On the development of the ethical content of Christianity, Bishop Ting said that many Christians felt that their priority was to go to heaven and paid little attention to giving witness in society. He hoped that his successors will work hard to solve these problems."[3] The Communist regime is trying to "solve these problems" by persecuting unregistered Protestant house churches and Catholics who remain in communion with Rome (rather than worshiping at the schismatic, state-approved "Patriotic Catholic Church").

In the summer 1997 issue of the *Journal of the United Religions Initiative*, the URI's magazine that was published in the late 1990s, URI activist Anke Kreutzer described four responses to the current spiritual crisis: fundamentalism, the ecological movement, the esoterics, and the spiritual movement. She said,

> Fundamentalism of all provinces, including pseudo-religious communities with fascist structures, satisfies those who cannot bear the freedom and responsibility of autonomous decision. The void in the sphere of collective norms and practices is thus filled with oversimplifying recipes by those who exploit it to satisfy their own sense of power and not rarely—financial profit. This trend is manifest on all levels of communal life, from the so-called theocracies to the rigorous regimes of small religious communities. It must also not be forgotten that it is also manifest in the inflexible insistence on outdated dogmas and hierarchical structures on the part of organized religions, for which a broad basis of consent has been lost a long time ago.[4]

This condemnation of fundamentalism puts cultists, Islamic theocracies, and traditional Christian churches in the same pejorative bin. Kreutzer could find no kind words for fundamentalism, but found things to praise in each of the three other alternatives (the ecological movement, the esoterics, and the spiritual movement).[5]

---

1. Jorge Aquino (Religion News Service), "A Bold Attempt to Close Breach Between Religions," *San Jose Mercury News*, p 11–E, June 29, 1996 (cited below as Aquino, "Bold Attempt to Close Breach Between Religions," 06/29/96).

2. Ibid.

3. Bob Chin, "Bishop Ting and the New Leadership of the China Christian Council," *Pacific Church News*, June/July 1997, p 37.

4. Anke Kreutzer, "An Experiment With Truth," *Journal of the United Religions Initiative*, issue 3, Summer 1997, p 11 (cited below as Kreutzer, "An Experiment With Truth").

5. Ibid. Regarding the ecological movement, Kreutzer said, "This trend is strongly felt as an argument for the commitment to the interfaith movement. . . . It is significant that this broad stream in the interfaith movement is often content with a consent about some fundamental ethical values as a common 'strategical basis,' leaving central questions of spiritual identity aside. It tends to adopt the conditions and methods of decision-making from the practice of political parties." Of the "esoterics," she said, "The 'fringe' of groups with a highly diverse profile, characterized by a radical break rather than grappling with their own religious traditions: a tendency for escapism into highly private and speculative, not seldom eclectic, modes of religious, magic, and occult practice, but with a refreshingly open minded, experimental attitude toward unorthodox ways of worship. In this rapidly growing spectrum a keen sense of personal experience beyond preconceived ideas is felt, combined with the demand that religious practice should involve the heart along with the head." Kreuzer said of the "spiritual movement," that "This equally growing number of people who greet the challenge of a pluralistic society and the access to virtually all religious and philosophical schools, accepts the dilemma of the individual being forced to find his or her own position in the excessive supply of information. Instead of discarding their tradition, they analyze and compare it with others to try and find a differentiated judgment. Their experimental attitude judges the modes of worship and contents of their faith by its fruit. They balance their desire for spiritual self-fulfillment with a sense of social responsibility." (Cont'd next page).

Interfaith leader Marcus Braybrooke says that fundamentalists

adopt an a-historical attitude to the central 'truths' of a religion. They are unchanging and not open to reinter-pretation in a changing world. Likewise, fundamentalists reject the idea of symbolism regarding their own truths—they take their particular myth as true in a literal sense. . . . For the fundamentalist, there is only one truth—which they possess. They cannot then accept a pluralistic society in which equal status is given to a vari-ety of truth claims. They are committed, by the logic of their belief, to work for the victory of their views. Many do so by honest democratic persuasion, but others seek to coerce their opponents.[1]

New Age author Neale Donald Walsch says, "I believe that URI can be successful only if the world comes to understand that the current separation of the world's exclusivist religions is a major problem and the largest causal factor in the political, economic and military crises faced by the earth's people today. I hope my work can help bring the world to this realization."[2]

Hatred of Christian orthodoxy is popular among Western liberals, and some global leaders with far more influence than Bishop Swing display this animus in their response to the threat of global war between Islam and the West.

On October 23, 2001, Antonio Garrigues Walker—deputy chairman of the European branch of the Trilateral Commission—told the *International Herald Tribune* that

The basic problem resides in the claim by every religion not merely to be the true religion but to be the only true religion. This claim reduces to a minimum, or eliminates altogether, any possibility of dialogue or understand-ing. It leads to an impasse and must be corrected. . . . The Christian churches should make every effort to show generosity to other religions by ensuring whenever possible—and it is almost always possible—that no emphasis is placed on questions that separate religions, and by encouraging the vast possibilities of cooperation on issues vital to humanity. . . . Relativism, thank goodness, is advancing. . . . Doors are opening into a new philosophical era in which we will have to survive without dogmatic bases and rid our minds of many traditional isms. In the end, the idea will prevail that dogmatism is bad and dialogue is essential for peaceful coexistence.[3]

The title for the Trilateralist's article says it all: "Church Dogma Harms Quest for Global Peace." This message fits perfectly with what Swing teaches—the only acceptable "ism" is relativism.

In like manner, Robert Reich, the former Secretary of Labor in the Clinton Administration, stated his hatred of religious orthodoxy in a mid-2004 article in a mainstream liberal magazine:

The great conflict of the 21st century will not be between the West and terrorism. Terrorism is a tactic, not a belief. The true battle will be between modern civilization and anti-modernists; between those who believe in the primacy of the individual and those who believe that human beings owe their allegiance and identity to a higher authority; between those who give priority to life in this world and those who believe that human life is mere preparation for an existence beyond life; between those who believe in science, reason, and logic and those who believe that truth is revealed through Scripture and religious dogma.[4]

Charles Upton criticizes Kreutzer's definition of "esoterics": "This is certainly not the definition of 'esoterism' according to the Traditionalist or Perennialist School (René Guénon, Frithjof Schuon, et. al.). Perennialist esoterism rejects magic, occult-ism and eclecticism, and requires commitment to a single religion in its most orthodox form; it also views certain types of contemporary 'fundamentalism' (Muslim, Christian, Jewish, Hindu) as ill-considered and unorthodox reactions to modern-ism. To the Traditionalists, true esoterism is only expressed in terms of the mystical or metaphysical core of *one* of the ortho-dox, revealed religions."

1. Marcus Braybrooke, *Faith and Interfaith in a Global Age*, CoNexus Press, 1998, pp 50–51 (cited below as Braybrooke, *Faith and Interfaith*).

2. E-mail from Neale Donald Walsch to Lee Penn, 11/20/02.

3. Antonio Garrigues Walker, "Church Dogma Harms Quest for Global Peace," *International Herald Tribune*, October 23, 2001, http://www.iht.com/cgi-bin/generic.cgi?template=articleprint.tmplh&ArticleId=36458, printed 02/19/03.

4. Robert B. Reich, "Bush's God," *The American Prospect*, July 2004, p 40.

With such logic, proponents of a post-modern form of "tolerance" may repress their religious opponents—and do so with an undisturbed conscience.

Such persecution has happened before—notably, under the Roman Empire. The issue then, as now, was Christian allegiance to a "higher authority" than the World and its gods. From the earliest persecution under Nero through the final pogroms under Diocletian, the justification was Christians' refusal to join pagan worship—even the seemingly perfunctory homage to the Emperor. As noted by historian Henry Chadwick, "A Christian defendant could gain release by offering incense on a pagan altar. The external act sufficed."[1] In his history of the Catholic Church, Thomas Bokenkotter explained, "The Christian Gospel proclaimed the reality of the one true God and hence demanded absolute rejection of the gods worshiped by Rome. Moreover, Christians took a relative view of the authority of the Emperor and Empire, which were only to be obeyed when they were in harmony with the will of the one true God, which had been revealed to his Church."[2]

A few URI supporters have understood that attacking "fundamentalism" is neither feasible nor just. At the 1996 State of the World Forum, Rabbi Arthur Herzberg said: "I must repeat, insistently: Let us not call upon the ancient communities to dissolve, for they will not. They will only turn more hostile as they feel more threatened. In the here and now, we must act as if the existence of each community, of each tradition, and especially of those with which we disagree most vehemently, is a good which we must help protect, and with which we must come to terms."[3]

In a similar vein, URI staff member Paul Andrews said in 1997 that Marxism and secular humanism could be as fundamentalist as any religion: "If you say that fundamentalism is the conviction that 'I have the answer; I don't need to listen to somebody else, and I'm not willing to change my beliefs and open up to the possibility of change,' then there is a whole lot more fundamentalism in the world than what's represented by religion. Marxism is a fundamentalism; secular humanism is a fundamentalism. . . . Never approach evil as if it is entirely outside yourself."[4]

Robert Traer, of the International Association for Religious Freedom, offered a more pointed criticism of smug anti-"fundamentalism":

Our vision of interfaith work is self-serving. It implies that those who organize interfaith activities have a 'higher goal' and thus, are more virtuous than those who are willing to 'live and let live' but make no bones about their dislike of certain religious traditions. We should acknowledge, however, that better intentions do not necessarily make us better people.[5]

He continued,

The language of interfaith conversation . . . seems to assume that thinking and talking about spirituality is the answer to religious intolerance. The implication is that religious leaders and communities who are unwilling to support interfaith activities are as responsible for religious conflict as the bigots and extremists who actually express their hatred through invective and violence. . . . Moreover, it is wrong for interfaith groups to assume that only an uncritical view of religious truth claims will foster the mutual respect among religious communities and the kind of spirituality among the members of these communities that are required to attain interfaith understanding and cooperation.[6]

---

1. Henry Chadwick, "The Early Christian Community," in John McManners, ed., *The Oxford Illustrated History of Christianity*, Oxford University Press, 1992, p 41.

2. Thomas Bokenkotter, *A Concise History of the Catholic Church*, Doubleday, 2004, rev. ed., p 38.

3. Rabbi Arthur Herzberg, "The Sins of Religion," address given at the 1996 State of the World Forum, as faxed by Forum staff to Lee Penn on 6/17/97 (cited below as Herzberg, "The Sins of Religion").

4. URI forum, Grace Cathedral, 02/02/97.

5. Traer, *Quest For Truth*, p 79.

6. Ibid., p 80.

He concluded, "The assumption of interfaith work seems to be that those not offering their support are part of the problem. I would suggest to my fellow interfaith organizers, however, that our pride and self-righteousness are great obstacles to the realization of our worthy goals. . . . Belief in ourselves is our sin. We are part of the problem and not merely the answer."[1]

Cardinal Ratzinger has rebuked the theologians whose definitions of fundamentalism are elastic and ever expanding: "instead of simply hammering away at fundamentalism—whose definition keeps getting broader and broader—theologians should ponder to what extent they are to blame for the fact that increasing numbers of people seek refuge in narrow or unhealthy forms of religion. When one no longer offers anything but questions and doesn't offer any positive way to faith, such flights are inevitable."[2]

Cardinal Ratzinger also showed the ominous implications of the rejection of Christian tradition:

> A new peril is also growing: the development of what you might call a modern world view that regards Christianity or the Catholic faith as an intolerant, antiquated affair unreconcilable with modernity and begins to apply pressure. I believe that this peril is already rather great, even though it still doesn't seem immediate. But the social pressure on the Church essentially to conform to today's accepted standards already exists now. . . . Of course, it is not yet persecution; it would be absurd to apply that expression to this case. But there are indeed areas of life— and not a few—in which, once again, it already takes courage to profess oneself a Christian. Above all there is a growing danger of assimilated forms of Christianity, which society then gladly holds up as humanistic forms of Christianity, as opposed to the alleged fundamentalism of those who don't want to be so streamlined. The danger of a dictatorship of opinion is growing, and anyone who doesn't share the prevailing opinion is excluded, so that even good people no longer dare to stand by such nonconformists. Any future anti-Christian dictatorship would probably be much more subtle than anything we have known until now. It will appear to be friendly to religion, but on the condition that its own models of behavior and thinking not be called into question.[3]

[III] LAYING THE GROUND FOR A NEW RELIGION OF THE "SACRED EARTH"

The third reason to stand against the URI is that statements over many years by URI leaders— including Bishop Swing—indicate that they are preparing the way for a New Religion, the religion of the "sacred earth." Rituals and symbols used in URI ceremonies and worship services demonstrate this syncretism in action.

Official URI documents firmly deny any intent of establishing a new religion or of promoting religious syncretism—which Cardinal Arinze describes as "the error of taking elements from the various religions in order to construct and serve up something new."[4] As its first principle, the URI Charter

1. Ibid., pp 80–81.
2. Joseph Cardinal Ratzinger, *Salt of the Earth: Christianity and the Catholic Church at the End of the Millennium—An Interview with Peter Seewald*, translated by Adrian Walker, Ignatius Press, San Francisco, 1997, p 137.
3. Ibid., pp 152–153.
4. Arinze, *Religions for Peace*, p 97. In another book, the Cardinal further defines syncretism and its related problems. He says, "Syncretism is the effort to put several religions together and to carve a new religion out of them. The effort may be guided by the desire to preserve all the factors that seem common to all the religions, a type of religious highest common denominator. It may be the desire not to offend any of the believers but rather to work out a pattern in which none of them feels threatened. It is not often that people would propose syncretism in theory as a new religion. Nevertheless, some have *de facto* engaged in syncretism by pulling, for example, some Christian beliefs into African Traditional Religion within Africa or in Latin America or vice versa. Others have coined 'new religions' in Europe by mixing up elements of Hinduism and Buddhism with Christianity and ancient pre-Christian religions. Syncretism may more often appear in particular practices such as interreligious prayer, when it does not respect the religious identity of the participants but presents them as members of one community of faith. . . . Syncretism is a danger that has to be watched in interreligious relations." (Arinze, *Meeting Other Believers*, pp 37–38.)

says, "The URI is a bridge-building organization, not a religion."[1]

In his 1998 book, Bishop Swing said, "In the same way that the United Nations is not a nation, the United Religions would not be a religion."[2] And in early 2003, Swing said, "Could we not, here and now, move beyond ancient hostilities to fresh ways of collaboration? Not by sacrificing unique religious beliefs and blending them into one foggy faith but by aspiring to a basic civility among believers of all faiths."[3] In early 2004, Swing continued his defense of the URI against accusations of syncretism: "I have on occasion asked people who called us that name to read our literature and show us where we fit that description. On no occasion has anyone written back to point at any of our literature and claim that it proves or suggests or even hints that we're syncretistic. I think that one goes away in time."[4]

Nevertheless, statements over many years by URI leaders and prominent supporters, from Bishop Swing on down, indicate that they are laying the foundations for a syncretic New Religion, a religion of the "sacred earth."

For some URI activists, (especially the cultists, New Age enthusiasts and Theosophists), this is the intended result; they know what they are doing, and why. Most other URI leaders appear to be building the foundation for syncretism unwittingly. As religious liberals, they are inveterate enthusiasts for reform. They do not understand the role of traditional texts, rites, creeds, and codes of conduct in sustaining a religious community. In the naïve assumption that ancient boundaries can be erased at will, and long-standing practices can be overturned without disorienting the faithful, these religious progressives undermine the foundations of belief for themselves and for their followers. Such has been the history of mainline American Protestantism since World War II, and of American Catholicism since the Second Vatican Council. If the old religions implode due to an excess of reform, the cultist True Believers will step in, creating a syncretic New Religion from the rubble.

BISHOP SWING

Bishop Swing has repeatedly predicted—and, at times, advocated—religious syncretism as the wave of the future. He knows that his views are controversial, and revels in the controversy: "I invite theological invective from people who hurl words like 'syncretist,' 'universalist' in my direction."[5]

In April 1996, Bishop Swing wrote,

Religions gave birth to a world they orphaned when the world grew up. They have become deadbeat fathers and mothers while their modern children walk around trying to piece enough religion together to make decisions about the future. They add a little yoga to the words of The Prophet. A little Catechism to a little Dharma. They will find their way eventually because humanity has always stretched to find its soul in new and foreign settings. One way or another, in Bangalore or in your grandchild, a United Religions will happen.[6]

Bishop Swing made United Religions the theme of his Christmas Eve, 1996 sermon. He proposed that: "For the sake of all the children of the world we are going to learn a new way for religions to interact. Jews, Muslims, Buddhists, Hindus, Christians—all—all of us will learn to live beside each

---

1. URI, "Charter," "Principles," principle 1, p 3.
2. Swing, *The Coming United Religions*, p 62.
3. Swing, "Import-Export of U.S. Religion," *PCN*, Winter 2003, p 6.
4. Dennis Delman, "Interview with Bishop William E. Swing, Founder and President of the United Religions Initiative," *Pacific Church News online*, February/March 2004, http://pcn.diocal.org/PCNO/pcn004-1/index.html, printed 02/24/04 (cited below as Delman, "Interview with Swing," *PCN* on-line, Feb./Mar. 2004).
5. Bishop William Swing, "Be All That You Can Be," sermon to ordinands, *A Swing with a Crosier*, Episcopal Diocese of California, 1999, p 68.
6. Bishop William Swing, "The United Religions Initiative," document issued in April 1996, p 10. (cited below as Swing, "The United Religions Initiative,"04/96).

other. Everyone will be invited to bring their best, richest, deepest stories to the common ground. And there we will build."[1] Thus, he invited his listeners to imagine building a new religious structure on a "common ground," using material from the "stories" from all religions.

In June of 1997, Bishop Swing gave an interview to the *San Francisco Chronicle* in which he called for a revision of the scriptures and theology of all the world's religions. He said, "Maybe we have to take a deeper look at theology. I think that religions are based on assumptions of truth being mediated from the creator to the created. These truths are divinely inspired and sacred for the people who hold them. I think all the religions of the world have a blind spot. If there's a United Religions pursuing a dialogue in depth, it begins to ask larger questions and force religions to make larger statements."[2] *Chronicle* reporter Don Lattin asked, "Isn't a lot of the problem that many sacred scriptures are full of violent, exclusionary rhetoric?" Swing replied, "That's right. And it's taught all week long, every place we go. The religions have to go back and read that one more time and ask if that is really what they believe. If you're sitting there with people from other religions at the table, you might come up with other conclusions."[3]

By 1998, Bishop Swing moved from predicting syncretism to advocating it. In *The Coming United Religions*, Bishop Swing stated,

> Originally I thought that the impetus for the coming together of religions would be finding a common moral voice and taking mutual action—without getting into the areas associated with spirituality: meditation, contemplative prayer, sacred writings, end-time hopes, wisdom, etc. But I no longer think that. If there is ever going to be a United Religions it will only happen because the Ultimate Ground of Being wills it. . . . A United Religions will either have a distinct spiritual momentum far beyond its own cleverness or it simply will not be.[4]

His comments throughout the rest of the book show what the "distinct spiritual momentum" would be.

In the same book, Swing described Alan Jones, Dean of Grace Cathedral in San Francisco, as one of the many "spiritual astronauts" of our time who are "pushing outward and upward following the embrace of the sacred."[5]

Jones, who is in charge of Swing's Episcopal cathedral, said: "There are absolutes that cannot be fully grasped or put into words . . . our struggle with language will never end. We are pilgrims of the Absolute. Some people are protectors of the Absolute rather than pilgrims of it. God doesn't need looking after . . . the Absolute exists not as turf to be defended or as proof of one's own superiority, but as the horizon toward which one is forever on pilgrimage."[6] Fr. Jones forgot to mention that "the Absolute" has a name and is incarnate in our Lord and Savior Jesus Christ. Christ is not "the horizon toward which one is forever on pilgrimage," but our Shepherd, Savior, God, and Lord; He calls us to love Him and obey Him. Jones' words mirror those of the apostate bishop described in C.S. Lewis' *The Great Divorce*: "For me there is no such thing as a final answer. The free wind of inquiry must *always* continue to blow through the mind, must it not? 'Prove all things' . . . to travel hopefully is better than to arrive."[7]

---

1. Bishop William Swing, "A Message for all the People," URI pamphlet, excerpt from a sermon delivered by Bishop Swing on Christmas Eve of 1996 at Grace Cathedral, p 2.

2. Don Lattin, interview with William Swing—"Bishop's Idea for a Leap of Faiths," *San Francisco Chronicle*, June 22, 1997, p 3/Z1 (cited below as Lattin, "Interview with Swing," *San Francisco Chronicle*, 06/22/97).

3. Ibid.

4. Swing, *The Coming United Religions*, p 22.

5. Ibid., p 60.

6. Ibid., p 61; ellipses are exactly as given in the original text.

7. C.S. Lewis, *The Great Divorce*, Macmillan Publishing Co., Inc., 1946, p 43; ellipses are in the original text.

Having quoted his spiritual astronauts, Bishop Swing then described a new spiritual unity that will arise via the United Religions:

"In the United Religions:

(a) *Silent respect would be rendered to every religion as each pursues its sacred path.*

(b) *That Which Binds Us Is Beyond Us.* As each religion renders silent respect to other religions, the rising mutual sympathy will lead to the discovery of a unifying mystery.

(c) *That Which Is Beyond Us Will Bind Us.* The unifying mystery that will be discovered will persuade religions of an ever-increasing kinship with each other and with all life."[1]

Bishop Swing did not name the "unifying mystery" that "will bind us." Instead, he calls for ultimate religious unity: "The time comes, though, when common language and a common purpose for all religions and spiritual movements must be discerned and agreed upon. Merely respecting and understanding other religions is not enough."[2] Since the purpose of religion is the service and worship of God, Bishop Swing's call for "all religions and spiritual movements" to have "common language and a common purpose" is, in effect, a call for all to worship a shared god.

In September 2002, Bishop Swing wrote that disestablishment of the Church of England would be "the last option, if absolutely necessary . . . Far more preferable, in my opinion, would be to expand the symbols, e.g., present an established Anglicanism that would be a new model of interfaith inclusion."[3] Thus, the Church of England would respond to religious diversity by keeping its ties to the state and becoming syncretic—rather than abandoning its claim to be the church for the whole nation, and remaining explicitly Christian.

Swing's vision of the religious future continues to expand, away from traditional Christianity. In early 2004, he said,

I'm sure that ten years from now the hot topic will be whether Jesus exclusively is the one and only person who saves. Or does God save in multiple ways, including Jesus; or as an outgrowth of Jesus; or as seen in Jesus. I think that all of us have learned our religions in tribal settings, and the day is coming quickly when we're going to have to understand our religion in global terms, and even in terms of an expanding universe. That is going to cause a radical form [sic] for every religion and in all theological thinking. Therefore, what we are about is part of the *avant garde* issue that everybody's going to be about in a strained and intense way in the future. Therefore a lot of the work we're doing right now is pioneering for the next religious explosion.[4]

OTHER URI LEADERS AND PROPONENTS

Other URI leaders and proponents have shown similar support for a New Religion as an outgrowth of the URI.

Bruno Barnhart said in the *Journal of the United Religions* that the 1993 Parliament of the World's Religions had:

1. Swing, *The Coming United Religions*, p 63.
2. Ibid., p 63.
3. Bishop William E. Swing, "A Swing Through the Diocese," *Pacific Church News online*, September 2002, http://www.dio cal.org/pcn/PCNO/pcn002-8/main.html, printed 10/12/02.
4. Delman, "Interview with Swing," *PCN* on-line, Feb./March 2004.

two great imperatives to communion, horizontal and vertical: vertical, however, in the sense of a spirituality which moves—with the Spirit in our time—not toward transcendence but toward incarnation. The community of religions and of peoples can only be achieved in the common ground of humanity—known in the voice of the oppressed. This human ground, I believe, is mysteriously one with the earth itself.[1] . . . The Parliament signals not only the birth of a community of religions in our time, but the recognition of this new revelation—common and convergent—from the ground.[2]

A non-transcendent "new revelation" "from the ground," the earth and humanity, moving "with the Spirit in our time"—such would be the basis for the New Religion.

Matthew Fox said, "There's no point in starting a new religion. That's the last thing we need. However, we do need to gather the essence from all the religions we do have, which is what I call 'deep ecumenism.' By blending the best of all our world religions, hopefully we'll distill a more universal truth. The human race is young, and we evolve as our religious consciousness evolves."[3] On another occasion, he said,

There's no such thing as a Jewish ocean and a Lutheran sun and a Buddhist river and a Taoist forest and a Roman Catholic cornfield. Once you move to the level of creation, you're into an era of deep ecumenism, and I think for mother earth to survive we need this awakening of wisdom from all world religions, and not just the five-thousand-year-old patriarchal ones, but the goddess religions, the religions of the native peoples of America, Africa, and Asia, and I think this and this alone is going to awaken the human race—this combination of mystical wisdom—to its own salvation. . . . God works through all religions, and that's why we have to draw forth the wisdom of all religions today, to recover our own divinity . . . Eckhart says God is a great underground river. So we come to this common ocean of being. This is why you have different wells of wisdom. There's the Jewish well and the Sufi well and the Buddhist well and the Catholic and Protestant, but they sink into one deep underground river. There's only one divine source of all this wisdom, you see.[4]

1. Charles Upton criticizes Barnhart's theology: "This is Incarnation at the expense of Resurrection and Ascension. If 'the community of religions and of peoples can only be achieved . . . in the voice of the oppressed,' then shouldn't we all pray that oppression never departs from this world? The 'poor' who shall 'see God' are not just the economically unlucky; if they were, anyone could achieve sainthood simply by losing all his or her money in the stock market. They are 'the poor in spirit,' those who have lost their lives for God, and found their lives in Him. This false identification of material with spiritual poverty is one of the central errors of Liberation Theology, which is where Barnhart gets this particular piece of rhetoric. The materially poor can be just as eaten up by sullen, rebellious pride as the rich often are by cruel, oppressive pride. Jesus did not identify himself exclusively with the cause of the materially oppressed. He ministered to Roman centurions, Pharisees and tax collectors *as well as* to prostitutes, laborers and beggars. Though he was critical of the privileged sects and classes—the Scribes, Pharisees, Sadducees and Herodians—and silent with regard to the Zealots, the anti-Roman revolutionary terrorists, the point of his social critique was most often directed against those who perverted true religion, not against those holding political power. And his words to Peter on the occasion of his arrest, 'those who live by the sword shall die by the sword,' certainly reveal what must have been his fundamental attitude toward the Zealots. (Jesus' words applied to the Romans as well—some of whom were within earshot—especially since the Roman name for the capital punishment he was about to suffer at their hands was *ius gladii*, 'judgment by the sword.') Jesus told the rich young man that his way to perfection was to give all he had to the poor, but he also required that the lepers 'give up' their leprosy, that the 5,000 give up their hunger and neediness, that Peter give up his faithlessness, that the attacked and offended give up their right to just retaliation. He was the enemy not of material riches per se, but of idolatry in all its forms. To Jesus, the common oppressors of both the materially rich and the materially poor were Sin and Death. It was these spiritual powers, not the worldly power of political or economic oppression, that he came to overthrow." (E-mail from Charles Upton to Lee Penn, 09/26/04).

2. Bruno Barnhart, "Book Review," *Journal of the United Religions Initiative*, Spring 1997, pp 12–13.

3. Virginia Lee, "Science and Spirit: Conversations with Matthew Fox, Ph.D. & Rupert Sheldrake, Ph.D.", *Common Ground On-Line*, http://www.commongroundmag.com/fox.html, printed 03/27/03. (cited below as V. Lee, "Conversations with Fox & Sheldrake."

4. Intuition Network, "Thinking Allowed: Conversations On The Leading Edge Of Knowledge and Discovery With Dr. Jeffrey Mishlove—Creation Spirituality with Matthew Fox, Ph. D.," http://www.intuition.org/txt/fox.htm, printed 03/28/03.

In 1997, URI Executive Director Charles Gibbs said that a URI planning conference held in New York City discussed how to "support sacred earth values in a variety of ways."[1]

In her 1998 book *Conscious Evolution*, Barbara Marx Hubbard said,

> Conscious evolution is the context for a 'meta-religio,' [sic] a new ground of the whole, calling upon spiritual leaders and practitioners of all faiths to create what Bishop William Swing, Episcopal bishop of California, calls a 'United Religions' to end the conflict among religions and to bring together the unique gifts of the faiths for the future of humanity. We need to move beyond ecumenical understanding to evolutionary fulfillment through the embodiment of the principles and the practices of the great faiths. We long not for a new religion, but for the evolution of religion, such that we embody the qualities of our master teachers and become conscious cocreators with the divine universal intelligence ourselves.[2]

Anglican Bishop Michael Ingham said in his 1999 "Christmas Message" that "I can imagine a time when the founders and saints of all the traditions—Moses, Jesus, Mohammed, Buddha, Guru Nanak, and so on—are honoured and cherished in all of them."[3]

Richard Kirby and Earl Brewer forecast the coming of a United Religions in their 1994 article, "Temples of Tomorrow," a portion of which was reprinted in the *Journal of the United Religions*.[4] (Brewer had been director of research at the National Council of Churches, and Kirby was, as of 1993, the president of the London Federation of the Theosophical Society.)[5] They likened the task of a "United Religions Organization" (URO) to creation of a "new covenant between God and humankind":

> These suggestions and programs amount to a kind of theological revolution that recalls the prophets of Israel. These prophets engendered new relationships with God, and in the fullness of time a new covenant. Now, in planetary crisis, that new covenant between God and humankind needs urgently to be extended to science, politics, government, and technology. The URO, perhaps over decades of research and discussion, will discern the nature of that covenant, and with it the responsibilities, rather than the rights, of planetary citizenship. The case for a United Religions Organization, in summary, is that it provides a conduit for divine power to bring healing and inspiration to Earth. The URO should also enlarge the religious vision of the human race as a whole and, hence, human decency.[6]

(An organization that would discern "the responsibilities, rather than the rights, of planetary citizenship"—what a strange thing to hope for, after a century in which tyrants have violated the rights of their subjects, recognizing no limits from God, law, or tradition on their ability to impose "responsibilities" on their citizens!)

"Temples of Tomorrow" also listed some of the characteristics that the authors expected religion to have in the future:

1. Charles Gibbs, "Regional Conferences Prepare for URI Global Summit," *Pacific Church News*, August/September 1997, p 23 (cited below as Gibbs, "Regional Conferences," *PCN*, August/September 1997). In their new book on the URI, Gibbs and Mahé report the same about this meeting. Members of a discussion group that "focused on 'Respect for Earth and All Her Creations' . . . pledged their support of the Earth Pledge and the Earth Charter and committed to circulating the UN Values Caucus' statement about Earth-based values, to bringing sacred Earth values to other meetings and caucuses, and to writing a column on Earth matters for the URI newsletter." (Gibbs/Mahé, *Birth of a Global Community*, p 93.)

2. Barbara Marx Hubbard, *Conscious Evolution: Awakening the Power of Our Social Potential*, New World Library, Novato, California, 1998, pp 89–90 (cited below as Marx Hubbard, *Conscious Evolution*).

3. Bishop Michael Ingham, "Christmas Message," http://www.prayerbook.ca/cann/1999/12/pblam861.htm, printed 04/08/03.

4. Richard Kirby, "Towards a United Religions Organization," *Journal of the United Religions Initiative*, Spring 1997, pp 8–9.

5. Richard Kirby and Earl Brewer, *The Temples of Tomorrow: World Religions and the Future*, Grey Seal Books, London, 1993, p iv (copyright notice and biographical page).

6. Richard Kirby and Earl D. C. Brewer, "Temples of Tomorrow," *The Futurist*, September-October 1994, pp 27–28.

The world religions are increasingly **working out the theoretical basis of a world theology,** such as a global philosophy of knowledge (epistemology). A mature, whole-earth theology will likely develop. Some groups are **preparing to send their religions into outer space,** and so to enter the space age. Churches are becoming like malls, serving as economic centers as well as religious ones. . . . The merging of two or more religious impulses, such as Hinduism and Christianity, is increasingly **producing hybrids,** such as Christian Yoga. **Faith and finance are converging** as religions enter the world of money with serious intent to reform it. . . . **The East is rediscovering a theistic orientation** in several contexts. For example, the Japanese have reclaimed the doctrine of the divinity of the Emperor. We will likely see a major Eastern contribution to the global doctrine of God, or the whole-earth concept of theism, in the twenty-first century. The religions are **rethinking their role as peacemakers,** and a world theology of peacemaking is emerging. The Green Movement and the world religions are converging. . . . **The feminine is increasingly partnering with the masculine** in religious thinking, leading to a fully integrated male/female world theology.[1]

Is this to be the New Religion of the year 2100, or a return to the Canaanite fertility cult of 2100 BC?

Kirby, a self-described "Esoteric Futurist," has praised the United Religions Initiative as part of the "roundtable of world religions in dialogue," from which would emerge the "Christ of the Third Millennium." He said,

Therefore the stock-in-trade of the spiritual scientist or esoteric futurist—the terms are almost synonymous in many ways—is to make sure that the spiritual sciences of the world are brought to the roundtable of discussion of exoteric philosophies and their bearing on the civil governance of the world. All the spiritual philosophies of the world are coming to the great Moot, the roundtable of world religions in dialogue. The United Religions Initiative is one of many associations promoting this dialogue. All the spiritual philosophies of the world are called to the discussion. The spiritual philosophies known as yoga or all the yogas are involved. The spiritual science of the Western Arthurian or Jungian or Alchemical traditions is invited. The Theosophy of the east and the Anthroposophy of the west are summoned to the great Conclave of spiritual science.[2] All of these have a contribution to make. Perhaps, as Jung and others have prophesied, we can foresee the emerging synthesis of these East-West traditions. We can term this the *Christosophy* of the 21st century. This could be the great synthesis of science, religion and philosophy of the 21st century. The Christ of the Third Millennium is from this viewpoint the goal, the center and the heart of the focus of Esoteric Futures studies and research.[3]

URI activist Anke Kreutzer wrote in the summer 1997 *Journal of the United Religions Initiative,* "While the strong inclination of proselytism among the religions tends to put off seekers against religion altogether, a united force in the search of the common God would no doubt attract many."[4]

Patricia Mische, co-founder of Global Education Associates (who attended the 1997 URI summit meeting[5] and spoke at the 1997 State of the World Forum on "Governance Structures for the 21st

---

1. Ibid., p28; "Forecasts for World Religions" side bar; emphasis as given in the original.
2. Charles Upton notes that Kirby is in error here. He warns, "To say 'The Theosophy of the east and the Anthroposophy of the west' is a clear reference to Blavatsky's Theosophical Society and the Anthroposophical Society of Rudolf Steiner, two occultist organizations originating in the West. 'Theosophy' is in no way 'of the East.' René Guénon makes clear in *Theosophy: The History of a Pseudo-Religion,* that despite its promiscuous borrowing of terms and concepts from eastern religions, the underlying assumptions on which the Theosophical Society is based are entirely western in origin. As for 'theosophy' in its generic meaning of 'divine wisdom,' this manifestation can in no way be exclusively identified with either the East or the West." (E-mail from Charles Upton to Lee Penn, 02/03/04; see also René Guénon, *Theosophy: The History of a Pseudo-Religion,* tr. by Alvin Moore Jr. et al., Sophia Perennis, 2001, cited below as Guénon, *Theosophy.*)
3. Richard Kirby (World Network of Religious Futurists), "The Focus of Esoteric Futures," http://www.wnrf.org/cms/esotericf.shtml, printed 04/25/03.
4. Kreutzer, "An Experiment With Truth," p13.
5. Paul Chaffee, "Ring of Breath Around the World: A Report of the United Religions Initiative Global Conference," issued in the summer of 1997 by the United Religions Initiative, p3.

Century")[1] says, "Our spiritual journey—our search for life in God—must be worked out now in a global context, in the midst of global crises and global community. Our spirituality must be a global spirituality."[2]

Robert Muller made it clear at the 1996 URI summit conference that the United Religions must tame "fundamentalism" and profess faithfulness "only to the global spirituality and to the health of this planet."[3] (In his view, the Earth is the divinity: "Hindus call our earth Brahma,[4] or God, for they rightly see no difference between our earth and the divine."[5] More recently, Muller has said, "When I appear before God I will probably discover that our supreme divinity is the Earth. She will smile at my surprise and say, 'I welcome you and give you my deepest thanks . . . Please sit next to me on my right and help me judge the national leaders, militaries and businessmen coming up from down there.'")[6]

Muller was still saying the same thing in 2004; in his newest book *Paradise Earth*, he wrote that with the United Religions, "all religions of the world will cooperate, define what they have in common, provide their wisdom on human behavior and morality, and right relations with nature, God's Creation and the universe thus ushering the world into a great Spiritual Renaissance. In the process they will hopefully reduce and progressively give up their fundamentalism in favor of a global spirituality."[7]

Br. Wayne Teasdale wrote in the *Journal of the United Religions* on behalf of a new, "enlarged consciousness" that "acts with the totality in mind":

> The Community of Religions, a term that expresses the living reality of the interfaith phenomenon, and which includes all of the religions taken together in their new and powerful identity, has to establish itself on the historic precedent of the prophetic function as we move towards the third millennium, and hopefully, a new, universal consciousness. . . . A new, universal awareness will dawn on the earth, and [sic] enlarged consciousness that acts with the totality in mind, and not merely vested interests as in the past. . . . It's high time for the religions to grow up, and take responsibility for the world, and the evolution of planetary civilization.[8]

In 1999, Neale Donald Walsch said that between 2000 and 2015, we will see "the emergence of a New Spirituality on a worldwide scale; a spiritual movement that embraces the highest thoughts ever held by human beings, discards the tenants [sic] of fear and exclusivity that have marked so many of the world's religions thus far, and produces a larger experience in our daily lives of Who We Really Are as

1. 1997 State of the World Forum, "Governance Structures for the 21st Century: Final Report." Mische spoke on "Panel II—Revitalizing and Reforming the United Nations," http://www.worldforum.org/1997forum/GlobalGovernance.html; printed in 1999, and no longer on the Net at this address. As of 2004, a copy of this web page is at http://web.archive.org/web/1999 0127151451/http://www.worldforum.org/1997forum/GlobalGovernance.html.

2. Patricia Mische, "Toward a Global Spirituality," in Joel Beversluis, ed., *Sourcebook of the World's Religions: An Interfaith Guide to Religion and Spirituality*, New World Library, 3rd ed., 2000, p237.

3. Aquino, "Bold Attempt to Close Breach Between Religions," 06/29/96.

4. Charles Upton comments, "Here again Muller reveals his ignorance of Hinduism. Brahma does not denote the earth, but rather God in His aspect of Creator; the word for the earth, personified as a goddess, is Bhumi." (E-mail from Charles Upton to Lee Penn, 02/03/04)

5. Robert Muller, *New Genesis: Shaping a Global Spirituality*, World Happiness and Cooperation, 1993, p49.

6. Robert Muller, *Ideas And Dreams for a Better World: 3001–3500, Volume VIII*, Idea 3046, http://www.robertmuller.org/volume/ideas3001.html, viewed 06/21/04.

7. Robert Muller, *Paradise Earth*, http://www.paradiseearth.us/pdf/PEFull.pdf, p18 (p. 26 of the PDF file), printed 05/31/04 (cited below as Muller, *Paradise Earth*).

8. Br. Wayne Teasdale, "The Interfaith Movement Must Be Based on Prophetic Courage," *Journal of the United Religions Initiative*, Spring 1997, p5. Although his statements have sweeping implications, Teasdale's particular concern was violation of human rights in Tibet. He said, "religious and spiritual leaders are curiously silent in the face of the PRC's blatant, and arrogant, abuse of human rights on the mainland, and especially Tibet. It is utterly indispensable to the immense opportunity of this moment in history that the Community of Religions confront the issue of Tibet squarely, and commit itself to the resolution of this painful, brutal tragedy. If it does not, it then has no moral credibility before the rest of the world."

Beings of Divine Heritage."[1] In 2002, his spirit guide repeated: "The world must create a New Spirituality;"[2] such a spirituality

> can present a new point of view, one that is not exclusivist, not elitist or separatist. It can invite people to seriously consider, for the first time in centuries, some new theological ideas. It can offer, for exploration and discussion, some New Revelations. The New Spirituality will open minds to larger concepts than present theologies embrace, to grander ideas than present theologies consider, and to greater opportunities for individual experience and expression than present theologies allow.[3]

In 2004, Walsch's familiar spirit said that the truth is "*every* where. It is in the Qur'an, and it is in the Upanishads. It is in the Bhagavad Gita, and it is in the Bible. It is in the portions of the Bible called the Torah and called the Psalms and called the New Testament. It is in the Book of Mormon and the Book of Hidden Words. Yet know this: It is found in Whole *nowhere*, and in Part *everywhere*."[4]

Interfaith scholar and URI activist Marcus Braybrooke has posed syncretism as a desirable alternative to "fundamentalism." He says,

> The pluralistic interfaith vision rests on radically different presuppositions. It assumes the possibility of those of different faiths respecting each other and affirming together certain basic moral values. It opens out also the possibility of theology becoming an inter-religious discipline and also the possibility of people of one faith absorbing into their spiritual life practices from another faith. In my view, the interfaith vision is in tune with the character of the emerging post-modern global society. Indeed, it offers the hope of a world civilization based on spiritual values, whereas the fundamentalist approach is likely only to lead to confrontation and conflict.[5]

Braybrooke described how Christians might attempt to "enter deeply into the spiritual depths of other faiths."[6] In the 1960s, he visited an ecumenical ashram in India that was led by an Anglican priest, Fr. Murray Rogers.[7] "I remember even more vividly being very moved that at the Eucharist, beside the expected readings from the Hebrew Bible and the New Testament, there were readings from the Vedas. The practice was maintained when the ashram moved to Jerusalem. I do not recall whether the reader said at the end of the lection from the Hindu scriptures, 'This is the Word of the Lord.' Yet the sort of global theology we are here envisaging suggests that authority belongs to all world scriptures."[8]

In an earlier book, Braybrooke had criticized the Theosophical Society, saying "The Theosophical Society should not be described as an interfaith organization. Its emphasis on the underlying unity of religions does not give the recognition to the separate identity of religions, which is a characteristic of interfaith organizations."[9] By this standard, it appears that Braybrooke—with his support for inter-religious theology, acceptance of the authority of "all world scriptures,"[10] and advocacy of "people of one faith absorbing into their spiritual life practices from another faith"[11]—is now promoting Theosophy.

1. Neale Donald Walsch, "Welcome to the New Millennium," *Magical Blend*, Issue 64, May 1999, p 46.
2. Neale Donald Walsch, *The New Revelations: A Conversation With God*, Atria Books, 2002, p 177.
3. Ibid., p 279.
4. Neale Donald Walsch, *Tomorrow's God: Our Greatest Spiritual Challenge*, Atria Books, 2004, p 208.
5. Braybrooke, *Faith and Interfaith*, p 51.
6. Ibid., p 110.
7. On Rogers' Anglican affiliation, see Judson B. Trapnell, "Abhishiktananada's Contemplative Vocation and Contemporary India," The College Theology Society, Annual Meeting, World Religions Section, May 31, 2002, in Jamaica New York, http://www.infinityfoundation.com/mandala/s_es/s_es_trapn_vocation.htm, printed 06/02/03.
8. Braybrooke, *Faith and Interfaith*, pp 109, 110.
9. Marcus Braybrooke, *Pilgrimage of Hope: One Hundred Years of Global Interfaith Dialogue*, Crossroad, 1992, p 267.
10. Braybrooke, *Faith and Interfaith*, pp 109, 110.
11. Ibid., p 51.

The United Communities of Spirit

The United Communities of Spirit (UCS), an on-line interfaith network which includes "members from every mainstream religion, an array of eclectic 'new agers' of all types—and pagans, and Wiccans, and humanists, and even atheists,"[1] supports the URI—and the development of a New Religion.

In his report on the 1997 URI summit conference, UCS leader Bruce Schuman said: "In many ways, the URI is intimately related to the United Communities of Spirit project. One might almost say our objectives are identical."[2] In the late 1990s, the UCS web site provided links to six "special organizations, who are leading the way in the emergence of a new spiritual understanding;" the URI was listed together with five New Age sites, including "The Summit Lighthouse" (Church Universal and Triumphant).[3] The UCS has said, "We are devising an array of programs intended to pursue the agenda of the URI, and doing what we can to lay the groundwork for a high-powered global network that can truly change the world."[4]

So, let's examine the objectives of the UCS, noting that Schuman and the UCS are still active supporters of the URI.[5]

A UCS document, "A Philosophy of Interfaith Harmony and Unity," stated:

> We see no need to develop one universal common religion for all of humanity—yet it seems clear to us that the global confluence of religions is, indeed, tending to create a new universal spirituality, that incorporates perspectives and insights from all traditions. . . . We are creating a forum for 'unity in diversity' that celebrates the unique merits of each particular approach to the divine energy, yet also provides a way that each of these approaches can be welded into a cohesive common framework.[6]

In a letter to Anke Kreutzer, another URI activist, Bruce Schuman said of celibacy that "It is not 'the answer,' at least for the 'large boat' religion that we must devise for the broad human future."[7] Regarding another UCS project, "World Scripture: A Comparative Anthology of Sacred Texts," Schuman said, "I tend to feel that World Scripture is the beginning of a global database of fundamental spiritual

---

1. United Communities of Spirit (UCS), "The United Religions Initiative as a Global Network," http://www.origin.org/ucs/text/uri2.cfm, printed 05/19/03 (cited below as UCS, "URI a Global Network").

2. Bruce Schuman, "All One People: A Common Flame burns for all," *The Light and Life Journal: An Exploration of the Spiritual Universe*, Autumn 1997, p 6 (cited below as Schuman, "All One People," *The Light and Life Journal*, Autumn 1997).

3. United Communities of Spirit, "Friends," http://origin.org/ucs/text/friends.htm, printed in 1998; no longer on the Net at this address. (As of 2004, a copy of this web page is at http://web.archive.org/web/19981205161613/http://origin.org/ucs/text/friends.htm.) The "Church Universal and Triumphant" is a Theosophical Society descendant which was headed until the late 1990s by Elizabeth Clare Prophet. (See Barrett, *The New Believers*, pp 373–380.)

4. UCS, "URI as a Global Network."

5. United Religions Initiative, "Affiliates," http://www.uri.org/regionalnews/affiliates/, printed 07/05/04. Schuman is listed as an affiliate member from North America. The United Communities of Spirit web site contains numerous pro-URI articles—see, for example, those listed on United Communities of Spirit (UCS), "Articles and Proposals," http://origin.org/ucs/text/vision.cfm, printed 04/30/03.

6. United Communities of Spirit, "A Philosophy of Interfaith Harmony and Unity," http://www.origin.org/ucs/text/review.cfm, printed 05/19/03.

7. Bruce Schuman, United Communities of Spirit, "Letter to Anke Kreutzer," January 17, 1998, http://origin.org/ucs/library/ucs100.htm. This page was printed in 1998, and is no longer on the Net at this address. As of 2004, a copy of this page is at http://web.archive.org/web/19980210062709/http://origin.org/ucs/library/ucs100.htm. Schuman's reference to celibacy did not pertain specifically to priestly celibacy, a long-standing discipline of the Roman Catholic Church. Schuman said that during a debate on human sexuality and spirituality in an on-line interfaith discussion group, "There were several voices I respect who took the classical view that the highest spirituality demands celibacy. And it's easy for me to agree with that, because I took that view myself for years, and see it in the lives of many saints that I admire. And yet—it doesn't seem enough. It is not 'the answer,' at least for the 'large boat' religion that we must devise for the broad human future."

principles that will eventually serve as the foundation for an emerging new global spirituality."[1] In a 1997 letter to Juliet Hollister, the founder of the Temple of Understanding, Schuman wrote that "the rapidly changing popular awareness of spirituality and religion" and "the explosive growth in global communications . . . contribute to the interfaith agenda a strong grass-roots drive towards syncretic or universal spirituality."[2]

Schuman also envisioned new prophets, new theology, and a new revival:

It's my feeling that today, the globalization of culture is leading to the transformation of religion, and I do believe that prophets of this new dispensation should and will arise, and will play a role in guiding the world community into a new era of globally enlightened spirituality. . . . I anticipate the emergence of a new form of global theology, that is grounded in the classical doctrines of the religions, but which reinterprets them through a common set of principles. . . . I am convinced we can and should develop a sophisticated and science-grounded new universal theology of the spirit . . . But I am also an advocate of grass-roots spiritual revival, the direct white-lightning mystical connectivity and personal energy-flow that can inspire and heal individuals and entire cultures.[3]

At the 1997 URI summit conference, Schuman discerned the spirit of a coming New Religion, "the vision of a Common Flame":

I am persuaded that this 'confluence' of cultural and ideational forces can lead to a profoundly illuminating general understanding of spiritual and religious truth—and that, indeed, something exactly like this is what is occurring in cultures today, in a vast creatively bubbling conversational process in which all participants are being illuminated and educated by all others. This kind of 'mutual edification' was an inherent part of the URI conference. Out of myriad conversations, there seemed to emerge something of a common vision, expressed from the podium by different voices at different times, but somehow conveying a common sense of destiny. Out of the center, there seemed to emerge the vision of a Common Flame, a white heat of the spirit into which all believers are being drawn, each from their own tradition and perspective.[4]

He also said,

a strong argument can be raised that syncretism is inevitable, and represents a constructive and illuminating tendency that should be encouraged.[5]

"Emerging new global spirituality," "universal spirituality," a "Common Flame," and a "large boat religion that we must devise;" new scriptures, new prophets, new theology, a new vision of mankind's destiny—if it walks like a New Religion and talks like a New Religion, it *is* a New Religion.

LEX ORANDI, LEX CREDENDI: THE SYNCRETIC LANGUAGE AND SYMBOLS OF THE URI

Many public statements of URI leaders and supporters point toward creation of a New Religion; the ceremonial language and symbols used by the URI at their worship services do the same. For those who understand how word, ceremony, and symbol shape religious belief, the meaning is unmistakable. As

1. Interfaith Voices for Peace and Justice, "Vision," http://interfaithvoices.org/ifv/text/vision.cfm, printed 04/25/01; no longer on the Net at this address. As of 2004, a copy of this page is at http://web.archive.org/web/20010309215740/http://interfaithvoices.org/ifv/text/vision.cfm.
2. Letter from Bruce Schuman to Juliet Hollister, July 28, 1997; http://origin.org.uri/files/uri010.cfm, printed in 1997; no longer on the Net.
3. Bruce Schuman, United Communities of Spirit, "The Bridge Across Consciousness," July 5, 1997—letter to Anke Kreutzer, http://origin.org/uri/files/uri005.cfm. Printed in 1998; no longer on the Net.
4. Schuman, "All One People," *The Light and Life Journal*, Autumn 1997, p7.
5. Ibid.

interfaith leader Marcus Braybrooke says, "Interfaith worship attracts strong opposition because it is the most powerful symbolic expression of the interfaith vision. Symbols always speak more eloquently than words."[1]

Words have definite and commonly understood meanings. If there were no intent on the part of the URI (or of a faction within it) to give birth to a new world religion, why not call the organization "Religious Coalition for Peace," "Religions United Against Violence," or a similar phrase that connotes peacemaking without implying a union of the religions? In response to a question asked from the floor at the January 26, 1997 URI forum—about the name of the URI and the similarity of this name with the UN's name—Executive Director Gibbs said that the name of the Initiative was discussed extensively at the June 1996 summit meeting, and "at this point in time, United Religions was still the best way of capturing in a couple of words what this was about."[2] The choice of the name "United Religions" is a deliberate and considered choice by the movement.

Symbols, hymns, and prayers used at URI worship ceremonies point in the same direction, toward syncretism. *Lex orandi, lex credendi*—the law of praying is the law of believing.

The *San Francisco Chronicle* reported that during the 1995 interfaith service at which Bishop Swing announced the URI, "prayers, chants, and incantations were offered to a dozen deities."[3] "Holy water from the Ganges, the Amazon, the Red Sea, the River Jordan, and other sacred streams"[4] was mingled "into a single 'bowl of unity'"[5] on the altar of Grace Cathedral. During the service, Bishop Swing made the meaning of the ritual clear. The *San Francisco Chronicle* reported: "'As these sacred waters find confluence here,' said Episcopal Bishop William Swing, 'may the city that chartered the nations of the world bring together the religions of the world.'"[6] The *San Jose Mercury News* reported, "Swing asked religious leaders to come together as one 'emerging soul' for peace."[7]

David Ponedel, Bishop of the Church of Divine Man, "oversaw the collection of the waters" used in this ceremony—a ceremony that has been used at other interfaith services since 1995,[8] including URI conferences.[9] Ponedel's text for the "Sacred Waters Ceremony," as used at the 1999 Parliament of World Religions in South Africa, states:

> Water has the power to purify, nourish, heal, replenish, dissolve, and transform. It is both an agent and a symbol for the uniting of opposites. . . . As an event in an interfaith setting, using water gathered at sacred sites from around the world, is a powerful act. . . . When this water is combined, a singular pool of energy is created,

1. Braybrooke, *Faith and Interfaith*, p 119.

2. Transcribed by Lee Penn from a tape of the January 26, 1997 URI forum at Grace Cathedral.

3. Don Lattin, "Religions of World Celebrated With Prayers to Dozen Deities," *San Francisco Chronicle*, June 26, 1995, p 1, front page section (cited below as Lattin, "Religions of World Celebrated," *San Francisco Chronicle*, 06/26/95).

4. Ibid.

5. Richard Scheinin, "Interfaith ceremony promotes world peace," *San Jose Mercury News*, June 26, 1995 (cited below as Scheinin, "Interfaith ceremony," 06/26/95).

6. Lattin, "Religions of World Celebrated," *San Francisco Chronicle*, 06/26/95, pp 1 and 11, section A (front page). Likewise, in early 1995 Swing described plans for the interfaith service at Grace Cathedral: "As waters from the sacred rivers of the world are poured together, those gathered will hear a young person representing the [Rediscovering Justice] conference offer a vision of the United Religions, and challenge the world's religions to commit to making such a vision a reality." (Bishop William Swing, "The Creation of the United Religions: An Overview," document released by the URI in 1995).

7. Scheinin, "Interfaith ceremony," *San Jose Mercury News*, 06/26/95.

8. E-mail from David Ponedel, Bishop of the Church of Divine Man, to Lee Penn, 11/11/02. He added, "As a participant over many months in the creation of this UN50 Interfaith Service, as well as the UN50 events 'Rediscovering Justice' at USF, and 'Celebrating the Spirit: Toward a Global Ethic' at UC Berkeley, that at no time was it proposed, discussed, or suggested by anyone that the religions of the world supplant one another, meld theology, or syncret [sic] into some sort of 'United Religion.'"

9. Interview of David Ponedel by Lee Penn, November 2002.

representing both the highest aspirations of the human family, and our shared understanding of the sacred relationship we hold with Life.[1]

At the 1997 URI summit conference, the public worship service included a procession of 15 banners with symbols representing the world's religions, including a banner for the Wiccans.[2] On the fifteenth banner was an empty circle, representing "the religions which are to come."[3] An array of 15 religious symbols (including the Wiccan pentagram and the empty circle for the religions of the future), was on the cover of Bishop Swing's 1998 book *The Coming United Religions*, and still appears (in a different form) on many URI publications.[4]

Schuman, the interfaith activist from the United Communities of Spirit, said in 1997:

And the last of these banners carried simply an empty circle—which Deborah [Moldow] described as representing 'the religions which are to come.' The next day, as we were breaking into our final groups of the conference, Deborah created a new category for discussion that invoked this spirit of emptiness—this 'empty center' that conference organizer Paul Andrews had spoken about. . . . I decided to join this group, because it seemed so deeply spiritual. Our group concentrated on meditation and inner receptivity. We began with silence, attuning ourselves to our 'inner guidance.' After a few minutes, I felt prompted to speak, and I mentioned why I had joined this group—which involved not only my sense of the creative unfolding from this 'empty center,' but also because I myself do not really have some 'tradition' or existing organization that I represent. I feel myself to be a representative of something new, something emerging, something not yet entirely defined, yet drawing its form from many sources—in a 'syncretic' way. Out of this 'empty center' there emerges—what?[5]

Syncretic religious observances have continued to mark URI gatherings since then.

• In April 2001, the Spiritual Alliance for the Earth, a URI Cooperation Circle, held an Earth Day interfaith service at Grace Cathedral. During the service, which was underwritten in part by Birkenstock,[6] "a Shinto Rite of Purification was performed, followed by a call to prayer by Native Americans," as well as "the Sufi's Salima and Taneen, a rabbi's song of lamentation for the destruction of Earth, a pagan's praise of Gaia, and the incredibly deep bass chants of Tibetan monks. The Cathedral's Dean, Alan Jones, provided a framework for interfaith prayers and blessings; the Rev. Sally Bingham gave a narrative that recognized the threat to Earth and our commitment to care for Her."[7]
• At the January 2002 URI "Latin American Assembly" in Oaxtepec, Mexico, "an ecumenical celebration of the Eucharist and an Aztec indigenous ceremony took place in the sulfur waters of the lake near the hotel."[8]

1. E-mail from David Ponedel, Bishop of the Church of Divine Man, to Lee Penn, 11/11/02.
2. Rowan Fairgrove, "Holy Brighid Holding the World in her Hands," http://www.conjure.com/inspired.html, printed 3/19/03 (cited below as Fairgrove, "Holy Brighid").
3. "Voices of the Light," No. 15, July 1, 1997; electronic newsletter of the United Communities of Spirit; http://www.origin.org/ucs/text/uri1.cfm, printed 10/3/02 (cited below as "Voices of the Light," 07/01/97); Fairgrove, "Holy Brighid."
4. In several URI publications issued in the fall of 2002, and on some of their Web pages posted in the same period, the 15 symbols are in a line, superimposed on a map of the globe.
5. "Voices of the Light," 07/01/97.
6. Grace Online, "A Song of Creation: Earth Day 2001 at Grace Cathedral," http://www.gracecathedral.org/enrichment/features/fea_20010515.shtml, printed 10/17/2001.
7. William Sadler, Ph. D., "Interfaith Alliance for Earth holds Inaugural Event," *EarthLight: The Magazine of Spiritual Ecology*, issue 42, Summer 2001, http://www.earthlight.org/essay42_safe.html, printed 02/17/2003. Capitalization is as given in the original text.
8. URI Latin American coordination team, "Latin American Assembly: 'Celebrating Our Identity, Building Bridges,'" *Pacific Church News*, Spring 2002, p35. A document on the URI web site as of July 2004 likewise indicates this: "The Sikhs offered their spiritual practices, the Catholics attended Mass, the Muslim performed suplicas, the Orixa tradition performed rituals, members of the Jewish faith prayed, *and there was an ecumenical celebration of the Eucharist and an Aztec indigenous ceremony in the sulfuric lake near the hotel.*" [emphasis added] (United Religions Initiative, "Latin America Regional Assembly: Celebrating Our Identity, We Build Bridges," http://www.uri.org/regionalnews/lamerica/lareg.asp, printed 07/16/04.)

• At the URI Global Assembly in Rio de Janeiro in 2002, there was an "interreligious ceremony of fire" attended by "approximately 200 persons, international guests and Brazilians," and held in "Parque da Cidade, one of the largest urban forests in the world."[1] A participant said, "A group of Amazon Indigenous sorcerers led a trail through the woods and with a group of shamans lit the fire. The ceremony also had a Wiccan and a Zoroastrian ritual."[2]

• On March 2, 2003, the URI joined "Grace Cathedral, the San Francisco Interfaith Council, the California Council of Churches/California Church IMPACT, Working Assets, and the National Council of Churches"[3] in sponsoring an interfaith anti-war prayer service. At this service, there was "a huge globe centered on the Cathedral's main altar."[4] Here, the Earth replaced the Cross and the Eucharist, the items that are usually at the center of Christian altars.

URI Global Council member Donald Frew, a Wiccan, said in March 2003, "Non-Christians who participate in interfaith activity never seem to incorporate elements of other religions into their own services. Only some of the Christians who are in the interfaith movement seem to do this. I think this is part of what makes interfaith work more threatening to traditional Christian groups."[5]

SYNCRETISM IN STONE:
DESIGNING AN INTERFAITH TEMPLE

In 2003, the San Francisco chapter of the American Institute of Architects, the Interfaith Center at the Presidio, and an art-oriented URI Cooperation Circle co-sponsored an "Interfaith Sacred Space Design Competition."[6] The planners explained their goal:

Is genuine interfaith space possible? What might a space designed to accommodate the needs of all faiths look like? An international 'ideas' competition is being launched to design sacred space where people from all religious traditions can feel comfortable, safe, and respected. As the interfaith movement grows, space will be needed for genuine interfaith dialogue and shared practice—not to change or compromise anyone but to cultivate friendship and common cause in the spirit of what we most value.[7]

Contestants were free to create a hypothetical site for their interfaith temple. Twenty-five designs, including the winners, were displayed at the July 2004 meeting of the Parliament of the World's Religions.[8] The sponsors sought designs that would:

• Provide opportunities for people to meet and share with others in ways that will expand their own understanding of what is sacred or divine.
• Offer an open, hospitable setting for people to experience the best of each other.
• Provide a setting for people of different religions to work cooperatively toward establishing peace and harmony, and to end religiously motivated violence.

1. United Religions Initiative, "URI Global Assembly 2002 News & Images," Wednesday, August 21, "Fire Ceremony in the Forest," http://www.uri.org/calendar/wednesday21.asp, printed 10/14/02.
2. Ibid.
3. Diocese of California, "In Time of War: March 2ⁿᵈ Interfaith Prayer Service Sought to Head Off War Effort," *Pacific Church News On-Line*, April/May 2003, Vol. 141, no. e3, http://pcn.diocal.org/PCNO/pcn003-3/index.html, printed 05/08/03 (cited below as March 2ⁿᵈ Interfaith Prayer Service," *PCN On-Line*, April/May 2003).
4. Ibid.
5. Interview of Donald Frew by Lee Penn, 3/28/03.
6. United Religions Initiative, *Interfaith Sacred Space Design Competition*, September 2, 2003, http://www.uri.org/design-comp/program.doc, p1, printed 07/17/04 (cited below as URI, *Interfaith Sacred Space Design Competition*, 09/02/03).
7. Ibid., p3.
8. United Religions Initiative, "URI CCs Help to Sponsor International Sacred Design Competition," *URI Update*, Issue 15, September 2004, p5 (cited below as URI, "CCs Sponsor International Sacred Design Competition," 09/04).

• Offer people throughout the world an opportunity to see and experience a model of interreligious cooperation that can be adapted for use in their own communities.
• Help religions achieve a base in world affairs by demonstrating their commitment to common values and their willingness to collaboratively use spiritual methods to promote world peace.
• Provide for the sacred space needs of all faiths."[1]

There were 160 designs from 17 countries[2] submitted for the competition, and URI Global Council member Donald Frew said that the entries "represent untold hours of work towards a dream of interfaith cooperation. They are the result of many more than 160 conversations all over the world about the nature of interfaith sacred space. We wanted to start a conversation. Well, the whole world has joined in."[3] There will be a new interfaith design contest in 2006.[4]

In February 2004, the URI and the Interfaith Center at the Presidio exhibited the designs for an interfaith temple. The *San Francisco Chronicle* reported:

There were 10 jurors and 16 religious advisers on hand to point out various design flaws that would make people of their respective faiths feel uncomfortable. Crosses were taboo, along with designs that seemed just a bit too Zen. . . . Another religious adviser, the Rev. Gerald O'Rourke from the Catholic Archdiocese of San Francisco, stood before a drawing of an altar holding symbols representing seven world religions. 'They are just trying to please us all, but that is virtual sacrilege,' O'Rourke said. 'Keep it simple. People just need a safe place where they can get together.' . . . Organizers say the reason for the contest is to stimulate interfaith ideas and interaction.[5]

Four contest winners were announced in March 2004,[6] along with seven honorable mentions.[7] Vivek Anand and Philip Sebastian, a San Francisco gay couple, were among the winning designers. The *San Jose Mercury News* reported,

Anand and Sebastian's design includes an underground cave, a passageway, a theater and a sanctuary. Scattered among them are a large tree, a garden, a piazza, a wooded labyrinth, a 'stations' wall, and a river with a lotus pond and two bridges. Overarching much of the space is a tent, 'reminiscent of the desert religions,' Sebastian said. 'It's a flowing design. I want people to wander through the whole thing,' Anand said. 'One of the reasons I didn't do one building is, that would just look like a beautiful church. For someone who's not Christian, it would still say 'church.' The competition's goal was to design a place where people could express their own faiths and come together with followers of other religions. 'It is providing an opportunity for engagement,' Anand said. 'You can't be condescending toward religions, just like you can't be condescending of humans.' . . . The common ground of spirituality is what inspired their design. Each element harks back to archetypes and symbols that can serve almost any religion. Pagans, American Indians or members of other religions that connect with the Earth and mankind's beginnings can find symbolism and sanctuary in the large, round cavern, with natural illumination from a skylight. Smaller side chambers, evocative of monks' cells, could be suitable for individual prayer, Buddhist meditation or Catholic confession. Similarly, niches in the horn-shaped passage could be used by individuals or small groups. Outdoor spaces, the theater or the piazza could accommodate Muslim prayer or ritual

1. URI, *Interfaith Sacred Space Design Competition*, 09/02/03, p 4.
2. URI, "CCs Sponsor International Sacred Dance Competition," 09/04, p 5.
3. Donald H. Frew, "Reflections on the Competition," http://www.interfaithdesign.org/pages/Frew_Article_01.html, printed 07/03/04.
4. Interfaith Sacred Space Design Competition, "Is Genuine Interfaith Space Possible?" http://www.interfaithdesign.org/, printed 07/03/04.
5. Don Lattin, "Interfaith contest designed to build common ground; Architects, visionaries draw up sacred space plans," *San Francisco Chronicle*, February 15, 2004, http://www.sfgate.com/cgi-bin/article.cgi?file=/chronicle/archive/2004/02/15/BAG90512UG1.DTL, viewed 07/17/04.
6. Interfaith Sacred Space Design Competition, "Winners (4)," http://www.interfaithdesign.org/2004_Competition/Pages_Thumb_Index/Thumb_Index_Win.html, printed 07/17/04.
7. Interfaith Sacred Space Design Competition, "Honorable Mentions (7)," http://www.interfaithdesign.org/2004_Competition/Pages_Thumb_Index/Thumb_Index_HM.html, printed 07/17/04.

dances. The Tree of Knowledge would make a pleasant place for Sunday school instruction or a Jewish wedding. River water can be used in religious rituals, serve as a symbol for life and replenishment, or just be a place for children to play.[1]

Such was the spirituality and world-view of this architectural contest co-sponsored by the URI and its allies in the interfaith movement: syncretism in wood and stone, and spiritual formlessness made physically manifest.

THE IMPLICATIONS OF RELIGIOUS SYNCRETISM

In the early stages of the development of the New Religion, the emphasis will be on acceptance of a "more inclusive set of global visions," with many religions and many gods, all on an equal footing. Gurudev Khalsa, who has led the Appreciative Inquiry process for several URI conferences,[2] said that one of the "major trends" affecting the creation of the URI was "movement toward a sense of global spirituality."[3] He described the process being used to build the URI: "Chartering does not depend on reaching a consensus of vision as much as it aims to create an ever widening, more inclusive set of global visions and relationships that enliven local action on behalf of the emerging United Religions. As such, it responds to the challenge of creating a transboundary organization in a postmodern world where imposing a single vision can only lead to failure."[4] Only later would the "more inclusive set of global visions" evolve toward what Bishop Swing describes as a "common purpose" for "all religions and all spiritual movements."[5] Then, we will learn the name of the entity that Bishop Swing hailed as "a spirit of colossal energy" being "born in the loins of the earth."[6]

Anglican Bishop Moses Tay of Singapore rebuked religious syncretism when he preached at Denver, Colorado in 1992. Nationally syndicated columnist Terry Mattingly quotes Bishop Tay's sermon:

> The bishop took as a text Revelation 2:12–16, in which the exalted Christ says to the angel of the Church of Pergamum, 'I know where you are living, where Satan's throne is.' Is it possible, asked the bishop, that Satan had set a throne in that Church? 'Would we be shocked if that is true, that Satan has his throne in some of our churches?' The text offers two danger signs, Tay noted. The first is the presence of corrupt teachers who bring other gods and idols into church life through forms of syncretistic worship. 'I believe this is . . . very prevalent within some quarters of the Anglican Communion,' he said. 'I say this with some shame and sadness, because this is the very thing that the Bible forbids.' Danger sign No. 2, he added, is compromise on issues of sexual immorality.[7]

By his writings and actions, Bishop Swing has ignored the Biblically based warning given by Bishop Tay, a fellow Anglican prelate.

---

1. Robin Evans, "A winning team," *San Jose Mercury News*, March 20, 2004. Printed from the web site http://www.mercurynews.com on 03/24/04.

2. "Peacemaker Voices," Gurudev Khalsa, http://perspectivesonpeacemaking.org/pmvoices.htm, printed 05/09/03.

3. Gurudev S. Khalsa and Kathryn M. Kaczmarski, "Chartering and Appreciative Future Search," http://ai.cwru.edu/gem/chartering.html, on-line copy printed 06/02/04. The article was published in volume 1, issue 2 of the *Journal of the GEM Initiative*. (This article is also cited as an abstract at Appreciative Inquiry Commons, "AI Written Works: Article Detail," http://appreciativeinquiry.cwru.edu/practice/bibAiArticlesDetail.cfm?coid=306, printed 05/09/03.)

4. Ibid.

5. Swing, *The Coming United Religions*, p 63.

6. Bishop William Swing, "Opening Address," United Religions Initiative, Stanford University, June 23–27, 1997, http://www.united-religions.org/youth/welcome/swingspeech.htm, printed 1997; no longer on the Net at this address (cited below as Swing, 1997 URI "Opening Address"). This passage from Swing's speech is also cited in Gibbs/Mahé, *Birth of a Global Community*, p 107.

7. Terry Mattingly, "Liturgical Dances With Wolves (1993): Ten Years As An Episcopalian—A Progress Report," http://tmatt.gospelcom.net/tmatt/freelance/wolves.htm, printed 04/08/03.

Jesus' Great Commission to the faithful is "Go therefore and make disciples of all nations, baptizing them in the name of the Father and of the Son and of the Holy Spirit, teaching them to observe all I have commanded you." (Matt. 28:19–20). The Great Commission is *not* "worship Ausar, Baal, Siva, Ishtar, and the Inner Light in common with thy neighbor, in order to understand his religion and make peace with him." Indeed, such common worship violates the First Commandment, "You shall have no other gods before me" (Deut. 5:7). Thus, what URI supporters see as accommodation to the needs of the times, orthodox Christians see as apostasy and idolatry.

When Christians participate in syncretic URI activities, or offer excuses for them, they are, in effect, trampling on the memory of the Christian martyrs of the Roman Empire. Catholic writers Carl Olson and Sandra Miesel summarized the origins of the Imperial persecutions: "Early Christianity was exclusive in nature. One reason the early Christians were persecuted so harshly by the Romans was their exclusive claims for Jesus. For the most part, Rome was willing to accommodate a variety of religious beliefs, as long as they took a syncretistic approach to other religions and paid special favor to the cult of the emperor. The Christians refused, insisting that Jesus, not the emperor, was God."[1] This was why "the Christians were disliked by pagans and accused of bizarre activities in their liturgies and gatherings. It is also why the Roman government eventually persecuted and killed large numbers of the early Christians."[2]

Those who favor development of a New Religion for the "new civilization" will find the URI to be a useful means by which to seek their goal. When this movement is built, money, bureaucratic influence, and political power can sway the United Religions Initiative in a direction never intended by some of its Christian founders. It would not be the first time for a liberal movement to be hijacked by others with a clear vision of where they want the movement to go.[3]

In a world with a successful United Religions Initiative, syncretism could win gradually, with religious orthodoxy being defined outside the bounds of polite discourse. What "political correctness" has done in Canada, the European Union, and some regions of the United States could be done worldwide, slowly but surely; global money power and global media power would lead a change in people's beliefs.[4]

1. Carl E. Olson and Sandra Miesel, *The Da Vinci Hoax: Exposing the Errors in The Da Vinci Code*, Ignatius Press, 2004, p166.

2. Ibid., p167.

3. In the 1920s, René Guénon described the use of such tactics by the Theosophists and their allies. He wrote, "We have already pointed out the existence of many auxiliary groups of the Theosophical Society, which allowed it to penetrate and work in the most diverse circles, usually without any reference being made to its special doctrines, and without setting forth any other goal than 'universal brotherhood' and certain moralizing tendencies which could hardly seem compromising. After all, one must be careful not to frighten with overly extravagant claims those whom one would like to attract imperceptibly as unwitting accomplices. The history of the Old-Catholic Church provides us with an example of this pretense. Theosophists are motivated by a keen desire for propaganda, which despite their contrary claims reveals just how Western they are, since the Eastern mentality, and the Hindu mentality in particular, has a deep repugnance for proselytism. And their methods for infiltration strangely recall those of many Protestant sects." (Guénon, *Theosophy*, p244.) He added, "If we examine the methods Theosophy employs for its diffusion, it is easy to see that they are identical to those used by Protestant sects. With the one as with the other there is the same proselytizing fury, the same insinuating suppleness used to reach the various targeted groups, which creates all sorts of associations that are more or less independent in appearance but are all intended to cooperate in the same task. . . . whether these organizations have an avowed aim of Theosophist propaganda, whether they proclaim themselves independent and open to all even while acknowledging their origin, or even whether they dissimulate their origin more or less carefully—all are in fact subject to a single direction; all are directly or indirectly consecrated to the 'service' of Theosophy, sometimes against the wishes of a great part of their membership, who are perfectly unconscious of the role they are made to play" (Guénon, ibid., pp268–269).

4. René Guénon predicted this trend in 1945, saying, "The anti-traditional action necessarily had to aim both at a change in the general mentality and at the destruction of all traditional institutions in the West, since the West is where it began to work first and most directly, while awaiting the proper time for an attempt to extend its operations over the whole world,

The preceding admonitions against religious syncretism are from an orthodox Christian perspective. For different reasons, the Sufi Muslim scholar Charles Upton denounces syncretism as a form of spiritual debauchery:

> The idea that the only alternative to inter-religious dialogue is inter-religious war, and that inter-religious dialogue is just another name for syncretism, is profoundly destructive and fundamentally absurd. Different religions may lead their devotees to God, but mixing elements from various religions into one shapeless conglomerate affects the spiritual life in the same way that invasive species affect an ecosystem: what is appropriate in its own context becomes terminally destructive when applied outside that context, destructive to both guest and host. Another man will love his wife, as I do my own—but to allow the devotees of another religion to worship at a shrine of my religion is like letting another man sleep with my wife. It is a form of promiscuity in the religious field that might be termed "god-swapping".[1]

[IV] FOSTERING DISSENT WITHIN TRADITIONAL RELIGIONS

The fourth reason to oppose the URI is that—by design—the URI is likely to foster dissent and division within traditional religions, especially within the Catholic Church.

In the fall of 2001, Swing told an interviewer for *The Witness* (a liberal Episcopal magazine) that

> when you're dealing at the grassroots level, there are a lot of people who say, I don't really go along with everything that my religion teaches and therefore that makes it possible for me to meet you and deal with you across the boundary lines. That's why we have more potential for dealing with those deeper differences. There are groups that have a very low esteem toward women, but then there are a lot of people in that group that have a high esteem toward women and they will join the URI.[2]

This aspect of the URI would give religious dissenters—such as supporters of ordaining women to the Catholic priesthood—additional support.

Swing appears to have carried forward an idea proposed in the late 1990s by Bruce Schuman, a long-time URI activist. Schuman believed that the URI can foster dialogue within religions as well as among them. For example, he envisioned the use of polls to redefine Catholic doctrine and belief, as a way to foster the dissenters within the Catholic Church:

> One way to define 'Catholicism,' for example, is by asking the question, 'What do people who say they are Catholics actually believe?' If we conducted a large-scale poll of religious people, and defined 'Catholicism' as 'what people who say they are Catholics actually believe,' we would have a potent and credible approach to the creation of a global interfaith organization, that would be grounded in the actual beliefs of religious people, rather than in some official but perhaps controversial doctrine. In the long run, this is probably the strongest approach.

using the Westerners duly prepared to become its instruments." (René Guénon, *The Reign of Quantity & The Signs of The Times*, orig. ed. 1945, reissued by Sophia Perennis et Universalis, 1995, p 231.)

1. Charles Upton, e-mail to Lee Penn, 05/27/04. Upton believes that the traditional religions (in particular, Judaism, Islam, Christianity, Hinduism, and Buddhism) each reflect a revelation of the one God, the one Absolute, to the adherents of each of those faiths. Each of these faiths is therefore, in its own right, a way to true communion with God. However, he says (as do others who believe in the "Transcendent Unity of Religions") that the beliefs and practices of each divinely revealed religion must be maintained in their integrity; the various religions cannot merge or unite in time, on Earth. Such unity as they have can only be experienced in eternity, before the face of God. Thus, Upton writes "We must remember, of course, that the 'gods' being swapped in such cases of syncretism are not actual independent deities, but rather human conceptions of the One God based on His providential Self-revelations to us, each of which is unique and incomparable. To add one to the other is both unnecessary and almost inconceivably foolish, like attempting to enter a room through two doors at once. The 'gods' possess no independent essence of their own; they are Names of the One."

2. Wortman, interview with Swing, *Witness*, 12/01, p 7.

Clearly, there may be significant tensions in a large religious organization. This is certainly true in the Catholic Church, where official Church doctrine may be seen as quite controversial by significant sub-groups within the Church. In an interfaith organization, do we give voice to these sub-groups and their agendas, or do we allow only the official representatives of the established hierarchy to represent their institution? It seems to me that the best approach is probably a compromise, that provides a channel for both (or multiple) points of view. Perhaps, as we are reconciling tensions *among* the various religions, we can also provide a forum that mediates the same kind of dialogue *within* existing religions.[1]

[v] A "NEW ETHIC" FOR THE NEW WORLD ORDER: HANS KÜNG'S GLOBAL ETHIC

The fifth reason to oppose the URI is that Bishop Swing and other prominent supporters of the URI presume that they can create a new "Global Ethic" that will be binding for us all.

A New Religion calls for a New Ethic, and a "Global Ethic" has been proposed by Hans Küng, a pro-URI Catholic theologian who was disciplined in 1979 by the Pope for his unorthodox teachings. Since 1993, the "Global Ethic" has been widely accepted by the international interfaith movement, including the URI.

Bishop Swing sees Küng's document, "Toward a Global Ethic," as a basis for a new ethic that will be created and sponsored by "all religions and spiritual movements."[2] The New Ethic would be defined after the URI is fully launched, because, as Bishop Swing says, "If a universal Declaration of a Global Ethos is brought forth without the underpinnings of an enduring global institution, it will lack gravity and binding power. A Declaration is derivative. Its creation and its continuance must rest on an abiding, global institution and on global acceptance."[3] With the URI, Swing says that "the path will exist for religions, together, to address the agonies and opportunities of the coming age."[4] Bishop Michael Ingham says of the 1993 "Global Ethic" that "It is hoped it might one day acquire the kind of status of United Nations charters such as those on Human Rights and the Environment."[5] An ethical charter, backed by "an abiding, global institution" and "global acceptance": in the New World Order, there would be no escape from the New Religion's New Ethic. As Küng wrote in 1998, "**There will be no new world order without a new world ethic**, a global or planetary ethic **despite** all dogmatic differences."[6]

Küng's "Declaration Toward A Global Ethic" was signed by most of the delegates to the 1993 Parliament of the World's Religions.[7] Interfaith activist Joel Beversluis wrote, "this effort of the 1993 Parliament was unprecedented in its scope and intent. Its primary value and lesson lies in the explicitly interreligious consensus on ethical principles and responsibilities."[8] Br. Wayne Teasdale, a Catholic URI supporter, offered similar praise for the new "Ethic": "The declaration contains general norms of behavior and responsibility that are universally acceptable and applicable. . . . A universal spirituality

---

1. Bruce Schuman, "A Global Network for the World Religions?: A Reply to Marcus Braybrooke," http://origin.org/uri/files/uri016.cfm, printed in 1998; no longer on the Net.

2. Swing, *The Coming United Religions*, p 27.

3. Ibid., p 44.

4. Ibid., p 45.

5. Ingham, "Is Tolerance Enough?"

6. Hans Küng, *A Global Ethic for Global Politics and Economics*, Oxford University Press, 1998, p 92.

7. Hans Küng, "Explanatory Remarks Concerning a 'Declaration of the Religions for a Global Ethic,'" http://astro.temple.edu/~dialogue/Antho/kung.htm, printed 05/08/03 (cited below as Küng, "Explanatory Remarks").

8. Joel Beversluis, "The Parliaments and the Quest for a Global Ethic," in Joel Beversluis, ed., *Sourcebook of the World's Religions: An Interfaith Guide to Religion and Spirituality*, New World Library, 2000, p 168 (cited below as Beversluis, "The Parliaments and the Quest for a Global Ethic").

would easily adopt the code of the Global Ethic."[1] Interfaith leader Marcus Braybrooke says, "The *Declaration* could well form the basis for a useful values or character education project, appropriately designed for young people. It may well be that it is through its educational applications that the *Declaration* will have its greatest impact."[2]

A successor document, "A Call to Our Guiding Institutions," which sought "to make the Global Ethic more specific and applicable"[3] was published by the Council for a Parliament of the World's Religions (CPWR) at the 1999 Parliament of the World's Religions.[4]

The URI and its allies continue to make use of the proposed "Global Ethic." On March 2, 2003, the URI, the National Council of Churches, and other liberal organizations co-sponsored an anti-war interfaith prayer service at Grace Cathedral. The Episcopal diocesan newsletter reported that there was "a huge globe centered on the Cathedral's main altar."[5] Before this totem, "six readers representing Buddhist, Christian, Islamic, and Jewish faiths, read passages from the Declaration, 'Towards a Global Ethic,' endorsed by the Parliament of the World's Religions' world assembly."[6] A URI Cooperation Circle, "URI Bridge CC," is engaged in a multi-year effort to promote acceptance of the "Global Ethic."[7]

Thus, the "Global Ethic" has proven itself to be acceptable to the major organizations in the interfaith movement since 1993.

The Global Ethic states: "there is already a consensus among the religions which can be the basis of a global ethic—a minimal *fundamental consensus* concerning binding *values*, irrevocable *standards*, and fundamental *moral attitudes*."[8] It claims that "the principles expressed in this global ethic can be affirmed by all persons with ethical convictions, whether religiously grounded or not."[9] It adds, "Rights without morality cannot long endure;" "*there will be no better global order without a global ethic*. By a global ethic we do not mean a global ideology or a single unified religion beyond all existing religions, and certainly not the domination of one religion over all others. By a global ethic we mean a fundamental consensus on binding values, irrevocable standards, and personal attitudes."[10]

The "Global Ethic" affirms that "*every human being must be treated humanely!* ... Humans must always be the subjects of rights, must be ends, never mere means ... No one stands 'above good and evil.'"[11] The "irrevocable, unconditional norm for all areas of life" must be based on the Golden Rule—stated positively as, "What you wish done to yourself, do to others!"[12] Much of this document is an extended discussion of themes taken from the Ten Commandments and the Beatitudes, and is consistent with 20th Century Catholic teaching on social issues.

However, the "Ethic" also contains open-ended rhetoric which could easily be used to define politically correct, collectivist liberalism as the only "authentically human" alternative:

---

1. Brother Wayne Teasdale, "Sacred Community at the Dawn of the Second Axial Age," in Joel Beversluis, ed., *Sourcebook of the World's Religions: An Interfaith Guide to Religion and Spirituality*, New World Library, 2000, p241.

2. Braybrooke, *Faith and Interfaith*, p87.

3. Beversluis, "The Parliaments and the Quest for a Global Ethic," p168.

4. Joel Beversluis, "The Quest for a Global Ethic," in Joel Beversluis, ed., *Sourcebook of the World's Religions: An Interfaith Guide to Religion and Spirituality*, New World Library, 2000, p173.

5. March 2nd Interfaith Prayer Service," *PCN On-Line*, April/May 2003.

6. Ibid.

7. United Religions Initiative, "URI Bridge CC," http://www.uribridgecc.org/, printed 06/04/04.

8. "Towards a Global Ethic: An Initial Declaration," in Joel Beversluis, ed., *Sourcebook of the World's Religions: An Interfaith Guide to Religion and Spirituality*, New World Library, 2000, pp175–176 (cited below as "Towards a Global Ethic: An Initial Declaration").

9. Ibid., p176.

10. Ibid., pp176–177.

11. Ibid., p177.

12. Ibid., p177.

Every form of egoism should be rejected: all selfishness, whether individual or collective, whether in the form of class thinking, racism, nationalism, or sexism. We condemn these because they prevent humans from being authentically human. Self-determination and self-realization are thoroughly legitimate so long as they are not separated from human self-responsibility and global responsibility, that is, from responsibility for fellow humans and for the planet Earth.[1]

(This denunciation of "every form of egoism" appears not to include those who claim that they can write a new, universal global ethic.)

The "Ethic" continues with four major ethical injunctions, but makes no reference to God in any way[2]—let alone explicitly acknowledging Him as the source of the moral law and of human dignity. The four points were:

1. "*You shall not kill!* Or, in positive terms, *Have respect for life!*. . . All people have the right to life, safety, and the free development of personality insofar as they do not injure the rights of others. . . . A human person is infinitely precious and must be unconditionally protected."[3]

2. "*You shall not steal!* Or in positive terms: *Deal honestly and fairly!* . . . No one has the right to rob or dispossess in any way whatsoever any other person or the commonweal. Further, no one has the right to use her or his possessions without concern for the needs of society and Earth."[4]

3. "All over the world we find endless lies and deceit, swindling and hypocrisy, ideology and demagoguery: [including] . . . Representatives of religions who dismiss other religions as of little value and who preach fanaticism and intolerance instead of respect and understanding. . . . *You shall not lie!* Or in positive terms: *Speak and act truthfully!*"[5]

4. "All over the world there are condemnable [sic] forms of patriarchy, domination of one sex over the other, exploitation of women, sexual misuse of children, and forced prostitution. . . . *You shall not commit sexual immorality!* Or in positive terms: *Respect and love one another!* . . . We have the duty to resist wherever the domination of one sex over the other is preached—even in the name of religious conviction. . . . Sexuality as a life-affirming shaper of community can only be effective when partners accept the responsibility of caring for one another's happiness. . . . Sexuality should express and reinforce a loving relationship lived by equal partners. . . . All lands and cultures should develop economic and social relationships which will enable marriage and family life worthy of human beings."[6]

The first of these four points contains a fatal weakness. It states, "A human person is infinitely precious and must be unconditionally protected."[7] However, Küng said of his "Ethic" that "Such a Declaration must be CAPABLE OF PRODUCING A CONSENSUS. Hence, statements must be avoided which a priori would be rejected by one of the great religions, and as a consequence disputed moral questions (like abortion or euthanasia) had to be excluded."[8] Therefore, under the New Ethic, those whose lives must be "unconditionally protected" do *not* include unwanted children in their mother's womb, or those tempted to end their lives to escape suffering. Covered by these two lethal loopholes in the "Ethic," the abortionists and the suicide doctors in the New World Order could continue their deadly trade unhindered.

1. Ibid., p178.
2. Braybrooke, *Faith and Interfaith*, p82. Braybrooke said that this was done because "the use of the word 'God,' however, created difficulties for Buddhists and might have alienated those who are non-religious."
3. "Towards a Global Ethic: An Initial Declaration," p178.
4. Ibid., p179.
5. Ibid., p180.
6. Ibid., p181.
7. Ibid., p178.
8. Küng, "Explanatory Remarks."

Cardinal Arinze warns against religious leaders creating such ethical loopholes: "If we want peace, we must defend life. . . . Religions will lay a necessary foundation for peace if they teach that human life should be respected in every moment of its existence, from conception right up to natural death."[1]

With their open-ended and high-flown language, the makers of the new ethic leave themselves much flexibility. They are not bound by any particular religion's scripture or tradition, nor are they bound by the legal precedents and protections which Americans (and other nations with a tradition of limited, constitutional government) have hitherto taken for granted.

Many other open questions remain about the application of the "Global Ethic."

• Does use of "possessions without concern for the needs of society" mean opposition to tax increases, new regulations, or Government confiscation of private property? Who defines the "needs of society" regarding use of property and income—the property owners or the rule-makers, the taxpayers or the tax gatherers?
• Who gets to define "racism"? Does racism include opposition to policies of open immigration or "affirmative action" racial quotas? Does racism include support for Zionism (which the UN General Assembly declared in 1975 to be "a form of racism")?
• Is patriotism, or even a desire for national sovereignty, included under the ban on "nationalism"?
• Do the condemnations of "sexism" and "patriarchy" mean that traditional Christians must accept women priests and abortion? Must Orthodox Jews accept women rabbis?
• Are Christian evangelism and orthodox preaching to be ended, on the grounds that they are "fanaticism and intolerance"?

A liberal supporter of interfaith dialogue criticizes the modern, Western presuppositions that are the basis of the "Global Ethic:"

> Some of its proponents assume too easily that religions ought to accept the authority of, or at least work with, secular international organizations. Former President Ali Khamenei of Iran stated, 'When we want to find out what is right and wrong, we do not go to the United Nations; we go to the Holy Koran.' He went on to say, more colourfully, 'For us the Universal Declaration of Human Rights is nothing but a collection of mumbo-jumbo by disciples of Satan.' His is far from the only view in contemporary Islam towards ethics, peace and human rights. Yet proponents of a global ethic need to understand and deal with the impulses that lead many religious people to say and believe such things; or else they will condemn their important project to sentimental, platitudinous irrelevance. . . . A further problem about the establishment of a global ethic could be that it might become the ethical equivalent of the pluralist theological agenda, constructing an agenda out there that is not only generalized and naïve but also fails to take seriously one's roots.[2]

The Catholic Church has warned strongly against such efforts to create a new, utopian "Global Ethic" divorced from Christian tradition and teaching.

In *Mit Brennender Sorge*, his 1937 encyclical against Nazism, Pope Pius XI warned that a New Morality without a basis on Christian faith couldn't succeed:

> It is on faith in God, preserved pure and stainless, that man's morality is based. All efforts to remove from under morality and the moral order the granite foundation of faith and to substitute for it the shifting sands of human regulations, sooner or later lead these individuals or societies to moral degradation. The fool who has said in his heart 'there is no God' goes straight to moral corruption (Psalms xiii. 1), and the number of these fools who today are out to sever morality from religion, is legion. They either do not see or refuse to see that the banishment of confessional Christianity, i.e., the clear and precise notion of Christianity, from teaching and education, from the organization of social and political life, spells spiritual spoliation and degradation. . . . To hand over the

---

1. Arinze, *Religions for Peace*, p75.
2. Martin Forward, *Inter-religious Dialogue: A Short Introduction*, Oneworld Publications, 2001, pp60, 61.

moral law to man's subjective opinion, which changes with the times, instead of anchoring it in the holy will of the eternal God and His commandments, is to open wide every door to the forces of destruction. The resulting dereliction of the eternal principles of an objective morality, which educates conscience and ennobles every department and organization of life, is a sin against the destiny of a nation, a sin whose bitter fruit will poison future generations.[1]

In his 1939 encyclical *Summi Pontificatus*, Pope Pius XII said,

Many perhaps, while abandoning the teaching of Christ, were not fully conscious of being led astray by a mirage of glittering phrases, which proclaimed such estrangement as an escape from the slavery in which they were before held; nor did they then foresee the bitter consequences of bartering the truth that sets free, for error which enslaves. They did not realize that, in renouncing the infinitely wise and paternal laws of God, and the unifying and elevating doctrines of Christ's love, they were resigning themselves to the whim of a poor, fickle human wisdom; they spoke of progress, when they were going back; of being raised, when they groveled; of arriving at man's estate, when they stooped to servility. They did not perceive the inability of all human effort to replace the law of Christ by anything equal to it; 'they became vain in their thoughts' (Rom. 1:21).[2]

Pius XII also warned that those who "divorce civil authority from every kind of dependence upon the Supreme Being" will

accord the civil authority an unrestricted field of action that is at the mercy of the changeful tide of human will, or of the dictates of casual historical claims, and of the interests of a few. Once the authority of God and the sway of His law are denied in this way, the civil authority as an inevitable result tends to attribute to itself that absolute autonomy which belongs exclusively to the Supreme Maker. It puts itself in the place of the Almighty and elevates the State or group into the last end of life, the supreme criterion of the moral and juridical order, and therefore forbids every appeal to the principles of natural reason and of the Christian conscience.[3]

This totalitarian peril remains, since prominent proponents of the Earth Charter say that "The protection of the Biosphere, as the Common Interest of Humanity, must not be subservient to the rules of state sovereignty, demands of the free market or individual rights. The idea of Global Sovereignty must be supported by a shift in values which recognize this Common Interest."[4]

In response to those who "talk of a common code of conduct, consensus morality, and agreed ethical standards,"[5] Cardinal Arinze warned, "ethical norms are built on belief systems and are nourished and invigorated by a religion that also sustains itself by ritual celebrations. The proposal of ethical norms based on the religion of nobody cannot carry anybody across the long and exacting pilgrimage of life. Indeed it smacks of secularism, which ignores or marginalizes all religions, or at least regards religion as a personal and private matter that should not be discussed in public."[6]

1. Pope Pius XI, *Mit Brennender Sorge*, (Encyclical on the Church and the German Reich), March 14, 1937, section 29; http://www.vatican.va/holy_father/pius_xi/encyclicals/documents/hf_p-xi_enc_14031937_mit-brennender-sorge_en.html, printed 02/23/03 (cited below as Pius XI, *Mit Brennender Sorge*).

2. Pope Pius XII, *Summi Pontificatus*, (Encyclical on the unity of human society, October 20, 1939), section 31, http://www.vatican.va/holy_father/pius_xii/encyclicals/documents/hf_p-xii_enc_20101939_summi-pontificatus_en.html, printed 04/24/03.

3. Ibid., sections 52–53.

4. Green Cross International, "The Green Cross Earth Charter Philosophy," Principle 14, "Global Sovereignty," http://www.gci.ch/GreenCrossPrograms/earthcharter/proposedtexts/EarthCharterPhilosophy.html, printed 04/24/03.

5. Arinze, *Religions for Peace*, pp 130–131.

6. Ibid., p 131.

[VI] SECULAR MILLENARIANISM

The sixth reason to stand against the URI is that the leaders of the URI seek an earthly utopia that the URI will help create.

At the 1995 interfaith service where the idea of the URI was first made public, the "Hymn for a New Age" was sung:

Through the long night we have come.
The sun is bright, the wars are done.
We will unite. We will be one. A new light has begun.
Smile, heaven, on our loving land,
shine blessings on our fair kingdom.
Enrich our time with growing love,
with joy abundant and long, prosperous days
Man's brotherhood is born again.[1]

Bishop Swing has issued a series of messianic proclamations about the URI since 1996. In April 1996, Swing wrote that the United Religions is needed

because there is no final place in the world to bring a spiritual grievance or to call for accountability among religions. . . . Because the creation of a United Religions would set the world's hope ablaze to imagine a religious, global sensitivity to all life instead of despairing over the present fragmentation that exists among the guardians of the world's soul. . . . Because some day, the ascendancy of militant fundamentalist voices of politically aspiring religions might be so pervasive that a United Religions will need to be created in order to save religions from their ethnic, tribal agendas.[2]

Swing told the June, 1996 URI summit conference:

I marvel that I am standing here talking about something that has never happened in the world and almost everyone who has had access to my ears has told me will never happen. . . . Today indeed is a special moment. Credulity trembles. And delirious hope gasps for a first breath. An entire new life for the world beckons us to step ahead. . . . A United Religions could end up being basically a spiritual resource for peace among religions, healing among nations, and wholeness in the realm of nature. . . . We want to enlist your imagination to become pioneers on a spiritual quest to serve all of God's creation beginning with religions and ending with religions. . . . The challenge ahead is to grow in understanding a world-wide calling. To attempt to expand the thinking patterns of religions is a daunting task of highest challenge. . . . Today is the first day of a long march toward coalition binding around the vision.[3]

In October 1996, Bishop Swing told the annual Diocesan convention, "I can see the year 2000 coming with soulful urgency, the world on the verge of the first global civilization, spiritual refugees wandering the earth seeking a symbol of hope. I do believe that at the bottom of religions there is a treasure chest of hope which the world yearns for. . . . I can see the day of a United Religions."[4]

In the letter that formally invited delegates to the summer 1997 summit conference, Bishop Swing wrote that United Religions would be "a deep new source of hope and healing for people and for the earth itself."[5]

---

1. June 25, 1995 service sheet for UN50 interfaith service, p2.
2. Swing, "The United Religions Initiative," p3.
3. Swing, opening speech for 1996 URI summit, pp1, 2, 4, 5.
4. Bishop William Swing, "Diocesan Convention Address," October 19, 1996, p12 (cited below as Swing, 10/19/96 address to Diocesan Convention).
5. Bishop William Swing, "Invitation Letter," *Journal of the United Religions Initiative*, issue 3, Summer 1997, p3.

In his opening address to the 1997 URI summit conference, Swing said: "If you come here because a spirit of colossal energy is being born in the loins of the earth, then come here and be a midwife. Assist, in awe, at the birth of a new hope."[1] The "new hope" will have the Earth—and not the Virgin Mary—as its mother. Swing added, "What is missing? What is missing is a global hope that could set the soul of the world ablaze. . . . Welcome to the long hard road of global hope. Welcome to the United Religions Initiative."[2]

When Swing spoke to the Japan Conference of Religious Representatives and Tendai Buddhists in Kyoto in 1997, he said, "The URI seeks to collect the world of religions in order to provide a global spiritual hope."[3]

Swing told an interviewer at the July 1998 Lambeth Conference (a worldwide meeting of Anglican bishops), "We are embarked on a mission to do something unprecedented in human history."[4]

In a sermon given while attending the 1999 Parliament of World Religions, Swing said, "What a time to wait on God . . . for the coming new light among religions, spiritual expressions, and indigenous traditions. The day is coming. . . . Prepare ye the way of the Lord."[5]

This "new light" will not be the light of Christ, and this "Lord" will be the "ruler of this world" (John 14:30). As Yeats asked,

And what rough beast, its hour come round at last,
Slouches towards Bethlehem to be born?[6]

URI supporter Barbara Marx Hubbard shares Swing's visions of earthly utopia: "In the past our glorious visions of the future—heaven, paradise, nirvana—were thought to happen after death. The newer thought is that we do not have to die to get there! We are not speaking here of life after death in some mythical heaven, but life more abundant in real time in history. We are speaking of the next stage of our social evolution."[7]

Jewish and Christian teachers warn us against such attempts to build heaven on earth with our own hands.

In a note of wisdom that is rare in URI documents, Rabbi Arthur Hertzberg, Vice President Emeritus of the World Jewish Congress, warned against utopianism: "I warn against the delusion that we can make a shining heaven on earth. That can happen only at the end of days, when God wills it."[8]

1. Swing, 1997 URI "Opening Address." This passage from his speech is also cited in Gibbs/Mahé, *Birth of a Global Community*, p107.

2. Ibid.

3. "Bishop Swing Asks for Religious Cease Fire at Japan Conference," *Pacific Church News*, December 1997/January 1998, p26.

4. Carol Barnwell, "'United Religions' is Bishop Swing's goal," *The Lambeth Daily*, Issue 4, 22 July 1998, http://justus.anglican.org/resources/Lambeth1998/Lambeth-Daily/22/UR.html, printed 04/22/03 (cited below as Barnwell, "United Religions.")

5. Delman, "Bishop Swing Preaches at Cape Town," *PCN*, Feb./March 2000, p25.

6. William Butler Yeats, "The Second Coming," 1921, in Alexander W. Allison, et. al., *The Norton Anthology of Poetry*, 3rd ed., W. W. Norton & Co., 1983, p883

7. Marx Hubbard, *Conscious Evolution*, p18. Charles Upton notes a contradiction within her ideology. "Barbara Marx Hubbard says elsewhere, 'We will soon be released from the fleeting imprisonment of mind by the material world.' [Barbara Marx Hubbard, *The Book of Co-Creation Part II—The Promise Will Be Kept: The Gospels, The Acts, the Epistles*, Foundation for Conscious Evolution, San Rafael, California, 1993 (privately published), p209] Yet here she denigrates 'life after death in some mythical heaven' and speaks in sanguine terms of the arrival of 'life more abundant in real time in history.' In the first passage she speaks as a modern-day Gnostic who sees no value in earthly life, and in the last two as a neo-Pagan who places all life and value in this world alone—apparently without noticing the contradiction. And it is precisely this contradiction that most clearly characterizes the New Age movement, which is not simply a modern form of Gnosticism, but rather an ambiguous hybrid of Gnosticism and Paganism." (E-mail from Charles Upton to Lee Penn, 02/03/04.)

8. Herzberg, "Sins of Religion." The address was also printed on pp6–8 of the Summer 1997 issue of the *Journal of the United Religions Initiative*.

The *Catechism of the Catholic Church* warns against globalism:

After the unity of the human race was shattered by sin God at once sought to save humanity part by part. The covenant with Noah after the flood gives expression to the principle of the divine economy toward the 'nations,' in other words, towards men grouped 'in their lands, each with [its] own language, by their families, in their nations.' This state of division into many nations is at once cosmic, social, and religious. It is intended to limit the pride of fallen humanity, united only in its perverse ambition to forge its own unity as at Babel.[1]

The only time that the world should be unified is when Christ returns to reign in glory. No organization, and no person other than the Son of Man, can be trusted with the title or power of a world ruler.

The *Catechism of the Catholic Church* also speaks against all earthly millennialism, including the New Age utopianism of the URI and its allies: "Ignorance of the fact that man has a wounded nature inclined to evil gives rise to serious errors in the areas of education, politics, social action, and morals."[2] Also,

Before Christ's second coming the Church must pass through a final trial that will shake the faith of many believers. The persecution that accompanies her pilgrimage on earth will unveil the 'mystery of iniquity' in the form of a religious deception offering men an apparent solution to their problems at the price of apostasy from the truth. The supreme religious deception is that of the Antichrist, a pseudo-messianism by which man glorifies himself in the place of God and of his Messiah come in the flesh. The Antichrist's deception already begins to take shape in the world every time the claim is made to realize within history that messianic hope which can be only realized beyond history through the eschatological judgment. The Church has rejected even modified forms of this falsification of the kingdom to come under the name of millenarianism,[3] especially the 'intrinsically perverse' political form of a secular messianism.[4]

The Eastern Orthodox repeat these admonitions. Bishop Kallistos Ware writes:

Scripture and Holy Tradition speak to us repeatedly about the Second Coming. They give us no grounds for supposing that, through a steady advance in 'civilization,' the world will grow gradually better and better until mankind succeeds in establishing God's kingdom on earth. The Christian view of world history is entirely opposed to this kind of evolutionary optimism. What we are taught to expect are disasters in the world of nature, increasingly destructive warfare between men, bewilderment and apostasy among those who call themselves Christians (see especially Matt. 24:3–27). This period of tribulation will culminate with the appearance of the 'man of sin' (2 Thess. 2:3–4), or Antichrist, who, according to the interpretation traditional in the Orthodox Church, will not be Satan himself, but a human being, a genuine man, in whom all the forces of evil will be concentrated and who will for a time hold the entire world in his sway. The brief reign of Antichrist will be abruptly terminated by the Second Coming of the Lord, this time not in a hidden way, as at his birth in Bethlehem, but 'sitting on the right hand of power, and drawing near upon the clouds of heaven' (Matt. 26:64). So the course of history will be brought to a sudden and dramatic end, through a direct intervention from the divine realm.[5]

---

1. *Catechism Of The Catholic Church*, Second Edition, Libreria Editrice Vaticana, 1997, sections 56–57, pp 20–21 (cited below as *Catechism*).

2. Ibid., section 407, p103.

3. This is 'chiliasm,' the belief in an earthly millennium of the latter days, which was condemned as heretical by the Second Ecumenical Council.

4. *Catechism*, sections 675–676, pp176–177.

5. Bishop Kallistos Ware, *The Orthodox Way*, St. Vladimir's Seminary Press, 1979, pp179–180. Another mainstream Eastern Orthodox commentator says the same: "In the Synoptic Apocalypse, there is no promise of better times to come. There are to be no worldly utopias. There will be a falling away from the faith; love will grow cold." (Fr. Columba Graham Flegg, *An Introduction to Reading the Apocalypse*, St. Vladimir's Seminary Press, 1999, p39.)

All should heed such warnings, even if the Parousia is 10,000 years in the future. These sobering teachings apply to all times and places until the Second Coming of Christ. Catholic evangelist Frank Sheed explains: "But if Anti-Christ is to be a real person and the Apostasy a real Apostasy coming at the end of the world, both Anti-Christ and Apostasy have their forerunners in every age of the world. For the truth is that just as every death is the end of the world in miniature, so every age is the last age in miniature. In that sense we are all in the last age. Anti-Christ is to come; but we have heard St. Paul say that 'the conspiracy of revolt is *already at work*.'" [1]

[VII] A FANCIFUL VIEW OF HISTORY

The seventh reason to oppose the URI is that its leaders appear not to understand either Church history or world history.

In the URI *Annual Report* for 2001, Bishop Swing said, "In the past the world has experienced religion causing wars, fueling wars, refusing to use its resources for truth and reconciliation." [2] In the spring of 1995, Swing had said the same: "there are 40 wars going on in the world today . . . and most of those wars are fueled by the great religions of the world." [3] Between 1995 and 1998, the URI's count of religion-caused wars increased. Bill Rankin, who was then the Vice President of Development for the URI, noted in 1998 that there have been "over 250 wars in this century, with nearly 110 millions killed as a result. . . . Religious differences have caused or aggravated much of this." [4]

This is a strange reading of the 20th century's history. World War I arose from the competing imperial and economic ambitions of the Great Powers, not a conflict between religions. The Nazi state was based on idolatry of race, nation, and the Führer, not on any form of religious orthodoxy. The Communist dictatorships have attempted to eradicate Judaism, Christianity, and Islam alike. It's hard to see how a United Religions could have prevented or mitigated wars due to imperial ambition (World War I), due to militant atheism (wars and atrocities caused by Communists), or due to revived paganism and aggressive nationalism (World War II).

In 1997, URI Executive Director Charles Gibbs said that "I was just in Oxford and we were talking about indigenous religions. Well, the indigenous religion there is the Druid faith." [5] This statement itself requires a leap of faith. The ancient "Druid faith"—which sacrificed people to the gods [6]—has been extinct in Britain since the isle was converted, over a millennium ago.

Bishop Swing said in 1998 that "The United Religions will not be a rejection of ancient religion but will be found buried in the depths of these religions." [7] Can Bishop Swing prove this from the depths of the Christian Faith—from Scripture and from the consistent teachings of the Church Fathers and the Ecumenical Councils? If United Religions were "buried in the depths" of Christianity, countless martyrs could have avoided agonizing deaths by burning incense before the statue of the Roman Emperor, and today's martyrs in Sudan and China could apostatize with a clear conscience.

1. Frank J. Sheed, *Theology and Sanity*, Ignatius Press, 1993, p353.

2. United Religions Initiative, "A Message of Hope from URI President, Bishop William E. Swing," *Annual Report* 2001, p3.

3. Bishop William Swing, "From Joppa to Caesarea: A Sermon for UN50," *Pacific Church News*, June/July 1995, p28.

4. Bill Rankin, "URI Fundraising—What is Our Role," *URI News Update*, fall 1998, p2.

5. Kristen Fairchild, "If a United Nations, Why Not a United Religions: An Interview With Charles Gibbs," *The Spire*, February 1997, part 2, http://www.gracecom.org/thespire/textures/gibbs2.html, printed 1997; no longer on the Net (cited below as Fairchild, interview with Charles Gibbs, 02/97).

6. Andrew Walls, "The Old Gods; Religions of Northern Europe," in Pat Alexander, ed., *Eerdmans' Handbook to the World's Religions*, Wm. B. Eerdmans Publishing Co., 1994, p118.

7. Swing, *The Coming United Religions*, p64.

Maybe martyrs are passé, anyhow. William Rankin said in 1998, "The United Religions Initiative exists to bring people together from all the religions of the world, to create a world where no one has to die because of God, or for God, any more."[1]

[VIII] RELIGIOUS RELATIVISM

The eighth reason to stand against the URI is that the URI (like the rest of the modern interfaith movement) promotes the notion that all religions and spiritual movements possess equivalent truth—an assumption that Cardinal Arinze denounces as a "theological error."[2]

From the beginning, Bishop Swing has set the philosophical tone for the URI. In the spring of 1996, Swing made a back-handed expression of faith in Christ: "I do believe that one can get to God by many ways. Nevertheless, when one gets to God, I believe that nothing about the Divine is contradicted by Jesus Christ."[3] In a speech to the San Francisco Deanery on September 11, 1996, Swing said, "We don't bring Christ to the world; Christ created the world. We [Christians] come with a community and a vocabulary."[4] (So, Christians are not to "make disciples of all nations" (Mt. 28:19), we are merely to offer "a community and a vocabulary" testifying to one of the "many ways" to get to God.)

In a July 1998 interview at the Lambeth conference of Anglican bishops, Bishop Swing equated the revelations offered by the different religions of the world, reducing Christ's saving acts to one story among many. He said, "The question is, can we stand the generosity of God in that he reveals himself to other people in the world through other symbols and through other stories?"[5]

In *The Coming United Religions*, Bishop Swing illustrated the nature of religion as he sees it. Six lines represent the major faiths—Christianity, Hinduism, Buddhism, Islam, Judaism, and the indigenous religions; like multiple paths up a mountain, these lines converge from below on a single point, a divine "unity which transcends the world."[6] At the top of the mountain are the esoteric believers from each faith; they "intuit that they were ultimately in unity with people of other religions because all come together at the apex, in the Divine. Everyone below the line would be identified as exoteric. These people in all religions would wed the form of faith to the content or final truth of their own faith. Thus, the forms of one's faith become absolutized because these forms, alone, are held to carry the truth."[7]

---

1. William Rankin, "The United Religions Initiative," The Center for Progressive Christianity, http://www.tcpc.org/resources/articles/united_religions.htm, printed 04/24/03; excerpts from lecture that he gave at the Claremont School of Theology, September 10, 1998 (cited below as Rankin, lecture at Claremont School of Theology, 09/10/98).

2. Arinze, *Religions for Peace*, p97. He said, "Relativism is the theological error that one religion is as good as another." In another book, he provided a similar definition of this error: "the mistake of those who say that all religions are roads to the same God, and that it does not matter to what religion a person chooses to belong, as long as the person has good will." (Arinze, *Meeting Other Believers*, pp36–37.)

3. Bishop William Swing, "Magellan Was Headed In The Right Direction," *Pacific Church News*, June/July 1996, p12.

4. From notes taken by Lee Penn of the speech given by Bishop Swing at the 9/11/96 meeting of the San Francisco Deanery for the Episcopal Diocese of California (cited below as Swing, speech to San Francisco Deanery, 09/11/96).

5. Barnwell, "'United Religions."

6. Swing, *The Coming United Religions*, pp58–59.

7. Ibid., p59. In like manner, Sarah McKechnie, president of the Lucis Trust, said "there is a transcendent point of unity which reveals the true spiritual 'common ground' towards which all religions can only point." (Letter to Lee Penn, 12/05/02.) Charles Upton contradicts these proponents of over-simplified universalism: "According to Swing, the exoterists are exclusivists, while the esoterists are universalists. According to metaphysician Frithjof Schuon, however, the fact that more than one religion is necessary in this manifest world is also an esoteric truth, which is why he characterizes the various Divine revelations as 'relatively Absolute.'" Most of the 'esoteric' sages produced by Judaism, Christianity and Islam have *not* been universalists—or perhaps we could say that their commitment to their own revelations was so all-consuming that it reduced

Thus, the Episcopal Bishop of California has demoted the Incarnate Word to one of the many "forms of one's faith." Swing assumes away the contradictory beliefs and world-views of the major religions, and advocates a form of religious relativism and syncretism that could hardly appeal to a dedicated believer in *any* of the faiths.

Other URI leaders and activists have followed where Swing leads.

At an interfaith festival in May 2002 in San Francisco, URI activist Paul Chaffee said, "different world spiritualities mirror God through a multitude of names and perceptions, but the one light is the same."[1]

In the summer 1997 issue of the URI *Journal*, Roger Corless, Professor of Buddhist Studies at Duke University, wrote:

> the detailed and sympathetic study of religions, a discipline that is not much more than a hundred years old, has uncovered not a universe but a polyverse, in which there exists a plurality of Absolutes. . . . It seriously challenges the paradigm, in which western philosophy has comfortably existed since the time of the pre-Socratics, that when we say Absolute we mean One and indeed, Unique. We cannot, we think, have more than one Absolute. Plurality implies Relativism, we are sure. But, it seems, the facts do not bear us out.[2]

In the same *Journal*, Anke Kreutzer wrote, "a United Religions must work for a shift from identification with individual religions to an awareness of one Divine manifest in all religions."[3]

Interfaith leader Marcus Braybrooke, a supporter of the URI, is dogmatically certain that "no creedal or doctrinal statement has absolute or permanent truth. Any such statement is the product of particular people who lived at a particular moment in history. The great truths of religion have a symbolic value. Absolute claims to religious truth fail to recognize the limitations of human knowledge."[4] He adds, "people of all faiths share a common quest. They seek the One Ultimate reality who is forever seeking them. This common quest is shown by the growing together of the life of the religious communities of the world, although this is often resisted, sometimes violently, by extremists. It is reflected in the beginnings of global theology, global ethics, and global spirituality."[5]

Regarding comparative religion, URI board member Rita Semel said in 1997: "Learning about other peoples' faith is not a detriment to living your own, but an enhancement. . . . The good part of any one of the faiths are replicated in the others; it's only the bad that we seem to be able to do all by ourselves. . . . In every faith in the world that I know of, there is some version of the Golden Rule. . . . If we could live by the Golden Rule, the rest is commentary."[6] However, there are three good things in the Christian faith that are not replicated in other faiths: God becoming incarnate as Man and

---

whatever universalism some of them may have espoused to comparative irrelevance." (E-mail from Charles Upton to Lee Penn, 02/03/04; see also Charles Upton, *The System of Antichrist: Truth & Falsehood in Postmodernism and the New Age*, Sophia Perennis, 2001, pp 62–63.)

1. Sharon Abercrombie, "Getting to know you: Followers of many faiths share their beliefs at the Presidio," *San Francisco Catholic*, May 17, 2002, p 3.

2. Roger Corless, "A Plurality of Absolutes," *Journal of the United Religions Initiative*, issue 3, Summer 1997, p 8. Charles Upton comments, "There is a contradiction between Paul Chaffee's and Roger Corless' statements. Chaffee says 'different world spiritualities mirror God through a multitude of names and perceptions, but the one light is the same.' This is the exact **opposite** of what Roger Corless is saying when he posits a 'polyverse, in which there exists a plurality of Absolutes.' Of course, 'a plurality of Absolutes' is absurd. Chaffee is trying to emphasize the universality of revelation, but he can't do it without somehow relativizing the various religions, treating them as 'equals,' and generally flattening them out. On the other hand, Corless vaguely understands that each religion is absolute in its own terms, but he can't express this without falling into the absurdity of a plurality of Absolutes." (E-mail from Charles Upton to Lee Penn, 03/11/04).

3. Kreutzer, "An Experiment with Truth," p 13.

4. Braybrooke, *Faith and Interfaith*, pp 47–48.

5. Ibid., p 120.

6. Transcribed by Lee Penn from tape of the February 2, 1997 URI Forum held at Grace Cathedral.

dwelling among us,[1] this *historically unique* God-Man dying on our behalf to redeem us from our sins, and this same God-Man rising from the dead, and promising the same for us.

Fr. Joseph Wainaina, a Catholic priest and URI activist in Kenya, likewise equated the value of all religions, saying in 1998 that "For me, there is no religion that is superior to another."[2]

And thus, farewell to logic, to reason, and to the First Commandment.

In 1997, Cardinal Arinze wrote: "To the error of religious relativism we therefore reply that one religion is not as good as another, that the religions are not all saying the same thing on every point at issue, and that every individual has personal responsibility, and therefore freedom, to look for objective religious truth."[3]

Against the false teachings of the relativists, Pope John Paul II reminds us of the teaching from the Bible: "Christ, the Redeemer of the world, *is the one mediator between God and men*, and there is no other name under heaven by which we can be saved (cf. Acts 4:12)."[4] Christians cannot compromise on this, unless we wish to betray the faith that the saints and martyrs have handed on to us.[5]

[IX] POPULATION CONTROL

The ninth reason to stand against the URI is that the movement, and its prominent allies, stand for population control, legal abortion, and artificial contraception—with a focus on the Third World.

At the Global Assembly of the URI in August 2002, the URI unanimously adopted a "Call to Global Healing" proposed by URI Cooperation Circles in Utah and at the UN headquarters.[6] This "Call" stated:

> We now call upon world leaders to implement the Earth and Faith agenda and use these principles to guide that implementation in creating a Culture of Global Healing: 1. All life is sacred and has intrinsic value regardless of the value judged by humans 2. Conserving biodiversity is in the best interest of both humans and other species 3. The human population must be stabilized to assure quality of life and to protect the rights of future generations.[7]

1. Charles Upton states that Hinduism also includes belief in the Incarnation of God: "The 10 avatars of Vishnu in Hinduism are also Incarnations of God, but not sacrificial ones. They teach, they enlighten, they sometimes heroically combat evil, they found spiritual cultures, but they do not die and rise to redeem the human race." Thus, he states that it is only the redemptive Passion of Christ, and the Resurrection, that are unique to the Christian faith. (E-mail from Charles Upton to Lee Penn, 03/11/04).

2. Andrea Useem, "Coming together: Interview with Fr. Joseph Wainaina," *Wajibu: A Journal of Social and Religious Concern*, Vol. 13, no. 3, 1998, http://www.peacelink.it/wajibu/4_issue/p2.html, printed 01/14/03.

3. Arinze, *Meeting Other Believers*, p37.

4. Pope John Paul II, *Tertio Millennio Adveniente: Apostolic Letter to the Bishops, Clergy, and Lay Faithful On Preparation for the Jubilee of the Year* 2000, Vatican translation, Pauline Books and Media, 1994, section 4, p10 (cited below as John Paul II, *Tertio Millennio Adveniente*).

5. Charles Upton says, "According to the philosophy of the transcendent unity of religions, the various true and revealed religions (and not everything that calls itself a religion *is* one) are in no way 'equal' to one another; each is unique, incomparable, and for its adherents, effectively absolute." (E-mail from Charles Upton to Lee Penn, 03/11/04) Thus, it is spiritually logical and necessary for the adherents of each of the traditional, revealed religions to uphold the unique and incomparable spiritual value of their own faith. Upton adds, "The URI and other interfaith activists can't seem to grant the validity of other religions without relativizing their own; they forget that a religion can only entail a real relationship between God and the human soul. To say either 'my religion is better than yours' or 'your religion is as good as mine' is to let your attention wander away from the essential relationship between God and the human soul. Outside of this God/soul relationship, all statements about religion—unless religion is reduced to the socio-historical or psychological—are effectively meaningless, or at least no longer statements about religion."

6. David Randle, "Utah Initiative Approved at Global Summit: URI Global Assembly Adopts Utah URI and UN URI Call to Global Healing," http://www.utahpop.org/utahinitiative.htm, printed 11/12/02.

7. Ibid.

With this action, the URI officially sided with the population controllers. This is consistent with the beliefs of URI leaders, as expressed since the organization was founded. URI leaders consider over-population to be a grave threat, and call upon the world's religions to change in response.

Bishop Swing has expressed the movement's dominant beliefs.

During Swing's global pilgrimage in 1996, he cited Pakistan as an example of overpopulation. He said: "Now the world is drowning in people. You can see it plainly. Pakistan is only the size of Texas, and yet it is the 8th most populated country in the world. . . . All through the middle of the earth, we are drowning in people. Ironically, the water shortage will tell us when the flood has begun. The great miracle of birth is, by sheer magnitude of numbers, reversing the Noah story."[1]

At the 1996 diocesan convention, Bishop Swing said, "On the negative side, I see a world deeply threatened by population explosion, by exploitation of the environment, by dark spiritual forces that treat people as commodities, and yet the religions of the world do not speak to one another to find a common voice or to take moral action."[2]

At the 1997 diocesan convention, Bishop Swing likened "the insane expansion of population" to exponential growth of algae in a lake. He explained, "Today, many people refer to the analogy of the twenty-ninth day, and these people are right to do so. Whenever a lake is taken over by algae, the algae doubles each day. This exponential growth takes thirty days to completely cover the lake and to remove all of the oxygen. Stepping backward to the twenty-ninth day, all seems to be benign and it appears to be 'business as usual.' What is not appreciated is the exponential fact that will blight [sic] out all life before daybreak."[3]

In his 1998 book *The Coming United Religions*, Bishop Swing asked, "Will the population problems of this earth ever be solved without the best wisdom, strengths, and actions of religions working together?"[4]

In April 2001, Swing told the Commonwealth Club of San Francisco, "I don't think the population question will ever be answered in a responsible way in this world unless the religions of the world come together and find a common voice."[5]

URI officials have agreed with Bishop Swing on this matter.

Iftekhar Hai, who has been on the URI board of directors since 1997, wrote in January 2000 that, among other problems, "the population explosion continues in the underdeveloped world, straining natural resources to the maximum. All these compelling conditions call for new global ethics."[6]

In April 2002, Paul Gundani, a Catholic who identified himself as "Director, United Religions Initiative, Zimbabwe," joined other liberal religious leaders in a public petition calling on President Bush to give full US funding to the United Nations Population Fund (UNFPA).[7] The letter to the President cited the Dalai Lama and Anglican Archbishop Desmond Tutu, two prominent URI supporters, as evidence of the morality of "planned parenthood": "Highly respected religious leaders have supported modern family planning as a moral good. The Dalai Lama has said that 'family planning is crucial, especially in the developing world.' Anglican Bishop Desmond Tutu stated, 'Planned parenthood is an

1. Bishop William Swing, "Journeying where the soul of this world was born," *Pacific Church News*, April/May 1996, p31.

2. Swing, 10/19/96 address to Diocesan Convention, p12

3. Bishop William Swing, "Excerpts: Bishop's Address" [to 1997 Diocesan convention], *Pacific Church News*, December 1997/January 1998, p34.

4. Swing, *The Coming United Religions*, p71.

5. Swing, Commonwealth Club speech, 04/25/01.

6. Iftekhar Hai, "Faith Community Must Take Lead in Resolving Global Problems," *San Francisco Chronicle*, January 5, 2000, pA17.

7. International Committee of Religious Leaders for Voluntary Family Planning, news release, "International Committee of Religious Leaders for Voluntary Family Planning Calls on President Bush to Release $34 Million for UNFPA," April 30, 2002, http://www.commondreams.org/news2002/0430-05.htm, printed 06/11/03.

obligation of those who are Christians. Our church thinks we should use scientific methods that assist in planning families."[1] Frances Kissling, president of Catholics for a Free Choice, asserted, "The Catholic leaders who have signed this letter to President Bush know that you can be Catholic and support family planning and they know that women's and children's lives are saved when voluntary family planning is available."[2]

Other prominent URI supporters, and the movement's globalist allies, have consistently stood for population control.

Matthew Fox, a leading New Age Episcopal priest in Swing's diocese, has said, "Obviously, excessive human population is a grave danger—and an issue of morality and immorality in our time. Again, it's one of the reasons I joined the Episcopal church, because of its open-minded and pragmatic view of birth control."[3] In *The Coming of the Cosmic Christ*, Matthew Fox took his anti-population enthusiasm even further, saying:

> It has been suggested that we call a United Species Conference—a conference far more representative than the United Nations is—and put this one question to the ten million representatives (one for each species): 'Should the human species be allowed to continue on this planet?' The vote would most likely be 9,999,999 to 1 that we humans, with our dualistic hatred of earth, of one another, and of our own existence, be banished to some distant place in the galaxy so that Mother Earth could continue her birthing of beauty, amazement, colors, and health.[4]

URI supporter Barbara Marx Hubbard wrote, "The vast effort of humanity to 'be fruitful and multiply' would have to be curtailed in our generation. One more doubling of the world population will destroy our life support system. Our Mother will not support us if we continue to grow in numbers!"[5] Her spirit guide said, "The population overgrowth on Earth must cease."[6]

URI supporter Robert Muller, a former Assistant Secretary-General of the UN, has given a UN imprimatur to efforts to reduce human population, and credits UN activities for preventing the birth of 2.2 billion people. He said,

> I am surprised that no one has as yet thought of creating a Pro-Earth, Humanity-challenging Organization which would put itself in the shoes of our Mother Earth and rejoice whenever humans diminish in numbers or consume less. It would give yearly prizes to people, events or institutions which achieve a reduction of the human population or of the consumption of Earth resources. The first prize should go to the United Nations which through its world population conferences and anti-population work has prevented 2 billion 200 million more people from being born between 1952 and the year 2000.[7]

As one of the steps toward a "democratic United Nations," Muller said that it is necessary to "make reproductive health and family planning information available to all people."[8] Muller also suggested a

---

1. Ibid.
2. Ibid.
3. V. Lee, "Conversations with Fox & Sheldrake."
4. Matthew Fox, *The Coming of the Cosmic Christ: The Healing of Mother Earth and the Birth of a Global Renaissance*, Harper San Francisco, 1988, p 15.
5. Barbara Marx Hubbard, *The Revelation: A Message of Hope for the New Millennium*, Nataraj Publishing, Novato, CA, 1995, p 45.
6. Ibid., p 224.
7. Robert Muller, *Ideas And Dreams For A Better World: 1001–1500, Volume III*, Idea 1024, 30 April 1997, http://www.robert-muller.org/volume/ideas1001.html, viewed 06/21/04.
8. Robert Muller and Douglas Roche, *Safe Passage into the Twenty-First Century: The United Nations' Quest for Peace, Equality, Justice, and Development*, Continuum, 1995, p 119 (cited below as Muller/Roche, *Safe Passage*).

"UN Marriage Certificate for the next Millennium."[1] Among other requirements, a couple would agree "to have only one or two children."[2] Indeed, a "proper Earth government" should define how many people each nation can support, and set policies accordingly—with special attention to "developing countries with a high rate of population growth." Muller says,

> In developing countries with a high rate of population growth the United Nations, the rich countries and the local countries should give 'small number of children's allowances' which would be stopped after a given small number of children. The parents would be incited to look for or be given means of controlling the result of their lovemaking. The UN should also consider population policies according to countries and regions that would be based on bio-regional considerations, namely, what can each country or region take in numbers of population? A proper Earth government would certainly have to raise such questions.[3]

Muller has urged the "white western world" to take up the cause of population control for racial reasons: "Business is not interested in population control: they are interested in growing numbers of consumers and new markets. But the white western world should be acutely interested, for within a few decades their children and children's children will be minimal in the world, close to disappearance."[4] Muller predicts this response to the problem: "The time might come when laws will be adopted in some poor countries that no couple should have more than two children while in the western countries allowances will be given for more children."[5]

In his newest book, Muller has retained his enthusiasm for population control. He says that "The United Nations should urgently consider several world emergency plans or conferences to halt the rapid decline of Planet Earth's life giving capacities and wealth," including "a world emergency plan to stop for at least five years the human population explosion."[6]

In a 1997 speech praising the Earth Charter at a UN forum, URI supporter Bishop James Ottley, who was then the Anglican Observer at the UN, listed human population growth as the *first* of seven "very severe consequences" of "breach of the communion among human beings with God and all of creation."[7] (The other evils included such things as pollution of the oceans, extinction of species, and weapons of mass destruction.)

The UN has long provided a public forum for anti-population ideologues. In a November 1991 interview with *The UNESCO Courier*, Jacques-Yves Cousteau said: "What should we do to eliminate suffering and disease? It's a wonderful idea but perhaps not altogether a beneficial one in the long run. If we try to implement it we may jeopardize the future of our species. It's terrible to have to say this. World population must be stabilized and to do that we must eliminate 350,000 people per day. This is so horrible to contemplate that we shouldn't even say it. But the general situation in which we are involved is lamentable."[8] Do the math on this requirement to "eliminate" 350,000 people per day. That's 127,750,000 "surplus" people per year, or 1.28 billion people to "eliminate" per decade.

Jan Fransen, a demographer and former staff member for the UN Population Fund, went further

1. Robert Muller, *Ideas And Dreams For A Better World: 501–1000, Volume II*, Idea 976, March 13, 1997, http://www.robert-muller.org/volume/ideas0501.html, viewed 06/21/04 (cited below as Muller, *Ideas And Dreams, Vol. II*).

2. Ibid., Idea 976, March 13, 1997.

3. Robert Muller, *Ideas And Dreams for a Better World: 1501–2000, Volume IV*, Idea 1732, http://www.robertmuller.org/volume/ideas1501.html, viewed 06/21/04.

4. Muller, *Ideas And Dreams, Vol. II*, Idea 773, 21 August 1996.

5. Robert Muller, *Ideas And Dreams for a Better World: 2001–2500, Volume VI*, Idea 2397, http://www.robertmuller.org/volume/ideas2001.html, viewed 06/21/04.

6. Robert Muller, *Paradise Earth*, p 27, (p. 35 of the PDF file).

7. Bishop James Ottley, "Redeeming Creation," June 27, 1997; http://www.aco.org/united-nations/earthsp.htm. Printed in 1997; no longer on the Net at this address.

8. Bahgat Elnadi and Adel Rifaat, "Interview With Jacques-Yves Cousteau," *The UNESCO Courier*, November 1991, p 13.

yet.[1] During an October 1999 population briefing for the European Parliament, he said, "I'm sorry that population has been reduced to reproductive health versus the micro-level of human rights." Fransen said that the real concern should be the number of "people which the earth can hold in a sustainable way;" he believed the earth's carrying capacity is 700 million to 1 billion people. He added that "the focus on human rights disturbs him because it draws attention away from this more pressing matter of the carrying capacity of the earth."

The URI Charter avows solidarity with "all living beings."[2] This concern does *not* include the least among us, babies in the wombs of their mothers.

In its support for population control, the URI has elite company—including Bill Gates, the Packard Foundation,[3] the Rockefeller Foundation, the World Bank, the UN Population Fund,[4] the Ford Foundation, the Hewlett Foundation, the Mellon Foundation,[5] Warren Buffett,[6] the MacArthur Foundation, George Soros' Open Society Institute,[7] and Ted Turner.[8]

Pope John Paul II has made a definitive reply to Bishop Swing, the URI, and the wealthy proponents of population control. In his 1995 encyclical letter *Evangelium Vitae*, the Pope said,

> The Pharaoh of old, haunted by the presence and increase of the children of Israel, submitted them to every kind of oppression and ordered that every male child born of the Hebrew women was to be killed (cf. Exod. 1:7–22). Today not a few of the powerful of the earth act in the same way. They too are haunted by the current demographic growth, and fear that the most prolific and poorest peoples represent a threat for the well-being and peace of their own countries. Consequently, rather than wishing to face and solve these serious problems with respect for the dignity of individuals and families and for every person's inviolable right to life, they prefer to promote and impose by whatever means a massive programme of birth control. Even the economic help which they would be ready to give is unjustly made conditional on the acceptance of an anti-birth policy.[9]

The Pope concluded that it is

> morally unacceptable to encourage, let alone impose, the use of methods such as contraception, sterilization and abortion in order to regulate births. The ways of solving the population problem are quite different. Governments and the various international agencies must above all strive to create economic, social, public health and cultural conditions which will enable married couples to make their choices about procreation in full freedom and with genuine responsibility. They must then make efforts to ensure 'greater opportunities and a fairer

1. Information in this paragraph is from Catholic Family and Human Rights Institute, "UNFPA Briefing Makes Light of High Mortality in Africa," October 15, 1999, *Friday Fax*, Vol. 2, no. 49, http://www.c-fam.org/FAX/fax_1999/faxv2n49.html, printed 06/17/04.)

2. URI, "Charter," "Preamble," paragraph 1, p2.

3. "The Coffee Bars Must Be Getting Crowded In Palo Alto & Seattle," "Scan" section, *The American Enterprise*, January-February 1999, Vol. 10, No. 1, pp15–16, on Gates and the Packard Foundation.

4. United Nations Population Fund (UNFPA), "Progress Report on UNFPA Support to Partners in Population and Development: Report of the Executive Director," July 10, 1998, http://www.unfpa.org/exbrd/partner.htm; printed 1998; no longer on the Net at this address; as of 2004, a copy of this page is at http://web.archive.org/web/19991004143025/http://www.unfpa.org/exbrd/partner.htm. Refers to the activities of the Rockefeller Foundation, the World Bank, and the UNFPA.

5. Zenit News Agency, "Private Foundations Fueling Family-Planning Programs," http://www.ewtn.com/vnews/getstory.asp?number=20542, printed 11/05/01. Refers to the activities of the Ford Foundation, the Mellon Foundation, and the Hewlett Foundation, among others.

6. Catholic World News, "Billionaire's Money Helps Population Control," April 4, 2001, http://www.ewtn.com/vnews/getstory.asp?number=13792, printed 04/03/01.

7. Life Research Institute, "Foundation Giving to Contraception and Abortion," *Population Research Institute Review*, September-October 2003, p8.

8. Catholic World News. "Turner Gives Another $21 Million to UN Population Control," July 27, 2000, http://www.ewtn.com/vnews/getstory.asp?number=5435, printed 07/28/2000.

9. Pope John Paul II, Encyclical Letter *Evangelium Vitae*, March 25, 1995, section 16; http://www.vatican.va/holy_father/john_paul_ii/encyclicals/documents/hf_jp-ii_enc_25031995_evangelium-vitae_en.html, printed 11/26/02.

distribution of wealth so that everyone can share equitably in the goods of creation. Solutions must be sought on the global level by establishing a true *economy of communion and sharing of goods,* in both the national and international order'.[1]

[X] A WORLDLY, UTILITARIAN VIEW OF RELIGION

The tenth reason to stand against the URI is that its leaders have a pragmatic, worldly, utilitarian view of religion.

Bishop Swing sets the tone for the movement, and has spoken in a consistent manner over the years.

In February 1996, Swing said, "We're on the threshold of the first global civilization. There's a global information network. There's a global financial network. There's a global ecology that we are now appreciating. But there is no global access to soul. . . . I think that as we become one global unit, we have to find out where religion is in regard to our global tribe."[2]

In his opening speech to the 1996 URI global summit meeting, Bishop Swing had said: "The sooner we can get religions to come together to serve the common good, the sooner global issues will have a chance for solution."[3]

Swing wrote in August 1996, "There is the approaching global civilization, and the one central body refusing to take responsibility at the table of global decision-making is religion."[4]

In September 1996, Swing told a gathering of Episcopal leaders in San Francisco, "We are at the threshold of the first global civilization, and we need to bring religion to the table. We can't get to a global civilization since religion is blocking the way."[5]

Swing stated in 1998 that "The United Religions Initiative will be inevitable when the world has run out of options. When it is clear that the missing ingredient in authentic diplomacy is religion. . . . The only reason there would ever be a United Religions is that the stark world demands it. The time of that demand is getting close."[6] He did not say what event would evoke the "demand," why he suspected that "the time of that demand is getting close," who will make the "demand," or how it will be enforced. Swing added that a United Religions "is inevitable. On the threshold of the first global civilization the world will insist that religions come together to see if they can find a common vocation."[7]

In April 2001, Swing told the San Francisco Commonwealth Club "The time will come when the world will see the potential of religion and be so frustrated by religion being stuck in the rut of violence that the world will demand a United Religions, and there will be one."[8] Swing added that when he presented the URI vision to diplomats, he has gotten a favorable response: "The ambassadors . . . say it would be so wonderful if religion would come out in the traffic and play where we play. If religion ever had anything to do with reconciliation or peace, what a difference it would make in the world."[9]

---

1. Ibid., section 91.

2. Richard Scheinin, "Bringing Together the 'United Religions': Episcopal Bishop Begins Tour to Build Support," *San Jose Mercury News,* February 3, 1996, p 11E.

3. Swing, opening speech for 1996 URI summit, p 5.

4. Bishop William Swing, "Seeking Peace Among Religions," *San Francisco Chronicle,* p A-17, August 22, 1996 (cited below as Swing, "Seeking Peace Among Religions," 08/22/96).

5. Swing, speech to San Francisco Deanery 09/11/96.

6. Bishop William Swing, "Unthinkable to Thinkable to Do-able to Inevitable," address to the World Congress of Faiths, July 22 1998, reprinted in *A Swing with a Crosier,* Episcopal Diocese of California, 1999, p 150.

7. Ibid., p 151.

8. Swing, Commonwealth Club speech, 04/25/01.

9. Ibid.

In the October 2001 issue of *Pacific Church News*, Swing said, "If people on this planet are going to have life and an earthly future, religions have got to be part of the solution rather than central to the problem." [1] Later that fall, Swing told the International Diplomacy Council: "We will change world history, because the world is going to get impatient with religion;" the world will want religion "to get your act together and make peace in the world."[2]

Other leading URI proponents have said the same.

The Rev. Charles Gibbs, Executive Director of the URI, said in 1997 that one of the reasons why the current attempt to form a United Religions would work—although previous efforts had failed—was secular leaders' desire for spiritual guidance in developing a "global civilization":

> There is increasingly a realization all around the world, not only among religious leaders but among politicians and scientists and business leaders, that if there is not a firm foundation in values, that if there isn't a deep spirituality that informs the choices we make and how we move into a global civilization, our time on earth may well be limited. We can't afford to continue to live the way we have been. All over you hear a call for religion and for deep spiritual values to join this dialogue.[3]

Bettina Gray, of the North American Interfaith Network, warned during the January 19, 1997 URI forum at Grace Cathedral that "Religion is standing before the bar of human need. . . . Society at large is looking at religion and saying, 'What are you doing, and why are you creating more difficulties and more antagonisms?'" [4] She added that "the hope for spirituality to continue and thrive on the planet" is based on the willingness of religious people to "cooperate *with* the world and *for* the world together."[5]

In 2001, Brother Wayne Teasdale, a Catholic supporter of the URI, proposed a new, worldly direction for the Church: "there are some voices in the Vatican that are looking for a new vision, and I think that the Church could be extremely effective and influential if it put its genius of organization to the service of the interfaith movement for justice, ecology, and peace."[6]

In "Preparing for the Next Millennium," URI supporter Robert Muller said: "The new age we are entering will be an age of communities and of cooperation: it will be an age of family (celebrated by the UN in 1994), and of the family of nations. The family of religions cannot be absent; its absence could mean the retrocession and evanescence of religions, left behind by rapidly growing political, economic, scientific, ecological, and sociological globalizations [sic] of the world."[7] Religions must use their "common heritages and institutional authority . . . combined with an emerging global spirituality" to make "enormous contributions to the challenges and details of creating a better world,"[8] or they will evanesce—which means "to dissipate like vapor."

This might be a gradual and peaceful disappearance, or it might be violent suppression of recalcitrant religions, as occurred during the French Revolution. Muller said,

1. Swing, "A Swing Through the Diocese," *PCN*, Oct./Nov. 2001, p5.

2. Dennis Delman, "Bishop Swing Given International Diplomacy Council Award," *Pacific Church News*, Winter 2002, p46.

3. Fairchild, interview with Charles Gibbs, 02/97, part 1.

4. Transcribed by Lee Penn from a tape of the January 19, 1997 URI forum held at Grace Cathedral (cited below as URI, forum at Grace Cathedral, 01/19/97).

5. Ibid.

6. Amy Edelstein, "Transforming the seeds of corruption: an interview with Brother Wayne Teasdale," *What Is Enlightenment? Magazine*, Spring/Summer 2001, p61.

7. Robert Muller, "Foreword: Preparing for the Next Millennium," in Joel Beversluis, ed., on-line version of *A Source Book for the Earth's Community of Religions*, http://www.origin.org/ucs/doc.cfm?e=0&ps=2&edit=1&fg=3176&fi=1089, printed 06/22/04.

8. Ibid.

Look at all the religious wars we had during the Middle Ages. Killing in the name of God was the rule. Religion was discredited to the point that the French Revolution abolished religions as the biggest troublemakers. Even today, many regard religions as troublemakers. This is why the common values between all religions should be expressed. They should cooperate in order to work on common values such as faith, prayer, compassion, charity, forgiveness, etc. With the Cold War over and the opposition to religion and spirituality ended in the former communist countries of Eastern Europe, we can move, we must move, to a global renaissance, to a global spirituality.[1]

Here, Muller posed two alternatives for the future of religions: being abolished as "troublemakers," or movement toward a new "global spirituality."[2]

Anglican Bishop James Ottley, a URI supporter, said in 1997, "Increasingly, the agenda of the world is shaped by global political, economic, environmental, and social forces. Because the world's agenda is the agenda of the church, we can no longer consider ourselves to be living in isolation from one another."[3] That's the central fallacy of the URI and similar movements: "the world's agenda is the agenda of the church." The goal of the URI is not to serve and glorify God, but to serve "global good"[4] by solving global problems.

The source of this fallacy may be that URI leaders have a definition of "religion" that is different from the one that most people—of any faith—would use. William Rankin, who was then the Vice-President of the URI, said in 1998, "J. M. Yinger defines religion as 'a system of beliefs and practices by means of which a group of people struggles with ultimate problems of human life. It expresses their refusal to capitulate to death, to give up in the face of frustration, to allow hostility to tear apart their human aspirations.' So far, so good."[5] After saying "so far, so good," Rankin did not progress to a God-centered definition of religion; he accepted Yinger's worldly definition without change. This reduces religion to psychology and social action.

By contrast, Cardinal Francis Arinze says, "the primary idea in religion is not the promotion of peace but the worship of God. Religion refers in the first place to the relationship of the creature to the Creator."[6] A mainstream secular authority agrees with this Catholic leader; *Webster's Dictionary* has as its first definition of religion, "the service and worship of God or the supernatural."[7]

[XI] THE POLITICAL AGENDA OF THE URI

The eleventh reason to stand against the URI is that, despite its claims to universality, the URI is committed to carry forward the agenda of secular Western liberalism.

URI leaders and supporters speak inconsistently when discussing the political agenda of the URI.

In 2003, URI Global Council member Donald Frew said, "The nature of the board, which includes many religions, makes it difficult for us to endorse any specific political position."[8] However, the URI Charter Preamble statement, "We unite in responsible cooperative action to bring the wisdom and

1. Muller/Roche, *Safe Passage*, p 28.

2. Unfortunately, the misdeeds and crimes of many Christians, Church hierarchs and laity alike, have provided a basis for such revolutionary hostility, the rage that became manifest in France in 1789, Russia in 1917, Spain in 1936, and on other occasions.

3. Anglican Communion Office at the United Nations, "The Ministry of the Anglican Communion Office at the United Nations—Annual Report 1997," http://www.aco.org/united-nations/annual97.htm, printed 1998; no longer on the Net at this address.

4. Swing, Commonwealth Club speech, 04/25/01.

5. Rankin, lecture at Claremont School of Theology, 09/10/98.

6. Arinze, *Religions for Peace*, p 10.

7. *Webster's Seventh New Collegiate Dictionary*, G. & C. Merriam Company, 1970, p 724.

8. Interview between Donald Frew and Lee Penn, 03/28/03.

values of our religions, spiritual expressions and indigenous traditions to bear on the economic, environmental, political and social challenges facing our Earth community,"[1] promises social and political action by the URI. At the end of the URI Global Assembly in Rio de Janeiro in 2002, Donald Frew told a large crowd that attended a peace rally,

> We all want to see change in the world. We want to see peace, justice, and healing for the Earth. Well, the only true change comes through changing people's minds. And nothing has the power over minds and souls that religion has. So any group like the URI, that is working to create understanding and cooperation between religions, to work for the betterment of all, has the potential to be the most powerful force for change on the planet. As a person of faith, called by my Gods to care for and protect the Earth, how can I not be involved?[2]

In line with the promise of the URI Charter, Frew saw much hope for global social change through the URI.

The URI's official support for the Earth Charter, and its leaders' support for population control, feminism, and the SIECUS sex education "declaration," firmly align the URI with the political Left.

On the one hand, Bishop Swing—who recently identified himself as a Republican[3]—said in 1996, "It would not be in the interest of the whole earth for a United Religions to become a political debating society with a right-wing or left-wing bias."[4] However, in an August 1996 speech about the URI to the North American Interfaith Network, Swing said, "At the bottom of capitalism, there is a spiritual bankruptcy which people everywhere are recognizing."[5] He said this at the close of a century in which leftist, *anti*-capitalist regimes had killed tens of millions of people.[6]

Ravi Peruman, who was then a member of the URI Board, said of the URI in 1997, "It's not an attempt to be political."[7] However, when asked in early 1997, "Is the United Religions intended to be a political movement? Will it be working with political leaders to help resolve conflict?," URI Executive Director Charles Gibbs replied, "I can't see how it would not be. . . . Ideally, a well-established United Religions and the values it would embody would have a powerful impact on the work politicians do."[8] Fr. O'Rourke, a former member of the URI board, likewise said in 2002 that the founders of the URI wanted to "influence people the world over—governments and politicians—to create cultures of peace and community."[9]

At the 1996 summit conference, Richard Barrett, from the World Bank, said, "It is important for the religions of the world to unite in order to have a unified voice of values which can be taken to the negotiating table in the major international organizations we have."[10] Gibbs reported that one of Barrett's requests was fulfilled at a May, 1997 URI conference in New York City; participants decided "to plan a gathering at the UN to explore the role the UR might have in advising and supporting global organizations such as the World Bank and the IMF [International Monetary Fund]."[11]

1. URI, "Charter," "Preamble," paragraph 10, p 2.

2. Donald Frew, "The Covenant of the Goddess & the Interfaith Movement," December 23, 2003, http://www.witchvox.com/white/coginterfaith.html, printed 08/04/04.

3. Bob Williams, "Swing marks 25th year as Bay Area bishop (Daybook)," *Episcopal News Service* interview of Bishop Swing, August 9, 2004, http://ecusa.anglican.org/3577_48087_ENG_HTM.htm, printed 08/10/04.

4. Swing, "The United Religions Initiative," 04/96, p 1.

5. Bishop Swing, August 10, 1996 speech before the North American Interfaith Network Conference, p 1.

6. Stéphane Courtois et al., *The Black Book of Communism: Crimes, Terror, Repression*, Harvard University Press, 1999.

7. URI, forum at Grace Cathedral, 01/19/97.

8. Fairchild, interview with Charles Gibbs," 02/97, part 1.

9. Patrick Joyce, "United Religions: Growing interfaith movement has roots in San Francisco," *Catholic San Francisco*, October 18, 2002, p 5.

10. Daniel Sneider, "United Nations of Clerics?: Religious Leaders Envision 'Spiritual UN'," *Christian Science Monitor*, July 18, 1996, p 3.

11. Gibbs, "Regional Conferences," *PCN*, Aug./Sept. 1997, p 23.

If the URI attains its goals, it will pursue a new, global symbiosis between politics and religion. Most URI proponents, and their globalist allies, see the world's religions as means to earthly ends: peace, social justice, and preservation of the biosphere. Their view of how to attain these ends is habitually partisan, corresponding closely to the platforms of socialist parties in Europe, the environmental movement, the feminist movement, and the liberal wing of the Democratic Party in the US. There's a problem here; much of mankind does not hold these beliefs. By what means will the URI and their allies obtain the acquiescence of the rest of us?

[XII] FEMINISM AND THE ORDINATION OF WOMEN

The twelfth reason to stand against the URI is that from the beginning, URI leaders have taken a feminist world-view for granted. As a result, they support elevation of women to religious leadership roles, even when this innovation is against a particular faith's long-held tradition.

In 1996, Bishop Swing said that the "new place and voice of women in religion" is one of the reasons why the URI could succeed although earlier, similar movements had failed.[1] Swing said in 1997 that one reason the URI expanded to include "modern spiritual movements" is that "If you go with the great religions, you have men only. If you go with modern spiritual movements, you have women as well."[2]

In April 2003, Bishop Swing made an ecumenical pilgrimage through Europe with Archbishop William Levada, of the Catholic Archdiocese of San Francisco, and with Metropolitan Anthony, of the Greek Orthodox Diocese of San Francisco. After his return, Swing posted a diary on his diocese's web site. Swing regretted that church leaders have been "telling our flocks about other churches and doing so in prejudicial and unfair ways. Education founded on respectful education [sic] is needed."[3] He then provided some examples of "respectful education" on the role of women in the Church, as he commented on differences among the Episcopal, Roman Catholic, and Orthodox churches.

Swing wrote, "Cardinal Kasper said wistfully, 'Women's ordination is a hard issue for us.' My reptile brain wanted to say, 'Our women are a problem for you. And you should know that your men are a problem for us.' Restraint prevailed."[4] In the same vein, he added, "The statement that the Pope made on women's ordination was just one degree less than a Papal Bull. Were it a Papal Bull and thus infallible it would have closed the question of women's ordination for 300 years into the future. At the last second, that Pope insisted on a slight bit of restraint. Therefore, it is a minor issue."[5] Swing continued,

Rome and Orthodoxy are very, very, very male. Also they both have high doctrines and devotion about the Blessed Virgin Mary. I find it difficult to utter the word 'Theotokos' in referring to Mary. Although I honor the devotion that Levada and Anthony have for Mary, I think that calling Mary the Mother of God moves close to idolatry. Jesus said, 'Who is my mother. . .? Those who do the will of my Father in heaven are my mother, brothers. . . .' And if she is the Mother of God, what relationship does she have with the one whom Jesus calls Abba, Father? Popular Islamic thinking is that Christians are polytheists: God, Jesus, His Mother. I can see where their impression comes from."[6]

1. Swing, "Seeking Peace Among Religions," 08/22/96.
2. Lattin, "Interview with Swing," *San Francisco Chronicle*, 06/22/97.
3. Bishop William Swing, "2003 Ecumenical Pilgrimage to London, Canterbury, Rome, Istanbul," "Footnotes and Afterthoughts," item 11, http://diocal.org/modules.php?op=modload&name=EasyContent&file=index&menu=122101&page_id=112,printed 06/03/04.
4. Ibid., item 15.
5. Ibid., item 16.
6. Ibid., item 18. The ellipses were in the original text.

Toward the end of his "afterthoughts," Swing observed, "In dealing with the Vatican and Orthodoxy, it is clear that time is on a different scale. They deal with centuries, mostly past centuries."[1]

The executive director of the URI wrote a poem to Sophia, a feminine "voice of God's Wisdom" in 1995; he presented it to the 1996 URI summit meeting.[2] The hymn was also part of a workbook used in URI planning conferences in 1996 and 1997.[3]

Annie Imbens-Fransen, a Catholic elected to the URI Global Council in 2002, describes herself as a "feminist theologian."[4] She wrote,

> If religious people use the right to freedom of thought, conscience and religion to discrimate [sic] women, they violate the human rights of women. In all these cases all people have the responsibility to stop this violence against people from another race and another sexe [sic]. . . . In many religious traditions women are not allowed to become religious leaders, such as rabbi, priest, minister, imam, monk, bishop, pope, etc. . . . In religions that are dominated by men women's consciousness is colonized by androcentric and patriarchal views on reality. It means that in these religions women's right to freedom of thought, conscience and religion has been obscured. In Christianity men constitute the dominant group; for centuries, they have thus appropriated the right to define how God must be viewed, how the world was created, and how that world should be ordered according to God's will.[5]

This feminist view of religion sees the priesthood and episcopacy, and other religious leadership posts, as offices for exercise of power. Therefore, religions that do not allow female leadership keep women powerless and violate human rights.

Speaking for the Catholic Church, Pope John Paul II said otherwise in the 1994 Apostolic Letter *Ordinatio Sacerdotalis*:

> the fact that the Blessed Virgin Mary, Mother of God and Mother of the Church, received neither the mission proper to the Apostles nor the ministerial priesthood clearly shows that the non-admission of women to priestly ordination cannot mean that women are of lesser dignity, nor can it be construed as discrimination against them. Rather, it is to be seen as the faithful observance of a plan to be ascribed to the wisdom of the Lord of the universe. . . . The greatest in the Kingdom of Heaven are not the ministers but the saints. . . . I declare that the Church has no authority whatsoever to confer priestly ordination on women and that this judgment is to be definitively held by all the Church's faithful.[6]

[XIII] PROMOTION OF THE NEW AGE MOVEMENT, PANTHEISM, AND THEOSOPHY

The thirteenth reason to oppose the URI is that the movement provides a global platform for New Age sects, Theosophists, and authoritarian cults (such as the Unification Church)—movements that are profoundly anti-Christian.

1. Ibid., item 26.

2. Gibbs/Mahé, *Birth of a Global Community*, p33.

3. United Religions Initiative, *Draft Workbook For Pilot Groups*, p36. (The history of the URI, stated on p4 of the workbook, appears to show that the workbook was written in 1996, after the initial URI summit meeting.)

4. Annie Imbens-Fransen, "Foundation for Pastoral Care for Women and United Religions Initiative," http://www.dwcw.org/e-symposium_1/cgi/wwwbbs.cgi?Symposium&194, printed 11/25/2002.

5. Ibid.

6. Pope John Paul II, Apostolic Letter *Ordinatio Sacerdotalis*, May 22, 1994, sections 3, 4; http://www.vatican.va/holy_fat her/john_paul_ii/apost_letters/documents/hf_jp-ii_apl_22051994_ordinatio-sacerdotalis_en.html, printed November 26, 2002.

With its close connection with New Age authors and New Age organizations, the URI promotes a movement that Pope John Paul II denounced in *Crossing the Threshold of Hope* as "*the return of ancient gnostic ideas under the guise of the so-called New Age.* We cannot delude ourselves that this will lead toward a renewal of religion. It is only a new way of practicing gnosticism—that attitude of the spirit that, in the name of a profound knowledge of God, results in distorting His Word and replacing it with purely human words."[1] The Pope said that Gnosticism "has always existed side by side with Christianity, sometimes taking the shape of a philosophical movement, but more often assuming the characteristics of a religion or para-religion in distinct, if not declared, conflict with all that is essentially Christian."[2]

In February 2003, the Vatican released a study of the New Age movement, *Jesus Christ, The Bearer of the Water of Life: A Christian Reflection on the "New Age."*[3] In presenting the document to the press, Cardinal Paul Poupard, president of the Vatican's Council for Culture, said: "The New Age proposes theories and doctrines about God, man, and the world, that are incompatible with the Christian faith. In addition, the New Age is both the symptom of a culture in deep crisis and the wrong answer to this situation of cultural crisis."[4]

In these admonitions, the Vatican has reiterated warnings given by prior popes.

In his 1937 encyclical against Nazism, Pope Pius XI warned against Pantheism and idolatrous speculation about God:

> The believer in God is not he who utters the name in his speech, but he for whom this sacred word stands for a true and worthy concept of the Divinity. Whoever identifies, by pantheistic confusion, God and the universe, by either lowering God to the dimensions of the world, or raising the world to the dimensions of God, is not a believer in God.[5]

Pope Pius XI added,

> Beware, Venerable Brethren, of that growing abuse, in speech as in writing, of the name of God as though it were a meaningless label, to be affixed to any creation, more or less arbitrary, of human speculation. Use your influence on the Faithful, that they refuse to yield to this aberration. Our God is the Personal God, supernatural, omnipotent, infinitely perfect, one in the Trinity of Persons, tri-personal in the unity of divine essence, the Creator of all existence. Lord, King and ultimate Consummator of the history of the world, who will not, and cannot, tolerate a rival God by His side.[6]

In 1919, under Pope Benedict XV, the Catholic Church had officially condemned Theosophy.[7] The Vatican's Holy Office (the predecessor to the Congregation for the Doctrine of the Faith), was asked for a ruling on Theosophy: [Question:] "Whether the doctrines, which today are called theosophical, can be in harmony with Catholic doctrine; and thus whether it is permitted to join theosophical societies, attend their meetings, and read their books, daily papers, journals, and writings." The *Reply* by the Holy Office was: "In the negative in all cases."

1. John Paul II, *Crossing the Threshold of Hope*, ed. by Vittorio Messori, Alfred A. Knopf, 1994, p 90.

2. Ibid.

3. Pontifical Council For Culture and Pontifical Council For Interreligious Dialogue, "Jesus Christ The Bearer Of The Water Of Life: A Christian reflection on the "New Age," 2003, http://www.vatican.va/roman_curia/pontifical_councils/interelg/documents/rc_pc_interelg_doc_20030203_new-age_en.html, printed 02/3/03.

4. Vatican Information Service (VIS) press release, "Vatican Offers Response To 'New Age' Ideology," *The Wanderer*, February 7–13, 2003, p 1.

5. Pope Pius XI, *Mit Brennender Sorge*, section 7.

6. Ibid., section 9.

7. Henry Denzinger, *The Sources of Catholic Dogma*, as translated by Roy J. Deferrari from the Thirtieth Edition of Henry Denzinger's *Enchiridion Symbolorum*, B. Herder Book Co., St. Louis and London, 1957, p 564, article 2189, titled "The Doctrines of Theosophy," a reply of the Holy Office, July 18, 1919.

Regarding the occult practices of the New Age movement, the Bible is clear: "You shall not practice augury or witchcraft. . . . Do not turn to mediums or wizards; do not seek them out, to be defiled by them: I am the LORD your God." (Lev. 19: 26, 31) The Catholic Church, in common with all orthodox Christians, condemns the practices that are common in New Age circles and among pagan adherents of "indigenous" faiths.

The *Catechism of the Catholic Church* states:

All forms of *divination* are to be rejected: recourse to Satan or demons, conjuring up the dead or other practices falsely supposed to 'unveil' the future. Consulting horoscopes, astrology, palm reading, interpretation of omens and lots, the phenomena of clairvoyance, and recourse to mediums all conceal a desire for power over time, history, and in the last analysis, other human beings, as well as a wish to conciliate hidden powers. They contradict the honor, respect, and loving fear that we owe to God alone. All practices of magic or sorcery, by which one attempts to tame occult powers, so as to place them at one's service and have a supernatural power over others—even if this were for the sake of restoring their health—are gravely contrary to the virtue of religion. . . . *Spiritism* often implies divination or magical practices; the Church for her part warns the faithful against it. Recourse to so-called traditional cures does not justify either the invocation of evil powers or the exploitation of another's credulity.[1]

In short, the Catholic Church, in common with orthodox Christians in all confessions, rejects the beliefs and practices of the new religious movements and "spiritual expressions" that the URI has welcomed to its table.

[XIV] THE UNITED RELIGIONS IS NOT REQUIRED BY THE CHRISTIAN CALL TO UNITY

The Christian response to the URI has been diverse, reflecting the divisions within Christianity itself. Support for the URI among the Evangelical Protestants and the Eastern Orthodox is scant. Mainline Protestantism in the industrialized nations supports the interfaith movement; such backing may go to the URI or to kindred interfaith organizations.

Within the Catholic Church—the largest and most powerful of the Christian Churches—the issue is still undecided. The Vatican remains aloof from the URI, but many Catholic dissenters are challenging this stance. The debate within the Catholic Church is ongoing, and it should be of interest to everyone to see why the Vatican believes as it does about this movement. Given the spiritual and organizational influence of the Catholic Church, the outcome of its current internal debate on the URI (and similar movements) will affect all Christians in all confessions.

Fr. Gerard O'Rourke, director of ecumenical affairs for the Catholic Archdiocese of San Francisco—and a former URI board member—has linked the URI to the Pope's ecumenical efforts: "John Paul II is constantly calling us as people of the world to come together at the completion of this millennium. There is a new movement of the Holy Spirit for us to begin to talk to each other."[2] Hence, Fr. O'Rourke believes that "If you are a Catholic, you know that you are now mandated to be a part of united religions. That's not the United Religions Initiative; Paul Andrews [a URI staff member in the late 1990s] would love if the Pope would say that in so many words, but he's saying it in other words."[3]

The Vatican office in charge of interreligious dialogue has decided otherwise, and has consistently held itself apart from the URI. The teaching documents of Vatican II and of the popes since Bl. John XXIII explain why the Catholic Church's authorities have done so.

Before Vatican II, Catholic teaching on the interfaith movement was clear and strict: stay away. As Pope Pius XI said in his 1928 encyclical *Mortalium Animos*, the proponents of the interfaith movement

---

1. *Catechism*, sections 2116–2117, pp 513–514.
2. Interview by Lee Penn of Fr. Gerard O'Rourke, May 4, 1998.
3. URI, forum at Grace Cathedral, 01/19/97.

hope that the nations, although they differ among themselves in certain religious matters, will without much difficulty come to agree as brethren in professing certain doctrines, which form as it were a common basis of the spiritual life. For which reason conventions, meetings and addresses are frequently arranged by these persons, at which a large number of listeners are present, and at which all without distinction are invited to join in the discussion, both infidels of every kind, and Christians, even those who have unhappily fallen away from Christ or who with obstinacy and pertinacity deny His divine nature and mission. Certainly such attempts can nowise be approved by Catholics, founded as they are on that false opinion which considers all religions to be more or less good and praiseworthy, since they all in different ways manifest and signify that sense which is inborn in us all, and by which we are led to God and to the obedient acknowledgment of His rule. Not only are those who hold this opinion in error and deceived, but also in distorting the idea of true religion they reject it, and little by little. turn aside to naturalism and atheism, as it is called; from which it clearly follows that one who supports those who hold these theories and attempt to realize them, is altogether abandoning the divinely revealed religion.[1]

THE DOCUMENTS OF VATICAN II

Vatican II signaled the opening of the Catholic Church to dialogue with other religions and to ecumenism with other Christians. However, the documents of Vatican II teach that it is the duty of Christians to evangelize and to follow Christ as Lord and Savior. No Vatican II document supports religious syncretism or relativism, the hallmarks of the URI.

The *Dogmatic Constitution on the Church* (*Lumen Gentium*) rejects the notion that all religions are equal as a means of salvation:

the Church, a pilgrim now on earth, is necessary for salvation: the one Christ is mediator and the way of salvation; he is present to us in his body which is the Church. He himself explicitly asserted the necessity of faith and baptism (cf. Mark 16:16, John 3:5), and thereby affirmed at the same time the necessity of the Church which men enter through baptism as through a door. Hence they could not be saved who, knowing that the Catholic Church was founded as necessary by God through Christ, would refuse to enter it, or to remain in it. . . . The Church knows that she is joined in many ways to the baptized who are honored by the name of Christian, but who however do not profess the Catholic faith in its entirety or have not preserved unity or communion under the successor of Peter. . . . Those who, through no fault of their own, do not know the Gospel of Christ or his Church, but who nevertheless seek God with a sincere heart and, moved by grace, try in their actions to do his will as they know it through the dictates of their own conscience—these too may achieve eternal salvation. Nor shall divine providence deny the assistance necessary for salvation to those who, without any fault of theirs, have not yet arrived at an explicit knowledge of God, and who, not without grace, strive to lead a good life. Whatever good or truth is found amongst them is considered by the Church to be a preparation for the Gospel and given by him who enlightens all men that they may at length have life. But very often, deceived by the Evil One, men have become vain in their reasonings, have exchanged the truth of God for a lie and served the world rather than the Creator (cf. Rom. 1:21 and 25). Or else, living and dying in this world without God, they are exposed to ultimate despair. Hence to procure the glory of God and the salvation of all these, the Church, mindful of the Lord's command, 'preach the Gospel to every creature' (Mark 16:16) takes zealous care to foster the missions.[2]

This decree upholds the value and obligation of evangelization:

By her proclamation of the Gospel, she draws her hearers to receive and profess the faith, she prepares them for baptism, snatches them from the slavery of error, and she incorporates them into Christ so that in love for

---

1. Pope Pius XI, *Mortalium Animos*, encyclical "On Religious Unity," January 6, 1928, http://www.vatican.va/holy_father/ pius_xi/encyclicals/documents/hf_p-xi_enc_19280106_mortalium-animos_en.html, paragraph 2, printed 05/18/04.

2. Vatican II; *Lumen Gentium*, sections 14–16, in Austin Flannery, O.P., General Editor, *Vatican Council II: The Conciliar and Post-Conciliar Documents*, 1992 rev. ed., Costello Publishing Company, Northpoint, New York, pp 365–368 (the Flannery volume is cited below as Flannery, *Vatican Council II*).

Him they may grow to full maturity. The effect of her work is that whatever good is found sown in the minds and hearts of men or in the rites and customs of peoples, these not only are preserved from destruction, but are purified, raised up, and perfected for the glory of God, the confusion of the devil, and the happiness of man. Each disciple of Christ has the obligation of spreading the faith, to the best of his ability.[1]

The *Decree on Ecumenism* (*Unitatis Redintegratio*)—which deals with unity among Christians, not unity among all religions—says, "Nothing is so foreign to the spirit of ecumenism as a false irenicism which harms the purity of Catholic doctrine and obscures its genuine and certain meaning."[2] This decree further states that imprudent zeal for Christian unity not based on Catholic faith is to be avoided: "This sacred Council urges the faithful to abstain from any frivolous or imprudent zeal, for these can cause harm to true progress toward unity. Their ecumenical activity cannot be other than fully and sincerely Catholic, that is, loyal to the truth we have received from the Apostles and the Fathers, and in harmony with the faith which the Catholic Church has always professed."[3] The decree's warnings should have even greater force in the context of dialogue with non-Christians.

The *Declaration on the Relation of the Church to Non-Christian Religions* (*Nostra Aetate*) states that

The Catholic Church rejects nothing of what is true and holy in these religions.[4] She has a high regard for the manner of life and conduct, the precepts and the doctrines which, although differing in many ways from her own teaching, nevertheless often reflect a ray of that truth which enlightens all men.[5] Yet she proclaims and is duty bound to proclaim without fail, Christ who is the way, the truth, and the life (John 1:6). In him, who reconciled all things to himself (2 Cor. 5:18–19), men find the fullness of their religious life.[6]

The Declaration restates the duty of the Church to proclaim Christ—and at the same time, to avoid religious discrimination:

It is the duty of the Church, therefore, in her preaching to proclaim the Cross of Christ as the sign of God's universal love and the source of all grace. We cannot truly pray to God the Father if we treat any people in other than brotherly fashion . . . There is no basis, therefore, in either theory or practice, for any discrimination between individual and individual, or between people and people arising either from human dignity or the rights which flow from it. Therefore, the Church reproves as foreign to the mind of Christ, any discrimination against people or any harassment of them on the basis of their race, color, condition of life, or religion.[7]

This decree says nothing in favor of syncretism, the equality of all religions as a way to salvation, or the need for a New Religion.

The *Declaration on Religious Liberty* (*Dignitatis Humanae*) firmly upholds religious freedom:

The Vatican Council declares that the human person has a right to religious freedom. Freedom of this kind means that all men should be immune from coercion on the part of individuals, social groups, and every human power so that, within due limits, nobody is forced to act against his convictions nor is anyone to be restrained from acting

1. Vatican II; *Lumen Gentium*, section 17, in Flannery, *Vatican Council II*, pp 368–369.
2. Vatican II; *Unitatis Redintegratio*, 21 November 1964, section 11, in Flannery, *Vatican Council II*, p 462.
3. Vatican II; *Unitatis Redintegratio*, 21 November 1964, section 24, in Flannery, *Vatican Council II*, p 470.
4. This is a reference to Hinduism, Buddhism, and 'other religions which are found throughout the world,' the religions discussed in the preceding paragraphs of the document.
5. Bishop William Swing cited a version of this sentence in his book, in order to show that Vatican II called for United Religions. (Swing, *The Coming United Religions*, p 17). Swing's translation is as follows: "The Catholic Church rejects nothing that is true and holy in these religions, (and) has high regard for their conduct and way of life for those precepts and doctrines which, although differing on many points from that (which) the Church believes and propounds, often reflect a ray of that truth that enlightens all men." Swing's citation of the Vatican II decree is disingenuous. He did not quote the very next sentence, which re-states the Church's duty to proclaim Christ, "without fail."
6. Vatican II; *Nostra Aetate*, 28 October 1965, section 2, in Flannery, *Vatican Council II*, p 739.
7. Vatican II; *Nostra Aetate*, 28 October 1965, sections 4–5, in Flannery, *Vatican Council II*, p 742.

in accordance with his conviction in religious matters in private or in public, alone or in association with others. The Council further declares that the right to religious freedom is based on the very dignity of the human person as known through the revealed word of God and by reason itself. This right of the human person to religious freedom itself must be given such recognition in the constitutional order of society as will make it a civil right.[1]

This same decree re-states the moral obligation of mankind to seek the truth:

All men are bound to seek the truth, especially in what concerns God and his Church, and to embrace it and hold onto it as they come to know it. The sacred Council likewise proclaims that these obligations bind man's conscience. Truth can impose itself on the mind of man only in virtue of its own truth, which wins over the mind with both gentleness and power. So while the religious freedom which men demand in fulfilling their obligation to worship God has to do with freedom from coercion in civil society, it leaves intact the traditional Catholic teaching on the moral duty of individuals and societies towards the true religion and the one Church of Christ.[2]

Papal Teachings Since Vatican II

Recent Popes have reaffirmed the teachings of Vatican II, restating the Catholic Church's opposition to religious syncretism or to compromise of the Catholic faith.

In 1964, Pope Paul VI wrote in his first encyclical *Ecclesiam Suam* that "honesty compels us to declare openly what we believe, namely that there is one true religion, the Christian religion, and that we hope that all who seek God and adore him, will come to acknowledge this."[3]

The document *On Dialog With Unbelievers (Humanae Personae Dignitatem)*, issued by the Vatican in 1968, called for dialog with all men, but contained cautionary statements that have not been heeded by the Christian supporters of the URI: "All Christians should do their best to promote dialogue between men of every class, as a duty of fraternal charity. . . . However, the nature and purpose of dialogue does not exclude other forms of communication, such as, among others, apologetics, contention, and controversy, nor does it rule out the defense of the rights of the human person."[4] "When engaging in dialogue, there must be no ambiguity about truth, as though it could be postponed until after dialogue, as some false forms of irenicism seem to do. Indeed, dialogue should originate in the common moral obligation of all to seek the truth, especially in the realm of religious problems."[5]

Finally, where there can be no agreement on ideology, it is possible that agreement can be reached with regard to practical matters. Certain conditions must be fulfilled, however, before consensus and cooperation can legitimately be achieved: the object of the dialogue must be good in itself or must be such that good may come from it; the agreement reached among the participants must not jeopardize a greater good, such as the integrity of doctrine, or personal rights such as civil, cultural, and religious liberty. In order to establish whether such conditions are verified of the dialogue to be undertaken, one must examine what the participants propose to do in the present and the future, and also what they did in the past.[6]

In 1990, John Paul II wrote to the bishops of Asia, reaffirming the duty of the Catholic Church to evangelize:

1. Vatican II; *Dignitatis Humanae*, 7 December 1965, section 2, in Flannery, *Vatican Council II*, p800.

2. Vatican II; *Dignitatis Humanae*, 7 December 1965, section 1, in Flannery, *Vatican Council II*, pp799–800.

3. Pope Paul VI, *Ecclesiam Suam*, as excerpted in Jacques Dupuis, ed. *The Christian Faith in the Doctrinal Documents of the Catholic Church*, 6th ed., Alba House, pp398–399 (the Dupuis book is cited below as Dupuis, *The Christian Faith*).

4. Vatican II; *Humanae Personae Dignitatem*, "Introduction," section 1, in Flannery, *Vatican Council II*, p1003.

5. Vatican II; *Humanae Personae Dignitatem*, "On Doctrinal Dialogue," section 1, in Flannery, *Vatican Council II*, p1007.

6. Secretariat for Unbelievers, *Humanae Personae Dignitatem*, "On Dialogue In Practical Affairs," in Flannery, *Vatican Council II*, pp1010–1011.

Although the Church gladly acknowledges whatever is true and holy in the religious traditions of Buddhism, Hinduism, and Islam as a reflection of that Truth which enlightens all people, this does not lessen her duty and resolve to proclaim without fail Jesus Christ who is 'the way, the truth, and the life' (John 14:6). . . . The fact that the followers of other religions can receive God's grace and be saved by Christ apart from the ordinary means which he has established does not thereby cancel the call to faith and to baptism which God wills for all people. It is a contradiction of the Gospel and of the Church's very nature to assert, as some do, that the Church is only one way of salvation among many, and that her mission towards the followers of other religions should be nothing more than to help them to be better followers of those religions.[1]

In the 1994 apostolic letter *Tertio Millennio Adveniente*, John Paul II prayed "that unity among all Christians of the various confessions will increase until they reach full communion."[2] The call for unity among all Christians is not the same as a quest for unity among all religions. The Pope also said that in Catholic Church-sponsored dialogue with "the leaders of the great world religions," care will always have to be taken to avoid "the risk of syncretism and of a facile and deceptive irenicism."[3]

In *Ut Unum Sint*, a 1995 encyclical dealing with unity among Christians, John Paul II said,

The unity willed by God can be attained only by the adherence of all to the content of revealed faith in its entirety. In matters of faith, compromise is in contradiction with God who is Truth. In the Body of Christ, 'the way, and the truth, and the life' (John 14:6), who could consider legitimate a reconciliation brought about at the expense of the truth? . . . A 'being together' which betrayed the truth would thus be opposed both to the nature of God who offers his communion and to the need for truth found in the depths of the human heart.[4]

In August 2000, the Vatican forcefully restated its opposition to religious relativism. The declaration *Dominus Iesus* was prepared by Cardinal Ratzinger, head of the Congregation for the Doctrine of the Faith. The Pope "ratified and confirmed this Declaration, adopted in Plenary Session and ordered its publication."[5]

In *Dominus Iesus*, the Catholic Church made the limits of interfaith dialogue clear. The Vatican said, "it must be firmly believed that, in the mystery of Jesus Christ, the Incarnate Son of God, who is 'the way, the truth, and the life' (John 14:6), the full revelation of divine truth is given."[6] It would "be contrary to the faith to consider the Church as one way of salvation alongside those constituted by the other religions, seen as complementary to the Church or substantially equivalent to her."[7] The "prayers and rituals" of other religions "may assume a role of preparation for the Gospel. . . . One cannot attribute to these, however, a divine origin or an *ex opere operato* salvific efficacy, which is proper to the Christian sacraments. Furthermore, it cannot be overlooked that other rituals, insofar as they depend on superstitions or other errors . . . constitute an obstacle to salvation."[8] "If it is true that the followers

1. Pope John Paul II, "Letter to the Bishops of Asia," January 23, 1990, section 4; as excerpted in Dupuis, *The Christian Faith*, p 415.

2. Pope John Paul II, *Tertio Millennio Adveniente*, section 16, p 23.

3. Ibid., section 53, p 56.

4. Pope John Paul II, *Ut Unum Sint: Encyclical Letter On Commitment to Ecumenism*, Pauline Books and Media, sect. 18, p 30.

5. Congregation for the Doctrine of the Faith (CDF), *Dominus Iesus: On the Unicity and Salvific Universality of Jesus Christ and the Church*, Pauline Books, "Conclusion," section 23, p 47 (cited below as CDF, *Dominus Iesus*).

6. Ibid., section 5, p 11. Speaking as a Traditionalist in the school of Schuon, Guénon, et. al., Charles Upton says, "The Traditionalists would agree that the unique revelation of God in Christ can have no equivalent, and that orthodox Christianity needs no complement since it provides all that is necessary to salvation. They would simply make the same claim for the Jewish, Muslim, Hindu and Buddhist revelations. As for 'I am the way, the truth and the life,' the Traditionalists accept this, but with the understanding that Jesus is speaking here as the Logos, the revelatory power behind all the true religions. They well know that this doctrine will not be accepted by most orthodox Christians, but see this very exclusivism as necessary to protect the depth and uniqueness of the Christian revelation." (E-mail from Charles Upton to Lee Penn, 11/03/04.)

7. CDF, *Dominus Iesus*, section 21, p 42.

8. Ibid., section 21, pp 42–43.

of other religions can receive divine grace, it is also certain that objectively speaking they are in a gravely deficient situation in comparison with those who, in the Church, have the fullness of the means of salvation."[1] "Because she believes in God's universal plan of salvation, the Church must be missionary."[2]

The Vatican also stated, "Equality, which is a presupposition of inter-religious dialogue, refers to the equal personal dignity of the parties in dialogue, not to doctrinal content, nor even less to the position of Jesus Christ—who is God himself made man—in relation to the founders of the other religions."[3] In interfaith dialogue, the Catholic Church deals with members of other religions as people with "equal personal dignity," without conceding that other religions are equally true.

In an Angelus message given on October 1 2000, the Pope reiterated the message of *Dominus Iesus*:

> With the Declaration *Dominus Iesus*—Jesus is Lord—approved by me in a special way at the height of the Jubilee Year, I wanted to invite all Christians to renew their fidelity to him in the joy of faith. . . . The Document clarifies essential Christian elements, which do not hinder dialogue but show its bases, because a dialogue without foundations would be destined to degenerate into empty wordiness. . . . The document thus expresses once again the same ecumenical passion that is the basis of my Encyclical *Ut Unum Sint*. I hope that this Declaration, which is close to my heart, can, after so many erroneous interpretations, finally fulfill its function both of clarification and of openness.[4]

In *Novo Millennio Ineunte*, an apostolic letter issued in early 2001 to direct the Catholic Church after the close of the Jubilee Year, Pope John Paul II re-stated the need for inter-religious dialogue to proceed—along with, and not in opposition to, evangelization. Re-stating the message of *Dominus Iesus*, he said:

> In the years of preparation for the Great Jubilee, the Church has sought to build, not least through a series of highly symbolic meetings, *a relationship of openness and dialogue with the followers of other religions*. This dialogue must continue. In the climate of increased cultural and religious pluralism which is expected to mark the society of the new millennium, it is obvious that this dialogue will be especially important in establishing a sure basis for peace and warding off the dread specter of those wars of religion which have so often bloodied human history. The name of the one God must become increasingly what it is: *a name of peace and a summons to peace*. Dialogue, however, cannot be based on religious indifferentism, and we Christians are in duty bound, while engaging in dialogue, to bear clear witness to the hope that is within us (cf. 1 Pt. 3:15). We should not fear that it will be considered an offense to the identity of others what is rather the joyful proclamation of a gift meant for all, and to be offered to all with the greatest respect for the freedom of each one: the gift of the revelation of the God who is Love, the God who 'so loved the world that he gave his only Son' (John 3:16). As the recent Declaration *Dominus Iesus* stressed, this cannot be the subject of a dialogue understood as negotiation, as if we considered it a matter of mere opinion: rather, it is a grace which fills us with joy, a message which we have a duty to proclaim. The Church therefore cannot forgo her missionary activity among the peoples of the world. It is the primary task of the *missio ad gentes* to announce that it is in Christ, 'the Way, and the Truth, and the Life' (John 14:6), that people find salvation. Interreligious dialogue 'cannot simply replace proclamation, but remains oriented towards proclamation'.[5]

The teachings of Vatican II and the encyclicals of recent Popes do *not* support the principles or practices of the URI. Nor do any post-conciliar Vatican rulings support Catholic participation in ventures (like the URI) that promote religious syncretism and relativism. No Catholic should support the URI, or view it as a legitimate means of attaining religious harmony, peace, or environmental preservation.

---

1. Ibid., section 22, p 43.
2. Ibid., section 22, p 44.
3. Ibid., section 22, pp 44–45.
4. Pope John Paul II, "Angelus—Sunday 1 October 2000," http://www.vatican.va/holy_father/john_paul_ii/angelus/2000/documents/hf_jp-ii_ang_20001001_en.html, printed 3/26/03.
5. Pope John Paul II, *Novo Millennio Ineunte: Apostolic Letter To the Bishops, Clergy, and Lay Faithful at the Close of the Great Jubilee of the Year* 2000, Pauline Books, 2001, sections 55–56, pp 71–72.

8

CLOSING THE CASE
AGAINST THE URI

SINCE 1995, the URI has moved from being the dream of one liberal Episcopal bishop to become a global movement of over 26,000 interfaith activists, with growing ties to the United Nations and with funding from major foundations.

The URI has grown with little controversy or active opposition, aside from the Vatican and from a few orthodox Protestants and Catholics. Most of those who instinctively reject the URI have assumed that the movement is too unrealistic to go far. Brooks Alexander, an Evangelical Christian expert on cults, explains the phenomenon: "That's New Age protective coloration. Unless the message gets across, it gets ignored. Unlike the early apostles of Christ, the preachers of the New Age don't stir up resistance wherever they go. If they are not understood and accepted, they are simply dismissed."[1] As the URI grows, attracting prominent adherents and million-dollar donors, the sanguine dismissal of the movement by many of its opponents is being proven unfounded.[2]

Other observers of the URI have favored the Gamaliel approach to the movement: "keep away from these men and let them alone; for if this plan or this undertaking is of men, it will fail; but if it is of God, you will not be able to overthrow them. You might even be found opposing God!" (Acts 5:38–39). In the long run, this will be true. Nevertheless, the Gamaliel strategy is no longer a good reason for a "wait and see" approach to the United Religions Initiative. The movement is taking root worldwide. Since 1789, many other utopian movements have done great damage before they were stopped. God rarely uses direct intervention to stop activities that are against His will. The ordinary means that God uses for this task are the discernment, labor, and prayers of the faithful, the members of the Body of Christ.

Ideas have consequences. Bad theology and bad philosophy matter. A movement like the URI, based on heretical theology and unrealistic philosophy, is out of touch with reality about God, human nature, and society. Giving credence and power to those out of touch with reality is dangerous; the history of the last century is an extended proof of this statement.

Many URI leaders and activists are worldly, liberal prelates, professors, and theologians. It might seem outlandish to worry that these people, whose spiritual forbears created the now-irrelevant World Council of Churches, could do anything as ominous as the creation of a New Religion that would synthesize ancient and modern heresies.

However, there *are* single-minded zealots within and around the URI—the cultists, Theosophists, and other members of new religious movements. These enthusiasts are the religious equivalent of the

---

1. Brooks Alexander, "Last Exit Before Judgment: Barbara Marx Hubbard and the 'Armageddon Alternative'," *Journal* of the Spiritual Counterfeits Project, Vol. 19:2–3, 1995, p 49, available through http://www.scp-inc.org.

2. René Guénon offered a similar reason for writing his exposé of Theosophy in 1921: "To all who are unprejudiced, Theosophy will probably appear more like a bad joke than something serious; but unfortunately this bad joke, far from being inoffensive, has taken many victims and continues to take more and more." (René Guénon, *Theosophy: History of a Pseudo-Religion*, tr. by Alvin Moore et al., orig. ed. 1921, rev. ed. Sophia Perennis, 2001, p 291).

Leninist activists in the anti-war movement of the 1960s. These spiritual Jacobins have missionary zeal aplenty, and an extensive track record of co-opting religious liberals—and liberal-run religious institutions. The liberal members of the traditional religions believe strongly in peace, equality, and tolerance; their credo is "Can't we all just get along?" This is not a belief system that inspires zeal or provides the basis for keeping control of an organization away from fanatics. You can't beat something with nothing.

The URI appears to be successful in overcoming potential tensions among its followers. Its proponents have included the Dalai Lama and churchmen from the state-approved churches in the People's Republic of China, pro-gay Episcopalians and anti-gay followers of the Rev. Moon, radical Muslims and radical feminists, as well as rich capitalist foundations and those who announce the spiritual bankruptcy of capitalism. Such is the URI's "unity in diversity." It may be that these people are united in their desire for religious peace. It may also be that they all oppose traditional Christianity more than they distrust each other, and so are willing to cooperate to marginalize orthodox Christianity.

Can the URI achieve its aims? Could an organization with 26,000 followers worldwide and annual revenues of less than $4 million spark the spiritual revolution that it desires? Bishop Swing seems to think so, if the conditions are right. In 1998, he said, "The United Religions Initiative will be inevitable when the world has run out of options. When it is clear that the missing ingredient in authentic diplomacy is religion. . . . The only reason there would ever be a United Religions is that the stark world demands it. The time of that demand is getting close."[1] Swing has said the same since then. Swing did not say what event would evoke the "demand," why he suspected that "the time of that demand is getting close," who will make the "demand," or how it will be enforced.

We cannot know whether (or when) a major, unexpected event favorable to the URI will occur. It may be that spiritual, economic, and political chaos from war or from mega-terrorism will spark the "demand" that Swing expects. Bishop Swing, or a charismatic successor, may succeed in getting the UN, the European Union, or other international bodies hostile to traditional Christianity to fully align themselves with the URI. Many other possibilities exist; history can make sudden, unexpected turns.

A successful United Religions Initiative would bring with it the spread of irrational New Age beliefs and practices, and would repopulate the "naked public square" of the West with a pantheon of idols. The collectivist "global ethic" fostered by the URI would provide a fig leaf of respectability for further expansion of national and international government power at the expense of individuals, families, and the Churches. Most of the URI's leaders, prominent supporters, and allies have a world-view and a cultural/political agenda inimical to traditional adherents of the three Abrahamic religions. If the URI succeeds in gaining global influence, it will become another opponent of Christ, another supporter of the relativist "culture of death."

A prayer card issued in 1996 by the URI contained an image of the birth of a new star, with the slogan, "Join a world waiting . . . for the birth of a new light . . . United Religions."[2] Christians do not need to "join a world waiting" for this "new light." We already have a light that cannot fail; Christ said, "I am the light of the world" (John 9:5). The world may wait for the birth of a false, new light; Christ gave us the response: "be of good cheer, I have overcome the world" (John 16:33).

On this matter, let's give Bishop Swing the last word. On September 11, 1996, he extolled the URI to a meeting of 281 San Francisco Episcopal lay leaders and clergy, saying: "We're talking about salvation history here. If I'm wrong, I'm dead wrong."[3] The Bishop has spoken; the case is closed.

---

1. "Bishop Swing Addresses World Congress of Faiths: Raises Possibility That URI Might Play A Role in Salt Lake City Olympics Opening Ceremony," *PCN*, Dec. 1998/Jan. 1999, p39; also, Swing, "Unthinkable to Thinkable to Do-able to Inevitable," address to World Congress of Faiths, 07/22/98, repr. in *A Swing with a Crosier*, Episcopal Diocese of Calif., 1999, p150.

2. URI, color prayer card issued in 1996, "Pray for the United Religions Assembly June 1996—June 1997."

3. From notes taken by Lee Penn of the speech given by Bishop Swing at the 9/11/96 meeting of the San Francisco Deanery for the Episcopal Diocese of California. The attendance total is from the 9/14/96 minutes of the San Francisco Deanery.

PART II

SERVANTS OF THE SHINING DARKNESS:
THE ANTI-GOSPEL OF THE NEW AGE MOVEMENT

The Macabre representation of the Tree of Knowledge and Death. Woodcut by Jost Amman, from Jacob Rueff's *De conceptu et generatione hominis*, printed by Peter Fabricus, Frankfurt, 1587.

"See to it that no one makes
a prey of you by philosophy and empty deceit,
according to human tradition, according to the
elemental spirits of the universe,
and not according to Christ."

St. Paul, Colossians 2:8

"The kingdom of God is not coming
with signs to be observed; nor will they say,
'Lo, here it is!' or 'There!' for behold, the kingdom
of God is in the midst of you."

Jesus, in Luke 17:20–21

POINT : COUNTERPOINT

Adam and Eve "are said to have committed Original Sin. I tell you this: it was the Original Blessing. For without this event, the partaking of the knowledge of good and evil, *you* would not even know the two possibilities existed!"[1]

————"GOD," TALKING WITH NEALE DONALD WALSCH, 1997

> The serpent said to the woman, 'You will not die. For God knows that when you eat of it your eyes will be opened, and you will be like God, knowing good and evil.' So when the woman saw that the tree was good for food, and that it was a delight to the eyes, and that the tree was to be desired to make one wise, she took of its fruit and ate; and she also gave some to her husband, and he ate.
>
> GENESIS 3:4–6————

> And to Adam he said, 'Because you have listened to the voice of your wife, and have eaten of the tree of which I commanded you, 'You shall not eat of it,' cursed is the ground because of you; in toil you shall eat of it all the days of your life; thorns and thistles it shall bring forth to you; and you shall eat the plants of the field. In the sweat of your face you shall eat bread till you return to the ground, for out of it you were taken; you are dust, and to dust you shall return.
>
> GENESIS 3:17–19————

The Secret Doctrine must some day become the just Karma of the Churches—more anti-Christian than the representative assemblies of the most confirmed Materialists and Atheists.[2]

————HELENA P. BLAVATSKY, *THE SECRET DOCTRINE*, 1888

> The ordinary detective discovers from a ledger or a diary that a crime has been committed. We discover from a book of sonnets that a crime will be committed. We have to trace the origin of those dreadful thoughts that drive men on at last to intellectual fanaticism and intellectual crime.[3]
>
> G. K. CHESTERTON, *THE MAN WHO WAS THURSDAY*————

The true communistic platform is sound; it is brotherhood in action and it does not—in its original platform—run counter to the spirit of Christ.[4]

————ALICE A. BAILEY, *THE RAYS AND THE INITIATIONS*, 1960 ED.

1. Neale Donald Walsch, *Conversations with God: An Uncommon Dialogue, Book* 2, Hampton Roads Publishing Company, Inc., 1997, p 57.

2. H. P. Blavatsky, *The Secret Doctrine: The Synthesis of Science, Religion, and Philosophy, Vol. II—Anthropogenesis*, Theosophical University Press, 1999 reprint of 1888 ed., p 228 (cited below as Blavatsky, *The Secret Doctrine, Vol. II*).

3. G. K. Chesterton, *The Man Who Was Thursday*, Perigee Books/G. P. Putnam's Sons, 1980, p 42 (cited below as Chesterton, *The Man Who Was Thursday*).

4. Alice A. Bailey, *The Rays and the Initiations: Volume V, A Treatise on the Seven Rays*, 1960, Lucis Publishing Company, p 680.

Highly evolved beings . . . share *everything*. With *everyone*. Not a being goes without. All the natural resources of their world, of their environment, are divided equally, and distributed to everyone."[1]

————"GOD," TALKING WITH NEALE DONALD WALSCH, 1998

The breakup of the 20th century procreative family structure is a vital perturbation needed for the breakthrough of the 21st century cocreative family structure.[2]

————BARBARA MARX HUBBARD, *CONSCIOUS EVOLUTION*, 1998

Your marriage vows, as you presently construct them, have you
making a very un-Godly statement.[3]

————"GOD," TALKING WITH NEALE DONALD WALSCH, 1998

> We deny the snobbish English assumption that the uneducated are the dangerous criminals. We remember the Roman Emperors. We remember the great poisoning princes of the Renaissance. We say that the dangerous criminal is the educated criminal. We say that the most dangerous criminal is the entirely lawless modern philosopher. Compared to him, burglars and bigamists are essentially moral men; my heart goes out to them. They accept the essential ideal of man; they merely seek it wrongly. Thieves respect property. They merely wish the property to become their property that they may more perfectly respect it. But philosophers dislike property as property; they wish to destroy the very idea of personal possession. Bigamists respect marriage, or they would not go through the highly ceremonial and even ritualistic formality of bigamy. But philosophers despise marriage as marriage.[4]
>
> G. K. CHESTERTON, *THE MAN WHO WAS THURSDAY*————

It has been suggested that we call a United Species Conference—a conference far more representative than the United Nations is—and put this one question to the ten million representatives (one for each species): 'Should the human species be allowed to continue on this planet?' The vote would most likely be 9,999,999 to 1 that we humans, with our dualistic hatred of earth, of one another, and of our own existence, be banished to some distant place in the galaxy so that Mother Earth could continue her birthing of beauty, amazement, colors, and health.[5]

————MATTHEW FOX, *THE COMING OF THE COSMIC CHRIST*, 1988

From democracy we will now move quickly to Gaiacracy or Earthcracy. From the power of government and the moneycracy of big business, we will now see the power of nature, of the Earth itself. The retribution will be terrible. The Earth will take revenge against her most advanced species which has begun to destroy her. She will retaliate with lack of oxygen, ultra-violet rays, lack of water, mounting cancers, the breakdown of the immune system of the human body, etc. God will not

1. Neale Donald Walsch, *Conversations with God: An Uncommon Dialogue, Book* 3, Hampton Roads Publishing Company, Inc., 1998, p 287 (cited below as Walsch, *Conversations/Book* 3).
2. Barbara Marx Hubbard, *Conscious Evolution: Awakening the Power of Our Social Potential*, New World Library, Novato, California, 1998, p 208.
3. Walsch, *Conversations/Book* 3, p 223.
4. G. K. Chesterton, *The Man Who Was Thursday*, p 43
5. Matthew Fox, *The Coming of the Cosmic Christ: The Healing of Mother Earth and the Birth of a Global Renaissance*, Harper San Francisco, 1988, p 15.

allow us to destroy His Creation and to put an end to the Earth's careful, miraculous evolution over billions of years. He is more likely to let humanity be destroyed.[1]

—————ROBERT MULLER, *IDEAS AND DREAMS FOR A BETTER WORLD*, 1998

> This is a vast philosophic movement, consisting of an outer and an inner ring. You might even call the outer ring the laity and the inner ring the priesthood. I prefer to call the outer ring the innocent section, the inner ring the supremely guilty section. The outer ring—the main mass of their supporters—are merely anarchists; that is, men who believe that rules and formulas have destroyed human happiness. They believe that all the evil results of human crime are the results of the system that has called it crime. . . . Naturally, therefore, these people talk about a 'happy time coming,' 'the paradise of the future,' 'mankind freed from the bondage of vice and the bondage of virtue,' and so on. And so also the men of the inner circle speak—the sacred priesthood. They also speak to applauding crowds of the happiness of the future, and of mankind freed at last. But in their mouths . . . these happy phrases have a horrible meaning. They are under no illusions; they are too intellectual to think that man upon this earth can ever be quite free of original sin and the struggle. And they mean death. When they say that mankind shall be free at last, they mean that mankind shall commit suicide. When they talk of a paradise without right or wrong, they mean the grave. They have but two objects, to destroy first humanity and then themselves.[2]
>
> G. K. CHESTERTON, *THE MAN WHO WAS THURSDAY*—————

The god of every exoteric religion, including Christianity, not withstanding its pretensions to mystery, is an idol, a fiction, and cannot be anything else."[3]

—————HELENA P. BLAVATSKY, *ISIS UNVEILED*, VOL. I, 1877

> See to it that no one makes a prey of you by philosophy and empty deceit, according to human tradition, according to the elemental spirits of the universe, and not according to Christ.
>
> ST. PAUL, COLOSSIANS 2:8—————

The various cosmogonies show that the Archæal Universal Soul was held by every nation as the 'mind' of the Demiurgic Creator, the *Sophia* of the Gnostics, or *the Holy Ghost as a female principle.*[4]

—————HELENA P. BLAVATSKY, *ISIS UNVEILED*, VOL. I, 1877

The voice of Sophia calls us out of bondage,
Held captive by Pharaoh and fearful of dawn,
She leads us in darkness through death to deliverance,
Then, into wilderness, come journey on. . . .
O voice of Sophia be spoken within us,
Enlighten our struggle from darkness to dawn,

---

1. Robert Muller, *Ideas And Dreams For A Better World: 1001–1500, Volume III*, Idea 1294, 25 January 1998, http://www.robertmuller.org/volume/ideas1001.html, viewed 06/17/04.

2. G.K. Chesterton, *The Man Who Was Thursday*, pp 45–46.

3. H.P. Blavatsky, *Isis Unveiled: Vol. I, Science*, Theosophical University Press, 1988 reprint of 1877 ed., p 307 (cited below as Blavatsky, *Isis Unveiled: Vol. I*).

4. Ibid., p 130.

Enliven the joy that is trembling within us,
Deep joy at your calling to come journey on.[1]

———Charles Gibbs, Executive Director of the URI,
"Hymn for a Hatching Heart,"1996

Now the Spirit expressly says that in later times some will depart from the faith by giving heed to
deceitful spirits and doctrines of demons.

St. Paul, 1 Timothy 4:1———

The present volumes have been written to small purpose if they have not shown, 1, that Jesus, the Christ-God, is a myth concocted two centuries after the real Hebrew Jesus died; 2, that, therefore, he never had any authority to give Peter, or anyone else, plenary power; 3, that, even if he had given such authority, the word Petra (rock) referred to the revealed truths of the Petroma, not to him who thrice denied him; and that besides, the apostolic succession is a gross and palpable fraud; 4, that the *Gospel according to Matthew* is a fabrication based on a wholly different manuscript. The whole thing, therefore, is an imposition alike upon priest and penitent.[2]

———Helena Blavatsky, *Isis Unveiled*, Vol. II, 1877

Christ and anti-Christ are the dualities of spirituality and materialism, both in the individual and in humanity as a whole. Or you can speak of God and the Devil with the same basic implications.[3]

———Alice A. Bailey, *The Externalisation of the Hierarchy*, 1957

I, Jesus Christ, was simply a first example of what you all can be. Since very few could actualize their full potential during the last two thousand years, I was deified and put above you. People worshipped me instead of actualizing themselves.[4]

———"Christ," speaking to Barbara Marx Hubbard, 1993

By this you know the Spirit of God: every spirit which confesses that Jesus Christ has come in the flesh is of God, and every spirit which does not confess Jesus is not of God. This is the spirit of antichrist, of which you heard that it was coming, and now it is in the world already.

St. John 1, John 4:2–3———

Those who fail and are disrupted by the impact of the powerful forces now flooding our earth will nevertheless have their vibration 'stepped up' to better things along with the mass of those who achieve, even if their physical vehicles are destroyed in the process.[5]

———Alice A. Bailey,
The Externalisation of the Hierarchy, 1957

1. United Religions Initiative, *Draft Workbook For Pilot Groups*, p36.
2. H.P. Blavatsky, *Isis Unveiled: Vol. II, Theology*, Theosophical University Press, 1988 reprint of 1877 ed., p544.
3. Alice A. Bailey, *The Externalisation of the Hierarchy*, 1957, Lucis Publishing Company, p137 (cited below as Bailey, *Externalisation of the Hierarchy*).
4. Barbara Marx Hubbard, *The Revelation: Our Crisis Is A Birth*, Foundation for Conscious Evolution, Sonoma CA, 1993, p304.
5. Bailey, *Externalisation of the Hierarchy*, p7.

There will be an evolutionary selection process based on your qualifications for co-creative power. . . . A Quantum Transformation is the time of selection of what evolves from what devolves. The species known as self-centered humanity will become extinct. The species known as whole-centered humanity will evolve.[1]

————A "higher voice," speaking to Barbara Marx Hubbard, 1995

All men at times obey their vices: but it is when cruelty, envy, and lust of power appear as the commands of a great super-personal force that they can be exercised with self-approval. The first symptom is in language. When to 'kill' becomes to 'liquidate' the process has begun. The pseudo-scientific word disinfects the thing of blood and tears, or pity and shame, and mercy itself can be regarded as a sort of untidiness.[2]

C. S. Lewis, "A Reply to Professor Haldane," in *Of This and Other Worlds*————

We are about to eat of the fruit of the Tree of Life and become godlike.[3]

————Barbara Marx Hubbard, 1995

From the point of view which is accepted in Hell, the whole history of our Earth had led up to this moment. There was now at last a real chance for fallen Man to shake off that limitation of his powers which mercy had imposed upon him as a protection from the full results of his fall.[4]

C. S. Lewis, *That Hideous Strength*————

Yours is a *race awakening*. Your time of fulfillment is at hand.[5]

————"God," speaking to Neale Donald Walsch, 1998

However far you went you would find the machines, the crowded cities, the empty thrones, the false writings, the barren beds: men maddened with false promises and soured with true miseries, worshipping the iron works of their own hands, cut off from Earth their mother and from the Father in Heaven.[6]

C. S. Lewis, *That Hideous Strength*————

A *progressive* democrat is not fundamentally different from a really progressive totalitarian.[7]

————Teilhard de Chardin, *Letters to Two Friends*, 1941

Everywhere and in every country men are being taught in their earliest years that they are not only individuals, not only members of a state, empire or nation, and not only people with an individual

---

1. Barbara Marx Hubbard, *The Revelation: A Message of Hope for the New Millennium*, Nataraj Publishing, Novato, CA, 1995, p 111 (cited below as Marx Hubbard, *Revelation/Hope*).

2. C. S. Lewis, "A Reply to Professor Haldane," in *Of This and Other Worlds*, Collins Fount Paperbacks, 1982, p 109.

3. Marx Hubbard, *Revelation/Hope*, p 82.

4. C. S. Lewis, *That Hideous Strength: A Modern Fairy-Tale for Grown-Ups*, Collier Books, Macmillan Publishing Company, 1946, 1965 ed., pp 203–204 (cited below as Lewis, *That Hideous Strength*).

5. Walsch, *Conversations/Book 3*, p 340.

6. Lewis, *That Hideous Strength*, p 293.

7. Pierre Teilhard de Chardin, *Letters to Two Friends* 1926–1952, The New American Library, 1968, p 154; letter of February 9, 1941 (cited below as Teilhard, *Letters to Two Friends*).

future, but that they are intended to be exponents of certain great group ideologies—Democratic, Totalitarian, or Communistic. . . . All this is very good and part of the ordained plan. Whether it is the democratic ideal, or the vision of the totalitarian state, or the dream of the communistic devotee, the effect upon the consciousness of humanity as a whole is definitely good. His sense of world awareness is definitely growing, his power to regard himself as part of a whole is rapidly developing and all this is desirable and right and contained within the divine plan.[1]

————ALICE A. BAILEY, *EDUCATION IN THE NEW AGE*, 1954

The process which, if not checked, will abolish Man, goes on apace among Communists and Democrats no less than among Fascists. The methods may (at first) differ in brutality. But many a mild-eyed scientist in pince-nez, many a popular dramatist, many an amateur philosopher in our midst, means in the long run just the same as the Nazi rulers of Germany. Traditional values are to be 'debunked' and mankind to be cut into some fresh shape at the will (which must, by hypothesis, be an arbitrary will) of some few lucky people in one lucky generation which has learned how to do it. The belief that we can invent 'ideologies' at pleasure, and the consequent treatment of mankind as mere ὕλη, specimens, preparations, begins to affect our very language. Once we killed bad men: now we liquidate unsocial elements[2]

C. S. LEWIS, *THE ABOLITION OF MAN*————

In my opinion, the world of tomorrow will be born out of the 'elected' group of those (arising from any direction and class, and confession in the human world) who will decide that there is something big waiting for us ahead, and give their life to reach it. People *have to* decide for or against progress, *now*. And those who say no have to just be dropped behind. And those who say yes will soon discover that they speak the same language and even worship the same God.[3]

————TEILHARD DE CHARDIN, *LETTERS TO TWO FRIENDS*, 1941

The enthronement of the gospel of progress necessarily required the final discrediting of the gospel of Christ, and the destruction of the whole edifice of ethics, law, culture, human relationships, and human behaviour constructed upon it. Our civilization, after all, began with the Christian revelation, not the theory of evolution, and we may be sure, will perish with it, too—if it has not already. Jesus of Nazareth was its founding father, not Charles Darwin; it was Paul of Tarsus who first carried its message to Europe, not Karl Marx, or even Lenin. Jesus, by dying on the Cross, abolished death-wishing; dying became thenceforth life's glory and fulfillment. So, when Jesus called on his followers to die in order to live, he created a tidal wave of joy and hope on which they have ridden for two thousand years. The gospel of progress represents the exact antithesis. It plays the Crucifixion backwards, as it were; in the beginning was the flesh, and the flesh became Word. In the light of this Logos in reverse, the quest for hope is the ultimate hopelessness; the pursuit of happiness, the certitude of despair; the lust for life, the embrace of death.[4]

MALCOLM MUGGERIDGE, "THE GREAT LIBERAL DEATH WISH"————

1. Alice A. Bailey, *Education in the New Age*, 1954, Lucis Publishing Company, pp 103–104.
2. C. S. Lewis, *The Abolition of Man*, Macmillan Publishing Co., Inc., 1947, paperback ed. 1955, p 85.
3. Teilhard, *Letters to Two Friends* p 154; letter of February 9, 1941.
4. Malcolm Muggeridge, "The Great Liberal Death Wish," reprinted in *The Portable Conservative Reader*, ed. Russell Kirk, Viking Penguin Inc., 1982, pp 613–614.

The tradition of the Dragon and the Sun is echoed in every part of the world, both in its civilized and semi-savage regions. It took rise in the whisperings about secret initiations among the profane, and was established universally through the once universal heliolatrous religion. There was a time when the four parts of the world were covered with the temples sacred to the Sun and the Dragon.[1]

————HELENA P. BLAVATSKY, *THE SECRET DOCTRINE*, VOL. II, 1888

The religion of the ancients is the religion of the future. A few centuries more, and there will linger no sectarian belief in either of the great religions of humanity. Brahmanism and Buddhism, Christianity and Mahometanism will all disappear before the mighty rush of *facts.* . . . But this can only come to pass when the world returns to the grand religion of the past; the *knowledge* of those majestic systems which preceded by far Brahmanism, and even the primitive monotheism of the ancient Chaldeans.[2]

————HELENA P. BLAVATSKY, *ISIS UNVEILED*, VOL. I, 1877

When the gods of the New Paganism come they will not be merely insufficient, as were the gods of Greece, nor merely false; they will be evil. One might put it in a sentence, and say that the New Paganism, foolishly expecting satisfaction, will fall, before it knows where it is, into Satanism.[3]

HILAIRE BELLOC, "THE NEW PAGANISM," IN *ESSAYS OF A CATHOLIC*, 1931————

1. Blavatsky, *The Secret Doctrine, Vol. II*, p378. She says almost exactly the same thing in *Isis Unveiled*: "This tradition of the Dragon and the Sun—occasionally replaced by the Moon—has awakened echoes in the remotest parts of the world. It may be accounted for with perfect readiness by the one universal heliolatrous religion. There was a time when Asia, Europe, Africa, and America were covered with the temples sacred to the sun and the dragons." (Blavatsky, *Isis Unveiled: Vol. I*, p550).
2. Blavatsky, *Isis Unveiled: Vol. I*, p613.
3. Hilaire Belloc, "The New Paganism," in *Essays of a Catholic*, TAN Books and Publishers, Inc., 1931, 1992 ed., p12.

9

THE NEW AGE MOVEMENT: FRIVOLOUS IN APPEARANCE, SINISTER IN SUBSTANCE

MOST OUTSIDE OBSERVERS OF THE NEW AGE MOVEMENT, conservatives and liberals alike, dismiss its teachings in the same way that *Newsweek* magazine described the writing of Neale Donald Walsch and James Van Praagh—as "a philosophy that can be summed up as religion without the hard parts. . . . R. Laurence Moore, a professor of history at Cornell, says that this is a familiar theme in American spiritualism, going back at least to the transcendentalists. 'If you read enough of it,' he says, 'it all reads the same: goofy, repetitive, goes down easy.'"[1] Most of those outside the New Age movement, if they take note of it at all, write it off as silly and harmless.

The truth is otherwise.

New Age and Theosophical teaching is *not* merely a collection of inane, comfortable bromides. Some of the leading authors from these movements have left us a collection of "hard sayings" that include:

• Praise for Lucifer, the light-bearer, because he awoke mankind in the Garden of Eden from its primal unconsciousness. For these New Age theorists, the Fall was really man's Ascent into knowledge and freedom.

• Proclaiming that we humans are gods, and that death is not real.

• Advocacy for population control—especially for the poor in the West and for the underdeveloped countries. This advocacy goes back to the late 1800s, when world population was a fraction of its current level.

• Contempt for traditional religions—with concentrated scorn directed at Judaism, evangelical Protestantism, and Roman Catholicism.

• Support for a new world order, a spiritualized form of Communism in which everyone will "share" everything.

• Apologetics for various and sundry dictators and authoritarian movements, of the extreme Right as well as the extreme Left.

• Acceptance of war and atomic weapons as instruments of human evolution.

• Forecasting a pending (and for them, desirable) "selection" of mankind, in which the progressives enter the New Age and the reactionaries face extinction. For the New Age apostles of "progressive" Social Darwinism, these casualties are a necessary price to pay for human evolution.

---

1. Jerry Adler, "Heaven's Gatekeepers—They give the people what they want: talkative spirits and a laid-back God," *Newsweek*, March 16, 1998, p65.

Christians worship one God, the Holy Trinity: the Father, the Son, and the Holy Spirit. In opposition, these New Age prophets propose an unholy trinity: human self-worship, Promethean religion that sometimes extends to praise of Lucifer, and a collectivist earthly Utopia.

It is likely enough, however, that little of this has come to the awareness of most New Age devotees. It's easy for those who seek spiritual consolation and community to pay attention to and internalize only the agreeable material in these writers' works, without attending to or consciously accepting the darker side of these beliefs. What the leaders have written is one matter; what their spiritually hungry followers may understand and accept is another matter altogether.

You might wonder: what does the aforementioned New Age nonsense have to do with the URI and its globalist allies? The answer is: quite a lot. Among the currently influential New Age writers who support the URI are Robert Muller, Barbara Marx Hubbard, and Neale Donald Walsch. All have been, to a greater or lesser extent, influenced by the teachings of Alice A. Bailey, a American Theosophist of the mid-20ᵗʰ Century. (Bailey's present-day followers at the Lucis Trust support the URI, as well.) Bailey, in turn, was a follower of Helena Petrovna Blavatsky, who first popularized Theosophy in Europe and North America after 1875. These New Age writers also praise the work of Teilhard de Chardin, a Jesuit whom the Catholic Church prohibited from publishing his writings during his lifetime. Teilhard's work, though nominally Catholic, has ominous similarities to the works of the Theosophists.

The pro-URI New Age activists apparently consider their beliefs to be consistent with the URI charter. The URI cannot say otherwise, and has no basis on which to exclude the New Age "gurus" from the movement.

New Age and Theosophist participation in the URI is but one example of the movement's growing influence in the Christian churches and in the world. For the last 125 years, New Age leaders worldwide have followed the false light of Theosophy; they now whisper sweet lies into the itching ears of the powerful—politicians, media moguls, UN officials, foundation grant-makers, and Anglican bishops alike. As the West moves deeper into apostasy from the Christian faith, the influence of the New Age movement spreads, among the elite as much as (or more than) among the rest of us.[1]

---

1. J. Gordon Melton, a historian of new religious movements, stated that the mass appeal of the New Age movement peaked in 1987–1988, around the time of the Harmonic Convergence celebrations and the release of a movie version of Shirley MacLaine's *Out on a Limb*. Since then, the movement "refocused and has continued, though with a quite varied appearance." (J. Gordon Melton, "The Future of the New Age Movement," in Eileen Barker and Margit Warburg, eds., *New Religions and New Religiosity*, Aarhus University Press, 1998, p140.) However, the present-day networking forums for the global business and political elite described in Part III of this book (the State of the World Forum and the World Economic Forum, among others) have consistently offered their constituency a diet of New Age spirituality at their meetings. Thus, it may be that as the New Age movement lost mass appeal, its influence increased among the global elite.

10

HELENA BLAVATSKY
AND THE THEOSOPHICAL SOCIETY

THEOSOPHY IS A BLEND OF distorted forms of Hinduism and Buddhism with Western occultism.[1] This spiritual movement took its modern form in 1875 in New York City, when Helena Petrovna Blavatsky founded the Theosophical Society.[2] Her two principal books were *Isis Unveiled* and *The Secret Doctrine*; she also began the magazine *Lucifer* in 1887.[3] A scholarly history of the Theosophical movement says of Blavatsky that "Everywhere she was involved with Freemasonry, Oriental secret societies, occult fraternities, and with the spiritualists who constituted, as it were, the exoteric 'church' from which doors opened to the more esoteric circles."[4] Influential 20th century Theosophists included Alice Bailey (founder of the Lucifer Publishing Company in New York City in 1922,[5] which is now known as the Lucis Trust), and Rudolf Steiner (founder of the Anthroposophical movement, a variant of Theosophy).[6]

At first glance, the stated aims of the Theosophical Society appear harmless:

• To form a nucleus of the universal brotherhood of humanity, without distinction of race, creed, sex, caste, or color.

1. Charles Upton states, "Blavatsky took for her own use little more than the terminology of Hinduism and Buddhism. Almost every application she made of concepts from these religions was erroneous." (E-mail from Charles Upton to Lee Penn, 03/23/04.)

2. For further information on the teachings of the Theosophical movement (Blavatsky, Alice Bailey, David Spangler, Neale Donald Walsch, Robert Muller, Barbara Marx Hubbard, and Benjamin Creme, see Lee Penn, "New Age and Globalist Strategies: Unity, Collectivism, & Control," *Journal* of the Spiritual Counterfeits Project, Vol. 23:4–24:1, 2000, pp42–70, and "Dark Apocalypse: Blood Lust of the Compassionate," *Journal* of the Spiritual Counterfeits Project, Vol. 24:2–24:3, 2000, pp8–31; obtainable through http://www.scp-inc.org.

3. Sylvia Cranston, *HPB: The Extraordinary Life and Influence of Helena Blavatsky, Founder of the Modern Theosophical Movement*, G. P. Putnam's Sons, 1994, p333 ff., on *Lucifer* magazine.

4. Joscelyn Godwin, *The Theosophical Enlightenment*, State University of New York Press, 1994, p281 (cited below as Godwin, *Theosophical Enlightenment*).

5. See, for example, the title page of Alice A. Bailey, *Initiation, Human and Solar*, First Edition, Lucifer Publishing Co., 135 Broadway, New York City, 1922.

6. The Steiner biography on the Anthroposophic Press web site does not mention the 1913 break between Steiner and Theosophy (Anthroposophic Press, "About Rudolf Steiner," http://www.anthropress.org/aboutrudolf.html, printed 03/24/04.) Instead, the document begins with Steiner's brief description of Anthroposophy, written in 1904, while Steiner was the head of the German branch of the Theosophical Society: "Anthroposophy is a path of knowledge, to guide the spiritual in the human being to the spiritual in the universe. It arises in people as a need of the heart and feeling life. Anthroposophy can be justified only to the degree that it satisfies this inner need. It may be acknowledged only by those who find within it what they themselves feel the need to seek. Therefore, anthroposophists are those who experience, as an essential need of life, certain questions on the nature of the human being and the universe, just as one experiences hunger and thirst.—Rudolf Steiner, *Anthroposophical Leading Thoughts*, 1904." This publishing house reprints Steiner's works, from his Theosophical period and from his post-1912 Anthroposophical period, without setting forth a philosophical break between the periods. The editor of Steiner's *Spiritualism, Madame Blavatsky, and Theosophy* says, "Rudolf Steiner's perhaps even greater contribution, as we shall

- To encourage the comparative study of religion, philosophy, and science.
- To investigate unexplained laws of nature and the powers latent in humanity.[1]

These principles were established in the 19th Century, and have been the foundation of Theosophy since then. However, in her writings—which the Theosophical movement still publishes and reveres—Madame Blavatsky showed the darker side of her world-view.

MANKIND AND NATURE AS "GODS"

For Blavatsky, the Lord is not God; mankind is. In *The Secret Doctrine*, she said: "esoteric philosophy shows that man is truly the manifested deity in both its aspects—good and evil."[2] Since mankind is god, it follows through the "law of spiritual development" that "mankind will become freed from its false gods, and find itself finally—*SELF-REDEEMED*."[3] Elsewhere in the same book, Blavatsky foreshadowed Gorbachev (who recently said "nature is my god"[4]) by claiming, "The silent worship of abstract or *noumenal* Nature, the only divine manifestation, is the one ennobling religion of Humanity."[5] Either way, for Blavatsky, God is not the Holy Trinity as revealed to Christians.

SYMPATHY FOR THE DEVIL

Throughout *The Secret Doctrine*, Blavatsky praised the Devil and belittled God.
In Volume I, *Cosmogenesis*, she wrote:

The devil is now called Darkness by the Church, whereas, in the Bible he is called the 'Son of God' (see Job), the bright star of early morning, Lucifer (see Isaiah). There is a whole philosophy of dogmatic craft in the reason why the first Archangel, who sprang from the depths of Chaos, was called Lux (Lucifer), the 'Luminous Son of the Morning,' or manvantaric Dawn. He was transformed by the Church into Lucifer or Satan, because he is higher and older than Jehovah, and had to be sacrificed to the new dogma.[6]

---

see, was to remove the dust of the past and Blavatsky's prejudices and place both method and teachings squarely in the evolutionary development of human consciousness. It is important to remember, however, that Rudolf Steiner did this as a Theosophist, within Theosophy. Anthroposophy, which he taught from the beginning, began as, and was for the first ten years of his public (and private) esoteric work, explicitly his contribution to Theosophy." (Christopher Bamford, "Introduction," pp 15–16, in Rudolf Steiner, *Spiritualism, Madam Blavatsky, and Theosophy: An Eyewitness View of Occult History*, ed. by Christopher Bamford, Anthroposophic Press, 2001.) [For further information on Rudolf Steiner, see Carrie Tomko, "Anthroposophy: The Occult Influences of Rudolf Steiner," *Journal* of the Spiritual Counterfeits Project, Part I, Vol. 25:2–25:3, 2001, pp 66–70, and Part II, Vol. 25:4–26:1, 2002, pp 60–70; obtainable through http://www.scp-inc.org.]

1. Theosophical Society in America, "Introduction to the Theosophical Society," http://www.theosophical.org/society/intro/index.html, printed 07/19/04.

2. H. P. Blavatsky, *The Secret Doctrine: The Synthesis of Science, Religion, and Philosophy, Vol. II—Anthropogenesis*, Theosophical University Press, 1999 reprint of 1888 ed., p 515 (cited below as Blavatsky, *Secret Doctrine, Vol. II*).

3. Ibid., p 420.

4. Fred Matser, "Nature Is My God," an interview with Mikhail Gorbachev, *Resurgence* 184, http://resurgence.gn.apc.org/184/gorbachev.htm, printed 07/19/04.

5. H. P. Blavatsky, *The Secret Doctrine: The Synthesis of Science, Religion, and Philosophy, Vol. I—Cosmogenesis*, Theosophical University Press, 1999 reprint of 1888 ed., p 381, footnote (cited below as Blavatsky, *Secret Doctrine, Vol. I*).

6. Ibid., pp 70–71.

Blavatsky went on to hail Satan as "Saviour" of man:

> Satan and his rebellious host would thus prove, when the meaning of the allegory is explained, to have refused to create physical man, only to become the direct Saviours and the Creators of 'divine Man'. . . . For, instead of remaining a mere blind, functioning medium, impelled and guided by fathomless Law, the 'rebellious' Angel claimed and enforced his right of independent judgment and will, his right of free-agency and responsibility, since man and angel are alike under Karmic Law.[1]

For her, Satan is the one who frees man from death: "Thus 'Satan' once he ceases to be viewed in the superstitious, dogmatic, un-philosophical spirit of the Churches, grows into the grandiose image of one who made of *terrestrial* a *divine* man; who gave him, throughout the long cycle of Mahâ-kalpa the law of the Spirit of Life, and made him free from the Sin of Ignorance, hence of death."[2]

In Volume II, *Anthropogenesis*, Blavatsky continued to exalt the Devil. She said: "Satan will now be shown, in the teaching of the Secret Doctrine, allegorized as Good, and Sacrifice, a God of Wisdom, under different names."[3] Blavatsky added,

> In this case it is but natural—even from the dead letter standpoint—to view *Satan*, the Serpent of Genesis, as the real creator and benefactor, the Father of Spiritual mankind. For it is he who was the 'Harbinger of Light,' bright radiant Lucifer, who opened the eyes of the automaton *created* by Jehovah, as alleged; and he who was the first to whisper: 'in the day ye eat thereof ye shall be as Elohim, knowing good and evil'—can only be regarded in the light of a Saviour. An 'adversary' to Jehovah the '*personating* spirit,' he still remains in esoteric truth the ever-loving 'Messenger' (the angel), the Seraphim and Cherubim who both *knew* well, and *loved* still more, and who conferred on us spiritual, instead of physical immortality—the latter a kind of *static* immortality that would have transformed man into an undying 'Wandering Jew.'[4]

In the end, Blavatsky raises up Satan as "the highest divine Spirit:"

> To make the point clear once for all: that which the clergy of every dogmatic religion—pre-eminently the Christian—points out as Satan, the enemy of God, is in reality, the highest divine Spirit—(occult Wisdom on Earth)—in its naturally antagonistic character to every worldly, evanescent illusion, dogmatic or ecclesiastical religions included. Thus, the Latin Church, intolerant, bigoted and cruel to all who do not choose to be its slaves; the Church which calls itself the bride of Christ, and the trustee at the same time of Peter, to whom the rebuke of the Master 'get thee behind me Satan' was justly addressed; and again the Protestant Church which, while calling itself Christian, paradoxically replaces the New Dispensation by the old 'Law of Moses' which Christ openly repudiated: both these Churches are fighting against divine Truth, when repudiating and slandering the Dragon of esoteric (because *divine*) Wisdom.'[5]

For her, "In antiquity and *reality*, Lucifer, or *Luciferus*, is the name of the angelic Entity presiding over the *light of truth* as over the light of the day."[6]

The logical consequence of these beliefs is that, for Blavatsky,

> The *Fall* was the *result of man's knowledge*, for his 'eyes were opened.' Indeed, he was taught Wisdom and the hidden knowledge by the 'Fallen Angel,' for the latter had become from that day his *Manas*, Mind and Self-Consciousness. . . . And now it stands proven that Satan, or the Red *Fiery* Dragon, the 'Lord of Phosphorus' (brimstone was a theological improvement), and *Lucifer*, or 'Light-Bearer,' is in us: it is our *Mind*—our tempter and Redeemer, our intelligent liberator and Saviour from pure animalism.[7]

1. Ibid., pp 193–194.
2. Ibid., p 198.
3. Blavatsky, *Secret Doctrine, Vol. II*, p 237.
4. Ibid., p 243.
5. Ibid., p 377.
6. Ibid., p 512
7. Ibid., p 513.

INVERTING CHRISTIAN TRADITION

With this theological foundation, Blavatsky raged against other aspects, great and small, of the Christian tradition.

Blavatsky dismissed the God of Abraham, Isaac, and Jacob as a "tribal god:"

History shows in every race and even tribe, especially in the Semitic nations, the natural impulse to exalt its own tribal deity above all others to the hegemony of the gods; and proves that the god of the Israelites was such a *tribal God*, and no more, even though the Christian Church, following the lead of the 'chosen' people, is pleased to enforce the worship of that one particular deity, and to anathematize all the others.[1]

She adds that

Jehovah has ever been in antiquity only 'a god *among* other *Gods*,' (lxxxii Psalm). The *Lord* appears to Abraham, and while saying, 'I am the *Almighty God*,' yet adds, 'I will establish my covenant to be *a* God unto thee' (Abraham) and unto his *seed after him* (Gen. xvii. 7)—not unto Aryan Europeans.[2]

("Aryan Europeans" did abandon the "tribal" worship of Jehovah during the last century. They idolized Hitler, the Aryan race, and the German nation instead—with gruesome results.)

Blavatsky moved on to assail Christ. In *Isis Unveiled*, Blavatsky said,

The present volumes have been written to small purpose if they have not shown, 1, that Jesus, the Christ-God, is a myth concocted two centuries after the real Hebrew Jesus died; 2, that, therefore, he never had any authority to give Peter, or anyone else, plenary power; 3, that, even if he had given such authority, the word Petra (rock) referred to the revealed truths of the Petroma, not to him who thrice denied him; and that besides, the apostolic succession is a gross and palpable fraud; 4, that the *Gospel according to Matthew* is a fabrication based on a wholly different manuscript. The whole thing, therefore, is an imposition alike upon priest and penitent.[3]

(With similar skepticism, Jack Spong, then serving as Bishop of the Episcopal Diocese of Newark, wrote in 1998: "Since God can no longer be conceived in theistic terms, it becomes nonsensical to seek to understand Jesus as the incarnation of the theistic deity. So the Christology of the ages is bankrupt."[4])

Blavatsky also claimed in 1877 that the miracles of Simon Magus, "the Great Power of God," were "more wonderful, more varied, and better attested than those either of the apostles or of the Galilean philosopher himself."[5] (Likewise, Bishop Spong, who considers himself to be a ground-breaking, reformist theologian, wrote in 1998, "The miracle stories of the New Testament can no longer be interpreted in a post-Newtonian world as supernatural events performed by an incarnate deity."[6])

Blavatsky's description of "Sophia" should give pause to those who invoke her as a female Third Person of the Godhead. In *Isis Unveiled*, she said,

The various cosmogonies show that the Archæal Universal Soul was held by every nation as the 'mind' of the Demiurgic Creator, the *Sophia* of the Gnostics, or *the Holy Ghost as a female principle*.[7] This may be the spiritual

---

1. Ibid., pp507–508.
2. Ibid., p508.
3. H.P. Blavatsky, *Isis Unveiled: Vol. II, Theology*, Theosophical University Press, 1988 reprint of 1877 ed., p544 (cited below as Blavatsky, *Isis Unveiled: Vol. II*).
4. Bishop John S. Spong, "A Call for a New Reformation," http://www.dioceseofnewark.org/vox20598.html, Thesis 2, printed 07/19/04 (cited below as Spong, "New Reformation").
5. Blavatsky, *Isis Unveiled: Vol. II, Theology*, p341.
6. Spong, "New Reformation," Thesis 5.
7. H.P. Blavatsky, *Isis Unveiled: Vol. I, Science*, Theosophical University Press, 1988 reprint of 1877 ed., p130 (cited below as Blavatsky, *Isis Unveiled: Vol. I*).

origin of "inclusive language" for the Third Person of the Trinity. In *The Secret Doctrine*, Blavatsky added: "In the great Valentian gospel *Pistis Sophia* (§ 361) it is taught that of the three Powers emanating from the Holy Names of the Three Τριδυναμεις, that of Sophia (the Holy Ghost according to these gnostics—the most cultured of all), resides in the planet Venus or Lucifer.[1]

The female "Sophia" resides in the planet Lucifer; you heard it here first.

Blavatsky said in 1877 that religious truth would be found in the aggregate of the religions: "Our examination of the multitudinous religious faiths that mankind, early and late, have professed, most assuredly indicates that they have all been derived from one primitive source. It would seem as if they were all but different modes of expressing the yearning of the imprisoned human soul for intercourse with supernal spheres. . . . Combined, their aggregate represents one eternal truth; separate, they are but shades of human error and the signs of imperfection."[2] She added, "It but needs the right perception of things objective to finally discover that the only world of reality is the subjective"[3] Maybe postmodernism is not so new, after all.

POPULATION CONTROL—IN 1888

In *The Secret Doctrine*, Blavatsky urged that an astrologically based form of natural family planning be taught to "the armies of the ragged and the poor:" "If instead of being taught in Sunday Schools useless lessons from the Bible, the armies of the ragged and the poor were taught Astrology—so far, at any rate, as the occult properties of the Moon and its hidden influences on generation are concerned, then there would be little need to fear increase of the population nor resort to the questionable literature of the Malthusians for its arrest."[4] (At the time, world population was about 1.6 billion people, roughly one-quarter of the current human population.) In the 20th Century, many others would follow the trail that Blavatsky blazed, and would concern themselves with limiting reproduction among the poor.

EVOLUTIONARY RACISM

Before 1950, New Age authors spoke more bluntly about race than is usual now.

In 1877, Blavatsky quoted anthropologist Alfred R. Wallace as saying, "it must inevitably follow that the higher—the more intellectual and moral—must displace the lower and more degraded races;" after a long period of "natural selection," the world will again be "inhabited by a single, nearly homogeneous race, no individual of which will be inferior *to the noblest specimens of existing humanity*."[5] Blavatsky approved of the opinions and "scientific methods" of this "great anthropologist," and added, "what he says above clashes in no way with our kabalistic assertions. Allow to ever-progressing nature, to the great law of the 'survival of the fittest,' one step beyond Mr. Wallace's deductions, and we have in the future the possibility—nay, the assurance of a race, which, like the Vril-ya of Bulwer-Lytton's *Coming Race*, will be but one remove from the primitive 'Sons of God.'"[6] (*The Coming Race* was an 1871 novel by a British occultist. It was based on the existence of a subterranean race, the Vril-ya, that were "psychically far in advance of the human species." Whoever mastered the energy of *vril* could "enjoy total mastery over all nature.")[7]

1. Blavatsky, *The Secret Doctrine, Vol. II*, p512.
2. Blavatsky, *Isis Unveiled: Vol. II,* p639.
3. Ibid., p639.
4. Blavatsky, *The Secret Doctrine, Vol. I.*, p228, footnote.
5. Blavatsky, *Isis Unveiled: Vol. I,* p296.
6. Ibid., p296.
7. Nicholas Goodrick-Clarke, *The Occult Roots of Nazism*, New York University Press, 1992, pp218–219.

In 1888, Blavatsky said,

Mankind is obviously divided into god-informed men and lower human creatures. The intellectual difference between the Aryan and other civilized nations and such savages as the South Sea Islanders, is inexplicable on any other grounds. No amount of culture, nor generations of training amid civilization, could raise such human specimens as the Bushmen, the Veddhas of Ceylon, and some African tribes, to the same intellectual level as the Aryans, the Semites, and the Turanians so called. The 'sacred spark' is missing in them and it is they who are the only *inferior* races of the globe, now happily—owing to the wise adjustment of nature which ever works in that direction—fast dying out. Verily mankind is 'of one blood,' *but not of the same essence.*[1]

She saw the extinction of "inferior races" as part of mankind's evolution:

a series of other less favoured groups—the failures of nature—will, like some individual men, vanish from the human family without even leaving a trace behind.[2]

A process of decimation is taking place all over the globe, among those races, whose 'time is up'—among just those stocks, be it remarked, which esoteric philosophy regards as the senile representatives of the archaic nations. It is inaccurate to maintain that the extinction of a lower race is *invariably* due to cruelties or abuses perpetrated by colonists. . . . Redskins, Eskimos, Papuans, Australians, Polynesians, etc., etc.—all are dying out. . . . The tide-wave of incarnating EGOS has rolled past them to harvest experience in more developed and less senile stocks; and their extinction is hence a Karmic necessity.[3]

No URI document says anything of this kind. However, there is a double standard in effect regarding the treatment of Blavatsky's writings. In today's mainstream public discourse, any conservative or traditionalist writer who ever said such things is dismissed as racist, and his entire body of work is considered unworthy of attention. However, Blavatsky, a spiritual predecessor of today's New Age movement, still gets respect from Theosophists and occultists; her followers are deemed to deserve a place at the interfaith table.

THE THEOSOPHICAL SWASTIKA

Part of Blavatsky's pantheon was the seven-headed "Serpent of Darkness" bearing the swastika on its crowns. She said,

And this 'true and perfect Serpent' is the seven-lettered God who is now credited with being Jehovah, and Jesus *One with him.* To this Seven-vowelled god the candidate for initiation is sent by Christos, in the *Pistis Sophia,* a work earlier than St. John's *Revelation,* and evidently of the same school. . . . These seven vowels are represented by the Swastika signs on the crowns of the seven heads of the Serpent of Eternity, in India, among esoteric Buddhists, in Egypt, in Chaldea, etc., etc., and among the Initiates of every other country. . . . The seven-headed serpent has more than one signification in the Arcane teachings. It is the seven-headed *Draco,* each of whose heads is a star of the Lesser Bear; but it was also, and pre-eminently, the Serpent of Darkness (i.e., inconceivable and incomprehensible) whose seven heads were the seven *Logoi,* the reflections of the one and first manifested Light—the universal LOGOS.[4]

The Bible describes a seven-headed animal, as well—but does so to warn against it rather than to

1. Blavatsky, *The Secret Doctrine, Vol. II,* p 421, footnote; see also pp 162, 168, 195, 196, 197, 249, 446, 779, and 780 for similar statements. On p 425, she contradicts these statements, and argues against "dividing humanity into *superior* and *inferior* races."

2. Ibid., p 446.

3. Ibid., pp 779–780.

4. Blavatsky, *The Secret Doctrine, Vol. I,* pp 410–411.

praise it. The book of Revelation portrays "a beast rising out of the sea, with ten horns and seven heads, with ten diadems upon its horns and a blasphemous name upon its heads," (Rev. 13:1) who receives its authority from the Dragon (Rev. 13:2, 4).[1]

The Theosophists have retained the swastika symbol. Since 1881,[2] the emblem of the Theosophical Society has included the image of a snake eating its tail, with an encircled swastika where the serpent's head meets its tail.[3] The Nazis borrowed the swastika symbol and ideas of Aryan racial supremacy from the Thule Society and other German occultists, and then made their own sanguinary adaptations to occultism.[4]

The premier historian of the occult roots of Nazism and neo-Nazism, Nicholas Goodrick-Clarke, explains the connection between Theosophy and Nazism:

> Even before the First World War, occult-racist *völkisch* sects in Austria and Germany had quarried the ideas of Theosophy for the Aryo-Germanic cult of Ariosophy. Notions of elite priesthoods, secret gnosis, a prehistoric golden age, the conspiracy of demonic racial inferiors and millennial prophecies of Aryan salvation all occur in the writings of Guido von List (1848–1919) and Jörg Lanz von Liebenfels (1874–1954) and their followers. Their ideas and symbols filtered through to several anti-Semitic and nationalist groups in late Wilhelmian Germany, from which the early Nazi Party emerged in Munich after the war. At least two Ariosophists were closely involved with Reichsführer Heinrich Himmler in the 1930s, contributing to his projects in Germanic prehistory, SS order ceremonial and his visionary plans for the Greater Germanic Reich in the third millennium. . . . Given the neo-pagan revivalism and frequent antipathy toward Christianity among fascists, Theosophy can offer such individuals a scheme of religious belief that ignores Christianity in favor of a mixture of mythical traditions and new scientific ideas from contemporary scholarship in anthropology, etymology, ancient history and comparative religion. In the nineteenth and early twentieth centuries, Theosophy itself tended to be associated with liberal and emancipatory causes by its leaders in Britain and India. Here one recalls Helena Blavatsky's support of Garibaldi's struggle in Italy and Annie Besant's championship of the Indian National Congress. However, the very structure of Theosophical beliefs can lend themselves to illiberal adoption. The implicit authority of the hidden mahatmas from a Lemuro-Atlantean dynasty with superhuman wisdom is easily transmogrified by racist enthusiasts into a new hierarchical social order based on the mystique of the blood. And the notion of an occult gnosis in Blavatskyan Theosophy, together with the charge that alien (Christian) beliefs have obscured this spiritual heritage, also fits the need to ascribe a prehistoric pedigree to modern racial nationalism.[5]

1. Charles Upton adds, "There is no better illustration of how mixing constellations-of-symbols integral to different religions can result in Satanic parodies. To assimilate to Jehovah and Christ the seven-headed cobra who overshadowed Gautama Buddha's meditation is, in Judeo-Christian terms, to assimilate Jehovah to Satan and Christ to Antichrist." (E-mail from Charles Upton to Lee Penn, 08/21/04).

2. Nicholas Goodrick-Clarke, *Hitler's Priestess: Savitri Devi, the Hindu-Aryan Myth, and Neo-Nazism*, New York University Press, 1998, p 35. He says, "Despite the universalism of Theosophy, its Aryans and swastika had a potent influence on mystical racism in Germany and Austria from the late 1890s onward."

3. Steven Heller, *The Swastika: Symbol Beyond Redemption?*, Allworth Press, 2000, pp 47–48; an example of this image is on p 48.

4. Nicholas Goodrick-Clarke, *The Occult Roots of Nazism*, New York University Press, 1992; Steven Heller, *The Swastika: Symbol Beyond Redemption?*, Allworth Press, 2000, pp 41–78.

5. Nicholas Goodrick-Clarke, *Black Sun: Aryan Cults, Esoteric Nazism, and the Politics of Identity*, New York University Press, 2002, pp 85–86. Another recent account by a journalist says the same: "The rationale behind many later Nazi projects can be traced back—through the writings of von List, von Sebottendorff, and von Liebenfels—to ideas first popularized by Blavatsky. A caste system of races, the importance of ancient alphabets (notably the runes), the superiority of the Aryans (a white race with its origins in the Himalayas), an 'initiated' version of astrology and astronomy, the cosmic truths coded within pagan myths . . . all of these and more can be found both in Blavatsky and in the Nazi Party itself, specifically in the ideology of its Dark Creature, the SS. It was, after all, Blavatsky who pointed out the supreme occult significance of the swastika. And it was a follower of Blavatsky who was instrumental in introducing the *Protocols of the Elders of Zion* to a Western European community eager for a scapegoat." (Peter Levenda, *Unholy Alliance: A History of Nazi Involvement with the Occult*, Continuum, 2002, p 40). The *Protocols* were an anti-Semitic forgery composed in France in the late 1800s, plagiarized and

DRAGON-WORSHIP:
THE RELIGION OF THE ANCIENTS—AND OF THE FUTURE

Blavatsky expected the current world religions to disappear; the

religion of the ancients is the religion of the future. A few centuries more, and there will linger no sectarian belief in either of the great religions of humanity. Brahmanism and Buddhism, Christianity and Mohammedanism will all disappear before the mighty rush of *facts.* . . . But this can only come to pass when the world returns to the grand religion of the past; the *knowledge* of those majestic systems which preceded by far Brahmanism, and even the primitive monotheism of the ancient Chaldeans.[1]

Blavatsky claimed that the universal "religion of the ancients" was the worship of the Dragon and the Sun. She said,

The tradition of the Dragon and the Sun is echoed in every part of the world, both in its civilized and semi-savage regions. It took rise in the whisperings about secret initiations among the profane, and was established universally through the once universal heliolatrous religion. There was a time when the four parts of the world were covered with the temples sacred to the Sun and the Dragon; but the cult is now preserved mostly in China and the Buddhist countries. . . . We find (a) the priests assuming the name of the gods they served; (b) the 'Dragons' held throughout all antiquity as the symbols of Immortality and Wisdom, of secret Knowledge and of Eternity; and (c) the hierophants of Egypt, of Babylon, and India, styling themselves generally the 'sons of the Dragon' and 'Serpents;' thus the teachings of the Secret Doctrine are thereby corroborated.[2]

The memory of this ancient religion was "the origin of the new *Satanic* myth" of Christians.[3]

The restored worship of the Dragon and the Sun is what Blavatsky expects to be the New Religion of the future. Thus, she predicted a literal fulfillment of the prophecy in Revelation that "Men worshiped the dragon, for he had given his authority to the beast" (Rev. 13:4).

modified from Maurice Joly's 1864 satire of the regime of Napoleon III, *Dialogue aux enfers entre Montesquieu et Machiavel.* James Webb, a historian of occult movements, says, "It is probable that the forgery entered Russia with Yuliana Glinka (1844–1918), the daughter of a Russian diplomat who spent her time in Paris and St. Petersburg and was a Theosophist devoted to Madame Blavatsky." (James Webb, *The Occult Establishment*, Open Court, 1976, p 217, for the quote and for the overview of the history of the *Protocols.*) Charles Upton comments, "The swastika is an ancient (Paleolithic) and nearly universal symbol of Divine action, with no sinister connotations until its use by the Nazis and their precursors. In modern times it appeared on Rudyard Kipling's books, and was even the emblem of the British War Savings Scheme during World War I. But its continued use by the Theosophical Society *after* World War II is as sinister as can be." (E-mail from Charles Upton to Lee Penn, 8/21/04).

  1. Blavatsky, *Isis Unveiled: Vol. I*, p 613.
  2. Blavatsky, *The Secret Doctrine, Vol. II*, pp 378–379. Charles Upton comments on Blavatsky's theological confusion: "It is true that many archaic Near Eastern religions, as well as Hinduism and Buddhism, took the serpent as a symbol of wisdom, a meaning which is undoubtedly reflected in the brazen serpent of Exodus. But the dominant meaning of the serpent in the Judeo-Christian tradition is clearly negative; it most often symbolizes not Divine Wisdom but rather a lower dualistic knowledge, the 'knowledge of good and evil,' which *obscures* Divine Wisdom. Furthermore, the essentially negative Judeo-Christian symbol of the dragon is derived from such Babylonian figures as Tiamat (equivalent in many ways to the Biblical Leviathan), the Chaos Monster who is slain in the Divine act of creation; this is basically what "dragon-slaying" has come to mean in the West. In China, on the other hand, the dragon is the Celestial Power, nearly equivalent to the Christian Holy Spirit. For Blavatsky to confuse the dragons of the East and the West shows "comparative religion" at its absolute worst, since it necessarily identifies the dragon of the Apocalypse with the Holy Spirit and the Celestial Dragon of China with Satan. One cannot presume to compare religions until one at least shows a willingness to understand them in their own terms." (E-mail from Charles Upton to Lee Penn, 08/21/04).
  3. Blavatsky, *The Secret Doctrine, Vol. II*, p 378.

HATRED FOR THE CHRISTIAN CHURCHES

Blavatsky's proclamation of "universal brotherhood" did not extend to Christians and their churches. In 1877, she said that *Isis Unveiled* was

> in particular directed against theological Christianity, the chief opponent of free thought. It contains not one word against the pure teachings of Jesus, but unsparingly denounces their debasement into pernicious ecclesiastical systems that are ruinous to man's faith in his immortality and his God, and subversive of all moral restraint. We cast our gauntlet at the dogmatic theologians who would enslave both history and science; and especially at the Vatican, whose despotic pretensions have become hateful to the greater portion of enlightened Christendom.[1]

In 1888, Blavatsky reiterated: "the Secret Doctrine must some day become the just Karma of the Churches—more anti-Christian than the representative assemblies of the most confirmed Materialists and Atheists."[2]

THE WORLDWIDE INFLUENCE OF
BLAVATSKY AND OF THEOSOPHY

Numerous authorities, from the Vatican to interfaith movement historians and scholarly supporters of Theosophy, confirm that Theosophy has decisively influenced occult, spiritualist, "New Thought," and New Age movements around the world since 1875. Blavatsky's work has borne plentiful dark fruit.

The Vatican's report on the New Age movement, released in early 2003, said that 19th-Century esotericism

> reached its clearest form in the ideas of Helena Blavatsky, a Russian medium who founded the *Theosophical Society* with Henry Olcott in New York in 1875. The Society aimed to fuse elements of Eastern and Western traditions in an evolutionary type of spiritualism. It had three main aims: 1. 'To form a nucleus of the Universal Brotherhood of Humanity, without distinction of race, creed, caste or colour.' 2. 'To encourage the study of comparative religion, philosophy and science.' 3. 'To investigate unexplained laws of Nature and the powers latent in man.' "The significance of these objectives . . . should be clear. The first objective implicitly rejects the 'irrational bigotry' and 'sectarianism' of traditional Christianity as perceived by spiritualists and theosophists. . . . It is not immediately obvious from the objectives themselves that, for theosophists, 'science' meant the occult sciences and philosophy, the *occulta philosophia*, that the laws of nature were of an occult or psychic nature, and that comparative religion was expected to unveil a 'primordial tradition' ultimately modelled on a Hermeticist *philosophia perennis*"[3]. . . . A prominent component of Mrs. Blavatsky's writings was the emancipation of women, which involved an attack on the 'male' God of Judaism, of Christianity and of Islam. She urged people to return to the mother-goddess of Hinduism and to the practice of feminine virtues. This continued under the

---

1. Blavatsky, *Isis Unveiled, Vol. II*, "Preface to Part II," p iv.
2. Blavatsky, *The Secret Doctrine, Vol. II*, p 228.
3. For the sentences inside the double quote marks, the Vatican was citing Wouter J. Hanegraaff, *New Age Religion and Western Culture: Esotericism in the Mirror of Secular Thought*, State University of New York Press, 1998, p 449. Charles Upton comments, "The Traditionalist School [Schuon, A. Coomaraswamy, Guénon, et al.] also speaks of a 'primordial tradition,' but denies that this tradition can function as a viable religious dispensation in our time. All religions ultimately spring from the same root; as the Jews and Muslims say, Adam was the first prophet. But the tree has branched since those times, symbolized in Genesis by the fall of the Tower of Babel and the 'confusion of tongues'; the only paths to God are now the various revealed religions. A revived 'religio perennis' can only be a counterfeit universalism leading to the regime of the Antichrist." (E-mail from Charles Upton to Lee Penn, 04/27/04).

guidance of Annie Besant, who was in the vanguard of the feminist movement. Wicca and 'women's spirituality' carry on this struggle against 'patriarchal' Christianity today.[1]

The authors of the *New Age Almanac* say,

Theosophy became the seedbed that nurtured the important new movements that would emerge so forcefully in the twentieth century. Several hundred new occult organizations can be traced directly to the Theosophical Society. For example, drawing upon the esoteric work initiated by Theosophy, ritual magicians have attempted to attain the mastery of the world through occult means in a measure only hinted at in theosophical circles. . . . Theosophy also nurtured a reborn astrology. . . . Beginning with minuscule astrological groups in the late nineteenth century, astrology made an astounding comeback to become the most pervasive popular occult practice in the latter part of the twentieth century. Theosophy also provided the prime channel through which Hinduism and Buddhism reached out to claim non-Asian supporters. Through theosophical literature, leaders, and centers, Eastern religious ideas flowed into the West. . . . Many of the early Buddhist groups in the West began in theosophical lodges. Ultimately, however, Theosophy proved itself more akin to Hinduism, and the new Hinduism of the Indian Renaissance of the nineteenth century used Theosophy effectively in its movement to Europe and North America. . . . Finally, through the success of theosophical disciples such as Edgar Cayce, reincarnation reached a popular audience beyond the Theosophical Society and earned the acceptance of the vast majority of the metaphysical community.[2]

Another observer of new religious movements says, "Rudolf Steiner's Anthroposophy, Krishnamurti, J. I. Gurdjieff, and P. D. Ouspensky all stem directly from the activities of the Theosophical Society, and the development of modern Buddhism, and especially in its indigenous form in present-day Sri Lanka, is largely due to Olcott's work."[3] (Olcott and Blavatsky were co-founders of the Theosophical Society.)

Marcus Braybrooke, a leading historian of the interfaith movement, said in 1992 that "Theosophists can claim to have been amongst the first to suggest a unity of religions."[4] He added,

The society insists that it is not offering a new system of thought, but merely underscoring certain universal concepts of God, nature and man that have been known to wise men in all ages and that may be found in the teachings of all the great religions. Emphasis is placed on mystical experience. A distinction is made between inner, or esoteric, and outer, or exoteric, teaching. It is said that all the historic world religions contain inner teaching which is essentially the same, despite external differences. This teaching is monistic in character, suggesting an underlying all-encompassing unity. Theosophy has also shown a preoccupation with the occult. . . . Theosophy has been a means of introducing many Westerners to the wisdom of the East. Some theosophists, notably Henry Steel Olcott and Annie Besant, played a part in the spiritual renaissance of Buddhism and Hinduism at the end of the last century and the beginning of this century. Besides the Theosophical Society, the teachings of theosophy have influenced Westerners through a variety of other organizations, such as Rosicrucianism, the Liberal Catholic Church, World Goodwill, and the Lucis Trust.[5]

1. Pontifical Council For Culture and Pontifical Council For Interreligious Dialogue, "Jesus Christ The Bearer Of The Water Of Life: A Christian reflection on the "New Age," 2003, section 2.3.2, http://www.vatican.va/roman_curia/pontifical_councils/interelg/documents/rc_pc_interelg_doc_20030203_new-age_en.html, printed 02/3/03.

2. J. Gordon Melton, Jerome Clark, and Aidan A. Kelly, *New Age Almanac*, Visible Ink Press, 1991, pp 6–7.

3. George D. Chryssides, *Exploring New Religions*, Cassell, 1999, p 87. Charles Upton notes, however, that "Gurdjieff probably lifted something from Blavatsky, but his core teachings stem from Sufi and Hesychast practices taken illegitimately out of context and mixed with other influences, notably hypnosis and psychic control. Krishnamurti as a young man was adopted by the Theosophical Society who trained him for the role of their new 'World Teacher,' a role he rejected. His own later teachings could be called the polar opposite of those of the Society." (E-mail from Charles Upton to Lee Penn, July 2, 2003.)

4. Marcus Braybrooke, *Pilgrimage of Hope: One Hundred Years of Global Interfaith Dialogue*, Crossroad, 1992, p 266.

5. Ibid., p 267.

Dr. Stephan Hoeller, Director of Studies for the Gnostic Society of Los Angeles, says, "C. G. Jung's statement that Blavatsky's Theosophy as well as Rudolf Steiner's Anthroposophy (a variant of Theosophy) were both pure Gnosticism in Hindu dress contains a large measure of truth."[1]

Historian K. Paul Johnson, who has written several scholarly histories of Theosophy, said:

A remarkable feature of Theosophy's history is the disparity between its miniscule membership and its vast and varied cultural influence. Blavatsky's ideas inspired leading figures in the development of modern art, most notably Wassily Kandinsky and Piet Mondrian. Theosophical influence in literature affected the Irish Literary Renaissance, in which William Butler Yeats and AE (George Russell) were prominent. Political activism in colonial India and Ceylon owed an immense debt to Theosophical influence. In the West, many social movements such as educational reform, women's suffrage, and abolition of capital punishment were advanced by the efforts of early Theosophists. But in no field of endeavor has Theosophy's influence been as great as in introducing Eastern religious ideas to the Western public.[2]

Joscelyn Godwin, author of *The Theosophical Enlightenment*, said that Theosophy and its offshoot movements were an historically unprecedented rejection by a civilization of its own tradition. Blavatsky believed that the West had better look to the East if it wanted to learn what real philosophy was (or to relearn what it once knew). With equal certainty she despised every form of institutional Christianity. As a result, her Society, its members, and its offshoots became the main vehicle for Buddhist and Hindu philosophies to enter the Western consciousness, not merely as an academic study but as something worth embracing. In so doing, they paved the way for the best and the worst of the oriental gurus who have taken up residence in the West. They introduced into the vernacular such concepts as karma and reincarnation, meditation, and the spiritual path. Together with the Western occult tradition, the Theosophists have provided almost all the underpinnings of the 'New Age' movement. . . . But these efforts themselves are something characteristically Western. . . . No previous civilization has ever had the interest, the resources, or the inner need to hold the entire world in its intellectual embrace; to take the terrifying step of renouncing, even blaspheming, its own religious tradition, in the quest for a more open and rational view; to publish freely those secrets that were formerly only given under the seal of initiation; and, in short, to plunge humanity into the spiritual alembic in which we find ourselves today.[3]

1. Stephan A. Hoeller, *Gnosticism: New Light on the Ancient Tradition of Inner Knowing*, Quest Books/Theosophical Publishing House, 2002, p 169.

2. K. Paul Johnson, *Initiates of Theosophical Masters*, State University of New York Press, 1995, p 113.

3. Godwin, *The Theosophical Enlightenment*, p 379. An alembic is a laboratory device used for distillation.

11

ALICE A. BAILEY
AND THE LUCIS TRUST

BETWEEN 1922 AND 1949, Alice Bailey published 24 books of "revelations," most of which she claimed to have channeled from the Tibetan ascended spiritual master Djwhal Khul. All these books remain in print through the Lucis Trust, and are widely available. A standard almanac on the New Age movement says, "The Arcane School and the books of Alice Bailey have contributed heavily to the concept and language of the New Age Movement."[1] A recent survey of new religious movements says that Bailey's group "is widespread in the Western world and membership is probably a few thousand people worldwide."[2]

The Rev. Betsy Stang (a Wittenberg Center interfaith minister who served on the URI Interim Global Council in 2000,[3] and who was a donor to the URI in 2002[4]), said of Alice Bailey's writings, "Some of Bailey's writing is really remarkable, very Gothic. You would put her with Blavatsky, Gurdjieff, and Steiner. She is historically very important. In my mind, Bailey has beautiful, poetic evocations in her books."[5]

Here follow some of Bailey's "beautiful, poetic evocations." As you read them, recall that Alice Bailey's present-day followers are public supporters of the URI, and have been donors to the movement. Note, as well, that World Goodwill, an affiliate of the Lucis Trust, enjoys UN recognition as a "Non-Governmental Organization." As World Goodwill says, "World Goodwill is an accredited non-governmental organization with the Department of Public Information of the United Nations. It maintains informal relations with certain of the Specialized Agencies and with a wide range of national and international non-governmental organisations. World Goodwill is an activity of the Lucis Trust, which is on the Roster of the United Nations Economic and Social Council."[6]

At the beginning of each of the Alice Bailey books that were—supposedly—dictated by the "Tibetan," there is this ambiguous disclaimer by the spirit guide:

> The books that I have written are sent out with no claim for their acceptance. They may, or may not, be correct, true and useful. It is for you to ascertain their truth by right practice and by the exercise of the intuition. Neither I nor A.A.B. is the least interested in having them acclaimed as inspired writings, or in having anyone speak of them (with bated breath) as being the work of one of the Masters. If they present truth in such a way that it follows sequentially upon that already offered in the world teachings, if the information given raises the aspiration

---

1. J. Gordon Melton, Jerome Clark, and Aidan A. Kelly, *New Age Almanac*, Visible Ink Press, 1991, p10.
2. Christopher Partridge, ed., *New Religions: A Guide—New Religious Movements, Sects, and Alternative Spiritualities*, Oxford University Press, 2004, p329 (cited below as Partridge, *New Religions*).
3. United Religions Initiative, "Interim Global Council Membership in 2000," *Annual Report* 2000, p8.
4. United Religions Initiative, "Honoring URI Donors and Volunteers," *Annual Report* 2002 leaflet.
5. The Rev. Betsy Stang (Wittenberg Center for Alternative Resources), telephone interview by Lee Penn, 12/10/97.
6. Lucis Trust, "World Goodwill," http://www.lucistrust.org/goodwill/index.shtml, printed 08/06/04.

and the will-to-serve from the plane of the emotions to that of the mind (the plane whereon the Masters can be found) then they will have served their purpose. If the teaching conveyed calls forth a response from the illumined mind of the worker in the world, and brings a flashing forth of his intuition, then let that teaching be accepted. But not otherwise.[1]

This is akin to a software warranty written by a crafty lawyer: you may use this, but we make no guarantee that it will be "useful." The "Tibetan" is correct about this: those who pursue the Theosophical way do so at their own risk.

CONTINUING BLAVATSKY'S WORK

Alice Bailey positioned herself as a follower of Blavatsky, and as her spiritual successor. Bailey praised Blavatsky on the acknowledgment page of *A Treatise On Cosmic Fire*, saying that the book is "dedicated with gratitude to Helena Petrovna Blavatsky, that great disciple who lighted her torch in the east and brought the light to Europe and America in 1875."[2] In *Running God's Plan*, her husband Foster Bailey likewise made it clear that Alice Bailey had followed Blavatsky's teachings, and claimed that both women had the same mentor, the Tibetan spirit guide Djwhal Khul:

Modern esotericism is a new phenomenon in the western world pioneered by the Tibetan teacher, Djwhal Khul, working with H. P. Blavatsky. Again, this time working with Alice Ann Bailey, the same master teacher has provided the interim teaching needed for conscious entry into the new Aquarian Age. The study of this new teaching in the books published under the name of Alice Bailey is producing a revival of esotericism and a new technique for self-development, this time with the selfless goal of world service.[3]

PRAISING THE FALLEN ANGELS
AND RE-DEFINING "666"

Bailey denied any opposition between God and the Devil, Christ and Anti-Christ: "Christ and anti-Christ are the dualities of spirituality and materialism, both in the individual and in humanity as a whole. Or you can speak of God and the Devil with the same basic implications."[4] Bailey describes Lucifer as the ruler of humanity, "Son of the Morning, The Prodigal Son."[5]

Therefore, the revolt of the angels against God was part of "the divine plan of evolution." [6] Bailey said that "the Great Law of Duality came into action, bringing about the 'fall of the angels,' as they descended from their sinless and free state of existence in order to develop full divine awareness upon earth, through the medium of material incarnation and the use of the principle of mind."[7] Bailey says that at the inception of the "divine plan," "there took place the original 'war in the heavens,' when the sons of God who responded to the divine urge to experience, to serve and to sacrifice, separated

1. Alice A. Bailey, *Esoteric Psychology—Volume II: A Treatise on the Seven Rays*, Lucis Publishing Company, 1942, p vii Blavatsky (cited below as A. Bailey, *Esoteric Psychology*).

2. Alice A. Bailey, *A Treatise on Cosmic Fire*, Lucis Publishing Company, 1925, p xi (cited below as A. Bailey, *A Treatise on Cosmic Fire*).

3. Foster Bailey, *Running God's Plan*, Lucis Publishing Company, 1972, p 27 (cited below as F. Bailey, *Running God's Plan*).

4. Alice A. Bailey, *The Externalisation of the Hierarchy*, 1957, Lucis Publishing Company, p 137 (cited below as A. Bailey, *Externalisation of the Hierarchy*).

5. Ibid., p 107.

6. Ibid., p 118.

7. Ibid., p 118.

themselves from the sons of God who responded to no such inspiration but who chose to stay in their original and high state of being."[1] In other words, the rebel angels were really the good guys.

Bailey re-interpreted the number 666 as the number of a "Heavenly Man;"[2] she also saw it as the number of "materialism, the number of the dominance of the three worlds prior to the process of reorientation and the expression of developed idealism and purpose. The third aspect expresses itself through pure materialism, and hence the three sixes."[3] She thus obscured a symbol which the Bible describes as "the number of the beast" (Rev. 13:18).

Alice Bailey said that "the Ancient of Days"[4] and the "Lord of the World, the One Initiator"[5] is a spirit named Sanat Kumara, "the Great Sacrifice."[6] He came to Earth from Venus[7] in "the middle of the Lemurian epoch, approximately eighteen million years ago" and "has remained with us ever since."[8]

Previously, Blavatsky had made clear her view of the nature and origin of Sanat Kumara.[9] Blavatsky had said that Sanat Kumara is one of "the 'mind-born Sons' of Brahmâ-Rudra (or Siva) the howling and terrific *destroyer of human passions and physical senses.*"[10] Venus, the planet from which Sanat Kumara came, "is our 'Lucifer,' the morning star."[11] The parent of Sanat Kumara is Siva, "the *destroyer;*" Siva is "the *creator* and the Saviour of Spiritual man, as he is the good gardener of nature. He weeds out the plants, human and cosmic, and kills the passions of the physical, to call to life the perceptions of the spiritual, man."[12] Blavatsky also noted that Christians call Sanat Kumara one of the fallen angels.[13] Therefore, Christians may conclude that the Theosophists' lord, whom they name Sanat Kumara, is a devil, a servant of the hostile power that Christ called "the ruler of this world" (John 14:30).

Alice Bailey believed that "for the first time" mankind is "intelligently participating and cooperating" in the "entire evolutionary process."[14] Therefore, the spiritual Hierarchy can "bring to an end the long silence which has persisted since Atlantean days" and "renew an ancient 'sharing of the secrets.'"[15]

1. Ibid., p 118.

2. A. Bailey, *A Treatise on Cosmic Fire*, p 306

3. Alice A. Bailey, *The Rays and the Initiations: Volume V, A Treatise on the Seven Rays*, 1960, Lucis Publishing Company, pp 79–80 (cited below as A. Bailey, *The Rays and the Initiations*).

4. A. Bailey, *A Treatise on Cosmic Fire*, p 211.

5. Alice A. Bailey, *Initiation, Human and Solar*, Lucis Publishing Company, 1922, p 29.

6. Ibid., p 28.

7. Ibid., p 129.

8. Ibid., p 28.

9. Charles Upton comments that the Theosophists appear to have erred in their characterization of Sanat Kumara. He says, "In Hindu doctrine, Sanat-Kumara is one of the four "mind-born sons" of Brahma the Creator. Madame Blavatsky and her Theosophical Society have distorted this figure in the following ways: 1) They name him as a son of Shiva, not Brahma. 2) They identify him with the Hebrew Ancient of Days, though he is actually a pictured as an eternal youth. 3) They consider him the 'Lord of the World' or 'planetary logos,' whereas in his original form he has nothing to do with world governance, but rather represents ascetic withdrawal from the world. 4) They claim that he came to Earth from Venus, a planet named after the Roman goddess of erotic love and identified with similar goddesses by both the Greek and the Mesopotamians, and a planet identified by the Hindus themselves with the god Shukra, analogous to the Greek Eros—and yet the Sanat-Kumara in Hindu belief is a brahmachari, a religious celibate. It's as if Blavatsky's sources were deliberately attempting to invert traditional Hindu doctrine." (E-mail from Charles Upton to Lee Penn, 08/13/04 and 10/09/04.)

10. H. P. Blavatsky, *The Secret Doctrine: The Synthesis of Science, Religion, and Philosophy, Vol. I—Cosmogenesis*, Theosophical University Press, 1999, reprint of 1888 ed., pp 458–459 (cited below as Blavatsky, *Secret Doctrine, Vol. 1*).

11. H. P. Blavatsky, *The Secret Doctrine: The Synthesis of Science, Religion, and Philosophy, Vol. II—Anthropogenesis*, Theosophical University Press, 1999, reprint of 1888 ed., p 45, footnote.

12. Blavatsky, *The Secret Doctrine, Vol. I*, p 459, footnote.

13. Ibid., p 458.

14. A. Bailey, *Externalisation of the Hierarchy*, p 685.

15. Ibid., p 685.

Thus, "in the immediate future," the "Masters will walk openly among men."[1] This "return to the situation which existed in Atlantean days,"[2] when "the Members of the spiritual Hierarchy were openly guiding and directing the affairs of humanity,"[3] carries with it certain dangers. As Bailey herself said,

> Then took place the great war between the Lords of Form and the Lords of Being, or between the Forces of Matter and the Great White Lodge. . . . The Forces of Light triumphed because the Hierarchy was forced to intervene potently. . . . They brought the Atlantean civilisation to an abrupt end after a long period of chaos and disaster. This took place through the medium of a culminating catastrophe which wiped hundreds of thousands of human beings off the face of the earth. This historical event has been preserved for us in the universal legend of the great flood.[4]

Bailey's "Hierarchy" wants mankind to return to a spiritual condition that last existed just before the Flood. Been there, done that; why would this work any better for mankind the second time than the first?

PROCLAIMING HUMAN DIVINITY
AND DENYING CHRIST

Like Barbara Marx Hubbard and Neale Donald Walsch, Bailey asserts human divinity. "We are all Gods, all the children of the One Father, as the latest of the Avatars, the Christ, has told us."[5]

There is a down-side to this exalted status, however. Bailey denies that Christ loves us: "The Son of God was called in The Old Testament a 'man of sorrows and acquainted with grief.' This did not in reality refer to His sufferings for poor miserable humanity (as orthodox theology so selfishly interprets it) but to the fact that He had to submit Himself to contact with humanity."[6] Nor does Christ's sacrifice save us. "It must be remembered that it is the teaching given by the Christ which saves humanity—not any symbolic death upon a cross. *Men must save themselves by their reaction and their response to the teaching given in its purity by the Christ.*"[7] Bailey denies hell; she therefore also denies salvation and grace: "There is, as you well know, no angry God, no hell, and no vicarious atonement. . . . As these erroneous ideas die out, the concept of hell will fade from man's recollection and its place will be taken by an understanding of the law which makes each man work out his salvation upon the physical plane, which leads him to right the wrongs which he may have perpetrated in his lives on Earth, and which enables him eventually to 'clean his own slate.'"[8] What a rotten deal Bailey offers! Instead of being saved and forgiven through Christ's death and resurrection and being told like the good thief, "Truly, I say to you, today you will be with me in Paradise" (Luke 23:43), we are left with the unforgiving law of karma and the requirement to right all the wrongs of all our past lives ourselves.

As befits a utopian social reformer, Bailey taught that Christ's Kingdom is of this world: "Christ taught also that the Kingdom of God is on Earth and told us to seek that Kingdom first and let all

1. Alice A. Bailey, *The Reappearance of the Christ*, Lucis Publishing Company, 1948, p121 (cited below as A. Bailey, *Reappearance of the Christ*).

2. Ibid., p121.

3. Ibid., p121.

4. A. Bailey, *The Externalisation of the Hierarchy*, pp122–123.

5. A. Bailey, *The Reappearance of the Christ*, p9.

6. Alice A. Bailey, *Externalisation of the Hierarchy*, p530.

7. Ibid., p635.

8. Alice A. Bailey, *Esoteric Healing—Volume IV: A Treatise on the Seven Rays*, Lucis Publishing Company, 1953, p393 (cited below as A. Bailey, *Esoteric Healing*).

things go for its sake."[1] Jesus Christ said otherwise to Pilate while He was on trial for His life: "My kingship is not of this world" (John 18:36).

Did Christ ascend to heaven to sit at the right hand of the Father? Not according to Bailey. "*He cannot return because He has always been here upon our Earth*, watching over the spiritual destiny of humanity; He has never left us. . . . He can only *reappear*,"[2] coming forth from "His present retreat in Central Asia."[3]

Bailey held that in the New Age, the sign of the Cross will be replaced by a new "mark" of "a new type of salvation." In *The Rays and the Initiations*, she said,

Recognition of the successful work of the New Group of World Servers will be accorded by the Hierarchy, and the testimony of the recognition will be the appearing of a symbol in the aura of the group—of the entire group. This will be a symbol projected by the Hierarchy, specifically by the Christ. . . . It is 'the mark of a Saviour' and it will embody the mark or indication (the signature as medieval occultists used to call it) of a new type of salvation or salvage. Up till now the mark of the Saviour has been the Cross ... The future holds within its silence other modes of saving humanity. The cup of sorrow and the agony of the Cross are well-nigh finished. Joy and strength will take their place.[4]

Bailey's prophecy of the replacement of the Cross by a new symbol appears to foreshadow the Rev. Sun Myung Moon's current "take down the cross" campaign.

Bailey supported progressive, evolutionary, liberal Christian theology. In her autobiography, she said,

there was really no reason because a priest or teacher six hundred years ago interpreted the Bible in one way (probably suitable for his time and age) that it should be acceptable now in a different time and age, under a different civilisation and with widely different problems. If God's truth is truth then it will be expansive and inclusive, and not reactionary and exclusive. If God is God, then His divinity will adapt itself to the emerging divinity of the sons of God, and a son of God today may be a very different expression of divinity from a son of God five thousand years ago.[5]

POPULATION CONTROL

In the 1940s—when world population was less than half what it is today—Alice Bailey said, "certain physical restrictions should be imposed, because it is now evident that *beyond a certain point the planet cannot support humanity*."[6] Bailey's proposed solutions were far-reaching: eugenics, and the reshaping of human sexuality so that people—like animals and plants—only mate and reproduce for a part of each year: "The emphasis in the future will shift from the urge to produce large families to that of producing *quality* and *intelligence* in the offspring. This will include that science of which eugenics is the distorted and exoteric indication."[7] "The real change in human consciousness which is needed will appear only as the race itself is brought under a rhythmic law—under which, for instance, the

1. Alice A. Bailey, *Externalisation of the Hierarchy*, p 603.

2. Ibid., p 597.

3. Ibid., p 590.

4. A. Bailey, *The Rays and the Initiations*, pp 233–234.

5. Alice A. Bailey, *The Unfinished Autobiography of Alice A. Bailey*, Lucis Publishing Company, 1951, p 142 (cited below as A. Bailey, *Unfinished Autobiography*).

6. Alice A. Bailey, *Education in the New Age*, 1954, Lucis Publishing Company, p 134 (cited below as A. Bailey, *Education in the New Age*).

7. Ibid., pp 133–134.

animal lives function, or the seasonal law under which forms in the vegetable kingdom operate—thus transferring the whole concept on to a higher turn of the evolutionary spiral."[1]

Bailey also said,

> One of the tasks of the educator of the future will be to teach the meaning of the Law of Rebirth, and thus bring about such a profound change in the racial attitude to life and sex, to birth and parenthood, that sex rhythm, cyclic experience, psychological preparation and directed, controlled body-building may go forward and supersede the present methods, which are based upon an uncontrolled response to the sex urge and desire, and the unthinking procreation of children. The vast population of the world today is the result of an animal response to these urges and of the general promiscuity, which is perhaps the outstanding factor, esoterically speaking and from the standpoint of the Hierarchy, of the present world distress, economic difficulties, and national aggressions.[2]

ASTROLOGICAL RACISM

In many of her books, Alice Bailey upheld occult racial theories, including the division of mankind into races that are on different points of the "ladder of evolution;" the Aryans and an emerging "new race" are the most-evolved. In *Education in the New Age*, Bailey predicted the use of occult racial theory in the schools of the future: "Young people will then be studied from the standpoint of their probable point upon the ladder of evolution and will be grouped as: a) Lemurians, with physical predispositions. b) Atlanteans, with emotional dominance. c) Aryans, with mental tendencies and inclinations. d) New race, with group qualities and consciousness and idealistic vision."[3]

In *Problems of Humanity*, Bailey stated that the races are unequal now, but that this is a temporary condition: "Under the great evolutionary process, men and races differ in mental development, in physical stamina, in creative possibilities, in understanding, in human perceptiveness and in their position upon the ladder of civilization; this, however, is temporary, for the same potentialities exist in all of us without exception, and will eventually display themselves."[4] She said, "The new race is forming in every land, but primarily in those lands where the fifth or Caucasian races are to be found."[5] In *The Destiny of the Nations*, Bailey predicted that "very low grade human bodies will disappear, causing a general shift in the racial types toward a higher standard."[6]

In *The Rays and the Initiations*, Bailey said that the "new race" will be distinguished by "a state of consciousness which is the Aryan or mental consciousness or state of thinking. . . . This state of consciousness will find its expression in people as far apart racially as the Japanese and the American or the Negro and the Russian."[7] Distinguishing herself from the Nazi race theorists, Bailey said in *Esoteric Psychology*, "I am not using the word Aryan as synonymous with Nordic but as descriptive of the intellectual goal of humanity, of which our Occidental civilisation is in the early stages, but which men of all time and all races have individually demonstrated. The Aryan state of consciousness is one into which all men eventually pass."[8]

1. Ibid., p136.
2. Ibid., p138.
3. Ibid., p71.
4. Alice A. Bailey, *Problems of Humanity*, 1947, Lucis Publishing Company, p90 (cited below as A. Bailey, *Problems of Humanity*).
5. A. Bailey, *Education in the New Age*, p118.
6. Alice A. Bailey, *The Destiny of the Nations*, 1949, Lucis Publishing Company, p125 (cited below as A. Bailey, *Destiny of the Nations*).
7. A. Bailey, *The Rays and the Initiations*, pp593–594.
8. A. Bailey, *Esoteric Psychology*, p379.

A quarter-century later, Foster Bailey—Alice Bailey's husband—proposed the same racial theories: "For millions of years the evolution of humanity has been going on.... We recognize three great stages of this human growth—Lemurian, Atlantean, and Aryan. We are now in the Aryan stage of the process of perfection. It is difficult to realise what a human being was like in Lemurian times."[1]

HUMAN INEQUALITY IN THE NEW AGE

Elitism and condescension would be the hallmarks of the planning and execution of Bailey's proposed New World Order. In *The Externalisation of the Hierarchy*, Bailey said, "The needed choices can now be made in cooperation, in consultation and with open eyes. The choice is clearly before the thinking people in every country, and upon their decision rests the fate of the less intelligent masses."[2] In *Education in the New Age*, she said,

> *Cooperative goodwill* is all that can, at this time, be expected from the masses, and this is the sublimation of forces released through civilisation. *Loving understanding* should be the hallmark of the cultured, wiser group, plus an ability to correlate the world of meaning with the world of outer effects. Ponder on this sentence. *Group love* is, and must be, the outstanding characteristic of the Illuminati of the world, and it is at this time the motivating power of the Masters of the Wisdom, until such time as enough disciples are expressive of this particular force.[3]

Inequality, based on "the new form of astrology" and "esoteric psychology" will be the basis of schooling in the New Age, as well. Bailey said,

> It will be apparent, then, that those to be taught will be gauged from the angles upon which I have touched: a) Those capable of being rightly civilised. This refers to the mass of men. b) Those capable of being carried forward into the world of culture. This includes a very large number. c) Those who can add to the assets of civilisation and culture 'the equipment' required for the process of functioning as conscious souls, not only in the three worlds of instinctual and intellectual living, but in the world of spiritual being also, and yet with complete continuity of consciousness and with complete triple integration. Not all can pass into the higher grades, and this must be appreciated. The gauging of ability will be based upon an understanding of the ray types (the science of esoteric psychology), on a comprehension of the condition of the glandular and physiological equipment, upon certain specific tests, and upon the new form of astrology.[4]

ANTI-SEMITISM

Bailey expressed hatred for Judaism in many of her books.[5]

In *The Rays And The Initiations*, Alice Bailey says,

> Symbolically, the Jews represent (from the point of view of the Hierarchy) that from which all Masters of the Wisdom and Lords of Compassion emerge: materialism, cruelty, and a spiritual conservatism, so that today they live in *Old Testament* times and are under the domination of the separative, selfish, lower concrete mind. But their opportunity will come again, and they may change all this when the fires of suffering at last succeed in

---

1. F. Bailey, *Running God's Plan*, p 154.
2. A. Bailey, *Externalisation of the Hierarchy*, pp 213–214.
3. A. Bailey, *Education in the New Age*, p 54.
4. Ibid., p 51.
5. In addition to the books cited below, other Bailey works contain anti-Semitic material: A. Bailey, *Problems of Humanity*, pp 86, 95–105, 141, and 172; also, A. Bailey, *Unfinished Autobiography*, pp 118–121; also, A. Bailey, *Destiny of the Nations*, pp 34–35.

purifying them and burning away their ancient crystallisation, thus liberating them to the extent that they can recognise their Messiah, Who will *not*, however, be the world Messiah. The Jews need humility more than any other nation. By humility they may learn something of value as well as a needed sense of proportion.[1]

In a tactic that is common for today's religious liberals, Bailey criticized St. Paul and separated his teachings from Christ. Her "contribution," as evident in two of her works, was to add a swipe at the Jews. In *The Rays and the Initiations*, Bailey said,

In the immediate past, the keynote of the Christian religion has been death, symbolised for us in the death of the Christ, and much distorted for us by St. Paul in his effort to blend the new religion which Christ gave us with the blood religion of the Jews.[2]

In a section of *The Externalisation of the Hierarchy* written in 1946,[3] Bailey reiterated:

the failure of Christianity can be traced to its Jewish background (emphasised by St. Paul), which made it full of propaganda instead of loving action, which taught the blood sacrifice instead of loving service, and which emphasised the existence of a wrathful God, needing to be placated by death, and which embodied the threats of the Old Testament Jehovah in the Christian teaching of hell fire.[4]

She added, "I have sought—with love and understanding—to point out the faults of the world religions, with their obsolete theologies and their lack of love, and to indicate the evils of Judaism. The present world faiths must return to their early simplicity, and orthodox Judaism, with its deep seated hate, must slowly disappear; all must be changed in preparation for the revelation which Christ will bring."[5]

In *The Reappearance of The Christ*, Bailey said,

Christ came to bring to an end the Jewish dispensation which should have climaxed and passed away as a religion with the movement of the sun out of Aries into Pisces. He, therefore, presented Himself to them as their Messiah, manifesting through the Jewish race. In the rejection of Christ as the Messiah, the Jewish race has remained symbolically and practically in the sign of Aries, the Scapegoat;[6] they have to pass—again speaking symbolically—into the sign, Pisces, the Fishes, and recognize their Messiah when He comes again in the sign Aquarius. Otherwise they will repeat their ancient sin of non-response to the evolutionary process. They rejected that which was new and spiritual in the desert; they did it again in Palestine two thousand years ago; will they do it again, as opportunity is offered to them? The difficulty with the Jew is that he remains satisfied with the religion of nearly five thousand years ago and shows as yet little desire to change.[7]

In the January 1939 section of *The Externalisation of the Hierarchy*,[8] Bailey wrote,

The solution will come, as I said, when the races regard the Jewish problem as a humanitarian problem but also when the Jew does his share of understanding, love, and right action. This he does not yet do, speaking racially. He must let go of his own separative tendencies and of his deep sense of persecution. He will do this latter with great facility, when he grasps, as a race, the significance, the significance and inevitability of the Law of Karma, and from a close study of the Old Testament and of the acts and deeds there claimed by him as his racial acts and

1. A. Bailey, *The Rays and the Initiations*, pp705–706. Other anti-Semitic material appears on pp 429–430, 534, 548, 634–637, and 679–681 of *The Rays and the Initiations*.

2. Ibid., p318.

3. A. Bailey, *Externalisation of the Hierarchy*, p541.

4. Ibid., p543.

5. Ibid., p543.

6. Charles Upton notes an error of Bailey's: "The symbol of Aries is the ram—a male sheep—not the goat. The astrological sign of the goat is Capricorn." (E-mail from Charles Upton to Lee Penn, 10/09/04.)

7. A. Bailey, *Reappearance of the Christ*, p81.

8. A. Bailey, *Externalisation of the Hierarchy*, pp71–79.

deeds (conquest, terrorism, and cruelty), realises that the law is working out and incidentally releasing him for a greater future. There must, at the same time, be a realisation by the Jew and Gentile of equal responsibility and equal liability for the present world difficulty.[1]

Bailey wrote this *after* the November 1938 Kristallnacht pogroms in Germany, and on the eve of the *Shoah*, the Nazi genocide.

At the same time, Bailey also gave a novel account of Jewish history—or, rather, pre-history:

those whom we now call the Jews . . . are the descendants of that earlier group which was held in pralaya between the first and second solar systems, If you will remember that the third ray governed that system and also governs the Jewish race, if you bear in mind that that system was occupied with the divine aspects of matter only and with external conditions, and that the Jews were the highest product of that system, you can come to an understanding of the Jew, his separateness, his desire for racial purity and his interest in all that is commercial and tangible.[2]

In *Esoteric Healing*, she wrote:

Their aggressive history as narrated in the Old Testament is on a par with present-day German accomplishment; yet Christ was a Jew and it was the Hebrew race which produced him. Let this never be forgotten. The Jews were great aggressors; they despoiled the Egyptians and they took the Promised Land at the point of the sword, sparing neither man, woman, nor child. Their religious history has been built around a materialistic Jehovah, possessive, greedy and endorsing and encouraging aggression.[3]

Today the law is working, and the Jews are paying the price, factually and symbolically, for all they have done in the past.[4]

Until, however, the Jews themselves face up to the situation and admit that there may be for them the working out of the retributive aspect of the Law of Cause and Effect, and until they endeavour to ascertain what it is in them, as a race, which has initiated their ancient and dire fate, this basic world issue will remain as it has been since the very night of time. . . . What I have said in no way mitigates the guilt of those who have so sorely abused the Jews. . . . Though much that has happened to the Jews originated in their past history and in their pronounced attitude of separativeness and nonassimilability, and in their emphasis upon material good, yet the agents who have brought the evil karma upon them equally incur the retributive aspects of the same law.[5]

When Bailey accused Jews of "separativeness" and "emphasis upon material good," she was making—in her own terms—the most serious accusation possible, since she said "the true nature of cosmic evil finds its major expression in wrong thinking, false values, and the supreme evil of materialistic selfishness and the sense of isolated separativeness."[6]

In a section of *The Rays and The Initiations* written in 1948[7]—after the *Shoah* —Bailey said that

The Jewish people have not only repudiated the Messiah (which their race produced), but they have forgotten their unique relation to humanity; they forget that millions in the world today have suffered as they have suffered and that—for instance—there are eighty per cent of other people in the concentration camps of Europe and only twenty per cent Jews. The Jew, however, fought only for himself, and largely ignored the sufferings of his fellowmen in the concentration camps.[8]

1. Ibid., p78.
2. Ibid., pp76–77. Other anti-Semitic material appears on pp74, 87, 88–89, 92, 544, 551, 615, and 637 of *Externalisation of the Hierarchy*.
3. A. Bailey, *Esoteric Healing*, p263.
4. Ibid., p264.
5. Ibid., pp265–266. Other anti-Semitic material appears on pp267–269 of *Esoteric Healing*.
6. A. Bailey, *The Rays and the Initiation*, p753.
7. Ibid., p620.
8. Ibid., p635.

Regarding the establishment of the State of Israel, Bailey said, "Today the Jewish people are engineering trouble, and it is interesting to note that the main contention of the past of Poland, lately of the Irish, and today of the Jews, is *territory*, thus evidencing a most distorted sense of values.... They are claiming a land to which they have no possible right and which the Jews have ignored for two thousand years."[1] She added, "The menace to world freedom today lies in the known policies of the rulers of the U.S.S.R. and in the devious and lying machinations of the Zionists."[2]

Instead of Zionism or religious orthodoxy, Bailey proposed assimilation as the solution to the "Jewish problem":

The Jewish problem will not be solved by taking possession of Palestine, by plaint and demand and by financial manipulations. That would be but the prolongation of ancient wrong and material possessiveness. The problem will be solved by the willingness of the Jew to conform to the civilisation, the cultural background and the standards of living of the nation to which—by the fact of birth and education—he is related and with which he should assimilate. It will come by the relinquishment of pride of race and of the concept of selectivity; it will come by renouncing dogmas and customs which are intrinsically obsolete and which create points of constant irritation to the matrix within which the Jew finds himself; it will come when selfishness in business relations and the pronounced manipulative tendencies of the Hebrew people are exchanged for more selfless and honest forms of activity.[3]

Bailey added that, on the part of Gentiles,

The growing anti-Semitic feeling in the world is inexcusable in the sight of God and man. I refer not here to the abominable cruelties of the obsessed German people. Behind that lies a history of Atlantean relationships into which it is needless for me to enter because I could not prove to you the truth of my statements. I refer to the history of the past two thousand years and to the everyday behaviour of Gentile people everywhere. There must be a definite effort on the part of the nationals of every country to assimilate the Jews, to inter-marry with them and to refuse to recognise as barriers old habits of thought and ancient bad relations.[4]

Give Bailey credit for this: she wanted to use non-violent means, assimilation and inter-marriage, as the Gentiles' solution to the "Jewish problem." She accurately distinguished between the Nazi genocide and the long-standing anti-Jewish prejudice in Christian and Islamic nations.[5] But as an explanation for the *Shoah*, "a history of Atlantean relationships" between the Germans and the Jews in their past lives is a true prize-winner.

A Lucis Trust/World Goodwill pamphlet, "The New Group of World Servers," says of world servers, those who put Theosophical principles into practice: "When active in the religious field, they heal differences and recognise the universality of truth. They attack no people, classes or systems, and under no circumstances do they ever condemn or criticise any race or nation."[6] It seems that Bailey would not meet the standards that her own followers at World Goodwill apply for membership in the "new group of world servers."

1. Ibid., p634.
2. Ibid., p680.
3. A. Bailey, *Esoteric Healing*, pp266–267.
4. Ibid., pp268–269.
5. Charles Upton comments, "This prejudice against Jews may have been of long standing, but was by no means universal. The history of Islam contains as many examples of Muslim-Jewish amity and cooperation as of Muslim-Jewish enmity. When Benjamin Disraeli became British Prime Minister, his opponents protested that he would be partial to Arab interests in the Middle East since he was a Jew." (E-mail from Charles Upton to Lee Penn, 04/27/04)
6. World Goodwill, "The New Group of World Servers," 1978, p4; from the New Religious Movements collection of the Graduate Theological Union Library in Berkeley, California (cited below as World Goodwill, "New Group of World Servers").

There is no evidence whatsoever that any URI leaders share Alice Bailey's anti-Semitic views. Nor have Robert Muller, Barbara Marx Hubbard, or Neale Donald Walsch repeated any of Bailey's diatribes about Judaism; they focus their scorn instead on orthodox, "fundamentalist" Christianity. Nevertheless, in most political and religious discourse since 1945 in Western Europe and North America, any hint of anti-Semitism has usually sufficed to make suspected writers, politicians, or religious leaders—*and their avowed followers*—outcast. As historian Philip Jenkins has said, "the anti-Semite is denounced in the United States and obliged to keep quiet."[1] It is noteworthy that this social sanction seems *not* to apply to Alice Bailey, her teachings, and her present-day Theosophist followers. This is not because Bailey's feculent writings are secret. On the contrary. All of the Bailey books remain in print; they are readily available in bookstores, and as a Lucis Trust CD-ROM of all 24 volumes.[2]

EQUAL-OPPORTUNITY CONTEMPT
FOR TRADITIONAL RELIGIONS

Bailey consigns traditional Judaism, Islam, and Christianity to the dustbin of history:

Palestine should no longer be called the Holy Land; its sacred places are only the passing relics of three dead and gone religions. . . . Judaism is old, obsolete, and separative and has no true message for the spiritually minded which cannot be better given by the newer faiths; the Moslem faith has served its purpose and all true Moslems await the coming of the Imam Mahdi who will lead them to light and to *spiritual* victory; the Christian faith also has served its purpose; its Founder seeks to bring a new Gospel and a new message that will enlighten all men everywhere. Therefore, Jerusalem stands for nothing of importance today, except for that which has passed away and should pass away. The 'Holy Land' is no longer holy, but is desecrated by selfish interests, and by a basically separative and conquering nation.[3]

Alice Bailey specifically hated the Vatican—enough to propose dropping the Bomb on the Holy See. In a section of *The Externalisation of the Hierarchy* dated April-May 1946, she wrote that

The atomic bomb does not belong to the three nations who perfected it and who own the secrets at present—the United States of America, Great Britain, and Canada. It belongs to the United Nations for use (or let us rather hope, simply for threatened use) when aggressive action on the part of any nation rears its ugly head. It does not essentially matter whether that aggression is the gesture of any particular nation or group of nations or whether it is generated by the political groups of any powerful religious organisation, such as the Church of Rome, who are as yet unable to leave politics alone.[4]

Bailey explained her animosity: "The churches are themselves great capitalistic systems, particularly the Roman Catholic Church, and show little evidence of the mind that was in Christ."[5] She said,

The Roman Catholic Church stands entrenched and unified against any new and evolutionary presentation of truth to the people; its roots are in the past but it is not growing into the light; its vast financial resources enable it to menace the future enlightenment of mankind under the cloak of paternalism, and a colorful outer appearance which hides a crystallization and an intellectual stupidity which must inevitably spell its eventual

1. ZENIT.org News Agency, "Historian Laments the New Anti-Catholicism in U.S.: Philip Jenkins, an Episcopalian, Faults the Intellectuals and Liberals," http://www.ewtn.com/vnews/getstory.asp?number=36317, printed 06/04/03.

2. Lucis Publishing Company, "US Online Secure Order Form," https://www.lucistrust.org/purchase/price.shtml, printed 06/04/03.

3. A. Bailey, *Rays and the Initiations*, p754.

4. A. Bailey, *Externalisation of the Hierarchy*, p548.

5. A. Bailey, *Problems of Humanity*, p169.

doom, unless the faint stirrings of new life following the advent of Pope John XXIII can be nourished and developed.[1]

Bailey despised the Russian Orthodox Church, as well. She praised the Bolsheviks for crushing the pre-1917 church and replacing it with a collaborationist, KGB-riddled structure:

> The Greek Orthodox Church reached such a high stage of corruption, graft, greed and sexual evil that, temporarily and under the Russian Revolution, it was abolished. This was a wise, needed and right action. . . . The refusal of the revolutionary party in Russia to recognize this corrupt church was wise and salutary. . . . The church in Russia has again received official recognition and faces a new opportunity. . . . The challenge of its environment is great and it cannot be reactionary as can—and are—the churches in other parts of the world.[2]

While Bailey condemns traditional Judaism and Christianity repeatedly in many of her books, she also aims a few shots at traditional Asian religions. "In the Oriental religions a disastrous negativity has prevailed; the truths given out have not sufficed to better the daily life of the believer or to anchor the truths creatively upon the physical plane. The effect of the Eastern doctrines is largely subjective and negative as to daily affairs. The negativity of the theological interpretations of the Buddhist and Hindu Scriptures have kept the people in a quiescent condition from which they are slowly beginning to emerge."[3] She added, "There is no indication that the great Oriental religions are taking an active lead in producing a new and better world."[4] She also said, "all the world Scriptures are now seen to be based on poor translations and no part of them—after thousands of years of translation—is as it originally was, if it ever existed as an original manuscript and was not in reality some man's recollection of what was said."[5] And so much for the *Koran* and all other religions' sacred texts.

In the early 1970s, Foster Bailey, who had been Alice Bailey's husband until her death in 1949, dismissed all the major religions with similar contempt. He said, "It is not reasonable that either Buddhism or Christianity, or any of the other old age organised religions, can transcend their perversions or that they have within themselves the qualities needed for world usefulness in the new Aquarian age. However, they still can have usefulness for the millions of human beings who are Atlantean in consciousness and who do not have the capacity to respond the new spiritual potencies of the Aquarian age."[6]

THE COMING NEW RELIGION

A New Religion would replace these outmoded beliefs. To establish the New Religion, Alice Bailey's New Age Christ has three current tasks:

> Therefore, we have isolated (if I may use such a word) three activities to which the Christ is at this time dedicated:
> 1. The reorganisation of the world religions—if in any way possible—so that their out-of-date theologies, their narrow-minded emphasis and their ridiculous belief that they know what is in the Mind of God may be offset, in order that the churches may eventually be the recipients of spiritual inspiration.

---

1. Ibid., p131. Bailey originally published this book in 1947, and died in 1949. The reference to Pope John XXIII is a posthumous emendation of the text by the Lucis Trust. It is noteworthy that they did *not* amend Bailey's cruel, totalitarian writings in the newer printings of her other works.
2. Ibid., p131.
3. Ibid., p129.
4. Ibid., p138.
5. Ibid., p126.
6. F. Bailey, *Running God's Plan*, p160.

2. The gradual dissolution—again, if in any way possible—of the orthodox Jewish faith, with its obsolete teaching, its separative emphasis, its hatred of the Gentiles and its failure to recognize the Christ. In saying this I do not fail to recognize those Jews throughout the world who acknowledge the evils and are not orthodox in their thinking; they belong to the aristocracy of spiritual belief to which the Hierarchy itself belongs.

3. Preparation for a new revelation which will inaugurate the new era and set the note for the new world religion.[1]

The New Religion proposed by Bailey would be based on magic, spiritual elitism, and the manipulation of the people: "The new religion will be one of Invocation and Evocation, of bringing together great spiritual energies and then stepping them down for the benefiting and the stimulation of the masses. The work of the new religion will be the distribution of spiritual energy and the protecting of humanity from energies and forces which they are not, at the particular time, fitted to receive."[2] In the New Religion, "the science of invocation and evocation will take the place of what we now call prayer and worship,"[3] because "as man progresses upon the Path he forgets worship; he loses all sense of fear, and adoration fails to engross his attention."[4] (By this standard, the seraphim, cherubim, and elders described in chapters 4 and 5 of the book of Revelation have not progressed far "upon the Path.")

There will be two levels of religious practice—one for the masses and one for the adepts of the New Age:

This new invocative work will be the keynote of the coming world religion and will fall into two parts. There will be the invocative work of the masses of the people, everywhere trained by the spiritually minded people of the world (working in the churches whenever possible under an enlightened clergy) to accept the fact of the approaching spiritual energies, focused through Christ and His spiritual Hierarchy, and trained also to voice their demand for light, liberation and understanding. There will also be the skilled work of invocation as practised by those who have trained their minds through right meditation, who know the potency of formulas, mantrams and invocations and who work consciously.[5]

The New Religion will work closely with the United Nations: "Thus the expressed aims and efforts of the United Nations will be eventually brought to fruition and a new church of God, gathered out of all religions and spiritual groups, will unitedly bring to an end the great heresy of separateness."[6] This foreshadows Robert Muller's writings about the religious role of the UN.

In April/May of 1946,[7] Bailey wrote that all of us must change our religious beliefs, since the alternative is "a religious war which will make the past war[8] appear like child's play."[9] She said, "That the Jews should be rid of fear is of major importance; that they should know and recognise the Christ as the Messiah, and therefore find for themselves that the religion they follow is destructive of many of the finer values, is likewise of major importance; that orthodox Judaism, along with all the other faiths, should . . . all move towards some loving synthesis and eliminate their mutual antagonisms and rivalries is equally urgent."[10] Bailey continued,

1. A. Bailey, *Externalisation of the Hierarchy*, pp 544–545.
2. Ibid., p 401.
3. Ibid., p 414.
4. Ibid., p 268.
5. A. Bailey, *Problems of Humanity*, p 159.
6. A. Bailey, *Destiny of the Nations*, p 152.
7. A. Bailey, *Externalisation of the Hierarchy*, p 541.
8. Bailey was referring here to World War II.
9. A. Bailey, *Externalisation of the Hierarchy*, p 545.
10. Ibid., p 545.

That the Vatican cease its political scheming, its exploitation of the masses and its emphasis on ignorance is as important; that the manifold divisions of the Protestant churches be bridged is imperative. If none of these things happen, humanity is headed towards a religious war which will make the past war appear like child's play; antagonisms and hatreds will embroil entire populations and the politicians of all the nations will take full advantage of the situation to precipitate a war which may well prove the end of humanity. There are no hatreds so great or so deep as those fostered by religion.[1]

Bishop Swing's warning, "What is a bigger terrorist threat than religion in the world today? There is none,"[2] echoes this statement by Bailey.

Bailey expected the New Religion, which she called the "Church Universal," to emerge by the close of the twentieth century—that is, just in time for the formation of the URI. She said, "Eventually, there will appear the Church Universal, and its definite outlines will appear towards the close of this century. In this connection, forget not the wise prophecy of H.P.B.[3] as touching events at the close of this century."[4] (Blavatsky had said, "In Century the Twentieth some disciple more informed, and far better fitted, may be sent by the Masters of Wisdom to give final and irrefutable proofs that . . . the source of all religions and philosophies now known to the world has been for many ages forgotten and lost to men, but is at last found."[5])

Bailey added, "I write for the generation which will come into active thought expression at the end of this century; they will inaugurate the framework, structure and fabric of the New Age which will *start* with certain premises which today are the dream of the more exalted dreamers and which will develop the civilisation of the Aquarian Age."[6] She said that "the problem before the Hierarchy" is to ensure that "the Plan can be rightly materialized and the close of this century and the beginning of the next see the purposes of God for the planet and for humanity assume right direction and proportion."[7]

Bailey said, "The day is dawning when all religions will be regarded as emanating from one great spiritual source; all will be seen as unitedly providing the one root out of which the universal world religion will inevitably emerge."[8] She added that

in the new world order, spirituality will supersede theology; living experience will take the place of theological acceptances. The spiritual realities will emerge with increasing clarity and the form aspect will recede into the background; dynamic, expressive truth will be the key-note of the new world religion. The living Christ will assume his rightful place in human consciousness and see the fruition of His plans, sacrifice, and service, but the hold of the ecclesiastical orders will weaken and disappear. Only those will remain as guides and leaders of the human spirit who speak from living experience, and who know no creedal barriers; they will recognise the onward march of revelation and the new emerging truths. These truths will be founded on the ancient realities but will be adapted to modern need and will manifest progressively the revelation of the divine nature and quality.[9]

Thus, liberal Protestants and modernist Catholics will have their dreams realized in the New Religion.

Bailey also said that mankind's adherence to the traditional religions is an accident of birth, and that old differences will be superseded by "One Humanity":

1. Ibid., pp545–546.
2. Coleen O'Connor, "Uniting Religions: Bishop Swing talks about religious terrorism, atomic bombs, and why we need a United Religions now," http://www.gracecathedral.org/enrichment/interviews/int_19990107.shtml, printed 2/4/03.
3. Bailey often abbreviated the name of Helena Petrovna Blavatsky to "H. P. B."
4. A. Bailey, *Externalisation of the Hierarchy*, p 510.
5. Blavatsky, *The Secret Doctrine, Vol. I*, p xxxviii.
6. A. Bailey, *The Rays and the Initiations*, p 109.
7. A. Bailey, *Destiny of the Nations*, p 11.
8. A. Bailey, *Problems of Humanity*, p 140.
9. A. Bailey, *Externalisation of the Hierarchy*, p 202.

World Unity will be a fact when the children of the world are taught that religious differences are largely a matter of birth; that if a man is born in Italy, the probability is that he will be a Roman Catholic; if he is born a Jew, he will follow the Jewish teaching; if born in Asia, he may be a Mohammedan, a Buddhist, or belong to one of the Hindu sects; if born in other countries, he may be a Protestant and so on. He will learn that religious differences are largely the result of man made quarrels over human interpretations of truth. Thus gradually, our quarrels and differences will be offset and the idea of the One Humanity will take their place.[1]

UPDATING FREEMASONRY
FOR THE NEW RELIGION

Alice Bailey said,

one of the things that will eventuate—when the new universal religion has sway and the nature of esotericism is understood—will be the utilisation of the banded esoteric organisms, the Masonic organism and the Church organism as initiating centres. These three groups converge as their inner sanctuaries are approached. There is no dissociation between the One Universal Church, the sacred inner Lodge of all true Masons, and the inner-most circles of the esoteric societies.[2]

Alice Bailey also predicted that Masonry would be a path to power in the new world order:

The *Masonic Movement* when it can be divorced from politics and social ends and from its present paralysing condition of inertia, will meet the need of those who can, and should, wield power. It is the custodian of the law; it is the home of the Mysteries and the seat of initiation. It holds in its symbolism the ritual of Deity, and the way of salvation is pictorially preserved in its work. The methods of Deity are demonstrated in its Temples, and under the All-Seeing Eye the work can go forward. It is a far more occult organisation than can be realised, and is intended to be the training school for the coming advanced occultists. . . . It meets the need of those who work on the first Ray of Will or Power.[3]

Her husband Foster Bailey, a 32nd degree Mason,[4] said that Masonry "is all that remains to us of the first world religion which flourished in an antiquity so old that it is impossible to affix a date. It was the first unified world religion. Then came the era of separation of many religions, and of sectarianism. Today we are working again towards a world universal religion. Again then, Masonry will come into its own, in some form or another."[5]

Alice Bailey held great hope for Masonry as a building-block for the religion of the future, but believed that Masonry would have to adapt to the times. Part of this adaptation would be the cleansing of Christian and Jewish imagery from Masonic rituals:

The time has now come, under cyclic law and in preparation for the New Age, for certain changes to be worked by Masons with spiritual understanding. The present Jewish colouring of Masonry is completely out of date and has been preserved far too long, for it is today either Jewish or Christian, and should be neither. The Blue Lodge degrees[6] are entirely Jewish in phrasing and wording, and this should be altered. The Higher Degrees are predominantly Christian, though permeated with Jewish names and words. This too should end. This Jewish

---

1. A. Bailey, *Education in the New Age*, p88.
2. A. Bailey, *Externalisation of the Hierarchy*, 1957, p513.
3. Ibid., p511.
4. Foster Bailey, *The Spirit of Masonry*, Lucis Publishing Company, 1957, p135.
5. Ibid., p29.
6. The "Blue Lodge" degrees are Enrolled Apprentice, Fellow Craft, and Master Mason. These degrees are universal throughout Masonry. Anyone who wishes to pursue the higher-level Masonic degrees in the Scottish Rite or York Rite must first attain the Master Mason degree. For the texts of the rites used in the "Blue Lodge," see Malcolm C. Duncan, *Duncan's Masonic Ritual and Monitor*, David McKay Co., Inc., 3rd ed., n. d. This book is widely available in paperback.

colouring is today one of the hindrances to the full expression of Masonic intention and should be changed, whilst preserving the facts and detail and structure of the Masonic symbolism intact.[1]

DEALING WITH "REACTIONARY FORCES"

Bailey believed that "conservative elements" and "reactionary forces" will be the opponents of the New Religion: "This inherent fanaticism (found ever in reactionary groups) will fight against the appearance of the coming world religion and the spread of esotericism. For this struggle certain of the well-organised churches, through their conservative elements (their most powerful elements), are already girding themselves."[2] Bailey offers a solution—to "arrest the reactionary forces in every nation": "If we can delay the crystallisation of the ancient evils which produced the world war, and arrest the reactionary forces in every nation, we shall be making way for that which is new and opening the door to the activities of the New Group of World Servers in every land—that group which is the agent of the Christ."[3] She left it unclear whether she meant to stop her opponents spiritually, or whether she was suggesting that the "reactionary forces" should be put under arrest on the physical plane.

Bailey said that the coming of "the new ideals, the new civilisation, the new modes of life, of education, of religious presentation and of government"[4] is inevitable. "They can, however, be delayed by the reactionary types of people, by the ultra-conservative and closed minds and by those who cling with adamantine determination to their beloved theories, their dreams and their visions, their interpretations and their peculiar and oft narrow understanding of the presented ideals. *They* are the ones who can and do hold back the hour of liberation."[5] It's not a giant step for a Theosophist to conclude that "the hour of liberation" should be hastened by getting "the reactionary types of people" out of the way.

BAILEY'S NEW WORLD ORDER: "A NEW POWER OF SACRIFICE"

With the New Religion and the "coming world state," there will be spiritual totalitarianism. As Alice Bailey said, "This coming age will be as predominantly the age of group interplay, group idealism, and group consciousness as the Piscean Age has been one of personality unfoldment and emphasis, personality focus and personality consciousness. Selfishness, as we now understand it, will gradually disappear, for the will of the individual will voluntarily be blended into the group will."[6] After all, the existence of separate persons is an illusion; we are all really part of The One. She said, "In the coming world state, the individual citizen—gladly and deliberately and with full consciousness of all that he is doing—will subordinate his personality to the good of the whole."[7] (As Orwell said of his protagonist, Winston, at the end of *1984*, "He had won the victory over himself. He loved Big Brother."[8])

Alice Bailey and her Lucis Trust associates have repeatedly praised revolutions and dictatorships,

1. A. Bailey, *The Rays and the Initiations*, p 418.
2. A. Bailey, *Externalisation of the Hierarchy*, p 453.
3. A. Bailey, *Reappearance of the Christ*, pp 188–189.
4. A. Bailey, *Externalisation of the Hierarchy*, pp 278–279.
5. Ibid., p 279.
6. A. Bailey, *The Rays and the Initiation*, p 109.
7. A. Bailey, *Education in the New Age*, p 122.
8. George Orwell, *1984*, New American Library edition, 1961, p 245.

approving them as part of the workings of "the Plan." In September 1939,[1] she said, "The men who inspired the initiating French revolution; the great conqueror, Napoleon; Bismarck, creator of a nation; Mussolini, the regenerator of his people; Hitler who lifted a distressed people upon his shoulders; Lenin, the idealist, Stalin and Franco" were "great and outstanding personalities who were peculiarly sensitive to the will-to-power and the will-to-change;" all were "expressions of the Shamballa force" (a force which Bailey extolled) and "emphasised increasingly the wider human values."[2]

Bailey explained that "There are disciples of Shamballa just as there are disciples of the Hierarchy.... It is wise and valuable to remember this. They are powerful, these disciples of Shamballa, headstrong and often cruel; they impose their will and dictate their desires; they make mistakes but they are nevertheless true disciples of Shamballa and are working out the Will of God as much as the disciples and Masters of the Hierarchy are working out the Love of God."[3] Bailey uses pseudo-mystical language to dismiss the victims of the dictators:

> If you study the nations of the world today from this angle, you will see this Shamballa energy of will working out potently through the agency of certain great outstanding personalities. The Lord of Shamballa in this time of urgency ... is sending forth this dynamic energy. It is form destroying and brings death to those material forms and organised bodies which hinder the free expression of the life of God, for they negate the new culture and render inactive the seeds of the coming civilization.[4]

Bailey viewed the dictatorships of her time as a positive part of human evolution, fostering humanity's "power to regard himself as part of a whole":

> Everywhere and in every country men are being taught in their earliest years that they are not only individuals, not only members of a state, empire or nation, and not only people with an individual future, but that they are intended to be exponents of certain great group ideologies—Democratic, Totalitarian, or Communistic.... All this is very good and part of the ordained plan. Whether it is the democratic ideal, or the vision of the totalitarian state, or the dream of the communistic devotee, the effect upon the consciousness of humanity as a whole is definitely good. His sense of world awareness is definitely growing, his power to regard himself as part of a whole is rapidly developing and all this is desirable and right and contained within the divine plan.[5]

(After World War II started, Bailey's writing strongly supported the Allies, favoring early US entry into the war against the Nazis.[6])

Bailey expected that "a spiritual Hierarchy" would appear and

> govern the people throughout the world and will embody in itself the best elements of the monarchial, the democratic, the totalitarian, and the communistic regimes. *Most of these groups of ideologies have latent in them much beauty, strength and wisdom, and also a profound and valuable contribution to make to the whole.* Each will eventually see its contribution embodied under the control of the Hierarchy of the Lords of Compassion and the Masters of the Wisdom.[7]

For Bailey, spiritual Communism was the objective:

> The Lord of the World, the 'Ancient of Days,' is releasing new energies into humanity, transmuted in the present furnace of pain and fiery agony. This transmutation will being about a new power of sacrifice, of inclusive

1. A. Bailey, *Externalisation of the Hierarchy*, p105.
2. Ibid., p133.
3. A. Bailey, *Destiny of the Nations*, p16.
4. Ibid., p17.
5. A. Bailey, *Education in the New Age*, pp103–104.
6. See, as one example, A. Bailey, *Externalisation of the Hierarchy*, pp229–240.
7. A. Bailey, *Destiny of the Nations*, pp11–12.

surrender, a clearer vision of the Whole and a cooperative spirit hitherto unknown and which will be the first expression of that great *principle of sharing*, so sorely needed today.[1]

WORLD WARS AND ATOM BOMBS:
ENGINES OF HUMAN EVOLUTION

There is no one so cruel as a utopian who sees traditionalists standing in the way of the March of History. In Bailey's view, war and genocide were part of God's plan, a divine house-cleaning to remove obstacles to the return of "the Christ" and the coming of the New Age.

Alice Bailey began writing about a coming "selection" as early as March 1934.[2] She said,

> Thus is the New Age dawning. . . . Ever the race is to the strong, and always the many are called and the few chosen. This is the occult law. . . . Lest this widespread upheaval and consequent disaster to so many should seem to you unfair, let me remind you that this one life is but a second of time in the larger and wider existence of the soul, and those who fail and are disrupted by the impact of the powerful forces now flooding our earth will nevertheless have their vibration 'stepped up' to better things along with the mass of those who achieve, even if their physical vehicles are destroyed in the process. The destruction of the body is not the worst disaster than can overcome a man.[3]

When Bailey wrote this, the Nazis had just taken power; man-made famine and political purges were occurring in the Soviet Union; Japan had begun its war against China. Many, many "physical vehicles" were being destroyed.

Bailey's dismissal of people as "vehicles" foreshadows the beliefs of the Heaven's Gate suicide cult. They viewed human bodies as temporary "vehicles," to be discarded in order to reach the higher plane of existence.[4] When the Hale-Bopp comet appeared in 1997, the cultists expected to be picked up by aliens and taken into the next kingdom. Therefore, 39 members of this group committed suicide together in a California mansion in March of that year in order to make a "spiritual" ascent.[5]

In September 1939,[6] Bailey wrote in *Externalisation of the Hierarchy* about the "beneficent and needed" aspects of the beginning of World War II, which she saw as a necessary step towards creating "new forms in the religious, political, educational and economic life of the race":

> Today we are watching the death of a civilisation or cycle of incarnation of humanity. In all fields of human expression, crystallisation and deterioration had set in. . . . there is everywhere a cry for change and for those new forms in the religious, political, educational and economic life of the race which will allow of freer and better spiritual expression. Such a change is rapidly coming and is regarded by some as death—terrible and to be avoided if possible. It is indeed death but it is beneficent and needed.[7]

She added,

---

1. Ibid., p95.
2. A. Bailey, *Externalisation of the Hierarchy*, p3.
3. Ibid., p7.
4. "Members of the group believed they were 'exiting their vehicles,' or their human bodies, to move onto a higher plane." (CNN, "Former Heaven's Gate member kills himself; another tries," May 6, 1997, http://www.cnn.com/US/9705/06/heavens.gate/, printed 06/04/03.)
5. For further information on this cult, see Partridge, *New Religions*, pp372, 391, 406.
6. A. Bailey, *Externalisation of the Hierarchy*, p105.
7. Ibid., pp114–115.

Pain has always been the purifying agent, employed by the Lords of Destiny, to bring about liberation. The accumulated pain of the present war and the inherited pain of the earlier stage (begun in 1914) is bringing about a salutary and changing world consciousness. The Lord of Pain has descended from His throne and is treading the ways of earth today, bringing distress, agony and terror to those who cannot interpret His ends.[1]

Bailey said in June 1947[2] that World War II, "with all its unspeakable horrors, its cruelties, and its cataclysmic disasters—was but the broom of the Father of all, sweeping away obstructions in the path of His returning Son."[3] (These "obstructions" are *people*, not impersonal forces or institutions.) She added, "It would have been well-nigh impossible to prepare for the coming in the face of the pre-war conditions. Upon these facts the new group of world servers must today take their stand."[4]

In *The Rays and the Initiations*, Bailey gave credit to the "Hierarchy" of ascended spiritual masters for "Their decision, taken early in this century, which precipitated—in the centre which we call 'the race of men'—those potencies and stimulating energies which produced that major destructive agency, the world war (1914–1945).[5] In April 1943,[6] Bailey said, "One of the purposes lying behind the present holocaust (World War II) has been the necessity for the destruction of inadequate forms. . . . Therefore the Law of destruction was permitted to work through humanity itself, and men are now destroying the forms through which many masses of men are functioning. This is both a good and a bad thing, viewed from the evolutionary angle"[7] ("Destroying the forms" does not mean shredding IRS paperwork; it is the Theosophist code phrase for killing.)

After the war, Bailey wrote in *Education in the New Age* that "the Custodians of God's Plan" viewed World War II as "in the nature of major surgical operation made in an effort to save the patient's life;" the operation had been "largely successful" in removing "a violent streptococcic germ and infection" that had "menaced the life of humanity."[8] The operation "was made in order to prolong opportunity and save life, *not* to save the form. The operation was largely successful."[9] Nevertheless, she warned that the two World Wars would be only the beginning of sorrows: "The germ, to be sure, is not eradicated and makes its presence felt in infected areas in the body of humanity. Another surgical operation may be necessary, not in order to destroy and end the present civilisation, but in order to dissipate the infection and get rid of the fever."[10] She added, "The next stage of human evolution will emerge as a result of the purificatory action of the World War."[11]

Bailey's romance with mass death extended to nuclear weapons. Regarding the origins of the Bomb, Bailey said, "The atomic bomb emerged from a first ray Ashram, working in conjunction with a fifth ray group; from the long range point of view, its intent was and is purely beneficent."[12]

1. Ibid., p116.
2. Ibid., p612.
3. Ibid., p618.
4. Ibid., p618.
5. A. Bailey, *The Rays and the Initiations*, p553.
6. Ibid., p76.
7. Ibid., pp75–76.
8. A. Bailey, *Education in the New Age*, p111.
9. Ibid., p111.

10. Ibid., pp111–112. Bailey's use of the germ/infection metaphor for people paralleled Himmler's speech to senior SS officers in Posen in 1943: "We have exterminated a bacterium because we do not want in the end to be infected by the bacterium and die of it. I will not see so much as a small area of sepsis appear here or gain a hold. Wherever it may form, we will cauterise it. All in all, however, we can say that we have carried out this most difficult of tasks in a spirit of love for our people. And we have suffered no harm in our inner being, our soul, our character." (Michael Burleigh, *The Third Reich: A New History*, Hill and Wang, 2000, p661).

11. A. Bailey, *Education in the New Age*, p149.

12. A. Bailey, *Externalisation of the Hierarchy*, p548. Bailey's teachings include the idea that there are seven "rays"—spiritual traits—that dominate human action.

In an essay titled "The Release of Atomic Energy," written on August 9, 1945, Bailey hailed "the release of atomic energy . . . this week, August 6, 1945, in connection with the bombing of Japan" as

the greatest spiritual event which has taken place since the fourth kingdom of nature, the human kingdom, appeared.[1]

She added:

You will now understand the meaning of the words used by so many of you in the second of the Great Invocations: *The hour of service of the saving force has now arrived.* This 'saving force' is the energy which science has released into the world for the destruction, first of all, of those who continue (if they do) to defy the Forces of Light working through the United Nations. Then—as time goes on—this liberated energy will usher in the new civilisation, the new and better world and the finer, more spiritual conditions.[2]

Bailey viewed the "first use of this energy" in "material destruction" (the atomic incineration of Hiroshima and Nagasaki) as "inevitable and desirable; old forms (obstructing the good) have had to be destroyed; the wrecking and disappearance of that which is bad and undesirable must ever precede the building of the good and desirable and the longed-for emergence of that which is new and better."[3] (It is an interesting coincidence that Bailey hated Christianity—and Nagasaki was the oldest Christian community in Japan.[4])

Perhaps Alice Bailey was channeling Dr. Strangelove on the Earth-plane. Her followers continue to do the same.

In 1990, Mary Bailey, the second wife of Foster Bailey,[5] published *A Learning Experience*, present-day reflections on the teachings of Alice Bailey. The book contained an essay, "Atomic Energy—Curse or Blessing?," written in response to the Chernobyl disaster. She reprinted most of Bailey's "Release of Atomic Energy" essay from 1945—including *all* the material quoted above. And she *defended* Alice Bailey's position:

It seems inevitable that, at this stage in its planetary evolution, humanity should be more aware of the destruction of form resulting from the use of two atomic bombs than with the liberation of the soul within the form. But this liberation and new opportunity, to the spiritual Hierarchy, is the real consequence of the bombs and their only justification because here the evolution of rootraces (and subraces) is concerned, with far-reaching implications.[6]

Bailey's calm acceptance of others' deaths arose from her beliefs about life and death, views reminiscent of Gnosticism that were expressed in *Education in the New Age*: "To the Custodians of God's Plan and to Those Who are working out the new developments, *the form side of life*, the outer tangible expression, is of entirely secondary importance. Your vision is oft distorted by the pain and suffering to which the form is subjected (either your own or that of others, individually or en masse)."[7] ("The form" is New Age-speak for a person.) She reiterated: "let us never forget that it is the *Life*, its purpose and its directed intentional destiny that is of importance; and also that when a form proves inade-

1. Ibid., p491; see also A. Bailey, *Problems of Humanity*, p81: "The release of the energy of the atom is definitely the inauguration of the New Age."
2. A. Bailey, *Externalisation of the Hierarchy*, p497.
3. Ibid., p498.
4. John McManners, *The Oxford Illustrated History of Christianity*, Oxford University Press, 1992, p515.
5. Biographical information is from Michael D. Robbins, "Alice A. Bailey," http://www.esotericastrologer.org/EA%20Essays/EAessaysMDR12.htm, printed 05/19/04. Mary Bailey married Foster Bailey after Alice Bailey, Foster's first wife, died in 1949.
6. Mary Bailey, *A Learning Experience*, 1990, Lucis Publishing Company, pp191–192.
7. A. Bailey, *Education in the New Age*, p111.

quate, or too diseased, or too crippled for the expression of that purpose, it is—from the point of view of the Hierarchy—no disaster when that form has to go. Death is not a disaster to be feared; the work of the Destroyer is not really cruel or undesirable."[1] Rather than being the "last enemy to be destroyed" (1 Cor. 15:26), Bailey says that "death is the great Liberator."[2] This is so because "*The domination of spirit (and its reflection, soul) by matter is what constitutes evil*."[3]

PRAISE FOR COMMUNISM: FROM LENIN TO MAO

Alice Bailey criticized the Stalinist regime in the USSR[4] but said that

> The true communistic platform is sound; it is brotherhood in action and it does not—in its original platform—run counter to the spirit of Christ. The imposition of intellectual and formal communism by a group of ambitious and sometimes evil men is *not* sound; it does not adhere to the true communistic platform, but is based on personal ambitions, love of power and on interpretations of the writings of Lenin and Marx which are also personal and run counter to the meaning of these two men.[5]

Like the Trotskyites, Bailey wished to defend the reputations of Marx and Lenin.

Bailey said that "true Communism" would "prove convincing to the world" after the fall of the Iron Curtain. In *The Rays and The Initiations*, she said,

> In Russia a world ideology is being wrought out which (when proven) can be presented to the world as a model system; this, however, will not come as a result of dictatorship, nor can it be presented aggressively to the world. Russia is in reality—whether she realises it or not—undertaking *a great experiment in education* and, in spite of evil methods and sinning against the soul of human freedom, eventually this educational process will prove convincing to the world and provide a world model. This can only take place when the present group of dictators and arrogant men have passed away or been forced out of power by an awakening people.[6]

She added, "when the present group of totalitarian rulers (behind what you call the 'iron curtain') die out a different state of affairs will gradually supervene and a true Communism (in the spiritual sense of the term) will take the place of the present wickedness."[7]

The economic system that Bailey proposed for the "new world order" will be built on global economic planning and wealth redistribution. In *The Externalisation of the Hierarchy*, she said,

> The new world order will recognise that the produce of the world, the natural resources of the planet and its riches, belong to no one nation but should be shared by all. There will be no nations under the category 'haves' and others under the opposite category. A fair and properly organised distribution of the wheat, the oil and the mineral wealth of the world will be developed, based upon the needs of each nation, upon its own internal resources and the requirements of its people. All this will be worked out in relation to the whole.[8]

1. Ibid., p112.
2. A. Bailey, *The Rays and the Initiation*, p607.
3. Ibid., p144.
4. She opposed Soviet "separateness," not totalitarianism. "The major sin of Russia, and that which has prostituted and warped the initial divine impulse underlying the ideology of that country, is the determination she demonstrates at this time to be separative and to shut the Russian people away from world contact, using the instruments of deception and the withholding of information. It is not the totalitarian nature of the Russian government which is the prime disaster; it is the refusal to develop the universal consciousness. . . . Russia is drifting into a pronounced expression of the great heresy of separateness." (A. Bailey, *The Rays and the Initiation*, p595; see also pp428 and 679 for similar criticisms.)
5. A. Bailey, *The Rays and the Initiations*, p680.
6. Ibid., p632.
7. Ibid., p745.
8. A. Bailey, *Externalisation of the Hierarchy*, p191.

The order of the day will be world central planning: "the entire economic problem and the institution of the needed rules and distributing agencies should be handled by an *economic league of nations*. In this league, all the nations will know their place; they will know their national requirements (based on population and internal resources, etc.) and will also know what they can contribute to the family of nations; all will be animated by a will to the general good."[1]

In *Problems of Humanity*, Bailey said that capitalism must go; "The world economic council (or whatever body represents the resources of the world) *must* free itself from fraudulent politics, capitalistic influence and its devious scheming; it *must* set the resources of the earth free for the use of humanity.... Sharing and cooperation must be taught instead of greed and competition."[2] She added, "The problem of distribution is no longer difficult once the food of the world is freed from politics and from capitalism."[3] Communism, which ruined the economies and the natural environment of the Soviet Union and Eastern Europe, would be attempted on a global scale.

Foster Bailey carried on Alice Bailey's work after his wife's death in 1949. In a 1972 Lucis Trust book, *Running God's Plan*, he praised the Russian Revolution: "Another hierarchical project approved at a centennial conference was to take action to raise the consciousness of the four hundred million mass of Russian people. In a few short years this effort has achieved amazing results and is already an outstanding hierarchical success. It has been demonstrated that hopeless, illiterate peasants when stimulated and given a chance become industrial workers."[4] Historians describe these same events as forced industrialization, coerced collectivization, and man-made famine. He also said, "History may well recognize Khrushchev as the greatest Russian liberator since Lenin"[5]—a telling definition of "liberation," given the totalitarian nature of the regime that Lenin founded.

Foster Bailey's spiritual "hierarchy" of ascended masters also approved of Maoism and the Chinese Cultural Revolution—which was still in progress when *Running God's Plan* was published. Foster Bailey said, "The cultural revolution in China was begun a few short years ago. This also is an hierarchical project. Amazing changes have been achieved in that short period. Chester Ronning, Canada's former Ambassador to China and an authority on China today, says that the Chinese people through revolution have changed their way of thinking. This is fundamental to national reform."[6] He added, "The change for the better in the life of the common people in China in the last few years is more than amazing. Seven hundred million human beings have been lifted into a new way of life."[7] Foster Bailey specifically praised the Cultural Revolution's practice of forcible rustication of city dwellers: "Today under Mao the mass of the people receive the greatest attention.... City dwellers are sent into the countryside to learn of the farmers. Not just how to farm but attitudes to life and to people."[8]

Foster Bailey's spirit guides also approved of the unification of Europe—by whatever means necessary: "Another approved hierarchical project is the uniting of the nations of Europe in one cooperating peaceful community.... One attempt was to begin by uniting the peoples living in the Rhine river valley using that river as a binding factor. It was an attempt by a disciple but did not work. Now another attempt is in full swing, namely the six nation European Common Market."[9] (This "disciple"

1. Ibid., p197.
2. A. Bailey, *Problems of Humanity*, p177.
3. Ibid., p175.
4. F. Bailey, *Running God's Plan*, p12.
5. Ibid., p45.
6. Ibid., pp12–13.
7. Ibid., p165.
8. Ibid., p166.
9. Ibid., pp14–15.

was probably Napoleon, whom Alice Bailey had hailed as a "great conqueror".)[1] Napoleon's principal legacy was death and destruction—"17 years of wars, perhaps six million Europeans dead, France bankrupt, her overseas colonies lost."[2]

Evidently, the Theosophists' spiritual masters in the "Hierarchy" condoned mass bloodshed to achieve their goals. According to the *Black Book of Communism*, there have been approximately 20 million killed under Soviet Communism, and 65 million slain by the Chinese Communists.[3] Many critics of New Age and Gnostic ideology have argued that these world-views are favorable to totalitarianism;[4] the writings of Alice and Foster Bailey bear this out.

How will the New World Order be brought about? In a 1978 pamphlet, Bailey's followers at World Goodwill divided mankind into four classes with varying levels of enlightenment, and stated that social change flows from the Hierarchy to the "New Group of World Servers," and then down to the rest of us:

People in the world at this time can be divided into four groups. . . :

First the uninformed masses. These through poverty, illiteracy, hunger, lack of employment, without leisure or means for cultural advancement are in an inflamed condition. They are, however, enough developed to respond to the mental suggestion and control of more advanced people.

1. A. Bailey, *Externalisation of the Hierarchy*, p133. Corinne McLaughlin and Gordon Davidson, followers of Alice Bailey and supporters of the URI, said, "Napoleon was following the guidance of the Adepts as he successfully began to unify Europe, but they warned him not to invade Russia. His own ego and lust for power overcame him, and he refused to listen. His obsession with power was dramatically expressed by demanding a coronation as emperor and then suddenly seizing the crown and placing it on his own head, rather than allowing the pope to crown him, as was the custom. This symbolized his supreme arrogance in setting himself above even the Pope as God's representative on Earth. By not following the spiritual guidance he was given, Napoleon cut himself off from further help and eventually brought disaster upon himself and his armies." (Corinne McLaughlin and Gordon Davidson, *Spiritual Politics: Changing the World from the Inside Out*, Ballantine Books, 1994, p243). Another Theosophist and follower of Alice Bailey, David Spangler, said the same: "Napoleon was an individual who was sent with a divine destiny to create in Europe something equivalent to the United States of America. His task was to lay a foundation for a United Europe, with one set of laws, one basic language, one coinage, and to eliminate the kind of strife that we have had for the past two hundred years in Europe. Unfortunately, as Napoleon gained power to do this, when he moved into the position where he was able to accomplish this, it went to his head. This was symbolically evident when it was time for him to be crowned Emperor and he seized the crown from the bishop and placed it on his own head. This is very symbolic of an individual's saying, 'It is I who am crowning myself. It is not God.' It was at this point that the spiritual powers of the world that had been backing him and had been responsible for many of his successes withdrew. It was at that point that Napoleon began to go downhill." (David Spangler, *Explorations: Emerging aspects of the new culture*, Findhorn publications lecture series, 1980, p102). Do these fans of tyranny channel information from the same sources, or do they copy each other on the material plane? (For more information on David Spangler, see Ron Rhodes, "The New Age Christ of David Spangler," *Journal* of the Spiritual Counterfeits Project, Vol. 23:2–23:3, 1999, pp20–29; available through http://www.scp-inc.org.)

2. Victor Davis Hansen, "The Little Tyrant: A review of *Napoleon: A Penguin Life*, by Paul Johnson," *Claremont Review of Books*, Summer 2003, http://www.claremont.org/writings/crb/summer2003/hanson.html, printed 06/06/03.

3. Stéphane Courtois et al., *The Black Book of Communism: Crimes, Terror, Repression*, Harvard University Press, 1999, p4.

4. The following works link totalitarianism to Gnosticism: Eric Voegelin, *The New Science of Politics: An Introduction*, University of Chicago Press, 1952; Eric Voegelin, *Science, Politics, and Gnosticism*, Regnery Publishing, 1997; Thomas Molnar, *Utopia: The Perennial Heresy*, Sheed and Ward, 1967; Stephen Muratore, "The Earth's End: Eschatology and the Perception of Nature," *Epiphany*, Vol. 6, no. 4, Summer 1986, pp40–49. However, Stephan A. Hoeller, a present-day Gnostic scholar, denies this link. He says, "All modern totalitarian ideologies are in some way spiritually related to Gnosticism, says Voegelin. Marxists, Nazis, and just about everybody else whom the good professor finds reprehensible are in reality Gnostics, engaged in 'immanentizing the eschaton' by reconstituting society into a heaven on earth. . . . At the same time, Voegelin has to admit that the Gnostics regard the earthly realm as unredeemably flawed. One wonders how such a realm could be turned into an earthly utopia. That Voegelin's supposed Gnostics have no knowledge of or sympathy with historical Gnosticism does not bother him either. Gnostics they are, and that is that. The confusion Voegelin created was made worse by a number of conservative political thinkers, mainly those with Catholic connections. Thomas Molnar, Tito Schabert, and Steven A. McKnight followed Voegelin's theories despite the obvious inconsistencies." (Stephan A. Hoeller, *Gnosticism: New Light on the Ancient Tradition of Inner Knowing*, Quest Books, Theosophical Publishing House, 2002, p183.)

Second, the middle classes—both higher and lower. These constitute the bulk of any nation—intelligent, diligent, often narrow-minded, enquiring, essentially religious; they are torn by economic and ideological conflicts and, because they can read and discuss and are beginning to think, they form the most powerful element in any nation.

Third, the thinkers everywhere. These are the intellectual, highly educated men and women who sense ideas and can formulate them into ideals. They utilise all the known methods to reach the general public. They stir the middle class to activity and, through them, arouse the masses. The part they play is of paramount importance. They are steadily influencing world affairs—sometimes for good and sometimes for selfish ends.

Fourth, the New Group of World Servers. These are the people who are building the new world order. They are all of them definitely serving humanity, and are, through the power of their response to the spiritual opportunity, tide and note, emerging out of every class, group, church, party, race and nation, and are therefore truly representative. . . . They own to no creed, save the creed of Brotherhood, based on the One Life. They recognise no authority save that of their own souls. . . .

Behind this four-fold division of humanity stand those Enlightened Ones whose right and privilege it is to watch over human evolution and to guide the destinies of men. In the West we call them Christ and His disciples. In the theologies of the East they are called by many names. They are also known as the Agents of God, or the Hierarchy of liberated souls, who seek ceaselessly to aid and help humanity. This they do through the implanting of ideas in the minds of the world thinkers, so that these ideas in due time receive recognition and eventually become controlling factors in human life.[1]

This theory of social class and social change gives a new meaning to the term "liberal elitism."

HUMAN CIVILIZATION: DESTRUCTION AND REBIRTH

Bailey wrote in the 1940s that the New Age, which she described as "the new heavens and the new earth," would be preceded by two kinds of "intense creative activity."[2] First would come "*A destructive cycle,* wherein the old order passes away and that which has been created—human civilization with its accompanying institutions—is destroyed. With this destructive action Humanity is today occupying itself—mostly unconsciously. The major creative agents are the intelligentsia of the race."[3] (She appears to have prophesied the global cultural revolution of the 1960s, and the role that the "chattering classes" have played in destabilizing traditional order.) Bailey said that after the destruction of the old order would come the building of the new, "*A cycle of restoration,* with many accompanying difficulties in which the mass of men take part, under the influence and inspiration of a regenerated intelligentsia."[4]

Bailey said that the spiritual Hierarchy has been busy with destruction since 1775. And when humanity achieves spiritual fusion with these entities, the result will be "the final act of destruction." In *The Externalisation of the Hierarchy,* she wrote,

---

1. World Goodwill, "The New Group of World Servers," pp6–7. This fourfold division of mankind is derived from A. Bailey, *Esoteric Psychology,* pp632–639. She listed the classes as "the ignorant masses," "the middle classes," "the thinkers of the world," and "the New Group of World Servers." Above all of these stand "Those Whose privilege and right it is to watch over human evolution and to guide the destinies of man." This material is on-line at http://beaskund.helloyou.ws/netnews/bk/psychology2/psyc2248.html, http://beaskund.helloyou.ws/netnews/bk/psychology2/psyc2249.html, and http://beaskund.helloyou.ws/netnews/bk/psychology2/psyc2250.html (printed 07/20/04); the web site has electronic copies of all the Bailey books.

2. A. Bailey, *The Rays and the Initiation,* p553.

3. Ibid., p553.

4. Ibid., p553.

It is interesting to note (though it is of no immediate moment) that the work of destruction initiated by the Hierarchy during the past one hundred and seventy-five years (therefore since the year 1775) has in it the seeds—as yet a long way from any germination—of the final act of destruction which will take place when the Hierarchy will be so completely fused and blended with Humanity that the hierarchical form will no longer be required. The three major centres will then become the two, and the Hierarchy will disappear and only Shamballa and Humanity will remain. . . . This event of final dissolution will take place only at the close of our planetary existence.[1]

THE END OF THE THEOSOPHICAL ROAD:
"THE CENTER OF PURE DARKNESS"

Bailey also set forth the results that individual seekers would attain from ever-growing closeness to the Hierarchy. Those who learn to meditate will see that "darkness is pure spirit."[2] Followers of Bailey's New Age path will find that "each contact with the Initiator leads the initiate closer to the centre of pure darkness—a darkness which is the very antithesis of darkness as the non-initiate and the unenlightened understand. It is a centre or point of such intense brilliance that everything fades out and *at the place of tension, and at that darkest point, let the group see a point of clear cold fire.*"[3] (Perhaps Dante was right when he described the center of Hell as ice.)[4] She urged her followers toward the "Great Renunciation," "the final great transference, based upon the renunciation of that which for aeons has connoted beauty, truth, and goodness."[5]

Dale McKechnie, Vice President of the Lucis Trust, said in 1998 that "The Bailey books carry one deeper into the relationship between Christ and God and the spiritual Hierarchy."[6] For those with eyes to see, the character of Bailey's "spiritual Hierarchy" is clear: individual intercourse with it leads to "the centre of pure darkness," and when mankind has blended with the Hierarchy, there will be a "final act of destruction."

McKechnie said in 1998 that the teachings of Alice Bailey "oppose what would be called orthodox Christianity. The one overshadows the other."[7] Given the nature of Bailey's teachings, that's an understatement.

---

1. A. Bailey, *Externalisation of the Hierarchy*, pp 566–567. Bailey says that there are now "three major planetary centres—Shamballa, Hierarchy, and Humanity." (Bailey, ibid., p 567) With the fusion of Hierarchy and Humanity, only Shamballa and Humanity, two "planetary centres," will remain.

2. A. Bailey, *The Rays and the Initiations*, p 174.

3. Ibid., p 174.

4. In contrast to Bailey's description of "the Initiator" as "pure darkness," the Apostle John wrote, "This is the message we have heard from him and proclaim to you, that God is light and in him is no darkness at all." (1 John 1:5) Charles Upton warns against Bailey's "clear cold fire." He says, "Fire without heat symbolizes knowledge without love — which, according to St. Augustine in *The City of God*, is precisely demonic knowledge."

5. A. Bailey, *The Rays and the Initiations*, p 224.

6. Telephone interview, April 24, 1998, by Lee Penn of Dale McKechnie, Vice-President of the Lucis Trust.

7. Ibid.

12

PRESENT-DAY
FOLLOWERS OF ALICE BAILEY

PATHWAYS TO PEACE AND ITS THEOSOPHICAL ASSOCIATES

PATHWAYS TO PEACE is listed as a URI Affiliate;[1] its president is Ms. Avon Mattison, who has donated to the URI for several years.[2] She was also a member of the URI "Organizational Design Team" that prepared the initial draft of the URI Charter in early 1998.[3] The vice-president and treasurer of Pathways to Peace, Masankho Banda,[4] is active in the URI.[5] Robert Muller is "Senior Adviser" for Pathways to Peace."[6] Other members of the "Council of Advisers" include Gordon Davidson, Corinne McLaughlin, Jean Houston, Barbara Marx Hubbard, and David Spangler, all of whom are prolific New Age authors.[7] Pathways To Peace says that it "has Consultative II Status with the United Nations Economic and Social Council, and works with the U.N. Centre for Human Rights, U.N. Centre for Human Settlements, UNESCO, UNICEF, and other Agencies. It is also an official Peace Messenger of the United Nations."[8]

Mattison, along with Gordon Davidson and Corinne McLaughlin (who also support the URI), are members of the "Steering Group" of the "World Service Intergroup" (WSI).[9] The WSI's stated purpose is to

> generate a focused, conscious and deliberate intergroup effort to specifically assist the Externalization of the Hierarchy and the Reappearance of the Christ. Hierarchy is a term used here to refer to those spiritual Masters of all traditions who have evolved through human experience to embody greater light, love-wisdom and spiritual power through ceaseless service to humanity and the Divine Plan. They have worked throughout the ages to further human evolution, and They are now in process of 'externalizing' or becoming known in public life. One of our tasks is to recognize them, and assist them by preparing humanity for the imminent reappearance of the World Teacher.[10]

---

1. United Religions Initiative, "Affiliates—North America," http://www.uri.org/regionalnews/affiliates/index.asp, printed 09/23/04.

2. United Religions Initiative, "Honoring Our Donors," *Annual Report* 2001, p10, and United Religions Initiative, "Honoring Our Donors," *Annual Report* 2000, p9.

3. URI on-line archive, e-mail from Sally Ackerly to URI leadership, February 27, 1998, http://origin.org/uri/txt/Org2Design.txt. Printed 1998; no longer on the Net.

4. Pathways to Peace, "Council of Directors," http://www.pathwaystopeace.org/pathways/executive_council.htm, printed 06/06/04 (cited below as Pathways to Peace, "Council of Directors").

5. Masankho Kamsis Banda, "Creating a worldwide Legacy of Peace Messengers" (biography), http://www.ucandanc.org/Biography.html, printed 04/11/03.

6. Pathways to Peace, "Council of Directors."

7. Ibid.

8. Pathways to Peace, "Mission," http://www.pathwaystopeace.org/pathways/organization_and_mission.htm, printed 04/11/03.

9. "World Service Intergroup," http://www.synthesis.tc/, printed 12/16/02 (cited below as "World Service Intergroup").

10. Ibid.

WSI members "study and honor all of the great spiritual teachings of the ages, especially the more modern presentations by H.P. Blavatsky, Alice Bailey, Helena Roerich and other teachers of the Ageless Wisdom."[1] The members of WSI's "Steering Group" are "representatives of esoteric organizations who are willing to dedicate major time and energy to the work of the World Service Intergroup.... All members are long-term students of the Tibetan[2] and have in-depth meditation and intergroup service experience."[3] In short, Mattison, Davidson, and McLaughlin are devotees of the teachings of Alice Bailey.

CORINNE MCLAUGHLIN AND GORDON DAVIDSON

The Dalai Lama wrote a laudatory foreword for McLaughlin and Davidson's *Spiritual Politics*, describing the book as "timely" and "a new approach for creating a happier, more peaceful world."[4] This is surprising, since the authors say that war can be a source of positive social change:

if peace is maintained at any price in order to continue vast injustices and materialistic, wasteful life-styles, then spiritual death may be the result. Physical death is only of the body, the form nature, which according to the Ageless Wisdom will be reborn again in another form. We must be cautious about a stubborn idealism that loves the ideal of peace more than it loves humanity's evolution. We can become so enamored of peace that it leads to inertia, stagnation, and above all else, an attachment to material comfort. Peace and war are not true opposites; peace and change are. War is only one form of change, and often the least effective. Yet there is a role for the right use of destruction when it is used against rigid and crystallized forms of thought and cultural patterns that prevent Life from evolving to its next step.[5]

This belies the Dalai Lama's statement that *Spiritual Politics* promotes a "more peaceful world." McLaughlin and Davidson wrote that

the next release of the Shamballa [sic] energy into human consciousness is planned for the year 2000 ... which will bring another cycle of major upheaval and change as we move into the next millennium. This high-voltage energy of synthesis will test every individual and institution to determine if they are aligned with the Higher Will.... If they are out of alignment, they will degenerate emotionally, physically, and mentally. This process has already begun, as we can see through the downfall of groups that are opposing evolution and synthesis, and will only accelerate in the years ahead.[6]

Shamballa[7] energy "destroys those material forms that have outlived their usefulness and that hinder the free expression of the Light of God.... Once the obstacles to its free expression have been removed, the unifying force released by Shamballa will ... create union and interdependence in religious, social, political, and economic fields."[8] In other words, the Shamballa energy will get the reactionaries out of the way, allowing global unity.

1. Ibid.
2. The Tibetan is the nickname of the spirit who (according to Alice Bailey, as she stated in her books) dictated Bailey's Theosophical books.
3. "World Service Intergroup."
4. Corinne McLaughlin and Gordon Davidson, *Spiritual Politics: Changing the World from the Inside Out*, Ballantine Books, 1994, foreword by His Holiness the Dalai Lama, p xiv (cited below as McLaughlin/Davidson, *Spiritual Politics*).
5. Ibid., p 51.
6. Ibid., p 255.
7. McLaughlin and Davidson mis-spell the term throughout their book; its correct spelling is Shambhala. (See, for example, Christopher Partridge, ed., *New Religions: A Guide—New Religious Movements, Sects, and Alternative Spiritualities*, Oxford University Press, 2004, p 210.)
8. McLaughlin/Davidson, *Spiritual Politics*, pp 252–253.

13

PIERRE TEILHARD DE CHARDIN

FR. PIERRE TEILHARD DE CHARDIN, S. J,. has been a respected teacher for the proponents of the United Religions Initiative and of the New Age movement.

Barbara Marx Hubbard described Teilhard de Chardin as "a spiritual godfather of conscious evolution."[1] Matthew Fox drew upon Teilhard de Chardin when writing about "the cosmic Christ."[2] In an essay titled "My Five Teilhardian Enlightenments," Robert Muller said, "Much of what I have observed in the world bears out the all-encompassing, global, forward-looking philosophy of Teilhard de Chardin."[3] Theosophist David Spangler said that "the life and writings of Pierre Teilhard de Chardin" are "a splendid example of revelation," and consistent with the "general release to the lay public of the mystery teachings" through "such avenues as the Theosophical Society, the Anthroposophical Society, New Thought movements and others."[4] Fr. Daniel Martin, who was the coordinator of the UN's Environmental Sabbath program, said in 1990: "The notion of the Earth being somehow *alive* is helping. It hearkens back to the French philosopher Teilhard de Chardin and subsequently Thomas Berry's thinking, that the whole process of cosmogenesis is a spiritual act; it's the manifestation of the Creator. . . . If you want to put it in a mystical way, we're talking about the birth of God."[5] A group of Teilhard's followers in the Netherlands, the Foundation Teilhard de Chardin in the Netherlands, lists the URI as one of its "Allied Organisations."[6] Ursula King, a founder of the Teilhard Centre in London, said, "Teilhard always sided with the modernists and progressives of any religion, never with the traditionalists. It was a *Neo*-Christianity, but also a *Neo*-Buddhism and a *Neo*-Hinduism, and other reform movements that took the modern world seriously, that in his view could perhaps show us to a spiritually helpful and enriching way forward."[7]

Therefore, Teilhard's views on theology and politics provide background and context for the present-day world-view and agenda of the URI and its New Age, globalist allies. Teilhard's message was consistent over the years; what he said to friends in private letters clarified his more general comments in his essays and addresses.

It should be noted that, however off-beat much of Teilhard's theology was, he remained Christian and loyal to the Catholic Church. In 1951, he wrote to his superior, the General of the Jesuits in Rome,

1. Barbara Marx Hubbard, *The Revelation: A Message of Hope for the New Millennium*, Nataraj Publishing, Novato, CA, 1995, p335.

2. Matthew Fox, *The Coming of the Cosmic Christ: The Healing of Mother Earth and the Birth of a Global Renaissance*, Harper San Francisco, 1988, pp77, 83, 137.

3. Robert Muller, *New Genesis: Shaping a Global Spirituality*, World Happiness and Cooperation, 1993, p160.

4. David Spangler, *Revelation: The Birth of a New Age*, Lorian Press, 1976 (5th Lorian Press printing 1984), p145.

5. Fr. Daniel Martin, "The Birth of God," *In Context*, issue 24, "Late Winter 1990," http://context.org/ICLIB/IC24/Griffin.htm, printed 07/20/04.

6. Foundation Teilhard de Chardin in the Netherlands, "Allied Organisations," http://home.worldonline.nl/~sttdc/alli.htm, printed 08/02/04.

7. Ursula King, *Christ In All Things: Exploring Spirituality with Teilhard de Chardin*, The 1996 Bampton Lectures, Orbis Books, 1997, p109.

that "I now feel more indissolubly bound to the hierarchical Church and to the Christ of the Gospel than ever before in my life. Never has Christ seemed to me more real, more personal, and more immense."[1] In a journal entry made within a week of his death in 1955, Teilhard said that Christ "is the most sustaining and only redeeming force."[2]

Despite the resemblances (noted below) between his writings and those of the Theosophists, Teilhard was not a Theosophist himself. In 1932, he said that the current "revival of theosophy and neo-Buddhism" in the West "appears to be founded upon a vast misunderstanding. . . . *In strict logic*, the Indian sage cannot concern himself with anything the life of the world has been, is, or will be. His European followers, I fear, are a long way from realizing this."[3] Teilhard wrote in 1934 that he aimed at "a general convergence of religions upon a universal Christ who fundamentally satisfies them all: that seems to me the only possible conversion of the world, and the only form in which a religion of the future can be conceived."[4] He viewed Theosophy as world-denying, and wished instead to affirm the divinely oriented evolution of the world.

Teilhard saw no contradiction between faith in God and faith in human and terrestrial evolution. He said, "The super-naturalising Christian Above is incorporated (not immersed) in the human Ahead! And at the same time Faith in God, in the very degree in which it assimilates and sublimates within its own spirit the spirit of Faith in the World, regains all its power to convert!"[5]

THE EMERGING "COMMON SOUL OF HUMANITY"

Foreshadowing Bishop Swing's chatter about the emergence of a "global soul,"[6] Teilhard de Chardin said in 1937,

> Under the combined effect of the material needs and spiritual affinities of life, humanity all around us is beginning to emerge from impersonality and assume some sort of heart and face. With the recording of this mysterious birth, the most general picture so far vouchsafed us of the biological current that is drawing us on is completed and disappears from sight. The organization of human energy, taken as a whole, is directed and pushes us towards the ultimate formation, over and above each personal element, *of a common soul of humanity.*[7]

(Did you know that you are a "personal element"?)

In March 1945, Teilhard said, "For men upon earth, all the earth, to learn to love one another, it is not enough that they should know themselves to be members of one and the same *thing*; in 'planetising' themselves they must acquire the consciousness, without losing themselves, of becoming one and

1. Pierre Teilhard de Chardin, *Letters from a Traveller*, Harper and Brothers Publishers, 1962, p43 (cited below as Teilhard, *Letters from a Traveller*).

2. As quoted in "Homily for the Mass of the tenth anniversary of the death of Pierre Teilhard de Chardin," delivered by Fr. André Ravier, Paris, March 25, 1965, in Pierre Teilhard de Chardin and Maurice Blondel, *Correspondence, With Notes and Commentary by Henri de Lubac, S.J.*, Herder and Herder, 1967, first pub. 1965, p169.

3. Pierre Teilhard de Chardin, "The Road of the West," in *Toward the Future*, translated by René Hague, Harvest/HBJ, 1973, pp44–45 (the essay collectioin is cited below as *Toward the Future*).

4. Pierre Teilhard de Chardin, "How I Believe," in *Christianity and Evolution*, translated by René Hague, Harcourt Brace Jovanovich, 1971, p130.

5. Pierre Teilhard de Chardin, "The Heart of the Problem," *The Future of Man*, translated by Norman Denny, Harper Torchbooks, 1969 ed., pp280–281 (the essay collection is cited below as *The Future of Man*).

6. Bishop William Swing, "What is missing is a global soul," *Pacific Church News*, August/September 1995, p5.

7. Pierre Teilhard de Chardin, "Human Energy," in *Human Energy*, translated by J.M. Cohen, Collins, 1969, first pub. 1962, p137 (the essay collectioin is cited below as *Human Energy*).

the same *person*."[1] This insistence that people merge their separated personhood into the One was recently restated by Neale Donald Walsch's spirit guide, who said, "The highest choice for the Self becomes the highest choice for another when the Self realizes that there is no one else,"[2] and that "*You must stop seeing God as separate from you, and you as separate from each other. The only solution is the Ultimate Truth: nothing exists in the universe that is separate from anything else.*"[3]

THE BLEAK ESCHATOLOGY OF THE "OMEGA POINT"

Although there's no evidence that Teilhard de Chardin was aware of (let alone a follower of) Alice Bailey, he appeared to share her view that death could be a liberation from material existence. In *Human Energy*, he asked in 1931, "How will the spiritual evolution of our planet end, we asked at the conclusion of the preceding chapter? Perhaps, we will now reply, in a psychic rather than material turning point—possibly like a death—which will in fact be a liberation from the material plane of history and elevation in God."[4]

Teilhard proposed in 1945 in *The Future of Man* that,

> Is it not conceivable that Mankind, at the end of its totalisation, its folding-in upon itself, may reach a critical level of maturity where, leaving the Earth and stars to lapse slowly back into the dwindling mass of primordial energy, it will detach itself from this planet and join the one true, irreversible essence of things, the Omega point? A phenomenon perhaps outwardly akin to death: but in reality a simple metamorphosis and arrival at the supreme synthesis. . . . In any event, of all the theories which we may evolve concerning the end of the Earth, it is the only one which affords a coherent prospect wherein, in the remote future, the deepest and most powerful currents of human consciousness may converge and culminate: intelligence and action, learning and religion.[5]

Teilhard has a reputation as an evolutionary optimist, but his eschatological vision is far bleaker than the Biblical promise of "a new heaven and a new earth," in which "the dwelling of God is with men," and God will "wipe away every tear from their eyes." (Rev. 21 : 1, 3, 4).

"FAITH IN PROGRESS"

Teilhard sometimes wrote as an ardent believer in human progress, and sometimes as one who looked beyond such temporal goals to Christ.

Teilhard wrote in 1941, "I am convinced that finally it is upon the idea of progress, and faith in progress, that Mankind, today so divided, must rely and can reshape itself."[6] In 1947, he said, "Let us not forget that faith in peace is not possible, not justifiable, except in a world dominated by faith in the future, *faith in Man* and the progress of Man."[7] Teilhard explained his zeal in a letter to a friend that year:

1. Pierre Teilhard de Chardin, "Life and the Planets: What is Happening at this Moment on Earth?," in *The Future of Man*, p120.

2. Neale Donald Walsch, *Conversations with God: An Uncommon Dialogue, Book 3*, Hampton Roads Publishing Company, Inc., 1998, p9.

3. Neale Donald Walsch, *Conversations with God: An Uncommon Dialogue, Book 2*, Hampton Roads Publishing Company, Inc., 1997, p173.

4. Pierre Teilhard de Chardin, "The Spirit of the Earth," in *Human Energy*, p47.

5. Pierre Teilhard de Chardin, "Life and the Planets: What is Happening at this Moment on Earth?," in *The Future of Man*, pp122–123.

6. Pierre Teilhard de Chardin, "Some Reflections on Progress," in *The Future of Man*, p81.

7. Pierre Teilhard de Chardin, "Faith in Peace," in *The Future of Man*, p154.

The Christian faith can recover and survive only by incorporating faith in human progress. And it is also my conviction that if this synthesis between faith in God and faith in Man were put into effect we would again see (and in much more universal and intense form) what has happened a few times in history (for example with Buddhism, Christianity, and Marxism); I mean the spreading like wildfire of a new state of mind. Is it not this climate and this new atmosphere that are necessary if our incredible technological resources are to succeed in producing their natural result of human unification?[1]

Nevertheless, in 1947 he told the French section of the World Congress of Faiths, "Correctly interpreted, I repeat, faith in Man can and indeed must cast us at the feet and into the arms of One who is greater than ourselves."[2] Teilhard warned that the idea of "Man, self-sufficient and wholly autonomous" was "the modern version of the heroic temptation of all time, that of the Titans, of Prometheus, of Babel and of Faust; that of Christ on the mountain."[3]

APOLOGETICS FOR TOTALITARIANISM

In his writings before, during, and after World War II, Teilhard explicitly and repeatedly favored totalitarianism. He was able to discern "contributions" to human evolution from the tyrants of his time, and did so in his public essays and in his private letters to friends.

Teilhard said in 1937 in *Human Energy*, the future economy "must be international and in the end totalitarian":

Seemingly, no less urgent than the question of sources of energy is the world-wide installation of a general economy of production and labour, reinforced by the establishment of a rational gold policy. Financial and social crises are at pains to remind us how confused our theories are in these matters and how barbarous our conduct. But when will men decide to recognize that no serious progress can be made in these directions except under two conditions: first that the proposed organization must be international and in the end totalitarian;[4] and secondly that it must be conceived on a very large scale.[5]

In March, 1939, Teilhard wrote that the time for "egotistical autonomy" had passed; "The individual, if he is to fulfil and preserve himself, must strive to break down every kind of barrier that prevents separate beings from uniting. His is the exaltation, not of egotistical autonomy but of communion with all others! Seen in this light the modern totalitarian regimes, whatever their initial defects, are neither heresies nor biological regressions: they are in line with the essential trend of 'cosmic' movement."[6] Furthermore,

In the totalitarian political systems, of which time will correct the excesses but will also, no doubt, accentuate the underlying tendencies or intuitions, the citizen finds his centre of gravity gradually transferred to, or at least aligned with, that of the national or ethnic group to which he belongs. This is not a return to primitive and undifferentiated cultural forms, but the emergence of a defined social system in which a purposeful organisation orders the masses and tends to impose a specialised function on each individual.[7]

1. Pierre Teilhard de Chardin, *Letters to Two Friends* 1926–1952, The New American Library, 1968, p102, letter of October 16, 1947 (cited below as Teilhard, *Letters to Two Friends*).

2. Pierre Teilhard de Chardin, "Faith in Man," in *The Future of Man*, p188.

3. Ibid., p188.

4. Here, Teilhard's editor inserted a footnote: "Obviously this adjective is intended to convey a general notion of totality, not a so-called 'totalitarian' regime." After reviewing Teilhard's other comments about totalitarian regimes, readers may reach their own conclusion about the accuracy of the editor's optimistic assessment of Teilhard's intent.

5. Pierre Teilhard de Chardin, "Human Energy," in *Human Energy*, pp133–134.

6. Pierre Teilhard de Chardin, "The Grand Option," in *The Future of Man*, p46.

7. Ibid., p39.

Teilhard concluded,

So there is no way out, if we wish to safeguard the pre-eminence of the spirit, except by taking the one road that remains to us, which leads to the preservation and further advance of consciousness—the road of unification. A convergent world, whatever sacrifice of freedom it may seem to demand of us, is the only one which can preserve the dignity and the aspirations of the living being. Therefore, *it must be true.* If we are to avoid total anarchy, the source and the sign of universal death, we can do no other than plunge resolutely forward, even though something in us perish, into the melting-pot of socialization.[1]

Teilhard expressed his boredom with the Allied cause in World War II in December 1939:

And still I cannot yet be really excited by this war. I realize its urgency, and its drama, and even the great Object it is to repel the reign of material force. But I have an obscure feeling that the Allies are fighting too much for quietness and stability (or rather immobility); and this point becomes always clearer in myself: the only fight in which I would like to mix and to die should be a battle for construction and movement ahead. . . . I still hope that some agreement may be reached without any major clash. . . . Whatever should be the end, the world needs a thorough readjustment under a more definite human common ideal.[2]

Within days of the French collapse in 1940, Teilhard wrote, "Since the beginning, I did not like this war; because I felt (maybe I told you) that, on the Allies' side, there was *not* any spirit of conquest and renovation: only fighting to keep going on an old-fashioned, 'bourgeoise,' [sic] conception of Man. There is something dreadfully primitive and narrow in the Hitler's [sic] religion and ideal. But the Germans had an internal flame, and *this* was too strong for us, much more than the tanks."[3]

In August 1940, Teilhard wrote to a friend that "the Germans deserve to win" the war:

Personally, I stick to my idea that we are watching the birth, more than the death, of a World. But the scandal, as you point it exactly, is that England and France should have come to this tragedy because they have sincerely tried the road of peace! But did they not precisely make a mistake on the true meaning of 'peace'? 'Peace' can not mean anything but a *higher process of conquest.* And, since 1919, France at least did scarcely more than to stick comfortably to the old routines. World is bound to belong to its most active elements. If we are defeated today by sheer brutal force, the reason is, I believe, that we did not, after the last war, find a spiritual and constructive outlet for force. Just now, the Germans deserve to win because, however bad or mixed is their spirit, they have more spirit than the rest of the world. It is easy to criticize and despise the fifth column. But no spiritual aim or energy will ever succeed, or even deserve to succeed, unless it proves able to spread and to keep spreading a fifth column. To incorporate spirit in Force (or either to sublimate Force into spirit), this is the problem, and this ought to be our dream. . . . In fact, I am even unable to understand what did really happen in June, and what this funny Pétain government really means.[4]

Teilhard's desire to unite spirit and Force calls to mind Daniel's prophecy concerning an eschatological tyrant: "But in his estate shall he honour the God of forces: and a god whom his fathers knew not shall he honour with gold, and silver, and with precious stones, and pleasant things." (Dan. 11:38, KJV)

Later that same month, Teilhard said, "Pétain government is full of good will; but, I am afraid, it has no spark, and the reforms it promotes have no clean roots in the country. . . . The great present crisis obliges everybody to face the major problem of constructing the World as a whole. Provided we escape the temptation to take refuge in the old shelters, nothing better could happen to drive us ahead."[5]

1. Ibid., p52.
2. Teilhard, *Letters to Two Friends*, p138, letter of December 13, 1939.
3. Ibid., p145, letter of June 18, 1940.
4. Ibid., pp146–147, letter of August 3, 1940. Nazi Germany had invaded and defeated France in May/June 1940, and forced the installation of a collaborationist government, headed by Pétain.
5. Ibid., p150, letter of August 18, 1940.

In September 1940, Teilhard wrote, "Of one thing I am certain: that you are reacting with all your strength to the defeat and are trying to find a way that will lead to a renaissance that will not be a bourgeois 'Restoration.' From this distance, it is the spectre of such a 'Restoration' that most disturbs me. Vichy's copy-book maxims for good children seem to be entirely to lack the fire which alone can bring about the virtues so rightly advocated."[1] What "virtues" did the collaborationist government advocate, and why would Teilhard have found "bourgeois restoration" more disturbing than the occupation of his country by the Nazis? (However, in October 1940, Teilhard wrote that it was "especially painful for me to 'swallow' some of Vichy's attitudes. The more I have always been since 1920 an advocate of a friendly understanding with Germany, the more repugnant to me now is a forced understanding which would entail a sort of betrayal of our real friends" in "the Anglo-Saxon circles."[2])

In February 1941, Teilhard wrote to a friend,

> My leading idea, just now, is that the true crisis of the world, today, does not lie exactly in a conflict between totalitarians and democrats, but between mobilists and fixists. If the democracies were not hampered by the heavy load of fixism which hides, and excuses (glorifies) itself among them, under the usurped name of Liberty, they would swallow in no time the powers of the Axis, or at least they would soon find a ground for mutual achievement. A *progressive* democrat is not fundamentally different from a really progressive totalitarian. Consequently, the main thing today, on the field of sound propaganda, is to make a campaign for the faith (a passionate and rational faith) in a well-understood human progress.[3]

At the end of the letter, he added, "I envy the Britons. . . . Not only do they save themselves. But, since Dunkirk, it would seem that they have stolen from the Nazis the moral leadership of the world."[4] (What manner of theologian would concede, even in the past tense, that the Nazis had *ever* had "the moral leadership of the world" that could be "stolen" from them?)

In March 1941, Teilhard wrote, "I am convinced that the present war is, at bottom, a conflict between 'mobilists' and 'immobilists,' and that it will stop the minute the mobilists, in each camp, will recognize each other and drop the political and religious immobilists."[5] He added that he was "greatly pleased by the booklet of Anne Lindbergh, 'The Wave of the Future.'"[6] (In that pamphlet, Lindbergh had written, "I cannot see this war, then, simply and purely, as a struggle between the 'Forces of Good' and the 'Forces of Evil.' If I could simplify it into a phrase at all, it would seem truer to say that the 'Forces of the Past' are fighting against the 'Forces of the Future.' The tragedy is, to the honest spectator, that there is so much that is good in the 'Forces of the Past,' and so much that is evil in the 'Forces of the Future.'"[7]) Teilhard had said the same in December 1940: "I strongly believe with Anne Lindbergh that this present war is only 'scum on the wave of the future.'"[8] Note the timing: the Jesuit theologian and the American writer perceived ambiguity in World War II at the time that the Nazis and the Soviets were still allies, and when Hitler was at the peak of his power in Europe.

In August 1941, Teilhard wrote,

> A profound source of personal irritation is my inability to take sides in the conflict. . . . Fundamentally, the only thing I believe in, the only thing I have chosen, is that one must believe in a Future of the Earth which will coincide with a 'totalisation' of Humanity. My 'enemies' are those who deny Progress. And this, by the way, is why

1. Teilhard, *Letters from a Traveller*, p 267, letter of September 20, 1940.
2. Ibid., pp 270–271, letter of October 30, 1940.
3. Teilhard, *Letters to Two Friends*, p 154, letter of February 9, 1941.
4. Ibid., p 155, letter of February 9, 1941. The ellipsis was in the original text.
5. Ibid., p 156, letter of March 21, 1941.
6. Ibid., p 156, letter of March 21, 1941.
7. Anne Morrow Lindbergh, *The Wave of the Future*, as quoted in John Lukacs, *The Last European War: September 1939/December 1941*, Yale University Press, 2001, p 514—including the footnote for the Lindbergh pamphlet.
8. Teilhard, *Letters to Two Friends*, p 153, letter of December 22, 1940.

since September 1939 I have not cared for this war which, from the French point of view, was merely a defense of egoism and the status quo. The constructive idealism, however distorted, was 'on the other side.' For the last year, fortunately, things have been changing, and the democracies are beginning to understand that freedom is a thing that is won by means of organized effort. But the separation of the elements is far from complete. . . . No one will ever dissuade me from thinking that the real divide, the real human conflict of today, is not between democrats, fascists, communists, and Christians, but between those who do and do not believe that there is a Humanity to be constructed over and above man (to save and complete Man, to be precise). It is a struggle between Stability and Movement.[1]

Concerning the Vichy regime, he added,

I have no taste for a pan-European serfdom that would lead us straight to the anthill (which it is biologically necessary to avoid). It seems that in the shadow of Vichy a sincere effort at reconstruction is under way which is not simply a reaction (that would be the end of everything!). Granting this, it seems evident from a distance that 'honor is lost' on that side. And I have no confidence in reforms, however timely, that are built on a foundation of cowardice. . . . Where are our fathers of '89! Actually I feel as if for the moment I no longer have a country. But there is still the Earth.[2]

In March 1945, Teilhard said,

I do not think we are yet in a position to judge recent totalitarian experiments fairly: that is to say, to decide whether, all things considered, they have produced a greater degree of enslavement or a higher level of spiritual energy. It is too early to say. But I believe this can be said, that in so far as these first attempts may seem to be tending dangerously towards the sub-human state of the ant-hill or the termitary, it is not the principle of totalisation that is at fault but the clumsy and incomplete way in which it has been applied.[3]

In December 1945, Teilhard proposed surrender to inevitable historic trends:

Although our individualistic instincts may rebel against this drive towards the collective, they do so in vain and wrongly. In vain, because no power in the world can enable us to escape from what is in itself the power of the world. And wrongly because the real nature of this impulse that is sweeping us toward a state of super-organisation is such as to make us more completely personalised and human. The very fact of us becoming aware of this profound ordering of things will enable human collectivisation to pass beyond the *enforced* phase, where it now is, into the *free* phase: that in which (men having at last understood that they are inseparably joined elements of a converging Whole, and having learnt in consequence to *love* the preordained forces that unite them) a natural union of affinity and sympathy will supersede the forces of compulsion.[4]

At the end, such was the fate of Winston, the central character of *1984*: "He had won the victory over himself. He loved Big Brother."[5]

In 1947, Teilhard predicted a convergence between Christianity and Marxism, equating the faith of the Stalinists to that of the Christians: "Take the two extremes confronting us at this moment, the Marxist and the Christian, each a convinced believer in his own particular doctrine, but each, we must suppose, fundamentally inspired with an equal faith in Man. . . . The divergence between them is in reality neither complete nor final. . . . Followed to their conclusion the two paths must certainly end by coming together: for in the nature of things everything that is faith must rise, and everything that

1. Ibid., pp99–100, letter of August 5, 1941.
2. Ibid., p100, letter of August 5, 1941.
3. Pierre Teilhard de Chardin, "Life and the Planets: What is Happening at this Moment on Earth?," in *The Future of Man*, pp118–119.
4. Pierre Teilhard de Chardin, "A Great Event Foreshadowed: the Planetisation of Mankind," in *The Future of Man*, pp124–125.
5. George Orwell, *1984*, New American Library edition, 1961, p245.

rises must converge."[1] He wrote this at the time that organized Marxism was, almost uniformly, explicitly Stalinist.

In 1949—when the USSR was imposing Communism on the East European nations, and when the crimes of the Nazis were known to all—Teilhard said that totalitarianism was one of the "natural components" needed for human progress, anthropogenesis:

> But does not the strange and persistent cleavage, so invariably manifest within so-called democratic movements in the opposed concepts of liberalism and *dirigisme* (or individualism and totalitarianism) explain itself when we realise that, although they may look like contradictory social ideals, they are in fact natural components (personalisation and totalisation) whose interaction biologically determines the essence and progress of anthropogenesis? On the one hand we have a system centred on the individual, and on the other a system centred on the group. . . . But there is really no contradiction in this. It is simply a matter of disconnection and disharmony which may even (why not?) be an inevitable and necessary alteration. Biologically, let me repeat, there can be no true Democracy without the balanced combination of these two complementary factors, which in their pure state are expressed, one by individualist and the other by authoritarian regimes.[2]

However, in May 1952, Teilhard wrote that the abatement of tension between the USSR and the US would not be possible "until the Russians stop telling lies (give up their 'morality of deception'), which is the root of the matter."[3]

In *The Phenomenon of Man*, Teilhard spoke more harshly against Communism and Nazism than he did elsewhere, but still said that "modern totalitarianism" is "really the distortion of something magnificent, and thus quite near to the truth":

> The Million in rank and file on the parade ground; the Million standardized in the factory; the Million motorised—and all this only ending up with Communism and National-Socialism and the most ghastly fetters. So we get the crystal instead of the cell; the ant-hill instead of brotherhood. Instead of the upsurge of consciousness which we expected, it is mechanisation that seems to emerge inevitably from totalisation. *'Eppur si muove!'*[4] In the presence of such a profound perversion of the rules of noogenesis,[5] I hold that our reaction should not be one of despair but of a determination to re-examine ourselves. When an energy runs amok, the engineer, far from questioning the power itself, simply works out his calculations afresh to see how it can be better brought under control. Monstrous as it is, is not modern totalitarianism really the distortion of something magnificent, and thus quite near to the truth?[6]

BALANCING "LAISSEZ FAIRE" WITH "FIRMNESS"

In the late 1940s, Teilhard offered the nascent UN an ambiguous perspective on human rights and individual freedom. He provided loopholes for those who would remake mankind, loopholes large enough to hold a Gulag.

1. Pierre Teilhard de Chardin, "Faith in Man," in *The Future of Man*, pp 191–192.
2. Pierre Teilhard de Chardin, "The Essence of the Democratic Idea: A Biological Approach," in *The Future of Man*, pp 241–242.
3. Pierre Teilhard de Chardin, *Letters from a Traveller*, p 328, letter of May 29, 1952.
4. "And yet it does move!," a legendary saying commonly ascribed to the astronomer Galileo. He supposedly said this under his breath at the end of his trial by the Inquisition, after being forced to recant the idea that the Earth revolves around the Sun.
5. Noogenesis is the rise of "a collective spirit of human consciousness encompassing the globe" (John Grim and Mary Evelyn Tucker, "Introduction," in Arthur Fabel and Donald St. John, eds., *Teilhard in the 21st Century: The Emerging Spirit of Earth*, Orbis Books, 2003, p 6 (cited below as *Teilhard in the 21st Century*).
6. Pierre Teilhard de Chardin, *The Phenomenon of Man*, Book Four, Chapter Two, "Beyond The Collective: the Hyper-Personal," Harper and Row, 1965 translation, pp 256–257 (cited below as Teilhard, *The Phenomenon of Man*).

In 1947, Teilhard told UNESCO that

the purpose of a new Declaration of the Rights of Man cannot be, as formerly, to ensure the highest possible degree of independence for the individual in society, but to define the conditions under which the inevitable totalisation of Mankind may be effected, not only without impairing but so as to enhance, I will not say the autonomy of each of us but (a quite different thing) the incommunicable singularity of being which each of us possesses. We must no longer seek to organise the world in favour of, and in terms of, the isolated individual; we must try to combine all things for the perfection ('personalisation') of the individual by his well-ordered integration with the unified group in which Mankind must eventually culminate, both organically and spiritually. . . . Whatever measures may be adopted to this end, there is one major principle which must be affirmed and always upheld: in no circumstances, and for no reason, must the forces of collectivity compel the individual to deform or falsify himself (by accepting as true what he sees to be false, for example, which is to lie to himself). Every limitation imposed on the autonomy of the element by the power of the group must, if it is to be justified, operate only in conformity with the free internal structure of the element. Otherwise a fundamental disharmony will arise in the very heart of the collective human organism. Three principles therefore: The absolute duty of the individual to develop his own personality. The relative right of the individual to be placed in circumstances as favourable as possible to his personal development. The absolute right of the individual, within the social organism, not to be deformed by external coercion but inwardly super-organised by persuasion, that is to say, in conformity with his personal endowments and aspirations.[1]

Teilhard said in 1949 that

There are two *general conditions* which must at all costs be observed in the planning of democratic institutions. The first of these is that the individual must be allowed the widest possible liberty of choice within which to develop his personal qualities (the one theoretical restriction being that his choice should be exercised in the direction of heightened powers of reflection and consciousness). The second, off-setting the first, is that everything must be done to promote and foster currents of convergence (collective organisations) within which alone, by the laws of anthropogenesis, individual action can achieve its fulfilment and full substance. In short, what is needed is a judicious mixture of *laissez-faire* and firmness. The problem is one of moderation, tact and 'art' for which no hard-and-fast rules can be laid down, but which, in each particular case, any body of people is perfectly capable of solving in its own way—provided its instinct of progress and 'super-humanisation' is sufficiently developed.[2]

"Firmness," of course, could include imposition of Soviet-style dictatorship, and local or national self-determination on these matters might be limited to those whose "instinct of progress" was adequate.

A PRAGMATIC, EVOLUTIONARY CASE
FOR EUTHANASIA AND EUGENICS

Teilhard de Chardin advanced a hard-line, Darwinian justification for euthanasia. In *Human Energy*, he said in 1937 that "the strong" needed to consider new ways to handle "life's rejects" in the hospitals:

How should we judge the efforts we lavish in all kinds of hospitals on saving what is so often no more than one of life's rejects? Something profoundly true and beautiful (I mean faith in the irreplaceable value and unpredictable resources contained in each personal unit) is evidently concealed in persistent sacrifice to save a human existence. But should not this solicitude of man for his individual neighbour be balanced by a higher passion, born of the faith in that other higher personality that is to be expected, as we shall see, from the world-wide

1. Pierre Teilhard de Chardin, "Some Reflections on the Rights of Man," in *The Future of Man*, pp194–195.
2. Pierre Teilhard de Chardin, "The Essence of the Democratic Idea: A Biological Approach," in *The Future of Man*, pp242–243.

achievements of our evolution? To what extent should not the development of the strong (to the extent that we can define this quality) take precedence over the preservation of the weak? How can we reconcile, in a state of maximum efficiency, the care lavished on the wounded with the more urgent necessities of battle?[1] In what does true charity consist?[2]

(Did you know that each of us is a "personal unit"? So much for the notion that we are all created in the image of God). Teilhard's beliefs are consistent with Alice Bailey's teaching that "when a form proves inadequate, or too diseased, or too crippled for the expression of that purpose, it is—from the point of view of the Hierarchy—no disaster when that form has to go."[3]

In *The Phenomenon of Man*, Teilhard made the case for eugenics as a planned response to the suppression of the *"crude forces of natural selection"* among mankind: "So far we have certainly allowed our race to develop at random, and we have given too little thought to the question of what medical and moral factors *must replace the crude forces of natural selection* should we suppress them. In the course of the coming centuries it is indispensable that a nobly human form of eugenics, on a standard worthy of our personalities, should be discovered and developed. Eugenics applied to individuals leads to eugenics applied to society."[4]

Likewise, in 1948, he said that after the seventeenth century, the

earth's population began to shoot up in an alarming fashion. . . . Now we suddenly see the saturation point ahead of us, and approaching at a dizzy speed. How are we to prevent this compression of Mankind on the closed surface of the planet (a thing that is good in itself, as we have seen, since it promotes social unification) from passing that critical point beyond which any increase in numbers will mean famine and suffocation? Above all, how are we to assure that the maximum population, when it is reached, shall be composed only of elements harmonious in themselves and blended as harmoniously as possible together? Individual eugenics[5] (breeding and education designed to produce only the best individual types) and racial eugenics (the grouping or intermixing of different ethnic types being not left to chance but effected as a controlled process in the proportions most beneficial to humanity as a whole) both, as I well know, come up against apparently insuperable difficulties, from the point of view of technical organisation and from that of psychological resistance. But this does not alter the fact that the problem of building a healthy Mankind already stares us in the face and is growing more acute every day.[6]

Teilhard saw the obstacles to eugenics (including "racial eugenics") as technical and "psychological resistance," not as moral laws forbidding such actions.

Teilhard's enthusiasm for eugenics was shared among authoritarians of the Right, the Center, and the Left during the last century. The US had taken the lead in these policies; starting in 1899, 35 states allowed the sterilization of the mentally handicapped. Michael Burleigh, a historian of the Third Reich, reported, "Wealthy philanthropists bore the costs of the eugenics laboratory at Cold Spring Harbor," the New York-based center of this movement, as well as for a eugenics institute in Munich under the Weimar Republic.[7] (This foreshadowed the zeal for contraception and population control among present-day American billionaires and foundations.) Burleigh continued, "German eugenicists

1. Here, Teilhard's editor inserted an exculpatory footnote: "Teilhard's constant efforts both to encourage the weak and inspire the strong prove that he knew how to make this reconciliation."
2. Pierre Teilhard de Chardin, "Human Energy," in *Human Energy*, p133.
3. Alice A. Bailey, *Education in the New Age*, 1954, Lucis Publishing Company, p112.
4. Teilhard, *The Phenomenon of Man*, Book Four, Chapter Three, "The Ultimate Earth," p282.
5. Here, Teilhard added a footnote: "The word is used here in its general and etymological sense of 'perfection in the continuance and fufilment of the species.'" (Pierre Teilhard de Chardin, "The Directions and Conditions of the Future," in *The Future of Man*, p243.)
6. Pierre Teilhard de Chardin, "The Directions and Conditions of the Future," in *The Future of Man*, pp242–243.
7. Michael Burleigh, *The Third Reich: A New History*, Hill and Wang, 2000, p346.

in turn enthused over American sterilisation laws and the 1924 Immigration Restriction Act.... American studies of 'poor white trash' families ... were effortlessly absorbed into the visual repertory of the National Socialists."[1] Nazi eugenics led to compulsory sterilization of the "unfit," and to the mass murder of the disabled and the chronically ill.[2]

Fabian socialists in Britain likewise favored eugenics. As Burleigh reports,

In Britain, where in 1931 a Labour MP endeavoured to introduce legislation permitting voluntary sterilisation, the Fabian Socialist Sidney Webb gave the game away about this enthusiasm, when he announced 'no consistent eugenicist can be a "laissez faire" individualist unless he throws up the game in despair. He must interfere, interfere, interfere!' Apart from a doctrinaire credulousness towards the prophylactic powers of modern science, some illiberal socialists wished to police and reform the lifestyles of those 'Lumpenproletarians' who did not conform to their ideals of what working-class people should be.[3]

In his 1928 manifesto *The Open Conspiracy*, the reformer H.G. Wells avowed the need for "directed breeding," adding that "the world community of our desires, the organised world community conducting and ensuring its own progress, requires a deliberate collective control of population as a primary condition."[4]

The Communists also supported eugenics. Robert Proctor, a historian of medicine under the Nazis, noted that "in 1931 the Communist Party of Germany expressed support for the sterilization of psychiatric patients under certain circumstances.... between 1931 and 1938 Germany and the Soviet Union shared a joint Institute for Racial Biology established in Moscow on the initiative of the German eugenicists Ludwig Aschoff and Oscar Vogt."[5] In 1932, the American Communist leader William Z. Foster wrote that "Communist society" will "turn its attention to the subjective factor, to the fundamental improvement of man himself" and will

go farther. It will scientifically regulate the growth of population. It will especially speed up the very evolution of man himself, his brain and body. Capitalism has checked the evolution of the human species, if it has not actually brought about a process of race degeneration. But Communism will systematically breed up mankind. Already the scientific knowledge is at hand to do this, but it is at present inapplicable because of the idiocy of the capitalist system, its planlessness, its antiquated moral codes, its warp and woof of exploitation.[6]

DARWINIAN RACISM

In a 1937 essay in *Human Energy*, Teilhard favored eugenics as a way for the "advancing wing of humanity" to deal with "fixed or definitely unprogressive ethnical groups":

In this field the apostles of birth control (although too often inspired by the narrow desire of relieving individual hardships) will have rendered us the service of opening our eyes to the anomaly of a society that concerns itself with everything except the recruitment of its own elements. Now eugenics does not confine itself to a simple control of births. All sorts of related questions, scarcely yet raised despite their urgency, are attached to it. What fundamental attitude, for example, should the advancing wing of humanity take to fixed or definitely unprogressive ethnical groups? The earth is a closed and limited surface. To what extent should it tolerate, racially or nationally, areas of lesser activity?[7]

1. Ibid., p 346.
2. Ibid., pp 345–404.
3. Ibid., pp 346–347.
4. H.G. Wells, *The Open Conspiracy: Blue Prints for a World Revolution*, Doubleday, 1928, pp 35–36.
5. Robert N. Proctor, *Racial Hygiene: Medicine under the Nazis*, Harvard University Press, 1988, p 23.
6. William Z. Foster, *Toward Soviet America*, International Publishers, 1932, pp 340–341.
7. Pierre Teilhard de Chardin, "Human Energy," *Human Energy*, pp 132–133.

Teilhard made some specific guesses about who these "fixed or definitely unprogressive ethnical groups" might be: Chinese, Indians, and Africans, among others. He did so despite describing "the doctrine of the selection and election of races" as "cynical and brutal theories in which, however, a noble passion may also stir," a "subtle deformation of a great truth" that would "disfigure or hide from our eyes the veritable contours of the noosphere[1] and render biologically impossible the formation of a veritable spirit of the earth."[2] Teilhard added that the "gates of the future, the entry into the super-human" will "open only to an advance of *all together*, in a direction in which *all together*[3] can join and find completion in a spiritual renovation of the earth."[4]

In August 1923, Teilhard wrote, "When I came to China I hoped to find a reservoir of thought and mysticism that would bring fresh youth to our West. I now have the impression that the reservoir is 'blocked'/emptied. The Chinese are primitive people (beneath their varnish of modernity or Confucianism); the Mongols are in gradual process of disappearance, and their lamas are coarse and dirty monks."[5]

In October 1923, Teilhard wrote of his travel through Asia, "For long weeks I have been submerged in the deep flood of the people of Asia. . . . Nowhere, among the men I met or heard about, have I discerned the smallest seed whose growth will benefit the future of mankind. Throughout my whole journey I have found nothing but absence of thought, senile thought, or infantile thought. . . . I am a pilgrim of the future on my way back from a journey made entirely in the past."[6]

In April 1927, he wrote:

In the light of the convergent evidence that I have gathered here from the most diverse men, I see an increasing possibility for another hypothesis, namely, that the Chinese are arrested primitives, victims of retarded development whose anthropological substance is inferior to ours. . . . Neither the Christian attitude of love for all mankind, nor humane hopes for an organized society must cause us to forget that the 'human stratum' may not be homogeneous. If it were not, it would be necessary to find for the Chinese, as for the Negroes, their special function, which may not (by *biological* impossibility) be that of the whites. I do not like these prospects. But they may some day become necessary. Is not the real way to conquer the world to utilize its faults, and not to deny them, *if* they are irremediable?[7]

In January 1929, Teilhard put the rural Somalis onto history's refuse pile. He said that the

human inhabitants would make an interesting study. Moreover, unlike the Chinese, they are well worth looking at: Tinkali, Hissa, Caragan, or Galla—they all have magnificent copper-coloured bodies, so that they really blend with the landscape and the fauna. . . . It's a survival of a splendid human type—but how ill-fitted, it would seem, to follow our forward march. They will merge or disappear—like the zebras and elephants. . . . Progress itself implies an unquenchable force that insists on the destruction of everything which has outlived its time.[8]

In September 1935, Teilhard indicated that he was not able to speak against the invasion of Ethiopia by Fascist Italy. He said,

1. For Teilhard, the noosphere is "a planetary 'thinking layer' composed of the collective sum of human cognition." (Arthur Fabel, "Teilhard 2000—The Vision of a Cosmic Genesis at the Millennium," in *Teilhard in the 21st Century*, p155.)
2. Teilhard, *The Phenomenon of Man*, Book Four, Chapter One, "The Collective Issue," pp238–239.
3. Here, Teilhard's text included this footnote, *verbatim* from p245 of *The Phenomenon of Man*: "Even if they do so only under the influence of a few, an *élite*."
4. Teilhard, *The Phenomenon of Man*, Book Four, Chapter One, "The Collective Issue," pp244–245.
5. Pierre Teilhard de Chardin, *Letters to Léontine Zanta*, intro. by Robert Garric and Henri de Lubac, tr. by Richard Wall, Harper and Row, 1969, p53, letter of August 7, 1923 (cited below as Teilhard, *Letters to Léontine Zanta*).
6. Teilhard, *Letters from a Traveller*, pp100–101, letter dated "at a deeper level, October."
7. Teilhard, *Letters to Two Friends*, pp67–68, letter of April 6, 1927.
8. Teilhard, *Letters from a Traveller*, pp149–150, letter of January 8, 1929.

In this mixed society you hear every sort of comment, from black to white, on the Abyssinian question: and I'm annoyed within myself as I realise my difficulty in finding a good reason for adopting any particular attitude. It's clear that we must tend toward a moral and biological organisation of the earth; but what should be the attitudes of human groups in relation to one another, seeing that their social values and capabilities differ so greatly? . . . The more I see of the East, the more I distrust the demagogue in international matters.[1]

As a biographer noted, "In early September [1935] he set sail for India. At Eritrea he watched with weary disinvolvement as regiments of sweating young Italians boarded troopships bound for Ethiopia."[2]

In December 1935, while traveling through India, Teilhard wrote: "There are, in fact, human groups that differ biologically and physically, and they can be 'converted' only by first transforming them within the human plane. I believe such convergence to be possible. So far as I have been able to form an opinion of them, the Hindus have been a disappointment to me. In them, too, the creative power seems in a pretty poor way, and you have to go to India to realise the numbing and deadening effect of a religion obsessed by material forms and ritualism."[3]

While traveling from Java to China in January 1936, Teilhard wrote:

As individuals, Indians are charming, but taken as a whole the country seems to be just as incapable of self-government as China or Malaya. Unfortunately, dislike of the English is general among the 'natives.' They want complete independence at all costs, even if it means death to the country. . . . The more I get around the world, the more I fear that Geneva (of which I am in my heart a great supporter), numbers of liberal Catholics, and especially my colleagues the 'Missiologues,'[4] are making a grave mistake in recognising the equality of races in the face of all the biological evidence. 'Universalism' is not democracy (= egalitarianism).[5]

In the same month, Teilhard expanded upon this in a letter to another friend: "The objective fact seems to me this (1) no international morality is possible without previous acceptance that there is an earth to be constructed which transcends states; (2) and once this construction has been agreed to, everything must give way; and as not all ethnic groups have the same value, they must be dominated (which does not mean they must be despised—quite the reverse.)"[6] As a comment on this, Teilhard added,

In other words, *at one and the same time* there should be official recognition of:
1. The priority/primacy of the earth over nations;
2. The inequality of peoples and races.
Now the *second* point is currently reviled by Communism . . . and the Church, and the *first* point is similarly reviled by the Fascist systems (and, of course, by less gifted peoples!).[7]

All of this had practical consequence. In a "war of construction," Teilhard recognized "the right of the earth to organise itself by reducing, even by *force*, the reactionary and backwards elements."[8] Therefore, "In this sense, in *last analysis*, I am with Mussolini against the liberals of the left and the missiologists."[9] Thus, in the "*last analysis*," Teilhard supported Fascist aggression against an African nation, an invasion that set the stage for the Berlin-Rome Axis.

1. Ibid., p 209, letter of September 14, 1935. The ellipsis is as it was given in the original.
2. Mary Lukas and Ellen Lukas, *Teilhard*, Doubleday and Co., 1977, p 139 (cited below as Lukas and Lukas, *Teilhard*).
3. Teilhard, *Letters from a Traveller*, p 216, letter of December 19, 1935.
4. "Missiology" is the study of Christian missionary work. A "missiologue" is a scholar or missionary who does such study.
5. Teilhard, *Letters from a Traveller*, pp 219–220, letter of January 21, 1936.
6. Teilhard, *Letters to Léontine Zanta*, pp 116–117, letter of January 26, 1936.
7. Ibid., p 117, letter of January 26, 1936. The ellipsis was in the original text.
8. Ibid., p 116, letter of January 26, 1936.
9. Ibid., p 116, letter of January 26, 1936.

In a 1948 essay, "My Fundamental Vision," Teilhard proclaimed that humanity must, "provided Heaven grant it life," continue its advance, characterized by "constantly increasing unification, centration, and spiritualization—the whole system rising unmistakably toward a critical point of final convergence."[1] He offered the preconditions for this prediction in a footnote following the words "provided Heaven grant it life:" the absence of "any astronomical or biological catastrophe which would destroy the earth or life on earth," a continued supply of "the natural resources available in the continents, which feed man's individual and social body;" and "(c) effective control, both in quantity and quality, of reproduction in order to avoid over-population of the earth or its invasion by a less satisfactory ethnic group."[2]

For Teilhard as with Blavatsky and Bailey, racism appeared to be consistent with evolutionary spirituality. However, unlike Alice Bailey, Teilhard eschewed anti-Semitism; in an August 1941 letter he described this prejudice as "odious imbecility."[3]

WORLD WAR II AS A "CRISIS OF BIRTH" FOR HUMANITY

Like Alice Bailey, Teilhard de Chardin hailed the World Wars as occasions for human unity and progress.

In May 1939, Teilhard did not expect war to come. However, he said that his "secret hope" was that "a deeper evolution, toward some sound internationalism, is going on in the masses, so that a new world will emerge. A mass experience (and unfortunately a mass suffering) seems to be the condition for a mass transformation."[4]

This "mass experience" began in September, 1939. Near the end of the war, in March 1945, Teilhard described World War II as "a crisis of birth" for a new humanity: "Finally, the present war; a war which for the first time in history is as widespread as the earth itself; a conflict in which human masses as great as continents clash together; a catastrophe in which we seem to be swept off our feet as individuals—what aspect can it wear to our awakened eyes except that of a crisis of birth, almost disproportionately small in relation to the vastness of what it is destined to bring forth?"[5] He thus anticipated the words that Barbara Marx Hubbard uses to describe humanity's current situation.

In December 1945, Teilhard described World War II as "this new stirring of the human dough." He held that this war, along with World War I, fostered human unity:

Ethnically, during the same period, there has been a vast and pitiless confusion of peoples, whole armies being removed from one hemisphere to the other, and tens of thousands of refugees beings scattered across the world like seed borne on the wind. Brutal and harsh though the circumstances have been, who can fail to perceive the inevitable consequences of this new stirring of the human dough? And economically and psychically the entire mass of Mankind, under the inexorable pressure of events and owing to the prodigious growth and speeding up of the means of communication, has found itself seized in the mould of a communal existence—large sections tightly encased in countless international organisations, the most ambitious the world has ever known; and the whole anxiously involved in the same passionate upheavals, the same problems, the same daily news. . . . Can anyone seriously suppose that we shall be able to rid ourselves of habits such as these? No; during these six years, despite the unleashing of so much hatred, the human block has not disintegrated. On the contrary, in its most rigid organic depths it has increased its vice-like grip upon us all. First 1914-1918 then 1939-1945—two successive

1. Teilhard, "My Fundamental Vision," in *Toward the Future*, pp 181–182.
2. Ibid., p 181, footnote.
3. Teilhard, *Letters to Two Friends*, p 99, letter of August 5, 1941.
4. Ibid., pp 131–132, letter of May 7, 1939.
5. Teilhard, "Life and the Planets: What is Happening at this Moment on Earth?," in *The Future of Man*, p 117.

turns of the screw. Every new war, embarked upon by the nations for the purpose of detaching themselves from one another, merely results in their being bound and mingled together in a more inextricable knot. The more we seek to thrust each other away, the more do we interpenetrate.[1]

In like manner, Alice Bailey had described the dislocation of people due to war and tyranny as "the institution of a process of blending" for mankind. In September 1939,[2] she had said,

Mussolini, the regenerator of his people; Hitler who lifted a distressed people upon his shoulders; Lenin, the idealist, Stalin and Franco are all expressions of the Shamballa force and of certain little understood energies. These have wrought significant changes in their day and generation and altered the face of Europe, incidentally affecting Asia and conditioning attitudes and policies in America. The results even when dangerous and terrible, have developed two vital characteristics in humanity. One has been the widespread development of the discriminating faculty, and secondly, a tendency to dispersion with its consequences of diffusing civilized and cultural values and the diverse gifts of the many people to the world soul. The drift of people to the colonies from Great Britain, the drift of the people from every nation in Europe to America, North and South, the dispersal of people within national boundaries as the result of war and expediency such as the evacuation of cities has brought about today, the removal of people out of Italy and of groups of people within Russia, and the constant moving onwards of the wandering Jews indicate a breaking down, upon a world-wide scale, of all outer boundaries and the institution of a process of blending and amalgamation such as the world has never seen before. It constitutes an educational system of untold value.[3]

ATOM BOMBS: HERALDING THE COMING OF THE "SPIRIT OF THE EARTH"

Soon after the bomb fell on Hiroshima, Teilhard exulted in *The Heart of Matter*, "In our recent mastery of the Atomic we have reached the primordial sources of the *Energy of Evolution*. . . . New powers call for new aspirations. If Mankind is to use its new access of physical power with balanced control, it cannot do without a rebound of intensity in its eagerness to act, to seek, to create."[4] Foreshadowing Barbara Marx Hubbard, he said in 1946, "In exploding the atom we took our first bite at the fruit of the great discovery, and this was enough for a taste to enter our mouths that can never be washed away: the taste for super-creativeness."[5]

In September 1946, after the US nuclear tests in the Pacific Ocean, Teilhard closed a paean to the Bomb by saying, "The atomic age is not the age of destruction but the age of union in research. For all their military trappings, the recent explosions at Bikini herald the birth into the world of a Mankind both inwardly and outwardly pacified. They proclaim the coming of the *Spirit of the Earth*."[6]

Like any god, the "spirit of the earth" will be jealous, demanding of zeal and sacrifice, finding expression through a "crisis of conversion." In a 1931 essay in *Human Energy*, Teilhard wrote:

To exert constant pressure on the whole area of reality, is this not the supreme sign of faith in Being, and therefore of worship? All this is ours if we learn not to stifle the spirit of earth in us. But let there be no mistake. He who wishes to share in this spirit must die and be reborn, to himself and to others. To reach the higher plane of humanity, he must not only reflect and see a particular situation intellectually, but also make a complete change

1. Teilhard, "A Great Event Foreshadowed: the Planetisation of Mankind," in *The Future of Man*, pp126–127.
2. Alice A. Bailey, *The Externalisation of the Hierarchy*, 1957, Lucis Publishing Company, p105.
3. Ibid., pp133–134.
4. Teilhard, *The Heart of Matter*, translated by René Hague, Collins, 1978, first pub. 1976, pp96–97.
5. Teilhard, "Some Reflections on the Spiritual Repercussions of the Atom Bomb," in *The Future of Man*, p146
6. Ibid., p147.

in his fundamental way of valuation and action. In him, *a new plane* (individual, social, and religious) *must eliminate another*. This entails inner tortures and persecutions. *The earth will only become conscious of itself through the crisis of conversion.*[1]

Teilhard's proclamation of the *spiritus mundi* foreshadowed Bishop Swing's announcement at the 1997 summit meeting of the URI that "If you come here because a spirit of colossal energy is being born in the loins of the earth, then come here and be a midwife. Assist, in awe, at the birth of a new hope."[2]

In 1937, Teilhard said that mankind might need to continue developing "ever greater and more destructive weapons," until "the spirit of discovery absorbs the whole vital force contained in the spirit of war":

> At present the majority of men do not yet understand force (the key and symbol of greater-being) except in its most primitive and savage form of war. This is perhaps why it is necessary for us to continue for some time still to manufacture ever greater and more destructive weapons. For we still, alas, need these machines to translate the vital sense of attack and victory into concrete experience. But may the moment come (and it will come) when the masses realize that the true human victories are those over the mysteries of matter and life. May the moment come when the man in the street understands that there is more poetry in a mighty machine for splitting the atom than in any artillery. A decisive hour will strike for man, when the spirit of discovery absorbs the whole vital force contained in the spirit of war.[3]

THE COMING "SEPARATION" OF REACTIONARIES AND PROGRESSIVES

Teilhard was, for decades, a zealot for Progress.

In December 1923, he wrote, "I have a ferocious belief in progress of some kind, and I hold those who deny it as evil-doers and heretics."[4]

In January 1941, Teilhard said, "It seems obvious to me that the moment has come when mankind is going to be divided (or will have to make the choice) between faith and non-faith in the earth's collective spiritual progress."[5]

In February 1941, Teilhard likewise said, "the world of tomorrow will be born out of the 'elected' group of those (arising from any direction and class, and confession in the human world) who will decide that there is something big waiting for us ahead, and give their life to reach it. People *have to* decide for or against progress, *now*. And those who say no have just to be dropped behind. And those who say yes will soon discover that they speak the same language and even worship the same God."[6]

He likewise prophesied in March 1945, "The profound cleavage in every kind of social group (families, countries, professions, creeds) which during the past century has become manifest in the form of two increasingly distinct and irreconcilable human types, those who believe in progress and those who do not—what does this portend except the separation and birth of a new stratum in the biosphere?"[7]

1. Teilhard, "The Spirit of the Earth," in *Human Energy*, p38.
2. Bishop William Swing, "Opening Address," United Religions Initiative, Stanford University, June 23–27, 1997, http://www.united-religions.org/youth/welcome/swingspeech.htm, printed 1997; no longer on the Net. This passage is also cited in Charles Gibbs and Sally Mahé, *United Religions Initiative, Birth of a Global Community: Appreciative Inquiry in Action*, Lakeshore Publishers, 2004, p107.
3. Pierre Teilhard de Chardin, "Human Energy," in *Human Energy*, pp135–136.
4. Teilhard, *Letters to Léontine Zanta*, p59, letter of December 12, 1923.
5. Teilhard, *Letters from a Traveller*, p275, letter of January 11, 1941.
6. Teilhard, *Letters to Two Friends*, p154, letter of February 9, 1941.
7. Teilhard, "Life and the Planets: What is Happening at this Moment on Earth?," in *The Future of Man*, p117.

This "separation" would divide the elect "elements of planetisation" from the "cast offs" who do not believe in progress. Teilhard said in December 1945,

It would seem, then, that the grand phenomenon which we are now witnessing represents a new and possibly final division of Mankind, based no longer on wealth but on belief in progress. The old Marxist conflict between producers and exploiters becomes out-dated—at the best a misplaced approximation. What finally divides the men of today into two camps is not class but an attitude of mind—the spirit of movement. On the one hand there are those who simply wish to make the world a comfortable dwelling-place; on the other hand, those who can only conceive of it as a machine for progress—or better, an organism that is progressing. One the one hand the 'bourgeois spirit' in its essence, and on the other the true 'toilers of the Earth,' those of whom we may safely predict that, without violence or hatred, simply by biological predominance, they will tomorrow constitute the human race. On one hand the cast-offs; on the other, the agents and elements of planetisation.[1]

Teilhard offered fewer specifics than Barbara Marx Hubbard about the coming division of mankind between evolution's elected and rejected, and his rhetoric was less brutal than that used by Alice Bailey. Nevertheless, all three authors have proposed the same fate for "reactionaries."

"THE AGE OF NATIONS HAS PASSED"

Like today's New Age and globalist writers, Teilhard proclaimed the obsolescence of the nation-state. He said in 1931,

Too much iron, too much wheat, too many automobiles—but also too many books, too many observations; and also too many diplomas, technicians, and workmen—and even too many children. The world cannot function without productive living beings, food, ideas. But its production is more and more patently exceeding its powers of absorption and assimilation. Here again, as in the case of love, we must ask what this excess production means. Is the world condemned, as it grows, to automatic death by stifling beneath its own excessive weight? Not at all, we would answer. It is in course of gathering to itself a new and higher body. At this crisis of birth, everything depends on the prompt emergence of a soul which by merely appearing will come to organize, lighten, and vitalize this mass of stagnant and confused matter. Now this soul, if it exists, can only be the 'conspiration' of individuals, associating to *raise* the edifice of life *to a new stage*. The resources at our disposal today, the powers that we have released, *could not possibly be absorbed* by the narrow system of individual or national units which the architects of the human earth have hitherto used. Our plan was to build a big house, larger but similar in design to our good old dwelling places. And now we have been led by the higher logic of progress which is in us, to collect components that are too big for the use we intended to make of them. *The age of nations has passed. Now, unless we wish to perish we must shake off our old prejudices and build the earth.*[2]

EXALTING "PLANNING" AND USE OF MAN'S POWER

Teilhard maintained a lifelong enthusiasm for "beneficent" use of human power. In September 1948, he commented that a reviewer of a book by Julian Huxley

criticized Huxley's warning that in the near future we shall be able to control genetically the products of human generation; because, the reviewer says, it is impossible or dangerous to decide what should be the 'best' human type. A very stupid criticism (probably expressing some anticommunist feeling), underestimating the fact that if Man really succeeds in controlling his own heredity, no force in the world will prevent him from using his new

1. Teilhard, "A Great Event Foreshadowed: the Planetisation of Mankind," in *The Future of Man*, pp138–139.
2. Teilhard, "The Spirit of the Earth," in *Human Energy*, p37.

power. I recognize that planning is always dangerous. But the question is not there. The question is to decide whether Man can avoid being forced to plan, by the very process of cosmic evolution. And the answer is that he *cannot*: because planning is the essence of Life.[1]

Comprehensive planning is to be applied worldwide. In *The Phenomenon of Man*, Teilhard said,

If there is a future for mankind, it can only be imagined in terms of a harmonious conciliation of what is free with what is planned and totalised. Points involved are: the distribution of the resources of the globe; the control of the trek towards unpopulated areas; the optimum use of the powers set free by mechanisation, the physiology of nations and races; geo-economy, geo-politics, geo-demography; the organisation of research developing into a reasoned organisation of the earth. Whether we like it or not, all the signs and all our needs converge in the same direction.[2]

Not even the horrors of the Third Reich's concentration camps could shake Teilhard's faith in human progress. A friendly biographer noted,

To some of his adversaries, Teilhard's optimistic viewpoint seemed more than a little naïve. Once in a debate with Gabriel Marcel on the subject of 'Science and Rationality,' he shocked his opponent by refusing to permit even the appalling evidence of the experiments of the doctors of Dachau to modify his faith in the inevitability of human progress. 'Man,' he asserted, 'to become fully man, must have tried everything. . . .' Of course, he added as a corollary, since the human species was still so young and still prone to fall back into the dark from which it came, the persistence of such evil was to be expected. But since, unlike the lower animals, man no longer acted purely out of instinct, he would presumably abandon every new experiment the moment he saw it did not lead him to greater personalization. . . . 'Prometheus,' Marcel had cried, articulating the astonishment of most of the audience. 'No,' Teilhard replied, 'only man as God has made him.[3]

EVOLUTIONARY UTOPIA:
"WAR IN A NATURALLY SUBLIMATED FORM"

Teilhard's view of the ideal human society was not one of peace and ordered liberty; it was, instead, a vision of an ongoing evolutionary struggle, "war in a naturally sublimated form." He said,

All hope of bourgeois tranquillity, the dreams of 'millenary' felicity in which we may be tempted to indulge, must be washed out, eliminated from our horizon. A perfectly-ordered society with everyone living in effortless ease within a fixed framework, a world in a state of tranquil repose, all this has nothing to do with our advancing Universe, apart from the fact that it would rapidly induce a state of deadly tedium. Although, as I believe, concord must of necessity prevail on earth, it can by our premises only take the form of some sort of tense cohesion pervaded and inspired with the same energies, now become harmonious, which were previously wasted in bloodshed: unanimity in search and conquest, sustained among us by the universal resolve to raise ourselves upwards, all straining shoulder to shoulder, towards ever greater heights of consciousness and freedom. In short, true peace, the only kind that is biologically possible, betokens neither the ending nor the reverse of warfare, but war in a naturally sublimated form. It reflects and corresponds to the normal state of Mankind become at last alive to the possibilities and demands of its evolution.[4]

C.S. Lewis spoke against such a cruel and Utopian view of the purpose of politics and human institutions. In *Mere Christianity* he said,

---

1. Teilhard, *Letters to Two Friends*, pp 186–187, letter of September 18, 1948.
2. Teilhard, *The Phenomenon of Man*, Book Four, Chapter Three, "The Ultimate Earth," p 283.
3. Lukas and Lukas, *Teilhard*, pp 237–238. The ellipses are as they appeared in the original text.
4. Teilhard, "Faith in Peace," in *The Future of Man*, pp 153–154.

The State exists simply to promote and to protect the ordinary happiness of human beings in this life. A husband and wife chatting over a fire, a couple of friends having a game of darts in a pub, a man reading a book in his own room or digging in his own garden—that is what the State is there for. And unless they are helping to increase and prolong and protect such moments, all the laws, parliaments, armies, courts, police, economics, etc., are simply a waste of time.[1]

THE VATICAN'S 1962 WARNING AGAINST TEILHARD'S WORKS

During his lifetime, Fr. Teilhard de Chardin was prohibited by his religious superiors from publishing his works. He obeyed, but continued to write. After his death in 1955, Teilhard's works began to be published, and attained wide popularity. In response, in 1962 the Vatican's Holy Office (the predecessor of the current Sacred Congregation for the Doctrine of the Faith) issued a *monitum*, an official warning against his writings:

> Several works of Fr. Pierre Teilhard de Chardin, some of which were posthumously published, are being edited and are gaining a good deal of success. Prescinding from a judgment about those points that concern the positive sciences, it is sufficiently clear that the above-mentioned works abound in such ambiguities and indeed even serious errors, as to offend Catholic doctrine. For this reason, the most eminent and most revered Fathers of the Holy Office exhort all Ordinaries as well as the superiors of Religious institutes, rectors of seminaries and presidents of universities, effectively to protect the minds, particularly of the youth, against the dangers presented by the works of Fr. Teilhard de Chardin and of his followers.[2]

In July 1981, the Holy See reiterated the concerns that it had raised in the 1962 warning.[3] Thus, the Vatican's doctrinal watchdogs under two Popes, John XXIII and John Paul II, held the line against Pierre Teilhard de Chardin. Given the nature of Teilhard's teachings, these warnings seem amply justified.

A PRESENT-DAY VATICAN "COMPROMISE" WITH TEILHARD?

In this context, it is disconcerting that the just-mentioned Holy Office document was, as of mid-2004, on-line at a conservative American Roman Catholic web site. It was *not* found at the official Vatican web site.

Teilhard's followers claim that he is being rehabilitated by the Catholic Church. The British Teilhard Association's on-line biography of Teilhard states that shortly after the 1962 warning from the Holy Office,

> the Jesuit General Jean-Baptiste Janssens authorised Teilhard's friend and confrère, the theologian (and later cardinal) Henri de Lubac, to publish a defence of Teilhard (*La pensée religieuse du Père Teilhard de Chardin*, 1962, published with imprimatur), saying it would be quite wrong to attach any value to an anonymous article. Pope John XXIII later described the incident of the *monitum* as 'most regrettable.' Both decree and *monitum* have long since been forgotten by all but Teilhard's bitterest opponents who, in the words of theologian Bruno de Solages,

1. C. S. Lewis, *Mere Christianity*, Macmillan Publishing Co., 1960, ch. 8, p169.
2. Sacred Congregation of the Holy Office, "Warning Regarding the Writings of Father Teilhard de Chardin," June 30, 1962, as published at http://www.ewtn.com/library/CURIA/CDFTEILH.HTM, printed 07/30/04.
3. Ibid.

quite simply cannot not see beyond their noses. . . . The process of 'rehabilitation' that had begun immediately after his death gathered pace on the centenary of his birth in 1981 with an important seminar on Teilhard at the Catholic Institute of Paris. In a letter to the Rector of the Institute written on behalf of Pope John Paul II Cardinal Casaroli spoke warmly [of] Teilhard's 'powerful poetic insight into the deep value of nature . . . his constant desire for dialogue with science' and, above all, his concern 'to honour both faith and reason.' And Pedro Arrupe SJ, General of the Society of Jesus, wrote to the Provincial of France: 'Teilhard's ideas proclaim the openness and concern with cultivating the world which characterised the teachings of the Council and of John XXIII and Paul VI and, today, John Paul II.' On 5 January 1983 Henri de Lubac was created cardinal. John Paul II honoured de Lubac in his own right but he also honoured, in a very real sense, Teilhard in the person of de Lubac who had been his great defender. And this was developed even further in 1995 on the fortieth anniversary of Teilhard's death in letters from Peter-Hans Kolvenbach SJ on behalf of the Jesuits and from Timothy Radcliffe OP on behalf of the Dominicans.[1]

A collection of letters from Teilhard to one of his friends earned a *Nihil obstat* and an *Imprimatur*, "a declaration that a book or pamphlet is considered to be free from doctrinal or moral error," in 1968 from the Catholic Archdiocese of Westminster, in England.[2] This was so, even though in this collection of letters, Teilhard had said: "*at one and the same time* there should be official recognition of: (1) The priority/primacy of the earth over nations; (2) The inequality of peoples and races. Now the *second* point is currently reviled by Communism . . . and the Church, and the *first* point is similarly reviled by the Fascist systems."[3]

Additionally, a mid-2004 search of the Vatican's home page, using the Vatican-provided search engine, revealed no English-language documents specifically criticizing Teilhard de Chardin's work, and three such documents with brief, favorable mention of him.[4]

Can it be that the Vatican is gradually "evolving," making a turn toward accepting the wayward Jesuit's theories—including the "totalisation" of humanity?

1. Siôn Cowell, "The Man," The British Teilhard Association, http://www.teilhard.org.uk/template.asp?pID=02&sub-PID=10, printed 07/30/04.

2. Teilhard, *Letters to Léontine Zanta*, p3 (copyright page).

3. Ibid., p117, letter of January 26, 1936. The ellipsis was in the original text.

4. In late 2001, Archbishop Agostino Marcetto, newly appointed by Pope John Paul II as the Secretary of the Pontifical Council for the Pastoral Care of Migrants and Itinerant People, wrote: "I will ask a mystic . . . the Jesuit Father Teilhard de Chardin, to be our teacher for a deeper 'knowledge' of the Word (the Son of God.) Here is the text that I have chosen for you." He then quoted Teilhard's "La Messe sur le monde" as his Christmas greeting to readers of the Pontifical Council's newsletter. (Pontifical Council for the Pastoral Care of Migrants and Itinerant People, "New Secretary at the Pontifical Council," *Apostolatus Maris*: The Church in the Maritime World, no. 75, 2001/IV, http://www.vatican.va/roman_curia/pontifical_councils/migrants/s_index_seafarers/stellamaris_bulletin/rc_pc_migrants_seaf_bol75eng.pdf, printed 07/30/04, p2.) In a document posted at the Vatican web site by the Pontifical Council for Culture, an American Jesuit wrote, "It is important that Catholics show respect for modern science. As an anthropologist, I am especially aware of this need in regard to evolution. Generally, we have a good record on this—Teilhard de Chardin, etc.—but the public has to be reminded of it." (William Biernatzki, SJ, "Tendencies Within US Culture," *Plenaria '97*, http://www.vatican.va/roman_curia/pontifical_councils/cultr/documents/rc_pc_cultr_01031995_doc_i-1995-ple_en.html, Section 3, printed 07/30/04.) In a document posted on the Vatican web site by the Pontifical Academy of Sciences, Paul Cardinal Poupard praised Teilhard's *Science and Christ* as a "very noteworthy attempt" in the direction of a "scientific Christology:" "it was a noble effort on the part of one of the twentieth century's great anthropologists to bring his scientific knowledge face to face with Christ. In his study of matter, this great Jesuit anthropologist perceived a strong urge to unification and synthesis, an excess of energy which enabled matter to transcend itself more and more. He saw this as evidence of a process which would culminate in Christ. Teilhard was obviously not so naïve as to try to deduce Christian doctrine from the simple study of the properties of matter. He wrote that science, left to itself, cannot discover Christ, but Christ fulfils the desires which arise in our hearts when we are at the school of Science. For Teilhard, Christ was so much a part of nature, as a unifying element, that he did not always acknowledge Christ's individuality. But at least he was looking in the right direction in his attempt to build a bridge between scientific research and the person of Christ." (Paul Cardinal Poupard, "Christ and Science," http://www.vatican.va/roman_curia/pontifical_academies/acdscien/documents/sv%209 9(50f5).pdf, pp486–487, printed 07/31/04.)

14

ROBERT MULLER

ROBERT MULLER DESCRIBES HIMSELF as a Catholic, "and considers himself a good one."[1] Indeed, Muller *claims* credit for "three visits by two Popes to the UN" and "the Assisi meetings of the Pope with religious leaders which I proposed to the Mayor of Assisi."[2] However, Muller's many writings are a veritable *Anti-Catechism*.

HETERODOX THEOLOGY AND COSMOLOGY

Like his New Age colleagues, Muller re-defines the story of mankind's fall: "As vividly described in the story of the Tree of Knowledge, having decided to become like God through knowledge and our attempt to understand the heavens and the earth, we have also become masters in deciding between good and bad; every invention of ours can be used for good or bad all along the above Copernican tapestry of our knowledge."[3]

Muller has declared his belief in Hindu astrophysics,[4] and in the Hindu concepts of *karma*,[5] "*prana*, 'the vital,'"[6] and reincarnation.[7] In his recent book *Paradise Earth*, Muller expressed these views in a poem that he wrote on July 4, 2003:

"I decide not to die
Not even to think of death,
To live forever
In God's and Mother Earth's marvelous paradise
In the endless eternal universe.
Yes, I want to live eternally.
I have lived before
In other forms,
I am part of a vast,

---

1. Robert Muller, *New Genesis: Shaping a Global Spirituality*, World Happiness and Cooperation, 1993, foreword by Pam Robbins, p xiii (cited below as Muller, *New Genesis*).

2. Robert Muller, "Spirituality in World Affairs," World Network of Religious Futurists, September 10, 1998, http://www.wnrf.org/cms/muller.shtml, printed 06/02/04.

3. The Robert Muller School, *The World Core Curriculum: Foundations, Implementation, and Resources*, 1991 (current edition, as provided by the School in November 2002), Arlington Texas, p 10 (essay by Robert Muller, "Spiritual Education: A World of Difference"); cited below as Robert Muller School, *World Core Curriculum: Foundations*.

4. Muller, *New Genesis*, pp 120–121.

5. Robert Muller and Douglas Roche, *Safe Passage into the Twenty-First Century: The United Nations' Quest for Peace, Equality, Justice, and Development*, Continuum (A Global Education Associates Book), 1995, p 102.

6. Robert Muller, *New Genesis*, p 125. Muller explains that "*prana*, 'the vital'" is "indeed a vital principle, the energy, the motor of the upward path of human civilization."

7. Ibid., p 126.

eternal, gigantic
living entity.
When I am buried
I will live again
In other life forms
And my soul will continue
To be part of the incredible
Cosmic meaning and transformation of creation.
I will simply never die.
To die is even more
incomprehensible than to live
Thank you dear Father God, Mother Earth and Uncle Sun
For this revelation
This morning you talked to me
And showed me the most wonderful, mysterious, incredible future
Thank you, thank you, thank you."[1]

Muller extols the linguistics and philosophy of the "Indigenous People," especially "the remarkable cosmologies of the Mayas [sic], Aztecs, Inkas [sic] and others;" there should be "a global spiritual Department to study the indigenous spiritualities and rituals derived from their intimate relation with nature and Creation."[2] Muller does not acknowledge that the "spiritualities and rituals" of the Mayans, the Aztecs, and the Incas incorporated human sacrifice. The Mayans also believed that natural disasters helped to reduce the population when necessary: "The ancient Maya in Central America believed that earthquakes were the gods' way of thinning out the population of humans when they became too numerous."[3]

In *My Testament to the UN*, Muller said, "The tremendous spiritual, cosmic forces remain largely unemployed because very few people turn to them, pray to them."[4] Jesus was one of many "great emissaries of the universe," who brought us messages "from outer-space."[5] Echoing Theosophist author Alice Bailey, he says that meditators become aware of "the outlines, and later the details of the hierarchical Plan."[6]

In 1998, Muller wrote, "It is becoming clear to me, dear God, that You cannot save us. It is us who must save ourselves, your miraculous nature and You, its Creator."[7]

God "cannot save us," but the UN might. Muller said in a 1995 interview with *World Goodwill*, a Theosophist newsletter issued by the Lucis Trust, that he considers the UN to be "one of the greatest institutions ever created by humans, a true meta-organism for the evolution of the human species and of the planet. In it converge all aspirations, dreams, differences, problems perceived by humans. . . .

---

1. Robert Muller, *Paradise Earth*, http://www.paradiseearth.us/pdf/PEFull.pdf, p 101, (p. 109 of the PDF file), printed 05/31/04 (cited below as Muller, *Paradise Earth*).

2. Robert Muller, *Ideas And Dreams for a Better World: 1001–1500, Volume III*, Idea 1043, May 19, 1997; http://www.robertmuller.org/volume/ideas1001.html, viewed 06/21/04 (cited below as Muller, *Ideas and Dreams, Vol. III*). Spelling is as given by Muller in his document. Muller praised the spirituality and cosmology of Aztecs, Incas, and Mayans in other "ideas" in the same series of documents: ideas 477 (October 30, 1995), 759 (August 7, 1996), 1040 (May 16, 1997), 1445 (June 26, 1998), 1517 (September 5, 1998), idea 1791, idea 2151, and idea 3090.

3. Walter A. Lyons, Ph.D., *The Handy Weather Answer Book*, Gale Research, 1997, p 253.

4. Robert Muller, *My Testament to the UN: A Contribution to the 50th Anniversary of the United Nations*, World Happiness and Cooperation, 1994, p 83 (cited below as Muller, *My Testament*).

5. Robert Muller, *Ideas And Dreams for a Better World: 501–1000, Volume II*, Idea 555, 16 January 1995, http://www.robertmuller.org/volume/ideas0501.html, viewed 06/21/04 (cited below as Muller, *Ideas and Dreams, Vol. II*).

6. Muller, *Ideas And Dreams, Vol. III*, Idea 1178, 1 October 1997.

7. Ibid., Idea 1444, 25 June 1998.

The UN is humanity's incipient global brain, and it is part of its global nervous system. . . . We still need a global heart . . . and we still need a global soul, namely our consciousness and fusion with the entire universe and stream of time."[1]

Muller's beliefs about Christ are not in line with traditional Christian teaching. He believes Jesus would say, "No human being on Earth, not even I in heaven am infallible, given all the killings and sufferings which were committed in my name."[2] After the second coming of Christ, Muller believes that "Christ" will leave again, telling us: "I will now make My peace with you and let you establish a perfect Earth. Farewell, My grownup children. At long last, you are on the right path, you have brought heaven down to earth and found your proper place in the universe. I will now leave you for a long journey, for I have to turn My sight to other troubled and unfinished celestial bodies. I now pronounce you Planet of God."[3]

Muller asserts that "The world's major religions in the end all want the same thing. . . . What the world needs today is a convergence of the different religions in the search for and definition of the cosmic or divine laws which ought to regulate our behavior on this planet. World-wide spiritual ecumenism, expressed in new forms of religious cooperation and institutions, would probably be closest to the heart of the resurrected Christ."[4] His "Christ" thus agreed with Alice Bailey, who wrote in 1947 that "the study of Comparative Religion has demonstrated that the foundational truths in every faith are identical."[5]

With heterodox theology, Muller also offers dissenting ideas on morality and Catholic Church discipline. "To foster a world spiritual renaissance I recommend that all religions should allow their clergies, male and female, to be married in order to increase the number of spiritual families and children raised in such families."[6] Muller had said previously

I have seen so many small village communities in Costa Rica with deserted churches and parish houses, due to the shortage of priests, that I begged His Holiness in two letters to allow Catholic sisters to officiate mass and religious ceremonies and to be the spiritual counselors of the people in these villages who need it so much. I had asked Costa Rican sisters if they would be ready to do it, and they said that they would do it enthusiastically. But my appeals to the Pope have remained unanswered.[7]

BUILDING A NEW WORLD ORDER AND ESTABLISHING "PROPER EARTH GOVERNMENT"

The implosion of the Soviet Empire did not dampen Muller's enthusiasm for world government and socialism. Muller knows that the idea of "world government" has an unsavory odor for many people.

1. World Goodwill, *World Goodwill Newsletter*, 1995, No. 2, "Interview with Robert Muller," http://www.lucistrust.org/goodwill/wgnl952.shtml, printed 05/29/03.

2. Muller, *Ideas And Dreams, Vol. III*, Idea 1263, Dec. 25, 1997.

3. Muller, *New Genesis*, p191. Muller's belief that Christ will depart once more after his reappearance on Earth is consistent with the beliefs of the Theosophist Alice Bailey, who said that Christ "will again appear and guide mankind" to a just civilization. She said that Christ "will—through the new group of world servers and the men of goodwill—complete His association with the Will of God (His Father's business) in such a manner that the eternal will-to-good will be translated by humanity into goodwill and right relations. Then His task will be done; He will be free again to leave us, this time not to return, but to leave the world of men in the hands of that great spiritual Server Who will be the new Head of the Hierarchy, the Church Invisible." (Alice A. Bailey, *The Externalisation of the Hierarchy*, 1957, Lucis Publishing Company, p609).

4. Muller, *New Genesis*, p126.

5. Alice A. Bailey, *Problems of Humanity*, Lucis Publishing Company, 1st ed. 1947; rev. ed. 1964, p156.

6. Robert Muller, *Ideas And Dreams for a Better World: 2001–2500, Volume VI*, Idea 2073, http://www.robertmuller.org/volume/ideas2001.html, viewed 06/21/04 (cited below as Muller, *Ideas and Dreams, Vol. VI*).

7. Muller, *Ideas And Dreams, Vol. III*, Idea 1157, Sept. 10, 1997.

Therefore, he advises, "since world government has been downgraded by a systematic campaign of extreme right parties claiming that it would lead to dictatorship, I recommend to use the words proper Earth government."[1] He promises, "We are on the threshold of an extraordinary, mind-boggling, new age of our human progress and evolution on planet Earth if we do not stick to obsolete beliefs, values, systems, institutions and laws."[2]

Muller has written, "We must learn to adjust our individual and group interests to the supreme interests, survival and apotheosis of the human race."[3] As individualism goes, so will go capitalism. "Historically it will be the privilege of capitalism to destroy the Earth in the 21st century unless government re-establishes its pre-eminent role and function for the people's and the Earth's fate."[4]

Muller favors using the European Union as the basis for "a World Union," unless the UN is "rapidly transformed" into "an effective world political union and administration."[5] Then, "since Russia reaches into the North of Asia, the old dream of Eurasia can be implemented. The plan of Robert Schuman who dreamt of integrating the African countries into Eurafrica can be implemented. . . . In the meantime, the US can organize the Americas from Alaska to the Tierra del Fuego and the two unions can be integrated into a World Union."[6] (This ought to be interesting news for Latin Americans and Africans who cherish their independence.)

European Union leaders are now thinking along similar lines. In an October 2001 speech to the College of Europe, Belgian Prime Minister Guy Verhofstadt said,

we now need a New World Order more than ever before. A world order in which American leadership will of course remain a key element, if only because it will remain the only country with a global military force until such time as Europe develops a defence capability of its own. But the other continents, and especially Europe, must make a major contribution to building this New World Order, too. They must take greater responsibility, and make a greater commitment. . . . We could order the world on the basis of existing regional cooperation organisations: the European Union, ASEAN, Mercosur, NAFTA, the African Union, the Arab League and SAARC in southern Asia.[7] In this context, we should also include countries like China, Russia and Japan, and the whole of Oceania. We need to take a first step down the path towards a global form of federalism, a structure where the reality of an increasingly interactive world is finally made a political reality too. In fact, a structure of this kind was already planned when the United Nations was created in 1945, but was never implemented after the Cold War. The New World Order could lead to a new G8, G9 or G10, with regular meetings between the delegates of the world's continents. . . . We need a global political vision, a political counterweight capable of reining in uncontrolled forces, be they market forces or ideological forces. The European Union is the model which shows this is possible. . . . What I have tried to do today is to prove that the European Union is the most generous political project on our continent, a project that can be held up as an example for a New World Order that will truly begin to close the gap between rich and poor. Now, as we stand on the threshold of the 21st century, I find it hard to imagine a greater political ambition. To all of you who are preparing for a European career I say that I hope, one day, we will achieve this goal together.[8]

1. Muller, *Paradise Earth*, p7, (p15 of the PDF file).
2. Ibid., p21, (p29 of the PDF file).
3. Muller, *New Genesis*, p185. "Apotheosis" means "elevation to divine status," according to *Webster's* dictionary.
4. Muller, *Ideas And Dreams, Vol. VI*, Idea 2049.
5. Robert Muller, *Ideas And Dreams for a Better World: 1–500, Volume I*, Idea 126, 13 November 1994, http://www.robertmuller.org/volume/ideas0001.html, viewed 06/21/04 (cited below as Muller, *Ideas and Dreams, Vol. I*).
6. Ibid., Idea 126, 13 November 1994.
7. ASEAN is the Association of Southeast Asian Nations. Mercosur (from the Spanish *mercado comun sur*) is a free-trade zone including Argentina, Brazil, Paraguay, and Uruguay. SAARC is the South Asian Association for Regional Cooperation, established in 1985 by Bangladesh, Bhutan, India, Maldives, Nepal, Pakistan and Sri Lanka.
8. Guy Verhofstadt, "The New World Order Since 11 September," October 23, 2001, web page of the Delegation of the European Commission to the United States, http://www.eurunion.org/partner/EUUSTerror/VerhofstadtSpWarsaw.htm, printed 08/03/04.

Muller recently wrote (in all caps, no less), "THE UNITED NATIONS MUST BE VASTLY STRENGTHENED TO RESOLVE THE MAJOR GLOBAL PROBLEMS HENCEFORTH INCREAS-INGLY CONFRONTING HUMANITY AND THE EARTH. IT MUST BE EMPOWERED TO ADOPT AND ENFORCE WORLD LAWS AND REGULATIONS.[1]

Such "world laws and regulations" would be intrusive, indeed. Muller's ideas for the world govern-ment would include "world-wide prohibition of alcoholic beverages.... As for smoking it should urgently be prohibited world-wide."[2] No more sodas, either:

My opposition to soft drinks was also because they contain carbon dioxide which we do not want to have in the air but which we let enter into our body. In September 1999, when spending a week at an Optimum Health Cen-ter in San Diego, California I learned that soft drinks leave health-damaging traces of toxic carbon dioxide on the walls of our intestines. I go therefore one step further and recommend that all carbonated so-called 'soft' drinks should be prohibited by the UN, World Health Organization and all governments in the world.[3]

In Muller's New World Order, there would be a "standard World Identity Card" for all,[4] centralized police and military forces under the control of "the Ministry of Peace"[5] (the same term that Orwell used in *1984* for Big Brother's military force),[6] a global secret service,[7] "world penal legislation,"[8] a glo-bal property record similar to "what the young French revolutionaries did for France,"[9] a "World Sus-tainable Consumption Commission,"[10] a "world taxation system"[11] (and income records for everyone on the planet),[12] and a comprehensive world database, a "Global Data and Optimum Design Agency where all data on our planet, on its environment and on humanity would be accessible."[13]

American cities would be totally re-designed: "The ideal US city of tomorrow: a big, concentrated round center with all the supermarkets and shopping centers conceivable, public services, health ser-vices, doctor's offices, schools and funeral homes around which dwellings and apartments are built concentrically in which people live who are stockholders of the totality."[14] Regarding academic free-dom, Muller says, "All University students on the planet should be required to take basic courses in planetary, cosmic and evolutionary consciousness, in ecology or Earth Science and on the United Nations."[15]

If this platform sounds like world Communism, Muller says that might not be altogether bad: "We should ask an honest man like Mikhail Gorbachev to tell us what was good in certain cases in commu-nism and which would be useful for humanity. Not everything is totally bad in any system. Even Hitler

1. Muller, *Paradise Earth*, p3, (p11 of the PDF file). The all-capitalization style is what Muller himself used in his book.

2. Muller, *Ideas And Dreams, Vol. III*, Idea 1410, 21 May 1998.

3. Muller, *Ideas And Dreams for a Better World: 2501–3000, Volume VII*, Idea 2699, http://www.robertmuller.org/volume/ ideas2501.html, viewed 06/21/04 (cited below as Muller, *Ideas and Dreams, Vol. VII*).

4. Muller, *Ideas And Dreams, Vol. III*, Idea 1001, 7 April 1997.

5. Muller, *Ideas And Dreams, Vol. I*, Idea 315, 21 May 1995.

6. George Orwell, *1984*, New American Library edition, 1961, p8.

7. Muller, *Ideas And Dreams, Vol. I*, Idea 413, 27 August 1995.

8. Muller, *Ideas And Dreams, Vol. III*, Idea 1377, 18 April 1998.

9. Muller, *Ideas And Dreams, Vol. I*, Idea 113, 31 October 1994.

10. Ibid., Idea 430, 13 September 1995.

11. Robert Muller, *Ideas And Dreams for a Better World*: 3001–3500, *Volume VIII*, Idea 3138, http://www.robertmuller.org/ volume/ideas3001.html, viewed 06/21/04 (cited below as Muller, *Ideas and Dreams, Vol. VIII*).

12. Muller, *Ideas And Dreams, Vol. I*, Idea 114, 1 November 1994.

13. Ibid., Idea 94, 12 October 1994.

14. Muller, *Ideas And Dreams for a Better World: 3501–4000, Volume IX*, Idea 3634, http://www.robertmuller.org/volume/ ideas3501.html, viewed 06/21/04.

15. Muller, *Ideas And Dreams, Vol. II*, Idea 573, 3 February 1996.

did something worthwhile, still existent today, when he asked for the building of the Volkswagen, the cheap, economic car for ordinary, low income people."[1]

(The historian William Shirer describes the Volkswagen as a "particular swindle perpetrated by Hitler on the German workers."[2] Hitler set the Volkswagen's price at 990 marks, and the workers were to pay for their car on the installment plan before it was produced or delivered to them. Shirer said, "Alas for the worker, not a single car was ever turned out for any customer during the Third Reich. Tens of millions of marks were paid in by the German wage earners, not a pfennig of which was ever to be refunded. By the time the war started the Volkswagen factory turned to the manufacture of goods more useful to the Army."[3])

Muller says that "both nationalisms and big, multinational corporations must be dismantled and replaced by something else. It has to come from an outside force, a people's revolution or a revolution of the scientists, thinkers, visionaries, prophets, globalists, futurologists and synthesizers of this planet."[4] He said, "As in the case of the French revolution, it is youth which must start that revolution. I will be happy to give them advice. But it is up to them, as the most advanced units of human evolution, to enter into action."[5]

Muller's revolutionary ideal does not include human equality as the West has understood it. He says: "I have more and more admiration for Hindu political science which observes that human societies are managed by a caste system: the kings or central government, the military, the merchants and the priests. The ordinary citizens are the lowest, servant caste, while there are alliances between the higher, ruling castes."[6]

Robert Muller also thinks that we may become extinct: "The Earth will take revenge against her most advanced species which has begun to destroy her. She will retaliate with lack of oxygen, ultraviolet rays, lack of water, mounting cancers, the breakdown of the immune system of the human body, etc. God will not allow us to destroy His Creation and to put an end to the Earth's careful, miraculous evolution over billions of years. He is more likely to let humanity be destroyed."[7]

In any event, Muller believes that liberty—as it has been understood in the past—is obsolete:

Since the Earth and nature have become a major preoccupation of humanity, it is imperative to reconsider notions such as liberty which was correct in an earlier period but no longer is. For example, the concept of free enterprise and full business freedom can now lead to substantial destructions [sic] of the Earth, of its natural resources and elements on which we live. This should become a major subject for debate in the United Nations. What was a justified moral concept yesterday may be today unethical and immoral.[8]

1. Ibid., Idea 776, 24 August 1996. More recently, Muller again praised Hitler's car: "Hitler has still left a small impact on the Earth: the Volkswagen, his people's car which is built to use the minimum of steel and gasoline is still very popular. It should be a dominant car in big cities and poor countries." (Muller, *Ideas And Dreams, Vol. VII*, Idea 2525).

2. William Shirer, *The Rise and Fall of the Third Reich: A History of Nazi Germany*, Pan Books, 1964, p331.

3. Ibid., p332.

4. Robert Muller, *Ideas And Dreams for a Better World: 1501–2000, Volume IV*, Idea 1634, 30 December 1998, http://www.robertmuller.org/volume/ideas1501.html, viewed 06/21/04 (cited below as Muller, *Ideas and Dreams, Vol. IV*).

5. Muller, *Ideas And Dreams, Vol. III*, Idea 1225, 17 November 1997.

6. Ibid., Idea 1095, 10 July 1997. Charles Upton says that "Muller's understanding of the Hindu castes, the *varnas*, is defective. The highest caste is that of the priests or *Brahmins*. Below them come the kings, the central government and the military, the *Kshatriyas*, who share a single caste. The merchants and artisans make up the third caste, the *Vaishyas*, while the fourth caste, the workers, are the *Shudras*. The higher castes do not form 'alliances,' but rather have specific duties and rights with respect to one another. For example, it is the duty of the *Kshatriyas*, the warrior caste, to defend the *Brahmins* in battle."

7. Muller, *Ideas And Dreams, Vol. III*, Idea 1294, 25 January 1998.

8. Muller, *Ideas And Dreams, Vol. IV*, Idea 1575, 2 November 1998.

He adds,

Within ten years governments will enforce laws requiring people to consume less. It will finally be realized that what is happening on this planet is a global, world war against nature. Governments don't want to recognize it today because they continue to believe in the illusion of endless economic growth, enrichment and power. But they will remember that during the first and second world war, people were asked to reduce their consumption because of the war effort. It will be the same situation once they recognize that there is an all out, possibly terminal war against the Earth.[1]

In his newest book, *Paradise Earth*, Muller quotes Machiavelli to set the theme for his chapter on "The Absolute, Urgent Need for Proper Earth Government." As Muller quotes from *The Prince and Other Discourses*: "There is nothing more difficult to take in hand, more perilous to conduct, or more uncertain in its success, than to take the lead in the introduction of a new order of things."[2]

That aphorism has a context, which Muller did not quote. The Italian political philosopher said,

And it ought to be remembered that there is nothing more difficult to take in hand, more perilous to conduct, or more uncertain in its success, then to take the lead in the introduction of a new order of things. Because the innovator has for enemies all those who have done well under the old conditions, and lukewarm defenders in those who may do well under the new. This coolness arises partly from fear of the opponents, who have the laws on their side, and partly from the incredulity of men, who do not readily believe in new things until they have had a long experience of them. Thus it happens that whenever those who are hostile have the opportunity to attack they do it like partisans, whilst the others defend lukewarmly, in such wise that the prince is endangered along with them. It is necessary, therefore . . . to inquire whether these innovators can rely on themselves or have to depend on others: that is to say, whether, to consummate their enterprise, have they to use prayers or can they use force? In the first instance they always succeed badly, and never compass anything; but when they can rely on themselves and use force, then they are rarely endangered. Hence it is that all armed prophets have conquered, and the unarmed ones have been destroyed. Besides the reasons mentioned, the nature of the people is variable, and whilst it is easy to persuade them, it is difficult to fix them in that persuasion. And thus it is necessary to take such measures that, when they believe no longer, it may be possible to make them believe by force.[3]

Such would be the reality of a New World Order, however idealistic its present-day propagandists; it could only be installed and maintained by force and "armed prophets."

THE FATE OF OPPONENTS: "A SPECIAL CORRAL OF THE UNIVERSE"

Muller loves humanity in general, but says "My only true friends in life were those who shared the same passion and concern for the world, for humanity, and for the United Nations. I was never able to cultivate any other real friendships."[4]

Muller says that "all those who hold contrary beliefs" to those favored in the "next phase of evolution" will "disappear."[5] He predicts a hellish destiny for those who balk at political and spiritual globalization: "Those who criticize the UN are anti-evolutionary, blind, self-serving people. Their souls will be parked in a special corral of the universe for having been retarding forces, true aberrations in the evolution and ascent of humanity."[6]

1. Ibid., Idea 1821.
2. Muller, *Paradise Earth*, p2 (p. 10 of the PDF file).
3. Niccolo Machiavelli, *The Prince*, on-line version from *The Literature Network*, http://www.online-literature.com/machiavelli/prince/6/, Chapter 6, "Concerning new principalities which are acquired by one's own arms and ability," printed 05/31/04.
4. Muller, *My Testament*, p124.
5. Muller, *Ideas And Dreams, Vol. IV*, Idea 1748.
6. Muller, *My Testament*, pp148–149.

Muller hails Ted Turner, saying "Thank you, dear Ted" for his billion dollar pledge to the UN.[1] Muller says that Gorbachev and Turner are the "only two persons on Earth who have a world-wide visibility and a deep faith in their destiny which is to change the course of this planet and avoid its destruction."[2]

The former UN official also has an abundance of self-esteem. He says that the Hopi Indians named him "Kogyun Deyo, Spider Boy with the task of making a big spiderweb to catch all evil in the world and then throw it far away into the universe."[3] He says, "Future history is likely to prove that Mr. Gorbachev and I were correct world diagnosticians and prophets."[4] He adds, "If I should ever be proclaimed a saint by the Catholic religion or by the United Religions Organization, I would like to be named or known as: Saint Robert of Mount Rasur."[5] Muller wrote in the late 1990s that one of his dreams was that "I will be appointed the Servant General of the World People's Assembly in 2000 and that the governmental UN General Assembly 2000 will honor me with the title Servant General Emeritus or Wise Elder of the United Nations."[6] Muller's dreams continue to expand; recently he has written, "My dream is to be the creator of the World Union and be remembered as the Father of the World."[7]

MULLER'S THEOSOPHICAL CONNECTIONS

Robert Muller's connections with the Theosophical movement are of long standing. Muller wrote the World Core Curriculum, now being taught in 43 Robert Muller Schools around the world.[8] He thinks that this curriculum "should be taught in all schools of Earth,"[9] and that it "could serve as a basic framework for a world employment policy" to be promoted by the UN's International Labor Organization.[10] In 1989, Muller won the UNESCO Prize for Peace Education for his work on this curriculum.[11] These schools drew praise in 2002 from former President Carter: "Rosalynn and I are pleased to congratulate you on receiving the Nuclear Age Peace Foundation's 2002 World Citizenship Award. . . . Your schools and books emphasize the increasing importance of global education."[12]

Gloria Crook, director of the Robert Muller School in Arlington, Texas, said in 1997 that the World Core Curriculum is "well accepted," but more so abroad than in the U.S. She noted that there is "wide objection" in the U.S. to any curriculum with a "religious sense."[13] Muller says that the "religious sense" of his curriculum is Mayan: "the world core curriculum . . . which I derived from my experience in the United Nations, is almost identical to the Mayan cosmology."[14]

1. Muller, *Ideas And Dreams, Vol. III*, Idea 1098, 13 July 1997.

2. Muller, *Ideas And Dreams, Vol. IV*, Idea 1883.

3. Muller, *Ideas And Dreams, Vol. III*, Idea 1220, 12 November 1997.

4. Muller, *Ideas And Dreams, Vol. I*, Idea 417, 31 August 1995.

5. Muller, *Ideas And Dreams, Vol. III*, Idea 1340, 12 March 1998.

6. Muller, *Ideas And Dreams, Vol. II*, Idea 857, 13 November 1996,.

7. Muller, *Ideas And Dreams, Vol. VIII*, Idea 3087.

8. The number of Robert Muller schools was provided by Muller in an interview with Lee Penn in November 2002.

9. Robert Muller, "An Open Letter to All Educators in the World," leaflet provided to Lee Penn by Muller in November 2002 (cited below as Muller, "Open Letter to All Educators").

10. Muller, *Ideas And Dreams, Vol. VI*, Idea 2021.

11. Muller, *New Genesis*, pp194–195 (biographic sketch).

12. Letter from Jimmy Carter to Robert Muller, October 24, 2002, as shown in Muller, *Paradise Earth*, introductory pages, (p7 of the PDF file).

13. Telephone interview by Lee Penn of Gloria Crook, Robert Muller School, June 1997.

14. Muller, *Ideas And Dreams, Vol. III*, Idea 1040, 16 May 1997.

The current manual for the World Core Curriculum says, "the underlying philosophy upon which The Robert Muller School is based will be found in the Teachings set forth in the books of Alice A. Bailey by the Tibetan Teacher, Djwhal Khul (published by Lucis Publishing Company) . . . and the Teachings of Morya as given in the Agni Yoga series books."[1]

What the Curriculum does for children, the media should do for adults. Muller says,

It is the media who are 'informing' us and should educate us about the major, very rapid changes which are taking place in the world. But the media do not recognize that they should be educators. They are simply communicators. Well, they should be the educators of our adult lives until death. This is why I have also couched the World Core Curriculum into a framework for World Media Coverage which I would like to see taught in all schools of journalism and hung on the walls of all media directors in the world, as a basis of their media coverage and programming.[2]

For many years, Muller has associated with two different branches of the Theosophical movement. One of these is Share International, a group that believes that "Maitreya," the "World Teacher," is about to return.[3] In March 1982, *Share International* printed one of Muller's articles, "The Future of the United Nations;" Muller gave *Share* his permission to post the article on its Web site in 1998.[4] Muller was interviewed in 1993 by Monte Leach for the same journal,[5] and the May 1999 issue included a reprint of a Muller lecture.[6] The organization interviewed Muller again in the summer of 2003.[7]

The second group of Theosophists that Muller cooperates with is the Lucis Trust. Muller spoke about "The Reappearance of Christ" in August 1979 to students at the Arcane School, (which is run by the Lucis Trust);[8] he reprinted this essay in his cornerstone book, *New Genesis: Shaping a Global Spirituality.*[9] Muller published seven articles between 1979 and 1984 in *The Beacon,*[10] which the Lucis Trust describes as "a magazine of esoteric philosophy presenting the principles of the Ageless Wisdom as a contemporary way of life."[11] A web site that promotes Muller's works offers a biography of him; at the

1. Robert Muller School, *World Core Curriculum: Foundation*, p1. Gloria Crook is President of this school. Robert Muller said, "History will prove that Gloria Crook, U Thant and the United Nations were right. The quicker all educators and media listen to them, the quicker we will get out of the present confusion and find a new and promising path of progress and evolution." (Muller, "Open Letter to All Educators.")

2. Robert Muller, "A Letter to All Educators in the World," http://www.unol.org/rms/rmltr.html, printed 06/21/04.

3. However, Share International—a Theosophical organization that sponsors Benjamin Creme as the prophet of "Maitreya," the soon-to-come "World Teacher," denies that the organization, its leaders, or members have been involved in the URI (E-mail from Cher Gilmore, Media Coordinator, Share International, to Lee Penn, 11/09/02).

4. Robert Muller, "The Future of the United Nations," posted on the Share International web site in 1998, http://www.shareintl.org/unfuturm.html; printed in 1998; no longer on the Net.

5. Monte Leach, "Robert Muller—a perennial optimist," *Share International*, December 1993, Vol. 12, no. 10, pp5–7.

6. Robert Muller, "When the human species decides, it will succeed," *Share International*, May 1999, p22.

7. Felicity Eliot, "Enter with hope for a better world: An interview with Dr. Robert Muller," *Share International Media Service*, July-August 2003, http://www.simedia.org/new/soc-econ-pol/for-the-united-nations.html, printed 08/28/03.

8. Lucis Trust, "The Arcane School," in Joel Beversluis, ed., *Sourcebook of the World's Religions: An Interfaith Guide to Religion and Spirituality*, New World Library, 3rd ed., 2000, p95.

9. Muller, *New Genesis*, p117; the book describes "The Reappearance of Christ" essay as a "Transcript of an address to the Arcane School Conference, New York, August 12, 1979."

10. The articles include: Robert Muller, "Prayer and Meditation at the United Nations," *The Beacon*, November/December 1978, pp376–378; Robert Muller, "A Moral and Spiritual Dimension," *The Beacon*, March/April 1980, pp249–251; Robert Muller, "The Future of the United Nations," *The Beacon*, July/August 1981, pp126–127; Robert Muller, "A World Core Curriculum, Part I," *The Beacon*, July/August 1982, pp298–302; Robert Muller, "A World Core Curriculum, Part II," *The Beacon*, September/October 1982, pp330–332; Robert Muller, "Of Right Global Relationships: Part I," *The Beacon*, January/February 1984 (the text of an address that he gave to the World Goodwill seminar in New York in October of 1982), pp208–211; and Robert Muller, "Of Right Global Relationships, Part II," *The Beacon*, March/April 1984, pp234–238.

11. Lucis Trust, "The Beacon," http://www.lucistrust.org/beacon/index.shtml, printed 03/27/03.

top of the web page, there is a quotation from two of Alice Bailey's books, *Education in the New Age*, and *The Externalisation of the Hierarchy*.[1]

Dale McKechnie, a vice president of the Lucis Trust, said in 1998, "Robert Muller apparently has been influenced by Alice Bailey's works. . . . He did speak at some of our conferences. . . . We have been a great supporter of his work. We've tried to support him and the United Nations and his current work at the Peace University in Costa Rica."[2] The Theosophists claim Muller as one of their own.

1. "Robert Muller's Exhortations and Ideas & Dreams for a Better World—Robert's Bio," *Earthpax*, http://www.earth-pax.net/Bio.htm, printed 02/12/04.

2. Telephone interview, April 24, 1998, by Lee Penn of Dale McKechnie, Vice-President of the Lucis Trust.

15

BARBARA MARX HUBBARD

B ARBARA M ARX H UBBARD has consistently delivered a Promethean, New Age message in books and lectures since the early 1980s. Some of her statements are her own words, and others are dictated by spirits that Marx Hubbard calls "higher voices" or "the Christ voice."[1]

INVERTED THEOLOGY: "WE ARE GODS!"

Marx Hubbard says, "We are immortal. We are not bound by the limits of the body."[2] She exults, "We can create new life forms and new worlds. We *are* gods!"[3] Since we are gods, there is no need for Christ to save us. Instead, "Multitudes of self-saviors is what we are, for those who have eyes to see."[4] Furthermore, Marx Hubbard's spirit guide told her, "Never again shall you have to return to the human condition. Henceforth you shall evolve consciously, aware at all times that you and God are one forever."[5]

The "Christ" who spoke to Marx Hubbard said, "I, Jesus Christ, was simply a first example of what you all can be. Since very few could actualize their full potential during the last two thousand years, I was deified and put above you. People worshipped me instead of actualizing themselves."[6] The spirit said, "I did not suffer on the cross and rise again on the third day to show you what I could do, but what *you* can do. *Yours* is the power. *Yours* is the glory. That is my message to you! . . . I manifest in time but I am not of time. I am eternal and evolving. And so, you are eternal and evolving."[7]

As Barbara Marx Hubbard continued her intercourse with her "inner teacher," she discovered that the "teacher" is—herself. She said,

All my life I have heard an inner voice and I tend to write in my journal and call the inner voice my Dearly Beloved. . . . In the last couple of months, the guidance from the Dearly Beloved is 'I Am You'. . . . Over a period of six weeks I started to invite what I call my universal self to take dominion within the household of selves that I am. . . . I have been experiencing an identity shift such that now I can say to you, 'I am the beloved that I seek.'

1. Barbara Marx Hubbard, *The Revelation: A Message of Hope for the New Millennium*, Nataraj Publishing, Novato, CA, 1995, p 11 ("Conventions Used in this Book") and p 15 (Preface) (cited below as Marx Hubbard, *Revelation/Hope*).

2. Barbara Marx Hubbard, *Conscious Evolution: Awakening the Power of Our Social Potential*, New World Library, Novato, California, 1998, p 212 (cited below as Marx Hubbard, *Conscious Evolution*).

3. Marx Hubbard, *Revelation/Hope*, p 312.

4. Barbara Marx Hubbard, *The Book of Co-Creation Part II—The Promise Will Be Kept: The Gospels, The Acts, the Epistles*, Foundation for Conscious Evolution, San Rafael, California, 1993 (privately published), p 143 (cited below as Marx Hubbard, *Book of Co-Creation*).

5. Marx Hubbard, *Revelation/Hope*, p 115.

6. Marx Hubbard, *The Revelation: Our Crisis Is A Birth*, Foundation for Conscious Evolution, Sonoma CA, 1993, p 304.

7. Marx Hubbard, *Revelation/Hope*, pp 100–101.

I am the universal human. . . . The local self has learned that there is no gratification in a deep way except through union with me.[1]

This fall into solipsism is a spiritual calamity that many New Age devotees mistake for growth. Barbara Marx Hubbard's condition *may* be a foretaste of Hell. As C. S. Lewis said, "The characteristic of lost souls is their rejection of everything that is not simply themselves;" after death, a lost soul "has his wish—to live wholly in the self and to make the best of what he finds there. And what he finds there is Hell."[2]

Marx Hubbard's view of ecclesiastical history is pure *Da Vinci Code* legend. She says that in the early Church,

> They shared. They attempted to become Christ-humans themselves. In these small circles men and women shared holy communion as co-equals. They had a new story, a new sacrament, and a new expectation of the transformation of the person and the body to life everlasting. They radiated their ecstatic vision and in the midst of a dying world they attracted new life. However, they were soon to be taken over by Constantine and it was at this point that they entered the power structure. The gnosis, the deeper mystical knowing of our potential for conscious evolution, was driven underground.[3]

Marx Hubbard's "inner voice" gave her this view of the spiritual history of the Christian era: "In the last two thousand years, planet Earth has been filled with volunteer old souls who chose to complete their education in whole-centeredness by working on a planet with the twin defects of carnivorous behavior and forgetfulness of God."[4]

Marx Hubbard's revision of the Lord's Prayer expresses her theology of self-worship:

OUR FATHER/MOTHER GOD…
WHICH ART IN HEAVEN…
HALLOWED BE *OUR* NAME…
OUR KINGDOM *IS* COME…
OUR WILL *IS* DONE…
GIVE US THIS DAY OUR DAILY BREAD…
FORGIVE US OUR TRESPASSES AS WE FORGIVE THOSE WHO TRESPASS AGAINST US…
LEAVE US NOT IN TEMPTATION BUT DELIVER US FROM EVIL…
FOR OURS IS THE KINGDOM, OURS THE POWER, OURS THE GLORY, FOR EVER AND EVER. AMEN[5]

Neale Donald Walsch's familiar spirit inverts the prayer in the same way, saying,

> Here is My message, the message I would seek to leave with the world: My Children, who art in Heaven, hallowed is your name. Your kingdom is come, and your will is done, on Earth as it is in Heaven. You are given this day your daily bread, and you are forgiven your debts, and your trespasses, exactly to the degree that you have

---

1. Wisdom Radio, transcript of interview of Barbara Marx Hubbard by Carolyn Craft, for the "Inner Wisdom" program. (This document is no longer on the Net.) Hubbard wrote similarly for her own newsletter in early 2000: "the inner voice, the guide, the 'Beloved' higher self that has been signaling me from afar for thirty-five years, is incarnating as me. . . . Starting only a year ago, my local self made a commitment to STOP and to invite the essential self, the inner Beloved, to take dominion within me. . . . In this process, I am learning to affirm: *I am the Beloved I have been seeking. I am the voice I have been hearing.*" (Barbara Marx Hubbard, *Voices of Conscious Evolution*, Foundation for Conscious Evolution Newsletter, Vol. 1, Winter 2000, p1.)
2. C.S. Lewis, *The Problem of Pain*, ch. 8, "Hell," Touchstone, 1996 reprint, pp109–110.
3. Marx Hubbard, *Revelation/Hope*, p18.
4. Ibid., p255.
5. Ibid., pp313–314. The ellipses are of Hubbard's meditation on each phrase of her prayer, and the italics and capitalization in the prayer are as given in the original text.

forgiven those who trespass against you. Lead your Self not into temptation, but deliver your Self from the evils you have created. For thine *is* the Kingdom, and the Power, and the Glory, forever. Amen. And Amen.[1]

Are these New Age writers trading notes on the Earth-plane, or are their spirit guides holding preternatural conference calls to coordinate their messages to humankind?

In the New Age, there is to be a new "Christ" and a New Religion. "Jesus" told Marx Hubbard, "The New Order of the Future will help emancipate Christ from the walls of the church to reveal him to be the potential in each man and woman on Earth."[2] All religions will be as one as we transcend orthodoxy; "The period of separate sects and dogmas gives way to the period of co-creative consciousness when everyone is attuning to the same pattern and is attracted to fulfilling their unique capacities to be Universal Humans."[3]

Her view of the Second Coming of Christ and the planetary awakening is this: "Christ, pure love and knowledge of God, marries Eve, human intellect. As the Second Couple they reach the Second Tree and enter the Second Garden at the time of the Second Coming, when the Christ within the people of Earth awakens simultaneously in a Planetary Pentecost."[4] The "Christ" spirit told Marx Hubbard, "My message is: *You* are King of Kings, *you* are Lord of Lords. I have no desire to return to Earth in the role of ruler over you. That is a failure. That is treating you as a regressive child."[5]

Marx Hubbard's higher voice says about God's judgment:

The 'second death' is for those of you who cannot evolve by choice, due to some deeply seated error in your understanding of the nature of reality.... The second death, for you, is a purification, an erasing of the memory of fear, through the shock of a fire.... Your misery will be soothed, your fear turned to love, your cynicism revealed to be the defensiveness of a sensitive and hurting soul ignorantly protecting itself from God. The second death is your next step toward eternal life.[6]

Like Alice Bailey, she considers the "material world" to be a prison, and looks to a hierarchy of "ascended masters." She says, "We will soon be released from the fleeting imprisonment of mind by the material world."[7] To foster spiritual evolution, her spirit guide says that we should "Call upon the full hierarchy of evolved beings to be with you now."[8] The entity adds, "Your highest spiritual beings, even now, are telling you that each of you has access to an inner teacher.... They tell you that through a process called 'initiation,' you can transform yourself into an 'ascended master'. They speak of the hierarchy of evolved beings."[9]

Regarding the Devil and the Fall, Marx Hubbard says, "Adam and Eve were symbolically the first couple. They joined the masculine and feminine together and made a whole being, wherein they reached the Tree of the Knowledge of Good and Evil, and separated from the animal world. To reach the Tree of Life, to have access to the powers of creation, each person must become whole, uniting the masculine and feminine, the yang and the yin, the rational and the intuitive."[10]

1. Neale Donald Walsch, *Conversations with God: An Uncommon Dialogue, Book* 3, Hampton Roads Publishing Company, Inc., 1998, p366.
2. Marx Hubbard, *Book of Co-Creation*, p67.
3. Marx Hubbard, *Revelation/Hope*, p194.
4. Marx Hubbard, *Book of Co-Creation*, p246.
5. Marx Hubbard, *Revelation/Hope*, pp235–236.
6. Ibid., p267.
7. Marx Hubbard, *Book of Co-Creation*, p209.
8. Ibid., p348.
9. Marx Hubbard, *Revelation/Hope* p281.
10. Marx Hubbard, *Conscious Evolution*, p213.

The serpent symbolizes an irresistible [sic] energy that is leading us toward life ever-evolving. First the serpent tempted Eve to eat of the Tree of Knowledge of Good and Evil. It attracted her beyond the animal/human world which knew no separation from the Creator. Then self-awareness came. We felt alone, different, afraid, guilty, incomplete. We forgot our Creator. We listened to inner voices, urging us to do more, be more, become more. The hunger of Eve awoke to re-unite with God.[1]

"Jesus" told Marx Hubbard to "Forgive Satan for fearing God. . . . Love Satan, my fallen brother, and do not let him make you reject God any more."[2] We are to similarly excuse Cain: "Forgive Cain, he knew not what he did. He was as a child, hurt by his father unwittingly."[3]

Marx Hubbard appears to have embraced a spiritual variant of social Darwinism: "'Evil' will appear to destroy—and indeed it will. It will destroy all those who cannot attune to the design at its coming stage, for life is future-oriented. Nature is less concerned about individual survival, than with the evolution of the whole to ever higher degrees of freedom, union, and consciousness of God."[4] She assigns the devil a key role in evolution: "Evil—the devil—is evolution's selection process that constantly weeds out the weaker from the stronger. It is the steady pressure of the forces of destruction, dis-integration, dissent, decay, devolution and death which test every body every instant of every day for weakness. When its pressure penetrates to a weak spot, it corrodes with the almighty force of God, destroying that which cannot endure to evolve."[5]

NEW MORALITY, FROM THE WOMB TO THE TOMB

In the new age envisioned by Marx Hubbard, contraception, abortion, sexual identity confusion, rampant divorce, and euthanasia will prevail.

She said that in the New Age, "Contra-ception becomes 'pro-ception.' Every child born is chosen, wanted, and adored. Birth defects are a nightmare of the past."[6] "Your adolescence will be a joy. You will be androgynous."[7] "You will choose to create another being only on very special occasions when the whole community of natural Christs sees the requirement."[8] "The breakup of the 20th century procreative family structure is a vital perturbation needed for the breakthrough of the 21st century cocreative family structure."[9] "Fidelity of the partners is to each other for the sake of their chosen act, whether it be a godly child or godly work in the universe. When the act is completed, the partnership is renewed if there is more to be done. It is lovingly ended if there is nothing more to be created by that particular couple. Each discovers the next partner, or partners, with no hint of sorrow, for nothing is separated among those totally connected with God."[10] "But if members of our family choose to remain where they are, we have no moral obligation to suppress our own potential on their behalf. In fact the suppression of potential is more 'immoral' than growing beyond our biological relationships."[11]

1. Marx Hubbard, *Book of Co-Creation*, p172.
2. Marx Hubbard, *Revelation/Hope*, p187.
3. Marx Hubbard, *Book of Co-Creation*, p8.
4. Barbara Marx Hubbard, *Happy Birth Day Planet Earth: The Instant of Co-Operation*, Ocean Tree Books, Santa Fe, New Mexico, 1986, pp26–27 (cited below as Marx Hubbard, *Happy Birth Day Planet Earth*).
5. Ibid., p22.
6. Barbara Marx Hubbard, *The Evolutionary Journey: A Personal Guide to a Positive Future*, Evolutionary Press, 1982, p90 (cited below as Marx Hubbard, *Evolutionary Journey*).
7. Marx Hubbard, *Revelation/Hope*, p165.
8. Ibid., p165.
9. Marx Hubbard, *Conscious Evolution*, p208.
10. Marx Hubbard, *Revelation/Hope*, p166.
11. Marx Hubbard, *Book of Co-Creation*, p60.

And to end it all, there is suicide. "Unchosen, involuntary death is surely a tyrant. Disease is a dictator. It is obscene to imagine a universal human suffering from death by cancer or heart disease, like a helpless animal. The dignity of humans requires death, and life, by choice not coercion."[1] "Those who have more to create choose to live on until they are finished with their work. When we feel that our creativity has run its course, we gracefully choose to die. In fact, it seems unethical and foolish to live on. . . . When we are old and tired of life and do not want to live on, we learn to die by choice, as some native people do."[2] Marx Hubbard says that such would be her own choice, when the time comes: "It is my preference that, when I feel complete with this life, I call in my beloveds, my family, my friends. In a momentous celebration I will prepare to enter the mystery of the next phase of life and seek the blessings of those I love. I choose to make my transition gracefully."[3]

THE COMING "SELECTION" OF MANKIND

As if the foregoing inverted theology and praise of the Culture of Death were not bad enough, Barbara Marx Hubbard calmly envisions a coming lethal "selection" of the human race. In 4 different books written over a 15-year period (*The Revelation: Alternative to Armageddon*; *Happy Birth Day, Planet Earth*; *The Revelation: A Message of Hope for the New Millennium*; and *The Book of Co-Creation*) Barbara Marx Hubbard has predicted "personal extinction"[4] for people who will not get with the New Age program and claim their "co-creative" power. "Either the good will prevail, connect, link, and magnetize the majority of humanity to act with love for life everlasting, or the violent selection of the self-centered will begin."[5] "There will be an evolutionary selection process based on your qualifications for co-creative power. . . . A Quantum Transformation is the time of selection of what evolves from what devolves. The species known as self-centered humanity will become extinct. The species known as whole-centered humanity will evolve."[6] "The selection process will exclude all who are exclusive."[7] (Had you believed that evolution was a *random* process? Think again.)

In her 1980 manuscript *The Revelation: Alternative to Armageddon,* Barbara Marx Hubbard's spirit guide proposed the destruction of one-quarter to one-half of humanity. It said,

Out of the full spectrum of human personality, one-fourth is electing to transcend with all their heart, mind, and spirit, One-fourth is ready to so choose, given the example of one other who has made the commitment, One-fourth is resistant to election. They are unattracted by life ever-evolving. Their higher self is unable to penetrate the density of their mammalian senses. They cannot be reached. They do not ask . . . yet they are good. They go about their business, eating, sleeping, reproducing, and dying. They are full-fledged animal/humans. One-fourth is destructive. They are born angry with God. They hate themselves. They project this hatred upon the world. They are defective seeds.[8]

1. Marx Hubbard, *Evolutionary Journey,* pp 84–85.

2. Marx Hubbard, *Conscious Evolution,* p 205.

3. Ibid., p 205.

4. Marx Hubbard, *Happy Birth Day Planet Earth,* p 31. She wrote: "Once the planetary quantum instant has occurred, there will be an irreversible distinction between those who have chosen personal evolution and those who have chosen personal extinction."

5. Marx Hubbard, *Revelation/Hope,* p 303.

6. Ibid., p 111.

7. Ibid., p 303.

8. Barbara Marx Hubbard, *The Book of Co-Creation: An Evolutionary Interpretation of the New Testament; Part III—The Revelation: Alternative to Armageddon,* New Visions, 1980, p 59. The ellipsis is as given from the original text.

The entity adds,

Now as we approach the quantum shift from creature-human to co-creative human—the human who is an inheritor of god-like powers—the destructive one-fourth must be eliminated from the social body. . . . One disconnected human, driven by an ego substituting for God, can hold the whole world in ransom. A single terrorist can now destroy a city, contaminate its water, spread poison gas in its air, unleash bio-organisms that cripple bodies with no compassion or care. Soon a single terrorist can wreak havoc everywhere through capture of one of your forthcoming manned orbiting platforms in space. Before this stage of power can be inherited by the God-centered members of the social body, the self-centered members must be destroyed. There is no alternative. Only the God-centered can evolve. Only the good endures.[1]

The spirit guide told Marx Hubbard in 1980: "Fortunately you, dearly beloveds, are not responsible for this act. We are. We are in charge of God's selection process for planet Earth. He selects, we destroy. We are the riders of the pale horse, Death. We come to bring death to those who are unable to know God. . . . The riders of the pale horse are about to pass among you. Grim reapers, they will separate the wheat from the chaff. This is the most painful period in the history of humanity."[2] Pronouncing the doom of half of mankind, the familiar spirit told Marx Hubbard, "Before the book of life can be opened, the selection process must be made so that only the God-conscious receive the power of co-creators. We will use whatever means we must to make this act of destruction as quick and painless as possible to the one-half of the world who are capable of evolving."[3] Note that the entity says that the "act of destruction" will be "as quick and painless as possible" for the survivors; it says nothing of what it will be like for the victims.

In 1993, Marx Hubbard repeated that mankind will not be in charge of the selection: "There will be a selection process not of our own doing, which will 'decide' what is capable of taking the next step of evolution, and eliminating what is destructive and unworthy of continuation."[4] "The 'reaper' is the harvester, the evolutionary selection process that separates those mutations which are favorable from those that are unfavorable. This selection process is not of human origin. It is the Divine Universal Intelligence that has been operative for billions of years. It is difficult for us to understand this at our immature stage. There are many forces of the larger system at work which we do not yet understand."[5] "Satan stands for separation from God. He is always probing every weakness to test for willingness to accept the illusion of separation. He is part of the selection process that will weed out the non-believers from the believers, that will bring forth the self-elected from the self-rejected, so that when the tribulations are over, only those connected to the whole survive."[6]

In 1995, Marx Hubbard said that the Four Horsemen of the Apocalypse "wait, holding in abeyance for one more instant the dreadful process of selection: The White Horse and the conqueror of creature/human nature, the Red Horse and the power to kill; the Black Horse and the power to destroy those who are in deficiency; the Pale Horse upon whom sits the rider called Death, poised to kill those

1. Ibid., (1980 ed.), p 60.
2. Ibid., (1980 ed.), pp 60–61.
3. Ibid., (1980 ed.), p 62.
4. Marx Hubbard, *Book of Co-Creation*, p 57. In saying that some lives are "unworthy of continuation," Marx Hubbard was using a phrase similar to one that had been chosen by previous evolutionary thinkers. In Germany in 1920, Karl Binding and Alfred Hoche published a defense of euthanasia, titled *Permission for the Destruction of Life Unworthy of Life*. That book influenced German doctors' beliefs before the Nazi seizure of power, and provided the theoretical rationale for the murder of handicapped persons in the euthanasia program after 1933. (Michael Burleigh, *Death And Deliverance: 'Euthanasia' in Germany*, 1900–1945, Cambridge University Press, 1994, pp 15–25.)
5. Marx Hubbard, *Book of Co-Creation*, p 56.
6. Ibid., p 299.

who choose to remain self-centered, with sword,[1] with hunger, with death, and with the beasts of the Earth. All are at the gate, ready to let loose the mighty force."[2]

For Marx Hubbard, the coming "selection" is a necessary part of evolution. "Those who do not evolve, those who do not believe in the potential for transformation" will "pass away forever from this strand of evolution—an extinct species like the dinosaurs."[3] "Those who are not sufficiently educated to align with the design, experience God's purification process as long as necessary, until they learn how to know God or the Intention of Creation experientially."[4] "All who choose not to evolve will die off; their souls will begin again within a different planetary system which will serve as kindergarten for the transition from self-centered to whole-centered being."[5] At the time of the quantum transformation, "All those humans capable of cooperating to self-transcend will do so. All those elements remaining in a state of self-centeredness, maintaining the illusion of separation, will become extinct. . . . Only that spectrum of human consciousness freely able to attune to the whole and hear the inner voice for God [sic] will survive. Just as Cro-Magnon and Neanderthal humans became extinct, so will selfish humans. This is necessary, for their temperament is not viable."[6] Like the totalitarians of the last century, Marx Hubbard refers to undesirable humans as "elements," and forecasts their elimination.

Marx Hubbard says that those who are "selected out" will never be reincarnated on Earth; "The second death is final as far as Earth is concerned. . . . The soul can learn elsewhere in the universe. When it is ready it will choose a planetary system at the right stage for the education it requires."[7] She adds that at "the great period of selection," "the self-transcenders will transcend and the non-transcenders will descend, devolve, and die to this particular planetary experience. Self-centered beings cannot survive in a synergistic world."[8]

Barbara Marx Hubbard praises John Spong, the retired Episcopal Bishop of New Jersey, as a reliable interpreter of the Bible.[9] He's the bishop who wrote in 1998 that "Theism, as a way of defining God is dead."[10] Her chatter about the coming "violent selection of the self-centered"[11] provides an ominous backdrop to Spong's statement that "The next generation will not be a time for the Christian Church to practice business as usual. Those who settle into such a path will be voting to die."[12] With similar rhetorical violence, a supporter of liberal revisions in the traditional teaching of the Episcopal Church said in 2000 that conservative bishops who threatened schism were "nothing more than ecclesiastical terrorists attempting to hold a gun to the head of the church;" he noted that "the international community long ago decided that there would be no negotiation with terrorists who threaten to blow up

---

1. Here, Hubbard's predictions about the mechanism of the "selection" contradict each other. In this 1995 prophecy, Hubbard says that the rider of the Pale Horse will use the "sword" as one of his means "to kill those who choose to remain self-centered." The "sword" refers to war and other violence—human actions, for which the participants are responsible. In 1993, as noted above, Hubbard had written, "There will be a selection process not of our own doing, which will 'decide' what is capable of taking the next step of evolution, and eliminating what is destructive and unworthy of continuation." A "selection process not of our own doing" refers to the elimination of people by natural causes rather than human action.

2. Barbara Marx Hubbard, *Revelation/Hope*, p173.

3. Marx Hubbard, *Book of Co-Creation*, p124.

4. Marx Hubbard, *Revelation/Hope*, p255.

5. Marx Hubbard, *Happy Birth Day Planet Earth*, p17.

6. Ibid., p23.

7. Marx Hubbard, *Revelation/Hope*, p255.

8. Ibid., p125.

9. Marx Hubbard, *Conscious Evolution*, p80.

10. Bishop John S. Spong, "A Call for a New Reformation," http://www.dioceseofnewark.org/vox20598.html, Thesis 1, printed 06/19/04.

11. Marx Hubbard, *Revelation/Hope*, p303.

12. Bishop John S. Spong, "Billy Graham: A Man of Integrity for Yesterday's World," *The Bishop's Voice*, http://newark.anglican.org/vox30399.html, printed 06/19/04.

an airplane if they do not get their way. This is no different."[1] Indeed—and we all know what is usually done with terrorists: execution or life in prison (if the terrorists survive long enough to be tried and convicted).

Survivors of the "selection" will be enthusiastic supporters of the "whole emerging system." As Marx Hubbard says, "Only those who have elected to use their powers well in their lifetime will be resurrected and reincorporated with genetic code and memories intact. Their bodies will be rematerialized. This is a universal law: Only the good evolves—'good' meaning that which is capable of aligning with the whole emerging system, by attuning to its overall design."[2] Marx Hubbard says that "the good which may be selected to proceed onward to the next step of evolution" will possess "the characteristics which will be essential for survival at the next stage of human development."[3] These are:

> One: The capacity for universal consciousness, in consistent attunement with the patterns in the process of evolution.
> Two: Love of freedom—the capacity to tolerate expanded choice, diversity, flexibility, ambiguity, uncertainty, responsibility, and response-*ability*.
> Three: The capacity to co-operate, unite, synergize and love everyone as a member of your body.
> Universal consciousness, expanded freedom of choice, love of unity-in-diversity appear to be characteristics of ourselves at the next stage.[4]

The inheritors of Marx Hubbard's new kingdom will pass all the current tests for political correctness.

The only way to prevent the "selection" would be for a critical mass of humanity to embrace New Age thinking. Marx Hubbard's spirit guide tells her and her allies that "What the angels are waiting for, dearly beloved, is you of my New Order of the Future. You represent the possibility of the avoidance of the painful process of selection, which means the destruction of the self-centered who cannot inherit the powers of co-creation."[5] In other words, if enough of us accept the god-like powers of co-creation, we can awaken into planetary consciousness and avert Armageddon.

ATOM BOMBS AND "CONSCIOUS EVOLUTION"

In 1995, Barbara Marx Hubbard wrote that the nuclear explosions of 1945 were an evolutionary turning point for humanity. "I saw the explosion of the atomic bomb as the beginning of our collective labor pains. It was the signal that the Cosmic Child, humanity, could either kill itself by remaining in self-centered consciousness in the womb of Earth, or instead emancipate itself for universal consciousness and action."[6] Three years later, in *Conscious Evolution*, Marx Hubbard emphasized the point: "An irreversible shift toward conscious evolution began in 1945 when the United States dropped atomic bombs on Hiroshima and Nagasaki. With this dreadful release of power we penetrated one of the invisible technologies of nature—the atom—and gained the power that we once attributed to the gods."[7] Like Alice Bailey and Teilhard de Chardin, Marx Hubbard writes with glowing optimism about mankind's destiny once we have learned to use our new god-like powers.

---

1. Nat Brown, "Bishops in the Playground," http://andromeda.rutgers.edu/~lcrew/assay45.html; posted as part of the discussion of the Episcopal Church's General Convention in 2000, on a site run by Louie Crew, a liberal gay activist in the Episcopal Church; printed 06/19/04.
2. Marx Hubbard, *Revelation/Hope*, p 111.
3. Marx Hubbard, *Book of Co-Creation*, p 120.
4. Ibid., p 120.
5. Marx Hubbard, *Revelation/Hope*, p 173.
6. Ibid., p 43.
7. Marx Hubbard, *Conscious Evolution*, p 9.

Barbara Marx Hubbard has said that the New Age is imminent: "We are at the threshold of a quantum shift in consciousness and action. We need just one more degree of connectedness to light up and link up the new world emerging in our midst."[1] In 1998, she expressed hope that the New Age would begin by 2008: "I do believe that within the next 10 years we can discover and commit to an evolutionary agenda. I believe we will have had a global awakening and will begin consciously and ethically to use our vast collective powers for the evolution of our species."[2] Since then, Marx Hubbard has extended the schedule for the arrival of the New Age. She now hopes for a "planetary Pentecost," a "planetary birth day party," by 2012 (which, as her interviewer for a New Age radio program noted, is an apocalyptic year according to the Mayan calendar.)[3]

THE NEW ORDER: "THE NEXT STAGE OF INDIVIDUALISM"

Marx Hubbard also offers prescriptions for a new political order. In the New Age, collectivism will be the new "individualism:" "Conscious evolution calls upon political leaders to move us toward a synergistic democracy that considers each of us as creative members of the whole community and ecology. We need to be guided toward the next stage of individualism.... Conscious evolution sets the stage for the next phase of individualism wherein we seek our uniqueness not through separation but through deeper participation in the whole."[4] Constitutional, limited government will also end: "As we graduate one by one, then finally collectively transcend the illusion of separation, we will go beyond the Constitution as an external document to the constitution as an internal document that is written in the consciousness of every co-creative person who is attuning to the evolutionary design."[5]

BARBARA MARX HUBBARD AND THEOSOPHY

Barbara Marx Hubbard closed a section of her 1998 book *Conscious Evolution* thus: "When asked what I choose to be the outcome of the book, my answer is that it serve the fulfillment of the plan. 'May Light and Love and Power restore the plan on Earth.' That is my prayer."[6] With this statement, she shows the influence of Alice Bailey's Theosophy on her work. The prayer that Barbara Marx Hubbard uttered is the final verse of "The Great Invocation," a Theosophical prayer written by Alice Bailey and still published by the Lucis Trust.[7] The entire prayer is this:

1. Barbara Marx Hubbard, *Live from the Peace Room*, December 1999 newsletter of the Foundation for Conscious Evolution, p1.

2. Marx Hubbard, *Conscious Evolution*, p4.

3. Michael Toms, August 9, 1999 interview with Barbara Marx Hubbard, Wisdom Radio, http://www.wisdomchannel.com/tvrd/transcripts/episode_transcript.asp; printed in 1999. The document is no longer on the Net.

4. Marx Hubbard, *Conscious Evolution*, p88.

5. Marx Hubbard, *Book of Co-Creation*, p80.

6. Marx Hubbard, *Conscious Evolution*, p216. The capitalization is as it was in her book—and is almost exactly as it is in the Lucis Trust's "Great Invocation."

7. The full text of this prayer is printed on a pale blue bookmark that is distributed with every volume of Alice Bailey's writings. It is also in Bailey's books—for example, Alice A. Bailey, *The Rays and the Initiations, Volume V: A Treatise on the Seven Rays*, Lucis Publishing Company, 1960, pvii (cited below as A. Bailey, *The Rays and the Initiations*).

From the point of Light within the Mind of God
Let light stream forth into the minds of men.
Let Light descend on Earth.

From the point of Love within the Heart of God
Let love stream forth into the hearts of men.
May Christ return to Earth.

From the centre where the Will of God is known
Let purpose guide the little wills of men—
The purpose which the Masters know and serve.

From the centre which we call the race of men
Let the Plan of Love and Light work out
And may it seal the door where evil dwells.

Let Light and Love and Power restore the Plan on Earth.[1]

Regarding the Great Invocation, Alice Bailey said, "This new Invocation, if given widespread distribution, can be to the new world religion what the Lord's Prayer has been to Christianity and the 23rd Psalm has been to the spiritually minded Jew."[2] Regarding the origin and purpose of "the Plan," Bailey says: "What you call 'the Plan' is the response of the Hierarchy to the inflowing purposeful will of the Lord of the World. Through Sanat Kumara, the Ancient of Days (as He is called in the Bible), flows the unknown energy."[3]

World Goodwill, an educational group associated with the Lucis Trust, explained the meaning of the Great Invocation's references to "the plan":

To bring in the new day and the human well-being which is our heritage, we do not need a further appraisal of the world condition based on a particular ideology or point of view. Rather, we need a deeper sense of reality based on spiritual values and a new perception of humanity as a unit of divine life within an ordered and purposive universe. There are six recognitions that can provide a basis for this deeper understanding:

One: Humanity is not following a haphazard or uncharted course—there is a Plan. This Plan has always existed and is part of the greater design of the Cosmos. The Plan has worked out through the evolutionary developments of the past and because of the special impetus given it from time to time by the great leaders, teachers and intuitives of the human race.

Two: There is an inner spiritual government of the planet, known under such different names as the spiritual Hierarchy, the society of Illumined Minds, or Christ and his Church, according to various religious traditions. Humanity is never left without spiritual guidance or direction under the Plan.

Three: The widespread expectation that we approach the 'Age of Maitreya,' as it is known in the East, when the World Teacher and present head of the spiritual Hierarchy, the Christ, will reappear among humanity to sound the keynote of the new age.

Four: There are millions of mentally alert men and women in all parts of the world who are in rapport with the Plan and work to give it expression. They are people in whom the consciousness of humanity as one interdependent unit is alive and active. They regard the many differing national, religious and social systems in which they serve as modes of expanding human consciousness and ways by which humanity learns needed lessons. Their

1. A. Bailey, *The Rays and the Initiations*, p vii; also, Lucis Trust, "The Great Invocation," http://www.lucistrust.org/invocation/, printed 06/19/04.

2. Alice A. Bailey, *The Reappearance of the Christ*, Lucis Publishing Company, 1948, p 32.

3. Alice A. Bailey, *The Rays and the Initiations*, p 130.

primary function is, through their living example, to give humanity a new and better vision of what life should be.

Five: The heart of humanity is sound. Our era is notable for the growth of goodwill and altruistic endeavour. All the crises, wars and catastrophes of the twentieth century have been unable to crush the human spirit.

Six: The Plan for humanity is based on the principles of sharing, cooperation, practical brotherhood, right relationships between all people and between nations, and goodwill in action.[1]

The open question is: how much of the rest of the teachings of Alice Bailey does Barbara Marx Hubbard uphold?

A WELL-CONNECTED "FUTURIST"

Barbara Marx Hubbard is active in the New Age network. She is an avowed admirer of Neale Donald Walsch, praising his "understanding and brilliant ability to communicate widely and broadly to masses of people about this work."[2] Walsch, whose New Age books have been on best-seller lists since the mid-1990s, has returned the favor. He describes Barbara Marx Hubbard as "a breathtaking visionary and a brilliant conceptualizer whose insights astonish and excite the human heart, and so, are sought after everywhere."[3] Walsch's spirit guide said in 2004 that at times, "I speak as her," and at other times, that Marx Hubbard "speaks as me."[4]

In *The Revelation: A Message of Hope for the New Millennium*, Marx Hubbard listed some "colleagues and teachers of conscious evolution:" Sri Aurobindo, Peter Caddy, Norman Cousins, Duane Elgin, Matthew Fox, R. Buckminster Fuller, Stanislas Grof, Willis Harman, Hazel Henderson, Jean Houston, Timothy Leary, John Mack, Abraham Maslow, Robert Mueller [sic], Michael Murphy, Theodore B. Roszak, Peter Russell, Rupert Sheldrake, David Spangler, Brian Swimme, Pierre Teilhard de Chardin, Michael and Justine Toms, Terry Cole Whittaker, and Gary Zukav.[5] Marx Hubbard also referred to Matthew Fox's *The Coming of the Cosmic Christ* as "a vision of the living Christ that connects us all."[6]

She also keeps company with other prominent people. In 1984, her name was "placed in nomination for the vice presidency of the United States at the Democratic National Convention."[7] Marx Hubbard is one of the directors of the World Future Society, along with Robert McNamara (formerly the U.S. Secretary of Defense and president of the World Bank), Maurice Strong (who was secretary general of the UN Conference on Environment and Development), and scholars from Georgetown University, George Washington University, and the University of Maryland.[8]

With colleagues and friends like these, Barbara Marx Hubbard can't be dismissed as a fringe writer, however bizarre and perverse her teachings are.

1. Lucis Trust, "World Goodwill," http://www.lucistrust.org/goodwill/, printed 06/19/04.
2. Marx Hubbard, *Conscious Evolution*, p viii.
3. Neale Donald Walsch, "Introduction," in Barbara Marx Hubbard, *Emergence: The Shift from Ego to Essence*, Hampton Roads, 2001, p xx.
4. Neale Donald Walsch, *Tomorrow's God: Our Greatest Spiritual Challenge*, Atria Books, 2004, pp 156–157.
5. Marx Hubbard, *Revelation/Hope*, p 349.
6. Ibid., p 345.
7. Foundation for the Future, "Board of Advisers—Barbara Marx Hubbard," http://www.futurefoundation.org/board/hubbard.html, printed 06/18/03.
8. World Future Society, "Frequently Asked Questions: Directors," http://www.wfs.org/faq.htm, printed 03/27/03.

16

NEALE DONALD WALSCH

NEALE DONALD WALSCH, meanwhile, has not been silent. About once a year, he cranks out new books, ongoing installments of his best-selling *Conversations With God* series.

Here follows some of what Walsch has learned from his familiar spirit. In some cases, Walsch is speaking directly for himself; in others, he quotes the "God" with whom he has his conversations.

WALSCH'S BLOB GOD, AN EVOLVING "GOD" OF GOOD AND EVIL

Walsch's spirit guide said, "All wisdom asks you to do is trust The Process. That is, *trust God*. Or if you wish, *trust yourself*, for Thou Art God."[1] Several years later, Walsch's ghostly companion repeated: "You are equal to God, and this equality with God is something that you yearn to experience. You are not inferior to God, nor to anything at all."[2]

Human equality with "God" follows from the "truth" of monism, that "All is One":[3] "*You must stop seeing God as separate from you, and you as separate from each other.* The *only* solution is the Ultimate Truth: nothing exists in the universe that is separate from anything else."[4] Recently, Walsch's "God" extended the Blob Principle further: "Everything is the same thing. There is only one energy, and that is the energy you call Life. The word 'God' may be used interchangeably here."[5] In case identifying "God" with "everything" and "energy" made "God" too specific, Walsch's spook added another layer of spiritual fog: "God is Life. Therefore, God Is Change. In one word, God Is Change. *God is a process.* Not a being, but a process. And that process is called change. Some of you might prefer the word evolution. God is the energy that evolves."[6]

Because "God" is changeable, there is no fixed truth, and there are no settled answers to ultimate questions. As Walsch's spirit guide says, "God is the Source of all that is creative. Answers are not creative. As soon as you think you have an answer, you stop creating. *Answers kill creation.* The last thing you want is the final answer to anything.... Stay within the question. Remain always with the inquiry."[7] Walsch's familiar spirit echoes the apostate bishop described in C.S. Lewis' *The Great Divorce*: "For me there is no such thing as a final answer ... to travel hopefully is better than to

1. Neale Donald Walsch, *Conversations with God: An Uncommon Dialogue, Book* 3, Hampton Roads Publishing Company, Inc., 1998, p350 (cited below as Walsch, *Conversations/Book* 3).

2. Neale Donald Walsch, *Communion with God*, G.P. Putnam's Sons, 2000, p161 (cited below as Walsch, *Communion with God*).

3. Neale Donald Walsch, *Conversations with God: An Uncommon Dialogue, Book* 2, Hampton Roads Publishing Company, Inc., 1997, p31 (cited below as Walsch, *Conversations/Book* 2).

4. Ibid., p173.

5. Walsch, *Communion with God*, p158.

6. Ibid., p158.

7. Neale Donald Walsch, *Tomorrow's God: Our Greatest Spiritual Challenge*, Atria Books, 2004, pp199–200 (cited below as Walsch, *Tomorrow's God*).

arrive."[1] Against this, the angelic spirit in Lewis' tale replied: "Thirst was made for water; inquiry for truth. What you now call the free play of inquiry has neither more nor less to do with the ends for which intelligence was given you than masturbation has to do with marriage."[2]

Walsch's "God" resides in "The Emptiness."[3] It says, "It is from The Emptiness that all wisdom will come and all healing will originate. It is from the void that I have come, and to the void that I will always return."[4] By announcing the void as its natural habitat, Walsch's spirit unwittingly indicates that it is not from Heaven.[5]

Walsch's "God" says of itself, "I am the Light, and I am the Darkness that creates the Light, and makes it possible. I am the Goodness Without End, and the 'Badness' which makes the 'Goodness' good. I am all of these things—the All of Everything—and I cannot experience any part of My Self without experiencing All of My Self.... Some part of Me must be *less* than magnificent for Me to choose the part of Me which *is* magnificent."[6] (Walsch's statement that "God" is "the Darkness that creates the Light, and makes it possible" mirrors Blavatsky, the founder of modern Theosophy. She said, "According to the tenets of Eastern Occultism, Darkness is the one true actuality, the basis and the root of light, without which the latter could never manifest itself, nor even exist. Light is matter, and Darkness pure Spirit."[7])

DEMOTING JESUS TO "HIGHLY EVOLVED BEING"

Walsch's "God" denies that Jesus is fully God and fully Man, demoting Him to the level of a "highly evolved being." "The spirit of that human you call Jesus was not of this Earth. That spirit simply filled a human body, allowed itself to learn as a child, became a man, and self-realized. He was not the only one to have done this. *All spirits* are 'not of this Earth.' *All souls* come from another realm, then enter the body. Yet not all souls self-realize in a particular 'lifetime.' Jesus did. He was a highly evolved being."[8]

According to Walsch's "God," "highly evolved beings"—ETs—are among us now. Walsch asked, "You're telling me that beings from outer space are helping us" with planetary change? His familiar spirit said: "Indeed. They are among you now, many of them. They have been helping for years.... The time will come when your consciousness will rise and your fear will subside, and then they will reveal themselves to you. Some of them have already done so—with a handful of people."[9]

Whatever Christ's nature and role might be, Walsch's "God" assigned an exalted position to Neale

1. C.S. Lewis, *The Great Divorce*, Macmillan Publishing Co., Inc., 1946, p43.

2. Ibid., p44.

3. Neale Donald Walsch, *Conversations with God for Teens*, Scholastic, Inc., 2001, p149 (cited below as Walsch, *Conversations with God for Teens*).

4. Ibid., p149.

5. Charles Upton comments, "The apophatic theology of St. Dionysius the Areopagite and other Christian mystical writers also speaks of the Godhead as an 'emptiness' or a 'divine desert.' But as St. Gregory Palamas points out, God is not limited to Non-Being; rather, He *transcends* both Being and Non-Being. The 'voidness' of God is not descriptive of His own nature, but of our human inability to comprehend Him except through His self-revelation to us. It is an extremely common satanic perversion of apophatic theology to see God's 'emptiness' as implying a privation on His part, as in Walsch's doctrine (discussed below) that God's nature contains 'Badness' or some aspect that is 'less than magnificent.'" (E-mail from Charles Upton to Lee Penn, 10/21/04.)

6. Walsch, *Conversations/Book* 3, pp10–11.

7. H.P. Blavatsky, *The Secret Doctrine: The Synthesis of Science, Religion, and Philosophy, Vol. I—Cosmogenesis*, Theosophical University Press, 1999 reprint of 1888 ed., p70.

8. Walsch, *Conversations/Book* 3, p329.

9. Walsch, *Conversations/Book* 2, p239.

Donald Walsch, anointing him in 2000 as "today's savior. You are My Beloved, in whom I am well pleased. You are the one I have sent to bring the others home."[1] (More recently, the spook said otherwise about "saviors:" "*Everyone else is as special as Moses, Jesus, and Mohammed.*"[2])

DENYING DEATH, PRAISING
THE "COSMIC WHEEL"

Walsch's familiar spirit denies death, saying, "There is no 'death.' Life goes on forever and ever. Life Is. You simply change form."[3] "God" explains to a teenage enquirer, "People do not die, Andrea, they just change form. For a time they exist in the form that you call 'human beings.' Then they take the form that you have called 'spirit beings.' They may turn to human form whenever they wish, and they may take other forms as well. You are all Divine Beings, eternally taking some form or another. You are Gods in formation."[4] Additionally, Walsch's spirit says, "*Nothing that you see is real. . . . you are living within an illusion of your own creation.*"[5]

Therefore, "Nothing is painful the moment you understand that nothing is real. This is as true of death as it is of life. When you understand that death, too, is an illusion, then you *can* say, 'O death, where is thy sting?' You can even *enjoy* death! You can even enjoy someone *else's* death."[6]

Human destiny after death is the eternal Cosmic Wheel: "After you experience the Oneness for an infinite time-no time, you will cease to experience it, because you cannot experience the Oneness as Oneness unless and until That Which Is Not One also exists. Understanding this, you will create, once again, the idea and the thought of separation, or disunity. Thus you will keep traveling the Cosmic Wheel, keep going, keep circling, keep on being, forever and ever, and even forever more."[7] Those of us who are un-enlightened will have to take Walsch's "God" at its word when it says, "This process— this Cosmic Wheel—is not a depressing treadmill. It is a glorious and continual reaffirmation of the utter magnificence of God, and all life—and there is nothing depressing about that at all."[8]

According to Walsch's spirit guide, birth is imprisonment in the body: "Birth itself is a death, and death a birth. For in birth, the soul finds itself constricted within the awful limitations of a body, and at death escapes those constrictions again. It does the same thing during sleep. Back to freedom the soul flies—and rejoices once again with the expression and experience of its true nature. Yet how can its true nature be expressed and experienced while *with* the body?"[9] (This is very similar to what the Theosophist Alice Bailey wrote: "If people but knew more, birth would be the experience which they would dread, and not death, for birth establishes the soul in the true prison, and physical death is only the first step towards liberation.")[10]

1. Walsch, *Communion with God*, p 168.

2. Neale Donald Walsch, *The New Revelations: A Conversation With God*, Atria Books, 2002, p 88 (cited below as Walsch, *New Revelations*).

3. Walsch, *Conversations/Book 2*, p 40.

4. Walsch, *Conversations with God for Teens*, p 260.

5. Walsch, *Communion with God*, p 119.

6. Walsch, *Conversations/Book 3*, p 143.

7. Ibid., p 98.

8. Ibid., p 103.

9. Ibid., p 201.

10. Alice A. Bailey, *Esoteric Healing—Volume IV: A Treatise on the Seven Rays*, Lucis Publishing Company, 1953, pp 392–393. Bailey said similar things in other books: *Education in the New Age*, 1954, Lucis Publishing Company, p 132 (cited below as A. Bailey, *Education in the New Age*), and *The Rays and the Initiations: Volume V, A Treatise on the Seven Rays*, 1960, Lucis Publishing Company, p 732 (cited below as A. Bailey, *The Rays and the Initiations*).

"HITLER WENT TO HEAVEN"

Denial of the goodness of the body leads to giving a "get out of Hell free" card to Hitler. Walsch's "God" says, "*Hitler went to heaven.*"[1] "There is no hell, so there is no place else for him to go."[2] (By the same logic, Walsch's *alter ego* says, "There is no devil."[3])

After all, Hitler was doing his victims a favor by killing them; his deeds were "mistakes," not crimes. Walsch's entity explains:

> Now your thought that Hitler was a monster is based on the fact that he ordered the killing of millions of people, correct? . . . Yet what if I told you that what you call 'death' is *the greatest thing that could happen to anyone*—what then? . . . You think that life on Earth is better than life in heaven? I tell you this, at the moment of your death you will realize the greatest freedom, the greatest peace, the greatest joy, and the greatest love you have ever known. Shall we therefore punish Bre'r Fox for throwing Bre'r Rabbit into the briar patch?[4]

The entity added:

> His actions were what you would call mistakes—the actions of an unevolved being—and mistakes are not punishable by condemnation, but dealt with by providing the chance for correction, for evolution. The mistakes Hitler made did no harm or damage to those whose deaths he caused. Those souls were released from their earthly bondage, like butterflies emerging from a cocoon. . . . Your statement that their deaths were nevertheless untimely, and therefore somehow 'wrong,' suggests that something could happen in the universe *when it is not supposed to.* Yet given Who and What I Am, that is impossible. Everything occurring in the universe is occurring perfectly. God hasn't made a mistake in a very long time. When you see the utter perfection in everything—not just in those things with which you agree, but (and perhaps especially) those things with which you disagree—you achieve mastery.[5]

"Hitler didn't *hurt* anyone. In a sense, he didn't *inflict* suffering, he *ended* it."[6] As Walsch says, "*There are no victims.*"[7] Indeed, "no soul joins the body, or leaves it, at a time that is inappropriate or wrong or 'too early' or 'too late.' The full agenda of the soul is not always known at the conscious level of the mind—nor can it be known or understood in the minds of others."[8] All of this seems to imply that the genocide victims of the last century got what their souls desired.

Walsch's "God" says that Hitler does not deserve condemnation for his acts—but the rest of humanity is responsible for allowing them to happen: "The purpose of the Hitler Experience was to show humanity to itself."[9] "The consciousness of separation, segregation, superiority—of 'we' versus 'they,' of 'us' and 'them,'—is what creates the Hitler Experience."[10] "God" also says that "group consciousness" created "the Hitler Experience":

> The Hitler Experience was made possible as a result of group consciousness. Many people want to say that Hitler manipulated a group—in this case, his countrymen—through the cunning and the mastery of his rhetoric. But this conveniently lays all the blame at Hitler's feet—which is exactly where the mass of people want it. But Hitler

1. Walsch, *Conversations/Book* 2, p35; also, Neale Donald Walsch, *Conversations with God: An Uncommon Dialogue, Book* 1, Hampton Roads Publishing Company, Inc., 1995, p61.

2. Walsch, *Conversations/Book* 2, p42.

3. Walsch, *Conversations/Book* 3, p6.

4. Walsch, *Conversations/Book* 2, p36.

5. Ibid., p42.

6. Ibid., p56.

7. Walsch, *Communion with God*, p160.

8. Walsch, *Conversations with God for Teens*, p268.

9. Walsch, *Conversations/Book* 2, p54.

10. Ibid., p55.

could do nothing without the cooperation and support and willing submission of millions of people. The sub-group which called itself Germans must assume an enormous burden of responsibility for the Holocaust. As must, to some degree, the larger group called Humans, which, if it did nothing else, allowed itself to remain indifferent and apathetic to the suffering in Germany until it reached so massive a scale that even the most cold-hearted isolationists could no longer ignore it.[1]

Maybe Hitler went to Heaven, but the German citizens and the "cold-hearted isolationists" did not; they get harsher words from Walsch's "God" than Hitler does.

Walsch's imp repeats what Alice Bailey said in September 1939, as World War II began:

Blame not the personalities involved or the men who produce these events before which we stand today bewildered and appalled. They are only the product of the past and the victims of the present. At the same time, they are the agents of destiny, the creators of the new order and the initiators of the new civilisation; they are the destroyers of what must be destroyed before humanity can go forward along the Lighted Way. *They are the embodiment of the personality of humanity.* Blame yourselves, therefore, for what is today transpiring and seek not to evade responsibility by placing it upon the shoulders of spectacular men or any statesmen, dictator, or upon any group.[2]

A similar argument has been common for a generation in American courtrooms: the criminal is not accountable for his evil deeds; instead, "society"—everybody else—is guilty.

A RELATIVIST, UTILITARIAN "GOD"

For Walsch's ghostly guide, truth is changeable. "Changing conditions create changing truth. Truth is nothing more than a word meaning 'what is so right now.' Yet what is so is always changing. Therefore, truth is always changing."[3] This view of the mutability of truth was put into practice when the Communists and the Nazis re-wrote history to fit the current needs of their regimes. Regarding the idea of "changing truth," George Orwell wrote: "The implied objective of this line of thought is a nightmare world in which the Leader, or some ruling clique, controls not only the future but *the past*. If the Leader says of such and such an event, 'It never happened'—well, it never happened. If he says that two and two are five—well, two and two are five."[4]

Walsch's spirit guide takes the creed of relativism and arbitrariness even further by saying, "there is no meaning to anything, *save the meaning you give it*. Life is meaningless. This is difficult for many humans to accept, yet it is My greatest gift. By rendering life meaningless, I give you the opportunity to decide what anything and everything means."[5]

If there is neither truth nor meaning, there can be no law. Walsch's celestial confidant told him that: "There's no such thing as the Ten Commandments.... God's Law is No Law. This is something you cannot understand. *I require nothing.*"[6] Walsch's spook sends all traditional moral codes, not just the Decalogue, into history's dust-bin: "'Right' and 'wrong' are figments of your imagination. They are judgments you are making, labels that you are creating as you go along.... When what you want changes, what you decide to call 'right' and 'wrong' changes. Your own history proves this."[7]

1. Ibid., p53.
2. Alice A. Bailey, *The Externalisation of the Hierarchy*, 1957, Lucis Publishing Company, p135 (cited below as A. Bailey, *Externalisation of the Hierarchy*).
3. Walsch, *Communion with God*, p158.
4. George Orwell, "Looking Back on the Spanish War," in George Orwell, *A Collection Of Essays*, Harcourt Brace, 1981, p199.
5. Walsch, *Communion with God*, p174.
6. Walsch, *Conversations/Book* 2, p167.
7. Walsch, *New Revelations*, p165.

"God" tells a teenage inquirer, "*I do not forgive anyone because there is nothing to forgive.*"[1] The spirit explains, "Forgiveness is never necessary, since no true offense can be committed by or against Divinity itself, given that Divinity itself is All That Is. This is something that advanced cultures understand."[2] Walsch's entity declares, "Obedience is not what I want from you. Obedience is not growth, and growth is what I desire."[3]

Therefore, the spirit guide told Walsch that the Fall was an "Original Blessing":

> *You* have declared that Hitler was 'wrong.' Good. By this measure you have come to define yourself, know more about yourself. Good. But don't condemn Hitler for *showing you that*. *Someone* had to. You cannot know cold unless there is hot, up unless there is down, left unless there is right. Do not condemn the one and bless the other. To do so is to fail to understand. For centuries people have been condemning Adam and Eve. They are said to have committed Original Sin. I tell you this: it was the Original Blessing. For without this event, the partaking of the knowledge of good and evil, *you* would not even know the two possibilities existed! Indeed, before the so-called Fall of Adam, the two possibilities *did not* exist. There was no 'evil.' Everyone and everything existed in a state of constant perfection. It was, literally, paradise. Yet you didn't *know* it was paradise—could not *experience* it as perfection—because you *knew nothing else*. Shall you then condemn Adam and Eve, or thank them?[4]

Speaking for himself, Walsch told a journalist, "Right and wrong are relative to what you are trying to accomplish. Moral choices are based on what works and doesn't work—on what is functional."[5] Walsch is absolutely, dogmatically certain that "The first step for us as a society as we evolve is to abandon our values. The people who have their feet in the mud, who are 'stuck,' are railing against this. They say that we are building a society without values, that we are abandoning our values. Well, we are abandoning our values. We ought to abandon our values. We ought to have only one value. What is it that's working? What works? And that assessment is dependent on what it is you're trying to do."[6] In this way, he raises up English utilitarianism and American pragmatism as the philosophical guideposts for mankind.

LIBERTINE THEOLOGY

Instead of self-denial and ascetic struggle, Walsch's spook offers an Epicurean alternative for spiritual growth:

> Now a lot of people are ridiculing this whole idea of 'doing what feels good.' They say this is the road to hell. Yet *I* say it is the road to *heaven*! Much depends, of course, on what you say 'feels good.' In other words, what kinds of experiences feel good to you? Yet I tell you this—no kind of evolution ever took place through *denial*. If you are to evolve, it will not be because you've been able to successfully *deny* yourself things that you *know* 'feel good,' but because you've *granted* yourself these pleasures—and found something even greater. For how can you know that something is 'greater' if you've never tasted the 'lesser'?[7]

In a similar vein, Walsch's entity allowed for enlightened selfishness among its devotees. It said, "The Highest Choice is not *always* the choice which seems to serve another."[8] Furthermore,

1. Walsch, *Conversations with God for Teens*, p 118.
2. Walsch, *Communion with God*, p 156.
3. Walsch, *Conversations/Book 2*, p 98.
4. Ibid., pp 56–57.
5. Don Lattin, "Chatting up the man who talks with God," *San Francisco Chronicle*, November 17, 2002, page E-2, downloaded 11/21/02 from http://www.sfgate.com (cited below as Lattin, "Chatting up the man who talks with God," 11/17/02).
6. Neale Donald Walsch and Dr. Brad Blanton, *Honest to God: A Change of Heart That Can Change the World*, Sparrowhawk Publications, 2002, pp 88–89 (cited below as Walsch/Blanton, *Honest to God*).
7. Walsch, *Conversations/Book 2*, p 79.
8. Ibid., p 97.

The biggest mistake people make in human relationships is to be concerned for what the other is wanting, being, doing, or having. Be concerned only for the Self. What is the Self being, doing, or having? What is the Self wanting, needing, choosing? What is the highest choice for the Self? . . . The highest choice for the Self becomes the highest choice for another when the Self realizes that there is no one else. The mistake, therefore, is not in *choosing* what is best for you, but rather, in not *knowing* what is best.[1]

As we become more highly evolved, guilt and shame disappear, according to Walsch's "God." Walsch asks it whether a highly evolved being "does not feel guilt or shame, no matter what he does?"[2] The entity replies: "No. Because guilt and shame is [sic] something which is imposed on a being from outside of itself. . . . No divine being (and all beings are divine) *ever* knows itself or anything it is doing to be 'shameful' or 'guilty' until someone outside of Itself labels it that way. . . . *The degree to which a culture is evolved is demonstrated by the degree to which it labels a being or an action 'shameful' or 'guilty'.*"[3]

"God" then reiterates to Walsch, "As I have already told you, there is no such thing as right and wrong."[4] "In truth, there is no such thing as a 'sinner,' for no one can be sinned against—least of all Me. That is why I say that I 'forgive' you. I use that phrase because it is one you seem to understand. In truth, I do *not* forgive you, and will not forgive you *ever*, for *anything*. I do not have to. There is nothing to forgive."[5]

LIBERTINE PRACTICE: FREE LOVE, COMMUNAL PARENTING, AND EUTHANASIA

As a result, Walsch's "God" has a hang-loose attitude about sexual ethics. Sexual activity by children and teenagers?

> Now in enlightened societies offspring are never discouraged, reprimanded, or 'corrected' when they begin to find early delight in the nature of their very being. . . . Sexual functions are also seen and treated as totally natural, totally wonderful, and totally okay. In some societies, parents couple in full view of their offspring—and what could give children a greater sense of the beauty and the wonder and the pure joy and the total okayness of the sexual expression of love than this?[6]

Walsch's familiar spirit does not state what the "offspring" in the "enlightened societies" are doing, and with whom.

To ensure that the kids get the message, Walsch's "God" says schools should replace the current "facts-based curriculum" with a "values-based curriculum," including courses on such things as "Celebrating Self, Valuing Others, Joyous Sexual Expression, Fairness, Tolerance, Diversities And Similarities, Ethical Economics, Creative Consciousness And Mind Power."[7] Walsch has proposed such a curriculum in two more recent books, as well: *Communion With God*[8] and *Conversations with God for Teens.*[9]

1. Walsch, *Conversations/Book* 3, p9.
2. Ibid., p301.
3. Ibid., p301.
4. Ibid., p302.
5. Ibid., p87.
6. Walsch, *Conversations/Book* 2, p105.
7. Ibid., p127.
8. Walsch, *Communion with God*, p107; the classes proposed included "freedom, full self-expression, joyous sexual celebration, human bonding, and diversity in oneness," among others.
9. Walsch, *Conversations with God for Teens*, p4. Here, Walsch asked, "You know that so much of the stuff they teach in school is pointless. Where are the classes in Sharing Power, Cooperative Living, Accepting Differences and Celebrating Diversity, Shameless Sexuality, Understanding Unconditional Love?"

In addition to "Joyous Sexual Expression," education in the New Age will teach children to develop their psychic powers. As the familiar spirit tells Walsch,

> An early message of the New Spirituality is that you create your own reality, and much time will be spent in Creation Education opening children to their natural abilities, including their psychic abilities and their manifestation abilities. . . . Meditation will soon be a part of the regular school day (it is in some schools right now), and early training in the psychic arts will follow. Young children will be encouraged to get in touch with their 'sixth sense,' and to train, use, and expand their psychic power.[1]

Along similar lines, Alice Bailey had said that in the New Age, "present day occultism will be the theme of world education in some modified form."[2]

Walsch's spirit guide says to a teenager, "Sex—and the beauty of sex, and the passion of sex, and the excitement of sex, and the wonder of sex, and the pure unbridled joy and *fun* of sex—is something that I have given you. To renounce it is to renounce me. Therefore do not renounce sex, nor any of the good and wonderful and fun things that I have given you in life. Simply renounce any addiction you may have to them."[3] With this call for youth to enjoy sex, the entity says nothing about reserving these pleasures for marriage. Instead, it subtly derides marriage: "Marriage is an institution that humans created and a state into which they enter in order, they say, to sanctify their love. Does this mean that love expressed outside of marriage is not sanctified? That is something only you can decide."[4]

"God's" only caveat about sexual expression is the standard set of criteria offered by present-day Western liberals: "Allow me to repeat, so that there can be no mistake about it, that responsible sex, with every health aspect understood, and every consequence considered, and every care taken and every joy expressed, is what is being discussed here."[5]

The spirit tells a teenage seeker why there is sexual abuse: "There is so much sexual abuse in the world because there is so much sexual repression in the world. Humans have been taught from the time they were very young to be ashamed of their body parts and embarrassed or guilty about their sexuality. The result is that millions of people have sexual hang-ups you wouldn't believe."[6] In other words, the way to prevent sexual depravity is to allow more sexual liberation, starting with the "very young." In 2004, Walsch's *alter ego* said the same: "Wherever you see sexual repression, you will see sexual crime and sexual dysfunction."[7]

Walsch's imp approves of mixing sex acts with occult rituals: "*Give yourself abundant pleasure, and you will have abundant pleasure to give others.* The masters of Tantric sex knew this. That's why they encourage masturbation,[8] which some of you actually call a sin."[9] It adds, "Mix what you call the sacred with the sacrilegious, for until you see your altars as the ultimate place for love, and your bedrooms as the ultimate place for worship, you see nothing at all."[10]

For the sake of the Divine Self, Walsch's "God" denounces fidelity and marriage vows: "Betrayal of

---

1. Walsch, *Tomorrow's God* p321.
2. A. Bailey, *The Externalisation of the Hierarchy*, p322.
3. Walsch, *Conversations with God for Teens*, p95.
4. Ibid., p301.
5. Ibid., p100.
6. Ibid., p12.
7. Walsch, *Tomorrow's God*, p361.
8. According to Charles Upton, Walsch's understanding of Tantrism is in error. Upton says, "Although Tantra is not to be strictly identified as 'the yoga of sex,' those practices which do include sexual union in no way 'encourage masturbation.' On the contrary, the usual practice is to suppress orgasm and ejaculation so as to refine, transmute and sublimate the sexual substances and energies."
9. Walsch, *Conversations /Book* 2, p77.
10. Walsch, *Conversations/Book* 3, p56.

yourself in order not to betray another is Betrayal nonetheless. It is the Highest Betrayal."[1] "Your marriage vows, as you presently construct them, have you making a very un-Godly statement."[2] "If you forfeit freedom, you forfeit your Self. And that is not a sacrament, that is a blasphemy."[3] (This may be a message that Walsch badly wanted to hear, since he "has been married five times."[4]) In 2004, Walsch's "God" stayed "on message" about marriage: "In the days of the New Spirituality love and freedom will be understood to be the same thing. This has important implications within the context of marriage currently understood and experienced by most of the human race."[5]

When Walsch has spoken for himself, rather than quoting "God," he said, "I envision a world where we can make love to anyone, anyway [sic] we wish to, at anytime, anywhere. (Of course they have to be willing and consent.) This concept is talked about in so many Utopian novels I read growing up. Please understand, I am not talking about sex, and yet at the same time, I am. What I am referring to is all the different ways that love can be expressed."[6] In 2004, Walsch's familiar spirit said the same: "In the days of the New Spirituality, human sexuality will be experienced as the joyous celebration of life and the glorious expression of Godliness that it was always meant to be, it will be expressed without embarrassment or shame or guilt and without restrictions or limitations of any kind, except those that are voluntarily self-imposed."[7]

Here's the practical result of Walsch's sexual morality in action. He wrote,

> My most romantic moments, by the way, were moments when I chose not to withhold anything. . . . I recall meeting a woman years ago at a party and I looked right at her and said, 'I want to go to bed with you. Sorry I've put it that way, but I've got only about five minutes here.' And she said, 'I wouldn't mind doing that with you, either.' And that was the most exciting weekend either of us had ever had. . . . We asked ourselves at the end of that weekend: Why can't we just do this all the time? By the way, we've never seen each other again since, and we knew that we probably wouldn't.[8]

Will acting on these principles mean that a "successful" Casanova leaves behind a trail of broken hearts, ruined marriages, neglected children, and venereal disease victims? Not to worry. "God" gives Walsch the creed that wolves would like to have sheep believe. With enlightenment, "You will know that you have never truly been victimized, and what you know, you will grow. Ultimately, you will realize that there are no victims. Always remember that."[9]

As a corollary to its hang-loose sexual ethic, Walsch's "God" proposed that parents should turn the care of their children over to the "entire community." It said, "In any society where producing offspring at a young age is not considered 'wrong'—because the tribal elders raise them and there is, therefore, no sense of overwhelming responsibility and burden—sexual repression is unheard of, and so is rape, deviance, and social-sexual dysfunction."[10] So, it recommended, "Place the raising of children in the hands of your respected Old Ones. Parents see their children whenever they wish, live with them if they choose, but are not solely responsible for their care and upbringing. The physical, social,

1. Walsch, *Conversations/Book* 2, p 97.
2. Walsch, *Conversations/Book* 3, p 223.
3. Ibid., p 210.
4. Walsch/Blanton, *Honest to God*, p 79.
5. Walsch, *Tomorrow's God*, p 343.
6. Kathy Close, "Interview with Neale Donald Walsch: Beginning A Dialog With The Divine," http://www.conversationswithgod.org/interview.htm; printed in 1999, and no longer on the Net at this address. As of 2004, a copy of this web page is at http://web.archive.org/web/19990220200021/http://conversationswithgod.org/interview.htm.
7. Walsch, *Tomorrow's God*, p 355.
8. Walsch/Blanton, *Honest to God*, p 195.
9. Walsch, *Communion with God*, p 160.
10. Walsch, *Conversations/Book* 3, pp 33–34.

and spiritual needs of the children are met by the entire community, with education and values offered by the elders."[1]

Walsch's poltergeist is of two minds about suffering. On one hand, suffering does not matter, since

At a very high metaphysical level, no one is 'disadvantaged,' for each soul creates for itself the exact people, events, and circumstances needed to accomplish what It wishes to accomplish. You choose everything. Your parents. Your country of birth. All the circumstances surrounding your re-entry. Similarly, throughout the days and times of your life you continue to choose and create people, events, and circumstances designed to bring you the exact, right, and perfect opportunities you now desire in order to know yourself as you *truly are*. In other words, no one is 'disadvantaged,' given what the *soul* wishes to accomplish. For example, the soul may *wish* to work with a handicapped body or in a repressive society or under enormous political and economic constraints, in order to produce the conditions needed to accomplish what it has set out to do. So we see that people *do* face 'disadvantages' in the *physical* sense, but that these are actually the right and perfect conditions *metaphysically*.[2]

On the other hand, suffering is such a great evil that euthanasia and suicide are justified as means to escape it: "It is insane to think that endless suffering is what God requires, and that a quick, humane end to the suffering is 'wrong.'"[3]

THE JUDGMENTS OF WALSCH'S TOLERANT GOD

For a non-judgmental deity, "God" shows some surprising lapses into prescriptive morality. In place of the three virtues of "faith, hope, love" (1 Cor. 13:13), Walsch's spook tells its followers, "Live your life according to the Core Concepts of Holistic Living: 1. Awareness 2. Honesty 3. Responsibility."[4] In another book, the spirit offers a different trinity of "Basic Principles of Life:" "Functionality, Adaptability, Sustainability."[5] This is Darwinian theory, applied to spirituality.

The entity dictates, "Even as I have told you to meditate every day so that you may quiet your mind and experience your Oneness with Me, now I tell you to exercise each day."[6] The goblin also condemns cigarette smoking, eating a "big hunk of red meat at every meal," lack of exercise, and overwork—just as strongly as it scorns war and belief in "doctrines and dogmas that are killing you."[7] All of this is quite a switch for this spook, which had told Walsch in 1997, "*I require nothing.*"[8] In the same book in which the entity denounces cigarettes, red meat, and dogma, it also says, "God demands nothing, commands nothing, requires nothing, compels nothing."[9] But then, Walsch's entity is not bound by the rules of logic in its messages.

Walsch's spook never says anything against abortion, which kills one-quarter of America's children in their own mother's wombs. However, it fulminates about environmental pollution, smoking, and other health risks:

You poison your system by inhaling carcinogens, you poison your system by eating food treated with chemicals that over the long run kill you, and you poison your system by breathing air that you have continually polluted. You poison your system in a hundred different ways over a thousand different moments, and you do this

1. Ibid., pp35–36.
2. Walsch, *Conversations/Book 2*, p156.
3. Walsch, *Conversations/Book 3*, p147.
4. Walsch, *Conversations with God for Teens*, p164.
5. Walsch, *New Revelations*, p223.
6. Walsch, *Communion with God*, p190.
7. Walsch, *New Revelations*, pp335–336.
8. Walsch, *Conversations/Book 2*, p167.
9. Walsch, *New Revelations*, p116.

knowing these substances are not good for you. But because it takes a longer time for them to kill you, *you commit suicide with impunity.*[1]

As an alternative to slow suicide, the spirit tells Walsch to "*listen to your body*" in order to know what to eat or drink. "You can come to this knowing by simply moving your hand slowly over the food. Your body will know at once all you need to know about whether that food is in harmony with your innermost intentions for the body and the soul. You will be able to pick up the vibration."[2]

Walsch's "God" is not consistent in its view of human sin. In the *New Revelations* of 2002, the spirit says, "As a group you are still dealing with the same problems that confronted you at the beginning. The problems of greed, envy, anger, righteousness, inequity, violence, and war."[3] However, in 1997, the spook had said, "Envy is a natural emotion urging you to strive to be more. . . . There is nothing wrong with envy. It is a motivator. It is pure desire. It gives birth to greatness."[4] And in another part of the 2002 *New Revelations*, the spirit praises anger: "Anger is not a negative emotion, it is a healer. Anger releases negative energy. That makes it a positive emotion, because it helps you get rid of something you don't want, and live a harmonious life."[5] It seems that Walsch's goblin is not bothered by contradicting itself; as a result, readers must decide for themselves whether envy and anger are virtues or vices.

Nor does Walsch's celestial buddy provide a consistent view of the human condition. In 2002, Walsch said that the world is "moving *closer to*, not further away from, total self-destruction."[6] In a book published in 2000, Walsch's spirit said otherwise: "It has been said that the human race is facing the same problems that it has faced since the dawn of recorded history—and this is true, but to a lesser degree all the time. Greed, violence, jealousy, and other behaviors that you believe do not benefit anyone are still displayed by members of your species, although now by the minority. This is a sign of your evolution."[7] In 2000, the spook also said that soon, "you will experience a quickening of the spirit, or what you might call a breakthrough, in which second-stage transformation begins. . . . Your race is at this breakthrough point now. Many humans felt a shift when you moved into your new millennium."[8] Perhaps "God" felt no need to be consistent over a 2-year period in its assessment of whether we are moving toward "total self-destruction" or toward a "breakthrough"—or, maybe, "God" in 2000 could not foresee the events of 2001.

GRAINS OF TRUTH AMIDST THE NEW AGE SEWAGE

Some of the dicta offered by Walsch and his "God" are reasonable as far as they go—a fact that may make these books more attractive to spiritually confused people.

For example, Walsch's "God" gives teenagers a firm, unambiguous warning against drug use: "Drugs start to control you from the very first use. You don't think so, but they do. The fact that you don't think so is *how* they do. Drugs stop you from thinking the way you usually think. Take enough of them and they stop you from thinking at all. 'Oh, I'll know when to stop' are the famous last words of thousands of people who have had their lives ruined by drugs. The same can be said about alcohol."[9]

1. Ibid., p168.
2. Walsch, *Communion with God*, pp192–193.
3. Walsch, *New Revelations*, p60.
4. Walsch, *Conversations/Book* 2, p209.
5. Walsch, *New Revelations*, p301.
6. Ibid., p343.
7. Walsch, *Communion with God*, p42.
8. Ibid., p106.
9. Walsch, *Conversations with God for Teens*, p203.

In reply to a teenager who is considering cheating on a test in a class, the entity urges him to remember, "you are deciding who you are;" in that context, "the question becomes, 'Is 'a cheater' who I really am? Am I a person who cannot be trusted? Is this who I want to be?"[1] This encourages the youth to look beyond his temptation to consider the character that he is forming by his choices.

To a 16-year-old girl who avows that she is "ready" for sex, Walsch's "God" says, "Really? Have you looked closely at all the possible outcomes? Have you explored, really explored, the consequences of deep love entanglements? Pregnancy? Sexually transmitted diseases—including AIDS?"[2] It then tells her to "talk to your parents."[3] While far from teaching chastity, the entity warns teenagers of some of the perils of promiscuity, and acknowledges the role that parents should play in guiding their children. "God" also tells a teenager that to avert a divorce, "your parents would have to believe that love is a decision, not a reaction. Then they would have to decide to love each other."[4] Such a response is one that traditionalist counselors might make, for love is indeed a choice and not an emotion.

To a teenager who grieves the loss of her father, the entity says, "Enormous sadness about something like the loss you've experienced can transform people into compassionate, sensitive, and deeply caring human beings"[5]—and such use of loss is a choice.[6] "God" tells a teenager, "If you are waiting for love in your life, *be* the love for which you are waiting. If you are waiting for compassion in your life, *be* the source of compassion for everyone whose life you touch. If you are waiting for laughter and fun to enter your life, bring that into the room when you *enter* the room."[7] The spook also says, "*What you seek from another, give to another. That which you wish to experience, cause another to experience.*"[8]

Walsch's "God" says, "it is natural for humans to experience themselves as part of a larger whole, and to know deeply that that is a thing called God. Atheism is a learned reaction; Deism is a natural response, an intuitive 'knowing,' a deep-seated awareness at the cellular level."[9] However far from the truth Walsch's monism is, he does make it clear that atheism is an aberration.

Walsch's spirit guide also says, "You are all merely stewards, seeking to take good care of that over which you have been given stewardship—including your bodies, the bodies of your mates and children, the land on which you live, and all else that you have in your care. These things are not your possessions, but simply articles that have been *placed in your care.*"[10] This is compatible with the Biblical injunction that Adam is to "till" and "keep" the Garden (Gen. 2:15), and with Jesus' distinctions between "faithful and wise" servants and their "wicked" opposites (Matt. 24:45–51).

These exhortations to good behavior and positive attitudes show that Walsch's "God" can sometimes urge what is right, in the same way that a stopped clock is right twice a day.

1. Ibid., p220.
2. Ibid., p106.
3. Ibid., p106.
4. Ibid., p222.
5. Ibid., p265.
6. Ibid., p266.
7. Ibid., p145.
8. Ibid., p232.
9. Walsch, *New Revelations*, p233.
10. Ibid., p256.

OVERTHROWING THE CHURCHES
AND PROCLAIMING THE NEW GOSPEL

Walsch, who describes himself as "one of those recovering Catholics,"[1] is a firm opponent of orthodox Christian churches—and of other traditional religions. He said in 2002, "I'm not impressed with exclusive, punitive organized religion. Elitist organized religion has done some good, but it has done more harm than good."[2] He suggests that "We should have a stamp on every church bulletin in the world like they do on cigarettes, you know: 'This Church is hazardous to your health.'"[3] Walsch's "God" tells a teenager, "nothing has done more to separate people from each other and from God than organized religion."[4] It tells a teenage religious believer, "go about living the answers you have, but never stop questioning the answers you are living."[5]

Furthermore, "there is no particular way that God 'wants' you to worship God. Nor, in fact, does God need to be 'worshiped' at all."[6] The spirit also says, "I do not need you to recognize that I exist or to pray to me or to have anything to do with me at all. And I will not punish you in the everlasting fires of hell if you do not."[7] It decrees, "No path to God is more direct than any other path. No religion is the 'one true religion,' no people are 'the chosen people,' and no prophet is 'the greatest prophet.'"[8]

Walsch's "God" mocks *all* the traditional religions: "There has not been a serious new theological construct presented to the human race in millennia. There has not been an expansion of your theologies in a hundred generations. *You have not challenged your God in a very long time.*"[9] The time line is interesting—if it has been 100 generations since mankind challenged God, and a traditional generation is 40 years, it means that we have not had a "serious new theological construct" since 2000 BC, around the time of the Call of Abraham. It also says, "One's religion is a product of one's birthplace and early teaching. It is a product not of eternal truth, but of cultural environment."[10] In two different books, the imp says, "Organizations are not, as a rule, interested in rendering themselves obsolete. This is as true of religions as it is of any other organized undertaking. Perhaps more so. The fact that a particular religion has been around for a very long time is not an indication of its effectiveness, but just the opposite."[11] The implication is that a New Religion would be better than the older religions—and perhaps the very Newest Religion (and the best one) would be the *New Revelations* proposed by Walsch's familiar spirit.

For those who are not satisfied with the Sermon on the Mount, Walsch's imp offers "a two-sentence gospel that would turn your planet on its ear. . . . 'We Are All One.' 'Ours is not a better way, ours is merely another way.'"[12] The spirit says that if these words were spoken by those with religious power, "The world would shake. The foundations of all the world's major religions—Separation and Betterness—would crumble!"[13]

---

1. Walsch/Blanton, *Honest to God*, p123.
2. Lattin, "Chatting up the man who talks with God," 11/17/02.
3. Walsch/Blanton, *Honest to God*, pp128–129.
4. Walsch, *Conversations with God for Teens*, p137.
5. Ibid., p137.
6. Ibid., p141.
7. Ibid., p187.
8. Walsch, *New Revelations*, pp97–98.
9. Ibid., p312.
10. Ibid., p186.
11. Walsch, *Conversations with God for Teens*, p140. The spirit repeats itself almost verbatim on p130 of *The New Revelations*.
12. Walsch, *New Revelations*, p210.
13. Ibid., p211.

As might be expected, Walsch's "God" has no use for "fundamentalism." It says, "Will you go back to the exact words and phrases and to-the-letter interpretations and literal applications of your old religions, as fundamentalists of every religion would have you do, or will you dare to explore, suggest, recommend, and create a *new* spirituality—one that does not reject everything about the old, but improves upon it, carrying humanity to grander heights?"[1] The new spirituality is to be our response to the call from "God" that "I am inviting you to create Tomorrow's God."[2]

As a progressive alternative to fundamentalism, Walsch's "God" says,

> You may want to consider the possibility that what would work for the world right now—given what the world says it wants to experience, which is peace and harmony—is a New Spirituality based upon New Revelations. . . . A spirituality that enlarges upon organized religion in its present form. For it is many of your old religions, with their inherent limitations, that stop you from experiencing God as God really is. They also stop you from experiencing peace, joy, and freedom—which are *other* words for God as God really is.[3]

Walsch's spirit guide says, "The world is hungry, the world is starving, for a new spiritual truth."[4]

Feminism will be integral to the New Spirituality. Walsch's entity refers to God using "he" and "she" interchangeably, and it says, "A big part of the New Spirituality will have to do with creating true equality for females, ending at last the disenfranchising and the outright abuse of one half the human race."[5] If Walsch's spook has its way, any religion whose tradition includes male leadership or use of male imagery for God will have to adapt—or else.

In 2002, Walsch's spirit guide said that the New Spirituality it offers

> can present a new point of view, one that is not exclusivist, not elitist or separatist. It can invite people to seriously consider, for the first time in centuries, some new theological ideas. It can offer, for exploration and discussion, some New Revelations. The New Spirituality will open minds to larger concepts than present theologies embrace, to grander ideas than present theologies consider, and to greater opportunities for individual experience and expression than present theologies allow.[6]

(Bishop Swing has a similar fondness for "enlarging" traditional religions. In 1997, he said, "If there's a United Religions pursuing a dialogue in depth, it begins to ask larger questions and force religions to make larger statements."[7])

In 2004, Walsch's "God" said that the spread of the New Spirituality "will be a *civil rights movement for the soul*, ending at last the oppression of humanity by its belief in a vain, violent, and vindictive God."[8]

Walsch gives his benediction to some religious movements that "teach of a God who is inclusive, and actually live that teaching:" the Unity Church, the United Church of Religious Science, and the Metropolitan Community Church, a predominantly gay denomination.[9] The only surprise here is that the Unitarian Universalists did not make the grade.

1. Ibid., p 64.
2. Walsch, *Tomorrow's God*, p 15.
3. Walsch, *New Revelations*, pp 142–143.
4. Ibid., p 258.
5. Ibid., p 200.
6. Ibid., p 279.
7. Don Lattin, "Bishop's Idea for a Leap of Faiths," *San Francisco Chronicle*, June 22, 1997, p 3/Z1.
8. Walsch, *Tomorrow's God*, p 243.
9. Walsch, *New Revelations*, pp 47–48.

THE APOCALYPTIC CHOICE: UTOPIA OR DOOM

In the late 1990s, Walsch's "God" had said, "Yours is a *race awakening*. Your time of fulfillment is at hand."[1] Since then, his utopianism has taken on a foreboding, apocalyptic edge.

Walsch and his bodiless *alter ego* now offer us a "New Gospel"[2] whose adoption will allow humanity to transcend the current "direst circumstance"[3] that threatens "the ultimate horror, which will be the end of *life* on earth."[4] In the final chapter of *The New Revelations*, Walsch warned: "Our world is still on the brink of global calamity, and it is moving *closer to*, not further away from, total self-destruction."[5] Walsch's "God" likewise told teenagers in 2001, "If things continue the way they are going, the world 'as you know it' could cease to exist within your lifetime."[6]

Despite their warnings of pending calamity, Walsch and his spirit guide continue to hold out the hope of utopia on earth. Walsch hailed his 2002 book, *The New Revelations: A Conversation With God*, as "a life-altering book. It contains New Revelations . . . lifting the whole human race to a new level of experience, to a new understanding of itself, to a new expression of its grandest vision."[7] If we change our beliefs in line with these New Revelations, Walsch's "God" says that "You are standing even now at the edge of a Golden Age, the beginning of a Thousand Years of Peace, which could lead to a greater glory for the human species than your heart can now hold the knowing of."[8]

Since *New Revelations* failed to work as desired, Walsch's spirit guide tried again with *Tomorrow's God* in 2004; it said, "This book is meant to save the world."[9] It also said that a "radical shift" in "humanity's understandings about God" could occur "Within three decades. Perhaps even faster than that," if we reach "critical mass," with "2 to 4 percent of the whole" population accepting the New Religion.[10]

(By contrast, in the same book, Walsch's spirit guide warned solemnly against making a "Bible" of the *Conversations with God* books. Walsch commented, "So the New Spirituality is not just a turning of the *Conversations with God* books into a 'new religion.'" The entity replied, "It is anything and everything BUT that. If that's what it was, I would tell you to burn those books and forget them forever. These books have great value—but only as the individual experience of one human being. Taken in that context, their value is inestimable. Turned into the 'official text' or the 'sacred source' of some new form of spiritual expression, they could be dangerous. And so could you." Walsch replied, "I have no intention of becoming dangerous."[11])

Walsch himself says, "a golden age of peace is within our reach. All that is needed now is the will to create it. All things are created with three basic tools—Understanding, Ability, and Will. We have, at last, the Understanding and the Ability. Will is the final element in every choice-making process. It is the ultimate tool of creation. When there is a Will there is a way."[12] It seems that Walsch proposes a "triumph of the will" as the pre-requisite for utopia. It follows that those who do not go along with the New Revelations are willfully recalcitrant, and are keeping humanity from its rightful, glorious destiny.

1. Walsch, *Conversations/Book* 3, p340.
2. Walsch, *New Revelations*, p210.
3. Ibid., p308.
4. Ibid., p307.
5. Ibid., p343.
6. Walsch, *Conversations with God for Teens*, p49.
7. Walsch, *New Revelations*, pviii.
8. Ibid., p26.
9. Walsch, *Tomorrow's God*, p5.
10. Ibid., pp16–17.
11. Ibid., p206.
12. Walsch, *New Revelations*, p345.

Walsch's guiding entity has warned that before the New Age begins, "there will be chaos, created largely by those who do not want to make the shift, who cannot accept the end of 'better' and The New Gospel of Oneness."[1] Unlike Barbara Marx Hubbard, Walsch never says that mankind will undergo a death-dealing "selection." However, he says: "Barbara Marx Hubbard—this incredible futurist, this breathtaking social seer—is the songbird of our new morning."[2] Hubbard's predictions, of course, include the "violent selection of the self-centered."[3]

Walsch does say that "Life will *change its form* (that is, adapt Itself to become sustainable) before it will allow any Part of Life to render Life Itself dysfunctional. And so you will see individuals who ignore the most important and functional messages of Life changing their form. To put this in your own terms, *they will die*."[4] Here, Walsch echoes what Alice Bailey said more bluntly decades ago: "it is the *Life*, its purpose and its directed intentional destiny that is of importance; and also that when a form proves inadequate, or too diseased, or too crippled for the expression of that purpose, it is—from the point of view of the Hierarchy—no disaster when that form has to go. Death is not a disaster to be feared; the work of the Destroyer is not really cruel or undesirable."[5]

War itself may be part of Life's "adjustment" process. Walsch says the activities of "Higher Life Forms" often "require Life Itself to make an adjustment, to adapt, in order to continue remaining sustainable. Individuals, families, nations, cultures, and societies all do this. Their 'adjustments' are often called 'war.'"[6] Again, Walsch is saying softly what Alice Bailey said harshly during the 1940s: "One of the purposes lying behind the present holocaust (World War II) has been the necessity for the destruction of inadequate forms."[7]

COMMUNISM AND WORLD GOVERNMENT, AS THE EXTRATERRESTRIALS DO IT

The New Spirituality of the New Revelations will be a collectivist religion, leading to a collectivist revolution that will usher in a collectivist world. Walsch's goblin says,

> Group action is what is required now. . . . The time for individual gurus who come along and change the world is over. The time for collective consciousness and collective action to change the collective reality is at hand. This is as it should be, for your present reality has been collectively created. It is now time for you to collectively re-create it anew. Work, then, in a collective. Do not follow individual masters, but master collective consciousness individually. Then work collectively to awaken the collective called Humanity.[8]

This is a call for a spiritual vanguard party to lead us all to a spiritual form of communism. In the end, the imp says that we should "all agree on one set of laws based on no religion in particular. . . . I mean, create a spiritual community as opposed to a religious community."[9] The ancient idea that Throne and Altar should act in concert will reappear in new guise; Walsch's entity said in 2004 that "In

1. Neale Donald Walsch, *Friendship with God: An Uncommon Dialogue*, G.P. Putnam's Sons, 1999, p 404.

2. Neale Donald Walsch, foreword for Barbara Marx Hubbard, *Conscious Evolution: Awakening the Power of Our Social Potential*, New World Library, Novato, California, 1998, p xi (cited below as Marx Hubbard, *Conscious Evolution*).

3. Barbara Marx Hubbard, *The Revelation: A Message of Hope for the New Millennium*, Nataraj Publishing, Novato, CA, 1995, p 303.

4. Walsch, *Tomorrow's God*, p 96.

5. A. Bailey, *Education in the New Age*, p 112.

6. Walsch, *Tomorrow's God*, p 103.

7. A. Bailey, *The Rays and the Initiations*, pp 75–76.

8. Walsch, *New Revelations*, p 313.

9. Ibid., pp 133–134.

the days of the New Spirituality the idea that politics and spirituality do not mix will be abandoned forever."[1] Furthermore, "In the days of the New Spirituality humanity will begin at last to hold more basic beliefs in common, creating a more uniform standard for all political expression around the world."[2]

Walsch's spirit guide proposes communism and world government as solutions to our social problems. It says that highly evolved beings—whom it describes as super-intelligent extra-terrestrials—practice pure communism: "They share *everything*. With *everyone*. Not a being goes without. All the natural resources of their world, of their environment, are divided equally, and distributed to everyone."[3] Walsch's imp says much the same to a teenager: "All that is required, Zoar, for every person to have sufficient food, clothing, and shelter is for the people of Earth to share and share alike. If they did, they would find that there is more than enough for everyone to live happily."[4]

The spirit's description of how the new social order would work will be familiar to anyone who has read what Marx and Lenin said about communism after the withering away of the state and the end of the class struggle: "In a community where there were no rules, no regulations, and no requirements, there would still be plenty of people who would do the things that need to be done. In fact, there would be very few who would not, for they would be uncomfortable being known as non-contributors. And that is what would change if there were no rules, regulations, or requirements."[5] (How does this "no rules, no regulations" ideal square with the entity's call for "one set of laws based on no religion in particular"?[6] Only the "Spirit" knows!)

Neale Donald Walsch's familiar spirit explains, "Social evolution is demonstrated by movement towards unity, not separatism."[7] "Another distinguishing and fascinating feature of highly evolved cultures is that within them there is no word or sound for, nor any way to communicate the meaning, the concept, of 'yours' and 'mine.' Personal possessives do not exist in their language."[8] "On your planet you have rejected out-of-hand any system which does not allow for the advancement of one being at the expense of another. If a system of governance or economics requires an attempt at equitable distribution, to 'all,' of the benefits *created* by 'all,' with the resources *belonging* to 'all,' you have said that system of governance violates the natural order. Yet in highly evolved cultures, the natural order IS *equitable sharing*."[9]

It also said, "the short-term solution to the world's foment [sic] may be a new social structure—a new, worldwide government."[10] Nations must disappear: "Highly evolved beings refuse to join together in nations. They believe in simply one nation."[11]

The "one-world government"[12] would have "a world court to settle disputes (one whose verdicts may not be ignored, as happens with the present World Court) and a world peacekeeping force to guarantee that no one nation—no matter how powerful or influential—can ever again aggress against another."[13] "The world government would include a Congress of Nations—two representatives from

1. Walsch, *Tomorrow's God*, p 245.
2. Ibid., p 255.
3. Walsch, *Conversations/Book* 3, p 287.
4. Walsch, *Conversations with God for Teens*, p 45.
5. Walsch, *Communion with God*, pp 146–147.
6. Walsch, *New Revelations*, p 133.
7. Walsch, *Conversations/Book* 3, p 260.
8. Ibid., pp 306–307.
9. Ibid., p 303.
10. Walsch, *Conversations/Book* 2, p 199.
11. Walsch, *Conversations/Book* 3, p 318.
12. Walsch, *Conversations/Book* 2, p 195.
13. Ibid., pp 195–196.

every nation on earth—and a People's Assembly—with representation in direct proportion to a nation's population."[1] Under this plan, the U.S. would have as many votes in the Congress of Nations as the Sudan, where Christians are sold into slavery or executed. The U.S. would have about one-fourth as many votes in the People's Assembly as the People's Republic of China, which persecutes Christians and enforces a one-child policy on families. Would anyone care to guess how long our traditional Constitutional protections of freedom of religion and freedom of speech (which are *already* under siege)[2] would survive?

In the future World State, there would still be war:

> Yet understand that there may still be violence upon the Earth. The peacekeeping force may *have* to use violence to get someone to *stop* doing so. As I noted in Book 1, failure to stop a despot empowers a despot. Sometimes the only way to *avoid* a war is to *have* a war. Sometimes you have to do what you don't *want* to do in order to ensure that you won't *have to keep on doing it!* This apparent contradiction is part of the Divine Dichotomy, which says that sometimes the only way to ultimately *Be* a thing—in this case, 'peaceful,'—may be, at first, to *not* be it! In other words, often the only way to know yourself as That Which You Are is to experience yourself as That Which You Are *Not*.[3]

Walsch's "God" is a master of the dialectic, "the Divine Dichotomy." So was the regime that George Orwell described in *1984*. There were "the three slogans of the Party: War Is Peace. Freedom Is Slavery. Ignorance Is Strength."[4] Perhaps Big Brother had concluded that "the only way to know yourself as That Which You Are is to experience yourself as That Which You Are *Not*."

Robert Cooper, a senior British diplomat, offered a practical application of the "Divine Dichotomy" in his April 2002 essay, "The post-modern state." He described the European Union as

> the most developed example of a postmodern system. It represents security through transparency, and transparency through interdependence. . . . European states are not the only members of the postmodern world. Outside Europe, Canada is certainly a postmodern state; Japan is by inclination a postmodern state, but its location prevents it developing more fully in this direction. The USA is the more doubtful case since it is not clear that the US government or Congress accepts either the necessity or desirability of interdependence, or its corollaries of openness, mutual surveillance and mutual interference, to the same extent as most European governments now do.[5]

He views "modern" states (those such as India, China, Pakistan,[6] and others who purse their national interest aggressively) and "failed states"—as potential security threats. Cooper proposes rough handling of those who do not fit the post-modern paradigm:

> The challenge to the postmodern world is to get used to the idea of double standards. Among ourselves, we operate on the basis of laws and open cooperative security. But when dealing with more old-fashioned kinds of states outside the postmodern continent of Europe, we need to revert to the rougher methods of an earlier era—force, pre-emptive attack, deception, whatever is necessary to deal with those who still live in the nineteenth century world of every state for itself. Among ourselves, we keep the law but when we are operating in the jungle, we must also use the laws of the jungle.[7]

---

1. Ibid., p 205.

2. See Lee Penn, "When the State Becomes God," *Journal* of the Spiritual Counterfeits Project, vol. 27:4–28:1, 2004, pp 24–51, and "The Soul Under Seige," *Journal* of the Spiritual Counterfeits Project, vol. 28:2–28:3, 2004, pp 4–21, for overviews of the developing threats to liberty in the US.

3. Walsch, *Conversations/Book* 2, p 196.

4. George Orwell, *1984*, New American Library edition, 1961, p 7.

5. Robert Cooper, "The post-modern state," *Observer Worldview Extra*, April 7, 2002, http://www.esiweb.org/pdf/esi_europeanraj_debate_id_2.pdf, p 3, printed 08/03/04.

6. Ibid., p 1.

7. Ibid., p 3.

If chaotic states such as Afghanistan "become too dangerous for established states to tolerate, it is possible to imagine a defensive imperialism. . . . What is needed then is a new kind of imperialism, one acceptable to a world of human rights and cosmopolitan values."[1] In the "right" hands, the Divine Dichotomy—a spiritual double standard—will be used to justify whatever the rulers of the future wish to do. (Note also that Cooper is ambiguous about the status of the US; are we part of the post-modern "zone of peace," or part of the modern-state "house of war?")

Walsch's familiar spirit urges,

> I dare you to throw out all your money, all your papers and coins and individual national currencies, and start over. Develop an international monetary system that is wide open, totally visible, immediately traceable, completely accountable. Establish a Worldwide Compensation System by which people would be given Credits for services rendered and products produced, and Debits for services used and products consumed. Everything would be on the system of Credits and Debits. Returns on investments, inheritances, winnings of wagers, salaries and wages, tips and gratuities, everything. And nothing could be purchased without Credits. There would be no other negotiable currency. And everyone's records would be open to everyone else.[2]

There is a Biblical warning against such a totalitarian economic system. St. John the Divine said that there would come a time when "no one can buy or sell unless he has the mark, that is, the name of the beast or the number of its name. This calls for wisdom: let him who has understanding reckon the number of the beast, for it is a human number, its number is 666." (Rev. 13:17-18)

The aforementioned social revolution only scratches the surface of the changes that Walsch's "God" foresees for the world. It says, "Everything about the New Spirituality is revolutionary. Your entire society will actually be reconstructed, from the ground up. In the days of the New Spirituality human relationships will be completely re-created in both purpose and process."[3] The last revolutionaries who tried to re-make *all* human relationships, and not merely overturn the old order in the Church and in the State, were Mao Zedong and Pol Pot.[4] Thus far in human history, the more radical the aims of the revolutionaries, the more blood has been shed to attain them.

The realization of Walsch's political ideals, pure communism and world government, would destroy freedom. This lays bare another contradiction within the guidance offered by Walsch's imp. On the one hand, it says: "Love grants freedom, fear takes it away."[5] The spirit also says that "freedom is the essence of God, and human rights—personal liberty, equality under the law, the fairness of trials—are

---

1. Ibid., p4.

2. Walsch, *Conversations/Book* 2, p186. Charles Upton notes that "In 'The Degeneration of Coinage,' a chapter of his book about the signs of the times, French metaphysician René Guénon speaks of the disappearance of money as a sign of the approaching dissolution of the present world." (See René Guénon, *The Reign of Quantity & the Signs of the Times*, orig. ed. 1945, reissued by Sophia Perennis, 1995, chap. 16, "The Degeneration of Coinage," pp133–139.)

3. Walsch, *Tomorrow's God*, p328.

4. Regarding Pol Pot and his Cambodian Communist government, political scientist Benjamin Valentino says, "Indeed, no drive to transform society has matched the scope, speed, and intrusiveness with which the Khmer Rouge thrust their peculiar brand of 'pure communism' on the Cambodian people. Khmer Rouge leaders adhered to a particularly radical variant of Maoist Marxism … that called for extraordinarily profound changes in the daily existence of Cambodians from all walks of life. Agricultural production was transformed. Major cities were emptied. Money, markets, and virtually all private property were eliminated. Former elites were stripped of power, and organized religion was abolished." (Benjamin A. Valentino, *Final Solutions: Mass Killing and Genocide in the Twentieth Century*, Cornell University Press, 2004, p133). Valentino continued, "Children were indoctrinated with Khmer Rouge political thought from a very early age. . . . To further the party's assault on all aspects of individualism, even the smallest vegetable gardens were banned. All traces of capitalism, including money, were abolished. A policy of communal eating was established on the farms, and family members were routinely separated to ensure that alternative loyalties to the regime could not take root." (Valentino, ibid., p137).

5. Walsch, *Communion with God*, p95.

expressions of that essence."[1] On the other hand, the goblin proposes social changes that would make Mao's China look libertarian by comparison.

René Guénon, a French metaphysician of the early 20th century, investigated the European spiritist movement of the 1920s. His assessment of the political philosophy of the New Age movement of his time is also on target for the effusions offered by Walsch's spirit guide: "It can be seen how closely related spiritist 'moralism' is to socialist and humanitarian utopias; all these people agree in situating their 'earthly paradise'—that is, the realization of their dreams of 'pacifism' and 'universal brotherhood'—in a more or less distant future. The spiritists simply add the further supposition that these things are already realized on other planets."[2]

WALSCH'S HEROES AND ALLIES

Given the moral squalor of the "God" whose words Walsch channels, it is sobering to note the entity's favorite world politicians, as of 1997.

> There have been those leaders among you who have been thoughtful enough and brave enough to propose the beginnings of such a new world order. Your George Bush,[3] whom history will judge to be a man of far greater wisdom, vision, compassion, and courage than contemporary society was willing or able to acknowledge, was such a leader. So was Soviet President Mikhail Gorbachev, the first communist head of state ever to win a Nobel Prize.[4]

Walsch inhabits the same spiritual hot tub as Robert Muller, Barbara Marx Hubbard, and other prominent supporters of the URI, the State of the World Forum, and similar ventures. Walsch told *Magical Blend* magazine that Robert Muller is one of the visionaries who "not merely see the future, but supply the vision to help create it," adding that Muller "has continually challenged our worldwide political reality, and now verges on altering it forever in a gloriously positive way."[5] In a foreword for Barbara Marx Hubbard's *Conscious Evolution*, Walsch described her as "the songbird of our new morning" and acclaimed her book as "beautiful music to wake up to."[6] He also extols Deepak Chopra, James Redfield,[7] Dr. Bernie Siegel, Marianne Williamson, and Gary Zukav,[8] saying that "their life work stands as testimony to the extraordinary brilliance of the light in all our souls."[9] Walsch also approves the works of Michael Lerner[10] and Jean Houston.[11] His familiar spirit endorses the works of

1. Walsch, *New Revelations*, p 174.

2. René Guénon, *The Spiritist Fallacy*, tr. by Alvin Moore, Jr. and Rama P. Coomaraswamy, Sophia Perennis, orig. ed. 1923, English ed. 2003, p 235.

3. This refers to the elder George Bush, who was President of the United States from 1989 to 1993.

4. Walsch, *Conversations/Book* 2, p 199.

5. Neale Donald Walsch, "Losing Patience, Finding Hope," *Magical Blend*, issue 57, October 1997, p 40.

6. Marx Hubbard, *Conscious Evolution*, p xi.

7. For further information on James Redfield, see John Moore, "The Mayan Gospel—The Mass Appeal of James Redfield's Celestine Prophecy," *Journal* of the Spiritual Counterfeits Project, Vol. 21:4–22:1, 1998, pp 32–43; obtainable through http://www.scp-inc.org.

8. For more information on Gary Zukav, see Tal Brooke, "Secrets of the Soul—Gary Zukav, putting God in small packages," *Journal* of the Spiritual Counterfeits Project, Vol. 22:4–23:1, 1999, pp 4–17; available through http://www.scp-inc.org.

9. Walsch, *Conversations/Book* 3, p 2 of the acknowledgments. Both Chopra and Williamson have attended State of the World Forum events.

10. Walsch/Blanton, *Honest to God*, p 184.

11. Ibid., p 60.

Matthew Fox,[1] Judith Schucman (whose channeled "Christ" speaks in the *Course in Miracles*),[2] Werner Erhard,[3] Sri Aurobindo, and Sai Baba.[4]

NEALE DONALD WALSCH AND THEOSOPHY

Neale Donald Walsch appears to be influenced by Theosophy. He says that *Spiritual Politics*, a popularization of the teachings of Alice Bailey, is "one of the most important books to appear in the marketplace of ideas in a very long time."[5] Walsch's "God" also urged people to read the writings of Rudolf Steiner and to study the methods of the Waldorf School that Steiner established.[6] Such is the spirituality of this prominent URI supporter.

1. Walsch, *Conversations/Book* 3, p 357.
2. Ibid., p 185.
3. Ibid., p 344.
4. Walsch, *Communion with God*, p 9.
5. Corinne McLaughlin and Gordon Davidson, *Spiritual Politics: Changing the World from the Inside Out*, Ballantine Books, 1994, front cover endorsement.
6. Walsch, *Conversations/Book* 2, p 129.

17

THE INVERTED
SPIRITUALITY AND POLITICS
OF THE NEW AGE MOVEMENT

BECAUSE THE NEW AGE ADEPTS extol each other's writings, speak at the same workshops, and share board memberships in the same organizations, it's fair to assess their teachings as a group. (If this is "guilt by association," it's an association that they have created for themselves.) As a group, the works of Helena Blavatsky, Alice Bailey and her followers, Teilhard de Chardin, Robert Muller, Barbara Marx Hubbard, and Neale Donald Walsch are a comprehensive anti-Gospel. These writers oppose the human dignity and liberty that derive from God creating mankind in His image (Gen. 1:27). Those who read New Age and Theosophical books with a discerning eye will find that these writers make clear their intentions for us all, just as Hitler did with *Mein Kampf* and as the Communists have done since Marx and Lenin. This time, let us heed the warning!

For public consumption, the "prophets" of the New Age announce a glittering future of human ease, freedom, power, and spiritual unity. In 1946, Teilhard de Chardin foresaw the technology of the 21st Century, including genetic engineering and nanotechnology. He said that "the release of nuclear energy, overwhelming and intoxicating though it was," was "simply the first act, even a mere prelude" in "a series of fantastic events" which would lead us to such feats as

> vitalisation of matter by the creation of super-molecules. The re-modelling of the human organism by means of hormones. Control of heredity and sex by the manipulation of genes and chromosomes. . . . The arousing and harnessing of the unfathomable intellectual and effective powers still latent in the human mass. . . . Is not every kind of effect produced by a suitable arrangement of matter? And have we not reason to hope that in the end we shall be able to arrange every kind of matter, following the results we have obtained in the nuclear field?[1]

Other New Age teachers have echoed this hymn to Prometheus, giving it a spiritual slant. Blavatsky said, "The majority of the future mankind will be composed of glorious Adepts."[2] In the mid-1990s, Robert Muller said, "from all perspectives—scientific, political, social, economic, and ideological— humanity finds itself in the pregnancy of an entirely new and promising age: the global, interdependent, universal age; a truly quantum jump; a cosmic event of the first importance that is perhaps unique in the universe: the birth of a global brain, heart, senses and soul to humanity."[3] Barbara Marx

---

1. Pierre Teilhard de Chardin, "Some Reflections on the Spiritual Repercussions of the Atom Bomb," in *The Future of Man*, translated by Norman Denny, Harper & Row, 1964, p144 (this essay collection is cited below as *The Future of Man*).

2. H.P. Blavatsky, *The Secret Doctrine: The Synthesis of Science, Religion, and Philosophy, Vol. II—Anthropogenesis*, Theosophical University Press, 1999 reprint of 1888 ed., p446

3. Robert Muller, "Foreword: Preparing for the Next Millennium," in Joel Beversluis, ed., on-line version of *A Source Book for the Earth's Community of Religions*, http://www.origin.org/ucs/doc.cfm?e=0&ps=2&edit=1&fg=3176&fi=1089, printed 06/22/04.

Hubbard likewise said, "We stand upon the threshold of the greatest age of human history."[1] Neale Donald Walsch's "God" proclaimed, "The twenty-first century will be the time of awakening, of meeting The Creator Within. . . . This will be the beginning of the golden age of the New Human."[2]

Nevertheless, the New Age promise of utopia is a lie. Blavatsky, Alice and Foster Bailey, Walsch, Muller, Marx Hubbard, and their New Age colleagues have barely concealed their hatred for God, their rejection of human tradition and morality, and their contempt for most of humanity. For the majority of us, these New Age teachers promise death.

For the spiritual elite, these New Age prophets promise power, secret knowledge, and membership in the "spiritual hierarchy." Teilhard de Chardin proposed that when mankind reaches "a critical level of maturity," the race will "detach itself from this planet and join the one true, irreversible essence of things, the Omega point. A phenomenon perhaps outwardly akin to death: but in reality a simple metamorphosis and arrival at the supreme synthesis."[3] Alice Bailey said that followers of her path will find that "each contact with the Initiator leads the initiate closer to the centre of pure darkness."[4] She urged her followers on toward the "Great Renunciation," "the final great transference, based upon the renunciation of that which for aeons has connoted beauty, truth, and goodness."[5]

In his apocalyptic novel *That Hideous Strength*, C. S. Lewis described the nature of this same temptation for Mark Studdock, who had sought initiation into an inner ring of scientific magicians: "Here, here surely at last (so his desire whispered to him) was the true inner circle of all, the circle whose centre was outside the human race—the ultimate secret, the supreme power, the last initiation. The fact that it was almost completely horrible did not in the least diminish its attraction."[6] Studdock's final initiation—if he went that far—would involve worship of "macrobes," spirits with far greater power and intelligence than any man. As his tempter described the macrobes, Studdock was simultaneously horrified and enticed: "These creatures . . . breathed death on the human race and on all joy. Not despite this but because of this, the terrible gravitation sucked and tugged and fascinated him towards them. Never before had he known the fruitful strength of the movement opposite to Nature which now had him in its grip; the impulse to reverse all reluctances and to draw every circle anti-clockwise."[7]

Bishop Swing, the founder of the URI, has said, "A United Religions will either have a distinct spiritual momentum far beyond its own cleverness or it simply will not be."[8] The macrobes, or beings worse than them, are the darkness at the end of the road, after the "distinct spiritual momentum" of the New Age movement has reached its goal.

In early 2003, the Vatican offered an incisive analysis of the origins and beliefs of the New Age movement, *Jesus Christ: The Bearer of the Water of Life*. The document warns specifically against the New Age ideas that are prevalent within the URI and among its utopian allies.

First, the New Age movement is not new; it is a revival of centuries-old anti-Christian traditions. The Vatican said,

1. Barbara Marx Hubbard, *The Evolutionary Journey: A Personal Guide to a Positive Future*, Evolutionary Press, San Francisco, 1982, p 11.

2. Neale Donald Walsch, *Friendship with God: An Uncommon Dialogue*, G. P. Putnam's Sons, 1999, p 295.

3. Pierre Teilhard de Chardin, "Life and the Planets: What is Happening at this Moment on Earth?," in *The Future of Man*, pp 122–123.

4. Alice A. Bailey, *The Rays and the Initiations: Volume V, A Treatise on the Seven Rays*, 1960, Lucis Publishing Company, p 174.

5. Ibid., p 224.

6. C. S. Lewis, *That Hideous Strength: A Modern Fairy-Tale for Grown-Ups*, Collier Books, Macmillan Publishing Company, 1946, pp 259–260.

7. Ibid., p 269.

8. Bishop William Swing, *The Coming United Religions*, United Religions Initiative and CoNexus Press, 1998, p 22.

When one examines many *New Age* traditions, it soon becomes clear that there is, in fact, little in the *New Age* that is new. The name seems to have gained currency through Rosicrucianism and Freemasonry, at the time of the French and American Revolutions, but the reality it denotes is a contemporary variant of Western esotericism. This dates back to Gnostic groups which grew up in the early days of Christianity, and gained momentum at the time of the Reformation in Europe. It has grown in parallel with scientific world-views, and acquired a rational justification through the eighteenth and nineteenth centuries. It has involved a progressive rejection of a personal God. . . . A powerful trend in modern Western culture which has given space to *New Age* ideas is the general acceptance of Darwinist evolutionary theory; this, alongside a focus on hidden spiritual powers or forces in nature, has been the backbone of much of what is now recognised as New Age theory.[1]

New Age is not a single, uniform movement, but rather a loose network of practitioners whose approach is to *think globally but act locally.*[2]

Against the claim by URI supporter Barbara Marx Hubbard that "We *are* gods!,"[3] and against Neale Donald Walsch's assertion that "You are not inferior to God, nor to anything at all,"[4] the Vatican replied, "This exaltation of humanity overturns the correct relationship between Creator and creature."[5]

Against the claims by supporters of world government that they are guardians of human rights and democracy, the Vatican replied, "The global brain needs institutions with which to rule, in other words, a world government. . . . there is much evidence that gnostic élitism and global governance coincide on many issues in international politics."[6]

Against the proponents of "global spirituality" and a "global ethic," the Vatican warned,

we are witnessing a spontaneous cultural change whose course is fairly determined by influences beyond human control. However, it is enough to point out that *New Age* shares with a number of internationally influential groups the goal of superseding or transcending particular religions in order to create space for a universal religion which could unite humanity. Closely related to this is a very concerted effort on the part of many institutions to invent a *Global Ethic*, an ethical framework which would reflect the global nature of contemporary culture, economics and politics. Further, the politicisation of ecological questions certainly colours the whole question of the Gaia hypothesis or worship of mother earth.[7]

Against the attempts to integrate some positive elements of New Age beliefs into Christianity, the Vatican warned,

The gnostic nature of this movement calls us to judge it in its entirety. From the point of view of Christian faith, it is not possible to isolate some elements of *New Age* religiosity as acceptable to Christians, while rejecting others. Since the *New Age* movement makes much of a communication with nature, of cosmic knowledge of a universal good—thereby negating the revealed contents of Christian faith—it cannot be viewed as positive or innocuous. In a cultural environment, marked by religious relativism, it is necessary to signal a warning against the attempt to place *New Age* religiosity on the same level as Christian faith, making the difference between faith and belief seem relative, thus creating greater confusion for the unwary.[8]

---

1. Pontifical Council For Culture and Pontifical Council For Interreligious Dialogue, "Jesus Christ The Bearer Of The Water Of Life: A Christian reflection on the "New Age," 2003, section 1.3, http://www.vatican.va/roman_curia/pontifical_councils/interelg/documents/rc_pc_interelg_doc_20030203_new-age_en.html, printed 02/3/03 (cited below as Vatican report on the "New Age," 02/3/03).

2. Ibid., section 2.

3. Barbara Marx Hubbard, *The Revelation: A Message of Hope for the New Millennium*, Nataraj Publishing, Novato, CA, 1995, p312.

4. Walsch, *Communion with God*, p161

5. Vatican report on the "New Age," 02/3/03, section 2.3.4.1.

6. Ibid., section 2.3.4.3.

7. Ibid., section 2.5.

8. Ibid., section 4.

The Vatican further warned against the anti-Christian aspect of the New Age movement:

New Age offers an alternative to the Judaeo-Christian heritage. The Age of Aquarius is conceived as one which will replace the predominantly Christian Age of Pisces. *New Age* thinkers are acutely aware of this; some of them are convinced that the coming change is inevitable, while others are actively committed to assisting its arrival. People who wonder if it is possible to believe in both Christ and Aquarius can only benefit from knowing that this is very much an 'either-or' situation. 'No servant can be the slave of two masters: he will either hate the first and love the second, or treat the first with respect and the second with scorn' (Luke 16:13). Christians have only to think of the difference between the wise men from the East and King Herod to recognise the powerful effects of choice for or against Christ. It must never be forgotten that many of the movements which have fed the New Age are explicitly anti-Christian. Their stance towards Christianity is not neutral, but neutralising: despite what is often said about openness to all religious standpoints, traditional Christianity is not sincerely regarded as an acceptable alternative. In fact, it is occasionally made abundantly clear that 'there is no tolerable place for true Christianity', and there are even arguments justifying anti-Christian behaviour.[1]

These present-day warnings repeat prior Catholic teachings against politicized idolatry. Against the German idolatry of race and nation in the Third Reich, Pope Pius XI wrote in 1937:

Whoever exalts race, or the people, or the State, or a particular form of State, or the depositories of power, or any other fundamental value of the human community—however necessary and honorable be their function in worldly things—whoever raises these notions above their standard value and divinizes them to an idolatrous level, distorts and perverts an order of the world planned and created by God; he is far from the true faith in God and from the concept of life which that faith upholds.[2]

The same warnings could apply to any movement that exalts any "fundamental value of the human community"—such as peace or environmental preservation—"above their standard value and divinizes them to an idolatrous level."

If the teachings of the New Age authors discussed above are put into practice for the whole society, we can expect that they will be enforced with zeal, for everyone. The spiritual leaders of that time will proclaim the virtues of spiritual unity and mass consciousness-change; they will forget their earlier advocacy of tolerance and "unity in diversity." In his 1920s investigation of occult movements, René Guénon predicted the same, based on the beliefs and behavior of the spiritists of his own time: "if they had the power they would impose their own ideas on all alike; for in practice no one is less tolerant than those who feel a need to preach tolerance and fraternity."[3] Those who follow these "spirits of the age" will find slavery, not freedom.

The popularity of the New Age movement is evidence of spiritual famine in America and other affluent nations. As Kenneth Woodward wrote for *Newsweek* in 2001, "What makes these bad best sellers noteworthy is what they tell us about the spiritual marketplace. Millions of seekers are looking for religious nourishment, but they can't tell authentic loaves of bread from the congealed mush put out by self-serving hustlers."[4] As a common saying goes among Evangelical Christians, "the cults are the unpaid bills of the Church."

Thus, a Christian response to the spread of this delusive form of spirituality needs to be twofold.

---

1. Ibid., section 6.1.

2. Pope Pius XI, *Mit Brennender Sorge*, (Encyclical on the Church and the German Reich), March 14, 1937, section 8; http://www.vatican.va/holy_father/pius_xi/encyclicals/documents/hf_p-xi_enc_14031937_mit-brennender-sorge_en.html, printed 02/23/03.

3. René Guénon, *The Spiritist Fallacy*, tr. by Alvin Moore, Jr. and Rama P. Coomaraswamy, Sophia Perennis, orig. ed. 1923, English ed. 2003, p 237 (cited below as Guénon, *The Spiritist Fallacy*).

4. Kenneth L. Woodward, "Platitudes or Prophecy?," *Newsweek*, August 27, 2001, as printed on 08/24/01 from *MSNBC.com*. No longer on the Net.

First, the Churches need to acknowledge and repent of their own failure to offer seekers the Gospel. Next comes ministry to the followers of the New Age movement—and to the movement's leaders, as well. The spiritually starved souls who follow New Age and Theosophical teachers are, each and all, people whom Christ loves and for whom He died and rose again. Christ desires that all be saved. It is a spiritual work of mercy to warn the people involved in these movements that they are rushing heedlessly toward the edge of a spiritual cliff, and to counsel those who seek aid. It is also essential to intercede in prayer on behalf of the leaders of the New Age movement, and their followers, that God might have mercy on them, and grant to them the graces of repentance, conversion, and true faith.

As may be obvious, I have offered the foregoing critique of the New Age movement from the perspective of a traditional Christian. However, the co-optation of religion by the spiritual scavengers of the New Age should be of concern to traditional believers in other faiths. As René Guénon said in 1921, traditional Hindus are "natural allies in this struggle.... Beyond the more particular reasons that Hindus have for profoundly detesting Theosophy, it is no more acceptable to them than to Christians ... or, in a general way, than it is to all who adhere to a truly traditional doctrine."[1]

To conclude, I would reiterate the warning against the New Age movement that René Guénon offered in the early 1920s:

What we see in all this, and more generally in spiritism and other analogous movements, are influences that incontestably come from what some have called 'the sphere of the Antichrist.' This designation can also be taken symbolically, but that changes nothing in reality and does not render the influences less ill-omened. Assuredly, those who participate in such movements, and even those who believe they direct them, may know nothing of these things. This is where the greatest danger lies, for quite certainly many of them would flee in horror if they knew they were servants of the 'powers of darkness.' But their blindness is often irremediable and their good faith even helps draw in other victims. Does this not allow us to say that the supreme craft of the devil, however he may be conceived, is to make us deny his existence?[2]

1. René Guénon, *Theosophy: History of a Pseudo-Religion*, tr. by Alvin Moore et al., orig. ed. 1921, rev. ed. Sophia Perennis, 2001, p 295.
2. Guénon, *The Spiritist Fallacy*, p 276.

PART III

LEVIATHAN RISING:
THE GLOBALIST ALLIES OF THE URI

The demons of Antichrist seducing men by bribe and the destruction of sacred images. Lyons, late 15th century.

"My kingship is not of this world. . . ."

Jesus, in John 18:36

"You know that those who are supposed
to rule over the Gentiles lord it over them,
and their great men exercise authority over them.
But it shall not be so among you; but whoever would be
great among you must be your servant, and whoever
would be first among you must be slave of all. For
the Son of man also came not to be served but
to serve, and to give his life as a
ransom for many."

Jesus, in Mark 10:42–45

POINT : COUNTERPOINT

Another hierarchical project approved at a centennial conference was to take action to raise the consciousness of the four hundred million mass of Russian people. In a few short years this effort has achieved amazing results and is already an outstanding hierarchical success. It has been demonstrated that hopeless, illiterate peasants when stimulated and given a chance become industrial workers.[1]

————FOSTER BAILEY, *RUNNING GOD'S PLAN*, 1972, APPROVING THE SOVIET REGIME

Now your thought that Hitler was a monster is based on the fact that he ordered the killing of millions of people, correct? . . . Yet what if I told you that what you call 'death' is *the greatest thing that could happen to anyone*—what then? . . . You think that life on Earth is better than life in heaven? I tell you this, at the moment of your death you will realize the greatest freedom, the greatest peace, the greatest joy, and the greatest love you have ever known. Shall we therefore punish Bre'r Fox for throwing Bre'r Rabbit into the briar patch?[2]

————"GOD," TALKING TO NEALE DONALD WALSCH ABOUT THE HOLOCAUST, 1997

Old forms (obstructing the good) have had to be destroyed; the wrecking and disappearance of that which is bad and undesirable must ever precede the building of the good and desirable and the longed-for emergence of that which is new and better.[3]

————ALICE BAILEY, *THE EXTERNALISATION OF THE HIERARCHY*,
APPROVING THE ATOMIC BOMBING OF JAPAN, 1945

The cultural revolution in China was begun a few short years ago. This also is an hierarchical project. Amazing changes have been achieved in that short period. Chester Ronning, Canada's former Ambassador to China and an authority on China today, says that the Chinese people through revolution have changed their way of thinking. This is fundamental to national reform.[4]

————FOSTER BAILEY, *RUNNING GOD'S PLAN*, 1972,
APPROVING THE CULTURAL REVOLUTION IN CHINA

In our time, political speech and writing are largely the defence of the indefensible. Things like the continuation of British rule in India, the Russian purges and deportations, the dropping of the atom bombs on Japan, can indeed be defended, but only by arguments which are too brutal for most people to face, and which do not square with the professed aims of political parties. Thus political language has to consist largely of euphemism, question-begging and sheer cloudy vagueness.

---

1. Foster Bailey, *Running God's Plan*, Lucis Publishing Company, 1972, p 12 (cited below as F. Bailey, *Running God's Plan*).
2. Walsch, *Conversations/Book 2*, p 36.
3. Alice A. Bailey, *The Externalisation of the Hierarchy*, 1957, Lucis Publishing Company, p 498 (cited below as A. Bailey, *Externalisation of the Hierarchy*).
4. F. Bailey, *Running God's Plan*, pp 12–13.

Defenceless villages are bombarded from the air, the inhabitants driven out into the countryside, the cattle machine-gunned, the huts set on fire with incendiary bullets: this is called *pacification*. Millions of peasants are robbed of their farms and sent trudging along the roads with no more than they can carry: this is called *transfer of population* or *rectification of frontiers*. People are imprisoned for years without trial, or shot in the back of the neck or sent to die of scurvy in Arctic lumber camps: this is called *elimination of unreliable elements*. Such phraseology is needed if one wants to name things without calling up mental pictures of them. Consider for instance some comfortable English professor defending Russian totalitarianism. He cannot say outright, 'I believe in killing off your opponents when you can get good results by doing so.' Probably, therefore, he will say something like this: 'While freely conceding that the Soviet régime exhibits certain features which the humanitarian may be inclined to deplore, we must, I think, agree that a certain curtailment of the right to political opposition is an unavoidable concomitant of transitional periods, and that the rigors which the Russian people have been called upon to undergo have been amply justified in the sphere of concrete achievement.' The inflated style is itself a kind of euphemism.[1]

GEORGE ORWELL, *"POLITICS AND THE ENGLISH LANGUAGE"*————

We do not want another committee. We have too many already. What we want is a man of sufficient stature to hold the allegiance of all people, and to lift us out of the economic morass in which we are sinking. Send us such a man and be he god or the devil, we will receive him.[2]

————PAUL-HENRI SPAAK, COUNCIL OF EUROPE, 1949

In any case, like it or not, the Commission has to respond to an active global social conscience. In the past people asked God to deliver them from evil. Today they look to international institutions— and in Europe that means the EU.[3]

————CHRIS PATTEN, EUROPEAN UNION EXTERNAL RELATIONS COMMISSIONER, 2000

Nothing can or ever has prevented mankind from a steady progress which has been from ignorance to knowledge and from darkness to light.[4]

————ALICE A. BAILEY, *PROBLEMS OF HUMANITY*, 1947

The Antichrist's deception already begins to take shape in the world every time the claim is made to realize within history that messianic hope which can be only realized beyond history through the eschatological judgment.[5]

CATECHISM OF THE CATHOLIC CHURCH, SECTION 676, 1997————

1. George Orwell, "Politics and the English Language," in George Orwell, *A Collection Of Essays*, Harcourt Brace, 1981, pp 166–167.

2. UK Independence Party, "Past Statements of Intent by champions of the E. U.," http://www.ukip-richmondpark.com/ EU%20statements.htm, printed 08/03/04. They describe Spaak as "the former Belgian Prime Minister, and President of the Consultative Assembly of the Council of Europe." Before World War II, Spaak had been a member of the Belgian Workers' Party, stated his admiration for "some of Hitler's magnificent achievements," and "declared in 1937 that 'the hour of Belgian national socialism has come.'" (John Laughland, *The Tainted Source: The Undemocratic Origins of the European Idea*, Warner Books, 1997, p 69.)

3. Chris Patten, "External Relations: Demands, Constraints and Priorities," October 6, 2000, http://coranet.radi-calparty.org/pressreview/print_right.php?func=detail&par=1882, printed 08/10/04.

4. Alice A. Bailey, *Problems of Humanity*, 1947, Lucis Publishing Company, p 153.

5. *Catechism Of The Catholic Church*, 2nd Ed., Libreria Editrice Vaticana, 1997, sec. 676, p 177 (cited below as *Catechism*).

As the 21st century unfolds, an ever more integrated global system demands an ever more inclusive and holistic approach to global governance.[1]

———STATE OF THE WORLD FORUM, COMMISSION ON GLOBAL GOVERNANCE, 2003

Weak if we were and foolish, not thus we failed, not thus; When that black Baal blocked the heavens he had no hymns from us."[2]

G. K. CHESTERTON, *THE MAN WHO WAS THURSDAY*———

Over the next 20 to 30 years, we are going to end up with world government. . . . It's inevitable.[3]

———JIM GARRISON, PRESIDENT OF THE STATE OF THE WORLD FORUM, 1995

The covenant with Noah after the flood gives expression to the principle of the divine economy toward the 'nations,' in other words, towards men grouped 'in their lands, each with [its] own language, by their families, in their nations.' This state of division into many nations is at once cosmic, social, and religious. It is intended to limit the pride of fallen humanity, united only in its perverse ambition to forge its own unity as at Babel.[4]

CATECHISM OF THE CATHOLIC CHURCH, SECTIONS 56–57, 1997———

In highly evolved societies there is neither 'marriage' nor 'business'—nor, for that matter, any of the artificial social constructions you have created to hold your society together."[5]

———"GOD," SPEAKING TO NEALE DONALD WALSCH, 1998

"Four reformers met under a bramble bush. They were all agreed the world must be changed. 'We must abolish property,' said one. 'We must abolish marriage,' said the second. 'We must abolish God,' said the third. 'I wish we could abolish work,' said the fourth. 'Do not let us get beyond practical politics,' said the first. 'The first thing is reduce men to a common level.' 'The first thing,' said the second, 'is to give freedom to the sexes.' 'The first thing,' said the third, 'is to find out how to do it.' 'The first step,' said the first, 'is to abolish the Bible.' 'The first thing,' said the second, 'is to abolish the laws,' 'The first thing,' said the third, 'is to abolish mankind.'"[6]

ROBERT LOUIS STEVENSON, "THE FOUR REFORMERS," 1888———

Many are preaching salvation of the individual through love. No one is proclaiming the other half of my message: the transformation of the species by the use of its collective scientific, cultural, and extraordinary individual capacities.[7]

———"CHRIST," TO BARBARA MARX HUBBARD, IN *THE BOOK OF CO-CREATION*

1. State of the World Forum—Commission on Globalisation, "Commission Overview: Strategic Context—The Challenge of Globalisation," http://www.commissionglobalization.org/overview/main.htm, printed 05/23/03.
2. G. K. Chesterton, *The Man Who Was Thursday*, Perigee Books/G. P. Putnam's Sons, 1980, p 2; "To Edmund Clerihew Bentley."
3. George Cothran, "One World, Under Gorby," *SF Weekly*, May 31–June 6, 1995, Vol. 14, no. 16, p 11.
4. *Catechism*, sections 56–57, pp 20–21.
5. Walsch, *Conversations/Book* 3, pp 218–219.
6. Robert Louis Stevenson, "The Four Reformers," reprinted in *The Portable Conservative Reader*, ed. Russell Kirk, Viking Penguin Inc., 1982, p 363.
7. Barbara Marx Hubbard, *The Book of Co-Creation Part II—The Promise Will Be Kept: The Gospels, The Acts, the Epistles*, Foundation for Conscious Evolution, San Rafael, California, 1993 (privately published), p 7.

There neither is nor can be any simple increase of power on Man's side. Each new power won *by* man is a power *over* man as well.[1]

C. S. LEWIS, *THE ABOLITION OF MAN*———

Humanity is poised to make inexorable progress toward creating a world that works for an increasing number of people. Indeed, in and through all the vicissitudes of contemporary history, a new cultural matrix is arising, one based on integration of all the dimensions of human life and with a new sense of personal and civic responsibility."[2]

———STATE OF THE WORLD FORUM, 1998

I see the great liberal death wish driving through the years ahead in triple harness with the gospel of progress and the pursuit of happiness. These our three Horsemen of the Apocalypse—progress, happiness, death. Under their auspices, the quest for total affluence leads to total deprivation; for total peace, to total war; for total education, to total illiteracy; for total sex, to total sterility; for total freedom, to total servitude.[3]

MALCOLM MUGGERIDGE, "THE GREAT LIBERAL DEATH WISH"———

Christ taught also that the Kingdom of God is on Earth and told us to seek that Kingdom first and let all things go for its sake.[4]

———ALICE A. BAILEY, *THE EXTERNALISATION OF THE HIERARCHY*, 1957

My kingship is not of this world. . . .

JESUS, IN JOHN 18:36———

THE COERCIVE UTOPIANS OF THE 21ST CENTURY

The teachings of Alice Bailey, Teilhard de Chardin, Robert Muller, Barbara Marx Hubbard, and Neale Donald Walsch set out the theory of government and economics under a leftist New World Order. The programs of Mikhail Gorbachev, the State of the World Forum, the Earth Charter movement, and their globalist allies describe the proposed practice. The rhetoric of Marxism-Leninism is gone; the plans for a new ant-hill society remain—a New Order with a "spiritual" veneer.

Gorbachev says, "*The socialist idea is inextinguishable*,"[5] and vowed in 2002 that "I intend to continue to contribute to building that new world order."[6] We should take Gorbachev and his visionary colleagues at their word, and not dismiss them as harmless cranks. They have money, media connections, and powerful allies—and deserve to be watched and opposed.

1. C.S. Lewis, *The Abolition of Man*, Macmillan Publishing Co., Inc., 1947, paperback ed. 1955, p71.
2. State of the World Forum, "Our Common Enterprise II: The Possibility," http://worldforum.percepticon.com/initiatives/our_common_enterprise_b.html, printed 06/16/04.
3. Malcolm Muggeridge, "The Great Liberal Death Wish," reprinted in *The Portable Conservative Reader*, ed. Russell Kirk, Viking Penguin Inc., 1982, p623.
4. A. Bailey, *Externalisation of the Hierarchy*, p603.
5. Mikhail Gorbachev, *On My Country And The World*, Columbia University Press, 2000, p68; the emphasis was as given in the original text.
6. Nick Hallissey, "Gorbachev plea to Yorkshire business," *ThisIsYork.co.uk*, 6/1/02, http://www.thisisyork.co.uk/york/archive/2002/06/01/york_news_local21ZM.html, printed 05/21/03. A similar report appeared in a 6/1/02 story reprinted by *Newsday.com*: "'Unfortunately,' he said, 'we wasted a lot of time after the end of the Cold War. Today we have to build a new world order step by step.'" (AP, "Gorbachev: Don't Americanize Cultures," *Newsday.com*, 6/2/02; no longer on the Net in original form.)

18

MIKHAIL GORBACHEV, "MAN WITH A STILL-UNFULFILLED DESTINY"

ALTHOUGH MIKHAIL GORBACHEV has been out of power for more than a decade, he retains global stature—and a collectivist, messianic vision of politics and society.

"THE SOCIALIST IDEA IS INEXTINGUISHABLE"

Gorbachev repudiates Stalinism, but he remains committed to the ideals of socialism and the October Revolution. In 2000, Gorbachev wrote, "*The October revolution undeniably reflected the most urgent demands of the broadest strata of the population for fundamental social change.*"[1] "To put it briefly, October played a civilizing role in the vast expanses of Asia and southeastern Europe."[2] "It should be noted that despite its weaknesses the system that was called socialist gave people (at least a majority of working people) a minimal income necessary for life and confidence in the future, which working people in the West as a rule do not know."[3] "The revolution—despite the price that was paid—brought historical renewal to Russia, freed it from the heritage of the feudal and absolutist past, and allowed the modernization of our country to begin."[4]

In Gorbachev's view, the creation of a "new civilization" requires a radical change in *everyone's* world view and behavior: "we need a radical turnaround in our thinking, one that is global, historically long-lasting, and humanist in the fullest and truest sense of the word. What is needed is a revolution in consciousness that would provide the grounds for and ensure a new approach to the basic way of life and forms of behavior of human beings in today's world."[5] He does not specify how he would gain popular assent to this "revolution in consciousness."

Gorbachev's New World Order would synthesize socialism and capitalism:

The socialist idea has not lost its significance or its historical relevance.[6] *... The socialist idea is inextinguishable.*[7]
.... I am convinced that a new civilization will inevitably take on certain features that are characteristic of, or inherent in, the socialist ideal. However, over the course of centuries, in both politics and social consciousness, a great number of differing ideas have been churned out—conservative and radical, liberal and socialist, individualist and collectivist. This is the reality encountered everywhere. An attempt to *synthesize* these views, trends,

---

1. Mikhail Gorbachev, *On My Country And The World*, Columbia University Press, 2000, p7; the emphasis was as given in the original text (cited below as Gorbachev, *On My Country And The World*).
2. Ibid., p29.
3. Ibid., p50.
4. Ibid., p77.
5. Ibid., p243.
6. Ibid., p67; the emphasis was as given in the original text.
7. Ibid., p68; the emphasis was as given in the original text.

and phenomena, an attempt to achieve an optimal interaction among them based on strictly humanist criteria—that is what will ensure movement toward a new civilization.[1]

In 1995, Gorbachev told the *San Francisco Chronicle*, "The continuation of building a new world order and new international relations—this will be a long and difficult process, but certainly we should build it up instead of destroying it by unwise moves."[2] He added, "We need a new information code that will affect the press and the information systems. And we need to address the problem of crime and terrorism."[3]

The New World Order would be brought about incrementally, rather than by revolution:

> The research we have conducted at the Gorbachev Foundation has led us to conclude that it is impossible to find a way out of the present transitional period by attempting to resolve only the current ongoing political problems.... It is necessary, in other words, to find roads leading to a new civilization.... We understand that building such a civilization is a long-term task (although on the scale of history a task that cannot be postponed). Few people in the world are ready for the profound, fundamental changes required for the creation of this civilization. What, then, should be done? We should not try to effect immediate all-embracing changes; rather, we should move toward such change step by step, finding urgent solutions where they are absolutely necessary, and partial solutions where nothing else can yet be done. Solutions will gradually enlarge the field of agreement and the range of possibilities for later, more substantial measures.[4]

He added, "Obviously, the goals of global management cannot be achieved all at once, in a single leap.... Thus it is necessary to approach this goal step by step, to try to enhance the role of existing institutions and encourage the coordination of the efforts of various governments. Above all, we are thinking about the United Nations."[5]

Part of Gorbachev's "global management" would be a new global planning agency. In 2000, he told the State of the World Forum, "When I was president [of the Soviet Union], I suggested to the United Nations that they strengthen the organization's environmental bodies, and create an economic body to oversee the world of finance. That did not happen. As a result, there has been great disappointment since the end of the Cold War."[6] In a book published the same year, Gorbachev said, "In the final analysis, a system for collective management of worldwide processes must be created, an effective form of collaboration based on equality among nations and peoples We must know how to combine and jointly subordinate national interests and actions for the sake of worldwide interests and actions."[7] He added, "What is important is that everyone must pursue the common goal: a genuine renewal of the life of the entire world community in order to arrive at new conditions of existence for the human race."[8]

1. Ibid., p74.

2. Jon Stewart, "MIKHAIL GORBACHEV: Once declared the 'man of the century' by Time magazine, the man who played a key role in ending the Cold War talks about the state of the world today," *San Francisco Chronicle*, September 24, 1995, page 3/Z1; Internet version, printed from http://www.sfgate.com on 05/13/03 (cited below as Stewart, "Mikhail Gorbachev," 09/24/95).

3. Ibid.

4. Gorbachev, *On My Country And The World*, p221.

5. Ibid., p227.

6. Mark Schapiro, State of the World Forum, "A Citizens' U. N.?," September 2000, http://www.simulconference.com/clients/sowf/dispatches/dispatch9.html, printed 05/24/03.

7. Gorbachev, *On My Country And The World*, p269.

8. Ibid., p277.

"NATURE IS MY GOD"

Gorbachev has condemned Western individualism and proposed the development of a new, nature-centered morality. He began by describing the Soviet experience as "something totally unacceptable to the civilized world: namely, humanity's alienation from property and power, making the individual a 'cog in the wheel' of a thoroughly ideologized machinery of the state."[1] Then Gorbachev said,

On the other hand, it is increasingly evident that the values of the Western world are becoming more and more anachronistic. Their Golden Age is in the past; they cannot assure a dependable future for the human race. We should take a sober and unprejudiced view of the strengths and weaknesses of collectivism, which is fraught with dictatorship. But what about the individualism of Western culture? At the very least, something will have to be done about its purely consumerist orientation that emphasizes 'having' rather than 'being,' acquiring and possessing rather than revealing the real potential of humanity. . . . The search for a new paradigm should be a search for synthesis, for what is common to and unites people, countries, and nations, rather than what divides them. The search for such a synthesis can succeed if the following conditions are met. First of all, we must return to the well-known human values that were embodied in the ideals of world religions and also in the socialist ideas that inherited much from those values. Further, we need to search for a new paradigm of development, based on those values and capable of leading us all toward a genuinely humanistic or, more precisely, humanistic-ecological culture of living. Finally, we need to develop methods of social action and policy that will direct society to a path consistent with the interests of both humanity and the rest of nature.[2]

Gorbachev also proposed,

At the same time, we must begin to define certain moral maxims or ethical commandments that constitute values common to all humankind. It is my view that the individual's attitude toward nature must become one of the principal criteria for ensuring the maintenance of morality. Today it is not enough to say 'Thou shalt not kill.' Ecological education implies, above all, respect and love for every living being. It is here that ecological culture interfaces with religion. . . . Honoring diversity and honoring the Earth create the basis for genuine unity.[3]

Naturalistic religion is consistent with Gorbachev's beliefs: "I believe in the cosmos. All of us are linked to the cosmos. Look at the sun. If there is no sun, then we cannot exist. So nature is my god. To me, nature is sacred. Trees are my temples and forests are my cathedrals."[4]

GORBACHEV'S SMALLPOX HOARD

Gorbachev's reverence for nature did not prevent him from massive violations of treaties against biological warfare; if we face a smallpox attack in the future, part of the credit will go to him. Soviet

1. Mikhail Gorbachev, "A call for new values," http://www.worldtrans.org/whole/gorbachev.html, printed 05/20/03 (cited below as Gorbachev, "A call for new values"). The site says, "This is an excerpt from Mikhail Gorbachev's new book *The Search for a New Beginning: Developing a New Civilization*, inspired by the 'State of the World Forum' in September 95 in San Francisco. This excerpt was printed in *Noetic Sciences Review*, Autumn edition."
2. Ibid.
3. Ibid.
4. Fred Matser, "Nature Is My God," an interview with Mikhail Gorbachev, *Resurgence* 184, http://resurgence.gn.apc.org/184/gorbachev.htm, printed 05/20/03. *Resurgence* describes itself as "the leading international forum for ecological and spiritual thinking, where you can explore the ideas of the great writers and thinkers of our time, both in print and on-line" (*Resurgence*, home page, http://resurgence.gn.apc.org/home.htm, printed 05/20/03). Matser was, as of 1997, the president of the Gorbachev Foundation in the Netherlands. (1997 State of the World Forum, "Participants," http://www.worldforum.org/1997forum/1997_Participants.html, printed in 1997; no longer on the Net.)

military forces supported the "socialist ideas"[1] of the USSR by violating the 1972 treaty banning germ weapons.[2] Soon after assuming power, Gorbachev signed

> a five-year plan, for 1985 to 1990, that brought the Soviet Union to its high point of developing an arsenal of deadly pathogens, including plague, brucellosis, tularemia, anthrax, and smallpox. . . . Under Gorbachev, there was no limit to the resources Moscow was prepared to invest. In 1990, $1 billion and more than sixty thousand skilled workers would be devoted to match deadly germs (often in vaccine-resistant strains) with missiles aimed at New York, Los Angeles, Chicago, and Seattle. At the same time U.S. scientists were collaborating with Russian counterparts to eradicate any trace of smallpox from the world (from which some 300 million people died during the twentieth century), the Soviet Union was secretly hoarding twenty tons of the germ for military use. New strains were being created. All this during glasnost.[3]

Gorbachev ordered a halt to the Soviet biological weapons program in 1990—18 *years* after the 1972 treaty and 5 *years* after he took power.[4] By the late 1980s, the USSR had loaded weapons-grade smallpox, anthrax, and plague onto ICBMs aimed at the US. The Soviet Union kept a stockpile of at least 20 tons of weapons-grade dry smallpox—at a time when smallpox viruses were supposed to be preserved in only two research sites worldwide. In 1990 and 1991, the last two years of Gorbachev's rule, Soviet researchers developed a new variant of smallpox weapons, a combination of smallpox and Venezuelan equine encephalitis. Arms reductions during 1991, the last days of the Soviet Union, "left alive the Soviet Union's germ empire, history's most pestilential arsenal."[5] There are indications that Russia has continued to work on these programs, despite additional halt-work orders issued in 1992 by Boris Yeltsin. Biopreparat, the agency under which the Soviets built their germ warfare arsenal from 1973 onwards, has reinvented itself as a state-run drug company.[6] Its military plants remain closed to outside inspection, and (as of 2001) the agency was directed by General Yuri Kalinin, who has run Biopreparat since 1979.[7]

THE "LAST REMAINING GLOBAL LEADER"?

Meanwhile, Gorbachev does not view himself as a lame duck politician. A May 1997 press release from Green Cross International says: "Gorbachev may be the last remaining global leader. He strikes those

1. Gorbachev, "A call for new values."

2. Derek Leebaert, *The Fifty-year Wound: How America's Cold War Victory Shapes Our World*, Little, Brown, and Co., 2002, p 456 (cited below as Leebaert, *Fifty-year Wound*).

3. Ibid., p 516.

4. Information in this paragraph, unless otherwise footnoted, is from Richard Preston, "The Bioweaponeers," *The New Yorker*, March 9, 1998, pp 52–65, Internet version, http://cryptome.org/bioweap.htm, printed 05/21/03. *ABC PrimeTime Live*, "Bacterial Weapons Warning," http://abcnews.go.com/sections/us/DailyNews/ptl0225.html, printed 05/21/03; the story states that US officials believe that Alibekov, "who provided this information, is credible about the structure of the Soviet biological weapons program from 1975 to 1991." Monterey Institute for International Studies, "CNS Occasional Papers: Former Soviet Biological Weapons Facilities in Kazakhstan: Past, Present, Future," http://cns.miis.edu/pubs/opapers/op1/op1.htm, printed 05/21/03. Al J. Venter, Jane's Information Group, "The invisible threat: what does Russia have up its biological warfare sleeve," *Jane's International Defense Review*, September 1998, http://www.janes.com/geopol/onlneproducts/chembio/features/features-idr_9-98.html; printed in 1998; no longer on the Net. Richard Preston, "The Demon in the Freezer," *The New Yorker*, July 12, 1999, pp 44–61. Reuters, "Soviet Smallpox Outbreak Report Worries Experts," June 15, 2002, http://www.vaccination-news.com/DailyNews/June2002/SovietSmallpoxEpidemic17.htm, printed 05/21/03.

5. Leebaert, *Fifty-year Wound*, p 600.

6. Ibid., pp 456, 603.

7. Ibid., pp 456, 603.

who meet him not as a has-been statesman relegated to the pages of history books, but rather as a man with a still-unfulfilled destiny."[1]

What could Gorbachev's "still-unfulfilled destiny" be? As Gorbachev told the *San Francisco Chronicle* in 1995, "I do believe that we need to move toward a new world order. . . . Actually, I've never left politics. I've continued to be active politically, but I think it's quite possible that my role might change. Let's live and see, let's wait and see."[2]

Gorbachev is making his intentions clear, with repeated pronouncements on behalf of building what he calls "a new world order." In 2001, Gorbachev said in response to the 9/11 attack, "It is now the responsibility of the world community to transform the coalition against terror into a coalition for a new, peaceful and just world order."[3]

In early 2002, in an interview with *Crisis*, a Republican Party-oriented Catholic magazine in the US, Gorbachev criticized President Clinton for failing to cooperate in building the new world order: "My relationship with President Clinton was quite strained, if not downright tense. Of course, it was not because of Monica Lewinsky. I was highly critical of his foreign policy. *He* is guilty for the fact that the U.S. has wasted those ten years following the end of the Cold War."[4] The interviewer, Deal Hudson, asked "What should he have done?," and Gorbachev replied, "I think he missed out on opportunities to develop a new world order."[5]

By contrast with Clinton, George H. W. Bush, "Bush the Elder," admired Gorbachev. He attested to this by giving Gorbachev the "George Bush Award for Excellence in Public Service" in 2001.[6]

"Bush I" shared Gorbachev's desire to build a new world order. On January 16, 1991, during the speech announcing the start of Gulf War I, Bush said, "We have before us the opportunity to forge for ourselves and for future generations a new world order, a world where the rule of law, not the law of the jungle, governs the conduct of nations. When we are successful, and we will be, we have a real chance at this new world order, an order in which a credible United Nations can use its peace-keeping role to fulfil the promise and vision of the U.N.'s founders."[7] He said the same in his State of the Union address of January 29, 1991:

> What is at stake is more than one small country, it is a big idea—a new world order, where diverse nations are drawn together in common cause to achieve the universal aspirations of mankind: peace and security, freedom,

1. Green Cross International, press release, "Global Viewpoint _ Mikhail Gorbachev," "dist. 5/5/97," http://web243.petrel. ch/GreenCrossFamily/gorby/newspeeches/pressrelease/pressrelease7.5.97.html, printed 05/13/03.

2. Stewart, "Mikhail Gorbachev," 09/24/95.

3. Mikhail Gorbachev, "The Peacemakers Speak," 10/19/01, http://www.thecommunity.com/crisis/gorbachev.html, printed 11/04/01.

4. Deal W. Hudson, "CRISIS Interview with Mikhail Gorbachev," *Crisis* Magazine, February 1, 2002, http://www.crisis-magazine.com/february2002/feature1.htm, printed 06/29/04; also, *Crisis* Magazine, February 2002, p 22.

5. Ibid.

6. George Bush Presidential Library Foundation, "The George Bush Award for Excellence in Public Service," http://www. georgebushfoundation.org/bush/asp/GeorgeBushAward/AwardRecipients.asp, printed 08/03/04. Bush praised Gorbachev thus: "for his extraordinary leadership in guiding the people of the former Soviet Union onto a path of economic and political reform. He was a partner in the peaceful termination of the Cold War, confirmed by his strong opposition to Iraq's aggression against Kuwait. His stewardship broke barriers that separated Europe, brought a new era of cooperation, and laid the foundation for peaceful change and economic prosperity in Europe. His commitment to arms control was s key ingredient in helping to build a more secure and stable world. His legacy will be shared by all future generations and his dedication to international peace and cooperation will serve as an inspiration to us all." (The George Bush Award for Excellence in Public Service, "Award Citation," 2001, http://www.georgebushfoundation.org/bush/html/GeorgeBushAward/BioMikhailGorbach ev.htm, printed 08/03/04.)

7. George H. W. Bush, speech announcing the Coalition attack on Iraq, January 16, 1991, http://www.famousquotes.me. uk/speeches/George_Bush/, printed 08/03/04. This is from a British archive of notable political speeches, from Queen Elizabeth I onward.

and the rule of law. Such is a world worthy of our struggle, and worthy of our children's future. . . . We will suc-ceed in the Gulf. And when we do, the world community will have sent an enduring warning to any dictator or despot, present or future, who contemplates outlaw aggression. The world can therefore seize this opportunity to fulfill the long-held promise of a new world order—where brutality will go unrewarded, and aggression will meet collective resistance.[1]

In 1992, Bush linked his quest for a New World Order to the European Union:

Half a millennium ago, Portugal and Spain helped chart a course towards a new world. Five hundred years later, European unity guides the way towards a new world order. Those early pioneers believed their mission was to probe the secrets of the world. Now we must explore the frontiers of common interest and common ground. . . . For almost 50 years, the West carried freedom's torch to protect the free world. Today, we stand at the shores of a new world order where diverse nations are drawn together in common cause to achieve the universal aspira-tions of mankind: peace and security, freedom and prosperity. A strong and united Europe offers the best hope for this united purpose and the best alliance for the United States.[2]

In mid-2002, Gorbachev told a business convention in the UK that "I intend to continue to contrib-ute to building that new world order."[3]

In October 2004, Gorbachev called for

a new world order that will be based on strong adherence to international law. . . . Gorbachev said the new world order he is advancing should adhere to international law, rely heavily on the United Nations and not seek to impose the views of one country or a group of countries on others. He said the new order should be more stable, more just and more humane. It will not deny the cultural and ethnic diversity in the world, and it will not ignore environmental challenges. 'World order does not mean world government,' he said, nor 'can you build a new world order on the basis of preemptive strikes'. . . . Any attempt at building the new world order will not succeed 'if we ignore poverty in the world,' Gorbachev said.[4]

When the former Soviet premier publicly and repeatedly calls for creation of a "new world order," it would be wise to assume that he means what says, and that he will do what he can to bring it about.

1. The American Presidency Project, George Bush—"Address Before a Joint Session of the Congress on the State of the Union," January 29, 1991, http://www.presidency.ucsb.edu/site/docs/doc_sou.php?admin=41&doc=3, printed 08/03/04.

2. George H. W. Bush, "Remarks at the Departure Ceremony for European Community Leaders Anibal Cavaco Silva and Jacques Delors," April 22, 1992, http://bushlibrary.tamu.edu/research/papers/1992/92042201.html, printed 08/03/04.

3. Nick Hallissey, "Gorbachev plea to Yorkshire business," *ThisIsYork.co.uk*, June 1, 2002, http://www.thisisyork.co.uk/york /archive/2002/06/01/york_news_local21ZM.html, printed 05/21/03. A similar report appeared in a June 1, 2002 story reprinted by *Newsday.com*: "'Unfortunately,' he said, 'we wasted a lot of time after the end of the Cold War. Today we have to build a new world order step by step.'" (Associated Press, "Gorbachev: Don't Americanize Cultures," *Newsday.com*, June 2, 2002; no longer on the Net in its original form.)

4. U.S. Newswire, "Gorbachev Calls for New World Order, Expresses Concern about Revival of Nuclear Arms Race," October 5, 2004, http://releases.usnewswire.com/GetRelease.asp?id=37523, printed 10/23/04.

19

THE STATE OF
THE WORLD FORUM

The State of the World Forum's luxurious meetings, held since 1995, were intended by Mikhail Gorbachev to establish "a kind of global brain trust to focus on the present and future of our civilization."[1] State of the World Forum (SWF) gatherings continue to attract an eclectic assortment of rich people, politicians, celebrities, social change activists, and spiritual "gurus."

AIMS: "RE-INVENTING THE WORLD" AND "GLOBAL GOVERNANCE"

Like Gorbachev, the SWF has a grandiose, worldwide mission. It "has sought over the years to contribute to the creation of a new approach required for the effective management of the global system" and intends "to establish a global leadership network across a multiplicity of disciplines and from around the world dedicated to working toward a sustainable civilization."[2] In 1997, Garrison said that the Forum's "mission is that of establishing a global network of leaders and change agents from across a spectrum of disciplines" who will be "given equal standing in deliberations which affect us all."[3] He also proposed to "create a new understanding of unity and diversity which must be so affirmative that it suggests a way to re-invent the world."[4] In 2003, the Forum's Commission on Globalisation stated that "As the 21st century unfolds, an ever more integrated global system demands an ever more inclusive and holistic approach to global governance."[5]

The SWF world-view is standard-issue 20th-Century collectivism, the belief that the ills afflicting humanity are "problems" that can be solved if the right people lead in setting goals and "exercising will." A statement issued by the SWF after its 1997 meeting, said:

This effort is being developed in the conviction that the process of globalization is in essence the challenge to envision and create the first global civilization; that the problems of the world are for the first time in history essentially manageable, given the scientific, political and social tools at our disposal; and that humanity, already cooperating in so many areas, stands potentially ready to envision and implement a common vision of the

1. State of the World Forum, "The World's Religions and The Emerging Global Civilization: An Interfaith Summit Conference June 24–28, 1996 San Francisco," *Pacific Church News*, April/May 1996, p33. A note at the end of the article says, "All quotes are from material distributed by the State of the World Forum."

2. State of the World Forum, "About Us," http://www.worldforum.org/about/main.htm, printed 05/20/03.

3. State of the World Forum, "Letter from the President," *Quarterly*, July-September 1997, Vol. 2, no. 3, p2.

4. State of the World Forum, *Toward a New Civilization*, May 1997, "The State of the World Forum Mission Statement," p7 (cited below as SWF, *Toward a New Civilization*, 05/97).

5. State of the World Forum—Commission on Globalisation, "Commission Overview: Strategic Context—The Challenge of Globalisation," http://www.commissiononglobalization.org/overview/main.htm, printed 05/23/03.

future. The question is not whether we can accomplish these things. We know we can. The question is that of setting priorities, reaching consensus, mobilizing resources and exercising will.[1]

Ted Turner, one of the co-chairs of the State of the World Forum,[2] told *E Magazine*: "You've got to be hopeful because I think that we're smarter than the opposition, because we are thinking long term. We're better educated and I put my money on the smart minority rather than the dumb majority. Wouldn't you?"[3] At a Time Warner Global Forum in Shanghai, China in September 1999, Turner had described himself as "a socialist at heart."[4] (As of the fall of 2004, Forbes estimated his net worth at $1.9 billion.)[5]

OUT WITH TRADITIONAL RELIGIONS; IN WITH THE NEW AGE

State of the World Forum speakers and supporters have repeatedly ridiculed traditional religions, particularly orthodox Christianity. This is consistent with the SWF's unyielding certainty that "at this unique transitional moment in history, questions are more important than answers, dialogue more constructive than dogma."[6]

Dr. Jim Garrison, President of the SWF and self-described follower of "inclusive Buddhism," said in 1998 that "the days of dogmatic religion are on the wane," adding: "I think that Judaism and Christianity and Islam have done real damage to the planet because they have too many answers."[7] Garrison attacked the Pope for "excluding women from the priesthood and talking about contraception as an evil;" he also condemned the Hasidic Jews for "killing people on the West Bank. And now they're arguing if you're a Jew but don't have a Jewish mother you're not a Jew."[8] Garrison concluded that "that the problems caused by subscribing to narrow dogma are shared by all the world's six major religions."[9] He said,

If my theology is an impediment I have to get rid of my theology. . . . I think the world needs to live in a spirit of inquiry and its [sic] out of inquiry that we learn tolerance. It's out of answers that we get dogmatic and we get violent and destructive with each other. I think history is moving beyond dogma. The conservative Jews and the

1. State of the World Forum, "1997 State of the World Forum," http://worldforum.percepticon.com/initiatives/our_comm on_enterprise_a.html, printed 06/16/04.

2. State of the World Forum, "Co-Chairs," http://www.worldforum.org/about/cochairs.htm, printed 06/02/04 (cited below as SWF, "Co-Chairs").

3. Tracey C. Rembert, "Ted Turner: Billionaire, Media Mogul... And Environmentalist" (Interview), *E Magazine*, January/February 1999, Volume X, number 1, p12 (cited below as Rembert, "Ted Turner: Billionaire... And Environmentalist," *E Magazine*).

4. Drudge Report, "Ted Turner: I Am A Socialist At Heart," September 29, 1999, http://www.drudgereport.com/matt2.html, printed in 1999; no longer on the Net.

5. *Forbes Magazine*, "The Forbes 400," "Spotlights," listing for Ted Turner, October 11, 2004, p130.

6. State of the World Forum, "Philosophy," http://www.worldforum.org/about/philosophy.htm, printed 05/20/03.

7. State of the World Forum, "A New Spirituality" article about Dr. Jim Garrison's October 27, 1998 presentation to the State of the World Forum; http://worldforum98.percepticon.com/spirit/article_spirit_.html, printed 05/22/03 (cited below as SWF, Garrison on "New Spirituality").

8. Ibid. Charles Upton notes that Garrison appears to be ignorant of the views of many Hasidic Jews about the state of Israel. Upton says, "This blanket condemnation of the Hasidic Jews ignores the large number of Orthodox Hasids who are and always have been anti-Zionist, considering a secular Jewish state to be a blasphemous usurpation of the function of the Messiah, who alone can lead the Jews back to their homeland. Hasidic rabbis with large followings, in the New York area and elsewhere, have in recent years actually made common cause with the Palestinians against Israel." (E-mail from Charles Upton to Lee Penn, 04/27/04).

9. SWF, Garrison on "New Spirituality."

conservative Christians and the conservative Imams they think what I'm saying is heresy, but I just say to these people, your box is too small, get into a bigger box.[1]

Garrison ended by saying that the SWF "is about honoring the mavericks and the heretics."[2] He added, "During times of transition orthodoxies fall and the heretics and the mavericks are the people creating the new orthodoxy."[3] Welcome to the New Religious Order, in which the only heresy will be orthodoxy.

Likewise, Ted Turner said in 1999, "Christianity is an eco-unfriendly religion."[4]

At the annual Forum meeting in 2000, Rabbi Zalman Schachter-Shalomi told the attendees that "All traditional systems—Moses, Jesus, Mohammed, Buddha—were embedded in the social and economic systems in which they arose. Their reality maps are a little obsolete."[5] He added that humanity needs a "messianic jump," a collective realization that we are "members of a larger body. The spirit of the Living God, the Shekinah, is waiting for us to grow up. There is the possibility of living heavenly days here on earth."[6] At the start of each day's events, there were blessings; these benedictions were provided by the founder of the Worldwide Indigenous Science Network, a rabbi who leads the Center for Engaged Spirituality at Naropa University, the head of the Sadhu Vaswani Mission (a Hindu organization), the head of the Sri Ramakrishna Spiritual Family, Deepak Chopra, Jonathan Granoff (an interfaith activist who is a follower of the "Sufi Master Bawa Muhaiyadeen," and the president of the Academy for Future Science.[7] Traditional Christianity and Judaism were conspicuous by their absence.

As an alternative to the traditional religions, the Forum has promoted New Age beliefs from its beginning. In 1995, the *San Francisco Chronicle* reported that at the first Forum, "Leaders of mainline Western religions or philosophies are mostly absent from the speakers' lineup, while unorthodox describes many on the list. These include forum speakers such as Willis Harman, president of the Institute of Noetic Sciences. As a Stanford University electrical engineering professor in the 1960s, he conducted experiments on the effects of psychedelic drugs on human creativity."[8]

Since then, Forum speakers have remained true to form, with New Age speakers outnumbering by far those who uphold traditional Christianity or Judaism. Speakers and participants at Forum events, virtually all of whom are New Age or "progressive," have included Caroline Myss,[9] Andrew Weil,[10] Deepak Chopra,[11] Marianne Williamson,[12] Jean Houston (one of Hillary Clinton's spiritual

1. Ibid.

2. Ibid.

3. Ibid.

4. Rembert, "Ted Turner: Billionaire… And Environmentalist," *E Magazine*, p 10.

5. Marc Ian Barasch, "Two for the Road: Religion's Path Ahead," Forum 2000, http://www.simulconference.com/clients/sowf/dispatches/dispatch23.html, printed 05/21/03.

6. Ibid.

7. State of the World Forum, *Forum 2000: 2000 and Beyond*, http://www.worldforum.org/conferences/swfandbeyond.pdf, pp 6–18, printed 06/27/04 (cited below as SWF, *Forum 2000: 2000 and Beyond*).

8. Edward Epstein, "Gorbachev Foundation's S. F. Meeting: Celebrities, scholars to discuss world's future," *San Francisco Chronicle*, September 25, 1995, p A-15, downloaded from http://www.sfgate.com on 05/23/03.

9. State of the World Forum, "Board of Directors," http://www.worldforum.org/about/bod.htm, printed 05/20/03 (cited below as SWF, "Board of Directors").

10. State of the World Forum, *Registry of Accomplishments: 1995–2000*, p 7 (cited below as SWF, *Registry of Accomplishments*).

11. Ibid., p 7.

12. Ibid., p 7. For more information on Marianne Williamson, see Tony Carnes, "Leaving Marianne Williamson & A Course in Miracles: An Insider Converts," *Journal* of the Spiritual Counterfeits Project, vol. 22:2–22:3, 1998, pp 18–33; see also Ron Rhodes, "America's Glitzy Guru—Marianne Williamson," *Journal* of the Spiritual Counterfeits Project, vol. 21:4–22:1, 1998, pp 22–31; available through http://www.scp-inc.org.

advisers),[1] Margot Anand,[2] Fritjof Capra,[3] Jesse Jackson,[4] Carl Sagan,[5] John Naisbitt,[6] Maurice Strong and Steven Rockefeller (Earth Charter movement leaders),[7] Riane Eisler (author of *Sacred Pleasures*),[8] the executive director of the World Federalist Movement,[9] Rupert Sheldrake,[10] Bella Abzug and Betty Friedan,[11] Maya Angelou,[12] Ervin Laszlo,[13] Brian Swimme,[14] Duane Elgin,[15] Barbara Marx Hubbard,[16] Stanislov Grof (a "transpersonal psychologist"),[17] Michael Lerner,[18] Faye Wattleton,[19] Sam Keen,[20] Barbara Streisand,[21] Michael Harner (president of the Foundation for Shamanic Studies),[22] Gerald Jampolsky,[23] Robert Jesse (president of the Council on Spiritual Practices, an organization that promotes use of "entheogens"—psychoactive plants and chemicals—for spiritual growth),[24] Frances Kissling (leader of "Catholics for a Free Choice," a pro-abortion lobby),[25] Patricia Mische,[26] Nick Bunick (described by the Forum as a "spiritual leader;" Bunick claims that he was the Apostle Paul in a past life),[27] Hal Puthoff (an

1. SWF, *Registry of Accomplishments: 1995–2000*, p7; for more information on Jean Houston, see Craig Branch, "Jean Houston: Profile of the New-Age Advisor to Hillary Clinton," *Journal* of the Spiritual Counterfeits Project, vol. 2:2–22:3, 1998, pp64–69; available through http://www.scp-inc.org. According to Robert Muller, Jean Houston remains close to the Clintons. He says that to ensure that a letter from him to Vice President Gore (written after the 2000 election) was received, "I sent it to Jean Houston who is very close to the Clintons suggesting that the proposal in the letter could also interest President Clinton. I was lucky: Jean Houston handed it personally to President Clinton." (Robert Muller, *Ideas And Dreams for a Better World*: 3501–4000, *Volume IX*, Idea 3607, http://www.robertmuller.org/volume/ideas3501.html, viewed 06/21/04).

2. SWF, *Registry of Accomplishments*, p7.

3. Ibid., p8.

4. Ibid., p8.

5. Ibid., p9.

6. Ibid., p10.

7. State of the World Forum, "Selected List of Forum 2000 Speakers," *Shaping Globalization: Convening the Community of Stakeholders: Schedule of Events, September 4–10, 2000*, p14.

8. State of the World Forum, "Forum 2000 Speakers and Participants," http://www.worldforum.org/forum2000/speakers.html, printed 02/04/01; no longer on the Net at this address (cited below as SWF, "Forum 2000 Speakers and Participants").

9. Ibid.

10. State of the World Forum, *The 5th Annual State of the World Forum, October 1–6, 1999*, p17 (cited below as SWF, *5th Annual State of the World Forum*, 10/99).

11. Ibid., p25.

12. State of the World Forum, "Forum Program Schedule 1997," *Quarterly*, July-September 1997, vol. 2, no. 3, p4 (cited below as SWF, "Forum Program Schedule 1997").

13. Ibid., p5.

14. Ibid., p5.

15. Ibid., p5.

16. Ibid., p5.

17. Ibid., p5.

18. Ibid., p7.

19. Ibid., p8.

20. Ibid., p8.

21. Ibid., p9.

22. 1997 State of the World Forum, "Participants," http://www.worldforum.org/1997forum/1997_Participants.html, printed in 1997; no longer on the Net (cited below as SWF, 1997 participants).

23. Ibid.

24. Ibid. On the agenda of the Council on Spiritual Practices, see Council on Spiritual Practices, "About CSP," http://www.csp.org/about.html, printed 06/10/03.

25. SWF, 1997 participants.

26. Ibid.

27. 1998 State of the World Forum, "People," http://www.worldforum98.org/people/letter_B.html; printed in 1998; no longer on the Net; a listing for Nick Bunick. Bunick's home page (http://www.fourfourfour.com/tgt/, printed 05/22/03) stated that he was invited to "give a three hour talk" to the Forum in the fall of 1998.) Bunick's home page claims that Bunick's story "began two thousand years ago when he lived as Paul the Apostle, and walked alongside Jesus." http://www.thegreattomorrow.org/book.html; printed 05/22/03).

ESP researcher),[1] Michael Murphy[2] and Steven Donovan (leaders of the Esalen Institute),[3] leaders of the Institute of Noetic Sciences,[4] Charlene Spretnak (of the Green Party),[5] Lynn Twist (of the Hunger Project),[6] Lester Brown (of the WorldWatch Institute),[7] Ram Dass,[8] Matthew Fox,[9] Huston Smith,[10] and Tony Robbins.[11] Forum President James Garrison worked for ten years at the Esalen Institute in Big Sur, California, including service from 1986 to 1990 as executive director of the Esalen Institute's Soviet-American exchange program.[12]

These adepts are enthusiastic about the Forum's activities. Fritjof Capra says, "The Forum's collective intellectual power and moral authority are awe-inspiring."[13] Marianne Williamson, proponent of *A Course in Miracles*[14] and author of *A Woman's Worth*, says, "The Forum is, for me, a very energizing experience—a kind of Central Headquarters for the Consciousness Revolution." [15] Marga Buhrig, former president of the World Council of Churches, said, "the Forum has a search for and a presence of spirituality, a hidden trend in a world full of contradiction. My own visions were deepened, widened, and confirmed."[16]

Marc Luyckx, member of the European Commission's "Forward Studies Initiative," says, "When I fly back to Europe, I feel enriched by the intellectual and spiritual energy of so many women and men who are silently creating a new culture and a new world."[17] In a May 1998 paper titled "Religion and Governance," Luyckx and co-author Harlan Cleveland quoted approvingly from Bishop Swing's book, *The Coming United Religions*;[18] they appear to have seen the URI as part of "a new culture and a new world."

1. SWF, 1997 participants.

2. SWF, "Forum Program Schedule 1997," p 8.

3. SWF, 1997 participants. Donovan was on the Forum's Board of Directors in the late 1990s; see SWF, *Toward a New Civilization*, May 1997, "Board of Directors," p 4.

4. SWF, 1997 participants. The Institute's participants in the Forum were Alise Agar, chief of operations; Winston Franklin, CEO; Thomas Hurley, director of education; Elise Miller, director of development; and Marisha Zeffer, development associate.

5. Ibid.

6. Ibid. Twist was on the Forum's Board of Directors in the late 1990s; see SWF, *Toward a New Civilization*, 05/97, "Board of Directors," p 4.

7. SWF, *Toward a New Civilization*, 05/97, "International Coordinating Council," p 5.

8. Ibid., "1996 Participant List," p 30.

9. Ibid., "1995 Participant List," p 22.

10. Ibid., "1995 Participant List," p 25.

11. Ibid., "1995 Participant List," p 25. For further information on Tony Robbins, see Ron Rhodes, "Anthony Robbins and the Quest for Unlimited Power," *Journal* of the Spiritual Counterfeits Project, vol. 22:2–22:3, 1998, pp 48–63; obtainable through http://www.scp-inc.org.

12. Marshall Kilduff, "Middle Man for a Meeting of the Minds," *San Francisco Chronicle*, Sunday, November 2, 1997, page 3/Z1; also SWF, "Board of Directors."

13. SWF, *Registry of Accomplishments*, p 8.

14. For additional information on Marianne Williamson, see Tony Carnes, "Leaving Marianne Williamson & A Course in Miracles, *Journal* of the Spiritual Counterfeits Project, vol. 22:2–22:3, 1998, pp 18–33.

15. SWF, *Registry of Accomplishments*, p 7.

16. Ibid., p 13.

17. State of the World Forum, "Testimonials," http://www.worldforum.org/history/testimon.html, printed 06/28/04.

18. World Network of Religious Futurists, "Religion and Governance," http://www.wnrf.org/cms/govern.shtml, printed 06/28/04.

"PROGRESSIVE" GLOBAL GOVERNANCE

The Forum has favored leftist solutions to political and economic problems, despite the appearance of conservatives such as George H. W. Bush,[1] Margaret Thatcher,[2] James Baker, and George Shultz[3] at these gatherings.

At the 2000 Forum, billionaire George Soros criticized Republicans and free markets, and called for international organizations, similar to the World Trade Organization, that can set binding rules for labor relations and environmental protection.[4] Gorbachev called for new structures to govern the world economy: "Globalization has been privatized. . . . Existing institutions are under the influence of certain powerful interests. We must begin thinking of some kind of government adequate to this changed global world. We need to develop mechanisms of interaction between nation-states and civil society against the maximizing of profits that downgrade the values of the human being."[5] A Forum reporter said, "George Soros suggested that a trans-national body, yet-to-be formed in shape or detail but perhaps the equal of the WTO, must be established to constrain the more destructive impacts of globalization. . . . [Soros added]: 'The environment and other common interests receive short shrift. The best way to strengthen protection of the common interest is through international structures of law.' Gorbachev responded with a call for a blueprint for such a body."[6]

Most speakers at Forum events have agreed that "global governance" and new UN agencies to manage the world economy are needed. The Forum has taken the deliberations of the UN and its conferences as a "global consensus around issues confronting the entire human community. They are thus a foundation from which all of us can begin to view the world and the future in a more integrated and holistic way."[7] The Forum also claimed that there was "a tremendous level of support for, and engagement with, Forum 2000 from many quarters of the United Nations."[8]

At the 1996 Forum, the session on "Educational Models for the 21st Century" stated that the objective of their efforts was "to create and sustain a life-long learning system, one that is globally-oriented, culturally adaptable and holistic. . . . The ultimate result would be the creation of a system built upon a 'new global citizen.'"[9]

In 1997, Forum speakers proposed creating a new "integral culture," saying that "The shift to integral culture must and will take place at all levels of interaction. All roles and relationships will be redefined: inner spiritual values, intimate family relationships (between men and women, and among adults, children, and elders); communities; nations, ethnic groups, and cultures; global institutions...

1. SWF, 5th *Annual State of the World Forum*, 10/99, p7.

2. State of the World Forum, "Global Broadcasts," http://www.worldforum.org/conferences/docs.htm, printed 05/21/03.

3. SWF, "Co-Chairs." Baker, US Secretary of State from 1989 to 1992, is one of the current co-chairs, and the document lists Schultz—and Maurice Strong—as among the original co-chairs in 1995.

4. George Soros, speech to the State of the World Forum 2000, September 5, 2000, http://www.soros.org/textfiles/speech es/090500_World_Forum.txt, printed 05/20/03.

5. Mark Schapiro, State of the World Forum, "A Citizens' U. N.?," September 2000, http://www.simulconference.com/clients/owf/dispatches/dispatch9.html, printed 05/24/03.

6. Ibid.

7. State of the World Forum, "Upcoming Events: United Nations 2000," http://www.worldforum.org/sections/upcoming/un2000.html, printed in 2000; no longer on the Net.

8. State of the World Forum, "Forum 2000: Relations with the United Nations," http://www.worldforum.org/forum2000/role_un.html, printed in 2000; no longer on the Net.

9. State of the World Forum, "1996 State of the World Forum: Educational Models for the 21st Century—Final Report," http://www.worldforum.org/1996forum/round_education.html, printed in 1998. No longer on the Net at this address. As of 2004, a copy of this page is at http://web.archive.org/web/19990203213230/http://worldforum.org/1996forum/round_educati on.html.

and the relationship of humans with the natural world and the larger living system."[1] (Not even the Soviets went so far.)

In 2004, Garrison proposed a similarly all-encompassing view of the change that we must make, a "leap of faith into a new age":

> Old beliefs and practices must be surrendered and new ways of living and relating embraced, but this requires a strength of spirit and fortitude of mind uncommon in ordinary times. Leadership during periods of historical turbulence and change is supremely challenging. It must enable the people to abandon what they hold as secure, but which is actually insufficient, and embrace what seems insecure but is potentially sufficient. This can only be done through a vision of the future that instills hope in human possibility. It can only be accomplished with an illumination of light so intense that people surrender their fear of the darkness and are emboldened to take a leap of faith into a new age.[2]

The last century saw tens of millions of people killed in order that "all roles and relationships" would "be redefined." In his historical study of genocide and mass killing, political scientist Benjamin Valentino found that

> Communist regimes probably have been responsible for the most violent mass killings in human history. Radical communist regimes have been so closely associated with mass killing because the changes they have sought to bring about in their societies have resulted in the nearly complete material dispossession of vast populations. Communist policies such as agricultural collectivization have stripped tens of millions of people of their homes and property and have obliterated traditional ways of life. In practice, few people have been willing to submit to such severe changes in the absence of violence and coercion. Communist leaders did not set out with the desire to exterminate millions of people, but they did not shy away from mass murder when they believed it was necessary to achieve their goals.[3]

This was the result of a "creative minority" urging mankind to "take a leap of faith into a new age." The present-day proponents of spiritual collectivism and an "integral culture" offer no reason why their planned experiment on mankind will work any better than previous efforts have done.

Participants in the 1997 Forum "Toward an Integral Global Paradigm" panel proposed a new, relativist definition of truth: "Meaning and information, grounded in specific contexts, become more significant than objective truths grounded in a view of absolute reality.... Truth becomes a way of knowing in which we learn to honor our woundedness and our dependency on others."[4]

All must accept the new, holistic world-view; the 1998 Forum session on "Our Common Enterprise" said,

> What is now needed is a Declaration of Integration: the articulation of a framework in which the different aspects of our lives—the individual and the communal, the scientific and the spiritual, the inner and the outer—can again cohere in a way that allows for a new sense of community to emerge. Only within the context of new community, and a new sense of integrated wholeness can the problems confronting us be solved. The future thus

1. State of the World Forum, "1997 State of the World Forum: 'Cosmology, Culture, and Social Change—Final Report,'" http://www.worldforum.org/1997forum/CosmologyandCulture.html, printed in 1998; no longer on the Net at this address. As of 2004, a copy of this page is at http://web.archive.org/web/19981206171003/http://www.worldforum.org/1997forum/CosmologyandCulture.html.

2. Jim Garrison, *America As Empire: Global Leader or Rogue Power?*, Berrett-Koehler Publishers, 2004, p 167 (cited below as Garrison, *America As Empire*).

3. Benjamin A. Valentino, *Final Solutions: Mass Killing and Genocide in the Twentieth Century*, Cornell Univ. Press, 2004, p 4.

4. State of the World Forum, "1997 State of the World Forum: 'Toward an Integral Global Paradigm: Honoring Multiple Ways of Knowing," http://www.worldforum.org/1997forum/IntegralGlobalParadigm.html, printed 1998. No longer on Net.

belongs to those who can see interconnections, who can appreciate the whole as well as the parts, and who can blend one aspect of life with another. To be authentic in the future will be to be integrated.[1]

And what, pray tell, will be the fate of the "inauthentic"?

At the year 2000 Forum, the utopian delusion remained intact. Forum planners forecast the emergence of a new "cultural matrix" and "global governance":

Humanity is poised to make extraordinary progress toward creating a world that works for an increasing number of people. Indeed, in and through all the vicissitudes of contemporary history, a new cultural matrix is arising based on the integration of all the dimensions of human life and a new sense of personal and civic responsibility. This mandates new thinking concerning global governance and the creation of new mechanisms and institutions whereby governments, the corporate sector, and civil society can interact creatively to solve common problems.[2]

IMPLEMENTING THE "POPULATION PLAN"

Robert Muller says of the Forum agenda,

since 1980 we have entered a third period—from now on the Earth is number one, and humanity is number two. Humanity is number two because we wish humans to decline on this planet. . . . I have just attended the Gorbachev meeting on the State of the World in San Francisco, and I have gained a lot of hope. They had the courage to get some of the best world experts to look into the state of the world and into the future, to create a vision of the society we want in the next millennium . . . and then do it. They want to implement the population plan, support simple and frugal lives, and get multinational corporations to acquire global consciousness. This gives me hope.[3]

Muller praised Gorbachev as "the prophet of a united human family, and the global architect who will give the world his vision, plan and proposals how the Earth and humanity can become the ultimate cosmic success of the universe and of God."[4]

The 1995 meeting of the State of the World Forum called on humanity to "create an ecumenical, ecological theology centered in a renewed sense of reverence for the environment that might provide a common denominator and rallying point for cooperation between the major world religions. There was strong agreement that religious institutions must wrestle with questions of sexuality, contraception, abortion, and family planning and take much greater responsibility for addressing the problem of controlling population growth."[5] In its report on the 2000 annual meeting, the Forum highlighted this dictum from actor Christopher Reeve: "Tolerance and diversity, acceptance, sharing, making the world a more equal place, these are very noble ideals. Yet we face a problem that if we don't solve it will make it very difficult to achieve. And that is simply the overpopulation of the world."[6]

1. State of the World Forum, "Our Common Enterprise II: The Possibility," http://worldforum.percepticon.com/initiatives/our_common_enterprise_b.html, printed 06/16/04.

2. State of the World Forum, "Forum 2000—Summary," http://www.worldforum.org/forum2000/summary.html, printed in 2000; no longer on the Net. A copy of this page is at http://www.21learn.org/acti/forum2000.html, printed 10/28/04.

3. Robert Muller, *Ideas And Dreams For A Better World: 1001–1500, Volume III*, "Ideas 1455 to 1466, 5 to 16 July 1998" reprint of a talk given by Muller at Findhorn in October 1995, http://www.robertmuller.org/volume/ideas1001.html, viewed 06/21/04.

4. Ibid., Idea 1081, 26 June 1997.

5. Sam Keen, Convener, "The Global Crisis of Spirit and the Search for Meaning," September 30, 1995, http://www.well.com/user/wforum/transcripts/themes/2spirit1.html; printed 03/28/98; no longer on the Net (cited below as Sam Keen, "The Global Crisis of Spirit," 09/30/95).

6. SWF, *Forum 2000: 2000 and Beyond*, p 18.

Gorbachev, the former premier of the USSR, got specific about "addressing the problem of controlling population growth"[1] in 1997. He said that "We will need a quick stabilization of global population and to do so we need to persuade the people through cultural and educational programs that for a certain transitional period families should limit themselves to one child and then following stabilization of global population to two children."[2] This would, in effect, be a global version of China's current one-child policy.

Ted Turner, one of the co-chairs of the State of the World Forum,[3] has proposed to go further, reducing world population from the current 6 billion to 2 billion. In an interview with *E Magazine*, an environmentalist publication, Turner explained:

The simplest answer is that the world's population should be about two billion, and we've got about six billion right now. I haven't done the actuarial tables, but if every woman in the world voluntarily stepped up and said, 'I'll only have one child,' and if we did that for the next 80 to 100 years, that would reduce the kind of suffering we're having. . . . We could have 10 billion people living below the poverty line, or we could have two billion people living well, and having color TVs and an automobile. The planet can support that number of people, and that's the way it was in 1930. You didn't have the global warming problem then, or all these problems that have occurred since the population has built up. And how you get there is very complicated. It's going to take a lot of education and improvements in health care. Personally, I think the population should be closer to when we had indigenous populations, back before the advent of farming. Fifteen thousand years ago, there was somewhere between 40 and 100 million people. But [population researchers] Paul and Anne Ehrlich have convinced me that if we're going to have a modern infrastructure, with commercial airlines and interstate highways around the world, we're going to need about two billion people to support it.[4]

Turner did not specify how this population plan would be enforced.

THE LIGHTER SIDE OF THE FORUM: NUDE MARCHES, TANTRIC SEX, AND ENTHEOGENS

The Forum has its lighter side, as well.

At a Forum discussion on nuclear disarmament in October 1999, Patch Adams told the gathering of 40 activists that "the only way to call attention to the Y2K danger of Russian nuclear warheads was for everybody to take off their clothes and march down Van Ness. The next thing you know, clothes were dropping—and forum folks were following Pied Piper Adams down the block, chanting anti-nuke slogans" (such as "Disrobe for disarmament")[5] while marching nude down a major street in downtown San Francisco.[6]

In 1998 and 1999, the Tantric sex teacher Margot Anand spread her message to Forum participants, including the usual swipe at Christianity. According to an account prepared by Forum staff in 1998,

1. Sam Keen, "The Global Crisis of Spirit," 09/30/95.

2. Mikhail Gorbachev, Green Cross International, "Finding Our Way Five Years After the Rio Earth Summit: 'A Vision for Environmental Sustainability," April 15, 1997, address to George Washington University, http://www.gci.ch/GreenCrossFamily/gorby/newspeeches/speeches/Georges%20WashUNI.5.97.html, printed 05/09/03.

3. SWF, "Co-Chairs."

4. Rembert, "Ted Turner: Billionaire… And Environmentalist," *E Magazine*, pp 10–11.

5. Ray Delgado, "Activists reveal naked truth about nuclear dangers," *San Francisco Examiner*, October 4, 1999, printed 5/21/03 from http://www.sfgate.com.

6. Philip Matier, Andrew Ross, "A's Deal With Pepsi Means Team May Stick in Oakland," *San Francisco Chronicle*, October 6, 1999; Internet version, downloaded 10/12/02 from http://www.sfgate.com.

Ms. Anand is a 'love and ecstasy trainer' and has developed a course of orgasmic training which is taught in nine institutions in several countries, producing 20,000 graduates to date. She said sex was at the root of all life, and its celebration and understanding was therefore vital to understanding and loving each other. Unfortunately, at present sex was not taken sufficiently seriously, and an 'anti-ecstatic conspiracy' had crashed the party. 'How can we love our planet and each other when the teaching of our dominant religion is that sex is somehow dirty and that we are conceived in original sin,' Ms. Anand said. The importance of sex in political terms should not be underestimated, she said. 'When healing takes place, sexual energy has enormous power.' Sex was also hugely important for leadership: 'You cannot be a good leader if you are sexually wounded.'[1]

At the 1999 Forum, Anand led a panel discussion on "Meditation, Power, and Politics," with participation by New Age luminaries Dean Ornish, Deepak Chopra, and Marianne Williamson.[2] Anand made a repeat appearance in 2000, leading a discussion of "Sex, Power, and Globalization."[3]

The "guru" of Tantra, however, has demonstrated the limits of her approach to ecstasy and enlightenment. When a journalist for a left-wing alternative newspaper contacted her for an interview, she "huffily declined to talk once she learned that she wasn't the sole subject" of a story about Tantric sex teachers in the San Francisco Bay area.[4] The journalist reported, "She also was upset at the idea of playing second banana to Joseph Kramer, who is profiled in the accompanying story, 'I'm more important than Joseph Kramer!' she shrieked in her French accent. 'I was the first on this scene. He is less important in scope!'. . . . Anand had a mantra alright, and it was 'What's in it for me?,' which she said quite a few times during our conversation."[5]

If nudity and forums on tantric sex did not provide sufficient stress relief to Forum participants, discussion of religious drug use might have done so. Over the years, the State of the World Forum has provided a high-status platform for advocates of "spiritual" use of hallucinogens. A 1996 Forum panel on "Drugs, Technology and the Mind in the 21st Century" involved a nostalgic look at the drug culture of the 1960s. The report was written by Ethan Nadelmann, director of the Lindesmith Center, a drug policy advocacy organization funded by George Soros.[6] The Forum panel's report said,

> Robert Jesse and Jeff Bronfman focused on the religious aspects of hallucinogenic drugs and discussed the implications of their work for drug policy. Other participants who included Ram Dass, Michael Aldrich, John Perry Barlow, Mitch Kapor, Steve Kubby and Howard Kornfeld, spoke about therapeutic uses of these drugs, their own and others' personal experiences, and the political responses which these drugs generate in the U.S. and other societies. The panel presented a remarkable opportunity to renew some of the discussions which proliferated a generation ago, but which then were lost as one of the casualties of the war on drugs.[7]

Seven contributors to two pro-entheogen books (*Entheogens and the Future of Religion*, and *Psychoactive Sacramentals: Essays on Entheogens and Religion*) attended or spoke at State of the World Forum

1. State of the World Forum, "Tantric Sex—the path to disarmament?," http://worldforum98.percepticon.com/spirit/article_2sex.html, printed 06/29/04.

2. "About Margot Anand," http://www.margotanand.com/AboutMargot.htm, printed 06/29/04.

3. SWF, *Forum 2000: 2000 and Beyond*, p 25.

4. Katy St. Clair, "A Touch of Tantra," *East Bay Express*, April 21, 2004, Vol. 26, no. 28, pp 26–27.

5. Ibid., p 27. Joseph Kramer is a sex therapist in the San Francisco Bay area.

6. Drug Policy Alliance, "The Nation Exclusive Profiles Soros/Nadelmann Role in Drug Policy; Magazine Article Extols Soros Funded Lindesmith Center and Its Director Ethan Nadelmann As Center Of Drug Policy Reform Movement," http://www.dpf.org/news/pressroom/pressrelease/pr_sep7_99.cfm, printed 06/02/04. Soros remains on the board of directors of the Drug Policy Alliance (Drug Policy Alliance, "About the Alliance: Board of Directors," http://www.dpf.org/about/keystaff/boardofdirec/, printed 06/02/04).

7. State of the World Forum, "1996 State of the World Forum: Creative Approaches to the Drug Crisis—Final Report by Ethan Nadelman [sic]," http://www.worldforum.org/1996forum/round_drugs.html; printed in 1997; no longer on the Net at this address (cited below as SWF, "Creative Approaches to the Drug Crisis," 1996). As of 2004, a copy of this page is at http://web.archive.org/web/19981206205353/http://www.worldforum.org/1996forum/round_drugs.html.

events in 1995, 1996, or 1997: Stanislav Grof, Robert Jesse, Jack Kornfield, Ann and Alexander Shulgin, Huston Smith, and Charles Tart.[1] At an October 30, 1998 forum on "Rogue Nukes: The Mafia and Drug Cartel Connection," former Senator Alan Cranston and Men's Wearhouse CEO George Zimmer proposed that we should "legalize marijuana, and re-examine laws on other drugs."[2]

"SIMPLE LIVING" FOR THE GLOBAL ELITE

At the 1995 State of the World Forum, the "Final Report of the Working Roundtable on the Environment" said, "All nations, but particularly the wealthiest ones, should adjust the present wasteful patterns of consumption.... The limited carrying capacity of our physical planet raises profound questions about the material lifestyles of the rich, about simpler and less energy intensive lifestyles all over the world, and about a major redistribution of future development opportunities."[3]

The Forum's call for simple living echoed the distress that Alice Bailey had expressed in 1948 about over-consumption in America:

One of the lessons to be learnt by humanity at the present time (a time which is the ante-chamber to the new age) is how few material things are really necessary to life and happiness. The lesson is not yet learnt. It is, however, essentially one of the values to be extracted out of this period of appalling deprivations through which men are every day passing. The real tragedy is that the Western Hemisphere, particularly the United States, will not share in this definite spiritual and vitalising process; they are at present too selfish to permit it to happen.[4]

While participants in the 1995 Forum were discussing "profound questions about the material lifestyles of the rich," they had the opportunity to experience such lifestyles. The September 28, 1995 *San Francisco Chronicle* reported: "Last night's meal [September 27] was prepared for the elite 500 attending the forum by chef Joyce Goldstein of Square One Restaurant. She was the first of a succession of celebrity chefs who will cook up a storm for the forum. Others will include Wolfgang Puck, Julian Serrano of Masa's, and Joachim Splichal of the Patina Restaurant in Los Angeles."[5] Goldstein's meal "featured a smoked trout salad, followed by filet of beef in shashlik marinade and a dessert of panna cotta with autumn fruit."[6]

Although Gorbachev's Green Cross International supports "a basic sustainable level of per capita material consumption,"[7] Gorbachev himself enjoyed the lifestyle of the rich and famous while he was

---

1. State of the World Forum, "Toward a New Civilization," May 1997 report on the 1995 and 1996 forums, list of those attending the 1995 conference, p22 and 25, and list of those attending the 1996 conference, p34. Also SWF, "Creative Approaches to the Drug Crisis," 1996; Robert Jesse, Alexander Shulgin, and Ann Shulgin were speakers for the session on "Drugs, Technology, and the Mind in the Twenty-First Century"; SWF, 1997 participants.

2. State of the World Forum, "1998 Schedule of Events: Friday Roundtables, October 30;" David Pasztor, "Stop the Spread of Nukes—Legalize Dope," *SF Weekly*, November 4, 1998, vol. 17, no. 39, p14.

3. Mahbub ul Haq, Convener, "The environment: Final Report of the Working Roundtables," September 30, 1995, http://www.well.com/user/wforum/transcripts/themes/6enviro1.html, printed 03/23/98. No longer available on the Net (cited below as SWF, report by Mahbub ul Haq on the environment, 1995).

4. Alice A. Bailey, *The Reappearance of the Christ*, Lucis Publishing Company, 1948, pp127–128.

5. Edward Epstein, "South African Official Warns About Cutting Into Foreign Aid: World luminaries turn out in S.F. at Gorbachev forum," *San Francisco Chronicle*, September 28, 1995, page A-6; retrieved from Internet archives at http://www.sfgate.com/; printed in 1999.

6. Edward Epstein, "Gorbachev Outlines Challenges to Planet in New Millennium: World luminaries turn out in S.F. for 5–day forum," *San Francisco Chronicle*, September 28, 1995, page A-6; retrieved from Internet archives at http://www.sfgate.com/; printed 03/25/98.

7. The Earth Charter Initiative, "Essays and Papers," "The Earth Charter: The Green Cross Philosophy," principle 7, http://www.earthcharter.org/files/resources/greencross.htm, printed 05/29/04.

at the 1995 Forum. On October 2, 1995, the society columnist for the *San Francisco Chronicle* wrote:

Photographer/author Proctor Jones and his wife, Martha, moved the furniture out of their living room Friday to make room for the dinner they hosted that evening for Raisa and Mikhail Gorbachev. The event ($5,000 a couple, more than 30 guests) was a benefit for Global Green. Gorby is founding president of Green Cross International, a partner of GG [Global Green]. Among the guests at dinner—filet mignon with watercress sauce, or salmon filets, followed by caterer Paula LeDuc's classic Grand Marnier souffles—were Annette Gellert, Indiana Governor Evan Bayh, art gallery owner Charles Campbell with wife Glenna, and the Joneses' neighbors, Ayse and Robert Kenmore, who hosted a reception (more than 200 [guests] at $250 a person) at their home before the dinner. The Kenmores gave the Gorbys a little gift: a pencil case that had belonged to Czar Alexander. Ayse had bought Czar Alexander's breakfast china set at a Sotheby's sale in London—'I'm such an egomaniac I buy anything with an A on it,' she said—and the case and a few other things were thrown in with it. Not thrown in with it: the pearl necklace with a diamond and sapphire pendant—the size of Czar Alexander's tablespoon—Ayse was wearing.[1]

Not bad "simpler and less energy intensive life styles"[2] if you can get them: catering by gourmet chefs, filet mignon, $5,000 fund-raising dinners, and jewels with a "diamond and sapphire pendant the size of Czar Alexander's tablespoon."

At the 1998 Forum, nuclear physicist Hans Peter Dürr, director of the Max-Planck Institute for Physics, said, "Europeans were using four times and Americans nearly seven times the amount of energy per person than the earth could sustain."[3] However, he justified his own jet set lifestyle: "His flight from Germany to San Francisco, for example, used up a year's supply of his suggested energy slave allocation. However, he said the benefits of sharing his thoughts on the overuse of energy with the corporate leaders attending the State of the World Forum outweighed the cost to the planet. 'To propagate this idea you have to travel around.'"[4] The bottom line: "we" should cut energy use by at least 75 percent; there would be an exemption from this mandate for the enlightened ones, whose global mission requires them to live high on the hog.

POST-MODERN SHAMANISM

At the 1995 Forum, multimedia technology meshed with ancient shamanism, the cries of apes, and champagne-drinking crowds of people in business suits. Anita Coolidge, writing for the *San Diego Earth Times*, reported:

The Native American contingent of Indigenous Peoples, led by Chief Oren Lyons, chose the perfect moment to introduce their main message. The 'cocktail party' setting was truly mind altering to begin with: two giant video screens had been set up at one end of the room as a demonstration of new multi media [sic] techniques. A computer linked a live video camera and a digitized imaging system for superimposed images that continually moved and changed on the screens. Two small altars containing fetishes and found objects were located between the screens, with burning candles adding to the palpable vortex created there. Music was played by a group of three or four musicians on instruments looking more like pieces of iron art than anything musical I've ever seen, with a distinctly harmonious, even celestial result. As the group in business suits mingled and mixed and plied themselves with champagne, Oren Lyons and others stepped forward to address them. A hush fell as a statement

1. Pat Steger, "The Social Scene—A Trinket From the Czar for the Visiting Gorbys: Fund raising brings them to the States," *San Francisco Chronicle*, October 2, 1995, p E-4. Printed from the Internet archives of sfgate.com on March 28, 1998.
2. SWF, report by Mahbub ul Haq on the environment, 1995.
3. State of the World Forum, "Slaves to Luxury," http://worldforum98.percepticon.com/sustainability/article_durr.html, printed 06/28/04.
4. Ibid.

was read, a sincere plea to be firm with major corporations to do business in ways that do not harm the environment, to save our environment for our children and our children's children. Moved by her own commitment to the environment and her thirty-five years of communion with chimpanzees, Jane Goodall stepped forward from the crowd and added a few words of her own, urging the crowd to heed the message just delivered. And, without pausing, as easily as she had spoken the words, she emitted a 'whoo-whoo-whoo' cry directly from the nation of chimps, startling sounds that surely galvanized the Natives' plea at the cellular level of all those present: to honor the earth and all the nations thereof.[1]

The Forum's mix of power and New Age spirituality continued to draw well-heeled crowds in 1997. Some joined a "ritualistic and experiential" shamanic ritual in a session titled "Remembrance: An Experiential Process to Regain the Indigenous, Integral Mind": "The three roundtables of the indigenous mind theme consisted of a Hawaiian Awa ceremony and private consultations in an indigenous meditation room. Sessions were ritualistic and experiential, each lead [sic] by a traditional healer and all aimed at awakening the awareness of indigenous (whole) mind and ancestral connectedness in participants." [2] Similar antics occurred at the 2000 Forum. "Working with the Worldwide Indigenous Science Network and the Ringing Rocks Foundation, a Ceremonial Room was constructed which offered a simulated Iroquois Long House and a Hawaiian ceremonial circle. As well as hosting a number of workshops, the Longhouse served as an open space where Forum participants could meditate, consult with healers, and take personal time."[3]

In 1997, inventor Lesley Danzinger told the Forum that she received the idea for a new light-bending material in a vision, and rebuked her audience for insensitivity to spirit and the Earth. At the end of her speech, "Lesley Danzinger received her final standing ovation. Shaking with fear and relief, Lesley was swept off the podium into a crowd of suits & ties that had just been slapped around by her. She was their leader. She had hit them where it counted. She had them. She was euphoric."[4]

In this manner, the "suits & ties" have hailed their own doom. Malcolm Muggeridge said of this phenomenon:

What but a death wish could bring about so complete a reversal of all the normal worldly considerations of good sense, self-interest and a desire to survive? I remember reading in Taine's *Origines de la France Contemporaine* of how, shortly before the Revolution, a party of affluent liberal intellectuals were discussing over their after-dinner cognac all the wonderful things that were going to happen when the Bourbon regime was abolished, and freedom à la Voltaire and Jean-Jacques Rousseau reigned supreme. One of the guests, hitherto silent, suddenly spoke up. Yes, he said, the Bourbon regime would indeed be overthrown, and in the process—pointing round—you and you and you will be carried screaming to the guillotine; you and you and you go into penurious exile, and—now pointing in the direction of some of the elegant ladies present—you and you and you will hawk your bodies round from sansculotte to sansculotte. There was a moment of silence while this, as it turned out, all too exact prophecy sank in, and then the previous conversation was resumed. I know several fashionable and affluent households in London and Washington and Paris where similar conversations take place, and where similarly exact prophecies might be made, without, as on the occasion Taine so appositely described, having the slightest impact.[5]

1. Anita Coolidge, "Ecology: The ultimate democracy—A report from the State of the World Forum," *San Diego Earth Times*, November 1995, http://www.sdearthtimes.com/et1195/et1195s3.html, printed 06/26/04.

2. State of the World Forum, "1997 State of the World Forum: 'Remembrance: An Experiential Process to Regain the Indigenous, Integral Mind—Final Report'," http://www.worldforum.org/1997forum/IndigenousMind.html, printed in 1998. No longer on the Net at this address; as of 2004, a copy of this page is at http://web.archive.org/web/19981205053554/http://www.worldforum.org/1997forum/IndigenousMind.html.

3. SWF, *Forum 2000: 2000 and Beyond*, p19.

4. Stephenie Hendricks, "The Science of Spirit," *Dispatches*, Grace Cathedral, http://www.gracecathedral.org/enrichment/dispatches/dis_19980706.shtml, printed 06/26/04.

5. Malcolm Muggeridge, "The Great Liberal Death Wish," reprinted in *The Portable Conservative Reader*, ed. Russell Kirk, Viking Penguin Inc., 1982, Viking Penguin Inc., 1982, p609.

THE FORUM'S ELITE SUPPORTERS

Given the spacey agenda of the Forum, it is sobering to note that numerous business leaders, politicians, and bureaucrats with global influence have participated in its events. Participants have included Zbigniew Brzezinski (national security adviser to President Carter),[1] Vicente Fox (president of Mexico),[2] George Soros,[3] Colin Powell,[4] John Sweeney (president of the AFL-CIO),[5] George Becker (president of the United Steelworkers of America),[6] executives from UNICEF, the UN Development Program, UNESCO, the UN Population Fund, the UN Environmental Program, the World Bank, the International Labor Organization, and the Commission on Global Governance,[7] Georges Berthoin (European Chairman of the Trilateral Commission from 1975 to 1992),[8] Walter Cronkite,[9] the director of the Jet Propulsion Laboratories at the California Institute of Technology,[10] the director of the American Medical Association,[11] and Maurice Strong, who is senior adviser to the UN Secretary General and to the World Bank.[12]

Prominent corporations and foundations likewise support the Forum, regardless of its New Age and utopian orientation. The Forum acknowledges "financial and programmatic support" since 1995 from many prominent foundations: the Koret Foundation, Fondazione Rispetto E Parita, the Charles Stewart Mott Foundation, the Ford Foundation, the Rockefeller Foundation, the Rockefeller Brothers Fund, the John Templeton Foundation, the John D. and Catherine T. MacArthur Foundation, the W. K. Kellogg Foundation, and the William and Flora Hewlett Foundation, and many others.[13] Corporate and governmental donors have included American Express, Archer Daniels Midland, Booz Allen Hamilton, General Motors Acceptance Corporation, Time Warner, Price Waterhouse Coopers, McKinsey & Co., the Royal Bank of Canada, CIGNA, Steelcase, the Conference Board, and the Canadian International Development Agency.[14] Other prominent foundations and corporations listed as "partners" by the SWF include the Abraham Fund, BBC World Television, British Airways, the Carnegie Corporation of New York, Chevron, the Club of Budapest, CNN, the *Economist*, the Fetzer Institute, the Gorbachev Foundation/Moscow, Harvard University, the Heinz Foundation, Hewlett-Packard, Johnson & Johnson, Kaiser Permanente, Louisiana Pacific, Macy's West, the Men's Wearhouse, the John Merck Fund, Montgomery Securities, NASDAQ, Occidental Petroleum, Oracle, and the Prince

1. SWF, *Registry of Accomplishments*, p9.

2. Ibid., p11.

3. SWF, "Forum 2000 Speakers and Participants."

4. Ibid.

5. Ibid.

6. Ibid.

7. Ibid. Also, numerous UN-related leaders of the Commission on Globalisation, "Co-Chairs & Commissioners," http://www.commissiononglobalization.org/leadership/cc_com.htm, printed 05/22/03 (cited below as Commission on Globalisation, "Co-Chairs & Commissioners").

8. Commission on Globalisation, "Co-Chairs & Commissioners." Forum president Jim Garrison dedicated his recent book to Berthoin, describing him as "one of the truly wise ones, who has mentored me in the ways of statecraft and governance" (Garrison, *America As Empire*, pv.)

9. SWF, 1997 participants.

10. Ibid.

11. Ibid.

12. SWF, *Toward a New Civilization*, 05/97, "1995 Schedule," p10. (For Strong's current positions, see Maurice Strong, *Where on Earth Are We Going*, Vintage Canada, 2001, p397.)

13. State of the World Forum, "Supporters," http://www.worldforum.org/about/supporters.htm, printed 06/29/04.

14. Ibid.

of Wales Business Leaders Forum.[1] The one major individual donor named on the SWF site is Joe Firmage,[2] who had resigned in 1999 from the billion-dollar Internet consulting firm that he had founded in order be free to "promote his belief that many of today's high-tech advancements, including semiconductors, fiber optics and lasers, came from aliens."[3]

A UN connection is built into the Forum's management structure; its 21 current co-chairs include Ruud Lubbers (UN High Commissioner for Refugees), Federico Mayor (Director General of UNESCO from 1987 to 1999), Gertrude Mongella (Secretary General of the UN World Conference on Women in Beijing), and Wally N'Dow (Secretary General of the UN Habitat II Conference in Istanbul).[4] The Forum lists the UN, UNICEF, and the UN Development Program among its partners.[5]

With leaders and supporters such as these, it would unwise to write off the State of the World Forum as a meaningless, California-style diversion for people with more money than common sense. The leaders of the SWF have a clear spiritual and political agenda. In the aftermath of a global crisis, they could realize their dreams.

1. State of the World Forum, "Partners," http://www.worldforum.org/about/partners.htm, printed 06/28/04 (cited below as SWF, "Partners").

2. State of the World Forum, "FAQs," http://www.worldforum.org/about/faq.htm, printed 06/28/04. The site states, "The Forum's largest contributors include Joe Firmage, the Fondazione Rispetto E Parita. . . ." et al.

3. Jon Swartz, "CEO Quits Job Over UFO Views: Advances in technology a gift of aliens, Silicon Valley pioneer believes," *San Francisco Chronicle*, January 9, 1999, page A-1.

4. SWF, "Co-Chairs."

5. SWF, "Partners."

20

THE EARTH CHARTER

The Earth Charter is the brainchild of Gorbachev (acting as chairman of Green Cross International) and Maurice Strong,[1] a wealthy and influential proponent of world government[2] and a former Executive Director of the United Nations Environment Program.[3] Gorbachev and Strong wrote the Charter to rectify what they saw as the excessively "anthropocentric emphasis" of the Declaration on the Environment produced at the 1992 UN conference in Rio de Janeiro.[4]

Gorbachev said of the Earth Charter: "We also need a new international environmental legal code rooted in an Earth charter—a covenant similar to the United Nations Declaration on Human Rights.... My hope is that this charter will be a kind of Ten Commandments, a 'Sermon on the Mount,' that provides a guide for human behavior toward the environment in the next century and beyond."[5] Maurice Strong said the same: "The **real goal** of the Earth Charter is that it will in fact become like the *Ten Commandments*, like the *Universal Declaration of Human Rights*. It will become a symbol of the aspirations and the commitments of people everywhere."[6] Gorbachev and Strong seem to view themselves as the lawgivers of the future, successors to Moses and Jesus. Steven Rockefeller, a leader in the Earth Charter movement, extended this apotheosis of the Charter. He told activists in 1998 that "One can think of the Earth Charter with its tripartite structure as a Tree of Life."[7]

1. The Earth Charter Initiative, "About Us: The Earth Charter Project, 1994–1999," http://www.earthcharter.org/aboutus/overview1994_1999.htm, printed 05/13/03.

2. Strong says in his autobiography that "world government is just not on; it is not necessary, not feasible, and not desirable." (Maurice Strong, *Where on Earth Are We Going*, Vintage Canada, 2001, p308.) Nevertheless, he proposes "management of global affairs" that will move in that direction; "The cause-and-effect relationships that determine the way our policies and actions interact to create our future are systematic in nature, and therefore must be managed systematically.... I have already said that we have to devise and accept global regulations that would impose constraints on our actions for the purpose of maximizing our long-term freedoms." (Maurice Strong, ibid., pp308, 309.) Among the changes that Strong favors are granting of taxing and borrowing power to the UN. (Maurice Strong, ibid., p328.)

3. Thomas Sieger Derr, "Global Eco-Logic," *First Things*, February 2000, p9.

4. The Earth Charter Initiative, "About Us: The Earth Charter Project, 1945–1992," http://www.earthcharter.org/aboutus/overview1945_1992.htm, printed 05/13/03.

5. Green Cross International, "Interview—Environment: 'Act Globally, not Nationally,'" *Los Angeles Times*, May 8, 1997, http://www.greencrossinternational.net/GreenCrossFamily/gorby/newspeeches/interviews/laTimes.html, printed 05/09/03. In recent years, Gorbachev has said the same, in less picturesque fashion: "The Earth Charter opens a new phase not only in ecological movement, but also in the world's public life. We must do everything we can, so that this Charter is accepted exactly as it was designed: a set of vitally important rules." (Mikhail Gorbachev, as quoted in The Earth Charter Initiative, *Biannual Report* 2002–2003, Earth Charter International Secretariat, http://www.earthcharter.org/files/resources/Biannual%20Report.pdf, p10, printed 06/22/04; this report is cited below as Earth Charter Initiative, *Biannual Report*, 2002–2003).

6. The Earth Council, "Papers and Speeches: Interview—Maurice Strong on a 'People's Earth Charter,'" March 5, 1998, http://www.ecouncil.ac.cr/about/speech/strong/mstrong.htm, printed 05/09/03.

7. Steven Rockefeller, "Update on Earth Charter Drafting Process," October 14, 1998; this is on the web page "International Environment Forum," 6–8 November 1998, http://www.bcca.org/ief/dchar98c.htm, printed 07/02/04. The same sentence is in the Earth Charter discussion, and is stated as "Adapted from Earth Council documents," in Gerald O. Barney et al., *Threshold 2000: Critical Issues and Spiritual Values for a Global Age*, Millennium Institute and CoNexus Press, 1998, p146.

Supporters of the Earth Charter have taken the "Ten Commandments" symbolism further. In 2001 they built an "Ark of Hope," a large wooden chest carried on poles and containing a copy of the Earth Charter on a papyrus scroll,[1] along with other environmental books. The Ark,

> created originally to honor the Earth Charter . . . is painted with indigenous symbolism celebrating Earth and all her living elements, animals and children. The five painted panels which form the sides and top of the Ark each represent the flora and fauna of the world as seen through the images of the world's traditional artists. Each panel visualizes a season, a direction, one of the five elements, and a universal symbol. Symbols of faith from traditional religions and indigenous societies surround the top panel of Spirit, which honors the children and young animals of the world. The carrying poles are fashioned like unicorn horns which, according to legend, render evil ineffective.[2]

Earth Charter supporters carried the Ark from Vermont to New York City in 2001; it was exhibited at the UN and at the New York Interfaith Center in early 2002.[3] The Ark then traveled to South Africa in August and September 2002 for the UN World Summit on Sustainable Development.[4] Since then, the Ark has traveled within the US; when it is not on the road, it is displayed at the Interfaith Center of New York.[5]

One of the changes that Gorbachev envisions is world government. When he founded Green Cross International, he said: "The emerging 'environmentalization' of our civilization and the need for vigorous action in the interest of the entire global community will inevitably have multiple political consequences. Perhaps the most important of them will be a gradual change in the status of the United Nations. Inevitably, it must assume some aspects of a world government. Indeed, such a process has already begun."[6]

Jim Garrison, President of the State of the World Forum, agreed. In 1995, he said, "Over the next 20 to 30 years, we are going to end up with world government. . . . It's inevitable;"[7] he likened opponents to Confederate secessionists and the Oklahoma City bombers.[8] In 2004, Garrison used bureaucratic language to describe the same globalist vision: "The current system of nation-states needs to be replaced by a transnational system of integrated global management. This will necessitate the development of network democracy and global issue networks . . . which enhance the power of governments by bringing the expertise of the civil society and business sectors to bear on specific issues of concern."[9] He stated that

> America must consciously view itself as a *transitional empire*, one whose destiny at this moment is to act as midwife to a democratically governed global system. Its great challenge is not to dominate but to catalyze. It must use its great strength and democratic heritage to establish integrating institutions and mechanisms to manage the emerging global system so that its own power is subsumed by the very edifice it helps to build. . . . If it attains

---

1. Earth Charter Initiative, "Ark of Hope Brings Message of Peace," http://www.earthcharter.org/events/arkofhope/release2.htm, printed 05/13/03.

2. Ibid.

3. The Ark of Hope, "The Ark of Hope," http://www.arkofhope.org/index.php?module=htmlpages&func=display&pid=1, printed 05/13/03 (cited below as "Ark of Hope").

4. Diane Gayer, "World Summit in South Africa," "The Ark of Hope travels to South Africa for the World Summit on Sustainable Development," http://www.arkofhope.org/modules.php?op=modload&name=News&file=article&sid=8&mode=thread&order=0&thold=0, printed 05/13/03.

5. "Ark of Hope." The travels of the ark between 2002 and the present are listed in the organization's calendar page, at http://arkofhope.org/index.php?module=PostCalendar.

6. Green Cross International, "The Founding Speech of Green Cross, by President Mikhail Gorbachev," Kyoto, Japan, April 20, 1993, http://www.greencrossinternational.net/GreenCrossFamily/gorby/FoundingspeechGorbi.html, printed 05/13/03.

7. George Cothran, "One World, Under Gorby," *SF Weekly*, May 31–June 6, 1995, Vol. 14, no. 16, p 11.

8. Ibid., p 12.

9. Jim Garrison, *America As Empire: Global Leader or Rogue Power?*, Berrett-Koehler Publishers, 2004, p 45.

this level of greatness, it could become the *final empire*, for it will have bequeathed to the world a democratic and integrated global system in which empire will no longer have a place or perform a role.[1]

Fr. Luis Dolan of the URI said that the future world government must have a religious basis: "Global governance is portrayed as essentially a civil ideal. It will not work, though, unless it is also presented as a religious ideal."[2]

Earth Charter Commissioners include Federico Mayor (former director general of UNESCO), Steven Rockefeller (chairman of the Rockefeller Brothers Fund), Ruud Lubbers (UN High Commissioner for Refugees), and Leonardo Boff (the Catholic proponent of liberation theology).[3]

The Earth Charter Initiative's aims are:

• To promote the dissemination, endorsement, and implementation of the Earth Charter by civil society, business, and government.
• To encourage and support the educational use of the Earth Charter.
• To seek endorsement of the Earth Charter by the UN.[4]

Once adopted by the UN, the Charter would be the starting point to create new, binding law—internationally, nationally, and locally. Steven Rockefeller, a key drafter of the Charter, explained,

> If the Earth Charter is endorsed by the UN General Assembly, it will begin to have the significance of a soft law document, like the UN Universal Declaration of Human Rights. Soft law documents are viewed as statements of intentions and aspirations and not as binding agreements. However, in the history of international law, soft law tends to become hard law over time. In this regard, the Earth Charter is being drafted in coordination with a hard law treaty that is designed to provide an integrated legal framework for all environmental and sustainable development law. This hard law treaty is being prepared by The World Conservation Union, IUCN, and is referred to as the Draft International Covenant on Environment and Development.[5]

This "hard law" would then govern the development and interpretation of local, state, and Federal laws. As Gorbachev said in 2000, "The ideas that inspired us in the Earth Charter are shaped there in the form of international law, based on which national legislation could be adopted. Also in the international court at The Hague, we could have an environmental tribunal that would take charge of implementation of that convention."[6]

Gorbachev and Strong had hoped to gain UN adoption of the Earth Charter in 2002, at the World Summit for Sustainable Development and then by the General Assembly.[7] This did not occur. Nevertheless, the Charter has won endorsement from UNESCO; the Earth Charter Initiative says, "More endorsements, including from UN agencies, are expected and the pursuit of this objective remains an

1. Ibid., p9.

2. Fr. Luis Dolan, "Development and Spirituality: Personal Reflections of a Catholic," (Global Education Associates), http://www.globaleduc.org/dolan.htm, printed 5/14/99.

3. The Earth Charter Initiative, "About Us: The Organization—Organization Structure," http://www.earthcharter.org/innerpg.cfm?id_menu=28, printed 06/22/04.

4. The Earth Charter Initiative, "Introduction," http://www.earthcharter.org/innerpg.cfm?id_menu=20, printed 06/18/04.

5. Steven Rockefeller, "An Introduction to the Text of the Earth Charter," Earth Charter Initiative, http://www.earthcharter.org/resources/speeches/ef_rockefeller.htm, printed 05/13/03. This "Draft International Covenant on Environment and Development," as proposed by the World Conservation Union, is on the Net at http://www.iucn.org/themes/law/pdfdocuments/EPLP31ENsecond.pdf, as of 05/13/03. Its contents and spirit mirror the Earth Charter, but the document contains language making it a binding treaty.

6. Mark Hertsgaard, State of the World Forum, "Interview with State of the World Forum Co-Chair Mikhail Gorbachev," September 2000, http://www.simulconference.com/clients/sowf/interviews/interview1.html, printed 05/23/03.

7. The Earth Charter Initiative, "The Earth Charter at the Johannesburg Summit," http://www.earthcharter.org/events/event.cfm?id_activity=458, printed 05/13/03.

important goal of the Initiative."[1] At the 2002 UN World Summit for Sustainable Development, heads of state (or their representatives) from Costa Rica, the Dominican Republic, Jamaica, Jordan, Mexico, Niger, Romania, and the Netherlands offered their support to the Earth Charter.[2]

Additionally, the Earth Charter continues to gain mainstream and liberal supporters: Valéry Giscard D'Estaing,[3] the United Nations University, the Florida League of Cities, the US Conference of Mayors, 220 cities and towns in Spain, 98 municipalities in Jordan, 23 towns and cities in Vermont (including Burlington and Montpelier), several campuses of Antioch University, Cairo University, Colgate University, the University of Connecticut, the International Association of Universities, Ben & Jerry's Foundation, the Lindbergh Foundation, the Brahma Kumaris World Spiritual University, the Council for a Parliament of the World's Religions, several nations' chapters of the Soka Gakkai, the Unitarian Universalists in the US, the Millennium Institute, the Natural Resources Defense Council, the Odd Fellows, the Sierra Club, Physicians for Social Responsibility, the Humane Society of the US, the World Federalist Association, the Club of Budapest, the city of Berkeley, California, the Senate of Puerto Rico, and the governments of Honduras and Bolivia.[4] The Charter is also popular among New Age, Theosophical, occult, and Sixties-style counterculture groups: the AMORC Rosicrucian order,[5] the association of Waldorf Schools in the United States, Findhorn, the Foundation for Conscious Evolution, Genesis Farm, the Great Barrington Rudolf Steiner School, a regional office of the Institute of Noetic Sciences, the Institute for Global Spirituality, the Institute for Planetary Synthesis, the Robert Muller School, the School of Ageless Wisdom, and World Goodwill.[6] Other odd groups support the Charter: Anarchist Action, the Association of Cymry Wiccae, Back-Rubs To Go.org, the Church of the Earth Nation, the Florida Cannabis Action Network, Great Old Broads for Wilderness, the Knights of Gaia, and the Pantheist Awareness Network.[7] The Charter has gained the endorsement of Pax Christi International and Pax Christi USA, the Canadian Catholic Organization for Development and Peace, the national board of the Leadership Conference of Women Religious, the National Coalition of American Nuns, and about 100 Catholic religious orders and houses—mostly nuns—worldwide.[8] In addition, two Catholic dioceses have endorsed the Earth Charter; the social justice offices in three other Catholic dioceses have also signed on as supporters.[9]

The proponents of the Earth Charter acknowledge that it represents a "moral revolution."[10] In a

1. Earth Charter Initiative, *Biannual Report* 2002–2003, p2.

2. Ibid., p8.

3. The Earth Charter Initiative, "January Newsflash," January 2003, http://www.earthcharter.org/events/event.cfm?id_acti vity=479&id_language=1, printed 05/13/03.

4. Earth Charter Initiative, list of organizations that have endorsed the Earth Charter, http://www.earthcharter.org/ endorse/endorsees.cfm, printed 06/18/04 (cited below as Earth Charter, list of endorsements).

5. The Earth Charter Initiative, "April Newsflash," April 2003, http://www.earthcharter.org/events/event.cfm?id_act ivity=507&id_language=1, printed 05/13/03; the Earth Charter is reprinted in AMORC's *Rosicrucian Digest*, Vol. 81, no. 1, 2003, pp8–12. The "Editor's Note," on p8 of the *Digest*, states, "We share this reprint of the Earth Charter with our readers because many points made by the Imperator in his preceding article clearly resonate with the Charter's main principles." (The "Imperator" is the current head of the Rosicrucian order.) The *Digest* is on-line at http://www.rosicrucian.org/publications/ digest/2003/2003digest_vol_81_1.pdf, printed 05/13/03.

6. Earth Charter, list of endorsements.

7. Ibid.

8. Ibid.

9. Ibid. The Catholic dioceses that support the Earth Charter include the Archdiocese of Louisville, Kentucky and the Diocese of Bathurst, in Australia. The two dioceses whose Offices of Justice and Peace have endorsed the Earth Charter are the Archdiocese of Portland, Oregon and the Diocese of St. Augustine, in Florida. In addition, the Social Concern Office of the Diocese of Jefferson City, Missouri supports the Charter.

10. Larry Rasmussen, "The Earth Charter, Globalization, and Sustainable Community," speech given 01/2001 for the panel "The Earth Charter and Christian Social Ethics," http://www.earthcharter.org/files/resources/rasmussen.htm, printed 12/20/04.

paper on the Earth Charter web site in 2004, a theologian at the Union Theological Seminary said,

the Earth Charter is an assault on the institutionalized anthropocentrism of reigning practices and their moral-ity. Even to say 'humanity is part of a vast evolving universe' and to view Earth as a remarkable niche in that uni-verse, and alive, because it is the bearer and sustainer of a unique community of life, is already to invert the orientation of prevailing ethics. In fact, the very moral universe that gave us universal human rights does not accord well with the Earth Charter ethic. The Earth Charter wants to de-center the sovereign human self (his-torically, an androcentric and white Western self) who is the moral legislator and whose very notion of freedom rests in giving ourselves the laws we live by. But the universal rights tradition combines the rightful assertion of human dignity as the norming norm with a practical and deeply institutionalized morality of the sovereign human subject as legislator over all else. The Charter does not accept this.[1]

THE EARTH CHARTER: A VELVET GLOVE

The basis of the Earth Charter is the belief that "Humanity is part of a vast evolving universe. Earth, our home, is alive with a unique community of life"[2]—a combination of the Gaia hypothesis and Teil-hard de Chardin's vision of cosmic evolution. The Charter states that "An unprecedented rise in human population has overburdened ecological and systems"[3]—the Malthusian "Population Bomb" argument.

The Preamble continues, "Fundamental changes are needed in our values, institutions, and ways of living."[4] To bring this about, "We urgently need a shared vision of basic values to provide an ethical foundation for the emerging world community. Therefore, together in hope we affirm the following interdependent principles for a sustainable way of life as a common standard by which the conduct of all individuals, organizations, businesses, governments, and transnational institutions is to be guided and assessed."[5] The Charter's scope is, by intent, all-encompassing.

The Charter sets forth four "broad commitments:" "1. Respect Earth and life in all its diversity. . . . 2. Care for the community of life with understanding, compassion, and love. . . . 3. Build democratic societies that are just, participatory, sustainable, and peaceful. . . . 4. Secure Earth's bounty for present and future generations."[6]

Realizing this vision would require comprehensive environmental regulation:

Adopt at all levels sustainable development plans and regulations that make environmental conservation and rehabilitation integral to all development initiatives. . . . Manage the use of renewable resources such as water, soil, forest products, and marine life in ways that do not exceed rates of regeneration and that protect the health of ecosystems. . . . Manage the extraction and use of non-renewable resources such as minerals and fossil fuels in ways that minimize depletion and cause no serious environmental damage.[7]

The Charter does not specify who will be doing this management, or to whom the New Managers will be accountable.

Whoever the future environmental planners are, they are called upon to "apply a precautionary approach:" "Take action to avoid the possibility of serious or irreversible environmental harm even

1. Ibid.
2. The Earth Charter Initiative, "The Earth Charter," Preamble, http://www.earthcharter.org/files/charter/charter.pdf, printed 03/24/04.
3. Ibid., Preamble.
4. Ibid., Preamble.
5. Ibid., Preamble.
6. Ibid., "I. Respect And Care for the Community of Life".
7. Ibid., "II. Ecological Integrity"—Article 5.

when scientific knowledge is incomplete or inconclusive. . . . Place the burden of proof on those who argue that a proposed activity will not cause significant harm, and make the responsible parties liable for environmental harm."[1] With this provision, the purveyors of alarmism and "junk science" would be able to tie the economy into knots.

The Charter asks us all to "Adopt patterns of production, consumption, and reproduction that safeguard Earth's regenerative capacities, human rights, and community well-being."[2] Some of the ideas—minimizing generation of waste products, fostering energy efficiency, and promoting the development and spread of environmentally sound technology—are reasonable. However, the proposal to "Internalize the full environmental and social costs of goods and services in the selling price"[3] opens the door to arbitrary, political price setting. And the killer idea—literally—in the Charter's "green" rhetoric is the call to "Ensure universal access to health care that fosters reproductive health and responsible reproduction."[4] In UN circles, "reproductive health" includes artificial contraception, abortion, and sterilization.

For Charter proponents, socialism is still a good idea. In order to "ensure that economic activities and institutions at all levels promote human development in an equitable and sustainable manner," the Charter urges us to "promote the equitable distribution of wealth within nations and among nations."[5] The Charter says that we should "require multinational corporations and international financial organizations to act transparently in the public good, and hold them accountable for the consequences of their activities."[6] So far, so good—but this call to transparency and accountability should also apply to foundations, international non-governmental bodies, national governments, and all international agencies.

The Charter commits itself to feminism, urging us all to "Affirm gender equality and equity as prerequisites to sustainable development and ensure universal access to education, health care, and economic opportunity. . . . Promote the active participation of women in all aspects of economic, political, civil, social, and cultural life as full and equal partners, decision makers, leaders, and beneficiaries."[7] The call for women to act as "decision makers, leaders" in all social and cultural institutions could become the basis of a demand for ordination of women priests and bishops in Catholic and Orthodox churches.

In one of the few references to gay rights in UN-related documents, the Charter calls for us to "Eliminate discrimination in all its forms, such as that based on race, color, sex, sexual orientation, religion, language, and national, ethnic or social origin."[8]

To implement these radical changes, education, the arts, the media, and religious teachers must step into line worldwide. The Charter proposes that we

integrate into formal education and life-long learning the knowledge, values, and skills needed for a sustainable way of life. . . . Provide all, especially children and youth, with educational opportunities that empower them to contribute actively to sustainable development. . . . Promote the contribution of the arts and humanities as well as the sciences in sustainability education. . . . Enhance the role of the mass media in raising awareness of ecological and social challenges. . . . Recognize the importance of moral and spiritual education for sustainable living.[9]

1. Ibid., "II. Ecological Integrity"—Article 6.
2. Ibid., "II. Ecological Integrity"—Article 7.
3. Ibid., "II. Ecological Integrity"—Article 7.
4. Ibid., "II. Ecological Integrity"—Article 7.
5. Ibid., "III. Social and Economic Justice"—Article 10.
6. Ibid., "III. Social and Economic Justice"—Article 10.
7. Ibid., "III. Social and Economic Justice"—Article 11.
8. Ibid., "III. Social and Economic Justice"—Article 12.
9. Ibid., "IV. Democracy, Nonviolence, and Peace"—Article 14.

All, children and adults alike, are to undergo lifelong catechesis in the principles of "sustainable living." Education is to change its role from transmitting traditional wisdom to the furtherance of a "sustainable way of life," and the media are to shift from the ideal of truthful reporting to the new goal of "raising awareness."

To bring about these changes, all "must commit ourselves to adopt and promote the values and objectives of the Charter. This requires a change of mind and heart. It requires a new sense of global interdependence and universal responsibility. We must imaginatively develop and apply the vision of a sustainable way of life locally, nationally, regionally, and globally."[1] The Charter adds, "we must find ways to harmonize diversity with unity, the exercise of freedom with the common good, short-term objectives with long-term goals."[2] This assumes that the human race is a unitary "we" that can harmonize these competing goals in a way that is acceptable to all.

With this ideological shift, there must also be political change.

> The partnership of government, civil society, and business is essential for effective governance. In order to build a sustainable global community, the nations of the world must renew their commitment to the United Nations, fulfill their obligations under existing international agreements, and support the implementation of Earth Charter principles with an international legally binding instrument on environment and development.[3]

That's the end point of all the rhetoric: having all social institutions work together to realize the new ecological and social ideals, and having the principles of the Earth Charter backed up by a "legally binding instrument."

The drafters of the Earth Charter *do* wish to "strengthen democratic institutions at all levels, and provide transparency and accountability in governance, inclusive participation in decision making, and access to justice," as well as to "protect the rights to freedom of opinion, expression, peaceful assembly, association, and dissent."[4] For those who value freedom, that's one of the few consolations in the document.

THE GREEN CROSS PHILOSOPHY: THE EARTH CHARTER'S IRON FIST

However, another document on the Earth Charter web site, "The Earth Charter: The Green Cross Philosophy," prepared by Gorbachev's Green Cross International, takes a much harder line. It makes explicit the totalitarian implications of the Earth Charter's vague, high-flown call for reform.[5]

First comes the call for "fundamental economic, social, and cultural changes:" "The current course of development is thus clearly unsustainable. Current problems cannot be solved by piecemeal measures. More of the same is not enough. Radical change from the current trajectory is not an option,

1. Ibid., "The Way Forward."
2. Ibid., "The Way Forward."
3. Ibid., "The Way Forward."
4. Ibid., "IV. Democracy, Nonviolence, and Peace"—Article 13.
5. The Earth Charter Initiative, "Essays and Papers," "The Earth Charter: The Green Cross Philosophy," http://www.earthcharter.org/files/resources/greencross.htm, printed 05/29/04. This paper, written in Moscow and Geneva in 1997, is described by its authors as "a synthesis document elaborated by Green Cross National Organizations and by individual experts during the process of consultations launched in 1996–1997." As such, it appears to reflect a consensus opinion within Green Cross, one of the principal supporters of the Earth Charter (this document is cited below as Earth Charter, "Green Cross Philosophy"). The same document is on the Green Cross web site. (Green Cross International, "The Green Cross Earth Charter Philosophy," October 14, 1998, http://www.gci.ch/GreenCrossPrograms/earthcharter/proposedtexts/EarthCharterPhilosophy.html, printed 05/29/04.)

but an absolute necessity. Fundamental economic, social, and cultural changes that address the root causes of poverty and environmental degradation are required and they are required now."[1]

Then comes a call for "Stabilization of the World's Population," and "Zero-Growth of Material Economy:"

Principle 6: Stabilization of the World's Population

(a) World population must stabilize. Such a balance can be reached through cooperation: an improvement in living conditions, quality of life, fairness, education, and the eradication of poverty.

Principle 7: Zero-Growth of Material Economy

(a) Even allowing for rapid technological improvements, resources are finite. A basic sustainable level of per capita material consumption will have to be reached in accordance with the Earth's natural resource constraints. This requires both increasing the material consumption of the people now living in poverty and reducing material over-consumption by the rich minority."[2]

Scientific uncertainty about the efficiency, efficacy, and necessity of radical environmental policies will not be allowed to interfere:

Principle 12: Precautionary Principle

(a) Precaution must be the basic organizing principle of environmental management. Scientific uncertainty should be used for objective assessment and not as an excuse for delaying action.

Principle 13: Prevention of Environmental Damage

(a) Protection of the environment is most effective when environmental harm is prevented rather than cured. End-of-pipe solutions are not sustainable and must be replaced by preventive action which stops problems before they arise. Prevention ensures a common inheritance for future generations."[3]

To enforce all this, the "Green Cross Philosophy" states that there must be "global sovereignty" which must not be "subservient to the rules of state sovereignty, demands of the free market or individual rights":

Principle 14: Global Sovereignty

(a) The protection of the Biosphere, as the Common Interest of Humanity, must not be subservient to the rules of state sovereignty, demands of the free market or individual rights. The idea of Global Sovereignty must be supported by a shift in values which recognize this Common Interest.

IMPLEMENTATION

1. The creation of an international body for the Sustainability of Human Life on the Earth. This body must have the independence and power to facilitate agreement between all societal actors to support the protection of the Biosphere as the Common Interest of Humanity."[4]

To put "a new social and economic system" in place, there must be new education:

4. To accelerate the implementation of a new social and economic system based on the respect of the existing limits of the Biosphere, priority must be given to Education and in particular, environmental education."[5]

---

1. Earth Charter, "Green Cross Philosophy," "Rationale," point 7.
2. Ibid., principles 6 and 7.
3. Ibid., principles 12 and 13.
4. Ibid., principle 14 and "Implementation," point 1.
5. Ibid., "Implementation," point 4.

Democratic institutions must not delay the Earth Charter revolution. At the 1995 State of the World Forum, Maurice Strong said, "We shouldn't wait until political democracy paves the way. We must act now."[1]

In this vein, it is notable that Strong's Earth Council has recently clashed with at least one democratic government. In 2003, the Costa Rican government sought a $1.65 million penalty for "what it alleged" was the Earth Council's "wrongful sale" of donated property.[2] As a result, the Earth Council said that it "is not possible for the Earth Council to function in Costa Rica until the situation is resolved and the financial viability of the Earth Council is re-established."[3] And unless the Costa Ricans come to heel, more international facilities may go; as the Earth Council says, "This unfortunate experience of the Earth Council will also affect the attitudes of other international organizations in deciding whether to locate in Costa Rica. It is therefore hoped and expected that this forced suspension will be of a temporary nature."[4]

Like Strong, Gorbachev is impatient for change. The former head of the USSR said, "the process of change is proceeding very slowly and from the standpoint of the global ecological situation it is proceeding too slowly. The Green Cross International must become the catalyst and an accelerator of this process."[5] He proposed a strategy of social change by pressure on the status quo from above and from below:

> any change in society is the result of the interaction of changes from above and from below. Changes from above are effected by leaders, by parliaments, by those who make decisions and approve laws and rules, who develop and define priorities and adopt budgets. The second category of changes are those implemented by ordinary citizens, social movements in the various parties, philosophers, by all those who accept and develop new ideas, by those who protest and those who defend their dreams, their visions. These changes are not always visible, but through interaction of human beings, through personal contacts and direct influence they transform the spiritual climate. The two lines of change are interrelated. They reinforce each other. The ideas coming from the bottom up must be accepted by the authorities above, but the decisions taken above cannot succeed without support from below. If from this standpoint you look at the ecological situation it becomes apparent that many things must happen along both of those lines of change and particularly in terms of their interaction. Helping to bring about this interaction is what the Green Cross International is going to do.[6]

Both Earth Charter leaders are determined to hurry us into a new, ecological society. Then, after the Charter is adopted and implemented—with or without a democratic process—the new "international body" will not "be subservient to the rules of state sovereignty, demands of the free market or individual rights." Such are the principles that Gorbachev and Strong (and their collaborators in the URI and elsewhere in the interfaith movement) would have us adopt as a new covenant with the earth, a new Ten Commandments.

1. Anita Coolidge, "Ecology—the ultimate democracy: A report from the State of the World Forum," *San Diego Earth Times*, November 1995, http://www.sdearthtimes.com/et1195/et1195s3.html, printed 05/08/03.

2. Earth Council, "The Earth Council and Costa Rica," December 2003, http://www.ecouncil.ac.cr/earth_council_and_costa_rica_website.pdf, p1. printed 05/26/04.

3. Ibid., p1.

4. Ibid., p4.

5. Green Cross International, "The Hague Speech by Mikhail Gorbachev," the Hague, 24 May 1993, "Extracts," http://www.greencrossinternational.net/GreenCrossFamily/gorby/hague.html, printed 05/13/03.

6. Ibid.

21

MAURICE STRONG

WHEN MAURICE STRONG SAYS ARROGANT THINGS, we should pay heed—for he keeps elite company. Until his retirement from the post in late 2002, Strong had been a member of the Foundation Board of the World Economic Forum (WEF)—along with the retired Archbishop of Canterbury (now known as Lord Carey of Clifton), Michael Dell (CEO of Dell Computer Corporation), Nobuyuki Idei (CEO of Sony Corporation), Heinrich von Pierer (CEO of Siemens), Peter Sutherland (Chairman of Goldman Sachs International), and other globally influential businessmen and politicians.[1] Strong had been active in the WEF since its founding in 1971.[2] In 2001, the UN Secretary-General Kofi Annan prepared a foreword for *Where on Earth Are We Going?*, Strong's newest book.[3] The biography for Strong on Amazon.com states, "Among the hats he currently wears are: Senior Advisor to UN Secretary General Kofi Annan; Senior Advisor to World Bank President James Wolfensohn; Chairman of the Earth Council; Chairman of the World Resources Institute; Co-Chairman of the Council of the World Economic Forum; member of Toyota's International Advisory Board."[4] In 2003, Strong was sent to North Korea by Kofi Annan to mediate the ongoing nuclear crisis.[5]

Strong has described himself as "a socialist in ideology, a capitalist in methodology."[6]

His spirituality is consistent with the URI vision. In 1978, Strong and his wife bought a large tract of land in the Baca/Crestone area of Colorado, and

learned that since antiquity, Indigenous Peoples' [sic] had revered this sacred land as a place for conducting their vision quests, receiving shamanic training and healing. It was prophesied that the world's religious traditions would gather here and help move the world toward a globally conscious and sustainable coexistence in balance with the Earth. The Strongs wholeheartedly embraced this vision. . . . Currently this community of world's religious traditions is the largest intentional interfaith community in North America. It has grown as a place for many of the world's wisdom traditions to be practiced, taught and preserved. The Manitou Foundation has supported many Indigenous Peoples initiatives. Groups that have received financial support and/or land grants,

1. World Economic Forum, "Foundation Board," updated December 20, 2002, http://www.weforum.org/site/homepublic.nsf/Content/Governance%5CFoundation+Board, printed 01/02/03.

2. World Economic Forum, *Annual Report* 2001/2002—"Solidarity in a Challenging Year," http://www.weforum.org/pdf/AnnualReport/annual_report_2001_2002.pdf, p 24. (provides the date that the WEF was founded), and p 29 (on Strong's retirement. The Foundation Board gave "heartfelt thanks" to Strong and to Raymond Barre "for the great contribution they have made to the development of the World Economic Forum since it was first created."), printed 06/18/04.

3. Maurice Strong, *Where on Earth Are We Going*, Vintage Canada, 2001, pp ix–x (cited below as Strong, *Where on Earth Are we Going*).

4. Maurice Strong, *Where on Earth Are We Going?*, Texere, 2001; listing from amazon.com—"Editorial Reviews: About the Author," printed 05/08/03.

5. CBC News, "Canadian diplomat returns from North Korea optimistic," January 18, 2003, http://www.cbc.ca/stories/2003/01/18/nkorea_strong030118, printed 05/19/03.

6. William Baue, "Rio + 10 Series: A Brief History of the Earth Summits—From Stockholm to Rio," SocialFunds.com, June 7, 2002, http://www.socialfunds.com/news/article.cgi/article858.html, printed 06/18/04 (cited below as Baue, "Brief History of the Earth Summits," 06/07/02).

include Native Americans; the three main Tibetan Buddhist lineages (including the High Lama of Bhutan); the Bon Tradition; Zen Buddhists; Shinto; Christian; Hindu; Jewish; Sufi; and Taoist organizations. Land was also given to Naropa College and Educo (an international environmental training organization).[1]

The Foundation's vision includes survival of a worldwide crisis, and renewal afterward:

> Groups and communities representing the great World Religions and the Wisdom of the Ages are settling here in order to embark on a unique experiment in human transformation and evolution. Colleges, places of worship and learning, healing centers, solar villages, projects in sustainable agriculture and cultural/artistic projects will provide a forum and example to which the world will be able to turn in times of crisis, transition and renewal."[2]

In his autobiography, Strong includes a fictional chapter written from the vantage point of 2031—a summary of the state of the world after global ecological disaster. He begins by avowing that life on Earth is all that there is; Earth is "the Prison of Life, and there is nothing beyond the gates of Planet Earth but the formless void. Since we cannot escape, we must endure, and since we cannot give up, we must continue the struggle."[3] Despite this Earth-bound perspective, Strong posits the emergence of a new movement for religious unity as a beacon of hope in this future time of trouble:

> One of the more dramatic events of the past year was the emergence of a new movement for spiritual unity under the charismatic leadership of the man who calls himself Tadi. As almost everyone by now knows, his message is deceptively simple, little more than an exhortation to people to return to the roots of their own religions, while tolerating and respecting all others as differing expressions of a universal spirituality that unites all people. . . . Ecumenism or unitarianism [sic] is not, of course, a new notion. What is new and remarkable is that people of all faiths have embraced Tadi's formulations. . . . The movement has also evoked vigorous and often hostile responses from fundamentalists of various religions.[4]

(Strong, like other liberal globalists, sees only two options: acceptance of a New Religion, or adherence to violent, judgmental "fundamentalism.")

In his tale of the future, Strong also sees a silver lining in the depopulation of the planet that would follow an ecological collapse:

> Certain worrying trends have even reversed—as a result not of good sense but of cataclysm. Population growth, for instance. . . . At the end of the decade, the best guesstimates of total world population is some 4.5 billion, fewer than at the beginning of this century. And experts have predicted that the reduction of the human population may well continue to the point that those who survive may not number more than the 1.61 billion people who inhabited the Earth at the beginning of the twentieth century. A consequence, yes, of death and destruction—but in the end a glimmer of hope for the future of our species and its potential for regeneration.[5]

A "universal spirituality" that could see "a glimmer of hope for the future of our species" in the death of three quarters of the world population is the spirituality of Moloch, not the spirituality of God.

---

1. The Manitou Foundation, "History," http://www.manitou.org/MF/history.html, printed 06/18/04.

2. The Manitou Foundation, "Mission & Vision," http://www.manitou.org/MF/mission.html, printed 06/18/04. In Strong's autobiography, there is a chapter with a vision of the global disasters that will occur if mankind does not change its direction. He says, from the perspective of 2031, "Still, other scattered islands of civility and order are to be found in many regions, beacons of civility and hope, playing the same role in our modern chaos as the medieval monasteries did in the Dark Ages, keeping alive the flickering embers of learning and wisdom. In Crestone, Colorado, for example, a community created as a spiritual retreat in recent materialistic times has proven to be a haven for the virtues of sustainability, harmony, and 'ethical husbandry.'" (Strong, *Where on Earth Are We Going*, p19.)

3. Strong, *Where on Earth Are We Going*, p7.

4. Ibid., pp20–21.

5. Ibid., p22.

When Strong moves from speculative fiction to straightforward autobiography, he maintains the same views. He said, "We are gods now, gods in charge of our own destiny, and gods can't be capricious."[1] Strong admired the Inuit, among whom he worked in 1945-1946. At one point, he noted that one of his friends, an old woman, was missing. As Strong describes it: "she had said goodbye to everybody she knew, to her family, and had walked out into a storm, never to return. . . . The Inuit were a nomadic people living in a savage environment, surviving on meagre resources, and it was an individual's duty to help the people survive. It was unthinkable to become a burden. And so they knew when it was time to go, when it was time to say goodbye."[2] Like Barbara Marx Hubbard and Neale Donald Walsch, Strong accepts euthanasia.

It's hardly a surprise, then, that Strong took instruction in Catholicism during his time with the Inuit, but "could not in the final analysis accept some of the fundamental beliefs of the Church."[3] Instead, Strong says,

> Universalist expressions of religious belief have always attracted me, as I have always seen that the innate spirituality of people, and the common values they share, are the essential foundations for a more peaceful, co-operative world. . . . I sense a continuity in our spiritual life paralleling that in the physical world: our physical bodies consist of elements that have always existed; they come together to give us our distinctive identity as human beings during our lifetime but return to the 'dust from which we come' after we die. So the spirit that resides in our individual souls emanates from the universal spirit, becomes incarnate within us during our lifetime, to be then subsumed into the universal source. . . . I have found the development of my inner spiritual resources one of my most constant challenges, and my connection with the cosmic forces that shape all existence has become central to me.[4]

Strong does not name these "cosmic forces," however.

Strong acknowledges conservative opposition to him and his agenda: "the right-wing media in the United States have recently been targeting me as a dangerous leader of a conspiracy to establish a world government that would subvert the sovereignty of the United States."[5] He adds,

> these are but the deluded and paranoid ravings of the Western far right, and I wouldn't normally trouble to mention them at all except that my reaction when I hear a few of these charges is that I wish I had a smidgen of the power (and money!) they say I have. I wish I could accomplish a few of the things they already attribute to me. Not all of them, of course—most I wouldn't like to see happen. I do wish I could assist my many friends and colleagues in all the organizations I belong to to [sic] remake the political and economic landscape.[6]

Notwithstanding his desire to "remake the political and economic landscape," Strong has had a "long and cordial relationship" with David Rockefeller,[7] and has been affiliated with the Rockefeller Foundation and Rockefeller University.[8] Strong also notes that Steven Rockefeller "has led the process of drafting and promulgating the Earth Charter."[9] At least one of America's richest families has no difficulty promoting the activities and beliefs of Strong, the "socialist in ideology."[10] Strong avows a "generally bipartisan" approach to US politics, since he donated over $100,000 to the Democratic

1. Ibid., p 29.
2. Ibid., p 65.
3. Ibid., p 66.
4. Ibid., pp 181–182.
5. Ibid., p 34–35.
6. Ibid., p 46–47.
7. Ibid., p 73.
8. Ibid., p 148.
9. Ibid., p 382.
10. Baue, "Brief History of the Earth Summits," 06/07/02.

campaign in 1988—and also, "out of friendship with some key Republicans," raised money for the Republican National Committee.[1] He and George H. W. Bush became friends while Bush was US Ambassador to the UN; as a result, in 1992, Bush did not oppose Strong's appointment as the head of the 1992 UN environmental summit meeting in Rio de Janeiro.[2] Despite Strong's belief that "the more wealthy societies—the privileged minority—would have to make the most profound—not to say revolutionary—changes, in attitudes, values and behaviour,"[3] he travels comfortably among the richest and most privileged people in the US.

1. Strong, *Where on Earth Are We Going*, p184.
2. Ibid., p184.
3. Ibid., pp132–133.

22

THE WORLD
ECONOMIC FORUM

The World Economic Forum (WEF) considers itself to be critical in setting each year's global agenda:

> It has become the premier gathering of international leaders from business, government, academia, media, non-governmental and other civil organizations. From its origins as a small business conference in the Swiss Alps, the Annual Meeting has grown to become the event where the leading issues confronting humanity are discussed and debated at the start of each calendar year. Traditionally held in Davos, Switzerland, the Annual Meeting covers a wide range of issues including global economic growth, trade, business management, the poverty gap, technology, health, religion and cultural understanding. . . . The Annual Meeting has played a key role in identifying new trends in the economic, political, social and cultural domains, and in shaping strategies and actions for corporations and countries to integrate these changes and maximize their potential. . . . The Forum believes that progress can best be achieved when governments and business can freely and productively discuss challenges and work together to mold solutions. The unique atmosphere of the Annual Meeting creates opportunities for the formation of global partnerships and alliances.[1]

In 2000, Paul Krugman (a liberal who says that "globalization is overwhelmingly, though not entirely, a good thing") nevertheless offered a colorful description of the WEF's meetings: "The scene at Davos—the superrich and their trophy wives schmoozing with officials elected and appointed, the lavish parties thrown by third-world nations, and so on—represents a sort of distilled essence of everything people love to hate about the New World Order."[2] The WEF continues to attract a well-placed crowd. Forbes reported that the 2004 annual meeting had "2,280 participants from 94 countries, including some 800 chairmen and chief executives, billionaires like Michael Dell and Bill Gates, 203 ambassadors and 31 heads of state and government."[3]

WEF leaders make it clear that they support "global governance." At a 2002 WEF panel discussion of "Global Governance: What Needs To Change," participants agreed that "US resistance to global governance[4] slows the system's progress but expressed hope that the terrorist attacks of 11 September would

---

1. World Economic Forum, "About the Annual Meeting," http://www.weforum.org/site/homepublic.nsf/Content/Annual+Meeting+2003%5CAbout+the+Annual+Meeting, printed 01/03/03.

2. Paul Krugman, "Reckonings: The Magic Mountain," *New York Times*, January 23, 2000, http://query.nytimes.com/search/restricted/article?res=F70D11FE3A590C708EDDA 80894D8404482, printed 05/08/03.

3. Michael Freedman, "World Economic Forum: Sunny Days in Snowy Davos," *Forbes.com*, January 21, 2004, http://www.forbes.com/2004/01/21/cz_mf_0121econdavos.ht ml, printed01/23/04.

4. It should be remembered that "global governance" has already made inroads into American sovereignty. In its June 2003 *Lawrence v. Texas* decision to overturn that state's anti-sodomy laws, the U. S. Supreme Court's majority opinion noted that the European Court of Human Rights (an organ of the European Union) had overturned similar British laws, based on standards set by the European Convention on Human Rights. Justice Anthony Kennedy wrote, "The right the petitioners seek in this case has been accepted as an integral part of human freedom in many other countries. There has been no showing

result in greater commitment to a multilateral system."[1] In the WEF's report on its 2002 annual meeting, Klaus Gretschmann, the Director-General of the Council of the European Union wrote, "For a new world order we need consistent policies, benchmarking of best practice and partnership in leadership. Law compliance, international standards, guaranteed but fair property rights, absence of bribery and corruption, business and government ethics, and human rights will have to form sound foundations."[2] However, in emergencies, the global "networks" might have to take their gloves off. Gretschmann said, "Rather than working top-down, like an international hegemony, networks are horizontal powers embedded in a system of checks and balances. This does not fully exclude, however, that in order to prevent barbarism and fend off atrocious fanaticism, networks may need to take on—temporarily and partially—the forms and functions of a—benign—global leviathan."[3]

Many business, political, and religious leaders attended the 2002 WEF Annual Meeting. Among them were Frank Griswold (the Presiding Bishop of the Episcopal Church in the US),[4] Cardinal Arinze, Archbishop Carey, Desmond Tutu, the president of the World Bank, the president of the Philippines, the prime ministers of Canada, Malaysia, and Romania, Secretary of State Colin Powell, Bill Gates, and the CEOs of the US Chamber of Commerce, the Saudi Arabian Investment Authority, McDonald's Corporation, and AOL Time Warner.[5] A similar cast of stars attended the 2004 WEF meeting in Davos, including Kofi Annan, the Secretary-General of the UN, US Attorney General John Ashcroft, Vice President Cheney, and the CEOs of Nestlé, Coca Cola, Hewlett Packard, Sony, Pfizer, Merck, Saudi Aramco, Nike, Siemens, and Chevron/Texaco.[6] George Soros, the President of the Council of the European Union, and the president of the AFL-CIO also attended.[7]

Since 2001, WEF meetings have included religious leaders in order to "discuss issues such as the role of religion in: (i) using moral resources internationally to build a genuine culture of dialogue, (ii) searching out common values to bridge divides among communities; and (iii) addressing the priority issues on the global agenda."[8] At the 2001 Forum, the assembled religious leaders had said, "Our goal

---

that in this country the governmental interest in circumscribing personal choice is somehow more legitimate or urgent." Human Rights Watch, which had filed a "friend of the court" brief in the case, hailed the decision: "*Lawrence v. Texas* is a landmark decision on the constitutional right to privacy of gays and lesbians in the United States; it may also prove to be an important decision for the incorporation of international human rights law into U.S. jurisprudence." With this decision, the Court crossed a key threshold: interpreting the Constitution with the aid of overseas laws, custom, and precedent, rather than basing its decision solely on U. S. tradition. This particular decision pleases liberals and libertarians—but the long-term price we pay in freedom may be high, since international law is often more authoritarian than U. S. custom. For example, much Constitutionally protected speech in the U. S. would be illegal overseas, under bans on "incitement to hatred," sectarianism, racism, and libel. (Quotations in this note are from Human Rights Watch, "*Lawrence v. Texas*: Constitutional right to privacy of gays and lesbians in the United States," *Human Rights News*, July 2, 2003, http://www.hrw.org/press/2003/07/hrw-amicus-bri ef.htm, printed 10/22/04.)

1. World Economic Forum, "Global Governance: What Needs to Change?," http://www.weforum.org/site/knowledgenavigator.nsf/Content/Global%20Governance:%20What%20Needs%20to%20Change%3F, printed 03/15/03.

2. Klaus Gretschmann, "Re-evaluating Leadership and Governance," World Economic Forum *Annual Meeting* 2002: *Global Agenda Monitor*, http://www.weforum.org/pdf/AM_2002/Global_Agenda_Monitor_2002.pdf, printed 05/08/03, p32.

3. Ibid.

4. Jan Nunley, "World's Religious Leaders at World Economic Forum," *Pacific Church News online*, February 2002, http://www.diocal.org/pcn/PCNO/pcn002-2.html, printed 10/12/02 (cited below as Nunley, "Religious Leaders at the World Economic Forum").

5. World Economic Forum, "Quotes from the Annual Meeting 2002," http://www.weforum.org/site/homepublic.nsf/Content/Annual+Meeting+2003%5CAnnual+Meeting+2002%5CQuotes+from+the+Annual+Meeting+2002, printed 01/03/03.

6. World Economic Forum, "List of Selected Participants," Annual Meeting 2004, http://www.weforum.org/site/homepublic.nsf/Content/Annual+Meeting+2004%5CList+of+Selected+Participants, printed 06/18/04.

7. Ibid.

8. World Economic Forum, "World Economic Forum Welcomes Religious Leaders to Annual Meeting 2002 in New York," http://www.weforum.org/site/homepublic.nsf/Content/World+Economic+Forum+Welcomes+Religious+Leaders+to+Annnual+Meeting+2002+in+New+York, printed 01/03/03.

is to inspire a spirit of universalism while respecting the integrity of particular traditions." [1]

There are no organizational ties between the URI and the WEF, but the WEF's religious agenda is compatible with that of the URI and other liberal, globalist movements. At the 2004 World Economic Forum meeting, one of the two discussion sessions that the WEF listed under "Spirituality and Religion" was "Organized Religion Takes On Its Taboos."[2] The content was similar to the spiritual fare that has been offered by the State of the World Forum. David Rosen, the International Director of Interreligious Affairs for the American Jewish Committee, said, "ways need to be devised to get organized religion to re-engage with what is happening in the world and to become a partner in improving the lot of humanity instead of being demonized as humanity's enemy." A cartoonist from South Africa showed some of the "cartoons he uses to challenge religious assumptions. One of his cartoons depicted the Pope trying to hold back a tidal wave of condoms. Another depicted God as a lesbian." A woman bishop from the Evangelical Church in Germany "lamented the way the Church had used religious texts to marginalize women." A chief executive from King's Fund in Britain said that organized religion "needs to become more inclusive," and to "become more open on the subject of sexuality." Lourdes Arizpe, Professor of Social Anthropology from the National University of Mexico, said that "Women are naturally taking a larger role in religion because for the first time in history, society's primary task is no longer procreation." She appeared to endorse the thesis advanced by the bestselling novel, *The Da Vinci Code*; "Arizpe also described how the modern New Testament appears, according to historical research, to have been selected by the Roman Emperor Constantine. In so doing, he omitted the Gnostic gospels and may have instead chosen gospels that are historically inaccurate. History, she said, shows that Mary Magdalene was much closer to Jesus than the Gospels indicate and may in fact have been one of the Apostles." The other religion-related session at Davos in 2004, "God in Politics," appears to have been an even-handed discussion of issues related to freedom of religion and the relationship between religion and the State; there was no apologetic for tradition in this session that would have counterbalanced the liberal, reformist bias of the "Taboos" discussion.[3]

The price tag for participating in the WEF is high. Companies with full membership in the WEF must have annual sales of $1 billion or more, and the cost—counting Forum dues, travel expenses, and the like—of attending the Davos Forum "can add up to $30,000 or $40,000 per head."[4] Some firms pay up to $250,000; these WEF "partners" are "heavily represented among speakers at the sessions. In addition, partner companies help choose session subjects and suggest participants."[5]

These are the people whom we are asked to trust with planning our future, a venture that Strong calls "cooperative globalism."[6]

1. Nunley, "Religious Leaders at World Economic Forum."

2. Information in this paragraph (unless otherwise footnoted) is from World Economic Forum, "Organized Religion Takes On Its Taboos," Annual Meeting 2004, January 23, 2004, http://www.weforum.org/site/knowledgenavigator.nsf/Content/Organized%20Religion%20Takes%20On%20Its%20Taboos_2004?open&event_id=, printed 06/18/04.

3. World Economic Forum, "God in Politics," Annual Meeting 2004, January 24, 2004, http://www.weforum.org/site/knowledgenavigator.nsf/Content/God%20in%20Politics_2004?open&topic_id=400850000&theme_id=400, printed 06/18/04.

4. Tad Szulc, "One of the greatest shows on earth," *Forbes*, December 2, 1996, p79.

5. Anne Swardson, "The Cost of Doing Business Extends to Davos," *Washington Post*, January 24, 2000, p A15.

6. Pranay Gupte, "Maurice Strong: Reaching out to broad range of constituencies for millennium," *Earth Times News Service*, http://www.earthtimes.org/trustees21/trustees21mauricestrongfeb21_98.htm, printed 4/15/98; no longer on the Net.

23

ARE THE NEW AGE AND GLOBALIST MOVEMENTS A CONSPIRACY?

THE SHORT ANSWER: NO.

Conspiracies are usually secretive associations with illegal objectives. New Age leaders and their utopian, globalist allies are open about their aims, and their activities are legal. The goals of the present-day New Agers and utopians match what radicals have sought since the French Revolution. This is not because of an organized plot among men that spans nations and decades. Rather, it shows the permanent vulnerability of mankind to temptation and sin.

God remains forever. He does not change; nor do his commandments. Human nature does not change, since mankind is created in God's image. The devil does not change; nor do the temptations he offers mankind. From the Garden of Eden to the séances of the Theosophists and the meeting-halls of Davos and New York, the message is the same: you will not die, and you will be like god. Human response to temptation does not change, either; apart from God's grace, we sin. The New Age and globalist movements offer bait that tempts many—freedom from the restrictions imposed by traditional morality, the ability to use spiritual power to attain worldly goals, and the delight of being in the inner circle of those who will create a new civilization.

Therefore, human rebellion against God follows a consistent pattern. People who wish to rebel against God will find collaborators and mentors to assist them, and to affirm that their choices are right. (Also, the religious and governmental authorities, by their oft-repeated injustices, put the same temptations, scandals, and stumbling blocks before their people, again and yet again.) What some over-enthusiastic observers see as multi-generational, international conspiracies are really just successive groups of fallen men following temptation to its logical conclusion. If New Age, globalist, and utopian movements show unity and consistent purpose internationally or over many years, it derives from the dark spirit they follow, wittingly or unwittingly—rather than from their own human, conspiratorial aptitude.

The New Age and globalist movements are not conspiracies. However, they are bearers of a worldview that is altogether opposed to the Christian faith and to the Western tradition of human freedom.

Some of the causes that the New Age and globalist movements support (such as protection of the environment from pollution and an end to inter-religious violence) are praiseworthy. Some of what the New Age and globalist movements oppose (for example, racial discrimination and imperialism) deserves Christian opposition. Thus, a knee-jerk reaction (i.e., if the New Age and globalist movements are for "X," Christians must oppose "X") is unwise. Christian opponents of the New Age and globalist movements should consider what injustices and spiritual hungers lead people to follow these movements, so that they might answer these real, unmet needs of their fellow men.

The New Age and globalist movements testify to the human desire for unity and order. In principle, these are not evil motives. As Brooks Alexander, of the Spiritual Counterfeits Project, said in 1983:

Evil mimics the kingdom of God in many of its external attributes, not the least of which is its cohesiveness. Human nature itself yearns for order and organization. As a race we bear the image of God, however distorted, and both unity and structure are among the deepest desires of the human heart. It is the intractable factor of fallenness that twists our best intended efforts at achievement. Under its influence our reach for totality inevitably becomes totalitarian.[1]

That's the problem with globalism; mankind's search for equity, order, and unity will most likely devolve into totalitarianism, if the lessons of history are any guide.

Benjamin Valentino, a political scientist who studied genocide in the 20th Century—including the crimes of the Nazis, the Communists, "ethnic cleansers," and combatants in guerrilla wars—said in 2004 that

History's most savage ideologies have been those that called for the extremely rapid and radical transformation of society. Such transformations have almost always come about at great cost in human life. It is impossible to rule out the advent of completely novel belief systems, but few contemporary ideological contenders seem ready to rival the bloody utopias of radical communism in their desire to rebuild society from the ground up. . . . One reason why radical communism became history's most deadly ideology was its contention that it could, indeed that it must, be applied to every society on earth.[2]

He also said,

Future communist mass killings are highly unlikely given the declining appeal of communist ideology since the end of the cold war. Nevertheless, we should remain vigilant of groups espousing similarly radical social changes, as this form of mass killing can have the bloodiest consequences of all.[3]

Valentino also examined the record of various Communist regimes, contrasting the most radical of these (the USSR under Stalin, China under Mao, and Cambodia under Pol Pot) with Marxist states that avoided committing genocide. He found that

Communist mass killing is more likely
- the higher the priority the communist leaders assign to the radical transformation of society
- the more the communization of society results in the dispossession of large numbers of people
- the more rapidly communist leaders seek to implement dispossessive policies
- the greater the physical capabilities for mass killing possessed by the regime
- the fewer and more difficult the options for victims of communist policies to flee to safety.[4]

With Valentino's analysis in mind, review what the New Age theorists and some of the globalists have said about the "new civilization" that they wish to create. It would be a collectivist society, more dedicated to "protection of the Biosphere"[5] than to "demands of the free market or individual rights."[6] The utopians warn that humanity is on the verge of self-destruction if we do not make "fundamental economic, social, and cultural changes"[7] *everywhere*, quickly. With a world government based on such

1. Brooks Alexander, "The Coming World Religion," Spiritual Counterfeits Project, 1983 pamphlet, p2.
2. Benjamin A. Valentino, *Final Solutions: Mass Killing and Genocide in the Twentieth Century*, Cornell University Press, 2004, pp150–151.
3. Ibid., p240.
4. Ibid., p74.
5. The Earth Charter Initiative, "Essays and Papers," "The Earth Charter: The Green Cross Philosophy," principle 14 and "Implementation," point 1, http://www.earthcharter.org/files/resources/greencross.htm, printed 05/29/04.
6. Ibid, principle 14 and "Implementation," point 1.
7. Ibid., "Rationale," point 7.

principles, there would be nowhere for opponents and members of disfavored classes to flee to. If these globalist visionaries gain power, they may shed their professorial niceness and commit mass murder to attain their goals. (Does this seem impossible and unprecedented? Think again. Would anyone who attended the Sorbonne with the future leaders of the Khmer Rouge have predicted that they would take over their country a quarter-century later, and proceed to kill one-fifth of the population?)

Despite the fall of the Third Reich and the Soviet Empire, secular messianism is still with us. Some people with such radical goals have a powerful audience, via the State of the World Forum, the Earth Charter movement, the World Economic Forum, and similar globalist organizations. "Utopia in power" has happened several times before in the last century; with the installation of a New World Order, it could happen again. This time, the killing fields could encompass the planet.

PART IV

IN CONCLUSION:
FROM THE "ANTI-TRADITION"
TO THE "COUNTER-TRADITION"

Albrecht Dürer, "The Apocalypse Of St. John," image of the seven-headed beast and the beast with lamb's horns (Rev. 13), 1496–98 woodcuts, from the Wetmore Print Collection at Connecticut College.

"How you are fallen from heaven,
O Day Star, son of Dawn! How you are cut down
to the ground, you who laid the nations low! You said in your heart,
'I will ascend to heaven; above the stars of God I will set my throne on
high; I will sit on the mount of assembly in the far north; I will ascend
above the heights of the clouds, I will make myself like
the Most High.' But you are brought down to Sheol,
to the depths of the Pit."

Isaiah 14:12–15

POINT : COUNTERPOINT

Let us allow the Father and Mother God to unite in sacred mystery. Let us build a world community in which all people have the opportunity to create meaning in their own lives.[1]

————Lauren Artress, *Walking a Sacred Path*, 1995

Everyone will be invited to bring their best, richest, deepest stories to the common ground. And there we will build.[2]

————Bishop Swing, Christmas Eve 1996 sermon on the URI

We unite to build cultures of peace and justice.[3]

————URI Charter Preamble, 2000

Unless the Lord builds the house, those who build it labor in vain.

Psalm 127:1————

Rather than working top-down, like an international hegemony, networks are horizontal powers embedded in a system of checks and balances. This does not fully exclude, however, that in order to prevent barbarism and fend off atrocious fanaticism, networks may need to take on—temporarily and partially—the forms and functions of a—benign—global leviathan.[4]

————Klaus Gretschmann, Director-General of the Council of the European Union, World Economic Forum, 2002

Then it came burning hot into my mind, whatever he said, and however he flattered, when he got me home to his house he would sell me for a slave.[5]

John Bunyan, *The Pilgrim's Progress*————

The protection of the Biosphere, as the Common Interest of Humanity, must not be subservient to the rules of state sovereignty, demands of the free market or individual rights. The idea of Global Sovereignty must be supported by a shift in values which recognize this Common Interest.[6]

————Earth Charter, "Green Cross Philosophy," 1996/1997

1. Lauren Artress, *Walking a Sacred Path: Rediscovering the Labyrinth as a Sacred Tool*, Riverhead Books, 1995, p161.
2. Bishop William Swing, "A Message for all the People," URI pamphlet, excerpt from a sermon delivered by Bishop Swing on Christmas Eve 1996 at Grace Cathedral, p2.
3. United Religions Initiative, "The United Religions Initiative Charter," http://www.uri.org/resources/publications/Charter%20PC%20format.doc, "Preamble," paragraph 6, p2; downloaded 07/07/04.
4. Klaus Gretschmann, "Re-evaluating Leadership and Governance," World Economic Forum *Annual Meeting* 2002*: Global Agenda Monitor*, http://www.weforum.org/pdf/AM_2002/Global_Agenda_Monitor_2002.pdf, printed 05/08/03, p32.
5. John Bunyan, *The Pilgrim's Progress*, Spire Books/Fleming H. Revell Co., 1972, ch. 5, p67.
6. The Earth Charter Initiative, "Essays and Papers," "The Earth Charter: The Green Cross Philosophy," principle 14 and "Implementation," point 1, http://www.earthcharter.org/files/resources/greencross.htm, printed 05/29/04.

What assurance have we that our masters will or can keep the promise which induced us to sell ourselves? Let us not be deceived by phrases about 'Man taking charge of his own destiny.' All that can really happen is that some men will take charge of the destiny of the others. They will be simply men; none perfect; some greedy, cruel and dishonest. The more completely we are planned the more powerful they will be. Have we discovered some new reason why, this time, power should not corrupt as it has done before?[1]

C. S. LEWIS, "IS PROGRESS POSSIBLE?"————

Let us never forget that it is the *Life*, its purpose and its directed intentional destiny that is of importance; and also that when a form proves inadequate, or too diseased, or too crippled for the expression of that purpose, it is—from the point of view of the Hierarchy—no disaster when that form has to go. Death is not a disaster to be feared; the work of the Destroyer is not really cruel or undesirable.[2]

————ALICE A. BAILEY, *EDUCATION IN THE NEW AGE*, 1954

The modern totalitarian regimes, whatever their initial defects, are neither heresies nor biological regressions: they are in line with the essential trend of 'cosmic' movement.[3]

————PIERRE TEILHARD DE CHARDIN, "THE GRAND OPTION," 1939 AND 1945

There will be a selection process not of our own doing, which will 'decide' what is capable of taking the next step of evolution, and eliminating what is destructive and unworthy of continuation.[4]

————BARBARA MARX HUBBARD, *THE BOOK OF CO-CREATION*, 1993

Detestation for any ethic which worships success is one of my chief reasons for disagreeing with most communists. In my experience, they tend, when all else fails, to tell me that I ought to forward the revolution because 'it is bound to come.' One dissuaded me from my own position on the shockingly irrelevant ground that if I continued to hold it I should, in good time, be 'mown down'—argued, as a cancer might argue if it could talk, that he must be right because he could kill me.[5]

C. S. LEWIS, "A REPLY TO PROFESSOR HALDANE"————

The majority of the future mankind will be composed of glorious Adepts.[6]

————HELENA P. BLAVATSKY, *THE SECRET DOCTRINE*, VOL. II, 1888

In the coming world state, the individual citizen—gladly and deliberately and with full consciousness

---

1. C. S. Lewis, "Is Progress Possible," in *God in the Dock—Essays on Theology and Ethics*, Walter Hooper, ed., Eerdmans, 1970, p316.
2. Alice A. Bailey, *Education in the New Age*, 1954, Lucis Publishing Company, p112 (cited below as A. Bailey, *Education in the New Age*).
3. Pierre Teilhard de Chardin, "The Grand Option," *The Future of Man*, translated by Norman Denny, Harper & Row, 1964, p46.
4. Barbara Marx Hubbard, *The Book of Co-Creation Part II—The Promise Will Be Kept: The Gospels, The Acts, the Epistles*, Foundation for Conscious Evolution, San Rafael, California, 1993 (privately published), p57.
5. C. S. Lewis, "A Reply to Professor Haldane," in *Of This and Other Worlds*, Walter Hooper, ed., Collins Fount Paperbacks, 1982, p97.
6. H. P. Blavatsky, *The Secret Doctrine: The Synthesis of Science, Religion, and Philosophy, Vol. II—Anthropogenesis*, Theosophical University Press, 1999 reprint of 1888 ed., p446.

of all that he is doing—will subordinate his personality to the good of the whole.[1]

———Alice A. Bailey, *Education in the New Age*, 1954

We stand upon the threshold of the greatest age of human history.[2]

———Barbara Marx Hubbard, *The Evolutionary Journey*, 1982

From all perspectives—scientific, political, social, economic, and ideological—humanity finds itself in the pregnancy of an entirely new and promising age: the global, interdependent, universal age; a truly quantum jump; a cosmic event of the first importance that is perhaps unique in the universe: the birth of a global brain, heart, senses and soul to humanity.[3]

———Robert Muller, "Preparing for the next millennium," 1994

The twenty-first century will be the time of awakening, of meeting The Creator Within. . . . This will be the beginning of the golden age of the New Human.[4]

———"God," talking to Neale Donald Walsch, 1999

The Hideous Strength confronts us and it is as in the days when Nimrod built a tower to reach heaven.[5]

C.S. Lewis, *That Hideous Strength*———

1. A. Bailey, *Education in the New Age*, p 122.

2. Barbara Marx Hubbard, *The Evolutionary Journey: A Personal Guide to a Positive Future*, Evolutionary Press, San Francisco, 1982, p 11.

3. Robert Muller, "Foreword: Preparing for the Next Millennium," in Joel Beversluis, ed., on-line version of *A Source Book for the Earth's Community of Religions*, http://www.origin.org/ucs/doc.cfm?e=0&ps=2&edit=1&fg=3176&fi=1089, printed 06/22/04.

4. Neale Donald Walsch, *Friendship with God: An Uncommon Dialogue*, G. P. Putnam's Sons, 1999, p 295.

5. C.S. Lewis, *That Hideous Strength: A Modern Fairy-Tale for Grown-Ups*, Collier Books, Macmillan Publishing Company, 1946, p 288 (cited below as Lewis, *That Hideous Strength*).

24

THE ASCENDANCY
OF THE "ANTI-TRADITION"

THE APPEAL OF THE URI and its New Age, globalist, utopian allies is based on some inescapable truths. Killing in the name of God is an abomination. Badly managed economic growth has harmed the natural environment. As globalization spreads, so does poverty. Many people and institutions have placed love of money and power above love of God and neighbor. The established religions are gravely tainted by hypocrisy, bigotry, and violence among their adherents and their leaders. People seek connection to God—and if this is not offered in the churches, they will justifiably go elsewhere.

These elements of truth in the URI's critique of the present world order may draw a wider audience for the more radical aspects of the agenda of the URI and its allies. This would fit the usual pattern of temptation; a mixture of lies and truth is likely to ensnare more people than a message that has no prima facie appeal or plausibility. So it has been from the beginning. It was not a rotten, worm-eaten fruit that the serpent offered to Eve in the Garden of Eden. Instead, "when the woman saw that the tree was good for food, and that it was a delight to the eyes, and that the tree was to be desired to make one wise, she took of its fruit and ate; and she also gave some to her husband, and he ate." (Gen. 3:6)

For many people, the activities and beliefs of the United Religions Initiative and their globalist, New Age allies are too bizarre to take seriously. Many secular and religious opinion makers and activists, people who instinctively reject the notion of building a utopian New World Order, take for granted that these visionary groups will remain a playground for cranks with too much time and money on their hands.

Such a view is excessively optimistic. With war, terrorism, and economic instability, we are in dangerous times; social and military disasters with global effects can occur anywhere with no warning. Traditional societies and traditional beliefs have been undermined everywhere over the last two centuries. The Enlightenment and other corrosive modern philosophies, the Industrial Revolution, the wars and ideologies of the 20th Century, and globalization (from the colonialism of the 19th century to the "free trade" imperialism of the 21st century) have done their work, cutting people adrift from the faith, family, and community that might once have sustained them and kept them sane during a crisis. As a result, the whole world is vulnerable to being destabilized via cataclysm. After one upheaval—or a series of them, in quick succession—the world's people, and their leaders, may turn to solutions that they would never have accepted before the crisis.

As the French metaphysician René Guénon said in 1945, "The world has even now reached a point where the security of 'ordinary life,' on which the whole outward organization of the modern world has rested up till now, runs serious risks of being troubled by unanticipated 'interferences.'"[1]

There is no lack of groups ready and willing to exploit such "interferences," should they arise. URI supporter Dee Hock warned in 2002:

---

1. René Guénon, *The Reign of Quantity & The Signs of The Times*, orig. ed. 1945, reissued by Sophia Perennis et Universalis, 1995, p 132.

I think we're on the knife's edge where we're going to undergo cataclysmic institutional failure. . . . I think if we do experience massive institutional failure, the first thing that will emerge, before we see the new forms, is almost total centralization of power and control, which will result in a widespread loss of liberty and freedom. That will last for a while, but it ultimately will not work, much like the Soviet Union. And when *that* collapses, then we're in for a second period of social carnage that will be unbelievable. [The interviewer asked: "So you're talking about a double cataclysm?"] Yes. And out of that, right from the ashes, may emerge the new forms of organization.[1]

The world's foundations tremble—and some of our religious and political leaders appear to be ready to give the old structure a push in order to foster their own anti-traditional agendas. Bishop Swing, Mikhail Gorbachev, Tony Blair, and President Bush's National Security Adviser Condoleezza Rice seem to share a view of how rapid social change happens: via a dramatic event that shapes a new consensus of what is possible and desirable. Groups and agencies that act as "the catalyst and an accelerator of this process"[2] (in Gorbachev's words) can build this new consensus, creating a New World Order from the rubble of the old regime. Ervin Laszlo, a prominent New Age author and activist, says that changing the world is "no longer utopian for the world is highly unstable and hence changeable, moreover the momentum for change is growing. The task before us is to reinforce the momentum and inform it so that it will head in a positive direction."[3]

In the view of Bishop Swing—who identifies himself as a Republican[4]—chaos is an essential part of creation; it was so at the beginning, and remains so as we approach "a new creation," a "new order." In 2004, he wrote:

In the first words of the Bible we read where the Spirit brooded over the chaos. . . . Chaos is the necessary ingredient that prompts the Creator's Spirit to be inventive. High praise for chaos. If Creation is an ongoing phenomenon and if chaos is a necessary ingredient beckoning to the Spirit, then we must be living on the edge of the Spirit's Pentecostal blast. Our world has more than enough of chaos. Surely the Spirit cannot be far behind. A new creation must be just ahead.[5]

He added, "In Eden the Spirit showed us delights and limitations. In Gethsemane the Spirit showed us restoration and the vast inclusive nature of the worldwide family of gardeners. Perhaps in the chaos of our own deaths and frightening uncertainties, the Spirit will bring us to a new order, for which at present we have no language or metaphors."[6] He got this right, at least: the New World Order, if it comes, will beggar description.

The Bible, however, testifies against Swing's ode to creative chaos. Through the prophet Isaiah, the LORD said, "For thus says the LORD, who created the heavens (he is God!), who formed the earth and made it (he established it; he did not create it a chaos, he formed it to be inhabited!): 'I am the LORD, and there is no other. I did not speak in secret, in a land of darkness; I did not say to the offspring of Jacob, 'Seek me in chaos.' I the LORD speak the truth, I declare what is right." (Is. 45:18–19).[7]

---

1. Dee Hock, "Transformation By Design," interview by Melissa Hoffman, *What Is Enlightenment?* magazine, Fall/Winter 2002, p139.

2. Green Cross International, "The Hague Speech by Mikhail Gorbachev," the Hague, 24 May 1993, "Extracts," http://www.greencrossinternational.net/GreenCrossFamily/gorby/hague.html, printed 05/13/03 (cited below as Gorbachev, Hague speech, 05/24/93).

3. Ervin Laszlo, *You Can Change the World: Action Handbook for the 21st Century*, Positive News Publishing, Ltd., 2002, p6.

4. Bob Williams, "Swing marks 25th year as Bay Area bishop (Daybook)," *Episcopal News Service* interview of Bishop Swing, August 9, 2004, http://ecusa.anglican.org/3577_48087_ENG_HTM.htm, printed 08/10/04.

5. Bishop William Swing, "The Holy Spirit and Two Creations, or Maybe Three," *Pacific Church News*, Summer 2004, p5.

6. Ibid., p6.

7. The parenthetical parts of these verses are as given in the Revised Standard Version translation.

One part of the New World Order would be a New Religious Order. Bishop Swing stated in 1998 that "The United Religions Initiative will be inevitable when the world has run out of options. When it is clear that the missing ingredient in authentic diplomacy is religion. . . . The only reason there would ever be a United Religions is that the stark world demands it. The time of that demand is getting close."[1] Swing did not say what event would evoke the "demand," why he suspected that "the time of that demand is getting close," who will make the "demand," or how it will be enforced. In the fall of 2001, Bishop Swing said the same to the International Diplomacy Council: "We will change world history, because the world is going to get impatient with religion;" the world will want religion "to get your act together and make peace in the world."[2] (The occasion for the speech was that the International Diplomacy Council, a group with close ties to the US State Department, had given Swing an award for promoting international understanding; President George W. Bush had sent Swing a letter praising him and the work of the URI.)[3]

In its 2003 Annual Report, the URI boasted of its growing international influence: "URI's successful grassroots engagement and its role as a catalyst for positive change is having an impact around the world and is engaging experts in Organizational Development, Conflict Transformation and International Relations—from the United Nations, NGOs and the international interfaith movement."[4] Like other proponents of the New World Order, the URI sees itself as a "catalyst for positive change."

Another part of the New World Order would be a New Economy, with the social order reconstructed to solve the ecological crisis. In 1993, Mikhail Gorbachev said, "the process of change is proceeding very slowly and from the standpoint of the global ecological situation it is proceeding too slowly. The Green Cross International must become the catalyst and an accelerator of this process."[5] The former ruler of the Soviet Union proposed a strategy of social change by pressure on the status quo from above and from below:

> any change in society is the result of the interaction of changes from above and from below. Changes from above are effected by leaders, by parliaments, by those who make decisions and approve laws and rules, who develop and define priorities and adopt budgets. The second category of changes are those implemented by ordinary citizens, social movements in the various parties, philosophers, by all those who accept and develop new ideas, by those who protest and those who defend their dreams, their visions. These changes are not always visible, but through interaction of human beings, through personal contacts and direct influence they transform the spiritual climate. The two lines of change are interrelated. They reinforce each other. The ideas coming from the bottom up must be accepted by the authorities above, but the decisions taken above cannot succeed without support from below. If from this standpoint you look at the ecological situation it becomes apparent that many things must happen along both of those lines of change and particularly in terms of their interaction. Helping to bring about this interaction is what the Green Cross International is going to do.[6]

As Gorbachev has proposed, many have acted. One of Gorbachev's allies, Maurice Strong's Earth Council, has proposed "a number of international campaigns and innovative catalytic programs,"

1. Bishop William Swing, "Unthinkable to Thinkable to Do-able to Inevitable," address to the World Congress of Faiths, July 22 1998, reprinted in *A Swing with a Crosier*, Episcopal Diocese of California, 1999, p150.

2. Dennis Delman, "Bishop Swing Given International Diplomacy Council Award," *Pacific Church News*, Winter 2002, p46.

3. International Diplomacy Council (IDC), letter from President Bush, November 6, 2002, http://www.diplomacy.org/idc11140101.html, printed 02/17/03.

4. United Religions Initiative, 2003: *Compassionate Actions for a Better World*, annual report; http://www.uri.org/resources/URI_Anual_Report_2003.pdf, viewed 09/24/04.

5. Gorbachev, Hague speech, 05/24/93.

6. Ibid.

including the Earth Charter, to foster "sustainable development at the global level."[1] And in 1998, Barbara Marx Hubbard described the world as "a system awaiting such catalytic action" as could be undertaken by the URI and similar movements "to grow and nurture a new world."[2]

The third leg of the New World Order would be a new political and security regime. Since 9/11, US and British political leaders have seen an opportunity to build such a new order.

At a Labor Party conference immediately after the September 11, 2001 terrorist attack, Tony Blair saw hope for global political and economic change: "This is a moment to seize. . . . The kaleidoscope has been shaken, the pieces are in flux, soon they will settle again. Before they do let us reorder this world around us and use modern science to provide prosperity for all. Science can't make that choice for us, only the moral power of a world acting as a community can."[3]

Condoleezza Rice, the National Security Adviser to President George W. Bush, likewise saw 9/11 as a catalytic event, one which "made possible" social change based on a "new consensus." In her April 2004 testimony to the Congressional committee investigating the September 11, 2001 attack on America, Rice said,

Now we have an opportunity and an obligation to move forward together. Bold and comprehensive changes are sometimes only possible in the wake of catastrophic events. Events which create a new consensus that allows us to transcend old ways of thinking and acting. And just as World War II led to a fundamental reorganization of our national defense structure and the creation of the National Security Council, so has Sept. 11 made possible sweeping changes in the ways we protect our homeland. President Bush is leading the country during this time of crisis and change. He has unified and streamlined our efforts to secure the American homeland by creating the Department of Homeland Security, established a new center to integrate and analyze threat information, terrorist threat information, directed the transformation of the F.B.I. into an agency dedicated to fighting terror, broken down the bureaucratic walls and legal barriers that prevent the sharing of vital information between our domestic law enforcement and foreign intelligence agencies, and working with Congress given [sic] officials new tools, such as the Patriot Act,[4] to find and stop terrorists.[5]

Rice said after 9/11 what the Project for a New American Century (PNAC) had said in September 2000: "the process of transformation, even if it brings revolutionary change, is likely to be a long one, absent some catastrophic and catalyzing event—like a new Pearl Harbor."[6] (The PNAC, like Gorbachev and Earth Council, seems to have an affinity for catalysts.)

1. Earth Council, "The Earth Council and Costa Rica," December 2003, http://www.ecouncil.ac.cr/earth_council_and_co sta_rica_website.pdf, pp1–2, printed 05/26/04.

2. Barbara Marx Hubbard, *Conscious Evolution: Awakening the Power of Our Social Potential*, New World Library, Novato, California, 1998, p194.

3. Michael White, "Let us reorder this world," *The Guardian*, October 3, 2001, http://politics.guardian.co.uk/labour2001/st ory/0,1414,562269,00.html, printed 08/03/04.

4. For assessments of the threat to liberty and the US Constitution posed by the provisions of the Patriot Act, see Nat Hentoff, *The War on the Bill of Rights and the Gathering Resistance*, Seven Stories Press, 2003, and James Bovard, *Terrorism and Tyranny: Trampling Freedom, Justice, and Peace to Rid the World of Evil*, Palgrave/Macmillan, 2003.

5. *New York Times*, "Testimony of Condoleezza Rice Before 9/11 Commission," published April 8, 2004, http://www.ny times.com/2004/04/08/politics/08RICE-TEXT.html?pagewanted=5&ei=5070&en=bca4334a5c2d5b51&ex=1082952000, page 5 of 36.

6. The Project for a New American Century, *Rebuilding America's Defenses: Strategy, Forces, and Resources For a New Century*, September 2000, ch. V, p51; on-line at http://www.newamericancentury.org/RebuildingAmericasDefenses.pdf, printed 05/11/04. Paul Wolfowitz was one of the participants in this project. In his novel *That Hideous Strength*, C.S. Lewis described—from the point of view of two planners for the N.I.C.E., a Satanic cult that sought to take total power in the realm, how a "catalyzing event" could occur: "'Emergency regulations,' said Feverstone. 'You'll never get the powers we want at Edgestow until the Government declares that a state of emergency exists there.' 'Exactly,' said Filostrato. 'It is folly to talk of peaceful revolutions. Not that the canaglia would always resist—often they have to be prodded into it—but until there is the disturbance, the firing, the barricades—no one gets the power to act effectively.'" (Lewis, *That Hideous Strength*, p130.)

We are accustomed to think that religious, business, and political leaders protect the social order in which they prospered, and uphold the values with which they were raised. Instead, some of the most influential people on Earth are themselves acting as change agents. As a result, previously inconceivable events—such as the creation of a powerful United Religions that would shape all the religions of the world—are now possible.

Multiple, complex agendas are at work here. The URI, like the rest of the interfaith movement, is an amalgam of liberals who are committed to peace, and of cultists and occultists who see this same movement as a vehicle to undermine traditional religions. The secular "powers that be," of the neo-conservative, capitalistic American Right and of the "Third Way" European Left, each seek to remake the world order in their own way. The Communists, who still wish to refashion the world, remain in the background waiting for their second chance. All of these political contenders appear to understand that traditional religious belief and mores stand in the way of their project of creating a New Humanity in a New World. Despite the fundamental differences among the contending secular forces, each will, for their own self-regarding motives, support anything that discredits and marginalizes traditional religions. That may be the explanation for the bizarre convergence of support for organizations such as the URI and the State of the World Forum. What, other than a common target, could align George H. W. Bush with Mikhail Gorbachev, George W. Bush with Gray Davis and George Soros, and the Dalai Lama with the kept churchmen of the Peoples' Republic of China? (This convergence of interest need not be conscious; it may be that all are being "drawn to the loadstone rock"[1] by spiritual forces that they do not perceive or understand.)

In his 1910 criticism of the Sillon, a radical French Catholic social action movement of the early 20th Century, Pope St. Pius X uttered a warning that could apply with equal or greater force to today's movements for religious globalism such as the United Religions Initiative:

> this organization which formerly afforded such promising expectations, this limpid and impetuous stream, has been harnessed in its course by the modern enemies of the Church, and is now no more than a miserable affluent of the great movement of apostasy being organized in every country for the establishment of a One-World Church which shall have neither dogmas, nor hierarchy, neither discipline for the mind, nor curb for the passions, and which, under the pretext of freedom and human dignity, would bring back to the world (if such a Church could overcome) the reign of legalized cunning and force, and the oppression of the weak, and of all those who toil and suffer.[2]

By undermining traditional Christianity and sovereign nation-states, the reformers in the URI and globalist movements are weakening critical barriers against an unprincipled global regime of force and spiritual deception.

1. Charles Dickens, "Book the Second," ch. 24, in *A Tale of Two Cities*.
2. Pope St. Pius X, *Notre Charge Apostolique (Our Apostolic Mandate)*, encyclical of August 25, 1910, section 40, http://www w.catholicculture.org/docs/doc_view.cfm?recnum=5456, printed 05/27/04. The translation is at a mainstream Catholic web site, Catholic Culture—not a schismatic or sedevacantist site. The original French text is this: "Hélas, lui qui donnait autrefois de si belles espérances, ce fleuve limpide et impétueux a été capté dans sa marche par les ennemis modernes de l'Église et ne forme plus dorénavant qu'un misérable affluent du grand mouvement d'apostasie organisé, dans tous les pays, pour l'établissement d'une Église universelle qui n'aura ni dogmes, ni monarchie, ni règle pour l'esprit, ni frein pour les passions et qui, sous prétexte de liberté et de dignité humaine, ramènerait dans le monde, si elle pouvait triompher, le règne légal de la ruse et de la force, et l'oppression des faibles, de ceux qui souffrent et qui travaillent." (Pie X, Pape, Lettre Encyclique De N.S.P. Le Pape Pie X Sur "Le Sillon," http://membres.lycos.fr/lesbonstextes/stpxnotrechargeapostolique.htm, printed 05/27/04.

25

A SPECULATIVE POSTSCRIPT: AFTER THE "ANTI-TRADITION," THE FINAL "COUNTER-TRADITION"?

AN ADVISORY

Allow me to begin this postscript with an advisory to my readers. As you have seen, most of this book is an analysis of the interfaith, New Age, and globalist movements, based on a detailed review of publicly available speeches, books, and news reports. I believe that the evidence exists for a definitive case against these movements, and have presented this to the best of my ability.

In this postscript, I move from data analysis to speculation about the future: if the "progressive" New World Order comes, what happens next? My aim is to give an initial warning and to raise awareness, not to offer definitive proof. Anyone who has a distaste for impressionistic futurism and eschatology may safely skip this postscript. If you have come away from the body of this book convinced that the interfaith, New Age, and globalist movements propose undesirable goals, and that these movements should be taken seriously, and that they deserve public scrutiny and opposition, then you have received the principal, urgent warning that I intended to convey.

It is, nevertheless, incumbent upon me to use this postscript to give an additional, longer-range (and admittedly speculative, impressionistic) alert. You might be prepared for an impending tempest, a storm coming from the Left, and may have already boarded up the windows as you hear the wind rise and see the sky darken. Beware! From over the horizon, there *may* approach a second and greater storm from the Right, a spiritual and political hurricane that could destroy whatever is left standing after the Left has done its work.

It might be that with discernment and prayer, one or both of these disasters—which would be a global replay of 1914-1945, on a larger scale—can be mitigated. But before people can react against these dangers, they first need to acknowledge their existence. We also need to remember that evil does not necessarily come from our identified enemies; it can arise amongst our friends and allies—and most perilously, from ourselves. Examination of conscience is essential to spiritual survival.

ABNORMAL TIMES

I now begin to look over the horizon, and to speculate about the implications and sequelae of the current push for a political, social, and religious New World Order.

It is not my intent to say, as a certainty, that the Apocalypse is upon us *now*. Still less do I intend the absurd exercise of setting the date for the Second Coming of Christ. Rather, I am arguing that *if* a New World Order is established (and various powerful forces are attempting to do this), the outcome will be far more complicated—with unexpected political and spiritual perils for the unwary—than most present-day traditionalist and conservative activists, commentators, visionaries, and novelists now expect.

Let's begin by stipulating that we are in abnormal times, and have been since at least 1914. In normal times, Anglican bishops would uphold the doctrine and discipline of their church, and would not raise their hands during a Wiccan-led invocation of Hekate and Hermes.[1] In normal times, billionaires would not declare themselves to be "socialist at heart,"[2] and would not fund movements that undermine the society within which they prospered. In normal times, the ravings of Helena Blavatsky, Alice Bailey, and their New Age followers would be of interest only to the physicians and ministers involved in healing the psyches and souls of these deluded people.

These are not normal times. Therefore, it is possible that, on the heels of a social, economic, or military disaster, the proponents of the New World Order—the URI and its interfaith associates, the globalist movements, and the devotees of Theosophy and the New Age movement—will have an opportunity to rebuild a shattered, disoriented world. Since some of our present-day political and spiritual leaders see themselves as midwives of radical change, we may be very close to such a forced-draft, global version of the Cultural Revolution. Abnormal times, indeed.

THE END OF THE AGE?—PAPAL WARNINGS AGAINST THE LEFT

Are we approaching the ultimate in abnormality, the end of the age? It's a useful question to ask, to examine the full extremity of the challenge that we *might* soon be facing. (Some day, of course, we certainly *will* face the end of the age.) An Italian Catholic commentator on the Apocalypse says, "it is completely licit for Christians to discern from various historical movements Satan's attempts to subvert the design of God's Providence through persecution and seduction. Every era can produce historical figures, political regimes, and ideologies which incarnate Satan's opposition to Christ. We can say that every historical era has its own Antichrist."[3]

Speculation about the end of the age and the Second Coming of Christ is as old as Christianity itself. Over the centuries, saints, lunatics, and charlatans alike have said, "the end is near." The saints who have expected the *Parousia* in their own time (or soon thereafter) have included St. Gregory the Great, who was Pope from 590 to 604,[4] St. Vincent Ferrer, a Dominican preacher who traveled through France and Spain calling for Church reform and warning, around 1400, that Antichrist was then alive,[5] and St. Faustina Kowalska,[6] a Polish nun and mystic of the 1930s who was canonized in 2000 by Pope John Paul II. I will pass over the charlatans and lunatics in silence. However, within the last 100 years, a series of Popes have warned of the approach of the final trial of mankind. With time, their warnings have become more urgent.

---

1. Donald Frew, Covenant of the Goddess, "1999–2000 Interfaith Report," http://www.cog.org/interfaith/cogdf00.html, printed 2/8/03.

2. Drudge Report, "Ted Turner: I Am A Socialist At Heart," September 29, 1999, http://www.drudgereport.com/matt2.html, printed in 1999; no longer on the Net.

3. Rev. Livio Fanzaga, *Wrath of God: The days of the Antichrist*, Roman Catholic Books, 1998, p 28 (cited below as Fanzaga, *Wrath of God*).

4. Bernard McGinn, *Antichrist: Two Thousand Years of the Human Fascination With Evil*, Harper San Francisco, 1994, pp 80–81 (cited below as McGinn, *Antichrist*).

5. Bernard J. McGinn, John J. Collins, and Stephen J. Stein, eds., *The Continuum History of Apocalypticism*, Continuum, 2003, pp 290–291.

6. Sister Faustina Kowalska, *Divine Mercy In My Soul*, Marian Press, 1987; see sections 83, 429, 474, 635, 793, 848, 965–966, 1146, 1155, 1589, and 1732.

Pope St. Pius X, in his first encyclical, warned in 1903 (more than a decade before the crisis of the West became manifest in a world war),

Who can fail to see that society is at the present time, more than in any past age, suffering from a terrible and deep-rooted malady which, developing every day and eating into its inmost being, is dragging it to destruction? You understand, Venerable Brethren, what this disease is—apostasy from God. . . . And as might be expected we find extinguished among the majority of men all respect for the Eternal God, and no regard paid in the manifestations of public and private life to the Supreme Will—nay, every effort and every artifice is used to destroy utterly the memory and the knowledge of God. When all this is considered there is good reason to fear lest this great perversity may be as it were a foretaste, and perhaps the beginning of those evils which are reserved for the last days; and that there may be already in the world the 'Son of Perdition' of whom the Apostle speaks (2 Thess. 2:3).[1]

In his 1928 encyclical on reparation to the Sacred Heart of Jesus, Pope Pius XI wrote:

error has crept in and has spread far and wide, so that it might well be feared that the fountains of Christian life might be in a manner dried up, where men are cut off from the love and knowledge of God. . . . in the last century, and in this present century, things have come to such a pass, that by the machinations of wicked men the sovereignty of Christ Our Lord has been denied and war is publicly waged against the Church, by passing laws and promoting plebiscites repugnant to Divine and natural law, nay more by holding assemblies of them that cry out, 'We will not have this man to reign over us' (Luke 19:14). . . . For from all sides the cry of the peoples who are mourning comes up to us, and their princes or rulers have indeed stood up and met together in one against the Lord and against His Church (Cf. Psalm ii, 2). Throughout those regions indeed, we see that all rights both human and Divine are confounded. Churches are thrown down and overturned, religious men and sacred virgins are torn from their homes and are afflicted with abuse, with barbarities, with hunger and imprisonment; bands of boys and girls are snatched from the bosom of their mother the Church, and are induced to renounce Christ, to blaspheme and to attempt the worst crimes of lust; the whole Christian people, sadly disheartened and disrupted, are continually in danger of falling away from the faith, or of suffering the most cruel death. These things in truth are so sad that you might say that such events foreshadow and portend the 'beginning of sorrows,' that is to say of those that shall be brought by the man of sin, 'who is lifted up above all that is called God or is worshipped' (2 Thessalonians 2:4). . . . And thus, even against our will, the thought rises in the mind that now those days draw near of which Our Lord prophesied: 'And because iniquity hath abounded, the charity of many shall grow cold' (Matt. 24:12).[2]

Pope Pius XII wrote in his 1951 encyclical on Catholic missions: "Venerable Brethren, you are well aware that almost the whole human race is today allowing itself to be driven into two opposing camps, for Christ or against Christ. The human race is involved today in a supreme crisis, which will issue in its salvation by Christ, or in its dire destruction."[3]

Pope John Paul II has warned of a pending "final confrontation" between the "Gospel and the anti-Gospel." In 1976, two years before his election to the Papacy, Karol Cardinal Wojtyla said in a speech in the United States,

---

1. Pope St. Pius X, *E Supremi*, Encyclical of Pope Pius X on the Restoration of All Things in Christ, October 4, 1903, http://www.vatican.va/holy_father/pius_x/encyclicals/documents/hf_p-x_enc_04101903_e-supremi_en.html, sections 3, 4, and 5; printed 04/27/04.

2. Pope Pius XI, *Miserentissimus Redemptor*, Encyclical of Pope Pius XI on Reparation to the Sacred Heart, May 8, 1928, http://www.vatican.va/holy_father/pius_xi/encyclicals/documents/hf_p-xi_enc_08051928_miserentissimus-redemptor_en.html, sections 1, 4, 15, and 17, printed 04/28/04.

3. Pope Pius XII, *Evangelii Praecones*, Encyclical of Pope Pius XII on Promotion of Catholic Missions, June 2, 1951, http://www.vatican.va/holy_father/pius_xii/encyclicals/documents/hf_p-xii_enc_02061951_evangelii-praecones_en.html, section 70, printed 04/27/04.

We are now standing in the face of the greatest historical confrontation humanity has gone through. I do not think that wide circles of the American society or wide circles of the Christian community realize this fully. We are now facing the final confrontation between the Church and the anti-Church, of the Gospel versus the anti-Gospel. This confrontation lies within the plans of divine Providence; it is a trial which the whole Church, and the Polish Church in particular, must take up. It is a trial of not only our nation and the Church, but in a sense a test of 2,000 years of culture and Christian civilization, with all of its consequences for human dignity, individual rights, human rights and the rights of nations.[1]

The context of the apocalyptic Papal warnings makes it clear that the Popes have been sounding the alarm about the rise of militant atheism, anti-clericalism, and materialism. In this view, the Antichrist is the beast who brazenly attacks traditional beliefs about God and Christ, who oppresses the faithful believers, and who makes war on the Church—primarily as an external enemy.

In the imagery of Revelation:

And I saw a beast rising out of the sea, with ten horns and seven heads, with ten diadems upon its horns and a blasphemous name upon its heads. And the beast that I saw was like a leopard, its feet were like a bear's, and its mouth was like a lion's mouth. And to it the dragon gave his power and his throne and great authority. One of its heads seemed to have a mortal wound, but its mortal wound was healed, and the whole earth followed the beast with wonder. Men worshiped the dragon, for he had given his authority to the beast, and they worshiped the beast, saying, 'Who is like the beast, and who can fight against it?' And the beast was given a mouth uttering haughty and blasphemous words, and it was allowed to exercise authority for forty-two months; it opened its mouth to utter blasphemies against God, blaspheming his name and his dwelling, that is, those who dwell in heaven. Also it was allowed to make war on the saints and to conquer them. And authority was given it over every tribe and people and tongue and nation, and all who dwell on earth will worship it, every one whose name has not been written before the foundation of the world in the book of life of the Lamb that was slain. (Rev. 13:1–8)

The "progressive" Theosophists of the Lucis Trust explain, from the standpoint of those who favor this development, how their "Christ" will come. A present-day document from "World Goodwill," an affiliate of the Lucis Trust, says:

In *The Reappearance of the Christ*, it is mentioned that the reappearance will not come as a result of some proclamation or some stupendous planetary event which will force human beings everywhere to say He is there! for that would evoke antagonism and laughter, resistance and fanatical credulity. We will know Him through potency in leadership, through dynamic but logical changes in world affairs, and through action taken by the masses of the people from the depths of their own consciousness.[2]

If this open onslaught from the Left were the totality of the final contest, it is one for which conservative and traditionalist Christians would be psychologically prepared. This is the assault against which the Popes of the last century warned; it would be the final conflict in the rear-guard action that traditionalists have been waging since the French Revolution. In this framework, the emergence and victory of the URI and other movements for religious syncretism, the rise of "progressive" globalist government, and the spread of anti-Christian occultism would be the immediate preparation for the rise of the beast with "seven horns and ten heads" (Rev. 13:1).

1. As quoted in "Notable and Quotable," *The Wall Street Journal*, November 9, 1978, page 30 (editorial page). This source indicates that the then-Cardinal Wojtyla made this statement in his last speech during his visit to the U.S., in September 1976.
2. World Goodwill, *The Problems of Humanity: Building Right Human Relations*, "Study Six: The Churches and Organised Religion," http://www.lucistrust.org/goodwill/pdf/poh6.pdf, p 25.

Popular Christian writers point their radar in the same leftward direction. Archbishop Fulton J. Sheen wrote in 1977, "We do know that at the end of time, when the great conflict between the forces of good and evil takes place, Satan will appear without the Cross, as the Great Philanthropist and Social Reformer to become the final temptation of mankind."[1] An English Catholic apologist of the last century, Ronald Knox, likewise said, "It seems probable enough that the Armageddon of the future lies between Catholicism and some form of humanitarianism—I mean the attempt (in some form) to produce a perfect humanity through the external pressure of breeding, education, and legal coercion."[2] Catholic and Protestant writers of apocalyptic fiction, from the dispensationalist Protestant *Left Behind* series[3] to the Catholic authors of *Lord of the World*[4] and *Father Elijah*,[5] have painted the Final Enemy as a man of the Left.

It may be that this is, indeed, the hour before the triumph of "progressive" religious and political globalists. Current American foreign policy has ranged most of the rest of the world against us; weapons of mass destruction and terrorist networks spread; Communist-ruled China is friendly with Russia now, and threatens to recover Taiwan by any means necessary; Russia retains a huge nuclear arsenal, and is led by a former KGB colonel;[6] imperialism, terror, and sex abuse with a religious cloak are discrediting traditional monotheist religions; capitalist economies worldwide are built on an unsustainable combination of public and private debt, imbalanced trade, concentration of wealth and power in few hands, and a race for the bottom in labor costs (a trend that may wipe out the middle classes that have been the bulwark of social stability in the industrialized nations). If this house of cards tumbles—or is pushed—then the globalist progressives will have their chance at creating a New World Order.

AN APOCALYPTIC THREAT FROM THE RIGHT, AS WELL?

As bad as this appears, we may face an even sterner challenge, one that will be the worse for being unexpected by most: a global theocratic reaction that follows the New World Order. Such a reaction could culminate in the appearance of a seemingly orthodox Christian wonder-worker, a leader who finally puts himself forward through the Church as the Anointed One, demanding worship as God (2 Thess. 2:4). This theocracy would establish a regime of legalism and "righteous" vengeance, responding to leftist antinomianism by fanatically enforcing its own laws, and by scapegoating *any* individuals or groups who might be plausibly blamed for installing or cooperating with the prior leftist, heretical "New World Order" regime. The new purge would begin where the Nazis left off.

A present-day Catholic mystic, who calls himself "Miguel de Portugal," sets forth this scenario in detail: a global war, followed by the creation of a "progressive" New World Order and an anti-Christian New Religion—and then, the rapid collapse of this system due to Divine intervention. He expects that immediately thereafter, there will be a time of massive conversions to the Christian faith—but the re-emergent Church would be swiftly captured by movements that pervert the Church into a totalitarian theocracy. In the name of enforcing religious orthodoxy, there would be a New Inquisition—and

---

1. Archbishop Fulton J. Sheen, *Life of Christ*, Image Books, 1977, p 10.
2. Ronald Knox, *The Belief of Catholics*, Ignatius Press, orig. ed. 1927; rev. ed. 2000, p 220.
3. Tim LaHaye and Jerry B. Jenkins, authors of a 12-book series beginning with *Left Behind* and ending with *Glorious Appearing*, Tyndale House Publishers, 1996–2004.
4. Robert Hugh Benson, *Lord of the World*, Wildside Press, 2002 ed.; this is a reprint of the book originally published in 1907.
5. Michael D. O'Brien, *Father Elijah: An Apocalypse*, Ignatius Press, 1996 (cited below as O'Brien, *Father Elijah*).
6. *abcNEWS.com*, "Reference—Newsmakers—Vladimir Putin," 2001, http://abcnews.go.com/reference/bios/putin.html, printed 04/27/04.

at the end, there would be a religious deceiver, a False Christ, who would ensnare most of the world. Soon after this, Jesus will return in power and glory to rescue his people from this final tyranny.[1]

The prophecies of "Miguel de Portugal" do not have ecclesiastical approval, and it remains to be seen whether future events will validate all his expectations. Many who may read his web site could be put off by his style, if not by his content.

Nevertheless, "Miguel" has given me—and perhaps, many others—an *essential* warning: as bad as a victory of leftist globalism would be, it would not necessarily be the end of our trials. History could well continue, with a global reaction toward a "Christianized" form of Fascism following the brief triumph of the leftist variant of the New World Order.

The Anglican writer C. S. Lewis describes what such a "religious" regime would be like: "The loftier the pretensions of the power, the more meddlesome, inhuman, and oppressive it will be. Theocracy is the worst of all possible governments. All political power is at best a necessary evil; but it is least evil when its sanctions are most modest and commonplace, when it claims no more than to be useful or convenient and sets itself strictly limited objectives."[2] He added, "The higher the pretensions of our rulers are, the more meddlesome and impertinent their rule is likely to be and the more the thing in whose name they rule will be defiled."[3] By exercising tyranny in the name of Christianity, a future rightist regime would perform an ultimate defilement. In an essay that was a sequel to the *Screwtape Letters*, Lewis' infernal contact at the "Tempters' Training College" exulted in the demonic potential of religion gone bad: "All said and done, my friends, it will be an ill day for us if what most humans mean by 'religion' ever vanishes from the Earth. It can still send us the truly delicious sins. The fine flower of unholiness can grow only in the close neighborhood of the Holy. Nowhere do we tempt so successfully as at the steps of the altar."[4]

In 1940, Lewis warned against "pseudo-theology" of the extreme Left *and* Right: "Fascism and Communism, like all other evils, are potent because of the good they contain or imitate. *Diabolus simius Dei*. And of course, their occasion is the failure of those who left humanity starved of that particular good. ... One of the things we must guard against is the penetration of both into Christianity. ... Mark my words: you will frequently see both a Leftist and a Rightist pseudo-theology developing—the abomination will stand where it ought not."[5]

Tolkien, a Roman Catholic, likewise offered a glimpse of what the Deceiver's religious dictatorship might be like. He pondered what might have occurred in the world of *The Lord of the Rings* if the good wizard Gandalf had accepted the temptation of using the evil One Ring, the talisman of power, to overthrow the Dark Lord Sauron. In a letter written to a reader in September 1963, Tolkien said, "Gandalf as Ring-Lord would have been far worse than Sauron. He would have remained 'righteous,' but self-righteous. ... Thus while Sauron multiplied ... evil, he left 'good' clearly distinguishable from it. Gandalf would have made good detestable and seem evil."[6] If a future regime makes "good detestable and seem evil," then the only help for humanity would be the Return of Christ.

1. The M+G+R Foundation, "The General Sequence of Events Leading to the End of These Times," November 28, 2003, http://www.mgr.org/sequence.html, printed 04/27/04; also, "The Spiritual Ambush of a Universal Religion: How It Will Be Used For the Manifestation of the False Christ," February 4, 2004, http://www.mdep.org/owr.html, printed 04/27/04.

2. C.S. Lewis, "Lilies That Fester," ch. 3 of *The World's Last Night And Other Essays*, Harcourt Brace Jovanovich, 1973, p40. This book is cited below as *World's Last Night*.

3. Ibid., p48.

4. C.S. Lewis, "Screwtape Proposes a Toast," ch. 4 of *World's Last Night*, p70.

5. C.S. Lewis, letter of January 17, 1940, in C.S. Lewis, *Letters of C.S. Lewis*, Walter Hooper, ed., Harcourt Brace, rev. ed. 1993, p336 (cited below as *Letters of C.S. Lewis*).

6. J.R.R. Tolkien, *The Letters of J.R.R. Tolkien*, ed. by Humphrey Carpenter and Christopher Tolkien, Houghton Mifflin Co., 1981, pp332–333; drafts of a letter to Mrs. Eileen Elgar, September 1963.

A present-day Evangelical Protestant expert on religious cultism, Brooks Alexander, also warns: "The mystery of iniquity evades any simplistic attempt to identify evil with chaos and disruption, or with vice and immorality."[1] The Final Deceiver will arrive on his own White Horse, a counterfeit of righteousness and justice.

The Russian Orthodox priest Alexander Men, assassinated in 1990 for his faith, warned, "When religion becomes an instrument in the hands of those in power, when its adherents use force, then faith loses its true nature and becomes the servant of political passions and the 'interests' of a particular social group. In many ways our present spiritual crisis bears traces of that counterfeit, that metamorphosis of religion, when religion is darkened by fanaticism and violence and becomes merged with interests of the state."[2] An Italian Catholic commentator on the Apocalypse restates the peril of politicized religion: "The recognition of the spiritual authority of the Church by the world in exchange for secular power has always been a subtle temptation and a form of blackmail. (Be very careful when political authorities begin to praise Christianity and speak well of it.)"[3]

What is the value of this warning? It alerts those who value Christian faith and human liberty that grave threats may come at us from multiple, unexpected directions—simultaneously or sequentially. In his novel *That Hideous Strength*, C.S. Lewis describes—from the point of view of the head of the secret police in the N. I. C. E., a Satanic group that attempts the takeover of England—how the Final Threat could transcend our usual political categories: "Isn't it absolutely essential to keep a fierce Left and a fierce Right, both on their toes and each terrified of the other? That's how we get things done. Any opposition to the N. I. C. E. is represented as a Left racket in the Right papers, and a Right racket in the Left papers. If it's properly done, you get each side outbidding the other in support of us—to refute the enemy slanders. *Of course* we're non-political. The real power always is."[4]

Therefore, our spiritual early warning systems should scan the entire horizon, not just the Left. We should not repeat the mistake that the French High Command made before World War II, when they expected the next attack from Germany to come as a frontal assault. In response, they built, and trusted, the "impregnable" Maginot Line—and were overwhelmed when Germany outflanked their defenses in 1940.

THE TWO-FOLD THREAT: LESSONS FROM HISTORY

It would be easily understandable that readers scoff at the notion that we face a two-fold, potentially apocalyptic threat to our faith and our freedom, from the extreme Right and the extreme Left alike. Below, I offer reasons (derived from theology, social theory, history, and human psychology) to take seriously the warning against an unexpected right-wing globalist aftermath of left-wing, URI/Gorbachev-style globalism.

Consider the lessons of human history—especially the experience of the 1914-1989 period. Fascism, it seems, has an enduring mass appeal. In Germany, the social-democratic revolution of 1918 faced an immediate, violent reaction from defenders of the old regime, including the rise of "Free Corps" militias in 1919 and a military coup attempt in 1920; the Nazi Party arose amidst this chaos. Throughout Europe, people reacted similarly, as a response to the threat of domestic Communism and subversion from Russia. The far Left evoked the authoritarian, Fascist Right. Additionally, as the Nazis seized

1. Brooks Alexander, "The Coming World Religion," Spiritual Counterfeits Project, 1983 pamphlet, p 2.
2. Alexander Men, *Christianity for the Twenty-First Century: The Prophetic Writings of Alexander Men*, Elizabeth Roberts and Ann Shukman, eds., Continuum, 1996, p 176.
3. Fanzaga, *Wrath of God*, p 63.
4. C.S. Lewis, *That Hideous Strength*, p 99; the speaker is Miss Hardcastle.

power, in 1933, "Hitler knew that masses of Socialist and Communist workers were deserting their parties in droves, many of them coming over to him easily and early."[1] Neo-Nazism in Germany is strongest in the former German Democratic Republic, the Soviet satellite state of 1945-1989.

In the aftermath of a future global leftist regime, those outraged by the horrors of the time may do as their European counterparts did between the World Wars, and turn toward an updated, religious form of Fascism. Recruits to the far right of the future may include many who helped to establish and manage the leftist "New World Order"; repentant and disillusioned leftists may become inveterate, illiberal, and fanatical anti-leftists in revulsion against their own earlier deeds. (This has happened before in the history of the Left; it can easily happen again.)[2] It's also true that persecution creates and ennobles martyrs; disreputable forces can align themselves with the persecuted, and cover themselves with borrowed glory after the end of the persecution. Exactly this occurred with the French Communists during and after World War II; it could happen again with cultic religious movements during and after a future leftist regime.

Another factor will be at work: a leftist New World Order will be, in practical terms, atheistic. Any spirituality that it fosters will be emotionally shallow and unsatisfying, akin to the spiritist pabulum now offered by Robert Muller, Neale Donald Walsch, and Barbara Marx Hubbard.

When the leftist regime collapses—whether by Divine or human action—people will seek a more "profound" spirituality. That will be the cue for those who plan a false restoration of tradition to offer their gilded wares to a disoriented, shell-shocked world. It is likely that multitudes will take the bait. The precedent for this is—again—the 1914–1989 period. Communism was established and maintained in Russia and China only by dint of civil war and repeated, massive purges; its atheism did not captivate the masses, or fully compensate them for their material sacrifices. By contrast, German Nazism took power without civil war. Hitler and the Nazis quickly won the adulation of the majority of the German people, and the Nazis remained popular *within Germany* until it was clear that Germany was losing the war.[3] The cult of blood and race, and a false restoration of *volkisch* tradition, was a part of the glue that held the Third Reich together until it was destroyed by the Allies. George Orwell wrote in 1937, "Fascism has been able to play upon every instinct that revolts against hedonism and a cheap

1. John Lukacs, *The Hitler of History*, Vintage Books, 1998, p106 (cited below as Lukacs, *The Hitler of History*).

2. Gordon Urquhart, a former member of Focolare, notes that recruitment of former leftists by new ecclesial movements has already proven successful: "Paradoxically, despite their right-wing position in church politics and their middle-class membership—at least in the western world—all three new movements [Focolare, Communion and Liberation, and the Neo-Catechumenal Way] have had considerable success in attracting recruits from the political far left. In fact, these two extremes have a great deal in common: the promise of a new world in the dim and distant future; the need for a tough, centralized, totalitarian but efficient structure in order to achieve the ambitious goals; the total obedience of individual members with no room for dissent.... Before the fall of communism, Lubich saw Focolare as a mirror image of the socialist world. 'We are made for them,' she would say. 'They have the right structures; all they need is our spirit to animate those structures.'" (Gordon Urquhart, *The Pope's Armada: Unlocking the Secrets of Mysterious and Powerful New Sects in the Church*, Prometheus Books, 1999, pp276–277). Chiara Lubich is the founder of Focolare (cited below as Urquhart, *The Pope's Armada*).

3. "In the Third Reich, the majority gave not only its passive but its active consent to the Führer." (Lukacs, *The Hitler of History*, p111). "For every two children born in 1932, three were born four years later. In 1938 and 1939, the highest marriage rates in *all* Europe were registered in Germany, surpassing even those among the prolific peoples of Eastern Europe." (ibid., p97) "From 1932 to 1939, the number of suicides committed by Germans under twenty dropped 80 *percent* during the first six years of the Hitler regime." (ibid., p98) Lukacs, a historian who wrote extensively on World War II and Hitler, ends his book thus: "That Hitler was the enemy of almost everything that was 'bourgeois' needs no further explanation. He belongs to the end of an age, and he was defeated, and—for a while—bourgeois civilization has been restored, at least in Western Europe and West Germany. But if Western civilization melts away, threatening to collapse, two dangers lie in the future. During a rising flood of barbarism, his reputation may rise in the eyes of orderly people, who may regard him as a kind of Diocletian, a tough last architect of an imperial order. At the same time he might be revered by at least some of the New Barbarians. But this book is the work of a historian, not of a prophet." (ibid., p268)

conception of 'progress.' It has been able to pose as the upholder of the European tradition, and to appeal to Christian belief, to patriotism, and to the military virtues."[1]

A new, global religious Fascism could do something like this, or worse.[2] The historian John Lukacs said, "Compared to the untruth of Stalin's Communism, Hitler's National Socialism may have been a half truth; but, as St. Thomas said, a half truth may be more evil than a lie. . . . A half truth is not equivalent to 50 percent of the truth. It means, instead, a 100 percent truth compounded with, and subordinated to, a 100 percent untruth, the result being an especially dangerous corruption of truth."[3] The same comparison could apply to the left-wing and right-wing variants of a future New World Order.

THE TWO-FOLD THREAT:
WARNINGS FROM SCRIPTURE AND PATRISTIC TRADITION

Consider the warnings that Christ issued against the Final Deceiver and his religious precursors. In the Sermon on the Mount, Jesus said, "Beware of false prophets, who come to you in sheep's clothing but inwardly are ravenous wolves." (Matt. 7:15) Jesus prophesied against the religious authorities who persecuted him for healing a man on the Sabbath (John 5:15–16): "But I know that you have not the love of God within you. I have come in my Father's name, and you do not receive me; if another comes in his own name, him you will receive." (John 5:42–43). In his apocalyptic discourse, given a few days before his Passion, Christ warned: "Take heed that no one leads you astray. For many will come in my name, saying, 'I am the Christ,' and they will lead many astray." (Matt. 24:4–5). He continued:

> And if those days had not been shortened, no human being would be saved; but for the sake of the elect those days will be shortened. Then if any one says to you, 'Lo, here is the Christ!' or 'There he is!' do not believe it. For false Christs and false prophets will arise and show great signs and wonders, so as to lead astray, if possible, even the elect. Lo, I have told you beforehand. So, if they say to you, 'Lo, he is in the wilderness,' do not go out; if they say, 'Lo, he is in the inner rooms,' do not believe it. For as the lightning comes from the east and shines as far as the west, so will be the coming of the Son of man." (Matt. 24:22–27).[4]

St. Paul likewise shows that Satan can act through seduction and false light: "even Satan disguises himself as an angel of light. So it is not strange if his servants also disguise themselves as servants of righteousness. (2 Cor. 11:14–15)

Taking these Biblical admonitions together, the nature of the Final Enemy becomes clearer. He will proclaim himself as the Christ, will build an "ecclesial movement" among the religious authorities and

---

1. George Orwell, *The Road to Wigan Pier*, 1937, as quoted in John Lukacs, *The Last European War: September 1939/December 1941*, Yale University Press, 2001, pp 305–306 (cited below as Lukacs, *The Last European War*).

2. John Lukacs himself drew out the parallel between Hitler and St. John's prophecy of the Final Deceiver. Lukacs said, "The Antichrist will not be horrid and devilish, incarnating some kind of frightful monster—hence recognizable immediately. He will not seem to be anti-Christian. He will be smiling, generous, popular, an idol, adored by masses of people because of the sunny prosperity he seems to have brought, a false father (or husband) to his people. Save for a small minority, Christians will believe in him and follow him. Like the Jews at the time of the First Coming, Christians at the time of the Antichrist—that is, before the Second Coming—will divide. Before the end of the world the superficial Christians will follow the Antichrist, and only a small minority will recognize his awful portents. Well, Hitler did not bring about the end of the world, but there was a time—not yet the time of the mass murders but the time of the Third Reich in the 1930s—when some of St. John's prophecies about the Antichrist accorded with this appearance and his appeal. And it may not be unreasonable to imagine that in the coming age of the masses he was but the first of Antichrist-like popular figures." (Lukacs, *The Hitler of History*, p 266, footnote).

3. Lukacs, *The Last European War*, p 325.

4. The same admonition appears in the other Synoptic Gospels, in Mark 13:5–6, Mark 13:20–23, Luke 17:22–23, and Luke 21:8.

rank-and-file Christians, and will rally many to his side with his false miracles, signs and wonders that counterfeit Christ's own actions. The Usurper will tempt even "the elect"—those who are (or consider themselves to be) orthodox and obedient Christians. Such will be the allure of the "Ape of Christ" that unless the time of trial were shortened by God, *everyone* would fall. This, then, will be a peril that could ensnare *anyone*—including traditionalists and conservatives. Contrast this with the New Age "Christs" such as Share International's "Maitreya,"[1] or with the secular utopias offered by Gorbachev and Maurice Strong, or with the silly syncretism of the United Religions Initiative and other interfaith movements. Many leftists, liberals, and New Age devotees love this stuff—but traditionalists of all kinds are instinctively disgusted. If the Last Trial is to test the faith of *everybody*, there will be a trap that could lure the Right as well as the Left.[2] In the time of the leftist New World Order, the Left will be tempted by seeing the realization of its own rebellious desires; in the succeeding time of the Deceiver, the orthodox and the rightists will be tempted via their own orthodoxy, religiosity, and instincts of obedience.

The tradition of the Church carries forward Christ's warning that mankind's final challenge may come at the hand of an imposter who acts in the name of Christ, and then falsely claims to be Him. The *Didache*, a summary of Church teaching from the end of the first century, warns of the final liar: "For in the last days the false prophets and the corrupters shall be multiplied, and the sheep shall be turned into wolves, and love shall change to hate. For as lawlessness increaseth they shall hate one another and persecute and betray, and then shall appear the deceiver of the world as a Son of God."[3]

In his scholarly history of the Christian traditions pertaining to Antichrist, Bernard McGinn says, "Antichrist as the false messiah, the 'pseudo-Christ,' is first and foremost the great deceiver, the archhypocrite."[4] St. Hippolytus of Rome wrote in the early part of the third century that "The Savior was manifested as a lamb, so he [Antichrist] too, in like manner, will appear as a lamb, though within he is a wolf."[5] McGinn comments,

1. The web site of this camera-shy Antichrist wanna-be is at Share International, http://www.shareintl.org; the beliefs of this organization are derived from Alice Bailey's Theosophy. The "John the Baptist" for this person is Benjamin Creme, who has traveled the world for more that two decades proclaiming the imminent public appearance of "Maitreya." The "World Teacher," however, has not shown his face, except for a few fleeting apparitions.

2. In 1921, René Guénon said, "In addition, today more than ever those claiming to be prophets and messiahs strangely abound in all those groups occupied with occultism. We have known a certain number of these apart from Alcyone and Theosophy, and still others are spreading in spiritist circles. Must this be seen as a sign of the times? Whatever the case and without venturing the least prediction, it is quite difficult in the presence of all these things not to recall the words of the Gospel, 'For false Christs and false prophets will arise and show great signs and wonders, so as to lead astray, if possible, even the elect.' Assuredly, we are not yet there; the false Messiahs we have seen until now have offered wonders of a very inferior quality, and those who have followed them were probably not very difficult to seduce, but who knows what the future holds in store? If one reflects that these false Messiahs have never been anything but more or less unconscious instruments in the hands of those who have raised them up, and if one looks at the series of attempts made by the Theosophists, one is led to think that these are no more than trials, experiments which will be renewed in various forms until success is achieved. In the meantime, these efforts always have the result of troubling some minds. We do not believe moreover that the Theosophists, any more than the occultists and the spiritists, have the strength to succeed in such an enterprise by themselves. But behind all these movements is there not something more fearsome, of which their leaders perhaps do not themselves know, and of which they are in their own turn merely the instruments? We merely raise this question without seeking to resolve it here." (René Guénon, *Theosophy: History of a Pseudo-Religion*, tr. by Alvin Moore et al., Sophia Perennis, 2001, pp271–272). When Guénon cited "Alcyone and Theosophy," he was referring to the promotion of Jeddu Krishnamurti as the coming World Teacher by the Theosophical Society in the early 1920s; "Alcyone" was the Theosophical movement's nickname for Krishnamurti.

3. "The Teaching of the Twelve Apostles to the Heathen," sec. XIII, vv. 3–4, in M. Basil Pennington, Alan Jones, and Mark Booth, eds., *The Living Testament: The Essential Writings of Christianity Since the Bible*, Harper and Row, 1985, p4. This text is also known as and cited below as the *Didache*.

4. McGinn, *Antichrist*, p5.

5. Ibid., p61, quoting from ch. 6 of Hippolytus' *On the Antichrist*.

The history of the Antichrist legend reveals, above all, how Christians have viewed the perversion of true religion, the masquerades that can be used to hide evil intent under the guise of religious probity.... Augustine of Hippo, preaching on the First Epistle of John, identified Antichrist with heretics and schismatics who departed from the true church, but he went on to speak also of Antichrists who remain within—those who confess Christ with their mouths but deny him by their deeds.[1]

McGinn concludes, "the dominant view of ultimate evil has not been one of cruel tyranny so much as one of deception, the masquerading of the lie that perverts the good that saves."[2]

Christian Scripture and Tradition together alert us to the ultimate peril: a foe who is the seductive Ape of Christ, and who will build his own religious and political kingdom on Earth.[3] As the Russian Orthodox theologian Vladimir Solovyov warned in 1900, "the closing scene in the tragedy of history will not be a mere infidelity to or a denial of Christianity, nor simply the triumph of materialism or anything similar to it, but that it will be a religious *imposture*. The name of Christ will be arrogated by forces in humanity that in their practice and in their very essence are alien, even inimical, to Christ and his Spirit."[4]

A FALSE HOPE: THE "GREAT KING" OF THE WEST AND A FUTURE "HOLY POPE"

There are traditions within the Catholic Church that may predispose some people to heed the Deceiver. Chief among these beliefs is the notion that a global upsurge of evil and a Divine chastisement will be followed by a time of peace and universal conversion to the Catholic Church. In this era, there would arise a Great King to restore order and justice worldwide; he would work in tandem with a Holy Pope, who will purify the Church and restore the ancient disciplines. In the words of one adherent of this theory:

The Great King to-be [sic] and the Holy Pontiff will reveal themselves to the world and fight Communism, thus prefiguring Henoch and Elias. Stones will fall from heaven; earthquakes and tidal waves will wreak havoc throughout the world; famines and epidemics will be widespread. Thus will come the end of the first stage, or 'the Good Friday of Christendom.' The resurrection will be spectacular; the Great King will be the Emperor of Western Europe, and anointed by the Holy Pontiff. Many Jews and all non-Catholic Christians will turn to the True Faith. The Mohammedans will embrace Christianity, as also the Chinese. In short, virtually the whole world will be Catholic. This universal preaching of the Gospel, in turn, will constitute the first sign of the second stage [leading to the rise of Antichrist and the end of the age].[5]

---

1. Ibid., p5.
2. Ibid., p279.
3. Charles Upton comments, "It is important to note here that this view of Antichrist is not limited to the Christian world. Islam—which has more strictly canonical material on *al-dajjal* than even Christianity, mostly from the prophetic traditions collected by Muslim, though *al-dajjal* does not appear in the Qur'an—sees the Antichrist as a kind of anti-*Mahdi*, destined to be slain by the Prophet Jesus when he returns at the end of time." (E-mail from Charles Upton to Lee Penn, 6/11/04).
4. Vladimir Solovyov, *War, Progress, and the End of History: Three Conversations—Including a Short Story of the Anti-Christ*, Lindisfarne Press, 1990, p120. These are the words of "Mr. Z," a viewpoint which Solovyov described as "absolutely religious and which will yet show its decisive value in the future," a viewpoint which Solovyov "unreservedly accept[s]." (Ibid., "Author's Preface," p20).
5. Yves Dupont, *Catholic Prophecy: The Coming Chastisement*, TAN Books and Publishers, Inc., 1973, p90 (cited below as Dupont, *Catholic Prophecy*).It should be noted that Dupont carries anti-Semitic baggage, as well. He says of the present day, "In fact, the so-called 'national prosperity' is in the hands of a very few, and it is no right-wing extremism to claim that money is controlled by a Judeo-Masonic clique" (ibid., p79).

The tradition of the Great King and the Holy Pope is based on apocalyptic speculation by saints and by anonymous writers,[1] from the fourth century onward.[2] It first emerged from the *Tiburtine Sibyl*, a work that may date back to AD 380–400.[3] However, expectations for a future Great Monarch and a Holy Pope are not defined in Scripture, or in any dogmatic Conciliar decrees, or in any other official teaching of the Catholic Church.[4] Rather, these hopes derive from private revelation—and Catholics are free to accept, or to reject, such visions and locutions according to the dictates of their own conscience and reason.[5] (Of course, Catholics are called upon to reject private revelations that are contrary to Scripture or to the traditional teaching of the Catholic Church.)

Those who await the Great Monarch and a Holy Pope *may* be ready to fall into the trap of the Deceiver, in a traumatized reaction against the preceding horrors of the left-wing globalist regime. Catholic writer Paul Thigpen warns, "Looking for the Great Monarch, then, who does not appear in Scripture, might lead to overlooking the Antichrist, who does. It might even lead—a more disturbing thought—to mistaking the Antichrist for the Great Monarch. After all, lesser antichrists of the past such as Hitler and Stalin have seduced followers with visions of grand and glorious earthly kingdoms. Surely the Antichrist of the last days will do the same."[6]

The French metaphysician René Guénon said likewise in 1945:

> One can already see sketched out, in various productions of indubitably 'counter-initiatic' origin or inspiration, the idea of an organization that would be like the counterpart, but by the same token also the counterfeit, of a traditional conception such as that of the 'Holy Roman Empire,' and some such organization must become the expression of the 'counter-tradition' in the social order; and for similar reasons the Antichrist must appear like something that could be called, using the language of the Hindu tradition, an inverted *Chakravarti*.[7] The reign of the 'counter-tradition' is in fact precisely what is known as the 'reign of Antichrist.'[8]

(For Guénon, spiritual growth within orthodox, traditional religions is a way to authentic "initiation,"

1. Paul Thigpen, *The Rapture Trap: A Catholic Response to 'End Times' Fever*, Ascension Press, 2001, p221 (cited below as Thigpen, *The Rapture Trap*). He says, "Visions and prophecies of this sort have been attributed to St. Caesar of Arles, Blessed Rubanus Maurus, St. Vincent Ferrer, St. Francis of Paola, St. Hildegard, Venerable Magdalene Porzat, and countless others of wise and holy reputation."

2. The books that set forth this tradition for a conservative Catholic audience include Edward Connor, *Prophecy for Today*, TAN Books and Publishers, Inc., orig. ed. 1956, rev. ed. 1984; Dupont, *Catholic Prophecy*; R. Gerald Culleton, *The Prophets and Our Times*, TAN Books and Publishers, Inc., orig. ed. 1941, rev. ed. 1974; R. Gerald Culleton, *The Reign of Antichrist*, TAN Books and Publishers, Inc., orig. ed. 1951, rev. ed. 1974. The 1956 Connor book carries an imprimatur from Bishop A. J. Willinger, of the Catholic Diocese of Monterey-Fresno; Culleton's 1941 *Prophets and Our Times* carries an imprimatur from Bishop Philip G. Scher, of the same Diocese. The 1941 Culleton book includes the following speculation: "Towards the end of the world the Jews are to commit some atrocious crime for which they will be gravely persecuted. Could this crime be a veering away of many Jews from the belief in a personal God and personal Messiah and all that such belief implies?" (R. Gerald Culleton, *The Prophets and Our Times*, ibid., p28). Culleton added, "The present war is causing great misery to the Jewish people. Its eventual effect upon Jewish aspirations to the Holy Land cannot well be forecast, but if its outcome opens up to them their ancient heritage, and we see at long last a Jewish state there, it means that interesting events in the history of the world are probably not too distant. The prophets do not necessarily forecast a universal Jewish migration, but certainly a Jewish Palestine." (R. Gerald Culleton, *The Prophets and Our Times*, ibid., pp34–35). The most modern of the books setting forth the "Great King" tradition is Desmond Birch, *Trial, Tribulation, and Triumph: Before, During, and After Antichrist*, Queenship Publishing Company, 1996. Birch's book is free of the anti-Semitic overtones of other books listed here.

3. McGinn, *Antichrist*, p89.

4. Thigpen, *The Rapture Trap*, pp223–224.

5. *Catechism Of The Catholic Church*, Second Edition, Libreria Editrice Vaticana, 1997, section 66–67, p23 (cited below as *Catechism*). See also Thigpen, *The Rapture Trap*, p216.

6. Thigpen, *The Rapture Trap*, p225.

7. *Chakravarti* is the Sanskrit word for "universal monarch," and literally means "turner of the wheel."

8. René Guénon, *The Reign of Quantity & The Signs of The Times*, orig. ed. 1945, reissued by Sophia Perennis et Universalis, 1995, p325 (cited below as Guénon, *Reign of Quantity*).

communion with God; those who are involved in "counter-initiation" are—knowingly or not—attaining communion with spiritual forces opposed to God.)

The desire for a "Great King" aligned with a "Holy Pope" to establish justice is understandable in these lawless times, when bureaucrats, venal time-servers, mountebanks, and charlatans dominate politics and churches. However, this is a yearning that will only find satisfaction when Christ returns. No one other than Him is fit to fill the roles that visionaries assign to idealized future Kings and Pontiffs.

RELIGIOUS SECTARIANISM:
LAYING THE FOUNDATION FOR THE FINAL DECEPTION

Additionally, sectarian religious movements[1] that seek political power are arising within and outside the churches. These movements may lay the groundwork for the "spiritual" reactionary regime that could follow the left-wing globalists.

In making the following criticism of right-wing sectarianism, I do not mean to disparage the sincerity or good will of these movements' present-day followers. Many members of these movements are—as one defender recently told me—people who are "trying to be good Catholics in these difficult times."[2] Like Lot, they are "greatly distressed by the licentiousness of the wicked" (2 Peter 2:7). Therefore, if they see a life raft that promises to carry them unscathed through the present ecclesiastical and social chaos, they climb on board. Criticism of these movements from the Left only makes this life raft look more appealing to beleaguered conservatives and traditionalists. Nevertheless, it would be spiri-

1. The classical list of criteria for brainwashing, and (by extension) religious cultism was put forward by Dr. Robert J. Lifton, in his book about the "thought reform" that prisoners of the Chinese Communists underwent during and after the Korean War. The criteria are these:

1. Milieu Control. This involves the control of information and communication both within the environment and, ultimately, within the individual, resulting in a significant degree of isolation from society at large.

2. Mystical Manipulation. There is manipulation of experiences that appear spontaneous but in fact were planned and orchestrated by the group or its leaders in order to demonstrate divine authority or spiritual advancement or some special gift or talent that will then allow the leader to reinterpret events, scripture, and experiences as he or she wishes.

3. Demand for Purity. The world is viewed as black and white and the members are constantly exhorted to conform to the ideology of the group and strive for perfection. The induction of guilt and/or shame is a powerful control device used here.

4. Confession. Sins, as defined by the group, are to be confessed either to a personal monitor or publicly to the group. There is no confidentiality; members' 'sins,' 'attitudes,' and 'faults' are discussed and exploited by the leaders.

5. Sacred Science. The group's doctrine or ideology is considered to be the ultimate Truth, beyond all questioning or dispute. Truth is not to be found outside the group. The leader, as the spokesperson for God or for all humanity, is likewise above criticism.

6. Loading the Language. The group interprets or uses words and phrases in new ways so that often the outside world does not understand. This jargon consists of thought-terminating clichés, which serve to alter members' thought processes to conform to the group's way of thinking.

7. Doctrine over person. Member's personal experiences are subordinated to the sacred science and any contrary experiences must be denied or reinterpreted to fit the ideology of the group.

8. Dispensing of existence. The group has the prerogative to decide who has the right to exist and who does not. This is usually not literal but means that those in the outside world are not saved, unenlightened, unconscious and they must be converted to the group's ideology. If they do not join the group or are critical of the group, then they must be rejected by the members. Thus, the outside world loses all credibility. In conjunction, should any member leave the group, he or she must be rejected also." (American Family Foundation, "Dr. Robert J. Lifton's Eight Criteria for Thought Reform," http://www.csj.org/studyindex/studymindctr/study_mindctr_lifton.htm, printed 05/28/04. A fuller explanation of these criteria is at the web page http://www.csj.org/infoserv_articles/lifton_robert_thoughtreform.htm, maintained by the same organization; printed 05/28/04.) These criteria were from Robert J. Lifton, *Thought Reform and the Psychology of Totalism: A Study of Brainwashing in China*, University of North Carolina Press, 1989, ch. 22. Anti-cult activists usually refer to these or similar criteria in analyzing the behavior of cults, sects, and new religious movements.

2. E-mail of 8/13/04 from a conservative defender of the New Ecclesial Movements in the Catholic Church.

tual malpractice for me to keep silent about the dangers that may come from this quarter, perils that few on the Right now perceive.

Five points, therefore:

• Sincerity and good will are positive attributes for souls, but I am not acting as a confessor for individuals. I am dealing with social movements, and the good or evil that may arise from these movements. There is abundant evidence in history that sincere zealots with praiseworthy intentions can do great harm—regardless of whether the fanatics are secular or religious, leftist or rightist.

• Bankers and art collectors know that the most dangerous counterfeits are those that seem real at first glance. The same is true for spiritual counterfeits. The more convincingly a cultic spiritual movement can present itself as a model of probity and orthodoxy, the more dangerous it is.

• Many of these movements' allies and adherents see what they want to see in the movements, and will never learn of or foster the full agenda of the organization. In this respect, they are like ordinary American Freemasons: sociable Protestant men who attend Lodge parties, do some old-fashioned rituals, and network for business—and who never discover, let alone approve of, the Theosophical and esoteric form of Masonry espoused by Foster Bailey, Manly Hall, and Memphis Rite Masonry.[1]

• The movements that I am criticizing appear to be trying to use money, political power, and spiritual manipulation to re-mold their followers, and to re-make the world. People of good will may enter the rank and file of these sectarian organizations, but *if* they are fully re-formed in the movement's image—or *if* they rise within the movement, approaching its "inner ring"[2]—how long will their sincerity and good will last? In Tolkien's *Lord of the Rings*, the wizard Gandalf warned the hobbit Frodo about the awful transformation that will befall any person who seeks to use the Ring of Power, even for good purposes: "Yes, sooner or later—later, if he is strong or well-meaning to begin with, but neither strength nor good purpose will last—sooner or later the dark power will devour him."[3]

• The groups that I name below appear to be preparing for a "utopia of the Right." However, they are not necessarily the ones who will build the final regime of the "counter-tradition." That dubious honor *may* fall to one of the present-day movements, or a coalition of these groups, or some yet-to-be established group that takes authoritarian pseudo-orthodoxy to its last extreme.

Outside the Catholic Church, rightist movements that explicitly seek to reunite Church and State include the followers of the Rev. Sun Myung Moon[4] and the Christian Reconstructionists[5] (whose ideal is a theocracy based on Old Testament Law).

Within the Catholic Church, these sectarian tendencies are exemplified now by Opus Dei, the Legionaries of Christ, the Neo-Catechumenal Way, and similar "new ecclesial movements." A

1. For a discussion of the irregular, occult, Theosophical branch of Masonry, see Lee Penn, "The Masonic Quest," *SCP Journal*, vol. 26:2–26:3, pp51–67. (This is the magazine issued by the Spiritual Counterfeits Project.)

2. C.S. Lewis, "The Inner Ring," in C.S. Lewis, *The Weight of Glory and Other Addresses*, Macmillan, 1980 ed., pp93–105.

3. J.R.R. Tolkien, "The Shadow of the Past," in *The Fellowship of the Ring*, 2nd ed., Houghton Mifflin Co., 1978, p56.

4. Moon has written, "Then what is God's Will? It does not mean the separation of church and state. It should be the unity of church and state," and has reiterated this position over the years. (The Rev. Sun Myung Moon, "The Way for the True Child," "The Providential Time and the Way of the Second Generation," http://www.unification.org/ucbooks/HDH/TC/TC3 b.html, printed 06/09/04.)

5. The center of this movement is the Chalcedon Foundation; see their web page, "Faith For All Life," http://www.chalcedon.edu/, printed 06/08/04. The Reconstructionist vision is this: "The role of every earthly government—including family government, church government, school government, vocational government, and civil government—is to submit to Biblical law. No government in any form can make men Christians or truly obedient; this is the work of God's sovereign grace. Much less should civil government try to impose Biblical law on an unbelieving society. Biblical law cannot be imposed; it must be embraced.... Though unapologetically Reformed, Chalcedon supports the kingdom work of all orthodox denominations and churches." (Chalcedon Foundation, "Chalcedon Vision Statement," http://www.chalcedon.edu/desk/vision_statement.sh tml, printed 06/08/04.)

scholarly observer of new religious movements says, "Each, from its own point of view, is promoting true spirituality, religious orthodoxy, and conservative morality."[1]

The new ecclesial movements are growing, and exist worldwide. The Legionaries of Christ have "500 priests, another 2,500 seminarians, 1,000 consecrated lay persons, and 30,000 active members in twenty nations."[2] As of 2001, Opus Dei had "82,443 laity and 1,763 priests" as members;[3] another 2,000 deacons and priests were in the closely related Priestly Society of the Holy Cross.[4] More than half of Opus Dei members, about 47,000, are in continental Europe.[5] The Neo-Catechumenal Way has "more than fifty 'Redemptoris Mater' seminaries throughout the world, from which thousands of priests have emerged and been juridically incardinated in the dioceses, but are often, in fact, at the exclusive service of the Way."[6] The "Way" has about one million members in 786 dioceses worldwide.[7] Focolare has "several million 'adherents' with 80,000 core members" in 1,500 dioceses in 190 countries.[8] Most of the youths who flock—in the hundreds of thousands—to Papal masses at Youth Day celebrations "do not come from the parishes, but from the movements: Focolare, the Neocatechumenal Way, the Charismatics. These are to a great extent made up of converts, of lukewarm Christians who have returned to a strong faith practice."[9]

All of these movements "are in practice largely autonomous from the local Churches."[10] A recent critique published by La Civiltà Cattolica—a paper whose contents are reviewed before printing by the Vatican's secretariat of state—warns of three dangers associated with the movements:

> The first danger: 'The tendency to make absolute their own Christian experience, holding it to be the only valid one, for which reason the 'true' Christians would be those who are part of their own movement.' The second: 'The tendency to close themselves off; that is, to follow their own pastoral plans and methods of formation for the members of the movement, to carry out their own apostolic activities, refusing to collaborate with other ecclesial organizations, or seeking to occupy all the territory themselves, leaving scarce resources for the activities of other associations.' The third: 'The tendency to cut themselves off from the local Church, making reference in their apostolic activity more to the methods of the movement and the directives of its leaders than to the directives and pastoral programs of the dioceses and parishes. From this arises the sometimes bitter tensions that can be created between the ecclesial movements and the bishops and pastors.'[11]

Opponents' accusations against these groups are the standard charges against cults: heretical teachings and rituals, secrecy, aggressive and deceptive methods of recruitment, rigidly separating young

---

1. David V. Barrett, *The New Believers: A Survey of Sects, Cults, and Alternative Religions*, Cassell & Co., 2001, p 203 (cited below as Barrett, *The New Believers*).

2. Sandro Magister, "The Legionaries of Christ: 'They're Accusing Us In Order to Attack the Pope,'" *L'espresso*, www.Chiesa, http://213.92.16.98/ESW_articolo/0,2393,41358,00.html, viewed 06/09/04.

3. John Allen, "The Word From Rome," "Opus Dei: No surprise it gets top billing in this papacy," *National Catholic Reporter*, November 9, 2001, http://www.nationalcatholicreporter.org/word/word1109.htm, viewed 06/09/04 (cited below as Allen, "Word from Rome," 11/09/01).

4. Barrett, *The New Believers*, p 200.

5. Ibid.

6. Sandro Magister, "The Seven Capital Vices of the Movements, According to 'La Civiltà Cattolica,'" *L'espresso*, www.Chiesa, http://213.92.16.98/ESW_articolo/0,2393,42202,00.html, printed 07/16/04 (cited below as Magister, "Seven Capital Vices of the Movements").

7. Urquhart, *The Pope's Armada*, p 7.

8. Ibid., p 6.

9. Sandro Magister, "Nomads of God: The New Paths of Religion in Europe," *L'espresso*, www.Chiesa, http://213.92.16.98/ESW_articolo/0,2393,42217,00.html, printed 08/17/04.

10. Sandro Magister, "Church or Little Churches? The Sectarian Threat of Catholic Movements," *L'espresso*, www.Chiesa, http://213.92.16.98/ESW_articolo/0,2393,41797,00.html, viewed 06/09/04 (cited below as Magister, "Church or Little Churches?").

11. Magister, "The Seven Capital Vices of the Movements."

adherents from their families, idolization of the founder of the movement, overemphasis on the virtue of obedience, methods of member formation that are akin to brainwashing, the teaching that salvation depends on loyalty to the movement, requiring members to make their confessions only to priests who are members of the movement, demanding public disclosure of faults (the "manifestation of conscience") in meetings with fellow-members and superiors, and (in the case of Opus Dei) use of flagellation and other harsh physical penances by some members.[1] It should be a red flag that these movements have spawned groups of bruised and disillusioned survivors, organizations such as the Opus Dei Awareness Network[2] and REGAIN,[3] and that these new ecclesial movements have a place on standard anti-cult web sites[4]—an "honor" not shared by traditional Catholic religious orders such as Benedictines, Dominicans, and Franciscans.

Defenders of the new ecclesial movements reply to these accusations with an appeal to authority. Fr. Rosino Gibellini, director of *Concilium*, a Catholic theological journal, said in 2003: "the movements are religious organizations. They are not sects, as above all, they refer to the authority of the Church. What is more, it could be said that they have a direct line with the leadership of the Church."[5] For *Concilium* to praise the new ecclesial movements is, perhaps, an unexpected instance of Left/Right unity within the Catholic Church's structure. *Concilium* says that it "exists to promote theological discussion in the spirit of Vatican II, out of which it was born. It is a catholic journal in the widest sense: rooted firmly in the Catholic heritage, open to other Christian traditions and the world's faiths."[6] Cardinal Schönbern, a conservative, made a similar defense of new ecclesial movements in 1997.[7] In 2000, Cardinal Stafford hailed the movements as "among the most beautiful fruits of the Council."[8]

Some Catholic bishops have acted against these groups. In 1981, Cardinal Hume, Archbishop of Westminster in the United Kingdom, gave credence to charges against Opus Dei by directing that in his diocese, they must refrain from enlisting members under 18 years of age, that they allow young people who wish to join Opus Dei to discuss the matter with their family, that people remain free "to join or leave the organization without undue pressure being exerted," that members have the freedom

1. For critiques of these movements, see Urquhart, *The Pope's Armada* (pertaining to Focolare, Communion and Liberation, and the Neo-Catechumenate); Jason Berry and Gerald Renner, *Vows of Silence: The Abuse of Power in the Papacy of John Paul II*, Free Press, 2004 (pertaining to the Legionaries of Christ); Maria del Carmen Tapia, *Beyond the Threshold: A Life In Opus Dei*, Continuum, 1997 (pertaining to Opus Dei); Fergal Bowers, *The Work: An Investigation into the History of Opus Dei and how it operates in Ireland Today*, Poolbeg Press (Ireland), 1989 (pertaining to Opus Dei); Michael Walsh, *The Secret World of Opus Dei*, Grafton Books (UK), 1989; reprinted in the US as *Opus Dei*, Harper San Francisco, 2004 (pertaining to Opus Dei); and Joan Estruch, *Saints and Schemers: Opus Dei and Its Paradoxes*, Oxford University Press, 1995. For a defense of the new ecclesial movements, and an argument that they are not "sects in the Catholic Church," see Cardinal Christoph Schönborn, "Are There Sects in the Catholic Church," *L'Osservatore Romano*, English language edition, 13/20 August 1997, p3; online at the web site for the Eternal Word Television Network, http://www.ewtn.com/library/CHRIST/ORSECTS.HTM, printed 08/03/04 (cited below as Schönborn, "Are There Sects in the Catholic Church"). The Cardinal said, "It is therefore wrong if communities which are approved by the Church are called sects (by institutions, individuals, or in media reports), or if a life according to the three evangelical counsels is seen as a sect-like practice."

2. Opus Dei Awareness Network (ODAN), "ODAN Home," http://www.odan.org/index.htm, printed 06/08/04.

3. Religious Groups Awareness International Network, http://www.regainnetwork.org/, printed 06/08/04. They say, "We have been able to assist many in their post legionary experience and inform others of the dangers that the Legion of Christ and the Regnum Christi pose to the Church and those who wish to be faithful to Her."

4. Opus Dei Awareness Network (ODAN), "Links," http://www.odan.org/links.htm, printed 06/08/04; this web page contains a list of ten anti-cult web sites.

5. ZENIT.org, "New Movements in Church Are Not Sects, Says Scientific Study; Researcher Thinks Groups Are Revitalizing Ecclesial Life," July 15, 2003, http://www.zenit.org/english/visualizza.phtml?sid=38882, printed 07/16/03.

6. *Concilium* English Edition, *Concilium*, http://www.concilium.org/english.htm, printed 08/03/04.

7. Schönborn, "Are There Sects in the Catholic Church."

8. Zenit.org, "26,000 attend Communion and Liberation Retreat," May 26, 2000, http://www.zenit.org/english/archive/0005/ZE000526.html, printed 08/13/04.

to choose a spiritual director inside or outside of the movement, and that Opus Dei activities be clearly advertised as such.[1] It's most unlikely that the Cardinal would have issued such directives if these practices were not common within Opus Dei. Historian Michael Walsh has said, "Popes before the present one can hardly be said to have been enthusiastic in their endorsement of Opus, and for every bishop who welcomes Opus into his diocese it is clear that there are many who either will not accept them, or are unhappy at finding them installed in their jurisdiction when they take up their appointments."[2] The Neo-Catechumenal Way "has been condemned by cardinals, bishops and important episcopal conferences."[3]

Nevertheless, these movements now have Papal favor. As Jason Berry and Gerald Renner explain, "John Paul saw the Legionaries as a sign of Catholic restoration in Latin America, akin to Opus Dei in Spain."[4] On the eve of Pentecost 2004, the Pope said, "The ecclesial movements and new communities are a providential answer, inspired by the Holy Spirit given the present need of new evangelization."[5]

There are two Legionary bishops: Bishop Brian Farrell, consecrated in 2003, who is second in command at the Pontifical Council for Promoting Christian Unity, and "Bishop Jorge Bernal, the prelate of Chetumal-Cancun in Mexico, who was consecrated in 1974."[6] In 1997, Pope John Paul II named Marcial Maciel as one of 21 Papal delegates for synod of the Catholic Church in the Americas.[7] In January 2001, the Pope praised the founder of the Legionaries: "With special affection I greet your beloved founder, Fr. Marcial Maciel, and extend to him my heartfelt congratulations. . . . I especially appreciated his confirmation of your characteristic fidelity to the successor of Peter."[8] In 2002, the Vatican's Congregation of Bishops held an orientation workshop for all bishops who had been ordained in the previous year. The event "was organized in cooperation with the Legionaries of Christ, and held at the Legionaries' university in Rome, Regina Apostolorum;" Cardinal Giovanni Battista Re, prefect of the Congregation, noted that "at the end of each daily Mass the bishops and the Legionaries had recited a prayer for the pope" which had been "written by Fr. Marcial Maciel Degollado, the founder of the Legionaries."[9] In 2003, John Allen commented, "Given the crisis in the United States and elsewhere provoked by the sex abuse scandals, John Paul's embrace of Maciel is noteworthy indeed."[10] (Allen found this to be "noteworthy" because there are unresolved, public accusations of sexual abuse against Maciel.[11])

The power of Opus Dei is also growing in the Vatican. The founder of Opus Dei, Josemaría Escrivá, was canonized, declared to be a saint, by John Paul II in October 2002. Escrivá was granted this status only 27 years after his death, the fastest canonization on record. The Pope's press spokesman is

1. Michael Walsh, *Opus Dei*, Harper San Francisco, 2004, pp165–166.

2. Ibid., p185.

3. Sandro Magister, "Saturday Night Masses for Everyone! Carmen and Kiko's Church of Many Rooms," *L'espresso*, www.Chiesa, http://213.92.16.98/ESW_articolo/0,2393,40205,00.html, viewed 06/09/04.

4. Jason Berry and Gerald Renner, *Vows of Silence: The Abuse of Power in the Papacy of John Paul II*, Free Press, 2004, p297 (cited below as Berry/Renner, *Vows of Silence*).

5. ZENIT, "Pope Calls New Movements a 'Providential Answer," May 30, 2004, http://www.zenit.org/english/visualizza.phtml?sid=54481, printed 05/31/04.

6. John Allen, "The Word From Rome," "The Trouble With Labels," *National Catholic Reporter*, January 10, 2003, http://www.nationalcatholicreporter.org/word/word0110.htm, viewed 06/09/04 (cited below as Allen, "Word from Rome," 01/10/03).

7. Berry/Renner, *Vows of Silence*, p203.

8. Jason Berry and Gerald Renner, "Sex-related case blocked in Vatican," *National Catholic Reporter*, December 7, 2001, http://www.natcath.com/NCR_Online/archives/120701/120701g.htm, viewed 06/09/04.

9. John Allen, "The Word From Rome," "Legionaries hold orientation for bishops," *National Catholic Reporter*, Sept. 27, 2002, http://www.nationalcatholicreporter.org/word/word0927.htm, viewed 06/09/04.

10. John Allen, "The Word From Rome," 01/10/03.

11. For details of these allegations, see Berry/Renner, *Vows of Silence*, pp209–221, 253, 289, 294–300.

Joaquín Navarro-Valls, a vowed lay member of the order; there are two Opus Dei Cardinals (Archbishop Juan Luis Cipriani Thorne of Lima, Peru, and Julián Herranz, the president of the Pontifical Council for Legislative Texts); supporters are rising in the congregations of the Curia, while opponents are marginalized or made to retire.[1] As John Allen noted, "Opus Dei does seem disproportionately represented in the Roman curia" for an organization of its size.[2]

The writings of the founder of Opus Dei, Josemaría Escrivá, express the tenor of much "new ecclesial movement" spirituality and practice. In *The Way*, he said, "When a layman sets himself up as an arbiter of morals, he frequently errs; laymen can only be disciples."[3] "The plane of the sanctity our Lord asks of us is determined by these three points: holy steadfastness, holy forcefulness and holy shamelessness."[4] "Steadfastness is not simply intransigence: it is 'holy intransigence.' Don't forget that there also exists a 'holy forcefulness.'"[5] "If, to save an earthly life, it is praiseworthy to use force to keep a man from committing suicide, are we not allowed to use the same coercion—'holy coercion'—to save the Lives (with a capital) of so many who are stupidly bent on killing their souls?"[6] "Who are you to judge the rightness of a superior's decision? Don't you see that he has more basis for judging than you? He has more experience; he has more upright, experienced, and impartial advisers; and above all, he has more grace, a special grace, the grace of his state, which is the light and powerful aid of God."[7] "Be slow to reveal the intimate details of your apostolate. Don't you see that the world in its selfishness will fail to understand?"[8] "There are many people, holy people, who don't understand your way. Don't strive to make them understand. It would be a waste of time and would give rise to indiscretions."[9] "Come on! Ridicule him! Tell him he's behind the times: it's incredible that there are still people who insist on regarding the stagecoach as a good means of transportation. That's for those who dig up musty, old fashioned 'Voltairianisms' or discredited liberal ideas of the nineteenth century."[10] "You have come to the apostolate to submit, to annihilate yourself, not to impose your own personal viewpoints."[11] "Obedience, the sure way. Blind obedience to your superior, the way of sanctity. Obedience in your apostolate, the only way: for, in a work of God, the spirit must be to obey or to leave."[12] "It is human nature to have little appreciation for what costs but little. That is why I recommended to you

1. Sandro Magister, "Vatican Letters—The Pope and His Court—A Thousand Curial Maneuvers," *L'espresso*, www.Chiesa, http://213.92.16.98/ESW_articolo/0,2393,41939,00.html, viewed 06/09/04.

2. Allen, "Word From Rome," 11/09/01.

3. Josemaría Escrivá, *The Way / Furrow / The Forge*, Scepter, n. d., maxim 61 from *The Way*, p 14 (cited below as Escrivá).

4. Ibid., maxim 387 from *The Way*, p 95.

5. Ibid., maxim 398 from *The Way*, p 97.

6. Ibid., maxim 399 from *The Way*, p 97.

7. Ibid., maxim 457 from *The Way*, p 110. Charles Upton comments, "The idea, implied here, that one's spiritual superior is necessarily superior in personal sanctity is clearly heretical in a Christian context. It may in fact be a mis-appropriation of the Hindu concept of the *satguru* (teacher whose essence is Truth), or the Shi'ite Muslim doctrine of the perfect Imam. Certainly the priest represents Christ, the one true Master for all Christians, and possesses as an objective fact the charisma of the Sacrament of Holy Orders. Just as certainly, he may be deluded on the psychological plane and/or in a state of mortal sin on the spiritual one. When Dante, in his *Inferno*, placed a pope in Hell, he was directly in line with traditional Christian doctrine as to such a possibility. It is true that one's spiritual master (a Sufi *shaikh*, Orthodox Christian *geron* or *staretz*, Hindu *satguru*, Zen *roshi*, or Tibetan Buddhist *vajraguru*) will indeed, if he is genuine, function as a direct manifestation of God for his disciple; but certainly not everyone who claims to be such a guide is in fact what he claims." (E-mail from Charles Upton to Lee Penn, 10/15/04.)

8. Escrivá, maxim 643 from *The Way*, p 160.

9. Ibid., maxim 650 from *The Way*, p 161.

10. Ibid., maxim 849 from *The Way*, p 214.

11. Ibid., maxim 936 from *The Way*, p 239.

12. Ibid., maxim 941 from *The Way*, p 239. Just as Escrivá upholds "blind obedience," the Rev. Sun Myung Moon holds out the necessity for "absolute obedience." Charles Upton comments: "As for 'blind' obedience, to be genuine it must be based on faith, 'the evidence of things not seen.' A 'disciple' is not a pawn, but someone who is being taught. In order to learn an art,

the 'apostolate of not giving.' Never fail to claim what is fairly and justly due to you from the practice of your profession, even if your profession is the instrument of your apostolate."[1]

The new ecclesial movements' approach to the sex abuse scandal in the Catholic Church (and to other human rights abuses) exemplifies their arrogance and indifference to the suffering of the powerless.

In August 2002, the conservative Catholic journalist Rod Dreher wrote in a column for the *Wall Street Journal* that unless the Pope took "dramatic action to restore the church to holiness—starting with deposing this legion of bad bishops—his criticism of modern society will ring hollow in the heart of this faithful American Catholic."[2] The prominent Opus Dei priest Fr. John McCloskey replied to the *Journal* that a "minuscule proportion" of "Catholic priests and bishops" were implicated in the scandal, and that "remedies are already being put into effect. I would hope that Mr. Dreher would be more patient in terms of the remedy. The church has a pretty good track record. Check in again in about another thousand years."[3]

Fr. McCloskey's millennial "let them eat cake" attitude toward the victims, families, and their supporters mirrors the stance that other prominent Opus Dei and Legionary priests, and their high-level allies, have taken. In March 2002, an Italian priest relied on Escrivá's maxims to attack a *Catholic World News* columnist's criticism of scandal-tainted priests. The priest also blamed parents for not teaching children to respect the Church hierarchy:

Unfortunately not all priests live in full harmony with the Church and with their sacred commitments. One of the prominent figures of the Church of the last century, Blessed Josemaría Escrivá, reminds us accurately of the fact that any priest—whoever he might be—is however always another Christ (*The Way*, 66). . . . Yes, there is a crisis in the Church in many countries. And yes, many priests continue to contribute to it, but this should inspire us to pray more for the priests and for their sanctification, rather than to publicly ridicule them as a group or even under pseudonyms. After all, even more responsible for the present crises are those parents who educate their children to all, but not Gospel values, including the lack of respect and devotion to the hierarchical structure given to the Church by Our Lord.[4]

In April 2002, Cardinal Herranz, an Opus Dei member whom John Allen describes as "the Vatican's attorney general," criticized "a climate of 'exaggeration, financial exploitation and nervousness' in the United States. Herranz also complained of a 'tenacious scandalistic style' in the American press."[5] In 2003, the Cardinal said, "pedophilia is only minimally identified with the Church, touching scarcely one percent of priests. Meanwhile for other categories of persons, the percentages are much higher."[6]

A layman associated with Opus Dei said in early 2002, in response to the then-emerging abuse scandal in Boston, "something will happen to America to protect the Church . . . any country that has historically persecuted the Church at the height of its power collapsed."[7] (In the same vein, in 2002

---

the apprentice must sometimes simply obey his master without yet understanding why—and this includes the art of contemplation. He obeys his master 'blindly,' however, not in order to remain blind, but that, God willing, he may learn how to *see*." (E-mail from Charles Upton to Lee Penn, 10/15/04.)

1. Escrivá, maxim 979 from *The Way*, p 249.

2. Rod Dreher, "The Pope Has Let Us Down," *The Wall Street Journal*, editorial page, August 25, 2002, http://www.opinion journal.com/extra/?id=110002177, printed 06/08/04.

3. Letter from Fr. McCloskey to the *Wall Street Journal*, as quoted in Amy Welborn's blog, at http://www.amywelborn. blogspot.com/2002_08_01_amywelborn_archive.html, viewed 06/08/04.

4. Letters to the Editor, "Criticizing priests," *Catholic World Report*, March 2003, http://www.catholic.net/rcc/Periodicals/ Igpress/2002-03/letters.html, printed 06/09/04.

5. John Allen, "The Word From Rome," "A Look at the New Cardinals," *National Catholic Reporter*, October 3, 2003, http:/ /www.nationalcatholicreporter.org/word/word100303.htm, viewed 06/09/04.

6. John Allen, "Vatican official comments on Geoghan murder," *National Catholic Reporter*, August 25, 2003, http:// nationalcatholicreporter.org/update/bn082503.htm, viewed 06/09/03.

7. From the printout of an on-line conversation between Lee Penn and an Opus Dei cooperator, 02/04/02.

Cardinal Oscar Rodriguez Maradiaga of Honduras, who is not a member of Opus Dei, decried "media 'persecution' of the Catholic church in the United States, comparing it to the times of Nero and Diocletian, and more recently, Stalin and Hitler."[1])

Eight former members of the Legionaries of Christ have formally accused the founder of the Legion, Fr. Marcial Maciel Degollado, of sexually molesting them in the 1950s and 1960s, and of "absolving" them afterward. Despite their pleas for justice, the Vatican has not investigated the charges.[2] Fr. Richard McBrien, a liberal critic of the Legion, said that if Maciel were an American priest facing similar charges by former students, "he would have been immediately removed from ministry under the U.S. bishops' 2002 charter for the protection of youth."[3]

In Peru, the diocese of Opus Dei Archbishop Cipriani had been the center of a brutal civil war between the Army and the terrorist Maoist group "Shining Path." Cipriani "consistently defended the armed forces against charges of atrocities, and argued that 'Most human rights organizations are just covering the tails of political movements, almost all of them Marxist or Maoist.'"[4] Such was his justification for refusing to allow the Catholic bishops' human rights groups to enter his jurisdiction.[5] In 2003, after peace was restored, the Peruvian Truth and Reconciliation Commission (TRC) paid "tribute to the role of the Churches, 'irrespective of theological or pastoral positions' in 'saving many lives and preventing many other abuses.'"[6] However, "the report made an explicit exception of the diocese of Ayacucho under its then archbishop, Juan Luis Cipriani, who 'placed obstacles in the way of church organisations working on human rights, and denied the existence of human rights violations.' Speaking at the Mass for the feast of St Rose of Lima on 30 August, Cardinal Cipriani said the TRC had not bothered to talk to him, and denounced its report as 'prejudiced, biased and petty.'"[7] It appears that Opus Dei clergy and prelates use similar language against those who criticize their role in abuse, whether the abuse is wartime atrocities or the cover-up of sexual crime.

Be that as it may, these "new ecclesial movements"—and high authorities within the Vatican—remain convinced that these organizations represent the future of the Catholic Church. Therefore, the movements and their elite supporters envision a complete reconstruction of the Catholic Church.

A Vatican reporter interviewed Cardinal James Francis Stafford, an American who headed the Pontifical Council for Laity in 2002; the Cardinal said, "Despite whatever rough edges these groups may possess, Stafford argued, what he hears from men and women involved in them is that they know how to build community. Hence, Stafford said, he hopes the American bishops will become more open to the movements."[8] Cardinal Stafford said the same in 2003 to a reporter from the newspaper of the Catholic Archdiocese of Boston:

1. John Allen, "The Word From Rome," "Cardinal Schotte's views on Dallas," *National Catholic Reporter*, June 14, 2002, http://www.nationalcatholicreporter.org/word/word0614.htm, viewed 06/09/04.

2. Sandro Magister, "The Confessions of an ex-Legionary: 'Why I Broke The Silence,'" *L'espresso*, www.Chiesa, http://213.92.16.98/ESW_articolo/0,2393,40388,00.html, viewed 06/09/04. See also Jason Berry, "Mahony Better Watch Out for Legion of Christ," *Los Angeles Times*, Sept. 26, 2004, http://www.latimes.com/news/printedition/opinion/la-op-berry26sep26,1,2822993.story?coll=la-news-comment, printed 09/27/04.

3. Rev. Richard P. McBrien, "The Legion of Christ," *The Tidings*, October 22, 2004, http://www.the-tidings.com/2004/1022/essays.htm, printed 10/22/04.

4. Philip Jenkins, *The Next Christendom: The Coming of Global Christianity*, Oxford University Press, 2002, p147.

5. World Church News, "New cardinals mirror John Paul's papacy," *The Tablet*, January 27, 2001, http://www.thetablet.co.uk/cgi-bin/citw.cgi/past-00005, printed 06/09/04.

6. World Church News, "The Americas," *The Tablet*, September 6, 2003, http://www.thetablet.co.uk/cgi-bin/citw.cgi/past-00144, printed 06/09/04.

7. Ibid.

8. John Allen, "The Word From Rome," "The 'Secret' Norms," *National Catholic Reporter*, November 29, 2002, http://www.nationalcatholicreporter.org/word/word1129.htm, viewed 06/09/04.

I sense that living forgiveness, that love, which is a tough love, to be very present in the ecclesial movements in a way that I don't sense them as strongly in the parishes. Also, the vision of the early communities after the ascension of Jesus, as expressed in Acts 2 and 4, are better expressed, better realized, in the new lay movements than I sense in most parishes. . . . I think one of the instruments that the Spirit has given to us would be these new lay communities, including the Neocatechumenate. Despite the fact that so many find objections to the Neocatechumenate in the United States, I am convinced that the means for renewal within the Church rests with the new communities and it also rests with the Neocatechumenate.[1]

Should American bishops open the door as requested, they may be letting a large and aggressive camel into the tent. As John Allen reported in 2003,

Spain is something of a laboratory for a redefinition of parish and diocesan structures. One staggering statistic from [Opus Dei priest] de la Hoz: Of Spanish Catholics who attend Mass at least once a month (roughly 18 percent of Spain's 37 million Catholics, or around 6.6 million people), more than 40 percent come from the movements. In other words, almost half of the practicing Catholics in Spain, some 3 million, belong to a movement. As this number continues to rise, I wondered, what will the impact be on parish life? Extrapolating from what Gordon and Munoz said, it seems one scenario is that the parish will not disappear, but it will play a very different role. Instead of being the center of Catholic life, the crucible in which one's spirituality is forged, it will function as a meeting place for the movements. The parish would become a sort of ecclesiastical piazza, in which adherents of the Neocatechumenate, Opus Dei, Regnum Cristi [sic], Catholic Action, Communion and Liberation, etc., meet to share experiences, to work on joint projects, and at least sometimes to worship together, before moving back down their different avenues. Under this scenario, the pastor becomes a facilitator rather than a shepherd in the traditional sense, someone whose task is to bring the movements into conversation and collaboration. The parish becomes the guarantor of communion, but the focus of Christian living will be inside the movements. A related question is what happens to bishops. When the primary identity of Catholics is defined in geographic terms, i.e., as a member of such-and-such as parish, the diocesan bishop is the key authority. But once Catholics understand themselves in terms of a charism or spirituality, one that crosses geographic boundaries, they become analogous to members of a religious order in the sense that they take their cues more from leadership of the group rather than bishops. Already one sees this process at work in Spain, where Kiko Arguello and Carmen Hernandez, co-founders of the Neocatechumenate, are higher-profile and more powerful figures than most Spanish bishops. Though Pope John Paul II has encouraged the movements, to what extent the institutional Church is prepared for the long-term implications of a shift from geography to charism as the locus of Catholic identity is an open question. Spain seems the place where this will be worked out first, and hence it bears watching.[2]

In 2004, Allen commented that the European Union's rejection of any mention of the Christian heritage of Europe in the proposed Union constitution

will probably push a few more European bishops to open their doors to new ecclesial realities such as Opus Dei, the Neocatechumenate, and the Legionaries of Christ. In a culture that often seems not just indifferent, but positively hostile, to organized religion, it may be that only disciplined, highly motivated groups operating outside traditional ecclesiastical structures will have the capacity to evangelize and catechize. If nothing else, the defeat on the constitution tells bishops that they need help.[3]

As an Italian commentator noted in 2003, the new ecclesial movements "refer directly to the pope as

1. ZENIT.com, "Cardinal Stafford on the Church's Crisis," August 23, 2003, http://www.zenit.org/english/visualizza.phtml?sid=39931, printed 08/03/04.

2. John Allen, "The Word From Rome," "New Movements changing Spain," *National Catholic Reporter*, May 9, 2003, http://www.nationalcatholicreporter.org/word/word0509.htm, viewed 06/09/04.

3. John Allen, "The Word From Rome," "Pope Displeased by Europe's rejection of Christian roots," *National Catholic Reporter*, June 25, 2004, http://www.nationalcatholicreporter.org/word/word062504.htm, printed 06/26/04.

their one connection to the Church. To different degrees they bear the distinctive features of a sect. The risk is that they will transform the Catholic Church into a body of memberships in juxtaposed groups that don't communicate with each other: each movement with its own liturgy, its own discipline, its own system of authority and beliefs."[1] The result of this trend would be the fragmentation of parish life,

> with the parish conceded to one of the movements. The ecclesial community finally coincides with a determined group, the sacraments become a service that is sometimes outsourced and sometimes produced from within, the parish pastoral council becomes a place for the groups to negotiate over the scarce remaining resources in the parish, intraecclesial associations lose their specific meaning, episcopal authority becomes evanescent (eventually replaced by the movement's authority), while papal authority is hailed as identifying, but is far removed and practically innocuous. At times, even administrative services (at the diocesan level as at the regional and national levels) tend to take on the movement's form.[2]

A former member of Focolare said the same: "A Church in which the movements predominate will no longer be recognizably Catholic. Even in the pre-conciliar period, the sense of a common faith was strong. In the Church of the future this sense of belonging, of identity could be fragmented into groups which have virtually nothing in common with one another."[3] He added, "It is ironic that the most pernicious and inhuman idea of the twentieth century, the deification of the collective, has found its last refuge and most passionate proponents in the very Catholics who fought communism so fiercely."[4]

If Catholic authorities restructure the Church based on the new ecclesial movements, Catholic parishes and dioceses would cease to embody the unity of the faithful. They would instead become recruiting grounds for competing authoritarian, politicized sects that claim allegiance to the Pope. This would be a radical revision of the structure and beliefs of the Catholic Church, a change that would eclipse the revisions in doctrine and discipline now being sought by Call to Action and other liberal dissenters.

Charles Upton draws out the parallels between the globalist syncretism of the URI and the new ecclesial movements' replacement of traditional, local Church structures with allegiance to a movement, its specialized spirituality, and its charismatic leader. He says,

> The proposed fragmentation of the once-unified Catholic Church into quasi-independent 'new ecclesiastical movements' appears as the reverse *mirror-image* of the syncretic ecumenism of the URI. The marginalization of geographically based communities such as the parish (which is seen as too 'parochial') or diocese is one of the watchwords of globalization. In line with the 'information culture' and the global, non-localized quality of cyberspace, both 'new ecclesial' and New Age networks tend to de-emphasize local and national cultures and communities while striving to be global in reach. Like so-called on-line 'communities,' New Age networks and the 'new ecclesial movements' lack the geographical, ethnic, cultural and historical common ground that would relate them to other 'communities' formed around other areas of interest. (So much for the 'unifying, community-building' claims made for the information culture's 'global brain' by its New Age proponents!) The resulting cultural and religious fragmentation inevitably evokes a desire for unity—consciously or otherwise. In the case of the 'new ecclesial movements' within Catholicism, this desire seems ready to express itself as the call for a totalitarian pope with the power to *impose* unity from above.[5]

---

1. Magister, "Church or Little Churches?"

2. Sandro Magister, "A Parish of the People, Not of the Elite. Italy Renews its Model of Church," *L'espresso*, www.Chiesa, http://213.92.16.98/ESW_articolo/0,2393,42028,00.html, viewed 06/09/04.

3. Urquhart, *The Pope's Armada*, p 409.

4. Ibid., p 413.

5. E-mail from Charles Upton to Lee Penn, 10/15/04.

SPIRITUAL VULNERABILITY:
THE FETISHES OF AUTHORITY AND OBEDIENCE

Could Catholics fall for such distortions of their ancient faith? Yes. (Here, the present heresies of the left-wing dissenters are not the issue.)

Among some conservative Catholics, *the* touchstone of the faith is obedience to ecclesiastical authority. Thus, one writer for a staunchly orthodox Catholic magazine claims that in the teachings of the early Church Fathers Clement of Rome, Ignatius of Antioch, Justin Martyr, and Irenaeus of Lyons, "we see the seed developing that later blossoms into the one doctrine that elevates the Catholic Faith above all others—Papal Infallibility."[1] Likewise, another book reviewer for the same magazine said, concerning a book that debated Catholic teachings on the Virgin Mary, that prospective converts to the Catholic Church must, "at some point," "cease examining each point of doctrine separately, confront the issue of authority, and simply assent to 'all that the Catholic Church believes and teaches.' This kind of assent is required for Catholic orthodoxy."[2] He added that the book's author "could have highlighted more the fact that Catholics accept the Marian dogmas because they first accept the authority of the Church. . . . For prior to the question of specific dogmas looms the question of where lies the authority on faith and morals for a Christian. And here we have the clearest signposts pointing us to Rome, and thus to what Rome teaches."[3]

In response to the priestly sex-abuse scandal and the ensuing public criticism of the Catholic hierarchy, various Catholic commentators propose *strict obedience* and respect for the hierarchy as the solution.

Archbishop Charles Chaput of the Archdiocese of Denver spoke for them when—as an antidote to the "prophetic" antics of rebels in religious orders—he proposed that we follow one of the "Rules for Thinking with the Church"[4] offered during the Reformation by St. Ignatius of Loyola. The "Thirteenth Rule," cited by the Archbishop, is:

> If we wish to proceed securely in all things, we must hold fast to the following principle: What seems to me white, I will believe black if the hierarchical Church so defines. For I must be convinced that in Christ our Lord, the Bridegroom, and in His spouse, the Church, only one Spirit holds sway, which governs and rules for the salvation of souls. For it is by the same Spirit and Lord who gave the Ten Commandments that our holy mother Church is ruled and governed.[5]

The Archbishop of Denver has put this viewpoint into practice in his dealing with lay critics. Rod Dreher, an orthodox Catholic who has written extensively about the Catholic sex abuse scandal, reports upon his correspondence with Chaput in early 2002, when the *Boston Globe* was breaking the news about the priestly sex assaults and ecclesiastical cover-up in Boston:

1. Thomas Ellis, book review of *Four Witnesses: The Early Church in Her Own Words*, in *New Oxford Review*, November 2003, p48. This statement exemplifies the institution-centered outlook of some Catholic apologists. However, *New Oxford Review* has carried prominent stories criticizing some of the Vatican's prudential judgments. For example, in March 2004, it ran a cover story by David Palm, titled "Catholic Confusion at the Very Top."

2. Thomas Storck, book review of *Mary: A Catholic-Evangelical Debate*, in *New Oxford Review*, July-August 2004, p45.

3. Ibid.

4. Ignatius Loyola, "Rules for Thinking with the Church," in "Readings from the Protestant and Counter Reformations," http://www.thecaveonline.com/APEH/reformdocument.html, printed 05/08/04; this version lists the first 13 of Ignatius' rules.

5. Archbishop Charles Chaput, "Consecrated life meant to be leaven in the Church," April 24, 2002, Archdiocese of Denver, http://www.archden.org/archbishop/docs/4_24_02_consecrated_life.htm, printed 05/08/04. This rule is part of the Spiritual Exercises of St. Ignatius of Loyola; the full set of eighteen rules may be found on-line at http://www.ccel.org/pager.cgi?file=i/ignatius/exercises/exercises1.0.html&up=i/ignatius/exercises/exercises.html&from=RTFToC159 and at http://www.fordham.edu/halsall/source/loyola-spirex.html, as of 05/19/04.

Then the Archbishop chastised me for making what he considered an unwarranted assumption that the Boston bishops were concerned about Geoghan, but not his victims. Chaput said, 'You don't know that.' He quoted a previous letter of mine in which I said, 'bishops don't seem to care, except insofar as it affects their finances.' His Excellency said—and this I will quote directly—'Well, I know bishops a lot better than you do, Rod, including their many weaknesses. To suggest that they protect their resources before they protect their people is not just insulting, but unjust and wrong. If you really believe that, why would you remain Catholic?'[1]

With this comment, Chaput placed belief in the hierarchy as the centerpiece of Catholic faith.

Leaders with such attitudes are capable of doing hideous things in times of great crisis, with the approval of their own conscience. As the Inner Party inquisitor told Winston, the dissident in Orwell's *1984*, "Whatever the Party holds to be truth *is* truth. It is impossible to see reality except by looking through the eyes of the Party."[2] Acceptance of this irrational mind-set (perhaps, after spiritual formation in a "new ecclesial movement") prepares the faithful to goose-step off a spiritual cliff, if a Deceiver should become Pope—or rather, anti-Pope.

In normal times, Catholics reject the idea that a Pope could be a heretic or an apostate—but we are here looking ahead into the Final Days, the most abnormal of times. And the *Catechism of the Catholic Church* says that in that brief time, the Church will follow the way of Christ, through her Passion to death and burial:

> Before Christ's second coming the Church must pass through a final trial that will shake the faith of many believers. The persecution that accompanies her pilgrimage on earth will unveil the 'mystery of iniquity' in the form of a religious deception offering men an apparent solution to their problems at the price of apostasy from the truth. The supreme religious deception is that of the Antichrist, a pseudo-messianism by which man glorifies himself in place of God and of his Messiah come in the flesh. . . . The Church will enter the glory of the kingdom only through this final Passover, when she will follow her Lord in his death and Resurrection. The kingdom will be fulfilled, then, not by a historic triumph of the Church through a progressive ascendancy, but only by God's victory over the final unleashing of evil, which will cause his Bride to come down from heaven. God's triumph over the revolt of evil will take the form of the Last Judgment after the final cosmic upheaval of this passing world.[3]

OUTSIDE THE CHURCH,
TWO WITNESSES TO THE DUAL PERIL

Scripture, Catholic tradition, and reason show the possibility that we face a twofold threat—and that the final test may be religious seduction under the leadership of a False Christ, not merely oppression by a tyrannical persecutor of Christians (akin to the Jacobins or the Communists). Two other witnesses testify to this same possibility—Friedrich Nietzsche, the apostle of atheism and nihilism, and René Guénon, a wise and insightful French traditionalist metaphysician who wrote in the middle of the last century.

THE NIHILIST'S DARK PROPHECIES:
FRIEDRICH NIETZSCHE

First, I present the testimony of Nietzsche, the declared foe of God. In 1885, in *Will to Power*, he saw the emergence of global politics and global governance: "Inexorably, hesitantly, terrible as fate, the great

1. Rod Dreher, as posted on April 16, 2004, in the discussion thread "Archbishop Chaput weighs in," at the web log *Open Book* (run by Amy Welborn), http://amywelborn.typepad.com/openbook/2004/04/archbishop_chap.html, printed 05/27/04.
2. George Orwell, *1984*, New American Library edition, 1961, p205.
3. *Catechism*, sections 675 and 677, pp176–177.

task and question is approaching: how shall earth as a whole be governed? And to what end shall 'man' as a whole—and no longer as a people, a race—be raised and trained?"[1]

Let's begin with Nietzsche's insights into the 20th Century.[2] In 1888, when it could hardly be imagined that the then-ruling European regimes could fall, he said in *Ecce Homo* that soon, "The concept of politics will have merged entirely with a war of spirits; all power structures of the old society will have been exploded—all of them are based on lies: there will be wars the like of which have never yet been seen on earth. It is only beginning with me that the earth knows *great politics*."[3] In *The Gay Science*, Nietzsche said in 1882, "I welcome all signs that a more manly, a warlike age is about to begin, an age which, above all, will give honor to valor once again."[4]

In *Ecce Homo*, Nietzsche promised, accurately, that "the uncovering of Christian morality is an event without parallel, a real catastrophe."[5] In the 1887 edition of *The Gay Science*, he elaborated: "The greatest recent event—that 'God is dead,' that the belief in the Christian God has ceased to be believable—is even now beginning to cast its first shadows over Europe;" however, few yet understood "what has really happened here, and what must collapse now that this belief has been undermined— all that was built upon it, leaned on it, grew into it: for example, our whole European morality."[6]

In *Untimely Meditations*, Nietzsche prophesied in 1874 about the effects of teaching moral relativism and the lack of a fundamental distinction between humans and animals:

> If, on the other hand, the doctrines of sovereign becoming, of the fluidity of all concepts, types and species, of the lack of any cardinal distinction between man and animal—doctrines which I consider true but deadly—are thrust upon the people for another generation with the rage for instruction that has by now become normal, no one should be surprised if the people perishes of petty egoism, ossification and greed, falls apart, and ceases to be a people; in its place systems of individualist egoism, brotherhoods for the rapacious exploitation of the non-brothers, and similar creations of utilitarian vulgarity may perhaps appear in the arena of the future.[7]

He wrote in 1877 of "this coming generation" that "Perhaps this generation as a whole will even seem more evil than the present generation—for, in wicked as in good things, it will be more *candid*; it is possible, indeed, that if its soul should speak out in free full tones it would shake and terrify our soul as would the voice of some hitherto concealed evil spirit of nature."[8]

In 1887, in *Will to Power*, Nietzsche wrote: "What I relate is the history of the next two centuries. I describe what is coming, what can no longer come differently: *the advent of nihilism*. . . . This future speaks even now in a hundred signs. . . . For some time now, our whole European culture has been moving as toward a catastrophe, with a tortured tension that is growing from decade to decade."[9]

Additionally, Nietzsche foresaw the strife that socialism and Communism would strew across Europe, and welcomed the failure of that social experiment. In 1885, Nietzsche wrote in *Will to Power*:

1. Friedrich Nietzsche, *The Will to Power*, tr. by Walter Kauffmann and R. J. Hollingdale, Vintage Books, 1968 (cited below as Nietzsche, *The Will to Power*), "Book four: Discipline and Breeding," section 957, p501.

2. This line of research was suggested by Tom Wolfe, in his 1996 essay: Tom Wolfe, "Sorry, but your soul just died," *Forbes ASAP*, December 2, 1996, pp211–223.

3. Friedrich Nietzsche, section 1 of "Why I Am a Destiny," in *Ecce Homo*, in the collection *On the Genealogy of Morals* and *Ecce Homo*, ed. and tr. by Walter Kaufmann, Vintage Books, 1969, p327 (cited below as Nietzsche, *Ecce Homo*).

4. Friedrich Nietzsche, section 283 of *The Gay Science*, in Walter Kaufmann, ed., *The Portable Nietzsche*, 1982 ed., p97 (this collection is cited below as *Portable Nietzsche*).

5. Nietzsche, section 7 of "Why I Am a Destiny," in *Ecce Homo*, p333.

6. Nietzsche, section 343 of Book V of *The Gay Science*, in *Portable Nietzsche*, p447.

7. Friedrich Nietzsche, section 9 of "On the uses and disadvantages of history for life," in *Untimely Meditations*, tr. by R. J. Hollingdale, Cambridge University Press, 1983, pp112–113 (cited below as *Untimely Meditations*).

8. Nietzsche, section 11 of "Richard Wagner in Bayreuth," in *Untimely Meditations*, p251.

9. Nietzsche, *The Will to Power*, "Preface," section 2, p3.

the Paris commune, which has its apologists and advocates in Germany too, was perhaps no more than a minor indigestion compared to what is coming. . . . I should wish that a few great experiments might prove that in a socialist society life negates itself, cuts off its own roots. The earth is large enough and man still sufficiently unexhausted; hence such a practical instruction and *demonstratio ad absurdum* would not strike me as undesirable, even if it were gained and paid for with a tremendous expenditure of human lives. In any case, even as a restless mole under the soil of a society that wallows in stupidity, socialism will be able to be something useful and therapeutic: it delays 'peace on earth' and the total mollification of the democratic herd animal; it forces the Europeans to retain spirit, namely cunning and cautious care, not to abjure manly and warlike virtues altogether.[1]

He continues: "the *barbarians* of the twentieth century . . . will come into view and consolidate themselves only after tremendous socialist crises—they will be the elements capable of the greatest severity toward themselves and able to guarantee the most enduring will."[2]

Total up the score: in the high noon of the Victorian era, the prophet of atheism discerned the coming of a Europe-wide catastrophe, unprecedented wars, moral collapse, nihilism, political fanaticism, the rise of "brotherhoods for the rapacious exploitation of the non-brothers," Communist victories followed by enormous bloodshed, and the rise of a generation that would seem to the men of the 19th century to speak with "the voice of some hitherto concealed evil spirit." That's the briefest possible summary of the history of the world since 1914, and it was a prospect that almost nobody of his time saw—aside from the Popes.[3]

Now, we can turn to what the anti-Apostle saw for the following era. After the time of war and catastrophe, Nietzsche saw a dark, majestic rebirth for humanity. After the destructive era of nihilism, Nietzsche expected the emergence of new values, to be defined by a new elite.

In 1887 in *Will to Power*, he said that there will be "a movement that in some future will take the place of this perfect nihilism—but presupposes it, logically and psychologically, and certainly can come only after it and out of it."[4] The nihilist phase "represents the ultimate logical conclusion of our great values and ideals—because we must experience nihilism before we can find out what value those 'values' really had."[5] In the reaction against the destruction of tradition, "new values"[6] would be set up to counterfeit and replace what was smashed. (Mikhail Gorbachev sounded a similar note in 1993: "Revaluation of values is basic to the evolution of civilization."[7])

In a section of *Will to Power* written in 1885, Nietzsche described how the New Elite, the commanding apostles of the New Values, would be formed: "A morality with such reverse intentions, which desires to train men for the heights, not for comfort and mediocrity, a morality with the intention of training a ruling caste—the future *masters of the earth*—must, if it is to be taught, appear in association with the prevailing moral laws, in the guise of their terms and forms."[8] Nietzsche found it

---

1. Ibid., "Book One: European Nihilism," section 125, pp77–78.
2. Ibid., "Book four: Discipline and Breeding," section 868, p465.
3. Papal warnings against the evils of Nietzsche's time (1844–1900) included the following encyclicals: Pius IX, *Quanta Cura* ("On Current Errors"), 1864; Leo III, *Diuturnum Ilud* ("On Government Authority"), 1881; Leo XIII, *Humanum Genus* ("On Freemasonry and Naturalism"), 1884; and Leo XIII, *Libertas Praestantissimum* ("On Human Liberty"), 1888. Even though Nietzsche and the Popes utterly disagreed on the cause, nature of, and cure for the disorders of their time, they were in agreement in diagnosing the society of their time as gravely ill. The reactionary Popes and the revolutionary philosopher both saw through the then-standing façade of Progress. All the Papal encyclicals just listed are in the following collection: Anthony J. Mioni, Jr., ed., *The Popes Against Modern Errors: 16 Papal Documents*, TAN Books and Publishers, 1999.
4. Nietzsche, *The Will to Power*, "Preface," section 2, pp3–4.
5. Ibid., "Preface," section 2, p4.
6. Ibid., "Preface," section 2, p4.
7. Green Cross International, "The Hague Speech by Mikhail Gorbachev," the Hague, 24 May 1993, "Extracts," http://www.greencrossinternational.net/GreenCrossFamily/gorby/hague.html, printed 05/13/03.
8. Nietzsche, *The Will to Power*, "Book four: Discipline and Breeding," section 957, p502.

"obvious" that "for this, however, many transitional means of deception must be devised, and that, because the lifetime of a single man signifies virtually nothing in relation to the accomplishment of such protracted tasks and aims, the very first thing to be done is the rearing of a new kind of man, in whom the duration of the necessary will and the necessary instinct will be guaranteed through many generations—a new master type and caste."[1] He added,

> From now on there will be more favorable preconditions for more comprehensive forms of dominion, whose like has never before existed. And even this is not the most important thing; the possibility has been established for the production of international racial unions whose task will be to rear a master race, the future 'masters of the earth';—a new, tremendous aristocracy, based on the severest self-legislation, in which the will of philosophical men of power and artist-tyrants will be made to endure for millennia—a higher kind of man who, thanks to their superiority in will, knowledge, riches, and influence, employ democratic Europe as their most pliant and supple instrument for getting hold of the destinies of the earth, so as to work as artists upon 'man' himself. Enough: the time is coming when politics will have a different meaning.[2]

Let's draw out the implications of these prophecies from the 19th Century. The creation of the New Elite, those who would rule after modernism and socialism have spent their fury, is a project that will take generations. These men will be trained to look as if they are "in association with the prevailing moral laws;" they, and their teachers, will be skilled users of many "transitional means of deception." The New Rulers would be formed strictly, "based on the severest self-legislation." The New Aristocrats will rise first in Europe, and will go from there to establish unprecedented, "comprehensive forms of dominion." Their strategy will be based on exploitation of their own "riches and influence," and will have as its goal the control of the planet's destiny and the artistic redesign of mankind. This is a summary of the strategy and aims of certain powerful, elite religious movements already in existence.

In *Ecce Homo*, Nietzsche said,

> Let us look ahead a century; let us suppose that my attempt to assassinate two millennia of antinature and desecration of man were to succeed. That new party of life which would tackle the greatest of all tasks, the attempt to raise humanity higher, including the relentless destruction of everything that was degenerating and parasitical, would again make possible that excess of life on Earth. . . . I promise a tragic age: the highest art in saying Yes to life, tragedy, will be reborn when humanity has weathered the consciousness of the hardest but most necessary wars without suffering from it.[3]

In 1887 in *Will to Power*, Nietzsche said that violence would give birth to "a stronger species" than the "pampered, weak of will" Europeans of the 19th Century;[4] a "dominating race can grow up only out of terrible and violent beginnings."[5] Hitherto, the world has looked for the barbarian "only in the depths. There exists also another type of barbarian, who comes from the heights: a species of conquering and ruling natures in search of material to mold."[6] In The *Gay Science*, he stated that the coming "manly" and "warlike" age (presumably, the 20th Century) "shall prepare the way for one yet higher, and it shall gather the strength which this higher age will need one day—this age which is to carry heroism into the pursuit of knowledge and *wage wars* for the sake of thoughts and their consequences."[7]

The new masters, those who come after the breakdown of the social system that proclaimed universal "equality" and "social justice," would live by the stern principles set forth in Nietzsche's 1888

1. Ibid., "Book four: Discipline and Breeding," section 957, pp 502–503.
2. Ibid., "Book four: Discipline and Breeding," section 960, p 504.
3. Nietzsche, section 4 of "The Birth of Tragedy," in *Ecce Homo*, p 274.
4. Nietzsche, *The Will to Power*, "Book four: Discipline and Breeding," section 868, p 464.
5. Ibid., "Book four: Discipline and Breeding," section 868, p 465.
6. Ibid., "Book four: Discipline and Breeding," section 900, p 479.
7. Nietzsche, section 283 of *The Gay Science*, in *Portable Nietzsche*, p 97.

Twilight of the Idols: "In order that there may be institutions, there must be a kind of will, instinct, or imperative, which is anti-liberal to the point of malice: the will to tradition, to authority, to responsibility for centuries to come, to the solidarity of chains of generations, forward and backward *ad infinitum*. When this will is present, something like the *imperium Romanum* is founded."[1]

The Coming Leaders foreseen by Nietzsche, the barbarians "from the heights," will "attempt to raise humanity higher," and will engage in "relentless destruction" of whatever, or whoever, opposes them or fails to meet their standard. Once again, it seems, there will be a time when "truth" will ride under Crusaders' arms, while "error"—no matter how narrow and distorted the perspective used to define it as such—will have no rights.

THE WARNINGS OF A
SUFI METAPHYSICIAN, RENÉ GUÉNON

In his 1945 book *The Reign of Quantity & The Signs of The Times*, the traditionalist metaphysician René Guénon warned of the approaching end of the age. He warned against the omnipresent materialism and artificial egalitarianism of the West, seeing these as symptoms of terminal illness: "One would have to be blind to fail to see the abyss which separates the normal from the modern civilization … that which the vast majority of men now living celebrate as 'progress' is exactly what is now presented to the reader as a profound decadence, continuously accelerated, which is dragging humanity towards the pit where pure quantity reigns."[2] He added, "the real goal of the tendency which is dragging men and things toward pure quantity can only be the final dissolution of the present world."[3] Furthermore, "the acceleration of time itself, as it becomes ever more pronounced and causes changes to be ever more rapid, seems to lead of its own accord towards dissolution."[4]

The universal corruption affects its opponents, as well: "those who most sincerely want to combat the modern spirit are almost all unwittingly affected by it, and all their efforts are therefore condemned to remain without any appreciable result."[5] Therefore, Guénon says, "the very idea of tradition has been destroyed to such an extent that those who seek to recover it no longer know which way to turn, and are only too ready to accept all the false ideas presented to them in its place and under its name."[6] He adds, "the work which has as its object to prevent all 'reaction' from aiming at anything further back than a return to a lesser disorder, while at the same time concealing the character of the lesser disorder so that it may pass as 'order,' fits in very exactly with the other work carried out with a view to securing the penetration of the modern spirit into the interior of whatever is left of traditional organization of any kind in the West."[7]

However, just before the end, Guénon sees a sudden, brief reversal of these trends. Instead of equality, there will be a new hierarchy. Instead of atheism and materialism, there will be spirituality and religion galore. Instead of the open war against tradition, there will be a false restoration of tradition, a recovery that is in fact a perverse, infernal inversion of authentic tradition. Antichrist will claim to bring the Millennium, "the 'golden age' into being through the reign of the 'counter-tradition,'" and will give it "an appearance of authenticity, purely deceitful and ephemeral though it be, by means of a

---

1. Nietzsche, section 39 of "Skirmishes of an Untimely Man," in *Twilight of the Idols*, in *Portable Nietzsche*, p542.
2. Guénon, *Reign of Quantity*, p77.
3. Ibid., p139.
4. Ibid., p198.
5. Ibid., pp208–209.
6. Ibid., p251.
7. Ibid., pp 255–256.

counterfeit of the traditional idea of the *Sanctum Regnum*."[1] In 1945, Guénon discerned only the "preliminary signs" of the "counter-tradition," "in the form of all the things that are striving to become counterfeits in one way or another of the traditional idea itself."[2] However destructive may be the "reign of quantity," the age of materialism and Godlessness, Guénon says that "the merely negative 'anti-tradition' only represented the necessary preparation"[3] for the emergence of the final "counter-tradition."

The Final Enemy

imitates in his own way, by altering and falsifying it so as always to make it serve his own ends, the very thing he sets out to oppose: thus, he will so manage matters that disorder takes on the appearance of a false order, he will hide the negation of all principles under the affirmation of false principles, and so on. Naturally, nothing of this kind can ever really be more than dissimulation and even caricature, but it is presented cleverly enough to induce an immense majority of men to allow themselves to be deceived by it.[4]

Guénon says of the reign of the Final Deceiver:

He will evidently be an 'imposter' (this is the meaning of the word *dajjâl* by which he is usually designated in Arabic) since his reign will be nothing other than the 'Great Parody' in its completest form, the 'satanic' imitation and caricature of everything that is truly traditional and spiritual. . . . His time will certainly no longer be the 'reign of quantity', which was itself only the end-point of the 'anti-tradition'; it will on the contrary be marked, under the pretext of a false 'spiritual restoration', by a sort of re-introduction of quality in all things, but of quality inverted with respect to its normal and legitimate significance. After the 'egalitarianism' of our times there will again be a visibly established hierarchy, but an inverted hierarchy, indeed a real 'counter-hierarchy', the summit of which will be occupied by the being who will in reality be situated nearer than any other being to the very bottom of the 'pit of Hell'. . . . by reason of his extreme opposition to the true in all its aspects, the Antichrist can adopt the very symbols of the Messiah, using them of course in an inverted sense.[5]

The servants of Antichrist will possess a dark, seductive sanctity: "The last degree of the 'counter-initiatic' hierarchy is occupied by what are called 'the saints of Satan' (*awilyâ esh-Shaytân*) who are in a sense the inverse of the true saints (*awilyâ er-Rahmân*), thus manifesting the most complete expression possible of 'inverted spirituality'."[6]

In the regime of Antichrist, "the setting up of the 'counter-tradition' and its apparent momentary triumph will in effect be the reign of what has been called 'inverted spirituality,'" a "parody of spirituality."[7] With the inversion of spirituality will come the inversion of traditional symbols: "The most diabolical trick of all is perhaps that which consists in attributing to the orthodox symbolism itself, as it exists in truly traditional organizations . . . the inverted interpretation which is specifically characteristic of the 'counter-initiation."[8]

Guénon concurs with Christian tradition in noting that the regime of Antichrist will be short: "all the prophecies (the word is of course used here in its rightful sense) indicate that the apparent triumph of the 'counter-tradition' will only be a passing one, and that at the very moment when it seems most complete it will be destroyed by the action of spiritual influences which will intervene at that point to prepare for the final reinstatement. Nothing less than a divine intervention of this kind would

1. Ibid., p331.
2. Ibid., p313.
3. Ibid., p319.
4. Ibid., p238.
5. Ibid., pp325–326.
6. Ibid., p358, note 162.
7. Ibid., p321.
8. Ibid., pp247–248.

in fact suffice to bring to an end, at the chosen time, the most formidable and the most truly 'satanic' of all the possibilities"[1] of the current age.

Charles Upton, a present-day metaphysician and comparative religion scholar, sums up the confusing and disorienting nature of the situation that we may be facing:

> The looming One World Government shows many signs of being the predicted regime of Antichrist. But . . . it's not quite that simple, since the 'tribal' forces reacting against globalism are ultimately part of the same system. According to one of many possible scenarios, the satanic forces operating at the end of the Aeon would be quite capable of establishing a One World Government only to set the stage for the emergence of Antichrist as the great leader of a world revolution *against* this government, which, if it triumphed, would be the *real* One World Government. Or the martyrdom of Antichrist at the hands of such a government might be a deliberate or even staged self-sacrifice, counterfeiting the death of Christ and leading to a counterfeit resurrection. I am not saying that this will happen; I am not prognosticating. I only wish to point out that Antichrist, as a counterfeit manifestation of the Divine universality, will have the capacity to use all sides in any conflict, including a global one, to build his power—except the ultimate Messianic Conflict, called Armageddon in the *Apocalypse*, which is initiated and concluded by God Himself.[2]

WHAT IS TO BE DONE?

How are we to respond to the dual perils before us—whether or not these constitute the Final Trial?

In part, and as the first step, by examining ourselves, repenting of our own sin and our participation in collective evil and deception. The prayer for our time, as for all earthly times, is "Lord Jesus Christ, Son of the Living God, have mercy on me, a sinner." Bernard McGinn ends his magisterial history of Antichrist thus:

> Contemporary forms of deception, especially deception on a worldwide scale never possible before, might spur our meditation on the meaning of the legend of Antichrist as the image of essential human evil. The dominance of appearance over substance may not have been invented in the electronic era, but some contemporary social critics remind us that deceit has reached a new level of sophistication as we approach the beginning of the third millennium. . . . If we are all part of a culture in which forms of deceit, both overt and covert, are present in many ways, we can admit that the most dangerous form of deceit is self-deceit, our ability to convince ourselves that we are doing what is best and for the best reasons, even when this is not the case—and somehow, however obscurely, we *know* it not to be the case. That is just another way of putting Augustine's ancient message: 'There you have the Antichrist—everyone who denies Christ by his works.'[3]

Having removed the logs from our own eyes, we may accurately discern the specks that are in the

---

1. Ibid., p314. Thomas Day, a current critic of the spiritual decay of the modern Church, discerned the present-day meaning of the trivialization and manipulation of religious symbols. After describing a liturgical horror that occurred in a Protestant church (at the end of a book that catalogued similar events in Catholic churches), he said, "What does it all mean? First of all it means that Roman Catholics are not the only ones capable of liturgical nuttiness. Secondly, it means prepare for the worst. We must surely be living in a dangerous era when any religion begins to treat human beings as if they were little kitsch toys—without yearnings, without imperfections, without imagination, without the gift of a soul, without art. We would expect dictators, radical political theorists, and others who have a low opinion of people to indulge in amusing games with symbols, as a sign of their contempt for the idiots called human beings, but in religion this sort of thing is bad news. It means the end of that idea of a special, creating human 'soul,' and the beginning of an age when people in churches will be manipulated as if they were stupid machines—easily turned on or off [with a gimmick] by smart machines. It means head for the hills." (Thomas Day, *Where Have You Gone, Michelangelo? The Loss of Soul in Catholic Culture*, Crossroad, 1993, p226.)

2. Charles Upton, *The System of Antichrist: Truth & Falsehood in Postmodernism and the New Age*, Sophia Perennis, 2001, pp506–507.

3. McGinn, *Antichrist*, pp279–280.

eyes of our opponents (Matt. 7:3–5). We should then pray on their behalf, for their salvation and conversion to the fullness of Truth; in doing this, we are asking God to bestow the greatest of blessings on them (Matt. 5:44). Such prayers may have great, unforeseen effect—results that may not be known to us until the Last Day.

In addition to repentance and prayer, it is also essential to be spiritually alert and to discern the signs of the times. As Jesus said, "Watch therefore, for you do not know on what day your Lord is coming." (Matt. 24:42) A holy priest in Michael O'Brien's apocalyptic novel *Father Elijah* reminds us of the difficulties associated with this discernment: "The apocalypse is not a melodrama. If it were, most people would wake up and see the danger they are in. That is our real peril. Our own times, no matter how troubled they may be, are our *idea* of what is real. It is almost impossible to step outside of it in order to see it for what it is. . . . The living apocalypse radiates a sense of normality. We are *inside* it."[1] To use a business cliché: we need to "think *out of the box.*" Prayer and repentance are the only way that we will see beyond the confines of the "box," to perceive what is really occurring.

Some who read this may have a calling to activism, in the churches and in the public square. I am not an organizer myself, neither a politician nor a cleric, neither a financier nor a senior executive. Therefore, I cannot venture a guess at an activist strategy that might successfully oppose or mitigate the present trends toward global religious deception, apostasy, and tyranny. (I am skeptical that social and political action can work any longer, but my assessment of the lateness of the hour may be incorrect. Such efforts *might* still turn the tide, and grant the world a season of peace and liberty.) Each reader who hears and receives these admonitions has his unique talents and station in life; the appropriate response will necessarily be different for everyone.

However anyone responds to these challenges, let it be a response based on love and humility. Everyone should reflect on the lessons that Solzhenitsyn learned while imprisoned in Stalin's gulag:

> In the intoxication of youthful successes I had felt myself to be infallible, and I was therefore cruel. In the surfeit of power I was a murderer, and an oppressor. In my most evil moments I was convinced that I was doing good, and I was well supplied with systematic arguments. And it was only when I lay there on rotting prison straw that I sensed within myself the first stirrings of good. Gradually it was disclosed to me that the line separating good and evil passes not through states, nor between classes, nor between political parties either—but right through every human heart—and through all human hearts. This line shifts. Inside us, it oscillates with the years. And even within hearts overwhelmed by evil, one small bridgehead of good is retained. And even in the best of all hearts, there remains . . . an un-uprooted small corner of evil. Since then I have come to understand the truth of all the religions of the world: They struggle with the evil *inside a human being* (inside every human being). It is impossible to expel evil from the world in its entirety, but it is possible to constrict it within each person. And since that time I have come to understand the falsehood of all the revolutions in history: They destroy only *those carriers* of evil contemporary with them (and also fail, out of haste, to discriminate the carriers of good, as well). And they then take to themselves as their heritage the actual evil itself, magnified still more.[2]

Let any of us, when tempted to be crusaders, heed this wisdom bought by Solzhenitsyn at so high a price!

---

1. O'Brien, *Father Elijah*, pp 156–157. The speaker is Father Elijah, the hero of the novel.

2. Aleksandr I. Solzhenitsyn, *The Gulag Archipelago* 1918–1956: *An Experiment in Literary Investigation*, vol. 2, tr. Thomas P. Whitney, Harper and Row, 1975, part IV, ch. 1, pp 615–616.

SED CONTRA:
AGAINST EXTREME-RIGHT "SOLUTIONS" TO THE CRISIS

At the beginning of the book, I replied to the objections to my thesis that might be raised by a challenger from the Left. I now reply to some possible—and very undesirable—extreme rightist responses to the present and pending crises.[1] As a literary convention, I allow the adherents of each of these positions to speak through one representative; he quotes his allies. I have named these zealots after Job's friends (Job 2:11 and 32:2).

The positions that I describe are held by relatively few people now, but such fanaticism can easily spread as traumatized people react to global upheaval. Who in Germany in 1913 would have foreseen what Germany became in 1933? Who in Russia in 1897 would have expected 1917?

Eliphaz: You have missed the point. You don't seem to understand that these *are* the times of the end, and America will stand or fall based on whether or not we support Israel to the hilt. "Israel is invincible, because it is flowing in the tide of divine prophecy."[2] A new Temple—located on the Temple Mount, where the Muslim Dome of the Rock now stands—is "an absolute necessity for the completion of the prophetic picture."[3] "If we want to be observers of prophecy we can, or we can be participants. We choose to be participants . . . doing everything we can to ensure the survival of Israel and . . . to support the building of the Temple."[4] "We shouldn't wait for God . . . but, as it were, hurry Him up. We should take up the burden first . . . and afterward He will agree and help us."[5] "When the Temple's rebuilt, it ushers in the Second Coming, but it also ushers in the Tribulation."[6] When prophecy is fulfilled, "God says he will lay the land of the Arabs waste and it will be desolate."[7] "Any attempt to divide the land of Palestine is contrary to God's word, for it has been set aside by God as the exclusive home for Israel."[8] "I see the rise of Islam to destroy Israel and take the land from the Jews and give East Jerusalem to [Palestinian Authority Chairman] Yasser Arafat. I see that as Satan's plan to prevent the return of Jesus Christ the Lord. . . . God says, 'I'm going to judge those who carve up the West Bank and Gaza Strip. . . . It's my land and keep your hands off it.'"[9] "Theologically, any Christian has to support Israel, simply because Jesus said to."[10] "If the US ever turns its back on Israel, we will no longer exist as a nation."[11]

---

1. In this section, I am speaking against extreme Zionism and premillennial dispensationalism, anti-Semitism, militia-style survivalism, neo-monarchism, and "traditionalist" religious cultism. Those who hold these positions generally self-identify with the Right, as they define it. However, all of these stances are antithetical to the humane, sober conservatism of Edmund Burke and his intellectual descendants, and are contrary to the American tradition established by the Founding Fathers, a balance of order and liberty in a Constitutional republic. The far-right stances that I debate in this section are not the conservatism of Robert Taft or Barry Goldwater.

2. An anonymous writer in 1974, as quoted by Paul Boyer, *When Time Shall Be No More: Prophecy Belief in Modern American Culture*, Harvard University Press, 1992, p195 (the book is cited below as Boyer, *When Time Shall Be No More*).

3. John Wesley White, 1980, as quoted by Boyer, *When Time Shall Be No More*, p199.

4. David Lewis, National Christian Leadership Conference for Israel, as quoted by Gershom Gorenberg, *The End of Days: Fundamentalism and the Struggle for the Temple Mount*, The Free Press, 2000, p127 (cited below as Gorenberg, *End of Days*).

5. Yehudah Etzion, an Israeli extremist, as quoted by Gorenberg, *End of Days* pp179–180.

6. A former high school pastor at Chuck Smith's Calvary Chapel, as quoted by Gorenberg, *End of Days*, p174.

7. Arthur Bloomfield, 1971, as quoted by Boyer, *When Time Shall Be No More*, pp201–202.

8. Lehman Strauss, 1965, as quoted by Boyer, *When Time Shall Be No More*, pp203–204.

9. Pat Robertson, as quoted in Associated Press, "Evangelist Pat Robertson leads pilgrims to Israel," *Haaretz.com*, October 4, 2004, http://www.haaretzdaily.com/hasen/spages/484433.html, printed 10/23/04.

10. Jerry Falwell, as quoted by Boyer, *When Time Shall Be No More*, p203.

11. Hal Lindsey, 1981, as quoted by Boyer, *When Time Shall Be No More*, p203.

Author: Maybe you're right, and we are in the very Final Days before the Second Coming of Christ. Even so, what you propose makes no sense—theologically or morally. The idea that God guaranteed the land of Palestine to a restored nation of Israel is not found anywhere in the New Testament or the Church Fathers. It is, as a Christian mass movement, a sectarian Protestant innovation dating to the early 1800s.[1]

Jews in Israel have the right to life and peace. So do the Arabs and Palestinians. (Some of them, by the way, are Christian.) No peace can be built on oppression and murder; "drive them into the desert" is as evil as "drive them into the sea."

The proponents of building the Third Temple are not part of the Israeli mainstream.[2] Every year, the Temple Mount Faithful attempt to carry a cornerstone to the Temple Mount to ceremonially begin the rebuilding; every year, they are intercepted and turned away by the Israeli police. A historian of the Dispensationalist prophecy movement notes, "In their obsession with the rebuilding of the Temple, these prophecy popularizers ignored the fact that most Israelis rejected the whole notion. Epithets like 'a bunch of nuts' and 'dangerous lunatics' routinely dotted Israeli press accounts of groups like the Temple Mount Faithful."[3]

The idea that we ought to "hurry Him up" to speed the Second Coming is presumption and blasphemy. The only way that we Christians should attempt to hasten the Kingdom of God is by faithful witness for Christ, works of love and mercy, and praying the Lord's Prayer, "Thy Kingdom come!"

It might be that a Third Temple is destined to be rebuilt on the site of Herod's Temple. *If* this is a true view of prophecy, then as Jesus said, "It is impossible but that offences will come: but woe *unto him*, through whom they come!" (Luke 17:1, KJV) It is not necessarily good to act in fulfillment of prophecy; Judas did so when he betrayed Christ, and Christ called him the "son of perdition" (John 17:12). How could God bless the rebuilding of a structure that He had said would be destroyed so that "there will not be left here one stone upon another, that will not be thrown down." (Matt. 24:2)—especially when that rebuilding could start a global religious war?

Those who wish to rebuild the Temple are following in the footsteps of Julian the Apostate the fourth-century Roman Emperor who sought to discredit Christ by rebuilding the structure upon which Christ had pronounced a sentence of doom. Julian ended the reconstruction after the Temple Mount was shaken by repeated earthquakes, and workers were killed by fires of unknown origin. Soon thereafter, the forsworn Emperor was killed on the battlefield.[4]

Bildad: Thanks for dealing with those Christian Zionists. But you have not looked at the real problem: the entire Jewish race! "It is no right-wing extremism to claim that money is controlled by a Judeo-

---

1. For refutations of pre-millennial Dispensationalism, the Christian heresy that is the basis of these extreme Zionist perspectives, see T. L. Frazier, *A Second Look at the Second Coming: Seeing Through the Speculation*, Conciliar Press, 1999 (Eastern Orthodox); Thigpen, *The Rapture Trap* (Roman Catholic); Carl E. Olson, *Will Catholics Be 'Left Behind'?: A Catholic Critique of the Rapture and Today's Prophecy Preachers*, Ignatius Press, 2003 (Roman Catholic). Many other such refutations exist from mainline and Evangelical Protestants, as well.

2. Charles Upton comments on the mainstream Jewish movement away from millennialist messianism in the last few centuries: "After the debacle of the false messiah Shabbetai Zevi in the 17th century, who electrified international Jewry before unexpectedly apostatizing to Islam, the consensus within Hasidism leaned toward a prohibition of 'pressing for the End.' The 'millennialist' attempt to bring about the advent of the Messiah and the Day of Judgment through human action on the stage of history was largely replaced by an emphasis on inner spiritual purification, by which the People of Israel would become worthy to receive the Messiah." (E-mail from Charles Upton to Lee Penn, 10/15/04).

3. Boyer, *When Time Shall Be No More*, p 199.

4. Warren Carroll, *The Building of Christendom: A History of Christendom*, Vol. 2, Christendom College Press, 1987, pp 53–54. The account of Julian's attempt to rebuild the Temple is from Ammianus Marcellinus, a pagan historian who served in the army under Julian in 363 and wrote of these events soon thereafter. Another account of these events, from the fifth century, is in the "Jewish History Sourcebook: Julian and the Jews 361–363 CE," at http://www.fordham.edu/halsall/jewish/julian-jews.html.

Masonic clique."[1] "There is, of course, convincing bibliographical evidence of a Judeo-Masonic plot from the 18th century onwards,"[2] a plot to destroy Christianity and morality. Indeed, "the Mystery of Iniquity will find its completion in the earthly kingdom of the Jews under Antichrist."[3] "God hates Evil, and the Jews after they had our Lord Jesus crucified, became the greatest evil. . . . the Jews are a band of thieves and murderers, and it is understandable that the just punishment of God is frequently bestowed upon them for their bloody misdeeds."[4] "Duns Scotus, the Doctor Subtilis, went still further than Thomas of Aquinas and proposed to Christianity a solution to the Jewish problem on the basis of the complete destruction of this devilish sect."[5] Therefore, "subjugation of the Jews is *the theologically, morally and politically correct, rational social policy*."[6] The times are with us, and against the Jews. "A vast and violent storm is rising up in the distance, a storm that will sweep away jewish [sic] control in Western civilization as surely as it was swept away in pre-WWII Germany . . . and for precisely the same reasons."[7]

Author: I regret the need to quote you, and do so only as evidence that there are those who think as you do. Although my response is brief, my revulsion against anti-Semitism and neo-Nazism is profound. I use an Eastern Orthodox manual for examination of conscience before going to confession, and it asks, "Have I honored God as my Heavenly Father by treating others as my brothers? . . . Have I defamed others who needed help, or failed to stand up for those unjustly treated? Have I been cruel to anyone? . . . Have I told lies, or added to or subtracted from the truth?"[8] These questions hold for *anyone*, and I can't imagine how the anti-Semitic opinions expressed above can pass muster.

Jesus, Mary, and the Apostles were all Jewish. Jesus told the Samaritan woman at the well, "Salvation is from the Jews." (John 4:22) St. Paul reminds us that "a hardening has come upon part of Israel, until the full number of the Gentiles come in, and so all Israel will be saved; as it is written, 'The Deliverer will come from Zion, he will banish ungodliness from Jacob;' 'and this will be my covenant with them when I take away their sins.' As regards the gospel they are enemies of God, for your sake; but as regards election they are beloved for the sake of their forefathers. For the gifts and the call of God are irrevocable. Just as you were once disobedient to God but now have received mercy because of their disobedience, so they have now been disobedient in order that by the mercy shown to you they also may receive mercy. For God has consigned all men to disobedience, that he may have mercy upon all." (Rom. 11:25–32) The story of salvation is not about "God hates Jews" (or "God hates fags"),[9] but about God's providence and mercy.

Furthermore, the Catholic Church opposes anti-Semitism and other forms of racism. In September 1938, Pope Pius XI told a group of Belgian pilgrims, "Anti-Semitism is unacceptable. Spiritually, we are all Semites."[10] (The Pope's view was shared by C.S. Lewis, an Anglican. Lewis said in 1955 that Christ's

1. Dupont, *Catholic Prophecy*, p79.
2. Ibid., p52.
3. Ibid., p53.
4. Maurice Pinay, *The Plot Against the Church*, 1st English ed. 1967, 2000 reprint, Christian Book Club of America, p644.
5. Ibid., pp642–643.
6. The Father Feeney Internet Archive, "The Necessary and Urgent Struggle of the Church against the Jew, and its Culmination in the Apocalypse," http://www.fatherfeeney.org/cain/cain13.htm, printed 08/07/04.
7. Edgar J. Steele, "That's *Mr.* Antisemite to You!," *Conspiracy Pen Pal Newsletter*, December 19, 2003, http://www.conspiracypenpal.com/columns/irving.htm, printed 08/12/04.
8. Antiochian Orthodox Christian Archdiocese, *A Pocket Prayer Book for Orthodox Christians*, 1956, 11th printing 1997, pp41–42.
9. There really is a web site of this name: http://www.godhatesfags.com/main/index.html—the home page of the Westboro Baptist Church, in Topeka, Kansas. They have another web site, as well, http://www.godhatesamerica.com/, and affirm there that "Ronald Reagan is in HELL!"
10. Pope Pius XI, address to Belgian pilgrims, September 6, 1938, as quoted in *We Remember: A Reflection on the Shoah*, a Vatican document issued on March 12, 1998, http://www.catholicherald.com/articles/00articles/shoah.htm, printed 08/16/04.

"shocking reply to the Syrophenician woman[1] (it came alright at the end) is to remind all us Gentile Christians—who forget it easily enough and even flirt with anti-Semitism—that the Hebrews are spiritually *senior* to us, that God *did* entrust the descendants of Abraham with the first revelation of Himself."[2])

What one Pope said privately before Vatican II was said authoritatively by the bishops of the entire Catholic Church at the Council.

In the decree *Nostra Aetate*, the Catholic Church declared:

The apostle Paul maintains that the Jews remain very dear to God, for the sake of the patriarchs, since God does not take back the gifts he bestowed or the choice he made. Together with the prophets and that same apostle, the Church awaits the day, known to God alone, when all peoples will call on God with one voice ... Even though the Jewish authorities and those who followed their lead pressed for the death of Christ (cf. John 19:6), neither all Jews indiscriminately at that time, nor Jews today, can be charged with the crimes committed during his passion. It is true that the Church is the new people of God, yet the Jews should not be spoken of as rejected or accursed, as if this followed from holy Scripture. Consequently, all must take care, lest in catechizing or in preaching the Word of God, they teach anything which is not in accord with the truth of the Gospel message or the spirit of Christ. Indeed, the Church reproves every form of persecution against whomsoever it may be directed. Remembering, then, her common heritage with the Jews and moved not by any political consideration, but solely by the religious motivation of Christian charity, she deplores all hatreds, persecutions, displays of antisemitism leveled at any time or from any source against the Jews.[3]

The Council Fathers added,

We cannot truly pray to God the Father of all if we treat any people in other than brotherly fashion, for all men are created in God's image. Man's relation to God the Father and man's relation to his fellow-men are so dependent on each other that the Scripture says: 'he who does not love does not know God' (1 John 4:8). There is no basis therefore, either in theory or in practice for any discrimination between individual and individual, or between people and people arising either from human dignity or from the rights which flow from it. Therefore the Church reproves, as foreign to the mind of Christ, any discrimination against people or any harassment of them on the basis of their race, color, condition in life, or religion.[4]

This Conciliar teaching should be heeded by all Christians, whether they are Catholic or not Its truth applies to all Christian confessions and denominations alike.

It might be that, before the end, there will be a "religious" neo-Nazi regime, presenting itself as a forceful and justified reaction against decadence and secularism. This "New Order" may imitate Hitler, and unleash a global anti-Semitic pogrom. This regime—if it comes—will serve Satan, not God.

Zophar: Those other guys are crazy, and you responded to them well. But you worry needlessly. America is a chosen nation, blessed and set apart by God as a "shining city on a hill." "God hath graciously patronized our cause, and taken us under his special care, as he did his ancient covenant

1. Lewis is referring to Christ's encounter with the Syropheonician woman, in Mark 7:24–30: "And from there he arose and went away to the region of Tyre and Sidon. And he entered a house, and would not have any one know it; yet he could not be hid. But immediately a woman, whose little daughter was possessed by an unclean spirit, heard of him, and came and fell down at his feet. Now the woman was a Greek, a Syrophoenician by birth. And she begged him to cast the demon out of her daughter. And he said to her, 'Let the children first be fed, for it is not right to take the children's bread and throw it to the dogs.' But she answered him, 'Yes, Lord; yet even the dogs under the table eat the children's crumbs.' And he said to her, 'For this saying you may go your way; the demon has left your daughter.' And she went home, and found the child lying in bed, and the demon gone."

2. C.S. Lewis, letter of May 14, 1955, in *Letters of C.S. Lewis*, pp 448–449.

3. Vatican II; *Nostra Aetate*, 28 October 1965, section 4, in Austin Flannery, O.P., General Editor, *Vatican Council II: The Conciliar and Post-Conciliar Documents*, 1992 rev. ed., Costello Publishing Company, Northpoint, New York, p741.

4. Vatican II; *Nostra Aetate*, 28 October 1965, section 5, in ibid., p742.

people."[1] As Lincoln said, "All the armies of Europe, Asia and Africa combined, with all the treasure of the earth (our own excepted) in their military chest; with a Buonaparte for a commander, could not by force, take a drink from the Ohio, or make a track on the Blue Ridge, in a trial of a thousand years. At what point then is the approach of danger to be expected? I answer, if it ever reach us, it must spring up amongst us. It cannot come from abroad. If destruction be our lot, we must ourselves be its author and finisher. As a nation of freemen, we must live through all time, or die by suicide."[2] America cannot fall.

But—even if the worst that you fear comes to pass, there are two answers. First, everyone should stockpile goods and prepare to retreat to the country if the Antichrist arises. Hole up and wait him out; Scripture says his reign will be short.

And if need be, we can terminate any tyrant, even the Antichrist, "with extreme prejudice." It's the American way. God, guts, and guns made America great, and will keep us so, till the end.

Author: I too love America. But the US, like all nations, is mortal. As C.S. Lewis said, "Nations, cultures, arts, civilisations—these are mortal, and their life is to ours as the life of a gnat."[3] Some day our nation, like all institutions and associations established by mankind, will come to an end. May that day be long delayed!

The idea of surviving the final Tribulation by guarding a hoard of goods in a rural retreat is an illusion. Prudence is one thing; the ideology of survivalism is quite another. When the Tribulation comes, it will be global. No one can say where the natural and social disasters, as symbolically described in the book of Revelation, will strike hardest. And there is nothing in the Gospel or the Epistles that commends the amassing of possessions as a hedge against disaster. The truth seems to be otherwise. Jesus offered a parable against "reasonable" avarice: "The land of a rich man brought forth plentifully; and he thought to himself, 'What shall I do, for I have nowhere to store my crops?' And he said, 'I will do this: I will pull down my barns, and build larger ones; and there I will store all my grain and my goods. And I will say to my soul, Soul, you have ample goods laid up for many years; take your ease, eat, drink, be merry.' But God said to him, 'Fool! This night your soul is required of you; and the things you have prepared, whose will they be?' So is he who lays up treasure for himself, and is not rich toward God." (Luke 12:16–21)

Nor does armed resistance offer a solution to an evil, apocalyptic tyranny. Again, Scripture offers a consistent witness, from the ministry of Jesus through the prophecy of Revelation. Jesus rejected violent resistance to his arrest by Roman soldiers and the masters of the Temple. "Simon Peter, having a sword, drew it and struck the high priest's slave and cut off his right ear. The slave's name was Malchus. Jesus said to Peter, 'Put your sword into its sheath; shall I not drink the cup which the Father has given me?'" (John 18:10–11). Additionally, "Jesus said, 'No more of this!' And he touched his ear and healed him." (Luke 22:51). He also warned: "all who take the sword will perish by the sword." (Matt. 26:52). Thus ended history's shortest war, and the most just, a war in defense of the Son of God:[4] Jesus healed his enemy, and told the first Pope to put his weapon down.

When the Roman Empire's first persecution of Christians began under Nero, the Epistles and Revelation did not sound a call to insurrection or to tyrannicide.

Peter—who was to be one of Nero's victims—said in a letter sent from Rome after the persecution began, "Be subject for the Lord's sake to every human institution, whether it be to the emperor as

---

1. A New Hampshire minister in 1788, as quoted by Boyer, *When Time Shall Be No More*, p75.
2. Abraham Lincoln, "Lyceum Address," January 27, 1838, http://showcase.netins.net/web/creative/lincoln/speeches/lyceum.htm, printed 08/12/04. The spelling "Buonaparte" (Napoleon) is as stated in the original.
3. C.S. Lewis, "The Weight of Glory," in C.S. Lewis, *The Weight of Glory and Other Addresses*, Macmillan, 1980 ed., p19.
4. A turn of phrase derived from Peter Kreeft, a Catholic author.

supreme, or to governors as sent by him to punish those who do wrong and to praise those who do right. For it is God's will that by doing right you should put to silence the ignorance of foolish men. Live as free men, yet without using your freedom as a pretext for evil; but live as servants of God." (1 Peter 2:13–16).

In the book of Revelation, it seems that an apparently mortal attack upon the Beast does not kill him; it merely gives the Deceiver an opportunity to show his power with a false "resurrection:" "And I saw a beast rising out of the sea, with ten horns and seven heads, with ten diadems upon its horns and a blasphemous name upon its heads. And the beast that I saw was like a leopard, its feet were like a bear's, and its mouth was like a lion's mouth. And to it the dragon gave his power and his throne and great authority. One of its heads seemed to have a mortal wound, but its mortal wound was healed, and the whole earth followed the beast with wonder. Men worshiped the dragon, for he had given his authority to the beast, and they worshiped the beast, saying, 'Who is like the beast, and who can fight against it?'" (Rev. 13:1–4).

Amidst the frightening and obscure symbols, the Revelator offered earthly advice: "If any one has an ear, let him hear: If any one is to be taken captive, to captivity he goes; if any one slays with the sword, with the sword must he be slain. Here is a call for the endurance and faith of the saints." (Rev. 13:9–10). This is a call to fidelity and to endure to the end—not a recommendation that the faithful should gather weapons for earthly battle. The absence of a call to arms in Revelation remains relevant, since most Biblical scholars—the orthodox as well as the Modernists—believe that the original "666" was the Emperor Nero.[1]

If we face the end times, the prudent and realistic World War II counsels of Reinhold Niebuhr and Dietrich Bonhoeffer would not hold.[2] We would be facing a different kind of battle, and would be called to use a different strategy.

Elihu: These other people are uncouth, Anglo-Saxon barbarians—Protestant heretics and Americanists, no doubt. They do not understand history or Catholic culture.

Yes, the Chastisement, and persecution of Christians, is coming soon. "The coming disaster will be of such magnitude that our whole civilization would be destroyed were it not for the presence of the Church. *It is the Church that will save civilization*."[3] The Church, as a visible and hierarchical institution, a "perfect society" led by the Pontiff, the Successor of Peter, *cannot* fail. Ever. Remember Christ's promise to Peter: "And I tell you, you are Peter, and on this rock I will build my church, and the powers of death shall not prevail against it. I will give you the keys of the kingdom of heaven, and whatever you bind on earth shall be bound in heaven, and whatever you loose on earth shall be loosed in heaven." (Matt. 16:18-19) The Roman See never has been, and never will be, heretical or apostate.

Even now, the ground is being prepared for a New Springtime of the Church, to be led by the New Ecclesial Movements: Opus Dei, the Legionaries of Christ, the Neo-Catechumenal Way, and other soldiers of God yet unrevealed. "If we consider the manner in which a handful of doctrinally well-trained and determined Bolsheviks took over Russia in 1917, and if we consider that there exists at present [1973] in Europe an equally well-trained and dedicated association of Catholics who are sparing no efforts to sow the seeds of renewal and are spreading the sound concepts of Catholic thinkers and philosophers who are just as unknown as Karl Marx was in 1850—but not less capable, one can see, then,

---

1. T.L. Frazier, *A Second Look at the Second Coming: Seeing Through the Speculation*, Conciliar Press, 1999, pp 238–242.

2. Dietrich Bonhoeffer, a Lutheran theologian, joined the underground resistance to Hitler, and was executed by the Nazis in the spring of 1945. Reinhold Niebuhr, an American theologian, battled against Christian pacifism in the late 1930s and 1940s, urging Christian support for the Allies in World War II.

3. Dupont, *Catholic Prophecy*, p 28.

that God has already set the stage for the marvelous renewal which He will work."[1] "To the extent possible, the Counter-Revolution should try to win over the multitudes. However, it should not make this its chief goal in the short run. . . . An objective view of history shows that the factor of mass is secondary; the principal factor is the formation of elites."[2]

Out from the coming chaos, there will be a *real* New Order, led by a victorious Great King and a Holy Pope—a Pope who will "rule with a rod of iron"[3] and "restore the former disciplines"[4] of the Roman Church. "The resurrection will be spectacular; the Great King will be the Emperor of Western Europe, and anointed by the Holy Pontiff. Many Jews and all non-Catholic Christians will turn to the True Faith. The Mohammedans will embrace Christianity, as also the Chinese. In short, virtually the whole world will be Catholic."[5] This "era of peace" may last a long time before a new apostasy ushers in the Antichrist.

So let us not be afraid, but rather follow the inspired teachings of St. Escrivá, the Founder of Opus Dei: "When a layman sets himself up as an arbiter of morals, he frequently errs; laymen can only be disciples."[6] "Obedience, the sure way. Blind obedience to your superior, the way of sanctity. Obedience in your apostolate, the only way: for, in a work of God, the spirit must be to obey or to leave."[7] The Church will lead; let us follow! We'll learn soon enough that secular government and separation of Church and State are Masonic delusions, "musty, old fashioned 'Voltairianisms' or discredited liberal ideas of the nineteenth century."[8] "If, to save an earthly life, it is praiseworthy to use force to keep a man from committing suicide, are we not allowed to use the same coercion—'holy coercion'—to save the Lives (with a capital) of so many who are stupidly bent on killing their souls?"[9]

The dark days of the Enlightenment will soon pass. "Liberalism is a mortal sin."[10] "If the Revolution is disorder, the Counter-Revolution is the restoration of order. And by order we mean the peace of Christ in the Reign of Christ, that is, Christian civilization, austere and hierarchical, fundamentally sacral, antiegalitarian, and antiliberal."[11]

Author: The promise of an Earthly utopia of the Right is a delusion, just as illusory as the idea of a leftist utopia. Go back and read this epilogue again, and *think*!

Note, as well, that there are parallels between the ideology of left-wing utopians and the beliefs of the right-wing zealots described here.

In the late 1930s, Escrivá wrote, "If, to save an earthly life, it is praiseworthy to use force to keep a man from committing suicide, are we not allowed to use the same coercion—'holy coercion'—to save the Lives (with a capital) of so many who are stupidly bent on killing their souls?"[12] The Theosophist Alice Bailey likewise exalted Life over individual lives (or, as she called them, "form"): "let us never forget that it is the *Life*, its purpose and its directed intentional destiny that is of importance; and also that when a form proves inadequate, or too diseased, or too crippled for the expression of that purpose, it is—from the point of view of the Hierarchy—no disaster when that form has to go."[13]

1. Ibid., p44.

2. Plinio Corrêa de Oliveira, *Revolution and Counter-Revolution*, The American Society for the Defense of Tradition, Family, and Property, 1993 ed., pp86–87 (cited below as Oliveira, *Revolution and Counter-Revolution*).

3. Dupont, *Catholic Prophecy*, p21.

4. Ibid., p21.

5. Ibid., p90.

6. Escrivá, maxim 61 from *The Way*, p14.

7. Ibid., maxim 941 from *The Way*, p239.

8. Ibid., maxim 849 from *The Way*, p214.

9. Ibid., maxim 399 from *The Way*, p97.

10. Don Felix Sarda Y Salvany, *What Is Liberalism*, tr. by Condé B. Pallen, TAN Books, 1979 reprint of 1899 ed., p27.

11. Oliveira, *Revolution and Counter-Revolution*, p75.

12. Escrivá, maxim 399 from *The Way*, p97.

13. Alice A. Bailey, *Education in the New Age*, 1954, Lucis Publishing Company, p112.

Plinio Corrêa de Oliveira (the right-wing Catholic founder of Tradition, Family, and Property) says, "An objective view of history shows that the factor of mass is secondary; the principal factor is the formation of elites."[1] Leninists, with their belief in the "vanguard party," a leader of Global Education Associates, with her belief in "creative minorities,"[2] and Ted Turner, with his disdain for the "dumb majority,"[3] would agree on him on sociology. Their only disagreement is the end toward which mankind is to be driven—for our own good, whether we like it or not.

If you continue as you appear to have begun, you will—however sincere you are now—go straight into the arms of the Final Deceiver, the one who will counterfeit Christ. Beware!

A CHALLENGE: IS ORTHODOXY BETTER THAN HERESY?

Additionally, I warn against a peril that is already emerging among those engaged in the "culture war": an apparent belief that use of bitter invective against enemies is proof of one's own zeal for the cause, that such epithets will rally the good against the evil, and that foes will be shocked to awareness and repentance by the strength of the curses hurled in their direction. Among some orthodox Christians, as throughout the world, the spirit of hatred runs free.

A few illustrations of this trend will suffice, drawn from some items recently published by those who ought to know better.

In its commentary on the deepening scandal of sexual abuse and cover-up in the Catholic Church, *New Oxford Review* (a steadfast, orthodox Catholic magazine) has taken to writing of "fag and/or fag-friendly priests"[4] and distinguishes itself from *Our Sunday Visitor*, a centrist Catholic publication, thus: "The *Visitor* 'respects the human dignity' of active homosexuals, but we at the NOR do not.... How can any Catholic *respect* their 'human dignity'?"[5]

Another orthodox Catholic magazine, *Culture Wars*, has recently gone off the deep end regarding the Jews. Its editor says,

> If salvation comes from the Jews who prepared the way for Christ and accepted him when he came, what comes from the Jews who rejected Christ? The answer is clear: what comes from this group is the opposite of salvation, namely, the work of Satan culminating in the arrival of the Antichrist. The answer is not only clear; there is no other possible answer to this question. . . . the Nazi attempt to exterminate the Jews was a reaction to Jewish Messianism (in the form of Bolshevism) every bit as much as the Chmielnicki pogroms flowed from the excesses of the Jewish tax farmers in the Ukraine. . . . Just as a small remnant of faithful Jews brought the Catholic Church into being after Christ's death and resurrection, so too a small number of Jews brought the 'synagogue of Satan' into existence at around the same time. The 'synagogue of Satan,' as its name implies, has as its purpose not preparing the world for the second coming of Christ but rather preparing the world for the coming of the Antichrist. Because of their rejection of Christ, the Jews who comprise the synagogue of Satan will have a special role to play in that event. . . . The contemporary Synagogue of Satan, whether in America or Israel, now poses the greatest threat to world peace.[6]

1. Oliveira, *Revolution and Counter-Revolution*, pp 86–87.

2. Patricia Mische, "Religion and World Order: Introduction and Overview," *Religion and World Order* 1994 *Symposium*, Global Education Associates, http://www.globaleduc.org/RWO3.pdf, printed 08/03/04.

3. Tracey C. Rembert, "Ted Turner: Billionaire, Media Mogul... And Environmentalist" (Interview), *E Magazine*, January /February 1999, Volume X, number 1, p 12.

4. Dale Vree, New Oxford Notes, "A Bigger Sin Than Buggery?," *New Oxford Review*, September 2003, p 22.

5. Dale Vree, New Oxford Notes, "Is Same-Sex 'Marriage' Inevitable," *New Oxford Review*, February 2004, p 18.

6. E. Michael Jones, "Salvation and the Jews," *Culture Wars*, February 2004, Vol. 23, no. 3, pp 40, 41, 43. Charles Upton comments, "Very similar rhetoric is often heard from certain Islamicist extremists. In view of the very real threat to the West

Catholic Answers, a mainstream group which engages in apologetics and evangelical outreach for Catholicism, sent out fundraising letters in early 2004 saying: "Islam is worse than Communism ever was.... Islam is and always has been a religion of violence.... it seeks to eliminate Christianity and Judaism.... The great threat of the twenty-first century is Islam."[1]

Such vituperation—and the attitude toward enemies that it manifests—will not bring victory for the cause of Christ. Instead, those who engage in it are fulfilling an apocalyptic prophecy of Christ: "And because wickedness is multiplied, most men's love will grow cold." (Mt. 24:12). They are also acting as predicted in the *Didache*: "the sheep shall be turned into wolves, and love shall change to hate. For as lawlessness increaseth they shall hate one another and persecute and betray...."[2]

A Catholic and a Protestant offer salutary warnings against being possessed by the spirit of hatred during the present (and pending) conflicts. Philip Trower, an orthodox Catholic, says in his history of the crisis in the Roman Catholic Church, "It is right to feel an abhorrence for heresy.... The faith has to be defended. But there are better and worse ways of doing it, and if one is not careful, love of the Church and faith can become entangled with natural bellicosity or the spirit of domination. We can forget that our opponents need prayers more than maledictions."[3] An evangelical Protestant writer for *Christianity Today* related an account of her meeting with a spiritually confused, heretical man who had been raised by a zealous mother, a preacher. She concluded her tale with a warning for us all, especially those of us who consider ourselves orthodox or faithful:

> For being so surrounded with Christianity, my friend knew nothing of the grace of God. All he heard and felt was judgment on his inadequacy: that he was not as fiery as mom, not as moral as church people, not as powerful as Catholics. Here was a man who needed more than anything the thoroughly orthodox word that his salvation comes by faith, not by works—in particular, not by religious works—but no one was speaking it to him. Why was the open fact of God's inviting love the one secret he didn't know about, and why were the heresies blazing in full neon color? I take it as a cautionary tale. If orthodoxy does not lead the hungry to the Bread of Life and the thirsty to living waters, is it any better than heresy?[4]

As we face multiple global perils that may test us to extremity, I ask all to remember these two warnings. "We can forget that our opponents need prayers more than maledictions,"[5] and, "If orthodoxy does not lead the hungry to the Bread of Life and the thirsty to living waters, is it any better than heresy?"[6]

KYRIE ELEISON! LORD, HAVE MERCY!
MARANA THA! OUR LORD, COME!

---

from such militants, who are sworn enemies of the State of Israel, one would have thought that anti-Semitism among conservative Christians would now be a thing of the past. Could its resurgence indicate an unconscious admiration by some conservative Christians for the Islamicists, who are willing and able to go to war in the name of religion—albeit by evil and essentially anti-religious means—against the same modernity that conservative Christians hate, but feel powerless to effectively oppose?" (E-mail from Charles Upton to Lee Penn, 10/15/04.)

1. From a fund-raising letter received twice in the spring of 2004, issued by Karl Keating, the president of Catholic Answers.

2. *Didache*, sec. XIII, vv. 3–4.

3. Philip Trower, *Turmoil & Truth: The Historical Roots of the Modern Crisis in the Catholic Church*, Ignatius Press and Family Publications/Oxford, 2003, p196 (cited below as Trower, *Turmoil & Truth*).

4. Sarah Hinlicky Wilson, "The Heresy Itch: Unlike gnosis, the gospel is not for the few, the proud, the knowledgeable," *Christianity Today*, January 2004, p67; the author is a doctoral student in systematic theology at Princeton Theological Seminary (cited below as Wilson, "The Heresy Itch.").

5. Trower, *Turmoil & Truth*, p196.

6. Wilson, "The Heresy Itch, p67.

APPENDIX I

The URI Charter's "Preamble, Purpose, and Principles"

The URI adopted its Charter in 2000, after 3 years of discussion. The initial section of the document, including the "Preamble, Purpose, and Principles," as it appears on the URI web site, is reproduced here:[1]

THE UNITED RELIGIONS INITIATIVE CHARTER

The United Religions Initiative (URI) is a growing global community dedicated to promoting enduring, daily interfaith cooperation, ending religiously motivated violence and creating cultures of peace, justice and healing for the Earth and all living beings.

Working on all continents and across continents, people from different religions, spiritual expressions and indigenous traditions are creating unprecedented levels of enduring global cooperation. Today, at its birth, people's hopes are rising with visions of a better world. It is a world where the values and teachings of the great wisdom traditions guide people's service, where people respect one another's beliefs, and where the resourcefulness and passion of people working together bring healing and a more hopeful future to the Earth community. The URI, in time, aspires to have the visibility and stature of the United Nations.

Since June 1996 thousands of people have shared their visions and worked together to create the URI. It is an organization for global good rooted in shared spiritual values. People from many different cultures and perspectives have worked to create an organization that is inclusive, non-hierarchical and decentralized; one that enhances cooperation, autonomy and individual opportunity. This co-creative work offered by people of many cultures has produced a unique organization composed of self-organizing groups which operate locally and are connected globally.

The URI's Charter has been spoken into being by a myriad of voices from around the world. Its essential spirit, values and vision are expressed in the Preamble, Purpose and Principles. Together, they inspire, ground and guide all URI activity. The Charter includes:

Preamble—the call that inspires us to create the URI now and continue to create it everyday;
Purpose—the statement that draws us together in common cause;
Principles—the fundamental beliefs that guide our structure, decisions and content;
Organization design—the way we organize to enhance cooperation and magnify spirit;
Guidelines for Action—an action agenda to inspire and guide our worldwide URI community.

The global URI organization will be born in June 2000. You are warmly invited to participate in the birth and the growth of the URI and become part of this extraordinary force for good in the world. This Charter is your invitation to participate in its on-going creation. Welcome!

---

1. United Religions Initiative, "The United Religions Initiative Charter," http://www.uri.org/resources/publications/Charter%20PC%20format.doc, printed 07/16/04.

We, people of diverse religions, spiritual expressions and indigenous traditions throughout the world, hereby establish the United Religions Initiative to promote enduring, daily interfaith cooperation, to end religiously motivated violence and to create cultures of peace, justice and healing for the Earth and all living beings.

We respect the uniqueness of each tradition, and differences of practice or belief.

We value voices that respect others, and believe that sharing our values and wisdom can lead us to act for the good of all.

We believe that our religious, spiritual lives, rather than dividing us, guide us to build community and respect for one another.

Therefore, as interdependent people rooted in our traditions, we now unite for the benefit of our Earth community.

We unite to build cultures of peace and justice.

We unite to heal and protect the Earth.

We unite to build safe places for conflict resolution, healing and reconciliation.

We unite to support freedom of religion and spiritual expression, and the rights of all individuals and peoples as set forth in international law.

We unite in responsible cooperative action to bring the wisdom and values of our religions, spiritual expressions and indigenous traditions to bear on the economic, environmental, political and social challenges facing our Earth community.

We unite to provide a global opportunity for participation by all people, especially by those whose voices are not often heard.

We unite to celebrate the joy of blessings and the light of wisdom in both movement and stillness.

We unite to use our combined resources only for nonviolent, compassionate action, to awaken to our deepest truths, and to manifest love and justice among all life in our Earth community.

PURPOSE

The purpose of the United Religions Initiative is to promote enduring, daily interfaith cooperation, to end religiously motivated violence and to create cultures of peace, justice and healing for the Earth and all living beings.

PRINCIPLES

1. The URI is a bridge-building organization, not a religion.
2. We respect the sacred wisdom of each religion, spiritual expression and indigenous tradition.
3. We respect the differences among religions, spiritual expressions and indigenous traditions.
4. We encourage our members to deepen their roots in their own tradition.
5. We listen and speak with respect to deepen mutual understanding and trust.
6. We give and receive hospitality.
7. We seek and welcome the gift of diversity and model practices that do not discriminate.
8. We practice equitable participation of women and men in all aspects of the URI.
9. We practice healing and reconciliation to resolve conflict without resorting to violence.
10. We act from sound ecological practices to protect and preserve the Earth for both present and future generations.
11. We seek and offer cooperation with other interfaith efforts.
12. We welcome as members all individuals, organizations and associations who subscribe to the Preamble, Purpose and Principles.

13. We have the authority to make decisions at the most local level that includes all the relevant and affected parties.

14. We have the right to organize in any manner, at any scale, in any area, and around any issue or activity which is relevant to and consistent with the Preamble, Purpose and Principles.

15. Our deliberations and decisions shall be made at every level by bodies and methods that fairly represent the diversity of affected interests and are not dominated by any.

16. We (each part of the URI) shall relinquish only such autonomy and resources as are essential to the pursuit of the Preamble, Purpose and Principles.

17. We have the responsibility to develop financial and other resources to meet the needs of our part, and to share financial and other resources to help meet the needs of other parts.

18. We maintain the highest standards of integrity and ethical conduct, prudent use of resources, and fair and accurate disclosure of information.

19. We are committed to organizational learning and adaptation.

20. We honor the richness and diversity of all languages and the right and responsibility of participants to translate and interpret the Charter, Articles, Bylaws and related documents in accordance with the Preamble, Purpose and Principles, and the spirit of the United Religions Initiative.

21. Members of the URI shall not be coerced to participate in any ritual or be proselytized.

APPENDIX II

URI's Global Leadership

In July 2002, the URI elected a new Global Council, a board of directors representing all URI Cooperation Circles worldwide. The document quoted below, from the URI web site, lists the 38 members as of June 30, 2004.[1] After each member's name, his religious affiliation appears in brackets.[2]

URI GLOBAL COUNCIL

"The URI Global Council is the decision-making body of the URI. In July 2002, a new Global Council was chosen. They will serve until July of 2005. Twenty-nine people from around the world were elected in URI's first democratic global elections. Others were selected to offer certain expertise or to represent other voices."[3]

Trustees of the Global Council

Founding Trustee: The Rt. Rev. William E. Swing, USA—*Council President* [Protestant—Episcopalian]
Executive Trustee: The Rev. Canon Charles P. Gibbs, USA [Protestant—Episcopalian]

Africa

Mr. Sabapathy Alagiah, Mozambique [Baha'i]
Ms. Despina Namwembe, Uganda [Orthodox Christian][4]
Mrs. Joyce Ng'oma, Malawi [Protestant—Presbyterian]

Asia

Fr. James Channan, Pakistan [Roman Catholic]
Ven. Dr. Jinwol Lee, Korea [Korean Buddhist]
Dr. Mohinder Singh, India [Sikh]

1. United Religions Initiative, "URI Global Council," http://www.uri.org/abouturi/globalcouncil, printed 06/30/04 (cited below as URI, "Global Council"); also, United Religions Initiative, "URI Global Council Trustees as of June 2003," *Annual Report* 2002 leaflet. Donald Frew provided two corrections to the document from the URI web site. Sam Srinivasan is an at-large member, not a regional member from North America, and Rabbi Kahn was erroneously listed twice in the URI document, once as Kahn and again as Khan. (Conversation between Donald Frew and Lee Penn, June 30, 2004.) The spelling of board member names is as given in the URI listing on its web page.

2. Religious affiliation data were provided by URI Global Council member Donald Frew in e-mail to Lee Penn on 11/18/02 and 4/4/03; he also provided a URI document listing Council members' religious affiliations in January 2004. This information was supplemented by research by Lee Penn, as documented in footnotes after the names.

3. URI, "Global Council."

4. She is a contact person for one of the Uganda Orthodox Church's anti-AIDS projects. The site says, "Uganda Orthodox Church—Works with women and youth from different faith backgrounds under the umbrella of the Inter-Religious Council of Uganda on programs for HIV/AIDS and adolescent reproductive health advocacy programs and awareness in the rural areas." Source: Communities Responding to the HIV/AIDS Epidemic, "Project on Gender, Faith, and Response to HIV/AIDS," http://www.corevaluesinitiative.org/leaders.cfm?Search=, printed 12/16/02.

EUROPE

Mrs. Annie Imbens-Fransen, Netherlands [Roman Catholic]
Mr. Deepak Naik, United Kingdom [Hindu]
Ms. Karimah Stauch, Germany [Muslim]

LATIN AMERICA AND THE CARIBBEAN

Dr. Gerardo Gonzalez Cortes, Chile [Roman Catholic][1]
Ms. Rosalia Gutierrez, Argentina [Indigenous—Argentine]
Mr. Jonathan Rose, Mexico—*Council Secretary* [Jewish]

MIDDLE EAST

Fr. Dr. George Khoury, Israel [Eastern Catholic]
Dr. Mohamed Mosaad, Egypt [Muslim]
Mr. Yehuda Stolov, Israel [Jewish]

NORTH AMERICA

Elder Donald H. Frew, USA—*Council Assistant Secretary* [Wiccan][2]
Rev. Kay Lindahl, USA [Protestant—Episcopalian; interfaith][3]
Rev. Heng Sure, USA [Buddhist]

THE PACIFIC

Rev. Dr. George Armstrong, New Zealand [Protestant—Anglican][4]
Ms. Shakuntala Moojani-Vaswani, Philippines [Hindu]
Mr. Bonifacio Amado M. Quirog, Jr., Philippines [Roman Catholic]

MULTIREGIONAL

Ms. Yoland Trevino, India ["Indigenous (Mayan) & Hindu"][5]
Rev. Jack W. Lundin, USA [Protestant—Lutheran]
Ms. Munirah Shahidi, Tajikistan [Muslim]—*Council Assistant Treasurer*

TRANSITION ADVISORY COMMITTEE

Mr. Iftekhar Hai, USA [Muslim]
Ms. Rita R. Semel, USA [Jewish]—*Council Chair*
Rabbi Doug Kahn, USA [Jewish]—*Council Treasurer*

---

1. In a conversation with Lee Penn on 06/30/04, Donald Frew indicated—as he had done previously in 2002 and 2003—that Gonzalez Cortes is Roman Catholic.

2. Frew has been "Wiccan priest (19yrs.); nine years on the Board of Covenant of the Goddess (CoG)—world's largest Wiccan organization—two as President; currently CoG's national interfaith representative." Rocky Mountain Chapter, United Religions Initiative, "Candidate Biographies—Donald H. Frew," http://tecwrk.com/RMC-URI/canidates.htm#four [sic], printed 12/15/02.

3. As described in e-mail from Donald Frew to Lee Penn, 11/08/02; see also the statement by ECUSA Bishop Robert M. Anderson, assistant in the Diocese of Los Angeles: "Lindahl, founder of The Listening Center in Laguna Niguel, Calif., is an Episcopalian who speaks out of years of spiritual practice. She has rich experience in leading ecumenical and interfaith dialogues both in her state and around the world;" from Listening Center, "The Art of Sacred Listening," http://www.sacredlistening.com/sal_review.htm, printed 12/02/02.

4. Victor Cheng, "Friends I Remember"—United Religions Initiative (URI) North American Summit, Salt Lake City, Utah, http://www.drby.net/post-events/uri/uri_friends_I_remember_pop.htm, printed 11/25/02; see also Armstrong's post at http://www.ascens.org/posta.htm (printed 11/25/02), in which he describes himself as "an Anglican parish priest and for 20 years taught also in a Seminary for priests." (Armstrong is described in an article on the URI web site as "Lecturer of the College of St. John the Evangelist in Auckland, New Zealand" (Marites Africa, "Pilgrims of Peace in Bali," http://www.uri.org/regionalnews/asiapacificassembly.asp, printed 12/5/2002).

5. As described in e-mail from Donald Frew to Lee Penn, 11/08/02.

The Global Council

"The purpose of the Global Council (GC) is to support URI's membership in making real the vision and values of the Preamble, Purpose and Principles. The Global Council's central spirit is not one of control, but rather one of service informed by deep listening to the hopes and aspirations of the whole URI community. The Global Council will inspire and support the URI worldwide community in cooperative global action. It is envisioned that their deliberations will be tempered with tenderness for one another and for the Earth community. It is envisioned that their actions will reflect a yearning to help people of the URI fulfill their aspirations to be a positive force for peace, justice, and healing in the world.

The Global Council is responsible to develop financial and other resources to meet the needs of the URI, Inc. The Global Council will accept eligible applicants for membership to the URI and manage the affairs of the URI, Inc."[3]

Global Council Trustees

"The term Trustee signifies that trustees carry the trust for the URI world membership. The Trustees of the URI will be exemplars who manifest the vision and values of the Preamble, Purpose and Principles, and who will model leadership and service by their actions. They will have a deep commitment to serve the whole of the URI community."[4]

1. As listed in a URI document, "URI Global Council Trustees 2002–2005," as provided by Donald Frew in January 2004.
2. As described by Donald Frew in a conversation with Lee Penn, 05/08/04.
3. URI, "Global Council."
4. Ibid.

A SELECTIVE
BIBLIOGRAPHY

This bibliography is designed to point readers to English language sources that they may use for their own investigation into the topics covered by this book; it is not merely a listing of the sources cited in the footnotes. This bibliography is a starting point for further research, and is not exhaustive. Web sites in this bibliography were valid as of August/September 2004. Most book publication information is from Amazon.com; it was supplemented as needed from Barnes and Noble and other on-line book sellers.

THE UNITED RELIGIONS INITIATIVE

HEADQUARTERS

United Religions Initiative, P. O. Box 29242, San Francisco, CA 94129-0242, USA, tel. (415) 561-2300, fax(415) 561-2313, office@uri.org.

BOOKS

Abu-Nimer, Mohammed, et al., *URI Interfaith Peacebuilding Guide*, United Religions Initiative e-book, 2004; order on-line at the link http://www.uri.org/peacebuilding/guide.

Gibbs, Charles and Mahé, Sally, *Birth of a Global Community: Appreciative Inquiry in Action*, Lakeshore Communications, Inc., 2004. (The present-day "official" history of the URI.)

Hock, Dee W., *Birth of the Chaordic Age*, Berrett-Koehler Publishers, 1999. (Hock was a key organizational designer for the URI.)

Sampson, Cynthia, et al., *Positive Approaches to Peacebuilding: A Resource for Innovators*, Pact Publications, 2003; order at the link http://www.pactpublications.com/item.asp?prod_cd=PDY001. (Includes a chapter on the URI.)

Swing, Bishop William E., *The Coming United Religions*, United Religions Initiative and CoNexus Press, 1998. (The "official" history of the URI as of 1998.)

PERIODICALS

United Religions Initiative, *e-Update Newsletter* and *Interfaith News.net* newsletter. These electronic letters are published several times a year. Go to http://www.uri.org/resources/ to sign up for these free e-mail subscriptions.

United Religions Initiative, *URI Update*. This hard copy newsletter has been published twice a year, and is available free by joining the URI mailing list. Contact the URI headquarters to do this.

WEB SITES

Acholi Religious Leaders Peace Initiative (ARLPI) home page—http://www.acholipeace.org; this is a URI Cooperation Circle.

Global AIDS Interfaith Alliance (GAIA) home page—http://www.thegaia.com; this is a URI Cooperation Circle.

Science and the Outer Streams web pages—http://www.fromusalive.com/outer/list.asp?iPage=3, and http://www.fromusalive.com/outer/list.asp?iPage=4. This site contains on-line videos of the URI charter-signing event in 2000.

United Religions Initiative home page—http://www.uri.org

United Religions Initiative home page for Latin America, in Spanish—http://www.uri.org/americalatina.

United Religions Initiative (United Kingdom) home page—http://www.uri.org.uk.

"Visions for Peace Among Religions"—http://interspirit.net/vpar/home.cfm; a discussion page for people active in this URI project.

THE EPISCOPAL DIOCESE OF CALIFORNIA

The headquarters of the URI is in this Diocese; their publications and web sites are valuable ways to track URI activity, and to monitor the development of New Age Anglicanism.

DIOCESAN OFFICE

Diocese of California, 1055 Taylor St., San Francisco, CA 94108, USA, tel.(415) 673-5015, fax(415) 673-9268, info@diocal.org

BOOKS PUBLISHED BY THE DIOCESE OF CALIFORNIA

Robinson, Mary Judith, *From Gold Rush to Millennium*, 2001; a history of the first 150 years of the Diocese of California. Order through the Diocese of California, by calling (415) 673-5015, or by mail at 1055 Taylor Street, San Francisco, CA 94108, Attn: Book Order. Further information on this book is available at http://diocal.org/modules.php?op=modload&name=Sections&file=index&req=viewarticle&artid=24.

Robinson, Mary Judith, ed., *Modern Profiles of an Ancient Faith*, 2001. The ordering information is the same as for *From Gold Rush to Millennium*.

Swing, Bishop William E., *A Swing With a Crosier: Sermons, Addresses, and Letters*, 1999. The ordering information is the same as for *From Gold Rush to Millennium*.

PERIODICALS

Pacific Church News Quarterly and *Pacific Church News Online*—the official newsletters of the Episcopal Diocese of California. A hard copy version of the quarterly magazine is available through the Diocese of California. Both newsletters are also available on-line at http://pcn.diocal.org.

WEB SITES

Diocese of California home page—http://diocal.org.

Grace Cathedral home page—http://www.gracecom.org. In addition, they have this web site: http://www.grace-cathedral.org.

APPRECIATIVE INQUIRY (AI)

BOOKS

Cooperrider, David, et al., *Appreciative Inquiry Handbook: The First in a Series of AI Workbooks for Leaders of Change*, Lakeshore Communications, 2003.

Cooperrider, David, ed., et al., *Appreciative Inquiry: Rethinking Human Organization Toward a Positive Theory of Change*, Stipes Publishing, 1999.

Cooperrider, David, and Whitney, Diana, *Collaborating for Change: Appreciative Inquiry*, Berrett-Koehler Publishers, 2000.

Paddock, Susan Star, *Appreciative Inquiry in the Catholic Church*, Thin Book Publishing Co., 2003.

Whitney, Diana, et al., *Encyclopedia of Positive Questions, Volume I: Using AI to Bring Out the Best in Your Organization*, Lakeshore Communications, 2001.

Whitney, Diana, et al., *The Power of Appreciative Inquiry: A Practical Guide to Positive Change*, Berrett-Koehler Publishers, 2003.

WEB SITES

Appreciative Inquiry Commons—http://appreciativeinquiry.cwru.edu. This is the home page for AI at Case Western Reserve University, where AI originated. An alternative web address is http://ai.cwru.edu.

Appreciative Inquiry in Great Britain—http://www.aradford.co.uk/; Anne Radford maintains this "AI Resource eCentre."

Philanthropic Quest International home page—http://www.appreciative-inquiry.org. The web master, Jim Lord, is an Appreciative Inquiry consultant. A related web site is http://www.lord.org.

Taos Institute home page—http://www.taosinstitute.net/; dedicated to "Creating Promising Futures Through Social Construction."

GLOBALIST LEADERS, ORGANIZATIONS, AND MOVEMENTS

GLOBALIST LEADERS

MIKHAIL GORBACHEV

BOOKS

Arrien, Angeles, and Gorbachev, Mikhail, *Working Together: Producing Synergy by Honoring Diversity*, Berrett-Koehler, 2001.

Gorbachev, Mikhail, *A Road to the Future: Complete Text of the December 7, 1988 United Nations Address*, Ocean Tree Books, 1990.

_____. *A Time for Peace*, Richardson & Steirman & Black, 1985.

_____. *At the Summit: A New Start in U.S.-Soviet Relations*, Eagle Publishing, 1988.

Gorbachev, Mikhail, and Mlynář, Zdeněk, *Conversations with Gorbachev: On Perestroika, the Prague Spring, and the Crossroads of Socialism*, Columbia University Press, 2002.

Gorbachev, Mikhail, *For a Nuclear-Free World: Speeches and Statements by the General Secretary of the CPSU Central Committee on Nuclear Disarmament Problems*, Victor Kamkin, 1987.

_____. *Gorbachev: Mandate for Peace*, PaperJacks, 1987.

_____. *Gorbachev: On My Country and the World*, Columbia University Press, 2000.

_____. et al., *Meaning of My Life: Perestroika*, Aspect Publications, 1990.

_____. *Memoirs*, Doubleday Books, 1996.

_____. *Peace Has No Alternative: Speeches, Articles, Interviews*, Stosius Inc/Advent Books Division, 1987.

_____. *Perestroika and Soviet-American Relations*, Sphinx Press, 1990.

_____. *Perestroika: Global Challenge: Our Common Future*, Dufour Editions, 1990.

_____. *Perestroika: New Thinking For Our Country and the World*, Collins, 1987.

_____. *Reykjavik: Results and Lessons*, Sphinx Press, 1987.

_____. *Socialism, Peace, and Democracy*, Pluto Press, 1998.

_____. *Socialism, Peace, and Democracy: Writings, Speeches, and Reports*, Harper Collins, 1988.

_____. *Speeches and writings (Leaders of the world)*, Pergamon Press, 1987.

_____. *State of the World*, Harper Collins, 1995.

_____. *The August Coup: The Truth and the Lessons*, Harper Collins, 1991. (Amazon gives the publication date of this book as October 1, 1991—less than 45 days after the coup.)

_____. *The Challenges of Our Time: Disarmament and Social Progress*, International Publishers, 1986.

_____. *The Coming Century of Peace*, Richardson and Steirman, 1986.

_____. *The Search for a New Beginning: Developing a New Civilization*, Harper San Francisco, 1995.

_____. *Toward a Better World*, Eagle Publishing Corporation, 1987.

_____. *Uncommon Opportunities: An Agenda for Peace and Equitable Development: Report of the International Commission on Peace and Food*, Zed Books, 1994.

Laszlo, Erwin, and Gorbachev, Mikhail, *You Can Change the World: An Action Handbook for the 21st Century*, Positive News, 2002.

Puledda, Salvatore, and Hurley, Andrew, and Gorbachev, Mikhail, *On Being Human: Interpretations of Humanism from the Renaissance to the Present (New Humanism Series)*, Latitude Press, 1997.

Yakovets, Yu V., and Gorbachev, Mikhail, *The Past and the Future of Civilizations (Studies in Russian Politics, Sociology, and Economics)*, The Edwin Mellen Press Ltd., 2000.

WEB SITES

Gorbachev's activities and speeches with Green Cross International—http://www.gci.ch/GreenCrossFamily/GORBY/activities.html.

Home page for the former Premier of the Soviet Union—http://www.mikhailgorbachev.org.

Another home page for Gorbachev—http://web243.petrel.ch/GreenCrossFamily/gorby/gorby.html

GEORGE SOROS

BOOKS

Notturno, Mark, and Soros, George, *Science and the Open Society: The Future of Karl Popper's Philosophy*, Central European University Press, 2000.

Soros, George, *George Soros on Globalization*, Public Affairs, 2002.

_____. *Open Society: Reforming Global Capitalism Reconsidered*, Public Affairs, 2000.

_____. *Opening the Soviet System*, Perseus Books, 1996.

_____. *Soros on Soros: Staying Ahead of the Curve*, Wiley, 1995.

Soros, George, and Volcker, Paul, *The Alchemy of Finance*, John Wiley & Sons, 2003 reprint.

Soros, George, *The Bubble of American Supremacy: Correcting the Misuse of American Power*, Public Affairs, 2003.

_____. *The Crisis of Global Capitalism: Open Society Endangered*, Public Affairs, 1998.

_____. *Underwriting Democracy: Encouraging Free Enterprise and Democratic Reform Among the Soviets and in Eastern Europe*, Perseus Books Group, 1991; 2004 reprint.

WEB SITES

George Soros' political home page and web log—http://www.georgesoros.com.

Open Society Institute and the Soros Foundations Network home page—http://www.soros.org.

MAURICE STRONG

BOOKS

Shah, Mahendra, and Strong, Maurice, *Food in the 21st Century: From Science to Sustainable Agriculture*, World Bank Publications, 2000.

Strong, Maurice, *Conference on the Human Environment: Founex Switzerland June 4-12 1971*, Walter De Gruyter, 1973.

Strong, Maurice, *Where On Earth Are We Going*, Vintage Canada 2001.

Ward, Barbara, and Strong, Maurice, ed., *Who Speaks for Earth?*, W. W. Norton and Co., 1973.

WEB SITES

UN University for Peace in Costa Rica home page—http://www.upeace.org; Strong is the President of the Council for the University for Peace.

GLOBALIST ORGANIZATIONS AND MOVEMENTS

THE EARTH CHARTER MOVEMENT

BOOKS

Casey, Helen M. and Morgante, Amy, eds., *Human Rights, Environmental Law, and the Earth Charter*, Boston Research Center for the 21st Century, 1998.

Casey, Helen M. and Morgante, Amy, eds., *Women's Views on the Earth Charter*, Boston Research Center for the 21st Century, 1997.

Commission on Global Governance, *Our Global Neighborhood: The Report of the Commission on Global Governance*, Oxford University Press, 1995; includes reference to the Earth Charter.

Morgante, Amy, ed., *Buddhist Perspectives on the Earth Charter*, Boston Research Center for the 21st Century, 1997.

United Nations, *Earth Summit Agenda 21: The United Nations Programme of Action From Rio*, United Nations Publications, 1993.

WEB SITES

Earth Charter Community Summits home page—http://www.earthchartersummits.org.

Earth Charter Initiative home page—http://www.earthcharter.org.

Earth Council home page—http://www.ecouncil.ac.cr.

Earth Charter USA home page—http://www.earthcharterusa.org.

THE "GLOBAL ETHIC" MOVEMENT

BOOKS

Braybrooke, Marcus, *Stepping Stones to a Global Ethic*, SCM Press, 1992.

Hodes, Nancy and Hays, Michael, eds., *United Nations and the World's Religions* (Proceedings of a Conference Held October 7, 1994, at Columbia University), Boston Research Center for the 21st Century, 1995.

Küng, Hans, *A Global Ethic for Global Politics and Global Economics*, Oxford University Press, 1998.

Küng, Hans, and Kuschel, Karl-Josef, eds., *A Global Ethic: The Declaration of the Parliament of the World's Religions*, Continuum, 1993.

Küng, Hans, and Schmidt, Helmut, *Global Ethic and Global Responsibilities: Two Declarations*, SCM Press, 1998.

Küng, Hans, *Global Responsibility: In Search of a New World Ethic*, Continuum, 1996.

————. *Yes to a Global Ethic*, Continuum, 1996.

Morgan, Peggy, and Braybrooke, Marcus, *Testing the Global Ethic: Voices from the Religions on Moral Values*, CoNexus Press, 1998.

Swidler, Leonard, *For All Life: Toward a Universal Declaration of a Global Ethic*, White Cloud Press, 1999.

WEB SITES

Center for Global Ethics home page—http://globalethic.org; an alternative site is at http://astro.temple.edu/~dialogue/geth.htm.

Council for a Parliament of the World's Religions (CPWR)—http://www.cpwr.org/resource/global_ethic.htm; their "global ethic" page.

Global Dialogue Institute home page—http://astro.temple.edu/~dialogue/anthocon.htm; a collection of essays and links by US supporters of the "global ethic."

Global Ethic Foundation home page—http://www.weltethos.org/dat_eng/index_e.htm; the home page for the movement worldwide.

Institute for Global Ethics home page—http://www.globalethics.org.

THE GORBACHEV FOUNDATION

WEB SITES

Gorbachev Foundation home page—http://www.gorby.ru/en/default.asp

Gorbachev Foundation of North America home page—http://www.gfna.net

GREEN CROSS INTERNATIONAL

WEB SITES

Global Green (Green Cross/USA) home page—http://www.globalgreen.org.

Green Cross International home page—http://www.greencrossinternational.net/index.asp.

STATE OF THE WORLD FORUM

BOOKS

Garrison, Jim, *America As Empire: Global Leader or Rogue Power?*, Berrett-Koehler Publishers, 2004. (Garrison is the Chairman and President of the State of the World Forum.)

_____. *Civilization and the Transformation of Power*, Paraview Press, 2000.

_____. *The Darkness of God: Theology After Hiroshima*, Eerdmans, 1983.

_____. *The Plutonium Culture: From Hiroshima to Harrisburg*, Continuum, 1981.

_____. *The Russian Threat: Myths and Realities*, Gateway, 1983.

Garrison, Jim, and Phipps, John-Francis, *The New Diplomats: Citizens As Ambassadors for Peace*, Green Books, 1991.

WEB SITES

State of the World Forum Commission on Globalization home page—http://www.commissiononglobalization.org.

State of the World Forum home page—http://www.worldforum.org.

State of the World Forum Simulconference 2000 home page—http://www.simulconference.com/clients/sowf; documents from the 2000 annual meeting.

State of the World Forum web pages for 1998 and 1999—http://worldforum.percepticon.com.

THE WORLD ECONOMIC FORUM

BOOKS

Schwab, Klaus, *The Global Competitiveness Report* 2003–2004, Oxford University Press, 2004. Similar reports for prior years are also available through on-line bookstores.

WEB SITES

World Economic Forum home page—http://www.weforum.org.

World Economic Forum web log—http://wef.typepad.com/blog.

OTHER GLOBALIST ORGANIZATIONS

WEB SITES

Club of Budapest home page—http://www.club-of-budapest.com.

Club of Rome home page—http://www.clubofrome.org.

European Union home page—http://europa.eu.int/index_en.htm.

Trilateral Commission home page—http://www.trilateral.org.

United Nations system web page—http://www.unsystem.org; a comprehensive index of organizations and web sites for the UN and related agencies.

THEOSOPHY AND THE NEW AGE MOVEMENT

THEOSOPHY

HELENA P. BLAVATSKY AND THE THEOSOPHICAL SOCIETY

BOOKS: BY BLAVATSKY

Blavatsky, H.P., *An Invitation to the Secret Doctrine*, Theosophical University Press, 1994.

_____. *Isis Unveiled*, 2 vol., Theosophical University Press, 1999 reprint of 1877 ed.

_____. *Lucifer: A Theosophical Magazine*; reprints of magazines issued from 1887 through 1897 are available through Amazon.

_____. *Nightmare Tales*, Society of Metaphysicians, 1998.

_____. *Practical Occultism*, Quest Books, 1967.

_____. *The Key To Theosophy*, Theosophical University Press, 1972.

_____. *The Secret Doctrine: The Synthesis of Science, Religion, and Philosophy* (Volumes 1 and 2), Theosophical University Press, 1999 reprint of 1888 ed. Additionally, there is a book-length index, published as a separate volume.

————. *The Voice of the Silence*, Theosophical University Press, 1992. Blavatsky, H. P. and Mead, G. R. S., *Theosophical Glossary*, Kessinger Publishing, reprint, 2003.

BIOGRAPHIES OF BLAVATSKY AND HISTORIES OF THEOSOPHY:

Balyoz, Harold, *Three Remarkable Women*, Altai Publishers, 1986. (Biographies of Blavatsky, Helena Roerich, and Alice Bailey, with excerpts from their work).

Caldwell, Daniel H., *The Esoteric World of Madame Blavatsky*, Quest Books, 2001. (Supportive of Theosophy)

Campbell, Bruce F., *Ancient Wisdom Revived: A History of the Theosophical Movement*, University of California Press, 1980. (Scholarly history; supportive of Theosophy)

Cranston, Sylvia, *H. P. B.: The Extraordinary Life & Influence of Helena Blavatsky*, Path Publishing House, 1998. (A detailed hagiography of Blavatsky)

Ellwood, Robert S., *Theosophy: A Modern Expression of the Wisdom of the Ages*, Quest Books, 1986. (A modern overview, by a Theosophist.)

Gilchrist, Cherry, *Theosophy: The Wisdom of the Ages*, Harper San Francisco, 1996. (A devotee's introduction to Theosophy).

Godwin, Joscelyn, *The Theosophical Enlightenment*, State University of New York Press, 1994. (Scholarly history).

Gomes, Michael, *The Dawning of the Theosophical Movement*, Quest Books, 1987. (Supportive of Theosophy)

Hanson, Virginia, *H.P. Blavatsky and the Secret Doctrine: Commentaries on Her Contribution to World Thought*, Quest Books, 1988. (Supportive of Blavatsky.)

Johnson, K. Paul, *Initiates of the Theosophical Masters*, State University of New York Press, 1995. (Scholarly history).

Johnson, K. Paul, *The Masters Revealed: Madam Blavatsky and the Myth of the Great White Lodge*, State University of New York Press, 1994. (Scholarly history).

Maroney, Tim, *The Book of Dzyan*, Chaosium, 2000. (Critical biography of Blavatsky by an occultist; includes an esoteric text that Blavatsky claimed was the source of *The Secret Doctrine*.)

Mills, Joy, 100 *Years of Theosophy: A History of the Theosophical Society in America*, Quest Books, 1987. (Supportive of Theosophy).

Murphet, Howard, *When daylight comes: A biography of Helena Petrovna Blavatsky*, Theosophical Publishing House, 1975. (Supportive of Theosophy)

Washington, Peter, *Madame Blavatsky's Baboon: A History of the Mystics, Mediums, and Misfits Who Brought Spiritualism to America*, Schocken Books, 1996. (Critical biography).

WEB SITES

Theosophical Society, Adyar—http://www.ts-adyar.org; this is the international headquarters of the movement that Blavatsky founded.

Theosophical Society in America home page—http://www.theosophical.org.

Theosophical Society in Pasadena, California—http://www.theosociety.org. Their Theosophical University Press publishes the works of Blavatsky, Annie Besant, and other Theosophists; the web page for the Press is http://www.theosociety.org/pasadena/ts/tup.htm.

United Lodge of Theosophists home page—http://www.ult.org/index.html.

ALICE A. BAILEY, FOSTER BAILEY, AND THE LUCIS TRUST

BOOKS

Bailey, Alice A., *A Treatise on Cosmic Fire*, Lucis Publishing Company, 1973.

————. *A Treatise on the Seven Rays, Vol. 1: Esoteric Psychology, Vol.* 1, Lucis Publishing Company, 2002.

————. *A Treatise on the Seven Rays, Vol. 2: Esoteric Psychology, Vol.* 2, Lucis Publishing Company, 1995.

————. *A Treatise on the Seven Rays, Vol. 3: Esoteric Astrology*, Lucis Publishing Company, 1998.

————. *A Treatise on the Seven Rays, Vol. 4: Esoteric Healing*, Lucis Publishing Company, 1999.

————. *A Treatise on the Seven Rays, Vol. 5: The Rays and the Initiations*, Lucis Publishing Company, 1971.

————. *A Treatise On White Magic, or The Way Of The Disciple*, Lucis Publishing Company, 1998.

————. *Discipleship in the New Age, Vol.* 1, Lucis Publishing Company, 1985.

_____. *Discipleship in the New Age, Vol.* 2, Lucis Publishing Company, 1995.

_____. *Education in the New Age*, Lucis Publishing Company, 1971.

_____. *From Bethlehem to Calvary*, Lucis Publishing Company, 1975.

_____. *Glamour: A World Problem*, Lucis Publishing Company, 1995.

_____. *Initiation, Human and Solar*, Lucis Publishing Company, 1997.

_____. *Letters on Occult Meditation*, Lucis Publishing Company, 1973.

_____. *Master Index of the Books of Alice Bailey*, Lucis Publishing Company, 1998.

_____. *Problems of Humanity*, Lucis Publishing Company, 3rd rev. ed. 1993.

_____. *Telepathy and the Etheric Vehicle*, Lucis Publishing Company, 1971.

_____. *The Consciousness of the Atom*, Lucis Publishing Company, 1972.

_____. *The Destiny of the Nations*, Lucis Publishing Company, 1987.

_____. *The Externalisation of the Hierarchy*, Lucis Publishing Company, 1983.

_____. *The Light of the Soul, Its Science and Effects: The Yoga Sutras of Patanjali*, Lucis Publishing Company, 1998.

_____. *The Labours of Hercules: An Astrological Interpretation*, Lucis Publishing Company, 1982.

_____. *The Reappearance of the Christ*, Lucis Publishing Company, 1978.

_____. *The Soul And Its Mechanism*, Lucis Publishing Company, 1971.

_____. *Unfinished Autobiography*, Lucis Publishing Company, 1994.

Bailey, Foster, *Changing Esoteric Values*, Lucis Publishing Company, 1995.

_____. *Reflections*, Lucis Publishing Company, 1979.

_____. *Running God's Plan*, Lucis Publishing Company, 1972.

_____. *The Spirit of Masonry*, Lucis Publishing Company, 1979.

_____. *Things To Come*, Lucis Publishing Company, 1979.

Bailey, Mary, *A Learning Experience*, Lucis Publishing Company, 1990.

Banks, Natalie, *Golden Thread: The Continuity of Esoteric Teaching*, Lucis Publishing Company, 1999.

Sinclair, John, *The Alice Bailey Inheritance*, Turnstone Press, 1985.

Additionally, the Lucis Trust has prepared some compilations of Alice Bailey's works: *A Compilation on Sex, Death: The Great Adventure, Ponder On This, Serving Humanity, Soul: The Quality of Life, The Seven Rays of Life*, and *The Seventh Ray: Revealer of the New Age*. They also offer a CD-ROM version of all of Bailey's works, with a master index, as well as a magazine, *The Beacon*.

WEB SITES

Lucis Trust home page—http://lucistrust.org/; also provides links to the Arcane School, World Goodwill, and the Lucis Publishing company. Their publications may be ordered through this site.

New Group of World Servers home page—http://www.ngws.org/index.htm.

Share International home page—http://www.shareintl.org. This group appears to be inspired by the teachings of Alice Bailey. Their public leader, Benjamin Creme, claims to be the advance man for "Maitreya," a camera-shy "World Teacher" whose appearance has been "imminent" since 1982. The Lucis Trust, however, has not accepted the claims of Maitreya and of Creme.

The works of Alice Bailey on-line—http://beaskund.helloyou.ws/netnews/bk/toc.html.

THE NEW AGE MOVEMENT

NEW AGE ANGLICANISM

MATTHEW FOX AND CREATION SPIRITUALITY

BOOKS

Fox, Matthew, *A Spirituality Named Compassion: Uniting Mystical Awareness with Social Justice*, Robert Bentley Publishers, 1999.

_____. *Breakthrough: Meister Eckhart's Creation Spirituality in New Translation*, Doubleday, 1980.

_____. *Confessions: The Making of a Post-Denominational Priest*, Harper San Francisco, 1997.

_____. *Creation Spirituality: Liberating Gifts for the Peoples of the Earth*, Harper San Francisco, 1991.

_____. *Creativity: Where the Divine and the Human Meet*, Jeremy P. Tarcher, 2002.

_____.*Hildegard of Bingen's Book of Divine Works With Music & Letters by Hildegard of Bingen*, Bear & Company, 1987.

_____. *Illuminations of Hildegard of Bingen*, Bear and Company, 2003.

_____. *Meditations With Meister Eckhart*, Bear & Company, 1982.

_____. *One River, Many Wells: Wisdom Springing from Global Faiths*, Jeremy P. Tarcher, 2004.

_____. *Original Blessing: A Primer in Creation Spirituality Presented in Four Paths, Twenty-Six Themes, and Two Questions*, Jeremy P. Tarcher, 2000.

_____. *Passion for Creation: The Earth-honoring Spirituality of Meister Eckhart*, Inner Traditions International, 2000.

_____. *Prayer: A Radical Response to Life*, Jeremy P. Tarcher, 2001. (Previously published in 1972 under the title *On Becoming a Musical, Mystical Bear: Spirituality American Style.*)

_____. *Sins of the Spirit, Blessings of the Flesh: Lessons for Transforming Evil in Soul and Society*, Three Rivers Press, 1999.

_____. *The Coming of the Cosmic Christ: The Healing of Mother Earth and the Birth of a Global Renaissance*, Harper San Francisco, 1988.

_____. *The Reinvention of Work: New Vision of Livelihood for Our Time*, Harper San Francisco, 1995.

_____. *Western Spirituality: Historical Roots, Ecumenical Routes*, Bear & Company, 1984.

_____. *Whee! We, Wee All the Way Home: A Guide to a Sensual Prophetic Spirituality*, Bear & Company, 1981.

_____. *Wrestling With the Prophets: Essays on Creation, Spirituality, and Everyday Life*, Jeremy P. Tarcher, 2003.

Fox, Matthew, and Hammond, Catherine, *Creation Spirituality and the Dreamtime*, Morehouse Publishers, 1991.

Fox, Matthew, and Sheldrake, Rupert, *Natural Grace: Dialogues on Creation, Darkness, and the Soul in Spirituality and Science*, Image Books, 1997.

_____. *Sheer Joy: Conversations With Thomas Aquinas on Creation Spirituality*, Jeremy P. Tarcher, 2003.

_____. *The Physics of Angels: Exploring the Realm Where Science and Spirit Meet*, Harper San Francisco, 1996.

Fox, Matthew, and Swimme, Brian, *Manifesto! for a Global Civilization*, Inner Traditions, 1991.

Fox, Matthew, and Tattersfield, Jane, *In the Beginning There Was Joy*, National Book Network, 1995. (A children's book; the description on Amazon is: "Mr. and Mrs. Joy (God) teach their children (us) to share and respect the beauty of all creation.")

WEB SITES

Friends of Creation Spirituality—http://www.matthewfox.org/sys-tmpl/door; Fox's home page.

Naropa University home page—http://www.naropa.edu; associated with the University of Creation Spirituality.

Techno Cosmic Mass home page—http://www.technocosmicmass.org, for information on Fox's drug-free rave liturgy.

University of Creation Spirituality home page—http://www.creationspirituality.com.

THE LABYRINTH MOVEMENT

BOOKS

Artress, Lauren, *The Sand Labyrinth: Meditation at Your Fingertips*, Journey Editions, 2000.

Artress, Lauren, *Walking a Sacred Path: Rediscovering the Labyrinth As a Spiritual Tool*, Riverhead Books, 1996.

Attali, Jacques, *Labyrinth in Culture and Society: Pathways to Wisdom*, North Atlantic Books, 1999.

Curry, Helen, *The Way of the Labyrinth: A Powerful Meditation for Everyday Life*, Penguin Compass, 2000.

McCullough, David, *The Unending Mystery: A Journey Through Labyrinths and Mazes*, Pantheon, 2004.

WEB SITES

Grace Cathedral Labyrinth Project home page—http://www.gracecathedral.org/labyrinth.

Veriditas home page—http://www.veriditas.net; "the voice of the labyrinth movement."

THE CATHEDRAL OF ST. JOHN THE DIVINE

WEB SITES

Episcopal Cathedral of St. John the Divine home page—http://www.stjohndivine.org.

PIERRE TEILHARD DE CHARDIN

BOOKS

Fabel, Arthur, and St. John, Donald, *Teilhard in the 21st Century: The Emerging Spirit of Earth*, Orbis Books, 2003.

King, Ursula, *Christ in All Things: Exploring Spirituality with Teilhard De Chardin*, Orbis Books, 1997.

Lubac, Henri de, *Teilhard De Chardin: The Man and His Meaning*, New American Library, 1968. (De Lubac, a supporter of Teilhard, was named as a Cardinal by Pope John Paul II in 1983, and continued in this post until his death in 1991.)

———. *Teilhard Explained*, Paulist Press, 1968.

———. *The Eternal Feminine: A Study on the Poem by Teilhard de Chardin*, Collins, 1971.

———. *The Religion of Teilhard de Chardin*, Image Books, 1968.

Lukas, Mary, *Teilhard: The Man, the Priest, the Scientist*, Doubleday, 1977.

Pierre Teilhard de Chardin Association, *Evolution, Marxism and Christianity: Studies in the Teilhardian Synthesis*, Garnstone, 1967.

Smith, Wolfgang, *Teilhardism and the New Religion: A Thorough Analysis of the Teachings of Pierre Teilhard De Chardin*, TAN Books and Publishers, 1988. (Traditional Catholic critique of the writings of Teilhard de Chardin.)

Teilhard de Chardin, Pierre, S. J., *Activation of Energy*, Harvest Books, 2002.

———. *Building the Earth*, Dimension Books, 2002.

———. *Christianity and Evolution*, Harvest Books, 2002.

———. *How I Believe*, Harper Collins, 1969.

———. *Human Energy*, Harcourt, 1972.

———. *Hymn of the Universe*, Harper Collins, 1969.

———. *Let Me Explain*, Collins, 1970.

———. *Letters From A Traveller*, Harper, 1962.

———. *Letters From Egypt*, 1905-1908, Herder and Herder, 1965.

———. *Letters From Hastings* 1908-1912, Herder and Herder, 1968.

———. *Letters From My Friend, Teilhard de Chardin*, 1948-1955: *Including Letters Written During His Final Years In America*, Paulist Press, 1980.

———. *Letters From Paris* 1912-1914, Herder and Herder, 1967.

———. *Letters to Léontine Zanta*, Collins, 1969.

———. *Letters To Two Friends*, 1926-1952, New American Library, 1968.

———. *Man's Place in Nature*, Harper Collins, 2000.

———. *On Happiness*, Collins, 1974.

———. *On Love and Happiness*, Harper Collins, 1984.

———. *On Suffering*, Collins, 1974.

———. *Science and Christ*, Harper and Row, 1965.

———. *The Appearance of Man*, Harper and Row, 1965.

———. *The Divine Milieu*, Perennial Classics, 2001.

———. *The Future of Man*, Image, 2004.

———. *The Heart of Matter*, Harvest Books, 2002.

———. *The Letters of Teilhard De Chardin & Lucile Swan*, University of Scranton Press, 2001.

———. *The Making of a Mind: Letters From a Soldier-Priest* 1914-1919, Harper and Row, 1965.

———. *The Phenomenon of Man*, Perennial, 1976; also a new translation, *The Human Phenomenon*.

————. *The Vision of the Past*, Harper, 1966.

————. *Toward the Future*, Harvest Books, 2002.

————. *Writings In Time of War*, Harper and Row, 1965.

Teilhard de Chardin, Pierre, S. J., and Blondel, Maurice, *Correspondence*, Herder and Herder, 1967.

BARBARA MARX HUBBARD

BOOKS

Marx Hubbard, Barbara, *Conscious Evolution: Awakening the Power of Our Social Potential*, New World Library, Novato, California, 1998

————. *Emergence: The Shift from Ego to Essence*, Walsch Books, Hampton Roads Publishing Co., Inc, Charlottesville, Virginia, 2001.

————. *Manual for Co-Creators of the Quantum Leap*, New Visions, n. d.

————. *Happy Birth Day Planet Earth: The Instant of Co-Operation*, Ocean Tree Books, Santa Fe, New Mexico, 1986.

————. *The Book of Co-Creation—The Revelation: Our Crisis Is A Birth*, 1st ed., Foundation for Conscious Evolution, Sonoma, California, 1993.

————. *The Book of Co-Creation Part II—The Promise Will Be Kept: The Gospels, The Acts, the Epistles*, Foundation for Conscious Evolution, Greenbrae, California, 1993 (privately published).

————. *The Evolutionary Journey: A Personal Guide to a Positive Future*, Evolutionary Press of the Institute for the Study of Conscious Evolution, San Francisco, 1982.

————. *The Hunger of Eve*, Stackpole Books, Harrisburg, Pennsylvania, 1976; updated editions were released in 1983 (Mindbody Communications, publisher) and 1989 (Island Pacific Northwest, publisher).

————. *The Revelation: A Message of Hope for the New Millennium*, 2nd ed., Nataraj Publishing, Novato, California, 1995.

WEB SITES

Foundation for Conscious Evolution home page, http://www.evolve.org—"A Global Community Center for Conscious Evolution."

CORINNE MCLAUGHLIN AND GORDON DAVIDSON

BOOKS

McLaughlin, Corinne and Davidson, Gordon, *Builders of the Dawn: Community Lifestyles in a Changing World*, The Book Publishing Company, 1990.

McLaughlin, Corinne and Davidson, Gordon, *Spiritual Politics: Changing the World from the Inside Out*, Ballantine Books, 1994.

WEB SITES

The Center for Visionary Leadership home page—http://www.visionarylead.org.

ROBERT MULLER

BOOKS

Gillies, Douglas, *Prophet: The Hatmaker's Son—The Life of Robert Muller*, East Beach Press, 2003.

Muller, Robert, 2000 *Ideas For A Better World: My Countdown on Dreams on Mt. Rasur to the Year* 2000 *for Your Thoughts and Action*, University for Peace, 1994.

————. *A Planet of Hope*, Amity House, 1985.

————. *A Testament to the Earth: Meditations and Reflections on Forty Years in the United Nations*, Amity House, 1987.

————. *Dialogues of Hope*, World Happiness and Cooperation, 1990.

_____. *First Lady of the World*, World Happiness and Cooperation, 1991.

_____. *Framework for preparation for the year* 2000, Albert Schweitzer Institute Press, 1994.

_____. *Most of All, They Taught Me Happiness*, Doubleday, 1978.

_____. *My Testament to the UN: A Contribution to the 50th Anniversary of the United Nations* 1995, World Happiness and Cooperation, 2nd ed. 1994.

_____. *New Genesis: Shaping a Global Spirituality*, World Happiness and Cooperation, orig. ed. 1982; 3rd printing 1993.

_____. *The Birth of a Global Civilization: With proposals for a new political system for Planet Earth*, World Happiness and Cooperation, orig. ed. 1991, 2nd printing 1992.

_____. *What War Taught Me About Peace*, Doubleday, 1985.

Muller, Robert, and Roche, Douglas, *Safe Passage into the Twenty-First Century: The United Nations' Quest for Peace, Equality, Justice, and Development*, Continuum (A Global Education Associates Book), New York, 1995.

Muller, Robert, and Zonneveld, Leo, eds. *The Desire To Be Human*, Mirananda Publishers, The Netherlands, 1983. (This is a collection of essays in honor of Teilhard de Chardin).

The Robert Muller School, *The World Core Curriculum: Foundations, Implementation, and Resources*, Arlington, Texas, 1991. (This is the most recent edition, as provided by the school in 2002.)

_____. *The World Core Curriculum Guidebook*, Arlington, Texas, 1993.

_____. *World Core Curriculum Manual (Overview)*, Arlington, Texas, 1986.

WEB SITES

Robert Muller (and his associates) have multiple web pages dedicated to his "ideas and dreams":

• http://www.earthpax.net—a web page with "Robert Muller's exhortations and ideas & dreams for a better world."

• http://www.goodmorningworld.org—a web page with recent writings by Muller.

• http://www.paradiseearth.us—"Robert Muller's Ideas and Dreams Nurturing Our Home." The text for Muller's newest book, Paradise Earth, is available for download here.

• http://www.robertmuller.org—the home page for Robert Muller; contains the text of his 4,000 "Ideas and Dreams for a Better World"

Robert Muller Schools International home page—http://www.unol.org/rms

NEALE DONALD WALSCH

BOOKS

Blanton, Brad, and Walsch, Neale Donald, *Honest to God: A Change of Hearts That Can Change the World*, Sparrowhawk Publications, 2002.

Walsch, Neale Donald, *Bringers of the Light*, Hampton Roads Publishing Company, Inc., 2000.

_____. *Communion with God*, G. P. Putnam's Sons, 2000.

_____. *Conversations with God: An Uncommon Dialogue*, Book 1, Putnam Publishing Group, 1996.

_____. *Conversations with God: Book* 1 *(Guidebook)*, Hampton Roads Publishing Company, Inc., 1996.

_____. *Conversations with God: An Uncommon Dialogue*, Book 2, Hampton Roads Publishing Company, Inc., 1997.

_____. *Conversations with God: An Uncommon Dialogue*, Book 3, Hampton Roads Publishing Company, Inc., 1998.

Walsch, Neale Donald, and Morissett, Alanis, *Conversations with God for Teens*, Scholastic, 2001.

Walsch, Neale Donald, *Friendship with God: An Uncommon Dialogue*, Putnam Publishing Group, 1998.

_____. *Moments of Grace*, Hampton Roads Publishing Company, Inc., 2001.

_____. *Neale Donald Walsch on Abundance and Right Livelihood*, Hampton Roads Publ. Company, Inc., 1999.

_____. *Neale Donald Walsch on Holistic Living*, Hampton Roads Publishing Company, Inc., 1999.

_____. *Neale Donald Walsch on Relationships*, Hampton Roads Publishing Company, Inc., 1999.

_____. *Questions and Answers on Conversations with God*, Hampton Roads Publishing Company Inc., 1999.

_____. *Re-Creating Your Self*, Neale Donald Walsch Pub., 2000.

————. *The Little Soul and the Sun: A Children's Parable Adapted from Conversations With God*, Young Spirit Books, 1998.

————. *The New Revelations: A Conversation with God*, Atria Books, 2002.

————. *Tomorrow's God: Our Greatest Spiritual Challenge*, Atria Books, 2004.

————. et al., *Wedding Vows from Conversations with God*, Hampton Roads Publishing Company Inc., 2000.

WEB SITES

Conversations With God Foundation home page—http://www.cwg.org.

Humanity's Team home page—http://www.humanitysteam.com/main.html.

The Changers home page—http://www.thechangers.org; a Walsch organization for teenagers.

OTHER GLOBALIST, NEW AGE AND UTOPIAN RESOURCES

WEB SITES

Alliance for a Responsible, Plural and United World home page—http://www.alliance21.org/2003/sommaire_en.php3.

Berkeley Psychic Institute home page—http://www.berkeleypsychic.com; affiliated with the Church of Divine Man.

Carter Center home page—http://www.cartercenter.org.

Citizens for Global Solutions home page—http://www.globalsolutions.org; this is the new name for the World Federalist Association.

Foundation for the Future home page—http://www.futurefoundation.org; Robert Muller and Barbara Marx Hubbard are on the Board of Advisers.

For The Common Good home page—http://www.global-forum.org; web page on globalization from an interfaith perspective, with essays by URI activist Josef Boehle.

Global Education Associates home page—http://www.globaleduc.org.

Jean Houston's home page—http://www.jeanhouston.org; she inspired Lauren Artress to start the Labyrinth Project at Grace Cathedral.

Millennium Institute home page—http://www.millenniuminstitute.net.

Pathways to Peace home page—http://pathwaystopeace.org.

The Mastery Foundation home page—http://www.masteryfoundation.org.

Wittenberg Center for Alternative Resources home page—http://www.wittenbergcenter.org; some of its leaders have been active in the URI.

World Social Forum home page for 2004—http://www.wsfindia.org.

Worldwatch home page—http://www.worldwatch.org.

ENTHEOGENS: THE INTERSECTION BETWEEN DRUGS AND RELIGION

BOOKS

Arthur, James, *Mushrooms and Mankind: The Impact of Mushrooms on Human Consciousness and Religion*, The Book Tree, 2003.

Clark, Heinrich, *Magic Mushrooms in Religion and Alchemy*, Park Street Press, 2002.

Davenport-Hines, Richard, *The Pursuit of Oblivion: A Global History of Narcotics*, W. W. Norton and Co., 2004.

DeKorne, Jim, *Psychedelic Shamanism: The Cultivation, Preparation and Shamanic Use of Psychotropic Plants*, Loompanics Unlimited, 1994.

Forte, Robert, et al., *Entheogens and the Future of Religion*, Pine Forge Press, 2000.

Grob, Charles S., *Hallucinogens: A Reader*, Jeremy P. Tarcher, 2002.

Lee, Martin A., and Shlain, Bruce, *Acid Dreams: The Complete Social History of LSD—The CIA, the Sixties, and Beyond*, Grove/Atlantic, 1986.

Masters, Robert, and Houston, Jean, *The Varieties of Psychedelic Experience*, Park Street Press, 2000 ed.

McKenna, Terence, *Food of the Gods: The Search for the Original Tree of Knowledge—A Radical History of Plants, Drugs, and Human Evolution*, Bantam, 1993.

Merkur, Daniel, *The Mystery of Manna: The Psychedelic Sacrament of the Bible*, Park Street Press, 2000.

_____. *The Psychedelic Sacrament: Manna, Meditation, and Mystical Experience*, Park Street Press, 2001.

Pinchbeck, Daniel, *Breaking Open the Head: A Psychedelic Journey into the Heart of Contemporary Shamanism*, Broadway, 2003.

Roberts, Thomas B., *Psychoactive Sacramentals: Essays on Entheogens and Religion*, Council on Spiritual Practices, 2001.

Russell, Dan, *Shamanism and the Drug Propaganda: The Birth of Patriarchy and the Drug War*, Kalyx.com, 1998.

Schultes, Richard Evans, *Plants of the Gods: Their Sacred, Healing and Hallucinogenic Powers*, Healing Art Press, 2002.

Shulgin, Alexander, *Pihkal: A Chemical Love Story*, Transform Press, 1991.

Smith, Huston, *Cleansing the Doors of Perception: The Religious Significance of Entheogenic Plants and Chemicals*, Sentient Publications, 2003.

Wasson, Gordon, et al., *Persephone's Quest: Entheogens and the Origins of Religion*, Yale University Press, 1992.

THE WESTERN OCCULT AND PSEUDO-CHRISTIAN TRADITION, FROM GNOSTICISM THROUGH THE NEW AGE

BOOKS

Aveni, Anthony, *Behind the Crystal Ball: Magic, Science, and the Occult from Antiquity Through the New Age*, University Press of Colorado, 2002.

Baigent, Michael, and Leigh, Richard, *The Elixir and the Stone: Unlocking the Ancient Mysteries of the Occult*, Penguin, 1997.

Bloom, Harold, *Omens of Millennium: The Gnosis of Angels, Dreams, and Resurrection*, Riverhead Books, 1997.

_____. *The American Religion: The Emergence of the Post-Christian Nation*, Simon and Schuster, 1992.

Burton, Dan, and Grandy, David, *Magic, Mystery, and Science: The Occult in Western Civilization*, Indiana University Press, 2003.

Butler, E. M., *The Myth of the Magus*, Cambridge University Press, 1993 ed.

Drury, Nevill, *Exploring the Labyrinth: Making Sense of the New Spirituality*, Continuum, 1999.

Ellis, Bill, *Lucifer Ascending: The Occult in Folklore and Popular Culture*, University Press of Kentucky, 2003.

Faivre, Antoine, *Access to Western Esotericism*, State University of New York Press, 1994.

_____. et al., *Modern Esoteric Spirituality*, Crossroad, 1995.

_____. *Theosophy, Imagination, Tradition: Studies in Western Esotericism*, State Univ. of New York Press, 2000.

Faivre, Antoine, and Hanegraaff, Wouter J., *Western Esotericism and the Science of Religion*, Peeters, 1998.

Ferguson, Marilyn, *The Aquarian Conspiracy: Personal and Social Transformation in the 1980s*, J.P. Tarcher, Inc., 1987.

Feuerstein, Georg, and Feuerstein, Trisha Lamb, *Voices on the Threshold of Tomorrow: 145 Views of the New Millennium*, Quest Books, 1993. (A collection of essays by a wide range of New Age authors.)

Gibbons, B. J., *Spirituality and the Occult: From the Renaissance to the Modern Age*, Routledge, 2001.

Hanegraaff, Wouter J., *New Age Religion and Western Culture: Esotericism in the Mirror of Secular Thought*, State University of New York Press, 1998.

Heelas, Paul, *The New Age Movement: The Celebration of the Self and the Sacralization of Modernity*, Blackwell Publishers, 1996.

Herrick, James A., *The Making of the New Spirituality: The Eclipse of the Western Religious Tradition*, InterVarsity Press, 2003. (Evangelical Christian critique of the New Age).

Hoeller, Stephan A., *Gnosticism: New Light on the Ancient Tradition of Inner Knowing*, Quest Books, 2002. (History of Gnosticism by an avowed Gnostic; published by a Theosophical press.)

_____. *Freedom: Alchemy for a Voluntary Society*, Quest Books, 1992. (Gnostic/Jungian view of freedom and its opponents)

Kerr, Howard, and Crow, Charles L., *The Occult in America: New Historical Perspectives*, Univ. of Illinois Press, 1986.

Kinney, Jay, *The Inner West: An Introduction to the Hidden Wisdom of the West*, Jeremy P. Tarcher, 2004.

Lewis, James R., and Melton, Gordon J., *Perspectives on the New Age*, State University of New York Press, 1992.

Lindholm, Lars B., *Pilgrims of the Night: Pathfinders of the Magical Way*, Llewellyn Publications, 1994.

Owen, Alex, *The Darkened Room: Women, Power, and Spiritualism in Late Victorian England*, University of Chicago Press, 2004.

————. *The Place of Enchantment: British Occultism and the Culture of the Modern*, University of Chicago Press, 2004.

Melton, J. Gordon, et al., *New Age Almanac*, Visible Ink Press, 1991.

Pauwels, Louis, and Bergier, Jacques, *The Morning of the Magicians*, Rowman & Littlefield Publishers, Inc., 1991.

Powell, Robert, *The Most Holy Trinosophia and the New Revelation of the Divine Feminine*, Anthroposophic Press, 2000.

Rudolph, Kurt, *Gnosis: The Nature and History of Gnosticism*, Harper San Francisco, 1987.

Smoley, Richard, *Inner Christianity: A Guide to the Esoteric Tradition*, Shambhala Publications, 2002.

Smoley, Richard, and Kinney, Jay, *Hidden Wisdom: A Guide to the Western Inner Traditions*, Penguin Books, 1999.

Styers, Randall, *Making Magic: Religion, Magic, and Science in the Modern World*, Oxford University Press, 2003.

Van Den Broek, R., et al., *Gnosis and Hermeticism from Antiquity to Modern Times*, State University of New York Press, 1997.

Versluis, Arthur, *Theosophia: Hidden Dimensions of Christianity*, Lindisfarne Books, 1994.

————. *Wisdom's Children: A Christian Esoteric Tradition*, State University of New York Press, 1999.

Webb, James, *The Occult Establishment*, Open Court Publishing Company, 1976.

————. *The Occult Underground*, Open Court Publishing Company, 1974.

Wilson, Colin, *The Occult: The Ultimate Book for Those Who Would Walk With the Gods*, Watkins Publishing, Ltd., 2nd ed., 2003.

COMPARATIVE RELIGION

BOOKS

Beaver, R. Pierce, et al., *Eerdmans' Handbook to the World's Religions*, Wm. B. Eerdmans Publishing Company, 1994.

Occhiogrosso, Peter, *The Joy of Sects*, Image Books, 1997.

Smith, Huston, *The World's Religions: Our Great Wisdom Traditions*, Harper San Francisco, 1991.

NEW RELIGIOUS MOVEMENTS, SECTS, AND CULTS

OVERVIEWS

BOOKS

Barker, Eilleen, and Warburg, Margit, *New Religions and New Religiosity*, David Brown Book Co., 2000.

Barrett, David V., *The New Believers: Sects, 'Cults' and Alternative Religions*, Cassell, 2003.

Chryssides, George D., *Exploring New Religions*, Cassell, 2000.

————. *Historical Dictionary of New Religious Movements*, Scarecrow Press, 2001.

Ellwood, Robert S., *Alternative Altars: Unconventional and Eastern Spirituality in America*, University of Chicago Press, 1981.

Jenkins, Philip, *Mystics and Messiahs: Cults and New Religions in American History*, Oxford University Press, 2001.

Kranenborg, Reender, and Rothstein, Mikael, *New Religions in a Postmodern World*, Aarhus University Press, 2003.

Lewis, James R., *Odd Gods: New Religions and the Cult Controversy*, Prometheus Books, 2001.

Lifton, Robert Jay, *Thought Reform and the Psychology of Totalism: A Study of Brainwashing in China*, University of North Carolina Press, 1989.

Melton, J. Gordon, *Encyclopedic Handbook of Cults in America*, Garland Publishing, 1992.

Miller, Timothy, ed., *America's Alternative Religions*, State University of New York Press, 1995.

Newport, John P., *The New Age Movement and the Biblical Worldview: Conflict and Dialogue*, Eerdmans, 1998.

Partridge, Christopher, *New Religions: A Guide—New Religious Movements, Sects and Alternative Spiritualities*, Oxford University Press, 2004.

Partridge, Christopher, and Groothuis, Douglas, *Dictionary of Contemporary Religion in the Western World: Exploring Living Faiths on Postmodern Contexts*, InterVarsity Press, 1998.

Pike, Sarah M., *New Age and Neopagan Religions in America*, Columbia University Press, 2004.

Rothstein, Mikael, *New Age Religion and Globalization*, Aarhus University Press, 2002.

Saliba, John A., S. J., *Perspectives on New Religious Movements*, Continuum, 1995.

Saliba, John A., S. J., and Melton, J. Gordon, *Understanding New Religious Movements*, Rowman and Littlefield, 2003.

Towler, Robert, et al., *New Religions & the New Europe*, David Brown Book Company, 1995.

Wilson, Bryan, *The Social Dimensions of Sectarianism: Sects and New Religious Movements in Contemporary Society*, Oxford University Press, 1990.

Wilson, Bryan, and Cresswell, Jamie, *New Religious Movements: Challenge and Response*, Routledge, 1999.

Wilson, Colin, *Rogue Messiahs: Tales of Self-Proclaimed Saviors*, Hampton Roads Publishing Company, 2000.

WEB SITES—ANTI-CULT

American Family Federation home page—http://www.cultinfobooks.com, and http://www.csj.org.

Apologetics Index home page—http://www.apologeticsindex.org; Evangelical critique of cults and new religious movements.

Christian Research Institute home page—http://www.equip.org. Evangelical Christian; part of its ministry includes analysis of cults and new religious movements. Anti-Catholic.

Cults and Mind Control News home page—http://www.trancenet.org.

Cult Information Centre home page—http://www.cultinformation.org.uk/home.html.

Cult Information and Family Support home page—http://www.cifs.org.au.

Ex-Cult Resource Center home page—http://www.ex-cult.org.

Fact Net home page—http://www.factnet.org; they say that they have been "Breaking News and Information on Cults and Mind Control since 1993."

Family Action Information and Resource Center home page—http://www.fair-cult-concern.co.uk.

Freedom of Mind Center home page—http://www.freedomofmind.com; Steven Alan Hassan, the web master, states that he has "27 years of frontline activism exposing destructive cults, providing counseling and training."

InfoCult home page—http://www.math.mcgill.ca/triples/infocult/ic-e1.html.

Recovering Former Cultists' Support Network—http://www.refocus.org.

Religious Movement Resource Center home page—http://lamar.colostate.edu/~ucm/rmrc1.htm.

Rick Ross home page—http://www.rickross.com; describes itself as an "institute for the study of destructive cults, controversial groups, and movements." He also has a blog with cult news at http://www.cultnews.com.

SIMPOS, a Netherlands anti-cult group, has resources on-line at http://www.stelling.nl/simpos/esotericism.htm and http://www.stelling.nl/simpos/esotericist_tendencies_m-z.htm#M.

Spiritual Counterfeits Project home page—http://www.scp-inc.org. This is an Evangelical Christian think tank that describes itself as a "frontline ministry confronting the occult, the cults, and the New Age movement and explaining why they are making an impact on our society." It publishes a journal twice a year, and shorter newsletters several times a year.

Triumphing Over London Cults home page—http://www.tolc.org; British anti-cult group.

Yahoo.com directory of anti-cult web pages—http://directory.google.com/Top/Society/Religion_and_Spirituality/Opposing_Views/Cults.

OTHER WEB SITES PERTAINING TO CULTS AND NEW RELIGIOUS MOVEMENTS

Anti-cult activists have accused these sites of being excessively sympathetic to cults and new religious movements.

Center for Studies on New Religions (CESNUR)—http://www.cesnur.org. (For an Evangelical critique, see the Apologetics Index web article on CESNUR, at http://www.apologeticsindex.org/c10.html.)

Cult Awareness Network home page (CAN)—http://www.cultawarenessnetwork.org. (For an Evangelical critique, see the Apologetics Index web article on CAN, at http://www.apologeticsindex.org/c19.html.)

Institute for the Study of American Religion (ISAR)—http://www.americanreligion.org. (For an Evangelical critique, see the Apologetics Index web article on J. Gordon Melton, the head of the ISAR, at http://www.apologeticsindex.org/m06.html.)

THE REV. SUN MYUNG MOON AND UNIFICATIONISM

BOOKS

Boettcher, Robert B., *Gifts of Deceit: Sun Myung Moon, Tongsun Park, and the Korean Scandal*, Holt, Rinehart and Winston, 1980. (Recommended by investigative reporter John Gorenfeld as "the only book dealing with Koreagate," the 1970s scandal.)

Case, Thomas W., *Moonie Buddhist Catholic: A Spiritual Odyssey*, White Horse Press, 1996. (Critique of Moon and Unificationism)

Chryssides, George W., *The Advent of Sun Myung Moon: The Origins, Beliefs and Practices of the Unification Church*, Palgrave Macmillan, 1991.

Hong, Nansook, *In the Shadow of the Moons: My Life in the Reverend Sun Myung Moon's Family*, Little, Brown, 1998. (Critique of Moon and Unificationism)

Horowitz, Irving Louis, *Science, Sin, and Scholarship: The Politics of Reverend Moon and the Unification Church*, MIT Press, 1978.

Introvigne, Massimo, *The Unification Church*, Signature Press, 2000.

Moon, Sun Myung, *Christianity in Crisis*, HSA Publications, 1977.

————. *Divine Principle*, HSA Publications, 1977.

————. *Exposition of the Divine Principle*, HSA Publications, 1996.

————. *God's Warning to the World*, Rose of Sharon Press, 1985.

————. *God's Warning To The World Book* 2, HSA Press, 1985.

————. *God's Will and the Ocean*, 1987.

————. *Home Church*, HSA Publications, 1983.

————. *Life of Prayer*, HSA Publications, n. d.

————. *New Hope: Twelve Talks by Sun Myung Moon*, HSA Publications, 1982.

————. *Science & Absolute Values: 10 Addresses*, ICF Press, 1982.

————. *The Life and Mission of Jesus Christ*, HSA Publications, 2001.

————. *True Family and World Peace: Speeches by the Reverend and Mrs. Sun Myung Moon in the Completed Testament Age*, HSA Publications, 2000.

————. *True Love*, HSA Publications, 1989.

————. *Way of God's Will*, HSA Publications, n. d.

————. *Way of Tradition, Vol.* 2, HSA Publications, n. d.

————. *Way of Tradition III*, HSA Publications, n. d.

————. *Way of Tradition IV*, HSA Publications, 1980.

Neufeld, K. Gordon, *Heartbreak and Rage: Ten Years Under Sun Myung Moon*, Vitualbookworm.com, 2002. (Critique of Moon and Unificationism)

Tillett, Gregory, *The Lord of the Second Coming: Sun Myung Moon and the Unification Movement*, Routledge, 1984.

Sherwood, Carlton, *Inquisition: The Persecution and Prosecution of the Reverend Sun Myung Moon*, Regnery Publishing, 1991. (Supportive of Moon; written by a former reporter for the *Washington Times*, and published by a leading US right-wing publisher.)

Underwood, Barbara, and Underwood, Betty, *Hostage to Heaven*, Random House, 1988. (Critique of Moon and Unificationism)

WEB SITES

Family Federation for World Peace and Unification home page—http://www.familyfed.org; Unificationist site

Family Federation for World Peace and Unification International—http://www.ffwpui.org; Unificationist site.

Freedom of Mind Center web page on Unificationism—http://www.freedomofmind.com/resourcecenter/groups/m/moonies; anti-cult site with information on Unificationism, by a former member.

John Gorenfeld's web page on the Moonies—http://www.iapprovethismessiah.com. Gorenfeld took the lead in exposing Moon's "coronation" as Messiah in March 2004 in Washington DC, and continues to add new information on the activities of this cult.

True Parents Organization home page—http://www.tparents.org; Unificationist site.

Unification home page—http://www.unification.net; Unificationist site.

Washington Times newspaper home page—http://www.washingtontimes.com; this is the Moon-owned conservative newspaper in Washington DC.

SECTARIAN AND CULTIC MOVEMENTS WITHIN THE CATHOLIC CHURCH

BOOKS

American Society for the Defense of Tradition, Family, and Property, *Tradition Family Property: Half a Century of Epic Anticommunism*, American Society for the Defense of Tradition, Family, and Property, 1981.

Arguello, Kiko, and Hernandez, Carmen, *Statute of the Neocatechumenal Way*, Hope Publishing House, 2003. (Arguello and Hernandez are the founders of the Neocatechumenal Way.)

Berglar, Peter, *Opus Dei: Life and Work of Its Founder, Josemaria Escriva*, Scepter Publications, 1995. (Supportive of Opus Dei; Scepter is an Opus Dei publisher)

Berry, Jason, and Renner, Robert, *Vows of Silence: The Abuse of Power in the Papacy of John Paul II*, Free Press, 2004. (Critique of the Legionaries of Christ)

Bowers, Fergal, *The Work: An Investigation into the History of Opus Dei and How It Operates in Ireland Today*, Dufour Editions, 1989. (Critique of Opus Dei)

Buzzi, Elisa, *A Generative Thought: An Introduction to the Works of Luigi Giussani*, McGill-Queen's University Press, 2004. (Giussani is the founder of Communion and Liberation.)

Conde, Angeles, and Murray, David J.P., *The Legion of Christ: a History*, Center for Integral Formation, 2003; order through the web site http://www.circlepressusa.com/interior02.phtml?se=001&ca=001&ar=177. This is a Regnum Christi publisher, so the book is pro-Legionary.

Coverdale, John F., *Uncommon Faith: The Early Years of Opus Dei, 1928-1943*, Scepter Publishers, 2002. (Supportive of Opus Dei)

de Oliveira, Plinio Correa, *Brainwashing: A Myth Exploited by the New "Therapeutic Inquisition"*, American Society for the Defense of Tradition, Family, and Property, 1985. (Oliveira is the founder of Tradition, Family, and Property)

_____. *Nobility and Analogous Traditional Elites: A Theme Illuminating American Social History*, Hamilton Press, 1993.

_____. *Revolution and Counter-Revolution*, American Society for the Defense of Tradition, Family, and Property, 1993.

_____. *The Way of the Cross*, America Needs Fatima, 1990.

de Oliveira, Plinio Correa, et al., *Our Lady at Fatima: Prophecies of Tragedy or Hope?*, American Society for the Defense of Tradition, Family, and Property, 1994.

del Carmen Tapia, Maria, *Beyond the Threshold: A Life in Opus Dei*, Continuum, 1999. (Critique of Opus Dei)

del Portillo, Alvaro, and Cavalleri, Cesare, *Immersed in God: Blessed Josemaría Escrivá, Founder of Opus Dei As Seen by His Successor, Bishop Alvaro Del Portillo*, Scepter Publishers, 1996. (Supportive of Opus Dei)

Escrivá, Josemaría, *Centennial Edition: The Complete Published Works of Saint Josemaría Escrivá*, Scepter Publishers, 2002. (Escrivá was the founder of Opus Dei).

_____. *Christ Is Passing By*, Scepter Publishers, 1974.

_____. *Conversations With Monsignor Josemaría Escrivá*, Scepter Publishers, 2002.

_____. *Friends of God: Homilies*, Scepter Publishers, 1997.

_____. *In Love With the Church*, Scepter Publishers, 1989.

_____. *The Way; The Furrow; The Forge* (single volume edition), Scepter Publications, 2001. (The key writings of the founder of Opus Dei.)

————. *The Way of the Cross*, Scepter Publishers, 2001.

Estruch, Joan, *Saints and Schemers: Opus Dei and Its Paradoxes*, Oxford University Press, 1995. (Critique of Opus Dei)

Gallagher, Jim, *Woman's Work: Chiara Lubich: A Biography of the Focolare Movement and Its Founder*, New City Press, 1997. (Supportive of Focolare)

Garvey, J. J. M., *Parents' Guide to Opus Dei*, Sicut Dixit Press, 1991. (Critique of Opus Dei).

————. *Prelature's Reaction: The Official Response from Opus Dei to "Parent's Guide to Opus Dei"*, Sicut Dixit Press, n. d. (Critique of Opus Dei).

Giussani, Luigi, *Morality: Memory and Desire*, Ignatius Press, 1986. (Giussani is the founder of Communion and Liberation.)

————. *The Psalms*, Crossroad Publishing Company, 2004.

————. *The Risk of Education*, Crossroad Publishing Company, 2001.

Giussani, Luigi, and Hewitt, Viviane, *At the Origin of the Christian Claim*, McGill-Queen's University Press, 1998.

Giussani, Luigi, and Hewitt, Viviane, *Why the Church?*, McGill-Queen's University Press, 2000.

Giussani, Luigi, and Zucchi, John, *The Religious Sense*, McGill-Queen's University Press, 1997.

Hearne, Jerry, *Unity Our Adventure: The Focolare Movement*, New City Press, 1987. (Supportive of Focolare)

Hutchison, Robert, *Their Kingdom Come: Inside the Secret World of Opus Dei*, Thomas Dunne Books, 1999. (Critique of Opus Dei)

Le Tourneau, Dominique, *What Is Opus Dei*, Scepter Publications, 1989. (Supportive of Opus Dei)

Lernoux, Penny. *People of God: The Struggle for World Catholicism*, Penguin, 1990. (Includes critiques of Opus Dei, Tradition, Family, and Property, and Communion and Liberation)

Lubich, Chiara, *Jesus: The Heart of His Message: Unity and Jesus Forsaken*, New City Press, 1985. (Lubich is the founder of Focolare.)

————. *The Cry: Jesus Crucified and Forsaken in the History and Life of the Focolare Movement, from Its Birth in 1943, Until the Dawn of the Third Millennium*, New City Press, 2001.

Lubich, Chiara, and Morneau, Bishop Robert F., *Only at Night We See the Stars: Finding Light in the Face of Darkness*, New City Press, 2002.

Lubich, Chiara, et al., *An Introduction to the ABBA School: Conversations from the Focolare's Interdisciplinary Study Center*, New City Press, 2002.

Maciel, Marcial, *Integral Formation of Catholic Priests*, Alba House, 1992. (Maciel is the founder of the Legionaries of Christ.)

Maciel, Marcial, and Colina, Jesus, *Christ Is My Life*, Sophia Institute Press, 2003.

Messori, Vittorio, *Opus Dei: Leadership and Vision in Today's Catholic Church*, Regnery, 1997. (Supportive of Opus Dei)

Ocariz, Fernando, *Canonical Path of Opus Dei: The History and Defense of a Charism*, Scepter Publishers, 1994.

Pasotti, Ezekiel, *The Neocatechumenal Way According to Paul VI and John Paul II*, St. Paul Publications, 1996. (Supportive of the Neocatechumenal Way.)

Rodriguez, Pedro, et al., *Opus Dei in the Church: An Ecclesiological Study of the Life and Apostolate of Opus Dei*, Scepter Press, 2003. (Released by an Opus Dei publisher.)

Romano, Giuseppe, *Opus Dei: Who? How? Why?*, Alba House, 1995. (Supportive of Opus Dei)

Rondoni, Davide, and Giussani, Luigi, *Communion and Liberation: A Movement in the Church*, McGill-Queen's University Press, 2000. (Supportive of Communion and Liberation.)

Urquhart, Gordon, *The Pope's Armada: Unlocking the Secrets of Mysterious and Powerful New Sects in the Church*, Prometheus Books, 1999. (Critique of Focolare, the Neo-Catechumenal Way, and Communion and Liberation.)

Walsh, Michael, *Opus Dei: An Investigation into the Powerful Secretive Society within the Catholic Church*, Harper San Francisco, 2004. (Critique of Opus Dei.)

WEB SITES: SUPPORTERS OF CATHOLIC "NEW ECCLESIAL MOVEMENTS"

American Society for the Defense of Tradition, Family, and Property home page—http://www.tfp.org; one of their ongoing public campaigns is "America Needs Fatima" (http://www.tfp.org/anf).

Communion and Liberation home page—http://www.clonline.org.

Focolare home page—http://www.focolare.org.

Legionaries of Christ home page—http://www.legionofchrist.org; also, http://www.legionariesofchrist.org. The home page of Regnum Christi, which is affiliated with the Legionaries, is http://www.regnumchristi.org. The Legionaries' official response to accusations against the group is at the Legionary Facts home page, http://www.legionaryfacts.org.

Neocatechumenal Way home page—http://www.camminoneocatecumenale.it/en.

WEB SITES: OPUS DEI AND ESCRIVÁ:

· Escrivá home page, devoted to the founder of Opus Dei—http://www.josemariaescriva.info.
· On-line works of the founder of Opus Dei—http://www.escrivaworks.org.
· Opus Dei USA home page—http://www.opusdei.org.
· *Romana* home page—http://en.romana.org; this is the "Bulletin of the Prelature of the Holy Cross and Opus Dei."

WEB SITES: CRITICS OF CATHOLIC "NEW ECCLESIAL MOVEMENTS"

CRITICS OF FOCOLARE:

· "Focolare Movement: Lights and Shadows" home page—http://www.focolare.net.

CRITICS OF THE LEGIONARIES OF CHRIST AND REGNUM CHRISTI:

· "Ex-Legionaries.com" home page for former members of the Legionaries of Christ and Regnum Christi—http://www.exlegionaries.com.
· Freedom of Mind Center web page on the Legionaries of Christ—http://www.freedomofmind.com/resource-center/groups/l/legion.
· Opponents of the Legionaries reply to the movement's self-defense at "Legionaryfacts.org;" their rebuttal is at http://www.legionaryfacts.com.
· Regain Network home page—http://www.regainnetwork.org; critical of the Legionaries of Christ and Regnum Christi.
· Rick Ross' anti-cult site has a web page on the Legionaries of Christ, at http://www.rickross.com/groups/loc.html.
· A conservative Catholic site, Unity Publishing, criticizes the Legionaries at this page: http://www.unitypublishing.com/Apparitions/LegionIndex.html.

CRITICS OF THE NEOCATECHUMENAL WAY:

· An opponent of the Way has gathered articles at the web site http://www.psychologue-clinicien.com/anglais/chemin.htm.
· An official report by the Roman Catholic Diocese of Clifton, in the United Kingdom, opposing the presence of the Way in three local parishes—http://ourworld.compuserve.com/homepages/ronald_haynes/nc-er2.htm.
· "Church Mouse" is an anti-Neocatechumenal web site in Australia, at http://church-mouse.net; they provide links to other sites at http://delorenzo.ozforces.com.au/links1.html.

CRITICS OF OPUS DEI:

· Freedom of Mind Center web page on Opus Dei—http://www.freedomofmind.com/resourcecenter/groups/o/opus.
· Opposing Views' collection of anti-Opus Dei web pages—http://www.opposing-religious-views.com/Christianity_Catholicism_Opus_Dei.html.
· Opus Dei Awareness Network home page—http://www.odan.org.
· Rick Ross' anti-cult site has a web page on Opus Dei, at http://www.rickross.com/groups/opus.html.
· "The Unofficial Opus Dei Home Page"—http://www.mond.at/opus.dei.

CRITICS OF TRADITION, FAMILY, AND PROPERTY (TFP):

· An Italian anti-cult group has extensive research on TFP and its allies at http://www.kelebekler.com/cesnur/eng.htm. Articles on this site include Miguel Martinez, "'Doctor Plinio' and his 'counter-revolutionary magisterium," at http://www.kelebekler.com/cesnur/storia/gb11.htm, and http://www.kelebekler.com/cesnur/storia/gb12.htm, and succeeding web pages.

- John Armour, "TFP: A Dangerous Cult," at http://www.sspx.ca/Angelus/1983_July/TFP_Dangerus.htm. This is an account published in 1983 in Angelus, the magazine of the Society of St. Pius X—which is itself a right-wing Catholic splinter group.

- Unity Publishing, "'America Needs Fatima': A Cult Using the Fatima Name," at http://www.unitypublishing.com/NewReligiousMovements/FatimaCult.html; written by a conservative Catholic.

Many other similar web pages exist; search Google for the name of each new ecclesial movement, with the terms "sect" or "cult" or "abuse."

WICCA AND NEO-PAGANISM

BOOKS

Adler, Margot, *Drawing Down the Moon: Witches, Druids, Goddess-Worshippers, and Other Pagans in America Today*, Penguin Books, 1997. (History and practice of Wicca, from a Neopagan perspective).

Alexander, Brooks, *Witchcraft Goes Mainstream*, Harvest House, 2004. (Scholarly Evangelical history and critique).

Ankarloo, Bengt, and Clark, Stuart, *Witchcraft and Magic in Europe: The Eighteenth and Nineteenth Centuries*, University of Pennsylvania Press, 1999. (Scholarly history).

_____. *Witchcraft and Magic in Europe: The Twentieth Century*, University of Pennsylvania Press, 1999. (Scholarly history).

Burnett, David, *Dawning of the Pagan Moon*, Thomas Nelson Inc., 1992. (History of witchcraft and Neopaganism; Evangelical Christian critique.)

Davis, Philip G., *Goddess Unmasked: The Rise of Neopagan Feminist Spirituality*, Spence Publishing Company, 1999. (Scholarly history; conservative Christian critique.)

DiZerega, Gus, *Pagans & Christians: The Personal Spiritual Experience*, Llewellyn Publications, 2001. (Neopagan call for Christian/Neopagan dialogue and mutual understanding).

Drury, Nevill, *Magic and Witchcraft: From Shamanism to the Technopagans*, Thames & Hudson, 2003.

Eliade, Mircea, *Occultism, Witchcraft, and Cultural Fashions: Essays in Comparative Religion*, University of Chicago Press, 1978. (Scholarly analysis).

Hutton, Ronald, *The Triumph of the Moon: A History of Modern Pagan Witchcraft*, Oxford University Press, 2001. (Scholarly history).

Lewis, James R., *Magical Religion and Modern Witchcraft*, State University of New York Press, 1996. (Scholarly essays by Neopagans).

Molnar, Thomas, *The Pagan Temptation*, Eerdmans, 1987. (Conservative Catholic critique).

Paris, Ginette, *The Sacrament of Abortion*, Spring Publications, Inc., 1992. (A Neopagan defense of abortion as a sacrifice.)

Pike, Sarah M., *Earthly Bodies, Magical Selves: Contemporary Pagans and the Search for Community*, University of California Press, 2001. (Anthropological study of Neopagan groups and practice.)

Russell, Jeffrey B., *A History of Witchcraft: Sorcerers, Heretics, and Pagans*, Thames & Hudson, 1982. (Scholarly history)

_____. *Mephistopheles: The Devil in the Modern World*, Cornell University Press, 1986. (Scholarly history)

_____. *The Prince of Darkness: Radical Evil and the Power of Good in History*, Cornell University Press, 1992. (Scholarly history)

_____. *Witchcraft in the Middle Ages*, Cornell University Press, 1984. (Scholarly history)

Starhawk, *The Spiral Dance*, Harper San Francisco, rev. ed., 1999.

Thornton, Bruce S., *Plagues of the Mind: The New Epidemic of False Knowledge*, ISI Books, 2004. (Conservative critique; includes a chapter on the ideology of the Goddess.)

Vale, V., and Sulak, John, *Modern Pagans: an Investigation of Contemporary Ritual*, RE/Search Publications, 2001. (Overview of Neopaganism, using primary sources.)

Ancient Ways Bookstore home page—http://www.ancientways.com; they put on the annual PantheaCon convention for Neopagans in February of each year.

Conjureworks—http://www.conjure.com; the home page of Rowan Fairgrove, a Wiccan who has long been active in the URI.

Covenant of the Goddess home page—http://www.cog.org; URI Global Council member Donald Frew, a Neopagan, is active in this organization.

THE INTERFAITH MOVEMENT

INTERFAITH ORGANIZATIONS

WEB SITES

CoNexus Multifaith Media home page—http://www.conexuspress.com; offers many books sympathetic to the interfaith movement.

Council for a Parliament of the World's Religions (CPWR) home page—http://www.cpwr.org.

Global Dialogue Institute (GDI) home page—http://astro.temple.edu/~dialogue, for information for 1995–1999, and http://global-dialogue.com for current information.

Ingrid Shafer's home page—http://ecumene.org; Shafer is an interfaith activist, and describes her site as "A Meeting Place for the World's Religions and Ideologies."

Interfaith Center at the Presidio home page—http://www.interfaith-presidio.org.

Interfaith Center of New York home page—http://www.interfaithcenter.org.

Interfaith Conference of Metropolitan Washington home page—http://www.interfaith-metrodc.org/ifc.htm.

Interfaith Network of the United Kingdom home page—http://www.interfaith.co.uk.

International Fellowship of Christians and Jews (IFCJ) home page—http://www.ifcj.org/site/PageServer.

Interfaith Youth Core (IYC) home page—http://www.ifyc.org.

International Association for Religious Freedom (IARF) home page—http://www.iarf.net.

International Council of Christians and Jews (ICCJ) home page—http://www.iccj.org/en.

International Interfaith Centre (IIC) home page—http://www.interfaith-center.org/oxford.

Inter-Religious Federation for World Peace (IRFWP) home page—http://www.irfwp.org. They state that they carry out their programs "through the Interreligious and International Federation for World Peace (IIFWP)," whose home page is http://www.iifwp.org. Both organizations are associated with the Unification Church, and were founded by the Rev. Sun Myung Moon.

Minorities of Europe (MoE) home page—http://www.moe-online.com/index.asp.

National Religious Partnership for the Environment (NRPE) home page—http://www.nrpe.org.

Network of International Interfaith Organizations (NIIO) web page—http://www.interfaith-center.org/oxford/network.htm.

North American Interfaith Network (NAIN) home page—http://www.nain.org.

Ontario Consultants on Religious Tolerance home page—http://www.religioustolerance.org.

Peace Council home page—http://www.peacecouncil.org.

Temple of Understanding (ToU) home page—http://www.templeofunderstanding.org.

Thanksgiving Square home page—http://www.thanksgiving.org.

The Interfaith Alliance (TIA) home page—http://www.tialliance.org.

Three Faiths Forum (TFF) home page—http://www.threefaithsforum.org.uk.

United Communities of Spirit (UCS) home page—http://origin.org/ucs/home.cfm.

World Conference of Religions for Peace (WCRP) home page—http://www.wcrp.org. (Previously, the group had been named the World Conference on Religion and Peace.)

World Congress of Faiths (WCF) home page—http://www.worldfaiths.org.

World Council of Churches (WCC) home page—http://www.wcc-coe.org; a Christian ecumenical body, but active in the interfaith movement.

World Council of Religious Leaders (WCRL) home page—http://www.millenniumpeacesummit.org. This grew out of the World Millennium Peace Summit of Religious and Spiritual Leaders, held in 2000 in New York.

World Faith Development Dialogue (WFDD) home page—http://www.wfdd.org.uk.

World Peace Prayer Society (WPPS) home page—http://www.worldpeace.org.

World Network of Religious Futurists (WNRF) home page—http://www.wnrf.org/cms/index.shtml.

ADVOCACY, HISTORY AND ANALYSIS OF THE INTERFAITH MOVEMENT

BOOKS

Barney, Gerald O., et al., *Threshold 2000: Critical Issues and Spiritual Values for a Global Age*, CoNexus Press, 1999.

Bassett, Libby, et al., *Earth and Faith: A Book of Reflection for Action*, United Nations Environment Program, 2000.

Beversluis, Joel, ed., *Sourcebook of the World's Religions: An Interfaith Guide to Religion and Spirituality*, 3rd ed., New World Library, 2000; contains essays by adherents of traditional and new religions, as well as UN documents and essays by interfaith movement leaders.

Braybrooke, Marcus, *Pilgrimage of Hope: One Hundred Years of Global Interfaith Dialogue*, Crossroad Publishing Co., 1992. Scholarly history of the interfaith movement from 1893 to 1991.

_____. *Faith and Interfaith in a Global Age*, CoNexus Press, 1998. History of the interfaith movement from 1993 to 1998.

_____. *Faiths in fellowship: A Short History of the World Congress of Faiths and Its Work*, World Congress of Faiths, 1976.

_____. *Inter-Faith Organizations, 1893-1979: An Historical Directory*, Edwin Mellen Press, 1980.

Cimino, Richard, and Lattin, Don, *Shopping for Faith: American Religion in the New Millennium*, Jossey-Bass, 2002. (Overview of religious trends in the US)

Coward, Harold, and Maguire, Daniel C., *Visions of a New Earth: Religious Perspectives on Population, Consumption, and Ecology*, State University of New York Press, 1999.

Forward, Martin, *Interfaith Dialogue: A Short Introduction*, Oneworld Publications, 2001.

Ingham, Archbishop Michael, *Mansions of the Spirit: The Gospel in a Multi-Faith World*, Anglican Book Centre, 1997.

Kirby, Richard, and Brewer, Earl, *The Temples of Tomorrow: World Religions and the Future*, Grey Seal Books, 1993.

Maguire, Daniel C., *Sacred Choices: The Right to Contraception and Abortion in Ten World Religions*, Augsburg Fortress Publishers, 2001. (Interfaith discussion by a "pro-choice" theologian.)

_____. *Sacred Energies: When the World's Religions Sit Down to Talk About the Future of Human Life and the Plight of This Planet*, Augsburg Fortress Publishers, 2000.

_____. *Sacred Rights: The Case for Contraception and Abortion in World Religions*, Oxford University Press, 2003.

Mische, Patricia M., and Merkling, Melissa, *Toward a Global Civilization? The Contribution of Religions*, Peter Lang Publishing, 2001.

Seager, Richard Hughes, *The Dawn of Religious Pluralism: Voices from the World's Parliament of Religions, 1893*, Open Court Publishing Co., 1993.

Storey, Celia and David, *Visions of an Interfaith Future*, International Interfaith Centre, 1994.

Teasdale, Wayne, et al., *The Community of Religions: Voices and Images of the Parliament of the World's Religions*, Continuum, 1996. (Pertains to the 1993 Parliament of the World's Religions)

Tobias, Michael, and Morrison, Jane, *A Parliament of Souls: In Search of Global Spirituality*, Bay Books, 1995. (Interviews with spiritual leaders at the 1993 Parliament of the World's Religions.)

Traer, Robert, *Faith, Belief, and Religion*, The Davies Group, 2001.

_____. *Faith in Human Rights: Support in Religious Traditions for a Global Struggle*, Georgetown University Press, 1991.

_____. *Quest for Truth: Critical Reflections on Interfaith Cooperation*, The Davies Group, 1999.

CATHOLIC PERSPECTIVES ON INTERRELIGIOUS DIALOGUE

Cardinal Arinze was President of the Pontifical Council for Interreligious Dialogue, the Vatican Curia department in charge of interfaith relations, from 1984 to 2002. In 2002, the Pope appointed Arinze as Prefect of Congregation for Divine Worship and the Discipline of the Sacraments.

BOOKS

Arinze, Cardinal Francis, *Building Bridges: Interreligious Dialogue on the Path to World Peace*, New City Press, 2004.

_____. *Meeting Other Believers: The Risks and Rewards of Interreligious Dialogue*, Our Sunday Visitor, 1998.

_____. *Religions for Peace: A Call for Solidarity to the Religions of the World*, Doubleday, 2002.

_____. *The Church in Dialogue: Walking With Other Believers*, Ignatius Press, 1990.

AUTHOR'S BIOGRAPHY

I am a health care information systems consultant and a journalist. I received a BA *cum laude* from Harvard in 1976, and master's degrees in business and in public health from the University of California at Berkeley in 1986. Since then, I have worked in finance and health care information systems—mostly as a consultant, assisting hospitals, health maintenance organizations, and other health care providers with automation and business planning. I was elected to Phi Beta Kappa as an undergraduate, and am listed in *Who's Who in America* (56th–59th editions) and *Who's Who in the World* (20th–22nd editions). I am a member of the American College of Health Care Executives and the Institute of Electrical and Electronics Engineers (IEEE).

As a journalist, I have written about the United Religions Initiative, cults, and the New Age movement since 1998, and have been published in various confessions' orthodox and conservative magazines:

- *The Christian Challenge* (Anglican)—19 by-lined stories from 1999 through 2004 on the URI, the New Age movement in the Episcopal Church, Anglican/Catholic relations, and pro-life issues.
- *Foundations* (Anglican)—2 articles on the URI: "The Globalism Blues" (September 1999) and "Amen, Swami: The URI Gets a Charter, But Not a Whole Lot Else" (August 2000).
- *HLI Reports* (Human Life International, a Catholic pro-life organization)—"The Case Against the United Religions Initiative," February 2001.
- *New Oxford Review* (Catholic)—4 feature stories between 1998 and 2000, including "The United Religions Initiative: A Bridge Back to Gnosticism" (December 1998) and "Beware! The New Age Movement is More Than Self-Indulgent Silliness" (July/August 2000).
- The *Journal* of the Spiritual Counterfeits Project (SCP), a front-line Reformed/Evangelical Protestant ministry whose mission is "confronting the occult, the cults, and the New Age movement." I have had 10 feature articles in the *Journal* since 1999: a 4-part series on the URI, globalism, and the New Age movement, a science fiction story ("The World Church of 2017"), a 3-part series on the history and beliefs of mainstream and fringe Freemasonry, and—in 2004—a 2-part series on the emerging police state. In addition, I co-authored "Neale Donald Walsch: Conversations With Myself" with Tal Brooke, the President of SCP. In 2004, this article won a "First Place" award in the "Critical Review" category from the Evangelical Press Association. (There were 500 contestants for this award.)
- *World Net Daily* (secular conservative)—Co-author, with SCP's Tal Brooke, of 2 articles in 2002: "How the State Confiscates Rights" (February 27, 2002) and "State Surveillance: Abolishing Freedom" (March 25, 2002).
- *The Wanderer* (Catholic)—Paul Likoudis' "United Religious Initiative Launched in Pittsburgh" (July 6, 2000) quoted extensively from my articles, as did several "From the Mail" columns: "Unscrambling the Labyrinth" (July 8, 1999), "The Transforming Power of the Labyrinth" (March 1, 2001), "The Endless Labyrinth" (April 12, 2001), and "Mapping the Scandals" (June 6, 2002).
- *Touchstone* (orthodox Christian, from all confessions)—"Midwives of a Common God: The Myriad Friends of the United Religions Initiative" (June 2000).
- The Catholic Family and Human Rights Institute, which acts as a pro-life advocate to the UN and other international bodies, published "The United Religions Initiative: An Organization Seeking to Undermine Traditional Religious Faith and Evangelization," in February 2005.

With this book, I hope to speak to a wider audience, to liberals as well as to conservatives, since the current and pending threats to liberty and to traditional religious belief come from both political extremes.

I was raised as an Episcopalian, but became atheist while in college. After a six-year detour into Marxism (as a member of the New American Movement, a "democratic-socialist" descendant of the Students for a Democratic Society), I returned to Christ in 1978. From 1979 to 1983, I was a member of a Methodist congregation in Oregon; from 1983 to 1995, I was an active member of the Episcopal Church in Bishop Swing's diocese, including serving on a San Francisco parish's Vestry, heading its Finance Committee, and participating in its Search Committee for a new rector in 1994.

I left the Episcopal Church in 1995—pushed away by Bishop Swing's establishment of the United Religions Initiative, his 1994 acceptance of Matthew Fox as an Episcopal priest, and the pro-abortion stance of the Episcopal Church. The last straw was when they started calling God "she" at my parish; by the next Sunday, I was seeking a new spiritual home, and began by worshiping at a Russian Orthodox parish. That year, I explored Catholicism and Eastern Orthodoxy—and was received into an Eastern Catholic parish that is in communion with Rome but worships, fasts, feasts, and prays in the Eastern Orthodox fashion. My spiritual home since 1995 has been the Christian East. My history is evidence that God is merciful to sinners, and shows that the writer of "Amazing Grace" was telling the truth.

INDEX

1984 (novel) 22, 101, 274, 292, 310, 344, 432

666 (number of the Beast) 130 n4, 260–262, 345, 445

9/11 (September 2001 attack on the U.S.) 25, 52, 81, 145, 363, 407

abortion 70, 82, 102, 208, 209, 217, 221, 319, 336, 368, 372, 385

abuse of children and teenagers, sexual 122, 334, 413, 425, 427–428, 431, 447

Acholi Religious Leaders' Peace Initiative (ARLPI) 74–75, 131, 142, 161 n3

Alexander, Brooks 235, 397, 415

al-Qaida 80–81

American exceptionalism 375, 443–444

Anand, Margot 368, 373

Andrews, Paul 62, 67 n5, 103, 131, 182, 187, 200, 229

angels, fallen 260–262

Anglicanism:
   and syncretism or the URI 18, 47, 53, 74 (also n2), 83, 98, 103, 140–146, 183, 191, 193, 196, 203, 212, 215, 218, 220, 224, 453
   New Age 146–156, 247, 410

Anthroposophy 131, 194 n2, 248 (also n6), 257–258, 286

anti-Catholicism 7, 23, 51 n4, 70, 123, 156, 188, 204–206, 246, 269–270, 339

Antichrist 3, 4, 213, 242, 254 n1, 256 n3, 352, 353, 356, 410, 412, 417–419, 432, 436–438, 442, 444, 446, 447

anti-Christianity 5, 6, 8, 9, 26, 33, 51, 52, 70, 89, 123, 124, 130 n4, 132, 148–149, 155, 176–177, 179, 180–182, 184–186, 188, 204, 205, 209, 214, 224 n2, 236, 239, 250, 251–252, 255 n2, 256–258, 266, 269–270, 273, 278, 283, 332, 339–340, 344, 349, 351, 366–367, 373, 396, 408, 410, 412, 415, 417 n2, 419, 432, 433, 442, 444

anti-Islamic prejudice 51, 78, 80 n5, 184, 214, 269, 366, 440, 448

anti–Semitism 70 n1, 121, 123, 124, 180, 182, 184, 265–269, 271, 273, 229, 330–331, 440 n1, 442–443, 447 (also n6)

apocalypse 255 n2, 321, 324, 341–342, 349, 358, 399, 409, 410–412, 415, 417–421, 439, 444; *see also*

Second Coming of Christ

Appreciative Inquiry 44, 56, 63–69, 203; *see also* SIGMA Project (Case Western Reserve Univ.)

Arinze, Cardinal Francis 51 n4, 52, 158, 159, 160, 173–174, 176, 181, 188, 209, 210, 215, 217, 244, 394

Ark of Hope 381

artificial contraception 17, 70, 82, 217–222, 295, 319, 366, 372, 385; *see also* family planning; population control

Artress, Lauren 103, 146–150, 401

Aryan, Aryans 251, 253, 254, 264–265

Assisi, interfaith meetings at 164, 306

astrology 229, 252, 254 n5, 257, 264–265

Atlantis, Atlanteans 254, 261–262, 264–265, 268, 270

atomic weapons; *see* nuclear weapons

Aztecs, as New Age spiritual models 200, 307

Bailey, Alice A. 15, 20–21, 29, 132, 133, 248, 259–285, 288, 295, 299, 300, 302, 307, 308, 315, 318, 323, 324–326, 331, 334, 342, 347, 348, 349, 355, 358, 375, 410, 418 n1, 446

Bailey, Foster 15, 20, 260, 265, 270, 273, 278, 280–281, 349, 355, 422

Bailey, Mary 278

Baker, James 25, 370

Barnhart, Bruno 191

Barrett, Richard 225

Bartlett, Rep. Roscoe 117

Belloc, Hilaire 245

Benedict XV, Pope 228

Benedict XVI, Pope 173

Besant, Annie 20, 29, 121 n13, 254, 257

Beversluis, Joel 40, 43, 70, 181, 206

biological warfare; *see* smallpox

birth, New Age view of 128, 155, 218, 264, 319, 329, 336

Blair, Tony 97, 405, 407

Blavatsky, Helena Petrovna (HPB) 17, 18–20, 29, 39, 40, 239, 241, 242, 245, 247, 248–258, 259–261, 272, 285, 299, 328, 348–349, 402, 410

Borg, Marcus 143

Brave New World (novel) 153

Braybrooke, Marcus 196, 199, 207, 216, 257

Brewer, Earl 193

Buddhism and the URI 48, 51, 54, 57, 77, 89, 108, 109, 137 n3, 164 n1, 167, 172, 180, 189, 207, 212, 215, 216, 366, 452, 453, 454

Bunyan, John 401

Bush, George H. W. (U.S. President,1989–1993) 24, 116, 363, 392, 408

Bush, George W. (U.S. President, 2001–) 5, 7, 13, 18, 25, 99, 100, 102, 406, 407, 408

Campbell, Joan Brown 52

Capitalism 5, 12, 38, 124, 225, 236, 280, 296, 309, 245, 359

Carey, Archbishop George (Anglican) 144, 146, 154

Carlyle Group 125

Carter, Jimmy 114, 313, 378

Cathedral of St. John the Divine (Episcopal) 38 n1, 145, 146, 150, 151

Catholic Family and Human Rights Institute (C–FAM) 51

censorship, press 76, 89

Chaffee, Paul 52, 65, 129, 134, 156, 158, 163, 183, 216

Chaput, Archbishop Charles (Catholic) 431

Charles, Bishop Otis (Episcopal) 84, 87, 162

Chesterton, G. K. 33, 239, 240, 241, 357

China, People's Republic of 5, 44, 51, 54, 98, 102, 142, 156–157, 185, 214, 280, 309, 344, 346, 355, 366, 373, 376, 397, 408, 413, 416

Chisthi, Ghulam Rasool 80, 82

Chopra, Deepak 111, 346, 367, 374

Christ; see Jesus

Christian Reconstructionists 422

Church of Scientology; see Scientology

civilization, destruction of 262, 276–279, 282–283, 309, 311, 331, 357, 390, 404–405

Clinton, Hillary 99, 135, 147, 367

Clinton, William J. (U.S. President, 1993–2001) 99, 132, 186, 363

Club of Budapest 97, 108, 378, 383

Club of Rome 24

coercion, religious 10–11, 175–176, 186, 231–232, 426, 446, 451

Common Market (Europe) 280; see also European Commission; European Union

Communion and Liberation 416 n2, 424 n1, 429

Communism, Marxist 7, 116, 134, 142 n11, 225, 279–282, 293, 296, 298, 305, 310, 343, 345 (also n4), 397, 414–417, 419, 430, 433, 448

Communism, spiritual 12, 132, 246, 275, 279–282, 310, 342–346

conspiracy and conspiracy theory 12, 16, 102, 214, 254, 391, 396–398

Constitution, U.S. 70, 73, 324, 344, 393 n4, 407 n4

contraception; see artificial contraception

Coomaraswamy, Rama 40 n5

Cooperrider, David 43–44, 46, 63–66, 79

Corless, Roger 172, 216

Corporations, as supporters of or participants in interfaith, New Age, and globalist movements:
    Appreciative Inquiry 64
    population control 221, 295
    State of the World Forum 25, 26, 368, 370, 374, 378
    World Economic Forum 17, 24, 389, 394
    World Millennium Peace Summit of Religious and Spiritual Leaders 50–51, 94, 111

Council for a Parliament of the World's Religions 39 n1, 42, 45, 53, 110, 112, 167, 207, 383

Council of All Beings 90–91

Council on Spiritual Practices 85, 86 n2, 368; see also Robert Jesse

Cousteau, Jacques-Yves 220

creation spirituality 152, 153, 155; see also Techno Cosmic Mass

Creme, Benjamin 248 n2, 314 n2, 418 n1

"crisis of birth" 299–300, 302

Cross, replacement of 201, 202, 262, 316, 413
    teachings of Alice Bailey 263
    teachings of Unification Church 123–124,

Crowley, Aleister 130 (also n4)

Crusades 1, 124

cults and sectarian religious movements 11–12, 36, 51, 75 n7, 115–126, 159 n1, 189, 192 n1, 194, 204 n3, 227–229, 235, 253–254, 256, 276, 407 n6, 408, 415–416, 421–430, 440 n1, 441, 442, 445–447; see also entries for the specific movement

Cultural Revolution, Chinese 280, 282, 355, 410

Dalai Lama, the 5, 47, 51, 98, 107, 110, 112, 114, 136, 180–181, 218, 236, 285, 408

Danzinger, Lesley 377

darkness, and Theosophy 241, 249, 253, 283, 328, 349

Davidson, Gordon 132–133, 281 n1, 284, 285–286

Davis, Gray 100, 408

Davis, Rep. Danny K. 117–118

Dawson, Christopher 42

Dayton, Sen. Mark 118

death, New Age view of 7, 33, 75, 128, 130, 212, 212 n7, 246, 250, 266, 277–279, 285, 288, 306–307, 318–323, 329, 330, 342, 349, 355, 390, 402, 405

Declaration of Independence, U.S. 13

Diocese of California Episcopal 5, 17, 35, 45, 86–87, 140, 141, 143, 153, 154, 165

Dispensationalism 414, 440 n1, 441

dissent, religious 159 n4, 160–174, 205–206, 229, 308, 416 n2, 430, 431

divinity, ascribed to mankind 7, 25, 34, 192, 193, 249, 250, 262–263, 316–319, 325, 329, 333, 350, 391

divorce 82, 319, 338

Dolan, Fr. Luis Catholic 94, 110, 111, 167, 169 n1, 382

Doonesbury (comic strip) 157

dragon, religion of the 130, 245, 250, 254, 255 (also n2), 412, 445

Dreher, Rod 427, 431

drug abuse 19, 82, 84–87, 101, 122 n4, 129, 130, 131, 147, 152, 154, 183, 337, 367, 374–375

Earth Charter movement 5, 12, 16–17, 24, 73, 50, 51, 96–97, 104, 126, 151, 193 n1, 210, 220, 225, 358, 368, 380–388, 391, 398, 401, 407

Eastern Orthodoxy 8, 11, 49, 89, 140, 158 n5, 213 (also n5), 229, 426 n7, 442

ecumenical movement, contrasted with interfaith movement 10–11

Eden, Garden of 7, 246, 396, 404, 405

education, New Age 21, 87–89, 128, 131, 243–244, 258, 264, 274, 276, 279, 295, 300, 313–314, 317, 322, 334, 336

Ehrlich, Paul and Anne 26, 373

entheogens (drug use for spiritual purposes) 84–87, 373–375

Episcopal Church 5, 8, 15, 17, 18, 20, 22, 35, 42, 44, 50, 56, 84, 86 (also n2), 87, 125, 131, 135, 135 n12, 140–147, 149, 151–159, 162–165, 178, 183, 189, 193, 199, 205, 207, 216, 219, 222, 226, 235, 236, 251, 322, 394, 452, 453, 456; *see also* Cathedral of St. John the Divine; Diocese of California; Grace Cathedral; National Cathedral

Epting, Bishop Christopher (Episcopal) 141 (also n5), 145

Erhard, Werner 137 n11, 162–163, 347

Escrivá, Fr. Josemaría (Catholic) 425–427, 446

Est, 163; *see also* Erhard, Werner

eugenics 7, 263, 294–296

European Commission (EC) 45, 46, 369

European Union (EU) 204, 236, 309, 344, 356, 393 n1, 394, 401, 429

Euthanasia 7, 101, 208, 294–296, 319, 321 n4, 333–336, 391

evangelization, religious 5, 6, 9, 38, 100, 158–159, 160, 175–182, 184, 209, 230–234, 235, 425, 429

evolution, New Age views of 7, 21, 22, 33, 34, 46, 65–66, 148, 167, 174, 192–193, 195, 212 (also n7), 213, 240–241, 243, 246, 248 n6, 252–253, 256, 260–262, 263–265, 269–270, 275, 276–279, 281–282 (also n1), 284, 285, 286, 287, 288, 289, 294–300, 302–303, 307–308, 309, 310, 311–312, 314 n1, 316, 317, 318–319, 320–324, 325–326, 327–328, 330, 332–333, 337, 343, 350, 357, 384, 390, 402, 403; *see also* progress, as New Age article of faith

exclusive religions 3, 70 n1, 177, 180–188, 195, 196, 204, 215 n7, 233 n6, 263, 320, 339, 340, 440

extinction, human 311, 390; *see also* "selection" of mankind, New Age concept of

extra-terrestrial beings 328, 343, 379

extreme-right politics and religion (Nazis, Fascists, Moonies, and rightist New Ecclesial Movements) 12, 110, 115–126, 178, 185, 209–210, 214, 228, 244, 254 (also n5), 263, 264, 267, 268, 275, 276, 281 n4, 289–293, 296, 297–298, 305, 310–311 (also n1), 321 n4, 331, 356 n2, 411–438, 440–448

Fairgrove, Rowan 48 (also n7), 129

fall of man, 7, 246, 258, 318, 332; *see also* Original Sin

families 12, 22, 25, 45, 50, 65, 70, 84, 117, 121, 124, 129, 208, 223, 240, 319, 345 n4, 370, 404, 422 n5, 424; *see also* marriage

family planning 98, 99, 102, 168, 218, 219, 252, 372; *see also* artificial contraception, population control

Fascism 12, 414–416

Faust (Goethe) 37

Feminism, 5, 66, 106, 166, 173, 225–227, 236, 257, 340, 385; *see also* ordination of women priests

Firmage, Joe 379

Fitzgerald, Archbishop Michael (Catholic) 159, 160

Flood (Biblical Deluge) 213, 218, 262, 357

Focolare 416 n2, 423, 430

Fonda, Jane 26

forgiveness of sins 50, 124, 163, 262, 317–318, 319, 332, 333, 429

foundations—supporters of or participants in interfaith, New Age, and globalist movements:
Appreciative Inquiry 64
population control, 218, 221
State of the World Forum 378–379
United Religions Initiative 58–62
World Economic Forum 394
World Millennium Peace Summit of Religious and Spiritual Leaders 25

Fox, Fr. Matthew (Episcopal) 18, 21, 146, 150, 152–

156, 192, 219, 240, 286, 326, 347, 369

Fransen, Jim 220–221, 227

freedom:
of religion 8, 10, 11, 70 (also n4), 112, 126, 176, 178–181, 217, 344, 415, 445
progressive/evolutionary, globalist and New Age redefinitions of 7, 33, 41, 88, 131, 182, 185, 227, 231–232, 246, 279, 292, 293–294, 303, 323, 329, 330, 335, 340, 345, 348, 355, 380 n2, 384, 355, 386, 396, 408

Freemasonry 19, 20, 21, 48, 137, 248, 273–274, 350, 419 n5, 422, 442, 446, 479

French Revolution 147, 223–224, 396, 412

Frew, Donald 16, 28, 36 n8, 41, 42, 44 n5, 49, 50, 52, 53n1, 54, 57, 58, 62, 63, 67, 69, 72, 74, 77, 81 (also n8), 82, 83, 87 n4, 90, 95, 102, 103 n1, 110, 113–114, 115, 125, 125 n3, 126 n7, 127, 128, 129, 129 n2, 139, 140, 141 n6, 158, 162, 175–176, 182, 201, 202, 224, 225, 452 n1, 453 (also nn 1, 2)

fundamentalism, religious 1, 6, 9–10, 36, 38, 50, 77n3, 79 (also n3), 107 n7, 134, 182–188, 195, 196, 211, 269, 340, 390

Garner, Sanford 125, 145 (also n4)

Garrison, James 357, 365–367, 369, 371, 378 n8, 381

Gates, Bill 17, 59, 62, 221, 393, 394

gay issues 5, 18 (also n5), 56 n5, 83–84, 119, 120, 122 n4, 130 n4, 143, 172, 180, 202, 236, 340, 385, 393 n4, 447

germ warfare; see smallpox

Gibbs, Fr. Charles (Episcopal) 34, 35, 38 n1, 50 n4, 53, 54, 55, 56, 79, 80, 82, 93, 95, 96, 100, 103, 115 n3, 125, 145, 169 n1, 179, 180, 193 n1, 199, 214, 223, 225, 242, 452, 455

Global AIDS Interfaith Alliance 56, 59, 74 (also n2)

global brain 308, 348, 350, 403, 430

Global Education Associates 43, 45, 167, 169, 172 n5, 194, 447

global ethic movement 6, 206–210, 216, 218, 236, 350

global governance 1, 7, 12, 16, 24, 93, 102–104, 350, 357, 365–366, 370–372, 393 (also n4), 432–433

Global Green, USA 151, 376; see also Green Cross International

global heart 308

global soul 37, 93, 287, 308; see also spirit of the earth

global spirituality 185, 195, 198, 203, 216, 223, 224, 350

globalist movement 353–398

globalization 355–398, 402–408, 410, 412–413; 419–

421, 445–447

political 7, 12, 15–17, 23–25, 26–27, 102–104, 125, 213, 224–226, 274–276, 279–282, 302, 308–312, 324, 342–345

religious 6, 9, 36, 37–38, 42–43, 134–136, 167, 182–205, 222–224, 255–256, 270–273, 287–288, 307–308, 339–340

Gnosticism 130, 212 n7, 228, 241, 251, 258, 278, 281 (also n4), 350, 395

Goldin Institute for International Partnership and Peace 57

Godwin, Joscelyn 358

Gorbachev Foundation 15–16, 24, 102 (also n8), 103 n13, 360, 361 n4, 378

Gorbachev, Mikhail 1, 15–16, 16 n2, 22, 23–24, 37, 98, 102, 103 n13, 104, 152, 249, 310, 313, 346, 358, 359–365, 370, 372–373, 375–376, 378, 380–382, 386, 405, 406, 407, 415, 418, 434

Grace Cathedral (Episcopal) 38 n1, 44, 52, 103, 112, 133, 136, 140, 145, 146, 148 n5, 150, 153, 164, 180, 183, 190, 199 (also n6), 200, 201, 207, 223

Gray, Bettina 110, 223

Great Invocation (Theosophical prayer) 22, 132, 278, 324, 325

Green Cross International and affiliates 15–16, 24, 152, 362, 375, 376, 380, 381, 386–388, 401, 406; see also Global Green, USA

Gretschmann, Klaus 394, 401

Griswold, Bishop Frank T. (Episcopal Presiding Bishop, 1997–)140–141, 141 n1, 143, 143 n5, 183, 394

Guénon, René 3, 4, 40 (also n7), 91 n4, 185n5, 194 n2, 204 nn3,4, 233 n6, 235 n2, 256 n3, 245 n2, 346, 351, 352, 404, 418 n2, 420–421, 432, 435–438

Gundani, Paul 168, 218

Gunderson, Gary 114, 156

Gutierrez, Rosalia 178 n1, 180, 453

Hai, Iftekhar 106, 164 n1, 218, 453

Han, Wenzao 156

Hare Krishna movement (ISKCON) 126

Hashish, use by Helena P. Blavatsky 19

Hekate (Pagan deity) 5, 49–50, 410

Hermes (Pagan deity) 5, 49–50, 410

Herzberg, Rabbi Arthur 187

hierarchy, spiritual, New Age concept of 261–265, 271, 272, 275, 277–284, 295, 308 n3, 318, 325, 342, 349, 402, 436–437, 446

highly evolved beings: see extra–terrestrial beings

Hinduism, and the URI 8, 36, 40 (also nn5,7), 41, 47, 51, 52 n4, 54, 57, 108, 109, 124, 137 n3, 152, 155 n2, 164 n1, 170 n8 176–177, 180–181, 194, 195, 196, 215, 306, 311 (also n6), 453–454

Hiroshima, atomic bombing of 278, 300, 323

Hitler, Adolf 23, 27, 117, 121, 251, 275, 290, 291, 300, 310–311 (also n1), 330–331, 332, 348, 355, 356 n2, 416, 416 n3, 417 (also n2), 420, 443, 445 n2

Hock, Dee 46, 56, 57, 103, 134, 404–405

Hoeller, Stefan 258, 281 n4

Hollister, Juliet 111, 198

Holocaust (genocide of the Jews during World War II) 36, 121, 267, 268, 330

Homosexuality: see gay issues

Houston, Jean 147, 284, 326, 346, 367, 368 n1

Hubbard, Barbara Marx 7, 21, 22, 23, 33, 34, 66, 85–86, 103, 115, 131, 134, 135, 150, 193, 212, (also n7), 219, 240, 242, 243, 247, 262, 269, 284, 286, 299, 300, 302, 316–326, 342, 346, 348, 349, 350, 357, 358, 368, 391, 402, 403, 407, 416

Huerta, Christian de la 83, 180

Huxley, Aldous 134, 153

Imbens-Fransen, Annie 166, 227, 453

Incas, as New Age spiritual models 307 (also n2)

individual identity, submergence of in New Age 66, 70, 90 n3, 243–244, 274–275, 289, 292, 294–295, 309, 319, 324, 342, 367, 387, 388, 391, 397, 401, 402–403, 446

Ingham, Bishop Michael (Anglican) 47, 141, 143, 183–184, 193, 206

Interfaith Center at the Presidio 156, 158, 163, 164 n1, 201, 202

Interfaith Center of New York 50, 103, 110, 145 n6, 150, 381

Interfaith curriculum for children, URI 76, 87–89

Interfaith movement, other than the United Religions Initiative: 6, 10–11, 26, 36, 39–44, 45–46, 50–52, 54 n8, 109–114, 115 n3, 124–126, 128–129, 134, 136, 138 nn10,11), 156, 163–164, 167, 185 n5, 187–188, 191–196, 199–200, 201–203, 206–207, 217 n5, 229–230, 233–234, 259, 367, 381, 389; see also names of specific interfaith organizations

Interfaith Sacred Space Design Competition 201–203

International Diplomacy Council 97, 99, 223, 406

Interreligious dialogue, orthodox Catholic position on: 9–11, 51 n4, 158–160, 164, 173–174, 176, 181–182, 187, 188, 213–215, 217, 224, 229–234, 408; see also Arinze, Cardinal

Islam:
   mainstream, and the URI, 44, 54, 56, 57, 74–75,

83, 100, 106–107, 137 n3, 164 n1, 200 n8, 453
   radical, and the URI, 77–82

Israel 36 n6, 44, 49, 53, 56, 82, 105 n2, 106, 107 n7, 120, 166, 169, 268, 399 n8, 440–441, 447 n6, 453; see also Palestine; Zionism

Jain, Bawa 50, 51, 103, 110

Jainism, and the URI 109

Jesse, Robert 86 n2, 368, 374, 375 (also n1); see also Council on Spiritual Practices; Rhythm Society

Jesus, the Christ:
   heterodox and New Age views on, 22, 88–89, 116, 120, 121, 123, 124, 130, 131 n13, 132, 143, 150, 155, 172–173, 174, 177, 179, 183–184, 190–191, 193, 194, 215–217, 226, 239, 241, 242, 250, 251–252, 253, 256, 260, 262–263, 266–267, 279, 282, 283, 288–289, 307–308, 316–318, 319, 325, 328–329, 347, 357, 358, 367, 368 n27, 395, 440
   traditional Christian views on, 9–10, 11, 32, 34, 160, 203–204, 210, 217, 230–234, 236, 238, 241, 242, 244, 351–352, 354, 441, 442–443, 444

Jesus Christ, the Bearer of the Water of Life (Vatican Document on the New Age) 228

Jewish Temple, plans to rebuild 440–441

John XXIII, Pope 229, 270 (also n1), 304, 305

John Paul II, Pope 122 n4, 163 n7, 184, 217, 221–222, 227, 228, 229, 232, 233, 234, 304, 305 (also n4), 410, 425, 429

Johnson, K. Paul 258

Jones, Fr. Alan (Episcopal) 103, 145, 164, 190, 200

Journal of the United Religions 185, 191–195

Judaism, and the URI 7, 8, 106, 214, 215, 246, 360

Karma 239, 256, 258, 262, 266, 267, 306

King, Ursula 286

Kirby, Richard 193

Kirby, Sr. Joan (Catholic) 110, 111, 168

Knitter, Paul 172

Knox, Ronald 413

Kreeft, Peter 444 n4

Kreutzer, Anke 185 (also n5), 194, 197, 216

Kucinich, Dennis 101

Küng, Hans 51 n10, 112, 173, 184, 206–210

Labyrinth movement 149–150, 171 n10

Lambeth Conference (Anglican), 1998 144 (also n11), 212, 215

Laszlo, Ervin 97, 368, 405

Latter-Day Saints, Church of (Mormons) 157–158, 196

Lattin, Don 190
Legionaries of Christ 422, 423, 424 n1, 425, 428–429, 445
Lemurians 261, 264, 265
Lenin, V.I. 27, 117, 122, 236, 244, 275, 279, 280, 300, 343, 348, 358, 447
Lerner, Michael (Catholic) 135, 346, 368
Lewis, C.S. 11, 13, 92, 190, 243, 244, 303–304, 317, 327–328, 349, 358, 402–403, 407 n6, 414, 415, 442–443, 444
liberalism, secular Western: 6–8, 16, 25, 50, 66, 71, 82–83, 100, 102, 224–226, 254, 293–294, 296, 298, 358, 359–360, 377, 383, 390, 393 (also n4), 408, 418
liberty: *see* freedom
Lord's Prayer, New Age versions of:
    Matthew Fox 155
    Barbara Marx Hubbard 317
    Interfaith Center at the Presidio 113
    Neale Donald Walsch 317–318
lowerarchy 92
Lucifer 7, 246–247, 249–250, 252, 260, 261; *see also* Satan
Lucifer Publishing Company 15, 20, 248
Lucis Trust 7, 15, 20, 21, 22, 60, 112, 131, 132, 215 n7, 247, 248, 257, 259–283, 307, 314, 315, 324, 412
Lucis Trust—related organizations:
    Arcane School 15, 20, 259, 314
    Lucis Publishing Company 20, 314
    World Goodwill 20, 132, 257, 259, 268, 281, 325, 383, 412
    World Service Fund 60, 131
Lukacs, John 414 n3, 417 (also n2)
Luyckx, Marc 369
Lyons, Oren 376

Machiavelli, Niccolo 312
Macy, Joanna 90
Maitreya (Theosophical) 26, 314 (also n3), 325, 418 (also n1)
marriage 18, 23, 52, 80 (also n5), 84, 119, 124, 125, 208, 219–220, 240, 268, 334–335, 357, 416 n3; *see also* families
Martin, Fr. Daniel (Catholic) 286
Marx, Karl 244, 445
Marxism 3, 122, 187, 281 n4, 289, 292–293, 302, 345 n4, 358, 397, 428; *see also* Communism
Masonry: *see* Freemasonry
Matser, Fred 361 n4
Mattison, Avon 103, 284–285
Mayans, as New Age spiritual models 49, 307, 313, 324

McCloskey, Fr. John (Catholic) 427
McGinn, Bernard 418, 438
McLaughlin, Corinne 132–133, 281 n1, 284, 285
McLennan, Scotty 157
Men, Fr. Alexander (Eastern Orthodox) 415
Miguel de Portugal 413–414
millenarianism 194, 195, 211–214, 223, 254, 285, 337, 339, 341–342, 372, 403, 427, 435, 436, 440–441
Mische, Patricia 43, 194–195, 368
modernism (heretical tendency within the Roman Catholic Church) 8, 174, 272, 386, 408
monism, as view of God and/or the universe 33, 327, 338
Moon, Sun Myung 5, 110, 116–126, 145 n4, 236, 263, 422, 426 n12
Moonies; *see* Unification Church and related organizations
Mormons: *see* Latter–Day Saints, Church of
Morton, James Parks 38 n1, 103, 110, 145 (also n6), 146, 150–152
Muggeridge, Malcolm 33, 244, 358, 377
Muller, Robert 7, 21, 50, 93, 101, 103, 111–112, 131, 132 n10, 133–134, 135, 184–185, 195 (also n4), 219, 220, 223–224, 241, 247, 269, 271, 284, 286, 306–315, 346, 348, 349, 358, 368 n1, 372, 383, 403, 416

Nagasaki, atomic bombing of 278, 323
National Cathedral, Washington DC (Episcopal) 125, 145, 150
National Council of Churches (US) 52, 112, 193, 201, 207
National Socialism: *see* Nazism
nation-state, obsolescence of 1, 12, 93–94, 119, 133–134, 213, 279–280, 298, 299–300, 302, 303, 305, 308–312, 342–346, 357, 360, 362–364, 370, 381–382, 444
nature–worship 24, 38 n1, 151, 188–201, 249, 361
Nazism 178, 209, 214, 228, 244, 254 (also n5), 264, 267, 268, 275, 276, 290 n4, 291, 293, 296, 321 n4, 331, 397, 413, 415, 416, 442, 443, 445n2, 447
Neocatechumenal Way 432
Neopaganism 28, 41, 127–128, 148, 162, 254; *see also* Wicca
Nesky, Andrew 48
Neuhaus, Fr. Richard (Catholic) 38
New Age movement 15, 18–23, 131–139, 146–156, 227–229, 237–352, 366–369, 373–375, 376–377, 396–398
"new civilization" 14, 15, 16, 24, 37 (also n5), 42–43, 182, 204, 359–360, 375 n1, 396, 397
New Group of World Servers 263, 268, 274, 277, 281,

282 (also n1), 308 n3

New Oxford Review 1, 431 n1, 447, 479

New Religion:

New Age and globalist predictions/proposals 34, 93–94, 255, 270–274, 286, 287–289, 306–308, 316–319, 339–342, 361, 366–369, 376–377, 389–391, 394–395, 404–406, 412

trends 37–38, 159–160, 206, 231, 413–415

URI and 71, 131, 132–136, 188–205, 235–236

new world order 7, 10, 14, 15, 26, 35, 38, 42–43, 103, 167, 206–211, 246, 265, 272, 273, 274–276, 279, 281, 282, 308–312, 346, 358 (also n6), 359, 360, 363–364, 393–394, 398, 404–407, 409–410, 413–414, 416–418, 480

Newman, Cardinal John Henry 34

Nietzsche, Friedrich 432–436

Nobel Peace Prize, predicted for the URI 44

nuclear war 1, 36, 278, 323, 355, 389

nuclear weapons 1, 7, 24, 36, 227, 246, 269, 277–278, 300, 323, 348, 373, 413

O'Brien, Michael 439

occultism; *see* Neopaganism; Theosophy

omega point 288, 349

one–world religion: *see* syncretism, religious; New Religion

Opus Dei 422–429, 445, 446

ordination of women priests 18, 82, 83, 172, 173, 205, 226–227, 385; *see also* feminism

Original Sin 239, 241, 332, 374; *see also* Fall of Man

O'Rourke, Fr. Gerard (Catholic) 139, 161, 161–165, 202, 225, 229

Orthodoxy, Eastern 8, 11, 49, 57 n3, 89, 140, 158, 158 n5, 213 (also n5), 229, 442, 480

Orwell, George 101, 274, 310, 331, 344, 356, 416–417, 432

Ottley, Bishop James (Anglican) 33, 142, 220, 224

Overpopulation: *see* population control and population reduction

Palestine 266, 268, 269, 420 n2, 440–441; *see also* Israel; Zionism

Pantheism 33, 227–229

Parliament of World Religions:

1893 6, 39–41, 43

1993 41–43, 128

1999 77, 199, 272

2004 110

Pathways to Peace 103, 138, 284–285

Patten, Chris 356

Paul VI, Pope 232, 305

Paul, the Apostle 9, 34, 214, 238, 241, 242, 244, 266, 368 (also n27), 417, 442, 443

persecution, religious 36, 52 n3, 70, 182–188, 204, 213, 344, 410, 416, 417–419, 427–428, 432, 443, 444–448

Peruman, Sri Ravi 108, 126 n3, 180, 225

Peter, the Apostle 192 n1, 230, 242, 250, 251, 421, 444–445

Pike, Bishop James (Episcopal) 18

Pius X, Pope 8, 174, 408 (also n2), 411

Pius XI, Pope 209–210, 228, 229–230, 351, 411, 442

Pius XII, Pope 210, 411

plan, hierarchical, New Age concept of 22, 244, 260, 275, 276, 324, 325

planning, as New Age article of faith 34, 279–280, 285, 294–296, 302–303, 355, 358, 360, 402

Ponedel, David 113, 136 n10, 199 (also n8)

population control 7, 98–99, 217–222, 225, 246, 252, 263–264, 295–296, 299, 384, 387; *see also* abortion; artificial contraception; family planning; population reduction

population reduction 26, 219–221, 307, 372–373, 390, 398

prayer, as a response to the present crisis 10, 27, 235, 352, 409, 438–439, 448

pre–millennial dispensationalism (Protestant eschatological belief) 440–447

progress, as New Age article of faith 7, 189, 244, 246, 252, 263, 272, 288–289, 291, 293, 294, 296, 297, 299, 301–303, 309, 314 n1, 340, 356, 367, 412; *see also* evolution, New Age views of

Project for a New American Century 407 (also n6)

proselytizing, religious 3, 40 n5, 41, 52, 173, 175–182, 194, 204 n3, 451

Protestantism—Evangelical churches 7, 20, 50 n5, 100, 140, 146, 151, 157, 183, 229, 235, 246, 351, 395, 415, 441 n1, 448

Protestantism—Mainline churches, other than Anglicans and Episcopalians 26, 140, 146, 229

Protestantism and the URI 11, 26, 57 n3, 100, 112, 140, 142, 156–158, 184, 452, 453, 454; *see also* Anglicanism; Episcopal Church

racism 123, 208, 252–253, 254 n2, 264–265, 196–299, 393n4, 441–443

radical social change, New Age calls for 263–264, 265, 270–273, 274–276, 279–283, 288–289, 294–296, 301–304, 308–313, 319–326, 332–336, 339–346, 348–352

Rangel, Rep. Charlie 119

Rankin, William 56 (also n5), 74 n2, 78, 82, 152 n4, 174, 214, 215, 224

Ratzinger, Cardinal Joseph 173, 188, 233

reactionaries, New Age proposals and predictions of fate of 7, 246, 269–270, 274, 276–279, 285, 297–298, 301–302, 312, 320–323, 341–342

Regnum Christi 424 n3

Reich, Robert 186

relativism, religious and philosophical 63–66, 186–187, 215–217, 230, 233–234, 236, 331–332, 350, 371–372, 433

reproductive rights; see abortion, artificial contraception, and population control

Republican Party, U.S. 5, 12–13, 18, 50, 100, 116, 363, 392

Rhythm Society 86 (also n2), 87; see also Jesse, Robert

Rice, Condoleezza 405, 407

Robert Muller Schools 21, 313–314, 383

Robinson, Gene 143

Rockefeller, David 391

Rockefeller, Laurance 150

Rockefeller, Steven 16–17, 368, 380, 382, 391

Roman Catholic Church:
    Catechism of the Catholic Church 11, 13, 213, 229, 356,357, 432
    Opponents of the URI 152, 158–160
    Supporters of the URI 160–174
    Archdiocese of San Francisco 162–165, 202, 209
    Members of the URI Global Council 452, 453
    Religious orders, male and female 169–172
    United States Conference of Catholic Bishops 165
    Supporters of the Earth Charter 382, 383 (also n9)see also Vatican, the

Ronning, Chester 280, 355

Rudolf Steiner Foundation 103

Ruse, Austin 51 (also n1), 52

Russia, 19, 24, 27, 53, 224 n2, 294 n5, 270, 279, 279 n4, 281, 300, 309, 359, 362, 413, 415, 416, 440, 445; see also Soviet Union

Russian Revolution 27, 270, 280

"sacred earth" 38 n1, 188–205

Sanat Kumara 261 (also n9), 325

Satan 31, 49, 116–117, 119, 120, 121, 203, 209, 213, 229, 249, 250, 254 n1, 255 n2, 319, 413, 417, 437, 440, 443, 447

Satanism 130, 245

Schuman, Robert 133, 309

Schuon, Frithjof 3, 178 n3, 185 n5, 215 n7, 225 n6, 256 n3

Scientology 126

Second Coming of Christ:
    heterodox and non–Christian views, 270–272, 284, 308, 318, 412
    orthodox Christian views, 13, 32, 213–214, 410–412, 417–419, 432; see also apocalypse

sects; see cults and sectarian religious movements

secular messianism 13, 213, 398

Seed, John 90–91

"selection" of mankind, New Age concept of 7, 243, 246, 252–253, 276, 297, 319, 320n1, 320–323, 342, 402

Semel, Rita 105, 164 n1, 183, 216

sexual ethics, New Age approach to 54, 129–131, 263–264, 319, 333–336, 338, 373–374

Sexual Information and Education Council of the US (SIECUS) 77, 82–83, 225

shamanism 16, 76, 90, 91 (also n4), 109, 130, 201, 368, 376–377, 389

Share International 26, 314 (also n3), 418

shari'a (Islamic law) 77 (also n3)

Sheed, Frank 214

Sheen, Archbishop Fulton J. (Catholic) 413

Shultz, George P. 99, 370 n3

SIGMA Project (Case Western Reserve University) 56, 63, 64; see also Appreciative Inquiry

Sikhism, and the URI 57, 108, 109, 200 n8, 452

Simon Magus 251

"simple living" and the State of the World Forum 375–377

smallpox, and Mikhail Gorbachev 23, 361–362

Smith, Huston, 23, 84–87

social Darwinism 7, 206, 319

social democracy 12

socialism 12, 24–25, 26, 226, 296, 308, 346, 356 n2, 358, 359–360, 361, 362, 366, 385, 389, 391, 410 (also n2), 417, 433, 434, 435

Solovyov, Vladimir 419 (also n4)

Sophia (female "Holy Spirit") 227, 241–242, 251–252

Soros, George 1, 5, 25, 61, 101–102, 221, 370, 374, 378, 394, 408

Soviet Union 15, 23–24, 276, 280, 293, 296, 360, 362, 363 n6, 373, 388, 397

Spaak, Paul-Henri 356 (also n2)

Spangler, David 248 n2, 281 n1, 284, 286, 326

spirit of the earth 12, 203, 212, 297, 300–301; see also global soul

Spiritual Counterfeits Project 397

Spong, Bishop Jack (Episcopal) 18, 143, 251, 322

Stafford, Cardinal James Francis 424, 428

Stalin, J. V. 117, 275, 300, 397, 417, 420, 428, 439

Stallings, G. Augustus 122 (also n4), 123, 124

Stang, Betsy 138 n11, 259

State Department, U. S. 7, 78 n5, 99, 406

State of the World Forum 5, 6, 16, 22, 24, 25, 26, 37, 103–104, 119, 187, 194, 346, 357, 358, 360, 365–379, 381, 388, 395, 398, 408

Steiner, Rudolf 61, 103, 131 (also n13), 194 n2, 248 (also n6), 257–258, 259, 383

Stevenson, Robert Louis 357

Strong, Maurice 16, 17, 24–25, 326, 368, 370 n3, 378, 380 (also n2), 388, 389–392, 406, 418

Suicide 78, 89 n2, 101, 208, 241, 276, 320, 336, 337, 391, 426, 446; *see also* euthanasia

Survivalism 444

swastika, in Theosophy and Nazism 253, 254 (also nn2,5)

Swidler, Leonard 173

Swing, Bishop William E. (Episcopal), 5, 12, 13, 15, 17–18, 33, 35–38, 42, 44–50, 52, 54, 56–58, 62–64, 66–68, 72, 76–79, 83–84, 86, 87, 93–94, 99–103, 106–107, 109–111, 113–115, 124–125, 127, 132 n10, 133, 135, 137, 140 (also n5), 144–146, 152–154, 157–165, 173–180, 182–186, 188–191, 199–200, 203, 205–206, 211–212, 214–216, 218–219, 221–227, 231, 236, 272, 287, 301, 340, 349, 369, 401, 405, 406, 452

syncretism, religious 3, 28, 84, 100, 151, 159, 164, 179, 188 (also n4), 189, 190, 196, 198–199, 201–205, 216, 230, 232–234, 412, 418, 430

Taliban 77, 79 (also nn 1, 2)

Tantra 16, 130, 334 (also n8), 373–374

Tay, Bishop Moses (Anglican) 203

Teasdale, Wayne 42, 173, 181, 195 (also n8), 206, 223

Techno Cosmic Mass 153–156; *see also* Fox, Fr. Matthew, creation spirituality, and University of Creation Spirituality

Teilhard de Chardin, S. J., Fr. Pierre (Catholic) 7, 21, 42–43, 134, 137, 243, 244, 247, 286–305, 323, 326, 348, 349, 358, 384, 402

Temple Mount Faithful 441

Temple of Understanding 15, 41, 45, 46, 109–113, 145 n6, 167–168, 198

Teresa, Mother (Catholic) 160

terrorism 1, 5, 36, 52, 77, 78–82, 89 n2, 178, 186, 192 n1, 236, 267, 272, 321, 322–323, 360, 363, 393–394, 404, 407, 413, 428

Thatcher, Margaret 370

Theosophical movement (spiritual movement founded in 1875 by H. P. Blavatsky) 3, 6, 7, 19–21, 29, 39, 40 nn1, 7, 48, 131–136, 259–285, 287, 324–326, 328, 347, 352, 410, 418 nn1, 2

Theosophical Society 7, 19–21, 39–40, 48, 131 n13, 193, 194 n2, 196, 197 n3, 204 n3, 248–258, 261 n9, 286, 418 n2

Thigpen, Paul 420

Third Reich: *see* Nazism

Ting, Bishop K. H. (Anglican) 142 (also n11), 185

Tolkien, J. R. R. 414, 422

Totalitarianism, New Age apologetics for 7, 210, 243, 244, 270 n1, 274–281, 289–294, 308–312, 322, 324, 330–331, 342–346, 359–360, 370–372, 386–388, 402

Warnings against 356, 397–398, 413–417, 430; *see also* Fascism; Nazism; Communism

Tradition, Family, and Property (TFP) 447

Traditionalist School (Schuon, Guénon, et al.) 3–4, 178 n3, 185 n5, 233 n6, 256 n3, 432, 436–438

Traer, Robert 51 n10, 54 n8, 176, 187

Trilateral Commission 186, 378

Trower, Philip 448

Turner, Ted 26–27, 51–52, 102, 221, 313, 366–367, 373, 447

Tutu, Archbishop Desmond (Anglican) 53, 98, 103, 143, 218–219, 394

United Nations (UN) 5, 6, 7, 15, 16, 17, 24, 26, 35–36, 44, 47, 50, 51, 53, 55, 64, 66, 70, 75, 78 (also n1), 79 n2, 81 n8, 82, 93–99, 103, 111, 112, 119, 124 n11, 125, 127 n8, 132–136, 139, 142, 152, 160, 161 nn4,9, 167, 181, 184, 189, 193 n1, 206, 209, 217–221, 223, 225, 235, 236, 240, 247, 259, 269, 271, 278, 284, 286, 293, 306–315, 336, 360, 363, 364, 370, 378 (also n7), 379–382, 385, 386, 389, 392, 394, 406, 449; *see also* UN agencies

UN agencies:
UNEP 96–97
UNESCO 21, 58 n10, 94, 95, 97–99, 132, 169, 220, 284, 294, 313, 378, 379, 382
UNFPA 98–99, 168 n1, 218 (also n7), 221 n4
UNICEF 95, 284, 378, 379

University for Peace, 21, 24, 125, 133

UN declaration on religious freedom (1981) 70

Unification Church and related organizations 7, 115–126, 227

Union of Soviet Socialist Republics (USSR); *see* Soviet Union

United Communities of Spirit 197–198, 200

United States Institute of Peace (USIP) 62, 99

"unity in diversity" 5, 33, 98, 109–114, 197, 236, 323, 351

University of Creation Spirituality 152

Upton, Charles 3–4, 9, 29, 37 n3, 40 n5, 70 n1, 77 n3, 80 n5, 89 n2, 91 n4, 106 n7, 155 n2, 178 n3, 181 n4, 183 nn4,5, 185 n5, 192 n1, 194 n2, 195 n4, 205 (also n1), 212 n7, 215 n7, 216 n2, 217 nn1,5, 233 n6, 248 n1, 254 nn1,5, 255 n2, 256 n3, 257 n3, 261 n9, 299 n6, 268 n5, 283 n4, 328 n5, 334 n8, 345 n2, 399 n8, 419 n3, 426 nn7,12, 430, 438, 441 n2, 447 n6

United Religions Initiative (URI):
    changes in strategy since 1996 66–68
    Charter 69–73, 449–451
    cultural radicalism 76–92
    funding sources 57–63
    Global Council members 452–454
    history 35–175
    political agenda 206–214, 217–222, 224–226
    powerful supporters 93–104
    reasons to oppose 76–92, 175–234
    situation as of 2004 53–55
    works of mercy 73–76

utilitarianism, religious 222–224, 331–332

utopianism 5, 6, 11, 13, 15, 27, 37, 42, 93, 102, 136, 209, 211–214, 235, 262–263, 276, 303–304, 335, 341–342, 349, 358, 372, 378, 396–397, 404–405, 446

Vatican, the 21, 45, 51 n4, 52, 74 n3, 80, 81, 140, 152, 158–160, 164, 165, 167, 173, 223, 227–229, 232–234, 235, 256, 269, 272, 304–305, 349–351, 423–428

Vatican II (Roman Catholic Church council, 1962–1965) 10, 173, 189, 229–231, 234, 424, 443

Vatican view of the New Age; see *Jesus Christ, the Bearer of the Water of Life*

Verhofstadt, Guy 310

Veriditas: *see* Labyrinth movement

Vichy regime (France under German occupation, World War II) 291–292

Volkswagen 311

Wainaina, Fr. Joseph (Catholic) 169, 217

Walker, Antonio Garrigues 186

Walsch, Neale Donald 7, 22–23, 43, 102, 115, 131, 135–136, 186, 195, 196, 239, 240, 243, 246, 247 (also n2), 262, 269, 288, 317–318, 236, 327–350, 355, 357, 358, 391, 403, 416

War on Terror 5, 100

war, as an occasion of progress 7, 246, 260–261, 276–279, 285, 291, 298–301, 303–304, 342, 344–345, 433–434

Ware, Bishop Kallistos (Eastern Orthodox) 213

Warner, Sen. John 118

wealthy supporters of or participants in interfaith, New Age, and globalist movements:
    New Age leaders 150
    population control 221
    radicals or socialists, self–avowed 1, 5, 16, 17, 24–25, 26–27, 51–52, 61, 101–102, 221, 313, 326, 366, 367, 368, 370 (also n3), 373, 374, 378, 380 (also n2), 388, 389–392, 394, 406, 408, 418, 447
    State of the World Forum 378
    United Religions Initiative 57–62
    World Economic Forum, 379
    World Millennium Peace Summit of Religious and Spiritual Leaders 51–52

Wicca 5, 12, 41, 48, 49, 57, 115 (also n3), 127–131, 162, 197, 200, 201, 257, 383, 410, 453 (also n2); *see also* Neopaganism

Williams, Archbishop Rowan (Anglican) 144

Wittenberg Center for Alternative Resources 138 (also n11), 259

Woodward, Kenneth 351

World Bank 24, 95, 221, 225, 326, 378, 389, 394

World Core Curriculum; *see* Robert Muller Schools

World Council of Churches 110, 112, 235, 369

World Economic Forum 5, 6, 17, 24, 25, 50, 111, 247 n1, 389, 392–396, 398, 401

world government 12, 220, 308–312, 342–346, 350, 357, 360, 364, 380–382, 391, 397–398, 438; *see also* global governance

World Millennium Peace Summit of Religious and Spiritual Leaders 50–54, 94, 111

World War I 21, 214, 299

World War II 21, 42, 148, 189, 214, 254 n5, 271 n8, 275–277, 289–291, 299–300, 331, 342, 346 n2, 407, 415, 416 (also n3), 445 (also n2)

Younghusband, Sir Francis 42

Zionism 209, 268, 366 n8, 440 n1, 441–442; *see also* Israel; Palestine

Zoroastrianism, and the URI 57, 91 n4, 108–109, 201, 454

Printed in Great Britain
by Amazon